P9-CBJ-470

The Fishing Lure Collector's Bible

The Most Comprehensive
Antique Fishing Lure
Identification & Value Guide Available

R.L. Streater
with Rick Edmisten
and Dudley Murphy

COLLECTOR BOOKS
A Division of Schroeder Publishing Co., Inc.

The current values in this book should be used only as a guide. They are not intended to set prices, which vary from one section of the country to another. Auction prices as well as dealer prices vary greatly and are affected by condition as well as demand. Neither the authors nor the publisher assumes responsibility for any losses that might be incurred as a result of consulting this guide.

Searching For A Publisher?

We are always looking for knowledgeable people considered to be experts within their fields. If you feel that there is a real need for a book on your collectible subject and have a large comprehensive collection, contact Collector Books.

Book design by R.L. Streater and Mary Ann Hudson

COLLECTOR BOOKS
P.O. Box 3009
Paducah, Kentucky 42002-3009

Contents

Acknowledgments

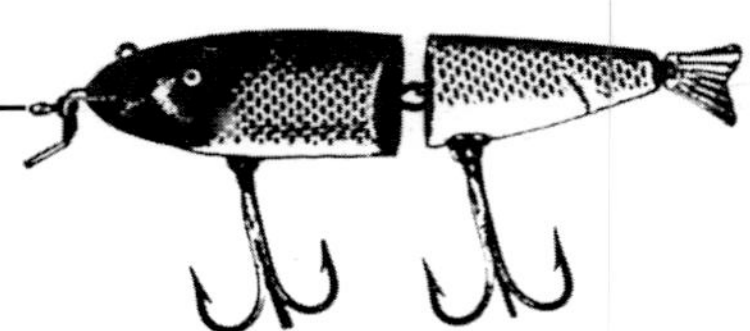

My thanks and appreciation to the many members of the NFLCC who shared with me their catalogs, old lures, and personal knowledge. Without their generous help, this book would not have been possible. We should all thank the founders of the National Fishing Lure Collectors Club. Without their efforts there would be no need for a book and very few collectors would know each other. Let's hear it for John Goodwin, Point Lookout, Missouri; Dudley Murphy, Springfield, Missouri; and Jerry Routh, Springfield, Missouri.

A very special thanks to my wife, Maryann, who put up with and encouraged me through the long months of work on this book. I feel lucky indeed, to have her as my silent partner.

Special thanks to Trig Lund of Dowagiac, Michigan, who allowed me to go through and research a wealth of lures and catalogs he had accumulated during many years in the fishing tackle industry; Janice Lewey for her great body work; Mark Ward for his friendship, support, and major editing help; and Debra Bandy for her guidance and advice.

Also a special thanks to Bruce Dyer, who taught me the meaning of doing research with an eye toward details that help to piece together the history of bait development.

Last, but certainly not least, I thank Tad Motoyama, Los Angeles, California, for his excellent Color Gallery photographs. — R.L. Streater

VET - WILL TELL
FISHING JOKES
FOR FOOD!
BASS

Introduction

It was in July of 1975 when I first met Dick Streater at an A&W Root Beer stand on the north side of Dowagiac, Michigan. During the spring of the previous year some of us had formed the National Fishing Lure Collectors Club at a historic gathering of lure collectors at the School of the Ozarks in Point Lookout, Missouri. Now it was time for our first national meeting and there before me stood Dick Streater, a lure collector with whom I had corresponded and shared information for several years but whom I had only just now come to know in person.

In the early years of lure collecting, very little information was available about the hobby. Most lure companies had ceased production years ago and with their primary emphasis being on lure sales, the archives of the few remaining lure companies were generally devoid of historical information. A few pocket catalogs and lure box inserts constituted the bulk of factual information. As collectors, we were geographically separated and largely uneducated regarding the history of the lures we sought. Buying and selling as a means of acquisition simply didn't exist, thus lure transactions focused on trading. Trading without information, without books. We were at the mercy of our own gut feelings and often made poor trades as a result of such ignorance. It would be some time before collectors would understand and appreciate the now popular phrase "knowledge is power."

When we discovered that Dick Streater was willing to allow collectors to make copies of a "lure scrapbook" which he had worked on for several years, it was as if a light had suddenly been turned on. That light was knowledge, and as it so often does, the light of knowledge illuminated the dark and obscure corners of our hobby with understanding. Lure collection could now begin in earnest. We no longer labored in complete ignorance. We had a reference book which Dick Streater would continue to refine, update, and later publish in limited numbers. It was the very first fishing lure collectors reference book and, despite the many excellent volumes by notable authors which followed, is still the most complete reference available.

One might infer that given time, someone else would have come forward with the first lure reference book, and arguably they would be right. But that was not the case. It was R.L. Streater who stepped up and brought forth that first book. The best technology of the day couldn't prevent Streater's book from being a little difficult to use, however, and updates, by their very nature, broke the continuity and flow of lure categories. Drawings and retouched copies of rare lures often had to suffice. *Streater's Reference Catalog of Old Fishing Lures* was a labor of love for the hobby and not undertaken for financial profit. It was the first attempt to satisfy the true collector's need to understand, to give shape and form to a previously ambiguous hobby.

In a phone conversation last year Rick Edmisten, my good friend and co-author of *Fishing Lure Collectibles,* confided in me that Dick Streater was planning to discontinue publishing his reference book. We were disturbed by the thought of the lure collecting hobby losing a vital component of its history. In agreement that Streater's book should not be relegated to oblivion, we persuaded Collector Books to publish this updated edition complete with lure values and a color section. Rick and I are honored to be involved with the *Fishing Lure Collector's Bible*, and we look forward to the continuing process of updating and revising this important volume.

Mankind defines history in terms of beginnings. The first tools, the first antibiotic, the first flight to the moon. Beginnings which set the pace for further developments. Beginnings which serve as benchmarks in shaping the future. If I could only own one antique fishing lure reference book, it would be *Streater's Reference Catalog of Old Fishing Lures*. It is the book which initially defined the lure collection hobby and now in revised form has cut a new benchmark into the mysterious history of fishing lure collectibles. For me it is a collectible in its own right. For the lure collection hobby, it is our beginning. —Dudley Murphy

About this Book

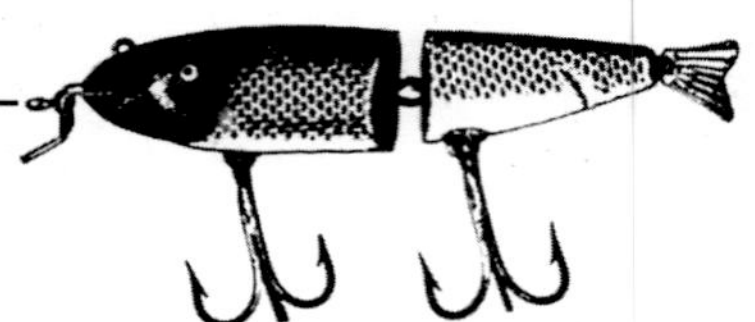

This book in intended to be a basic textbook for identifying old fishing lures. This identification is a never ending search. Note that I have enclosed each lure in a drawn line box. I use a small, pressure sensitive silver ¼" dot to indicate the lures I have in my collection. You could also use another color dot to show the lures you are looking for. That method then becomes your personal inventory of both your own collection and also your want list. In case of changes, the dots are easily removed.

The current values in this book should be used only as a guide. They are not intended to set prices, which vary from one section of the country to another. Auction prices as well as dealer prices vary greatly and are affected by physical condition as well as demand. Neither the authors nor the publisher assumes responsibility for any losses that might be incurred as a result of consulting this guide.

Some lures cannot be accurately valued since they do not exist in sufficient quantities to create a history of transactions which might establish a value scale. It should be remembered that values are arbitrary, and true current market values can only be determined when someone is willing to pay the seller's price, or when the seller accepts the buyer's offer. Listed values therefore are based on what a lure should bring in an average market.

In the past few years sensationalized auction prices have tended to create the impression that all "old lures" are valuable, and while certain lures are indeed valuable, the vast majority of antique fishing lures are quite affordable and available in adequate quantities to allow collectors to comfortably enjoy the hobby. High auction prices have caused sellers to bring lures "out of the woodwork" in hopes of matching the publicized prices, but when rare lures begin to become available in large quantities, their value tends to decrease dramatically. Record-setting lures simply do not exist in quantities of 50 or 60 but rather in quantities of usually a dozen or less. There must be a quantity sufficient to establish a consistency and desire, but few enough to prove rarity.

While most lures are still readily affordable, there are a good number that exceed the limits of casual affordability. It must be remembered that lure prices can vary as widely as pork bellies in the commodity market. The state of the national economy and the variables of eye appeal, such as color, version, condition, and desirability, based on factors such as rarity and vintage, all tend to prevent values from crystallizing into a predictable pattern. Values rise and fall and collectors learn to expect these fluctuations and adapt in a manner that allows them to continue collecting.

Ideas and Tips on Lure Display and other Collecting Trivia

Make your display cases portable, or you'll wish you had. I fabricate mine from ¼" plexiglass with white backs and clear covers. They are hung on the wall by two screws into the wall studs with the cases drilled "keyhole" style so they can be easily removed.

You can hang lures closer together without crowding if you unscrew the screw eyes until the hooks hang straight down the side of the lure instead of at a 45° angle in their normal position. You can add interest to your displays by attaching a couple of rare or interesting lure boxes to your case.

A simple way to identify and dress up your cases is to buy small plastic letters to title your cases. A well-stocked sign shop will have them, or they can be ordered. I try to use the same style letter used in the early company logos or advertising. One prime example is **Heddon's "Dowagiac" Minnows.**

I use a thin aluminum pop rivet (3/32") to hang up my lures. Clinch them up tight, hang the lure through the line tie, and bend them over double so the lure can't come unhooked. To freeze a lure in a fixed position, put a second pop rivet in one of the hook hangers. Certain lures hang and look better horizontally or at a 45° angle. Don't get committed to just a vertical hang.

Some guys have made an interesting display using an old stump or a chunk of driftwood. Frogs and mice lend themselves to this sort of arrangement.

Another interesting variation is to have one case with lures in-the-box. Some of the early boxes were works of art and the creative merchandising genius of their producers. A real prize here would be a lure in one of the old wooden boxes.

Look for other fishing related items to spice up your display. Rods, reels, and tackle boxes all fill the bill. My two favorites are a hand-operated trolling motor and a brass/oak line drier.

Try to go to the NFLCC annual meeting every year. You can learn more there in two days than you will the rest of the year in your local area.

I keep a large file folder for each collector I write. On the outside I record all the trades we make, so they are there for quick recall.

R.L. Streater's Original Condition Rating of Old Plugs – The NFLCC uses a slightly revised version today.

1. **New-In-Box:** The older the plug, the more interesting and valuable.
2. **Mint:** "New-In-Box" without the box. Any defects must be virtually undetectable.
3. **Excellent:** very minor defects, chips, scratches, etc., with good bright paint.
4. **Good:** generally good condition. Could have some minor problems, but will look good hanging up.
5. **Average:** starting to show age or problems. I use a mental sliding scale on this: the older the plug, the poorer the condition to still retain an average.
6. **Fair:** major visible defects, lost paint, rust, cracks.
7. **Poor:** still recognizable as to color, etc. A plug you might hang up but would try to replace soon.
8. **Repainted:** either in full or partially touched up. If it can be stripped of the paint, it could improve the rating. Techniques will be forthcoming.
9. **Beater:** so far gone that it should be stripped for parts, saving the hook hardware, eyes, hooks, and metal lips.
10. **Plug Body**: stripped down body, ready to be used for repainting and fishing use.

General Comments

Always be specific when commenting on condition. Use examples such as worm burn one side, missing weed guard, rusty hooks. An obviously never fished mint plug should not be downgraded for checked paint. After all, it adds character.

Ethically speaking, it is a good idea to tell when you are trading for a plug that you intend to trade it to another person.

For cleaning plugs I use Bon Ami Powder. Some others use toothpaste, denture cleaners, and the like. I would hope a future newsletter of the NFLCC would go into this in detail. If you don't have experience with lure cleaning, it is best to leave the job for someone who does. Over-cleaning can seriously reduce the value of a lure.

A word about the dating system that I have used in the catalog. When you see a date circled 1910, that means I can place that bait in that time frame, maybe because of an ad, or a dated catalog. If you see the word "new," that means it was being introduced to the trade in that time. The term "Patented" or "Patent applied for" means they are actually patented. Also patents of a part of a bait, such as lip or hook rig, may be shown on the bait, but not date the bait itself.

Zip codes were introduced in 1959, so any manufacturer showing a zip code was in business after 1959.

I don't think we can always go by what is known about the manufacturer's hardware and hook rigs. In discussions with some of the old-timers, they said they often borrowed from each other when they were short on an item. Also put yourself in the shoes of the metal stamped parts salesman...wouldn't you try to sell all of the bait manufacturers your wares?

When I show a length, and in most cases when the manufacturer's data shows a length, it is of the body itself, exclusive of all hardware.

Many of us have thought that baits with a square swivel indicated an older bait. Patent information shows that Al Wilson patented a round swivel in 1902. So much for that theory.

We could classify lures as to time frame:

A. Pre-World War I, 1800s – 1917
B. World War I, World War II – 1918 – 1945
C. Post WW II, 1945 – present

or

A. Pre-1900 – Basically spoons
B. 1900 – 1910 – The classic era
C. 1911 – 1920 – Age of innovation
D. 1921 – 1930 – Many new baits appear
E. 1931 – 1940 – For many, collectibility ends here
F. 1941 – present – Age of modern collectible lures

Reference Books

One cannot overemphasize the need for the serious collector to read everything available about lures if a thorough knowledge is to be gained. The following books should proved helpful additions in the reader's library of research materials: *Fishing Lure Collectibles*, Murphy & Edmisten, Collector Books, Paducah, KY; *Early Fishing Plugs of the U.S.A.*, Kimball, Art and Scott, 1989, Aardvark Publications, Inc., P.O. Box 252, Boulder Junction, WI 54512; *Old Fishing Lures and Tackle*, Third Edition, Carl F. Luckey, 1991, Books Americana, Inc., P.O. Box 2326, Florence, AL 35630; *Fishing Tackle Antiques*, Karl White, 1992, P.O. Box 169, Arcadia, OK 73007; *Fred C. Keeling & Co.*, Jack Looney, 1993, 20201 16th Street North, Independence, MO 64056; *Creek Chub Bait Company*, Harold Smith, 1992, 3366 Eskew Rd., Boonville, Indiana 47601.

Color Gallery

South Bend "SALTS" and Musky Baits
The 6 – 4½" King Orenos shown are the last production bearing that name, and were made specifically for the Northwest salmon market place. Two colors not shown are pink and red head/white. The single hook model shown is called the Coast Oreno. Also shown is the 4½" No. 976 Musk-Oreno and the 6½" Troll Oreno. See pages 385 – 409. R.L. Streater collection.

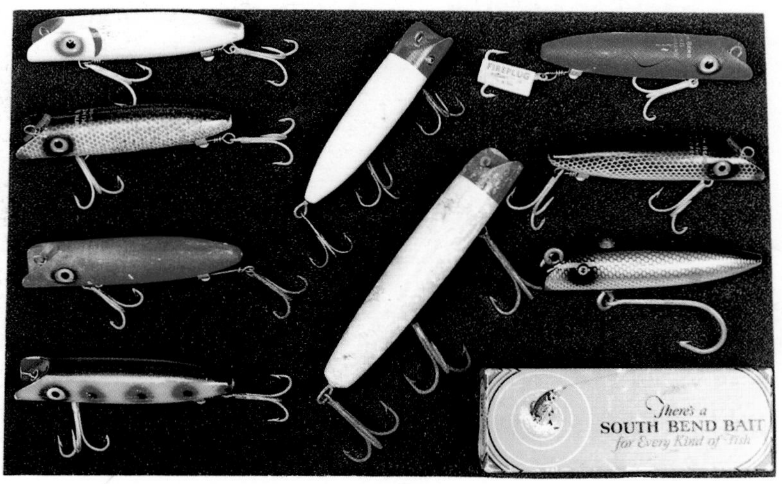
There's a
SOUTH BEND BAIT
for Every Kind of Fish

The Pflueger "Scramble" Paint Finish
It was made in the glass eyed era and also in the later pressed/painted eye time frame. A good item for "color collectors" in that they would never get two alike. The blue "canoe" box was stamped on the end: No. 5039 Scramble Finish. H.L. Musselman collection.

Color collection of CCBCo. #100 Wigglers. See pages 88 and 100. Steve Ellis collection.

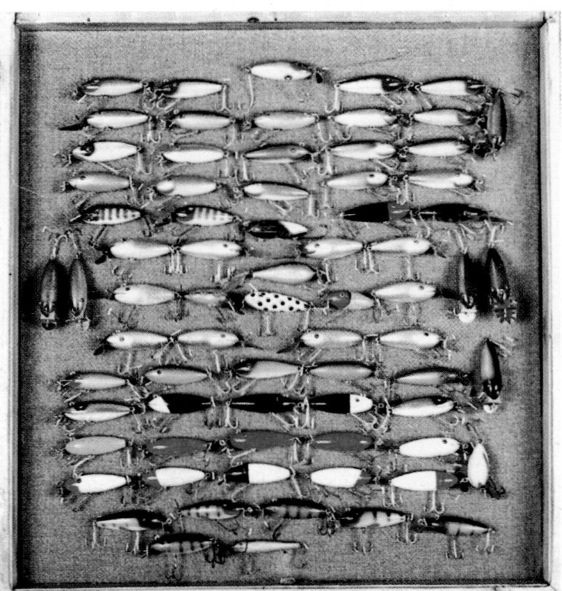

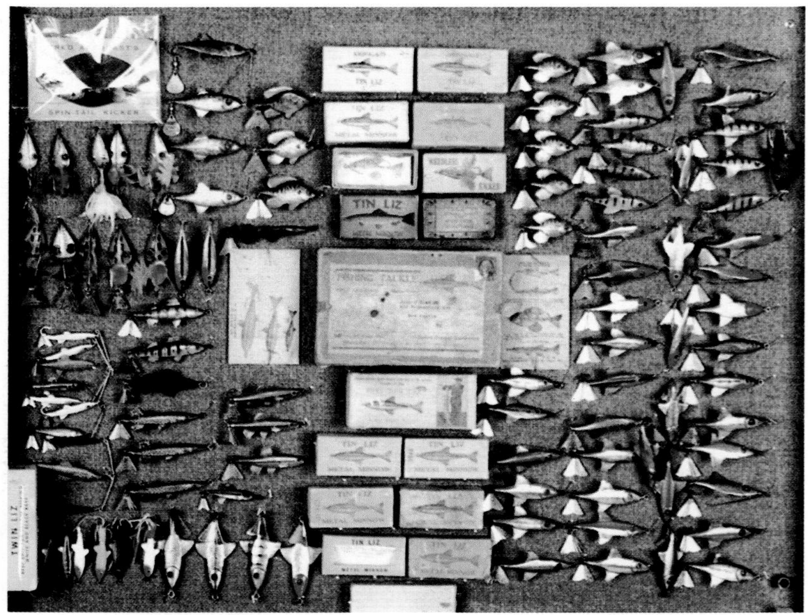
SPIN-TAIL KICKER
TIN LIZ
TWIN LIZ

Fred Arbogast lure collection. See page 54.
Steve Ellis collection.

Smokin', Drinkin' and Fishin' Lure collection
Another fun collection to acquire, and don't forget to ask the question... "What fish do you catch on the King Edward Cigar Bait?" The answer is: Smoked Salmon! $5.00 – 40.00. R.L. Streater collection.

Budweiser
Coors
Blitz
7

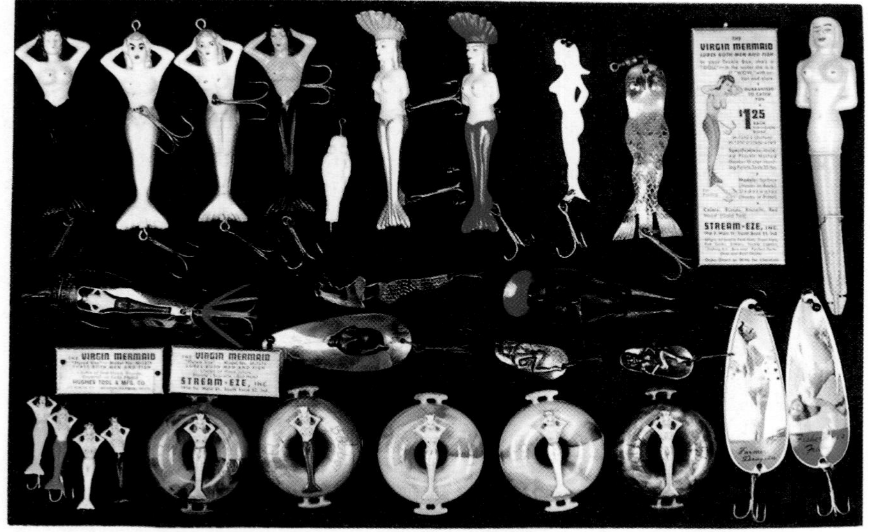
VIRGIN MERMAID
STREAM-EZE, INC.
$1.25
HUGHES TOOL & MFG. CO.

A Mermaid or Girly Lure collection
This would include any lure with a woman figure on it and hopefully not obscene in any way. The illustrated "Mermaid" lures are becoming quite collectible. $5.00 – 50.00.
Note the variations: flyrod, spoon, bobber, colors, and shapes. See pages 266 and 411. R.L. Streater collection.

BURGER KING
AC
O.F.R.A
BP
GOODYEAR
DEKALB
NOVELTY
LURE
COLLECTORS
1996

An Advertising Novelty Lure collection.
A collection like this can be a lot of fun to accumulate, many of the lures were given free as premiums or as part of a sales promotion. Others were sold by mail order or in novelty gift shops. $5.00 – 25.00. R.L. Streater collection.

MOSQUITO CHASER
ANTI SKEETER
FLIT LOTION
ANTI SKEETER TALC
SKEETER CHASER
MOSQUITO LOTION
GREEN-O
ED'S NO. 1-A HEADNET
ED. CUMINGS, INC.
SKAT
SPRAYER
FLAG
GREEN-O
SHU-BUG
NO-MO SKEETS
INSECT REPELLENT
COACHELLA VALLEY MOSQUITO ABATEMENT DISTRICT
Skram
INSECT REPELLENT
SHU-BUG

A partial display of the Streater Mosquito Repellent Collection. A lot of these can be found in the bottoms of old tackle boxes and in old lake cabins. Anything bug related would qualify; note the head net and sprayer, along with creams, lotions, and burnable scented sticks.
Collecting mosquito stuff is a relatively new thing and values are hard to assess. A base of $5.00 and a top end in the $25.00 to $35.00 range would seem adequate at this time as there is no way to know how rare or scarce the various items are. As in lures and tackle, having the original box would add to the value.

Shur Strike Minnows by Creek Chub Bait Co.
In the late 1920s up until the 1970s, there was real need for lower priced baits. Paw Paw was turning out low cost baits. So Bend made their "Best-O-Luck line," and Pflueger made three different price levels, so Creek Chub created the Shur Strikes. Most literature we have found indicated that CCB Co. didn't want to publicize their tie-in with Shur Strike and just used numbers for ID of their baits. They did use distinctive colors not used by CCBCo. so we were able to gradually assemble the full picture. The names assigned were done by collectors, and in many cases, by R.L. Streater. They also made lures for private label companies such as Sears Roebuck, Western Auto, Herter, Uncle Tom, and Gateway. The four main boxes are shown plus the Gateway box. The original background for the display was a Shur Strike Dealer Counter Card. R.L. Streater collection.

SHUR-STRIKE MINNOWS
SHUR-STRIKE
LOW IN PRICE
MINNOWS
HIGH IN QUALITY
"Catch the Fish"
SHUR-STRIKE MINNOWS
"CATCH THE FISH"
SHUR-STRIKE MINNOWS
SHUR-STRIKE
minnows

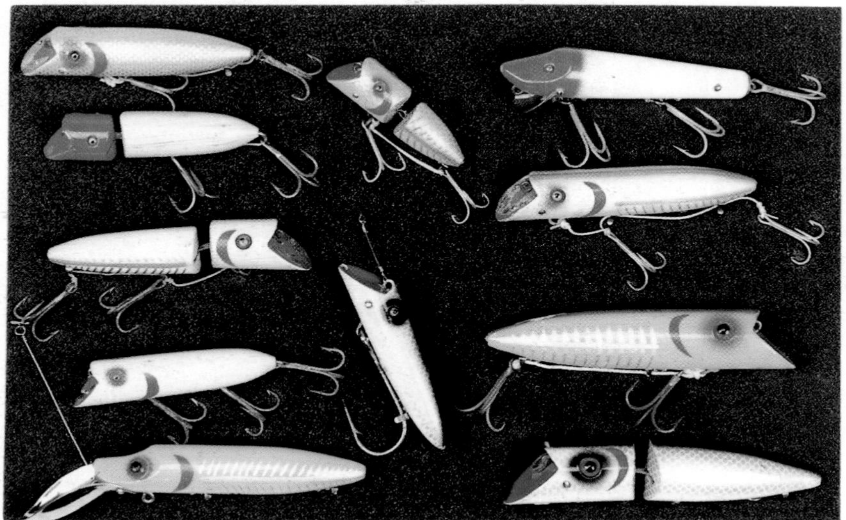

The Heddon "Salmon Salts" collection
The Northwest Salmon Plug has a unique place in fishing history and thus lure collection also. This photo shows Heddon's attempt to get a piece of the action by modifying their existing plugs with H.D. Hook Rigs specifically for salmon fishing. Shown here are the Heddon Bassers, Zig-Wags, King Bassers, King Zig-Wags, Great Vamp, and the Salmon River Runt. Note the special colors for salmon fishing. When one of these plugs shows up in a color like Pike or Perch, it is tougher to find and more valuable to color collectors. $40.00 – 150.00. See pages 169, 172 – 174, 184, 189 – 191. R.L. Streater collection.

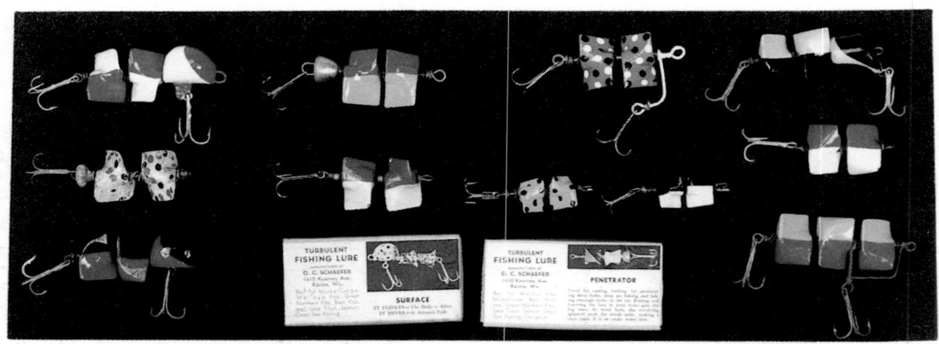
TURBULENT
FISHING LURE
O. C. SCHAEFER
SURFACE
TURBULENT
FISHING LURE
O. C. SCHAEFER
PENETRATOR

The Turbulent Fishing Lures, by O.C. Schaefer, Racine, Wisconsin
These handpainted and hand carved lures featured counter-rotating sections to create the fish attraction "turbulence." There is no name printed on these lures, but their shape and color are an easy identifier. $40.00 – 75.00. See page 359. R.L. Streater collection.

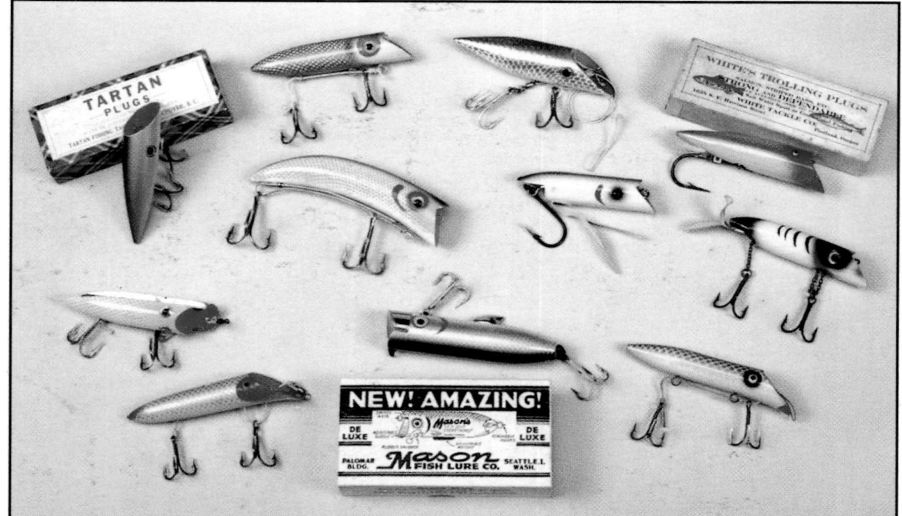
TARTAN
PLUGS
WHITE'S TROLLING PLUGS
WHITE TACKLE CO.
NEW! AMAZING!
DE LUXE
DE LUXE
PALOMAR BLDG.
Mason
FISH LURE CO.
SEATTLE I, WASH.

Northwest Salmon Plugs
This photo shows some of the more distinctive salmon lures made in Oregon, Washington, Alaska, and British Columbia, Canada. Much like Florida which had its own tackle makers, so did the Pacific Northwest. These plugs, along with the accompanying value guide are from the Jim Lone collection, Seattle, WA.
From top to bottom: Row A: Tartan Plug, Ross Reflecto, Harris; Row B: Derby, Nelson Banana, Mason Deluxe, Row C; Bill's Action, Perfect Action; Row D: White's Trolling, Lunker Lure, Presley.

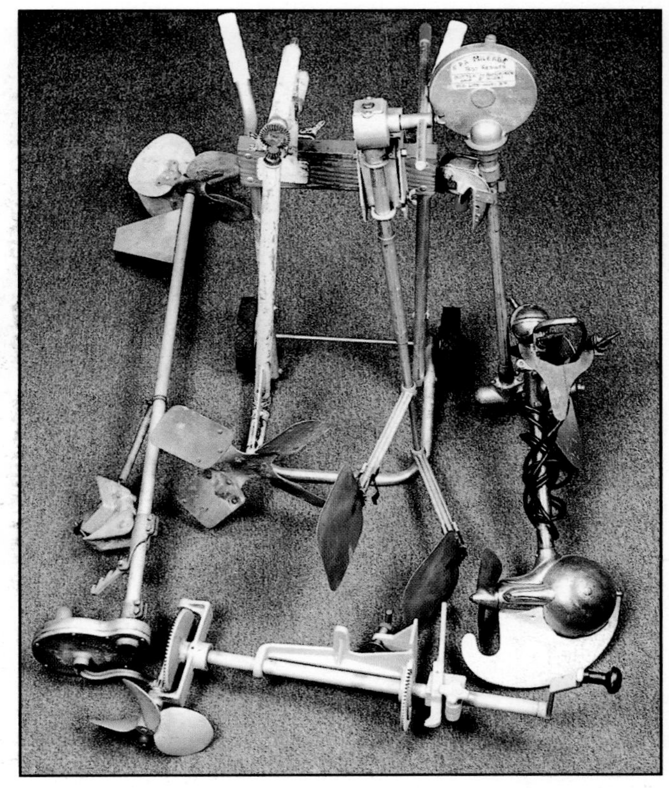

Hand or foot powered trolling motors, plus early electric
This is a new area for fishing collectors. Shown here are five motors: on the stand (left) is the Sanborn Troller, (right) The Twin Fins; on the floor (left) Bray's Silent Kreeper, (bottom) Handi-Troll, (right) Submerged Electric Motor (1902 patent). Most motors of this type were made in the late 1930s and then again after the end of W.W. II. R.L. Streater collection.

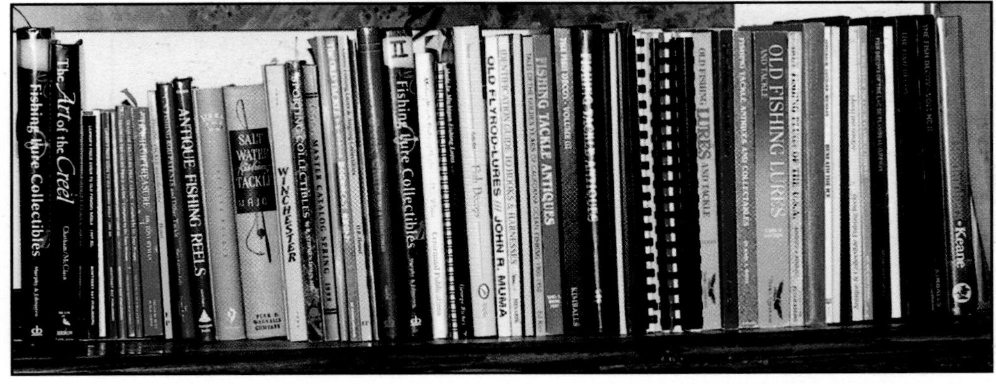
Fishing Lure Collectibles
The Art of the Creel
ANTIQUE FISHING REELS
WINCHESTER
Fishing Lure Collectibles
FISHING TACKLE ANTIQUES
OLD FISHING LURES
OLD FISHING LURES AND TACKLE
Keane

Knowledge is the key — over 50 books on antique and collectible fishing tackle.

NFLCC
1995
COLLECTORS
NFLCC
1995
TACKLE
COLLECTORS
NFLCC
1995
TACKLE
COLLECTORS

The Jamison Coaxer is a true classic collectible. Patent applied for on April 18, 1904, and awarded on January 3, 1905. A white cork body with red feathers or bucktail with felt ears was the most common model. The tougher colors are frog, aluminum, and all red. See pages 215 – 216. R.L. Streater collection.

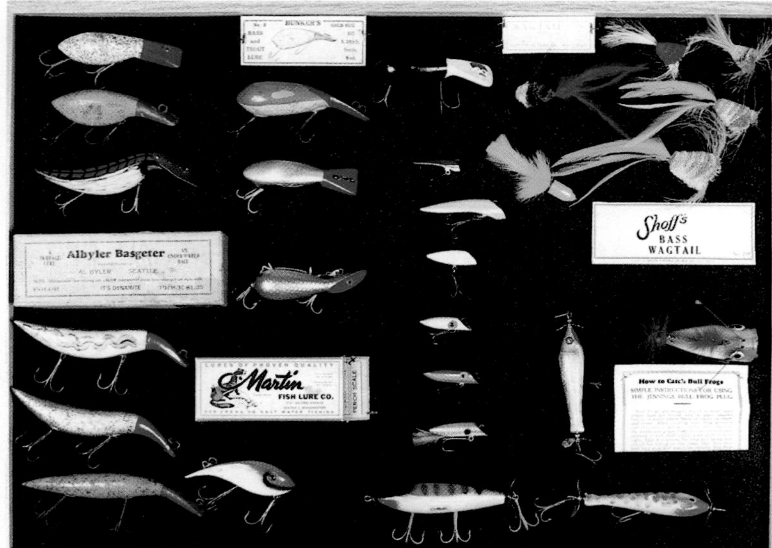
Albyler Basgeter
Shoff's
BASS
WAGTAIL
Martin
FISH LURE CO.
How to Catch Bull Frogs

Made in Washington state lure collection
This is a great idea for any collector, collect the lures and tackle made in your own home state. They should be easier to find and less expensive than the lures that are sought after nationally. This photo features Washington-made lures by Al Byler, Martin Tackle Co., Clarence Shoff Tackle Co., Bunker Lures, and Dr. Jennings Baits. $10.00 – 75.00. R.L Streater collection.

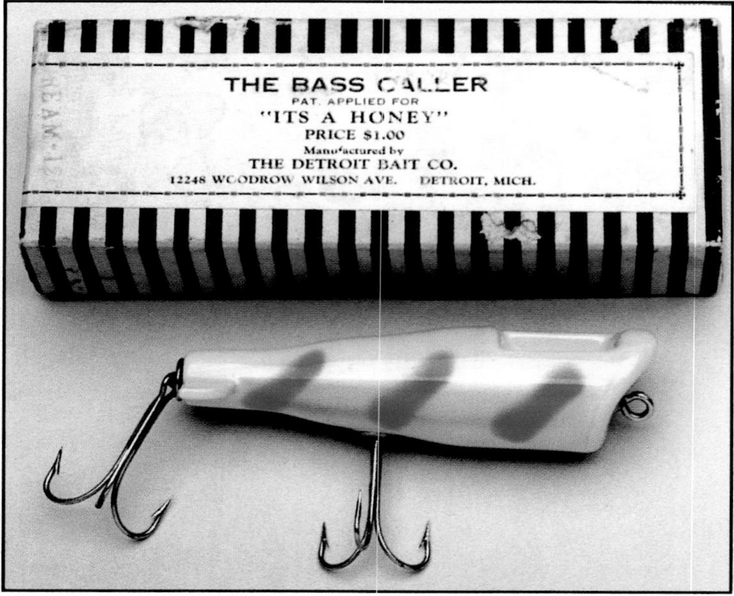
THE BASS CALLER
PAT. APPLIED FOR
"ITS A HONEY"
PRICE $1.00
Manufactured by
THE DETROIT BAIT CO.
12248 WOODROW WILSON AVE. DETROIT, MICH.

Bass Caller with original box, Detroit Bait Co., 1940s– 1950s. See page 135.

THE HEAD ROTATES
VAUGHN'S LURE
VAUGHN TACKLE COMPANY
CHEBOYGAN, MICHIGAN
PATENT PEND.
Price 1.20

Vaughn's Lure with original box, Vaughn Tackle Co., c. 1940s – 1950s. See page 428.

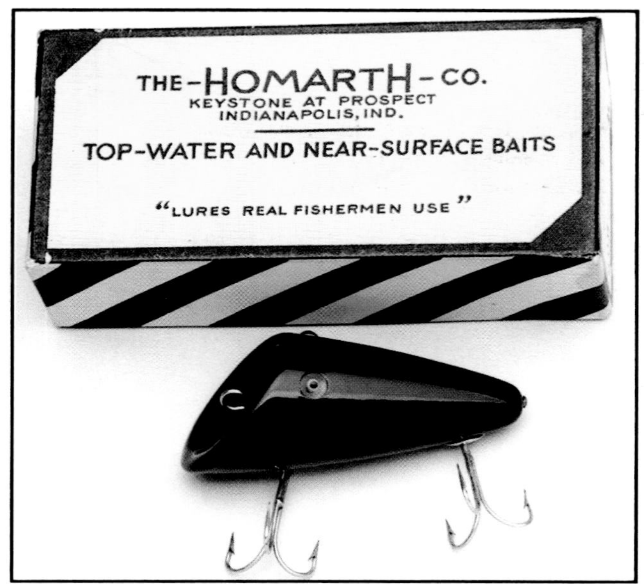
THE-HOMARTH-CO.
KEYSTONE AT PROSPECT
INDIANAPOLIS, IND.
TOP-WATER AND NEAR-SURFACE BAITS
"LURES REAL FISHERMEN USE"

Homarth Bait with original box, c. 1935.

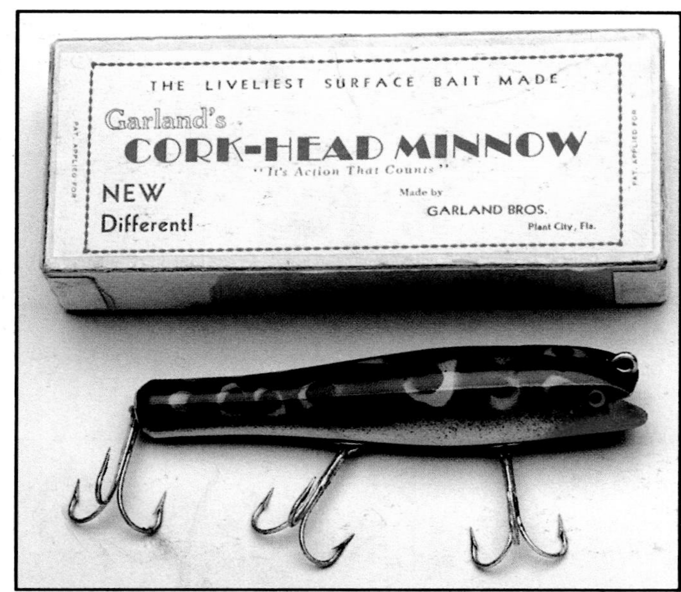
THE LIVELIEST SURFACE BAIT MADE
Garland's
CORK-HEAD MINNOW
"It's Action That Counts"
NEW
Different!
Made by
GARLAND BROS.
Plant City, Fla.

Cork-Head Minnow "Darter," with original box, c. 1936. See page 155.

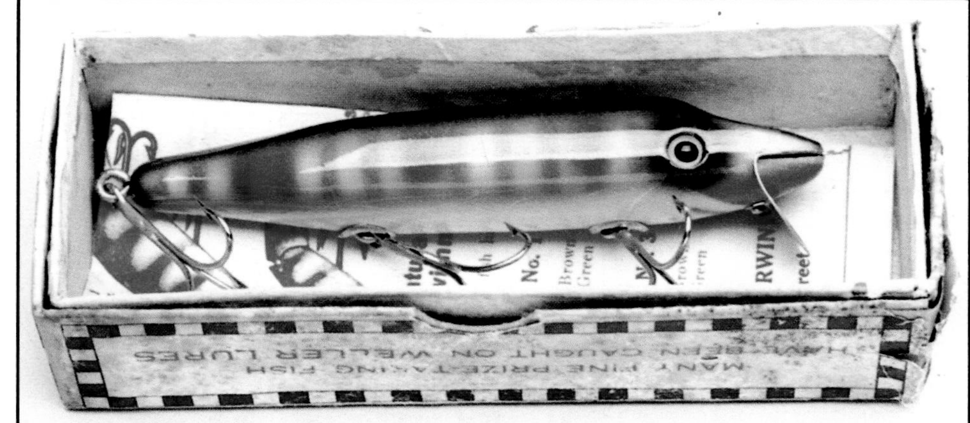
MANY FINE PRIZE-TAKING FISH
HAVE BEEN CAUGHT ON WELLER LURES

Weller Minnow with original box, Erwin Weller Co. See pages 445 – 446.

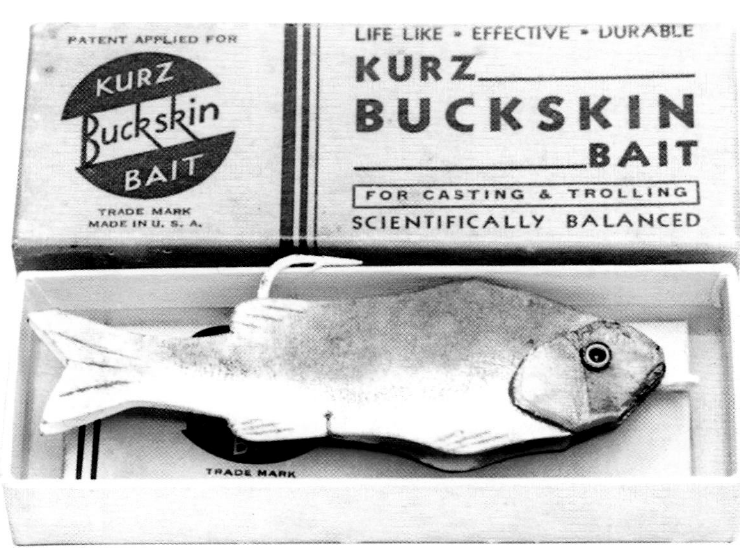
PATENT APPLIED FOR
KURZ
Buckskin
BAIT
TRADE MARK
MADE IN U. S. A.
LIFE LIKE • EFFECTIVE • DURABLE
KURZ
BUCKSKIN
BAIT
FOR CASTING & TROLLING
SCIENTIFICALLY BALANCED
TRADE MARK

Kurz Buckskin Bait with original box, c. 1940s – 1950s. See page 243.

Fish Spotter, A.J. Kumm, 1933. See page 237.

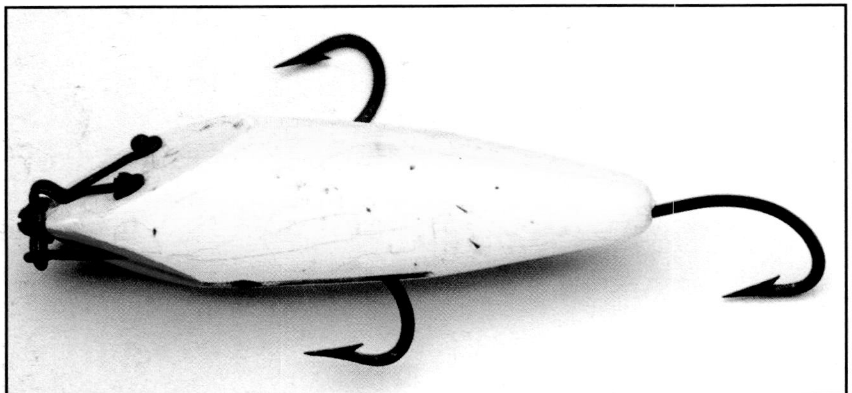

Woggle Bug, Payne Bait Co., c. 1915. See page 339.

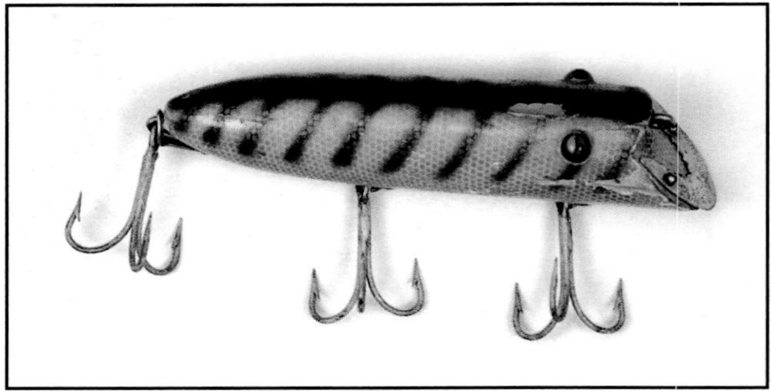

Heddon Basser, rare color, special order. See page 173.

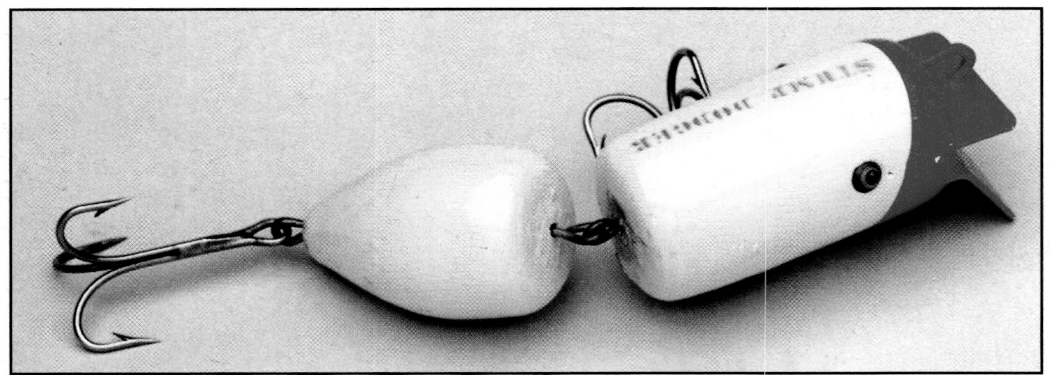

Rare jointed Musky Stump Dodger, c. 1914. See page 360.

Creek Chub
Nature Lures
Catch More Fish

Collection of CCBCo. lures, c. 1920s – 1950s. Fisherman's Spot collection. See pages 97 – 109.

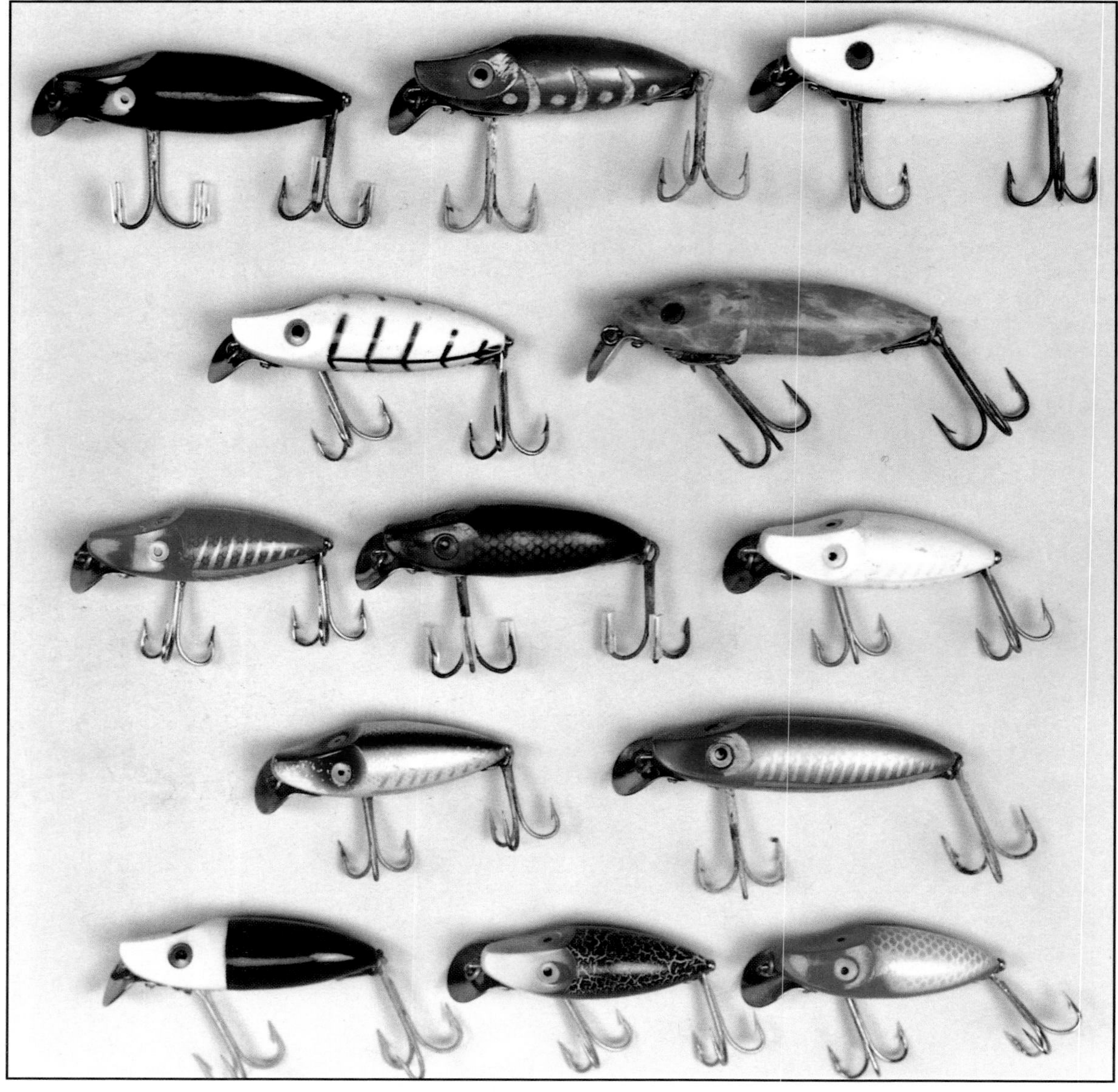

Heddon River Spooks – The Tough Colors

Heddon River Runt Spooks (plastic) are becoming a popular collectible. They were made for many years, in many models and sizes, with many colors. This makes them moderately easy to find, but how about the tough colors? They are for the most part uncataloged for River Runts. Above are photos and descriptions of the rare colors Runts have been found in. Because we don't know the color numbers, we have used color descriptions. (GE – gold eye), (DE – dark eye).

Top row: solid black, GE; glow worm, 2 pc., GE; solid white, 2 pc., DE.
2nd row: white, black ribs, GE; water wave, red/white mixed, 2 pc., DE.
3rd row: red scale/silver shore, GE; green scale, 2 pc., DE; white, green shore, WE.
4th row: blue back, white scale/silver shore, GE; blue back, white shore, 2 pc., GE.
5th row: white head/black, 2 pc., GE; slate crackle back, GE; Allen Stripey, GE.

1st row: gray scale, black gill, GE; fluorescent orange, GE.
2nd row: white scale, black dots, GE; fluorescent green, GE; fluorescent yellow, GE.
3rd row: black, white/yellow/red dots, GE; fluorescent orange red/black dots, GE; fluorescent purple, GE.
4th row: pearl white, GE; clear white scale, 2 pc., DE; no lip; salt, red/gold scale, GE.
5th row: this first lure is the #S-9400 series; silver-salmon-runt, scoop lip, bar rig w/split rings, white shore/red gill. This lure is almost always 100% shrunk-up; white, red eye and tail, 2 pc. GE; dace scale, 2 pc., GE. See page 183.

Some general observations about River Runt Spooks. The introduction year for the sinker was 1933. Because they were made from an unstable plastic, most if not all of them have disintegrated. The floater came along in 1935, with the same problem. The strangest color Heddon made was called the "Water Wave" (1938) in red and white, yellow and black, green and black, with the two colors swirled together. In 1950 Heddon got into fluorescent paints with the Spook-Ray colors. We find them today in what we call "pink shore" and another with a black head with yellow shore. Both are faded from their original bright colors and had the letters SR in front of the number. In 1951 they came out with the Spook Glow (SG) finishes, and added the Go-Deeper SG series in 1952. The four colors, fluorescent orange/yellow shore, fluorescent green/yellow shore, fluorescent yellow/silver shore, fluorescent red/black shore, were made just a couple of years. Conclusion: collect River Runt Spooks. There are lots of them, and you can either trade or buy. See pages 171 and 183.

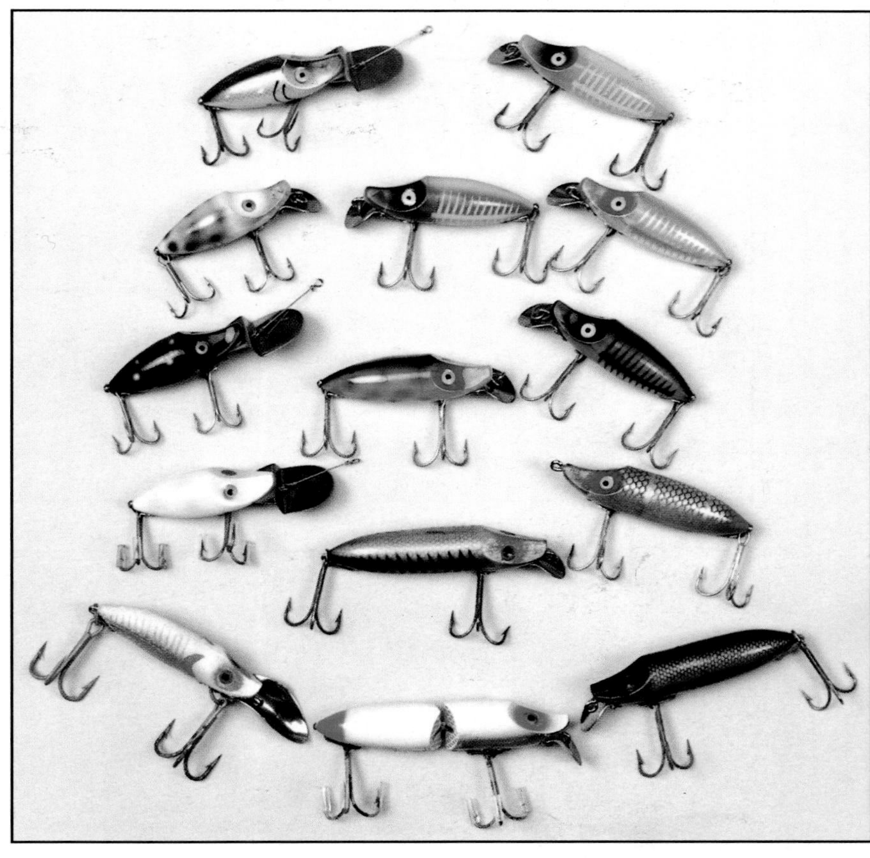

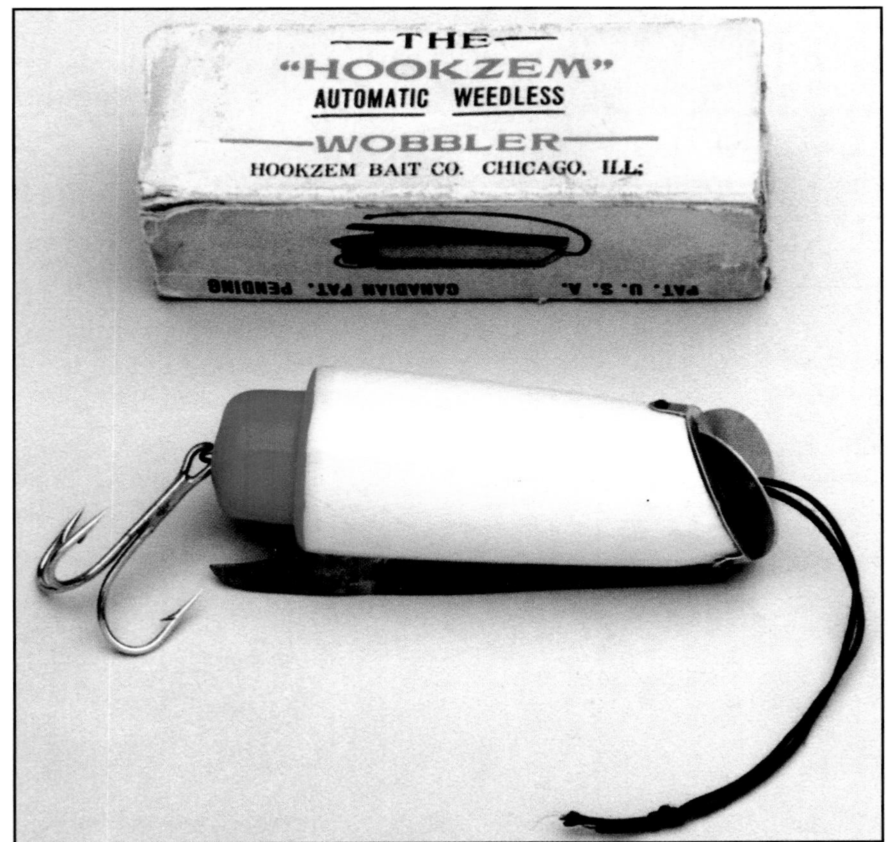
—THE—
"HOOKZEM"
AUTOMATIC WEEDLESS
—WOBBLER—
HOOKZEM BAIT CO. CHICAGO, ILL.
PAT. U. S. A.
CANADIAN PAT. PENDING

Hookzem Automatic Weedless Wobbler, c. 1922. See page 212.

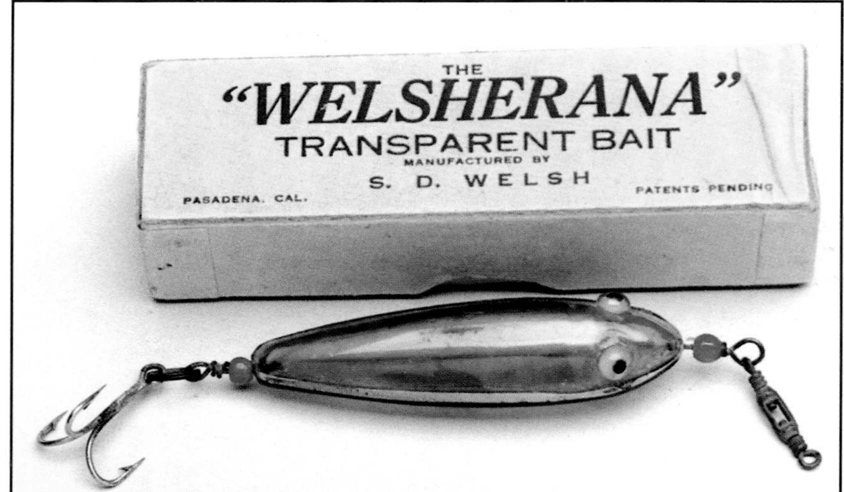
THE
"WELSHERANA"
TRANSPARENT BAIT
MANUFACTURED BY
S. D. WELSH
PASADENA, CAL.
PATENTS PENDING

Welsherana Bait with box, c. 1920s – 1940s. See pages 443 and 453.

OUTING MFG. CO.
Elkhart-Indiana
Outing's
Getum - hollow metal
Lure
with detachable hooks
HOOK HOLDER

Outing's Getum Lure with box, c. 1925. See page 275.

EWERT'S ARTIFICIAL BAIT
That Incomparable, Reliable Game Fish Getter
THE REVOLVING WHEELS - AN AMERICAN TRIUMPH
Patented August 19, 1919
EWERT'S ARTIFICIAL BAIT
The Revolving Wheels — An American Triumph

"Ewert's Artificial Bait" with box, Walter Scott Ewert, c. 1919. See page 140.

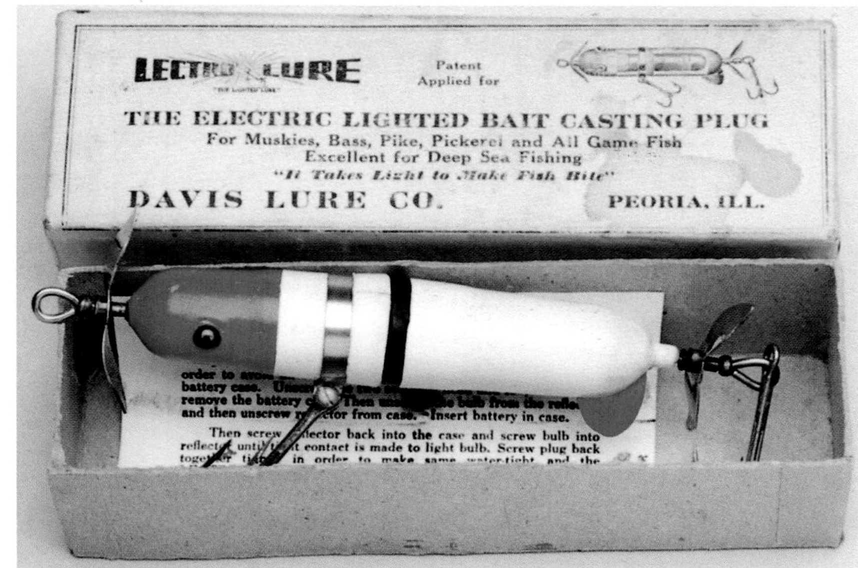
LECTRO LURE
Patent Applied for
THE ELECTRIC LIGHTED BAIT CASTING PLUG
For Muskies, Bass, Pike, Pickerel and All Game Fish
Excellent for Deep Sea Fishing
"It Takes Light to Make Fish Bite"
DAVIS LURE CO.
PEORIA, ILL.

Lectro Lure, Davis Lure Co., c. 1931. See page 133.

Pontiac Radium Minnow, Pontiac Manufacturing Co., c. 1909. See page 346.

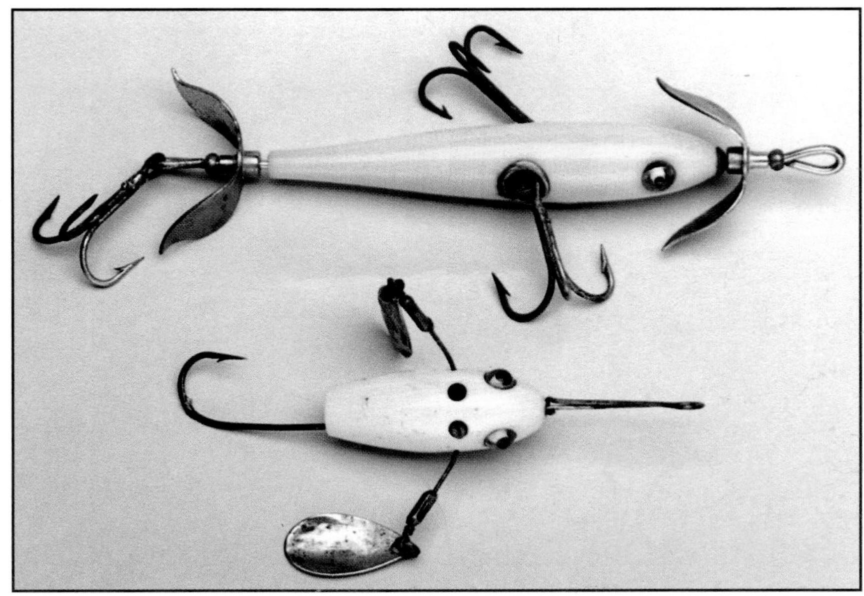

Top: Nixon Ivory Minnow, c. 1914. See page 272. Bottom: Unidentified bait bearing qualities typical of Nixon lures.

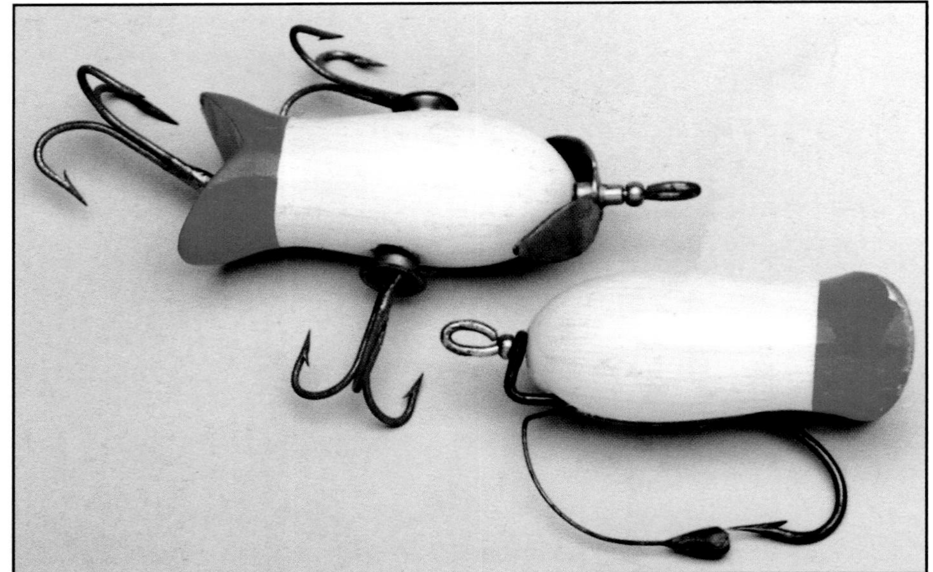

Top: Tooley's Spinnered Bunty, c. 1913; bottom: Tooley's Weedless Bunty, c. 1913, L.S. Tooley Co. See page 423.

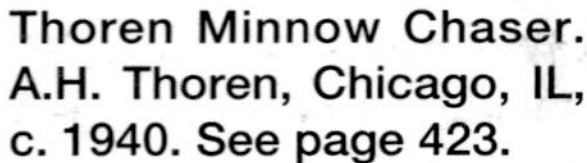

Thoren Minnow Chaser. A.H. Thoren, Chicago, IL, c. 1940. See page 423.

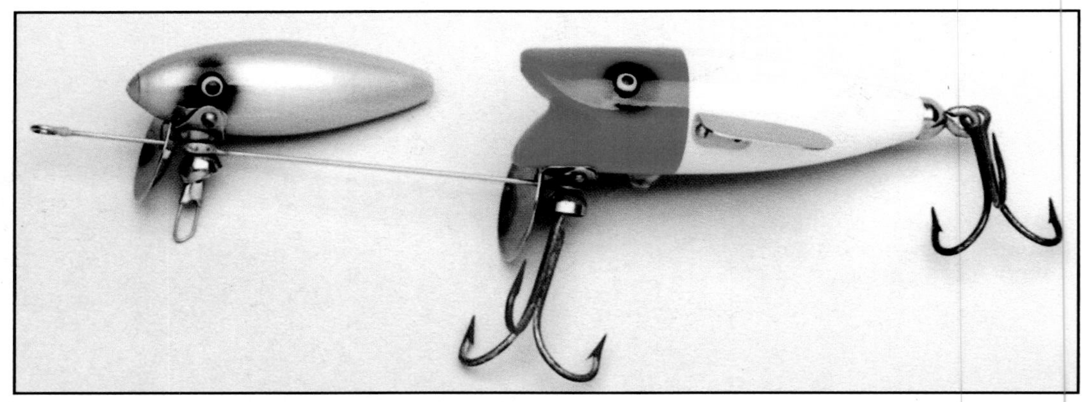

Top: Little Wonder, c. 1913; bottom: Champion Bait, c. 1912. See page 449.

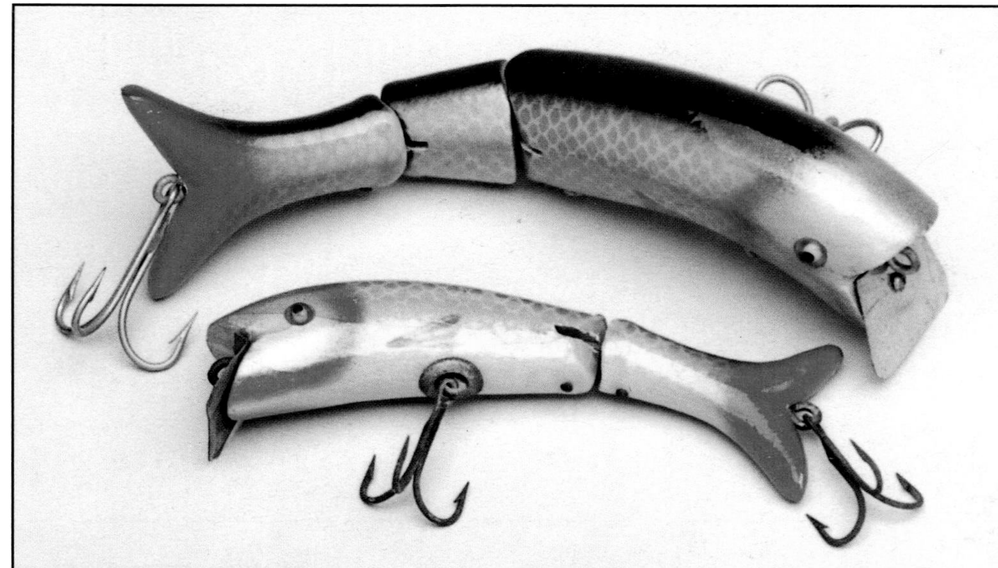

Goble Baits, Tulsa, OK, c. 1930.

Two 5-hook Winchester Minnows, Winchester Repeating Arms Co., c. 1921. Top lure features a realistic decal scale finish. See page 440.

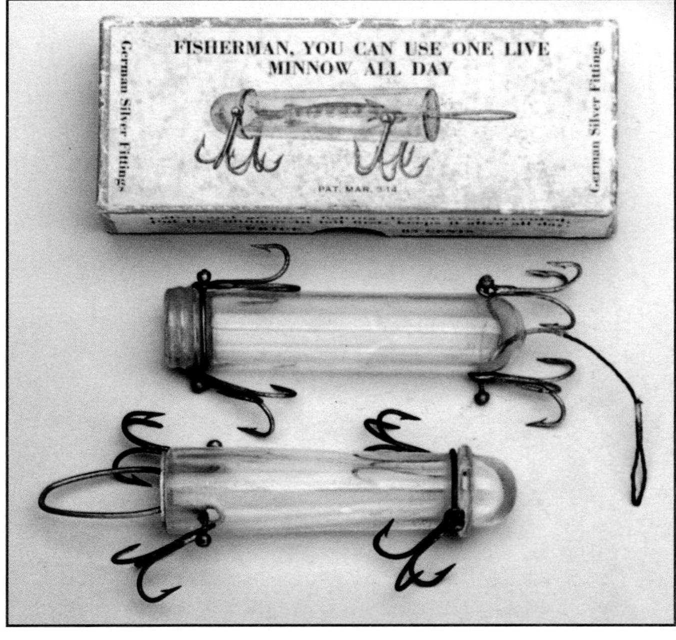
FISHERMAN, YOU CAN USE ONE LIVE
MINNOW ALL DAY
German Silver Fittings
German Silver Fittings

Detroit Glass Minnow Tube with box, c. 1914. See page 135.

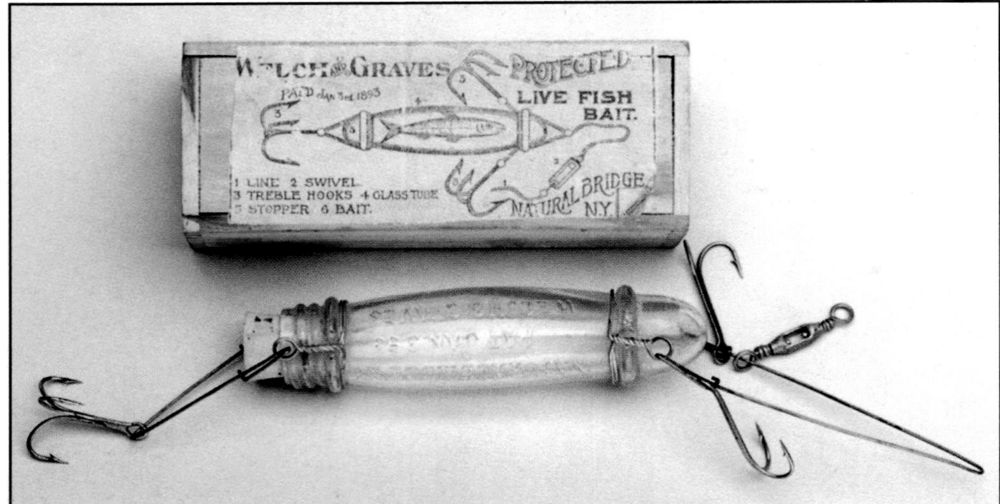
PROTECTED
LIVE FISH
BAIT.
1 LINE 2 SWIVEL
3 TREBLE HOOKS 4 GLASS TUBE
5 STOPPER 6 BAIT.
NATURAL BRIDGE
N.Y.

Welch and Graves glass minnow tube with box, c. 1893. See page 152.

Pfeiffer's Live Bait Holder with box, c. 1916. See page 339.

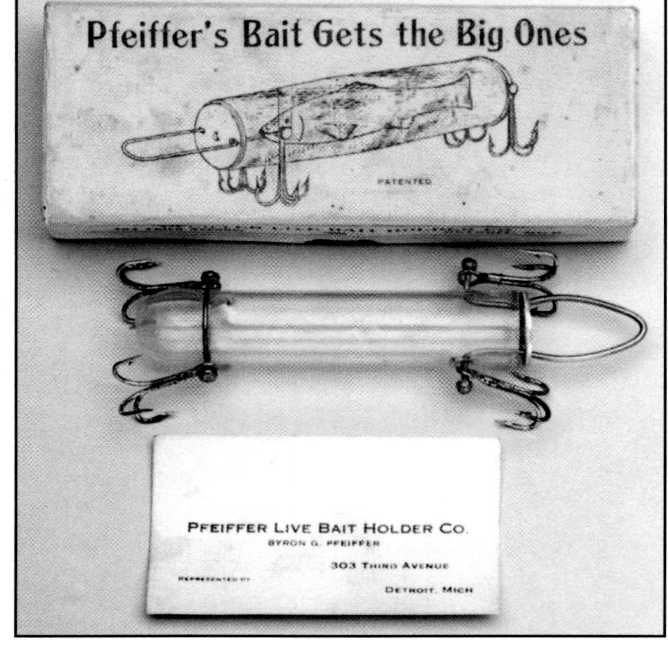
Pfeiffer's Bait Gets the Big Ones
PATENTED
PFEIFFER LIVE BAIT HOLDER CO.
BYRON G. PFEIFFER
303 THIRD AVENUE
DETROIT, MICH

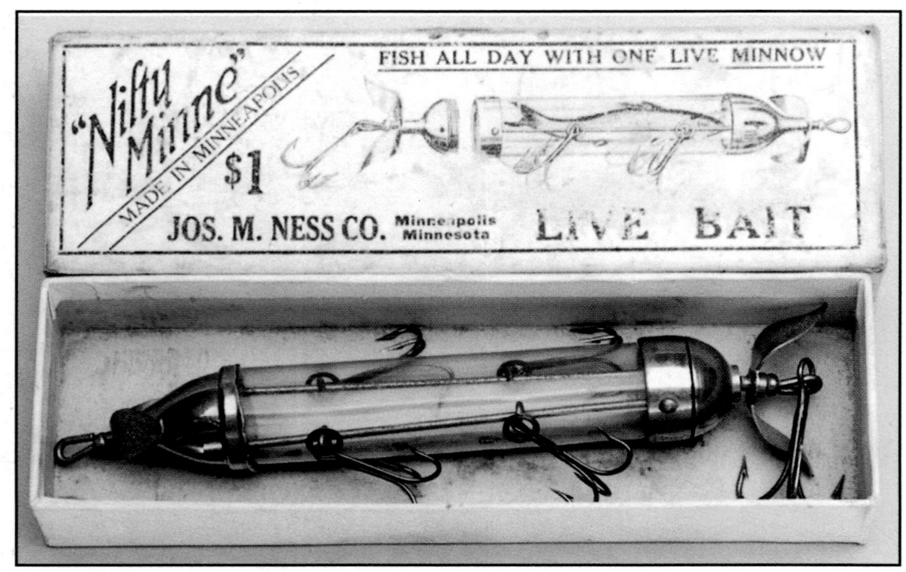
"Nifty Minne"
MADE IN MINNEAPOLIS
$1
FISH ALL DAY WITH ONE LIVE MINNOW
JOS. M. NESS CO. Minneapolis Minnesota
LIVE BAIT

Ness Nifty Minne with box, c. 1913. See pages 272 and 274.

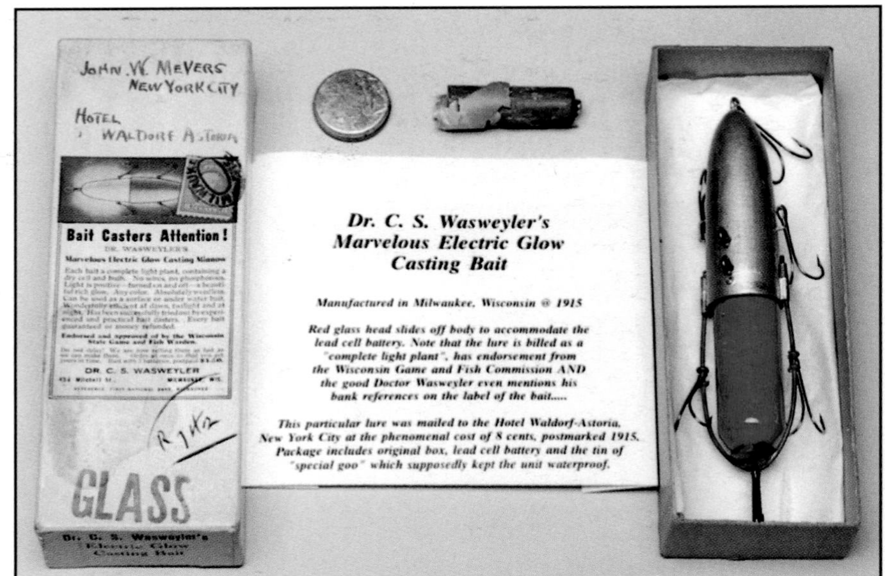
JOHN W. MEYERS
NEW YORK CITY
HOTEL
WALDORF ASTORIA
Bait Casters Attention!
DR. C. S. WASWEYLER
GLASS
Dr. C. S. Wasweyler's
Electric Glow
Casting Bait
Dr. C. S. Wasweyler's
Marvelous Electric Glow
Casting Bait
Manufactured in Milwaukee, Wisconsin @ 1915
Red glass head slides off body to accommodate the lead cell battery. Note that the lure is billed as a "complete light plant", has endorsement from the Wisconsin Game and Fish Commission AND the good Doctor Wasweyler even mentions his bank references on the label of the bait.....
This particular lure was mailed to the Hotel Waldorf-Astoria, New York City at the phenomenal cost of 8 cents, postmarked 1915. Package includes original box, lead cell battery and the tin of "special goo" which supposedly kept the unit waterproof.

Dr. Wasweyler's Marvelous Electric Glow Casting Minnow, c. 1915. See page 453.

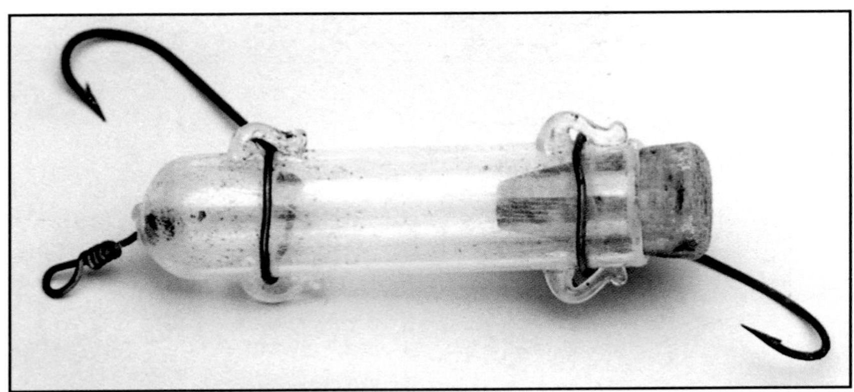

Nicely made unidentified glass minnow tube. Possibly homemade.

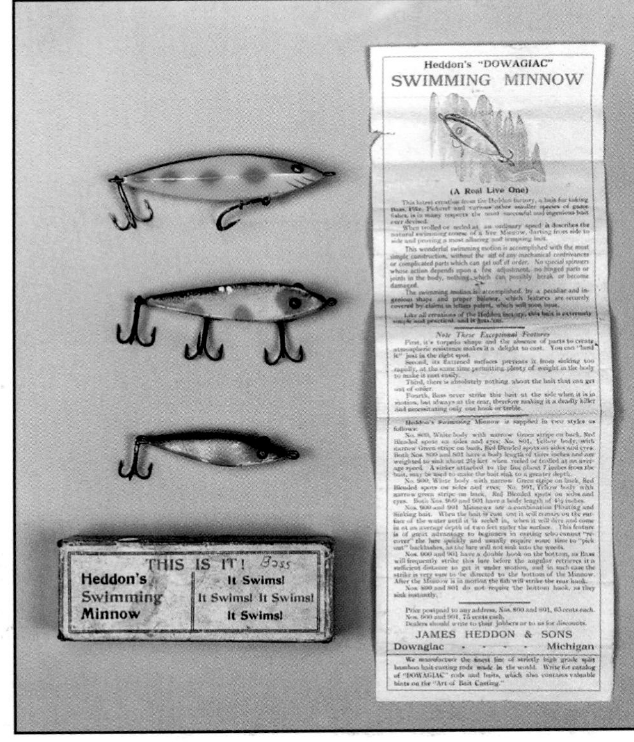
Heddon's "DOWAGIAC"
SWIMMING MINNOW
(A Real Live One)
JAMES HEDDON & SONS
Dowagiac - - - - Michigan
THIS IS IT!
Heddon's
Swimming
Minnow
It Swims!
It Swims! It Swims!
It Swims!

A Heddon 2550. When you have all three sizes of the Heddon Swimming Minnow, the 800 + the 850 + the 900 = 2550. Also adding to this great three-piece set is the very early original box and two-color brochure. See page 166. H.L. Musselman collection.

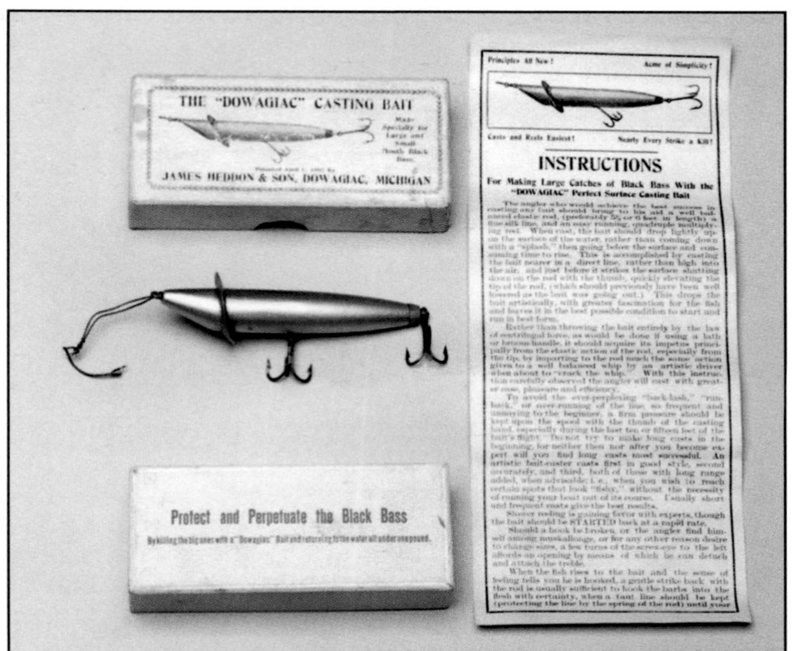
THE "DOWAGIAC" CASTING BAIT
JAMES HEDDON & SON, DOWAGIAC, MICHIGAN
INSTRUCTIONS
Protect and Perpetuate the Black Bass

Heddon Dowagiac Casting Bait, c. 1904. Aluminum paint finish is unusual. See pages 160 – 194.

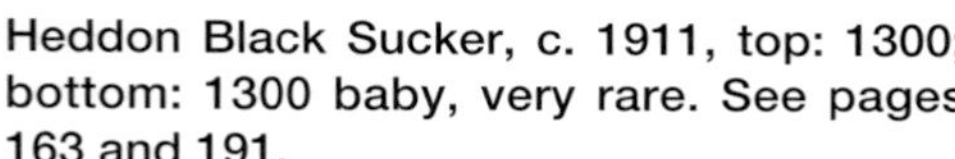

Heddon Black Sucker, c. 1911, top: 1300; bottom: 1300 baby, very rare. See pages 163 and 191.

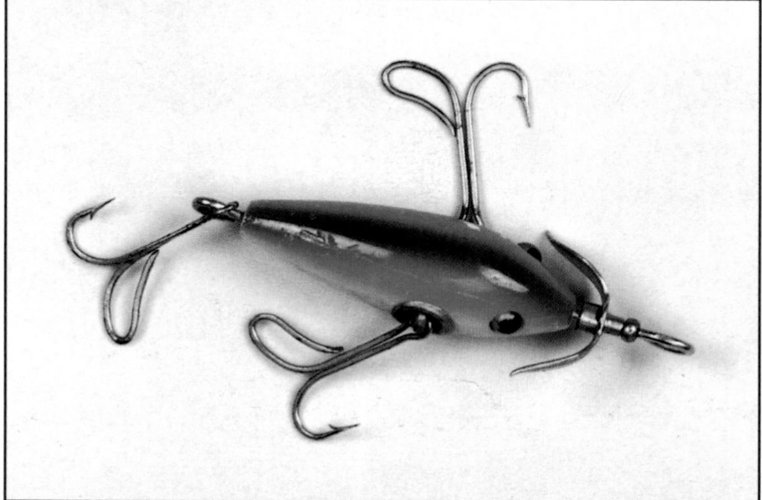

A very rare Heddon No. 20 Baby Dowagiac Minnow with smaller double dummy hooks. Rainbow color, cup rig, GE, name on prop. An observation by Streater: "If all the manufacturers printed complete catalogs with all the variations included, they would have used twice as much paper and ink as they did." See page 164.

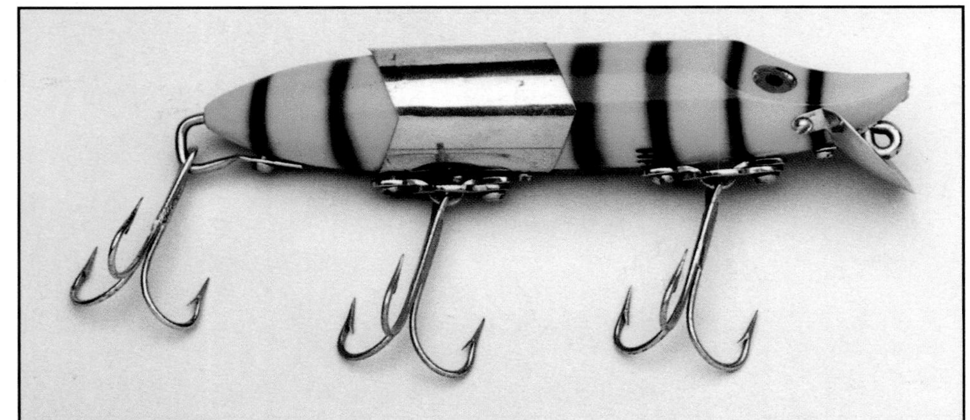

Heddon King-fish Vamp Spook, c. 1935. See page 171.

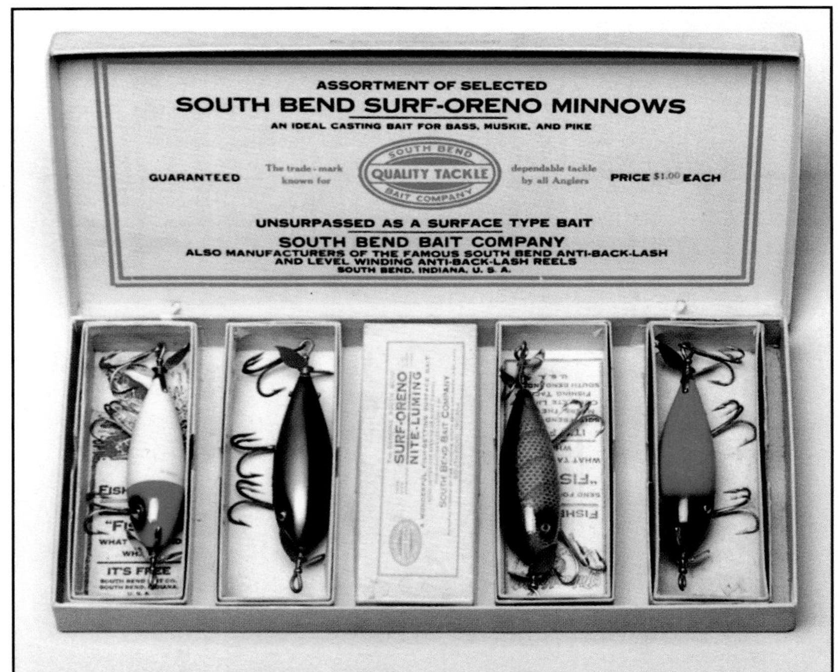
ASSORTMENT OF SELECTED
SOUTH BEND SURF-ORENO MINNOWS
AN IDEAL CASTING BAIT FOR BASS, MUSKIE, AND PIKE
GUARANTEED
The trade-mark known for
SOUTH BEND
QUALITY TACKLE
BAIT COMPANY
dependable tackle by all Anglers
PRICE $1.00 EACH
UNSURPASSED AS A SURFACE TYPE BAIT
SOUTH BEND BAIT COMPANY
ALSO MANUFACTURERS OF THE FAMOUS SOUTH BEND ANTI-BACK-LASH AND LEVEL WINDING ANTI-BACK-LASH REELS
SOUTH BEND, INDIANA, U. S. A.
SURF-ORENO
NITE-LUMINO
SOUTH BEND BAIT COMPANY

South Bend display, six-pack, (missing one box), c. 1928. See page 389.

SOUTH BEND
QUALITY TACKLE
BAIT COMPANY
THE GENUINE
SOUTH BEND MINNOW
FOR GAME FISH
MANUFACTURED EXCLUSIVELY BY
SOUTH BEND BAIT COMPANY
MANUFACTURERS OF THE FAMOUS SOUTH BEND ANTI-BACK-LASH REEL
SOUTH BEND, INDIANA

Uncataloged South Bend "Coast Minnow" type lure, c. 1926. See South Bend lures, pages 385 – 409.

South Bend Underwater Minnow, c. 1920s. This thin bodied version appears fo have been made for distribution by hardware companies. See pages 386 – 387.

"PFLUEGER BUCKTAIL"
BASS FLY

A color collection of Pflueger "Surprise" Minnows, c. 1915. See page 297.

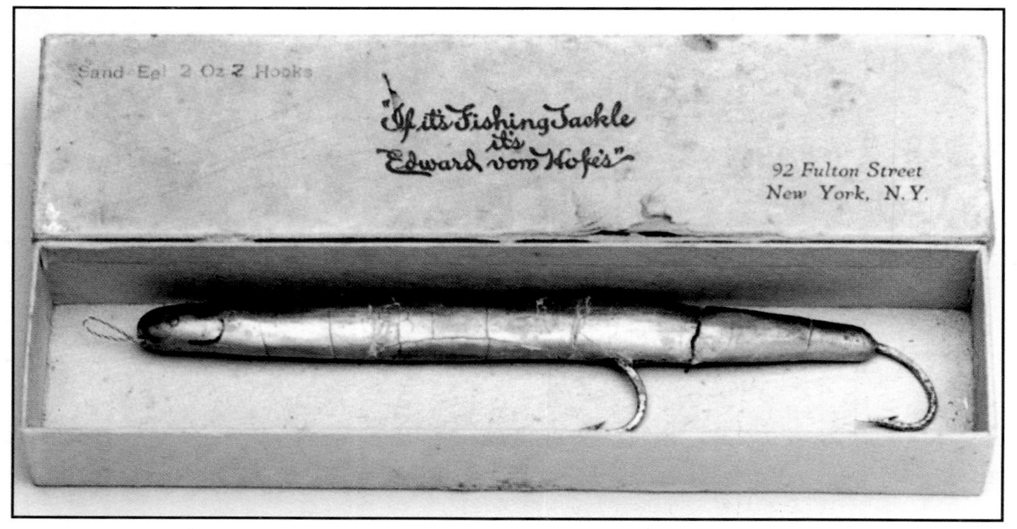
Sand Eel 2 Oz 2 Hooks
"If it's Fishing Tackle
it's
Edward vom Hofe's"
92 Fulton Street
New York, N.Y.

Sand Eel, Edward vom Hofe, c. 1920.

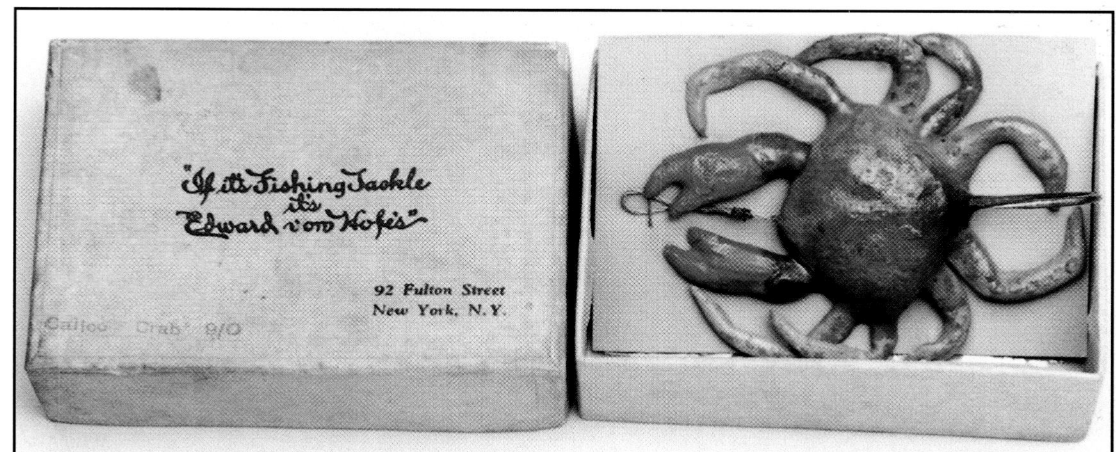
"If it's Fishing Tackle it's Edward vom Hofe's"
92 Fulton Street
New York, N.Y.
Calico Crab 9/0

Calico Crab, Edward vom Hofe, c. 1920.

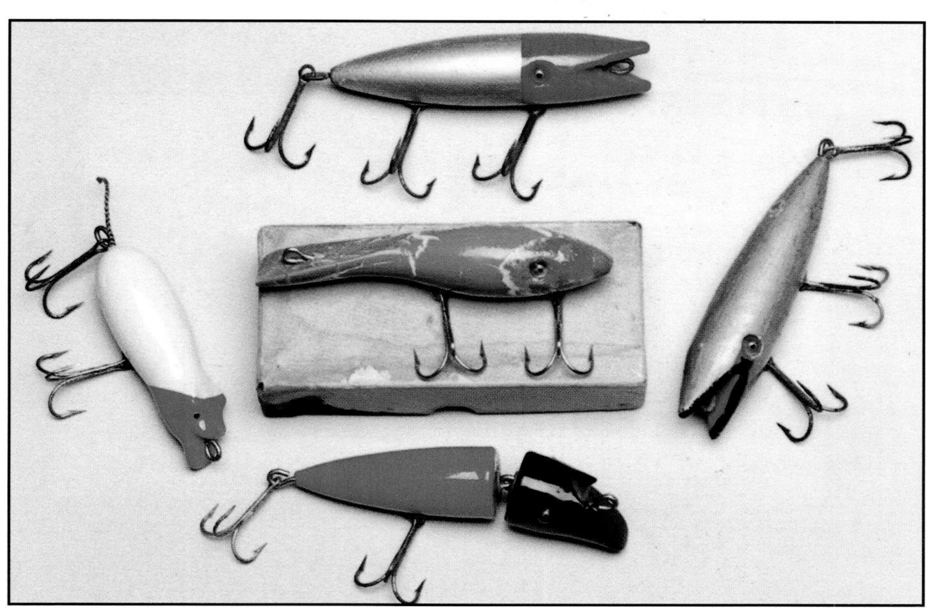

Lures made by the Winchester Bait and Mfg. Co., Winchester, IN, c. 1930. See page 442.

Maker's Name
Maker's Address
Mfg'r Name of Article MODEL PAKRON MINNOW
Stock No.
Size
Rec'd From H.K.
Address E.M.Co.
Date Rec'd
Per
JOB 16259
Filed in Dept.
E. M. CO. SAMPLE No.

Pflueger Pakron, Pflueger factory tag, c. 1925. See page 282.

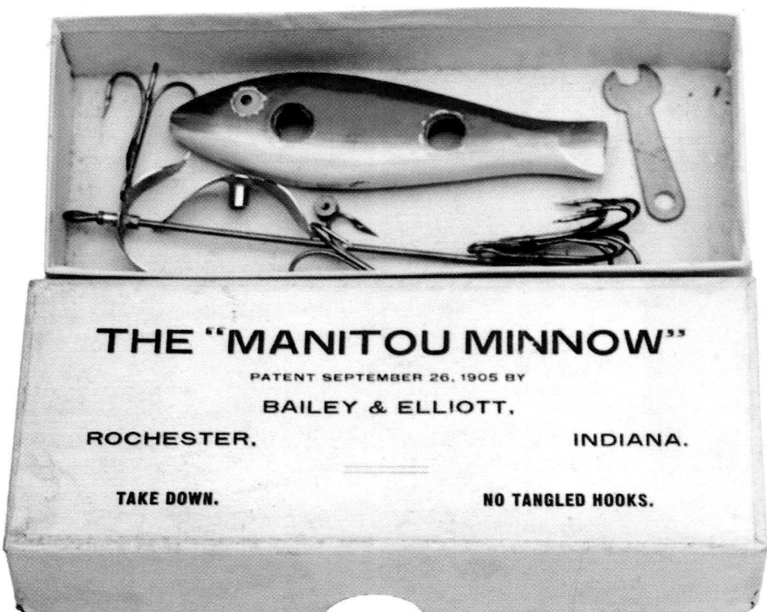
THE "MANITOU MINNOW"
PATENT SEPTEMBER 26, 1905 BY
BAILEY & ELLIOTT,
ROCHESTER, INDIANA.
TAKE DOWN.
NO TANGLED HOOKS.

"Manitou Minnow," with box and hook wrench, c. 1905. See page 67.

Folk art lures of high quality and workmanship, c. 1920 – 1930.

Jacobs Horse Fly, c. 1930. See page 224.

Fred Arbogast "Walleye", c. 1920 – 1930, top: Walleye Liz; center: Big Tin Liz; bottom: snake. See page 54.

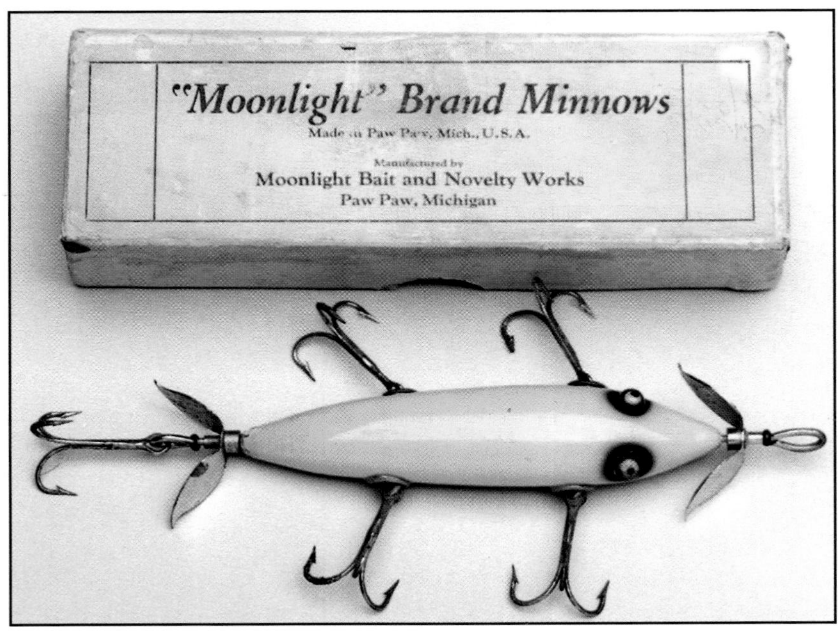
"Moonlight" Brand Minnows
Made in Paw Paw, Mich., U.S.A.
Manufactured by
Moonlight Bait and Novelty Works
Paw Paw, Michigan

Moonlight Floating Minnow #1200 with box, c. 1925. See page 254.

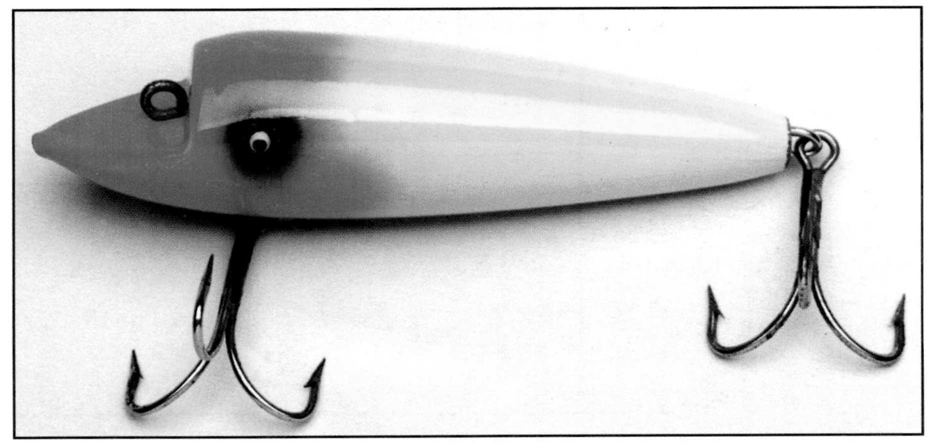

Musky size Little Wonder, Moonlight Bait Co., c. 1925. See page 253.

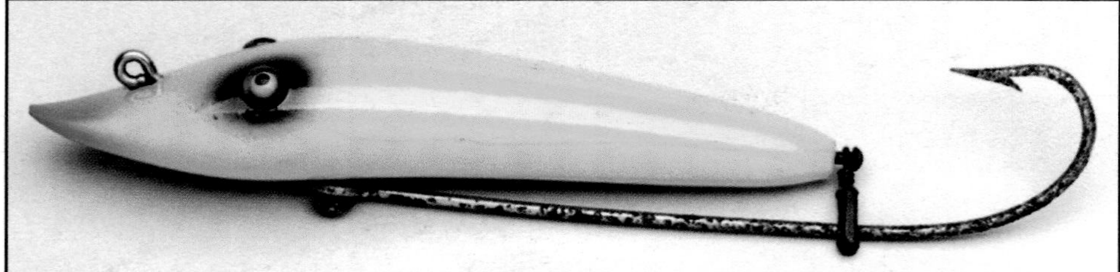

Moonlight #2500 single hook Pikaroon, c. 1923. See page 257.

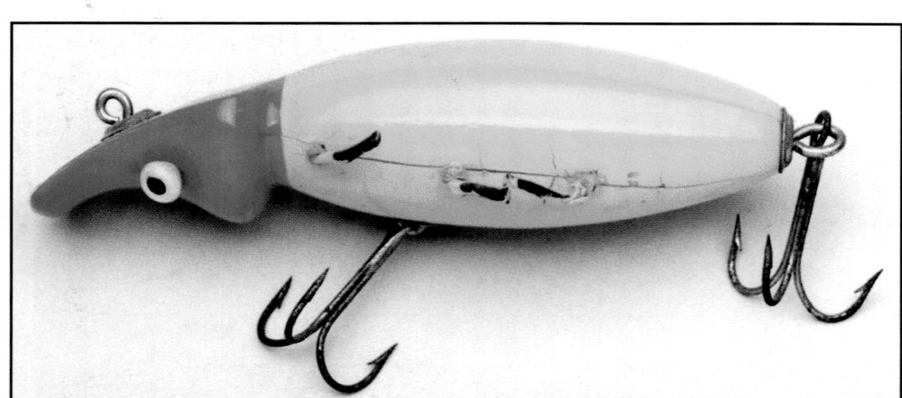

Moonlight Ladybug Wiggler, c. 1916. See page 252.

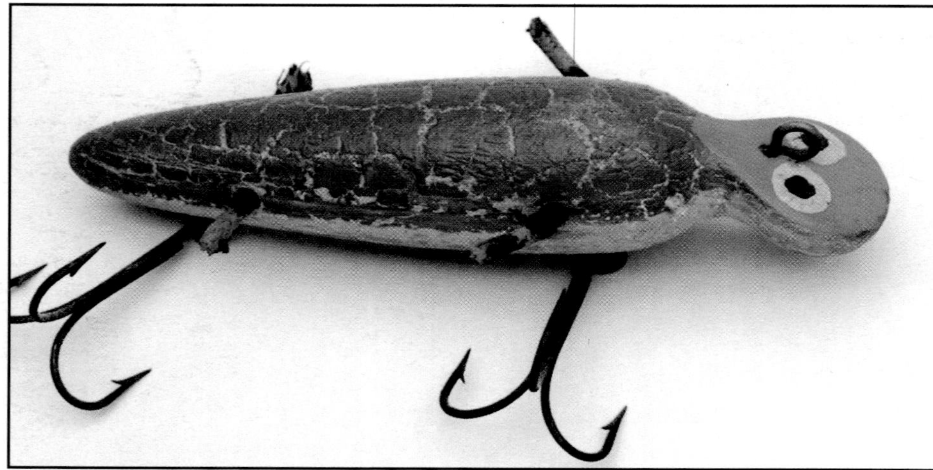

Pepper Roman Spider, Joe Pepper, Rome, NY, c. 1915. See pages 341 and 343.

THE HARKAUF

Harkauf Buck Tail Wooden Minnow, c. 1904. See page 213.

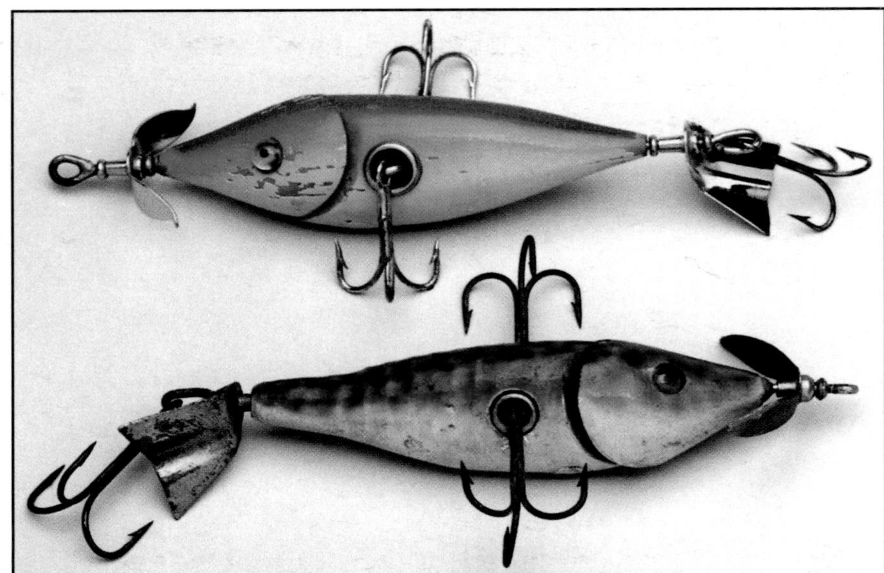

"Wilcox Wiggler," E.C. Campbell, top: Stage III; bottom: Stage II, c. 1907 – 1915.

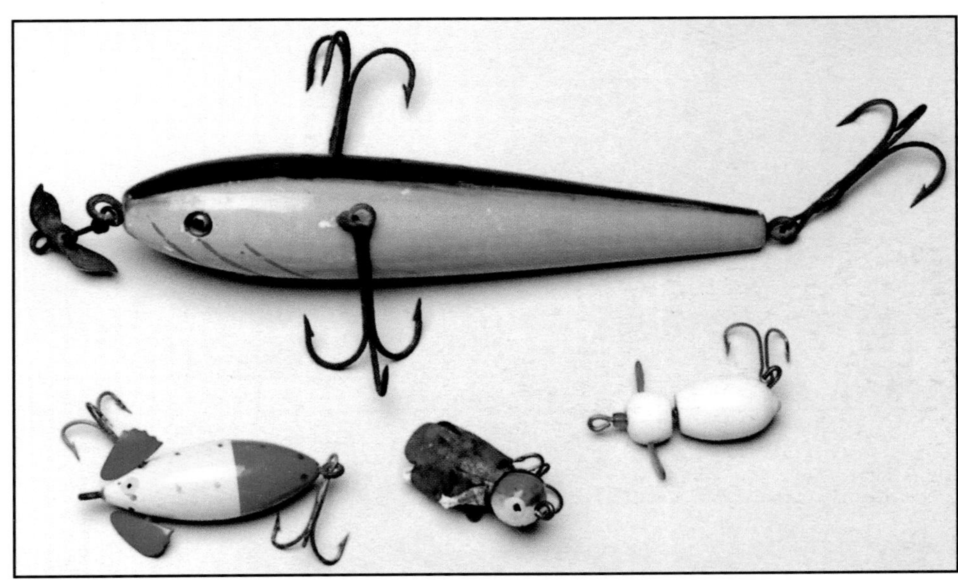

Top: 8" Musky; bottom left: Roman Diving Bait; center: Mystic Bug; bottom right: Floating Bass Bait. J. Pepper, Rome, NY, c. 1915 – 1920s. See pages 341 – 342.

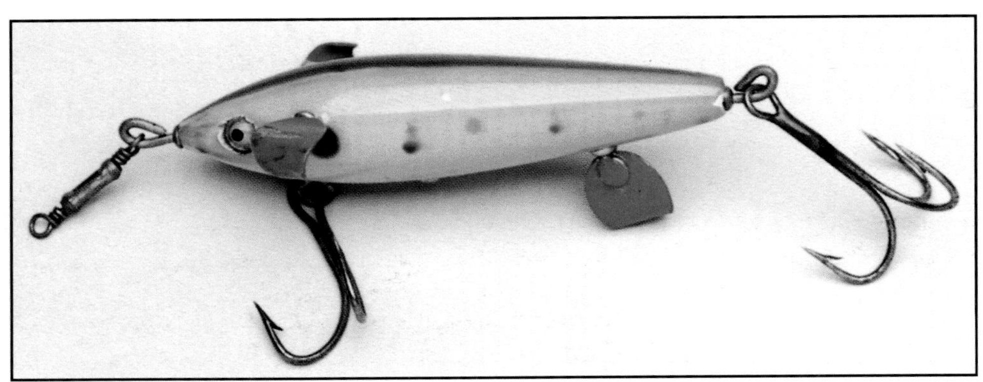

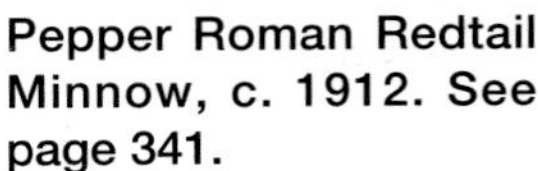

Pepper Roman Redtail Minnow, c. 1912. See page 341.

Green-Wyle Co., Klipon Minnow, c. 1930. Notice the unusual clip-on hook hangers. See page 156.

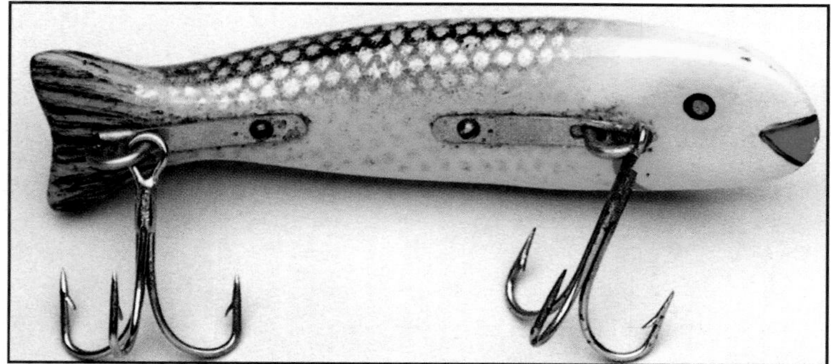

Klipon Minnow, c. 1930. See page 156.

William E. Davis lures, c. 1909, top: Ideal Minnow; bottom: Jersey Expert. See pages 132 and 223.

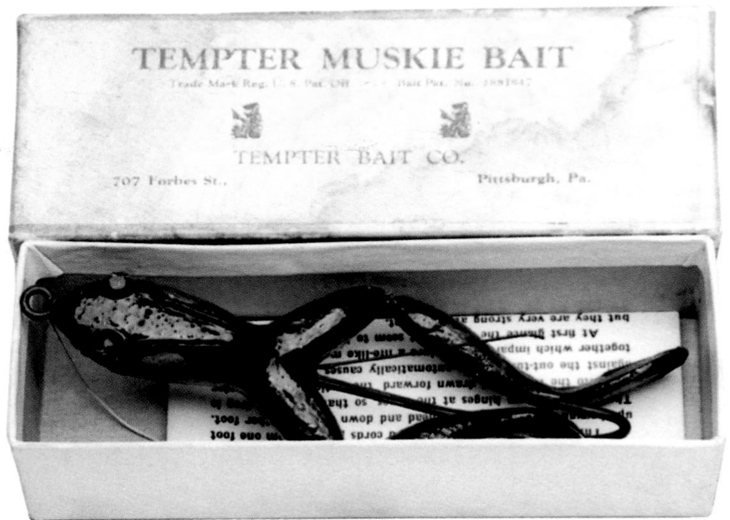
TEMPTER MUSKIE BAIT
TEMPTER BAIT CO.
707 Forbes St.
Pittsburgh, Pa.

Tempter muskie frog, c. 1928. See page 354.

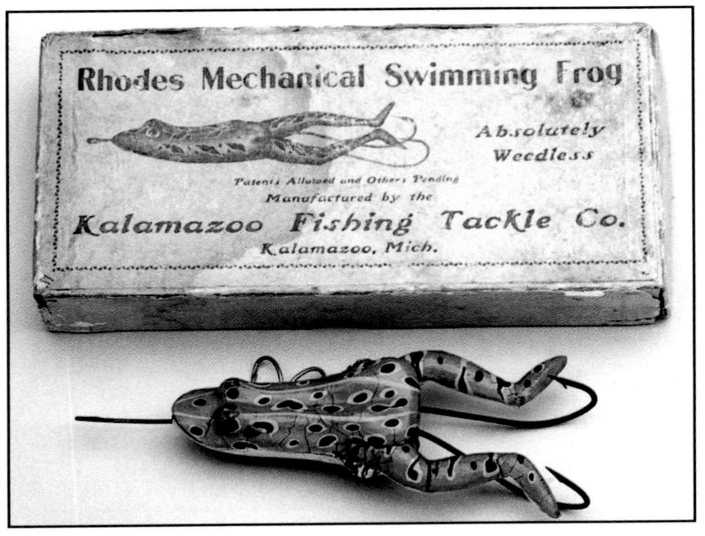
Rhodes Mechanical Swimming Frog
Absolutely Weedless
Patents Allowed and Others Pending
Manufactured by the
Kalamazoo Fishing Tackle Co.
Kalamazoo, Mich.

Rhodes Mechanical Swimming Frog, c. 1906. See pages 369 and 378.

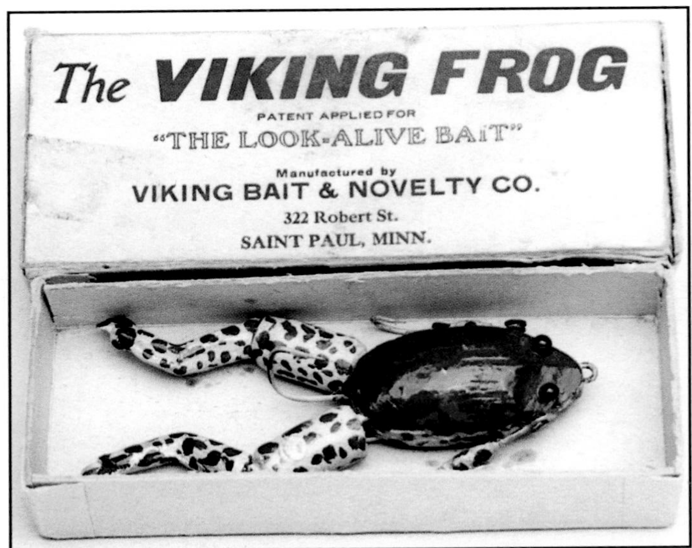
The VIKING FROG
PATENT APPLIED FOR
"THE LOOK-ALIVE BAIT"
Manufactured by
VIKING BAIT & NOVELTY CO.
322 Robert St.
SAINT PAUL, MINN.

Viking Frog with box, c. 1920.

HASTING'S
WEEDLESS RUBBER FROG
HOLLOW SOFT RUBBER
Absolutely Weedless
The only Pure Rubber Frog made. Painted in exact imitation of meadow frog. A great bait for all game fish. Can be used as surface or underwater bait. For underwater use, hold frog under water and squeeze out the air, and the frog will fill with water.
Manufactured only by THE W. J. JAMISON CO., Chicago, Ill.

Hastings Weedless Rubber Frog, W.J. Jamison Co., c. 1915. See page 217.

Can anyone identify this beautiful frog?

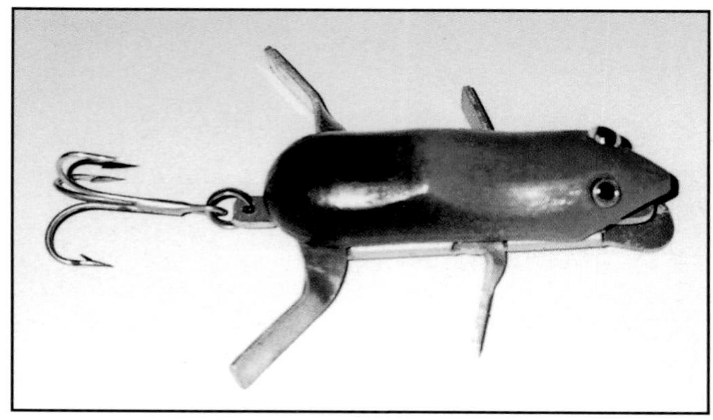

Keen Kicker Frog, H.O. Kuehn, Detroit, MI, 2" body, Keen Kicker Pat. Pend. on belly, c. 1932. Frank Baron collection, Livonia, MI.

Unknown composition material frog, c. 1930s, Michigan area? Frank Baron collection, Livonia, MI.

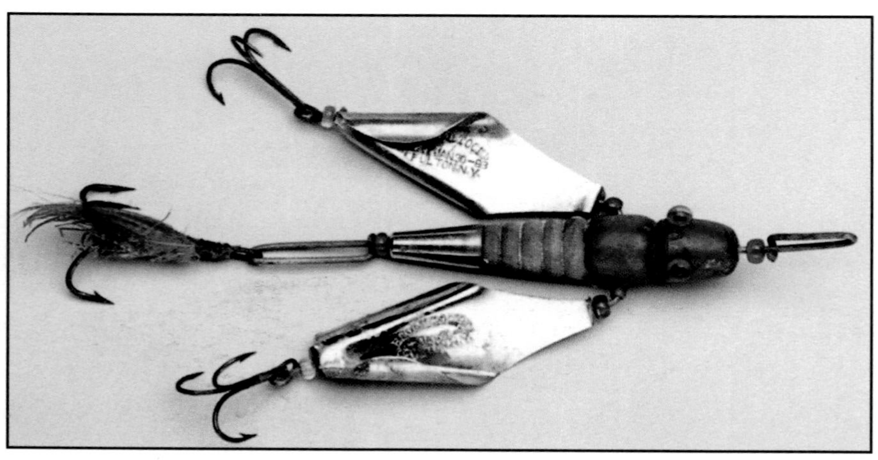

"Flying Helgramite," Harry Comstock, c. 1880s. See pages 114 and 292.

Bonafide Aluminum Minnow, Bonafide Mfg. Co., c. 1908. See page 70.

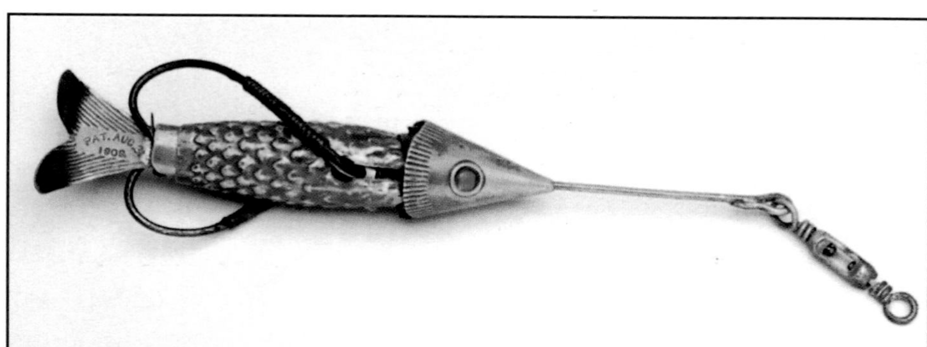
PAT. AUG.
1908

Chautauqua Trolling Hook, hollow metal with painted eyes, A.J. Krantz and G.E. Smith, Jamestown, NY, c. 1909. See page 241.

Pflueger May Bug Spoon, c. 1890. See page 289.

Haskell Minnow, Riley Haskell, Painesville, Ohio, c. 1859. See page 211.

Burgess Artificial Minnow, c. 1910 – 1915, broken rear hook. See page 68.

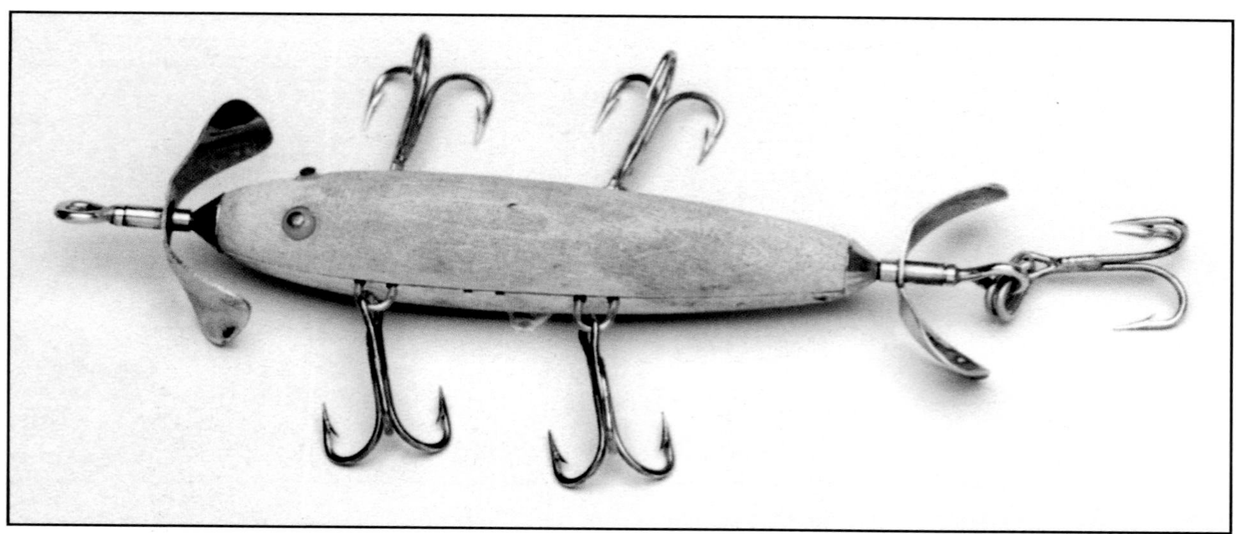

Ackerman Minnow, elaborate rare minnow, J.L. Ackerman, Monticello, IN, c. 1906. Sold unpainted.

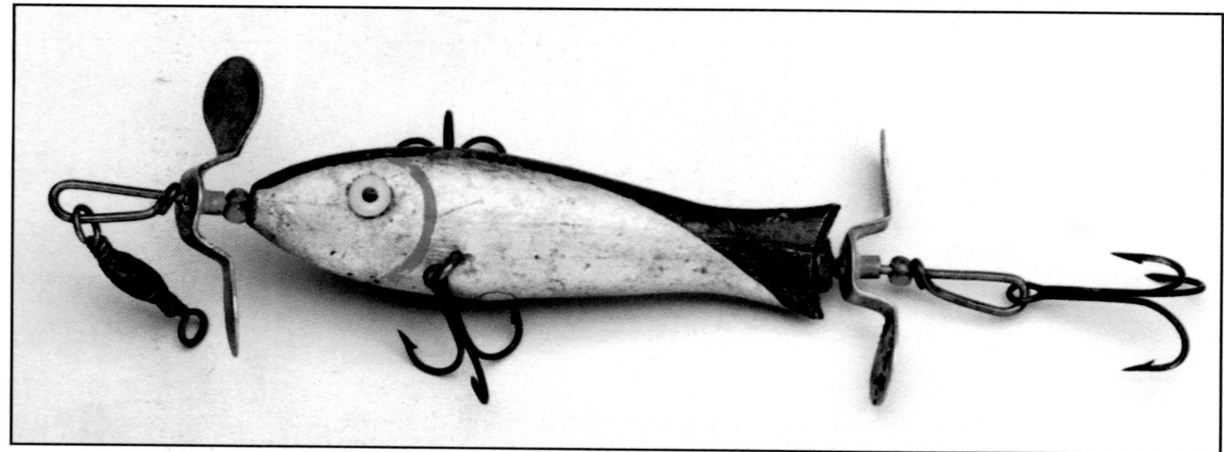

The Kent Double Spinner Artificial Minnow, Fred A. Pardee and Co., c. 1902. See pages 280 and 348.

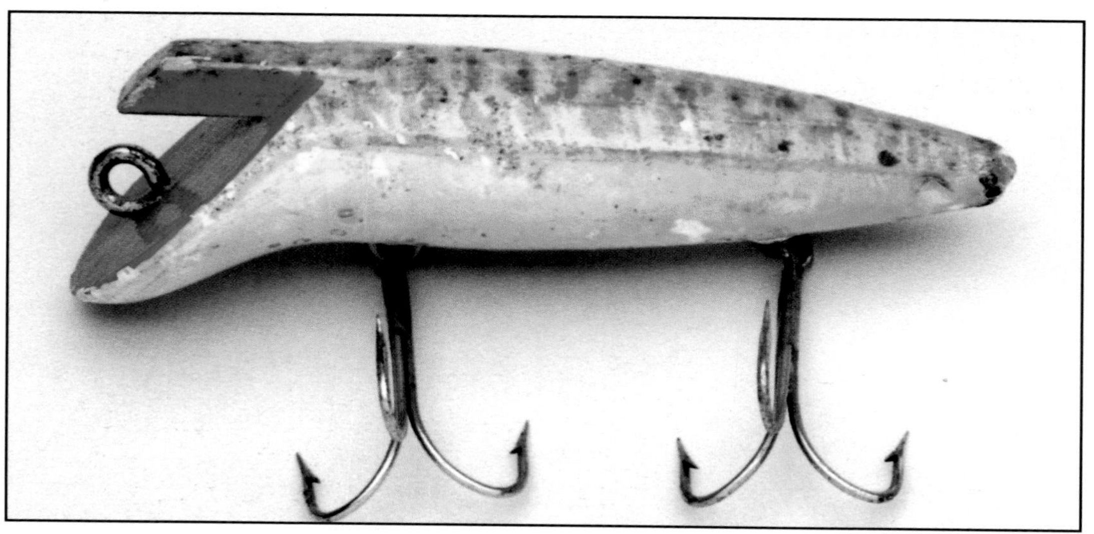

Hanson Irresistible Minnow, c. 1919. See pages 205 and 211.

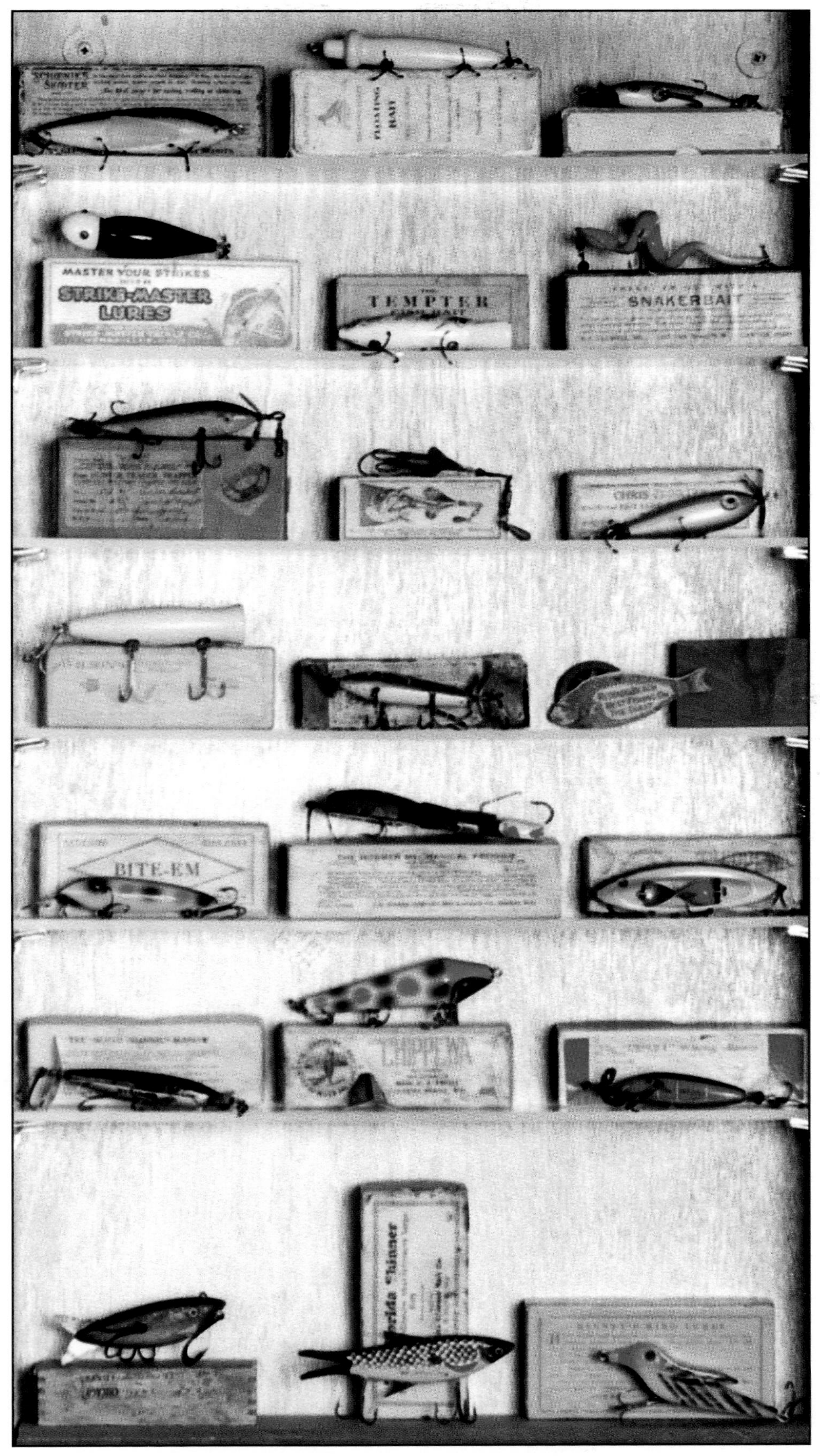
MASTER YOUR STRIKES
STRIKE-MASTER
LURES
TEMPTER
SNAKERBAIT
BITE-EM
CHIPPEWA

Lures in boxes with paperwork have become desirable and valuable.

LLOYD & COMPANY · CHIGAGO
Hungry-Jack
PATENT APPLIED FOR
GETS THE BIG ONES ·
LLOYD & COMPANY

Hungry-Jack lure with box, c. 1939. Made of wood, the rear portion is a "plunker" hinged to a "pinkie." See page 251.

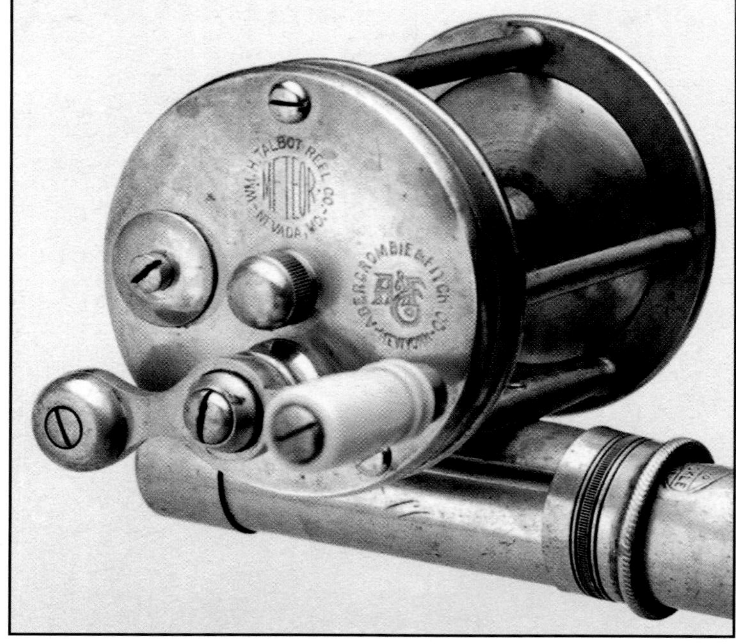

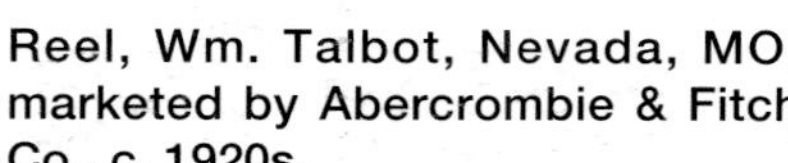

Reel, Wm. Talbot, Nevada, MO, marketed by Abercrombie & Fitch Co., c. 1920s.

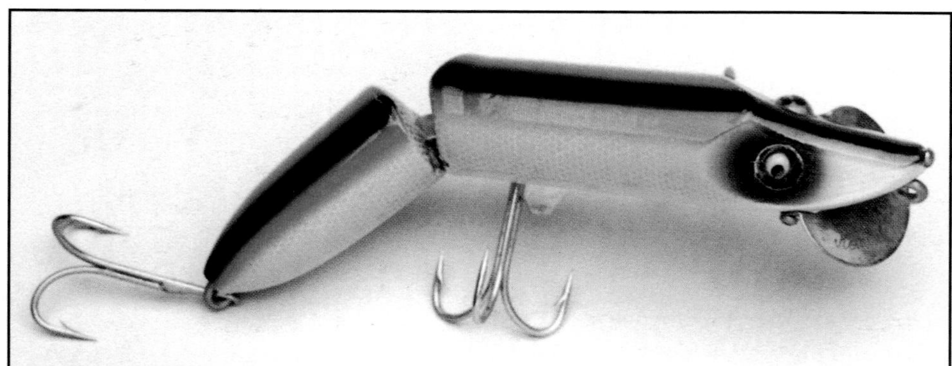

Heddon Rainbow Scale Vamp, a rare color. See page 171.

Early baitcasting and fly reels, 1860s – 1920s. Some of the top names are Meek, Milam, Leonard, Talbot, Horton, Gayle, Heddon, Sage, Snyder, E. vom Hofe, Deally. $100.00 – 1,000.00+.

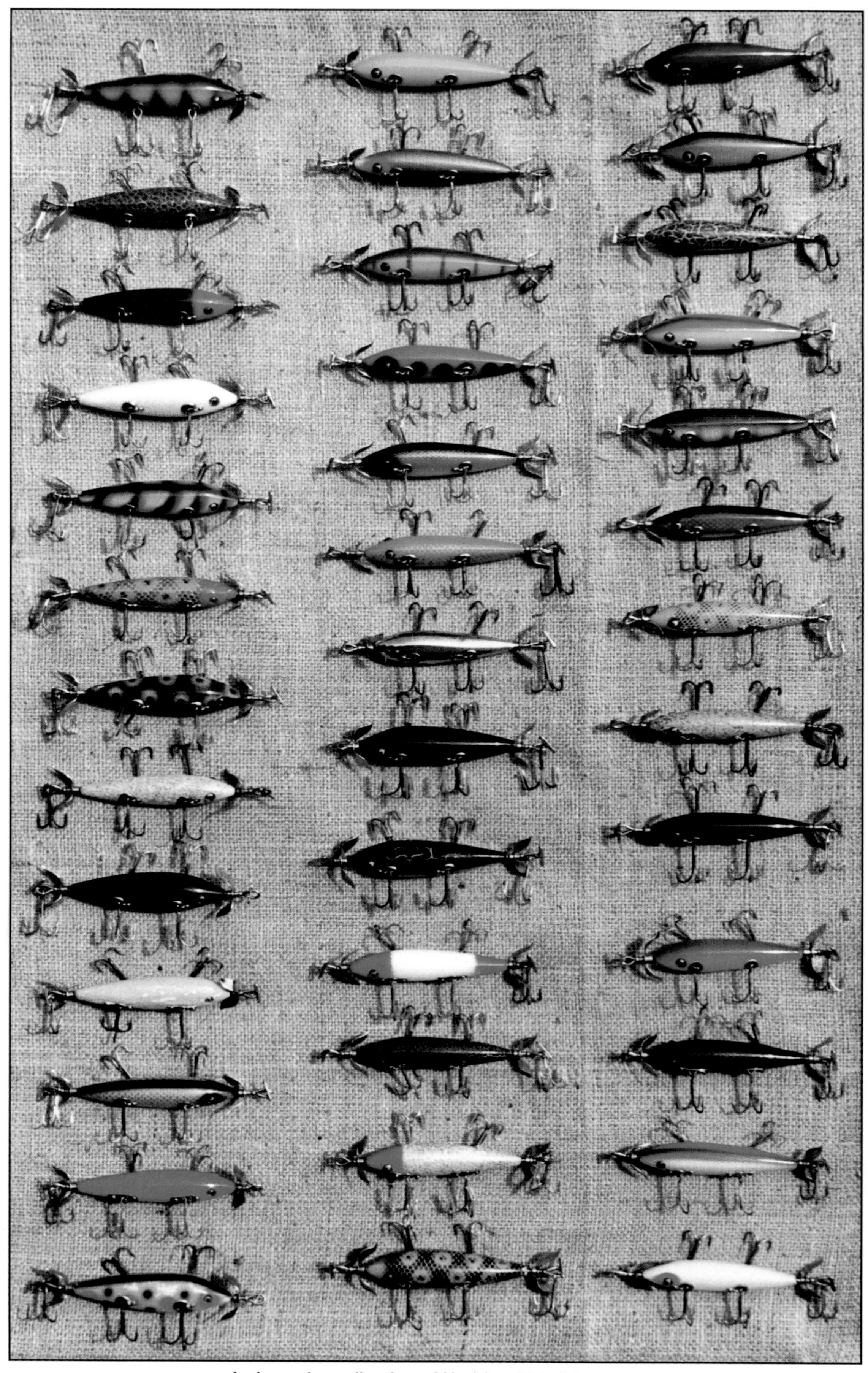

A nice color collection of Heddon #150 Minnows.

Heddon Color Chart

Left row	Center row	Right row
1. yellow perch	1. solid yellow	1. blended red
2. sienna fancy back	2. copper	2. rainbow (early)
3. red-head fancy back	3. perch (variation)	3. fancy back (early green)
4. solid white	4. orange with black spots	4. rainbow
5. bar perch	5. red dace	5. perch (variation)
6. red-head frogscale	6. goldfish scale	6. red scale (black back-cream belly)
7. frogspot	7. nickel metal plated	7. frogscale
8. saltwater (silver)	8. red scale (scale on belly)	8. saltwater (gold)
9. green scale (scale on belly)	9. fancy back (black)	9. solid black
10. solid luminous	10. red-white-redi	10. wilburn special
11. shiner scale dace	11. fancy back (green)	11. green scale (black back-cream belly)
12. solid red	12. red-head saltwater	12. rainbow
13. strawberry	13. frogscale	13. white (red around eyes)

Sami Taylor collection.

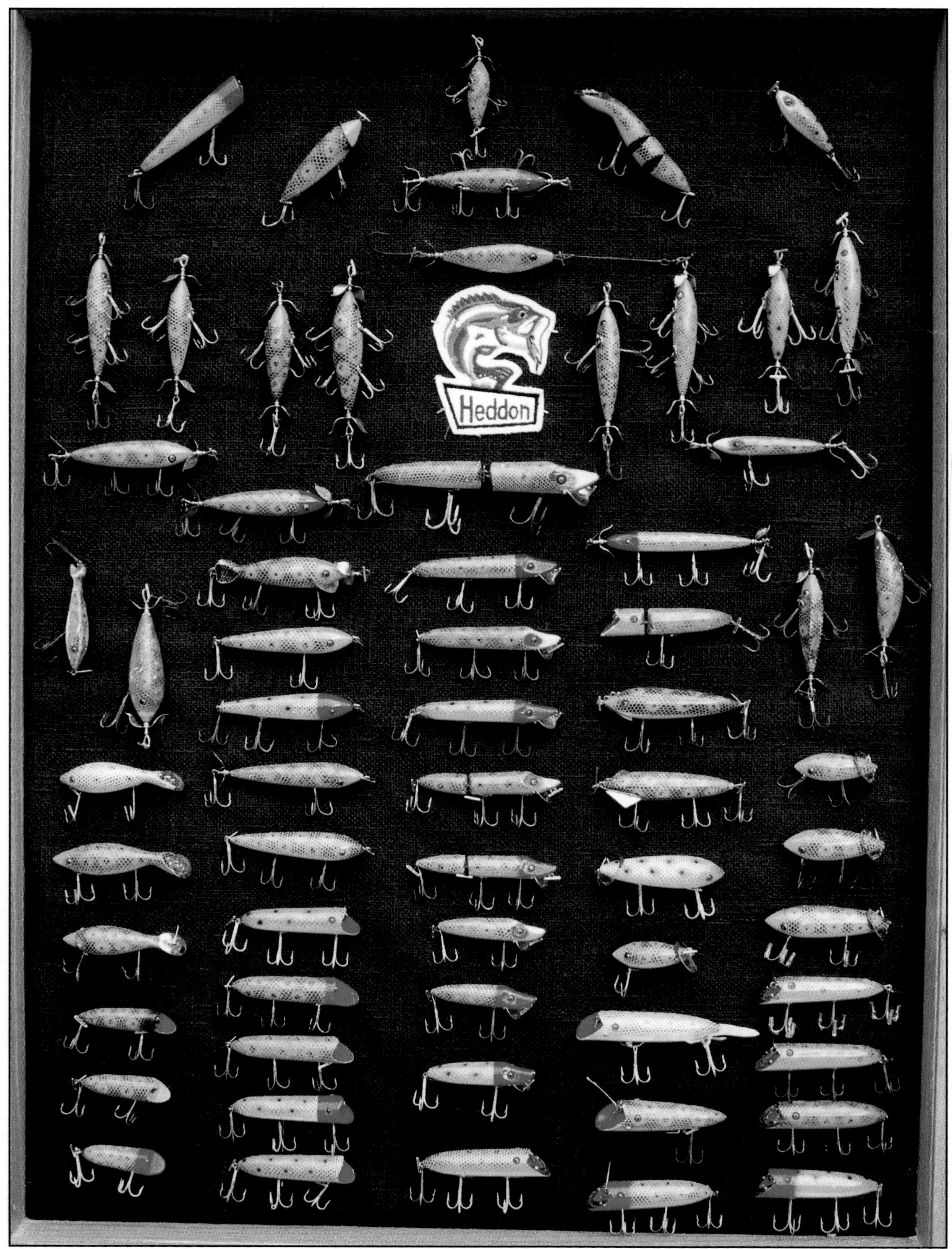
Heddon

A collection of Heddon lures in frog scale finish. Sami Taylor collection.

Shakespeare Evolution Minnow with box, c. 1902. See page 375.

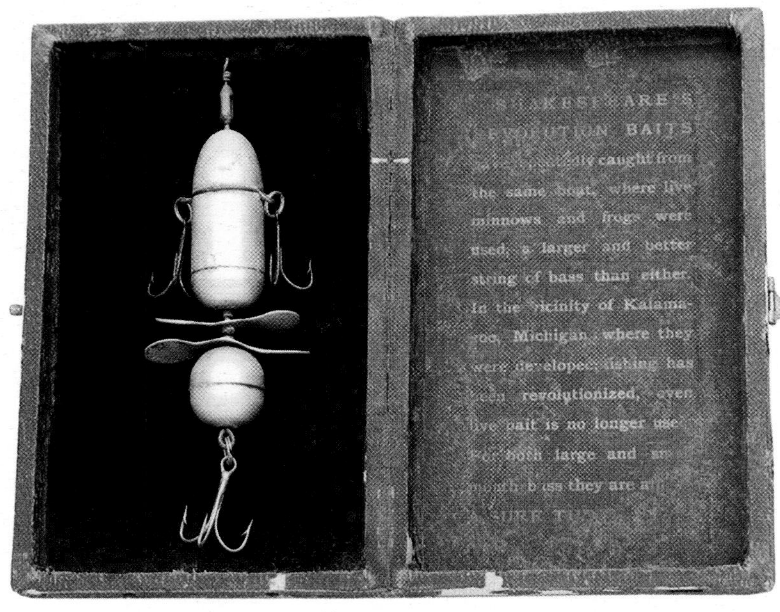
SHAKESPEARE'S
EVOLUTION BAITS
the same boat, where live
minnows and frogs were
used, a larger and better
string of bass than either.
In the vicinity of Kalamazoo, Michigan, where they
were developed, fishing has
been revolutionized, even
live bait is no longer used.
For both large and
mouth bass they are a

Shakespeare Revolution with presentation box, c. 1902. See pages 364 and 373.

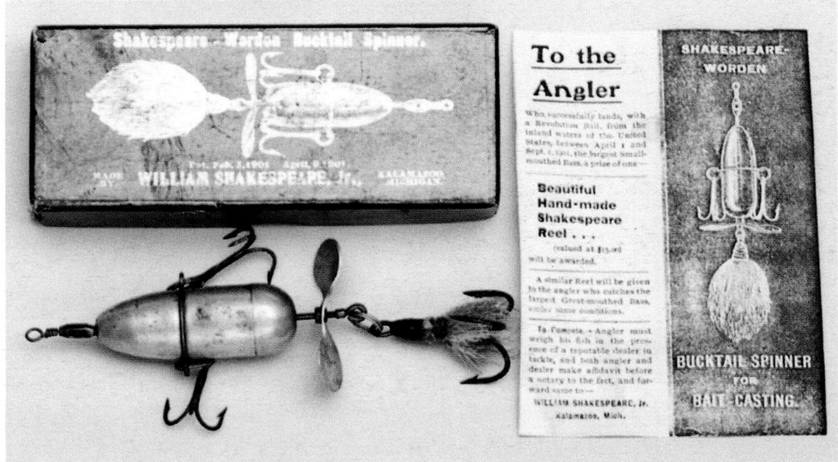
WILLIAM SHAKESPEARE, Jr.
To the Angler
Beautiful Hand-made Shakespeare Reel . . .
SHAKESPEARE-WORDEN
BUCKTAIL SPINNER FOR BAIT-CASTING.

Shakespeare Worden Bucktail Spinner. c. 1902. See pages 364 and 373.

Shakespeare Saltwater special (top) and Sardinia (bottom) lures, c. 1925. See pages 372 and 380.

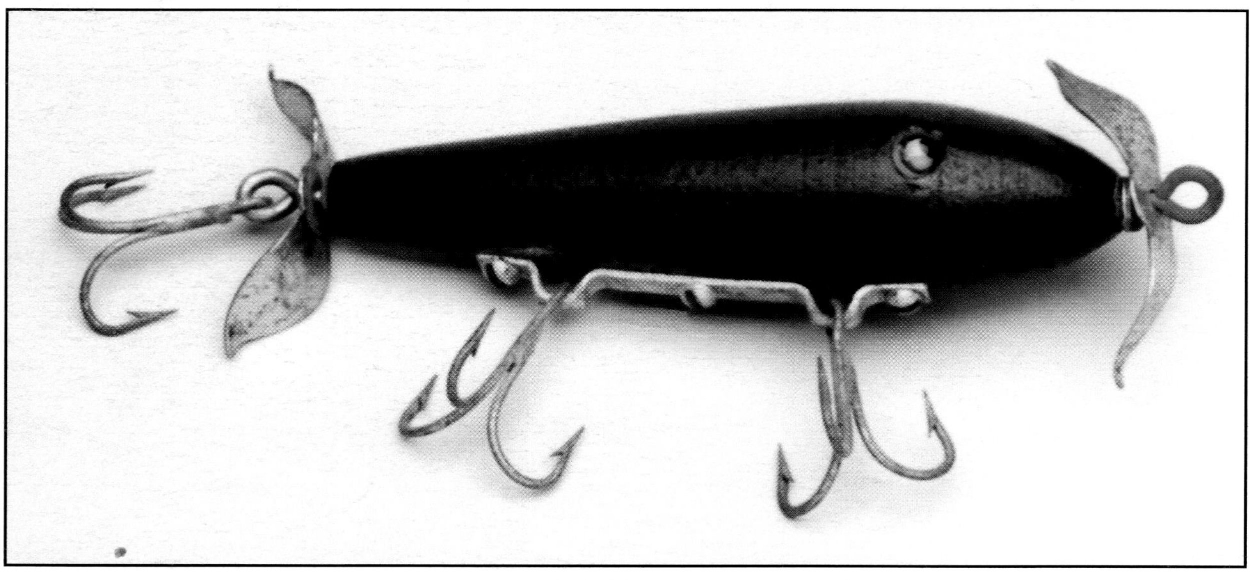

Shakespeare long-staple hook rig shown on a Jim Dandy Floating Minnow, c. 1930. Jim Dandy was Shakespeare's economy line of lures.

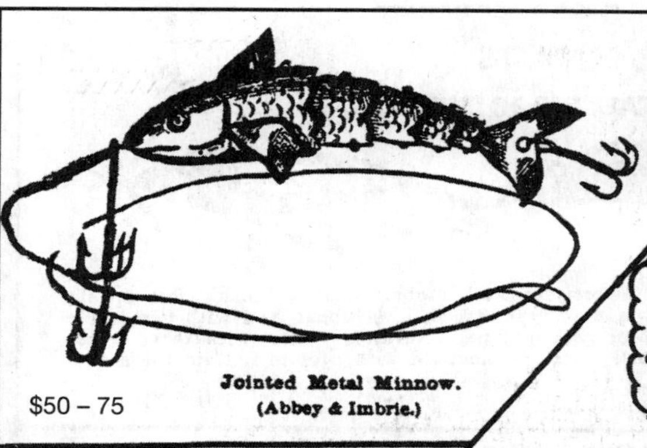

Jointed Metal Minnow.
(Abbey & Imbrie.)

$50 – 75

Abbey & Imbrie

NEW YORK, N.Y. **Established 1820**

INTRO. IN 1920 AS A CENTENNIAL LURE.

THE "GLOWBODY" MINNOW 3¼"–3½"

$30 – 40

$50 – 60

(Patent applied for)
"PERMANENTLY LUMINOUS"

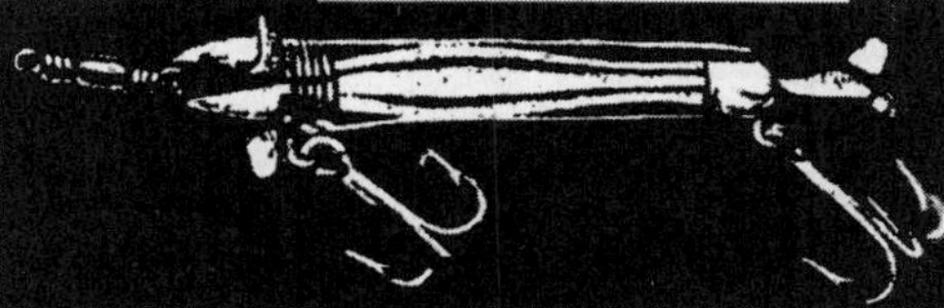

The "Glowbody" Minnow has nickel plated head and tail, with fins and propeller, and two detachable double hooks; latter can be easily detached and single hook used if desired. Its crystal body contains a tube of permanently luminous material. It is equally adapted to night or day fishing, as deep waters are always dark. The luminous body is protected top and bottom by wires to which the hooks are secured by a ring or loop. Length including head and tail, 3¼ to 3½ inches.

No. 1. Glowbody Minnow ....

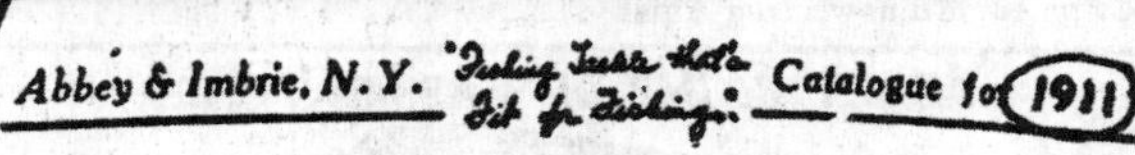

Abbey & Imbrie, N.Y. "Fishing Tackle that's Fit for Fishing" Catalogue for 1911

The "Octopus" Wooden Minnows

$150 – 200

NO. 1 – 3½" 5 TREBLES
NO. 2 – 2½" 3 TREBLES & 1 SPINNER.
NO. 1
(EARLY PFLUEGER – IN WOOD BOX)

The Hiawatha Wood Minnow.

$125 – 150

A&I 1914

Made from selected cedar, perfectly shaped and ballasted. Before applying the brilliant porcelain enamel finish, the cedar is carefully treated to prevent the absorption of water, so that the enamel will not peel or flake off. The spinner blades revolve in opposite directions rendering the use of swivels unnecessary. All metal fittings, including treble hooks, are heavily nickel plated.

Style No. 1100—
With 3 Detachable Treble Hooks and 2 Spinners.
Body 2½ in. long. Weight, about ¾ oz.

1100	Fancy Back	1104	Red
1101	Rainbow	1108	Blended Green
1102	White	1109	Yellow Perch

Style No. 1150—
With 5 Detachable Treble Hooks and 2 Spinners.
Body 3½ in. long. Weight, about 1 oz.

1150	Fancy Back	1154	Red
1151	Rainbow	1158	Blended Green
1152	White	1159	Yellow Perch

I WONDER IF THESE ARE HEDDON'S – NOTE THE NUMBERS – 1(100) & 1(150) – I WOULDN'T BET AGAINST IT.

BOOK OF THE BLACK BASS.

$50 – 75

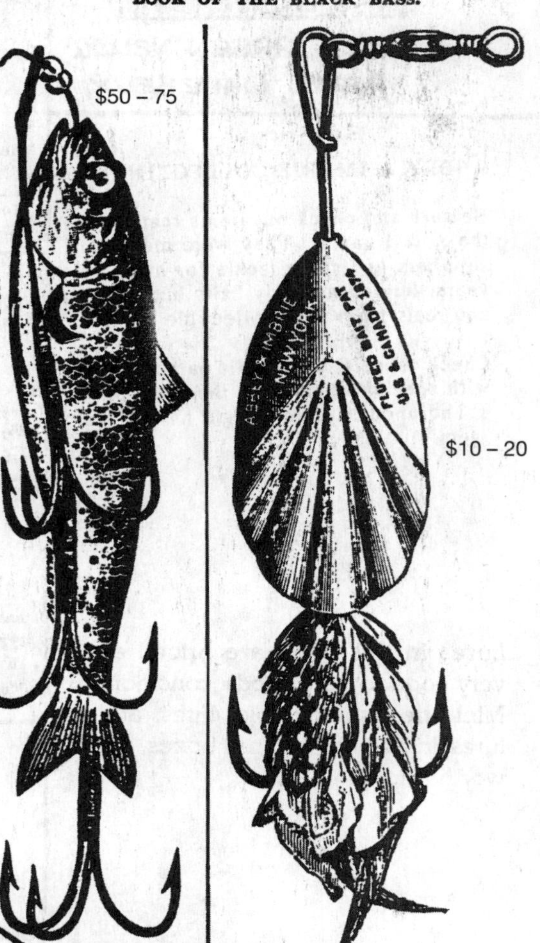

No 9.
ABBEY & IMBRIE NEW YORK
FLUTED BAIT PAT. U.S. & CANADA 1899

$10 – 20

$40 – 60

2½" **"ABBEY" IRIDESCENT PEARL MINNOW**

1910

Gets the big ones in deep water. Its iridescent whiteness in very deep water attracts fish where duller baits fail. Length of minnow, 2½ inches.

THIS IS THE "MAGNET PEARL MINNOW – S. DOERING & CO. BROOKLYN, N.Y.

WHAT CAN I SAY ABOUT THESE GEMS? THEY MAY BE 1920-1930 MOONLITE-THEN PAW-PAW.

A & I MARKETED A LINE CALLED THE "MINNEHAHA WOOD MINNOW" AN INEXPENSIVE LURE- 2½"-TREBLE OR SINGLE HOOKS (3)

SOLD FOR .15¢ IN 1914.

RED, GREEN, WHITE & YELLOW.

$40 – 50

Empire City
Fishing Tackle
THE MINNEHAHA
WOOD MINNOW
A dependable trolling and casting bait for Black Bass.

RED, GREEN, YELLOW BACKS, WHITE BELLY.

ABBEY & IMBRIE COLLECTING

Be sure and check out items that bare the A & I name. They were major suppliers of fishing tackle for many years, buying not only baits but rods and reels from very collectible firms.

Check especially the split bamboo rods with special attention to the short ones 8' and under......you might have a real "gem".

Lures in this book are priced as very good to very good+ condition. Mint lures, special color lures, and lures in correct original boxes are worth more.

Abbey & Imbrie—FISHING TACKLE—New York, N. Y.

(1929)

BAITS

RIDEAU WOOD MINNOW

4" 3½"

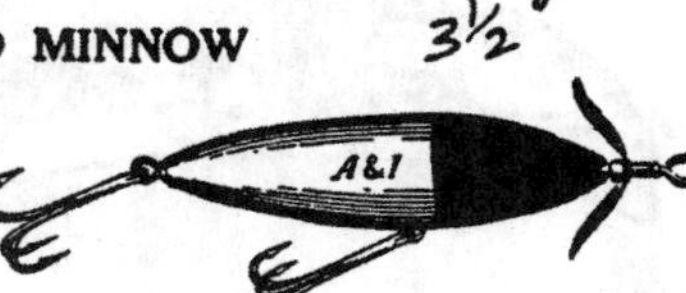

An exceptionally attractive assortment with highest quality finish. Put up six in a counter display box. Three spinner type, 3½ inch, ⅝ ounce, and with two treble hooks for surface fishing and three zig-zag type, 4 inch, ¾ ounce, with three treble hooks for under water fishing. All baits are mounted with eyes to imitate the actual minnow. Assorted colors.

No. 75. Rideau Assortment .... $20 – 30

ABBEY & IMBRIE CRIPPLED MINNOWS

$50 – 60

A real lifelike crippled minnow that can be made to imitate the splashing struggles of an injured shiner. A Killer for bass and pickerel. Length 4 inch, ¾ ounce. Mounted with two treble hooks.

No. 3404. Crippled Minnow, white, red head.......................

No. 3406. Crippled Minnow, silver scale finish.......................

No. 3408. Crippled Minnow, frog finish ....

4"

ABBEY & IMBRIE BASS-CATCHER

3½" $40 – 50

A successful wiggling bait for bass, perch, pickerel, etc. The finish of No. 2704 closely resembles the light reflection from chubs or shiners darting in the sun. 3½ inch, 1 oz. Mounted with 1 inch heavy wire leader and two treble hooks.

No. 2704. Bass Catcher, white, red head.............................

No. 2707. Bass Catcher, gold scale finish.............................

No. 2704M. Bass Catcher, silver, red head.............................

ABBEY & IMBRIE MOUSE

2½" $40 – 50

Looks and swims like a field mouse, and is entirely different in shape and action from the ordinary lure. An attractive and killing bait, especially for bass. Length 2½ inch, ⅝ ounce. Mounted with treble tail hook.

No. 59. Mouse, gray color..............

ABBEY & IMBRIE ASTRA WOOD MINNOW

2½" $20 – 30

While the lowest priced wood bait, it is a real killer and looks like any other dollar bait. Made in one pattern only. White body with red head. Zig-zag under water type. Length 2½ inches, weight ¼ ounce. Mounted with one double hook. Packed in glassine envelope, three dozen in a box.

No. 15. Astra Wood Minnow...............................

ABBEY & IMBRIE CLEARWATER WOOD MINNOW

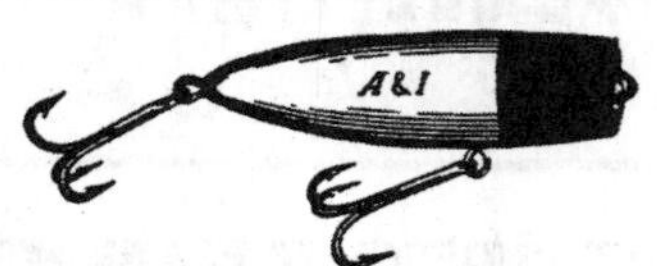

4" $20 – 30

A surface floating minnow of the "plunker" type. Assorted colors, white body, red head; yellow-red; red-black; white-blue. Mounted with two treble hooks. Length 4 inches, weight ½ ounce.

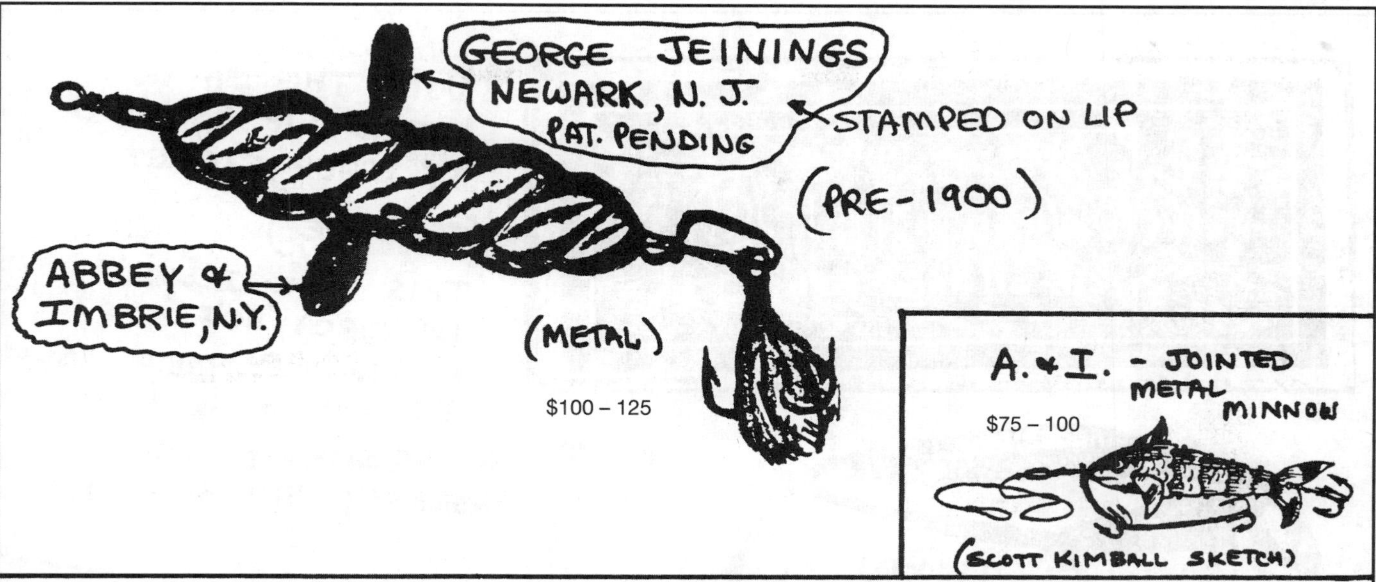
GEORGE JEININGS
NEWARK, N.J.
PAT. PENDING
STAMPED ON LIP
(PRE-1900)
ABBEY & IMBRIE, N.Y.
(METAL)
A. & I. - JOINTED METAL MINNOW
(SCOTT KIMBALL SKETCH)

$100 – 125

$75 – 100

Celluloid Minnow.

1885

$40 – 50

This Minnow is Practically INDESTRUCTIBLE.

In the most substantial manner on hooks particularly adapted to AMERICAN WATERS. This cut shows the exact size of a No. 7. We keep the follow-
in stock:

Nos.	4	5	6	7	8	9
Inches long.	2	2½	3	3½	4	4½

your dealer does not keep our goods in stock, or will not order them for you, send 50 cents for our 120-page Illustrated Catalogue.

ABBIE & IMBRIE, Manufacturers of Fine Fishing Tackle.

18 VESEY STREET (FOURTH DOOR FROM ASTOR HOUSE), NEW YORK CITY.

"THE FAIRY" MINNOW.

$20 –40

IMBRIE'S
FAIRY NO.7

NO.	4	5	6	7	8	9
INCH	2	2½	3	3½	4	4½

AD: FOREST & STREAM WITH ROD & GUN MAGAZINE - AUG. 13, 1885

Abbey & Imbrie
Fishing Tackle that's Fit for Fishing
GO-GETTERS
For all Game-Fish

NOTE THE SAME METAL LIP AS USED BY SHUR STRIKE.

(TACK EYE.)

THIS BOX ILLUS. IS CIRCA '30'S-'40'S. AND WAS PROBABLY MADE BY SHUR STRIKE (CCBCO)

A&I NO. 66SHS - WHICH WAS PROBABLY SHINER-SCALE.

(WOOD)

$20 – 30

"A. & I." Phantom Minnows—With Swivel

(Lengths given below include head and tail.)

(1920) "SILK"

$20 – 40

Bodies made of ribbon silk, beautifully mottled and striped in Blue, Brown or Silver.

Nos.	1	2	3	4	5	6	7	8
Code	(071)	(072)	(073)	(074)	(075)	(076)	(077)	(078)
Inches	2	2¼	2½	2¾	3¼	3½	4¼	4½
For	Trout				Black Bass		Pike Pickerel, etc.	

Values in this book are based on lures in very good to very good+ condition.

PORPOISE HIDE PHANTOM MINNOWS—WITH SWIVEL (1920)

Very durable and extra strong. Blue or Silver. For heavy fishing in Southern waters, such as Sea Trout, Crevalle, Red Drum, etc. Heavy treble hooks on 6-ply gut.

Nos.	5	6	7	8
Code	(025)	(026)	(027)	(028)
Inches	3½	4	4¼	4½

The Soldier Bait (18)

A brightly shining, light and indestructible minnow for Bass and Ouananiche trolling. Excellent for small Bluefish (Snappers). Made of German silver, heavily plated, 3¼ inches long.
No. 4 (017) With Treble Hook
No. 5 (018) With Single Hook

(VERY THIN BAIT)

$20 – 30

MFG'D. BY: C. KAUSCH
"SILVER SOLDIER" BATH, N.Y. - EARLY 1900'S-1925

THIS BAIT IS A VERY OLD CLASSIC - AND SHOULD BE RATED HIGHER THAN IT IS.

NOTE: THE A&I BAITS SHOWN ON PAGES 7 & 8 WERE MADE BY MOONLIGHT 1ST - THEN PAW PAW.

KING OF BAITS
No 1000

No. 1000 Bait Assortment — Three dozen assorted medium priced wood minnows on wire rack. The rack is made so the baits cannot fall off — and in fact can be locked on. It's a permanent store fixture. Complete assortment of baits for all sections of the country. Each with treble hooks. Weight 3¼ lbs.

No. 1001 Wire Rack — As used on No. 1000 Asst. without baits. Weight 2½ lbs.

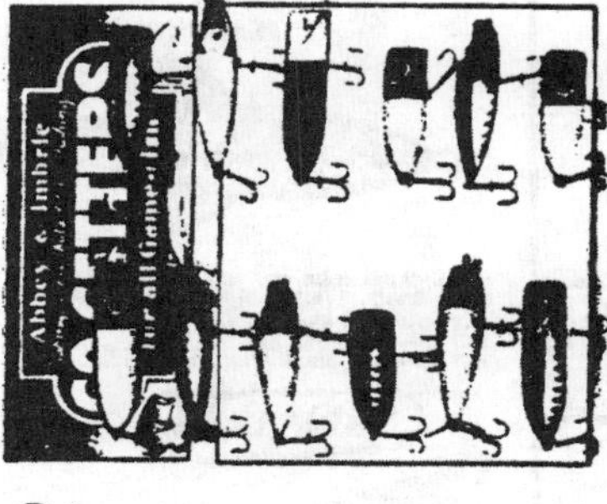

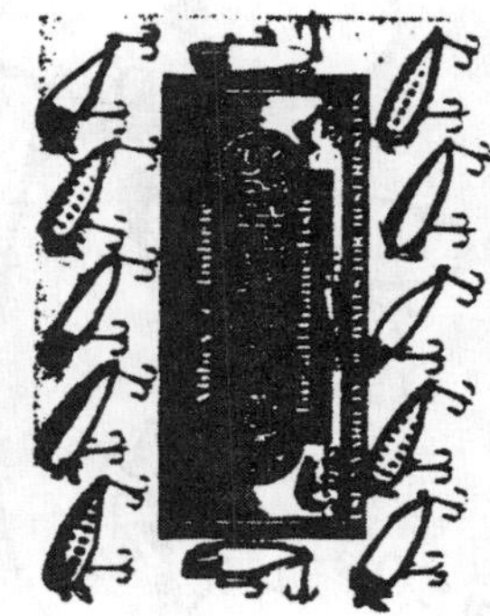

A & I MARKETED A LINE OF LURES IN THE '20'S, CALLED THE "GO-GETTERS" FULL LINE OF TYPES, INCLUDING THE RIGHTS TO PRODUCE THE RUSH TANGO PATENTS.

Abbey & Imbrie—FISHING TACKLE—New York, N. Y.

BAITS

WOOD MINNOWS

After exhaustive research and experimenting, Abbey & Imbrie present for the first time a line of Abbey & Imbrie wood minnows, covering the complete field. It has been the desire to include a range that would include the lowest possible prices. The baits are well made, finely finished and fitted with imported hooks. Breaking strength of eyes and hooks tested to fifty pounds.

ABBEY & IMBRIE WHIPPET

$40 – 50

An effective bait for trolling and casting as it gets down into the deep and quiet haunts where the big ones lurk, flashing the sunlight from its two spinners in an irresistible manner. Especially popular in Southern waters. Length 4 inch, ⅝ ounce. Mounted with two treble hooks.

No. 2404. Whippet, white, red head..
No. 2407. Whippet, gold, scale finish.
No. 2409. Whippet, perch finish .

ABBEY & IMBRIE FLASH-HEAD WOBBLER

ALSO: WHITE BODY W. THIN BARBER POLE RED STRIPE

$30 – 40

An ideal bait for deep water fishing when pike and bass have left the shoals and taken to deeper water. The nickel plated metal head quickly sinks to any desired depth with zig-zag wobbling motion. Length 3½ inch, 1 ounce. Mounted with two treble hooks.

No. 3707. Flash-head Wobbler, gold scale.
No. 3708. Flash-head Wobbler, frog finish.

ABBEY & IMBRIE WHIRLING CHUB

$75 – 100

Made in natural body shape with fan tail which makes it a close imitation to a live minnow in looks and action. It really seems like a fish and has been successfully used in landing bass, pike, pickerel and musky. Mounted with head spinner and two treble hooks. Length 4½ inch, 1 ounce.

No. 3204. Whirling-Chub white, red head...
No. 3206. Whirling-Chub, silver scale finish.
No. 3208. Whirling-Chub, frog finish .

EZY-KATCH WOOD MINNOW

$20 – 30

Made of the best material, finely finished. Put up six assorted colors in a counter display box. Three spinner type, weight ½ ounce, for surface fishing, and three zig-zag type, weight ⅝ ounce, for under water fishing. Length 3½ inch. Mounted with two treble hooks.

No. 50. Ezy-Katch

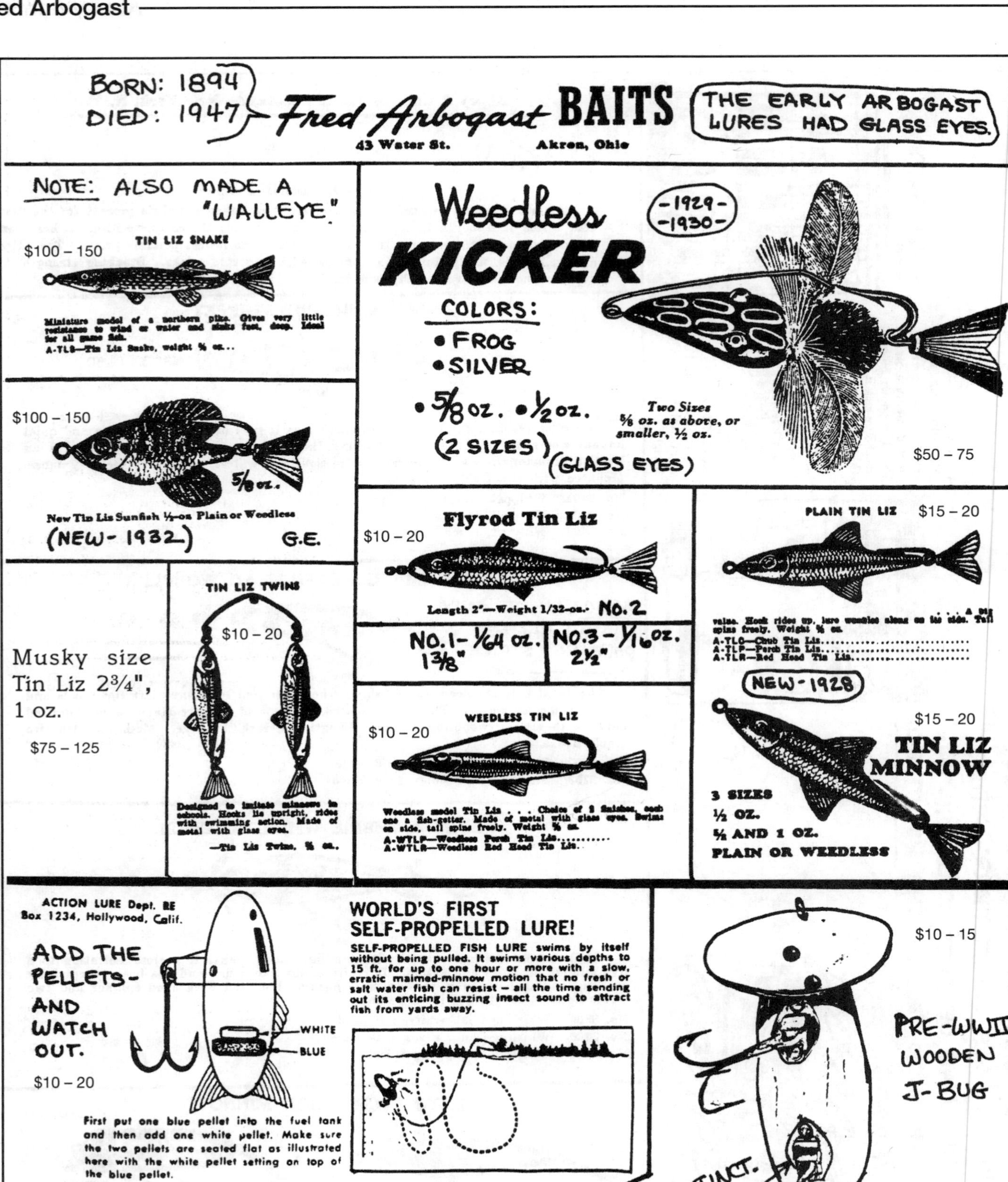
BORN: 1894
DIED: 1947
Fred Arbogast BAITS
43 Water St. Akron, Ohio
THE EARLY ARBOGAST LURES HAD GLASS EYES.
NOTE: ALSO MADE A "WALLEYE."
TIN LIZ SNAKE
$100 – 150
$100 – 150
5/8 oz.
New Tin Liz Sunfish ½-oz Plain or Weedless
(NEW- 1932)
G.E.
Weedless KICKER
-1929- -1930-
COLORS:
• FROG
• SILVER
• 5/8 OZ. • ½ OZ.
(2 SIZES)
(GLASS EYES)
Two Sizes 5/8 oz. as above, or smaller, ½ oz.
$50 – 75
Flyrod Tin Liz
$10 – 20
Length 2"—Weight 1/32-oz.- NO. 2
NO. 1- 1/64 OZ. 1 3/8"
NO. 3 - 1/16 OZ. 2½"
PLAIN TIN LIZ
$15 – 20
(NEW-1928)
$15 – 20
TIN LIZ MINNOW
3 SIZES
½ OZ.
¾ AND 1 OZ.
PLAIN OR WEEDLESS
TIN LIZ TWINS
$10 – 20
Musky size Tin Liz 2¾", 1 oz.
$75 – 125
—Tin Liz Twins, ⅝ oz.
WEEDLESS TIN LIZ
$10 – 20
ACTION LURE Dept. RE
Box 1234, Hollywood, Calif.
ADD THE PELLETS- AND WATCH OUT.
$10 – 20
WHITE
BLUE
WORLD'S FIRST SELF-PROPELLED LURE!
SELF-PROPELLED FISH LURE swims by itself without being pulled. It swims various depths to 15 ft. for up to one hour or more with a slow, erratic maimed-minnow motion that no fresh or salt water fish can resist – all the time sending out its enticing buzzing insect sound to attract fish from yards away.
First put one blue pellet into the fuel tank and then add one white pellet. Make sure the two pellets are seated flat as illustrated here with the white pellet setting on top of the blue pellet.
Keep your pellets dry and out of direct sunlight. Also keep the blue tablets and the white tablets in their respective containers until ready for use. They should not be stored in the same container.
$10 – 15
PRE-WWII WOODEN J-BUG
NOTE THE DISTINCT. HOOK RIG
2 SIZES: 2⅛" - 2¾"

BILL ADCOCK OF BATON ROUGE, LA. DEVELOPED THE "NOTCHED LINE TIE" TO MAKE THE RIVER RUNT A FASTER SWIMMER. THE LINE HELD TIGHT ON THE LINE TIE NOTCH. (1930'S)

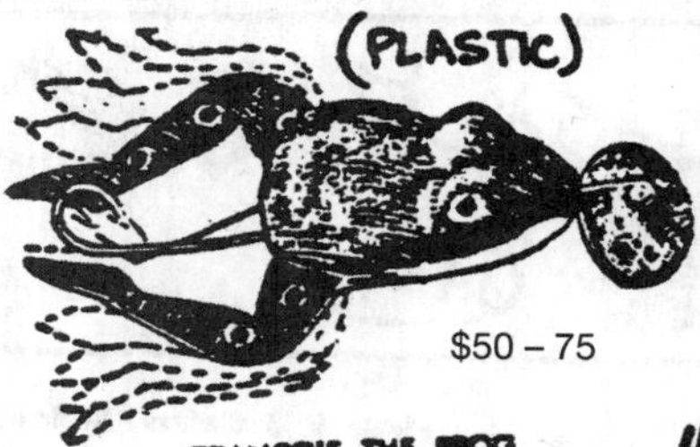
(PLASTIC)
FRANCOIS THE FROG

$50 – 75

ONE OF MANY ANIMATED FROG BAITS. 1949

ANDERSON ANIMATED CO.
"FRANCOIS THE FROG"

Lure values are based on as very good to very good+ condition.

FRED ARBOGAST UPDATE

- HE STARTED MAKING LURES IN 1924.
- THE TIN LIZ WAS 1ST LURE.
- HE ALSO INVENTED THE RUBBER SKIRT.
- THE JITTERBUG WAS INTRO. IN 1937, AND FOR A SHORT TIME WAS MADE OF CEDAR – WITH GLASS EYES. A LATER WWII VARIATION HAD A PLASTIC LIP. (IN COLORS)
- IN THE OPINION OF THE AUTHOR, THE COLLECTABILITY OF ARBOGAST ENDS WITH THIS LURE, AND FOR MANY – BEFORE THIS JITTERBUG.

1931

NICKEL – COPPER – BRASS

$5 – 10

Allen's Jig Bug

Weedless Wonder FISHING LURE

RELEASED

$10 – 20

COCKED

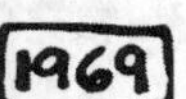
1969

The Only 100% Weedless Fishing Plug in the World!

You can now catch fish in the weeds where the big lunkers live. Developed, used, and tested 6 years before large scale manufacturing.

Fish 100% of your favorite fishing grounds—not just the open water.

The construction makes it safe to use—never fear about hooking your children or your companion while casting.

Save money on lures! Since this is a floating, weedless lure, you don't snag up and lose it along with a valuable piece of line.

Body made of Balsa wood, and all metal parts, nickel plated or stainless steel. Never any corrosion or rusting. Will give you reliable, dependable fishing year after year.

Does not tangle in your tackle box.

Comes in a variety of colors; Red & White, Green back & Black back.

*Pat. No. [illegible] DEALER INQUIRIES INVITED

ANDERSON & SON, INC.,
Box 416, Dept. FA69,
Hope Valley, Rhode Island 02832

A. B. TRICKY TROLL

$5 – 10

Something NEW has been added: "C.F.R.A.," it has sensational magnetic force toward fish. It's A. B. TRICKY TROLL, the lure that stands back of its name. Guaranteed to catch 14 different salt water fish variety for good fishing.

TRY

A. B. TRICKY TROLL

A. B. SUPPLY COMPANY
Mechanicville, New York

1958 I WONDER WHAT "C.F.R.A." IS? ANYWAY, IT'S A SALT WATER BAIT.

"CATCH FISH RIGHT AWAY"

MORE TONY ACCETTA

- THE JIGOLET PREV. ILLUS. AS WEEDLESS, WAS ALSO RIGGED CONVENTIONAL W/2 TREBLES. PAT. #2208827.
- IN 1957, CO. NAME WAS TONY ACCETTA & SON.

—the only jig with the built-in fish-getting action!

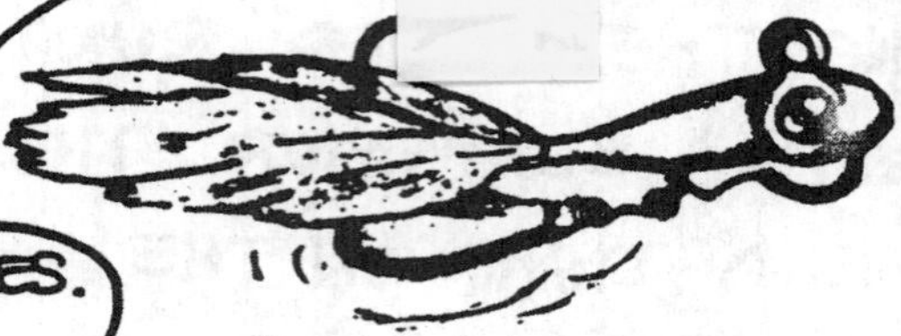

1957

JIGAROO

(FROM 1/8 OZ. TO 3½ OZ)

$5 – 10

JIGIT & SKIRT
No. 2/0 Hook
Shown Actual Size
1951

$5 – 10

SUPER-MOP SEA WORM
(FROM 3/4 OZ. TO 3 OZ.)
Made in 3 Colors: Yellow, Blue, Yellow & Green

$5 – 10

No. 21 HOBO Actual Size
½ oz.
Tony Accetta
"HOBO"

$5 – 10

NO. 5 – 2¼" – 3/8 OZ.
NO. 7 – 2¾" – 5/8 OZ.

NEW WEED DODGER

QUICK CHANGE HULA SKIRT LINK

PATENT NO. 2,208,827

(CHROME PLATED)
THE ACCETTA SPOON.

$5 – 10

Accetta JIGIT-EEL

The original nylon eel lure —simulates many eel skins. Gives more eel action to get Blues, Stripers, Kings, Etc. Rigged and non-rigged.

JIG-IT EEL (1938)

$5 – 10

Accetta HOLLO-HEAD

Attracts fish by sound waves and fast wiggling, erratic action. For all fresh-water and small salt-water fish. ½ oz. 2" long. Spinning or trolling. $1.35 in popular colors.

HOLLO-HEAD – 1938 BY ACCETTA

$5 – 10

Mint lures, original boxed lures, and special color lures are worth more.

Tony Accetta 853 E. 144th. ST. CLEVELAND. O.
TONY ACCETTA
BUG SPOON

$5

(TENITE)

"JIGOLET"

SNAGLESS

NEW-1941

No. 34 RW 5/8 oz.
SNAGLESS

2¾"

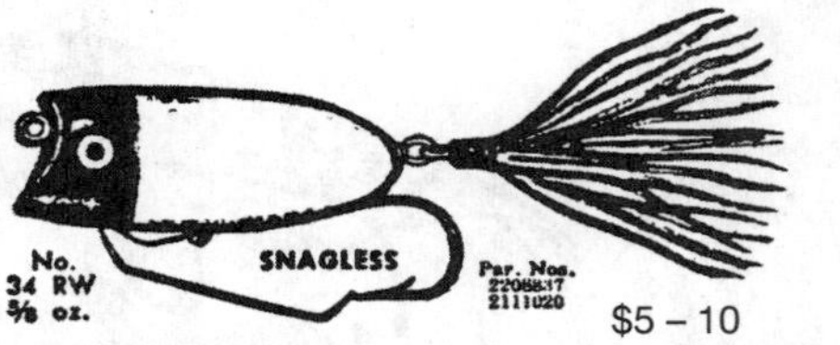

$5 – 10

BUG SPOONET
FLY ROD LURE

$5

TONY ACCETTA
NEW
RIVER DEVIL

3-3/8"

GREEN SPOON

A proven killer for striped bass and other small salt water game. Very effective trolling for land-locked salmon, lake trout, pike, musky. Nickel finish spoon.
3⅜ in. length by ½ in. wide
No. 801 $5

TONY ACCETTA WAS THE U.S. PROFESSIONAL CASTING CHAMPION.

TONY ACCETTA NEW RIVER DEVIL

(1937)

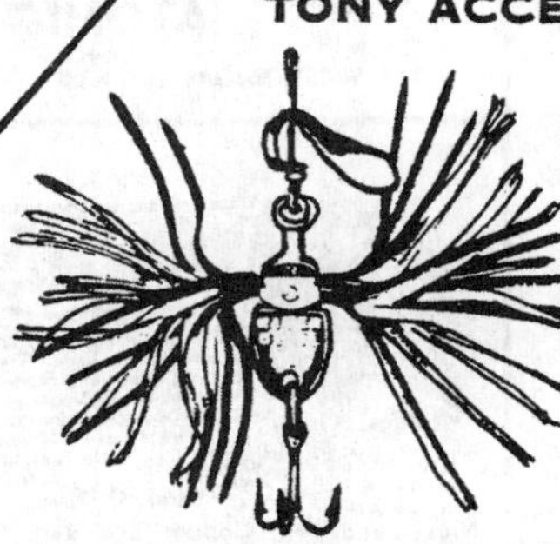

The new River Devil with rubber Hula skirts is a life like imitation of a crawling, creeping spider. Runs deep and the wiggling action of the skirt, plus the natural action of the spinner makes this a real fish-getter. Should be reeled in slow, with short jerks of the rod. This causes the creeping, crawling action of the rubber legs. Bait is balanced to ride upright at all times. It is weedless and can be fished in any waters. 2½ inches long, weighs ⅝ ounce. Two standard colors in skirts: Red and White, or Black and White.

Illustration shows treble hooks but comes with single hook

No. 8SR—New River Devil......

2½" – 5/8 oz.

$5

Lures in this book are priced as very good to very good+ condition. Mint lures, special color lures and lures in correct original boxes are worth lots more.

TONY ACCETTA PET SPOON

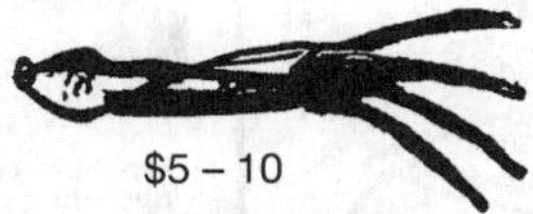

$5 – 10

A spoon bait for all conditions. Deep or shallow water; spring, summer, or fall the Pet will catch fish. Cast it in the lily pads, over the logs, anywhere except on the bank. Chrome finish with either Yellow, Black, or White feather. Absolutely weedless.

No. 15GF—Pet Spoon. 3¼ inches long, weight ½ ounce, with feather.......
No. 14GF—Pet Spoon. 2¼ inches long, weight ¼ ounce, with feather.......
No. 15WG—Pet Spoon. Same as 15GF, without feather....................
No. 14WG—Pet Spoon. Same as 14GF, without feather....................

"PET" FLY ROD SPOON – 1½" – 1/24 oz.

SEA KING
Trolling Spoon

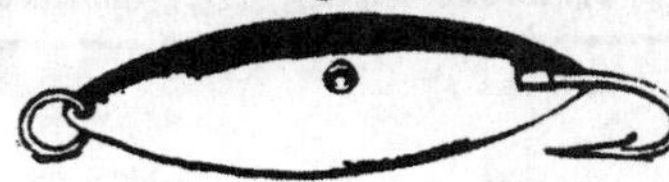

For salt water and fresh water fishing. For lake trout and other game fish. Length overall 3½ in. Length spoon 2¾". Nickel Finish.
No. 4413—Each $5

TONY ACCETTA WEED DODGER

One of the positive rules in fishing is to put the lure where the fish are. With many lures this is not possible because they are not weedless. The Weed Dodger is and can be cast in the thickest of weeds, around tree stumps, and along brushy banks without hanging up. And best of all it is a sure hooker. A real killer with its fast wiggling, wobbling action. Furnished in three colors: All nickel; red with white stripe, reverse side nickel; black with white stripe, reverse side nickel. Two sizes.

No. 5—Weed Dodger. 2/0 hook, weight ⅜ ounce....................
No. 6—Weed Dodger. 4/0 hook, weight ½ ounce....................
No. 7—Weed Dodger. With feather streamer. This lure has been unusually effective. Same size as No. 6 but heavier, weighing ⅝ ounce. Nickel finish only with following color streamers: Black, White, and Yellow......................

$5

Lure collecting is fun, tell a friend.

META-LURE SPOON

3½" $5

For casting and trolling. Has six flat reflecting surfaces which scatter a much greater reflection

$5

WEEDLESS SPIN DODGER

As above with spinner attached, for more action, flash and wiggle. Choice Black, Red or Yellow streamer feather tail.
No. 6630—
State color streamer

2¾" – 5/8 oz.

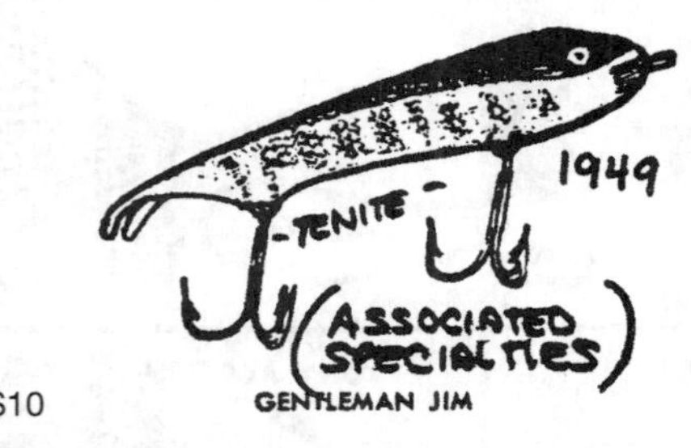
1949
TENITE
(ASSOCIATED SPECIALTIES)

$10

GENTLEMAN JIM

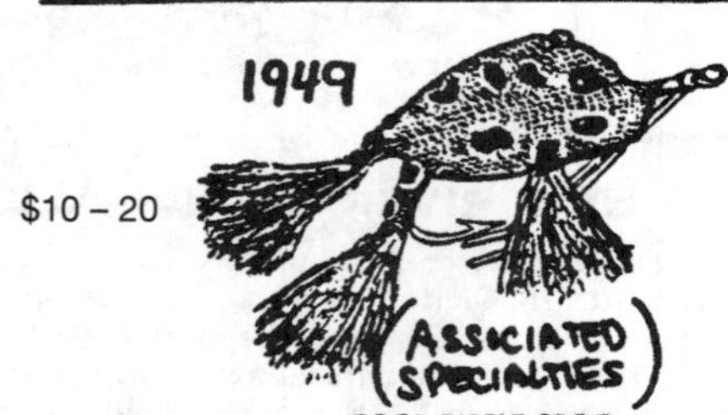
1949
(ASSOCIATED SPECIALTIES)

$10 – 20

COOL RIPPLE FROG

MADE FROM RAYON AND NYLON.

ANY BODY KNOW ADDRESS OF: ASSOCIATED SPECIALTIES

(SEE COOL RIPPLE)

FOR MORE SURE STRIKES USE THE WEEDLESS *TRIP-LURE*

$10

A little wonder that works like magic. This triple threat lure gets right into the weed beds and lily patches where the foxy old whoppers lurk. A strike sets off trip action which springs hooks outward embedding them in fish's jaw.

FISH JUST CAN'T GET AWAY FROM THE *TRIP-LURE*

In casting position hooks are held in place so that points are concealed, making it impossible for them to snag weeds or other objects in the water. When fish strikes side hooks snap sharply into his mouth.

TRIP-LURE, patent pending

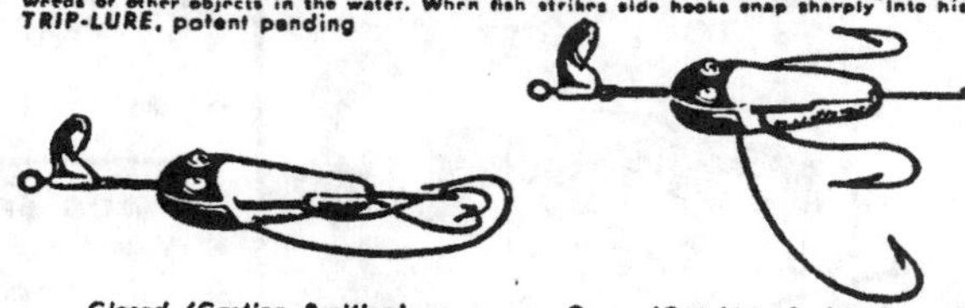

DEALERS WANTED

Closed (Casting Position) *Open (Catching Position)*

(1946)

FEATURES:

- Revolutionary weedless principle.
- Hair trigger, gaffing action.
- Weaving, teasing motion produced by spinner.
- Body made of tenite offering toughness and durability.
- Hooks specially designed to sink securely in fish's mouth.
- Supplied in red and white, and other attractive colors.
- All metal parts non-rusting and non-corrosive.

Available at your sporting goods store or order direct.

Send check, cash, or money order to:

ATOMIC FISHING TACKLE DIVISION

S. & G. PRODUCTS, INC.

213 WEST SHORE AVENUE BOGOTA, N. J.

$10

The ONLY New BAIT
WIGGLY-WRIGGLER 1932
A real, sure-fire fish getter combining all the features you've ever wanted in a lure. The phantom body is in constant motion, reflecting light from every angle. Weighs ½ ounce, yet casts beautifully into the strongest wind because there is no air resistance. Lights on the water without splashing. Always rides upright and can not twist your line. Normal reeling runs bait about 10 inches under surface, over the weeds where the big boys lie. Variable reel speeds will place it anywhere from the surface to the bottom.
ing positive hooking. Every real fisherman wants more of these effective lures—so irresistible to pickerel and pike. Send your remittance and order today and make your tackle box up-to-date.
Two attractive finishes—Nickel and Red—Copper and Red—Postpaid
DEPT. NO.
THE ALLIANCE MANUFACTURING COMPANY, Alliance, Ohio

ARNOLD'S IMITATION PORK BAIT

$5

-1927-

Arnold's Imitation Pork Bait is made of specially prepared pure white rubber; is clean to use; is odorless; is properly shaped so as to correctly imitate the action of a live minnow, and does not have the "flip" at the end, making a trailer hook necessary.

It can be easily cleaned by wiping off with a cloth saturated with gasoline. This makes it possible to re-use this bait many times.

It is not bulky to carry, it does not tip over in your tackle box and ruin all your tackle, and will produce results.

Color: White body with red head.

1917→

ARNOLD'S PAT'D — ARNOLD'S

"Handy" Casting Weight
Attachable from either end. Kidney shaped. Weedless. Non-kinkable. Will not come open in use. Three sizes—½ oz., ⅓ oz., 3-16 oz.

IMITATION PORK BAIT
Perfect in action. Made of specially prepared white rubber with white and red heads. No. 1, for Fly Casting, No. 2, for Bait Casting, 60c per dozen. No. 3, for Surf Casting or Trolling.

Dealers and Jobbers Wanted

S. ARNOLD, Mfgr. 2328-A Brooklyn Kansas City, Mo.

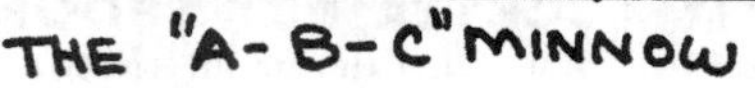

THE "A-B-C" MINNOW

$100 – 150 $75 – 100

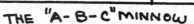

WHITE RED GREEN — RED GREEN

No. 100 No. 200

NO. 100 4" - HAS EYES & MOUTH

NO. 200 NO EYES - 3½" NO MOUTH

COLORS: RED, GREEN, WHITE

NOTE: TURNING THE SCREW EYE MAKES THE BODY SECTIONS INTERCHANGEABLE.

(1923) DETROIT, MICH. (SOME G.E.)

Lures in excellent to mint condition, in correct original boxes, and in special order colors are worth more.

AUTOMATIC WEEDLESS BAIT

$5

A weedless lure that is as effective in hooking a fish as an open hook. Has 3/0 hook with single spoon. It can be cast as far and as accurately as a plug and never tangles. Furnished in four colors: Natural bucktail, red, white

KRAZY MINNOW®
FISHING LURES
U.S. Patent #3,123,932
MFG. IN U.S.A. BY
AITKEN-WARNER CORPORATION
P. O. BOX 215
GREEN CAMP, OHIO 43322

$5

METAL

3 SIZES:
PEPPY – SPINNING
TIPPY – CASTING (3¼")
LAZY – TROLLING

THIS BAIT CAN BE MADE TO RUN DEEP, SHALLOW, OR SURFACE BY SWITCHING THE 2 METAL SECTIONS, VIA SPLIT RINGS

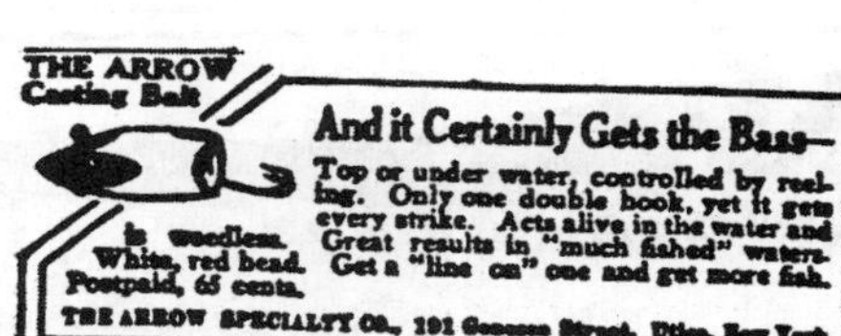
THE ARROW
Casting Bait
And it Certainly Gets the Bass—
Top or under water, controlled by reeling. Only one double hook, yet it gets every strike. Acts alive in the water and is weedless. Great results in "much fished" waters. Get a "line on" one and get more fish.
White, red bead. Postpaid, 65 cents.
THE ARROW SPECIALTY CO., 191 Genesee Street, Utica, New York

ARROW CASTING BAIT
1 DOUBLE HOOK
RH/WHITE
1915
ARROW SPECIALTY CO.
UTICA, N.Y.

$20 – 30

"ATTENTION FISHERMEN"
Make every cast a weedless cast, with
MASTER WEEDLESS WIGGLERS
A true weedless all metal bait.
Here is a bait that ... weeds, whether ... or under water, and has ... alluring action that they just cannot resist it.
Made by AUGIE'S BAIT CO.
1821 W. Greenfield Ave.,
Milwaukee, Wis.

AUGIES BAIT CO.
MILWAUKEE, WIS.
1928
• 9/16 OZ.
• 5/8 OZ

$5

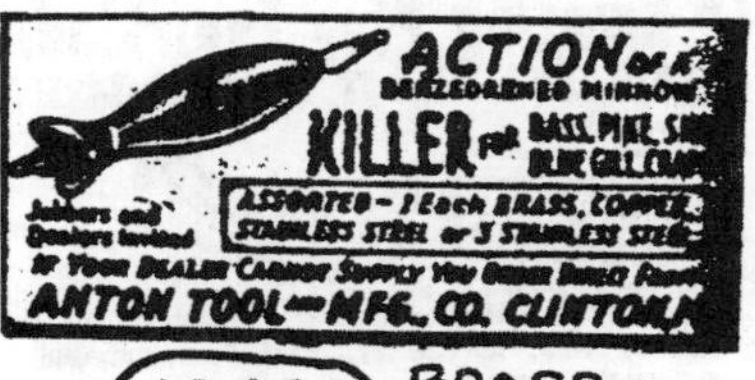
ACTION
KILLER
ASSORTED – 1 Each BRASS, COPPER, STAINLESS STEEL or 3 STAINLESS STEEL
ANTON TOOL MFG. CO. CLINTON

1948
BRASS –
COPPER –
STAINLESS –

$5

$250 – 300

Michigan Life Like Minnows

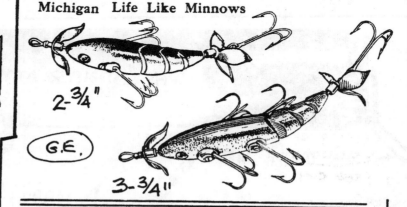

2-¾"

G.E.

3-¾"

AFTER a long experience and careful study of Bait Casting and Trolling, we have gotten up this Bait, or in other words, this "Fisherman's Friend." It is made from selected Cedar, very strong and durable, and to represent a live minnow swimming. The improvement on this minnow over other makes is the Jointed Tail portion, which is flexible, and when being drawn through the water the Three-Blade Propeller wiggles the Jointed Tail portion, and makes an excellent imitation of a live minnow while swimming.

It has been pronounced to be the most perfect casting and trolling bait ever put on the market and beats live bait.

The hooks are very easily detachable, and cannot possibly tangle or interlock, as they cannot swing forward. They can be replaced by any common treble hook, of any size or shape.

The bait is beautifully finished with a Special Water Proof Finish, which prevents it from soaking water or peeling off. All spinners and hooks are heavily nickeled, thus preventing rust.

Manufactured by

ADOLPH ARNTZ

Fishing Tackle, Guns, Sporting Goods, Bicycles, Etc.

26 W. WESTERN AVENUE MUSKEGON, MICHIGAN

Sent to any place in the United States or Canada postage prepaid upon receipt of price.

MICHIGAN LIFE LIKE MINNOW - Colors Available

Light Green, Speckled Back, White Belly....Dark Green, Speckled Back, White Belly....Dark Back, Aluminum Belly....Perch....Dark Back, Yellow Belly....Brook Trout....All Aluminum....Green Back, Yellow Sides, Red Belly....Natural Wood.

PATENT DATE: FEB. 28, 1908

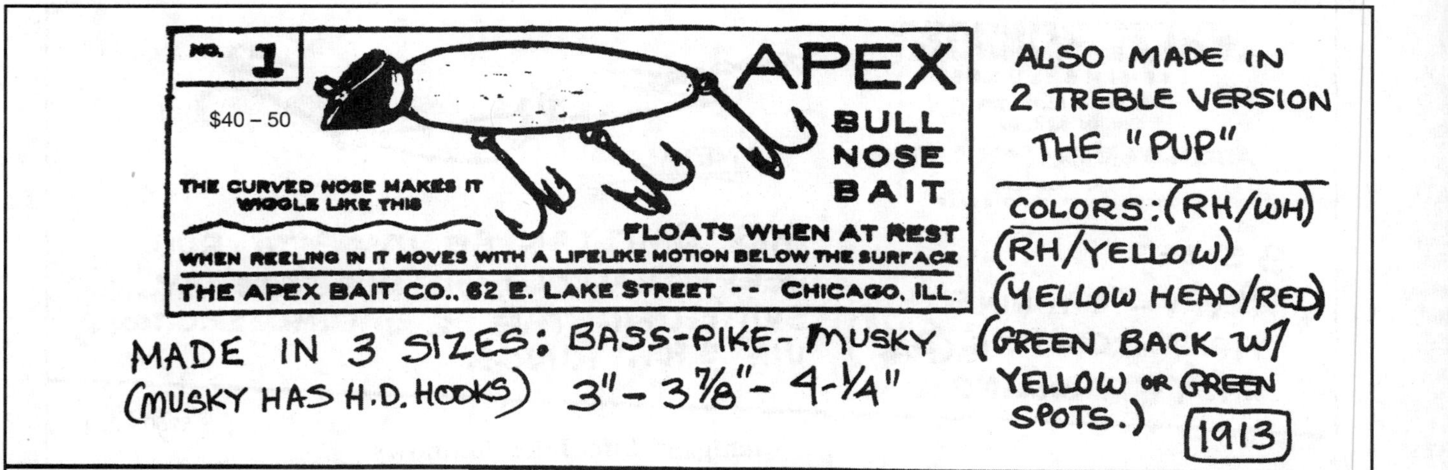

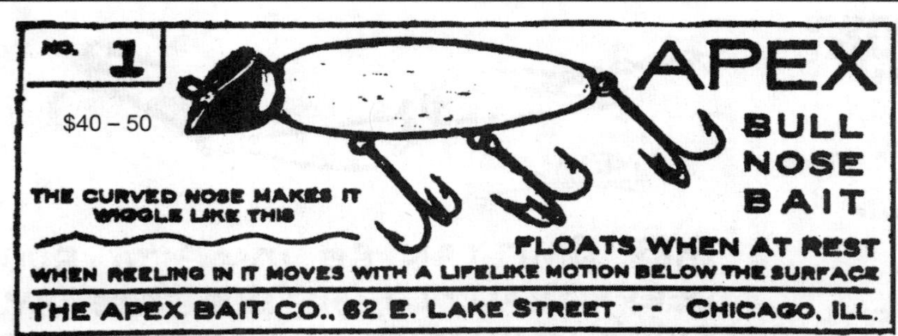
NO. 1
APEX
BULL NOSE BAIT
THE CURVED NOSE MAKES IT WIGGLE LIKE THIS
FLOATS WHEN AT REST
WHEN REELING IN IT MOVES WITH A LIFELIKE MOTION BELOW THE SURFACE
THE APEX BAIT CO., 62 E. LAKE STREET -- CHICAGO, ILL.

$40 – 50

ALSO MADE IN 2 TREBLE VERSION THE "PUP"

COLORS: (RH/WH) (RH/YELLOW) (YELLOW HEAD/RED) (GREEN BACK W/ YELLOW OR GREEN SPOTS.)

1913

MADE IN 3 SIZES: BASS-PIKE-MUSKY (MUSKY HAS H.D. HOOKS) 3" – 3 7/8" – 4-1/4"

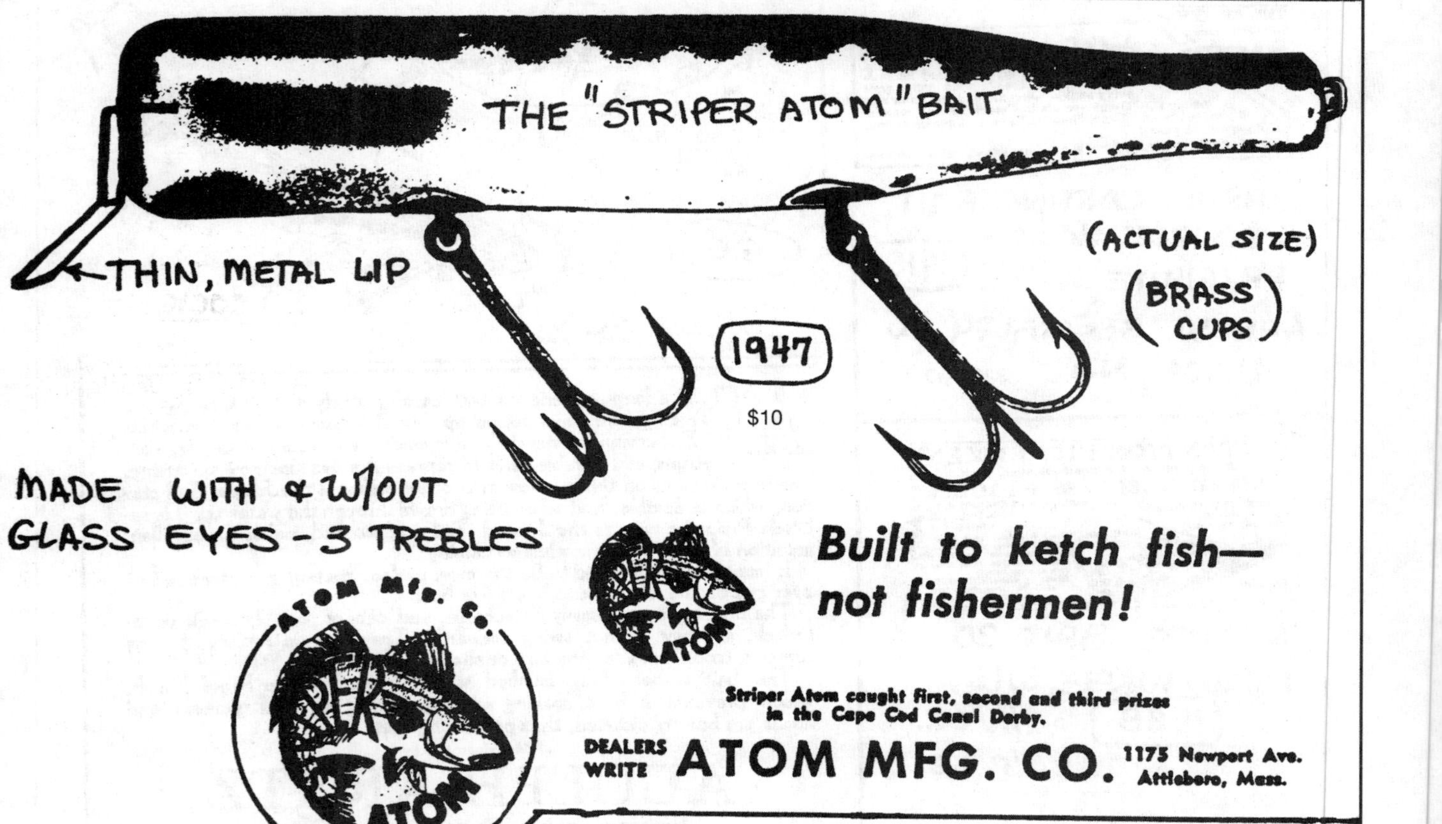

THE "STRIPER ATOM" BAIT

THIN, METAL LIP

(ACTUAL SIZE)

(BRASS CUPS)

1947

$10

MADE WITH & W/OUT GLASS EYES – 3 TREBLES

ATOM Mfg. Co. Attleboro, Mass.

ATOM

Built to ketch fish— not fishermen!

Striper Atom caught first, second and third prizes in the Cape Cod Canal Derby.

DEALERS WRITE ATOM MFG. CO. 1175 Newport Ave. Attleboro, Mass.

FISHERMEN! Here Is The Most Amazing Plug Ever Made

IT FLOATS! IT SINKS! IT'S WEEDLESS! IT CATCHES FISH!

(7/8 oz.) Anderson MINNOW

1949

Patent Applied For

SNAPS OPEN WHEN FISH STRIKES

So Tricky—Game Laws Prohibit Use in Minnesota, Missouri, and Pennsylvania

Barb is protected in lure while casting
Available in Perch, Frog and Red Head
Weight 7/8 oz.

SEND COUPON

ANDERSON BAIT CO.
1324 Henderson St., Chicago 13, Ill.
Please send ☐ R.H. ☐ PERCH ☐ FROG
NAME
ADDRESS
CITY STATE

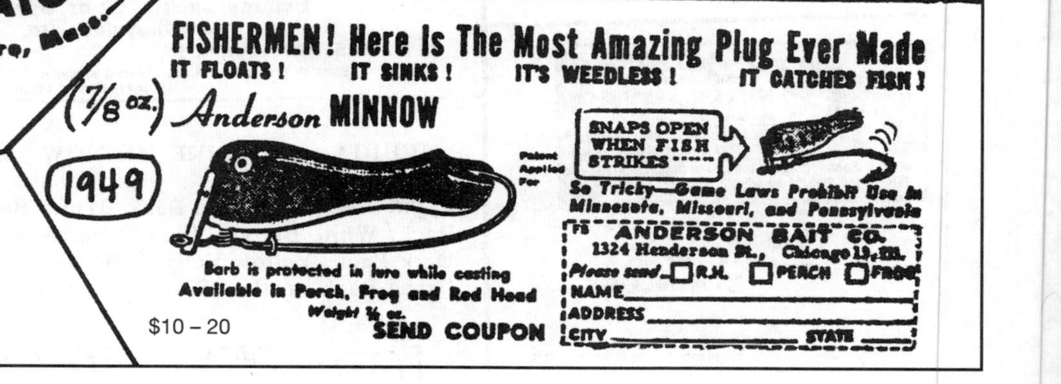

Condition = value.

$10 – 20

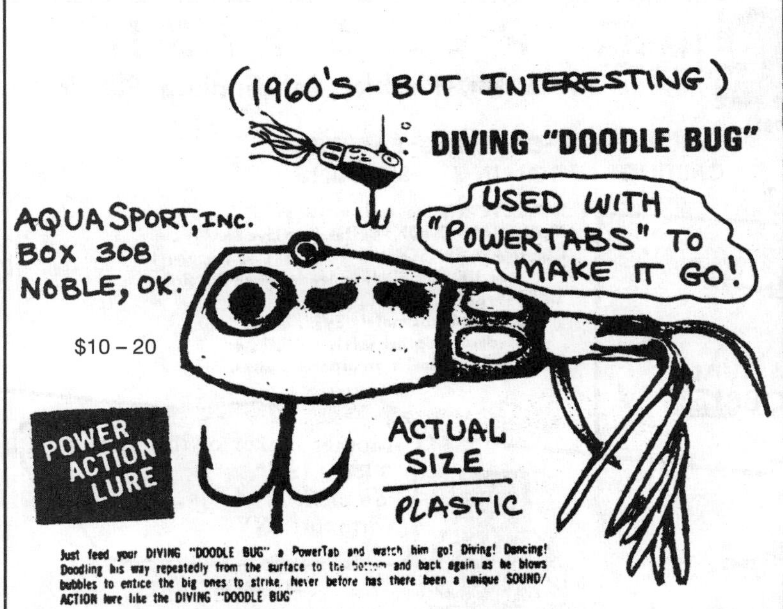

(1960'S - BUT INTERESTING)
DIVING "DOODLE BUG"
USED WITH "POWERTABS" TO MAKE IT GO!
AQUA SPORT, INC.
BOX 308
NOBLE, OK.
POWER ACTION LURE
ACTUAL SIZE
PLASTIC
Just feed your DIVING "DOODLE BUG" a PowerTab and watch him go! Diving! Dancing! Doodling his way repeatedly from the surface to the bottom and back again as he blows bubbles to entice the big ones to strike. Never before has there been a unique SOUND/ACTION lure like the DIVING "DOODLE BUG"

$10 – 20

LUCKY BUNNY $15

1954

3-3/4"

3"

2 1/8"

PLASTIC BODY (RED) (GREEN) (YELLOW)

REAL RABBIT FOOT BODY

2 SIZES
- SPINNING SIZE
- BAIT CASTING SIZES

MFG. BY:
AMERICAN ROD AND GUN
STAMFORD, CONN.

UBANGI $10

MFG. BY:
FORREST ALLEN
STAMFORD, CONN.
(1955)

$100 – 150

OSCAR THE FROG (1947)

One of the finest bass and pike lures on the market. OSCAR is a versatile, animated frog that can do just about everything his live counterpart can. He swims, dives or skims the surface, depending on how you fish him. OSCAR has movable arms and legs, and his actions in the water belie the fact that he is a mechanical bait. OSCAR is ideal for either trolling or casting.

Sturdily constructed with ample tensile strength—OSCAR can catch big fish as well as small.

OSCAR has a substantial treble hook on his belly and an accepted bass-size hook on either leg, one up and one down. Painted in natural colors, OSCAR has eye-appeal as well as fish appeal. He's a natural.

T. F. AU CLAIRE AND ASSOC. INC. 279 HIGHLAND AVE. DETROIT 3, MICHIGAN

ALLCOCK $5 – 10

METAL BALLS ROTATE ON A WIRE.

WATER WITCH

1 1/4" - 1 1/2" - 2" - 2 1/2" SIZES

$100 – 150

LATER NOTE: ALSO MADE BY THE GEE-WIZ BAIT CO. RICHLAND CENTER, WISC.

- ALSO MADE IN A MUSKY SIZE – EARLY MODEL – (5") HAD DARK BROWN LEGS.

(1931)

GEE-WIZ FROG LURE

Gee Wiz!

$40 – 50

The Most Life-Like Lure Made—*Unique, Deadly!*

This will prove to be the BAIT SENSATION for 1931. The greatest contribution to angling in many decades. It's the kick that gets the fish. This lure does all that a live frog can do—and more!

Made In 2 Sizes—
Our No. 23 B—Red and white ....
Our No. 23 A—Musky size, natural green ..
Our No. 23 B—In natural green ....

Recommended by Leading Authorities on Angling—At Your Dealer, or Direct

ALL STAR BAIT CO. 1303 West Jackson Blvd. **CHICAGO, ILL.**

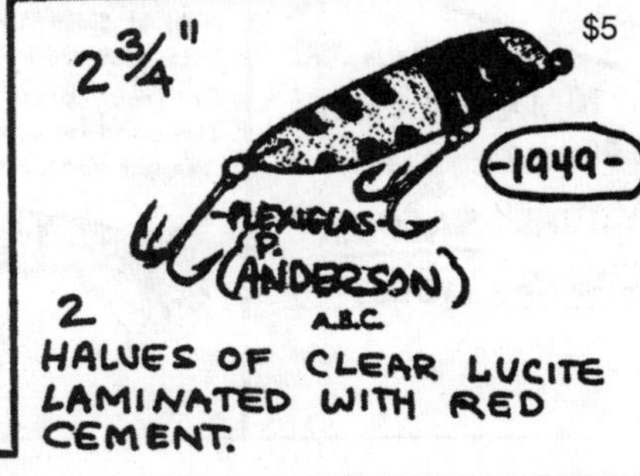

PLEXIGLAS
P. ANDERSON
A.B.C.

$5

2 3/4"

(1949)

2 HALVES OF CLEAR LUCITE LAMINATED WITH RED CEMENT.

ACTUAL LURE

1950

REAL FISH

In Tough, Pliable, Self-Sealing Plastic

ACTUAL LURES are manufactured under U. S. A. Pat. No. 2169811

COLD SPRING HARBOR
LONG ISLAND, N.Y.

THE BEST FISH-CATCHING BAIT FOR
CASTING - TROLLING - SPINNING

REAL EYE - Natural scale markings-
REAL FISH ACTION - Better Than Live Bait!
USE IT ALL SEASON! One Actual Lure has caught over 100 fish. Rides up leader when fish strikes.
SIZES (Wobbler and Skip-Dip):
Small, approximately 3½", ⅝ oz.
Medium, approximately 4¾", ⅞ oz.
Individually packed in transparent tubes.

$10

ACTUAL
WOBBLER

S54 Small
S58 Small (wounded)
S55 Medium
S59 Medium (wounded)

Another maker of this type was:
"TRU-FISH"
Pomonok Products, Inc.
Northport, NY

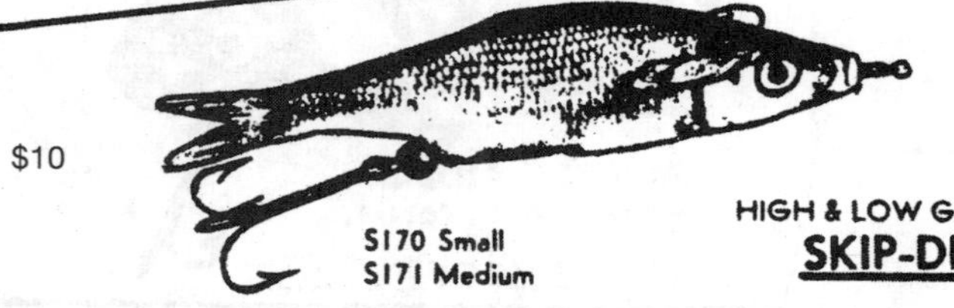

$10

HIGH & LOW GLIDING
SKIP-DIP

S170 Small
S171 Medium

SKIP-DIP ACTION

Attached parallel plane fins give it the skip & dip motion. Fish it on the surface - over the weeds. By adding weight, fish it deep with same porpoise-like action.

Tiny-Trouter

A REAL FISH - Especially Selected for FLY ROD!

$10

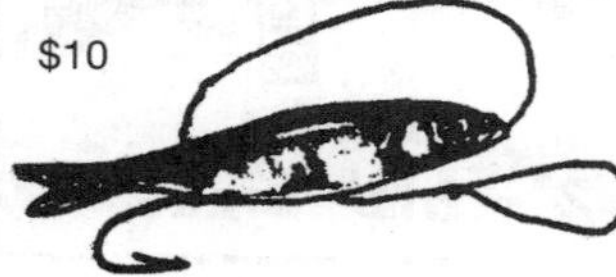

An ideal small bait for pan fish!

S60 Tiny Trouter
S61 Tiny Trouter (wounded)
Weight approx. ¼ oz. Size approx. 2½".

THE Spin-ster

A REAL FISH for Spinning

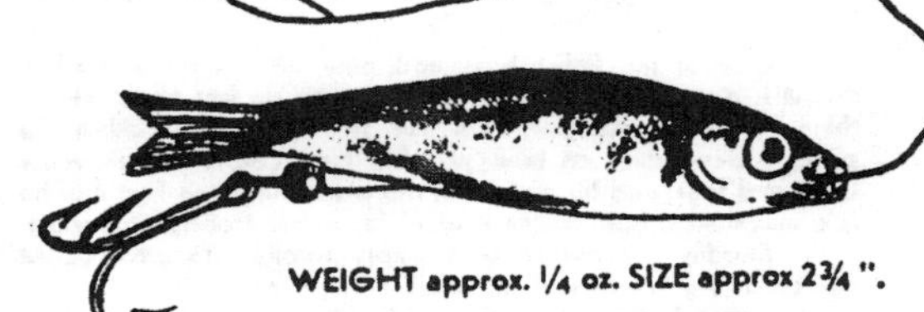

WEIGHT approx. ¼ oz. SIZE approx 2¾".

$10

S265 Actual Spin-ster
S266 Wounded Spin-ster
S267 Skip-Dip Spin-ster

CRICKET

$5

ALSO MADE:
REGULAR
"FISH EGGS"
*

* THEY ALSO MADE A COMB. SPINNER AND ACTUAL SALMON EGGS LURE.

SMALL golden brown SHRIMP

A REAL SHRIMP IN TOUGH, PLIABLE, SELF-SEALING PLASTIC

For Trout - Bass - Pike and all other game fish.
Designed for Spinning and Fly Rod.
Weight ¼oz. Approximately 3" long.

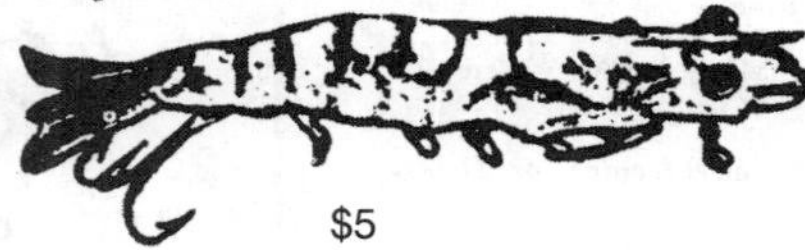

$5

The REAL - ACTUAL
Golden Brown SHRIMP

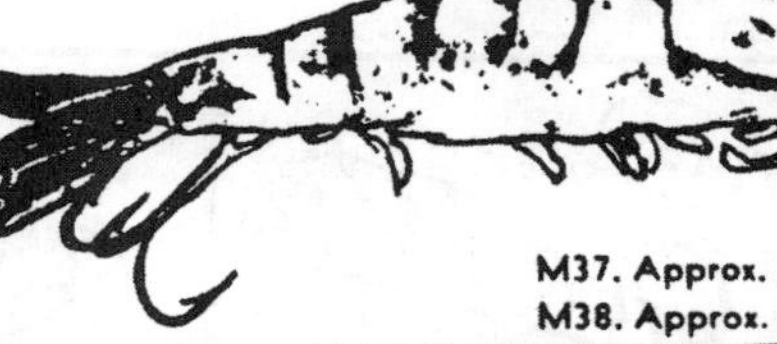

$10

M37. Approx. 3¾".
M38. Approx. 4¾".

$5

ACTUAL 'HOPPER

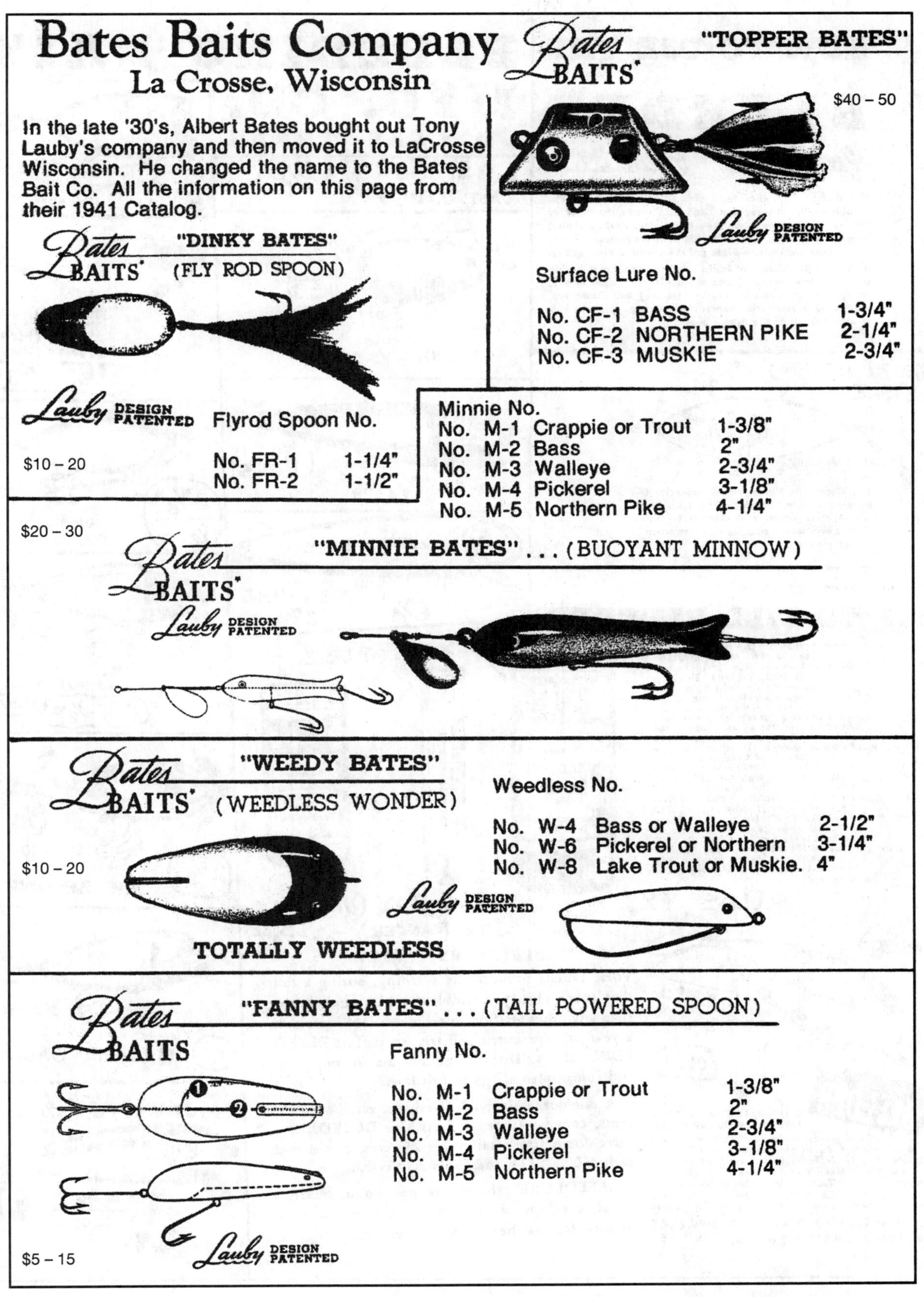
Bates Baits Company
La Crosse, Wisconsin
In the late '30's, Albert Bates bought out Tony Lauby's company and then moved it to LaCrosse Wisconsin. He changed the name to the Bates Bait Co. All the information on this page from their 1941 Catalog.
Bates BAITS
"DINKY BATES"
(FLY ROD SPOON)
Lauby DESIGN PATENTED
Flyrod Spoon No.
$10 – 20
No. FR-1 1-1/4"
No. FR-2 1-1/2"
Bates BAITS
"TOPPER BATES"
$40 – 50
Lauby DESIGN PATENTED
Surface Lure No.
No. CF-1 BASS 1-3/4"
No. CF-2 NORTHERN PIKE 2-1/4"
No. CF-3 MUSKIE 2-3/4"
Minnie No.
No. M-1 Crappie or Trout 1-3/8"
No. M-2 Bass 2"
No. M-3 Walleye 2-3/4"
No. M-4 Pickerel 3-1/8"
No. M-5 Northern Pike 4-1/4"
$20 – 30
Bates BAITS
"MINNIE BATES" . . . (BUOYANT MINNOW)
Lauby DESIGN PATENTED
Bates BAITS
"WEEDY BATES"
(WEEDLESS WONDER)
Weedless No.
No. W-4 Bass or Walleye 2-1/2"
No. W-6 Pickerel or Northern 3-1/4"
No. W-8 Lake Trout or Muskie. 4"
$10 – 20
Lauby DESIGN PATENTED
TOTALLY WEEDLESS
Bates BAITS
"FANNY BATES" . . . (TAIL POWERED SPOON)
Fanny No.
No. M-1 Crappie or Trout 1-3/8"
No. M-2 Bass 2"
No. M-3 Walleye 2-3/4"
No. M-4 Pickerel 3-1/8"
No. M-5 Northern Pike 4-1/4"
$5 – 15
Lauby DESIGN PATENTED

HOW TO USE THE BLEEDER

for Best Results

The BLEEDER, when used with BLEEDLURE Tablets, should not be worked fast. Rod movements, to right or left, or up or down, should be fairly easy. Reeling should be moderately slow. All BLEEDER Baits are buoyant, lively, and respond instantly to slight rod movement or easy reeling.

Cast the BLEEDER out in the usual manner. Let it remain still for a few seconds. Move rod tip left and right slowly, or up and down easily, as the case may be. Count ten, make a quick short jerk. Repeat this operation until the bait is retrieved out of the fishing zone.

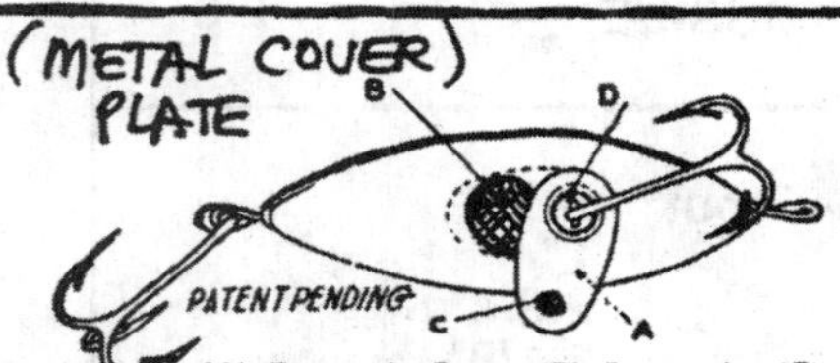
(METAL COVER)
PLATE
B
D
PATENT PENDING
C
A

(A) Receptacle Cover. (B) Receptacle. (C) Receptacle Hole, usually sufficient for bleeding in clear water. (D) Receptacle Hinge. Dotted line shows position of cover when in casting position.

HOW TO FILL BLEEDER

Hold the bait in the palm of your hand, back down. Move receptacle cover (A) to one side far enough to receive the BLEEDLURE Tablets. Move receptacle cover back in position, leaving a small opening at the side. This permits the water to start the dissolving process of the tablets. After two or three casts, adjust the opening according to the amount of bleeding desired. In clear water a smaller amount of bleeding will be needed than in murky water. After a little experience with the BLEEDER, you will learn for yourself how to regulate the bleeding feature for best results in all water. Always use TWO BLEEDLURE Tablets at a time. These will last from 20 to 35 minutes in actual casting.

KEEP IN MIND that the BLEEDER simulates small prey, badly wounded, and *profuse bleeding is not necessary.*

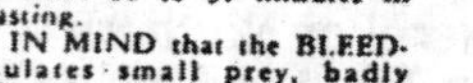
DALLAS, TX.

(RANGER)

IT BLEEDS

1939

BLEEDER

ONLY BAIT THAT BLEEDS LIKE LIVE WOUNDED PREY

"Tried Bleeder in the bay. Caught several cod and red snappers. You've got something there."—F. W. Webber, Reg. Guide, Bellingham, Wash. Letters pouring in. Cut shows Ranger—dives with crazy side-to-side action. Bleed-lure Tablets fit in bait belly—leave realistic stream of "blood." Each Bleeder comes with 1 doz. tablets. Get your Bleeder now and be ready for record catches.

At Your Dealer's or Direct
BLEEDING BAIT MFG. CO.

DEALERS WRITE TODAY

BLEEDING BAIT MFG. CO.

DALLAS, TEXAS

B.P.S. 100 - 4" - 3/4 oz. (NOT ILLUS.)

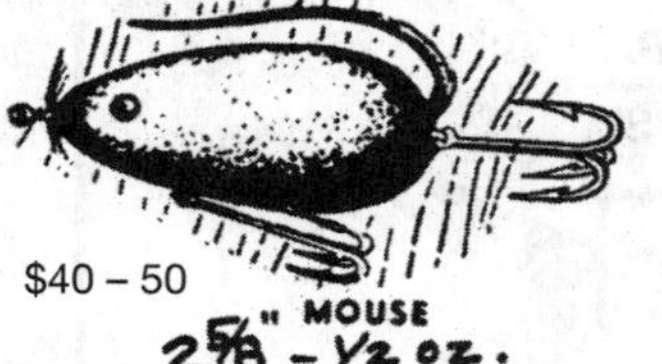

$40 – 50

MOUSE 2 5/8" - 1/2 oz.

(NO HOOKS)

$50 – 75

TEASER

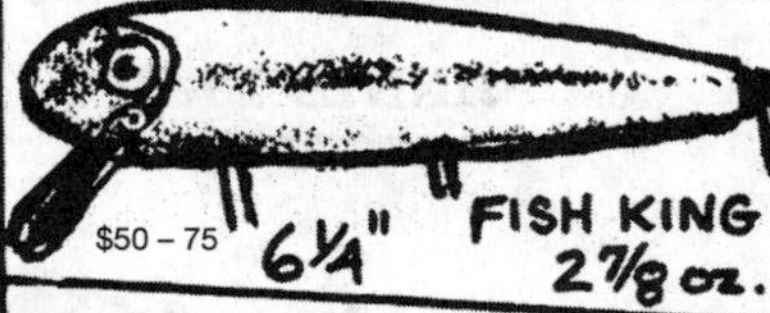

$50 – 75

FISH KING 6 1/4" 2 7/8 oz.

BLOOD TABLETS

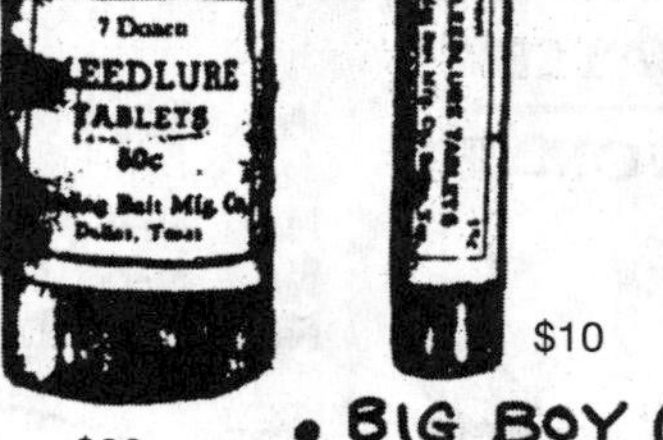
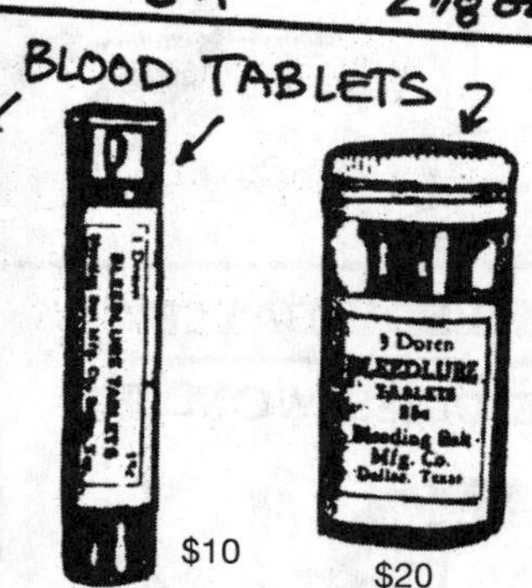
7 Dozen
BLEEDLURE
TABLETS
80c
Dallas, Texas

$20

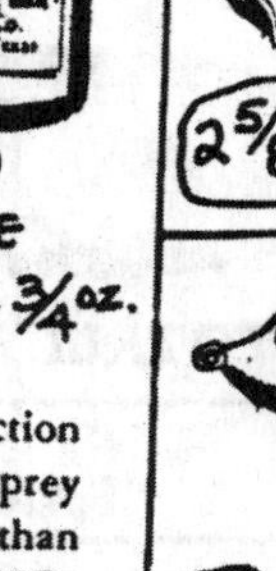

$10

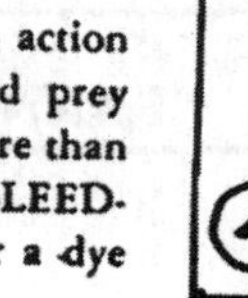
3 Dozen
BLEEDLURE
TABLETS
Bleeding Bait Mfg. Co.
Dallas, Texas

$20

• BIG BOY (LARGE SIZE RANGER) - 4" - 3/4 oz.

BLEEDLURE TABLETS

These tablets produce the bleeding, oozing action that more closely resembles live, wounded prey than any other artificial lure. It required more than a year of experiment and trial to perfect BLEEDLURE tablets. They are neither a stain nor a dye and conform to all game fish laws.

A one-dozen size vial of tablets, retail value 15 cents, comes with each bass size BLEEDER. A three-dozen size, retail value 25 cents, comes with each MUSKYITE and FISH KING bait.

BLEEDLURE tablets are packed in moisture proof, break-proof vials. When empty, they may be used for matches, hooks, sinkers, etc.

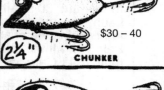

2 1/4" CHUNKER $30 – 40

$30 – 40

(FLOATER) BUBBLER (Sinker) 2 5/8" – 5/8 oz.

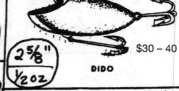

2 5/8" 1/2 oz. DIDO $30 – 40

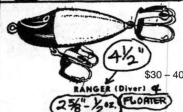

4 1/2" RANGER (Diver) & FLOATER 2 5/8" - 1/2 oz. $30 – 40

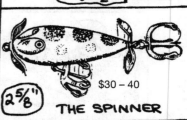

2 5/8" THE SPINNER $30 – 40

4" BROKEN BACK $30 – 50

MUSKYITE $50 – 75

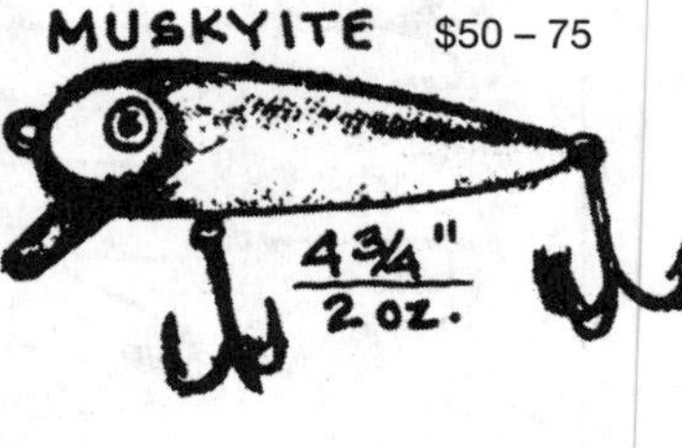
4 3/4"
2 oz.

$20 – 30

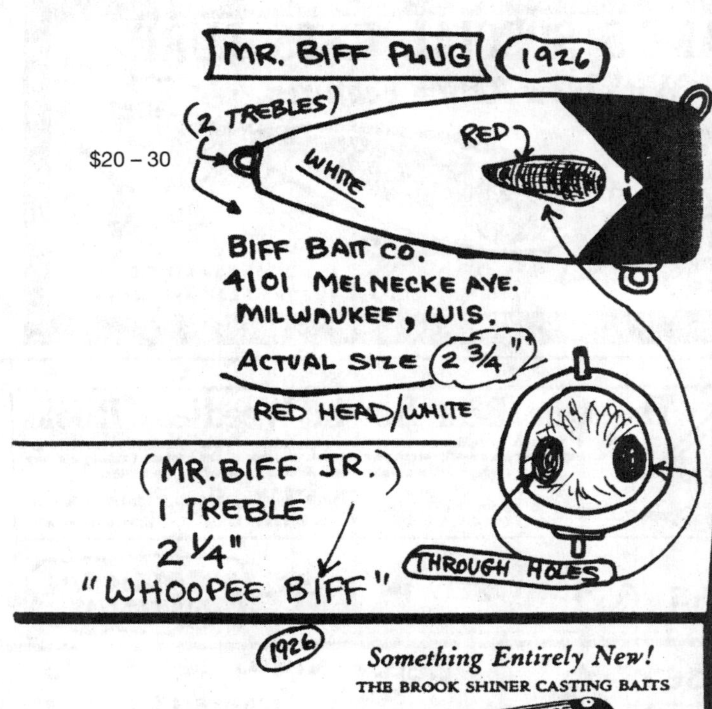
MR. BIFF PLUG
1926
(2 TREBLES)
RED
WHITE
BIFF BAIT CO.
4101 MELNECKE AVE.
MILWAUKEE, WIS.
ACTUAL SIZE 2 3/4"
RED HEAD/WHITE
(MR. BIFF JR.)
1 TREBLE
2 1/4"
"WHOOPEE BIFF"
THROUGH HOLES

1925

BIFF BAITS

BIFF GOES THAT SASEY BASSEY

CORK

Ptd. Dec. 22, 1925

$25

BASSEY BIFF SURFACE SINGLE WOBBLER

No. 777—Green and White, 1/4 ounce
No. 778—Red and White, 1/4 ounce

Made of hard-drawn, highly polished aluminum, two propeller blades and a bent spoon to which cork float is fastened. Corks are coated with a high gloss water-proof indestructible celluloid process finish.

One nickel-plated extra strong treble hook securely fastened to bait. The balance weight located in front of bait serves several purposes, primarily it does away with the use of a swivel or leader and positively prevents snarling and twisting of your line and interference with the churning and spattering motion while passing through the water. Made in two colors which are blended, two inches in length and weighs 1/4 ounce.

1926

$40 – 50

Something Entirely New!

THE BROOK SHINER CASTING BAITS

PATENT PENDING

Two Casting Baits

Special Introductory Price for this Month
REGULARLY PRICED

2 SIZES

- LARGE BAIT for pickerel, wall eyed and great northern pike — muskies.
- SMALL BAIT for large and small mouthed bass — white bass.

We guarantee the Brook Shiner Baits to catch more fish than any bait you ever owned. Money refunded and $5.00 for any fishless Brook Shiner Bait—Tried out and O. K.'d by old timers.

Exclusive Features—adjusting aluminum tongue and tail will make baits shimmy— wiggle, dart or immitate a shiner in fear and distress. Every strike a fish, because of unique hook attachment.

DO IT NOW! Remember our absolute iron clad guarantee. You want this bait at any price. SLIP US A DOLLAR BILL--NOW!

THE BROOK SHINER BAIT COMPANY
627 Sixth Avenue Milwaukee, Wis.

BIG BASS BITER
Streater tells the story on how this bait was invented to catch dormant, sleeping bass. You lower the teeth and they see a sleeping fish -and bites it- the bass wakes up with a reflex action bites back....fish-on! Go get a set of Uncle Harry's discarded dentures & make yourself this "super secret lure".

$5 – 15

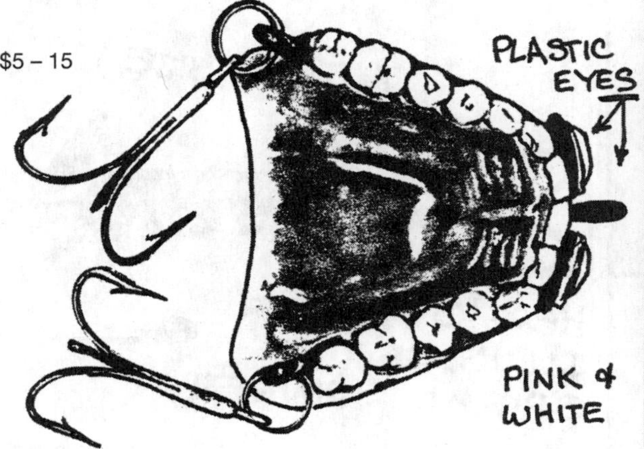
PLASTIC
EYES
PINK &
WHITE

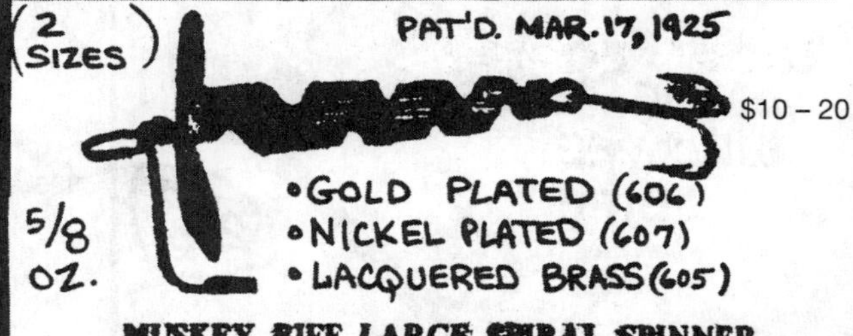
(2 SIZES)
PAT'D. MAR. 17, 1925
5/8 OZ.
•GOLD PLATED (606)
•NICKEL PLATED (607)
•LACQUERED BRASS (605)

$10 – 20

MUSKEY BIFF LARGE SPIRAL SPINNER

606 - GOLD - 3"
607 - NICKEL - 3"
605 - BRASS

PIKEY BIFF SMALL SPIRAL SPINNER

Weight 1/2 Ounce

No. 666—Nickel-Plated, two-inch size.

May be used in fresh and salt waters. Here is a deep water bait that is entirely different from all other types of spinners for the reason that it is absolutely reliable.

A Spiral Spinner can be operated at almost any depth of water, by merely regulating the speed of reeling. The balance weight located in front of the bait does away with the use of a swivel or leader, prevents snarling of line and back lashing when casting, and interference with spinning while passing over logs and rocks. While drifting the bass may be allowed to settle in deep water, then reeling slowly the bait will travel over the bottom. This is a very good way to [illegible] the big game fish. Made of strong spring brass and spring wire [illegible] will not rust or corrode. Nickel-plated on the outside and red enameled on the inside. Made in two sizes—two and three inches. Large size is an ideal bait for Muskies and Wall-eyed Pike. Small size is adapted for catching Sand and Grass Pike, Black Bass, Silver Pickerel, Rock Bass and large size Perch.

- MUSKY BIFF - 3" - 5/8 oz. $20 – 30
- PIKEY BIFF - 2" - 1/2 oz. $15 – 20

THE TACKLE BOX
LAND O'LAKES,
WISCONSIN.

$20 – 30 A RATHER NON-DESCRIPT TACK EYE WOOD BAIT. – 3 3/8" PROBABLY 40'S-50'S.

BAKE'S SPECIAL BASS LURE
With New Action Features
ROLLS WITH MOTION OF THE WATER
DUAL BEARINGS INSURE FREE SPINNING

$5 – 10

(1912 BING'S AD)

The One Best Bet in Weedless Hooks

Bing's famous weedless attachment, placed onto absolutely hand forged O'Shaughnessy hooks—the strongest hooks in the world, the best that money can buy. Plain weedless, each, 10c. Weighted weedless, each, 15c.

Sizes, No. 1, 1/0, 2/0, 3/0, 4/0, 5/0.

Bing's Weedless Fishhook Co.
Loan & Trust Bldg. Milwaukee, Wis.

BING'S O'SHAUGHNESSY

BING'S CASTING SPOON WAS PAT'D. JULY 17, 1906.

THE FIXED TAIL HOOK MODEL WAS ADVERTISED IN 1905 – (NEMAHBIN MINNOW)

$20 – 30

"THE WHOOPEE BIFF" (2 1/8")

"BASSEY" 1920'S

BELLY VIEW OF BIFF'S BAIT. (NAME IS STAMPED ON BELLY METAL)

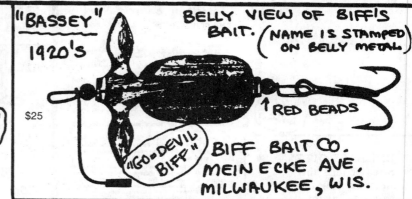

$25

RED BEADS

("GO-DEVIL BIFF")

BIFF BAIT CO.
MEINECKE AVE,
MILWAUKEE, WIS.

$20 – 30
$30 – 40 for musky

NOTE: ALSO MADE A MUSKY SIZE

MR. BIFF PLUG

MUSKY/PIKE BIFF SPIRAL SPINNER

$20 – 30

(PIKE – SIZE)

HERE'S A BETTER ILLUS. OF THE SPIRAL SPINNER.

$10

1952

Cork-bodied flies and spinning lures. Boone Baits are BEST. They're "Florida Fashioned."
BOONE BAIT CO.
WINTER PARK FLORIDA

MANITOU MINNOW

Patented: September 26, 1905

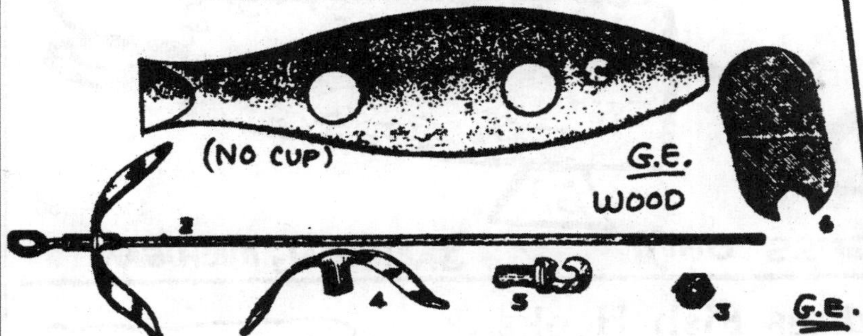
(NO CUP)
G.E.
WOOD
2
4
5
3
6
G.E.

FOLLOW THESE DIRECTIONS

To assemble, take body (No. 1) and insert rod (No. 2) in head of body to first hole and insert same through treble hooks, then to second hole and insert treble hooks and push rod entirley through body, then screw locknut (No. 3) to end of threads on (No. 2) place spinner (No. 4) on nipple (No. 5) and screw nipple (No. 5) on end of (No. 2) until the end of rod (No. 2) shows in opening of nipple (No. 5) then place treble hooks in hook at end of nipple (No. 5) then take wrench (No. 6) and hold locknut (No. 3) and screw nipple (No. 5) tightly to locknut (No 3).

IN 1905–A DO-IT-YOURSELF LURE KIT!

BAILEY & ELLIOTT,
ROCHESTER, INDIANA

$500 – 600

Wig-Wag

TRADE  MARK
ROYAL BRAND
FISHING TACKLE

KNOWN BY ALL ANGLERS
FOR QUALITY AND DEPENDABLE TACKLE

PATENT PENDING

The Royal Brand *Wig-Wag* Wood Minnows
are
Exclusively Manufactured by
A. J. BUKOSKE & SON
Winnipeg, Man.

(SLIGHT RIDGE IN HEAD)
CUP – 2 TREBLES
2½" – 3"
3 TREBLES
3½" – 4" – 4½" – 5"

$15

MINNOW SOCKS

1958

Patent Pending

NOW—STILL FISH, TROLL, CAST WITH LIVE MINNOWS, BALAO, EELS, MULLET, LARGE SHRIMP, FROGS, ETC.
Chinese handcuff principle holds bait securely, keeps alive indefinitely. Simply slide bait head-first into "SOCK" from either end.
In still fishing "SOCK" allows bait to swim naturally. Use with all bait rigs. Troll sock alone or attach to spoon. Ideal for spinning, surf casting, many other uses.
Hand woven of nylon coated, stainless stee. wire.
3 sizes, 4 cards:

3 Large ....8/0 and/or 10/0 hooks $1.90
4 Medium ....3/0 —— 6/0 hooks $2.00
6 Small ....4 ——. 3/0 hooks $1.90
3 Assorted $2.15

Check or M.O., No C.O.D.'s

BAIT'S ALIVE! Box 93 Postal Sta. K Toronto

$5

BLIMP'S
fishing tackle co.

P.O. BOX 437 • MANCHESTER, KY. 40962 • (606) 596-5873

SQUEAKY
Mr.
Mouse

THE HEAD REVOLVES AND IT SQUEAKS!

(THIS IS NOT OLD (70's) BUT IT'S NEAT!)

$20 – 40

(HEAD UNSCREWS)

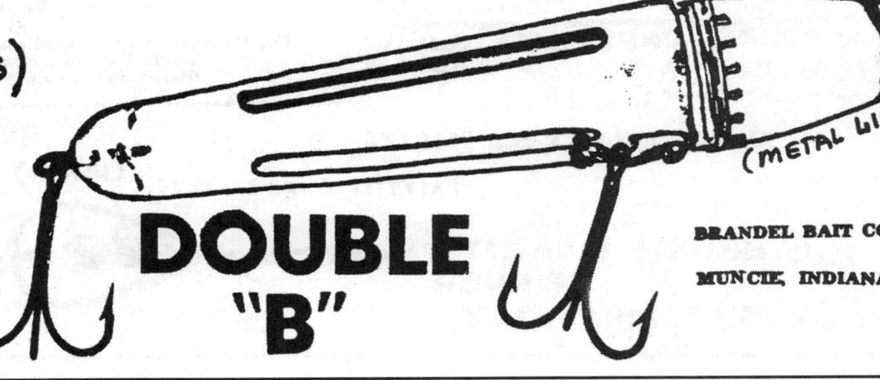
(METAL LIP)

CLEAR PLASTIC MINNOW TUBE

DOUBLE "B"

BRANDEL BAIT CO.
MUNCIE, INDIANA

$15

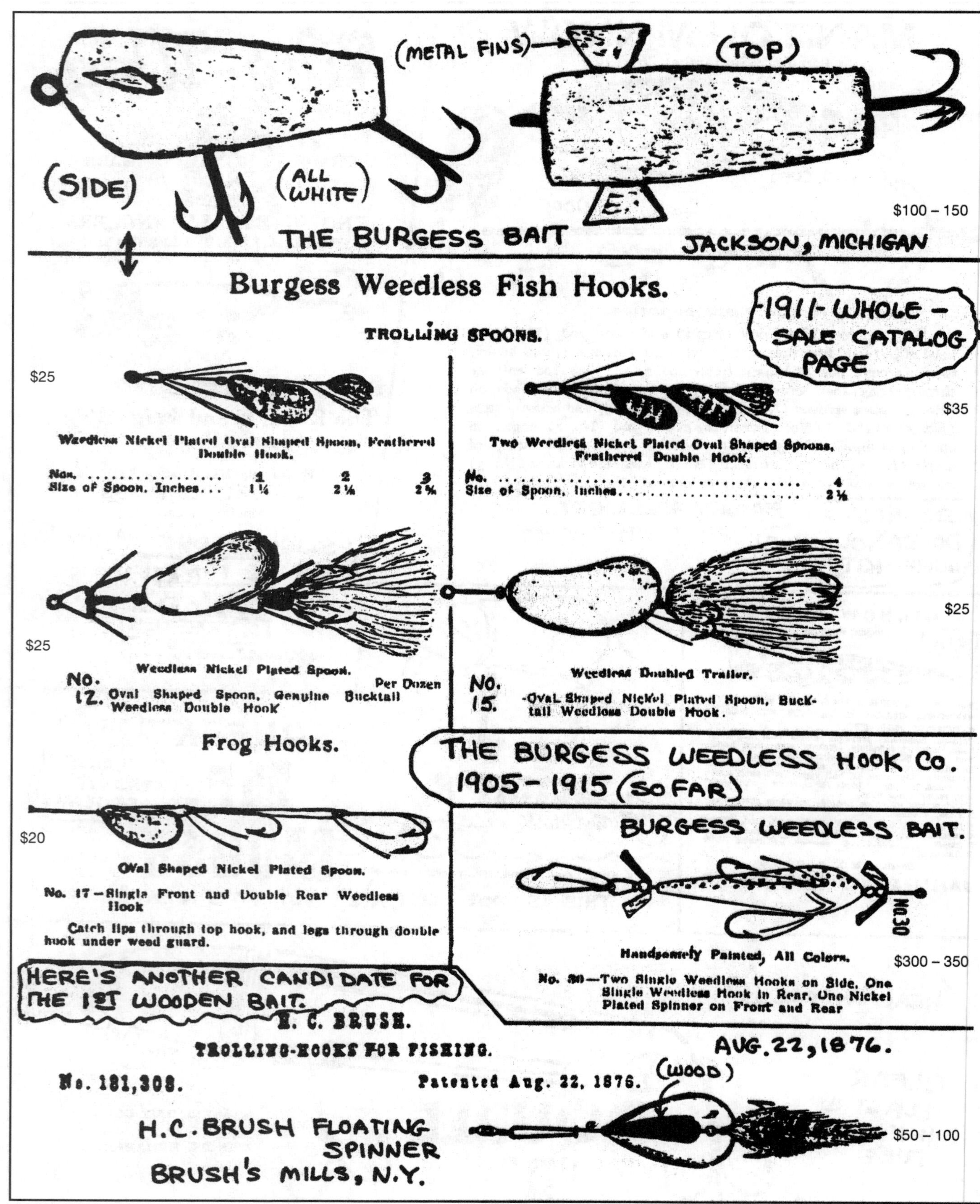
(METAL FINS)
(TOP)
(SIDE)
(ALL WHITE)
$100 – 150
THE BURGESS BAIT
JACKSON, MICHIGAN
Burgess Weedless Fish Hooks.
-1911- WHOLE-SALE CATALOG PAGE
TROLLING SPOONS.
$25
Weedless Nickel Plated Oval Shaped Spoon, Feathered Double Hook.
Nos. 1 2 3
Size of Spoon, Inches 1¼ 2⅛ 2⅝
$35
Two Weedless Nickel Plated Oval Shaped Spoons, Feathered Double Hook.
No. 4
Size of Spoon, Inches 2⅛
$25
$25
Weedless Nickel Plated Spoon.
Per Dozen
No. 12. Oval Shaped Spoon, Genuine Bucktail Weedless Double Hook
Weedless Doubled Trailer.
No. 15. Oval Shaped Nickel Plated Spoon, Bucktail Weedless Double Hook.
Frog Hooks.
THE BURGESS WEEDLESS HOOK Co. 1905-1915 (SO FAR)
$20
Oval Shaped Nickel Plated Spoon.
No. 17 – Single Front and Double Rear Weedless Hook
Catch lips through top hook, and legs through double hook under weed guard.
BURGESS WEEDLESS BAIT.
NO.30
Handsomely Painted, All Colors.
$300 – 350
No. 30—Two Single Weedless Hooks on Side, One Single Weedless Hook in Rear, One Nickel Plated Spinner on Front and Rear
HERE'S ANOTHER CANDIDATE FOR THE 1ST WOODEN BAIT.
H. C. BRUSH.
TROLLING-HOOKS FOR FISHING.
AUG. 22, 1876.
No. 181,308.
Patented Aug. 22, 1876.
(WOOD)
H.C. BRUSH FLOATING SPINNER
BRUSH'S MILLS, N.Y.
$50 – 100

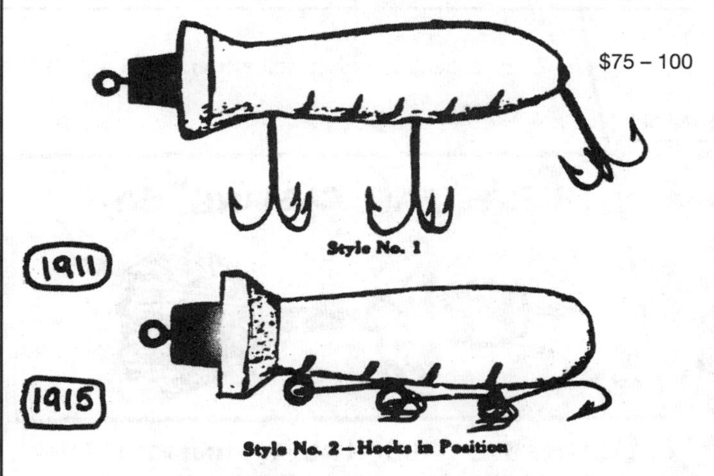
$75 – 100
Style No. 1
1911
1915
Style No. 2—Hooks in Position

INSTRUCTIONS:—Cast near shore or near weeds or among opening-in weeds in from 1 to 4 feet of water. Retrieve *more rapidly* than with ordinary baits, and the greatest success will be attained.

T. J. BOULTON

32 Lauderdale Street DETROIT, MICHIGAN

THE BASS HOG THE GREATEST BASS BAIT KNOWN

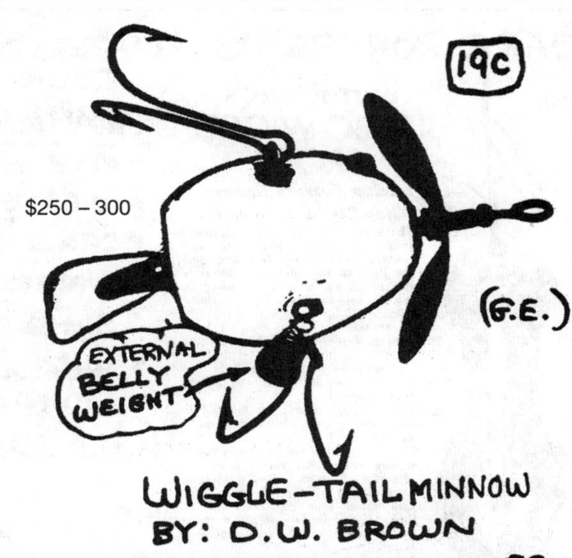
19C
$250 – 300
(G.E.)
EXTERNAL BELLY WEIGHT

WIGGLE-TAIL MINNOW
BY: D.W. BROWN

- AS THE PROP REVOLVES, THE TAIL WAGS. HAS AN "EXTERIOR" BELLY WEIGHT—SO MUST BE OLD.

$75 – 100

1925
(TOP)

BOLTON'S A-B-C MINNOW
DETROIT, MICH.

A SCREW EYE ALLOWED THE REMOVAL OF THE TOP PC.

For Bass, Pickerel and Pike use

BILL BAILER'S

B-K BAIT

(Made by a fisherman and guaranteed to catch fish)

$10 – 20 Patented July 25, 1925

Double Spinner B-K Bait
Combination Gold and Nickel Plated Spinner

Single B-K Bait
Gold or Nickel Plated Spinner,

Silk Wound Bass Bug with Buck Tail Wings
The IDEAL Casting Bait
and a real fish getter. Keel weight keeps hook upright avoiding weeds and snags, also makes hook more effective when fish strike. One user says he caught 27 Small Mouth Bass out of 31 casts made with B-K Bait (name on request). *If your dealer does not carry this wonderful bait, send direct to*
W. S. BAILER, 436 Breckenridge St., BUFFALO, N. Y.

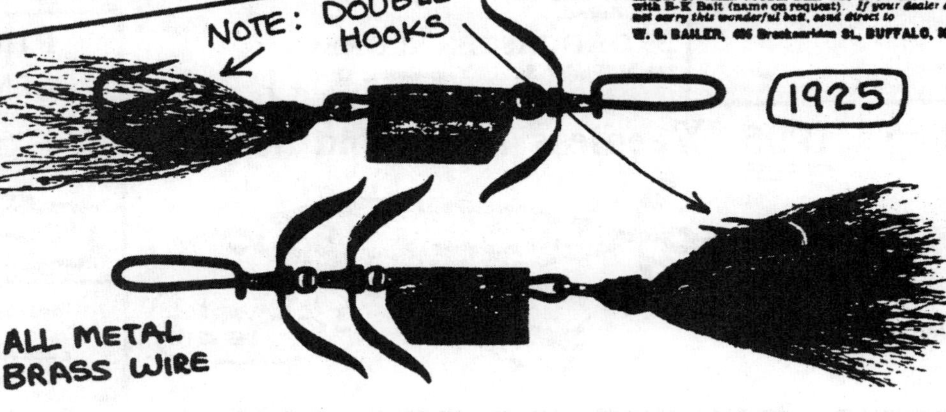
NOTE: DOUBLE HOOKS
1925
ALL METAL BRASS WIRE

Better condition means higher values.

BARR-ROYERS CO. – WATERLOO, IOWA.

$10

Barr-Royers
JUMBO WIGGLE FROG

(1931) *Action Extraordinary*
They Strike It to Eat

The true to life kicking, wiggling, swimming action, the color and conformation of the live frog and the flash of the spinner is irresistible to all game fish. Finished in brown meadow and green pond frog.

(Three sizes.)

- Length 4 inches, Weight 1 ounce, Spinner sized for best results,
- Length 3 inches, Weight ½ ounce with spinner,
- Length 1½ inches, Weight 1/10 ounce with baby June Bug spinner for fly rod.

If your jobber or dealer cannot supply you, order direct from us.

Forty Years of Angling have taught us that to catch fish, give them true reproductions of their regular foods—attach a spinner to excite their curiosity and anger.

Send for free literature describing our Fish Hound—Wiggle Frog—Craw Dad—Water Puppy—Sand Toad—and Wiggle Fin Minnow.

BARR-ROYER CO.

THEY ALSO MADE:

- FISH HOUND
- WIGGLE FROG
- CRAW DAD
- WATER PUPPY
- SAND TOAD
- WIGGLE FIN MINNOW

(NEED ILLUS.)

Lure collecting is fun, tell a friend.

BUEL'S "FAR CASTING" BAIT

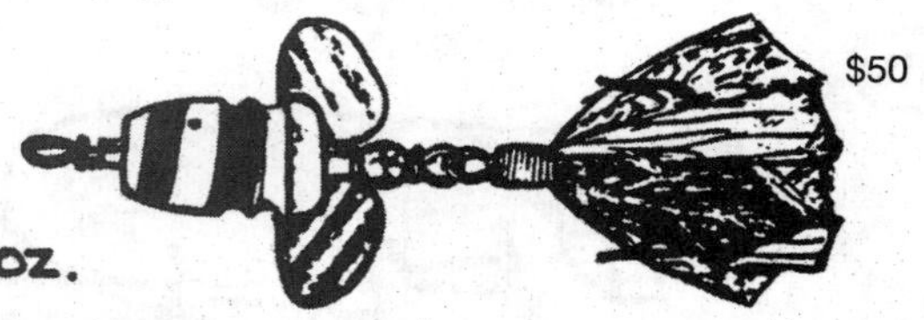

$50

½ oz.

BONAFIDE ALUMINUM MINNOW $1,000+

BONAFIDE MFG. CO. PLYMOUTH, MICHIGAN

(1908)

(WIRE LEADER INSIDE)

NOTE: 2 HALVES OF CAST SOLID ALUMINUM – HELD W/BRASS SCREW

(RUBBER) (1913)

BURKE'S BASS BAIT NO. 4 $30 – 40

A hollow bait made of soft rubber, which admits water. Similar in action to Burke's Bass Bait, No. T13327, except that it is a wobbler. Complete with two hooks, one double and one treble.

Lures in this book are priced as very good to very good+ condition. Better condition, special color, and original box add much more value.

Four Lures for the PRICE of ONE

WHEN You Buy the NEW

(1933) 4-IN-1 $25 – 50

BROADCASTER

THE LURE YOU'VE DREAMED ABOUT

PATENTED

It is a surface teaser, a woozy wiggler, a darting demon, or a deep diving killer. A simple adjustment of the PATENTED NOSEPIECE regulates the action and depth.

The BROADCASTER is the only lure made with EASILY REMOVABLE HOOKS that can never work loose, can never pull out.

- Two hook size—3½", weighs ½ oz.
- Three hook size—4½", weighs ¾ oz.

Buy it from your dealer. If he can't supply you, we will send it postpaid anywhere in U. S. Three hook size, Specify colors desired.

BROADCASTER LURES
224 N. Phelps St. Youngstown, Ohio

RUBBER

BURKE'S BUG BAIT $20 – 30

A weedless Bass Bait made of soft white rubber with fancy colorings, 2¼ inches long. Can be filled with water and regulated same as T13327.

2¼"

RUBBER (1921)

BURKE'S BASS BAIT $20 – 30

This bait is made of soft rubber, is hollow, and admits water; the amount of water admitted controls the buoyancy of the bait and adds more or less weight to it. By holding bait under water and pressing with the thumb and finger the inflowing water may be cut off to make the bait any weight desired. The amount of water admitted causes the bait to ride high or low in the water.

Bing's 1906 Weedless Nemahbin Minnow

BING'S

(UNDER WATER)

5½"-OVERALL LENGTH

$150 – 200

BING'S WEEDLESS NEMAHBIN MINNOW

4¼" OVERALL

BING'S

$250 – 300

Manufactured and For Sale By
A. F. BINGENHEIMER
142 Second St. Milwaukee, Wis.

THE BITE-EM-BATE

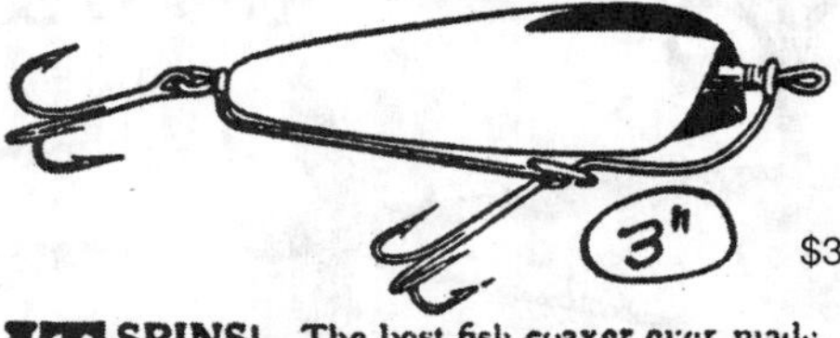
3"

$30 – 40

IT SPINS DIPS DIVES DARTS | The best fish coaxer ever made. Some day it will be your "Old Reliable." Why not now? no more, no less. At dealers or direct.

The Bite-Em-Bate Co., Warsaw, Ind.

THE 1ST
BITE-EM

1917
NOTE LINE TIES

BITE-EM-BATE COMPANY, WARSAW, IND.

Bite-Em-Bate

This is the original member of the family, and one of the most popular lures ever produced. There is nothing like it in construction or efficiency. By trying one, you will greatly improve your batting average.

PATENT PENDING
Bite-Em Bate
1920

1920

$35

Bite-Em-Bate Mole

Bite-Em-Water-Mole

The water mole is intended primarily as a surface lure although, by tying the line in the upper line hitch (not shown in the illustration) the bait can be made to ride from a few inches to several feet under water, depending on your reeling. Casting, it goes out like a bullet, and is as accurate as the casting baits used by experts.

1920

$30

PATENT PENDING

Bite-Em-Bate, Wiggler

Bite-Em-Wiggler

The rear spoon makes this lure very active, causing it to dip, dive or skitter at the will of user. It also adds to the attractiveness of the bait, thereby hooks many tardy rear biters which other wise would be lost. This is the plug that made Bite-Em-Bates famous. It is built on the same principle as the well-known "spoon" bait.

NEW WEEDLESS LURE

"WEEDLESS BUT NOT FISHLESS"

$10

A
B

U. S. PAT. 2261066

AT LAST! A weedless bait that works. No more snags when the big ones strike. No more losses with tricky but fishless gadgets. A fisherman inventor has perfected the INVADER to help you get into the spots infested with weeds and pond lilies . . . favorite haunts of the big fellows. Yes indeed, this bait is "weedless but not fishless."

THIS DEPENDABLE weedless plug has internally disposed sliding treblehook, for setting (see diagram A). The instant it is compressed, hooks are exposed through slots (see diagram B). A twitch of the rod pulls hook forward setting it securely.

Head finishes in five popular colors:
Red Black Green White Yellow

B & M PRODUCTS COMPANY
P. O. Box No. 469, NORWALK, CONN.

Here is my $.......... cash, money order, check for ...... INVADERS, colors Red ☐, Black ☐, Green ☐, White ☐, Yellow ☐.

THE "INVADER"

1946

Fish for Sure with an OZARKA LURE

$5

1947

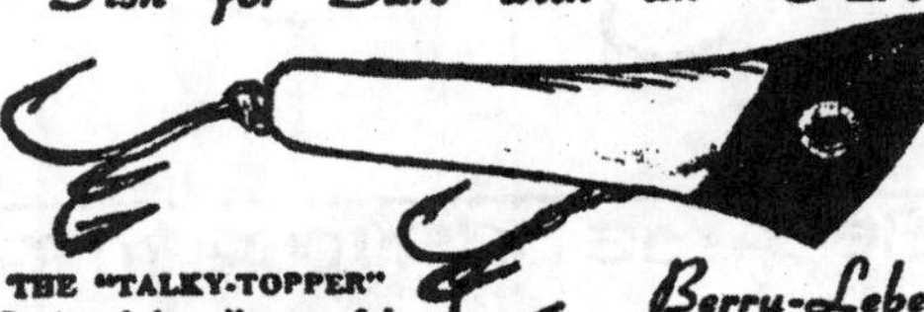

THE "TALKY-TOPPER"
Designed for all game fish

Favorite of the famous Ozark fishing country, here's the dual-action, no-foul, easy-to-use surface lure you'll want! Can be "popped"; it'll wiggle and swish. Nothing like it; 12 colors.

At Your Dealer or Order Direct

Berry-Lebeck Manufacturing Co.
CALIFORNIA, MO.

BON-NET

OWN A GENUINE BON-NET LURE— FIELD AND STREAM WINNER 1952 MUSKY CONTEST

$25

G.E. (6 TREBLES)

A tantalizing surface bait that gurgles, sputters, and jingles as it skims through the water. Irresistible to MUSKIES, large bass, and northern.

If your dealer cannot supply you, send check, or money order.

Exclusive distributor for BON-NET baits.
W. H. Hobbs Supply Co.
Eau Claire, Wis.

1952

Check Color
☐ Red & White ☐ Perch
☐ Orange spot ☐ Frog

MFG. IN MICHIGAN FOR DISTRIBUTORS IN WISC. (EAU CLAIRE AND STEVENS POINT) 10,000 BAITS PER ORDER – 50/50.

BOSHEARS TACKLE CO.
LITTLE ROCK ARK.

$5

RAZZLE DAZZLE

MINETTE

BATES PROD. CARLISLE, MASS.

$5

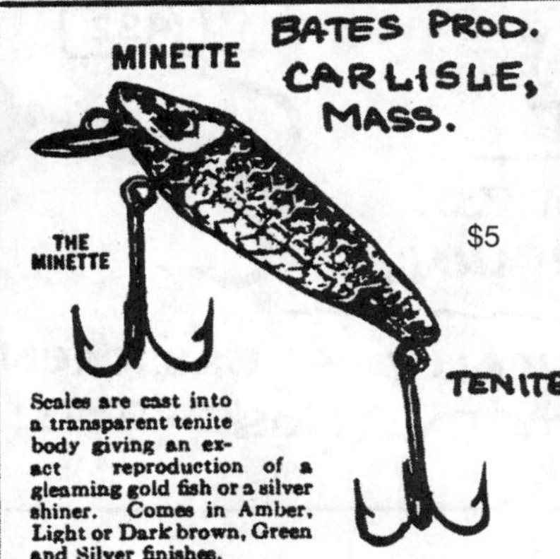
THE MINETTE

TENITE

Scales are cast into a transparent tenite body giving an exact reproduction of a gleaming gold fish or a silver shiner. Comes in Amber, Light or Dark brown, Green and Silver finishes.

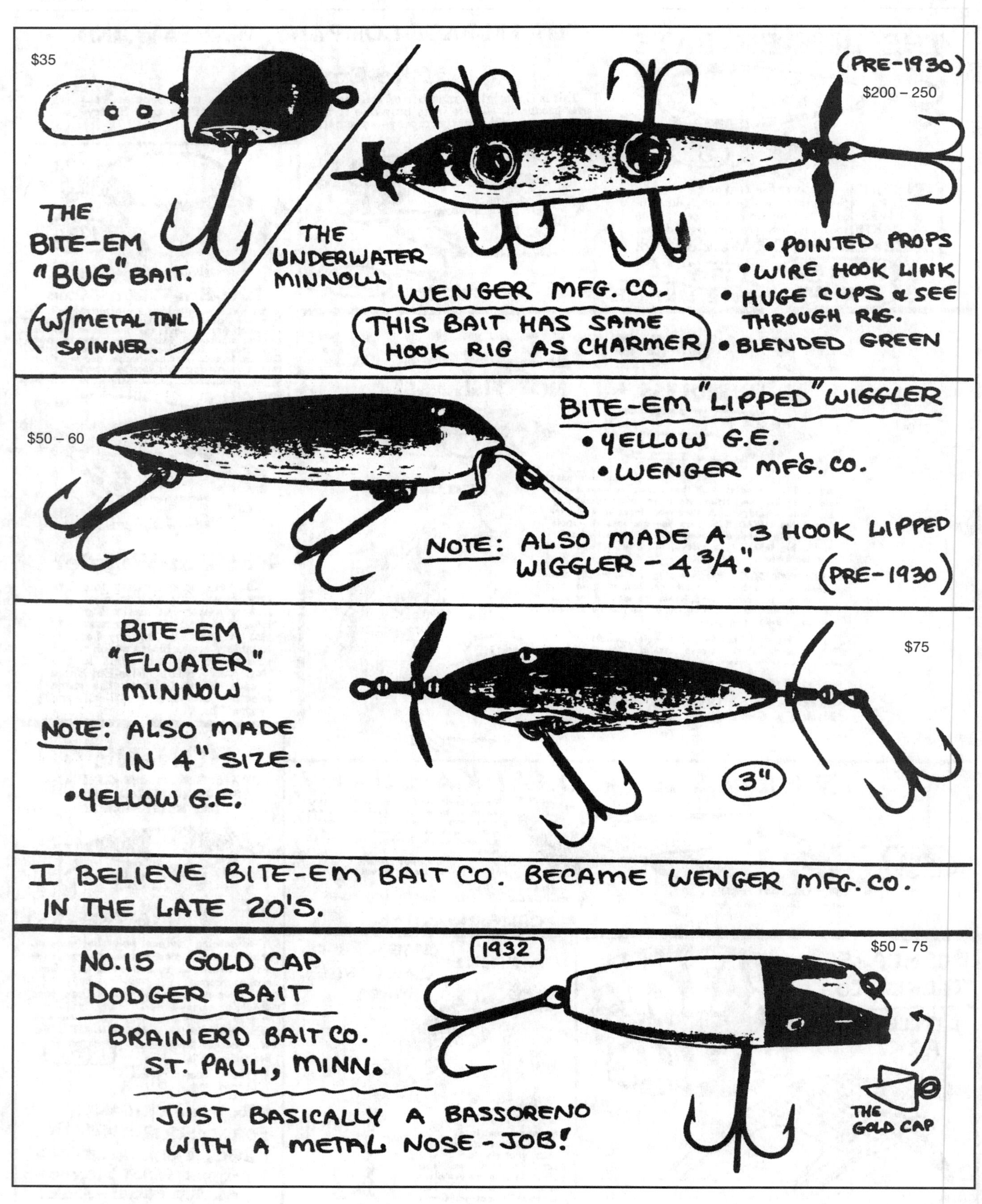
$35
THE BITE-EM "BUG" BAIT.
(W/METAL TAIL SPINNER.
THE UNDERWATER MINNOW
WENGER MFG. CO.
THIS BAIT HAS SAME HOOK RIG AS CHARMER
(PRE-1930)
$200 – 250
• POINTED PROPS
• WIRE HOOK LINK
• HUGE CUPS & SEE THROUGH RIG.
• BLENDED GREEN
$50 – 60
BITE-EM "LIPPED" WIGGLER
• YELLOW G.E.
• WENGER MFG. CO.
NOTE: ALSO MADE A 3 HOOK LIPPED WIGGLER - 4 3/4".
(PRE-1930)
BITE-EM "FLOATER" MINNOW
NOTE: ALSO MADE IN 4" SIZE.
• YELLOW G.E.
$75
3"
I BELIEVE BITE-EM BAIT CO. BECAME WENGER MFG. CO. IN THE LATE 20'S.
NO.15 GOLD CAP DODGER BAIT
1932
$50 – 75
BRAINERD BAIT CO. ST. PAUL, MINN.
JUST BASICALLY A BASSORENO WITH A METAL NOSE-JOB!
THE GOLD CAP

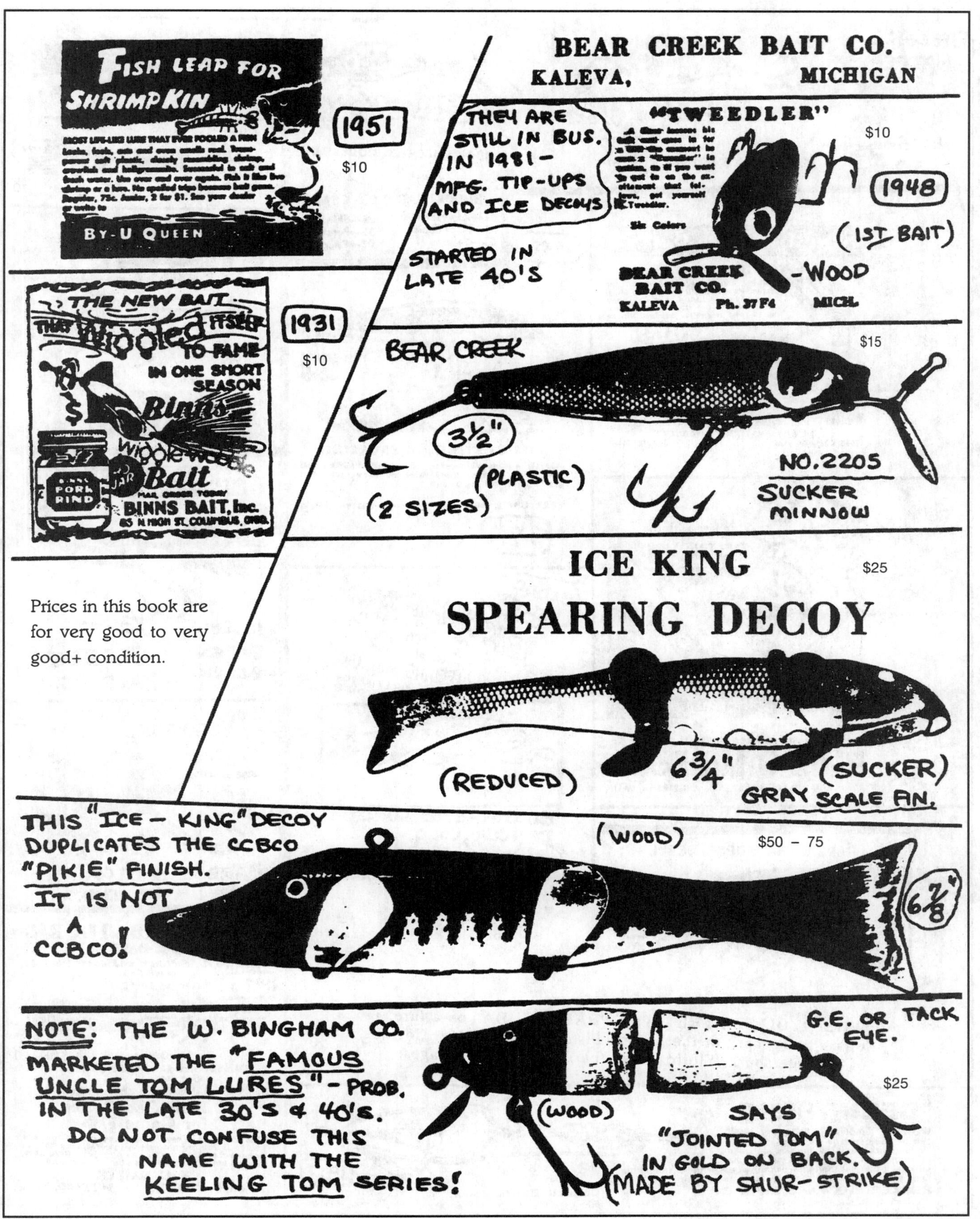
FISH LEAP FOR SHRIMP KIN
BY-U QUEEN
1951
$10
THE NEW BAIT THAT WIGGLED ITSELF TO FAME IN ONE SHORT SEASON
Binns Wiggle-Woggle Bait
PORK RIND
BINNS BAIT, Inc.
1931
$10
BEAR CREEK BAIT CO.
KALEVA, MICHIGAN
THEY ARE STILL IN BUS. IN 1981 - MFG. TIP-UPS AND ICE DECOYS
STARTED IN LATE 40'S
"TWEEDLER"
Six Colors
BEAR CREEK BAIT CO.
KALEVA Ph. 37F4 MICH.
$10
1948
(1ST BAIT)
-WOOD
BEAR CREEK
$15
3½"
(PLASTIC)
(2 SIZES)
NO. 2205
SUCKER MINNOW
ICE KING
SPEARING DECOY
$25
(REDUCED)
6¾"
(SUCKER)
GRAY SCALE FIN.
Prices in this book are for very good to very good+ condition.
THIS "ICE - KING" DECOY DUPLICATES THE CCBCO "PIKIE" FINISH.
IT IS NOT A CCBCO!
(WOOD)
$50 – 75
6⅞"
NOTE: THE W. BINGHAM CO. MARKETED THE "FAMOUS UNCLE TOM LURES" - PROB. IN THE LATE 30'S & 40'S.
DO NOT CONFUSE THIS NAME WITH THE KEELING TOM SERIES!
G.E. OR TACK EYE.
$25
(WOOD)
SAYS "JOINTED TOM" IN GOLD ON BACK.
(MADE BY SHUR-STRIKE)

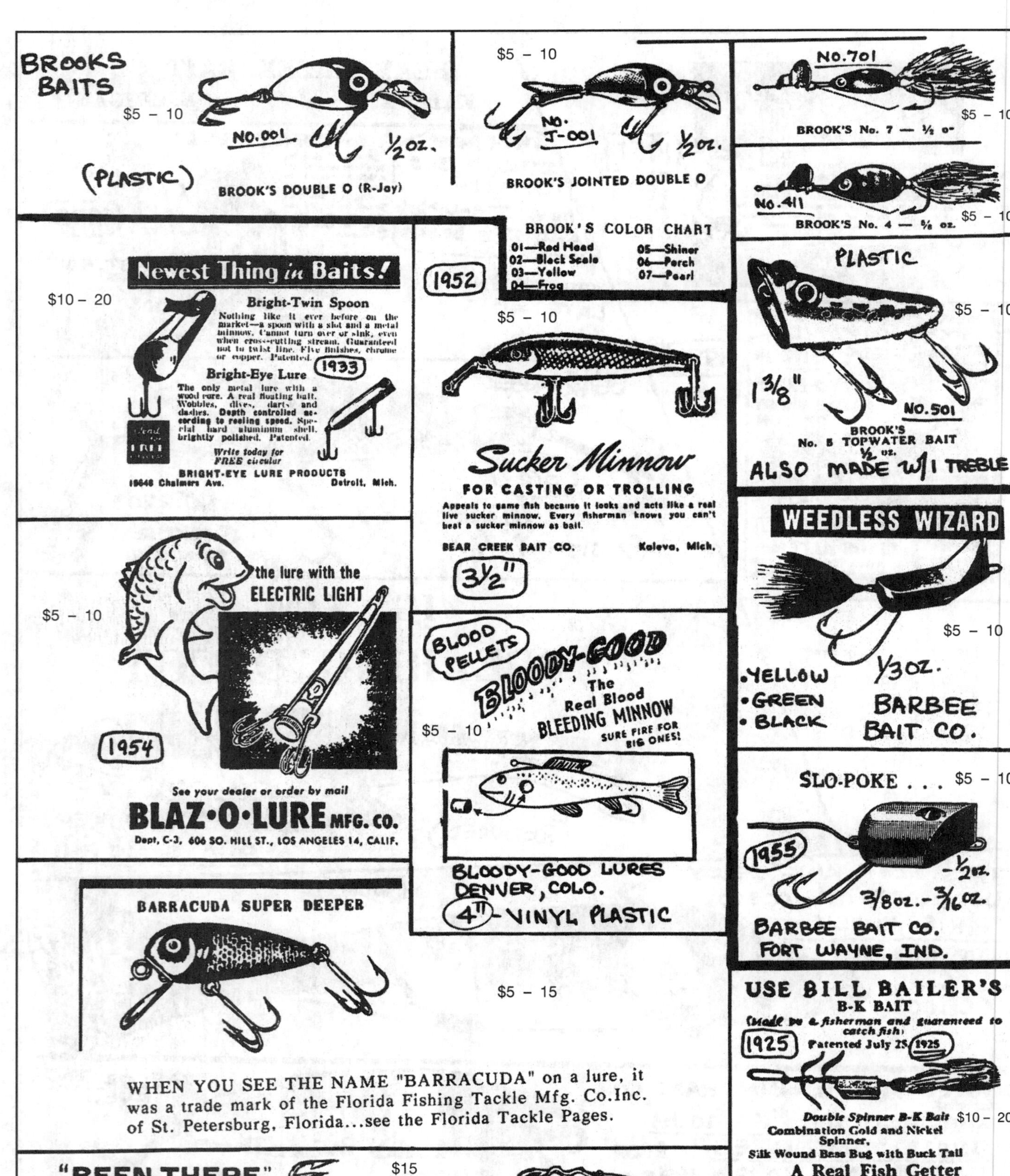
BROOKS BAITS
$5 – 10
NO.001
½ oz.
(PLASTIC)
BROOK'S DOUBLE O (R-Jay)
$5 – 10
NO. J-001
½ oz.
BROOK'S JOINTED DOUBLE O
NO.701
$5 – 10
BROOK'S No. 7 — ½ oz.
NO.411
BROOK'S No. 4 — ⅜ oz.
$5 – 10
BROOK'S COLOR CHART
01—Red Head
02—Black Scale
03—Yellow
04—Frog
05—Shiner
06—Perch
07—Pearl
1952
Newest Thing in Baits!
$10 – 20
Bright-Twin Spoon
Nothing like it ever before on the market—a spoon with a slot and a metal minnow. Cannot turn over or sink, even when cross-cutting stream. Guaranteed not to twist line. Five finishes, chrome or copper. Patented.
Bright-Eye Lure
1933
The only metal lure with a wood core. A real floating bait. Wobbles, dives, darts and dashes. Depth controlled according to reeling speed. Special hard aluminum shell, brightly polished. Patented.
Write today for FREE circular
BRIGHT-EYE LURE PRODUCTS
19648 Chalmers Ave. Detroit, Mich.
$5 – 10
Sucker Minnow
FOR CASTING OR TROLLING
Appeals to game fish because it looks and acts like a real live sucker minnow. Every fisherman knows you can't beat a sucker minnow as bait.
BEAR CREEK BAIT CO. Kaleva, Mich.
3½"
PLASTIC
$5 – 10
1⅜"
NO.501
BROOK'S No. 5 TOPWATER BAIT ½ oz.
ALSO MADE W/1 TREBLE
$5 – 10
the lure with the ELECTRIC LIGHT
1954
See your dealer or order by mail
BLAZ·O·LURE MFG. CO.
Dept. C-3, 606 SO. HILL ST., LOS ANGELES 14, CALIF.
WEEDLESS WIZARD
$5 – 10
•YELLOW
•GREEN
•BLACK
⅓ OZ.
BARBEE BAIT CO.
BLOOD PELLETS
BLOODY-GOOD
The Real Blood BLEEDING MINNOW
SURE FIRE FOR BIG ONES!
$5 – 10
BLOODY-GOOD LURES DENVER, COLO.
4" - VINYL PLASTIC
SLO-POKE . . .
$5 – 10
1955
-½ oz.
⅜ oz. - 3/16 oz.
BARBEE BAIT CO. FORT WAYNE, IND.
BARRACUDA SUPER DEEPER
$5 – 15
WHEN YOU SEE THE NAME "BARRACUDA" on a lure, it was a trade mark of the Florida Fishing Tackle Mfg. Co.Inc. of St. Petersburg, Florida...see the Florida Tackle Pages.
USE BILL BAILER'S B-K BAIT
(Made by a fisherman and guaranteed to catch fish)
1925
Patented July 25, 1925
Double Spinner B-K Bait
$10 – 20
Combination Gold and Nickel Spinner.
Silk Wound Bass Bug with Buck Tail
A Real Fish Getter for Game Fish
This Bait must be seen to be appreciated. Order one today. If you are not satisfied your Money Will Be Refunded or Send for One on Approval. Once used, you will never be without this bait in your outfit.
W. C. BAILER
Breckenridge St. BUFFALO, N. Y.
"BEEN THERE"
$15
Weedless Tandem Bait Casting Hook can be used with frogs, minnows, pork rind and other suitable natural bait. An all-round good hook which can be cast into thick lily-pads and underwater weeds without snagging. Send your order today. Satisfaction guaranteed.
BECKER SHEWARD MFG. CO. - - - Council Bluffs, Iowa
1917

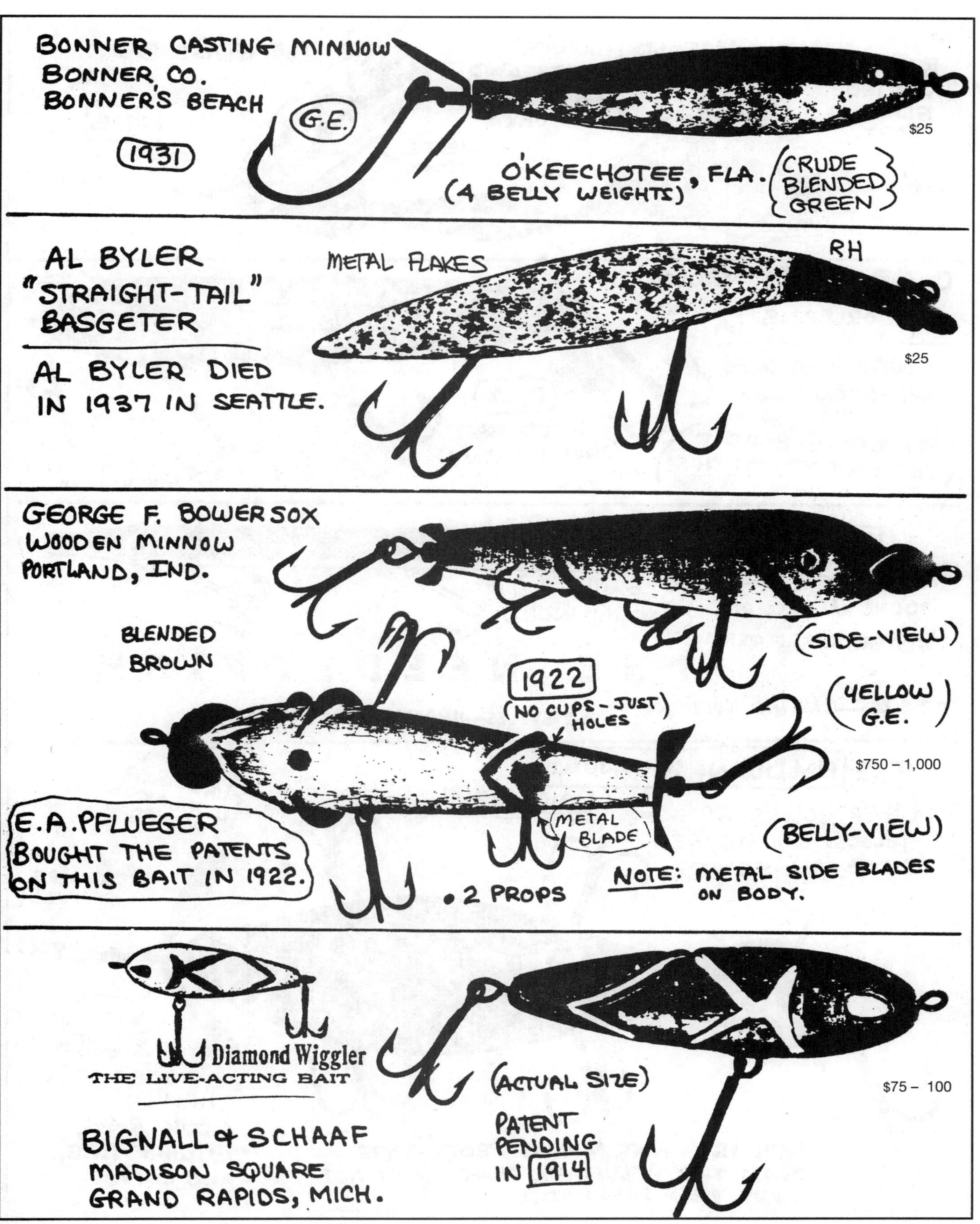
BONNER CASTING MINNOW
BONNER, CO.
BONNER'S BEACH
G.E.
1931
O'KEECHOTEE, FLA.
(4 BELLY WEIGHTS)
CRUDE BLENDED GREEN
$25
AL BYLER
"STRAIGHT-TAIL"
BASGETER
AL BYLER DIED IN 1937 IN SEATTLE.
METAL FLAKES
RH
$25
GEORGE F. BOWERSOX
WOODEN MINNOW
PORTLAND, IND.
BLENDED BROWN
(SIDE-VIEW)
1922
(NO CUPS - JUST) HOLES
(YELLOW G.E.)
$750 – 1,000
E.A. PFLUEGER BOUGHT THE PATENTS ON THIS BAIT IN 1922.
METAL BLADE
(BELLY-VIEW)
• 2 PROPS
NOTE: METAL SIDE BLADES ON BODY.
Diamond Wiggler
THE LIVE-ACTING BAIT
BIGNALL & SCHAAF
MADISON SQUARE
GRAND RAPIDS, MICH.
(ACTUAL SIZE)
PATENT PENDING IN 1914
$75 – 100

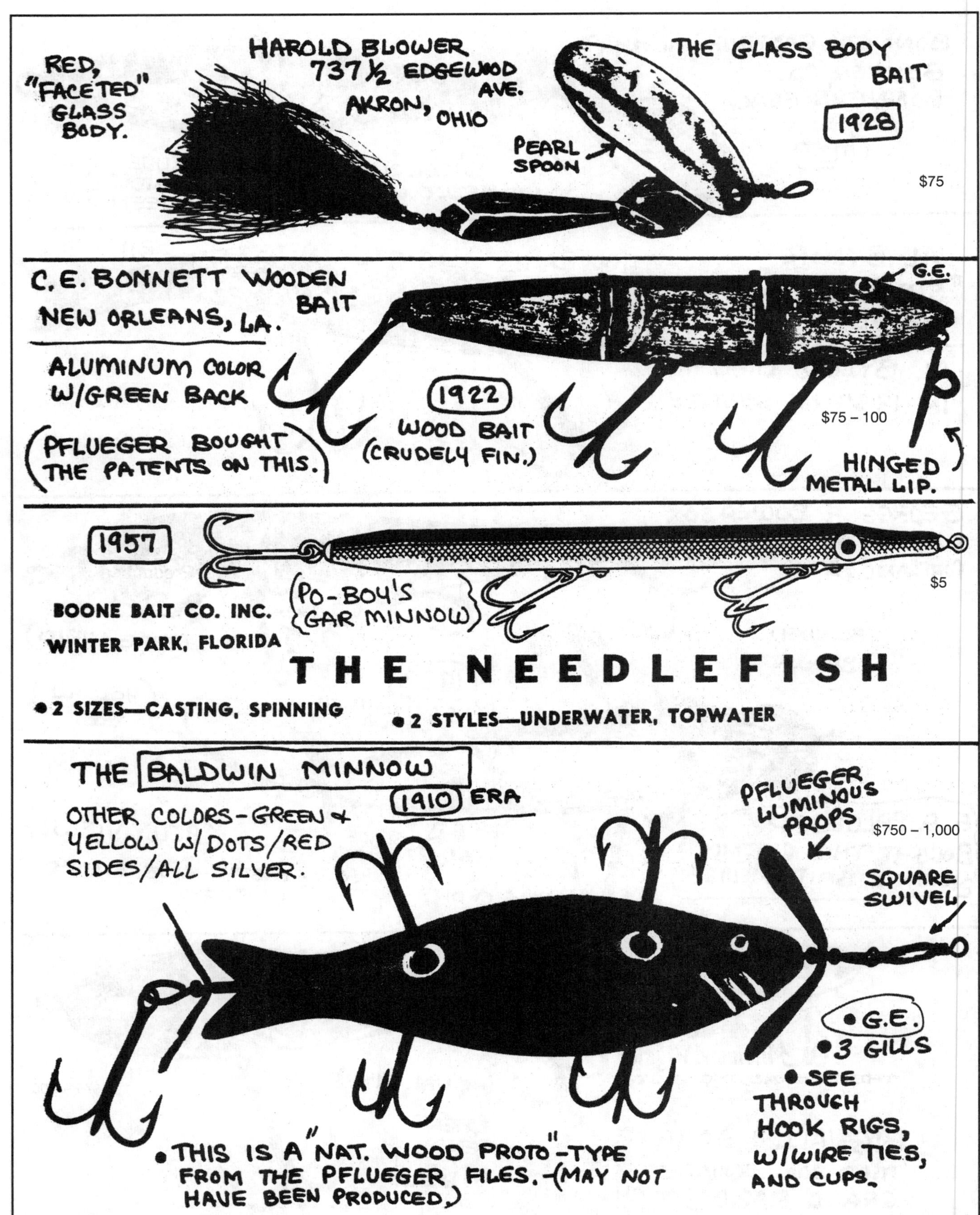
HAROLD BLOWER
737½ EDGEWOOD AVE.
AKRON, OHIO
RED, "FACETED" GLASS BODY.
THE GLASS BODY BAIT
1928
PEARL SPOON
$75
C.E. BONNETT WOODEN BAIT
NEW ORLEANS, LA.
ALUMINUM COLOR W/GREEN BACK
(PFLUEGER BOUGHT THE PATENTS ON THIS.)
1922
WOOD BAIT (CRUDELY FIN.)
G.E.
$75 – 100
HINGED METAL LIP.
1957
(PO-BOY'S GAR MINNOW)
BOONE BAIT CO. INC.
WINTER PARK, FLORIDA
$5
THE NEEDLEFISH
• 2 SIZES—CASTING, SPINNING
• 2 STYLES—UNDERWATER, TOPWATER
THE BALDWIN MINNOW
1910 ERA
OTHER COLORS-GREEN & YELLOW W/DOTS/RED SIDES/ALL SILVER.
PFLUEGER LUMINOUS PROPS
$750 – 1,000
SQUARE SWIVEL
• G.E.
• 3 GILLS
• SEE THROUGH HOOK RIGS, W/WIRE TIES, AND CUPS.
• THIS IS A "NAT. WOOD PROTO"-TYPE FROM THE PFLUEGER FILES. (MAY NOT HAVE BEEN PRODUCED.)

BROWN'S FISHERETTO AND WEEDLESS ATTACHMENT

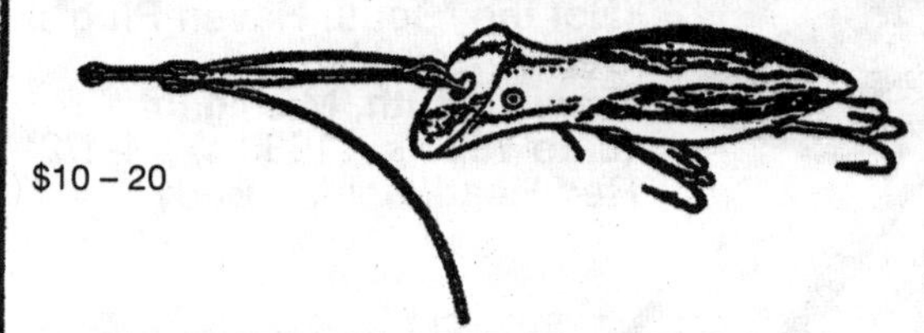

$10 – 20

One of each for 50c or
2 of each for $1.00
Bill Postpaid
BROWN'S
FISHERETTO CO. MFG.
Alexandria, Minn.

$10 – 20

Brown's Weedless Attachment Leaders

Can be Used on Practically All Bass Lures and Plugs for Casting and Trolling

PRICE 39c EACH

Manufactured by Brown's Fisheretto Co., Alexandria, Minnesota

$25

The Brown brothers opened a general store in Osakis, Minnesota in the late teens. This is one of Minnesota's prime lake areas better known by the town of Alexandria. S. J. Brown patented the "Fisheretto" bait in 1920. Their quality of production was just a click or two above home-made or folk art with crude paint jobs and basic screw eye and washer hook rigs. They also made a surface bait and a couple of ice spearing decoys. Production probably ended around WW II.

S. J. BROWN.
FISH BAIT OR LURE.
APPLICATION FILED OCT. 30, 1918.

1,331,618. Patented Feb. 24, 1920.

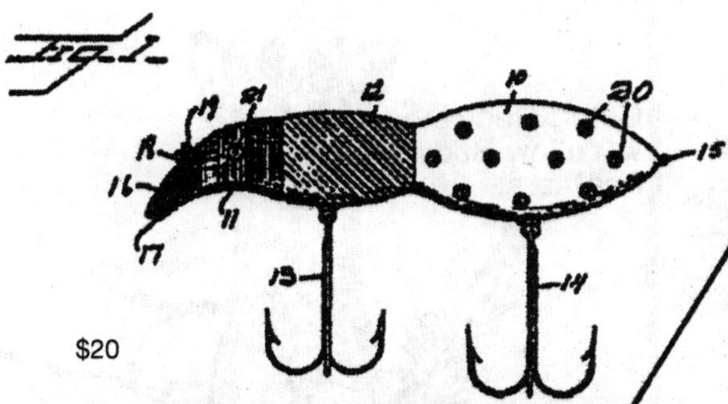

Fig. 1.
19
21
12
10
20
18
15
16
11
17
13
14

$20

See ya later alligator!

Outer's Magazine -August, 1912

$10 – 20

Alligator Tongue Bait

The newest, oddest, most effective lure on the market. White as milk, tougher than leather, soft and flexible as silk. Lasts forever. Dries up as hard as a board when not in use, and softens with a little soaking. You can leave it in your tackle box from one year to another, put it in water when you want it and have a soft, white, flexible bait in a few minutes. It is shaped almost like a minnow, and comes in all sizes.

35c each, or four (assorted sizes) for $1.00

A. S. BROWN. 60 Hathaway Building Milwaukee, Wisconsin

Another Alexandria, Minnesota item from the same era as the Brown Fisherettos. Outer's Magazine of May, 1913.

The Hook With the Live Guard

$5

BAKER WEEDLESS Plain or Weighted, 15 cents

Spoon or Buck Tail hooks at 30 cents. Your dealer has them, or we will send one by mail prepaid.
BAKER WEEDLESS FISH HOOK COMPANY. Alexandria, Minn.

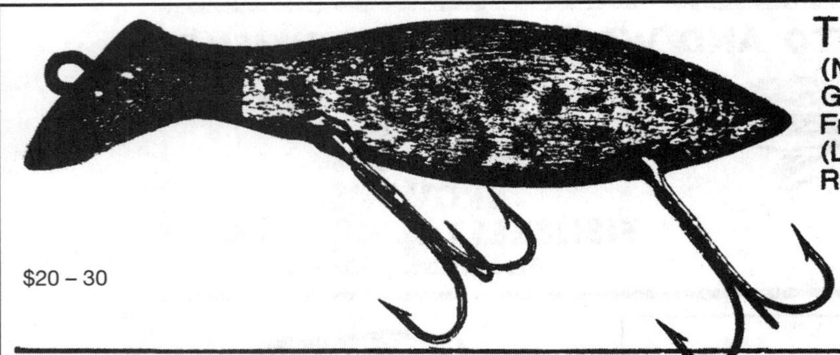

The Beyerlein Lure

(Not the "South Haven Plug")
Gus B. Beyerlein
Frankenmuth, Michigan
(Late 1920's - 1930's) 4-1/2"
Red Head/Golden Body

$20 – 30

THE BASS BOMB

May Be Used Two Ways
by Reversing the Position
of the Tail Hook.

Manufactured by the
BASS BOMB BAIT COMPANY
DIGHTON, MASS.

Patent Pending - 1949
6-1/4" 3-3/4 Oz.

BASS
BOMB
BAIT
CO.
Reg. Trade Mark

$10 – 20

Wood Striper Plug - Color Silver w/Red Blotches

CRAWDADS No. 321

Blackman & Betz
Cheney, Wash.

Top Cover of Actual Box

CRAWDADS
MANUFACTURED
—BY—
BLACKMAN & BETZ
CHENEY, WASH.
NO. 321
PRICE 75 CENTS
PATENT APPLIED FOR

Side view of 2 pc. box top w/label

Color: Red Head w/Yellow Body & Feathers.

$50

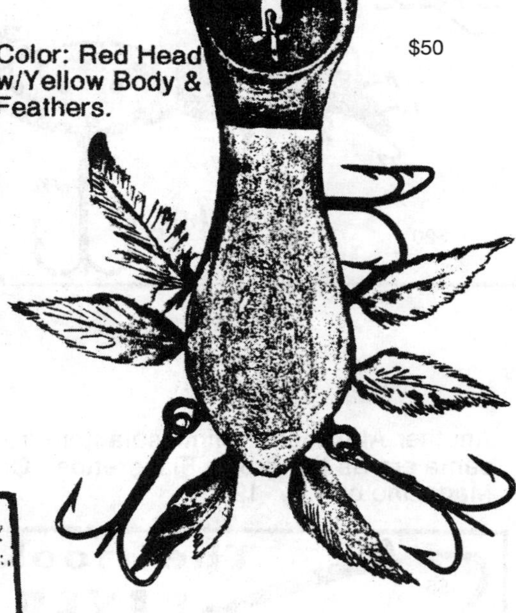

PATENT APPLIED FOR (1920's)

THE GOLD BUG
BUNKER AND BYLER - two individuals in the Seattle, WA area, making bass baits for a very limited bass fishing population in the 30's. They did not leave much information to study today.
BUNKER'S
No. 2
BASS and TROUT LURE
GOLD BUG
465 N. 38th St. Seattle, Wash.
$10 – 20
BUNKER NO. 1 4"
$10 – 20
$25
"BASGETER" UNDERWATER
$25
BUNKER GOLD-BUG
3" NO. 2
AL BYLER WAS A CRIPPLED MAN THAT LIVED IN A HOTEL IN SEATTLE.
HE MFG'D. THESE LURES IN THE BASEMENT OF THE HOTEL - IN THE 1930'S
$25
$20 – 30
AL BYLER (1 TREBLE) UNDERWATER
"BASGETER" SURFACE
NOTE: THESE ILLUSTRATIONS WERE MADE BY A COPY MACHINE. USE THIS TECHNIQUE TO RELAY INFORMATION.
A SURFACE LURE
Albyler Basgeter
AN UNDERWATER BAIT
MANUFACTURED BY
AL BYLER SEATTLE
NOTE - Most successful when retrieving with a SLOW intermittent motion, head submerged, tail above water.
COLOR A
IT'S DYNAMITE

CREEK CHUB BAIT CO. (CCBCO) COLOR CHART

(PRE-PLASTIC ERA)

CCBCO developed the scale finish as we know it. First color was a handsome combination of green, silver, and a pinkish red.(Original OO) This number became Nat. Pikie Scale.

00 Natural Pikie Scale
01 Perch Scale
02 Red Head/White and (Blended Red Head & Tail)
03 Silver Shiner Scale
04 Golden Shiner Scale
05 Dace Scale or (Red Side Scale)
06 Goldfish or (Gold Scale)
07 Natural Mullet Scale
08 Rainbow
09 Brilliant Green Back Scale (Over Gold Base)
10 Blue Head/White
11 White Head/Black - (Nite Glo Head Option) (1968 = Purple)
12 All Red
13 All Black
14 Yellow Spotted
15 Tan Crab (Crawdad Finish)
16 River Peeler (Steel Blue - Crawdad)
17 Coachdog (Old was Luminous)
18 Silver Flash (New in 1926)
19 Frog
20 Green Gar (Gar Minnow)
21 Day-N-Nite (Silver Flash & Luminous) (Fluorescent Red)
22 Luminous White W/Red Head (Fluorescent Green)
23. Fluorescent Yellow
24 Red Wing (Black & Red)
25. White Scale
26. White & Red with Wings (Tiny Tim)
27 Spotted (Tiny Tim)
28 Gray (Tiny Tim)
29 V for Victory (Yellow or White W/Red Dots & Black Back Stripe
30 Black Spots on Orange (Red Head Optional)
31 Rainbow Fire
32 Fire Plug (Gantron - Black Back, Bright Green Sides, Orange Belly)
33 Black Scale
34 Blue Flash
35 Purple Eel
36 Black Sucker (Spin Deepster)
37 Yellow Flash
38 Pearl (Glo-Pearl)

V-355 Skunk-Custom Black/White made for Western Auto Stores

00 Natural Crab Shell (Crawdad)
00 Bug Finishes

OOY Pickerel Pikie/Yellow Tail
OOR Pickerel Pikie/Red Tail

50 Yellow Beetle (Yellow W/Green Wings & Black Dots)
51 Green Beetle (Lite Greenish Gold W/Yellow Wings & Black Dots)
52 Red & White Beetle (White W/Red Wings & Black Dots)
53 Orange Beetle (Orange W/Red Wings & Black Dots)
54 Gold Beetle (Gold Body W/Black Wings)
55 Black Beetle (Black Body W/Red Wings & Yellow Dots)

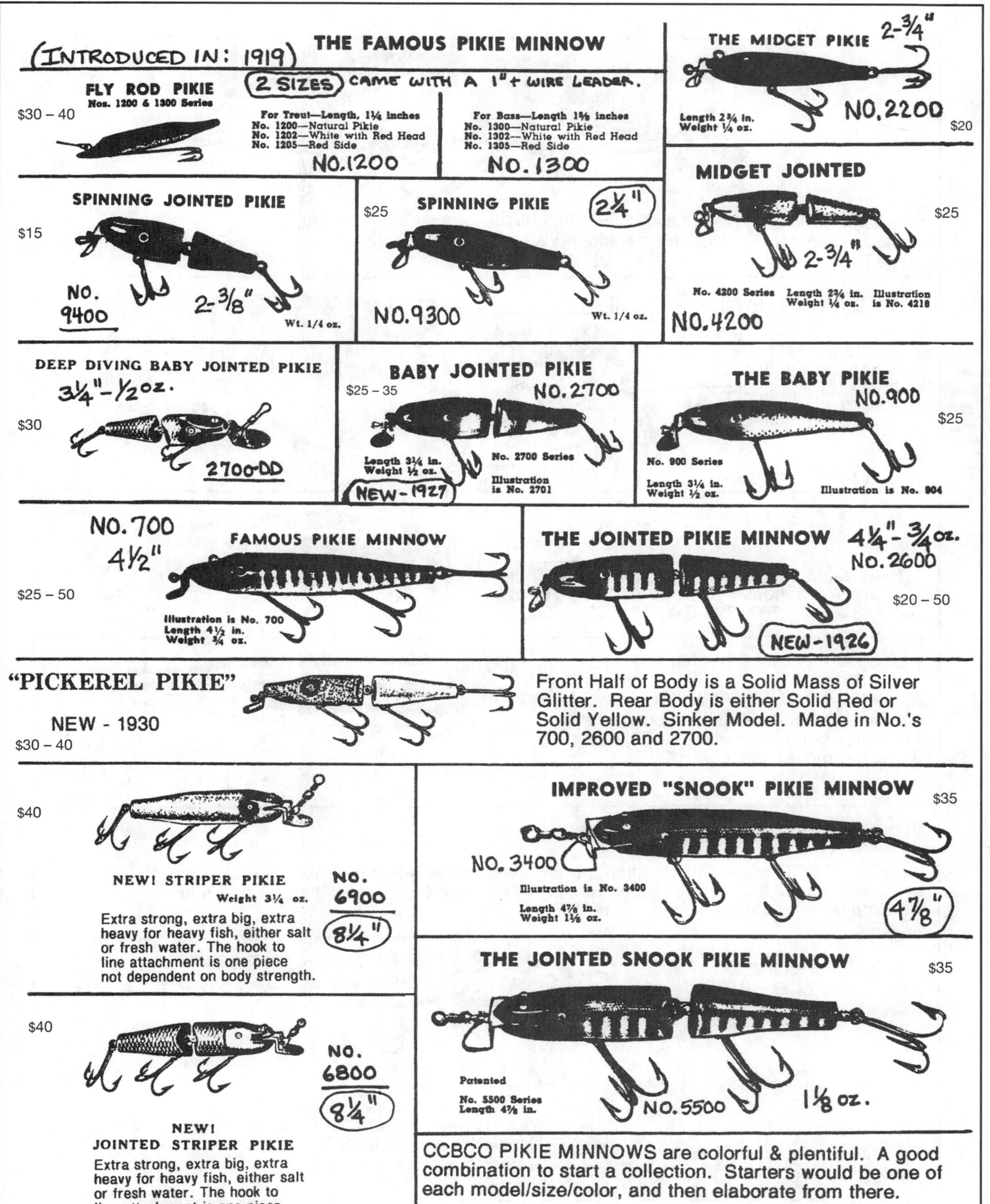

(INTRODUCED IN: 1919)
THE FAMOUS PIKIE MINNOW
FLY ROD PIKIE
Nos. 1200 & 1300 Series
2 SIZES CAME WITH A 1" + WIRE LEADER.
$30 – 40
For Trout—Length, 1¼ inches
No. 1200—Natural Pikie
No. 1202—White with Red Head
No. 1205—Red Side
NO. 1200
For Bass—Length 1⅝ inches
No. 1300—Natural Pikie
No. 1302—White with Red Head
No. 1305—Red Side
NO. 1300
THE MIDGET PIKIE 2-¾"
Length 2¾ in.
Weight ¼ oz.
NO. 2200
$20
SPINNING JOINTED PIKIE
$15
NO. 9400
2-⅜"
Wt. 1/4 oz.
$25
SPINNING PIKIE
2¼"
NO. 9300
Wt. 1/4 oz.
MIDGET JOINTED
$25
2-¾"
No. 4200 Series Length 2¾ in. Weight ¼ oz. Illustration is No. 4218
NO. 4200
DEEP DIVING BABY JOINTED PIKIE
3¼"-½oz.
$30
2700-DD
BABY JOINTED PIKIE
$25 – 35
NO. 2700
Length 3¼ in.
Weight ½ oz.
No. 2700 Series
Illustration is No. 2701
NEW-1927
THE BABY PIKIE
NO. 900
$25
No. 900 Series
Length 3¼ in.
Weight ½ oz.
Illustration is No. 904
NO. 700
4½"
FAMOUS PIKIE MINNOW
$25 – 50
Illustration is No. 700
Length 4½ in.
Weight ¾ oz.
THE JOINTED PIKIE MINNOW 4¼"-¾oz.
NO. 2600
$20 – 50
NEW-1926
"PICKEREL PIKIE"
NEW - 1930
$30 – 40
Front Half of Body is a Solid Mass of Silver Glitter. Rear Body is either Solid Red or Solid Yellow. Sinker Model. Made in No.'s 700, 2600 and 2700.
$40
NEW! STRIPER PIKIE
Weight 3¼ oz.
NO. 6900
8¼"
Extra strong, extra big, extra heavy for heavy fish, either salt or fresh water. The hook to line attachment is one piece not dependent on body strength.
IMPROVED "SNOOK" PIKIE MINNOW
$35
NO. 3400
Illustration is No. 3400
Length 4⅞ in.
Weight 1⅛ oz.
4⅞"
THE JOINTED SNOOK PIKIE MINNOW
$35
$40
NO. 6800
8¼"
NEW!
JOINTED STRIPER PIKIE
Extra strong, extra big, extra heavy for heavy fish, either salt or fresh water. The hook to line attachment is one piece not dependent on body strength.
Patented
No. 5500 Series
Length 4⅞ in.
NO. 5500
1⅛ oz.
CCBCO PIKIE MINNOWS are colorful & plentiful. A good combination to start a collection. Starters would be one of each model/size/color, and then elaborate from there.

DOUBLE JOINTED PIKIE

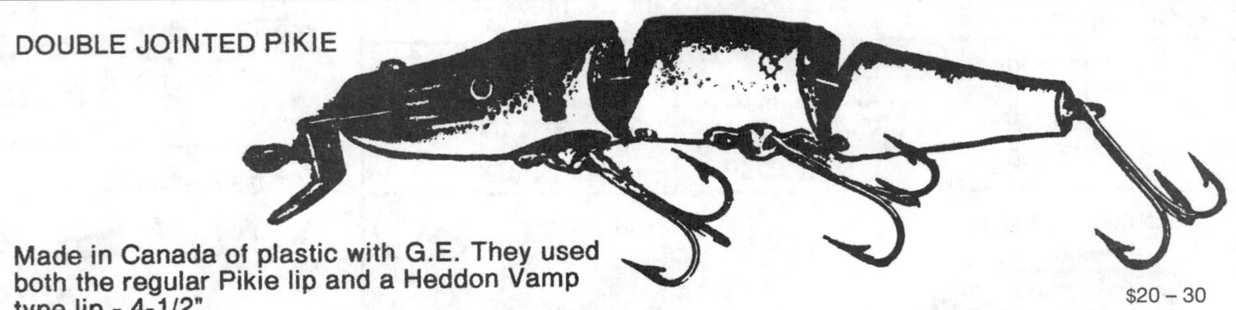

Made in Canada of plastic with G.E. They used both the regular Pikie lip and a Heddon Vamp type lip - 4-1/2".

$20 – 30

ROUND NOSE PIKIE

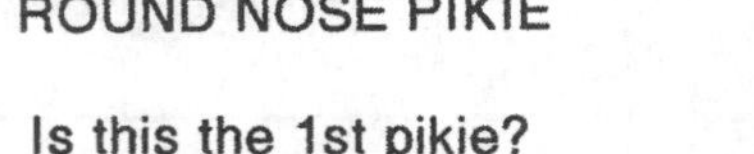

Is this the 1st pikie? It has more the face of the Wiggler, which was CCBCO's 1st bait.

G.E.
H.P.G.M.

$25 – 150

SALT WATER PIKIE (1957)

$35

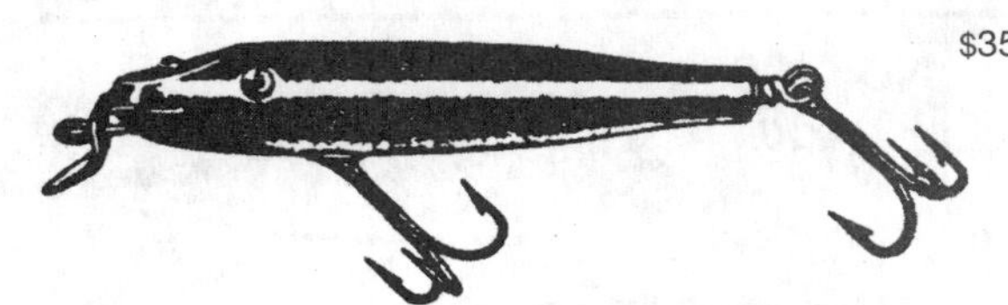

Extra sturdy, through-wire construction. Two strong treble hooks. Colors: 702-SW, 707-SW, 718-SW, 734-SW, 735-SW. 6-1/2" 1 Oz.

NO. 6000 GIANT STRAIGHT PIKIE

$35

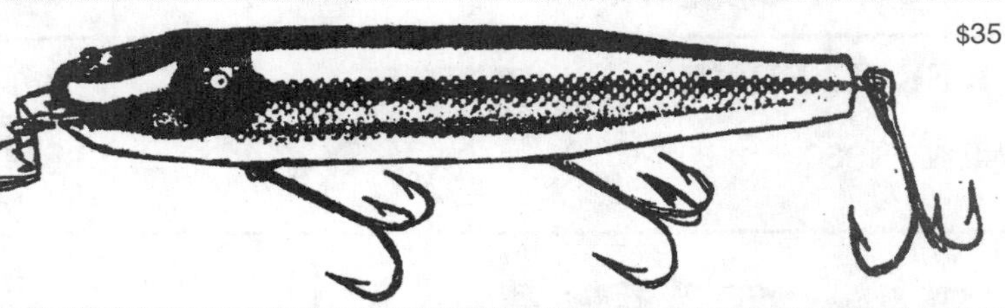

Made from 1961 - 1978, I assume this bait was added to capitalize on the Pikies big fish reputation. 8" & 3-1/2 Oz. makes this one H.D. Bait.

NO. KF118 - KINGFISH PIKIE MINNOW

$50 – 75

In 1939, CCBCO made this bait and probably continued with it until WW II ended it. I say that because like other Kingfish Baits made for the Gulf Coast, it had a 2" metal teardrop plate on the back. 5" 3 H.D. Trebles

NO. 2800-P JOINTED THREE SECTION PIKIE MINNOW
(Made of Plastic Only)

$20 – 30

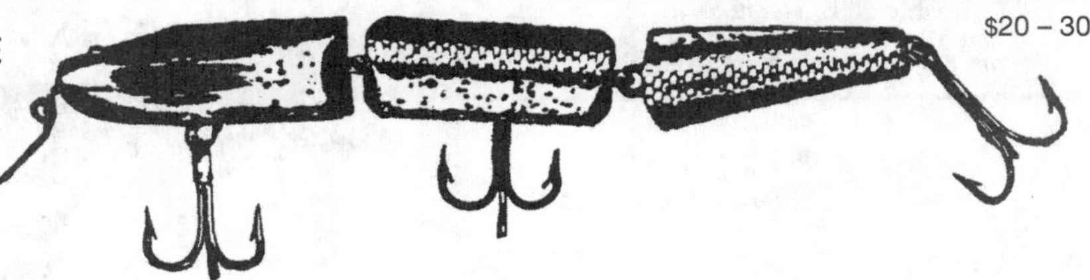

Was made in the late 1960's and into the 1970's. This was made by CCBCO in Indiana, unlike the Canadian version above. Had the DD (Deep Dive) Lip.

NO. 2300 - SW HUSKY PIKIE MINNOW GE 6"

$35

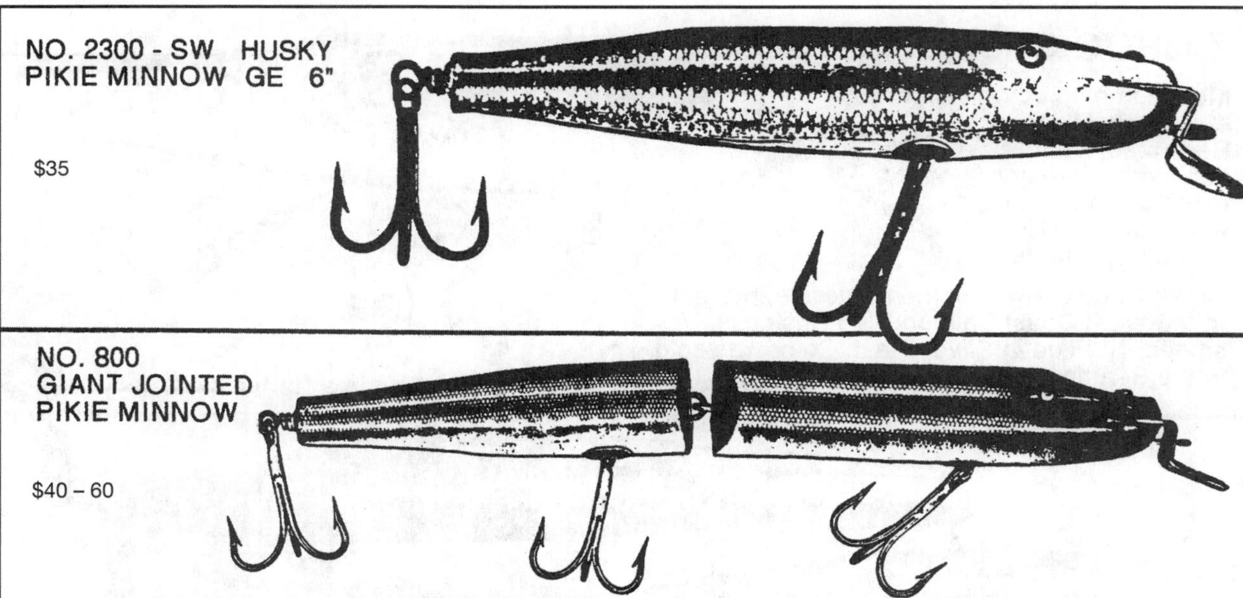

NO. 800
GIANT JOINTED PIKIE MINNOW

$40 – 60

Late 1950's through 1970. Made first in G.E. and later in T.E. with the "Improved" construction which was the thru-body wire rig with a reinforced lip. 10-1/2"

$30 – 50

SALTWATER TEASER PIKIE

South Bend pretty much had this segment of the market tied up with their line of Teasers, but CCBCO made some at least. They used the No. 6000 Giant Pikie Body, put on a Surfster lip and of course left off the treble hooks. 8" T.E. 3-1/2 Oz. Red Head/White

The New Giant JOINTED PIKIE
ANOTHER FISHING SENSATION FROM
Creek Chub
13 inches of giant-killer! A real mouthful for any game fish . . . fresh or salt water.
The new Creek Chub Giant Pikie was developed because of demand. It's become a sensation . . . the fastest selling bait we've ever launched. Reports of catches are coming in . . . and they're good! They call it a "lunker bait."
Try it for trolling or surf casting. Thirteen inches in length, 4 ounces of dynamite, six finishes. Every tackle box needs one. See your sporting goods dealer.
Write to Dept. SW-9 Garrett, Indiana
Free COLORFUL FOLDER
Creek Chub Baits
CATCH MORE PRIZE FISH
Manufactured in Canada by Allcock, Laight and Westwood Company, Ltd., Toronto

This 1958 Ad shows the NEW Giant Jtd. Pikie @ 13". It has also been found @ 14", and 4 Oz. Made in G.E. and T.E. versions. The ad did suggest trolling or surf casting, the latter so the angler can get a "run" into the cast of this big, big lure!

$35

Prices in this book are for very good to very good+ condition.

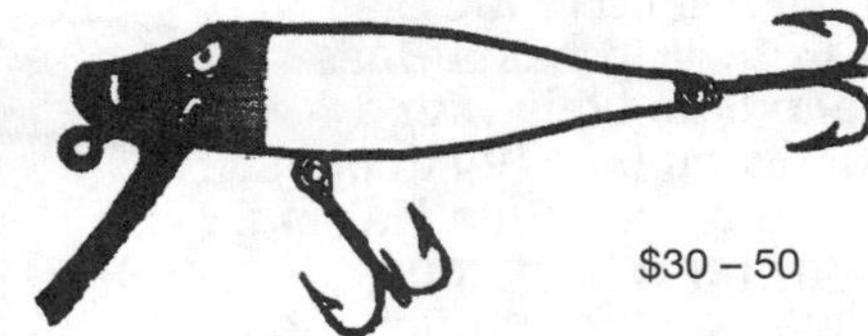

$30 – 50

No. 9300 ULTRA-LITE PIKIE

This little plastic bait came out in the early 1960's The main feature is the oversize plastic lip. 1-13/16" size. As long as we are showing "Pikies"-I had to show this one.

Note: Also made a jointed model....No. 9400-UL-P
1961 - 1970's 1-5/8"

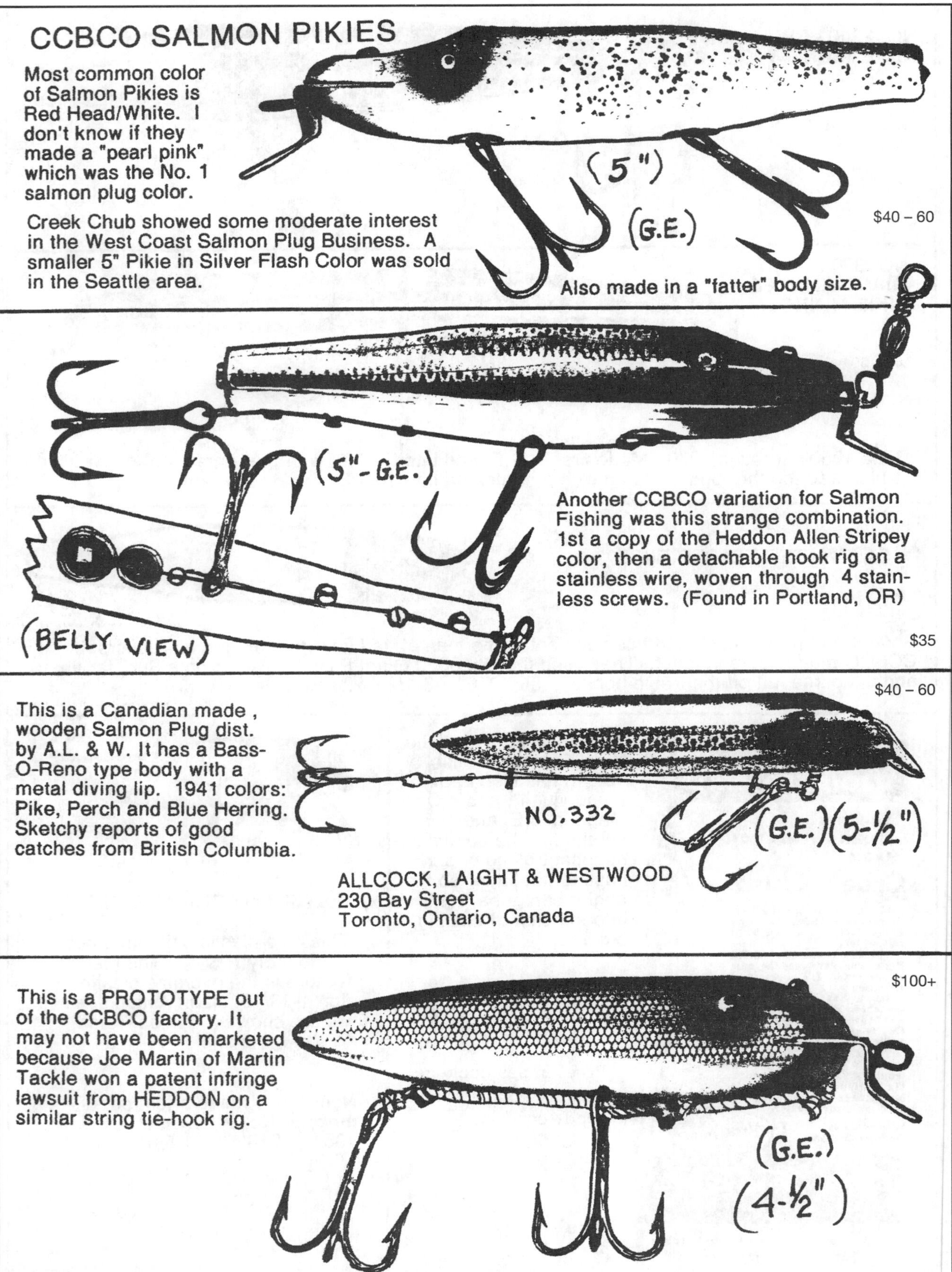
(5")
(G.E.)
(5"-G.E.)
(BELLY VIEW)
NO. 332
(G.E.)(5-1/2")
(G.E.)
(4-1/2")

CCBCO SALMON PIKIES

Most common color of Salmon Pikies is Red Head/White. I don't know if they made a "pearl pink" which was the No. 1 salmon plug color.

Creek Chub showed some moderate interest in the West Coast Salmon Plug Business. A smaller 5" Pikie in Silver Flash Color was sold in the Seattle area.

$40 – 60

Also made in a "fatter" body size.

Another CCBCO variation for Salmon Fishing was this strange combination. 1st a copy of the Heddon Allen Stripey color, then a detachable hook rig on a stainless wire, woven through 4 stainless screws. (Found in Portland, OR)

$35

$40 – 60

This is a Canadian made , wooden Salmon Plug dist. by A.L. & W. It has a Bass-O-Reno type body with a metal diving lip. 1941 colors: Pike, Perch and Blue Herring. Sketchy reports of good catches from British Columbia.

ALLCOCK, LAIGHT & WESTWOOD
230 Bay Street
Toronto, Ontario, Canada

$100+

This is a PROTOTYPE out of the CCBCO factory. It may not have been marketed because Joe Martin of Martin Tackle won a patent infringe lawsuit from HEDDON on a similar string tie-hook rig.

The CCBCO Pikie Minnow had a well deserved reputation as a "fish catcher". Because of this, they were able to make this bait in every imaginable size and combination of features. Combine that with their many colors, plus their flexible policy on special order, custom colors & your work is cut out for you as a Pikie Collector!

$35

IMPROVED HUSKY PIKIE MINNOW

Illustration is No. 2301
Length 6 in.
Weight 1½ oz.
(2301)
Patented
No. 2300 Series

IMPROVED JOINTED HUSKY PIKIE MINNOW $30

Illustration is No. 3000
Length 6 in.
Weight 1½ oz.
(3000)
Patented
No. 3000 Series

NEW! DEEP DIVING CREEK CHUB LURES

Certain Creek Chub Lures are now made with a DEEP DIVING MOUTHPIECE

$25

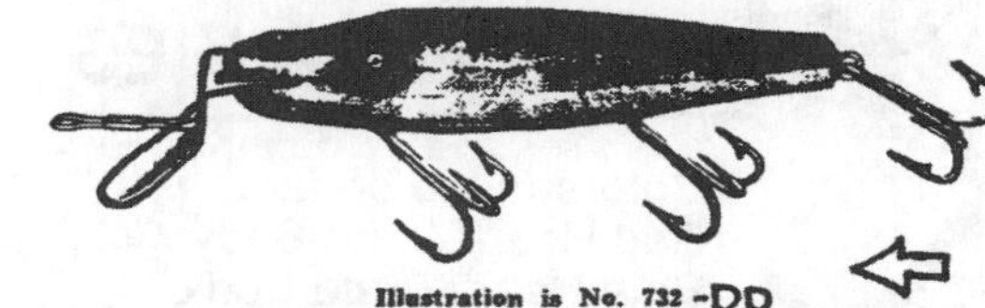

Illustration is No. 732 -DD

DEEP DIVE LIPS- ADD "DD" TO NUMBER.

NO. 7400 **NEW SALT "SURFSTER"** *NOTE BELOW

$35

Length 7¼"
Wt. 2½ oz.
(7¼")

The largest of the new "Surfsters"—this floating, wriggling, wagging lure is pure dynamite on those bigger salt water fish!

No. 7400—Pikie Scale
No. 7401—Perch Scale
No. 7402—White & Red
No. 7418—Silver Flash
No. 7434R—Blue Flash
No. 7435R—Purple Eel
No. 7437—Yellow Flash

3 DIFF. MODELS

No. 7300 Surfster Series

Length 6" Weight 1⅞ oz.

Its new wriggling and wagging action—on the surface—gets the bigger fish. A beautiful top lure for Pike and Muskie—and a popular size for salt water spinning, too! Same finishes as No. 7400 Series.

T.E. (6")

NO. 7200 SURFSTER SERIES

LENGTH - (4¼") G.E. & T.E.

THE CREEK CHUB "TARPON PIKIE"

$50 – 75

Patented (#4000)

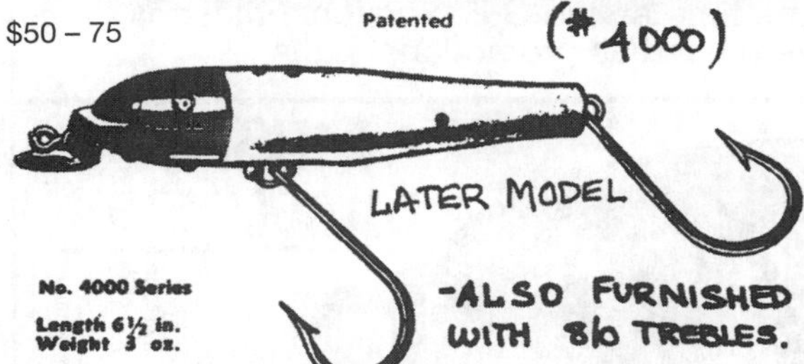
LATER MODEL
No. 4000 Series
Length 6½ in.
Weight 3 oz.
-ALSO FURNISHED WITH 8/0 TREBLES.

*There are what we call "HYBRID" Surfsters out there. They were made from the "parts" after the lines were discontinued using 700 and 6900 bodies, T.E. 7200 & 7300 Sizes.

Condition + age = value.

Special Equipment

No Extra Charge

We equip our lures with one or more hooks when so ordered. Below we show some very effective one and three hook lures. Other lures can be equipped in like manner, but we warrant the following to be exceptionally good:

$20 – 40

DELUXE WAG TAIL CHUB

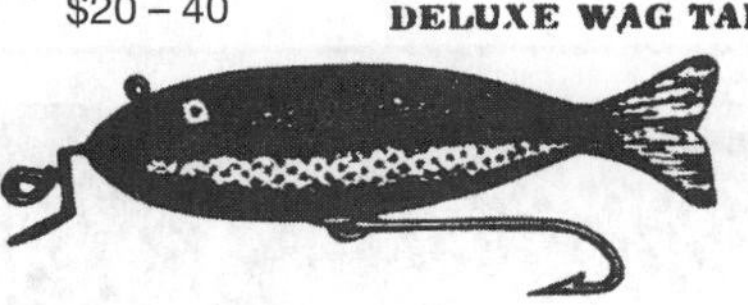

Order 800, 801, 803, 804, 808 Special.

$20

BABY PIKIE MINNOW

Order 900, 903, 904, 905 and 906 Special.

$20 – 50

PIKIE MINNOW

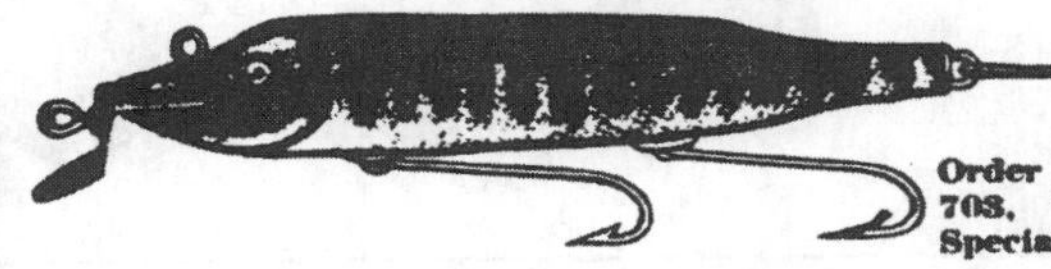

Order 700, 701, 702, 703, 704, 705, 706 Special.

TARPON PIKIE

1931

G.E. - 6-3/8"
REINFORCED ON CORNERS OF LIP.

$50 – 75

NO-EYE PIKIES

$20

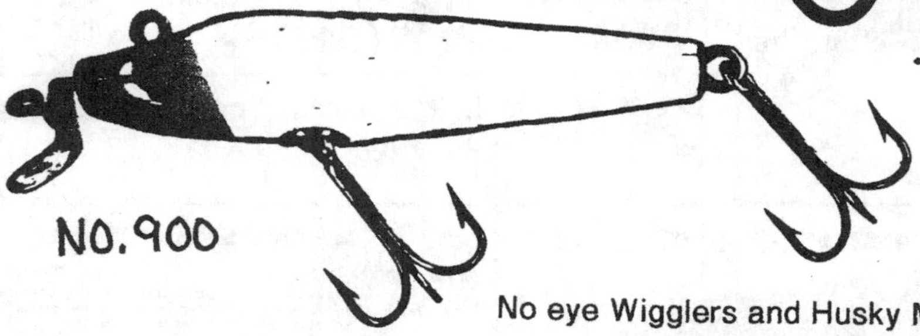

NO. 900

Colors found so far
Red Head/White Body
Blue Head/White Body
Black Head/White Body
White Head/Black Body

No eye Wigglers and Husky Muskies have also been found

$25

NO. 700

The NO-EYED Pikies were apparently made at the same time as the G.E. versions. Most of them seem to have an inferior finish, so maybe they were used as promotional baits.

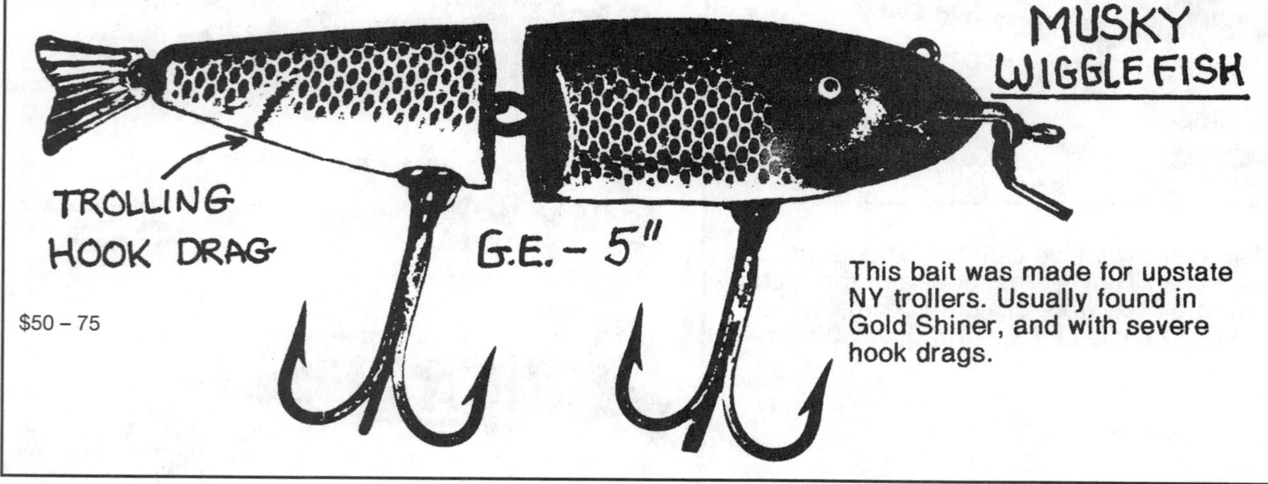
MUSKY
WIGGLEFISH
TROLLING
HOOK DRAG
G.E. - 5"

$50 – 75

This bait was made for upstate NY trollers. Usually found in Gold Shiner, and with severe hook drags.

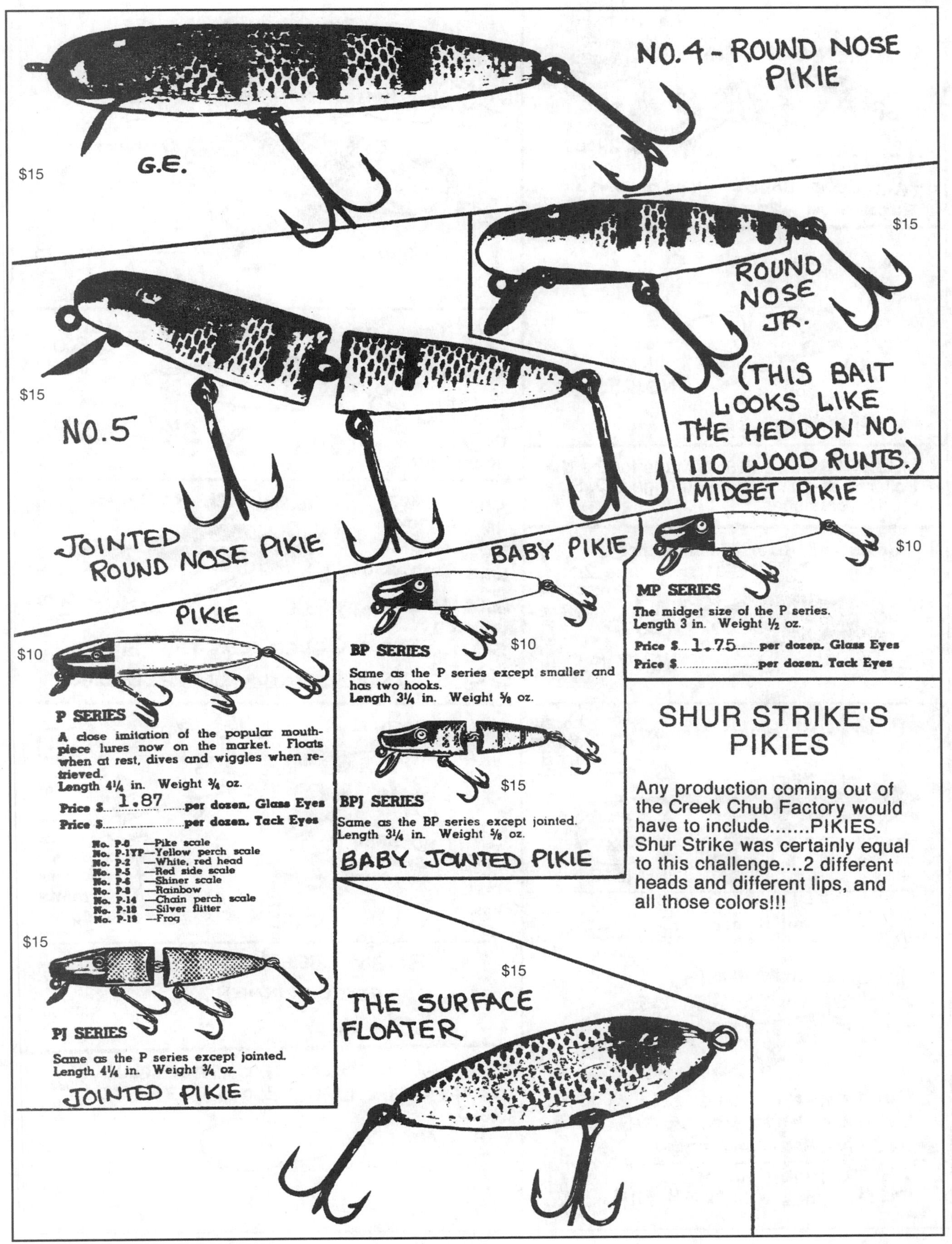

NO.4 - ROUND NOSE PIKIE
G.E.
$15
$15
ROUND NOSE JR.
(THIS BAIT LOOKS LIKE THE HEDDON NO. 110 WOOD RUNTS.)
$15
NO.5
JOINTED ROUND NOSE PIKIE
MIDGET PIKIE
$10
BABY PIKIE
MP SERIES
The midget size of the P series.
Length 3 in. Weight 1/2 oz.
Price $ 1.75 per dozen. Glass Eyes
Price $ per dozen. Tack Eyes
PIKIE
$10
BP SERIES
$10
Same as the P series except smaller and has two hooks.
Length 3¼ in. Weight 5/8 oz.
P SERIES
A close imitation of the popular mouthpiece lures now on the market. Floats when at rest, dives and wiggles when retrieved.
Length 4¼ in. Weight ¾ oz.
Price $ 1.87 per dozen. Glass Eyes
Price $ per dozen. Tack Eyes
No. P-0 —Pike scale
No. P-1YP—Yellow perch scale
No. P-2 —White, red head
No. P-5 —Red side scale
No. P-6 —Shiner scale
No. P-8 —Rainbow
No. P-14 —Chain perch scale
No. P-18 —Silver flitter
No. P-19 —Frog
$15
BPJ SERIES
Same as the BP series except jointed.
Length 3¼ in. Weight 5/8 oz.
BABY JOINTED PIKIE
$15
$15
PJ SERIES
Same as the P series except jointed.
Length 4¼ in. Weight ¾ oz.
JOINTED PIKIE
THE SURFACE FLOATER

SHUR STRIKE'S PIKIES

Any production coming out of the Creek Chub Factory would have to include.......PIKIES. Shur Strike was certainly equal to this challenge....2 different heads and different lips, and all those colors!!!

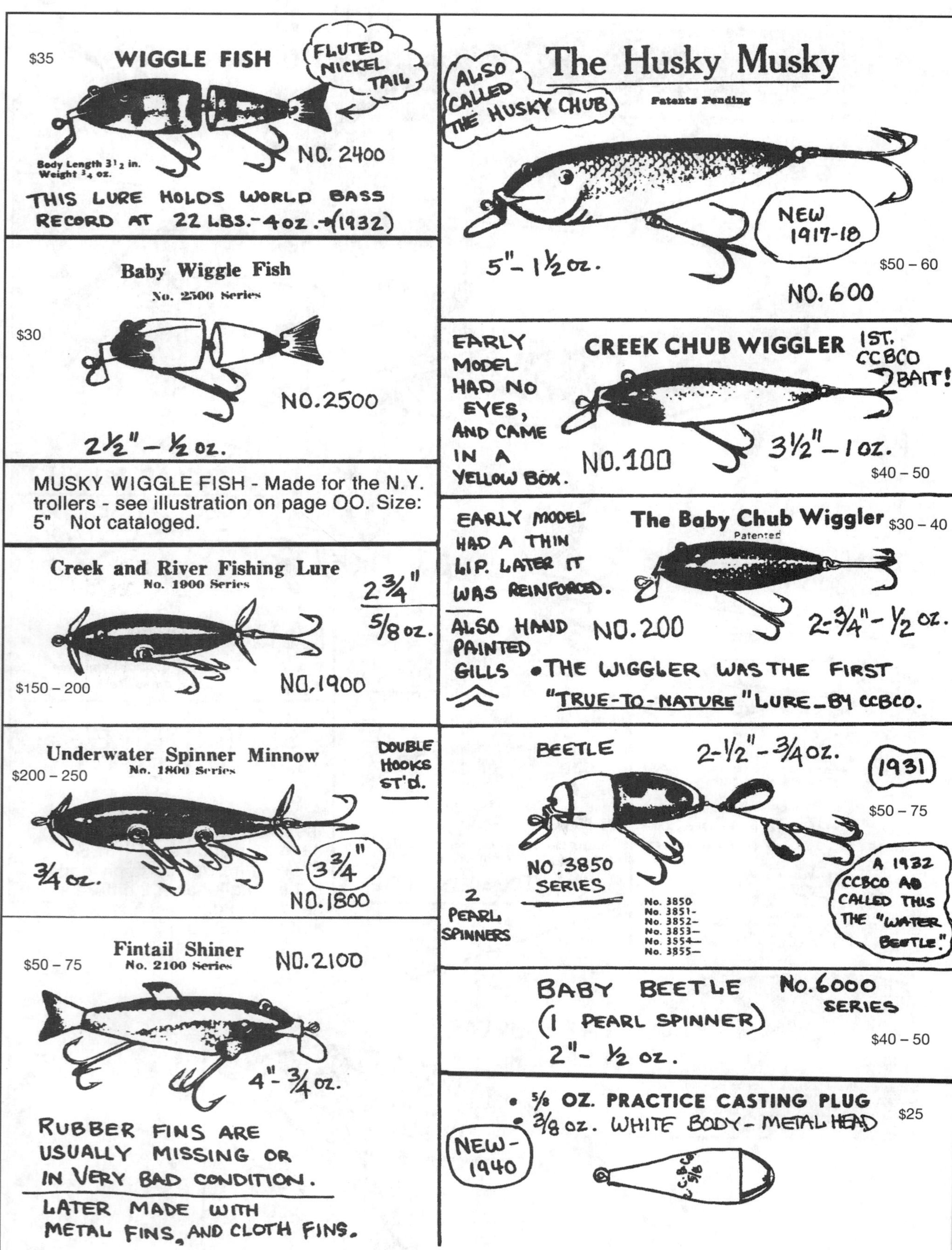
$35
WIGGLE FISH
FLUTED NICKEL TAIL
Body Length 3 1/2 in.
Weight 3/4 oz.
NO. 2400
THIS LURE HOLDS WORLD BASS RECORD AT 22 LBS.-4oz.→(1932)
Baby Wiggle Fish
No. 2500 Series
$30
NO.2500
2½" – ½ oz.
MUSKY WIGGLE FISH - Made for the N.Y. trollers - see illustration on page OO. Size: 5" Not cataloged.
Creek and River Fishing Lure
No. 1900 Series
2¾"
5/8 oz.
$150 – 200
NO.1900
Underwater Spinner Minnow
No. 1800 Series
$200 – 250
DOUBLE HOOKS ST'D.
¾ oz.
-3¾"
NO.1800
Fintail Shiner
No. 2100 Series
$50 – 75
NO.2100
4"- ¾ oz.
RUBBER FINS ARE USUALLY MISSING OR IN VERY BAD CONDITION.
LATER MADE WITH METAL FINS, AND CLOTH FINS.
ALSO CALLED THE HUSKY CHUB
The Husky Musky
Patents Pending
NEW 1917-18
5"- 1½ oz.
$50 – 60
NO. 600
EARLY MODEL HAD NO EYES, AND CAME IN A YELLOW BOX.
CREEK CHUB WIGGLER
1ST. CCBCO BAIT!
NO.100
3½"- 1 oz.
$40 – 50
EARLY MODEL HAD A THIN LIP. LATER IT WAS REINFORCED.
The Baby Chub Wiggler
Patented
$30 – 40
ALSO HAND PAINTED GILLS
NO.200
2-¾"- ½ oz.
•THE WIGGLER WAS THE FIRST "TRUE-TO-NATURE" LURE_BY CCBCO.
BEETLE
2-½"-¾ oz.
1931
$50 – 75
NO.3850 SERIES
2 PEARL SPINNERS
No. 3850
No. 3851-
No. 3852-
No. 3853-
No. 3854-
No. 3855-
A 1932 CCBCO AD CALLED THIS THE "WATER BEETLE."
BABY BEETLE
No.6000 SERIES
(1 PEARL SPINNER)
2"- ½ oz.
$40 – 50
• 5/8 OZ. PRACTICE CASTING PLUG
• 3/8 oz. WHITE BODY - METAL HEAD
$25
NEW- 1940
C.C.B.Co 5/8

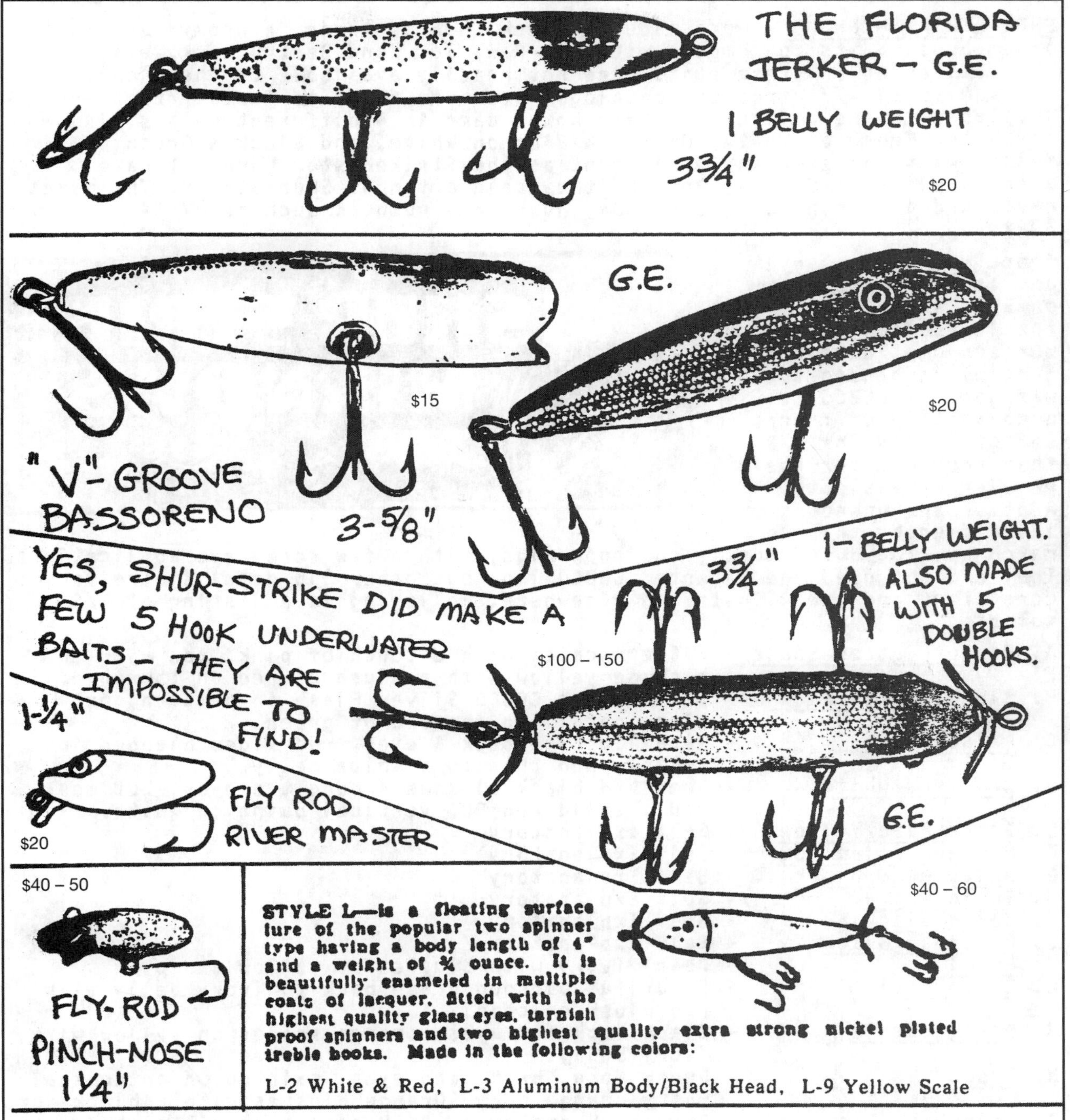
THE FLORIDA JERKER - G.E.
1 BELLY WEIGHT
3¾"
$20
G.E.
$15
$20
"V"-GROOVE BASSORENO
3-5/8"
1-BELLY WEIGHT.
3¾"
ALSO MADE WITH 5 DOUBLE HOOKS.
YES, SHUR-STRIKE DID MAKE A FEW 5 HOOK UNDERWATER BAITS - THEY ARE IMPOSSIBLE TO FIND!
$100 – 150
1-¼"
FLY ROD RIVER MASTER
$20
G.E.
$40 – 50
$40 – 60
FLY-ROD PINCH-NOSE 1¼"

STYLE L—is a floating surface lure of the popular two spinner type having a body length of 4" and a weight of ¾ ounce. It is beautifully enameled in multiple coats of lacquer, fitted with the highest quality glass eyes, tarnish proof spinners and two highest quality extra strong nickel plated treble hooks. Made in the following colors:

L-2 White & Red, L-3 Aluminum Body/Black Head, L-9 Yellow Scale

SHUR STRIKE BOXES - COLORS & NAMES

Shur Strike made 4 different color boxes: 1. Blue & White 2. Green & White 3. Orange, Blue & White 4. Green, Black & Yellow (This box sometimes is found with the NRA stamp which stood for the National Relief Association from 1933 - 1935).

Other distributors bought Shur Strike Minnows and put them in their own boxes:
Edward K. Tryon Co.- "Kingfisher", Sears-Roebuck-"Meadow Brook", "Bass-A-Lure", Western Auto-""Western", Hibbard-Spencer-Bartlett Co.-"True Value", W. Bingham Co.- "Uncle Tom", Gateway-"Gateway", Montgomery Ward-"Hawthorne","Sport King", and "Fish-Ketcher"

SHUR-STRIKE MINNOWS - were made by Creek Chub as their "economy" and mail order house baits to compete with Paw-Paw, So. Bend Best O'Luck, etc. The cataloging on these baits were not readily available to the public, but some dealer/distributor catalogs have been found to further the info available to the collector. Their boxes came in 4 different colors,Blue on White, Green on White, Orange & Blue on White, and Black & Green on Yellow with the same style of print as the StrikeMaster Lures. I have also displayed a Gateway Box and they sold a ton of Shur Strike. The boxes never had a lure name on the ends, just some numbers such as HV-14 and BO-2.

SHUR-STRIKE
MINNOWS

There was a glass-eye and tack eye producion on S/S, and alot of the lures look anything but economy, some are just plain handsome. It was good of CCBCO to use a completely different set of colors for S/S than they did for their regular Pikies, etc. Alot of the unknowns are identified by this color match-up. They used mostly cup hook rigs, with a few screw eye applications. They did not used the patented CCBCO lip, but other lip details were very consistant and are illustrated elsewhere. Following is a listing of S/S colors:

A. Peanut Butter Scale - Silver scales with a touch of pink, tan eyes and back on yellow with a blush of red on the chin.
B. Black Silver Flash - same as the CCBCO Silver Flash in pattern, but black detailing instead of green.
C. Rainbow - Metallic blue back & eyes, red sides blended into yellow, and then to a white belly.
D. Red Head/White - Some had black blushes around the eyes, but most had a solid red 90' vertical paint on white.
E. Black Head/Yellow - Self explanatory
F. Red Head/Aluminum - Self Explanatory
G. White Head/Black - Self Explanatory
H. Solid White - Self Explanatory
I. Solid Black - Self Explanatory
J. Red Head/Black - Self Explanatory
K. Pearl - Pearl Ivory with blushes of yellow and pink
L. Green Scale - Beautiful blended green back to ivory belly with red blush on chin.
M. Orange Scale - Black back and eyes, orange scales on yellow with ivory belly.
N. Frog - Green Nose, back, and eyes, painted on an unusual rusty orange body. Orange blushes with a black dot.
O. Greenback Dace - Greenback and eyes, Pink scales on silver body blended out to ivory belly
P. Gray Shiner Scale - Your basic shiner scale, black eye & back, red blush on chin on gray body.
Q. Blackened Gold Scale- Blackish Olive Drab back and eye, scaled over gold with a greenish ivory belly and red chin blush.
R. Yellow Shiner Scale - Your basic shiner scale with a dark green back and eyes, but printed on yellow.
S. Green Sided Perch - Black back & eyes, solid green area on sides, & vertical black and red bars over a yellow scale and yellow belly.

T. Yellow Pikie Scale -Your Basic Pikie Scale colors, but printed on a yellow body with a red eye blush.

U. Yellow Pike Scale -Black back & eyes, then a vertical yellow scale pattern on yellow blended to white belly, Some black vertical is present also.

V. Blackfaced small/ scaled green shiner -Black back & eyes & face, very small scales of yellow on green with a pink scale side stripe, blending into a white belly with red chin blush.

W. Florida Vertical Red Bars -This bait was obviously aimed at the Florida Mkt. White body, black back stripe and vertical solid red bars and eyes.

There were also some special colors for the Crab Wiggler, the Flatfish type and the 1941 Small Dude bait. That's really an awesome line-up of colors for a cheapo-line of baits!

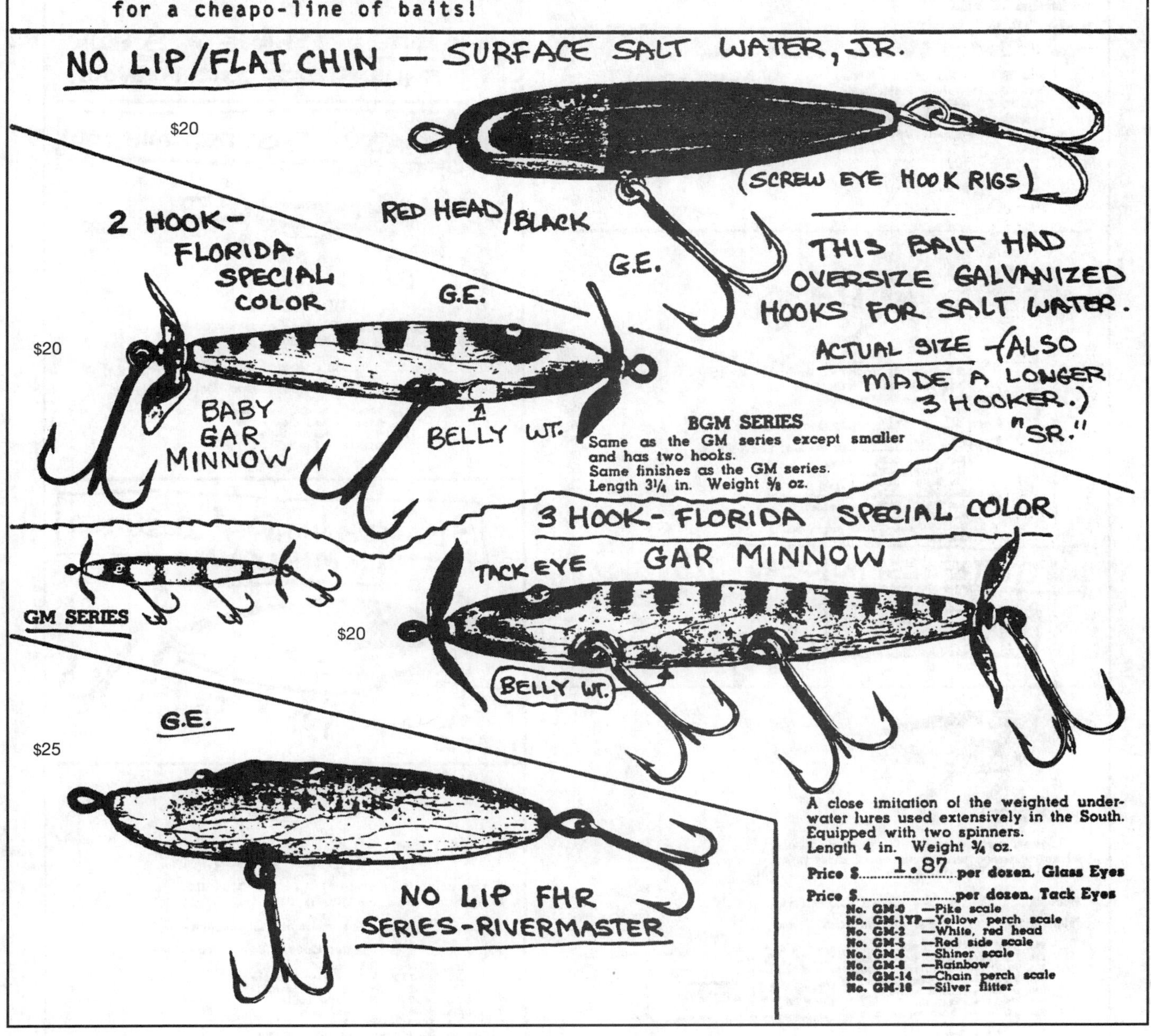
NO LIP/FLAT CHIN — SURFACE SALT WATER, JR.
$20
(SCREW EYE HOOK RIGS)
RED HEAD/BLACK
G.E.
THIS BAIT HAD OVERSIZE GALVANIZED HOOKS FOR SALT WATER.
ACTUAL SIZE (ALSO MADE A LONGER 3 HOOKER.) "SR."
2 HOOK- FLORIDA SPECIAL COLOR
G.E.
$20
BABY GAR MINNOW
BELLY WT.
3 HOOK- FLORIDA SPECIAL COLOR
GAR MINNOW
TACK EYE
GM SERIES
$20
BELLY WT.
G.E.
$25
NO LIP FHR SERIES-RIVERMASTER

BGM SERIES
Same as the GM series except smaller and has two hooks.
Same finishes as the GM series.
Length 3¼ in. Weight ⅝ oz.

A close imitation of the weighted underwater lures used extensively in the South. Equipped with two spinners.
Length 4 in. Weight ¾ oz.

Price $ 1.87 per dozen. Glass Eyes
Price $........ per dozen. Tack Eyes

No. GM-0 —Pike scale
No. GM-1YP—Yellow perch scale
No. GM-2 —White, red head
No. GM-5 —Red side scale
No. GM-6 —Shiner scale
No. GM-8 —Rainbow
No. GM-14 —Chain perch scale
No. GM-18 —Silver flitter

NEW SHUR-STRIKES for 1941

$10 – 20

THE "SMALL DUDE"

SD SERIES

A very small, weighted, fast wiggling, sinking lure for all game fish in stream or lake.

Length 1⅞ in. Weight ½ oz.

Price $ 1.70 per dozen. Painted Eyes Only

No. SD-0 —Natural Pike Scale
No. SD-1YP—Yellow Perch Scale
No. SD-2 —White with Red Head
No. SD-5 —Red Side Scale
No. SD-18 —Silver Flitter
No. SD-19 —Frog
No. SD-20 —White Scale
No. SD-41 —Blue Back
No. SD-42 —Goldfish
No. SD-43 —Spotted

$10

PS SERIES

A small sinking underwater lure. Weighted body equipped with two spinners.
Length 1¾ in. Weight ½ oz.

Price $ 1.87 per dozen. Glass Eyes
Price $........ per dozen. Tack Eyes

No. PS-0 —Pike scale
No. PS-1YP—Yellow perch scale
No. PS-2 —White, red head
No. PS-5 —Red side scale
No. PS-6 —Shiner scale
No. PS-8 —Rainbow
No. PS-14 —Chain perch scale
No. PS-18 —Silver flitter

"PETITE SPINNER" OR "MIDGET"

$15

PL SERIES

A floating surface lure which pops and bobs when retrieved with a series of short jerks.
Length 3 in. Weight ½ oz.

Price $ 1.75 per dozen. Glass Eyes
Price $........ per dozen. Tack Eyes

No. PL-0 —Pike scale
No. PL-1YP—Yellow perch scale
No. PL-2 —White, red head
No. PL-5 —Red side scale
No. PL-6 —Shiner scale
No. PL-8 —Rainbow
No. PL-14 —Chain perch scale
No. PL-18 —Silver flitter
No. PL-19 —Frog

S/S- "PLUNKER"

NOTE: SPEC. ORDER - NO PROPS.

"INJURED MINNOW"

$20

IM SERIES

A double spinner, floating surface lure for bass.
Length 3¾ in. Weight ¾ oz.

Price $ 1.87 per dozen. Glass Eyes
Price $........ per dozen. Tack Eyes

No. IM-2 —White, red head
No. IM-5 —Red side scale
No. IM-18—Silver flitter
No. IM-19 —Frog

NOTE: I HAVE A 3 HOOK SHUR STRIKE INJ. MINNOW.

"BABY" INJURED MINNOW

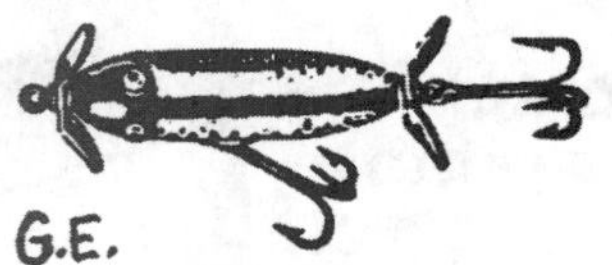

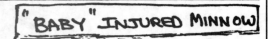

$20

G.E.

BIM SERIES

Same as the IM series except smaller.
Length 2¾ in. Weight ½ oz.

Price $ 1.87 per dozen. Glass Eyes
Price $........ per dozen. Tack Eyes

No. BIM-2 —White, red head
No. BIM-5 —Red side scale
No. BIM-18—Silver flitter
No. BIM-19 —Frog

S/S-"SPINNING" INJURED MINNOW

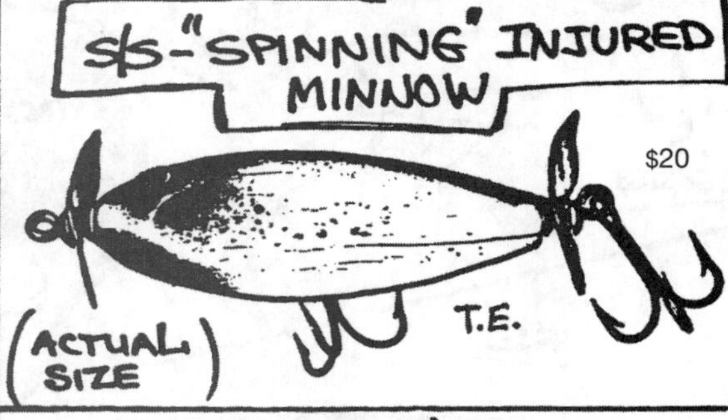

$20

T.E.

(ACTUAL SIZE)

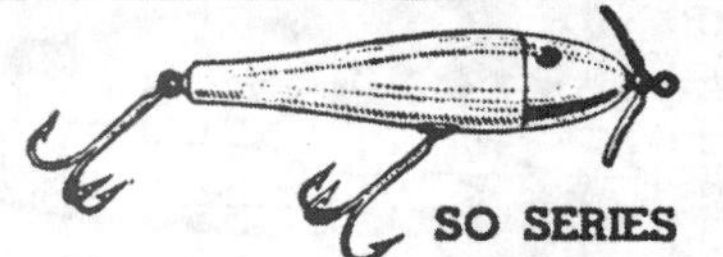

$20

SO SERIES

A rather chunky spinner type surface lure.
Length 2¾ in. Weight ⅝ oz.

Price $ 1.80 per dozen. Glass Eyes
Price $........ per dozen. Tack Eyes

No. SO-0 —Pike scale
No. SO-1YP—Yellow perch scale
No. SO-2 —White, red head
No. SO-5 —Red side scale
No. SO-6 —Shiner scale
No. SO-8 —Rainbow
No. SO-14 —Chain perch scale
No. SO-18 —Silver flitter
No. SO-19 —Frog

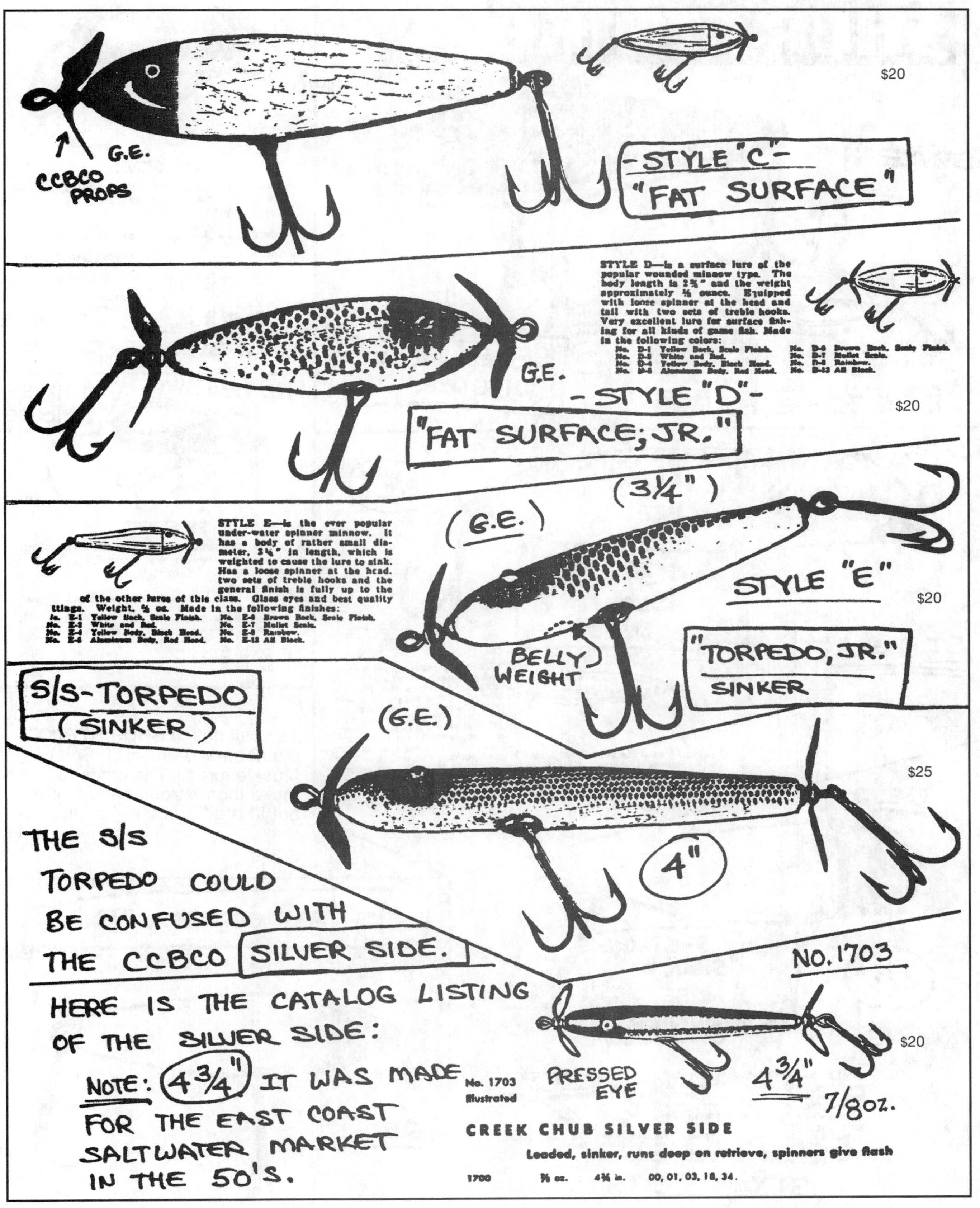
$20
CCBCO PROPS
G.E.
-STYLE "C"-
"FAT SURFACE"
STYLE D—is a surface lure of the popular wounded minnow type. The body length is 2¾" and the weight approximately ⅓ ounce. Equipped with loose spinner at the head and tail with two sets of treble hooks. Very excellent lure for surface fishing for all kinds of game fish. Made in the following colors:
No. D-1 Yellow Back, Scale Finish.
No. D-2 White and Red.
No. D-4 Yellow Body, Black Head.
No. D-5 Aluminum Body, Red Head.
No. D-6 Brown Back, Scale Finish.
No. D-7 Mullet Scale.
No. D-8 Rainbow.
No. D-13 All Black.
G.E.
-STYLE "D"-
$20
"FAT SURFACE; JR."
(3¼")
(G.E.)
STYLE E—is the ever popular under-water spinner minnow. It has a body of rather small diameter, 3¼" in length, which is weighted to cause the lure to sink. Has a loose spinner at the head, two sets of treble hooks and the general finish is fully up to the of the other lures of this class. Glass eyes and best quality ttings. Weight, ½ oz. Made in the following finishes:
No. E-1 Yellow Back, Scale Finish.
No. E-2 White and Red.
No. E-4 Yellow Body, Black Head.
No. E-5 Aluminum Body, Red Head.
No. E-6 Brown Back, Scale Finish.
No. E-7 Mullet Scale.
No. E-8 Rainbow.
No. E-13 All Black.
STYLE "E"
$20
BELLY WEIGHT
"TORPEDO, JR." SINKER
S/S-TORPEDO (SINKER)
(G.E.)
$25
THE S/S TORPEDO COULD BE CONFUSED WITH THE CCBCO SILVER SIDE.
4"
NO. 1703
HERE IS THE CATALOG LISTING OF THE SILVER SIDE:
$20
NOTE: 4¾" IT WAS MADE FOR THE EAST COAST SALTWATER MARKET IN THE 50'S.
No. 1703 Illustrated
PRESSED EYE
4¾"
7/8oz.
CREEK CHUB SILVER SIDE
Leaded, sinker, runs deep on retrieve, spinners give flash
1700 ⅞ oz. 4¾ in. 00, 01, 03, 18, 34.

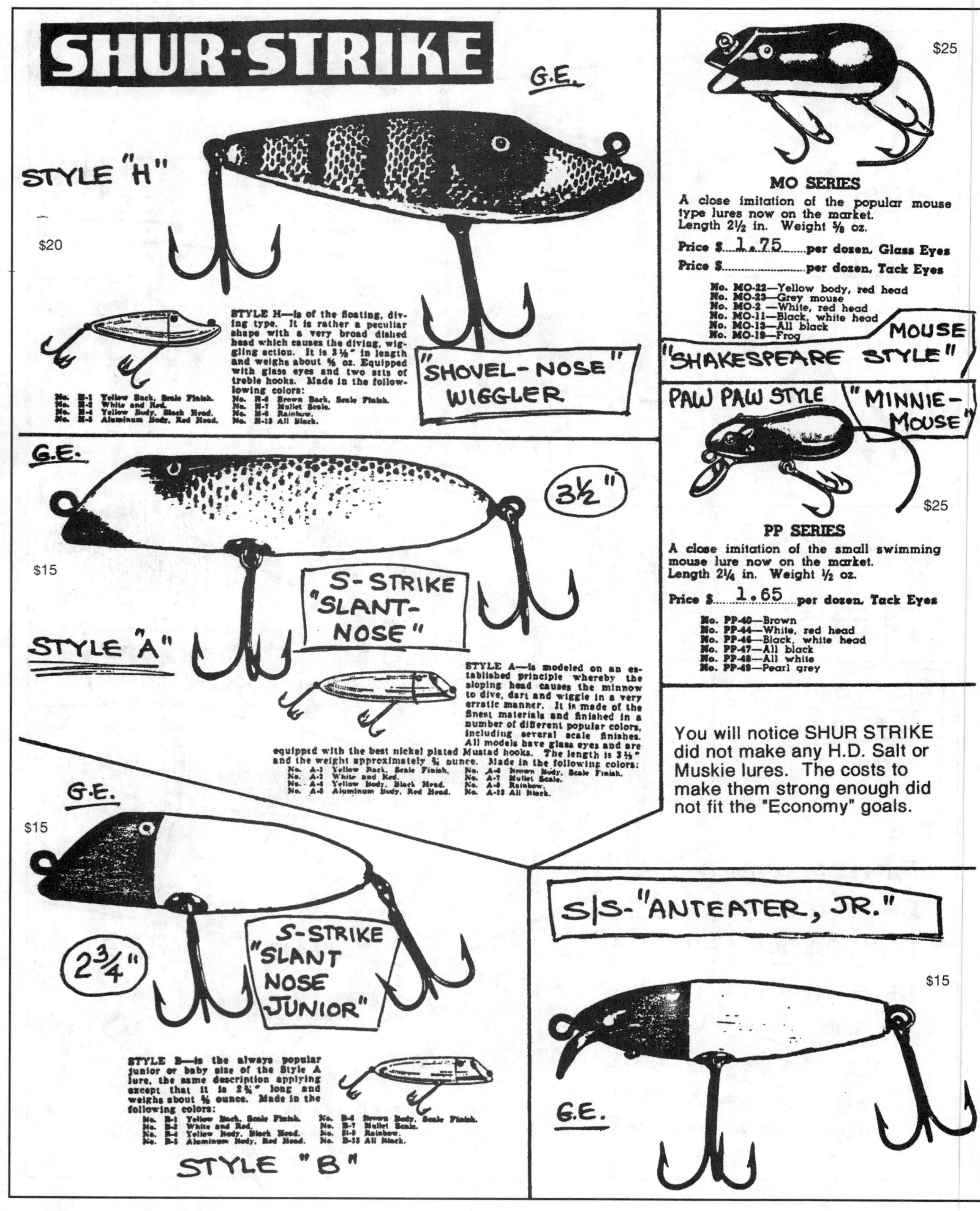

SHUR-STRIKE

G.E.

STYLE "H"

$20

"SHOVEL-NOSE" WIGGLER

STYLE H—is of the floating, diving type. It is rather a peculiar shape with a very broad dished head which causes the diving, wiggling action. It is 3½" in length and weighs about ⅝ oz. Equipped with glass eyes and two sets of treble hooks. Made in the following colors:

No. H-1 Yellow Back, Scale Finish.
No. H-2 White and Red.
No. H-4 Yellow Body, Black Head.
No. H-5 Aluminum Body, Red Head.
No. H-6 Brown Back, Scale Finish.
No. H-7 Mullet Scale.
No. H-8 Rainbow.
No. H-13 All Black.

$25

MO SERIES

A close imitation of the popular mouse type lures now on the market. Length 2½ in. Weight ⅝ oz.

Price $ 1.75 per dozen, Glass Eyes
Price $........ per dozen, Tack Eyes

No. MO-22—Yellow body, red head
No. MO-23—Grey mouse
No. MO-2 —White, red head
No. MO-11—Black, white head
No. MO-13—All black
No. MO-19—Frog

"SHAKESPEARE MOUSE STYLE"

G.E.

3½"

$15

S-STRIKE "SLANT-NOSE"

STYLE "A"

STYLE A—is modeled on an established principle whereby the sloping head causes the minnow to dive, dart and wiggle in a very erratic manner. It is made of the finest materials and finished in a number of different popular colors, including several scale finishes. All models have glass eyes and are equipped with the best nickel plated Mustad hooks. The length is 3½" and the weight approximately ¾ ounce. Made in the following colors:

No. A-1 Yellow Back, Scale Finish.
No. A-2 White and Red.
No. A-4 Yellow Body, Black Head.
No. A-5 Aluminum Body, Red Head.
No. A-6 Brown Body, Scale Finish.
No. A-7 Mullet Scale.
No. A-8 Rainbow.
No. A-13 All Black.

PAW PAW STYLE "MINNIE-MOUSE"

$25

PP SERIES

A close imitation of the small swimming mouse lure now on the market. Length 2¼ in. Weight ½ oz.

Price $ 1.65 per dozen, Tack Eyes

No. PP-40—Brown
No. PP-44—White, red head
No. PP-46—Black, white head
No. PP-47—All black
No. PP-48—All white
No. PP-49—Pearl grey

You will notice SHUR STRIKE did not make any H.D. Salt or Muskie lures. The costs to make them strong enough did not fit the "Economy" goals.

G.E.

$15

2¾"

S-STRIKE "SLANT NOSE JUNIOR"

STYLE B—is the always popular junior or baby size of the Style A lure, the same description applying except that it is 2¾" long and weighs about ⅝ ounce. Made in the following colors:

No. B-1 Yellow Back, Scale Finish.
No. B-2 White and Red.
No. B-4 Yellow Body, Black Head.
No. B-5 Aluminum Body, Red Head.
No. B-6 Brown Body, Scale Finish.
No. B-7 Mullet Scale.
No. B-8 Rainbow.
No. B-13 All Black.

STYLE "B"

S/S-"ANTEATER, JR."

$15

G.E.

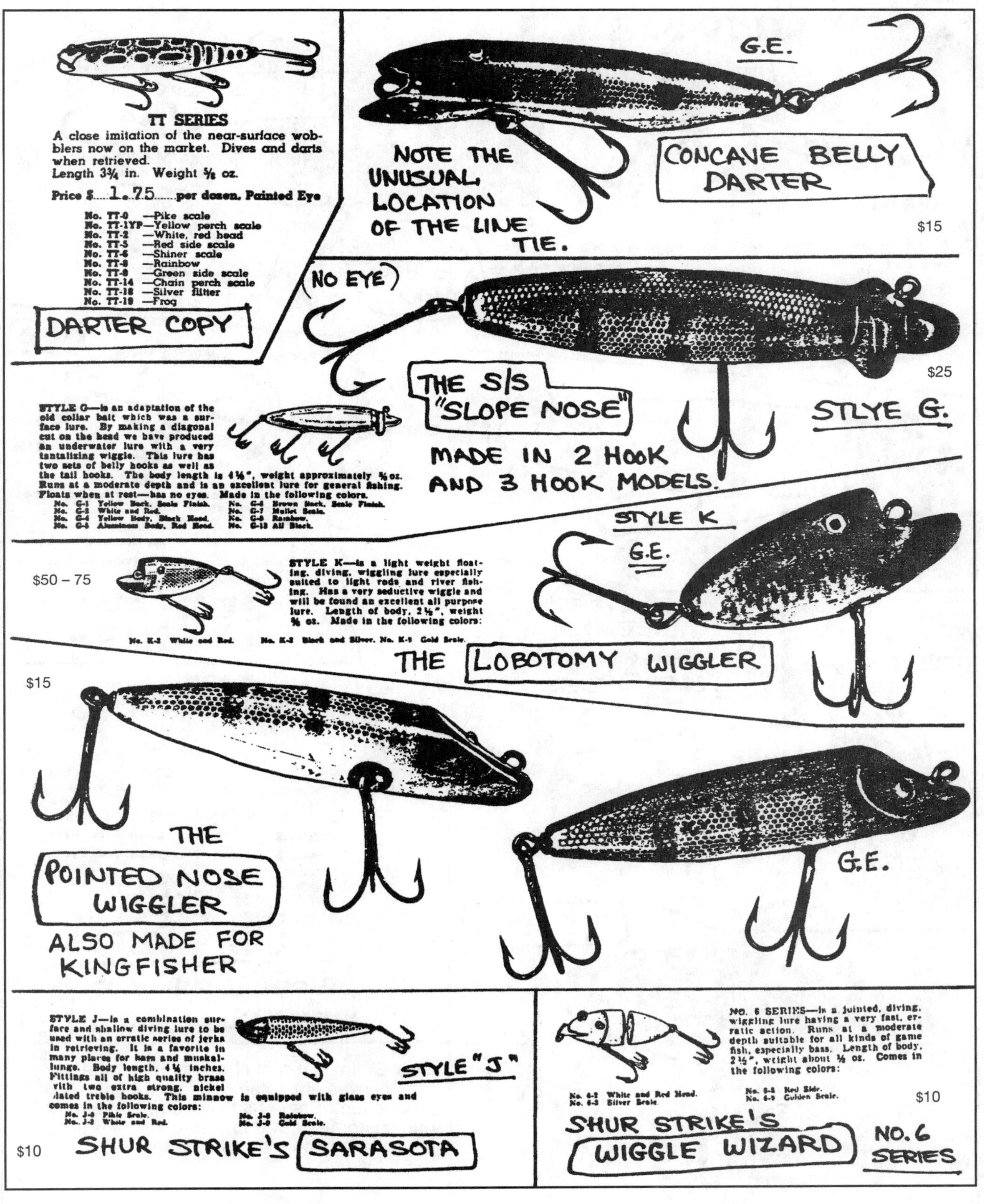
TT SERIES
A close imitation of the near-surface wobblers now on the market. Dives and darts when retrieved.
Length 3¾ in. Weight ⅝ oz.
Price $ 1.75 per dozen. Painted Eye
No. TT-0 —Pike scale
No. TT-1YP—Yellow perch scale
No. TT-2 —White, red head
No. TT-5 —Red side scale
No. TT-6 —Shiner scale
No. TT-8 —Rainbow
No. TT-9 —Green side scale
No. TT-14 —Chain perch scale
No. TT-18 —Silver flitter
No. TT-19 —Frog
DARTER COPY
G.E.
NOTE THE UNUSUAL LOCATION OF THE LINE TIE.
CONCAVE BELLY DARTER
$15
(NO EYE)
THE S/S "SLOPE NOSE"
$25
STLYE G.
MADE IN 2 HOOK AND 3 HOOK MODELS.
STYLE G—is an adaptation of the old collar bait which was a surface lure. By making a diagonal cut on the head we have produced an underwater lure with a very tantalizing wiggle. This lure has two sets of belly hooks as well as the tail hooks. The body length is 4⅛", weight approximately ⅝ oz. Runs at a moderate depth and is an excellent lure for general fishing. Floats when at rest—has no eyes. Made in the following colors.
No. G-1 Yellow Back, Scale Finish. No. G-6 Brown Back, Scale Finish.
No. G-2 White and Red. No. G-7 Mullet Scale.
No. G-4 Yellow Body, Black Head. No. G-8 Rainbow.
No. G-5 Aluminum Body, Red Head. No. G-13 All Black.
STYLE K
G.E.
$50 – 75
STYLE K—is a light weight floating, diving, wiggling lure especially suited to light rods and river fishing. Has a very seductive wiggle and will be found an excellent all purpose lure. Length of body, 2⅛", weight ⅝ oz. Made in the following colors:
No. K-2 White and Red. No. K-3 Black and Silver. No. K-9 Gold Scale.
THE LOBOTOMY WIGGLER
$15
THE POINTED NOSE WIGGLER
ALSO MADE FOR KINGFISHER
G.E.
STYLE J—is a combination surface and shallow diving lure to be used with an erratic series of jerks in retrieving. It is a favorite in many places for bass and muskallunge. Body length, 4¼ inches. Fittings all of high quality brass with two extra strong, nickel plated treble hooks. This minnow is equipped with glass eyes and comes in the following colors:
No. J-0 Pike Scale. No. J-8 Rainbow.
No. J-2 White and Red. No. J-9 Gold Scale.
STYLE "J"
$10
SHUR STRIKE'S SARASOTA
NO. 6 SERIES—is a jointed, diving, wiggling lure having a very fast, erratic action. Runs at a moderate depth suitable for all kinds of game fish, especially bass. Length of body, 2½", weight about ½ oz. Comes in the following colors:
No. 6-2 White and Red Head.
No. 6-3 Silver Scale.
No. 6-5 Red Side.
No. 6-9 Golden Scale.
$10
SHUR STRIKE'S WIGGLE WIZARD
NO. 6 SERIES

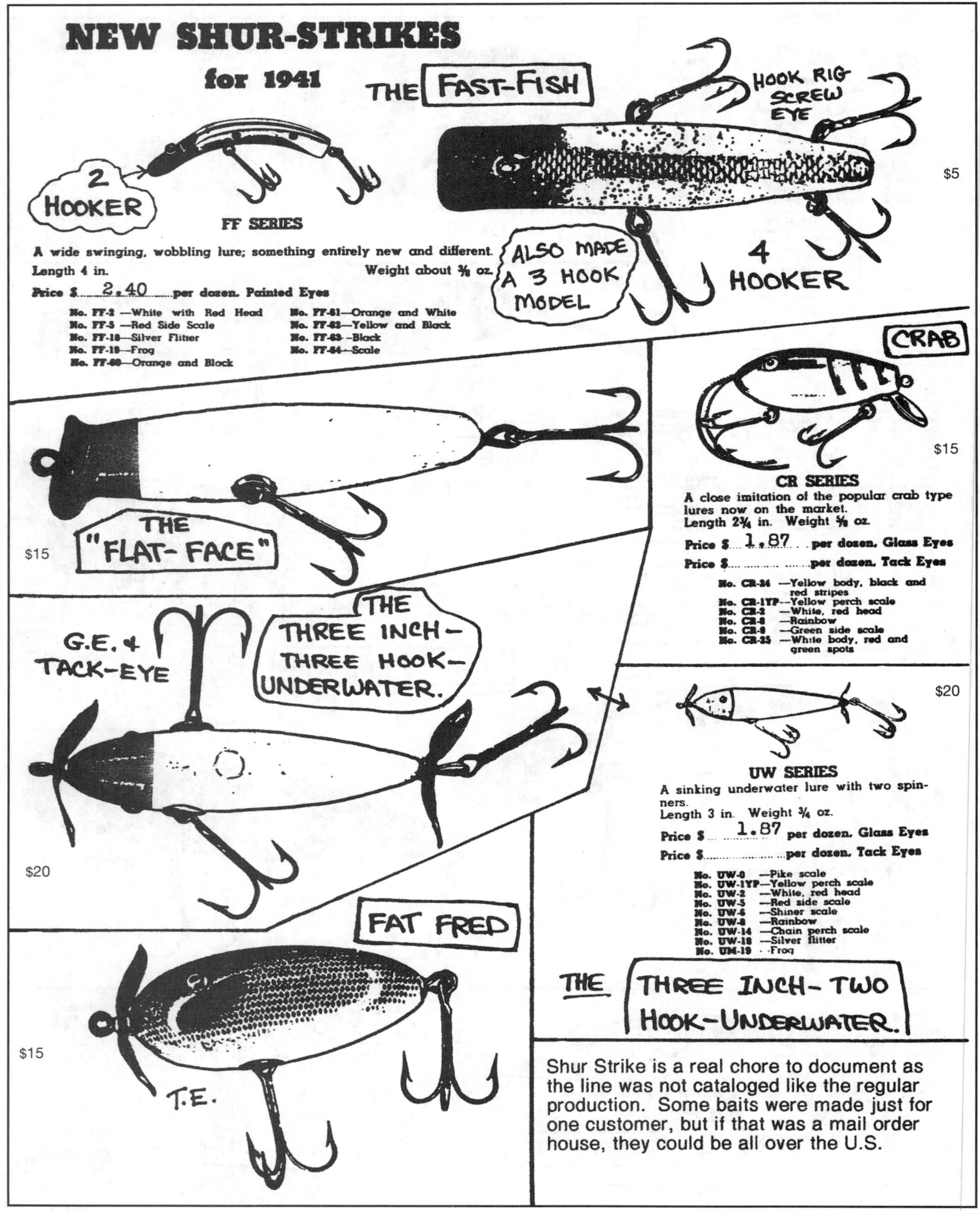
THE FAST-FISH
HOOK RIG SCREW EYE
$5
2 HOOKER
ALSO MADE A 3 HOOK MODEL
4 HOOKER
CRAB
$15
THE "FLAT-FACE"
$15
G.E. & TACK-EYE
THE THREE INCH-THREE HOOK-UNDERWATER.
$20
$20
FAT FRED
$15
T.E.
THE THREE INCH-TWO HOOK-UNDERWATER.

NEW SHUR-STRIKES

for 1941

FF SERIES

A wide swinging, wobbling lure; something entirely new and different.

Length 4 in. Weight about 3/8 oz.

Price $ 2.40 per dozen. Painted Eyes

No. FF-2 —White with Red Head
No. FF-5 —Red Side Scale
No. FF-18—Silver Flitter
No. FF-19—Frog
No. FF-80—Orange and Black
No. FF-81—Orange and White
No. FF-82—Yellow and Black
No. FF-83—Black
No. FF-84—Scale

CR SERIES

A close imitation of the popular crab type lures now on the market.

Length 2¾ in. Weight 3/8 oz.

Price $ 1.87 per dozen. Glass Eyes

Price $........ per dozen. Tack Eyes

No. CR-34 —Yellow body, black and red stripes
No. CR-1YP—Yellow perch scale
No. CR-2 —White, red head
No. CR-8 —Rainbow
No. CR-9 —Green side scale
No. CR-35 —White body, red and green spots

UW SERIES

A sinking underwater lure with two spinners.

Length 3 in. Weight ¾ oz.

Price $ 1.87 per dozen. Glass Eyes

Price $........ per dozen. Tack Eyes

No. UW-0 —Pike scale
No. UW-1YP—Yellow perch scale
No. UW-2 —White, red head
No. UW-5 —Red side scale
No. UW-6 —Shiner scale
No. UW-8 —Rainbow
No. UW-14 —Chain perch scale
No. UW-18 —Silver flitter
No. UM-19 —Frog

Shur Strike is a real chore to document as the line was not cataloged like the regular production. Some baits were made just for one customer, but if that was a mail order house, they could be all over the U.S.

CREEK
CHUB
BAITS
CATCH
MORE
FISH!

MUSKY DARTER- 4¼"
2-H.D. HOOKS

Creek "Darter"

THE "TWO THOUSAND"

NO. 2000 (3¾")

Length 3¾ in.
Weight ½ oz.

$15

THE MIDGET "DARTER"

$10 NO. 8000 (3")

Length 3 in.
Weight ⅜ oz.

NOTE: 2 TREBLE HOOKS OR 3 TREBLE HOOKS

SPINNERED "DARTER"

(3¾")

$15

No. 2000-S Series — Length 3¾ in. — Weight ½ oz.

Just the same as the No. 2000, except equipped with a rear spinner. Made in following finishes:

No. 2000-S—Natural Pikie
No. 2001-S—Natural Perch
No. 2002-S—White and Red
No. 2014-S—Yellow Spotted
No. 2018-S—Silver Flash
No. 2019-S—Frog

NO. 2000C

THE JOINTED "DARTER"

$15

NO. 4900

Length 3¾ in.
Weight ½ oz.

3 TREBLE HOOKS

3¾"

SPINNING DARTER

$10

NO. 9000

2-½"

No. 9000 Series — Wt. 1/4 oz.

Wiggles, wobbles, dives with a lifelike, near-the-surface darting action. Gets the big ones! Made in the following finishes:

No. 9014–Yellow Spotted No. 9018–Silver Flash No. 9019–Frog

THE DARTER IS A VERY OLD LURE— BUT WAS NOT MADE WITH GLASS EYES_ IN ANY QUANTITY.

"SURF DARTER"

$20

• 7" LENGTH • 3¾ OZ.
• 2-H.D. RIGGED TREBLES

NO. 7600

GIANT MUSKY DARTER

$25

5½"- 3 H.D. TREBLES

Creek Chub's INJURED MINNOWS

NO. 7700 — CALLED THE "SALT SPIN" DARTER

2 OZ.

$20

The Original Injured Minnow

"THE CRIP"

NO. 1500

3¾"

Length 3¾ in.
Weight ¾ oz.

$10 – 35

The Baby Injured Minnow

No. 1600 Series

Length 2¾ in.
Weight ½ oz.

NO. 1600

$10 – 25

(2¾")

EARLY 1500 WAS CALLED THE "FLAT SIDE CHUB." IT HAD A THINNER BODY THAN ALL LATER MODELS.

EARLY 1600 WAS CALLED THE "BABY FLAT SIDE CHUB." – AGAIN IN THAT EARLY CCBCO FINISH — GREEN, SILVER, & RED SCALE. (THE EARLY MODELS WERE REALLY FLAT-SIDED!)

SPINNING INJURED MINNOW

¼ OZ.

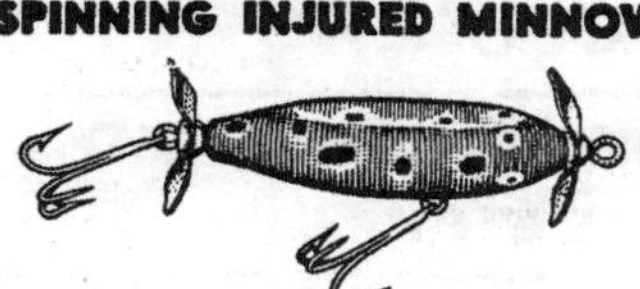

$10

(2½")

No. 9500 Series

NO. 9500

Husky Injured Minnow

$30 – 50

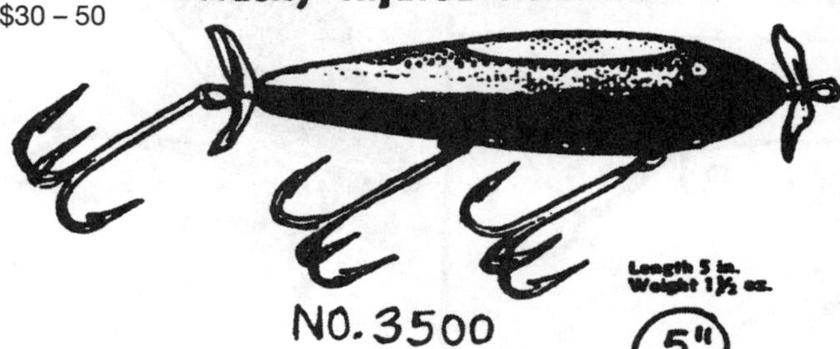

Length 5 in.
Weight 1½ oz.

NO. 3500

(5")

Flyrod Injured Minnow

$20 – 30

NO. F-90

(2¼") - SILVER FLASH FINISH ONLY.
- PLASTIC FINS

NEW-1926

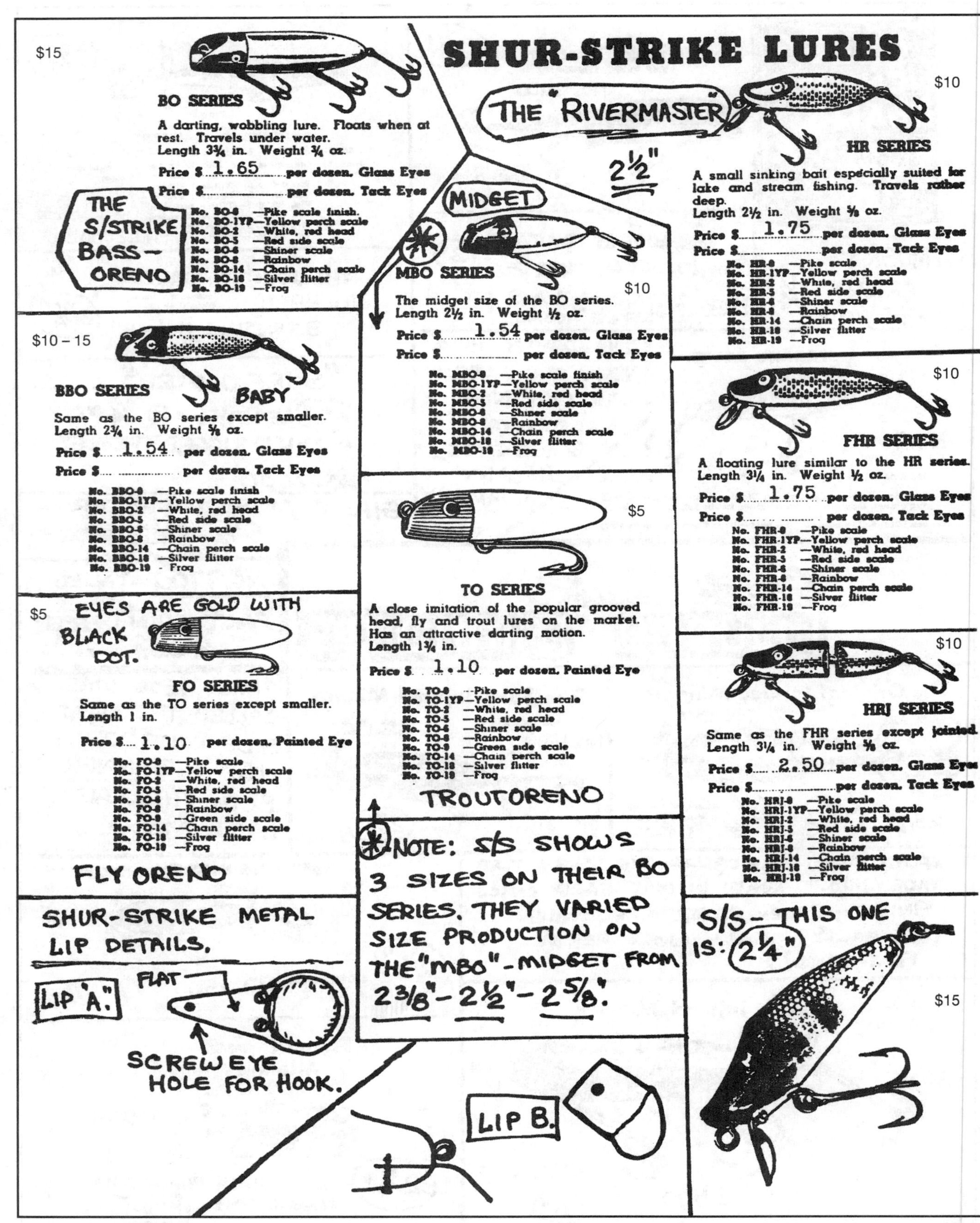
$15
SHUR-STRIKE LURES
BO SERIES
A darting, wobbling lure. Floats when at rest. Travels under water.
Length 3¾ in. Weight ¾ oz.
Price $ 1.65 per dozen. Glass Eyes
Price $ per dozen. Tack Eyes
THE S/STRIKE BASS-ORENO
No. BO-0 —Pike scale finish.
No. BO-1YP—Yellow perch scale
No. BO-2 —White, red head
No. BO-5 —Red side scale
No. BO-6 —Shiner scale
No. BO-8 —Rainbow
No. BO-14 —Chain perch scale
No. BO-18 —Silver flitter
No. BO-19 —Frog
$10
THE "RIVERMASTER"
2½"
HR SERIES
A small sinking bait especially suited for lake and stream fishing. Travels rather deep.
Length 2½ in. Weight ⅜ oz.
Price $ 1.75 per dozen. Glass Eyes
Price $ per dozen. Tack Eyes
No. HR-0 —Pike scale
No. HR-1YP—Yellow perch scale
No. HR-2 —White, red head
No. HR-5 —Red side scale
No. HR-6 —Shiner scale
No. HR-8 —Rainbow
No. HR-14 —Chain perch scale
No. HR-18 —Silver flitter
No. HR-19 —Frog
MIDGET
MBO SERIES
$10
The midget size of the BO series.
Length 2½ in. Weight ½ oz.
Price $ 1.54 per dozen. Glass Eyes
Price $ per dozen. Tack Eyes
No. MBO-0 —Pike scale finish
No. MBO-1YP—Yellow perch scale
No. MBO-2 —White, red head
No. MBO-5 —Red side scale
No. MBO-6 —Shiner scale
No. MBO-8 —Rainbow
No. MBO-14 —Chain perch scale
No. MBO-18 —Silver flitter
No. MBO-19 —Frog
$10 – 15
BBO SERIES
BABY
Same as the BO series except smaller.
Length 2¾ in. Weight ⅝ oz.
Price $ 1.54 per dozen. Glass Eyes
Price $ per dozen. Tack Eyes
No. BBO-0 —Pike scale finish
No. BBO-1YP—Yellow perch scale
No. BBO-2 —White, red head
No. BBO-5 —Red side scale
No. BBO-6 —Shiner scale
No. BBO-8 —Rainbow
No. BBO-14 —Chain perch scale
No. BBO-18 —Silver flitter
No. BBO-19 - Frog
$10
FHR SERIES
A floating lure similar to the HR series.
Length 3¼ in. Weight ½ oz.
Price $ 1.75 per dozen. Glass Eyes
Price $ per dozen. Tack Eyes
No. FHR-0 —Pike scale
No. FHR-1YP—Yellow perch scale
No. FHR-2 —White, red head
No. FHR-5 —Red side scale
No. FHR-6 —Shiner scale
No. FHR-8 —Rainbow
No. FHR-14 —Chain perch scale
No. FHR-18 —Silver flitter
No. FHR-19 —Frog
$5
TO SERIES
A close imitation of the popular grooved head, fly and trout lures on the market. Has an attractive darting motion.
Length 1¾ in.
Price $ 1.10 per dozen. Painted Eye
No. TO-0 —Pike scale
No. TO-1YP—Yellow perch scale
No. TO-2 —White, red head
No. TO-5 —Red side scale
No. TO-6 —Shiner scale
No. TO-8 —Rainbow
No. TO-9 —Green side scale
No. TO-14 —Chain perch scale
No. TO-18 —Silver flitter
No. TO-19 —Frog
TROUTORENO
$5
EYES ARE GOLD WITH BLACK DOT.
FO SERIES
Same as the TO series except smaller.
Length 1 in.
Price $ 1.10 per dozen. Painted Eye
No. FO-0 —Pike scale
No. FO-1YP—Yellow perch scale
No. FO-2 —White, red head
No. FO-5 —Red side scale
No. FO-6 —Shiner scale
No. FO-8 —Rainbow
No. FO-9 —Green side scale
No. FO-14 —Chain perch scale
No. FO-18 —Silver flitter
No. FO-19 —Frog
FLY ORENO
$10
HRJ SERIES
Same as the FHR series except jointed.
Length 3¼ in. Weight ⅝ oz.
Price $ 2.50 per dozen. Glass Eyes
Price $ per dozen. Tack Eyes
No. HRJ-0 —Pike scale
No. HRJ-1YP—Yellow perch scale
No. HRJ-2 —White, red head
No. HRJ-5 —Red side scale
No. HRJ-6 —Shiner scale
No. HRJ-8 —Rainbow
No. HRJ-14 —Chain perch scale
No. HRJ-18 —Silver flitter
No. HRJ-19 —Frog
*NOTE: S/S SHOWS 3 SIZES ON THEIR BO SERIES. THEY VARIED SIZE PRODUCTION ON THE "MBO"-MIDGET FROM 2⅜"-2½"-2⅝".
SHUR-STRIKE METAL LIP DETAILS.
LIP "A."
FLAT
SCREW EYE HOLE FOR HOOK.
LIP B.
S/S-THIS ONE IS: 2¼"
$15

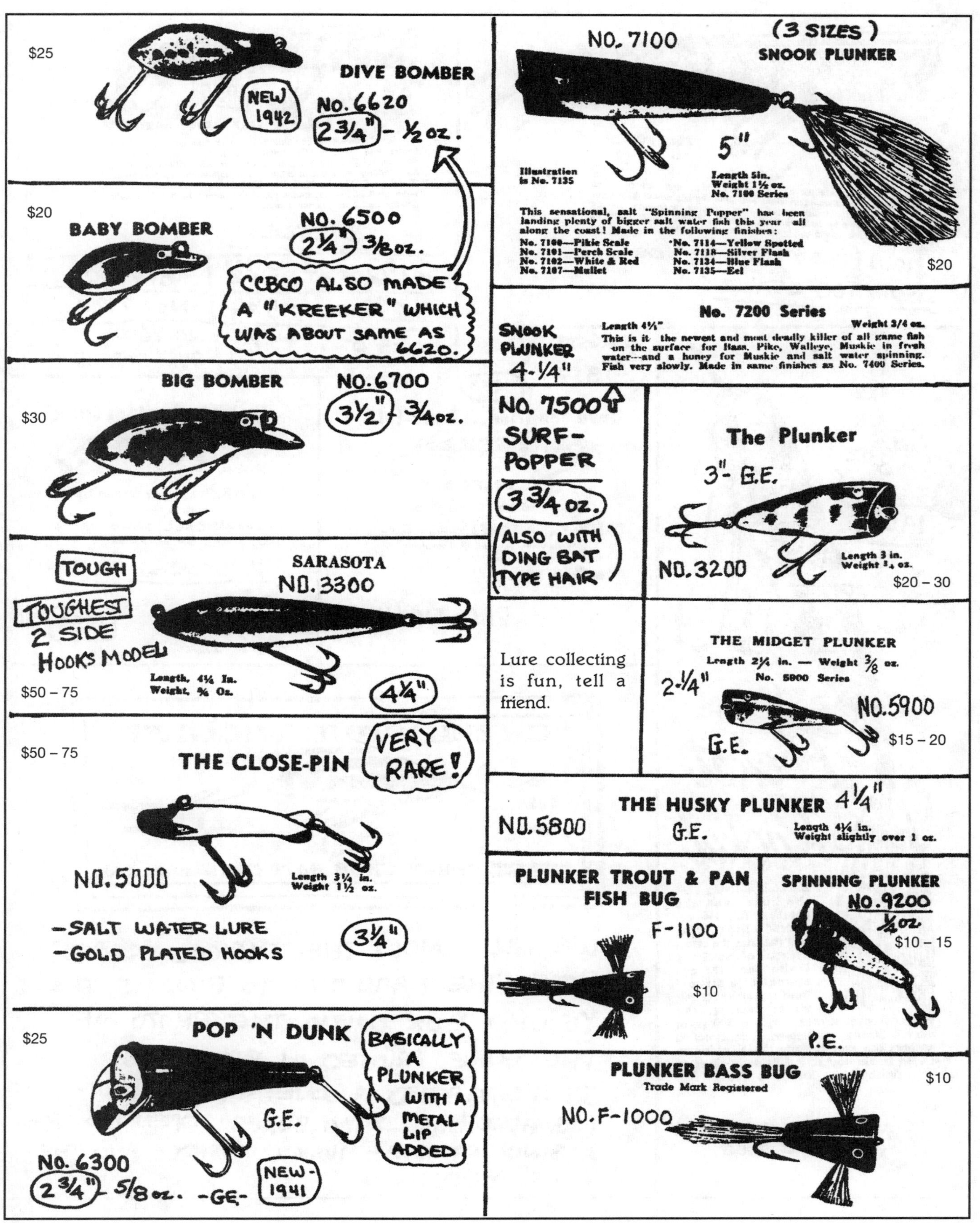
$25
DIVE BOMBER
NEW 1942
NO. 6620
2¾" - ½ oz.
$20
BABY BOMBER
NO. 6500
2¼" 3/8 oz.
CCBCO ALSO MADE A "KREEKER" WHICH WAS ABOUT SAME AS 6620.
BIG BOMBER
NO. 6700
$30
3½" 3/4 oz.
TOUGH
TOUGHEST
2 SIDE HOOKS MODEL
SARASOTA
NO. 3300
Length, 4¼ In.
Weight, ⅝ Oz.
$50 – 75
4¼"
$50 – 75
THE CLOSE-PIN
VERY RARE!
NO. 5000
Length 3¼ in.
Weight 1½ oz.
-SALT WATER LURE
-GOLD PLATED HOOKS
3¼"
$25
POP 'N DUNK
BASICALLY A PLUNKER WITH A METAL LIP ADDED
G.E.
NO. 6300
2¾" 5/8 oz. -GE-
NEW-1941
NO. 7100
(3 SIZES)
SNOOK PLUNKER
5"
Illustration is No. 7135
Length 5in.
Weight 1½ oz.
No. 7100 Series
This sensational, salt "Spinning Popper" has been landing plenty of bigger salt water fish this year all along the coast! Made in the following finishes:
No. 7100—Pikie Scale
No. 7101—Perch Scale
No. 7102—White & Red
No. 7107—Mullet
No. 7114—Yellow Spotted
No. 7118—Silver Flash
No. 7134—Blue Flash
No. 7135—Eel
$20
No. 7200 Series
SNOOK PLUNKER 4-1/4"
Length 4¼"
Weight 3/4 oz.
This is it the newest and most deadly killer of all game fish on the surface for Bass, Pike, Walleye, Muskie in fresh water—and a honey for Muskie and salt water spinning. Fish very slowly. Made in same finishes as No. 7400 Series.
NO. 7500
SURF-POPPER
3¾ oz.
(ALSO WITH DING BAT TYPE HAIR)
The Plunker
3" G.E.
NO. 3200
Length 3 in.
Weight ¾ oz.
$20 – 30
Lure collecting is fun, tell a friend.
THE MIDGET PLUNKER
Length 2¼ in. — Weight ⅜ oz.
No. 5900 Series
2-¼"
NO. 5900
G.E.
$15 – 20
THE HUSKY PLUNKER 4¼"
NO. 5800
G.E.
Length 4¼ in.
Weight slightly over 1 oz.
PLUNKER TROUT & PAN FISH BUG
F-1100
$10
SPINNING PLUNKER
NO. 9200
½ oz.
$10 – 15
P.E.
PLUNKER BASS BUG
Trade Mark Registered
$10
NO. F-1000

$15

SURF POPPER

Fast and accurate on a cast, reaches way out. Dives, pops to the surface, splashes—tantalizes and gets the big ones! Through-wire construction; strong hooks. New leading increases weight to 4 oz. Available in finishes 7502L, 7507L, 7518L, 7534L, 7535L, and 7437. Order yours today and get more big fish.

NOW (1957) WT. = 4 OZ.
NO. 7500 SERIES

$20

P.E. 1955

SALT WATER DARTER

New leading makes this bait streak like an arrow right where you want it. On retrieve, it zigs, it zags, it darts. 5½" long. Weight: 1 oz. with unusual tail loading to make its darting action possible. Through-wire construction. Finishes: 2002-SW, 2007-SW, 2018-SW, 2034-SW, 2035-SW. Also built in 2¼ oz. and 4 oz. sizes, known as the Salt Spin Darter and Surf Darter, respectively.

3 SIZES:

• 1½ oz. — 5½"	NO. 7700
• 2¼ oz. — 5¾"	NO. 7700
• 4 oz. — 7"	NO. 7600 SURF DARTER

$15

(1⅛ OZ)

1957

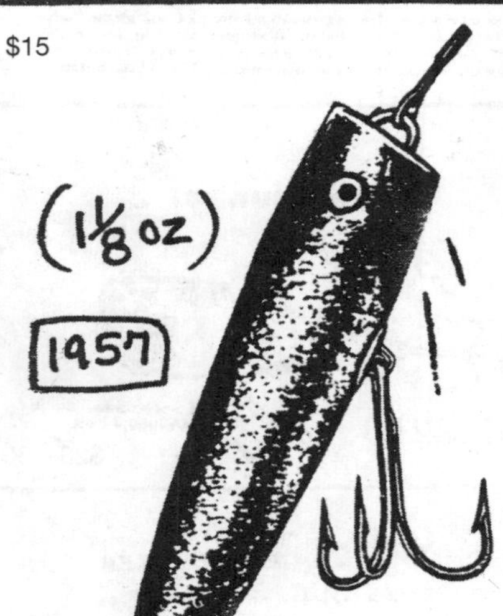

IT'S THE *Pocket Rocket*

Bucktail a-flying . . . she bucks and she pops! A full 1⅛ oz. of deadly fish catching bait that has the effectiveness of an Izaak Walton and the eye appeal of a circus! Built especially for salt water casting, the Pocket Rocket streaks 'way out 300 ft. or more. Strong through-wire construction anchors the exceptionally tough, cadmium plated treble hooks. Available in silver or finish (Nos. 7018 and 7034).

NO. 7018 – SILVER
NO. 7034 – BLUE

LARGEST (3/8 OZ.) 1958

Have you tried...Snark-Eel?

BRAND NEW . . .

But now at most tackle shops.

CREEK CHUB LURES, Garrett, Indiana
Write today for free 1958 catalog.

• 3/8 OZ.

PLASTIC (ALL 3)

$10

Tiny bait for Fly and Spin Casting!

TWO SIZES: ⅛-¼ oz.

SNARKIE... be sure to try it!

Write for Free Catalog.

Creek Chub Baits
Dept. HH-6 Garrett, Indiana

$10

2 SIZES:
• ⅛ OZ.
• ¼ OZ.

1959

"CREEK CHUB WIGGLER"
PAT. PENDING
Wiggler
Wobbler
Splatter
Surface
Near Surface
Deep
Manufactured only by CREEK CHUB BAIT CO., Garrett, Ind.

WE ALL KNOW THE TYPICAL CCBCO BOX – THE HARD ONE TO FIND IS THE YELLOW BOX WITH THE PHOTO OF THE LURE PRINTED IN BLACK, AS ILLUSTRATED ABOVE. THE FOLLOWING ALSO HAD INTRO. BOXES: OPEN MOUTH – ALBINO CRAWDAD – HUSKY MUSKY – AND THE PIKIE MINNOW.

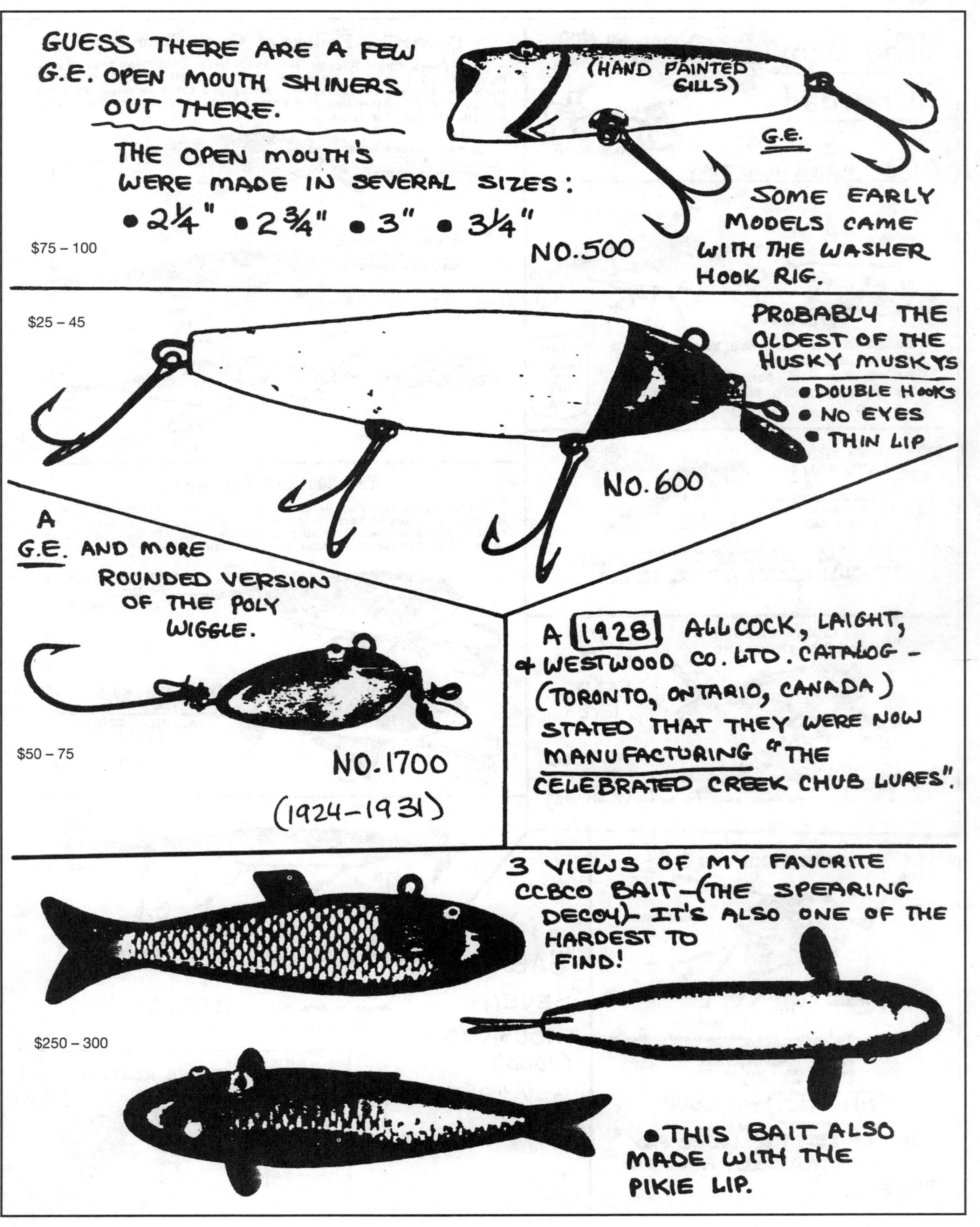
GUESS THERE ARE A FEW G.E. OPEN MOUTH SHINERS OUT THERE.
THE OPEN MOUTH'S WERE MADE IN SEVERAL SIZES:
• 2¼" • 2¾" • 3" • 3¼"
(HAND PAINTED GILLS)
G.E.
SOME EARLY MODELS CAME WITH THE WASHER HOOK RIG.
NO.500
PROBABLY THE OLDEST OF THE HUSKY MUSKYS
• DOUBLE HOOKS
• NO EYES
• THIN LIP
NO. 600
A G.E. AND MORE ROUNDED VERSION OF THE POLY WIGGLE.
NO. 1700
(1924–1931)
A 1928 ALLCOCK, LAIGHT, & WESTWOOD CO. LTD. CATALOG – (TORONTO, ONTARIO, CANADA) STATED THAT THEY WERE NOW MANUFACTURING "THE CELEBRATED CREEK CHUB LURES".
3 VIEWS OF MY FAVORITE CCBCO BAIT – (THE SPEARING DECOY) – IT'S ALSO ONE OF THE HARDEST TO FIND!
• THIS BAIT ALSO MADE WITH THE PIKIE LIP.

$75 – 100

$25 – 45

$50 – 75

$250 – 300

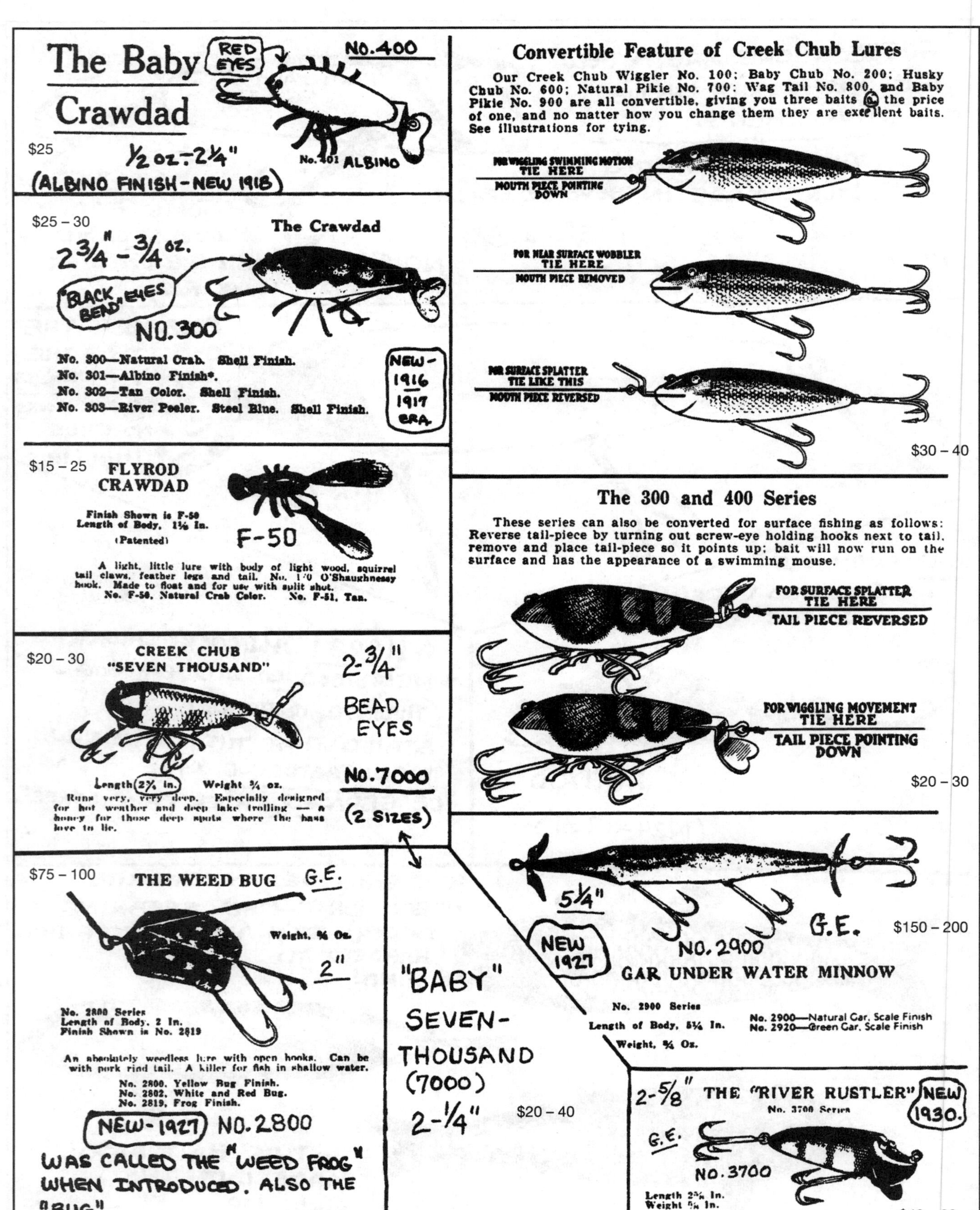

The Baby Crawdad

RED EYES

NO. 400

$25

1/2 oz. - 2 1/4"

No. 401 ALBINO

(ALBINO FINISH - NEW 1918)

$25 – 30

The Crawdad

2 3/4" - 3/4 oz.

"BLACK BEND" EYES

NO. 300

No. 300—Natural Crab. Shell Finish.
No. 301—Albino Finish*.
No. 302—Tan Color. Shell Finish.
No. 303—River Peeler. Steel Blue. Shell Finish.

NEW - 1916 1917 ERA

$15 – 25

FLYROD CRAWDAD

Finish Shown is F-50
Length of Body, 1 1/8 In.
(Patented)

F-50

A light, little lure with body of light wood, squirrel tail claws, feather legs and tail. No. 1/0 O'Shaughnessy hook. Made to float and for use with split shot.
No. F-50, Natural Crab Color. No. F-51, Tan.

$20 – 30

CREEK CHUB "SEVEN THOUSAND"

2-3/4"

BEAD EYES

Length 2 3/4 in. Weight 3/4 oz.

Runs very, very deep. Especially designed for hot weather and deep lake trolling — a honey for those deep spots where the bass love to lie.

NO. 7000

(2 SIZES)

$75 – 100

THE WEED BUG G.E.

Weight, 5/8 Oz.

2"

No. 2800 Series
Length of Body, 2 In.
Finish Shown is No. 2819

An absolutely weedless lure with open hooks. Can be with pork rind tail. A killer for fish in shallow water.

No. 2800, Yellow Bug Finish.
No. 2802, White and Red Bug.
No. 2819, Frog Finish.

NEW - 1927 NO. 2800

WAS CALLED THE "WEED FROG" WHEN INTRODUCED. ALSO THE "BUG".

"BABY" SEVEN-THOUSAND (7000) 2-1/4"

$20 – 40

Convertible Feature of Creek Chub Lures

Our Creek Chub Wiggler No. 100; Baby Chub No. 200; Husky Chub No. 600; Natural Pikie No. 700; Wag Tail No. 800, and Baby Pikie No. 900 are all convertible, giving you three baits at the price of one, and no matter how you change them they are excellent baits. See illustrations for tying.

FOR WIGGLING SWIMMING MOTION TIE HERE
MOUTH PIECE POINTING DOWN

FOR NEAR SURFACE WOBBLER TIE HERE
MOUTH PIECE REMOVED

FOR SURFACE SPLATTER TIE LIKE THIS
MOUTH PIECE REVERSED

$30 – 40

The 300 and 400 Series

These series can also be converted for surface fishing as follows: Reverse tail-piece by turning out screw-eye holding hooks next to tail, remove and place tail-piece so it points up; bait will now run on the surface and has the appearance of a swimming mouse.

FOR SURFACE SPLATTER TIE HERE
TAIL PIECE REVERSED

FOR WIGGLING MOVEMENT TIE HERE
TAIL PIECE POINTING DOWN

$20 – 30

5 1/4"

G.E.

$150 – 200

NEW 1927

NO. 2900

GAR UNDER WATER MINNOW

No. 2900 Series
Length of Body, 5 1/4 In.
Weight, 3/4 Oz.

No. 2900—Natural Gar, Scale Finish
No. 2920—Green Gar, Scale Finish

2-5/8" THE "RIVER RUSTLER" NEW 1930.
No. 3700 Series

G.E.

NO. 3700

Length 2 5/8 In.
Weight 5/8 In.

$40 – 60

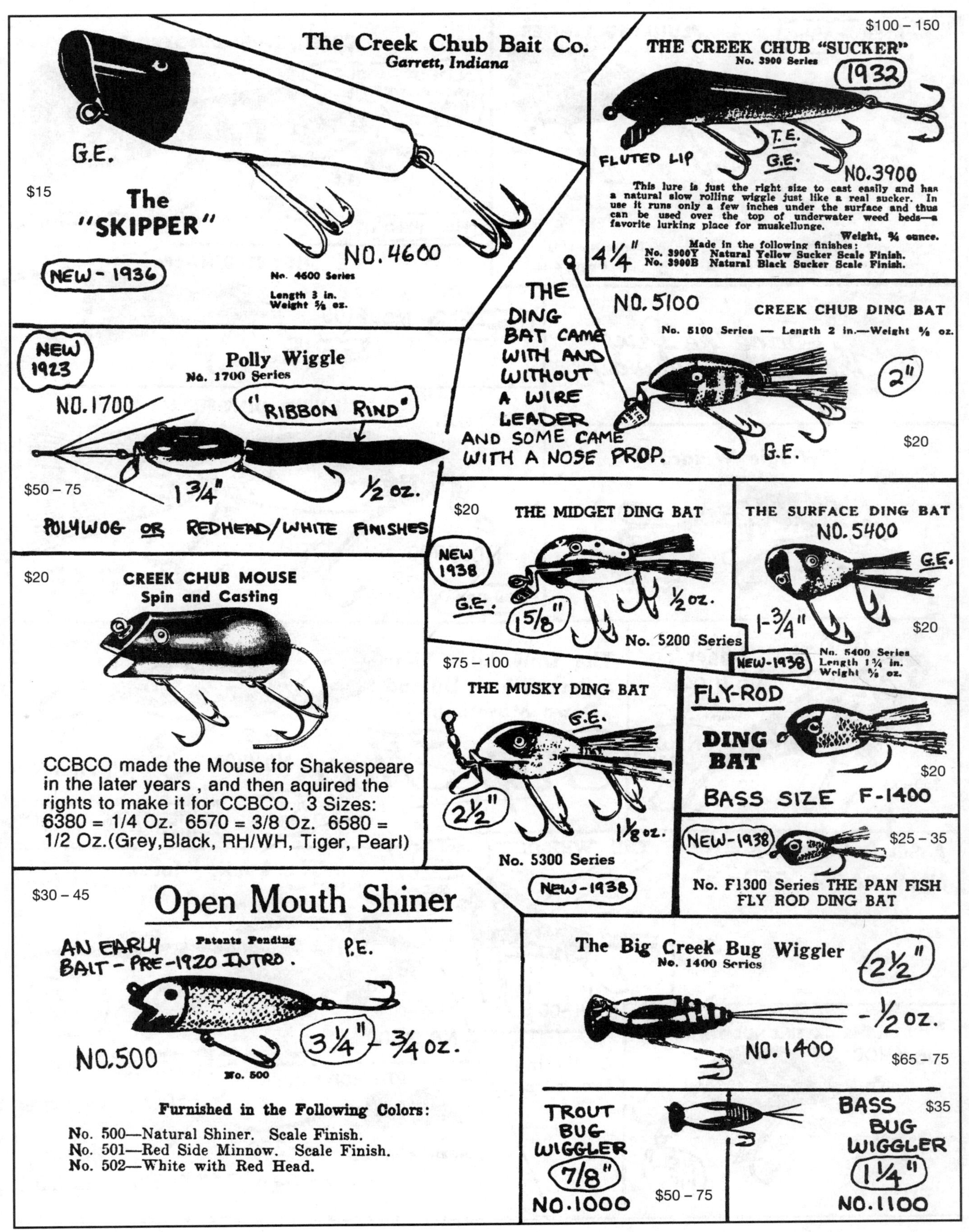

The Creek Chub Bait Co.
Garrett, Indiana
G.E.
$15
The "SKIPPER"
NEW - 1936
NO. 4600
No. 4600 Series
Length 3 in.
Weight 5/8 oz.
$100 – 150
THE CREEK CHUB "SUCKER"
No. 3900 Series
1932
FLUTED LIP
T.E.
G.E.
NO. 3900
This lure is just the right size to cast easily and has a natural slow rolling wiggle just like a real sucker. In use it runs only a few inches under the surface and thus can be used over the top of underwater weed beds—a favorite lurking place for muskellunge.
Weight, 3/4 ounce.
Made in the following finishes:
4 1/4"
No. 3900Y Natural Yellow Sucker Scale Finish.
No. 3900B Natural Black Sucker Scale Finish.
NEW 1923
Polly Wiggle
No. 1700 Series
NO. 1700
"RIBBON RIND"
$50 – 75
1 3/4"
1/2 oz.
POLYWOG OR REDHEAD/WHITE FINISHES
THE DING BAT CAME WITH AND WITHOUT A WIRE LEADER AND SOME CAME WITH A NOSE PROP.
NO. 5100
CREEK CHUB DING BAT
No. 5100 Series — Length 2 in.—Weight 5/8 oz.
2"
G.E.
$20
$20
THE MIDGET DING BAT
NEW 1938
G.E.
1 5/8"
1/2 oz.
No. 5200 Series
THE SURFACE DING BAT
NO. 5400
G.E.
1-3/4"
$20
NEW-1938
No. 5400 Series
Length 1 3/4 in.
Weight 5/8 oz.
$20
CREEK CHUB MOUSE
Spin and Casting
CCBCO made the Mouse for Shakespeare in the later years , and then aquired the rights to make it for CCBCO. 3 Sizes: 6380 = 1/4 Oz. 6570 = 3/8 Oz. 6580 = 1/2 Oz.(Grey,Black, RH/WH, Tiger, Pearl)
$75 – 100
THE MUSKY DING BAT
G.E.
2 1/2"
1 1/8 oz.
No. 5300 Series
NEW-1938
FLY-ROD
DING BAT
$20
BASS SIZE F-1400
NEW-1938
$25 – 35
No. F1300 Series THE PAN FISH FLY ROD DING BAT
$30 – 45
Open Mouth Shiner
AN EARLY BAIT - PRE-1920 INTRO.
Patents Pending
P.E.
NO.500
3 1/4"
3/4 oz.
No. 500
Furnished in the Following Colors:
No. 500—Natural Shiner. Scale Finish.
No. 501—Red Side Minnow. Scale Finish.
No. 502—White with Red Head.
The Big Creek Bug Wiggler
No. 1400 Series
2 1/2"
-1/2 oz.
NO. 1400
$65 – 75
TROUT BUG WIGGLER
7/8"
NO.1000
$50 – 75
BASS BUG WIGGLER
$35
1 1/4"
NO.1100

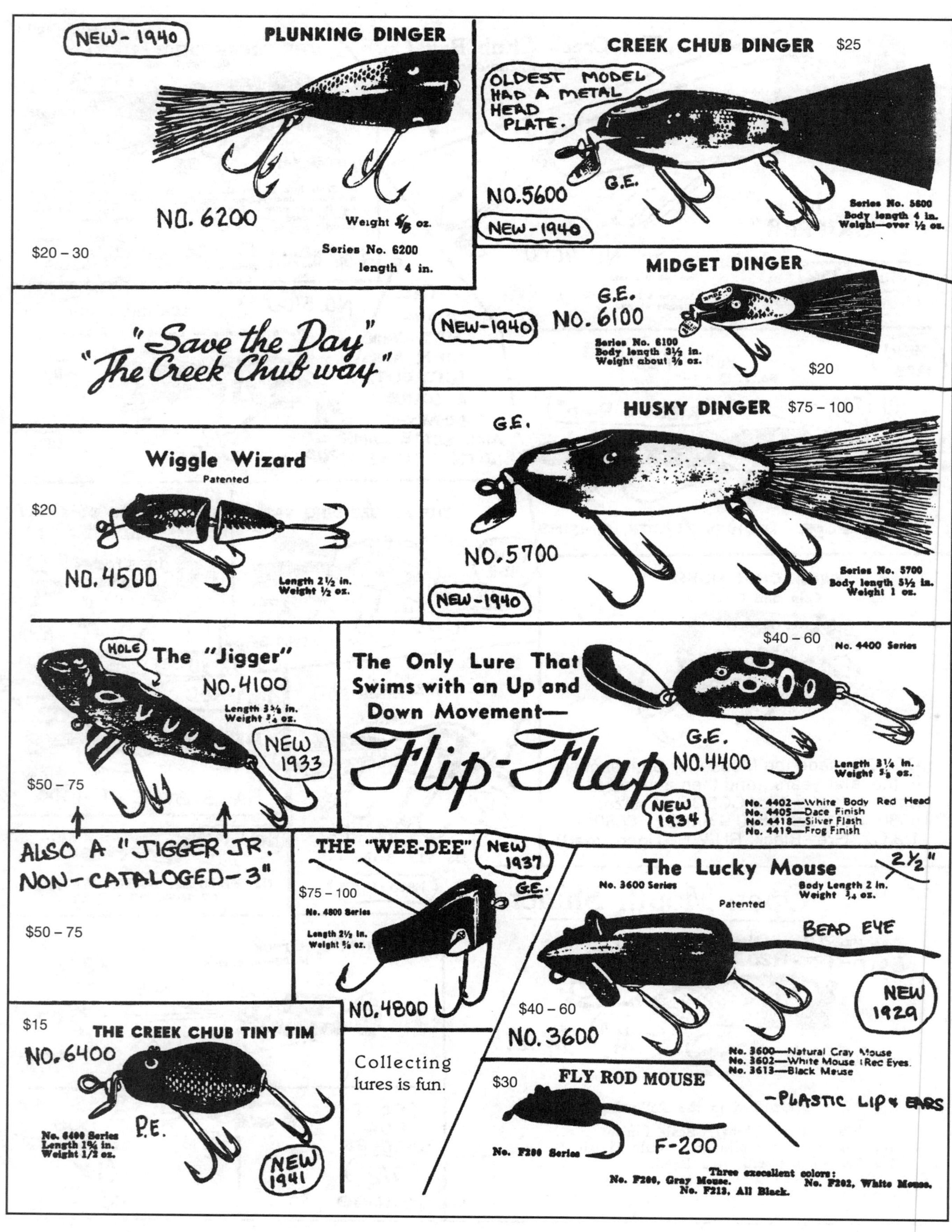
NEW-1940
PLUNKING DINGER
NO. 6200
Weight 5/8 oz.
Series No. 6200
length 4 in.
$20 – 30
CREEK CHUB DINGER
$25
OLDEST MODEL HAD A METAL HEAD PLATE.
NO.5600
G.E.
NEW-1940
Series No. 5600
Body length 4 in.
Weight—over 1/2 oz.
MIDGET DINGER
G.E.
NEW-1940
NO. 6100
Series No. 6100
Body length 3½ in.
Weight about 3/8 oz.
$20
"Save the Day"
"The Creek Chub way"
HUSKY DINGER
$75 – 100
G.E.
NO.5700
NEW-1940
Series No. 5700
Body length 5½ in.
Weight 1 oz.
Wiggle Wizard
Patented
$20
NO.4500
Length 2½ in.
Weight ½ oz.
HOLE
The "Jigger"
NO.4100
NEW 1933
$50 – 75
ALSO A "JIGGER JR. NON-CATALOGED-3"
$50 – 75
$40 – 60
No. 4400 Series
The Only Lure That Swims with an Up and Down Movement—
Flip-Flap
G.E.
NO.4400
Length 3¼ in.
NEW 1934
No. 4402—White Body Red Head
No. 4405—Dace Finish
No. 4418—Silver Flash
No. 4419—Frog Finish
THE "WEE-DEE"
NEW 1937
G.E.
$75 – 100
No. 4800 Series
Length 2½ in.
NO.4800
The Lucky Mouse
2½"
No. 3600 Series
Body Length 2 in.
Patented
BEAD EYE
NEW 1929
$40 – 60
NO. 3600
No. 3600—Natural Gray Mouse
No. 3602—White Mouse Red Eyes.
No. 3613—Black Mouse
$15
THE CREEK CHUB TINY TIM
NO. 6400
P.E.
No. 6400 Series
Length 1¾ in.
Weight 1/2 oz.
NEW 1941
Collecting lures is fun.
$30
FLY ROD MOUSE
-PLASTIC LIP & EARS
F-200
No. F200 Series
Three excellent colors:
No. F200, Gray Mouse.
No. F202, White Mouse.
No. F213, All Black.

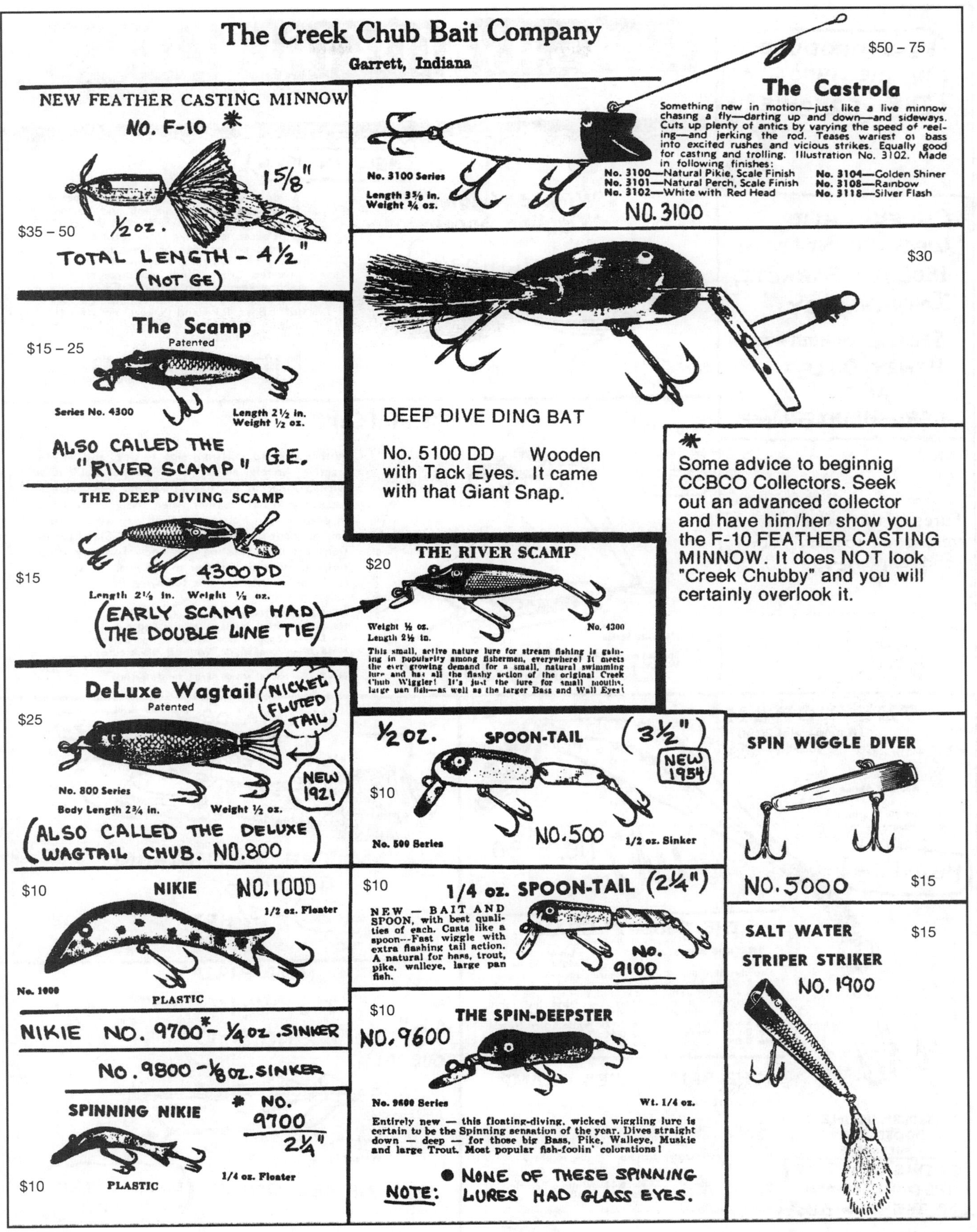

The Creek Chub Bait Company

Garrett, Indiana

NEW FEATHER CASTING MINNOW

NO. F-10 *

1 5/8"

1/2 oz.

$35 – 50

TOTAL LENGTH - 4 1/2"

(NOT GE)

$50 – 75

The Castrola

Something new in motion—just like a live minnow chasing a fly—darting up and down—and sideways. Cuts up plenty of antics by varying the speed of reeling—and jerking the rod. Teases wariest of bass into excited rushes and vicious strikes. Equally good for casting and trolling. Illustration No. 3102. Made in following finishes:

No. 3100—Natural Pikie, Scale Finish
No. 3101—Natural Perch, Scale Finish
No. 3102—White with Red Head
No. 3104—Golden Shiner
No. 3108—Rainbow
No. 3118—Silver Flash

No. 3100 Series

Length 3⅝ in.
Weight ¾ oz.

NO. 3100

$30

DEEP DIVE DING BAT

No. 5100 DD Wooden with Tack Eyes. It came with that Giant Snap.

The Scamp

Patented

$15 – 25

Series No. 4300

Length 2½ in.
Weight ½ oz.

ALSO CALLED THE "RIVER SCAMP" G.E.

THE DEEP DIVING SCAMP

$15

4300DD

Length 2½ in. Weight ½ oz.

(EARLY SCAMP HAD THE DOUBLE LINE TIE)

*

Some advice to beginnig CCBCO Collectors. Seek out an advanced collector and have him/her show you the F-10 FEATHER CASTING MINNOW. It does NOT look "Creek Chubby" and you will certainly overlook it.

$20

THE RIVER SCAMP

Weight ½ oz.
Length 2½ in.

No. 4300

This small, active nature lure for stream fishing is gaining in popularity among fishermen, everywhere! It meets the ever growing demand for a small, natural swimming lure and has all the flashy action of the original Creek Chub Wiggler! It's just the lure for small mouths, large pan fish—as well as the larger Bass and Wall Eyes!

DeLuxe Wagtail

Patented

(NICKEL FLUTED TAIL)

$25

NEW 1921

No. 800 Series

Body Length 2¾ in. Weight ½ oz.

(ALSO CALLED THE DELUXE WAGTAIL CHUB. NO.800)

1/2 OZ. SPOON-TAIL (3 1/2")

NEW 1954

$10

No. 500 Series

NO.500

1/2 oz. Sinker

SPIN WIGGLE DIVER

NO. 5000

$15

$10

NIKIE NO. 1000

1/2 oz. Floater

No. 1000

PLASTIC

$10

1/4 oz. SPOON-TAIL (2 1/4")

NEW — BAIT AND SPOON, with best qualities of each. Casts like a spoon—Fast wiggle with extra flashing tail action. A natural for bass, trout, pike, walleye, large pan fish.

NO. 9100

SALT WATER

$15

STRIPER STRIKER

NO. 1900

NIKIE NO. 9700* - 1/4 OZ. SINKER

NO. 9800 - 1/8 OZ. SINKER

$10

THE SPIN-DEEPSTER

NO. 9600

No. 9600 Series

Wt. 1/4 oz.

Entirely new — this floating-diving, wicked wiggling lure is certain to be the Spinning sensation of the year. Dives straight down — deep — for those big Bass, Pike, Walleye, Muskie and large Trout. Most popular fish-foolin' colorations!

SPINNING NIKIE

* NO. 9700

2 1/4"

$10

PLASTIC

1/4 oz. Floater

NOTE: • NONE OF THESE SPINNING LURES HAD GLASS EYES.

RE-INTRODUCED IN THE 1970'S AS THE "COHOKIE" -

CREEK CHUB WAS FOUNDED IN 1906 IN GARRETT, INDIANA – BY GEORGE SCHULTHESS HENRY DILLS AND CARL HEINZERLING

Lures in this book are for very good to very good+ condition.

FLASHY METAL LURES

NEW IN 1926

"Wicked Wiggler" Wiggling Spoon

Patented

No. S-1 Series Length 2¼ in. Weight ¾ oz.

2¾"

$15 – 20

NO. S-1

Made of heavy brass, with durable nickel finish and stamped on top and bottom with large scales. The "Wicked Wiggler" is an exceptional "big fish" getting spoon! does not revolve or twist the line—has a fast wiggling movement with the inverted Creek Chub mouthpiece! Fast reeling keeps it on surface. Casts easily and wiggles a pork rind something "awful"! Bass, Pike and Pickerel go after it, plenty. Illustration is No. S-1. Made in following finishes:

No. S-1—Equipped with feathered treble
No. S-2—Equipped with snap for pork rind
No. S-3—Equipped with rigid single hook.

"Sinful Sal"

$10 – 30

1930

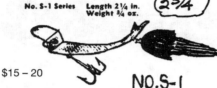

With a decided roll from side to side, and an attractive wobble all its own, "Sinful Sal" is a wicked killer of big bass, pike and muskellunge, especially in hot weather when the fish are lying in deep water. You can troll all day with "Sinful Sal" without danger of a kinked line. Stabilizer in front prevents twisting the line. For very deep trolling, use with a sinker in the line. Illustration is No. S-22. Made in the following finishes:

Patented
No. S-20 Series

Spoon Length 2¾ in.
Weight ¾ oz.

NO. S-20

No. S-20—All Nickel
No. S-21—Nickel inside, White & Red outside
No. S-22—Copper inside, White & Red outside
No. S-23—Nickel inside, White & Black outside
No. S-24—Nickel inside, Yellow Spotted outside
No. S-25—Nickel inside, Frog finish outside

THE "CHAMP"

(A new metal Pikie)

$10 – 15

Patented

No. S-30 Series

Length 3¼ in.
Weight ⅝ oz.

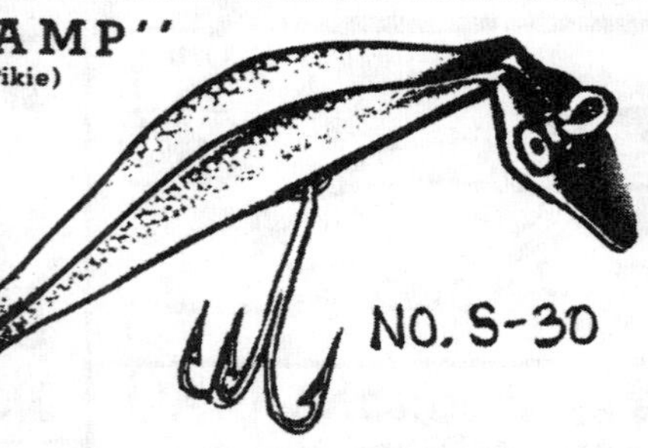

NO. S-30

NEW-1936

THE "MUSKY" CHAMP

No. S-40 Series Length 5 in. Weight 1½ oz.

Exactly like the Champ described above, except the body is 5-in. long and is equipped with quadruple strength treble hooks. Suitable for lake trout, muskellunge, great northern pike and light salt water fish. Made in following color combinations:

No. S-40 -Pikie
No. S-40N Nickel
No. S-40C -Copper
No. S-42 -White & Red Head
No. S-44 Yellow Scale
No. S-49 Green Scale

THE SALT WATER CHAMP

No. S-50 Series Length 5 in. Weight 3 oz.

Equipped with No. 8/0 imported tarpon hook or with No. 9/0 extra strength treble. Please specify which is desired. Strong enough and suitable for heaviest salt water fishing. Made in the following finishes:

No. S-50N Nickel
No. S-50C Copper
No. S-52 White & Red Head
No. S-57 Mullett

INDESTRUCTIBLE HOOKS CAN'T PULL OUT!

IS THIS PART OF THE DEVELOPMENT OF THE SPOON PLUG?

IN CATALOG → NEW IN 1936 -BUT- NONE EVER FOUND!

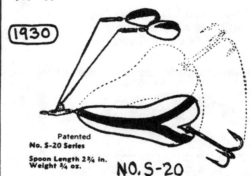

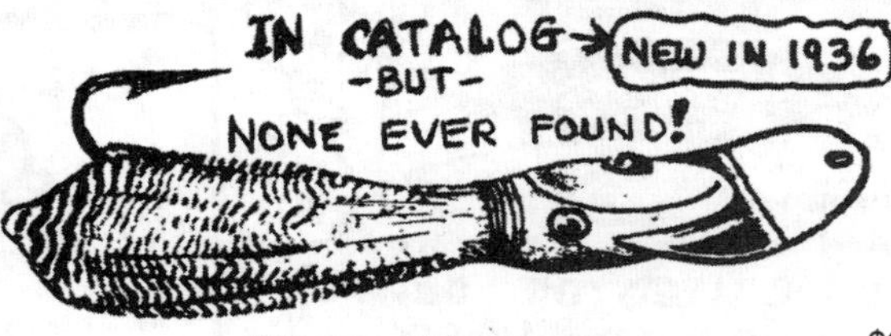

THE FETHI-MIN
NO. 4700
3" – 3/4 oz.

$20 – 50

(NEW - 1929)

The "Wigl-Y-Rind"

NO. S-10

2½"
4⅛" OVERALL

$15 – 25

No. S-10
Weight ⅝ oz.

- NICKEL ONLY

WITH 2 SETS OF HOOKS

CREEK CHUB FLY ROD LURES

FLOATING FLY ROD MINNOW

No. F-1200

$10

F-1200

White cedar body. Buck hair wings and tail. No. 1 hollow point hook. A surface fly rod minnow that always rides right side up, skitters over the surface and lifts easily. Very durable and will outlast any other wood or cork body lure made.

The above bugs are made in the following finishes:

No. F-1000	No. F-1100	No. F-1200—All White
No. F-1001	No. F-1101	No. F-1201—All Red
No. F-1002	No. F-1102	No. F-1202—All Gray
No. F-1003	No. F-1103	No. F-1203—Black & Yellow
No. F-1004	No. F-1104	No. F-1204—Gray & Brown
No. F-1005	No. F-1105	No. F-1205—Red & White

Fly Rod Flexible Floating Feather Minnow

No. F-1 Series

F-1

$10

Has hook carrying feathers loosely attached to body, giving more movement and a better hooker. Put up one in a box or set of eight in counter display. Illustration is No. F-1.

Made in the following Finishes

No. F-1—Creek Chub, Scale Finish	No. F-5—All Red
No. F-2—Pikie, Scale Finish	No. F-6—Manchester
No. F-3—Gold Fish, Scale Finish	No. F-7—Lord Baltimore
No. F-4—White and Red	No. F-8—Silver Doctor

"POP-IT" LURE F-100

NEW 1926

No. F-100 Series.

Patented

Made with cork body; No. 1 Hollow Point Hook, bucktail and mallard feathers. Feathers and buck tail permanently attached to body without the use of thread; guaranteed to stick tighter than if thread tied. Here is a lure which will get the bass when pulled so as to make the bait go pop-pop on the surface. The reason it is such a killer is, that though it is a very small and light lure, when jerked it makes a big fuss on the surface, which the bass can't resist. When pulled fast, it has a wiggling movement like a minnow hustling for his life. Illustration is No. F-101. Made in the following finishes:

No. F-100—Chub No. F-101—Perch
No. F-102—Brown Bug

$10

The Bug-A-Moth

$10

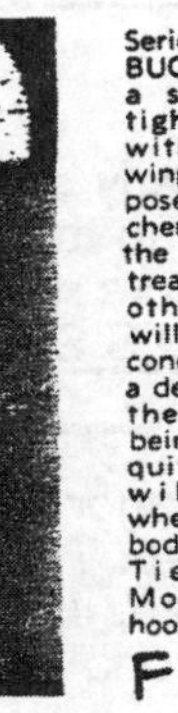

Series No. F-500, BUG-A-MOTH, is a small bodied, tightly tied lure with prominent wings. Body composed of hair and chenille treated by the same chemical treatment as the other lures and will float under all conditions. Makes a decided riffle on the water when being retrieved and quite frequently will take fish when other larger bodied lures fail. Tied on No. 1 Model perfect hook.

F-500

No. F-500—All White	No. F-503—Black & Yellow
No. F-501—All Red	No. F-504—Gray & Brown
No. F-502—All Gray	No. F-505—Red & White

The Bug-A-Boo

$10

- BASS SIZE
  No. F-400 (No. 1 Hook)
- TROUT & PANFISH
  NO. F-700 (No. 6 Hook)
  No. F-800 (No. 8 Hook)

THE "HUM-BIRD"

Patented

No. F-300 Series

F-300

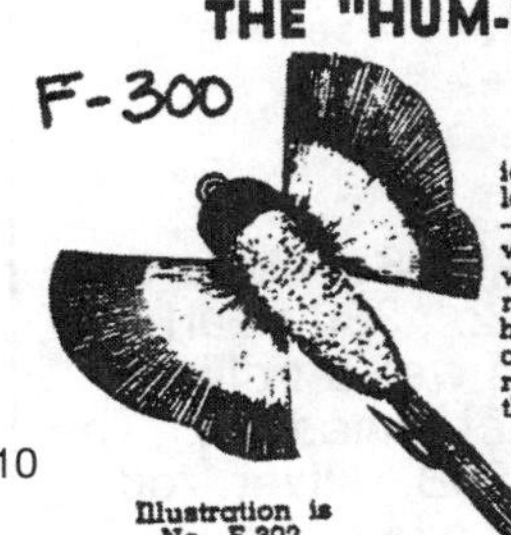

$10

Illustration is No. F-302.

This new cork bodied flat wing Bass Fly looks like a butterfly—floats high on the water, easy to lift without straining the rod—and unlike many hair bodied lures—cannot absorb or carry any water. The thin, flat stiff hair wings cause the lure to sail through the air and light on the water like a living insect. Twitching the rod creates a natural flutter, which attracts and gets bass, trout, and pan fish. Illustration is No. F-302. Made in following color combinations:

No. F-300—Red Wing Red Body
No. F-301—White Wing White Body
No. F-302—Red & Yellow Wing Yellow Body
No. F-303—Green & White Wing White Body
No. F-304—Red & White Wing Red Body
No. F-305—Green & Yellow Wing Green Body
No. F-306—Black & Yellow Wing Black Body
No. F-307—Black & White Wing Green Body

The Bug-A-Bass

$10

F-600

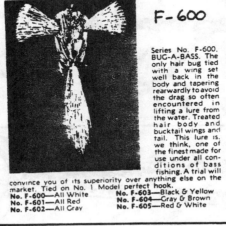

Series No. F-600, BUG-A-BASS. The only hair bug tied with a wing set well back in the body and tapering rearwardly to avoid the drag so often encountered in lifting a lure from the water. Treated hair body and bucktail wings and tail. This lure is, we think, one of the finest made for use under all conditions of bass fishing. A trial will convince you of its superiority over anything else on the market. Tied on No. 1 Model perfect hook.

No. F-600—All White	No. F-603—Black & Yellow
No. F-601—All Red	No. F-604—Gray & Brown
No. F-602—All Gray	No. F-605—Red & White

Other Fly Rod Lures

F-1000 Plunker Bass Bug
F-1100 Plunker Trout & Panfish Bug
Fly Rod Plunker - a very small version of the 3200

Fly Rod Darter - like the fly rod pikie

FLYROD FROGGIE

F-80

$15 – 25

F-81

Finish Shown is No. F-80
Length of Body, 1 In.

Looks and acts just like a frog. Flexible rubber legs protect point of hook, making it weedless—and help it kick around like a frog. Floats.

No. F-80, Green Meadow Frog.
No. F-81, Brown Meadow Frog.

THE BULL PUP

Length 1 in.

$10

F-900

No. F-900 Series

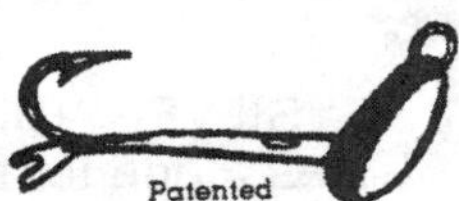

Patented

(OVERSIZE ILLUS.) ACTUAL 1"

1/40 OZ.

SINGLE HOOK

CCBCO'S NON-CATALOGED & SPECIAL ORDER BAITS

$40

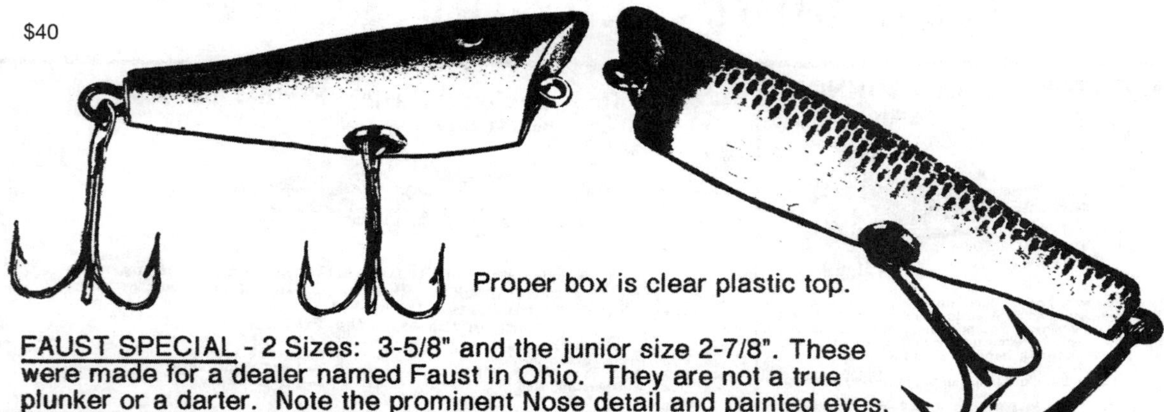

Proper box is clear plastic top.

FAUST SPECIAL - 2 Sizes: 3-5/8" and the junior size 2-7/8". These were made for a dealer named Faust in Ohio. They are not a true plunker or a darter. Note the prominent Nose detail and painted eyes. I have seen them in Red Head, Frog, Golden Shiner and Goldfish.

$30 – 50

The Simmons Hardware Company of St, Louis, MO had CCBCO make a Plunker-like bait 2-1/2", with a flat face rather than the cupped face of the #3200 Plunker, PE and wood, they did stay in the CCBCO colors rather than dropping down to the Shur Strike quality. Collectors call it "THE SIMMON'S SPECIAL".

Another mystery bait in this category is the "MORGAN SPECIAL". Again made for a customer named Morgan in Ohio. This is more of a Darter with a very pointed nose on top of the bait. PE and 3-3/4" in size, its probably going to be found in the local Ohio - Indiana area because there was no national distribution.

$30 – 50

$40 – 50

G.E.-4½"

PETER'S SPECIAL - Special order by: H. L. Peters Co., 330 Pearl St. Buffalo, N.Y. This was a trolling lure, thus the metal, fluted tail. The color shown is 2600B,,,silver, red blush throat, black eye circle.

#1700 Silver Sides

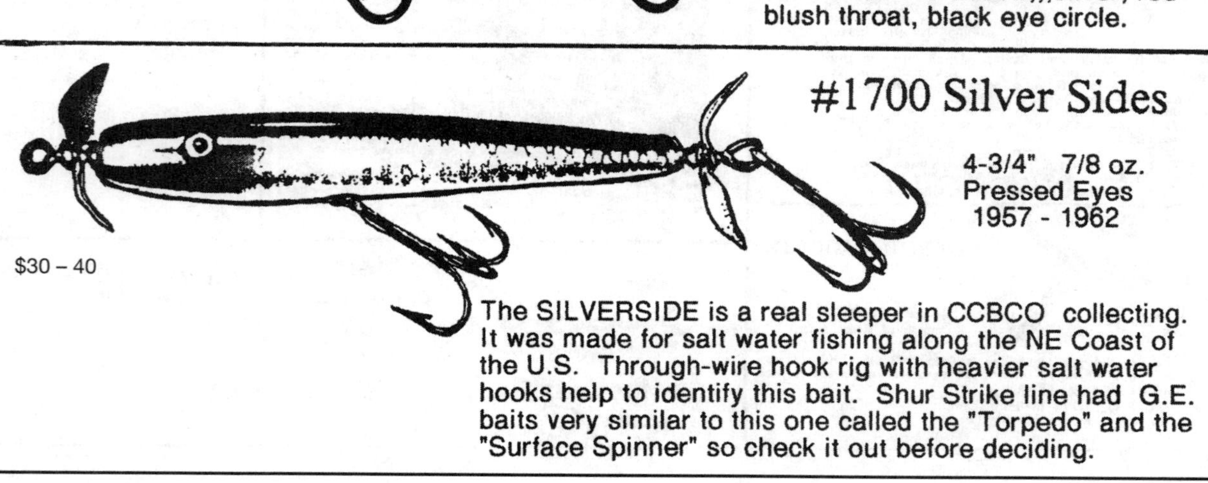

4-3/4" 7/8 oz.
Pressed Eyes
1957 - 1962

$30 – 40

The SILVERSIDE is a real sleeper in CCBCO collecting. It was made for salt water fishing along the NE Coast of the U.S. Through-wire hook rig with heavier salt water hooks help to identify this bait. Shur Strike line had G.E. baits very similar to this one called the "Torpedo" and the "Surface Spinner" so check it out before deciding.

The Original Patent for CCBCO'S Scale Finish

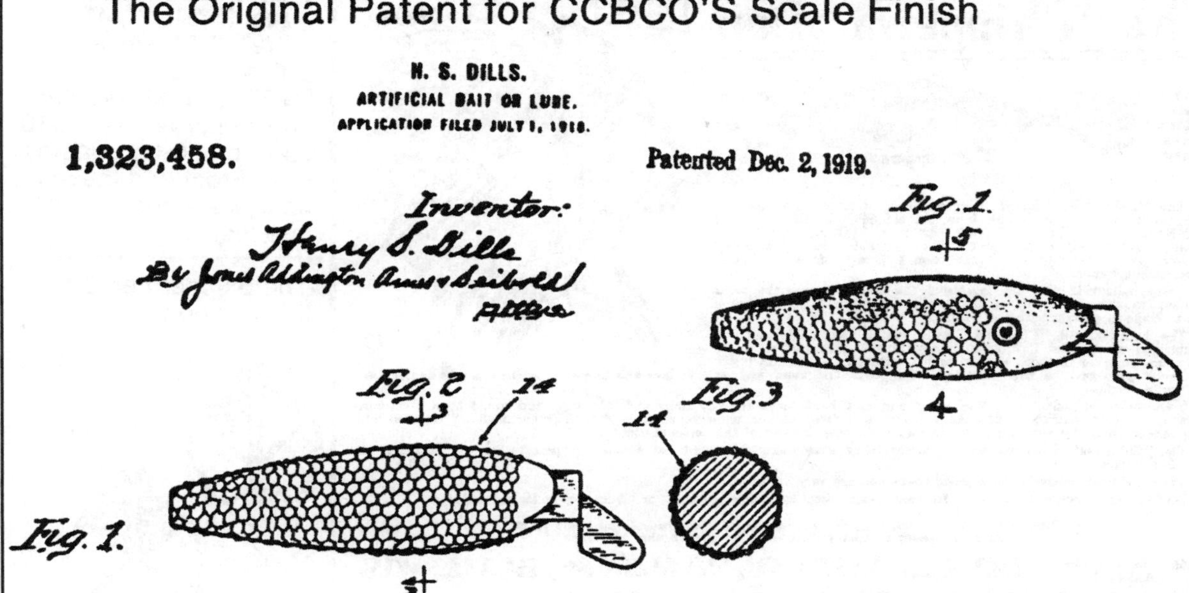
H. S. DILLS.
ARTIFICIAL BAIT OR LURE.
1,323,458.
Patented Dec. 2, 1919.
Inventor:
Henry S. Dills
Fig. 1.
Fig. 2
Fig. 3
14
4

CCBCO - NON-ILLUSTRATED COMMENTS & RESEARCH

HISTORY.......based on a conversation with Harry Heinzerling, son of founder Carl Heinzerling. His thought was that the Wiggler was being fished and tested prior to 1906, and was being exposed locally by the principals who then were just fishermen. When the more formal marketing began in 1906, Carl H. would take the early production baits to Florida for testing and evaluating new colors.

Cowen Street was the site of the first factory which initially employed 5 women and soon up to10. Around 1911-12 the company bought a three story brick building. In 1916 they added a 2 story brick wing addition to accomodate their growing sales volume.The patent on the scale finish was the real breakthrough for CCBCO, and they licensed Heddon, So. Bend, Jamison and others to paint scale finishes.The Co. always stressed quality and used the best in hooks, hardware and paint. Their patented "Lip" was claimed to give their baits the "Natural Minnow Action".

During the depression, their plant was running 5 and sometimes 6 days a week. Harry thought this was because with so many people out of work, they went fishing to put some food on the table. ("Catch & release would have to wait for Ray Scott & B.A.S.S.")

1. Creek Chub was the name of an actual species of minnow used locally for bait.
2. CCBCO used a sequential numbering system during the early days, starting with the 1st Wigglers @ No. 100, and the Baby Wiggler @ No. 200, etc.
3. There are 2 different dates stamped for patent dates of the CCBCO Lips: 9-7-20 and 9-27-20. Remind everyone that these dates are the patent dates for the lips.....and does NOT make every bait a 1920 bait!
4. An early hook rig was just a screw eye and a washer. I have an early Crawdad with a small washer and a Baby Wiggler with a larger one much like the washer on the early Wilson Wobblers.
5. It is thought that the early baits were made concurrently with and without glass eyes in the 100, 200, 600, 700, which would help to explain some of the weird combinations.
6. Most Creek Chub Baits will be found without hand painted gill marks (HPGM).
7. The 1920 catalog showed the NEW Pikie Minnow, and the 1924 catalog introduced a line of fly rod baits.
8. Henry Dills, the main designer, experimented with an external belly wire hook rig on their Husky Musky & Husky Pikie, perhaps as a forerunner to the through-the-body rig.

The "Chippewa" Bait

1913
$150 – 200

The "CHIPPEWA" BASS BAIT

CHIEF of RIVER and LAKE

The "CHIPPEWA" Bait is a combination of an artificial minnow with the most attractive of all lures, the old SPOON HOOK. The SPINNER of the "CHIPPEWA" bait is a SPOON; placed horizontally in the body of the minnow it casts a glitter to each side and downward and will attract the fish from a greater distance than a perpendicular spinner.

These baits ride near the surface of the water and with the hooks attached to the under side of the bait a fish striking from below is sure to come in contact with the hooks.

The hooks of the "Chippewa" baits are all detachable and can be changed or replaced if broken. They are also reversible so as to throw the point of the hook upward and by attaching a weedless treble rear hook you have a bait that will ride over the moss and is practically weedless.

It gets the SAVAGE strike that lands the fish

These baits are made from Red cedar and half hard brass, securely fastened to the wood and bound by a brass wire binder that extends entirely around the bait and is soldered to the screweye at front end. The hooks are all fastened into loops formed from this wire binder which makes the stripping out of the hooks impossible.

The "Chippewa" Baits are no experiment; they were thoroughly tried out during the past season and proved to be great fish getters.

They are nicely enameled in blended colors and are very attractive.

Made in three sizes,—3-inch body for bass, 4-inch body for pike or pickerel, and 5-inch body for muscallonge.

Price.—Bass bait $1.00, Pike or pickerel bait $1.10, Muscallonge bait $1.25.
At your dealer's or by mail postpaid upon receipt of price.

(Write for descriptive folder) **IMMELL BAIT CO., 28 Main St., BLAIR, WIS.**

Chippewas made in 5 sizes: 3",3-1/2", 4", 4-1/2", & 5", sinkers & floaters, B=Bass, P=Pike, M=Musky.Pat. on spinner is 11-1-1910. Later marketing was by C. J. Frost and these 2 baits were done by the late teens.

The Skipper had 2 diff. lips as shown.

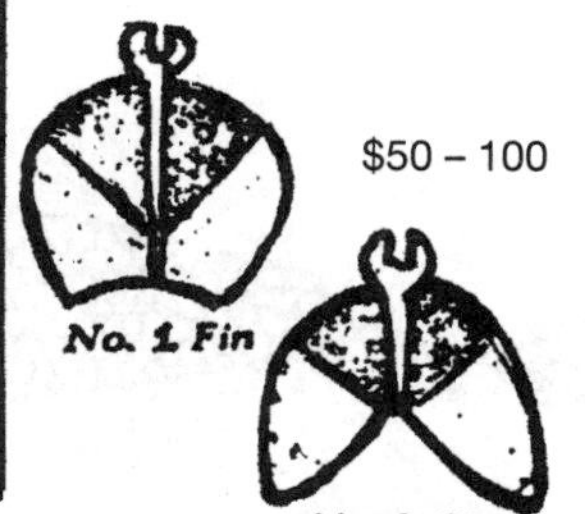
$50 – 100
No. 1 Fin
No. 2 Fin

$100 – 150

EVER USE A SKIPPER?

If you never have you are missing the biggest thrill that ever traveled back to you over your casting line. Just think of casting a bait that strikes the surface with the same little splash as that of a frog leaping into the water, starts off, in response to your reel, with the motion of a frog, produces a sound in the water exactly like a frog, making a quick "get away" from a dangerous locality, looks like a frog, acts like a frog, and makes the bass think it is a real frog. What happens? It's the strike right there before your eyes while you are watching the bait. You see the rise, hear the splash and you are ready for the strike when the line goes taut.

No other bait will give you as much real pleasure on your next fishing trip as a Skipper. ,The bait with the SECRET balance, producing a motion that's a tempter.

Cast this bait into the lily pads and watch it come through. You'll wonder how it does it. That's the SECRET we won't tell, but we'll let you use this secret on the end of your casting line all season. Get a Skipper and get the fish.

Finished in Two Colors: { **S-76 Fancy Spotted** / **S-77 Green and White**

1916

Price 75c at Your Dealers or by Mail Postpaid

C. J. FROST, Dept. 10 - - - STEVENS POINT, WIS.

GOING FISHING?

1914

$75 – 100

THE ROTARY-MARVEL, $1.00

Doesn't it stand to reason that a lure which attracts fish from a much greater area than any other bait will g-t MORE strikes? The revolving, nickel-plated head of the Rotary-Marvel flashes an irresistible challenge that arouses fish to strike from a distance at which they would not notice a dull, painted bait. It will increase your catches from 25% to 50%. ¶An entry blank for our 1914 Prize Fishing Contest is in every box. Send $1.00 by return mail for a Rotary-Marvel AND GET MORE STRIKES.

CASE BAIT CO., 212 E. Ferry Av., Detroit, Mich.

Here is another great Michigan Bait....THE ROTARY MARVEL. It has a Chrome Plated Head & 3 body colors: Red, Yellow, and White. A few have been found with polka-dots also, which along with most of them having the Pflueger Neverfail Hook Hangers implies some sort of connection with that fishing standard.....the Pflueger "Globe". 1 size: 3".

$100 – 150

THE CHARMER MINNOW

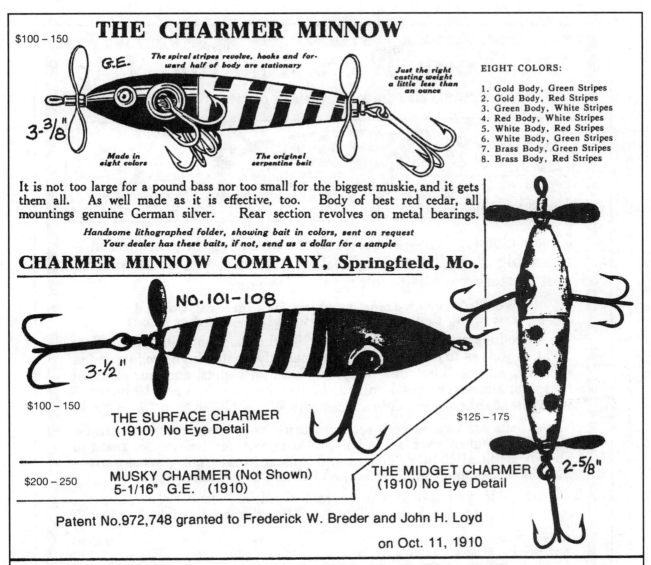

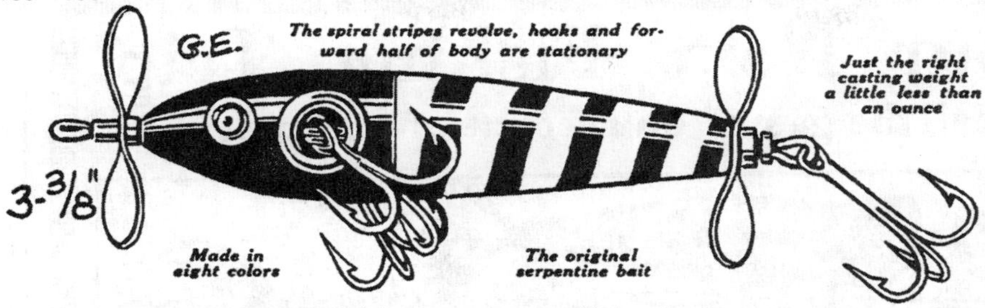

G.E.

The spiral stripes revolve, hooks and forward half of body are stationary

Just the right casting weight a little less than an ounce

3-3/8"

Made in eight colors

The original serpentine bait

EIGHT COLORS:

1. Gold Body, Green Stripes
2. Gold Body, Red Stripes
3. Green Body, White Stripes
4. Red Body, White Stripes
5. White Body, Red Stripes
6. White Body, Green Stripes
7. Brass Body, Green Stripes
8. Brass Body, Red Stripes

It is not too large for a pound bass nor too small for the biggest muskie, and it gets them all. As well made as it is effective, too. Body of best red cedar, all mountings genuine German silver. Rear section revolves on metal bearings.

Handsome lithographed folder, showing bait in colors, sent on request
Your dealer has these baits, if not, send us a dollar for a sample

CHARMER MINNOW COMPANY, Springfield, Mo.

NO. 101-108

3-1/2"

$100 – 150

THE SURFACE CHARMER
(1910) No Eye Detail

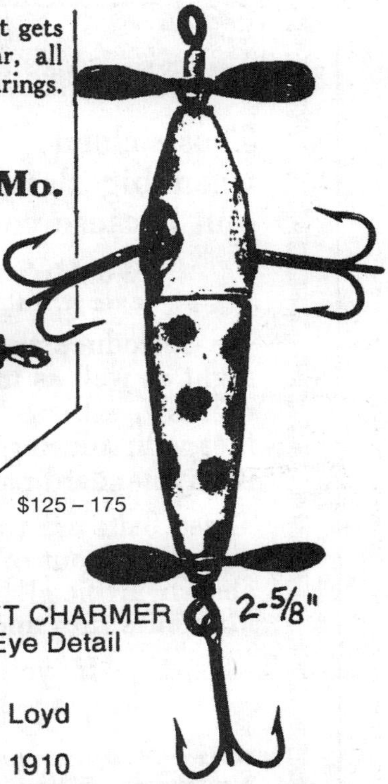

$125 – 175

THE MIDGET CHARMER 2-5/8"
(1910) No Eye Detail

$200 – 250 MUSKY CHARMER (Not Shown)
5-1/16" G.E. (1910)

Patent No.972,748 granted to Frederick W. Breder and John H. Loyd on Oct. 11, 1910

$20

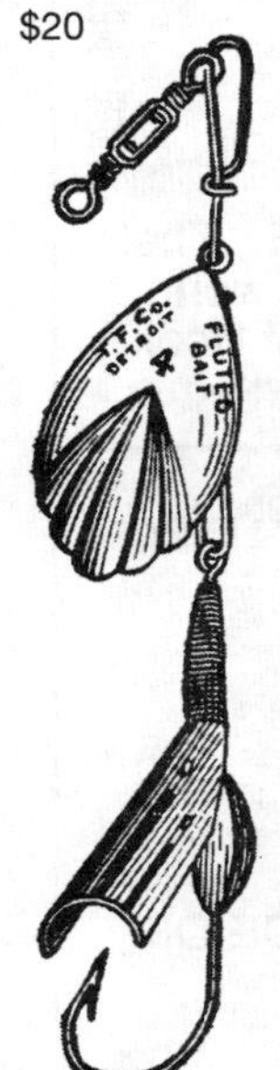

WEEDLESS TROLLING SPOON

The cut here shown is of Cooper's "Weedless Trolling Spoon," a new product of The Fisherman Company, known by all our readers as makers of their "Weedless Porker." This trolling spoon being weedless will be of especial interest to bass and pickerel anglers, as a spoon that could be trolled through weedy places and over weedy pockets is what we have long desired. It's also a good muskie bait.

The Fisherman Company issue a very interesting catalog which not only shows their full line, but gives some valuable information regarding pork rind casting. This catalog they will gladly send our readers.

THE COOPER'S WEEDLESS TROLLING SPOON & COOPER'S WEEDLESS PORKER. (1910 - 1911 era) They made a shaped rubber weed guard which was supported by a pc. of spring steel. A good idea!!

ABSOLUTELY WEEDLESS

$10

Rubber protector, supported by steel spring, makes the Porker a hook which can be safely cast in the thickest rushes. One hook will last a season.

OUR COMBINATION OFFER

3 Porkers, 1 Box Salted Pork Rind, and 1 Phosphor Bronze Wire Leader with Patent Snap attached, postpaid, $1.00.

Stamp gets catalogue with casting instructions

THE FISHERMAN CO., Ypsilanti, Mich.

On Your Next Fishing Trip

Don't "call the game" on account of darkness:

Those cloudy days—in the early morning or late afternoon—when big Bass, Trout and Muskies are busy, you don't want to quit because your bait isn't right. Do you?

Wouldn't you give most anything for a lure that would do everything that any other one would do—and then some?

We introduce the new Marvelite 100%-plus bait that will catch 'em at night as well as in the daytime—our specially treated high grade wooden minnow, with its luminous belly and luminous spots, and our artificial flies with alluring bright luminous bodies, on Nos. 6, 8 and 10 hooks—in any standard pattern. We suggest the White Miller on a No. 8 hook.

These baits are treated with real **radium**—not phosphorus, and can be taken right out of your tackle box and used without waiting for them to absorb artificial light. The phosphorus baits are not **permanent**—Marvelite flies and minnows are, and **that's** the advantage.

If you would like a real thrill, try landing a gamy black Bass, Trout or Muscallonge at night.

Prices

Marvelite Minnow - - - - - - - - - **$3.00**
Marvelite Flies - - - - - - - - - - **1.00**

COLD LIGHT MANUFACTURING COMPANY
50 Union Square, New York City

This ad was published in the May, 1919 issue of FIELD & STREAM MAGAZINE. Their "MARVELITE" Minnow was treated with REAL RADIUM! What a great place to work. Looking at the ad enlarged about 40% brings out what appears to be a Neverfail Hook Hanger, so they probably bought their baits from Pflueger. $75 – 100

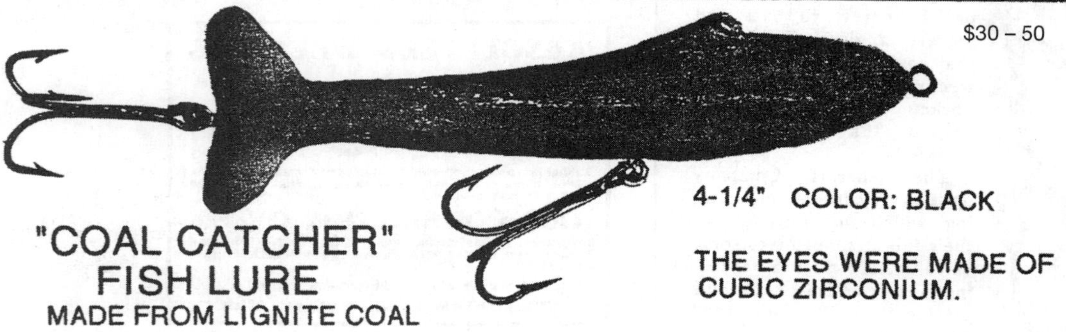
$30 – 50
4-1/4" COLOR: BLACK
"COAL CATCHER"
FISH LURE
MADE FROM LIGNITE COAL
THE EYES WERE MADE OF
CUBIC ZIRCONIUM.

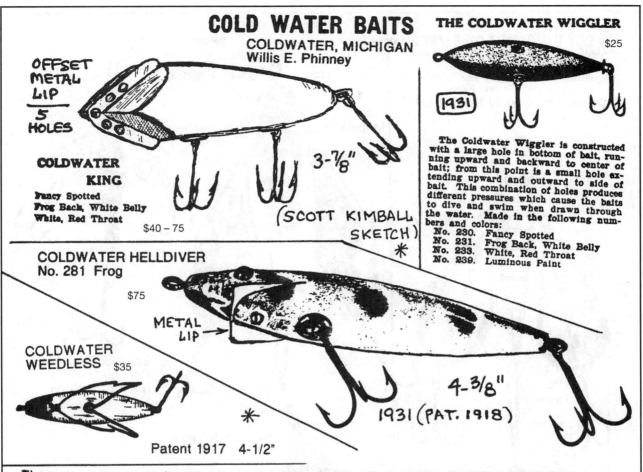

COLD WATER BAITS

COLDWATER, MICHIGAN
Willis E. Phinney

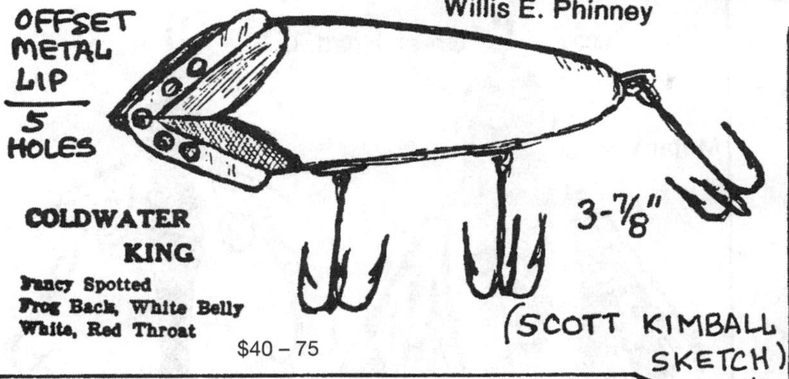

OFFSET METAL LIP
5 HOLES

COLDWATER KING

Fancy Spotted
Frog Back, White Belly
White, Red Throat

$40 – 75

3-7/8"

(SCOTT KIMBALL SKETCH)

THE COLDWATER WIGGLER

$25

1931

The Coldwater Wiggler is constructed with a large hole in bottom of bait, running upward and backward to center of bait; from this point is a small hole extending upward and outward to side of bait. This combination of holes produces different pressures which cause the baits to dive and swim when drawn through the water. Made in the following numbers and colors:

No. 230. Fancy Spotted
No. 231. Frog Back, White Belly
No. 233. White, Red Throat
No. 239. Luminous Paint

COLDWATER HELLDIVER
No. 281 Frog

$75

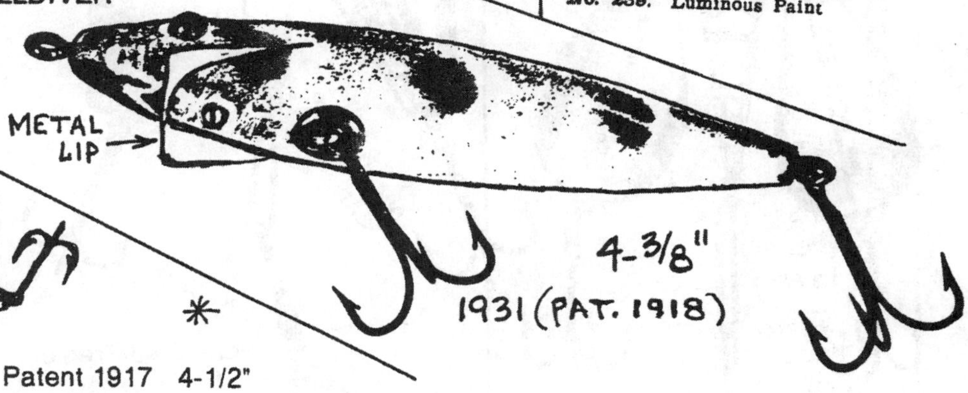

METAL LIP

4-3/8"

1931 (PAT. 1918)

COLDWATER WEEDLESS $35

Patent 1917 4-1/2"

There was some sort of a relationship between Samual O. Larrabee (EUREKA BAIT CO.) and the COLDWATER Bait Co of W. E. Phinney. The illustrated 1931 ad for the Wiggler is actually the Eureka Wiggler. What we do know is they both lived in Coldwater, MI and were active inventing baits in the 1914 - 1918 era. (See Eureka)

When we first started collecting old fishing lures, metal baits were pretty much passed over like a YUGO in a used car lot. What we didn't know was that W. D. Chapman was making handsome, innovative metal baits in the 1870's and 80's. Luckily for us, he was proud of his lures and always marked his name on them. This is just one example of a line of products he manufactured.

CHAPMAN'S BAITS STILL AHEAD!

"THE NEW COMBINATION," Just Out. See Cut.

W. D. Chapman & Son, Theresa, N. Y.

$100 – 150

(1885 AD)

(Patent Applied For and Allowed.)

In Three Sizes for PIKE, PICKEREL, BASS, TROUT & MUSCALONGE.

THEFLYING HELGRAMITE!

ARTIFICIAL BAIT,
Especially for Bass, Pike, Pickerel and all Game Fish.
H. Comstock's Patent, Jan. 30, 1883, Fulton, N. Y.

$1,500+

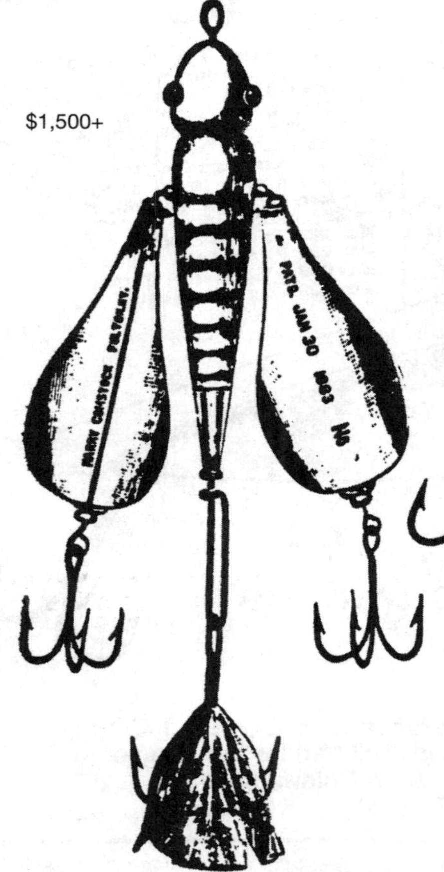
HARRY COMSTOCK FULTON, N.Y.
PATD. JAN 30 1883
No

WILL NOT SINK AND SNAG!
Exactly Like Life!
Price, No. 1, $1. No. 2, $1.15. No. 3, $1.25.
A LIBERAL DISCOUNT TO THE TRADE.
If your dealer does not keep this bait, I will send prepaid to any address upon receipt of price.
Address
HARRY COMSTOCK,
Fulton, N. Y.

$750 – 1,000

Green Head, G.E.

Metal Wings

METAL CAP

Feathered Treble

$1,500+

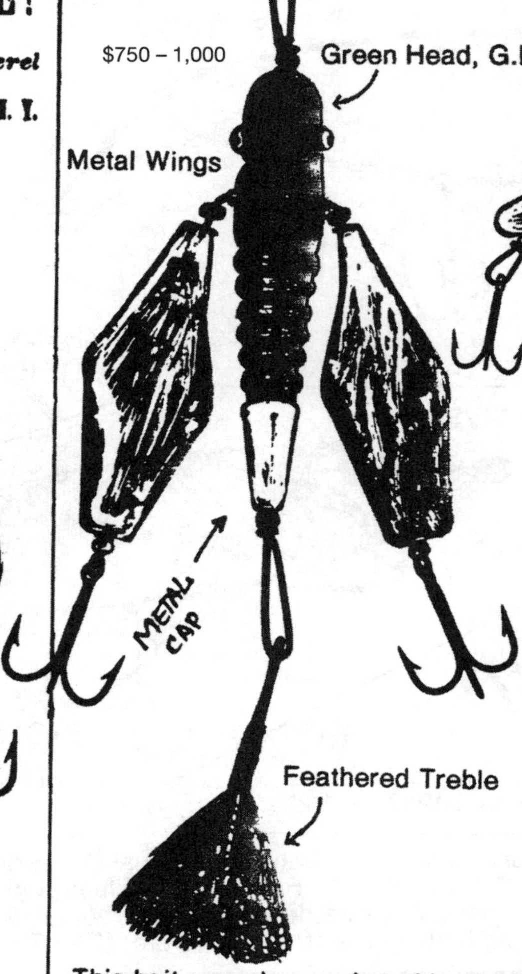

Basic or Plain Model
Reduced from 3"
No. 2 on 1 Wing

This bait was also marketed by the PFLUEGER CO. in a "Luminous" version. Note: 3 different shapes of the metal wings shown. The 2 not in the ad were copies made from the actual baits.

This ad ran in the June 14, 1883 edition of the AMERICAN ANGLER WEEKLY. Note that it states there are 3 models: No. 1 - No. 2 - No. 3. This bait had a wooden body, which was a breakthrough for that era.

$15 – 20

comstock weedless chunk
WORK THIS BAIT SLOWLY
Manufactured By
Wheeler-Lunbeck Manufacturing Co.
VALPARAISO, INDIANA

F. E. COMSTOCK
Valparaiso, Indiana
Patented May 25, 1926

Made in 2 Colors
Red Head/White
All White

This bait was also marketed by Moonlight and Paw Paw as the 99% Weedles Bait.

THE "BABY" FLYING HELGRAMITE

$1,500+

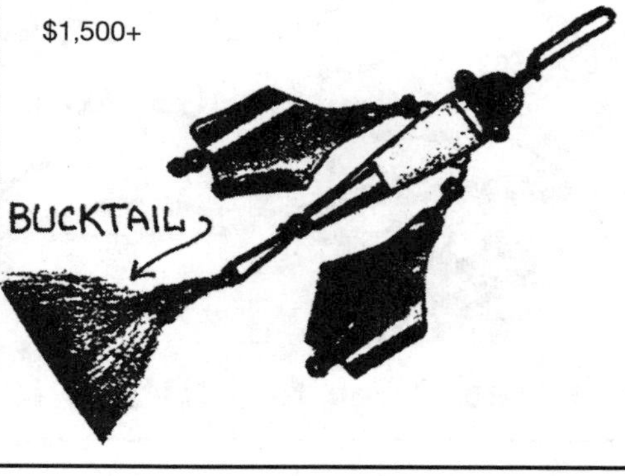

BUCKTAIL

$20 – 40

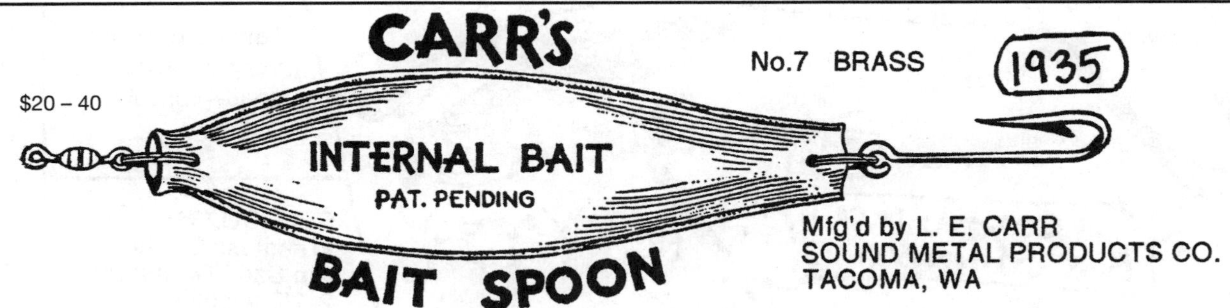
CARR'S
INTERNAL BAIT
PAT. PENDING
BAIT SPOON
1935

No.7 BRASS

Mfg'd by L. E. CARR
SOUND METAL PRODUCTS CO.
TACOMA, WA

SOMETHING NEW IN FISHING........SENSE OF SMELL AND SIGHT
Instructions: To fill, use a grease gun or sausage filler, or fill by hand with salmon eggs, ground liver, or whatever the fish are feeding on like ground-up herring.

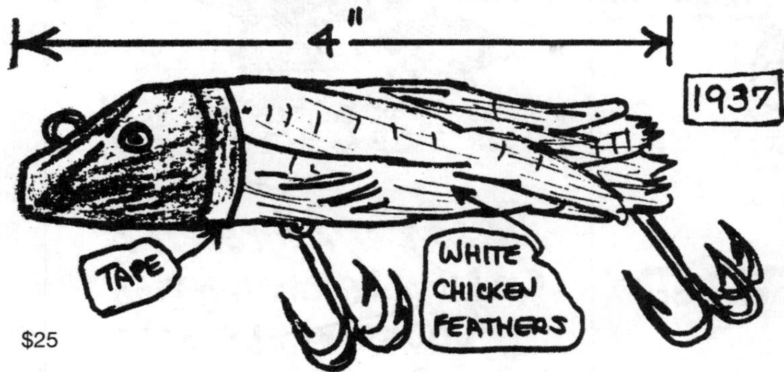
ED'S HULA HULA
IT FLOATS — IT DIVES — IT WOBBLES
FOR BAIT RODS
PAT. PENDING
ED. CUMINGS, INC., FLINT, MICHIGAN.
4"
1937
TAPE
WHITE CHICKEN FEATHERS

$25

Ed Cumings, Inc.

The HULA HULA has a BassOreno type head with a feathered body - 4"
A. Red head, White feather body
B. Black head, White feather body
C. Yellow head, Red & Yellow body
D. Green head, White & green body
E. White head, Red & White body
F. Red head, Black & white body
G.E. - 1/2 oz. - Ind. Box (Illus.)

NOTE: Cumings also made a line of Fly Rod Baits called EVERFLOAT TROUTERS. Cork Heads with body feathers.
1. Red Head, White feather body
2. Green Head, Gray feather body
3. Red Head, Gray feather body
4. Yellow Head, Green feather body
5. Black Head, White feather body
6. White Head, Green feather body

$25

Length 9"
WAIKIKI
dia. head 1¾" For Salt Water Fishing

The WAIKIKI BAIT was originally designed for salt water fishing ......but their 1937 Catalog stated that it has become a "killer" for Muskies & Northern Pike. 2 - 7/0 plated trebles. Head is Red Enamel, G.E., body is White Goose Feathers. Different color combinations can be special ordered.

$25

HONOLULU BELLE
For Salt Water Fishing
Length 14", dia. head 2½"
Length 9", dia. head 1¾"

The HONOLULU BELLE was made with a Port Orford Cedar Head, G.E., Red Head. NO HOOKS ARE FURNISHED, but 2 copper tubes are inserted through the wood part in 2 different directions, that enables the fisherman to install copper wire and the kind of hooks and positioning for each type of fish being pursued. Note that there are two sizes.

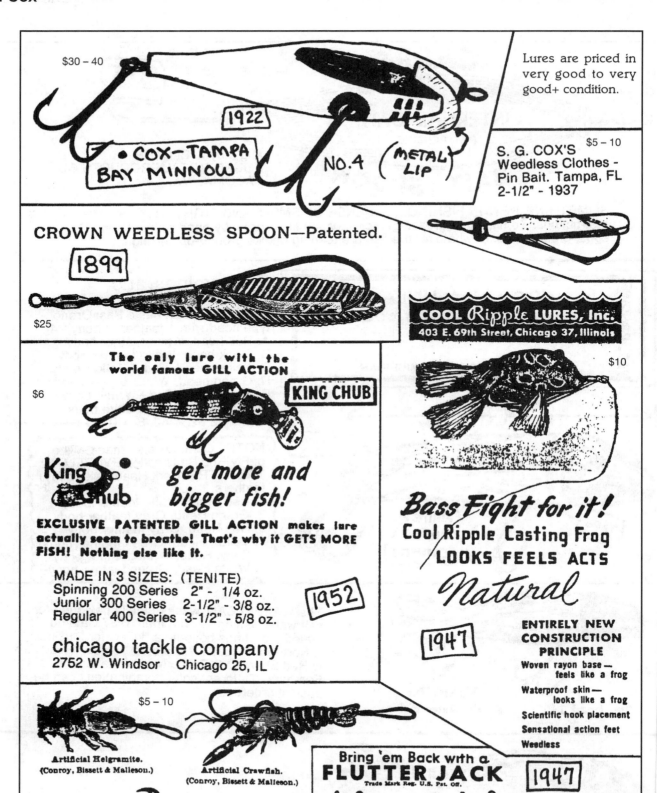

$30 – 40

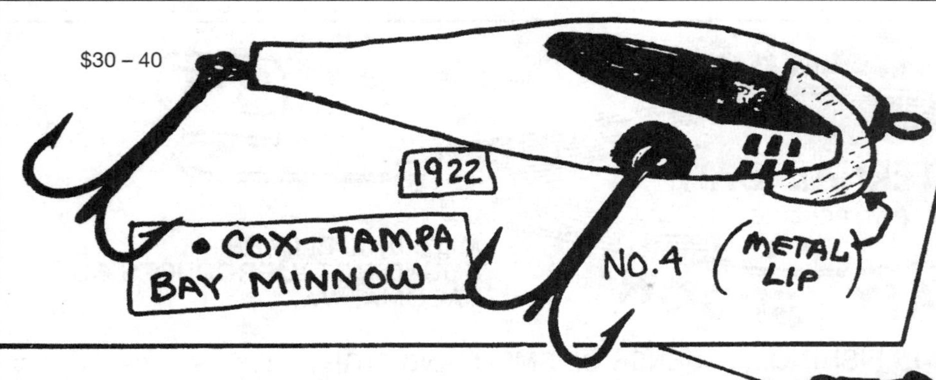
1922
• COX-TAMPA BAY MINNOW
NO.4 (METAL LIP)

Lures are priced in very good to very good+ condition.

$5 – 10

S. G. COX'S Weedless Clothes-Pin Bait. Tampa, FL 2-1/2" - 1937

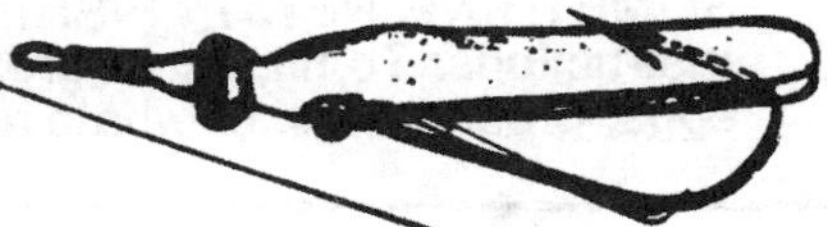

CROWN WEEDLESS SPOON—Patented.

1899

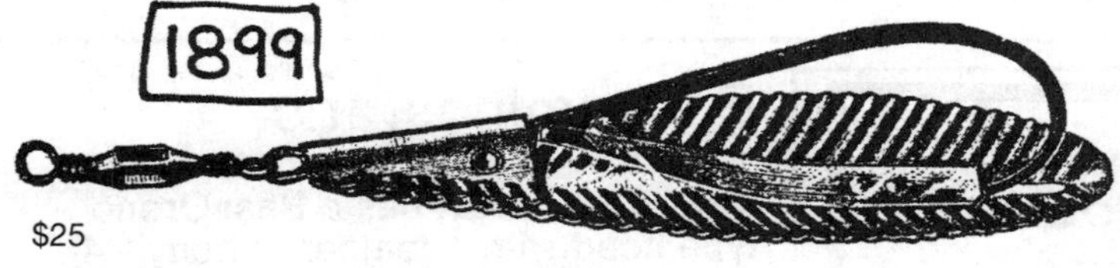

$25

COOL Ripple LURES, Inc.
403 E. 69th Street, Chicago 37, Illinois

$10

Bass Fight for it!
Cool Ripple Casting Frog
LOOKS FEELS ACTS
Natural

1947

ENTIRELY NEW CONSTRUCTION PRINCIPLE
Woven rayon base—feels like a frog
Waterproof skin—looks like a frog
Scientific hook placement
Sensational action feet
Weedless

The only lure with the world famous GILL ACTION

$6

KING CHUB

King Chub get more and bigger fish!

EXCLUSIVE PATENTED GILL ACTION makes lure actually seem to breathe! That's why it GETS MORE FISH! Nothing else like it.

MADE IN 3 SIZES: (TENITE)
Spinning 200 Series 2" - 1/4 oz.
Junior 300 Series 2-1/2" - 3/8 oz.
Regular 400 Series 3-1/2" - 5/8 oz.

1952

chicago tackle company
2752 W. Windsor Chicago 25, IL

$5 – 10

Artificial Helgramite.
(Conroy, Bissett & Malleson.)

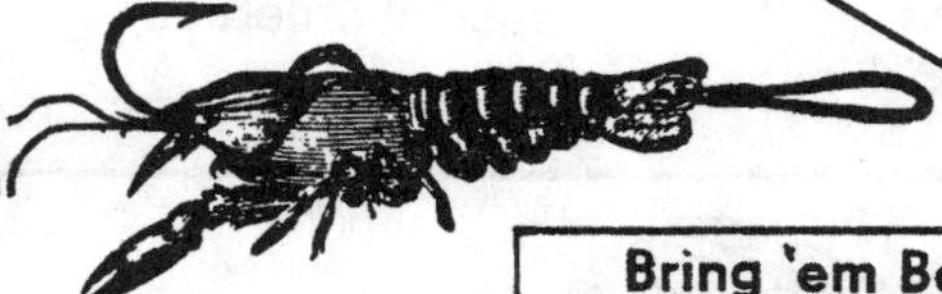

Artificial Crawfish.
(Conroy, Bissett & Malleson.)

$5 – 10

Artificial Flexible Minnow.
(Conroy, Bissett & Malleson.)

Bring 'em Back with a FLUTTER JACK
Trade Mark Reg. U.S. Pat. Off.

1947

Sr. Jr.

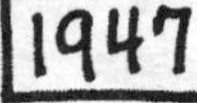

AT YOUR DEALER'S
Deep or top water casting lure for any season. Bright chrome plated. Choice of 15 bucktail colors.

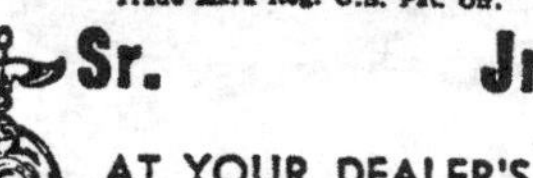

L. B. COOK BAIT MFG. CO.
401-A Rutherford St. Shreveport, La.

• 3/8 oz.
• 1/2 oz.

$5

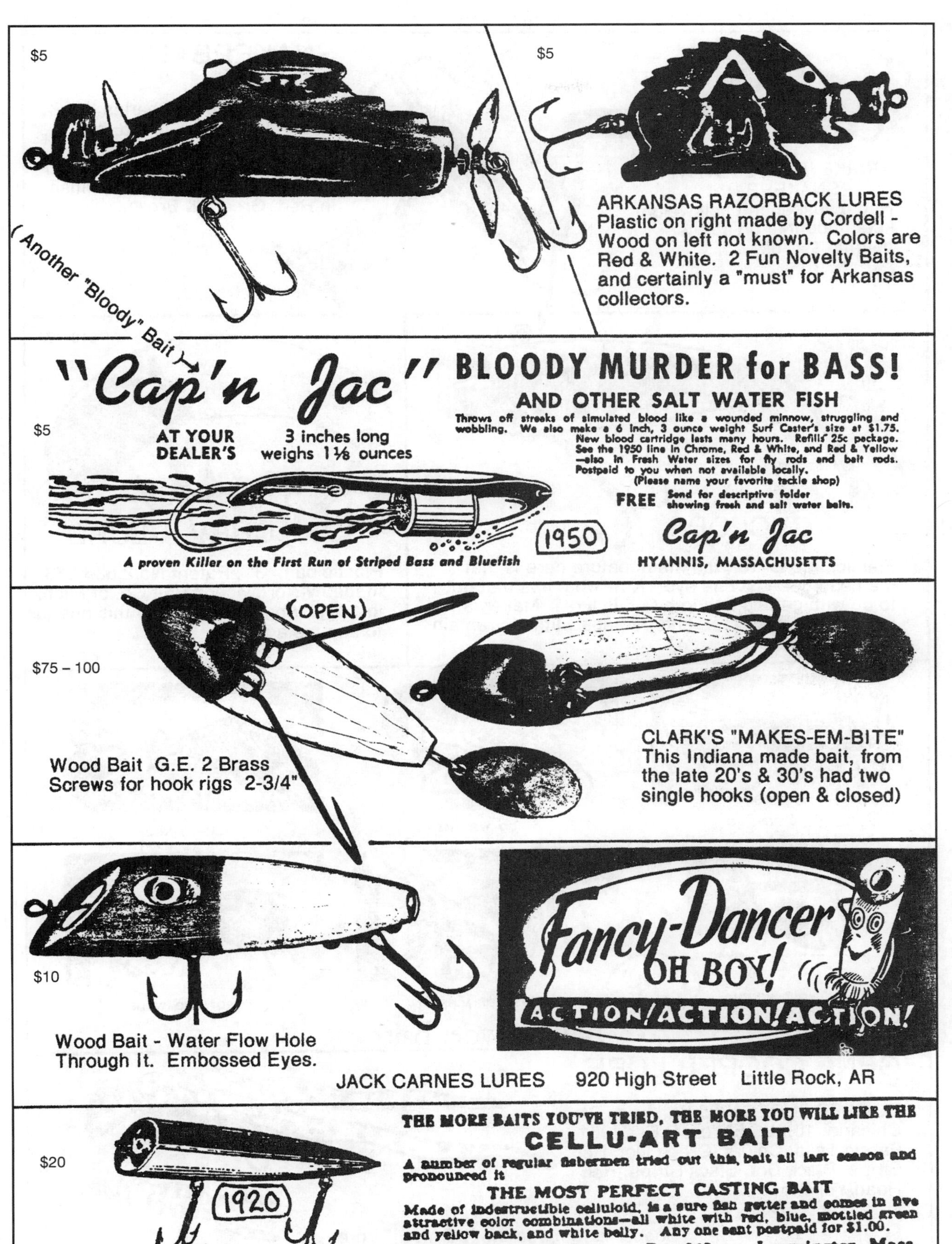
$5
$5
ARKANSAS RAZORBACK LURES
Plastic on right made by Cordell - Wood on left not known. Colors are Red & White. 2 Fun Novelty Baits, and certainly a "must" for Arkansas collectors.
(Another "Bloody" Bait)
"Cap'n Jac"
BLOODY MURDER for BASS!
AND OTHER SALT WATER FISH
Throws off streaks of simulated blood like a wounded minnow, struggling and wobbling. We also make a 6 inch, 3 ounce weight Surf Caster's size at $1.75. New blood cartridge lasts many hours. Refills 25c package. See the 1950 line in Chrome, Red & White, and Red & Yellow —also in Fresh Water sizes for fly rods and bait rods. Postpaid to you when not available locally.
(Please name your favorite tackle shop)
$5
AT YOUR DEALER'S
3 inches long weighs 1⅛ ounces
FREE Send for descriptive folder showing fresh and salt water baits.
1950
Cap'n Jac
HYANNIS, MASSACHUSETTS
A proven Killer on the First Run of Striped Bass and Bluefish
(OPEN)
$75 – 100
Wood Bait G.E. 2 Brass Screws for hook rigs 2-3/4"
CLARK'S "MAKES-EM-BITE"
This Indiana made bait, from the late 20's & 30's had two single hooks (open & closed)
$10
Wood Bait - Water Flow Hole Through It. Embossed Eyes.
Fancy-Dancer
OH BOY!
ACTION/ACTION/ACTION!
JACK CARNES LURES 920 High Street Little Rock, AR
$20
1920
THE MORE BAITS YOU'VE TRIED, THE MORE YOU WILL LIKE THE
CELLU-ART BAIT
A number of regular fishermen tried out this bait all last season and pronounced it
THE MOST PERFECT CASTING BAIT
Made of indestructible celluloid, is a sure fish getter and comes in five attractive color combinations—all white with red, blue, mottled green and yellow back, and white belly. Any one sent postpaid for $1.00.
THE CELLU-ART CO. Box 248 Leominster, Mass.

SNAKERBAIT

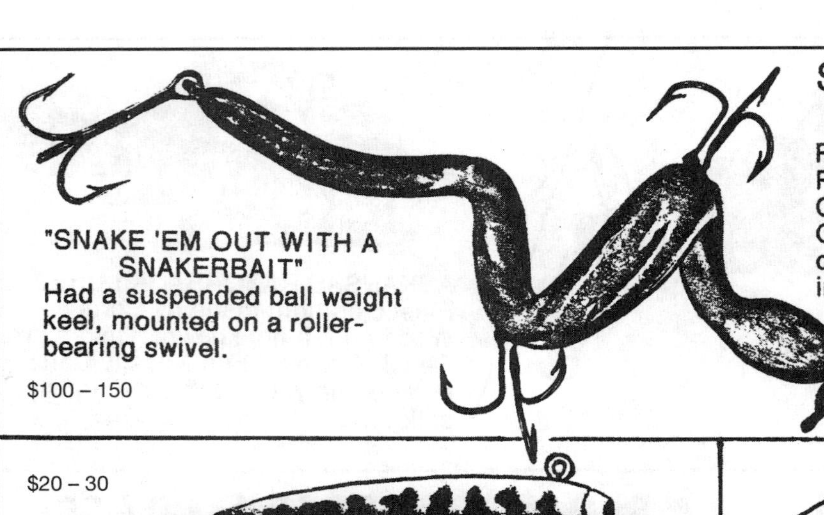

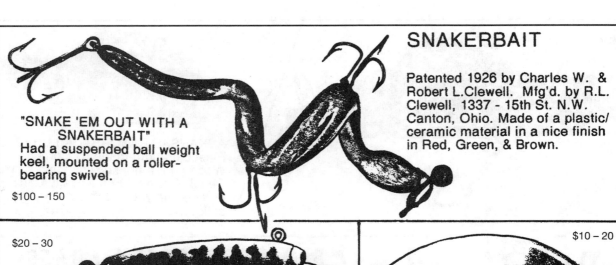

Patented 1926 by Charles W. & Robert L.Clewell. Mfg'd. by R.L. Clewell, 1337 - 15th St. N.W. Canton, Ohio. Made of a plastic/ ceramic material in a nice finish in Red, Green, & Brown.

"SNAKE 'EM OUT WITH A SNAKERBAIT"
Had a suspended ball weight keel, mounted on a roller-bearing swivel.

$100 – 150

$20 – 30

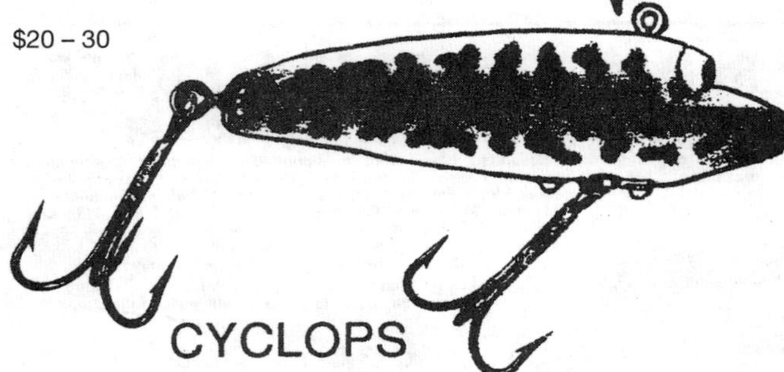

CYCLOPS

Plastic bait, 2-7/8", the main feature here is that the head has just one eye! Now what has that got to do with getting fish to bite this lure? Maker is unknown at this time, and perhaps wants to remain anonymous?

$10 – 20

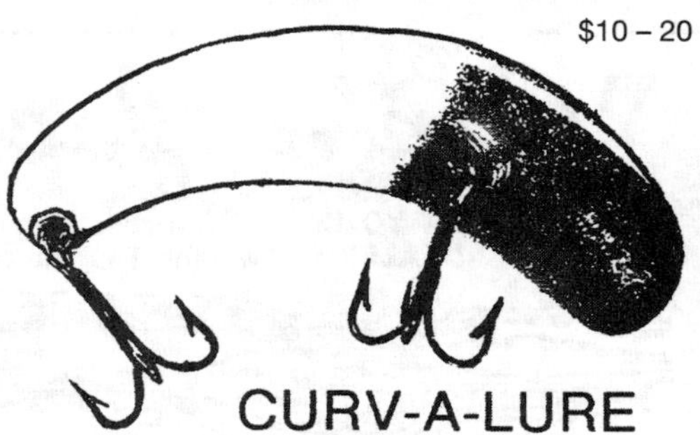

CURV-A-LURE

Plastic bait, 3" , Patent No.2,536,553, made by Northwoods Bait Co. of Mich. in 1951. Anglers might buy this one jus to see the action!

BIG JERK

DO WEE GEE

FLASH MINNOW

LOUD MOUTH

(1-3/4")

PLASTERED MINNOW

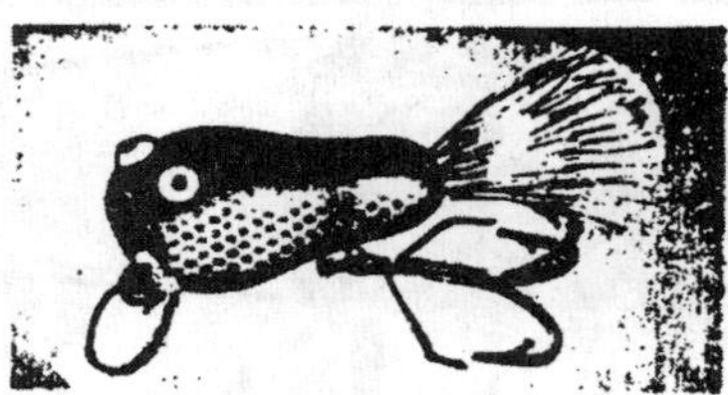

WOBBLING WILLIE

$10 each

Bill Crowder Baits

GENE COOPER LURE

COOPER LURES, 325 W. Huron St. Chicago 10, IL. 5/8 oz. P.E. 1951 Fabric Tails, Colors: Green Dot, Red Stripe, Black Dot, Black Stripe, Red Head/Yellow.

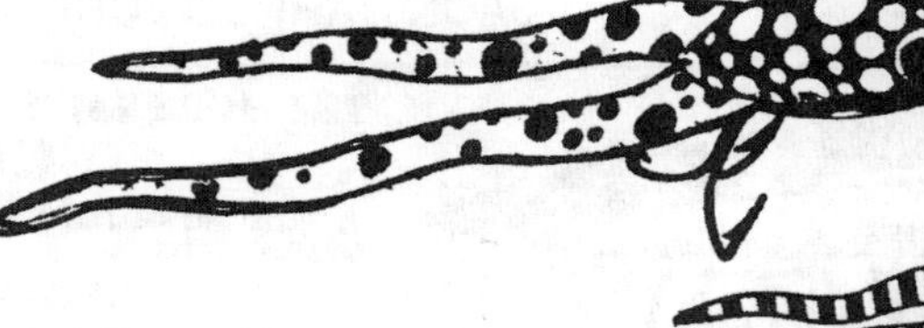

PATENTED

$5

Cooper also made the "UBANGI" Lure

$5
2 Models: Spoon Up-Spoon Down
4 Sizes: Fly Rod, Spinning, Regular, Muskie
6 Colors: Green Frog/Red & White/ Black/Yellow Frog/Black & Orange/ and Scale
CATCH-ALL INC.
Sales Office: 2028 N. THIRD ST., MILWAUKEE 12, WISCONSIN.
Factory: HILES, WISCONSIN.
CHAMPION LURES
WARWICK , RHODE ISLAND
Wood, Pressed Eye, 5-1/4", Hook Link Rig, Looks alot like a Musky "Jinx", but it is just another Striper Plug.
"Surf Bug"
$10
CAPTIVATED LURES, INC.
First in Self-Propelled Fishing Lures
P. O. Drawer 16875
Jacksonville, Fla. 32216
LULU has a small electric motor that runs on pen light batteries. It is designed for topwater use, and can run up to 300 feet on its own power.
A big advantage of LULU is that you don't have to reel it all the way back to the boat or shore. Let LULU stay out where the fish are. An injured minnow effect can be made by stopping the line feed while the lure is still "pulling".
Here Comes LULU tm
LULU IS SOLD ON A 30 DAY MONEY BACK GUARANTEE!
$10 – 20
MOTOR
PEN LIGHT BATTERY
SWITCH
BRASS RIB
PROPELLER SEALS
O RING
SWITCH SEALS
MOTOR CONTACT

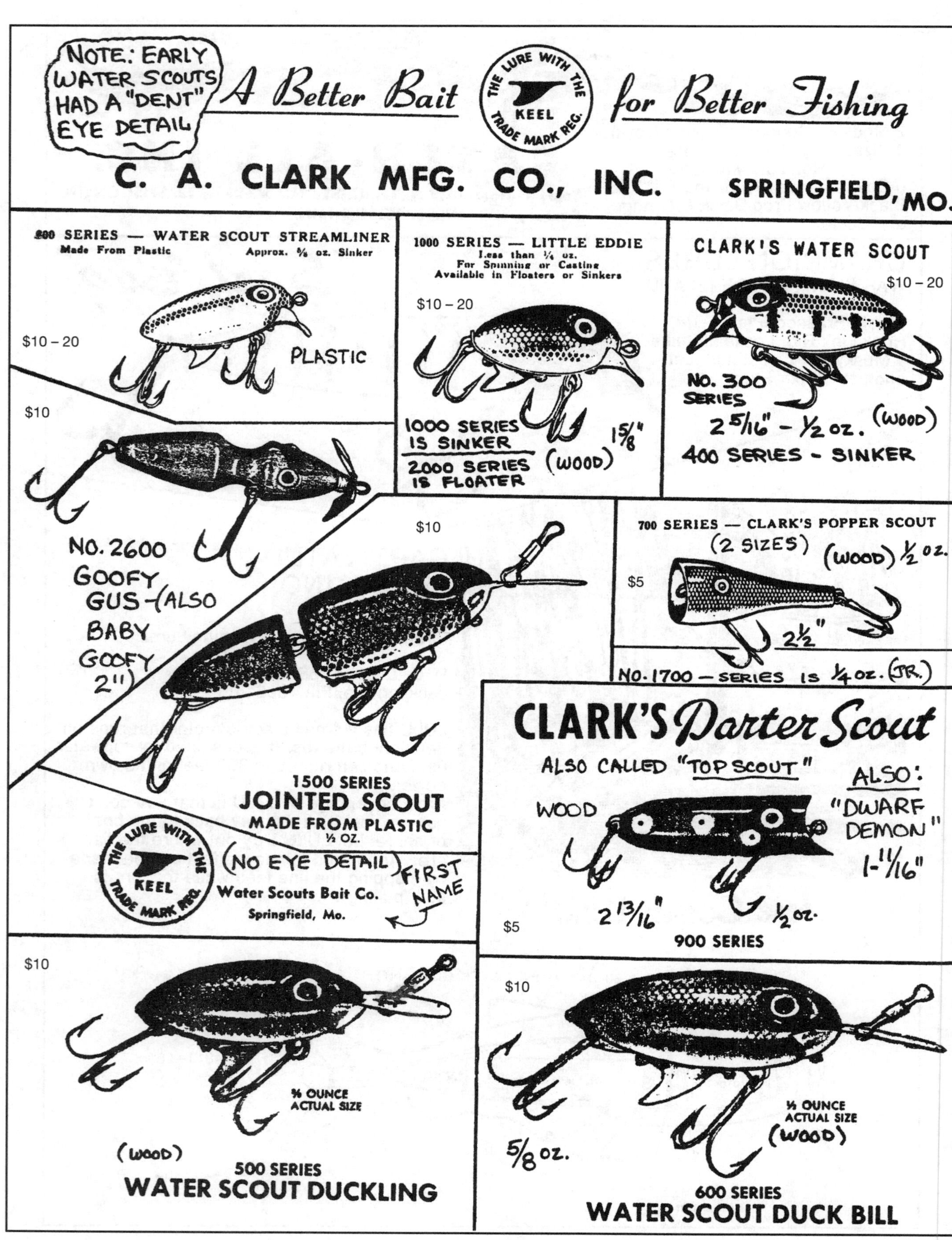
NOTE: EARLY WATER SCOUTS HAD A "DENT" EYE DETAIL
A Better Bait
THE LURE WITH THE KEEL TRADE MARK REG.
for Better Fishing
C. A. CLARK MFG. CO., INC. SPRINGFIELD, MO.
800 SERIES — WATER SCOUT STREAMLINER
Made From Plastic
Approx. ⅝ oz. Sinker
$10 – 20
PLASTIC
1000 SERIES — LITTLE EDDIE
Less than ¼ oz.
For Spinning or Casting
Available in Floaters or Sinkers
$10 – 20
1000 SERIES IS SINKER
2000 SERIES IS FLOATER
(WOOD)
1⅝"
CLARK'S WATER SCOUT
$10 – 20
NO. 300 SERIES
2 5/16" - ½ oz.
(WOOD)
400 SERIES - SINKER
$10
NO. 2600 GOOFY GUS - (ALSO BABY GOOFY 2")
$10
700 SERIES — CLARK'S POPPER SCOUT
(2 SIZES)
(WOOD) ½ oz.
$5
2½"
NO. 1700 — SERIES IS ¼ oz. (JR.)
1500 SERIES
JOINTED SCOUT
MADE FROM PLASTIC
½ OZ.
THE LURE WITH THE KEEL TRADE MARK REG.
(NO EYE DETAIL)
Water Scouts Bait Co.
Springfield, Mo.
FIRST NAME
CLARK'S Darter Scout
ALSO CALLED "TOP SCOUT"
WOOD
ALSO: "DWARF DEMON" 1-11/16"
2 13/16"
½ oz.
$5
900 SERIES
$10
⅜ OUNCE ACTUAL SIZE
(WOOD)
500 SERIES
WATER SCOUT DUCKLING
$10
½ OUNCE ACTUAL SIZE
(WOOD)
⅝ oz.
600 SERIES
WATER SCOUT DUCK BILL

CARTER'S BESTEVER BAITS

Carter Lures

Sell better with dealers because they get more fish than other lures

1923
AD

$15 – 20

Jobbers and dealers everywhere are stocking Carter Baits. Order now and put in stock a bait that sells itself.

Our new ½-oz. single hook surface and underwater weedless lure is having a wonderful sale for both day and night fishing; will not hook up casting in weeds, over logs or in drift.

Made in three sizes—¾-oz. and ⅝-oz. with two treble or double hooks; ½-oz. with one treble, double or single (weedless attachment) hook.

Write for discount and illustrated circulars

CARTER'S BESTEVER BAIT CO.
25½ West Washington St. Indianapolis, Ind.

Another Carter Address was:
CARTER BAIT COMPANY
23 Cordova Building
Indianapolis, Indiana (1927)

The BLACK Bait

CARTER BAITS

$15 – 20

Carter's
"OLD BLACKJOE"

CARTER COLORS

Red Head, White
Red Head, Aluminum
Red Head, Gold
Red Head, Yellow
All Red & All Black

No. 30 Large Size 3-5/8"

No. 20 Medium Size 3-1/8"

No. 10 Midget Size 2-5/8"

Baby Carter Fly Rod Lure 1-1/4"

SOME CARTER COMMENTS:

One Old Black Joe Copy was called: "The Black Ace"
Suman & Co. Inc.
Richmond, Ind.

The original Carters were not glass eyed, Some of the Dunks era were G.E.

There are some pressed eye Carter look alikes out there called:
RED'S OLD TIMERS
Jasonville, Ind.

Who is DUNK?
Milton S. Dunkelberger
Dayton, Ohio
He patented Dunk's Dubble-Header on Jan. 26, 1932.

One Baby Carter Model had a mouse finish, G.E. and a string tail.

The last word in a single hook surface and underwater lure

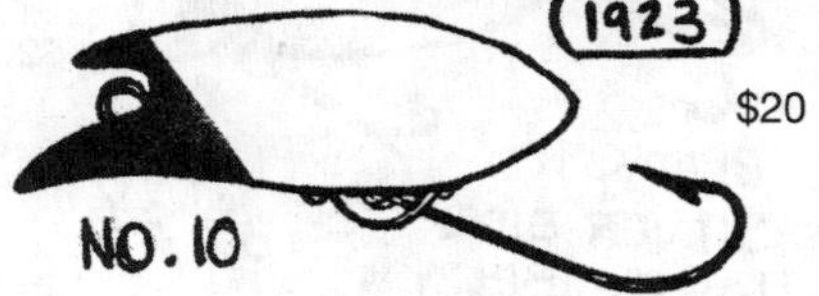
1923
NO.10

$20

Thomas J. Carter was making baits & applied for a patent on April 3, 1919, it was granted on Feb. 12, 1924. They apparently ceased business in 1932, and were aquired by American Display (Dunks) who then listed baits in their 1933 Catalog. All the baits were cup rigged/screw eye hook rigged. Customer could order either double (D) or treble (T) hooks.

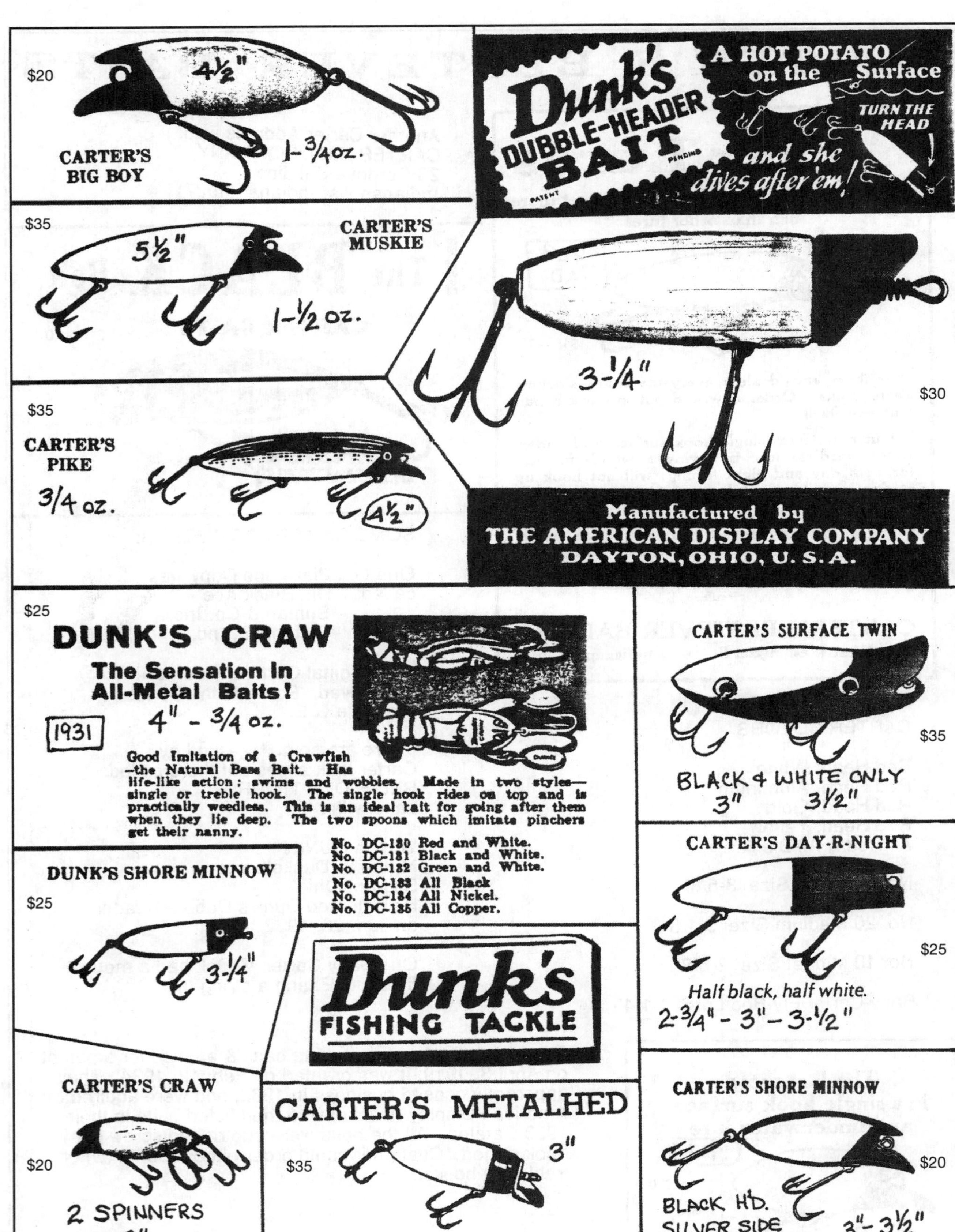
$20
4½"
CARTER'S BIG BOY
1-3/4 oz.
Dunk's DUBBLE-HEADER BAIT
PATENT PENDING
A HOT POTATO on the Surface
TURN THE HEAD
and she dives after 'em!
$35
5½"
CARTER'S MUSKIE
1-½ oz.
3-¼"
$30
$35
CARTER'S PIKE
¾ oz.
4½"
Manufactured by
THE AMERICAN DISPLAY COMPANY
DAYTON, OHIO, U. S. A.
$25
DUNK'S CRAW
The Sensation In All-Metal Baits!
1931
4" - ¾ oz.
Good Imitation of a Crawfish —the Natural Bass Bait. Has life-like action; swims and wobbles. Made in two styles—single or treble hook. The single hook rides on top and is practically weedless. This is an ideal bait for going after them when they lie deep. The two spoons which imitate pinchers get their nanny.
No. DC-180 Red and White.
No. DC-181 Black and White.
No. DC-182 Green and White.
No. DC-183 All Black
No. DC-184 All Nickel.
No. DC-185 All Copper.
CARTER'S SURFACE TWIN
$35
BLACK & WHITE ONLY
3" 3½"
CARTER'S DAY-R-NIGHT
$25
Half black, half white.
2-¾" - 3" - 3-½"
DUNK'S SHORE MINNOW
$25
3-¼"
Dunk's FISHING TACKLE
CARTER'S CRAW
$20
2 SPINNERS
3"
CARTER'S METALHED
$35
3"
CARTER'S SHORE MINNOW
$20
BLACK H'D.
SILVER SIDE
WHITE BELLY
3"- 3½"

No.461 Muskie Size 4-3/8"
No.462 Medium Size 3-1/2"
No.463 Baby Size 2-7/8"
No.464 Single Hook 2-3/4"

LOOKS AND ACTS LIKE A CRIPPLED BLUEGILL.

$5 each

Spoonfish

(Patents Applied for)

PAT. PEND
Dunk's
Spoonfish

DUNK'S

$30

DUBBLE-HEADER
MIDGET – 2"
MEDIUM – 2½"

NOTE: METAL REVERSIBLE LIP ON THIS LATER MODEL.

Worry-Wart

(Patents Applied for)

$5

A New Lure for a New Way of Fishing!

You get SPINNING ACTION going down and coming up.

No. WW-46
Weight
⅞ ounce
Price $1.00

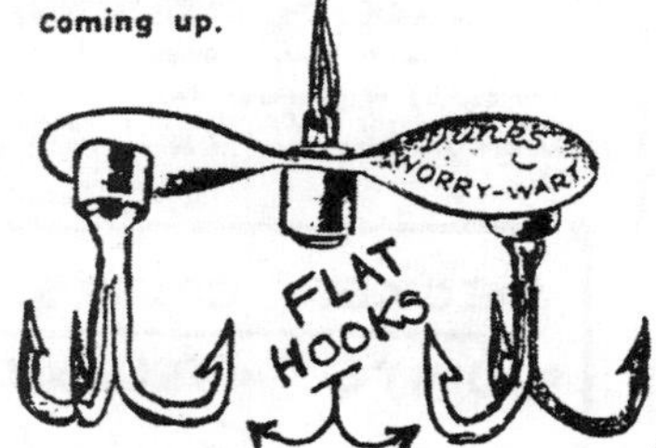
Dunk's
WORRY-WART
FLAT
HOOKS

$40

CARTER'S MOUSE

Length 2¾", weight ½ oz. Price 85c.

Grey back, white belly, red lower lip.

All black.

All grey.

DUNK'S DUNKIT

$30

A REAL ALARM CLOCK FOR SLEEPY BASS

2-½"

$10

STUBBY'S HYDROPLUG BAIT

(1923)

Entirely a new principle in artificial baits. Water is used for the casting weight. Has wonderful wiggling movement in water. Weighs ⅝ ounce when ready to cast. Used with Pork Rind, Buck Tail, Feathers or Live Bait. Body finished Bright Red and Aluminum.

$20

DUNK'S PRACTICE CASTING PLUG - 4 Colors: Official Size
PP-170 Red Head, White
PP-171 Green Head, White
PP-172 Red Head, Yellow
PP-173 Green Head, Yellow

THE CHIPMUNK

$50 – 75

4-½"
NO.11
1
2
3
4
5
6
7
8
9
10
11

Swim-a-lure

DUNK'S Came out with 11 lures in 1941 called Swim-a-lures. Bad timing with WW II just around the corner.

1. SUNFISH 2"
2. BLUEGILL 2-1/2"
3. BIG CHUB 3-1/4"
4. STRIPED MINNOW 3"
5. RED SHRIMP 2-1/2"
6. JOINTED PIKE 4"
7. YELLOW JACKET 3-1/2"
8. FROG 2-1/8"
9. BABY DUCK 3"
10. PIKE 4-1/4"
11. CHIPMUNK 4-1/2"

Note the distinctive metal lip that will help you identify this group of lures.

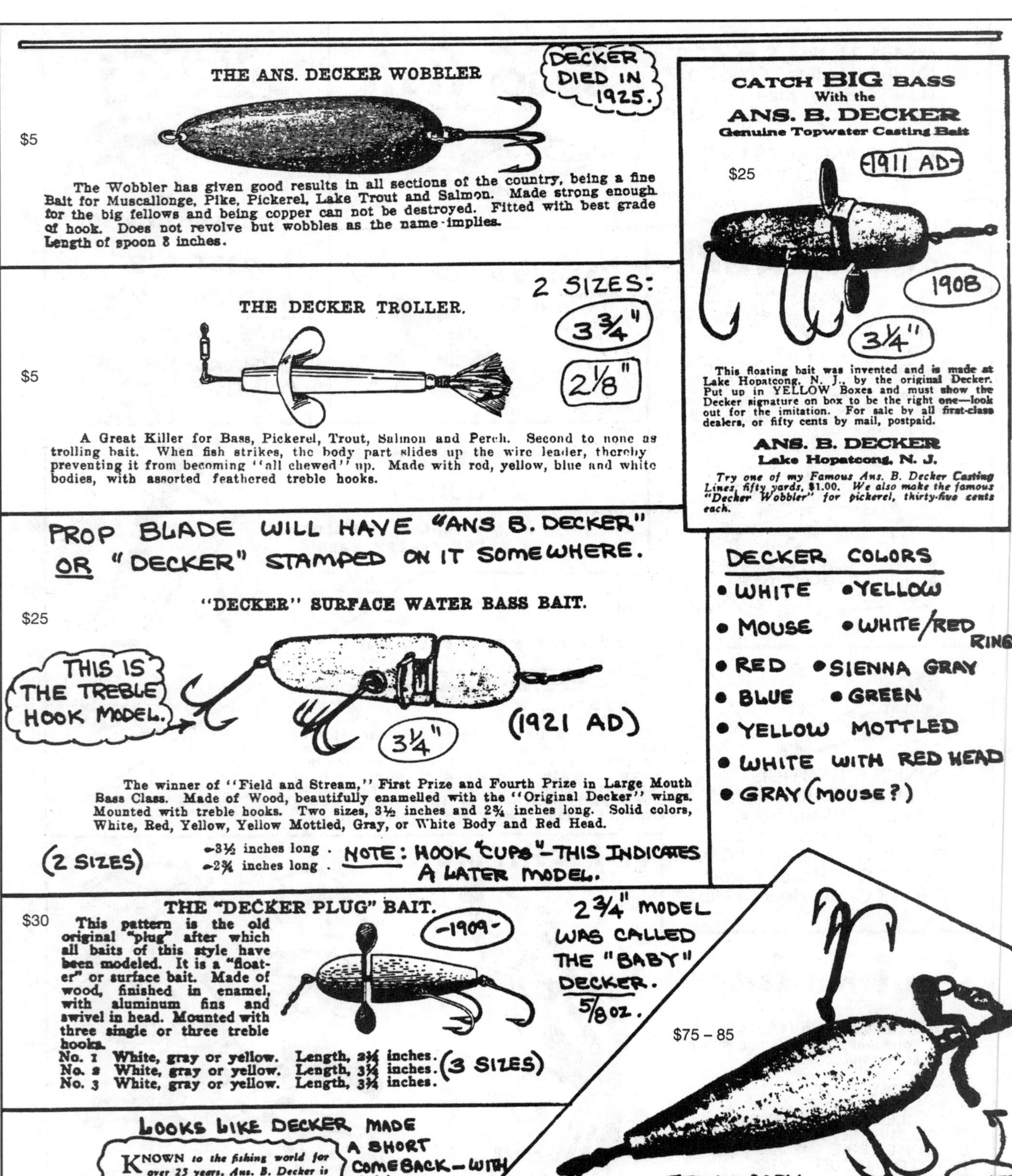

THE ANS. DECKER WOBBLER

DECKER DIED IN 1925.

$5

The Wobbler has given good results in all sections of the country, being a fine Bait for Muscallonge, Pike, Pickerel, Lake Trout and Salmon. Made strong enough for the big fellows and being copper can not be destroyed. Fitted with best grade of hook. Does not revolve but wobbles as the name implies. Length of spoon 3 inches.

THE DECKER TROLLER.

2 SIZES: 3 3/4" 2 1/8"

$5

A Great Killer for Bass, Pickerel, Trout, Salmon and Perch. Second to none as trolling bait. When fish strikes, the body part slides up the wire leader, thereby preventing it from becoming "all chewed" up. Made with red, yellow, blue and white bodies, with assorted feathered treble hooks.

CATCH BIG BASS
With the
ANS. B. DECKER
Genuine Topwater Casting Bait

$25

1911 AD

1908

3 1/4"

This floating bait was invented and is made at Lake Hopatcong, N. J., by the original Decker. Put up in YELLOW Boxes and must show the Decker signature on box to be the right one—look out for the imitation. For sale by all first-class dealers, or fifty cents by mail, postpaid.

ANS. B. DECKER
Lake Hopatcong, N. J.

Try one of my Famous Ans. B. Decker Casting Lines, fifty yards, $1.00. We also make the famous "Decker Wobbler" for pickerel, thirty-five cents each.

PROP BLADE WILL HAVE "ANS B. DECKER" OR "DECKER" STAMPED ON IT SOMEWHERE.

"DECKER" SURFACE WATER BASS BAIT.

$25

THIS IS THE TREBLE HOOK MODEL.

3 1/4"

(1921 AD)

The winner of "Field and Stream," First Prize and Fourth Prize in Large Mouth Bass Class. Made of Wood, beautifully enamelled with the "Original Decker" wings. Mounted with treble hooks. Two sizes, 3½ inches and 2¾ inches long. Solid colors, White, Red, Yellow, Yellow Mottled, Gray, or White Body and Red Head.

(2 SIZES)

- 3½ inches long.
- 2¾ inches long.

NOTE: HOOK "CUPS"—THIS INDICATES A LATER MODEL.

DECKER COLORS

- WHITE
- YELLOW
- MOUSE
- WHITE/RED RINGS
- RED
- SIENNA GRAY
- BLUE
- GREEN
- YELLOW MOTTLED
- WHITE WITH RED HEAD
- GRAY (MOUSE?)

THE "DECKER PLUG" BAIT.

$30

-1909-

This pattern is the old original "plug" after which all baits of this style have been modeled. It is a "floater" or surface bait. Made of wood, finished in enamel, with aluminum fins and swivel in head. Mounted with three single or three treble hooks.

No. 1 White, gray or yellow. Length, 2¾ inches.
No. 2 White, gray or yellow. Length, 3¼ inches.
No. 3 White, gray or yellow. Length, 3¾ inches.

(3 SIZES)

2 3/4" MODEL WAS CALLED THE "BABY" DECKER. 5/8 OZ.

LOOKS LIKE DECKER MADE A SHORT COMEBACK—WITH NEW ADDRESS.

KNOWN to the fishing world for over 25 years, Ans. B. Decker is again President of his company and has an active interest in the manufacture of his famous baits.

Ans. B. Decker, Inc.
P.O. Box 52 Mt. Arlington, N. J.

$75 – 85

ZEROX COPY (ACTUAL SIZE) OF A LITTLE KNOWN DECKER MODEL.

DECKER ON PROP

- A.B. DECKER'S FIRST NAME WAS ANSON.
  - DECKER HAD A CLOSE RELATIVE THAT WAS A FAMOUS FISHING GUIDE ON LAKE HOPATONG, N.J. IN THE 1877 – 1883 TIME FRAME.
- A 1912 DECKER AD USED THIS ADDRESS: THE DECKER BAIT CO. 48 Willoughby St. Brooklyn, N. Y.

BABY SIZE, DECKER CASTING BAIT

For Users of Lighter Tackle

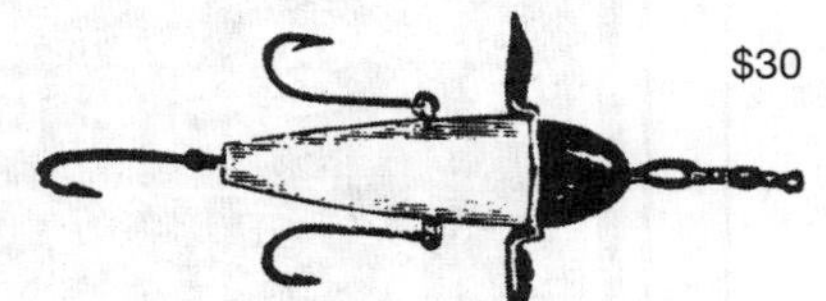

$30

Length, 2¾ inches. Fitted with Cincinnati Bass Hooks No. 22 or Treble Hooks No. 4. Aluminum Wings. Colors: White, Yellow, Mouse, White with Red Wings, White with Red Head and White with Red Head and Wings.

(1931 AD)

THIS 1905 AD ⟹ THROWS ANOTHER HAT IN THE DECKER RING. I HOPE JACOB MICK WAS A DISTRIB. FOR DECKER. (3 HOOK-N.J. RIG)

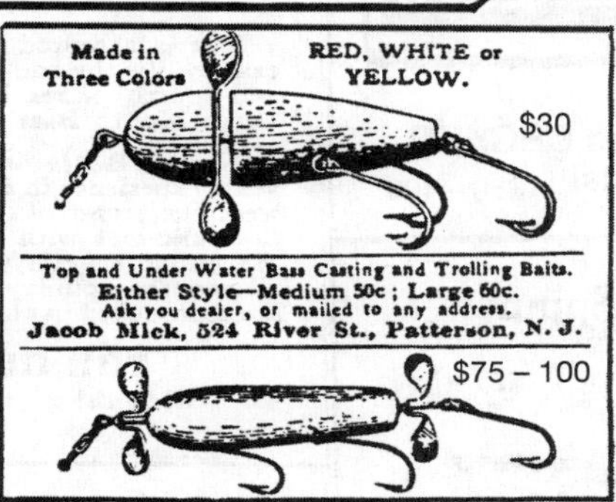

Made in Three Colors — RED, WHITE or YELLOW.

$30

Top and Under Water Bass Casting and Trolling Baits. Either Style—Medium 50c; Large 60c. Ask you dealer, or mailed to any address. Jacob Mick, 524 River St., Patterson, N. J.

$75 – 100

- THE YELLOW KID COLORS:
  - YELLOW / GOLD SPOTS
  - RED HEAD / YELLOW
  - WHITE BODY / GOLD SPOTS
- ALSO A "LONG" SLIM YELLOW KID – 3½" (1915)

THE MANHATTAN Under Water Casting Bait — It's a Sure Winner

Just toss it out in a likely looking bass or trout hiding place, and right off you will get action. The revolving fins cause just the right excitement to assure you of a strike if there is a fish in the immediate neighborhood. Cost only 85c each and your money back if they don't prove up to all we say.

S. J. MEYER CO. 1110 Longwood Ave., Bronx, N. Y.

$75 – 100

1922 AD – LOOKS LIKE MY ILLUS. OF THE LITTLE KNOWN UNDERWATER DECKER – (WHAT DO WE DO NOW – PUNT!)

LIVINGSTON S. HINCKLEY OF NEWARK, N. J. IS CREDITED WITH THE PATENT ON THE N.J. ALUMINUM PHANTOM. (1896 – 1897)

- THE NEW JERSEY ALUMINUM PHANTOM ALSO WAS MADE IN A SMALLER MODEL – NO. 4 WITH NO SIDE HOOKS – JUST A BUCKTAIL TREBLE. HAS THE SAME JAN. 12, 1897 DATE ON THE SPINNER. THIS WOULD ALSO COMPLY WITH THE NEW JERSEY 3 HOOK POINT LAW. (2½")

- A 1909 AD SHOWED THIS BAIT IN 3 SIZES:
  - 3¾"
  - 3"
  - 2"

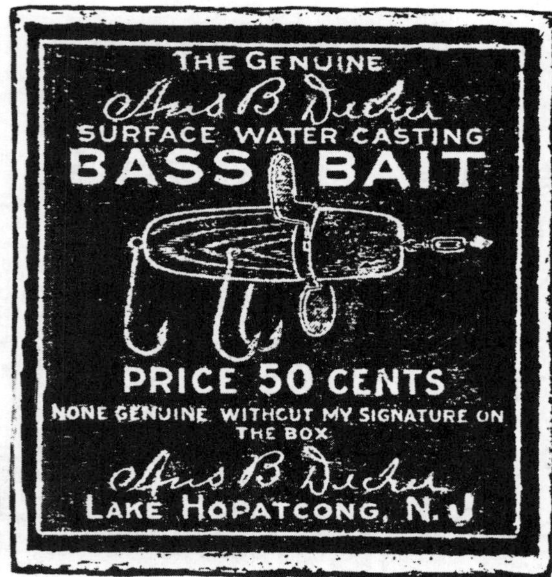
THE GENUINE
Ans B Decker
SURFACE WATER CASTING
BASS BAIT
PRICE 50 CENTS
NONE GENUINE WITHOUT MY SIGNATURE ON THE BOX
Ans B Decker
LAKE HOPATCONG, N.J

Blue Labeled, unusual shaped DECKER BOX. What a buy at 50 cents! $50 – 100

Useful Hints to Bass Fishermen

and

The History of the Wooden Bait

By Ans. B. Decker

is some of the valuable information contained in the **Decker Bait** catalog which will be mailed **FREE** on request. Kindly mention your dealer.

$30 – 40

This is a reproduction of a **Decker Bait.** It is exactly like the one used by the winner of the first and fourth prizes in the Field & Stream contest, Large Mouth Bass class.

Decker Baits are the product of (35) thirty-five years experience in Bass fishing as a business. They were the secret of the Decker family for two generations and met with instant success when offered to the public several years ago. Read what fishermen all over the country think. Some interesting letters are reproduced in our catalog. Send for it at once.

THE DECKER BAIT CO.

45 Willoughby St. Brooklyn, N. Y.

Note: Another address for Decker shown in this April, 1912 Ad from Outers Book. Also there is a time frame for their years guiding on Lake Hopatcong. 1912 - 35 years = started guiding in 1877, through the two generations.

Decker's Double End Spinner

$75 – 85

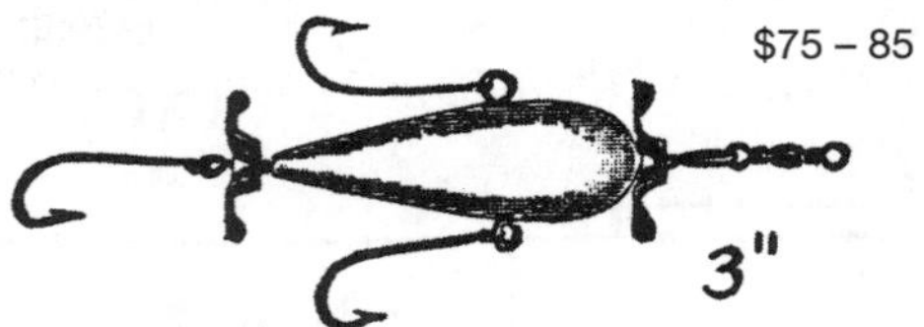
3"

Length 3 inches. Fitted with Cincinnati Bass Hooks No. 20 or Treble Hooks No. 3. Brass, nickle plated wings. Used for surface, or underwater casting. Under Water trolling highly successful for small mouth Bass.

Seven Colors: White, Yellow, Mouse, Sumac, Green, White with Red Head and Red.

Retails for 75 cents each

$30 – 40

Ans. B. Decker

GENUINE TOP WATER CASTING BAIT

Treble and Single Hooks

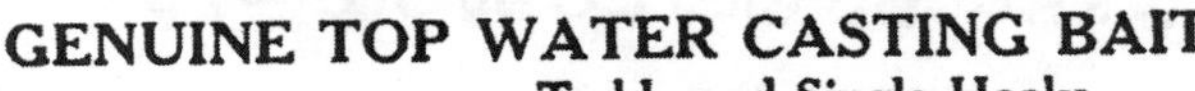

We are now sole distributors to the trade of this popular and well-tested floating bait. This is the original and genuine Decker bait—packed in YELLOW Boxes, bearing the "Decker" signature. Stock carried in New York City for immediate shipment. Where bass baits are bought there will be a demand for the "Decker." Advertised in outdoor magazines. If not in stock order a supply immediately.

MANCALL SPECIALTY COMPANY, 82 Duane Street, New York, N. Y.

Distributors of Mancall and Maximus Brand of Snell Hooks, Leaders, Tackle Boxes and Lines

This June 1923 ad introduced some new information. The box color changed to Yellow. Retail went up to .75 cents. An exclusive sole distributorship was awarded to Mancall Specialty Co. of New York. They must have sold to all the bait and tackle stores in the area.

I PROVED in the contest last year that my Bait would catch the big BASS. Now as one good sized fish will put twenty-five small ones in the shade, why not purchase your bait accordingly?

$30 – 40

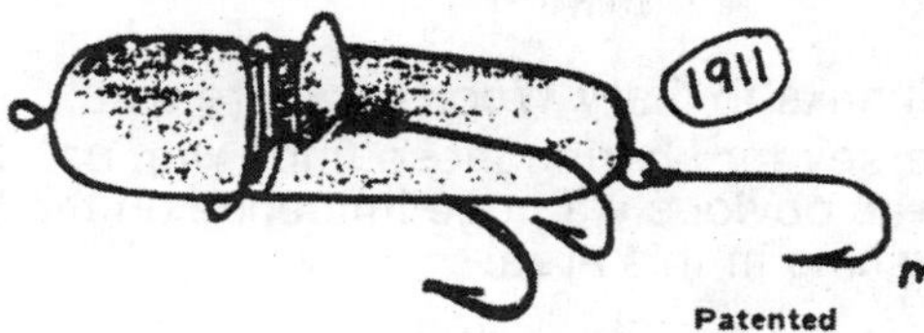
1911
Patented

Come on, MR. CHAMPION!

$1,000.00 against $500.00 I can catch more Bass over 14 inches than you can!

Look for the BLUE BOX and the name DECKER, HOPATCONG, stamped on the wings.
For sale by all up-to-date dealers, or by mail, **FIFTY CENTS, cash or money order.**

In 1914, Decker was making what he called the "Red Head" series. 3 treble hooks and a swivel w/bright red head and white enameled body.

The New Jersey game laws allowed only 3 hook points, and became known as the JERSEY RIG.

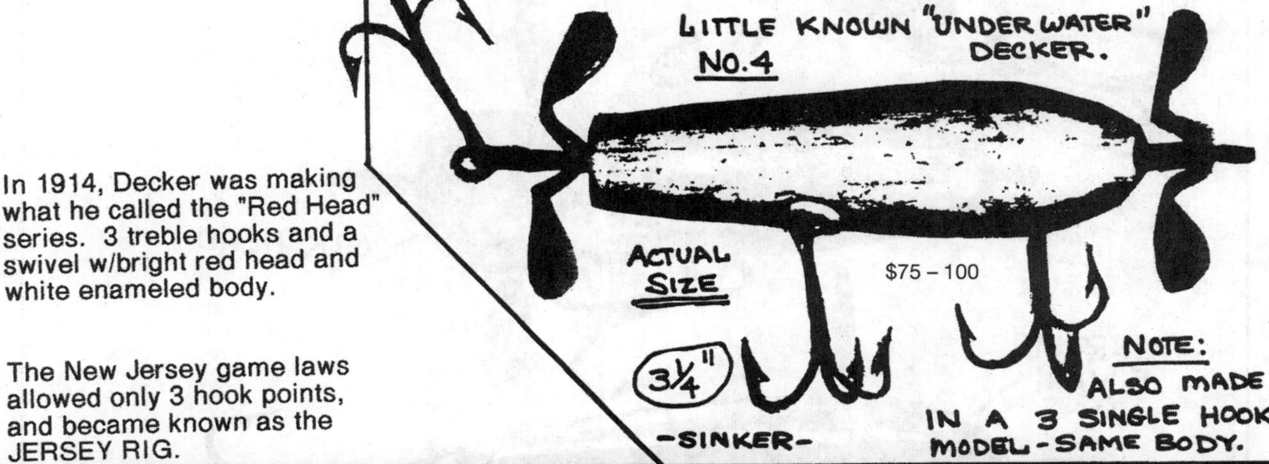
LITTLE KNOWN "UNDER WATER" DECKER.
No. 4
ACTUAL SIZE
3¼"
-SINKER-
NOTE:
ALSO MADE IN A 3 SINGLE HOOK MODEL - SAME BODY.

$75 – 100

$150 – 250

"The Griffiths" Minnow

(1923)

This Minnow is supplied with a body having a screwed head and several detachable fins of different colors, the object of which is to suit varying weather and water conditions. If the weather is bright and the water clear, a dark fin, such as copper, should be used; if the day is rather cloudy and dull, the brass fin should be used as it is a little brighter; but if it is a very dull day, or very colored water, the silver fin should be mounted, which will be found to be very deadly. The fin mounted on the body is already bent up to what is considered the best position, the others, however, are left flat for the angler to experiment with. It will be found that an angle of about 45° with the body will give the best results. It is a good plan to have one fin bent in the reverse direction to reverse the spin, and thus unkink the line should it become kinked. The fins are so constructed that they give the maximum spin with the minimum of motion through the water, and the advantage of this method of fixing them is that they can be adjusted to suit the volume and pressure of the water.

The 1 inch size is made with one treble hook (as illustrated), the larger sizes having 2 treble hooks, tandem style.

Inches		Inches	
1	For Trout......	2½	Bass ....
2	Trout and Bass.	3	Pickerel .

2½"

Lures within are priced in very good to very good+ condition. Condition = value.

$20 – 30

Here is an "unknown" bait in the same style......metal head with a wood body....cup hook rigged.

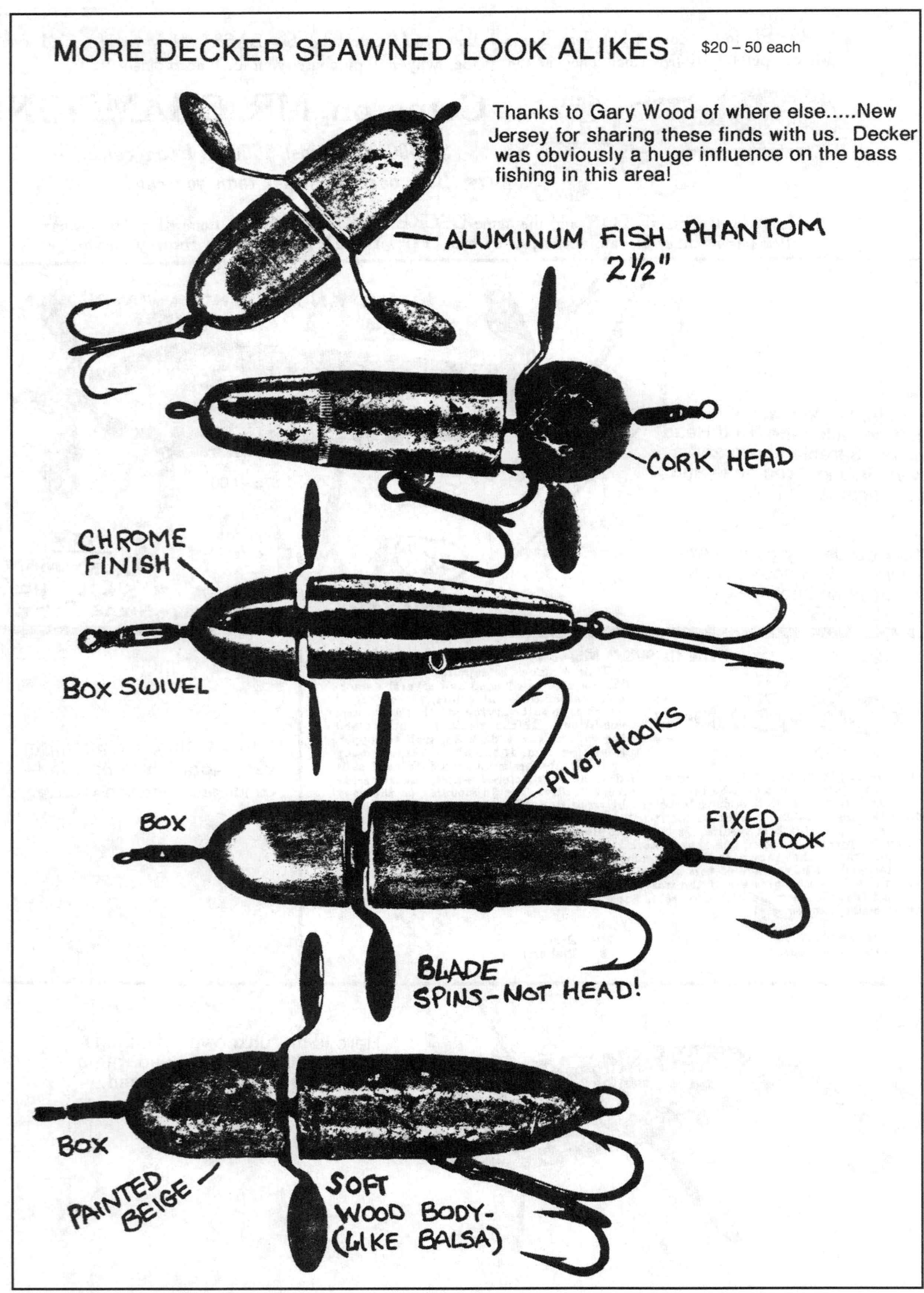
MORE DECKER SPAWNED LOOK ALIKES
$20 – 50 each
Thanks to Gary Wood of where else.....New Jersey for sharing these finds with us. Decker was obviously a huge influence on the bass fishing in this area!
ALUMINUM FISH PHANTOM
2½"
CORK HEAD
CHROME FINISH
BOX SWIVEL
PIVOT HOOKS
BOX
FIXED HOOK
BLADE SPINS-NOT HEAD!
BOX
PAINTED BEIGE
SOFT WOOD BODY- (LIKE BALSA)

THERE IS A BUNCH OF THESE DECKER LOOK ALIKES - SOME ARE TOUGH TO SORT OUT - SOME MAY BE THE SAME LURE WITH A DIFFERENT NAME.

ALUMINUM "KILLER" BAIT.

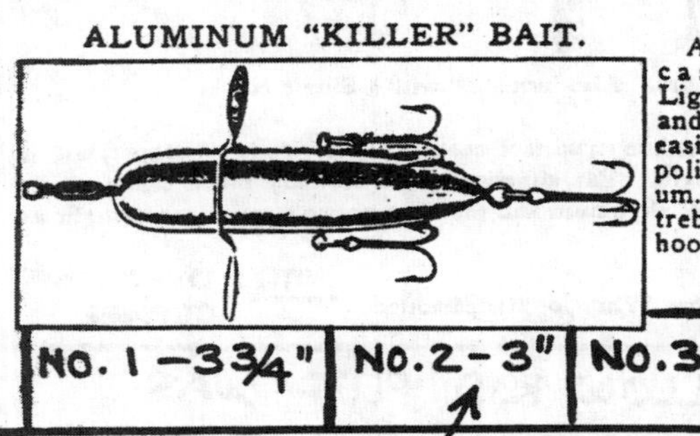

A fine surface casting bait. Light in weight and plays very easily. Bright polished aluminum. Fitted with treble or single hooks.

NO. 1 – 3¾"	NO. 2 – 3"	NO. 3 – 2"

IN 1907, VOM HOFE CATALOG CALLED THE 3" MODEL THE "YELLOW DEVIL."

$35

THE SNYDER SPINNER.

1904

$30

Air Tight, Nickel Plated Blade, Three Treble Hooks, Brass Box Swivel.
Snyder Spinner—Enameled Yellow and Spotted with Gold Leaf.

THE "TORPEDO" BAIT. -1909- $100 – 150

A new bait and likely to find favor as a bass lure. Made of "Silverine," and will not tarnish. Will float on the surface and spins very readily. Fitted with one feathered treble hook. Fins have holes drilled to attach other hooks if desired.

$35 – 45

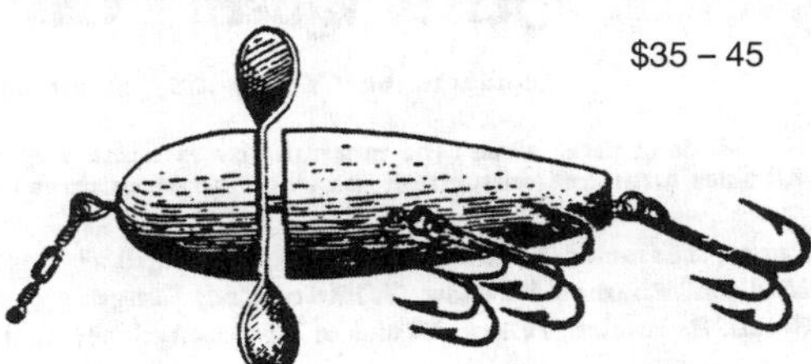

MANHATTAN TOP WATER BAIT.

This is a Wooden Floating Bait, made in three sizes, either White, Yellow or Mouse Colors. State style desired. Mounted with either single or treble hooks.

Nos.	D 42-1	D 43-2	D 44-3
Length inches	2¾	3¼	3¾

THE NEW JERSEY ALUMINUM PHANTOM.

$35

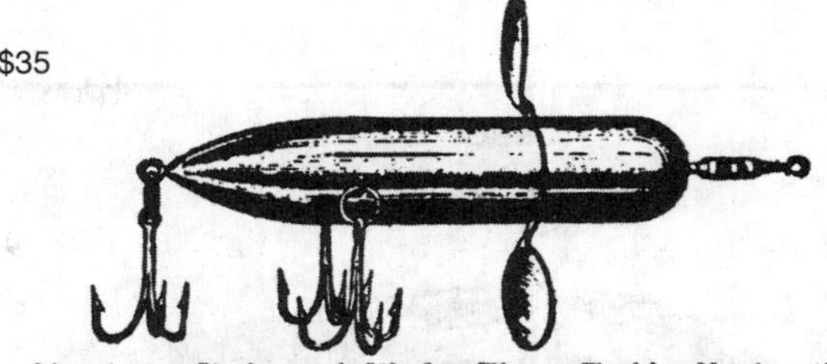

Aluminum Body and Blade, Three Treble Hooks, Split Steel Rings, Brass Box Swivel.

Nos.	4	3
Inches	2½"	3"

PATENT DATE - JAN. 12, 1897 - IS ON ONE PROPELLER BLADE.

$35

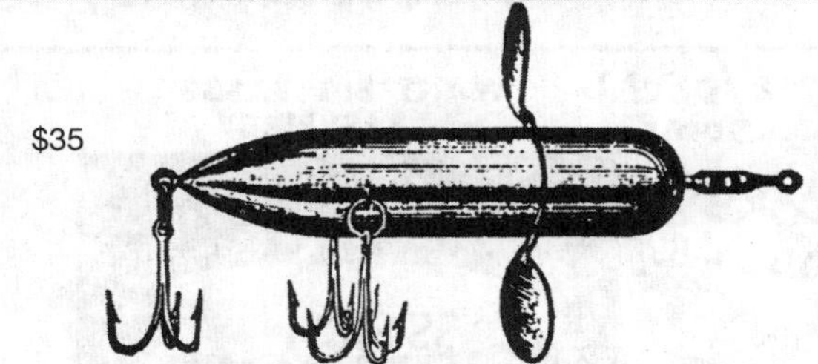

NO. 1 – 4¼"　NO. 3 – 3"
NO. 2 – 3¾"　NO. 4 – 2½"

THE ALUMINUM FISH PHANTOM

THESE ARE PROBABLY THE SAME - MFG'D. BY THE NEW JERSEY ALUMINUM CO. - IT WAS ALSO CALLED THE "FLYING GO-DEVIL".

THE "YELLOW BIRD PHANTOM" WAS SAME AS ABOVE EXCEPT YELLOW WITH GOLD SPOTS. ADD Y- TO NUMBERS ABOVE.

THE SUCCESS SPINNER

Hand Made, Air Tight, Floats and Will Not Twist Line

$30

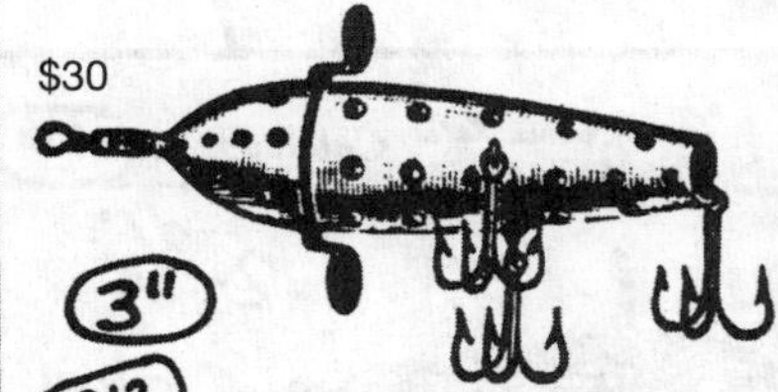

3"

1912

ALSO WITH 3 SINGLE HOOKS.

HOLLOW METAL CONSTRUCTION.

1910 - 20's

The Success Spinner is hand-made, air-tight, floats, and will not twist line. Length 3⅛ inches. Enameled yellow and spotted with gold leaf. Also enameled in brown and green with gold spots.
The Success Spinner will catch more bass than any artificial bait made.

No. 40—Yellow, gold spots
No. 41—Yellow, red head
No. 42—White, gold spots
No. 43—White, red head
No. 44—Green, gold spots
No. 45—Brown, gold spots

YELLOW, WHITE SPOTS

BROWN & GREEN WITH GOLD SPOTS.

Lures in excellent to mint condition are worth more.

JERSEY EXPERT.

$30

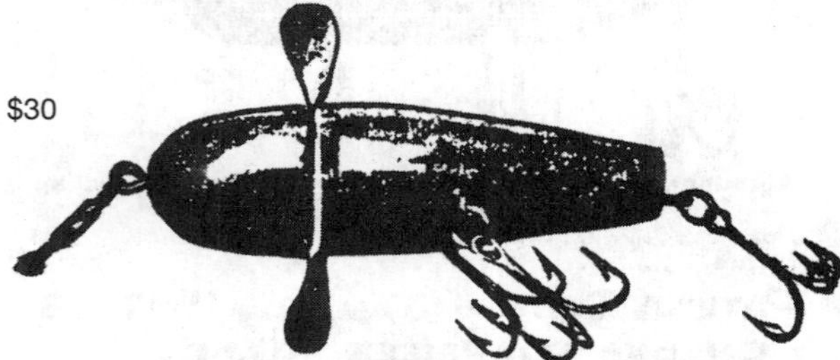

Colors white, yellow and mouse. (RED)

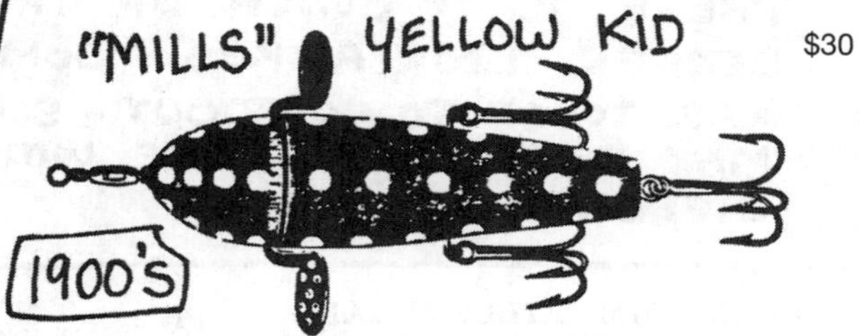
"MILLS" YELLOW KID
1900'S

$30

⅔ size. Also furnished with 3 Single Hooks.

One of the best known surface casting baits. Made of copper, and is absolutely watertight. Far superior to the ordinary metal casting baits (which are made of aluminum and therefore not so strong or watertight as the Yellow Kid).

Furnished in Yellow, White, or Red, Spotted. NOTE: MADE OF COPPER

THE YELLOW KID PLUG WAS NAMED AFTER A CHARACTER IN A POPULAR SUNDAY PAPER COMIC. IT WAS DRAWN BY R.F. OUTCAULT. (DIST. BY WM. MILLS & SON - NEW YORK.)

NAME/DECAL ON SOME.

WANT BIG BASS? try "BASSBIRD"

LOOKS OLD - BUT ISN'T!

BASS BIRD

$15

(1946)

Full production soon

Mechanically synchronized, precision machined and balanced for trouble free casting and twistless trolling.

AN UNBELIEVABLY SMOOTH PERFORMING BASS GETTER.

THIS BAIT WILL BRING THEM OUT—

You must bring them in

Distributors Wanted

J. J. GILL & ASSOCIATES

820 W. 105th St. Los Angeles 44, Calif.

MADE IN 2 SIZES

"JERSEY QUEEN" CASTING BAITS

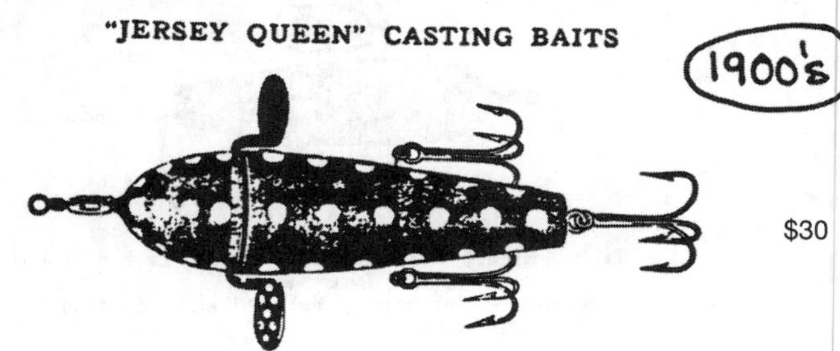
1900's

$30

Also furnished with 3 Single Hooks

One of the best known surface casting baits. They are made of wood, nicely enameled, white or yellow, and yellow with gold spots. They are made in three sizes: large, 3¾ inches; medium, 3¼ inches; small, 2¾ inches. All sizes are furnished with either three treble hooks or three single hooks.

Size		
Large,	Yellow or White.	Yellow, gold spotted.
Medium,	Yellow or White.	Yellow, gold spotted.
Small,	Yellow or White.	Yellow, gold spotted.

The above lures are particularly desirable for fishing in New Jersey and other nearby waters.

Values in this book are based on lures in very good to very good+ condition. Upgraded condition, special colors, and original boxes increase lures' values.

"Jersey Queen" Casting Baits.

Similar to the "Yellow Kid," only made of Red Cedar.

Made in three sizes; the medium size is same size as "Yellow Kid." All sizes furnished with either the treble hooks or three single hooks.

Large, Enameled Yellow, White or Red, Length 2¾ inches........

Medium, Enameled Yellow, White or Red, Length 3¼ inches.....

Small, Enameled Yellow, White or Red, Length 3¾ inches........

The above lines are particularly desirable for fishing in New Jersey and other near-by waters.

No. 5500—Yellow, gold spots.
No. 5510—Yellow, red head.
No. 5506—White, gold spots.
No. 5514—White, red head.
No. 5408—Mouse color.
No. 5400—Solid yellow.
No. 5516—Solid white.
No. 5401—Yellow, gold spots, mounted with 3 single hooks instead of trebles, for Jersey fishing.

Abbey & Imbrie, N. Y. *"Fishing Tackle that's Fit for Fishing."* *Catalogue for 1914*

$30

2-¾"

3¼"

The Topwater Casting Bait.

A wooden floating Casting Bait. Treble hooks, as illustrated—or single hooks. Only the head revolves when trolled. State style desired.

Colors—Yellow with gold spots; plain white.

1	2
2¾	3¼

JIM DONALY BAITS

JAMES L. DONALY

139 - Chester Ave. Bloomfield, N.J.
137 - Court St. Newark, N.J.
P.O. Box 283 Newark, N.J.
(all Donaly advertised addresses)

COLORS: NO. 27-1S WHITE WITH RED BAND. NO. 37 - GREEN BACK, WHITE BELLY. NO. 47 - WHITE, WITH RED STRIPES

REDFIN MINNOW BAIT.

1908

$250 – 300+

3-1/4"

3¼ in. long. Weighs 15 pwt....................... White belly, red stripes; or white body, red stripes.

(ALSO IN MOUSE FINISH,)

REDFIN FLOATING BAIT.

NO. 57 (4")

$150 – 200

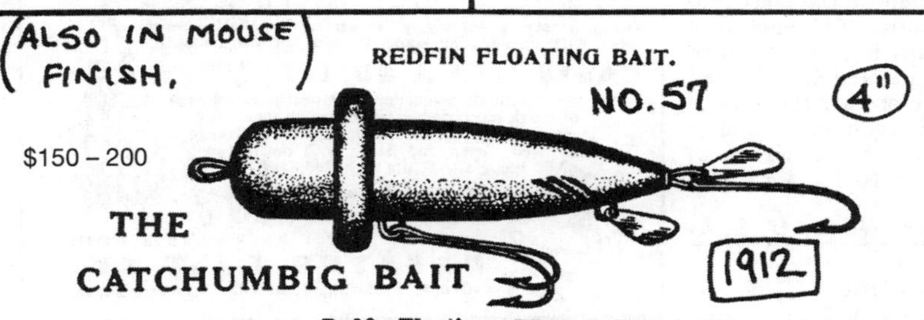

THE CATCHUMBIG BAIT

1912

Redfin Floating. White body, red collar. 4 in. long. Weighs 15 pwt. ....
The above can be had with two nickel plated treble hooks, or Jersey style, three hooks.

A FIELD AND STREAM PRIZE WINNER

THE REDFIN MINNOW

No. 27 (Pat. April 21, 1914)

REDFIN WEEDLESS BAIT. (3¼")

$150 – 250

NO. 67 (1915)

Redfin Weedless. White enamel body, 3¼ in. long, red stripe, nickel fins. Detachable belly hooks, nickel plated.

Floating Bait

REDFIN

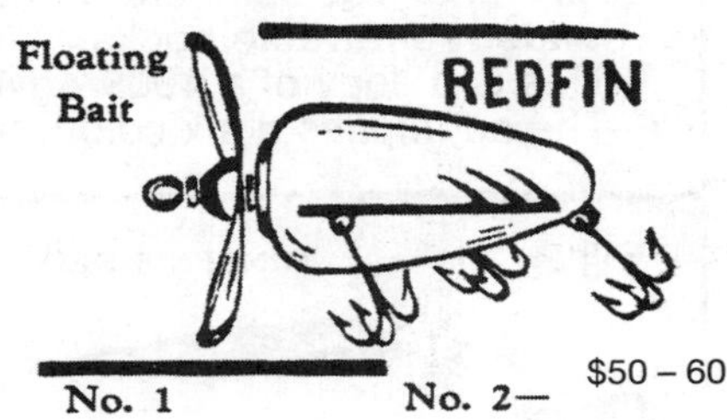

No. 1 No. 2— $50 – 60

Sizes—No. 1, Body, 2⅞ in. No. 2, 2¼ in.
Colors—Red, Yellow, Gray, White, Black.
Hooks—Three Treble or Three Single Hooks

I met a man in Seattle that lived next to Jim Donaly. As a kid he would go next door & up to the bathroom to watch Donaly test each WOW Bait that he had made. He rigged a dowel with line and a snap and would pull the baits at different speeds through the bath water.

Most all Donalys were hand painted. Careful if cleaning - they can get "tacky". The WOW was made for 10 years and then sold to Heddon. The WOW was in 1937 catalog.

Donaly Mouse

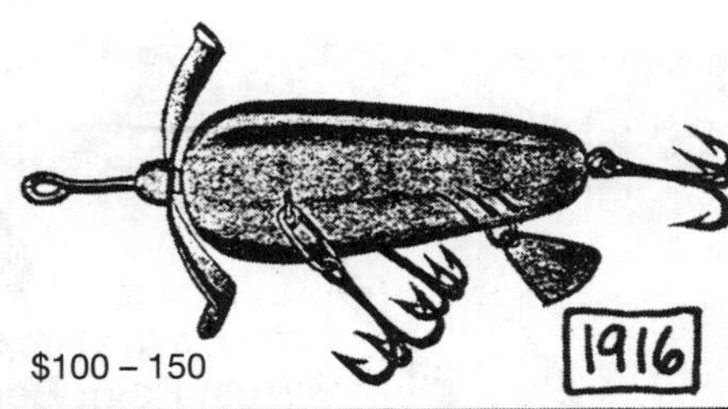

$100 – 150

1916

$100 – 150

DIVER

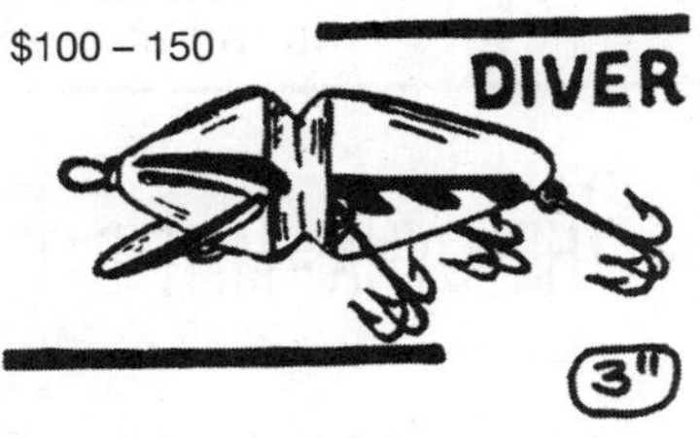

(3")

Size—Three-inch Body.
Colors—Yellow and Green, both with White belly and red and black striping.
Hooks—Three Treble or Three Single Hooks

$50 – 60

Floating Bait

WOW

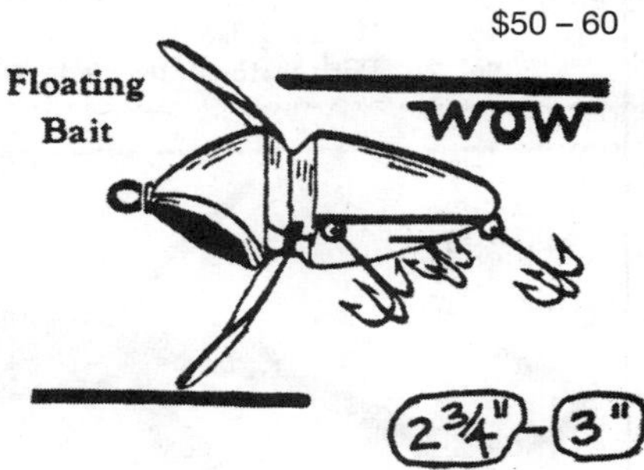

(2¾")-(3")

Sizes—No. 1, Body, 3 in. No. 2, 2¾ in.
Colors—Red, Yellow, Gray, White, Black.
Hooks—Three Treble or Three Single Hooks

(I BELIEVE THIS WAS THE ORIGINAL PATENT FOR THE "CRAZY CRAWLER.")

Floating Bait

JERSEY WOW

$50 – 60

(3")

$300 – 350+

The IDEAL MINNOW

New in principle. A sure killer whether in casting or trolling. The small pair of spinners shown in front of cut is bright red, revolves very freely and has a resilient attachment to the body representing neutral fin-movement of a live minnow. The hooks are instantly removed by pressing a spring, and any hook with an eye may be used. The back is of wood nicely painted and blended in colors that will stand water test. Never before has there been offered to the angling fraternity an article of such value and is manufactured and sold direct to fisherman upon the recipience of a postal or express order. One minimum. Price $0.50. Half dozen in select colors. Price $2.75. Manufactured by
Wm. E. Davis, 41 Bank St. Morristown, N. J., U. S. A.

Has small red spinners up front & spring loaded removable hooks. Wood with G.E. This is a copy of a 1909 Advertisement. The ad implies a six color selection.

Cradle Action
The New
Magic FISH
KILLER
1944
It rocks, it jitters, it wiggles—an action so tantalizing it stirs the fighting instinct of all game fish. Hooks slung cradle fashion creates a new wiggly "rocker" action that's irresistible—with no dangling hooks to miss the fish's mouth.
CASTS LIKE A BULLET and retrieves beautifully,
fast or slow; with deadly action, any depth. Handmade of tough hardwood—strong enough for musky—small enough for bass. Colors: Yellow, Orange, Red, Green and Black with contrasting spots; also White with Red head.
Special Introductory Price Only $1
GUARANTEED FISH GETTER
OR YOUR MONEY BACK—ORDER NOW!
DECATUR BAIT CO.
1076 W. Main St., Dept. 147 • Decatur 24, Ill.

$20

$35 – 50

DINEEN'S SPINNING MINNOW.

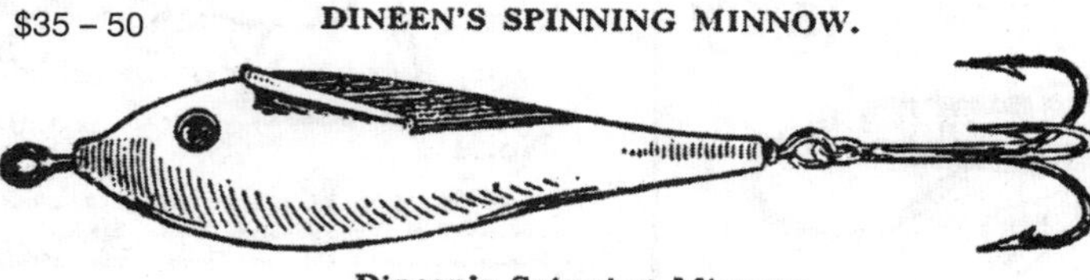

Dineen's Spinning Minnow.

Length of body 3½ inches.

No. 1.	With regular treble hook........................each,	**$0.50**
No. 2.	With feathered treble hook..................... "	**.60**

Known as JOHN DINEEN'S 1911 SPINNING MINNOW. Made of hollow brass, 3-1/2", also with a nose swivel and a feathered treble. Colors: Brass, Copper, Nickel, Red Back/White Belly, Green Back/White Belly. John Dineen
559 - So. State Street
Chicago, Illinois

$20 – 40

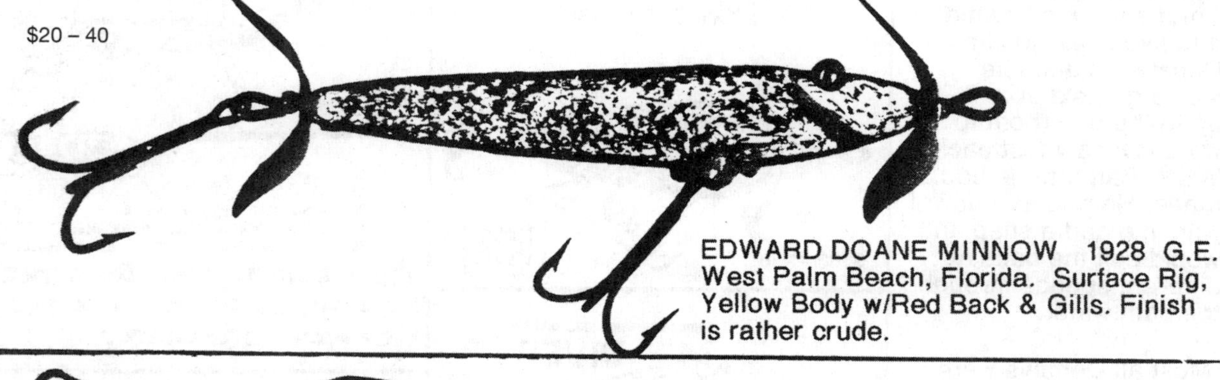

EDWARD DOANE MINNOW 1928 G.E. West Palm Beach, Florida. Surface Rig, Yellow Body w/Red Back & Gills. Finish is rather crude.

$5

THE DYNA - MITE BAIT DYNA TACKLE CO.
3204 - Gaston Ave.
Dallas 1, Texas

A popular bait for White Bass in the 40's & 50's. It was designed by a dentist. It was promoted as "A Perfect Trolling & Casting Bait".

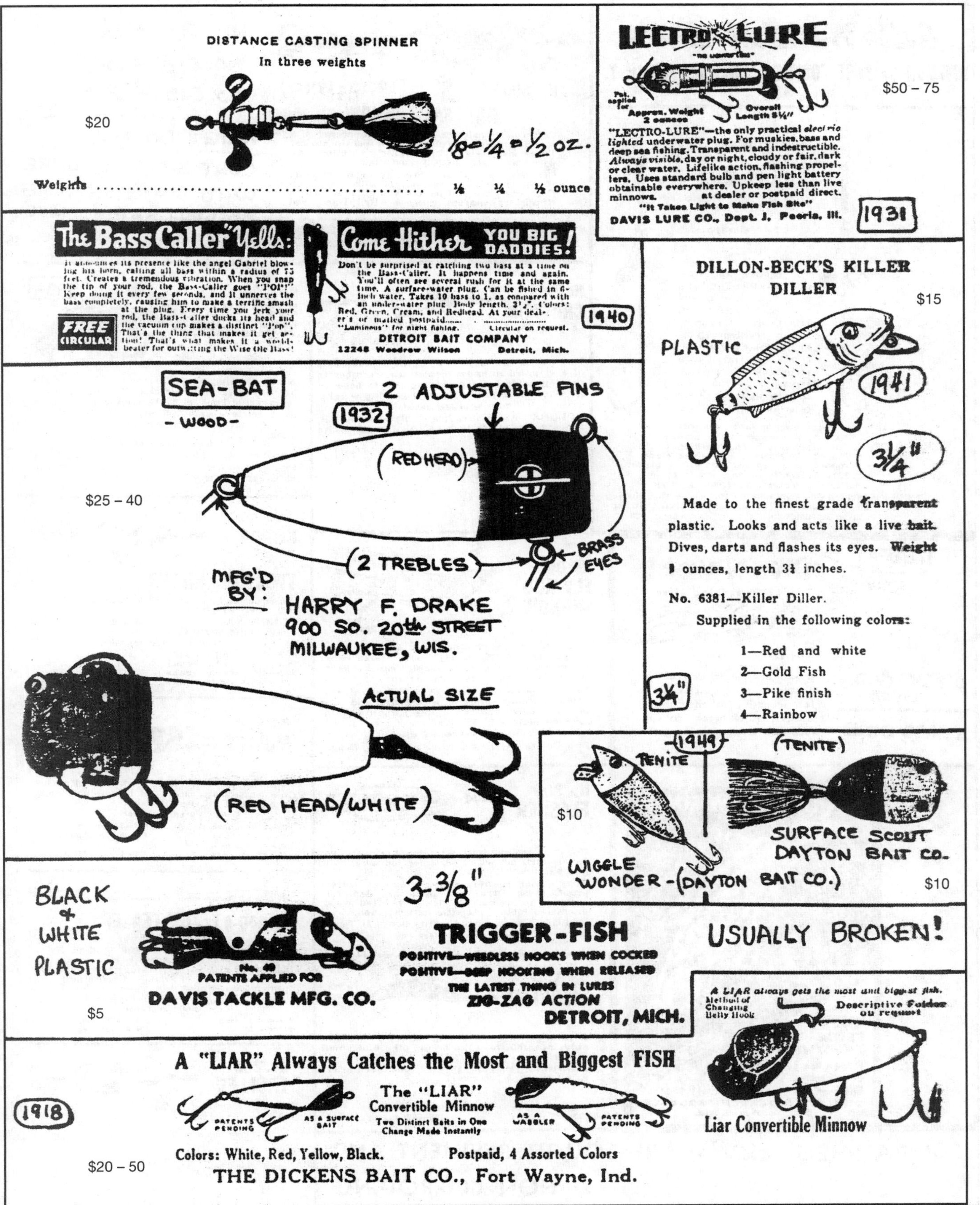
DISTANCE CASTING SPINNER
In three weights
$20
1/8 – 1/4 – 1/2 OZ.
Weights .... 1/8 1/4 1/2 ounce
LECTRO LURE
Pat. applied for
Approx. Weight 2 ounces
Overall Length 5 1/4"
"LECTRO-LURE"—the only practical electric lighted underwater plug. For muskies, bass and deep sea fishing. Transparent and indestructible. Always visible, day or night, cloudy or fair, dark or clear water. Lifelike action, flashing propellers. Uses standard bulb and pen light battery obtainable everywhere. Upkeep less than live minnows. at dealer or postpaid direct.
"It Takes Light to Make Fish Bite"
DAVIS LURE CO., Dept. J, Peoria, Ill.
1931
$50 – 75
The Bass Caller" Yells:
It announces its presence like the angel Gabriel blowing his horn, calling all bass within a radius of 75 feet. Creates a tremendous vibration. When you snap the tip of your rod, the Bass-Caller goes "POP!" Keep doing it every few seconds, and it unnerves the bass completely, causing him to make a terrific smash at the plug. Every time you jerk your rod, the Bass-Caller ducks its head and the vacuum cup makes a distinct "Pop". That's the thing that makes it get action! That's what makes it a world-beater for outwitting the Wise Ole Bass!
FREE CIRCULAR
Come Hither YOU BIG DADDIES!
Don't be surprised at catching two bass at a time on the Bass-Caller. It happens time and again. You'll often see several rush for it at the same time. A surface-water plug. Can be fished in 6-inch water. Takes 10 bass to 1, as compared with an under-water plug. Body length, 3 1/2". Colors: Red, Green, Cream, and Redhead. At your dealer's or mailed postpaid......
"Luminous" for night fishing. Circular on request.
DETROIT BAIT COMPANY
12248 Woodrow Wilson Detroit, Mich.
1940
DILLON-BECK'S KILLER DILLER
$15
PLASTIC
1941
3 1/4"
Made to the finest grade transparent plastic. Looks and acts like a live bait. Dives, darts and flashes its eyes. Weight ounces, length 3 1/4 inches.
No. 6381—Killer Diller.
Supplied in the following colors:
1—Red and white
2—Gold Fish
3—Pike finish
4—Rainbow
3 1/4"
SEA-BAT
- WOOD -
1932
2 ADJUSTABLE FINS
(RED HEAD)
$25 – 40
(2 TREBLES)
BRASS EYES
MFG'D BY:
HARRY F. DRAKE
900 SO. 20th STREET
MILWAUKEE, WIS.
ACTUAL SIZE
(RED HEAD/WHITE)
1949
TENITE
(TENITE)
$10
SURFACE SCOUT
DAYTON BAIT CO.
WIGGLE WONDER - (DAYTON BAIT CO.)
$10
BLACK & WHITE PLASTIC
3-3/8"
No. 40
PATENTS APPLIED FOR
DAVIS TACKLE MFG. CO.
$5
TRIGGER-FISH
POSITIVE—WEEDLESS HOOKS WHEN COCKED
POSITIVE—DEEP HOOKING WHEN RELEASED
THE LATEST THING IN LURES
ZIG-ZAG ACTION
DETROIT, MICH.
USUALLY BROKEN!
A LIAR always gets the most and biggest fish.
Method of Changing Belly Hook
Descriptive Folder on request
Liar Convertible Minnow
A "LIAR" Always Catches the Most and Biggest FISH
1918
PATENTS PENDING
AS A SURFACE BAIT
The "LIAR" Convertible Minnow
Two Distinct Baits in One Change Made Instantly
AS A WABBLER
PATENTS PENDING
Colors: White, Red, Yellow, Black.
Postpaid, 4 Assorted Colors
$20 – 50
THE DICKENS BAIT CO., Fort Wayne, Ind.

Bill De Witt Baits

DIVISION OF SHOE FORM CO. INC., AUBURN, N.Y.

No. 500 (1930-1940)

NATURAL MINNOW

Colorful, translucent, with all iridescence of a real live minnow. You can even feel the scales! Three sizes, six colors. Whirling action. All wire parts are entirely rustproof.

COLORS: A, Yellow Perch, transparent gills; B, Silver Shiner, transparent gills; C, Green Pike, red gills; D, Goldfish, red gills; E, Brown Chub, transparent gills; F, Red Dace, red gills.

(I.D NAME ON PLASTIC FINS)

NO. 512 – 2½"
NO. 513 – 3½"
NO. 515 – 5"

NOTE: DO NOT CONFUSE THIS LURE WITH THE "FISH MASTER" OF WOLLASTON, MASS.

$5

$5

Nos. 700 and 701 BASS BUG SPINNER

1½" Blades

For casting and trolling. A killer for bass, pike and pickerel and equally effective for lake trout and salmon. Heavy resilient Pyra-Shell blades, permanent colors, rust proof construction. Mounted on individual cards with interchangeable Carlisle hooks 4/0 and 9/0.

Order by number and color

700—A, Red head, white blades.
700—B, White head, red blades.
700—C, One black, one white blade.
700—D, One red and one white blade.
701—E, White blades, red inlay.
701—F, White blades, black inlay.

Pattern 701 when in action gives the illusion of inner and outer blades revolving in opposite directions.

No. 900 CRIP-MIN

4¼" body

Has all of the erratic wriggling movements of a crippled minnow. Sealed air chamber in the top holds the top side up. Holes beneath let water in to provide proper casting weight.

Order by number and color.

COLORS: A, White head, black body; B, Black head, white body; C, Red head, white body.

$5

No. 1000 DUCK BILL WRIGGLER

1939

3½" long

$5

A new floating plug of correct casting weight but having a large air chamber that gives it remarkable buoyancy. Wriggling action on a light retrieve and fast diving with a heavy pull. Remarkably sensitive and yet extremely durable.

Order by number and color

COLORS: A, All black; B, All white; C, White top, red bottom; D, Red top, white bottom; E, Green mottle.

Dive-N-Wobl

1943

Like Something Alive

WOBBLES DARTS DIVES

$5

Brand new — a demon for action — rests quietly for a few seconds . . . then plunges, dodges, quick-breaks to surface with a splash and gurgle.

• FLY ROD SIZE

• BASS SIZE

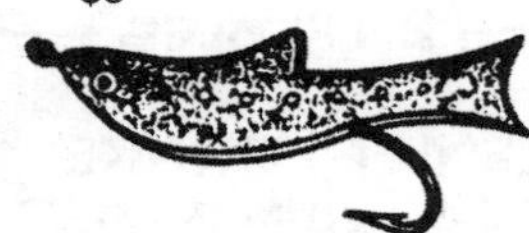

No. 600 FLY ROD MINNOW

$5

A featherweight minnow for fly rod use. Weighs only 3/100 oz. 1½" long. Finish cannot crack or chip, semi-pliable, can be bent under warm water to vary action.

The laminated construction of these featherweight minnows adds both strength and pliability. Hooks are of the finest quality from our own factory in England.

Order by number and color

Two Colors: A, Brook trout green; B, Pearl.

No. 400 TWISTING KILLER

$5

An effective lure for trolling and also for casting when weighted.

COLORS: A, Black head, white body; B, Red head, white body; C, Pearl.

Order by number and color.

402—2½" single hook.
403—3½" treble hooks.
404—4½" treble hooks.
405—5¾" treble hooks.

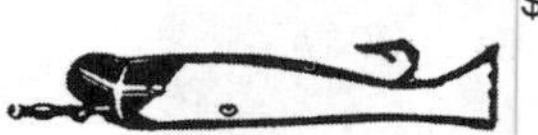

No. 800 MULLET

$5

Made in ten sizes from 3" to 18". Red head and white body other color combinations can be supplied on special order.

Order by Number

803—3", one hook . . .
804—4", one hook . . .
805—5", one hook . . .
806—6", one hook . . . .
807—7", one hook . . . .
808—8", two hooks . . .
809—9", two hooks . . .

$5

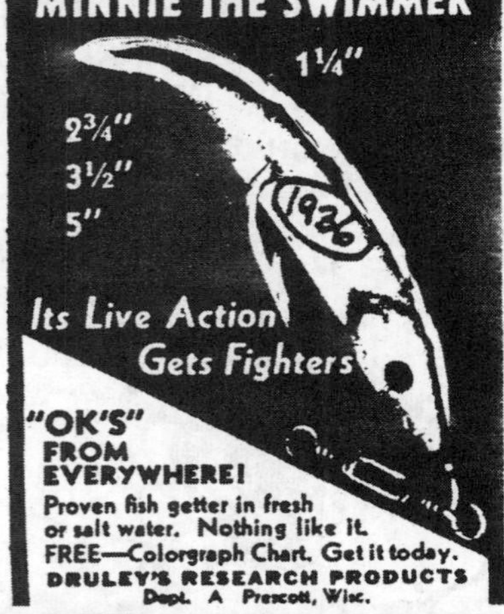

MINNIE THE SWIMMER
1¼"
2¾"
3½"
5"
1926
Its Live Action Gets Fighters
"OK'S" FROM EVERYWHERE!
Proven fish getter in fresh or salt water. Nothing like it.
FREE—Colorgraph Chart. Get it today.
DRULEY'S RESEARCH PRODUCTS
Dept. A Prescott, Wisc.

No. 300 FLASHER

$5

For deep trolling with wire or other deep line. Lively darting action. A killer for lake trout and salmon. 3⅜" blade.

Tough, non-rusting and completely waterproof, these Pyra-Shell baits are definitely superior to similar articles of painted wood, enameled metal or brittle natural shell.

COLORS: A, Red head, white body; B, Pearl.

Order by number and color

No. 100 WOBBLER

$5

A rolling, wobbling action makes it practicably infallible for lake trout, pike and small salt water fish.

COLORS: A, all gold; D, white body, red head; E, all silver; F, all pearl.

Order by number and color.

102—2" blade.
103—3" blade.
104—4" blade.
105—5" blade.

No. 800-A TEZUM TEASER

(HOOKLESS)

$5

A sea-going relative of The Mullet. Towed astern, it creates a surface commotion that brings game fish streaking for your bait. Doubles chances of strikes. Used singly or in tandem as illustrated above. Tough and flexible. Red Head and White Body.

Order by Number

812-A—12" long . . . .
816-A—16" long
820-A—20" long
824-A—24" long

No. 200 TROLLER

3-¾"

$5

PYRA SHELL *Baits* ARE TOUGH, RESILIENT AND NON-CORRODING

DICKENS'
Game Fish Getters

$20

DICKENS' WEEDLESS WONDER

This DECKER concoction may have worked, but the product name needs help!

YOPTECADLE A natural fish lure. One drop on live bait minnow or frog will double your catch and guarantee you a big string on so-called "*off days.*"

ONE DOLLAR BY MAIL

ANS B. DECKER, Lake Hopatcong, N. J.

1911 Ad - National Sportsman

BASS CALLER BAIT(Pat.1939)
Detroit Bait Co. Detroit, Mich.
Hollowed out area top of head.
3-1/2" N.E.

$15 – 25

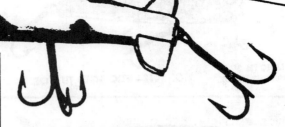

118—Luminous (For Night Fishing)
119—Red Head—White Body—Silver Side
120—Cream Body—Silver Side—Orange Stripe
121—Green Body—Yellow Side—Black Stripe
122—Red Body—Yellow Side—Black Stripe

You Can Use One Live Minnow All Day

PATENT PENDING

$100 – 200

Price, 85 Cents
German Silver Fittings

A Minnow-Tube is a transparent glass receptacle that magnifies a live minnow two or three times its size; affords free circulation of water for the minnow and keeps it alive a whole day, no matter how many times he may be cast.

DIRECTIONS.

Press ends of bail and slip the stopper up; put in live minnow tail first. Worms, water-bugs, etc., may also be used, but a live minnow is most desirable and effective.

For the many anglers who prefer the pole and line and who have no confidence in wooden minnows, spinners and other contraptions, this device will soon pay for itself in minnows.

There is no question of the superiority of live bait, as fish will strike at it while utterly refusing to attack any form of artificial lure.

Heretofore no plan has ever been devised to keep a minnow alive.

Think what an invention of this kind means. Any one who has ever used it is at once convinced that for the angler it is as far superior to the dummy wooden decoy bait and other contraptions as a live duck is superior to a dummy wooden decoy duck for duck shooters. Think then also how much time will be saved "experimenting" with wooden baits and contraptions to determine which will be the most successful colors under the "conditions," and what it means to have a bait that will last indefinitely, free from paint and enamel to become dead and peel off. That it is no longer necessary for the angler to load down his tackle box with fancy but useless lures.

It is of proper shape and material to meet the least of atmospheric resistance when cast.

It is the greatest attractor ever invented and yet always appeals to the anglers in a true and sportsman-like manner, as it is not necessary to impale a live minnow upon a hook.

When you are through fishing for the day the minnow may, and rightly should, be returned to the water.

Detroit Glass Minnow Tube Company
54-56 Lafayette Boulevard
DETROIT, MICHIGAN

THE THREE BEST LIVE MINNOW BAITS

Live Minnow Hook, held by top fin
Price 25c

Minnow not harnessed, hooked nor mutilated—remains alive and active.

1914

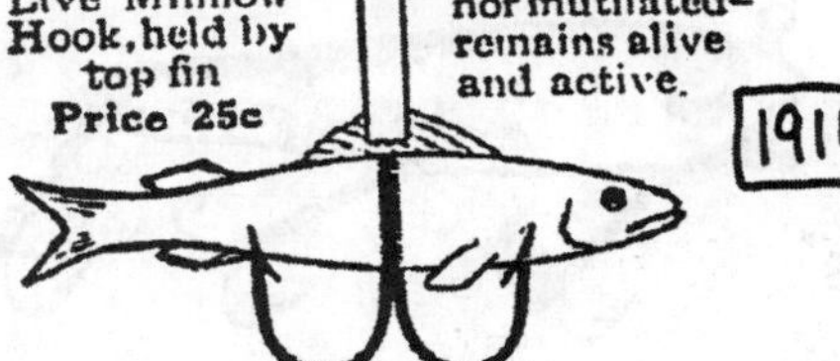

$20 – 30

$75 – 100

Price 85c

Magnifying Glass Minnow Tube
Minnow will remain alive all day

$100 – 125

Live Minnow Cage
Price 50c

Ask your dealer or by mail prepaid from
DETROIT GLASS MINNOW TUBE CO.
59 W. Lafayette Blvd., Detroit, Mich.

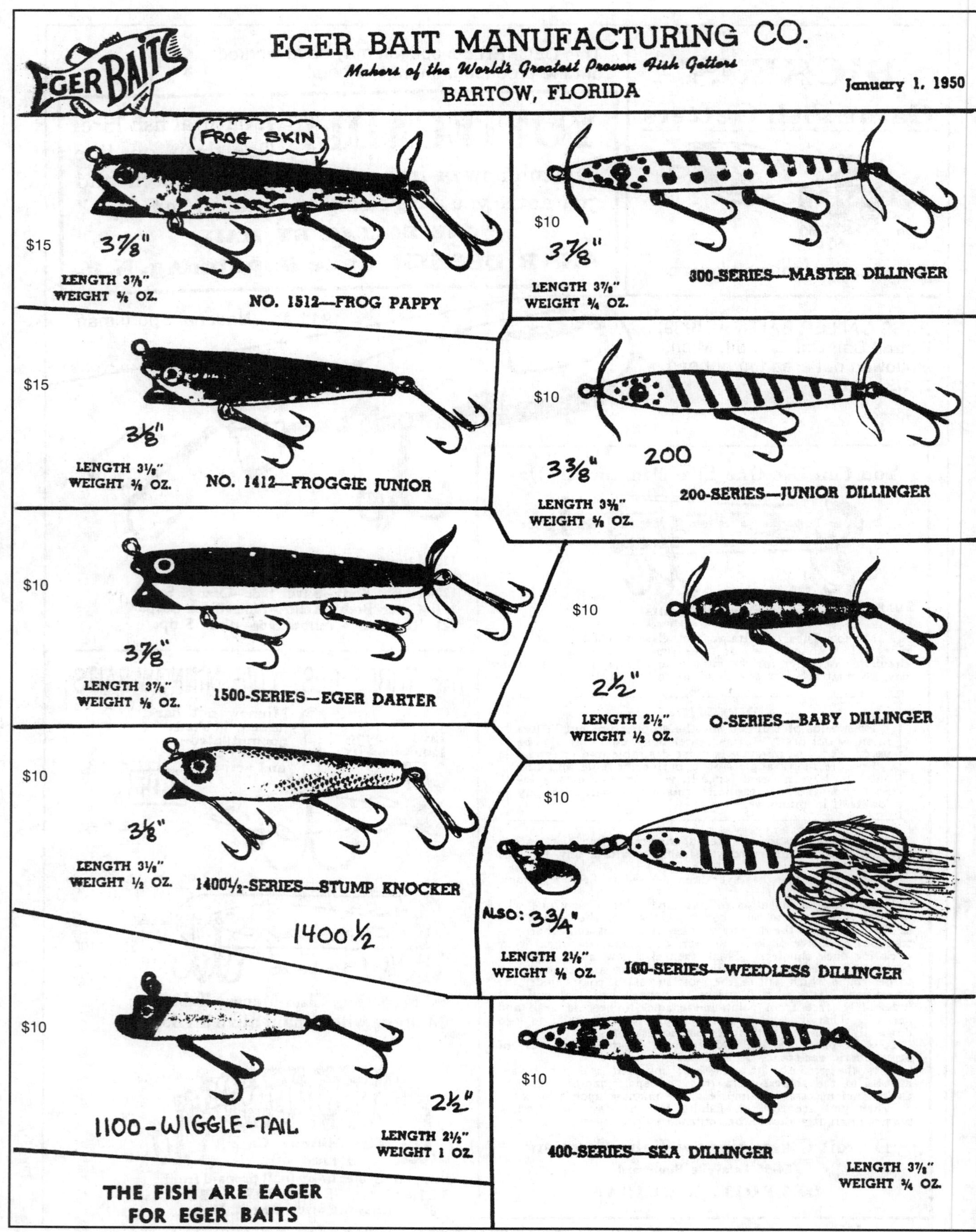
EGER BAITS
EGER BAIT MANUFACTURING CO.
Makers of the World's Greatest Proven Fish Getters
BARTOW, FLORIDA
January 1, 1950
FROG SKIN
$15
3 7/8"
LENGTH 3 7/8"
WEIGHT 5/8 OZ.
NO. 1512—FROG PAPPY
$10
3 7/8"
LENGTH 3 7/8"
WEIGHT 3/4 OZ.
300-SERIES—MASTER DILLINGER
$15
3 1/8"
LENGTH 3 1/8"
WEIGHT 5/8 OZ.
NO. 1412—FROGGIE JUNIOR
$10
200
3 3/8"
LENGTH 3 3/8"
WEIGHT 5/8 OZ.
200-SERIES—JUNIOR DILLINGER
$10
3 7/8"
LENGTH 3 7/8"
WEIGHT 5/8 OZ.
1500-SERIES—EGER DARTER
$10
2 1/2"
LENGTH 2 1/2"
WEIGHT 1/2 OZ.
O-SERIES—BABY DILLINGER
$10
3 1/8"
LENGTH 3 1/8"
WEIGHT 1/2 OZ.
1400 1/2-SERIES—STUMP KNOCKER
1400 1/2
$10
ALSO: 3 3/4"
LENGTH 2 1/2"
WEIGHT 5/8 OZ.
100-SERIES—WEEDLESS DILLINGER
$10
2 1/2"
1100-WIGGLE-TAIL
LENGTH 2 1/2"
WEIGHT 1 OZ.
$10
400-SERIES—SEA DILLINGER
LENGTH 3 7/8"
WEIGHT 3/4 OZ.
THE FISH ARE EAGER
FOR EGER BAITS

EGER BAITS

CATCH MORE AND BIGGER FISH

(CONT.)

EGER'S GENUINE FROGSKIN PATENTED TOPWATER BAITS

NO. 1312—BULL NOSE FROG

A surface plunker of extraordinary appeal, covered with genuine frogskin. Amazingly lifelike in the water and irresistible in action. An ideal spinning bait. U.S. Pat. No. 2092304.

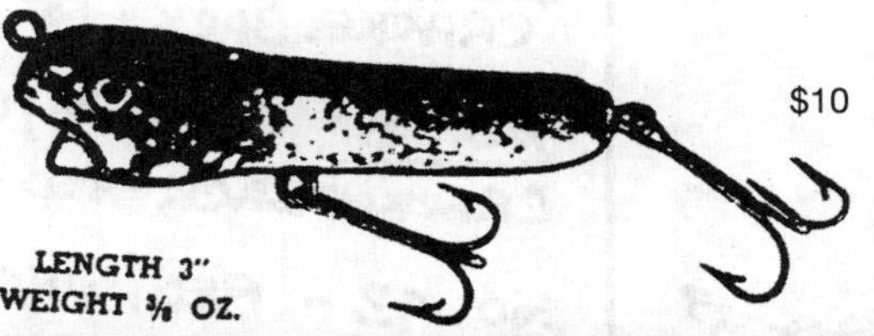

$10

LENGTH 3"
WEIGHT ⅜ OZ.

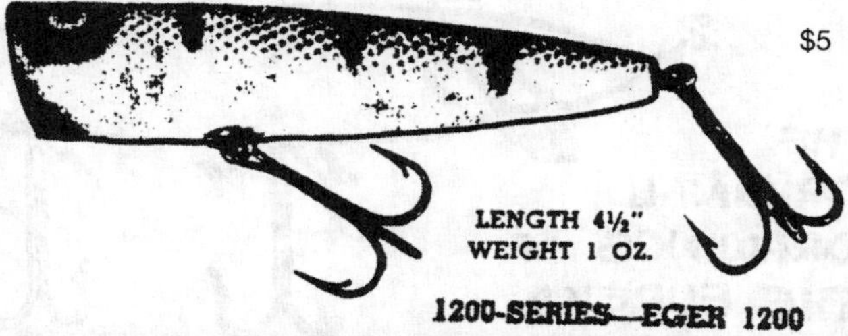

$5

LENGTH 4½"
WEIGHT 1 OZ.

1200-SERIES—EGER 1200

1915

Electric Luminous Submarine Bait

"THE GLOW WORM"

The Game Warden has approved this electric lighted, minnow-shaped Fish-Lure, which can be used as a regular bait, but with greater success. *The Electric Luminous Submarine Bait* gets the big ones and doubles the pleasure of fishing. A neat, tiny electric lamp and battery housed inside, throws the light outward. Reversing the battery; you then throw the light towards the rear through small port-holes. The greatest thing for dark days, among the lily-pads or at night. Simple, durable and practical. Price complete with extra cell, $1.50, with weedless hooks and spinners, $2.00. Send order today subject to our money back guarantee.

We have an exceptionally interesting proposition for dealers

The Electric Luminous Submarine Bait Co.
666 C Forest Home Avenue Milwaukee, Wisconsin

$100 – 150

$10

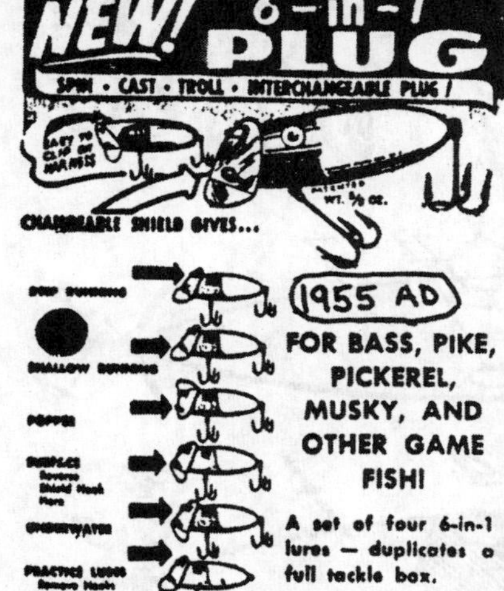
NEW! 6-in-1 PLUG
SPIN • CAST • TROLL • INTERCHANGEABLE PLUG!
CHANGEABLE SHIELD GIVES...
1955 AD
FOR BASS, PIKE, PICKEREL, MUSKY, AND OTHER GAME FISH!
A set of four 6-in-1 lures — duplicates a full tackle box.
Colors: Redhead, Perch, Pike, & Frog finishes.

ESSENTIAL PRODUCTS COMPANY
210 Fifth Avenue New York 10, N.Y.

RED HEAD/WHITE

1946

(PLASTIC)

$5

HELGA-DEVIL

ETCHEN TACKLE CO.
1014 Penobscot Bldg.
Detroit 26, Michigan

$10

(3 SIZES)
• 1½"
• 2¼"
• 2¾"

(EARLY 1900'S)

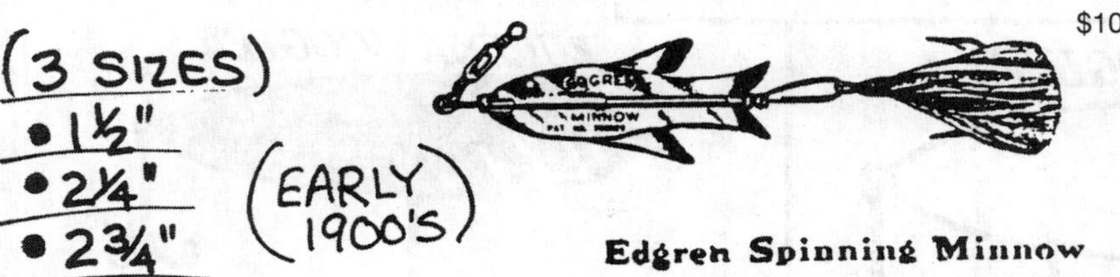
EDGREN MINNOW

Edgren Spinning Minnow

Operates on a center and always carries the treble hook directly back of itself. It revolves at so high a speed that it looks round and very much alive. It is made of the very best of material, heavily nickel plated and is guaranteed to give satisfaction as a fish getter. Made in three sizes.

No. 2002—Length of body, 1½ inches.
No. 2003—Length of body, 2¼ inches.
No. 2004—Length of body, 2¾ inches.

EDGREN MFG. CO.
CHICAGO, ILL.

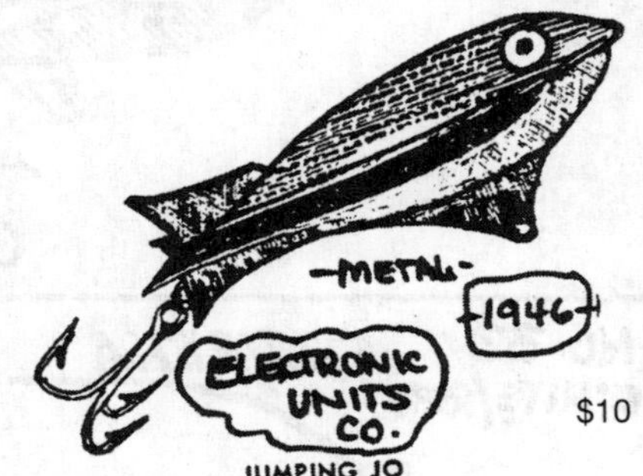
-METAL-
1946

ELECTRONIC UNITS CO.

$10

JUMPING JO

DAYTON, OHIO
NO. 4
3¾" - ⅔ OZ.

"CLEARS THE WATER WHEN JERKED"

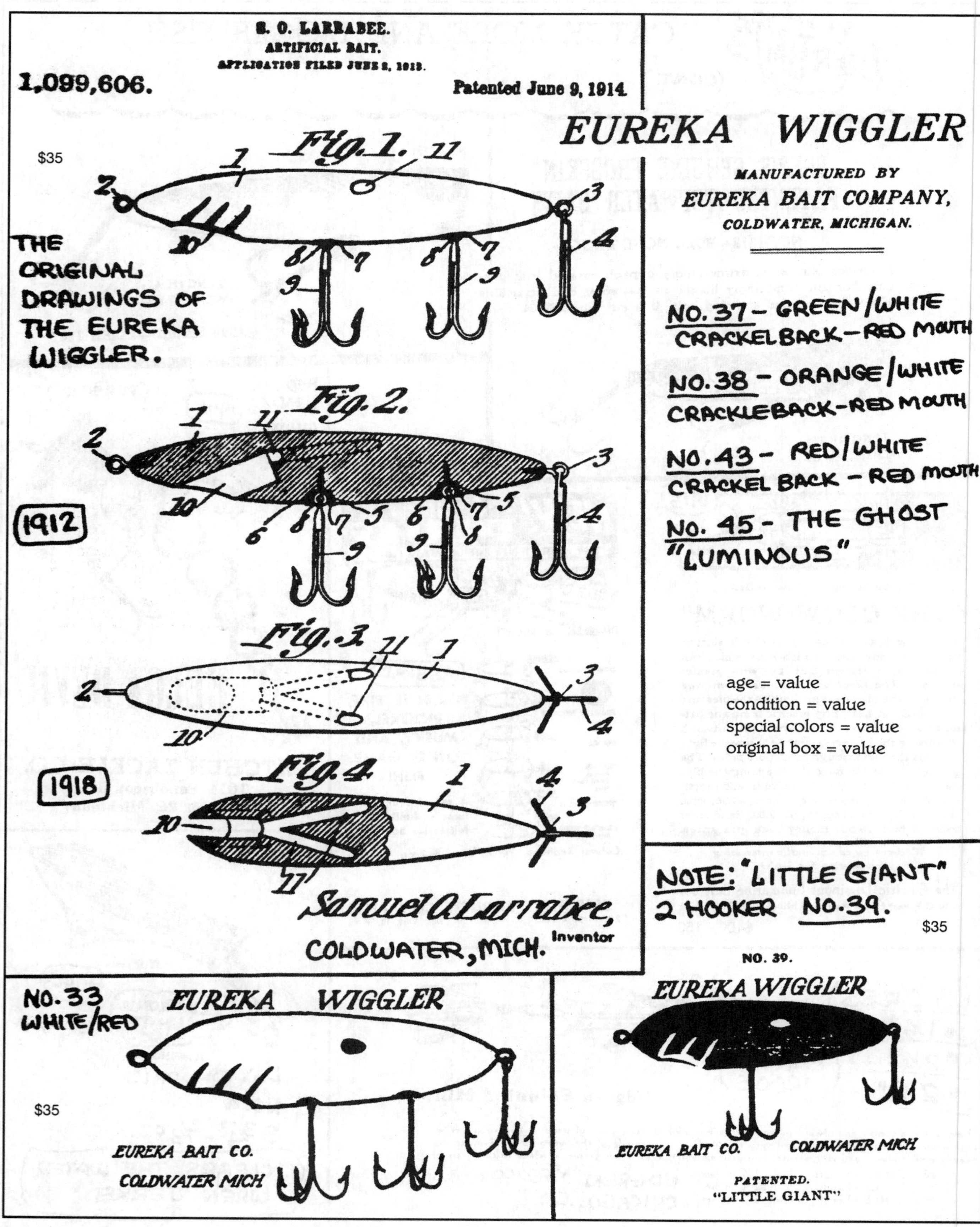
S. O. LARRABEE.
ARTIFICIAL BAIT.
APPLICATION FILED JUNE 2, 1913.
1,099,606.
Patented June 9, 1914.
$35
Fig. 1.
THE ORIGINAL DRAWINGS OF THE EUREKA WIGGLER.
Fig. 2.
1912
Fig. 3.
1918
Fig. 4.
Samuel A. Larrabee,
COLDWATER, MICH.
Inventor
EUREKA WIGGLER
MANUFACTURED BY
EUREKA BAIT COMPANY,
COLDWATER, MICHIGAN.
NO. 37 - GREEN/WHITE CRACKELBACK - RED MOUTH
NO. 38 - ORANGE/WHITE CRACKLEBACK - RED MOUTH
NO. 43 - RED/WHITE CRACKEL BACK - RED MOUTH
NO. 45 - THE GHOST "LUMINOUS"
NOTE: "LITTLE GIANT" 2 HOOKER NO. 39.
$35
NO. 39.
EUREKA WIGGLER
EUREKA BAIT CO.
COLDWATER MICH
PATENTED.
"LITTLE GIANT"
NO. 33 WHITE/RED
EUREKA WIGGLER
$35
EUREKA BAIT CO.
COLDWATER MICH

age = value
condition = value
special colors = value
original box = value

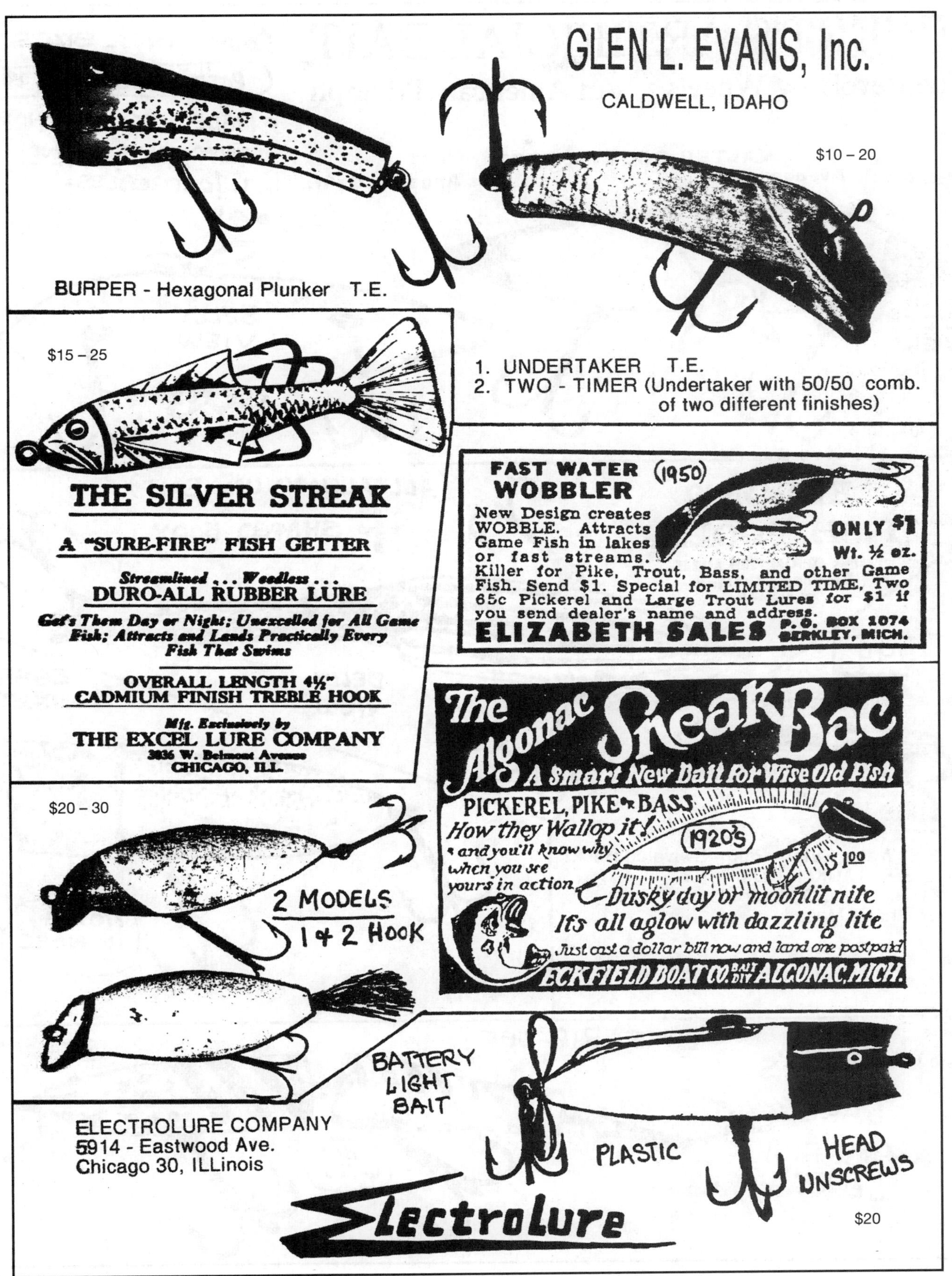
GLEN L. EVANS, Inc.
CALDWELL, IDAHO
$10 – 20
BURPER - Hexagonal Plunker T.E.
1. UNDERTAKER T.E.
2. TWO - TIMER (Undertaker with 50/50 comb. of two different finishes)
$15 – 25
THE SILVER STREAK
A "SURE-FIRE" FISH GETTER
Streamlined ... Weedless ...
DURO-ALL RUBBER LURE
Get's Them Day or Night; Unexcelled for All Game Fish; Attracts and Lands Practically Every Fish That Swims
OVERALL LENGTH 4½"
CADMIUM FINISH TREBLE HOOK
Mfg. Exclusively by
THE EXCEL LURE COMPANY
3836 W. Belmont Avenue
CHICAGO, ILL.
FAST WATER WOBBLER
(1950)
New Design creates WOBBLE. Attracts Game Fish in lakes or fast streams.
ONLY $1
Wt. ½ oz.
Killer for Pike, Trout, Bass, and other Game Fish. Send $1. Special for LIMITED TIME, Two 65c Pickerel and Large Trout Lures for $1 if you send dealer's name and address.
ELIZABETH SALES
P. O. BOX 1074
BERKLEY, MICH.
The Algonac Sneak Bac
A Smart New Bait for Wise Old Fish
PICKEREL, PIKE & BASS
How they Wallop it!
& and you'll know why when you see yours in action
1920'S
$1.00
Dusky day or moonlit nite
It's all aglow with dazzling lite
Just cast a dollar bill now and land one postpaid
ECKFIELD BOAT CO. BAIT DIV. ALGONAC, MICH.
$20 – 30
2 MODELS
1 & 2 HOOK
BATTERY LIGHT BAIT
ELECTROLURE COMPANY
5914 - Eastwood Ave.
Chicago 30, ILLinois
PLASTIC
HEAD UNSCREWS
Electrolure
$20

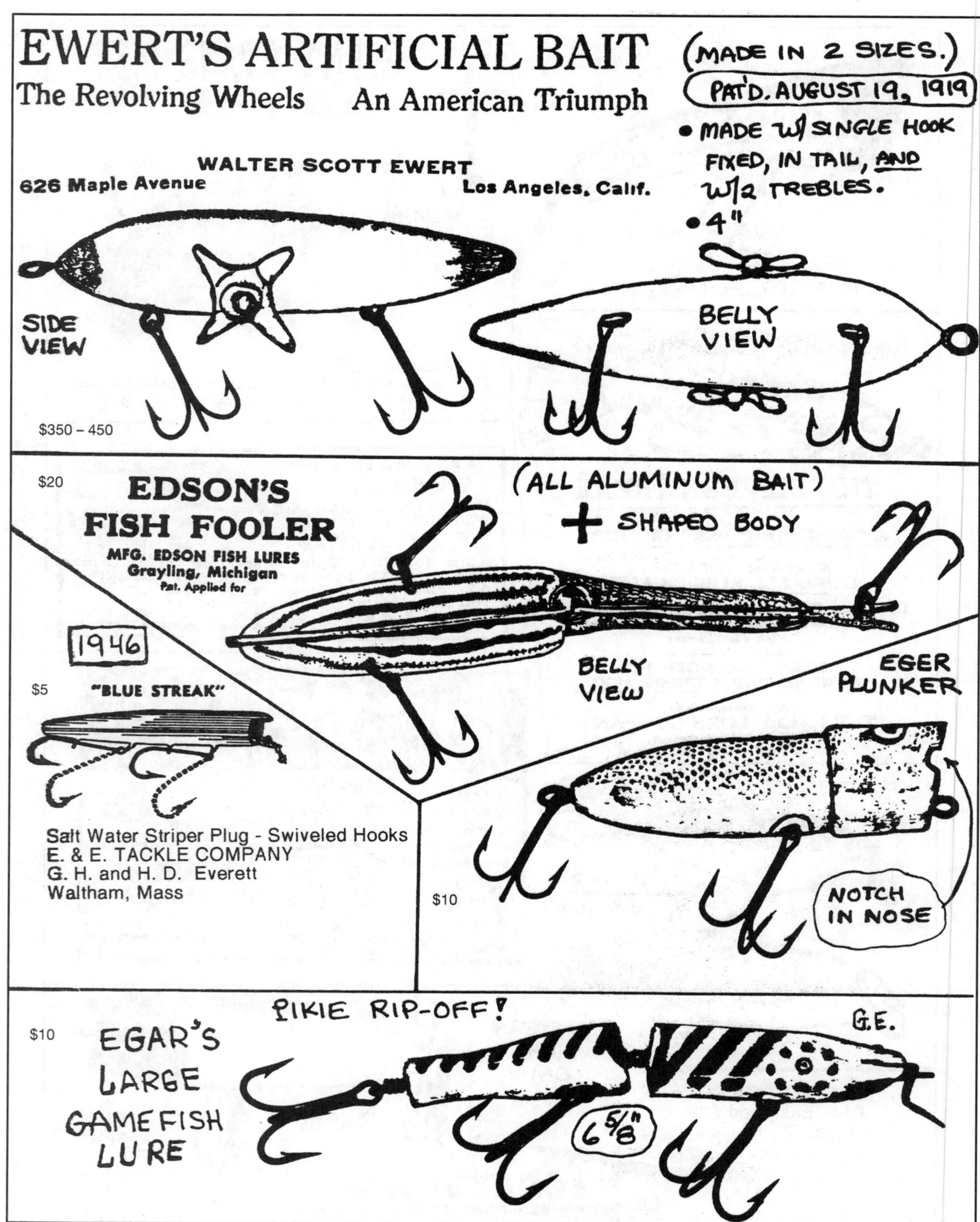
EWERT'S ARTIFICIAL BAIT
The Revolving Wheels An American Triumph
(MADE IN 2 SIZES.)
PAT'D. AUGUST 19, 1919
• MADE W/ SINGLE HOOK FIXED, IN TAIL, AND W/2 TREBLES.
• 4"
WALTER SCOTT EWERT
626 Maple Avenue
Los Angeles, Calif.
SIDE VIEW
BELLY VIEW
$350 – 450
$20
EDSON'S FISH FOOLER
MFG. EDSON FISH LURES
Grayling, Michigan
Pat. Applied for
(ALL ALUMINUM BAIT)
+ SHAPED BODY
1946
BELLY VIEW
EGER PLUNKER
$5
"BLUE STREAK"
Salt Water Striper Plug - Swiveled Hooks
E. & E. TACKLE COMPANY
G. H. and H. D. Everett
Waltham, Mass
$10
NOTCH IN NOSE
PIKIE RIP-OFF!
G.E.
$10
EGAR'S LARGE GAME FISH LURE
6 5/8"

NOTE: 3 DIFF. NAMES AND 3 DIFF. SPINNER DETAILS.

Little Egypt Wiggler

For deep water. Hook rides upright, making it nearly weedless.
Each ....

$15

THE EGYPT WIGGLER

A highly successful Black Bass Bait used with pork rind strips

$15

½ OZ.

NICKEL PLATED BRASS

$15

NEW EGYPT WIGGLER

All brass, nickel plated or natural brass finish if ordered. Weight, ½ oz.; 3/0 hook. Larger or smaller hooks will be furnished on request. Hook detachable.

The New Egypt is equipped with our new spinner, same as used on the Dixie Wiggler. See Page 4 for description.

The Skidder

For shallow water. Rides like the Little Egypt, but not as heavy.

$15

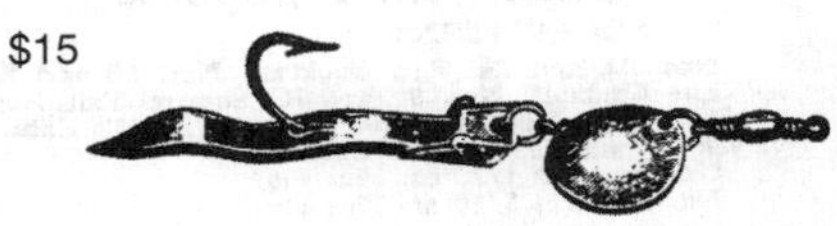

IN RESEARCHING THE EGYPT WIGGLER AND THE SKIDDER – I FOUND MUCH OVERLAP AND DUPLICATION, IDENTICAL ILLUSTRATIONS WITH DIFFERENT NAMES. I'M NOT SURE THE MFG. WAS ALL THAT CONSISTANT– SO WE SHOULDN'T WORRY ABOUT IT.

Some People

Little Egypt Wiggler, Weight, ½ oz.

are still ploughing with a crooked stick, others continue to fish with wooden plugs, covered with GANG HOOKS, while the "live ones" are fishing with Al. Foss Pork Rind Minnows.

Now, Mr. Fisherman, does not common sense tell you that if you are continually changing from one lure to another, that there is a screw loose, somewhere, and you have not found the right one yet?

Those who use Al. Foss Pork Rind Minnows simply lack the will power to change lures, but spend the time fishing that they formerly consumed in trying to find one that they could catch fish with.

1917 AD

$20

No 3 Oriental Wiggler, Solid Celluloid, Weight, ⅝ oz
No. 4 Oriental Wiggler, Solid Celluloid, Weight ½ oz.

Last year, about this time, we deposited $500.00 and issued a challenge to other manufacturers of artificial lures, for a competitive fishing contest, our lures against theirs, and while they all make strong claims about the fish-taking qualities of their goods they would not dare enter a contest of this kind.

The Oriental Wiggler and Little Egypt Wiggler for bait-casting and trolling, the Skidder for shallow and weedy water.

We put up pork rind strips, cut the correct size for these lures, they are thin and flexible, free from grease, and the genuine bear our label.

We would prefer to sell you through your dealer, BUT if he is "asleep at the switch" send in your remittance for samples, or better still send for a full set and one extra bottle of pork rinds which will last you all season.

$15

Skidder, Weight, ½ oz.

SKIDDER–

Made by

AL. FOSS

1716 to 1736 Columbus Road, Cleveland, O.

THE AL FOSS ORIENTAL WIGGLER WAS ONE OF THE FIRST– IF NOT THE FIRST– ALL PLASTIC LURES.

(3 MODELS) GLASS EYES

SOMETIMES FURNISHED WITH WIRE WEED GUARD.

COLORS:
- ALL WHITE
- ALL RED
- RED & WHITE

CELLULOID – THEN MADE OF PYRALIN.

PAT'D. APRIL 30, 1918

$20

Oriental Wiggler

The bodies of the Oriental Baits are made of Pyralin and are furnished in Red and White, Yellow and White, or Black and White.

Pork Rind is attached by impaling on the hook and buttoning the forward end to little button as per illustration. Our Pork Rind strips are punctured at the proper places for ready attachment. Hook detachable.

Other size hooks furnished if specified.

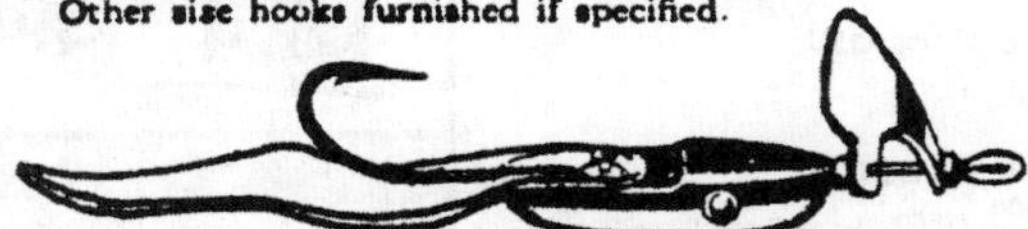

No. 3—Weight—5/8 ounce, 3/0 Hook.......

Baby Oriental Wiggler

No. 4—Weight—1/2 ounce, 1/0 Hook.....

Musky Oriental Wiggler (NO. 3M)

Re-enforced and strengthened to use on Musky, Tarpon, Tuna, and all large salt water fish.

Used in conjunction with our Musky Pork Rind Strips.

Musky Oriental—Weight—5/8 ounce, 5/0 Hook

AL FOSS Pork Rind Lures

Dixie Wiggler

Red and white bucktail standard, also furnished in red, white, black, brown, yellow or orange. The Dixie has a very low center of gravity and the design makes it practically weedless. Enamel decorated.

TRUE TEMPER MODEL HAD A "PONCA" SPINNER. PAT. APRIL 17, 1928

NEW-1929

$15

No. 13—Weight—5/8 ounce, 3/0 Hook.
No. 14—Weight—1/2 ounce, 1/0 Hook.

The Mouse

Red and white bucktail standard, also furnished in white, red, brown, black, yellow or orange. The mouse is the most recent addition to our line and has a very attractive motion in the water. Fishermen have been more than enthusiastic about the results obtained with this lure.

LATER, THE TRUE TEMPER MODEL HAD THE "PONCA" DOUBLE BLADE — UNBALANCED, SPINNER.

NEW IN 1931

$20

No. 15—Weight—5/8 ounce, 3/0 Hook.

FOSS FROG WIGGLER

2 SIZES

The very last word in an artificial bait casting or trolling lure. It will outwiggle anything that you have ever tied to your line. It is practically weedless and snagproof. One bucktail and one plain hook furnished with each bait. Made in two sizes:

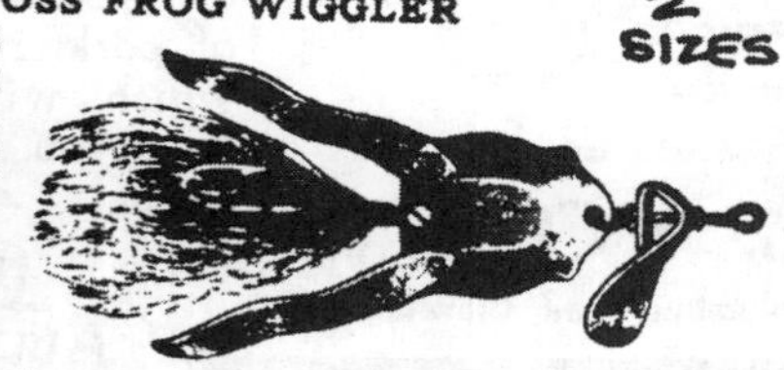

$20

No. 11—weight ⅝ oz.—3/0 Hook
No. 12—weight ½ oz.—1/0 Hook.

FOSS JAZZ WIGGLER

(2 SIZES)
NO. 9 – 5/8 oz.
NO. 10 – 1/2 oz.

JAZZ WIGGLER

1/2 OR 5/8 OZ.

JAZZ WIGGLER

$15

Shimmy Wiggler

Red and white bucktail standard, also furnished in white, red, brown, black, yellow or orange. A composite lure combining all the good things that have ever happened in a successful fish lure—the spinner, the spoon, the fly, and the deadly pork rind.

PAT'D.- 1918

$15

NICKEL SILVER OR GOLD

No. 5—Weght—5/8 ounce, 3/0 Hook.
No. 6—Weight—1/2 ounce, 1/0 Hook.

$15

Shimmyette Fly-Rod Wiggler,

A miniature Pork Rind Wiggler. Body and spinner made of nickel silver—spinner shaft of music wire. No. 7 with a No. 3 Sproat hook—weight 1/16 oz. No. 8 with a No. 6 Sproat hook—weight 1/20 oz. Owing to its peculiar construction lifts off the water with perfect ease.

An excellent lure for bass, trout and other game fish.

Used either with or without our fly-rod pork rind. More effective with the pork.

$15

Shimmyette Fly Spinner

SIX PATTERNS–

Nos. 8A and 7A, Red Bucktail; Nos. 8B and 7B White Bucktail; Nos. 8C and 7C, Squirrel Tail; Nos. 8D and 7D, Red Ibis; Nos. 8E and 7E, Al's Cahill; Nos. 8F and 7F, Caster's Choice.

No. 8 weight 1/20 oz. Plus Fly.
No. 7 weight 1/16 oz. Plus Fly.

$15

NO. 10 SHIMMY SPOON

NO. 9 SHIMMY SPOON

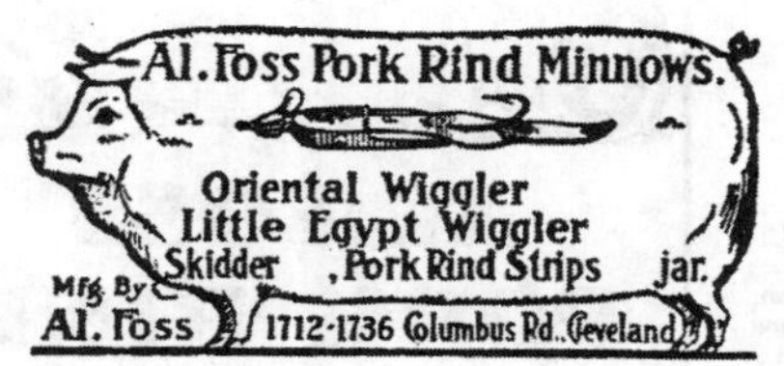
Al. Foss Pork Rind Minnows.
Oriental Wiggler
Little Egypt Wiggler
Skidder , Pork Rind Strips jar.
Mfg. By
Al. Foss
1712-1736 Columbus Rd., Cleveland

(2 SIZES)

$10

FLY ROD

NEW "DOC" PATTERN

A new True Temper light weight fly spinner. Will spin with a minimum of motion.

No. 34 Large No. 3 Sneck hook
No. 35 Small No. 6 Sneck hook

(2 SIZES)

NO. 27 – 5/8 oz.

$10

AL FOSS HELL CAT

A casting spoon with improved spinner and weed guard. A real bass lure. Red bucktail only. Wt. 5/8 oz. 5/0 hook.

No. 28 1/2 oz.

EXTRA BUCKTAILS FOR

AL FOSS LURES

	Colors:	
Red	Red and White	No. AF3— Size 3/0 Hook...
Natural	Black and Yellow	
Black	White	No. AF1— Size 1/0 Hook....
Yellow	Black and White	

NO. 32

$10

FLITTER SPOON No. 32

FLITTER SPOON — A combination of our Flitter fly spoon with 12 inch stainless wire leader, and casting weight. Bright finish. A very effective deep running bait especially recommended for White Bass, Wall-Eyed Pike and Small Mouth Bass.
No. 32

$10

AL FOSS

HELL CAT'S JERRY

New fast sinking lure for deep water fishing. Lively action. Wt. 1/2 oz. 3/0 hook. Red bucktail only.
No. 30—

(DIVER)

$10

NO. 29 TOM 1/2 oz.

CAN BE USED AS A "SKIPPER"

AL FOSS BELIEVED IN HIS PRODUCTS. IN A 1921 AD HE SAID – "ALMOST EVERY DEALER HAS AL FOSS MINNOWS. IF YOURS IS DEAD FROM THE NECK UP, HUNT UP A NEW DEALER OR SEND US HIS NAME AND WE WILL SUPPLY YOU DIRECT!"

AL FOSS LURES CAME IN UNIQUE METAL BOXES.

COLLECTING TIPS:

- THE EARLY MODELS MADE BY AL FOSS, HAD THE NAME AL FOSS AND A PATENT DATE ON IT, IN SMALL PRINT.
- THE LATER VINTAGE AL FOSS WAS MFG'D. BY

  TRUE TEMPER PRODUCTS
  THE AMERICAN FORK & HOE CO.
  SPORTING GOODS DIVISION
  GENEVA, OHIO

  AND HAD A LARGER SIZE AL FOSS-ONLY ON THE SPINNERS.

BASS—4 3/8 inches long, 1/2-inch wide, 12 strips per bottle.
SIDESTEPPER—3 1/4 inches long, 1/2-inch wide. 12 strips per bottle.
FLY ROD—2 inches long, 1/4-inch wide. 24 strips per bottle.
MUSKY—5 1/4 inches long, 5/8-inch wide. 6 strips per bottle.
THE FROG—3 inches long, 3/4-inch wide. 6 strips per bottle.

THE FROG

The new Frog Pork Rind Strip is a sure fire bait. We have been experimenting with the design for over a year. Experts, who have tried it, have, without exception, been enthusiastic over it. Don't fail to have a bottle in your tackle box if you want to be sure of getting fish.

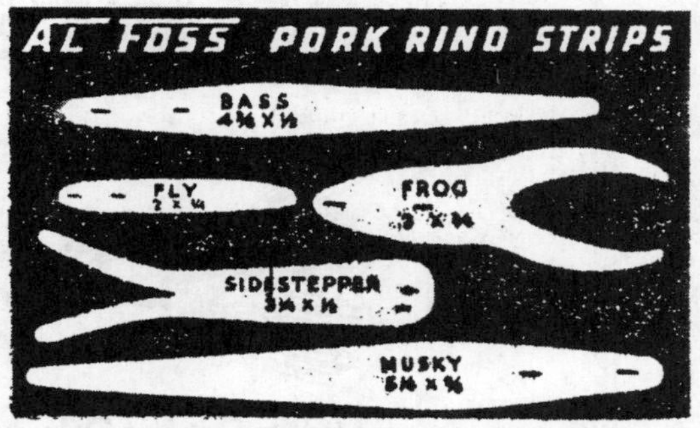
AL FOSS PORK RIND STRIPS
BASS 4 3/8 X 1/2
FLY 2 X 1/4
FROG 3 X 3/4
SIDESTEPPER 3 1/4 X 1/2
MUSKY 5 1/4 X 5/8

(ACTUAL SIZE)

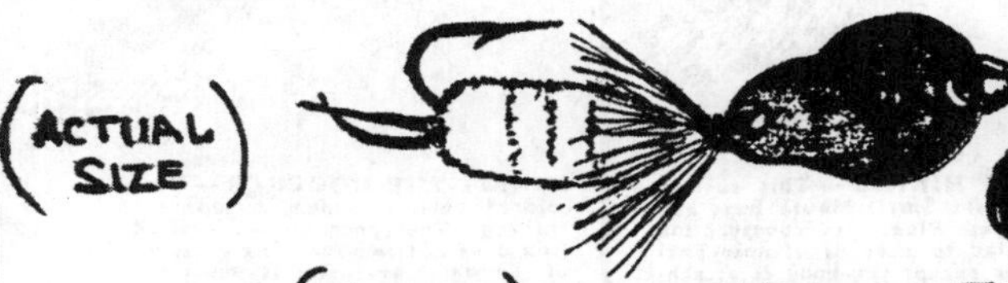

$15

(ILLUS.) → • SHIMMY, JR. NO. 7
• SHIMMY, JR. NO. 8

ALSO MADE A SHIMMY SPINNER – NO. 8. (SPINNING SIZE)

$10

2 SIZES

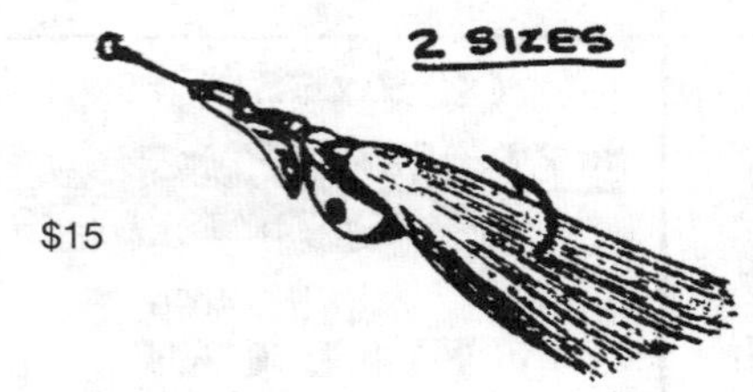

$15

Al Foss Pork Rind

THE SHEIK — One of the most successful baits ever introduced. The Big Mouth Bass of Florida and Tiger Muskies of Height of Land Lakes in Northern Ontario, take it with equal fierceness. Statically and dynamically balanced, it casts like a bullet even into a strong head wind.

No. 19 — Weight ⅝ oz. 5/0 hook, red bucktail.......

No. 20 — Weight ½ oz. 3/0 hook, red bucktail.......

$15

AL FOSS

FAN DANCER

Small teaser spoon mounted on hook provides added attraction. For all game fish. Red and white bucktail only. Can be converted to deep or shallow water fishing.

No. 18—Wt. ⅜ oz. 3/0 hook....

AL.FOSS PORK RIND MINNOWS

Manufactured by

AL.FOSS ... CLEVELAND ... O.

NO.33 AL FOSS RUBBER FROG

$15

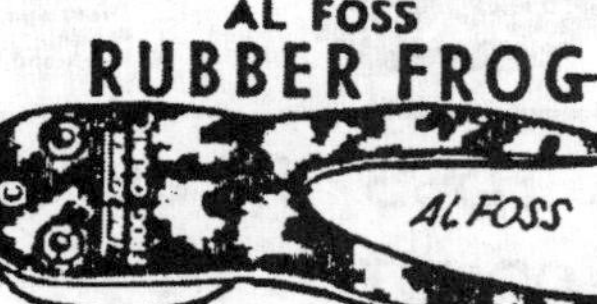
AL FOSS

Attach to Al Foss, Johnson, Liotta Single hook casting lures. Fish can't resist the wiggling action. An extra casting bait can be made by attaching frog to casting weight with long shank hook and spinner attached.

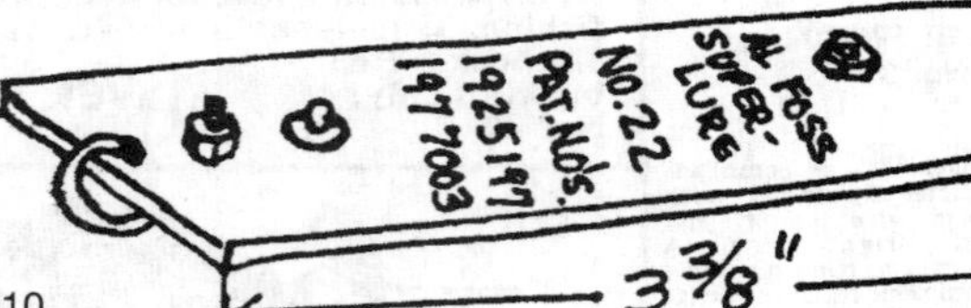
AL FOSS
SUPER-LURE
NO. 22
PAT. NOS.
1925197
1977003
3⅜"

$10

HEAVY METAL SPOON NO. 22 "SUPER-LURE"

AL FOSS *Bass* POP CASTING BAIT

NEW-1941

A chugging surface lure. Weedless. Action of a frog swimming on surface. A real killer for large and small mouth bass. Wt. ⅝ oz.

No. 31 — Chrome spoon with rubber frog chunk. Size 5/0 hook.

$15

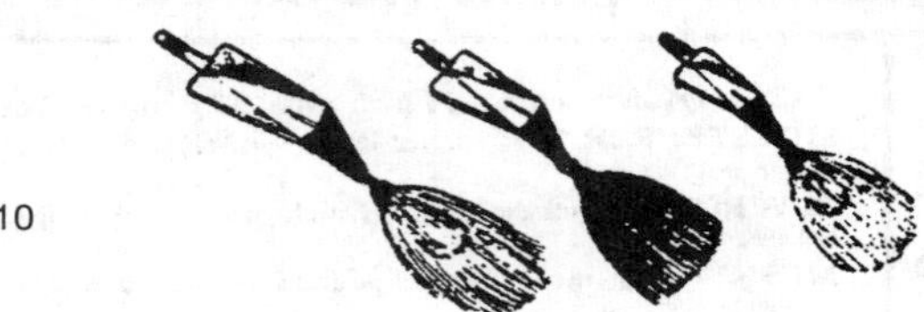

$10

FLITTER FLY

THE FLITTER FLY — This is a new fly rod lure that is packed with action for Bass and Trout.

No. 24—For Bass and Large Trout. Length 3", weight 1/20 oz., polished blade, bucktail fly with No. 3 Sproat hook.

No. 25 — For Bass and Trout. Length 2¼", weight 1/24 oz., polished blade, bucktail fly with No. 6 Sneck hook.

No. 26 — For Trout, Bluegills and Panfish. Length 1½", weight 1/36 oz., polished blade, bucktail fly with No. 6 Sneck hook.

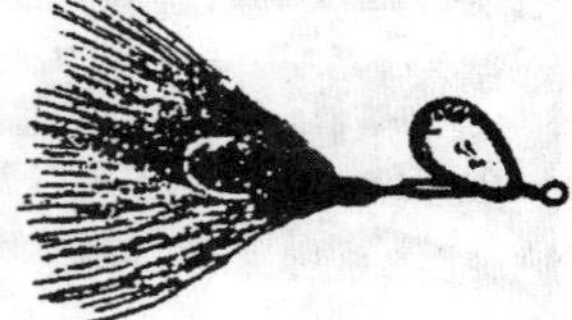

$10

Made In One Size Only

No. 1 hardened silver blade highly polished, solid round brass bead, strong short music wire shaft with *quick hook change*—No. 3 Sneck ribbed waterproof hook; red and white bucktail standard but can be furnished in white, red, yellow, orange, brown or black.

No. 1 Bucktail Fly Spinner

MINNIE-THE-MOOCHER

A jointed spoon lure for casting; has a wiggling motion no solid bait can have. Can be used with bucktail or pork rind strip. Plated and enamel finish.

$15

LITTLE MINNIE — This casting spoon is for Small Mouth Bass and Wall-Eyed Pike. Its construction is similar to that of Minnie-The-Moocher except the hook is attached directly to the forward section. Price each ....

No. 17 — Weight ⅜ oz. 3/0 hook, red and white bucktail—nickle plated.

No. 17R — Weight ⅜ oz. 3/0 hook, red and white bucktail — red and white enamel.

No. 17B — Weight ⅜ oz. 3/0 hook, red and white bucktail — black and white enamel.

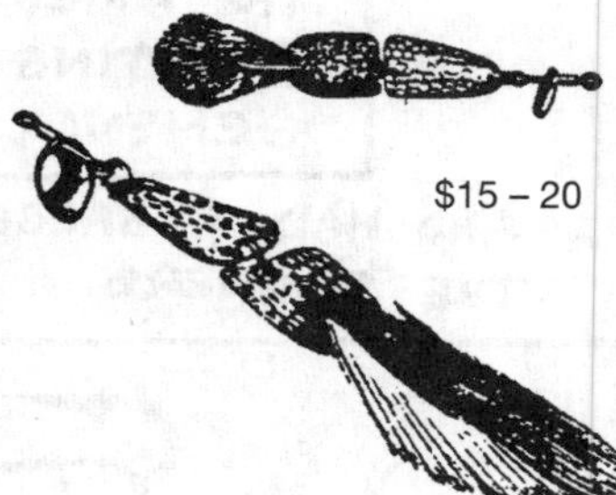

$15 – 20

MINNIE-THE-MOOCHER — This jointed casting spoon is tops for trolling. The spoon on the forward link does not revolve. The pressure of the water against this imparts a wiggling motion to the bait which gives it great attracting power for Pike and Large Mouth Bass. each ....

No. 16 — Weight ⅝ oz. 3/0 hook, red and white bucktail—nickle plated.

No. 16R — Weight ⅝ oz. 3/0 hook, red and white bucktail — red and white enamel.

No. 15B — Weight ⅝ oz. 3/0 hook, red and white bucktail — black and white enamel.

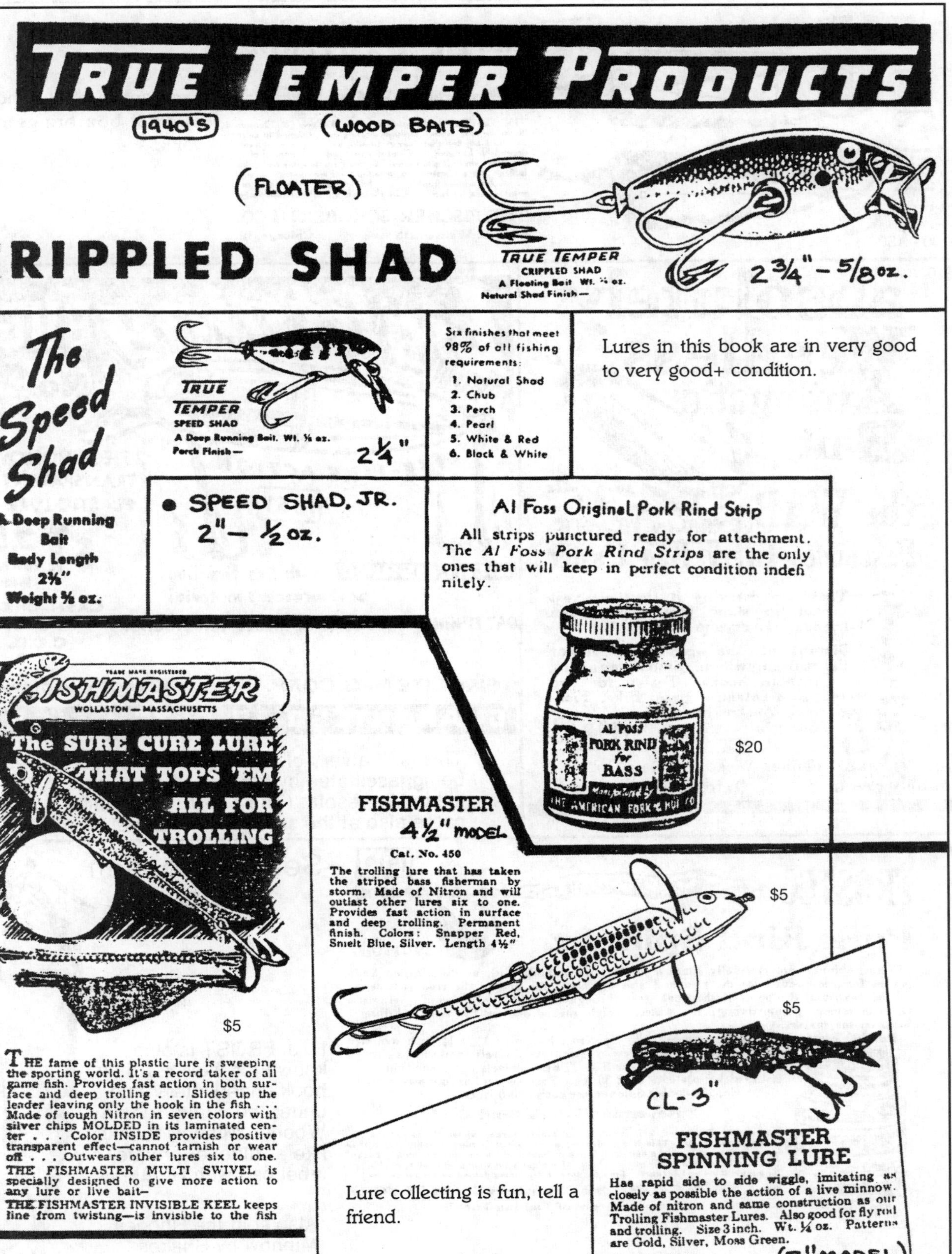
TRUE TEMPER PRODUCTS
(1940'S)
(WOOD BAITS)
$5
(FLOATER)
CRIPPLED SHAD
TRUE TEMPER
CRIPPLED SHAD
A Floating Bait
Natural Shad Finish—
2 3/4" – 5/8 oz.
$5
The Speed Shad
A Deep Running Bait
Body Length 2⅝"
Weight ⅜ oz.
TRUE TEMPER
SPEED SHAD
A Deep Running Bait. Wt. ⅜ oz.
Perch Finish—
2 1/4"
Six finishes that meet 98% of all fishing requirements:
1. Natural Shad
2. Chub
3. Perch
4. Pearl
5. White & Red
6. Black & White
Lures in this book are in very good to very good+ condition.
• SPEED SHAD, JR.
2" – 1/2 oz.
Al Foss Original Pork Rind Strip
All strips punctured ready for attachment. The Al Foss Pork Rind Strips are the only ones that will keep in perfect condition indefinitely.
AL FOSS
PORK RIND
for
BASS
THE AMERICAN FORK & HOE CO
$20
TRADE MARK REGISTERED
FISHMASTER
WOLLASTON — MASSACHUSETTS
The SURE CURE LURE THAT TOPS 'EM ALL FOR TROLLING
$5
THE fame of this plastic lure is sweeping the sporting world. It's a record taker of all game fish. Provides fast action in both surface and deep trolling . . . Slides up the leader leaving only the hook in the fish . . . Made of tough Nitron in seven colors with silver chips MOLDED in its laminated center . . . Color INSIDE provides positive transparent effect—cannot tarnish or wear off . . . Outwears other lures six to one.
THE FISHMASTER MULTI SWIVEL is specially designed to give more action to any lure or live bait—
THE FISHMASTER INVISIBLE KEEL keeps line from twisting—is invisible to the fish
FISHMASTER
4 1/2" MODEL
Cat. No. 450
The trolling lure that has taken the striped bass fisherman by storm. Made of Nitron and will outlast other lures six to one. Provides fast action in surface and deep trolling. Permanent finish. Colors: Snapper Red, Smelt Blue, Silver. Length 4½"
$5
$5
CL-3"
FISHMASTER SPINNING LURE
Has rapid side to side wiggle, imitating as closely as possible the action of a live minnow. Made of nitron and same construction as our Trolling Fishmaster Lures. Also good for fly rod and trolling. Size 3 inch. Wt. ¼ oz. Patterns are Gold, Silver, Moss Green.
Cat. No. CL 3
(3" MODEL)
Lure collecting is fun, tell a friend.

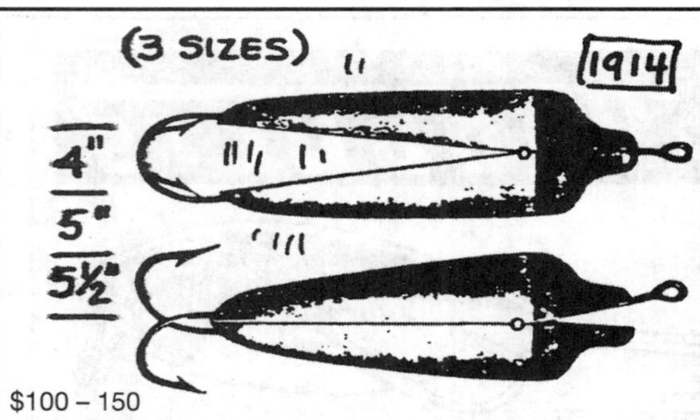
(3 SIZES)
1914
4"
5"
5½"

"THE CAPTOR"

(PAT PENDING)

The New Artificial Weedless Floating Bait

THE CAPTOR the invention of J. B. Fischer of Chicago, Ill., is the only perfect weedless floating lure, designed to catch and hold any fish that attempts to take it. If you want a real dependable lure give the Captor a trial and be convinced of its superiority over all other lures. If you want to enjoy real game fishing get a Captor. Write today for free catalog or send for regular finish— for luminous finish—state size wanted, 4 in. for Bass, 5 in. for Pickerel, 5½ in. for Muskalonge.

THE FISCHER-SCHUBERTH CO.
5820 S. Wentworth Ave. Chicago, Ill.

$100 – 150

Excellent to mint condition original box brings more value.

$15

absolutely Weedless Automatic Bait

When the fish bites it it looks like this.

the WAB (PYRALIN) PLASTIC

Fascinates Every Bait Caster

They are carrying it in their vest pocket to show their fishing fan friends. Everyone wants it.

Slam it into the weed bed, rushes or lily pads anywhere. Smooth as a plug without hooks. Tested for two years catching Bass, Pike, Pickerel, Muskies and even Sunfish.

1924

Fenner Weedless Bait Co.
Oxford, Wis.

Lightning BUG No. 2

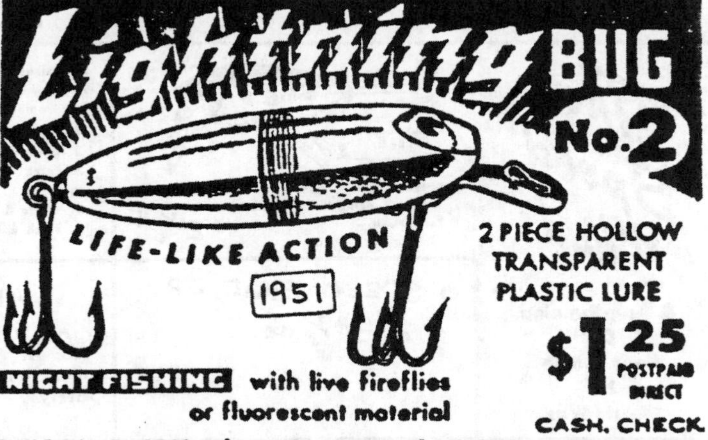
LIFE-LIKE ACTION
1951

2 PIECE HOLLOW TRANSPARENT PLASTIC LURE

$1.25 POSTPAID DIRECT

NIGHT FISHING with live fireflies or fluorescent material

DAY FISHING -1001 color or insect combinations

CASH, CHECK M. O. OR C.O.D.

FIRE-LITE MFG. CORP. GOSPORT, INDIANA

GUARANTEED TO CATCH FISH!

This isn't a very old bait, but I remember being fascinated by fireflies when I was a kid in Minnesota. (The $?*&/!! Mosquitos came also at the same time. (Lots of them)

$10

$15 – 25

1919

FROSTCO Pork Rind Spinner

NO. 100

These spinners are especially adapted for the use of pork rind, as the Frostco Snap is used for a connection for the rind and also the hook; the end of the rind is fastened by the snap and the point of the hook goes through the middle of the rind, giving it a wavy movement going through the water, which makes one of the most "killing" lures on the market.

No. 100 has a single blade, pear-shaped, German silver, size 1¼ x ¾ inch mounted between two of the new Neverkink Swivels and hand-forged O'Shaughnessy hook No. 3/0. These swivels are made from brass balls, nickel-plated. Test 30 lbs. Each swivel has four swivel ball.

No. 101 double Spinner, see cut on rind label.

"Nevermiss" Pork Rind Bait

Nevermiss Pork Rind Bait is cut in the proper shape and weight to get the best action in the water. This is a rind only, which makes it more durable. One strip naturally lasts as long as a bait, as it is almost impossible to tear out the hook. Packed 10 strips in a glass jar. If you can't get from your dealer, send for sample Rind and Spinner. *Send for booklet describing fishing tackle specialties.*

PORK RIND

ACTUAL SIZE

H. J. FROST & CO., 92 Chambers St., NEW YORK
Manufacturers of Fishing Tackle

Senate Wooden Minnow

$150 – 200

H. J. FROST is also known for their 3 & 5 hook underwaters sold under the name Senate Wooden Minnow. Looks like a Pflueger private label bait with HPGM.

Also sold the Rhodes Minnow by Shakespeare at one time.

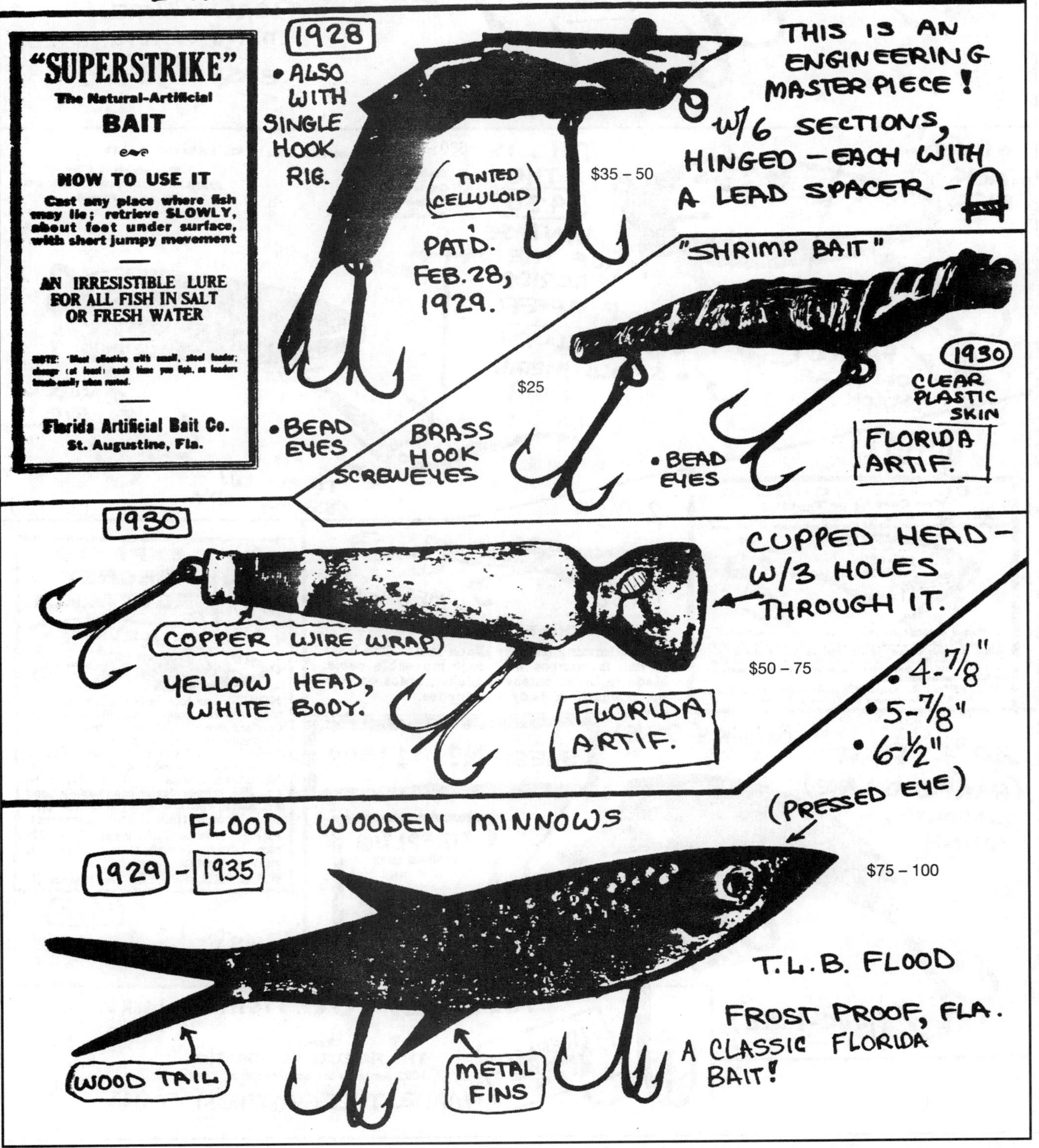
FLORIDA HAD THEIR OWN BAIT MFG'. INDUSTRY - ALOT OF THEIR INVENTIONS WERE LATER MARKETED NATIONALLY.
"SUPERSTRIKE"
The Natural-Artificial
BAIT
HOW TO USE IT
Cast any place where fish may lie; retrieve SLOWLY, about foot under surface, with short jumpy movement
AN IRRESISTIBLE LURE FOR ALL FISH IN SALT OR FRESH WATER
Florida Artificial Bait Co.
St. Augustine, Fla.
1928
• ALSO WITH SINGLE HOOK RIG.
TINTED CELLULOID
PAT'D. FEB. 28, 1929.
• BEAD EYES
$35 – 50
THIS IS AN ENGINEERING MASTER PIECE!
W/6 SECTIONS, HINGED - EACH WITH A LEAD SPACER -
"SHRIMP BAIT"
1930
CLEAR PLASTIC SKIN
FLORIDA ARTIF.
$25
BRASS HOOK SCREWEYES
• BEAD EYES
1930
CUPPED HEAD - W/3 HOLES THROUGH IT.
COPPER WIRE WRAP
YELLOW HEAD, WHITE BODY.
FLORIDA ARTIF.
$50 – 75
• 4-7/8"
• 5-7/8"
• 6-1/2"
FLOOD WOODEN MINNOWS
1929 - 1935
(PRESSED EYE)
$75 – 100
T.L.B. FLOOD
FROST PROOF, FLA.
A CLASSIC FLORIDA BAIT!
WOOD TAIL
METAL FINS

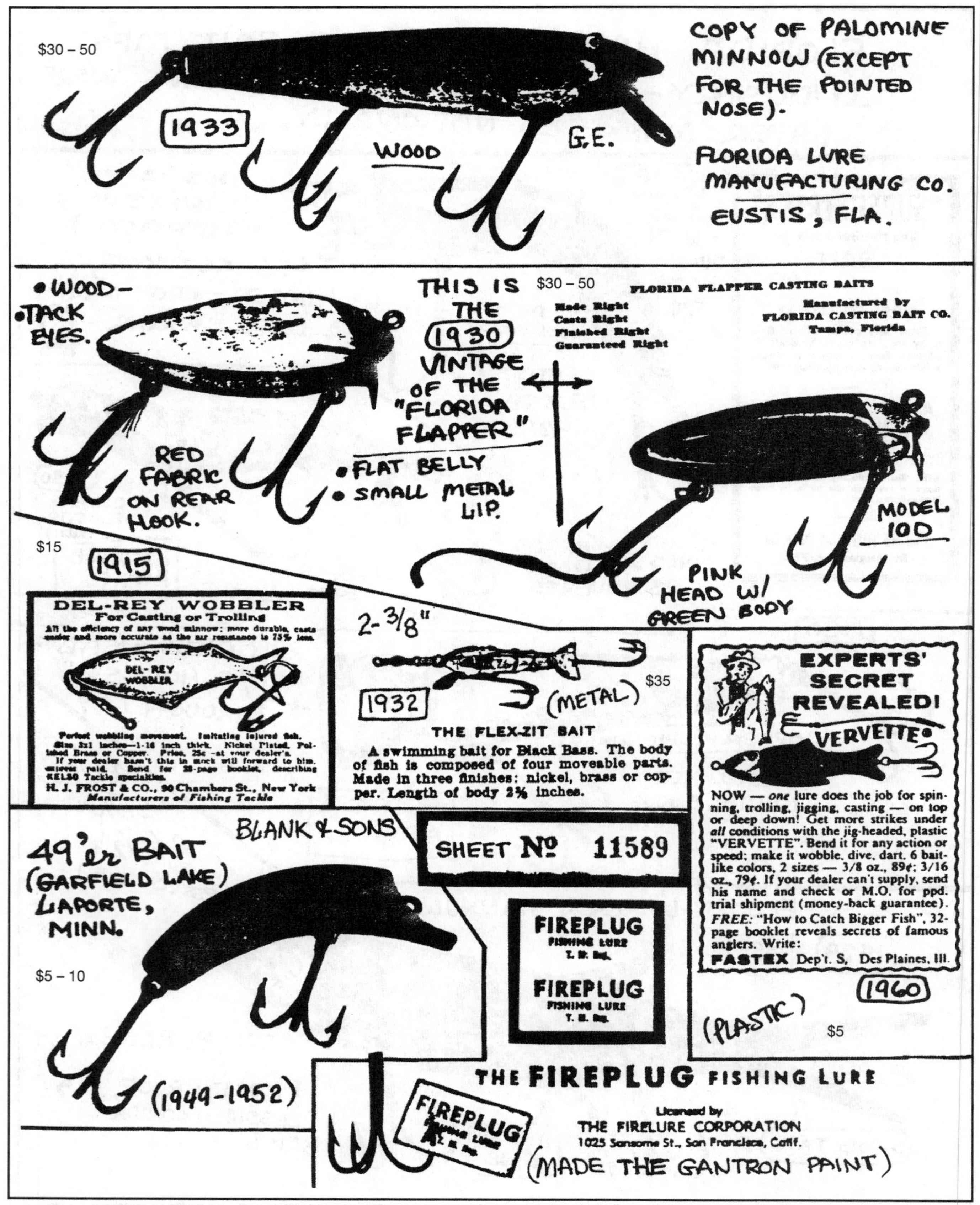
$30 – 50
1933
WOOD
G.E.
COPY OF PALOMINE MINNOW (EXCEPT FOR THE POINTED NOSE).
FLORIDA LURE MANUFACTURING CO.
EUSTIS, FLA.
• WOOD-
• TACK EYES.
THIS IS THE 1930 VINTAGE OF THE "FLORIDA FLAPPER"
$30 – 50
FLORIDA FLAPPER CASTING BAITS
Made Right
Casts Right
Finished Right
Guaranteed Right
Manufactured by
FLORIDA CASTING BAIT CO.
Tampa, Florida
RED FABRIC ON REAR HOOK.
• FLAT BELLY
• SMALL METAL LIP.
MODEL 100
PINK HEAD W/ GREEN BODY
$15
1915
DEL-REY WOBBLER
For Casting or Trolling
All the efficiency of any wood minnow; more durable, casts easier and more accurate as the air resistance is 75% less.
DEL-REY WOBBLER
Perfect wobbling movement. Imitating injured fish. Size 3x1 inches—1-16 inch thick. Nickel Plated, Polished Brass or Copper. Price, 25c at your dealer's.
If your dealer hasn't this in stock will forward to him, express paid. Send for 28-page booklet, describing KELSO Tackle specialties.
H. J. FROST & CO., 90 Chambers St., New York
Manufacturers of Fishing Tackle
2-3/8"
1932
(METAL)
$35
THE FLEX-ZIT BAIT
A swimming bait for Black Bass. The body of fish is composed of four moveable parts. Made in three finishes: nickel, brass or copper. Length of body 2⅜ inches.
EXPERTS' SECRET REVEALED!
VERVETTE
NOW — one lure does the job for spinning, trolling, jigging, casting — on top or deep down! Get more strikes under all conditions with the jig-headed, plastic "VERVETTE". Bend it for any action or speed; make it wobble, dive, dart. 6 bait-like colors, 2 sizes — 3/8 oz., 89¢; 3/16 oz., 79¢. If your dealer can't supply, send his name and check or M.O. for ppd. trial shipment (money-back guarantee).
FREE: "How to Catch Bigger Fish", 32-page booklet reveals secrets of famous anglers. Write:
FASTEX Dep't. S, Des Plaines, Ill.
1960
(PLASTIC)
$5
BLANK & SONS
SHEET № 11589
49'er BAIT (GARFIELD LAKE) LAPORTE, MINN.
$5 – 10
(1949-1952)
FIREPLUG FISHING LURE T. M. Reg.
FIREPLUG FISHING LURE T. M. Reg.
THE FIREPLUG FISHING LURE
Licensed by
THE FIRELURE CORPORATION
1025 Sansome St., San Francisco, Calif.
(MADE THE GANTRON PAINT)

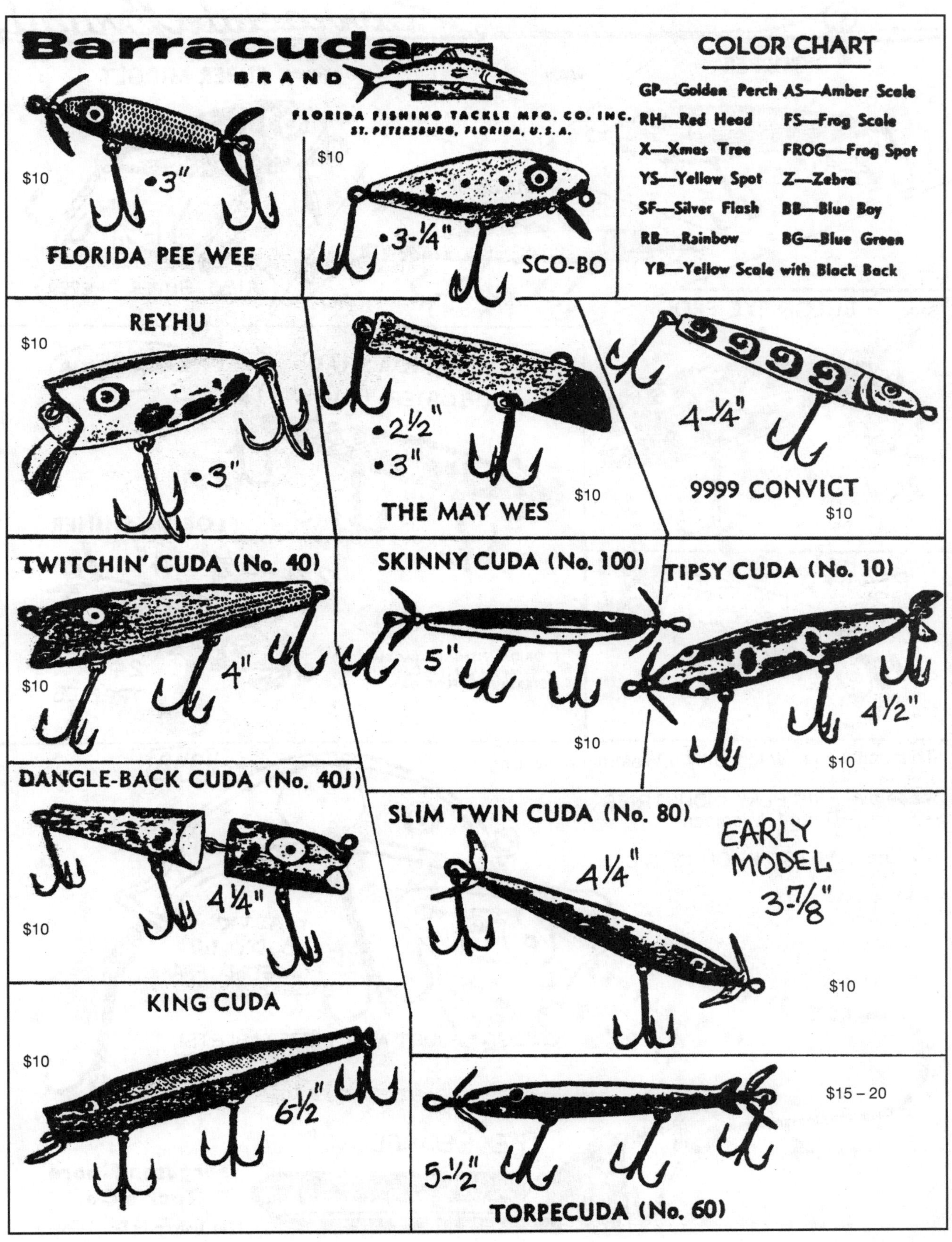
Barracuda
BRAND
FLORIDA FISHING TACKLE MFG. CO. INC.
ST. PETERSBURG, FLORIDA, U.S.A.
COLOR CHART
GP—Golden Perch AS—Amber Scale
RH—Red Head FS—Frog Scale
X—Xmas Tree FROG—Frog Spot
YS—Yellow Spot Z—Zebra
SF—Silver Flash BB—Blue Boy
RB—Rainbow BG—Blue Green
YB—Yellow Scale with Black Back
$10
•3"
FLORIDA PEE WEE
$10
•3-1/4"
SCO-BO
REYHU
$10
•3"
•2½"
•3"
THE MAY WES
$10
4-1/4"
9999 CONVICT
$10
TWITCHIN' CUDA (No. 40)
$10
4"
SKINNY CUDA (No. 100)
5"
$10
TIPSY CUDA (No. 10)
4½"
$10
DANGLE-BACK CUDA (No. 40J)
4¼"
$10
SLIM TWIN CUDA (No. 80)
4¼"
EARLY MODEL 3-7/8"
$10
KING CUDA
$10
6-½"
$15 – 20
5-½"
TORPECUDA (No. 60)

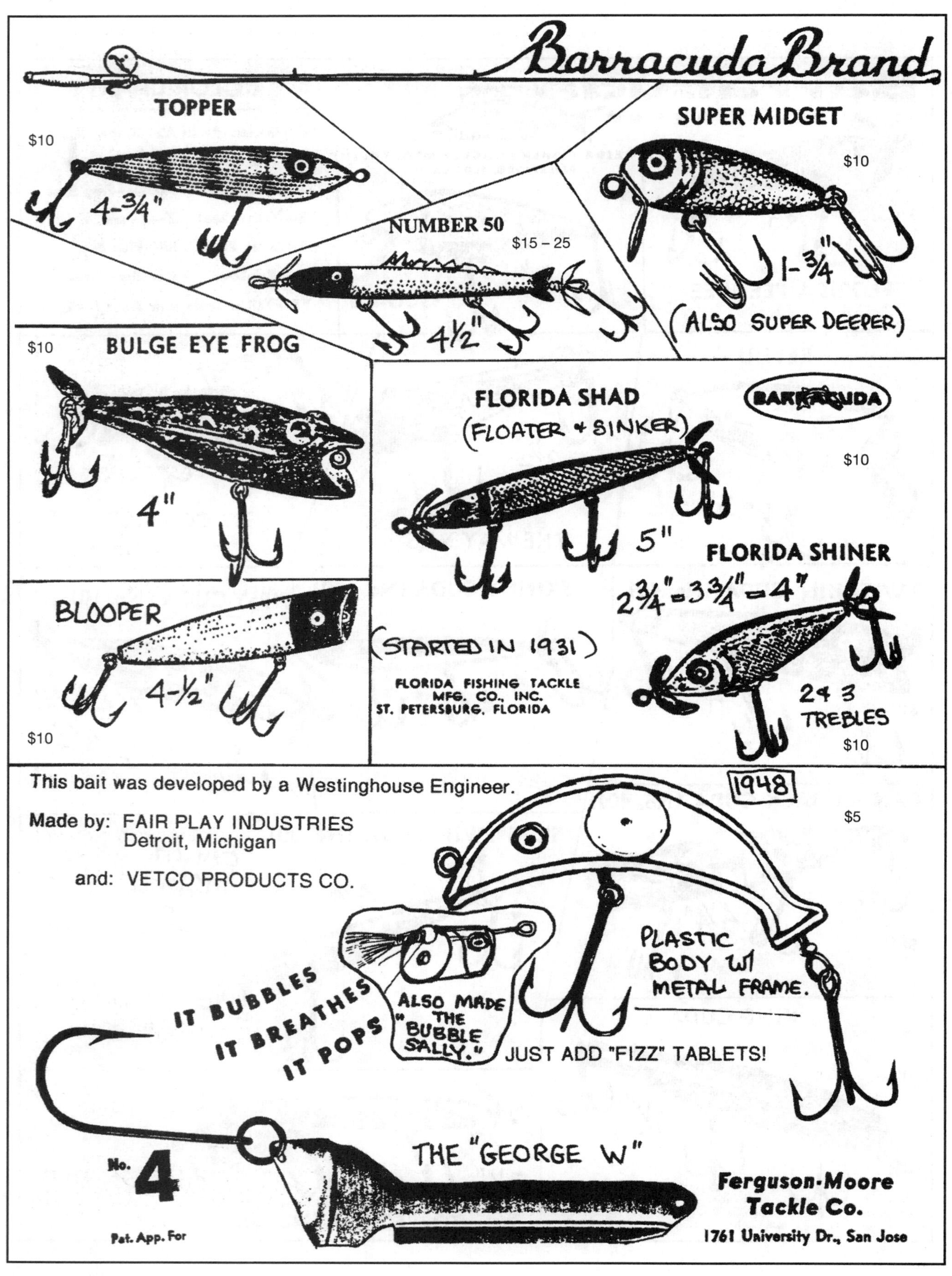
Barracuda Brand
TOPPER
$10
4-3/4"
SUPER MIDGET
$10
1-3/4"
(ALSO SUPER DEEPER)
NUMBER 50
$15 – 25
4½"
$10
BULGE EYE FROG
4"
FLORIDA SHAD
(FLOATER + SINKER)
BARRACUDA
$10
5"
FLORIDA SHINER
2¾"-3¾"-4"
2 & 3
TREBLES
$10
BLOOPER
4-½"
$10
(STARTED IN 1931)
FLORIDA FISHING TACKLE
MFG. CO., INC.
ST. PETERSBURG, FLORIDA
This bait was developed by a Westinghouse Engineer.
1948
$5
Made by: FAIR PLAY INDUSTRIES
Detroit, Michigan
and: VETCO PRODUCTS CO.
PLASTIC
BODY W/
METAL FRAME.
IT BUBBLES
IT BREATHES
IT POPS
ALSO MADE
THE
"BUBBLE
SALLY."
JUST ADD "FIZZ" TABLETS!
THE "GEORGE W"
No.
4
Pat. App. For
Ferguson-Moore
Tackle Co.
1761 University Dr., San Jose

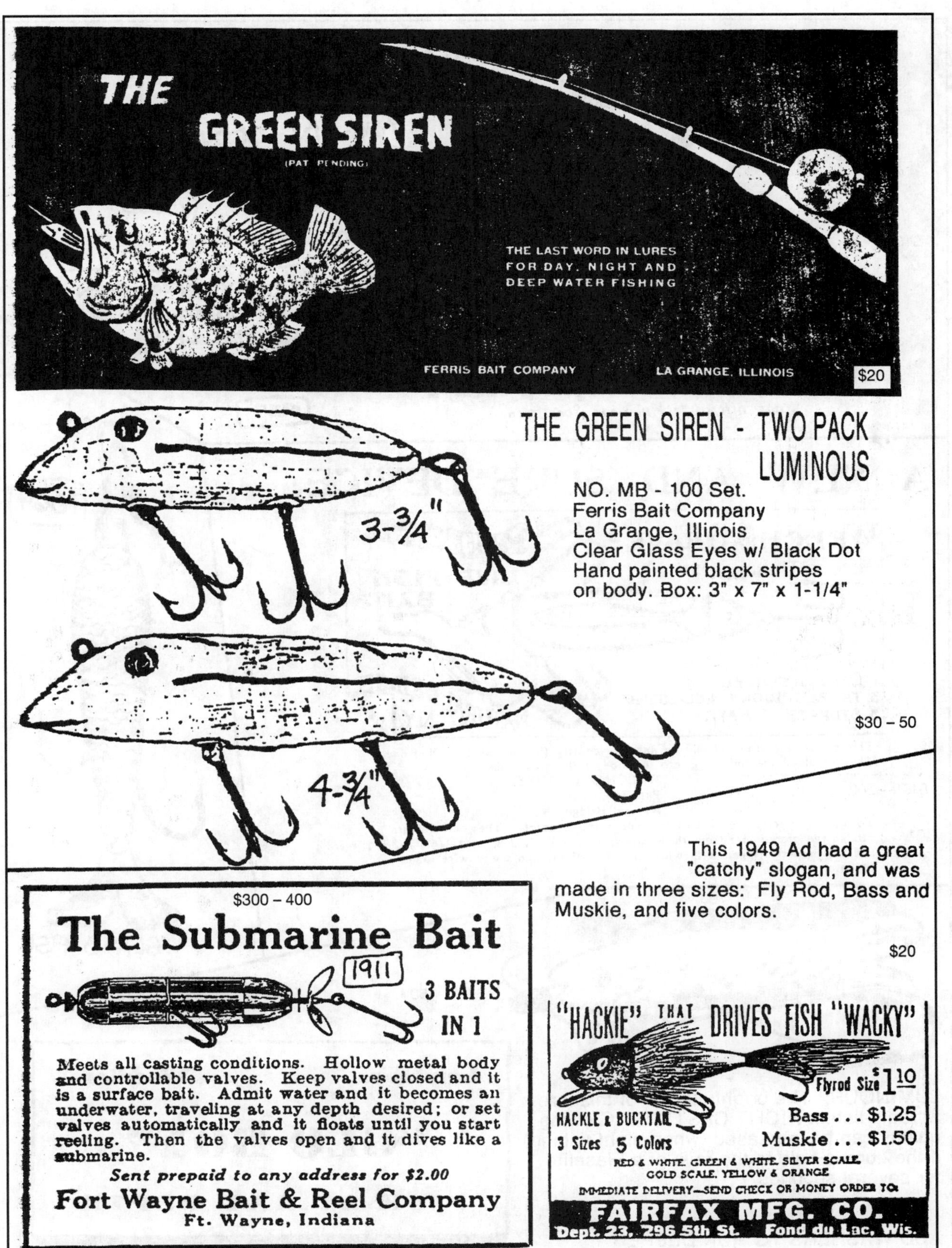
THE
GREEN SIREN
(PAT PENDING)
THE LAST WORD IN LURES
FOR DAY, NIGHT AND
DEEP WATER FISHING
FERRIS BAIT COMPANY
LA GRANGE, ILLINOIS
3-3/4"
4-3/4"
The Submarine Bait
1911
3 BAITS
IN 1
Meets all casting conditions. Hollow metal body and controllable valves. Keep valves closed and it is a surface bait. Admit water and it becomes an underwater, traveling at any depth desired; or set valves automatically and it floats until you start reeling. Then the valves open and it dives like a submarine.
Sent prepaid to any address for $2.00
Fort Wayne Bait & Reel Company
Ft. Wayne, Indiana
"HACKIE" THAT DRIVES FISH "WACKY"
Flyrod Size $1.10
HACKLE & BUCKTAIL
Bass . . . $1.25
3 Sizes 5 Colors
Muskie . . . $1.50
RED & WHITE, GREEN & WHITE, SILVER SCALE, GOLD SCALE, YELLOW & ORANGE
IMMEDIATE DELIVERY—SEND CHECK OR MONEY ORDER TO:
FAIRFAX MFG. CO.
Dept. 23, 296 5th St. Fond du Lac, Wis.

$20

THE GREEN SIREN - TWO PACK LUMINOUS

NO. MB - 100 Set.
Ferris Bait Company
La Grange, Illinois
Clear Glass Eyes w/ Black Dot
Hand painted black stripes on body. Box: 3" x 7" x 1-1/4"

$30 – 50

$300 – 400

This 1949 Ad had a great "catchy" slogan, and was made in three sizes: Fly Rod, Bass and Muskie, and five colors.

$20

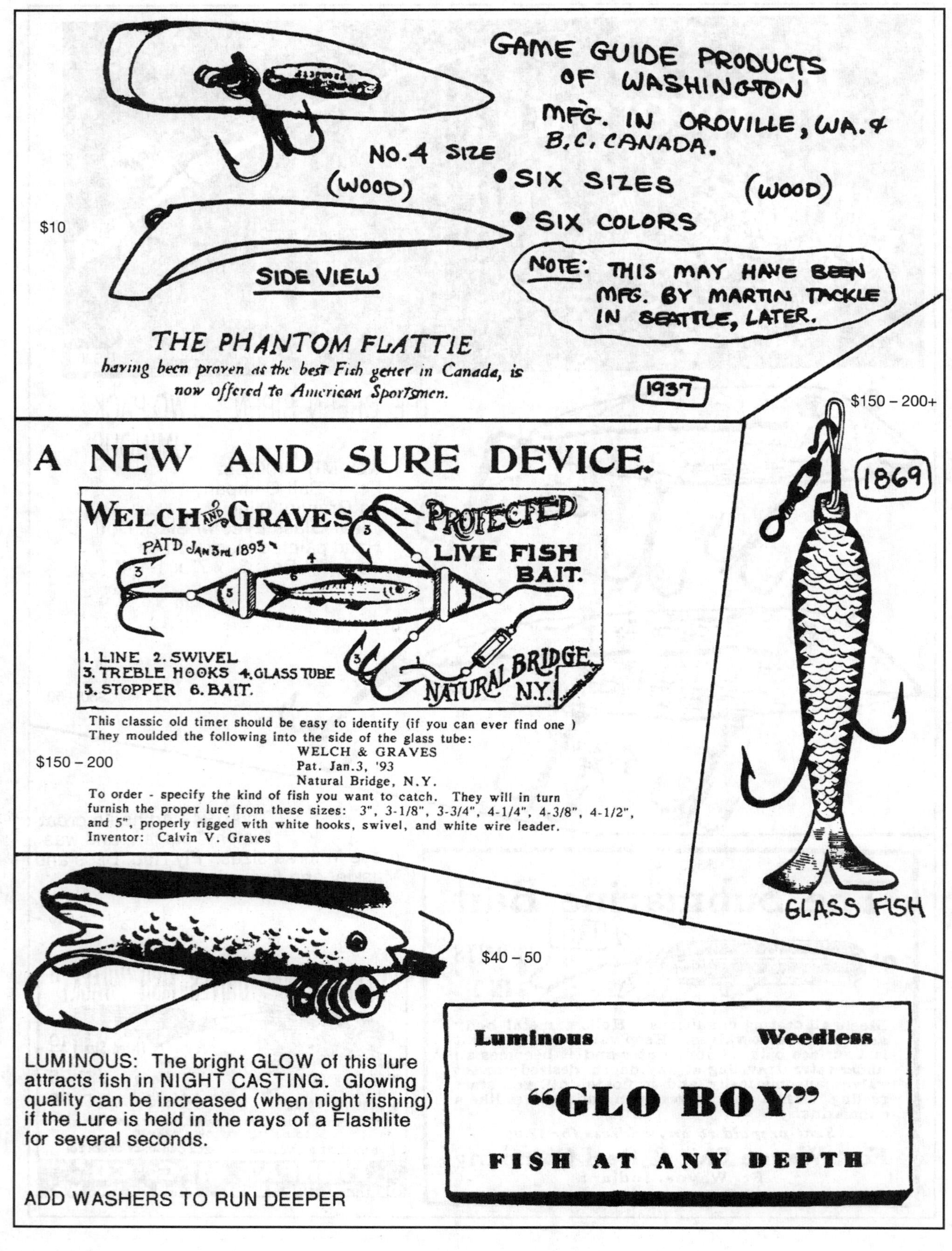
GAME GUIDE PRODUCTS
OF WASHINGTON
MFG. IN OROVILLE, WA. &
B.C. CANADA.
NO. 4 SIZE
(WOOD)
• SIX SIZES
(WOOD)
• SIX COLORS
$10
SIDE VIEW
NOTE: THIS MAY HAVE BEEN MFG. BY MARTIN TACKLE IN SEATTLE, LATER.
THE PHANTOM FLATTIE
having been proven as the best Fish getter in Canada, is now offered to American Sportsmen.
1937
$150 – 200+
A NEW AND SURE DEVICE.
1869
WELCH AND GRAVES PROTECTED
PATD JAN 3rd 1893
LIVE FISH BAIT.
1. LINE 2. SWIVEL
3. TREBLE HOOKS 4. GLASS TUBE
5. STOPPER 6. BAIT.
NATURAL BRIDGE N.Y.
This classic old timer should be easy to identify (if you can ever find one)
They moulded the following into the side of the glass tube:
WELCH & GRAVES
Pat. Jan.3, '93
Natural Bridge, N.Y.
$150 – 200
To order - specify the kind of fish you want to catch. They will in turn furnish the proper lure from these sizes: 3", 3-1/8", 3-3/4", 4-1/4", 4-3/8", 4-1/2", and 5", properly rigged with white hooks, swivel, and white wire leader.
Inventor: Calvin V. Graves
GLASS FISH
$40 – 50
LUMINOUS: The bright GLOW of this lure attracts fish in NIGHT CASTING. Glowing quality can be increased (when night fishing) if the Lure is held in the rays of a Flashlite for several seconds.
Luminous
Weedless
"GLO BOY"
FISH AT ANY DEPTH
ADD WASHERS TO RUN DEEPER

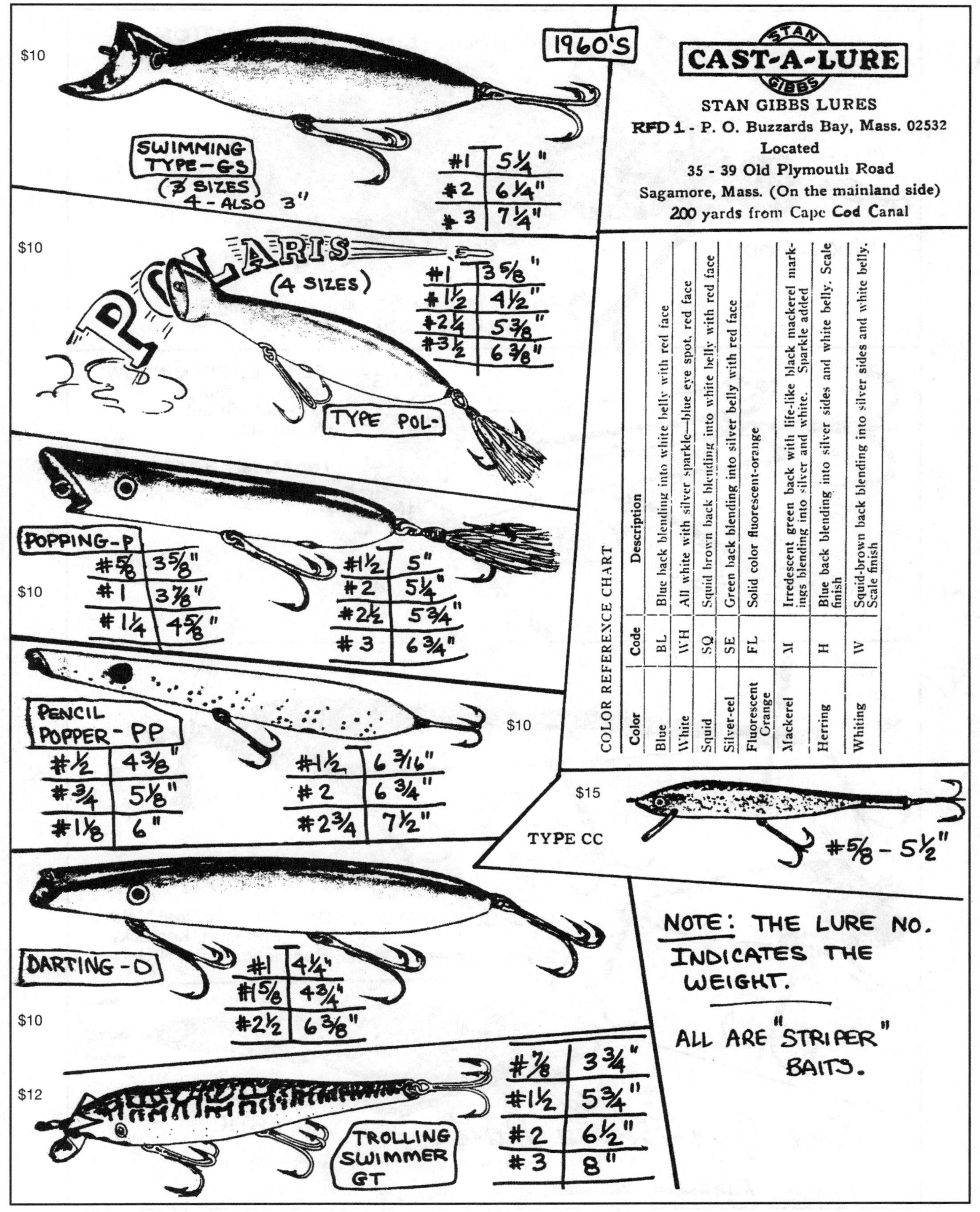

1960'S

CAST-A-LURE

STAN GIBBS

STAN GIBBS LURES
RFD 1 - P. O. Buzzards Bay, Mass. 02532
Located
35 - 39 Old Plymouth Road
Sagamore, Mass. (On the mainland side)
200 yards from Cape Cod Canal

$10

SWIMMING TYPE—GS (3 SIZES) 4 - ALSO 3"

#1	5¼"
#2	6¼"
#3	7¼"

$10

POLARIS (4 SIZES)

TYPE POL-

#1	3⅝"
#1½	4½"
#2¼	5⅜"
#3½	6⅜"

$10

POPPING-P

#⅝	3⅝"
#1	3⅞"
#1¼	4⅝"
#1½	5"
#2	5¼"
#2½	5¾"
#3	6¾"

$10

PENCIL POPPER - PP

#½	4⅜"
#¾	5⅛"
#1⅛	6"
#1½	6 3/16"
#2	6¾"
#2¾	7½"

COLOR REFERENCE CHART

Color	Code	Description
Blue	BL	Blue back blending into white belly with red face
White	WH	All white with silver sparkle—blue eye spot, red face
Squid	SQ	Squid brown back blending into white belly with red face
Silver-eel	SE	Green back blending into silver belly with red face
Fluorescent Orange	FL	Solid color fluorescent-orange
Mackerel	M	Irredescent green back with life-like black mackerel markings blending into silver and white. Sparkle added
Herring	H	Blue back blending into silver sides and white belly. Scale finish
Whiting	W	Squid-brown back blending into silver sides and white belly. Scale finish

$15

TYPE CC

#⅝ - 5½"

$10

DARTING - D

#1	4¼"
#1⅝	4¾"
#2½	6⅜"

$12

TROLLING SWIMMER GT

#⅞	3¾"
#1½	5¾"
#2	6½"
#3	8"

NOTE: THE LURE NO. INDICATES THE WEIGHT.

ALL ARE "STRIPER" BAITS.

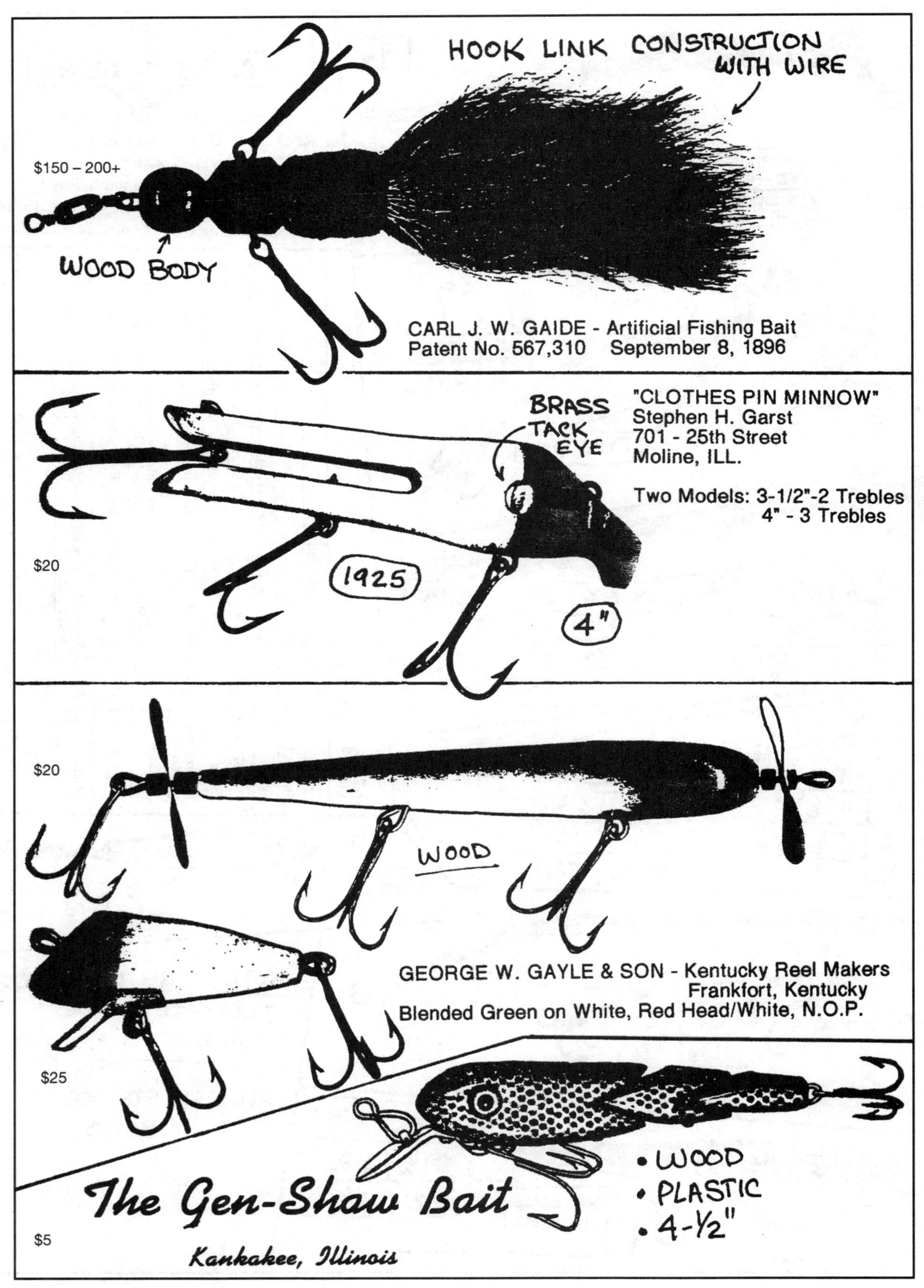
HOOK LINK CONSTRUCTION WITH WIRE
$150 – 200+
WOOD BODY
CARL J. W. GAIDE - Artificial Fishing Bait
Patent No. 567,310 September 8, 1896
BRASS TACK EYE
"CLOTHES PIN MINNOW"
Stephen H. Garst
701 - 25th Street
Moline, ILL.
Two Models: 3-1/2"-2 Trebles
4" - 3 Trebles
$20
1925
4"
$20
WOOD
GEORGE W. GAYLE & SON - Kentucky Reel Makers
Frankfort, Kentucky
Blended Green on White, Red Head/White, N.O.P.
$25
The Gen-Shaw Bait
Kankakee, Illinois
• WOOD
• PLASTIC
• 4-1/2"
$5

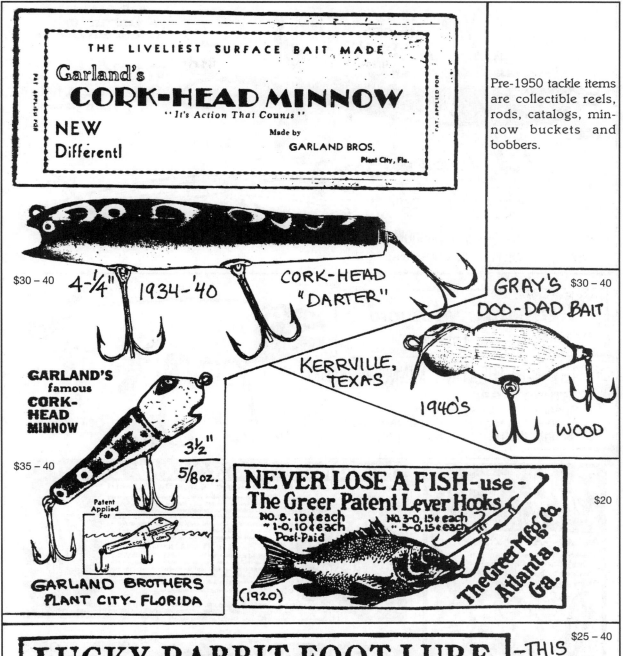

THE LIVELIEST SURFACE BAIT MADE

Garland's

CORK-HEAD MINNOW

"It's Action That Counts"

NEW

Different!

Made by

GARLAND BROS.

Plant City, Fla.

PAT. APPLIED FOR

Pre-1950 tackle items are collectible reels, rods, catalogs, minnow buckets and bobbers.

$30 – 40

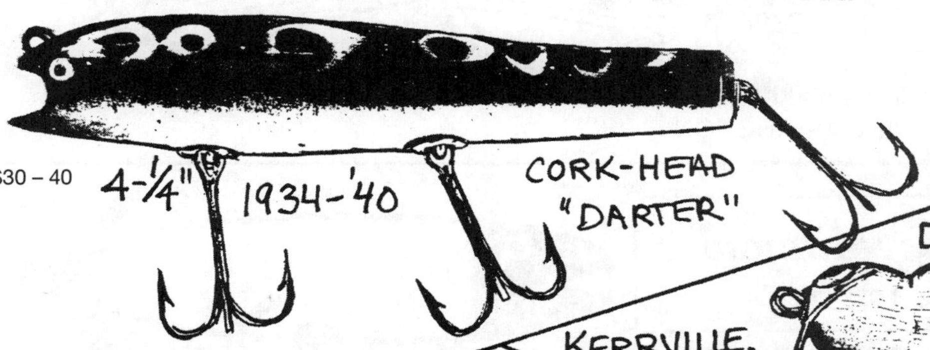

4-1/4" 1934-'40 CORK-HEAD "DARTER"

GRAY'S DOO-DAD BAIT $30 – 40

KERRVILLE, TEXAS

1940'S

WOOD

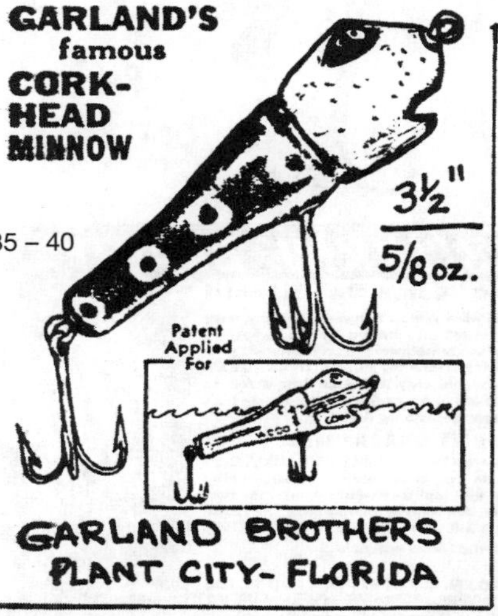

GARLAND'S famous CORK-HEAD MINNOW

3½" 5/8 oz.

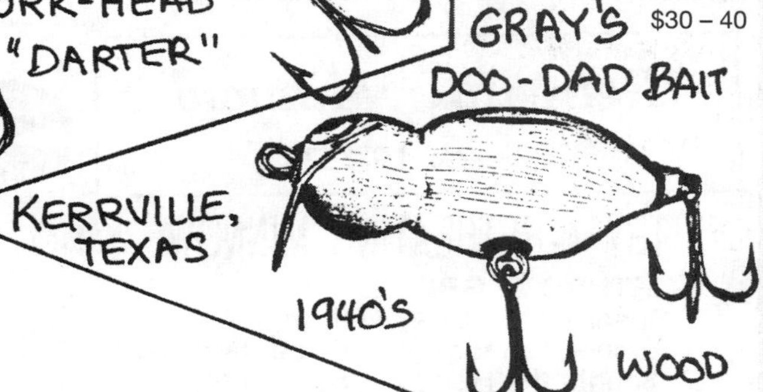

$35 – 40

Patent Applied For

GARLAND BROTHERS PLANT CITY- FLORIDA

NEVER LOSE A FISH-use-

The Greer Patent Lever Hooks

NO. 8. 10¢ each
" 1-0, 10¢ each
Post-Paid

NO. 3-0, 15¢ each
" .5-0, 15¢ each

The Greer Mfg. Co. Atlanta, Ga.

(1920)

$20

$25 – 40

LUCKY RABBIT FOOT LURE

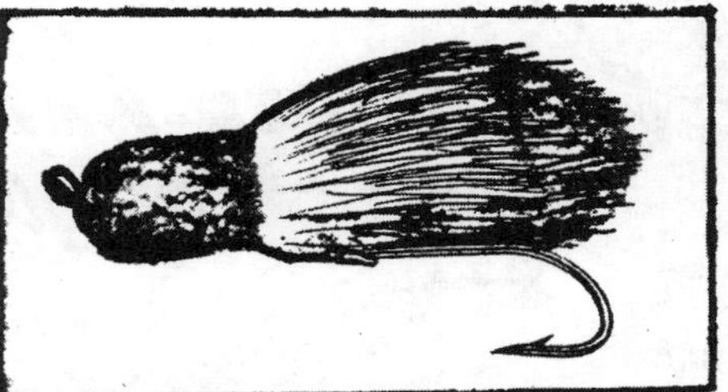

This "natural" keeps Lady Luck smiling at you. For all game fish. Only genuine rabbit foot lure on market. Red, black, brown. Length about 2 inches. 75 cents each, 3 for $2.00.

GARDI, 246 Fifth Avenue, New York City

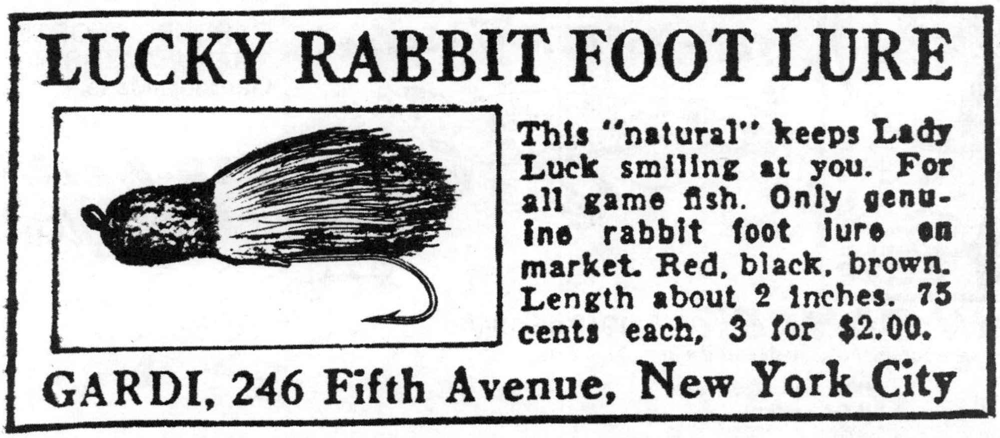

-THIS BAIT IS EARLIER THAN THE LUCKY BUNNY.

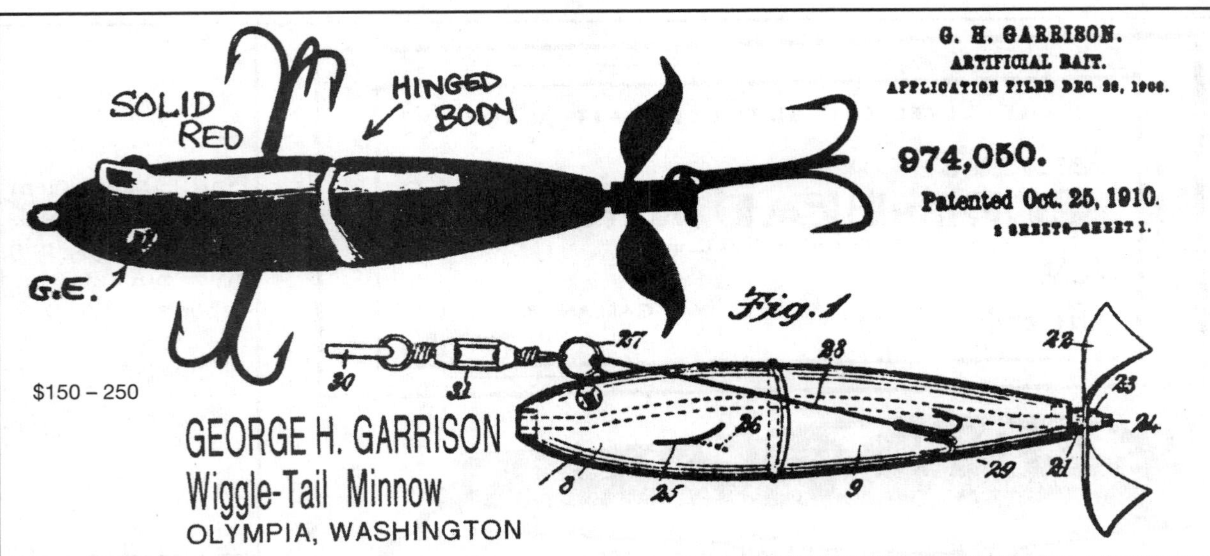
SOLID RED
HINGED BODY
G.E.
G. H. GARRISON.
ARTIFICIAL BAIT.
APPLICATION FILED DEC. 28, 1908.
974,050.
Patented Oct. 25, 1910.
2 SHEETS—SHEET 1.
Fig. 1

$150 – 250

GEORGE H. GARRISON
Wiggle-Tail Minnow
OLYMPIA, WASHINGTON

Retreating Minnow

Patent No. 1,933,170

TRY A RETREATING MINNOW
JETHRO A. GREIDER
Spear Lake - Cromwell, Ind.
(Fishermen took his advice, but they bought the Heddon Crab Wiggler)

PAT'D.
OCT. 31 - '33

$100 – 150

KLIPON
LURES FOR ALL FRESH WATER GAME FISH
At Last—A Hookless Plug
Hooks clip on easily and instantly—scientifically designed—balanced to insure life-like motion—durability guaranteed.
1930
4 Other models, 12 finishes
"Good News For the Angler— Bad News For the Fish"
At Your Dealer Or Direct From GREEN-WYLE CO. 3002 Emmons Ave. Brooklyn, N. Y.
Revolutionary New "BLINKIN' BEAUTY"
Its Radiant Light Keeps Blinking a "Come On" Signal!!
You'll be amazed when you see how even those shy, wary fellows are hypnotized into striking by the compelling blinking action of this sensational plug. A fluorescent plastic spinner revolving around the BLINKIN' BEAUTY'S super-bright luminous body makes its light appear to blink on and off. Tests prove our finny friends simply can't resist this ingenious, devastating device.
RESULTS GUARANTEED
Nothing else lands 'em like a BLINKIN' BEAUTY. Casting or trolling... in fresh or salt water, it's guaranteed to hook catches that will "top" the wildest dreams of the most ardent anglers...or, double your money back. Once tried, you'll never again fish without a BLINKIN' BEAUTY.
Order yours today! Sent postpaid
WORLD'S GREATEST FISH CATCHER ...Bar None!
GLO-LURE CO., DEPT. S 3405 N. CLARK ST., CHICAGO 13, ILL.
PATENT PEND
Made with "Super-Bright" LUMINOUS PLASTIC
TOP-WATER "Gurgler"
UNDER-WATER "Wiggler"
TWIN-DANCER
available in 7 colors fishy scales and all:
• White Belly Frog
• Yellow with Red Head
• Shiner
• Black
• White with Red Head
• All Green Frog
• Perch

$5

GARDNER SPORTS MANUFACTURING
Gardner, Mass.

$100 – 150

1940's - 1948

$5 – 10

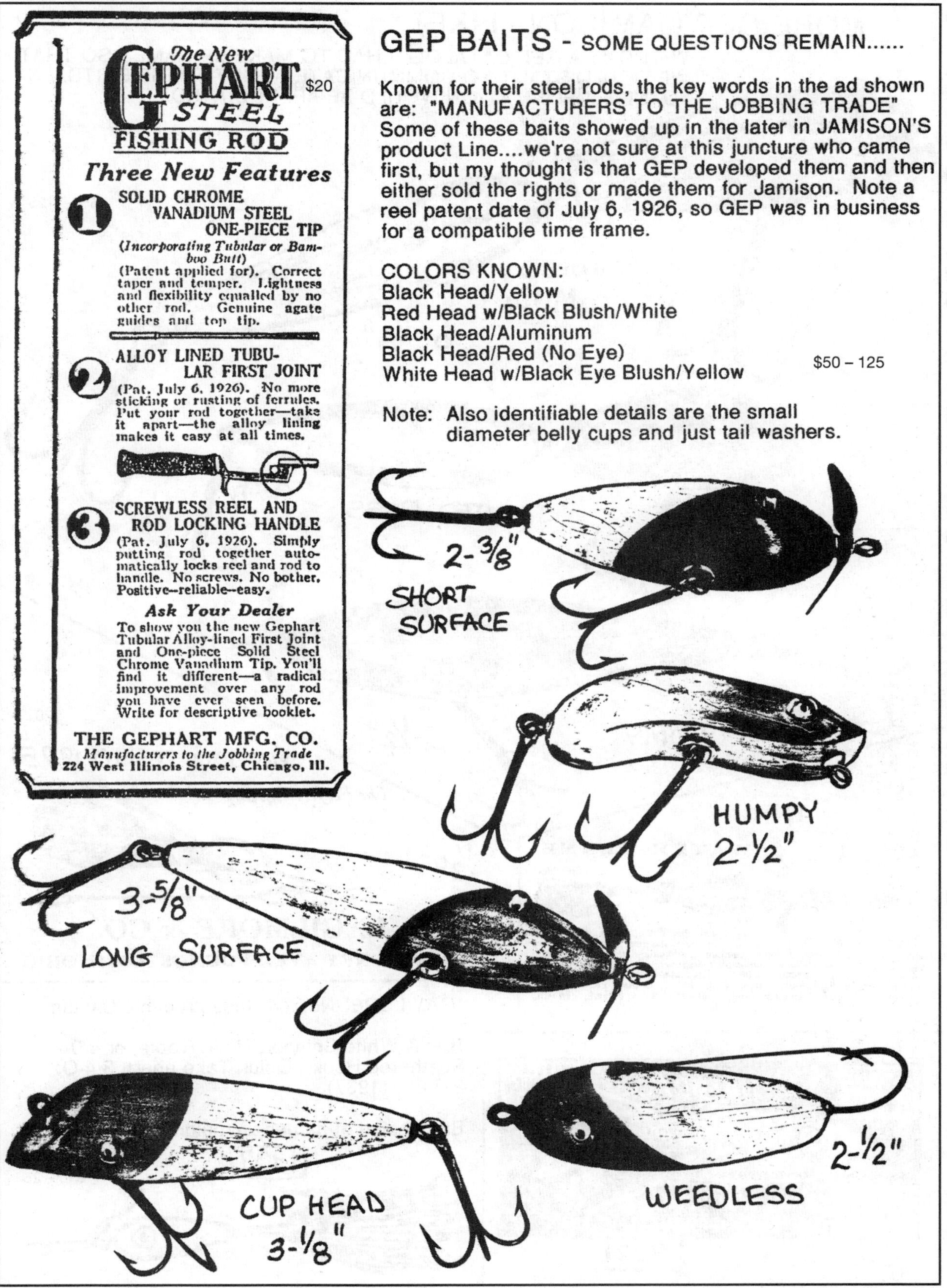
The New
GEPHART
STEEL
FISHING ROD
$20
Three New Features
1 SOLID CHROME VANADIUM STEEL ONE-PIECE TIP
(Incorporating Tubular or Bamboo Butt)
(Patent applied for). Correct taper and temper. Lightness and flexibility equalled by no other rod. Genuine agate guides and top tip.
2 ALLOY LINED TUBULAR FIRST JOINT
(Pat. July 6, 1926). No more sticking or rusting of ferrules. Put your rod together—take it apart—the alloy lining makes it easy at all times.
3 SCREWLESS REEL AND ROD LOCKING HANDLE
(Pat. July 6, 1926). Simply putting rod together automatically locks reel and rod to handle. No screws. No bother. Positive--reliable--easy.
Ask Your Dealer
To show you the new Gephart Tubular Alloy-lined First Joint and One-piece Solid Steel Chrome Vanadium Tip. You'll find it different—a radical improvement over any rod you have ever seen before. Write for descriptive booklet.
THE GEPHART MFG. CO.
Manufacturers to the Jobbing Trade
224 West Illinois Street, Chicago, Ill.

GEP BAITS - SOME QUESTIONS REMAIN......

Known for their steel rods, the key words in the ad shown are: "MANUFACTURERS TO THE JOBBING TRADE" Some of these baits showed up in the later in JAMISON'S product Line....we're not sure at this juncture who came first, but my thought is that GEP developed them and then either sold the rights or made them for Jamison. Note a reel patent date of July 6, 1926, so GEP was in business for a compatible time frame.

COLORS KNOWN:
Black Head/Yellow
Red Head w/Black Blush/White
Black Head/Aluminum
Black Head/Red (No Eye)
White Head w/Black Eye Blush/Yellow

$50 – 125

Note: Also identifiable details are the small diameter belly cups and just tail washers.

2-3/8"
SHORT SURFACE
HUMPY
2-1/2"
3-5/8"
LONG SURFACE
CUP HEAD
3-1/8"
2-1/2"
WEEDLESS

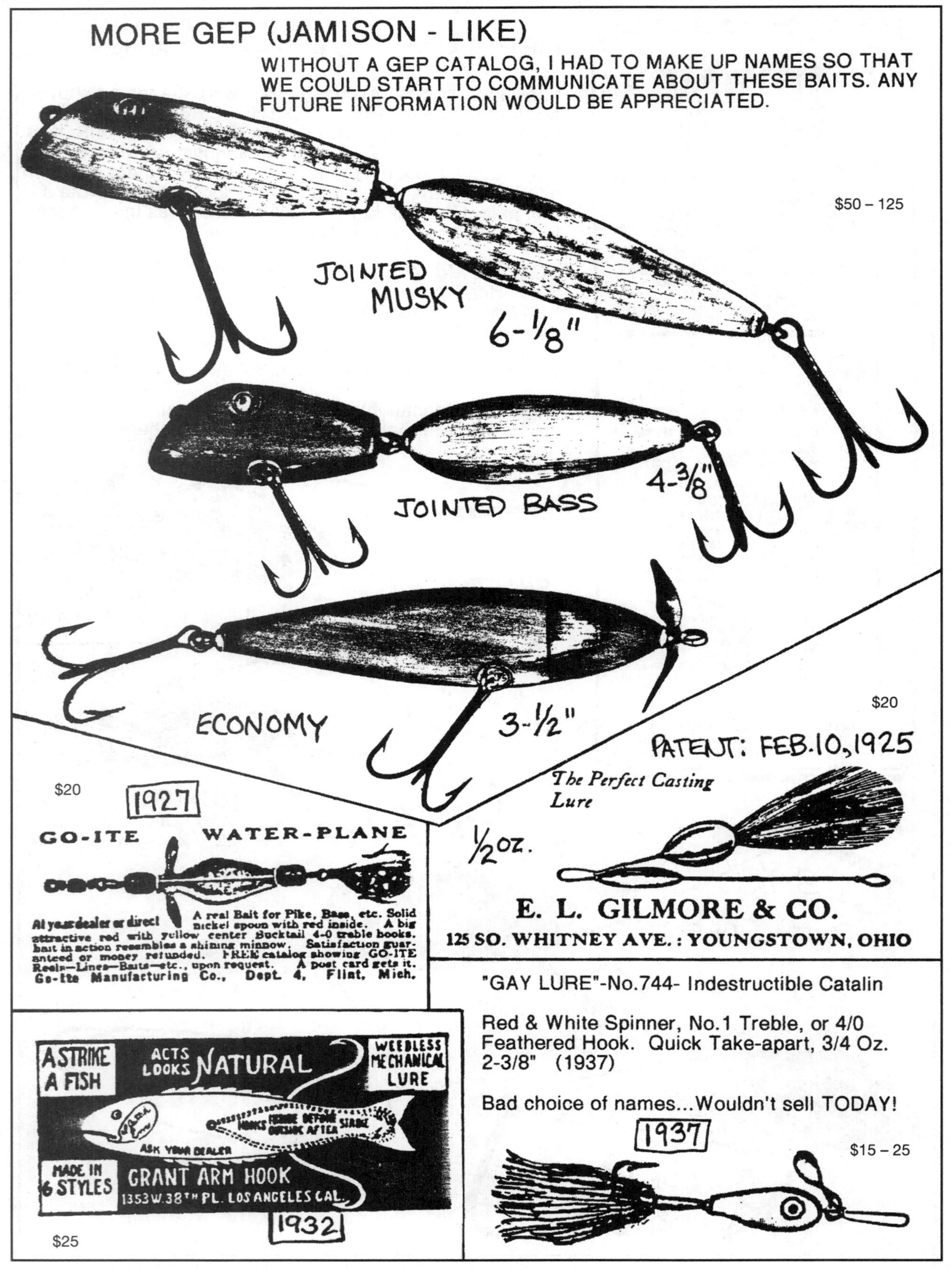
MORE GEP (JAMISON - LIKE)
WITHOUT A GEP CATALOG, I HAD TO MAKE UP NAMES SO THAT WE COULD START TO COMMUNICATE ABOUT THESE BAITS. ANY FUTURE INFORMATION WOULD BE APPRECIATED.
$50 – 125
JOINTED MUSKY
6-1/8"
JOINTED BASS
4-3/8"
ECONOMY
3-1/2"
$20
PATENT: FEB. 10, 1925
The Perfect Casting Lure
1/2 OZ.
E. L. GILMORE & CO.
125 SO. WHITNEY AVE. : YOUNGSTOWN, OHIO
$20
1927
GO-ITE WATER-PLANE
At your dealer or direct
A real Bait for Pike, Bass, etc. Solid nickel spoon with red inside. A big attractive red with yellow center Bucktail 4-0 treble hooks. bait in action resembles a shining minnow. Satisfaction guaranteed or money refunded. FREE catalog showing GO-ITE Reels—Lines—Baits—etc., upon request. A post card gets it.
Go-Ite Manufacturing Co., Dept. 4, Flint, Mich.
"GAY LURE"-No.744- Indestructible Catalin
Red & White Spinner, No.1 Treble, or 4/0 Feathered Hook. Quick Take-apart, 3/4 Oz. 2-3/8" (1937)
Bad choice of names...Wouldn't sell TODAY!
1937
$15 – 25
A STRIKE A FISH
ACTS LOOKS NATURAL
WEEDLESS MECHANICAL LURE
ASK YOUR DEALER
MADE IN 6 STYLES
GRANT ARM HOOK
1353 W. 38TH PL. LOS ANGELES CAL.
1932
$25

HOME OF HEDDON'S "DOWAGIAC" Rods and Minnows

1911

The factory illustrated above, thirty by one-hundred feet, three stories and basement, is devoted exclusively to the manufacture of Heddon Bait-Casting Rods and Artificial Minnows.

There is no factory in the world as well equipped with machinery and tools for the exclusive manufacture of these specialties. Much of the machinery has been designed and built under our own roof and there is no mechanical device lacking which would contribute to accuracy and economy in their production.

Every part entering into the Rods or Minnows which it is practical for us to produce is made under this roof from the raw material.

IN 1889, JAMES HEDDON TOSSED A WHITTLED PC. OF WOOD INTO DOWAGIAC CREEK. POW..... A BASS HIT IT, AND HEDDON WAS BORN. IN 1902, A FACTORY WAS BUILT TO PRODUCE BAITS IN VOLUME. LATER CAME 2 MORE GENERATIONS – CHARLES HEDDON AND JOHN HEDDON TO BECOME THE LARGEST PRODUCER OF ARTIFICIAL BAITS IN THEIR TIME.

(1990) → NOTE: SOME OF HEDDON'S CURRENT LITERATURE SAYS "1894."

1907

DOWAGIAC "ARTISTIC" MINNOW

APPROX. ACTUAL SIZE

BODY – 1 3/4" – 1/2 OZ.
1 TREBLE – IN BUCKTAIL FLY
NO. 50 – YELLOW BODY, FANCY MOTTLED BACK
NO. 51 – GOLD BODY, GREENISH BACK
(SOME W/GOLD HARDWARE)

WEIGHT BUOY (LEAD COLOR)
– WOOD W/ LEAD PLUG – 1/4 OZ.
TO BE ATTACHED 3" ABOVE THE BAIT.

$100 – 150

THE DOWAGIAC "ARTISTIC" MINNOW

With 1 Treble Hook and 1 Spinner. "Weight buoy" with each bait. Length of body, 1¾ inches. Weight without buoy, ½ ounce, with buoy ¾ ounce. This bait carries with it a novelty termed a "weight buoy." It is enameled dark lead color and can be attached on the line 3 inches above the minnow, thereby giving additional weight when desired for casting and to prevent the minnow from sinking too rapidly in shallow water.

No. 50 Yellow body, fancy mottled back.
No. 51 Gold body and greenish cast back.

NOTE: IT IS SOMETIMES HARD TO TELL THE PFLUEGER FROM THE HEDDON.

THIS IS A HARD TO FIND ITEM, EVEN HARDER TO FIND BOTH – TO COMPLETE THE SET.

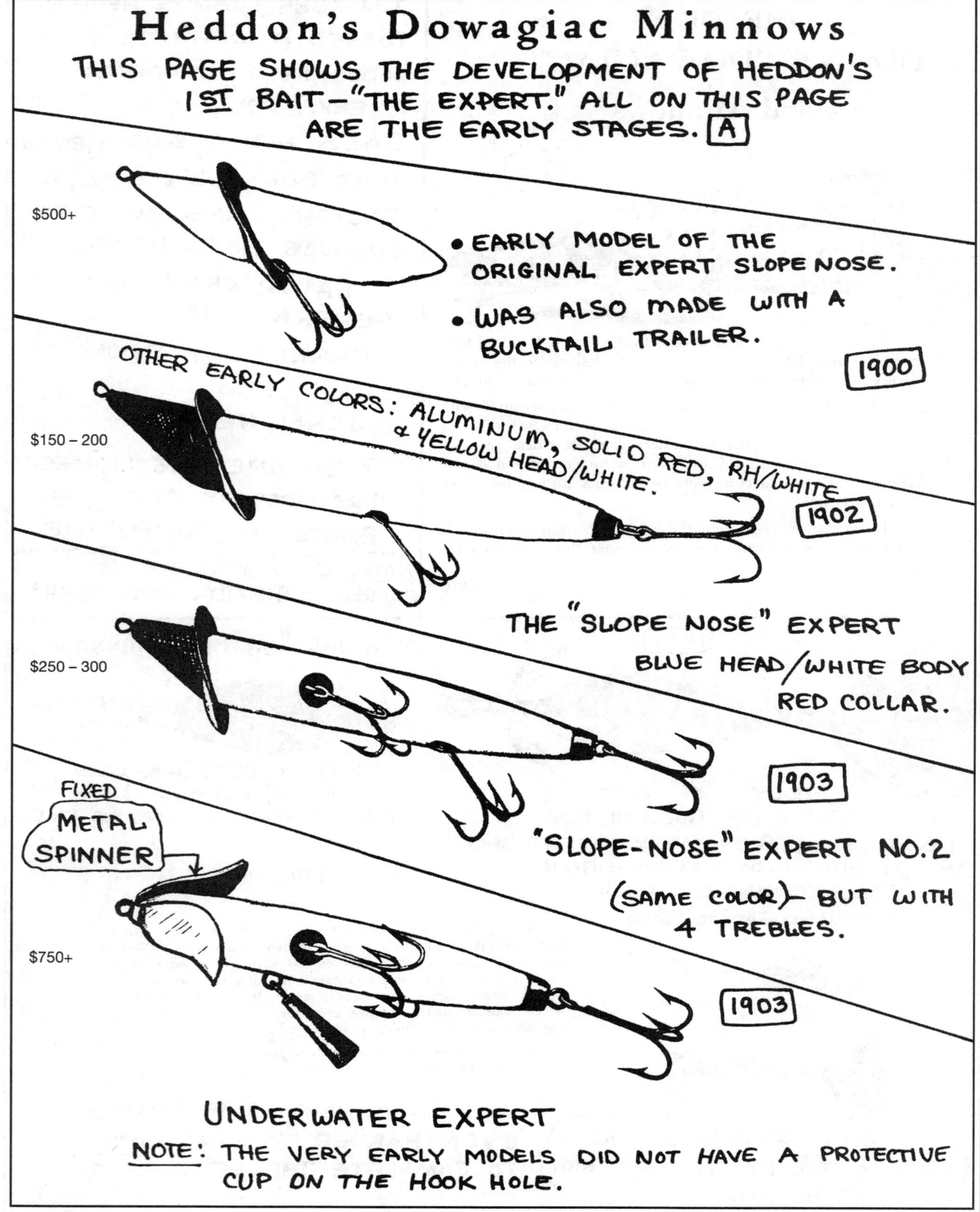
Heddon's Dowagiac Minnows
THIS PAGE SHOWS THE DEVELOPMENT OF HEDDON'S 1ST BAIT—"THE EXPERT." ALL ON THIS PAGE ARE THE EARLY STAGES. A
$500+
• EARLY MODEL OF THE ORIGINAL EXPERT SLOPE NOSE.
• WAS ALSO MADE WITH A BUCKTAIL TRAILER.
1900
OTHER EARLY COLORS: ALUMINUM, SOLID RED, RH/WHITE & YELLOW HEAD/WHITE.
$150 – 200
1902
THE "SLOPE NOSE" EXPERT
BLUE HEAD/WHITE BODY
RED COLLAR.
$250 – 300
1903
FIXED
METAL
SPINNER
"SLOPE-NOSE" EXPERT NO.2
(SAME COLOR)– BUT WITH 4 TREBLES.
$750+
1903
UNDERWATER EXPERT
NOTE: THE VERY EARLY MODELS DID NOT HAVE A PROTECTIVE CUP ON THE HOOK HOLE.

Heddon Surface Bait

No. 200 Special

$150 – 200

NO. 200 (SPECIAL)

This is the old reliable Heddon Expert, made only in the winning combination of colors shown in illustration. This is a Surface lure used preferably for casting, but also adaptable to "skittering" or "bobbing." It operates beautifully upon the surface of the water and avoids weeds to a considerable exent. It can be used among lily pads and rushes if properly handled and is a great attractor and practically sure killer of all of the smaller species of surface biting game fishes.

Has no spinners and is regularly supplied with three treble hooks, as illustrated. Is also supplied with two treble hooks, if preferred.

Weight, approximately 12 pwts; length of body 4 3-4 in.

NOTE: THIS OLDTIMER WAS ALSO MADE WITH 2 TREBLES OR 3 DOUBLE HOOKS AS SHOWN BELOW.

NOTE: ALL OF THE LURES IN THIS PERIOD WERE CUP HOOK RIGGED, AND HAD THE METAL TAIL CAP AS SHOWN.

THE COLLARS WERE PAINTED RED.

TO GIVE THIS SHAPE A "TIME FRAME" – IT IS STAGE [B].

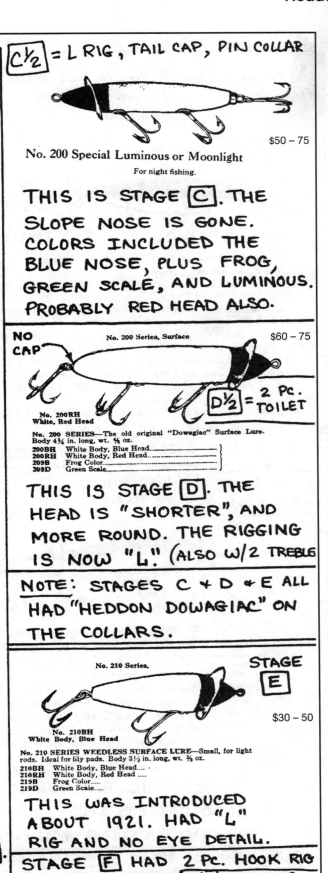

[C½] = L RIG, TAIL CAP, PIN COLLAR

$50 – 75

No. 200 Special Luminous or Moonlight

For night fishing.

THIS IS STAGE [C]. THE SLOPE NOSE IS GONE. COLORS INCLUDED THE BLUE NOSE, PLUS FROG, GREEN SCALE, AND LUMINOUS. PROBABLY RED HEAD ALSO.

NO CAP

No. 200 Series, Surface

$60 – 75

[D½] = 2 Pc. TOILET

No. 200RH
White, Red Head

No. 200 SERIES—The old original "Dowagiac" Surface Lure. Body 4¾ in. long, wt. ⅘ oz.

200BH	White Body, Blue Head
200RH	White Body, Red Head
209B	Frog Color
209D	Green Scale

THIS IS STAGE [D]. THE HEAD IS "SHORTER", AND MORE ROUND. THE RIGGING IS NOW "L." (ALSO W/2 TREBLE

NOTE: STAGES C + D + E ALL HAD "HEDDON DOWAGIAC" ON THE COLLARS.

No. 210 Series,

STAGE [E]

$30 – 50

No. 210BH
White Body, Blue Head

No. 210 SERIES WEEDLESS SURFACE LURE—Small, for light rods. Ideal for lily pads. Body 3½ in. long, wt. ⅗ oz.

210BH	White Body, Blue Head
210RH	White Body, Red Head
219B	Frog Color
219D	Green Scale

THIS WAS INTRODUCED ABOUT 1921. HAD "L" RIG AND NO EYE DETAIL.

STAGE [F] HAD 2 Pc. HOOK RIG AND GLASS EYES. [F½] = NO EYE.

Heddon Muskollonge or Salt Water Minnow

No. 700 Series

NO. 707

$400 – 500

(1911)

Illustrated above in No. 707 style of decoration is also supplied in the following colors:

Fancy Green back, White belly, No. 700. Yellow Perch, No. 709-A. Other colors on special order.

This Minnow is designed specially for catching Muskollonge and the smaller species of salt water game fishes. It is entirely too heavy for bait casting, unless thrown with a great deal of care upon a very heavy stiff Rod. Its weight and general construction are best adapted to trolling and it is designed to attract and hold the "big ones." Has two spinners and three extra strong No. 1-0, best possible quality hollow point nickel plated treble hooks.

Weight, approximately 3 ounces. Length of body 5 in.

- OTHER SIZES: 4¾" – 5½"
- ALSO RIGGED WITH 5 TREBLES

Heddon Minnow

SAME LENGTH AS THE 150.

No. 175 Series

(1911)

$200 – 250

No. 175 Series

3¾" – 1¼ oz.

This series of Minnows, illustrated above in Fancy Green Back finish, No. 175, is also supplied in the following colors:

Rainbow colors, consisting of Green Back, Pink and Yellow Sides and White belly, No. 176; Pure White Body with Slate colored Back, No. 177. Other colors on special order.

This series has two spinners and three No. 1-0, very large, hollow point treble hooks, which will hold the heaviest and largest fish which can be taken on a Casting Rod. Weight, approximately 18 pwts; length of body 3 3-4 inches. Has about the same sinking tendency as the No. 150 series previously described.

This series is designed specially for holding the "big ones."

NOTE: THIS BAIT WAS ALSO CALLED THE "HEAVY CASTING MINNOW"

NOTE: SOME HAVE OVERSIZE CUPS.

HEDDON HOOK RIGS.

FROM THE OUTSET, THEY GAVE SPECIAL ATTENTION TO THIS DETAIL.

BECAUSE OF THIS, THE COLLECTOR CAN "DATE" HIS FINDS MUCH EASIER WITH HEDDON THAN OTHER MFG'S.

NO. 1 — 1901 ERA

HEDDON'S 1ST HOOK RIG – OPEN SCREW EYE AND NO METAL CUP. DESIGNED TO NOT TANGLE, SCRATCH THE PAINT, AND REMAIN AT THE PROPER HOOKING ANGLE.

NO. 2 THE SAME RIG AS ABOVE, WITH THE ADDED DETAIL OF A NARROW CUP.

NO. 3 NEXT CAME A CONVENTIONAL CUP RIG, VERY SIMILAR TO CCBCO. THIS LASTED UNTIL 1915 TO 1917.

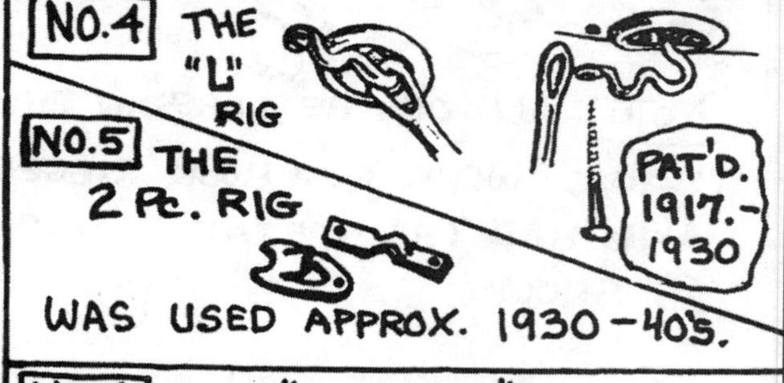

NO. 4 THE "L" RIG — PAT'D. 1917.–1930

NO. 5 THE 2 PC. RIG WAS USED APPROX. 1930–40'S.

NO. 6 THE "SURFACE" OR 1 PC. RIG. USED IN LATE 1940'S.

DOWAGIAC MINNOWS.

No. 1400
3"
G.E.

$1,000+

"DOWAGIAC" SINGLE HOOK MINNOW

This is a new type of Minnow, which has but one single detachable hook on the belly, being designed for compliance with State Laws prohibiting the use of more than one hook, or, for the use of anglers who prefer to use only one hook on a Bait. The one hook is located in the best possible position for effectiveness and an extra detachable hook is included in the box which may be put on at the rear if desired. Sinking Bait, two spinners, length of body 3 in. No. 1400. White body, with Red, Green and Black Spotted effect. No. 1401. Yellow body, with Red, Green and Black spotted effect.

NO. 1400 – SINGLE HOOK MINNOW.

THIS IS A LITTLE KNOWN VARIATION OF THE NO. 0 DOWAGIAC MINNOW.

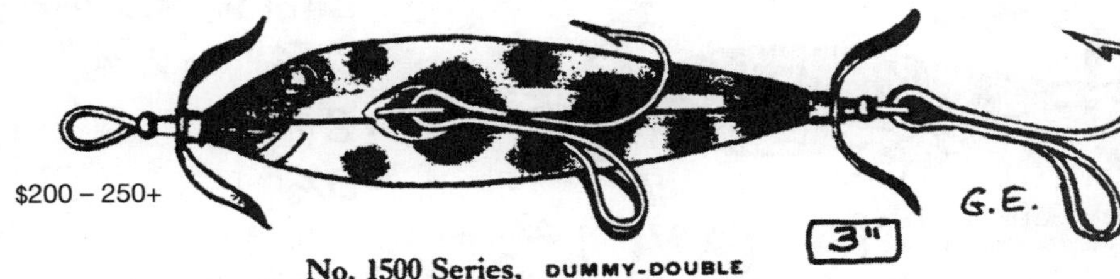
G.E.
3"

$200 – 250+

No. 1500 Series, DUMMY-DOUBLE

This is Heddon's latest product, having new style of detachable hook fastening and the Heddon new patented Dummy-Double type of hook, doing away with treble hooks and guaranteed to increase killing certainty. Sinking Bait, two spinners, three Dummy-Double Hooks. Length of body 3 inches.

No. 1500, White body with Red, Green and Yellow Spotted effect; No. 1501, Yellow body with Red, Green and Yellow Spotted effect; No. 1503, Fancy Green back, White belly.

THIS RARE ITEM WAS MADE IN THESE COLORS:

- WHITE BODY, RED & GR'N. SPOTS
- YELLOW BODY, RED & GR'N. SPOTS
- FANCY GREEN BACK
- BLENDED RED
- RAINBOW

SHOWN AS A SEMI-WEEDLESS LURE – A GREAT IMPROVEMENT AS IT PULLS OVER SNAGS WITH THE POINT OF THE HOOK FACING UP.

NO. 0

Heddon's "Dowagiac" Minnows

No. 0 (SUPERIOR FINISH)

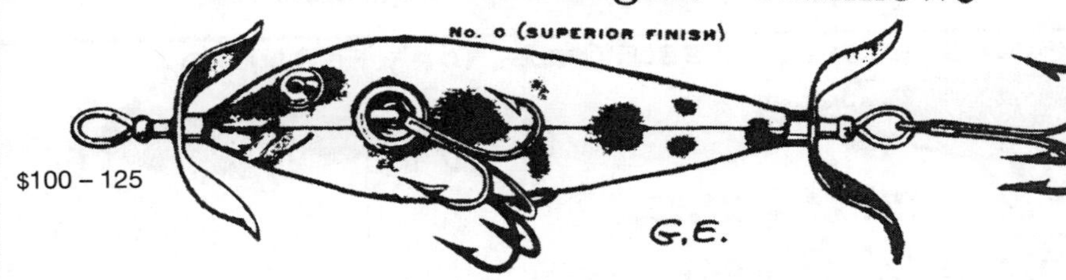
G.E.

$100 – 125

"DOWAGIAC" MINNOW, NOS. 0 AND 00 SERIES

This is a new design with five flat surfaces and side hooks mounted on a ridge with body of Minnow sloping away from the hooks, leaving them in the clearest possible position for efficiency. Two spinners, extra strong "DOWAGIAC" design nickel plated treble hooks, supplied in either three treble hook pattern or five treble hook pattern as follows: Three treble hook pattern weighs 13 pwts., length of body 3 inches. Colors No. 0, White Body, Red and Green Decorations. No. 01, Yellow body, Red, Green and Black Decorations. No. 02, Red Body with Black Decorations.

Five treble hook pattern weighs 16 pwts., length of body 3 1-2 inches. Colors, No. 00, White Body, Red and Green Decorations. No. 001, Yellow Body, Red, Green and Black Decorations. No. 002, Red Body with Black Decorations.

NOTE:

THIS HEX SHAPE WAS NOT THE 1ST BODY SHAPE. IT WAS INTRODUCED AFTER THE ROUND BODY IN ABOUT 1906–1907?

- HAS BEEN FOUND IN TOILET-SEAT RIG

NO. 00

3½" – 3⅞"

1¼ oz.

(5 TREBLES)

$100 – 150

Heddon's "Dowagiac" Minnow, No. 00 Series

NO. 1300 (1911)

5¾" – 2½ oz.

HEDDON'S BLACK SUCKER

$400 – 500

G.E.

No. 1300 Series, "DOWAGIAC" BLACK SUCKER MINNOW

The body of this Minnow is formed in exact imitation of the Black Sucker and the coloration is true to life of this fish, which is the natural food of the Muskollonge.

This bait is designed specially for trolling for Muskollonge, or can be cast upon a very heavy stiff Rod. Has one specially designed extra strong Hollow Point Treble Hook on either side and one extra strong No. 5-0 Hollow Point Treble Hook at the rear. All of the metal construction is extra heavy.

Has one spinner at the front; weighs approximately 2¼ ounces; length of body 5¾ inches.

MOST ARE BLACK SUCKER FINISH

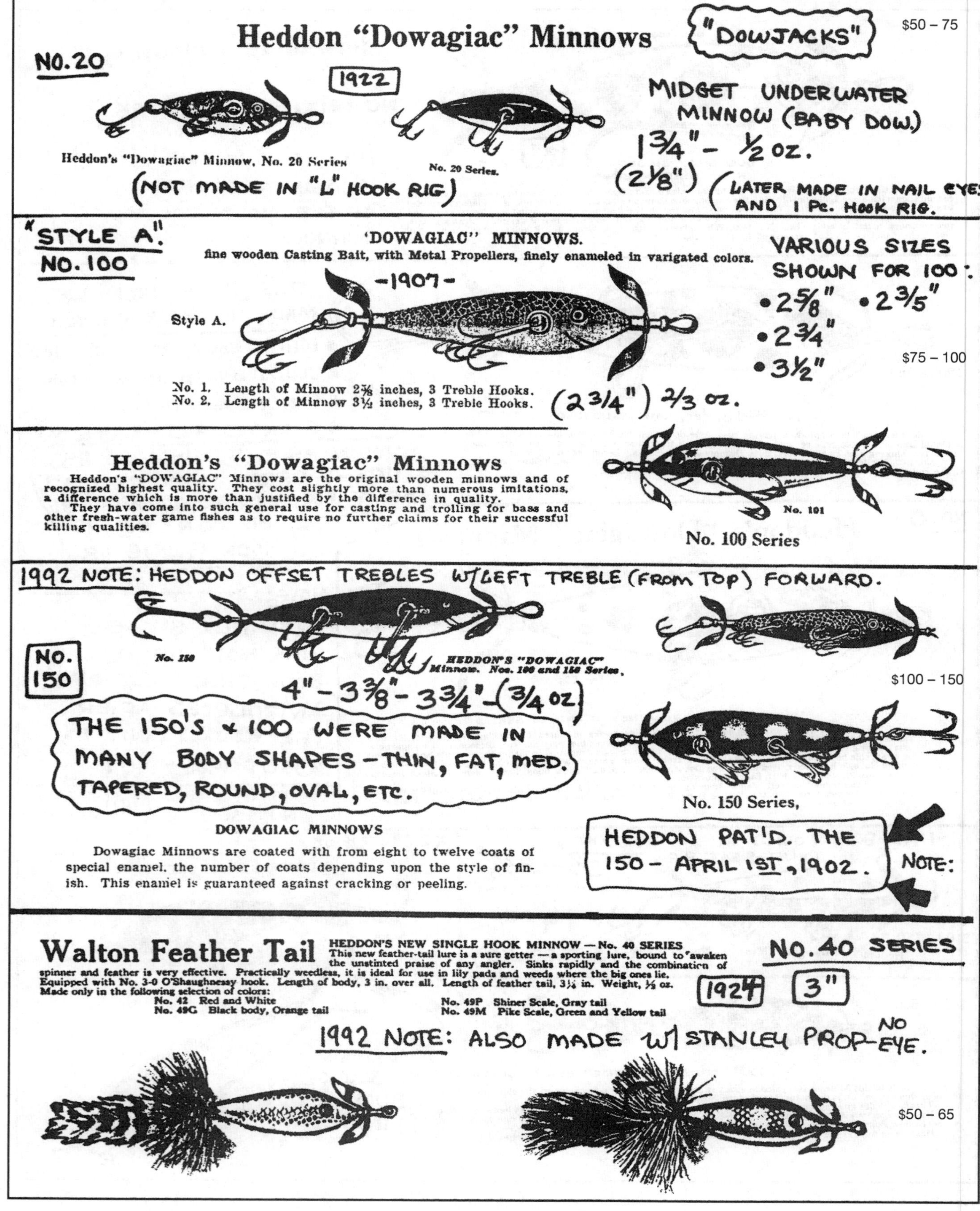
Heddon "Dowagiac" Minnows
"DOWJACKS"
$50 – 75
NO.20
1922
MIDGET UNDERWATER MINNOW (BABY DOW.)
1 3/4" - 1/2 OZ.
(2 1/8")
Heddon's "Dowagiac" Minnow, No. 20 Series
No. 20 Series.
(NOT MADE IN "L" HOOK RIG)
(LATER MADE IN NAIL EYE AND 1 PC. HOOK RIG.
"STYLE A".
NO. 100
'DOWAGIAC" MINNOWS.
fine wooden Casting Bait, with Metal Propellers, finely enameled in varigated colors.
VARIOUS SIZES SHOWN FOR 100:
• 2 5/8" • 2 3/5"
• 2 3/4"
• 3 1/2"
-1907-
Style A.
$75 – 100
No. 1. Length of Minnow 2 5/8 inches, 3 Treble Hooks.
No. 2. Length of Minnow 3 1/2 inches, 3 Treble Hooks.
(2 3/4") 2/3 oz.
Heddon's "Dowagiac" Minnows
Heddon's "DOWAGIAC" Minnows are the original wooden minnows and of recognized highest quality. They cost slightly more than numerous imitations, a difference which is more than justified by the difference in quality.
They have come into such general use for casting and trolling for bass and other fresh-water game fishes as to require no further claims for their successful killing qualities.
No. 101
No. 100 Series
1992 NOTE: HEDDON OFFSET TREBLES W/LEFT TREBLE (FROM TOP) FORWARD.
NO. 150
No. 150
HEDDON'S "DOWAGIAC" Minnow. Nos. 100 and 150 Series.
$100 – 150
4" - 3 5/8" - 3 3/4" - (3/4 OZ.)
THE 150'S + 100 WERE MADE IN MANY BODY SHAPES - THIN, FAT, MED. TAPERED, ROUND, OVAL, ETC.
No. 150 Series,
DOWAGIAC MINNOWS
Dowagiac Minnows are coated with from eight to twelve coats of special enamel, the number of coats depending upon the style of finish. This enamel is guaranteed against cracking or peeling.
HEDDON PAT'D. THE 150 - APRIL 1ST, 1902.
NOTE:
Walton Feather Tail
HEDDON'S NEW SINGLE HOOK MINNOW — No. 40 SERIES
This new feather-tail lure is a sure getter — a sporting lure, bound to awaken the unstinted praise of any angler. Sinks rapidly and the combination of spinner and feather is very effective. Practically weedless, it is ideal for use in lily pads and weeds where the big ones lie. Equipped with No. 3-0 O'Shaughnessy hook. Length of body, 3 in. over all. Length of feather tail, 3 1/4 in. Weight, 1/2 oz.
Made only in the following selection of colors:
No. 42 Red and White
No. 49G Black body, Orange tail
No. 49P Shiner Scale, Gray tail
No. 49M Pike Scale, Green and Yellow tail
NO. 40 SERIES
1924
3"
1992 NOTE: ALSO MADE W/ STANLEY PROP- NO EYE.
$50 – 65

HEDDON'S DOWAGIAC

No. 1600 Series—Deep Diving

When cast upon the water this bait will float until retrieved, when it dives under the water from three to four feet and has a wobbling motion closely resembling the movements of a live fish. Length 4¼ inches; weight ¾ oz. All scale finish colors on request. Finished in the following colors:

No. 1600	Fancy mottled green back, white belly
No. 1600S	White body with red and green spotted effect
No. 1602	White body with red head
No. 1605	Yellow body with red and green spots
No. 1609A	Imitation yellow perch
No. 1609B	Frog coloration

$75 – 100

NO. 1600
WIGGLER
NOTE: 2 TYPES OF RIGGING. (3 TREBLES)

SMALL METAL LIP

No. 1700 Series
Near Surface

1700

Floats when at rest, dives and describes a most alluring wiggling movement when in action, running near the surface, closely resembling the movements of a live fish. Has three treble hooks; 4¼ inches long; weighs ¾ oz. All scale finish colors on request. Finished in the following colors:

No. 1700	Fancy green back, white belly
No. 1700S	White body with red and green spotted effect
No. 1702	White body with red head
No. 1705	Yellow body with red and green spots, green back
No. 1709A	Imitation yellow perch
No. 1709B	Frog coloration

THESE 2 WIGGLERS WERE INTRODUCED IN 1915. THEY WERE THE FIRST HEDDON LURES TO UTILIZE THE "L" TYPE HOOK RIG THAT WAS PATENTED IN 1917.

$75 – 125

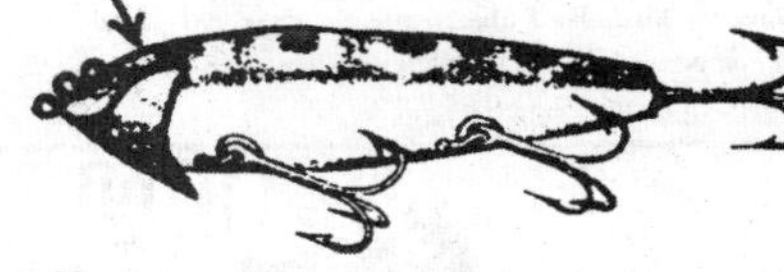

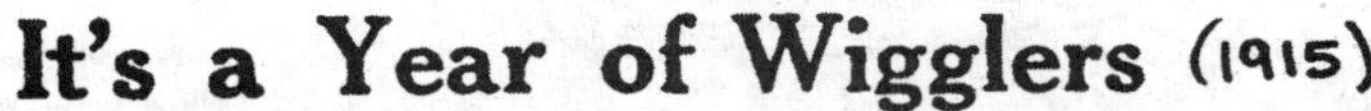

It's a Year of Wigglers (1915)

Wiggling, diving baits have the call this season—more will be used than all other styles put together. They have proved their effectiveness. Even hard-shell "live baiters" have become converted to them. The pioneer Dowagiac "Wigglers" will naturally be in the big majority. It was Jim Heddon, you know, who put out the first diving and swimming minnow, half a dozen years ago.

(2 SIZES)

NO. 1000
MOONLIGHT BAIT

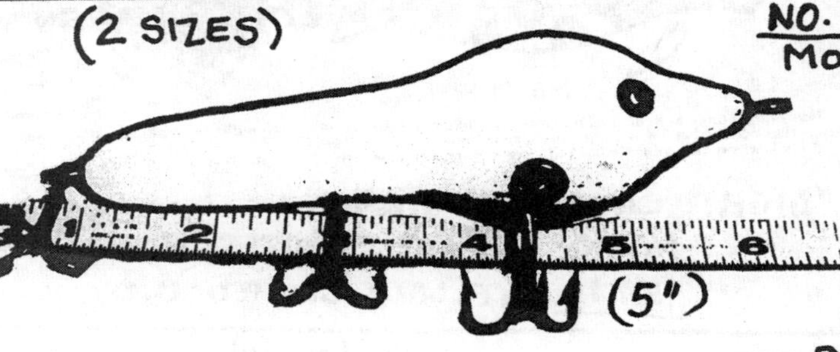
(5")
Heddon's Night-Radiant Moonlight Bait
Makes 'Em "Bite at Night"
Manufactured by JAMES HEDDON & SONS Dowagiac, Mich.
Read directions inside

$1,000+

DON'T KNOW IF THIS LURE WAS EVER PUBLISHED IN A HEDDON CATALOG. I WOULD ESTIMATE IT WAS MADE IN 1912–'15 ERA. MAYBE EARLIER.

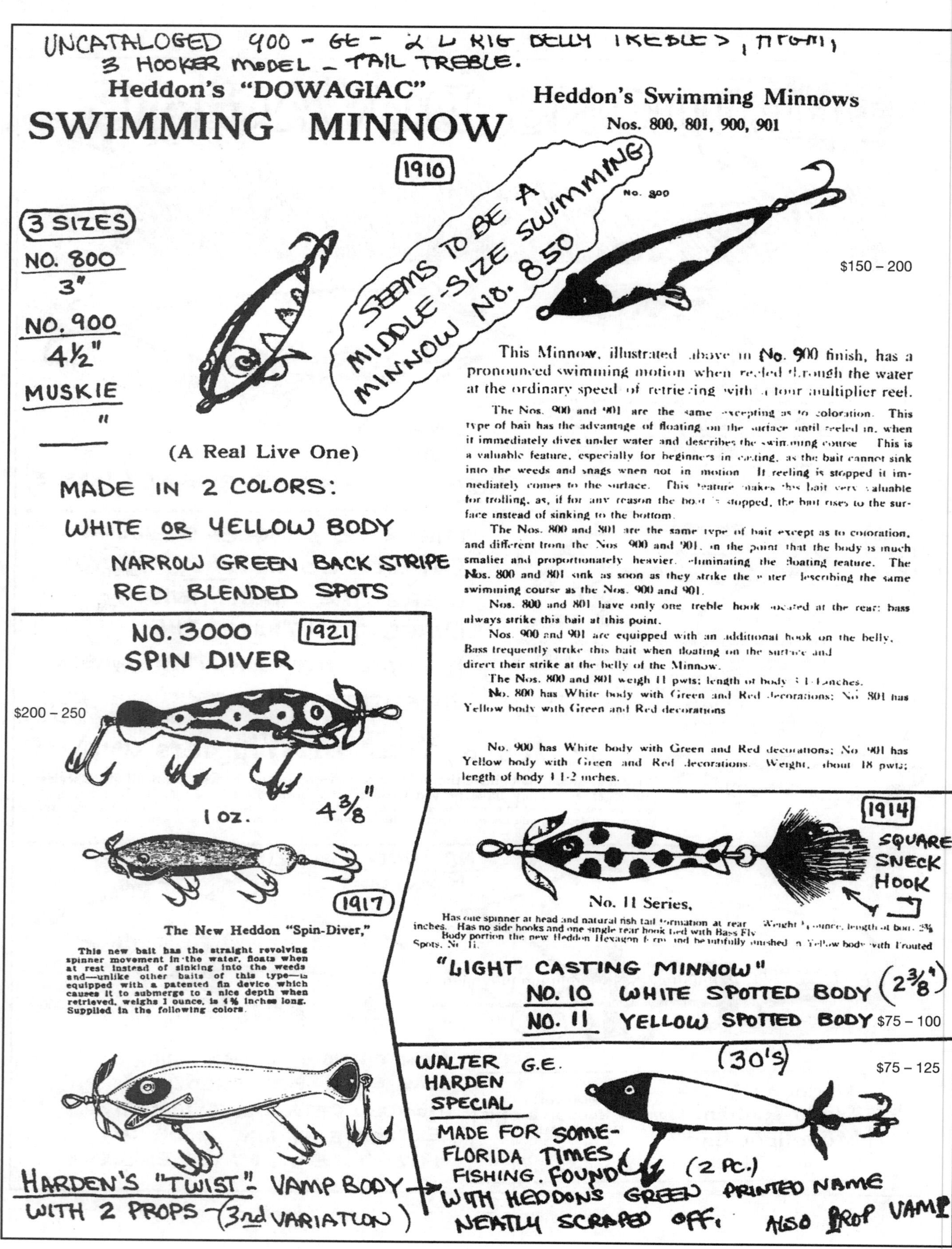

UNCATALOGED 900 - GE - 2 L RIG BELLY TREBLES, HTGM, 3 HOOKER MODEL - TAIL TREBLE.

Heddon's "DOWAGIAC"

SWIMMING MINNOW

1910

3 SIZES

NO. 800 3"

NO. 900 4½"

MUSKIE "

SEEMS TO BE A MIDDLE-SIZE SWIMMING MINNOW NO. 850

(A Real Live One)

MADE IN 2 COLORS:

WHITE OR YELLOW BODY

NARROW GREEN BACK STRIPE

RED BLENDED SPOTS

Heddon's Swimming Minnows

Nos. 800, 801, 900, 901

No. 800

$150 – 200

This Minnow, illustrated above in No. 900 finish, has a pronounced swimming motion when reeled through the water at the ordinary speed of retrieving with a four multiplier reel.

The Nos. 900 and 901 are the same excepting as to coloration. This type of bait has the advantage of floating on the surface until reeled in, when it immediately dives under water and describes the swimming course. This is a valuable feature, especially for beginners in casting, as the bait cannot sink into the weeds and snags when not in motion. If reeling is stopped it immediately comes to the surface. This feature makes this bait very valuable for trolling, as, if for any reason the boat is stopped, the bait rises to the surface instead of sinking to the bottom.

The Nos. 800 and 801 are the same type of bait except as to coloration, and different from the Nos. 900 and 901, in the point that the body is much smaller and proportionately heavier, eliminating the floating feature. The Nos. 800 and 801 sink as soon as they strike the water describing the same swimming course as the Nos. 900 and 901.

Nos. 800 and 801 have only one treble hook located at the rear; bass always strike this bait at this point.

Nos. 900 and 901 are equipped with an additional hook on the belly. Bass frequently strike this bait when floating on the surface and direct their strike at the belly of the Minnow.

The Nos. 800 and 801 weigh 11 pwts; length of body 3 1-4 inches.

No. 800 has White body with Green and Red decorations; No. 801 has Yellow body with Green and Red decorations.

No. 900 has White body with Green and Red decorations; No. 901 has Yellow body with Green and Red decorations. Weight, about 18 pwts; length of body 4 1-2 inches.

NO. 3000 SPIN DIVER 1921

$200 – 250

1 oz. 4⅜"

1917

The New Heddon "Spin-Diver,"

This new bait has the straight revolving spinner movement in the water, floats when at rest instead of sinking into the weeds and—unlike other baits of this type—is equipped with a patented fin device which causes it to submerge to a nice depth when retrieved, weighs 1 ounce, is 4⅜ inches long. Supplied in the following colors.

1914

SQUARE SNECK HOOK

No. 11 Series,

Has one spinner at head and natural fish tail formation at rear. Weight ¼ ounce, length of body 2⅜ inches. Has no side hooks and one single rear hook tied with Bass Fly. Body portion the new Heddon Hexagon form and beautifully finished in Yellow body with Frouted Spots, No. 11.

"LIGHT CASTING MINNOW"

NO. 10 WHITE SPOTTED BODY (2⅜")

NO. 11 YELLOW SPOTTED BODY $75 – 100

HARDEN'S "TWIST" - VAMP BODY WITH 2 PROPS (3rd VARIATION)

WALTER HARDEN SPECIAL G.E. (30's)

$75 – 125

MADE FOR SOME FLORIDA TIMES FISHING. FOUND (2 PC.) WITH HEDDONS GREEN PRINTED NAME NEATLY SCRAPED OFF. ALSO PROP VAMP

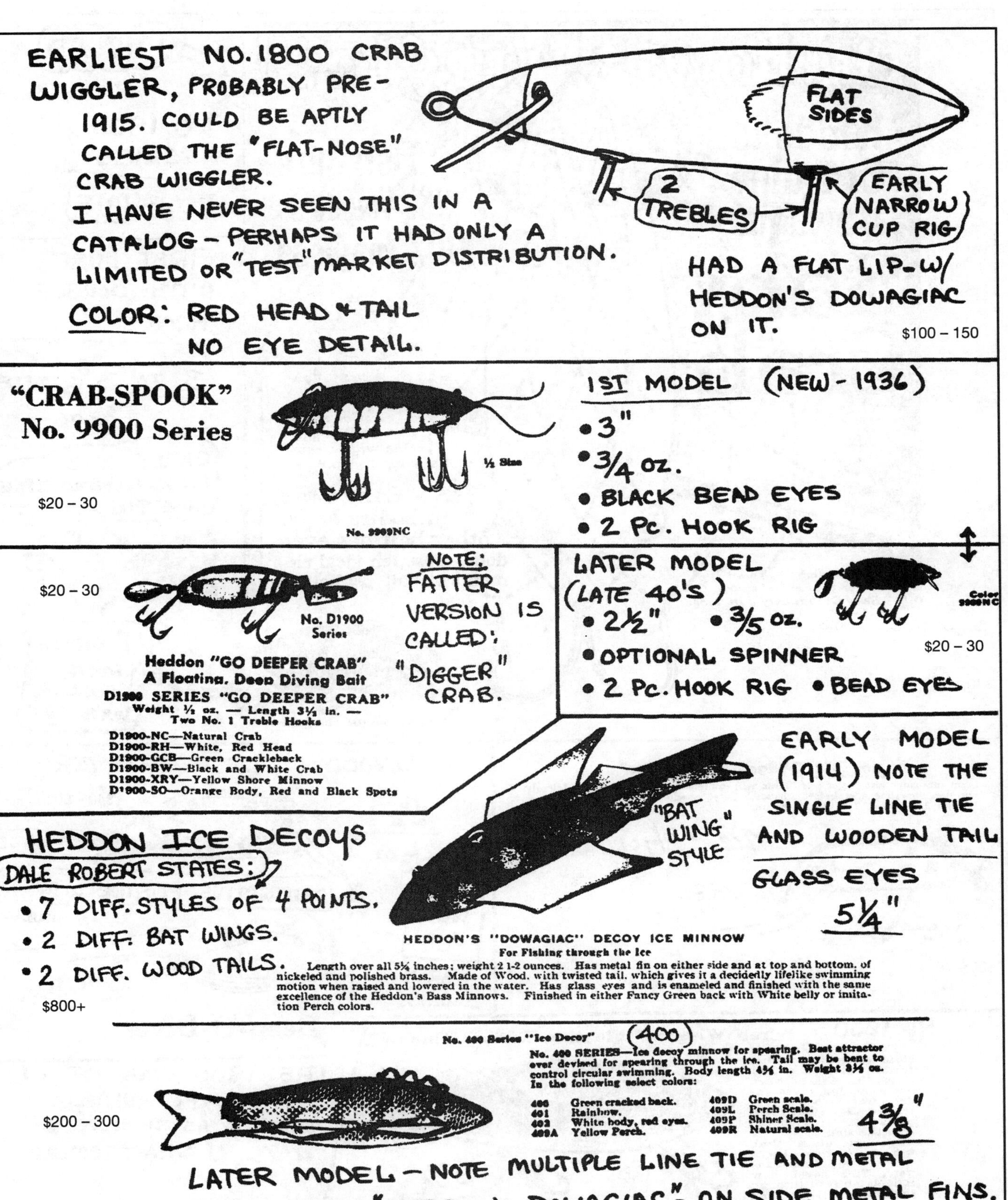
EARLIEST NO. 1800 CRAB WIGGLER, PROBABLY PRE-1915. COULD BE APTLY CALLED THE "FLAT-NOSE" CRAB WIGGLER.
I HAVE NEVER SEEN THIS IN A CATALOG – PERHAPS IT HAD ONLY A LIMITED OR "TEST" MARKET DISTRIBUTION.
COLOR: RED HEAD & TAIL NO EYE DETAIL.
FLAT SIDES
2 TREBLES
EARLY NARROW CUP RIG
HAD A FLAT LIP-W/ HEDDON'S DOWAGIAC ON IT.
$100 – 150
"CRAB-SPOOK"
No. 9900 Series
½ Size
No. 9900NC
$20 – 30
1ST MODEL (NEW - 1936)
• 3"
• 3/4 OZ.
• BLACK BEAD EYES
• 2 PC. HOOK RIG
$20 – 30
No. D1900 Series
Heddon "GO DEEPER CRAB"
A Floating, Deep Diving Bait
D1900 SERIES "GO DEEPER CRAB"
Weight ½ oz. — Length 3½ in. —
Two No. 1 Treble Hooks
D1900-NC—Natural Crab
D1900-RH—White, Red Head
D1900-GCB—Green Crackleback
D1900-BW—Black and White Crab
D1900-XRY—Yellow Shore Minnow
D1900-SO—Orange Body, Red and Black Spots
NOTE: FATTER VERSION IS CALLED: "DIGGER" CRAB.
LATER MODEL (LATE 40'S)
• 2½" • 3/5 OZ.
• OPTIONAL SPINNER
• 2 PC. HOOK RIG • BEAD EYES
Color 9900NC
$20 – 30
EARLY MODEL (1914) NOTE THE SINGLE LINE TIE AND WOODEN TAIL
GLASS EYES
5¼"
"BAT WING" STYLE
HEDDON ICE DECOYS
DALE ROBERT STATES:
• 7 DIFF. STYLES OF 4 POINTS.
• 2 DIFF. BAT WINGS.
• 2 DIFF. WOOD TAILS.
HEDDON'S "DOWAGIAC" DECOY ICE MINNOW
For Fishing through the Ice
Length over all 5¼ inches; weight 2 1-2 ounces. Has metal fin on either side and at top and bottom, of nickeled and polished brass. Made of Wood, with twisted tail, which gives it a decidedly lifelike swimming motion when raised and lowered in the water. Has glass eyes and is enameled and finished with the same excellence of the Heddon's Bass Minnows. Finished in either Fancy Green back with White belly or imitation Perch colors.
$800+
No. 400 Series "Ice Decoy"
(400)
No. 400 SERIES—Ice decoy minnow for spearing. Best attractor ever devised for spearing through the ice. Tail may be bent to control circular swimming. Body length 4⅜ in. Weight 3½ oz. In the following select colors:
400 Green cracked back.
401 Rainbow.
402 White body, red eyes.
409A Yellow Perch.
409D Green scale.
409L Perch Scale.
409P Shiner Scale.
409R Natural scale.
4⅜"
$200 – 300
LATER MODEL – NOTE MULTIPLE LINE TIE AND METAL TAIL – SAYS "HEDDON – DOWAGIAC" ON SIDE METAL FINS.
• CALLED "4 POINT" STYLE.

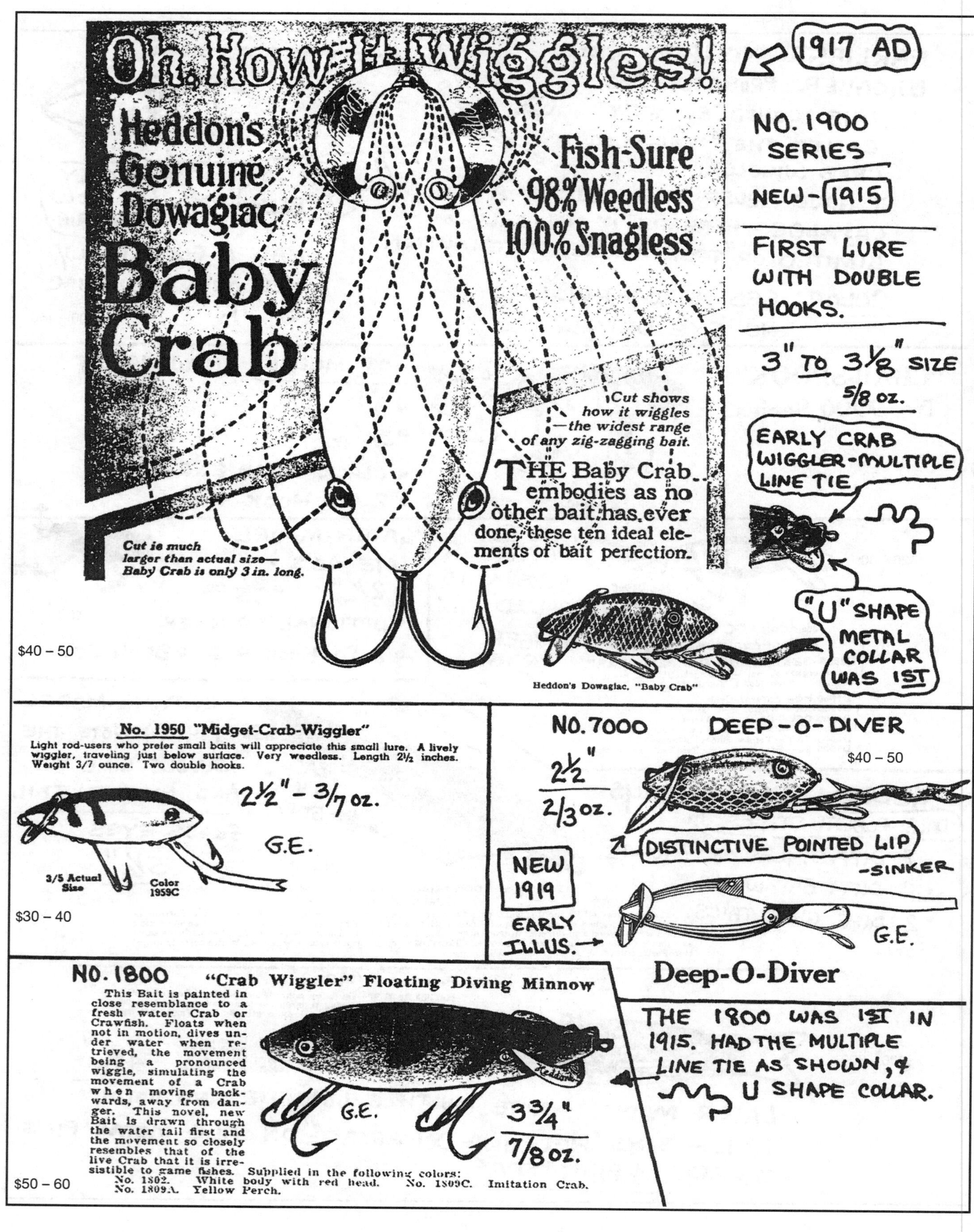
Oh, How it Wiggles!
Heddon's Genuine Dowagiac
Baby Crab
Fish-Sure
98% Weedless
100% Snagless
Cut shows how it wiggles —the widest range of any zig-zagging bait.
THE Baby Crab embodies as no other bait has ever done, these ten ideal elements of bait perfection.
Cut is much larger than actual size—Baby Crab is only 3 in. long.
1917 AD
NO. 1900 SERIES
NEW-1915
FIRST LURE WITH DOUBLE HOOKS.
3" TO 3 1/8" SIZE
5/8 oz.
EARLY CRAB WIGGLER-MULTIPLE LINE TIE
"U" SHAPE METAL COLLAR WAS 1ST
Heddon's Dowagiac, "Baby Crab"
$40 – 50
No. 1950 "Midget-Crab-Wiggler"
Light rod-users who prefer small baits will appreciate this small lure. A lively wiggler, traveling just below surface. Very weedless. Length 2½ inches. Weight 3/7 ounce. Two double hooks.
2½" - 3/7 oz.
G.E.
3/5 Actual Size
Color 1959C
$30 – 40
NO. 7000
DEEP-O-DIVER
2½"
2/3 oz.
$40 – 50
DISTINCTIVE POINTED LIP
-SINKER
NEW 1919
EARLY ILLUS.
G.E.
Deep-O-Diver
NO. 1800
"Crab Wiggler" Floating Diving Minnow
This Bait is painted in close resemblance to a fresh water Crab or Crawfish. Floats when not in motion, dives under water when retrieved, the movement being a pronounced wiggle, simulating the movement of a Crab when moving backwards, away from danger. This novel, new Bait is drawn through the water tail first and the movement so closely resembles that of the live Crab that it is irresistible to game fishes. Supplied in the following colors:
No. 1802. White body with red head. No. 1809C. Imitation Crab.
No. 1809A. Yellow Perch.
G.E.
3¾"
7/8 oz.
THE 1800 WAS 1ST IN 1915. HAD THE MULTIPLE LINE TIE AS SHOWN, & U SHAPE COLLAR.
$50 – 60

1925

Baby Game Fisher

Baby Game Fisher No. 5400 Series

NO. 5400 - 4"-½ oz.

(ALSO IN PIKE SCALE)

"Out-Natures Nature in Lifelike Movement"

$20 – 30

"Out-natures nature in lifelike movements"
No. 5509P

NEW 1923

"Game Fisher"

No. 5500 Series

The "Game Fisher," floating while at rest, draws below the surface in a zigzagging motion. No scurrying crab, nor escaping minnow can match the oscillating, wiggling, erratic extremes of movement so naturally accomplished by this masterpiece of Heddon construction. It casts just right yet offers no tiring resistance in retrieving. The construction permits the famous Heddon sure-catch hook presentation and has the patented fastening. While unlike other wooden baits, the flexible body offers the hooked fish no purchase for shaking loose the barbs.

Invented, patented and exclusively held by Heddon. This Lure is built to withstand the most savage attacks of large game fish. Wonderful records made on Bass, Pike and Muskies. Length of body, 4¾ inches. Weight, ¾ ounce. Made only in the following colors:

No. 5501 Rainbow
No. 5502 White Body, Red Head and Tail.
No. 5509D Green scale
No. 5509P Shiner scale

4¾" - ¾ oz.

THIS WAS ONE OF THE FIRST - IF NOT THE 1ST JOINTED LURE. IT WAS ALSO AN UN-OFFICIAL "SONIC" LURE.... GIVING OFF A SOUND AS THE BODY PARTS CLACKED TOGETHER.

UNQUESTIONABLY the most important and farthest reaching innovation and wooden-bait improvement that the Heddon factory in all its years of originativeness and pioneering has developed for the angler.

This amazing new principle of compound flexible movement revolutionizes every previous conception in lifelike moving lures.

Nature itself seems outdone. No scurrying crab, panicky frog or escaping minnow can surpass the excessive sidesweeping, erratic extremes of luring movement that follow the lightest pull of this bait through the water.

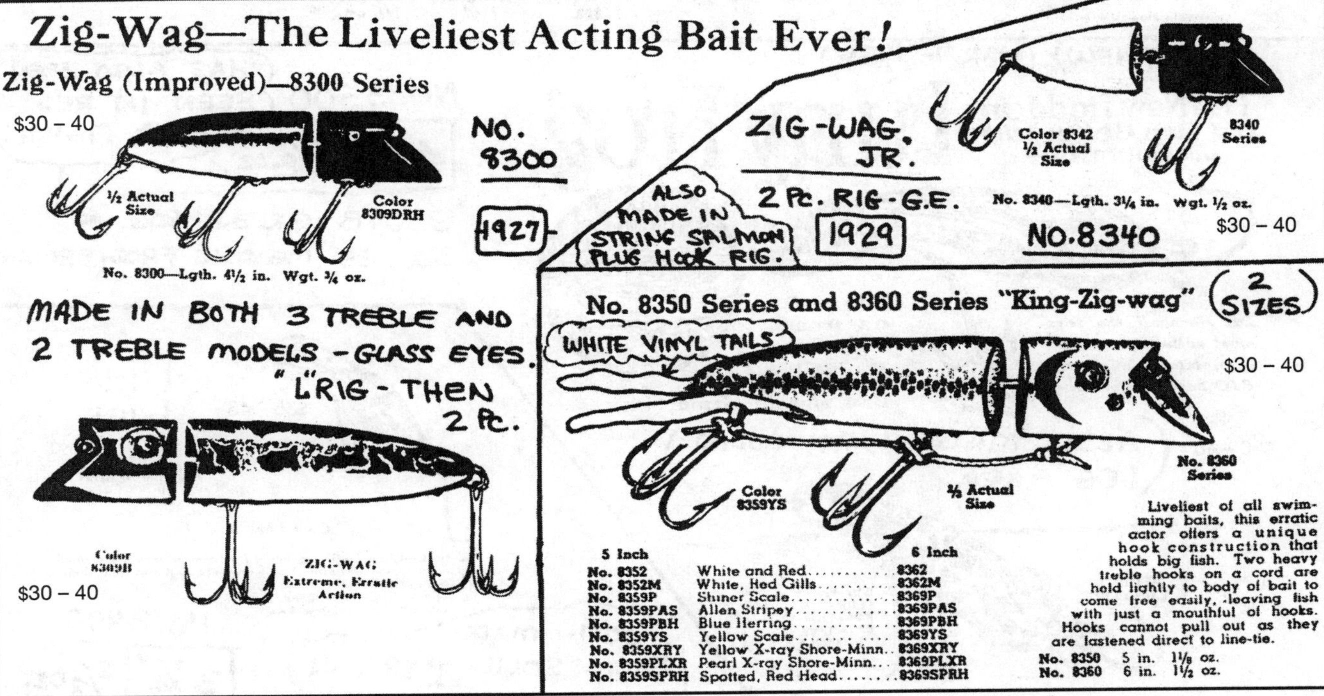

Zig-Wag—The Liveliest Acting Bait Ever!

Zig-Wag (Improved)—8300 Series

$30 – 40

NO. 8300

½ Actual Size

Color 8309DRH

1927

No. 8300—Lgth. 4½ in. Wgt. ¾ oz.

MADE IN BOTH 3 TREBLE AND 2 TREBLE MODELS - GLASS EYES. "L" RIG - THEN 2 Pc.

Color 8309H

ZIG-WAG Extreme, Erratic Action

$30 – 40

ZIG-WAG JR.

2 Pc. RIG - G.E.

ALSO MADE IN STRING SALMON PLUG HOOK RIG.

1929

Color 8342 ½ Actual Size

8340 Series

No. 8340—Lgth. 3¼ in. Wgt. ½ oz.

NO. 8340

$30 – 40

No. 8350 Series and 8360 Series "King-Zig-wag" (2 SIZES)

WHITE VINYL TAILS

$30 – 40

Color 8359YS

⅔ Actual Size

No. 8360 Series

5 Inch		6 Inch
No. 8352	White and Red	8362
No. 8352M	White, Hed Gills	8362M
No. 8359P	Shuner Scale	8369P
No. 8359PAS	Allen Stripey	8369PAS
No. 8359PBH	Blue Herring	8369PBH
No. 8359YS	Yellow Scale	8369YS
No. 8359XRY	Yellow X-ray Shore-Minn.	8369XRY
No. 8359PLXR	Pearl X-ray Shore-Minn.	8369PLXR
No. 8359SPRH	Spotted, Red Head	8369SPRH

Liveliest of all swimming baits, this erratic actor offers a unique hook construction that holds big fish. Two heavy treble hooks on a cord are hold lightly to body of bait to come free easily, leaving fish with just a mouthful of hooks. Hooks cannot pull out as they are lastened direct to line-tie.

No. 8350 5 in. 1⅛ oz.
No. 8360 6 in. 1½ oz.

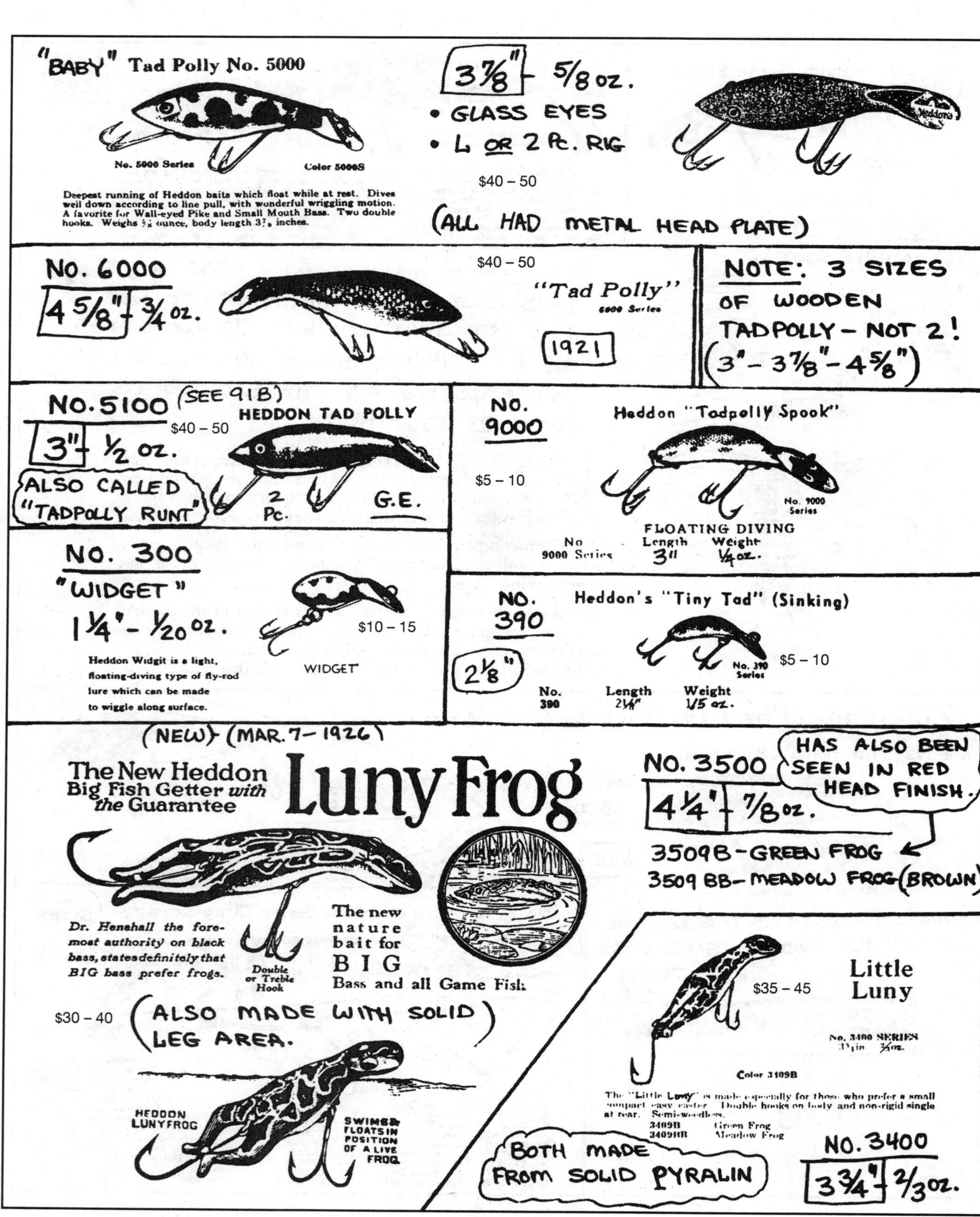
"BABY" Tad Polly No. 5000
No. 5000 Series
Color 5000S
Deepest running of Heddon baits which float while at rest. Dives well down according to line pull, with wonderful wriggling motion. A favorite for Wall-eyed Pike and Small Mouth Bass. Two double hooks.
3 7/8" - 5/8 oz.
• GLASS EYES
• L OR 2 PC. RIG
$40 – 50
(ALL HAD METAL HEAD PLATE)
NO. 6000
4 5/8" - 3/4 oz.
$40 – 50
"Tad Polly"
6000 Series
1921
NOTE: 3 SIZES OF WOODEN TADPOLLY - NOT 2!
(3" - 3 7/8" - 4 5/8")
NO. 5100 (SEE 91B)
HEDDON TAD POLLY
3" - 1/2 oz.
$40 – 50
ALSO CALLED "TADPOLLY RUNT"
2 Pc.
G.E.
NO. 9000
Heddon "Tadpolly Spook"
$5 – 10
No. 9000 Series
FLOATING DIVING
No 9000 Series
Length 3"
Weight 1/4 oz.
NO. 300
"WIDGET"
1 1/4" - 1/20 oz.
$10 – 15
Heddon Widgit is a light, floating-diving type of fly-rod lure which can be made to wiggle along surface.
WIDGET
NO. 390
Heddon's "Tiny Tad" (Sinking)
2 1/8"
No. 390 Series
$5 – 10
No. 390
Length 2 1/8"
Weight 1/5 oz.
(NEW) - (MAR. 7 - 1926)
The New Heddon Big Fish Getter with the Guarantee
Luny Frog
Dr. Henshall the foremost authority on black bass, states definitely that BIG bass prefer frogs.
Double or Treble Hook
The new nature bait for BIG Bass and all Game Fish
$30 – 40
(ALSO MADE WITH SOLID LEG AREA.)
HEDDON LUNYFROG
SWIMS & FLOATS IN POSITION OF A LIVE FROG
NO. 3500
4 1/4" - 7/8 oz.
HAS ALSO BEEN SEEN IN RED HEAD FINISH.
3509B - GREEN FROG
3509 BB - MEADOW FROG (BROWN)
$35 – 45
Little Luny
No. 3400 SERIES
Color 3409B
3409B Green Frog
3409BB Meadow Frog
BOTH MADE FROM SOLID PYRALIN
NO. 3400
3 3/4" - 2/3 oz.

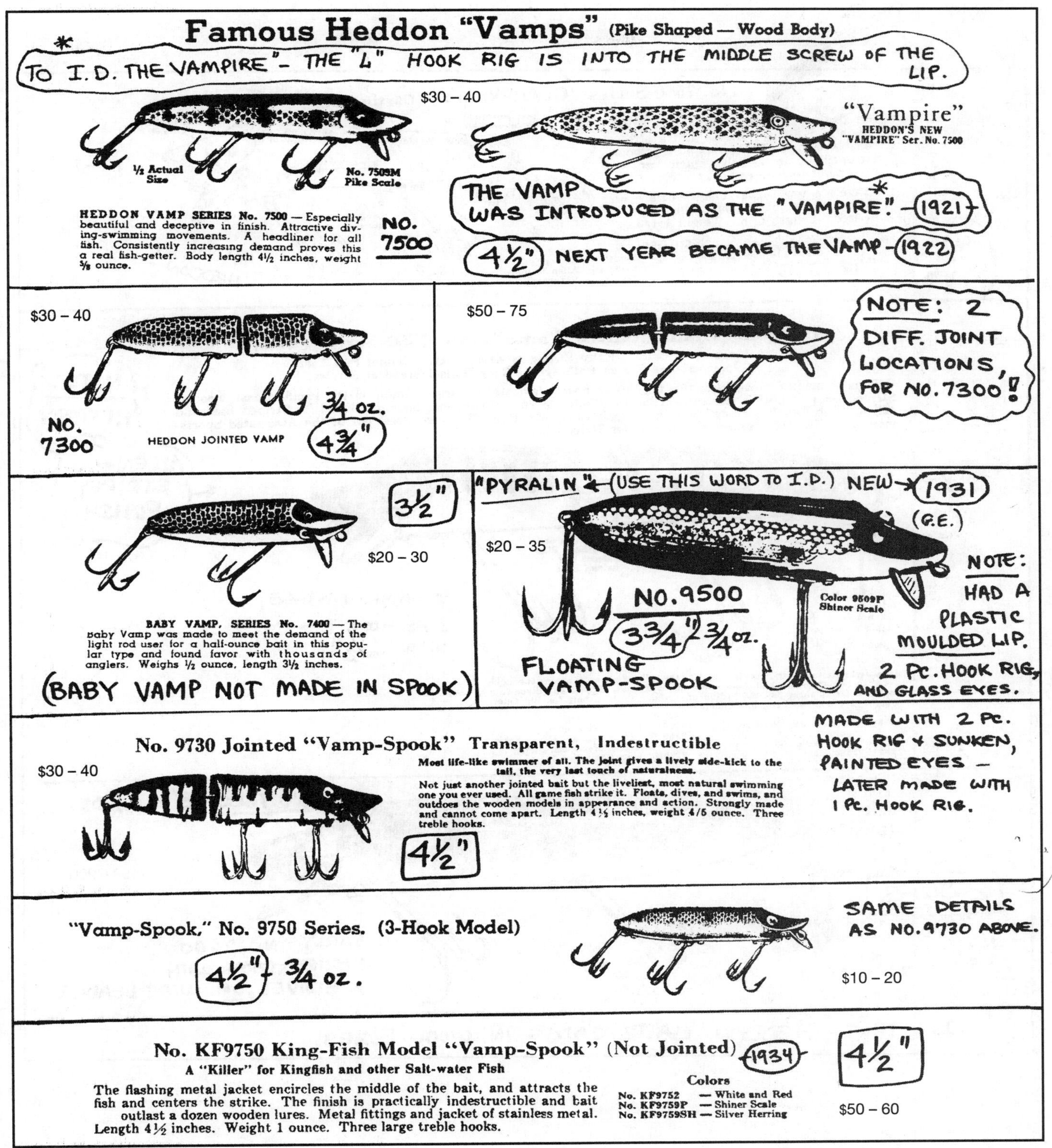
Famous Heddon "Vamps" (Pike Shaped — Wood Body)
* TO I.D. THE VAMPIRE" - THE "L" HOOK RIG IS INTO THE MIDDLE SCREW OF THE LIP.
$30 – 40
½ Actual Size
No. 7509M Pike Scale
HEDDON VAMP SERIES No. 7500 — Especially beautiful and deceptive in finish. Attractive diving-swimming movements. A headliner for all fish. Consistently increasing demand proves this a real fish-getter. Body length 4½ inches, weight ⅝ ounce.
NO. 7500
"Vampire"
HEDDON'S NEW "VAMPIRE" Ser. No. 7500
THE VAMP
WAS INTRODUCED AS THE "VAMPIRE".* 1921
4½" NEXT YEAR BECAME THE VAMP 1922
$30 – 40
¾ oz.
NO. 7300
HEDDON JOINTED VAMP
4¾"
$50 – 75
NOTE: 2 DIFF. JOINT LOCATIONS, FOR NO. 7300!
3½"
$20 – 30
BABY VAMP. SERIES No. 7400 — The Baby Vamp was made to meet the demand of the light rod user for a half-ounce bait in this popular type and found favor with thousands of anglers. Weighs ½ ounce, length 3½ inches.
(BABY VAMP NOT MADE IN SPOOK)
"PYRALIN" ← (USE THIS WORD TO I.D.) NEW → 1931
(G.E.)
$20 – 35
NO. 9500
3¾" ¾ oz.
Color 9509P Shiner Scale
FLOATING VAMP-SPOOK
NOTE: HAD A PLASTIC MOULDED LIP. 2 PC. HOOK RIG, AND GLASS EYES.
No. 9730 Jointed "Vamp-Spook" Transparent, Indestructible
Most life-like swimmer of all. The joint gives a lively side-kick to the tail, the very last touch of naturalness.
Not just another jointed bait but the liveliest, most natural swimming one you ever used. All game fish strike it. Floats, dives, and swims, and outdoes the wooden models in appearance and action. Strongly made and cannot come apart. Length 4½ inches, weight 4/5 ounce. Three treble hooks.
$30 – 40
4½"
MADE WITH 2 PC. HOOK RIG & SUNKEN, PAINTED EYES — LATER MADE WITH 1 PC. HOOK RIG.
"Vamp-Spook," No. 9750 Series. (3-Hook Model)
4½" ¾ oz.
SAME DETAILS AS NO. 9730 ABOVE.
$10 – 20
No. KF9750 King-Fish Model "Vamp-Spook" (Not Jointed) 1934
4½"
A "Killer" for Kingfish and other Salt-water Fish
The flashing metal jacket encircles the middle of the bait, and attracts the fish and centers the strike. The finish is practically indestructible and bait outlast a dozen wooden lures. Metal fittings and jacket of stainless metal. Length 4½ inches. Weight 1 ounce. Three large treble hooks.
Colors
No. KF9752 — White and Red
No. KF9759P — Shiner Scale
No. KF9759SH — Silver Herring
$50 – 60

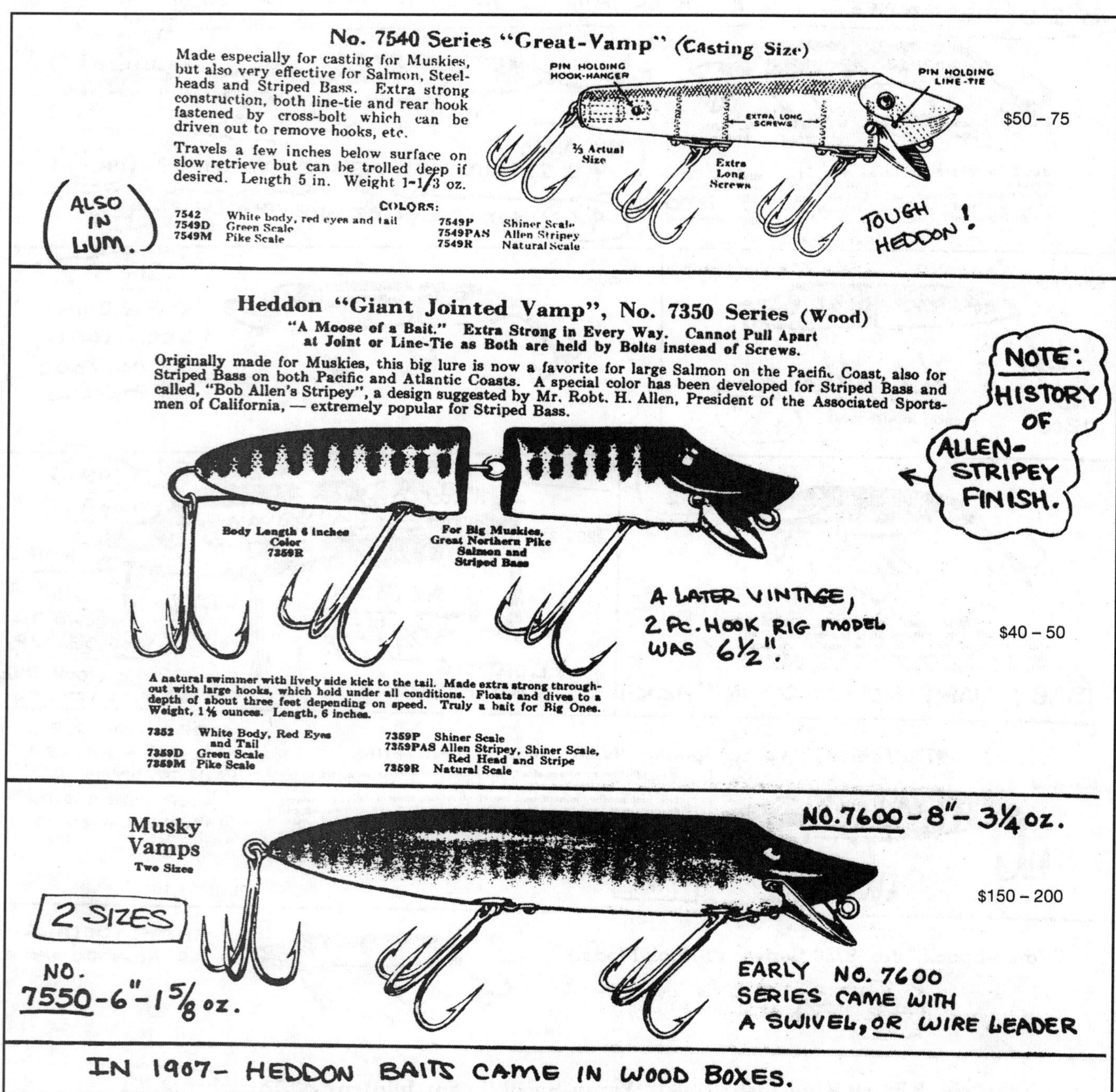

No. 7540 Series "Great-Vamp" (Casting Size)

Made especially for casting for Muskies, but also very effective for Salmon, Steelheads and Striped Bass. Extra strong construction, both line-tie and rear hook fastened by cross-bolt which can be driven out to remove hooks, etc.

Travels a few inches below surface on slow retrieve but can be trolled deep if desired. Length 5 in. Weight 1-1/3 oz.

PIN HOLDING HOOK-HANGER
PIN HOLDING LINE-TIE
EXTRA LONG SCREWS
⅔ Actual Size
Extra Long Screws

COLORS:

7542 White body, red eyes and tail
7549D Green Scale
7549M Pike Scale
7549P Shiner Scale
7549PAS Allen Stripey
7549R Natural Scale

ALSO IN LUM.

TOUGH HEDDON!

$50 – 75

Heddon "Giant Jointed Vamp", No. 7350 Series (Wood)

"A Moose of a Bait." Extra Strong in Every Way. Cannot Pull Apart at Joint or Line-Tie as Both are held by Bolts instead of Screws.

Originally made for Muskies, this big lure is now a favorite for large Salmon on the Pacific Coast, also for Striped Bass on both Pacific and Atlantic Coasts. A special color has been developed for Striped Bass and called, "Bob Allen's Stripey", a design suggested by Mr. Robt. H. Allen, President of the Associated Sportsmen of California, — extremely popular for Striped Bass.

NOTE: HISTORY OF ALLEN-STRIPEY FINISH.

Body Length 6 inches
Color
7359R
For Big Muskies, Great Northern Pike Salmon and Striped Bass

A LATER VINTAGE, 2 PC. HOOK RIG MODEL WAS 6½".

$40 – 50

A natural swimmer with lively side kick to the tail. Made extra strong throughout with large hooks, which hold under all conditions. Floats and dives to a depth of about three feet depending on speed. Truly a bait for Big Ones. Weight, 1⅝ ounces. Length, 6 inches.

7352 White Body, Red Eyes and Tail
7359D Green Scale
7359M Pike Scale
7359P Shiner Scale
7359PAS Allen Stripey, Shiner Scale, Red Head and Stripe
7359R Natural Scale

Musky Vamps
Two Sizes

NO. 7600 – 8" – 3¼ oz.

$150 – 200

2 SIZES

NO. 7550 – 6" – 1⅝ oz.

EARLY NO. 7600 SERIES CAME WITH A SWIVEL, OR WIRE LEADER

IN 1907 – HEDDON BAITS CAME IN WOOD BOXES.

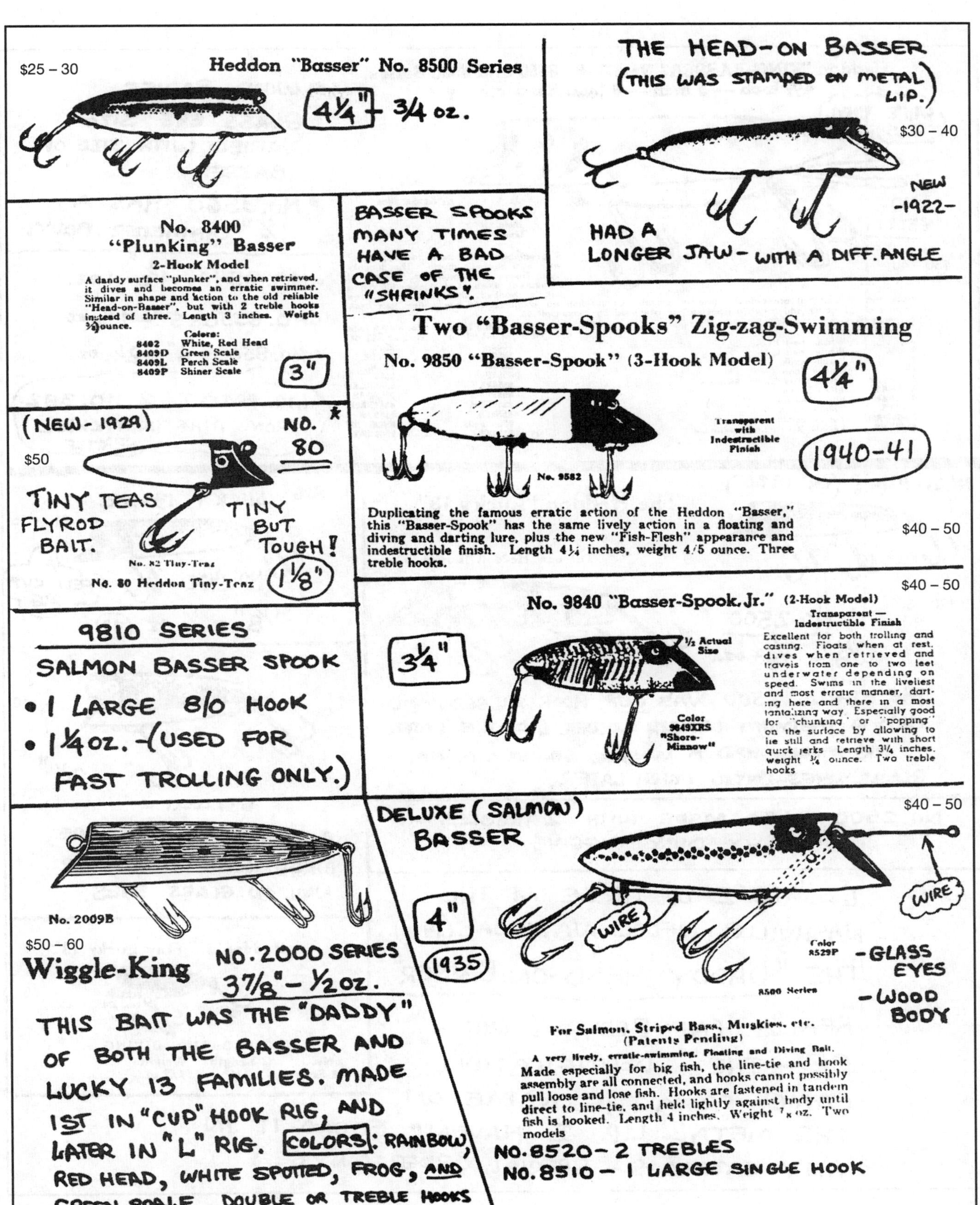
$25 – 30

Heddon "Basser" No. 8500 Series

4 1/4" – 3/4 oz.

THE HEAD-ON BASSER
(THIS WAS STAMPED ON METAL LIP.)

$30 – 40

NEW -1922-

HAD A LONGER JAW – WITH A DIFF. ANGLE

No. 8400
"Plunking" Basser
2-Hook Model

A dandy surface "plunker", and when retrieved, it dives and becomes an erratic swimmer. Similar in shape and action to the old reliable "Head-on-Basser", but with 2 treble hooks instead of three. Length 3 inches. Weight 3/5 ounce.

Colors:

8402	White, Red Head
8409D	Green Scale
8409L	Perch Scale
8409P	Shiner Scale

3"

BASSER SPOOKS MANY TIMES HAVE A BAD CASE OF THE "SHRINKS"!

Two "Basser-Spooks" Zig-zag-Swimming

No. 9850 "Basser-Spook" (3-Hook Model)

4 1/4"

Transparent with Indestructible Finish

1940-41

No. 9582

Duplicating the famous erratic action of the Heddon "Basser," this "Basser-Spook" has the same lively action in a floating and diving and darting lure, plus the new "Fish-Flesh" appearance and indestructible finish. Length 4 1/4 inches, weight 4/5 ounce. Three treble hooks.

$40 – 50

(NEW-1929)

NO. 80 *

$50

TINY TEAS FLYROD BAIT.

TINY BUT TOUGH!

No. 82 Tiny-Teaz

No. 80 Heddon Tiny-Teaz

1 1/8"

$40 – 50

No. 9840 "Basser-Spook. Jr." (2-Hook Model)

Transparent — Indestructible Finish

3 1/4"

1/2 Actual Size

Color 9849XRS "Shore-Minnow"

Excellent for both trolling and casting. Floats when at rest, dives when retrieved and travels from one to two feet underwater depending on speed. Swims in the liveliest and most erratic manner, darting here and there in a most tantalizing way. Especially good for "chunking" or "popping" on the surface by allowing to lie still and retrieve with short quick jerks. Length 3 1/4 inches, weight 3/4 ounce. Two treble hooks

9810 SERIES

SALMON BASSER SPOOK

- 1 LARGE 8/0 HOOK
- 1 1/4 OZ. -(USED FOR FAST TROLLING ONLY.)

No. 2009B

$50 – 60

Wiggle-King

NO. 2000 SERIES
3 7/8" – 1/2 OZ.

THIS BAIT WAS THE "DADDY" OF BOTH THE BASSER AND LUCKY 13 FAMILIES. MADE 1ST IN "CUP" HOOK RIG, AND LATER IN "L" RIG. COLORS: RAINBOW, RED HEAD, WHITE SPOTTED, FROG, AND GREEN SCALE. DOUBLE OR TREBLE HOOKS

DELUXE (SALMON) BASSER

$40 – 50

4"

1935

WIRE

WIRE

Color 8529P

- GLASS EYES
- WOOD BODY

8500 Series

For Salmon, Striped Bass, Muskies, etc.
(Patents Pending)

A very lively, erratic-swimming, Floating and Diving Bait.

Made especially for big fish, the line-tie and hook assembly are all connected, and hooks cannot possibly pull loose and lose fish. Hooks are fastened in tandem direct to line-tie, and held lightly against body until fish is hooked. Length 4 inches. Weight 7/8 oz. Two models

NO. 8520 – 2 TREBLES
NO. 8510 – 1 LARGE SINGLE HOOK

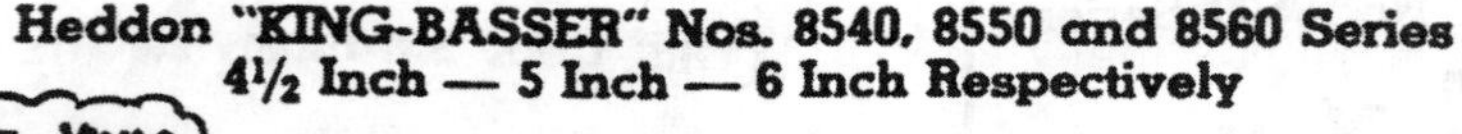

Heddon "KING-BASSER" Nos. 8540, 8550 and 8560 Series
4½ Inch — 5 Inch — 6 Inch Respectively

WHITE VINYL TAILS
NO. 8552M
Cross-bolt Holding Line-Tie.
½ Actual Size

$30 – 40

- WOOD BODIES
- GLASS EYE SIZE VARIED WITH SIZE OF BASSER.
- NO. 8560 HAS A 1¼" DIAMETER BODY.

- NO. 8540 - 4½" - 1 oz.
- NO. 8550 - 5" - 1 1/10 oz.
- NO. 8560 - 6" - 2¼ oz.

LIC. PATENT 2,110,382 FROM MARTIN TACKLE_ SEATTLE.

A great bait for salmon-trolling, either with row boat or motor. The loosely hung hooks give maximum freedom of movement, even at slow speed. When fish is hooked, the hooks come free from rear of bait but are held by line tie thereby giving fish no leverage and preventing fish from getting off. Line-tie and forward hook station are held by cross-bolt.

No. 8540 4½ Inch Weight 1 oz.		No. 8550 5 Inch Weight 1-1/10 oz	No. 8560 6 Inch Weight 2¼ oz
8542	White, Red Head	8552	8562
8542M	White, Red Gills	8552M	8562M
8549L	Perch Scale	8559L	8569L
8549P	Shiner Scale	8559P	8569P
8549PLXR	Pearl X-ray Shore Minnow	8559PLXR	8569PLXR
8549PAS	Allen Stripe	8559PAS	8569PAS
8549PBH	Blue Herring	8559PBH	8569PBH
8549YS	Yellow Scale	8559YS	8569YS
8549SPRH	Yellow Spotted	8559SPRH	8569SPRH
8549XRY	Yellow X-ray Shore Minnow	8559XRY	8569XRY

NEW - 1919? (OR 1920)

The Heddon "Lucky 13"

$20 – 30

The new Heddon "Lucky 13"

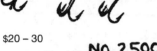

NO. 2500

3⅞" - ⅝+ oz.

THE EARLY 2500 WAS CUP HOOK RIGGED, AND HAD A MEDIUM LENGTH LOWER LIP. THE LATER L RIG MODEL HAD A LONGER LOWER LIP. NO GLASS EYES UNTIL MUCH LATER.

NO. 2500 ALSO MADE WITH 2 TREBLES AND HEAVY DUTY RIGGING.

I SAW 2 OF THESE AT THE NASHVILLE NFLCC NATIONAL (1990) THE "DADDY HEAD-ON BASSER"

REALLY FAT BODY - L RIG - G.E. - THE IDENTIFICATION CAME FROM THE NAME ON THE METAL LIP. I HAVEN'T FOUND IT IN ANY CATALOGS - SPECIAL ORDER MAYBE?

"L" RIG LUCKY 13-JR.

$10 – 15

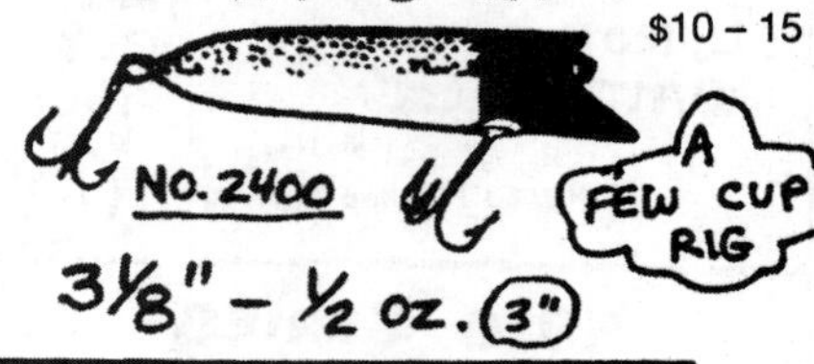
NO. 2400
A FEW CUP RIG

3⅛" - ½ oz. (3")

2½"

$10

BABY LUCKY 13

A LATER VINTAGE LURE, MADE WITH PAINTED OR NAIL ON GLASS EYES.

Heddon's "Tiny Lucky 13"

No. 370 Series

$5

FLOATING-DIVING

No.	Length	Weight
370 Series	1⅞"	1/5 oz.

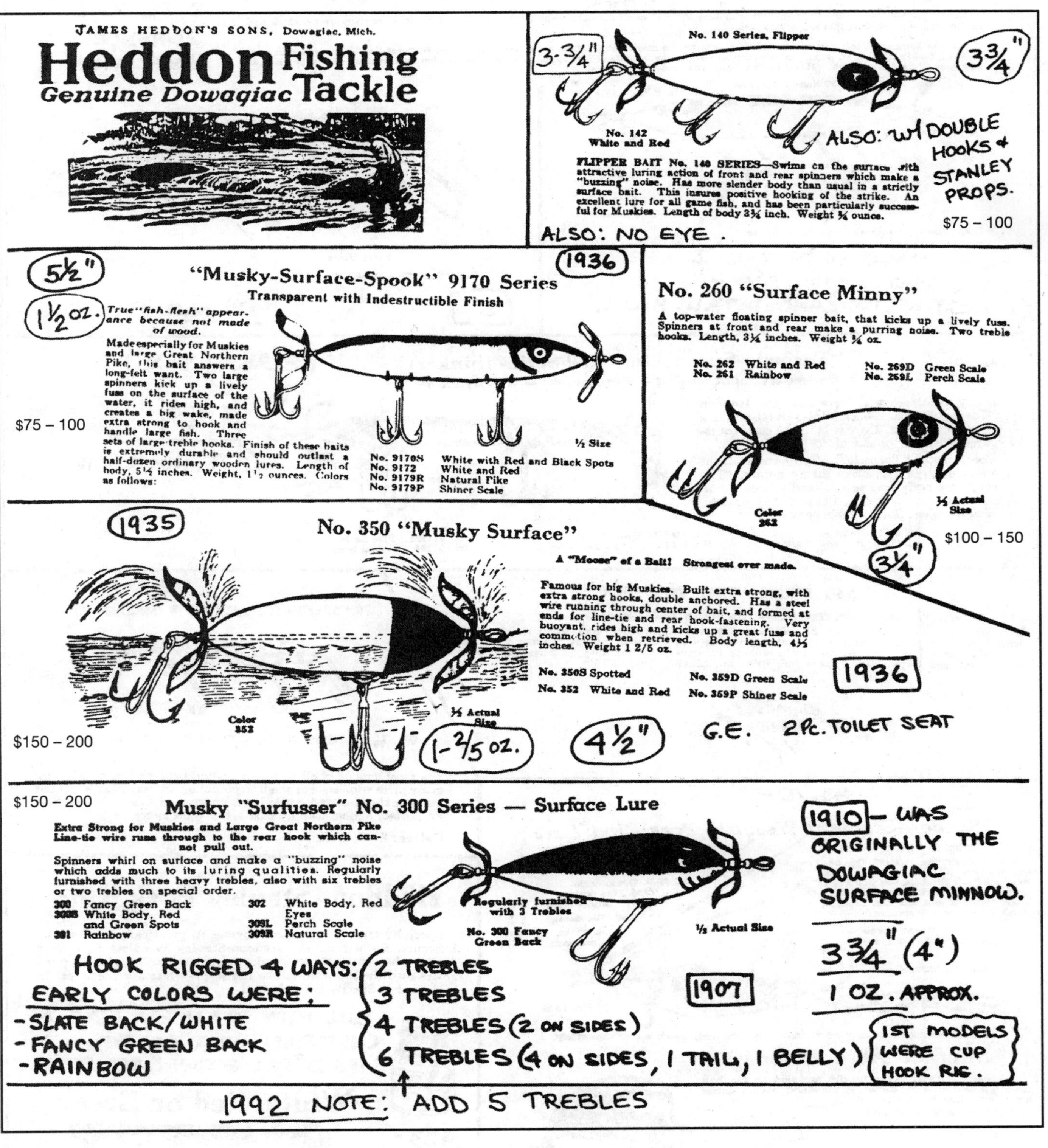

JAMES HEDDON'S SONS, Dowagiac, Mich.

Heddon Fishing Tackle

Genuine Dowagiac **Tackle**

No. 140 Series, Flipper

3-3/4"

3¾"

No. 142 White and Red

ALSO: W/ DOUBLE HOOKS & STANLEY PROPS.

FLIPPER BAIT No. 140 SERIES—Swims on the surface with attractive luring action of front and rear spinners which make a "buzzing" noise. Has more slender body than usual in a strictly surface bait. This insures positive hooking of the strike. An excellent lure for all game fish, and has been particularly successful for Muskies. Length of body 3¾ inch. Weight ¾ ounce.

$75 – 100

ALSO: NO EYE.

5½"

1936

"Musky-Surface-Spook" 9170 Series

Transparent with Indestructible Finish

1½ oz.

True "fish-flesh" appearance because not made of wood.

Made especially for Muskies and large Great Northern Pike, this bait answers a long-felt want. Two large spinners kick up a lively fuss on the surface of the water, it rides high, and creates a big wake, made extra strong to hook and handle large fish. Three sets of large treble hooks. Finish of these baits is extremely durable and should outlast a half-dozen ordinary wooden lures. Length of body, 5¼ inches. Weight, 1½ ounces. Colors as follows:

½ Size

$75 – 100

No. 9170S	White with Red and Black Spots
No. 9172	White and Red
No. 9179R	Natural Pike
No. 9179P	Shiner Scale

No. 260 "Surface Minny"

A top-water floating spinner bait, that kicks up a lively fuss. Spinners at front and rear make a purring noise. Two treble hooks. Length, 3¼ inches. Weight ¾ oz.

No. 262	White and Red	No. 269D	Green Scale
No. 261	Rainbow	No. 269L	Perch Scale

Color 262

⅓ Actual Size

$100 – 150

3¼"

1935

No. 350 "Musky Surface"

A "Moose" of a Bait! Strongest ever made.

Famous for big Muskies. Built extra strong, with extra strong hooks, double anchored. Has a steel wire running through center of bait, and formed at ends for line-tie and rear hook-fastening. Very buoyant, rides high and kicks up a great fuss and commotion when retrieved. Body length, 4½ inches. Weight 1 2/5 oz.

No. 350S	Spotted	No. 359D	Green Scale
No. 352	White and Red	No. 359P	Shiner Scale

1936

Color 352

⅓ Actual Size

$150 – 200

1-2/5 oz.

4½"

G.E. 2Pc. TOILET SEAT

$150 – 200

Musky "Surfusser" No. 300 Series — Surface Lure

1910 – WAS ORIGINALLY THE DOWAGIAC SURFACE MINNOW.

Extra Strong for Muskies and Large Great Northern Pike Line-tie wire runs through to the rear hook which cannot pull out.

Spinners whirl on surface and make a "buzzing" noise which adds much to its luring qualities. Regularly furnished with three heavy trebles, also with six trebles or two trebles on special order.

300	Fancy Green Back	302	White Body, Red Eyes
300S	White Body, Red and Green Spots	309L	Perch Scale
301	Rainbow	309R	Natural Scale

Regularly furnished with 3 Trebles

No. 300 Fancy Green Back

½ Actual Size

3¾" (4")

1 OZ. APPROX.

1907

HOOK RIGGED 4 WAYS:
- 2 TREBLES
- 3 TREBLES
- 4 TREBLES (2 ON SIDES)
- 6 TREBLES (4 ON SIDES, 1 TAIL, 1 BELLY)

EARLY COLORS WERE:
- SLATE BACK/WHITE
- FANCY GREEN BACK
- RAINBOW

1ST MODELS WERE CUP HOOK RIG.

1992 NOTE: ADD 5 TREBLES

Heddon "Torpedo"—Underwater

MADE IN "L", 2 Pc. AND SURFACE HOOK RIGS.

These Torpedo Lures are sinking minnows with long body of small diameter — believed by many to be an advantage over a thick body in hooking and holding hard-mouthed fish.

A favorite because of the ease with which it shoots to the mark—straight as an arrow. Has a weird "crawling" appearance in water and is a fine "actor" in streams. In contrast to cheaply made baits of like type, note the full Heddon construction—eyes, patent hook fastening, superlative finish. Made in two sizes, two and three hooks.

No. 130 Series, Torpedo

$30 – 50

No. 139Z Rainbow Scale

NO. 130

Large Size (Three Hook) 4½ in. ¾ ounce.

ALSO MADE WITH THE 2 SIDE TREBLE HOOK RIG—(LIKE THE 100) AND 1 TAIL HOOK.

No. 120 Series, Torpedo

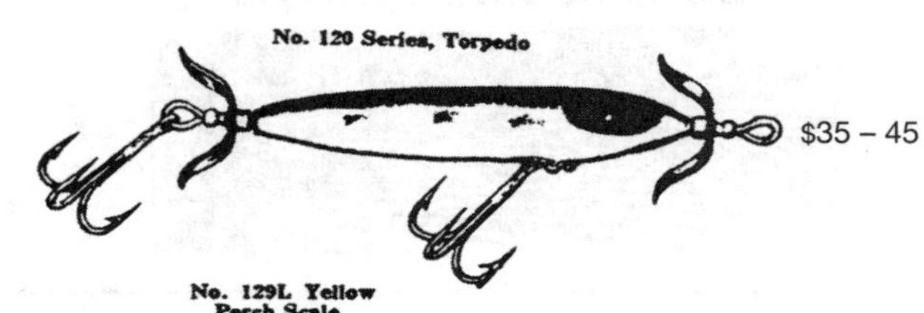

$35 – 45

No. 129L Yellow Perch Scale

Small Size (Two Hook) 3 in. ½ ounce.

3"

NO. 120

$50 – 75

"Torpedo-Spook" No. 9130 Series (Sinker)

Underwater Spinner Bait — Transparent — Indestructible

(GLASS EYES)

Many fishermen who have used the Heddon "Torpedo" (No. 130 and 150 series) prefer a slim bodied bait. Here it is in the new transparent "Spook" material.

The famous "Torpedo." Spinners at front and rear give attractive luring action. The very slim body makes it a deadly hooker and an excellent caster. Length 4¾ inches. Weight, ¾ oz. Three treble hooks.

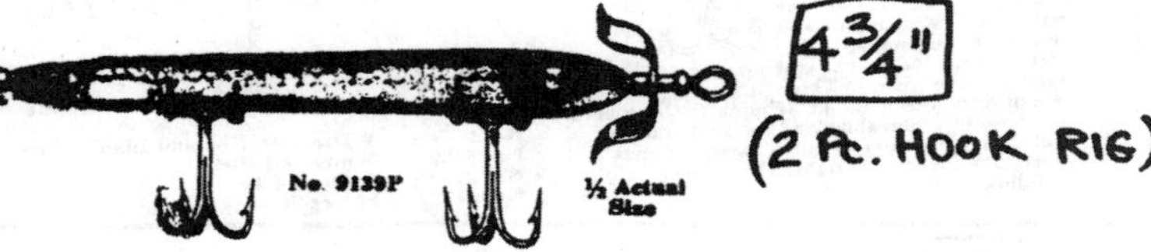

No. 9139P ½ Actual Size

4¾"

(2 Pc. HOOK RIG)

No. 9131 Rainbow
No. 9132 Red and White
No. 9139D Green Scale
No. 9139L Yellow Perch Scale
No. 9139M Pike Scale
No. 9139P Shiner Scale

360 SERIES "TINY TORPEDO"

Wt. 1/5 oz. — Lgt. 2½ in. — Two No. 6 Treble Hooks —

This lure is a topwater version of the famous Heddon "Torpedo" and when slowly retrieved, with a series of jerks of the rod tip, imitates a struggling wounded minnow. When a fast retrieve is used, it acts like a scared minnow streaking for cover. Outstanding for bass, pike, crappies, white bass and large trout. Colors: BF, RHF, RH, L, XRS, XRW, XBW

$5 – 10

30 "SALTWATER TORPEDO"® (SINKING)

P.E. $15 – 20

G.E. $30 – 40

Wt. ⅞ oz.—Lgt. 4⅛ in.—Three No. 1 Treble Hooks

The most famous of all saltwater casting baits and responsible for many prize winners. For small tarpon, channel bass, bluefish, snook and weakfish (saltwater trout), it is unexcelled. Correctly weighted for perfect action. Can be cast extreme distances.

Colors: XWB, XWR

$15 – 20

—NO. 70—

"Heddon-Stanley" Weedless Pork Rind Lure

No. 70 Series

Body of pyralin, weight ½ oz., length over all 3½ inches. This weedless Pork Rind Lure is positively the last word in Pork Rind Baits, absolutely weedless and snagless. Special Stanley type double spinner.

Weedless always furnished unless "Plain" is specified.

Weedless illustrated

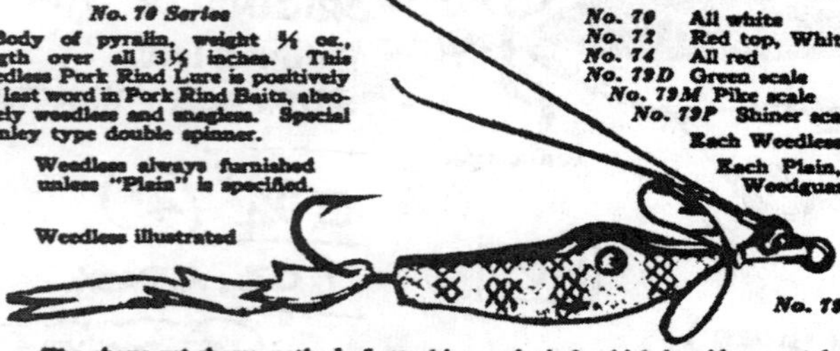

No. 70 All white
No. 72 Red top, White bottom
No. 74 All red
No. 79D Green scale
No. 79M Pike scale
No. 79P Shiner scale
Each Weedless,
Each Plain, without Weedguard.

No. 79M

The above cut shows method of attaching pork rind, which is sold separately.

Surface Attachment

A pair of metal wings readily attached to the bait, causing it to ride on the surface of the water, with a skittering effect when being retrieved.

(Cut is one-half actual size.)

(NEW - 1923)

The above Pork Rind illustration shows the shape and special slitting. Actual length of strip, 3½ inches. Specially designed for use on Heddon Stanley No. 70

Heddon-Stanley Pork Rind—

Specially cut for animated movement, practically non-fouling. Designed for use on the Heddon-Stanley Weedless Pork-Rind Lures—the new Ace and Stanley Weedless Hooks. Red or green colors furnished in addition to the staple white are the latest in pork-rinds. Specify color desired.

Pork Rind

WILLIAM STANLEY WAS A CHAMPION BAIT CASTER AND MFG'D "PERFECTION WEEDLESS HKS

—White, Red or Green

1923—HEDDON BOUGHT STANLEY.

Showing How This Pork Strip Looks in Water

$10

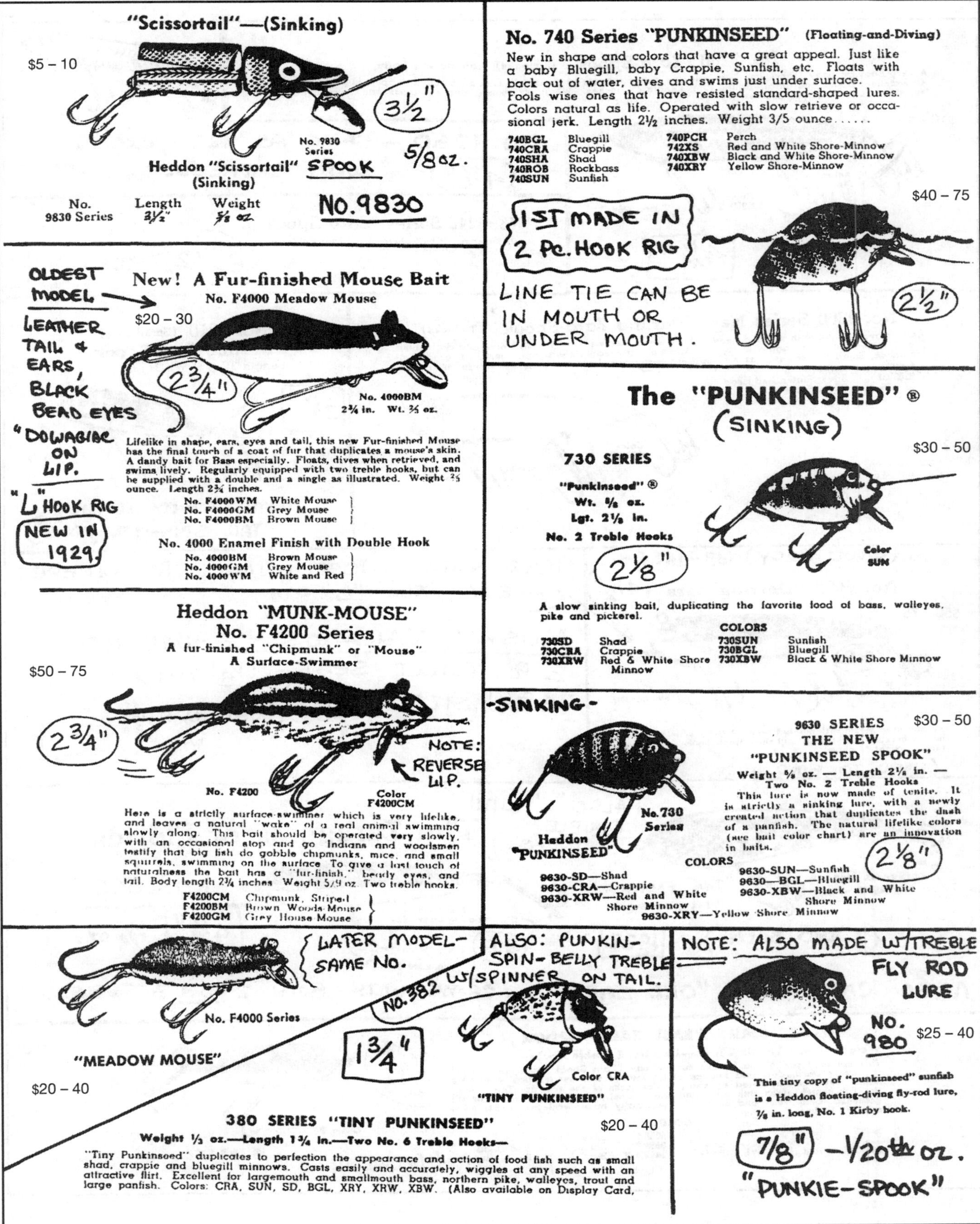

"Scissortail"—(Sinking)

$5 – 10

3 1/2"

No. 9830 Series SPOOK

5/8 oz.

Heddon "Scissortail" (Sinking)

No.	Length	Weight
9830 Series	3 1/2"	5/8 oz.

NO. 9830

No. 740 Series "PUNKINSEED" (Floating-and-Diving)

New in shape and colors that have a great appeal. Just like a baby Bluegill, baby Crappie, Sunfish, etc. Floats with back out of water, dives and swims just under surface. Fools wise ones that have resisted standard-shaped lures. Colors natural as life. Operated with slow retrieve or occasional jerk. Length 2 1/2 inches. Weight 3/5 ounce......

740BGL Bluegill
740CRA Crappie
740SHA Shad
740ROB Rockbass
740SUN Sunfish
740PCH Perch
742XS Red and White Shore-Minnow
740XBW Black and White Shore-Minnow
740XRY Yellow Shore-Minnow

$40 – 75

1ST MADE IN 2 PC. HOOK RIG

LINE TIE CAN BE IN MOUTH OR UNDER MOUTH.

2 1/2"

OLDEST MODEL →

New! A Fur-finished Mouse Bait

No. F4000 Meadow Mouse

$20 – 30

LEATHER TAIL & EARS, BLACK BEAD EYES

"DOWAGIAC" ON LIP.

"L" HOOK RIG

NEW IN 1929.

2 3/4"

No. 4000BM
2 3/4 in. Wt. 2/5 oz.

Lifelike in shape, ears, eyes and tail, this new Fur-finished Mouse has the final touch of a coat of fur that duplicates a mouse's skin. A dandy bait for Bass especially. Floats, dives when retrieved, and swims lively. Regularly equipped with two treble hooks, but can be supplied with a double and a single as illustrated. Weight 2/5 ounce. Length 2 3/4 inches.

No. F4000WM White Mouse
No. F4000GM Grey Mouse
No. F4000BM Brown Mouse

No. 4000 Enamel Finish with Double Hook

No. 4000BM Brown Mouse
No. 4000GM Grey Mouse
No. 4000WM White and Red

Heddon "MUNK-MOUSE"
No. F4200 Series
A fur-finished "Chipmunk" or "Mouse"
A Surface-Swimmer

$50 – 75

2 3/4"

NOTE: REVERSE LIP.

No. F4200

Color F4200CM

Here is a strictly surface-swimmer which is very lifelike, and leaves a natural "wake" of a real animal swimming slowly along. This bait should be operated very slowly, with an occasional stop and go. Indians and woodsmen testify that big fish do gobble chipmunks, mice, and small squirrels, swimming on the surface. To give a last touch of naturalness the bait has a "fur-finish," beady eyes, and tail. Body length 2 3/4 inches. Weight 5/9 oz. Two treble hooks.

F4200CM Chipmunk, Striped
F4200BM Brown Woods Mouse
F4200GM Grey House Mouse

The "PUNKINSEED"®
(SINKING)

$30 – 50

730 SERIES

"Punkinseed"®
Wt. 5/8 oz.
Lgt. 2 1/8 in.
No. 2 Treble Hooks

Color SUN

2 1/8"

A slow sinking bait, duplicating the favorite food of bass, walleyes, pike and pickerel.

COLORS

730SD Shad
730CRA Crappie
730XRW Red & White Shore Minnow
730SUN Sunfish
730BGL Bluegill
730XBW Black & White Shore Minnow

-SINKING-

No. 730 Series

Heddon "PUNKINSEED"

9630 SERIES
THE NEW
"PUNKINSEED SPOOK"

$30 – 50

Weight 5/8 oz. — Length 2 1/8 in. — Two No. 2 Treble Hooks

This lure is now made of tenite. It is strictly a sinking lure, with a newly created action that duplicates the dash of a panfish. The natural lifelike colors (see bait color chart) are an innovation in baits.

2 1/8"

COLORS

9630-SD—Shad
9630-CRA—Crappie
9630-XRW—Red and White Shore Minnow
9630-XRY—Yellow Shore Minnow
9630-SUN—Sunfish
9630—BGL—Bluegill
9630-XBW—Black and White Shore Minnow

LATER MODEL- SAME NO.

No. F4000 Series

"MEADOW MOUSE"

$20 – 40

ALSO: PUNKIN-SPIN- BELLY TREBLE ON TAIL.

NO. 382 W/SPINNER

1 3/4"

Color CRA

"TINY PUNKINSEED"

380 SERIES "TINY PUNKINSEED"

$20 – 40

Weight 1/3 oz.—Length 1 3/4 in.—Two No. 6 Treble Hooks—

"Tiny Punkinseed" duplicates to perfection the appearance and action of food fish such as small shad, crappie and bluegill minnows. Casts easily and accurately, wiggles at any speed with an attractive flirt. Excellent for largemouth and smallmouth bass, northern pike, walleyes, trout and large panfish. Colors: CRA, SUN, SD, BGL, XRY, XRW, XBW. (Also available on Display Card,

NOTE: ALSO MADE W/TREBLE

FLY ROD LURE

NO. 980

$25 – 40

This tiny copy of "punkinseed" sunfish is a Heddon floating-diving fly-rod lure, 7/8 in. long, No. 1 Kirby hook.

7/8" -1/20th oz.

"PUNKIE-SPOOK"

No. 9260 "Zara-Spook" (3 Hooks) Transparent body.

A very buoyant body makes this bait bob and dance when rod is jerked. Can be made to leap nearly half out of water. An excellent caster and an all-around lure. Length 4¼ inches. Weight 4/5 ounce and equipped with 3 strong treble hooks. No. 9250 is same size but has two trebles

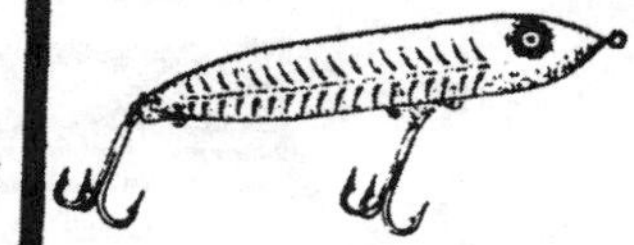

$10 – 15

½ Actual Size

Color 9269XRG

No. 9260 Series

4¼"

NO. 9250 – SAME AS 9260, EXCEPT (4¼") WITH 2 TREBLES.

$10 – 15

No. 9240 Series "Zara-Spook Jr."

Length 3 inches. Weight ⅜ ounce. Two trebles. Same colors as others.

3" 2 TREBLES

No. 9200 Series New "Darting Zara-Spook" (3 Hooks)

An improved model with notched head, which when "jerked" rapidly, will dive and dart about 6 or 8 inches and jump again to top. Should be retrieved in short quick jerks. A great bait for Snook, Small Tarpon, etc., as well as fresh-water fish. Length 4¼ inches. Weight 4/5 ounce

9209BF Bull-Frog
9209RH Silver Flitter, Red Head
9209SS Silver Scale

$25 – 50

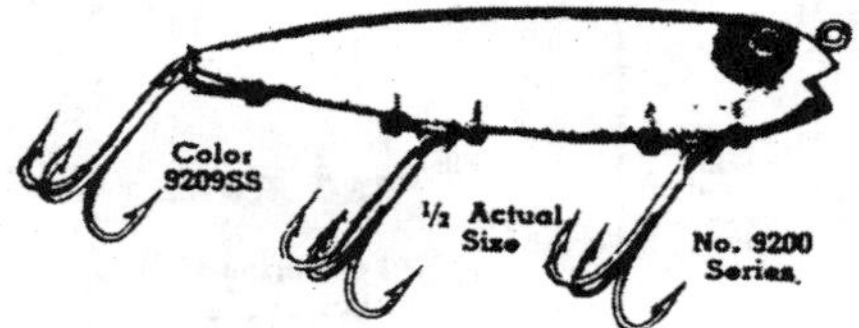

Color 9209SS

½ Actual Size

No. 9200 Series.

No. 9210 (Small Size) Darting-Zara-Spook

Length 3⅛ in. Wt. 3/5 oz.

3⅛"

$15

WITH OR WITHOUT THE TAIL SPINNER. (ADD'S.)

(WOOD BODY) 1933–1934 –

No. 6600 "Darting Zara" (4½")

$50 – 75

G.E.

Color No. 6609BF

An improved model with notched head. A lively actor and a sure hooker because of slim body and three treble hooks. Length 4½ inches, weight ⅝ ounce.

(HARD TO FIND LURE)

G.E.

(1992 NOTE: MOSTLY IN 2 PC. – THERE ARE A FEW "L" RIG.

MUSKY ZARAGOSSA – HUGE H.D. 2 PC. TOILET SEAT – 1⅛" THICK – 4 3/4" SIZE. RED HEAD/WHITE.

The Zaragossa of Florida

$75 – 150

(ALSO "L" WITH DOUBLE HOOKS.)

Zaragossa Minnow No. 6500 Series

"THE FLORIDA WONDER"

(WOOD BODY) 1922

No. 6509 D Illustration ½ actual size

G.E.

No. 6500 Series

NO. 6500

4½" – ¾ oz.

ALSO CALLED THE "OLD ZARA" — CAME WITH BOTH 2 and 3 TREBLES.

365 SERIES "BABY ZARA" SPOOK

Weight ⅜ oz.—Length 2⅞ in.—Two No. 2 Treble Hooks—

This spinning size of the famous casting size "Zara Spook" is a natural! All the lively dash, dart and bounce of an injured minnow frantically seeking safety, when manipulated by short, quick jerks of the rod tip. The size of the fish which slash this lure, and their ferocity, will amaze you. For all gamefish, both fresh and saltwater, especially bass, walleyes, trout, pike, and white bass.

COLORS

365BF	Bullfrog	365SS	Silver Flitter
365XRY	Yellow Shore Minnow	365PRH	Shiner Scale, Red Head
365RH	Red Head, White Body	365XBW	Black & White Shore Minnow

2⅞"

$10

Color BF

SURFACE

(DECAL EYE)

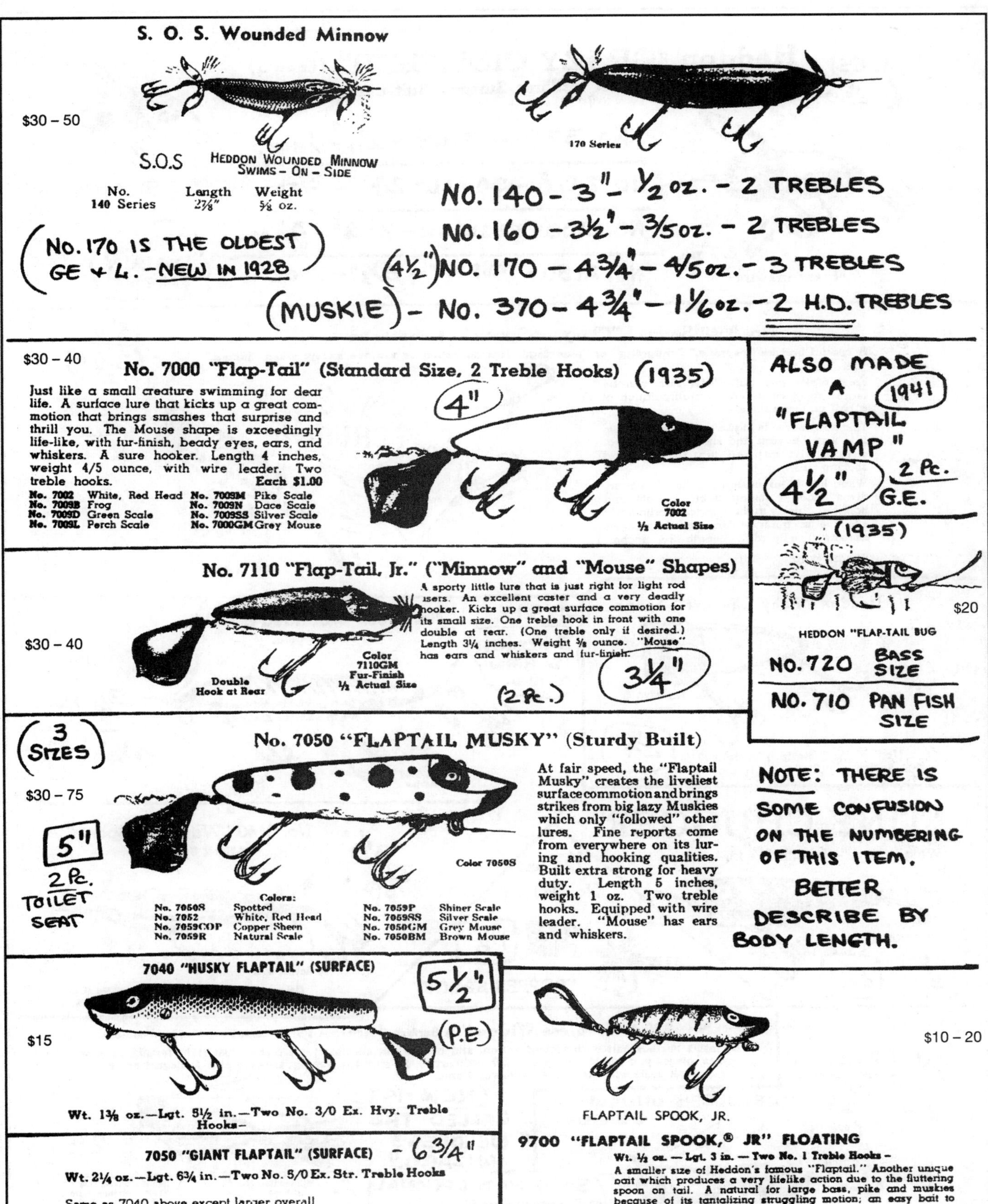
S. O. S. Wounded Minnow
$30 – 50
S.O.S HEDDON WOUNDED MINNOW SWIMS – ON – SIDE
No. 140 Series Length 2⅞" Weight ⅝ oz.
170 Series
NO. 140 – 3" – ½ oz. – 2 TREBLES
NO. 160 – 3½" – 3/5 oz. – 2 TREBLES
(4½") NO. 170 – 4¾" – 4/5 oz. – 3 TREBLES
(MUSKIE) – NO. 370 – 4¾" – 1⅙ oz. – 2 H.D. TREBLES
(NO. 170 IS THE OLDEST GE + L. – NEW IN 1928)
$30 – 40
No. 7000 "Flap-Tail" (Standard Size, 2 Treble Hooks) (1935)
(4")
Just like a small creature swimming for dear life. A surface lure that kicks up a great commotion that brings smashes that surprise and thrill you. The Mouse shape is exceedingly life-like, with fur-finish, beady eyes, ears, and whiskers. A sure hooker. Length 4 inches, weight 4/5 ounce, with wire leader. Two treble hooks. Each $1.00
No. 7002 White, Red Head No. 7009M Pike Scale
No. 7009B Frog No. 7009N Dace Scale
No. 7009D Green Scale No. 7009SS Silver Scale
No. 7009L Perch Scale No. 7000GM Grey Mouse
Color 7002
½ Actual Size
ALSO MADE A (1941) "FLAPTAIL VAMP" (4½") 2 Pc. G.E.
(1935)
$20
HEDDON "FLAP-TAIL BUG
NO. 720 BASS SIZE
NO. 710 PAN FISH SIZE
No. 7110 "Flap-Tail, Jr." ("Minnow" and "Mouse" Shapes)
$30 – 40
A sporty little lure that is just right for light rod users. An excellent caster and a very deadly hooker. Kicks up a great surface commotion for its small size. One treble hook in front with one double at rear. (One treble only if desired.) Length 3¼ inches. Weight ⅝ ounce. "Mouse" has ears and whiskers and fur-finish.
Double Hook at Rear
Color 7110GM Fur-Finish
½ Actual Size
(3¼")
(2 Pc.)
(3 SIZES)
No. 7050 "FLAPTAIL MUSKY" (Sturdy Built)
$30 – 75
(5")
2 Pc. TOILET SEAT
At fair speed, the "Flaptail Musky" creates the liveliest surface commotion and brings strikes from big lazy Muskies which only "followed" other lures. Fine reports come from everywhere on its luring and hooking qualities. Built extra strong for heavy duty. Length 5 inches, weight 1 oz. Two treble hooks. Equipped with wire leader. "Mouse" has ears and whiskers.
Color 7050S
Colors:
No. 7050S Spotted No. 7059P Shiner Scale
No. 7052 White, Red Head No. 7059SS Silver Scale
No. 7059COP Copper Sheen No. 7050GM Grey Mouse
No. 7059R Natural Scale No. 7050BM Brown Mouse
NOTE: THERE IS SOME CONFUSION ON THE NUMBERING OF THIS ITEM. BETTER DESCRIBE BY BODY LENGTH.
7040 "HUSKY FLAPTAIL" (SURFACE)
(5½")
(P.E)
$15
Wt. 1⅜ oz.—Lgt. 5½ in.—Two No. 3/0 Ex. Hvy. Treble Hooks—
7050 "GIANT FLAPTAIL" (SURFACE) – 6¾"
Wt. 2¼ oz.—Lgt. 6¾ in.—Two No. 5/0 Ex. Str. Treble Hooks
Same as 7040 above except larger overall
$10 – 20
FLAPTAIL SPOOK, JR.
9700 "FLAPTAIL SPOOK,® JR" FLOATING
Wt. ½ oz. — Lgt. 3 in. — Two No. 1 Treble Hooks —
A smaller size of Heddon's famous "Flaptail." Another unique bait which produces a very lifelike action due to the fluttering spoon on tail. A natural for large bass, pike and muskies because of its tantalizing struggling motion; an easy bait to use because it works itself.

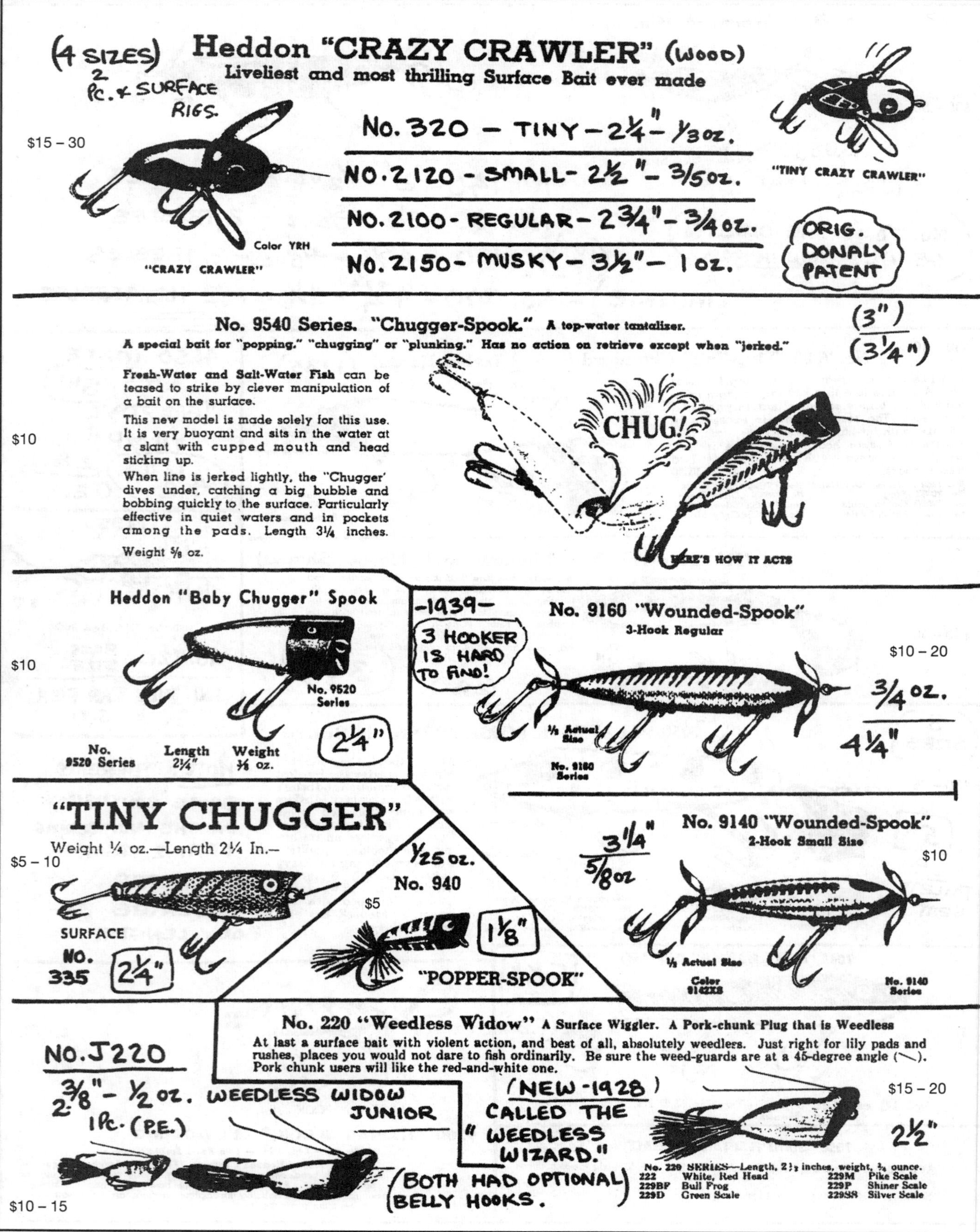
(4 SIZES) Heddon "CRAZY CRAWLER" (WOOD)
Liveliest and most thrilling Surface Bait ever made
2 Pc. & SURFACE RIGS.
$15 – 30
No. 320 – TINY – 2¼" – ⅓ oz.
NO. 2120 – SMALL – 2½" – 3/5 oz.
NO. 2100 – REGULAR – 2¾" – ¾ oz.
NO. 2150 – MUSKY – 3½" – 1 oz.
Color YRH
"CRAZY CRAWLER"
"TINY CRAZY CRAWLER"
ORIG. DONALY PATENT
No. 9540 Series. "Chugger-Spook." A top-water tantalizer.
A special bait for "popping," "chugging" or "plunking." Has no action on retrieve except when "jerked."
(3") (3¼")
Fresh-Water and Salt-Water Fish can be teased to strike by clever manipulation of a bait on the surface.
This new model is made solely for this use. It is very buoyant and sits in the water at a slant with cupped mouth and head sticking up.
When line is jerked lightly, the "Chugger" dives under, catching a big bubble and bobbing quickly to the surface. Particularly effective in quiet waters and in pockets among the pads. Length 3¼ inches.
Weight ⅝ oz.
$10
CHUG!
HERE'S HOW IT ACTS
Heddon "Baby Chugger" Spook
$10
No. 9520 Series
No. 9520 Series
Length 2¼"
Weight ⅜ oz.
2¼"
-1939-
3 HOOKER IS HARD TO FIND!
No. 9160 "Wounded-Spook"
3-Hook Regular
$10 – 20
¾ oz.
4¼"
⅓ Actual Size
No. 9160 Series
"TINY CHUGGER"
Weight ¼ oz.—Length 2¼ In.—
$5 – 10
SURFACE
NO. 335
2¼"
1/25 oz.
No. 940
$5
1⅛"
"POPPER-SPOOK"
3¼"
⅝ oz
No. 9140 "Wounded-Spook"
2-Hook Small Size
$10
⅓ Actual Size
Color 9142XS
No. 9140 Series
No. 220 "Weedless Widow" A Surface Wiggler. A Pork-chunk Plug that is Weedless
At last a surface bait with violent action, and best of all, absolutely weedless. Just right for lily pads and rushes, places you would not dare to fish ordinarily. Be sure the weed-guards are at a 45-degree angle (⟍). Pork chunk users will like the red-and-white one.
NO. J220
2⅜" – ½ oz. WEEDLESS WIDOW JUNIOR
1 Pc. (P.E.)
(NEW-1928) CALLED THE "WEEDLESS WIZARD."
(BOTH HAD OPTIONAL BELLY HOOKS.
$15 – 20
2½"
$10 – 15
No. 220 SERIES—Length, 2½ inches, weight, ⅔ ounce.
222 White, Red Head
229BF Bull Frog
229D Green Scale
229M Pike Scale
229P Shiner Scale
229SS Silver Scale

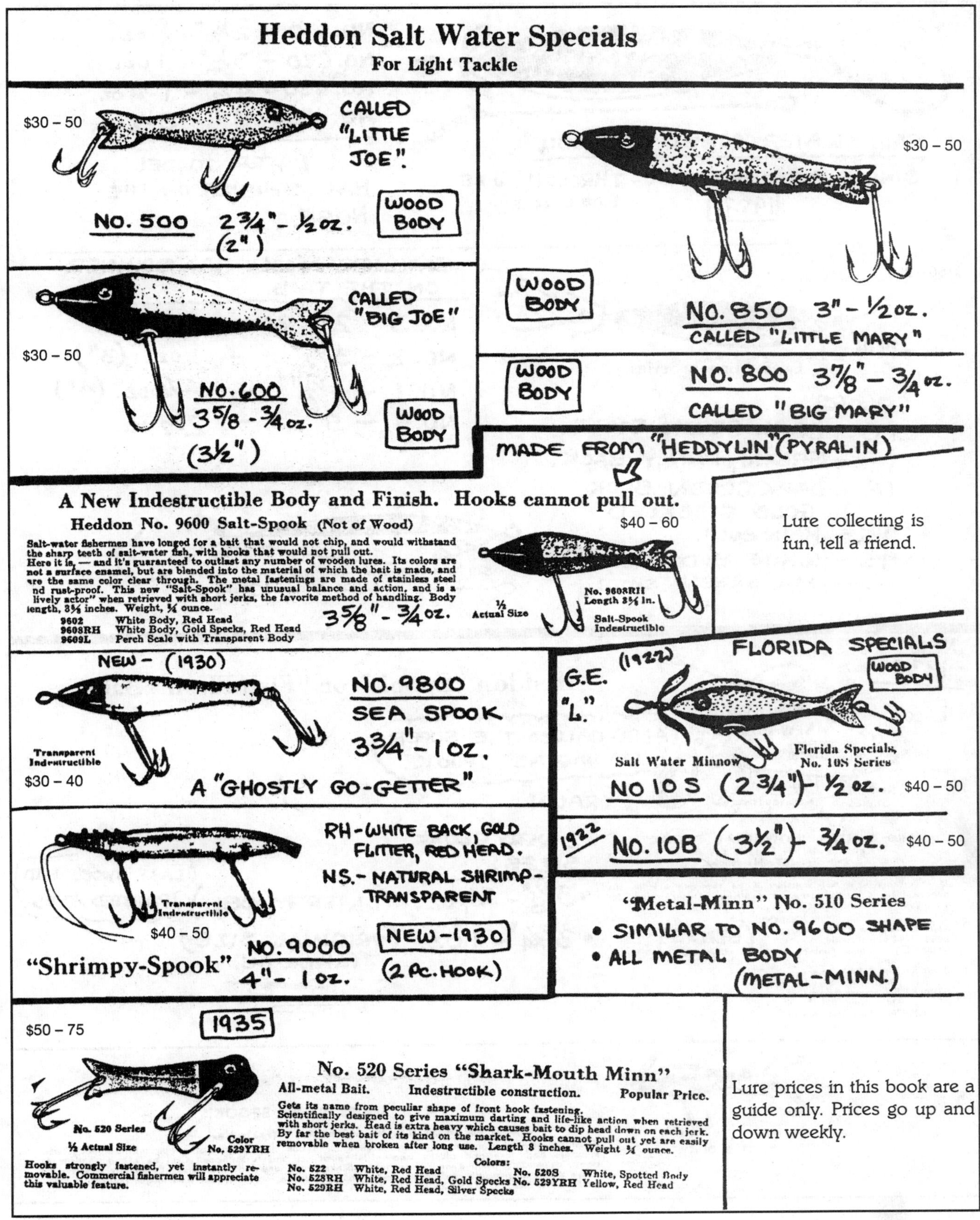

Heddon Salt Water Specials

For Light Tackle

$30 – 50

CALLED "LITTLE JOE".

NO. 500 2¾" - ½ oz. (2")

WOOD BODY

$30 – 50

WOOD BODY

NO. 850 3" - ½ oz.

CALLED "LITTLE MARY"

$30 – 50

CALLED "BIG JOE"

NO. 600 3⅝ - ¾ oz. (3½")

WOOD BODY

WOOD BODY

NO. 800 3⅞" – ¾ oz.

CALLED "BIG MARY"

MADE FROM "HEDDYLIN" (PYRALIN)

A New Indestructible Body and Finish. Hooks cannot pull out.

Heddon No. 9600 Salt-Spook (Not of Wood)

Salt-water fishermen have longed for a bait that would not chip, and would withstand the sharp teeth of salt-water fish, with hooks that would not pull out. Here it is, — and it's guaranteed to outlast any number of wooden lures. Its colors are not a surface enamel, but are blended into the material of which the bait is made, and are the same color clear through. The metal fastenings are made of stainless steel and rust-proof. This new "Salt-Spook" has unusual balance and action, and is a lively actor" when retrieved with short jerks, the favorite method of handling. Body length, 3⅝ inches. Weight, ¾ ounce.

9602	White Body, Red Head
9608RH	White Body, Gold Specks, Red Head
9609L	Perch Scale with Transparent Body

3⅝" - ¾ oz.

$40 – 60

½ Actual Size

No. 9608RH Length 3⅝ in. Salt-Spook Indestructible

Lure collecting is fun, tell a friend.

NEW - (1930)

NO. 9800 SEA SPOOK 3¾" - 1 oz.

Transparent Indestructible

$30 – 40

A "GHOSTLY GO-GETTER"

FLORIDA SPECIALS

(1922) G.E. "L."

WOOD BODY

Salt Water Minnow

Florida Specials, No. 10S Series

NO 10 S (2¾") - ½ oz. $40 – 50

1922 NO. 10B (3½") - ¾ oz. $40 – 50

RH - WHITE BACK, GOLD FLITTER, RED HEAD.

NS. - NATURAL SHRIMP - TRANSPARENT

Transparent Indestructible

$40 – 50

"Shrimpy-Spook" NO. 9000 4" - 1 oz.

NEW - 1930 (2 PC. HOOK)

"Metal-Minn" No. 510 Series

- SIMILAR TO NO. 9600 SHAPE
- ALL METAL BODY (METAL-MINN.)

$50 – 75

1935

No. 520 Series

½ Actual Size

Color No. 529YRH

Hooks strongly fastened, yet instantly removable. Commercial fishermen will appreciate this valuable feature.

No. 520 Series "Shark-Mouth Minn"

All-metal Bait. Indestructible construction. Popular Price.

Gets its name from peculiar shape of front hook fastening. Scientifically designed to give maximum darting and life-like action when retrieved with short jerks. Head is extra heavy which causes bait to dip head down on each jerk. By far the best bait of its kind on the market. Hooks cannot pull out yet are easily removable when broken after long use. Length 3 inches. Weight ¾ ounce.

Colors:

No. 522	White, Red Head
No. 528RH	White, Red Head, Gold Specks
No. 529RH	White, Red Head, Silver Specks
No. 520S	White, Spotted Body
No. 529YRH	Yellow, Red Head

Lure prices in this book are a guide only. Prices go up and down weekly.

$150 – 250

SALT WATER COAST MINNOW

SINGLE ABERDEEN HOOK – THROUGH WIRE HOOK RIG

1922

NO. 610 – 2½" – ½ oz.
NO. 620 – 3½" – 1 oz.
NO. 630 – 4½" – 1¾ oz.
NO. 640 – 5" – 3½ oz.

LATER MODEL HAD SPINNER ON THE NOSE.

$150 – 200

–1914–

Coast Minnow Series,

EARLIER MODEL HAD SPINNER ON THE TAIL.

NO. 3 – 2½" BODY – ½ oz.
NO. 2 – 3½" – 1 oz. (3")
NO. 1 – 4½" – 1¾ oz. (4")
NO. 4 – 5" – 2½ oz.

COLORS:
1D – DARK GREEN SCALE.
1F – GREEN, FANCY BACK.
1G – DARK GREEN BACK, GOLD SPECKLED.
1R – RAINBOW.
1S – WHITE BODY, RED AND GREEN SPOTS.

Salt Water Minnow—Coast Series

NEW
–1930–

Heddon "Spook" or "Fish-Flesh" Baits

$10 – 20

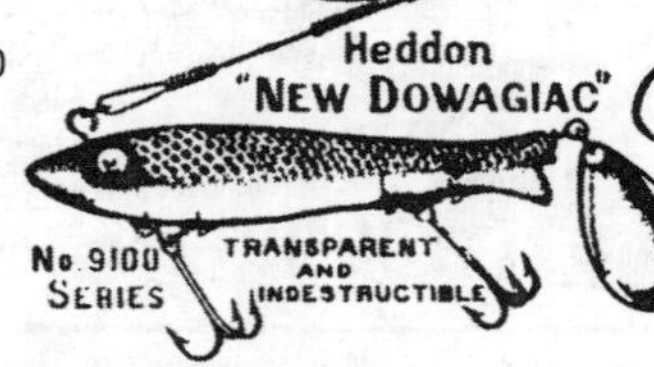
Heddon
"NEW DOWAGIAC"
No. 9100
SERIES
TRANSPARENT
AND
INDESTRUCTIBLE

ALSO CALLED THE SUPER DOWAGIAC SPOOK.

–PYRALIN

9100 SERIES "DOWAGIAC SPOOK"
Weight ¾ oz. — Length 3⅛ in. —
Two No. 1 Treble Hooks

A deep-sinking lure with a spinner at front and rear. Most effective in hot weather when the fish are in the depths. Ideal for casting or trolling. Outstanding for walleyes, lake trout and all deep water fish.

COLORS
9100-L—Yellow Perch Scale
9100-P—Shiner Scale
9100-RET—White, Red Eyes and Tail
9100-XRY—Yellow Shore Minnow
9100-XRS—Silver Shore Minnow
9100-XRW—Red and White Shore Minnow

(GLASS EYES)

2 VERY CLOSE SIZES:
• 3⅛" – ¾ oz. (LATER MODEL) (LAST MODEL HAD PAINTED EYES)
• 3¾" – 1 oz. (ORIGINAL SIZE)
2 Pc. HOOK-G.E.

$5

"TINY SPOOK"

310 SERIES "TINY SPOOK"

Wt. ¼ oz. — Lgt. 1⅞ In. — Two No. 6 Treble Hooks —

Spinning size of the long famous "Dowagiac Spook", with natural shape minnow body, and spinners both fore and aft to create lifelike action and turbulence. Can be fished shallow or deep, depending upon speed of retrieve. Sinks about one foot a second. Especially effective on large trout, largemouth and small mouth bass, walleyes, northern pike and larger panfish. Colors: CRA, SUN, BGL, L, XRY, XBW, RH, XRS

Heddon "RIVER RUNT"

$5 – 20

No. 9110
Series

(SINKING)

9110 SERIES
Standard
"River Runt Spook" ®
Wt. ½ oz. — Lgt. 2⅛ in.
No. 1 Treble Hooks

Heddon "River-Runt-Spook"
(Sinking)

(SINKING)

9010 SERIES $5 – 20
Midget
"River Runt Spook" ®
Wt. ⅜ oz. — Lgt. 2⅛ in.
No. 2 Treble Hooks

Transparent
Indestructible
Finish
No. 9010
Series

Heddon
"MIDGET RIVER-RUNT-SPOOK"

$5 – 20

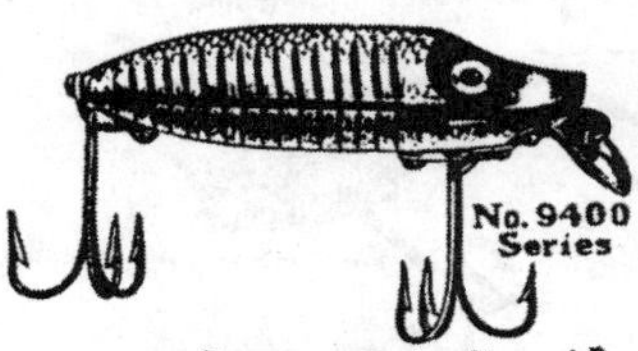

9400 SERIES
Floating "River Runt Spook" ®
Wt. ½ oz.—Lgt. 3 in.
No. 1 Treble Hooks

No. 9400
Series

Heddon "River-Runt Spook"
(Floating)

Heddon Midget Digit

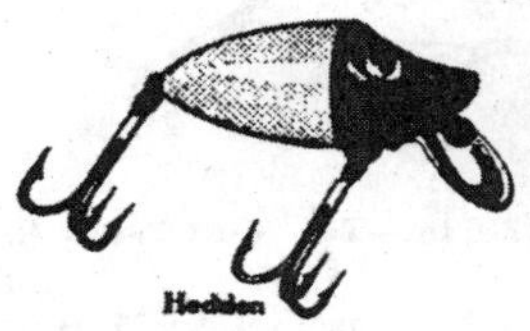
Heddon

WOOD BODY

(SINKING)

$5 – 20

NO. B-110 Length 1½" Weight 2/5 oz.

TWO JOINTED MODELS:
No. 9430 "Floating Jointed River-Runt-Spook"
Transparent Body. Indestructible Finish
Similar to the "Floating River-Runt-Spook," in a jointed model; a very lively swimmer with a side kick to the tail. Dives when retrieved about two feet deep. Strongly jointed. Length 3¾ inches. Weight ¾ ounce.

(1934) 3¾" – ¾ oz. – (FLOATING)

$5 – 20

9020 SERIES
"Midgit Digit"*
"River Runt Spook"*
Weight ⅜ oz. — Length 1⅝ in.
No. 6 Treble Hooks
A sinking bait, the smallest of the "River Runt" family. Excellent for bass and panfish.

No. 9020
Series

Heddon
"MIDGIT DIGIT RIVER-RUNT-SPOOK"

9330 SERIES
Jointed
"River Runt Spooks"*
9330—Sinking Model

$5 – 20

2¾" – 4/7 oz.
(SINKING)

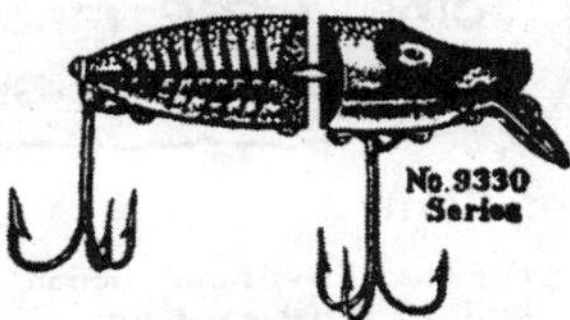
No. 9330
Series

Heddon "RIVER-RUNT-SPOOK"
(Jointed Sinking)

No. 750 Series

$5 – 20

"RIVER-RUNTIE"
(WOOD BODY)

$5 – 20

"RIVER-RUNTIE-SPOOK"
No. 950 Series
1¼" – 1/25 oz.

"NO-SNAG — RIVER-RUNT-SPOOK" — No. N-9110 Series
A Dead-sure Hooker. Weedless and Snagless.

BODY – 2½"
5/8 oz.

$10 – 25

1941

$5 – 20

Color XRW
"TINY RUNT"

NO. 340
2⅜" – ¼ oz.
(FLOATING)

$5 – 20

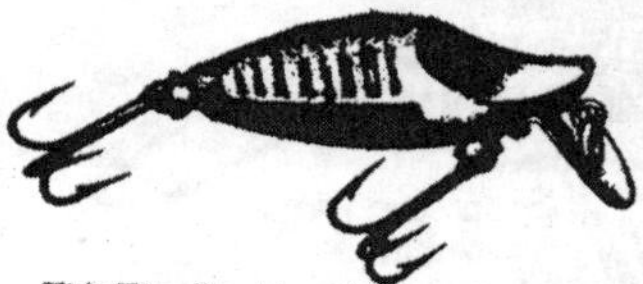

NO. 350
2⅛" – ⅕ oz.
(SINKING)

This Tiny Runt is a sinking, wiggling lure, #350 Heddon, ⅕ oz.

SCOOP LIP – 1939

NOTE: FIRST MODELS OF GO-DEEPERS HAD A "SCOOP" SHAPED LIP, SHOWN HERE.

$10 – 25 HEDDON "GO-DEEPER-RUNT"

No. D9010 Series
"Midget GO-DEEPER River-Runt" 3⅛" – 3/7 oz.

No. D9110 "Standard Size GO-DEEPER
Same as above except a little larger. Length overall 3½ in. Weight 3/5 oz.

$5 – 20

"GO DEEPER" "TINY RUNT"

NOT MADE IN SCOOP LIP.

D350 SERIES "GO DEEPER" "TINY RUNT"
Wt. ¼ oz. — Lgt. 2¾ in. — Two No. 6 Treble Hooks —

$5 – 10

GO-DEEPER
• NO. D-9010
MIDGET - 3⅛"
• NO. D-9110
STANDARD
3½" - ⅝ oz.

$5 – 10

D9430 SERIES
JOINTED "GO DEEPER"
"RIVER RUNT SPOOK"
Weight ⅝ oz. — Length 4¼ in.
Two No. 1 Treble Hooks

LATER MODEL GO-DEEPERS HAD FLAT LIPS (ILLUS.)

D9430
Series

Heddon Jointed "Go Deeper" "River Runt Spook"

L-10 "LAGUNA RUNT" (SINKING)

$20 – 25

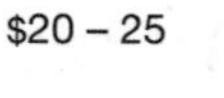

Wt. ½ oz.—Lgt. 2⅝ in.—Two No. 1 Treble Hooks

This bait has the body of the original wooden "River Runt" with the metal lip removed and an extra weight added. The smallest and lightest of all saltwater casting lures. A great "killer" for weakfish (saltwater trout) and pompano.

610 "SEA RUNT" (SINKING)

$20 – 30

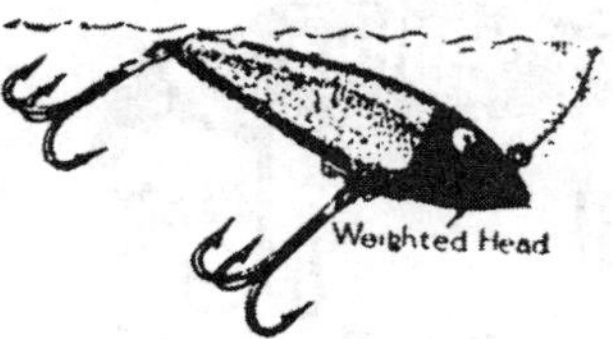
Weighted Head

Wt. ⅝ oz.—Lgt. 2⅝ in.—Two No. 1 Treble Hooks

Especially deadly for weakfish (saltwater trout). A heavy lead weight perfectly balanced in the head causes it to dive at a sharp angle with the quiver of a minnow. Lure darts in a lifelike manner when jerked.

Original "River-Runt" No. 110 Series

$10 – 40

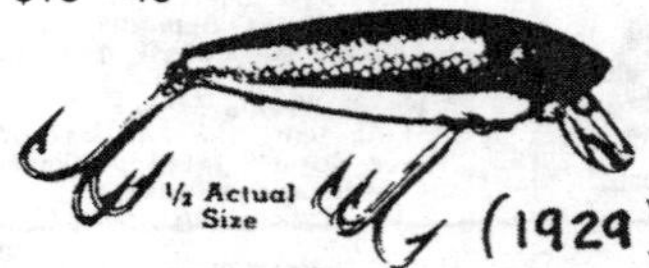
½ Actual Size

WOOD BODY
2⅝" - ½ oz. - G.E.
(1929) (SINKER) "L"

NOTE: EARLY RIVER RUNT (1933) SPOOKS HAD SUNKEN EYES, AND THE 2 PC. HOOK RIGS. SOME WERE MADE FROM UN-STABLE PLASTIC - AND "SHRUNK".

No. 7510 Series "Giant River-Runt"

SCREW HOLDING HOOK-HANGER
PIN HOLDING LINE-TIE
EXTRA LONG SCREWS
3¼"

$50 – 100

⅔ Actual Size **No. 7519P**

Famous "River-Runt" action in a big bait for Muskies, Large G. N. Pike, Salmon, etc. Looks much bigger than it is in the water, and entire bait is taken inside mouth by average fish, thereby insuring hooking. Floats easily with wire-leader. Dives on retrieve and swims lively. Weight just over 1 oz. Length 3¼ inches. Two trebles. Built extra strong.

7512 White and Red 7519P Shiner Scale
7519M Pike Scale 7519PAS Allen Stripey

NOTE: LOOK AT GARCIA ABU HI-LOW-(ADJ. RACHET-JAW LIP.) MADE BY HEDDON, ALSO SOLD AS A R.-RUNT W/HEDDON (9400 SIZE) NAME.

"SALMON—RIVER-RUNT"
For Salmon and Striped BASS

$30 – 45

STRING
Spoon and Plug Combined
Loosely Hung Hooks

Combines Spoon-flash and Live Minnow Swim
(Note the large "Go-Deeper" Metal Lip.)

LARGE "TEDDY-BEAR" GLASS EYES.
NO. 8850
5" - 1⅖ oz.
WOOD BODY

HAD 3 DIFF. METAL LIPS -
① SCOOP LIP (ILLUS.)
② MUSKY VAMP LIP
③ SPECIAL ⇨ ......
(NOSE NAIL)
H.D. BRASS SWIVEL

$15 – 20

No. S-9400 Series
"SILVER-SALMON—RUNT"
Transparent Body and Indestructible Finish
Great for Silver Salmon and Steelheads

Transparent Body
No. S-9400 Series
NOTE: MOST HAVE "SHRUNK"

Heddon "SILVER-SALMON-RUNT"
With large "Go-Deeper" collar

• LENGTH: 3" - ⅝ oz.
• MADE FROM 9400 SPOOK BODY. HOOKS HUNG ON RINGS.

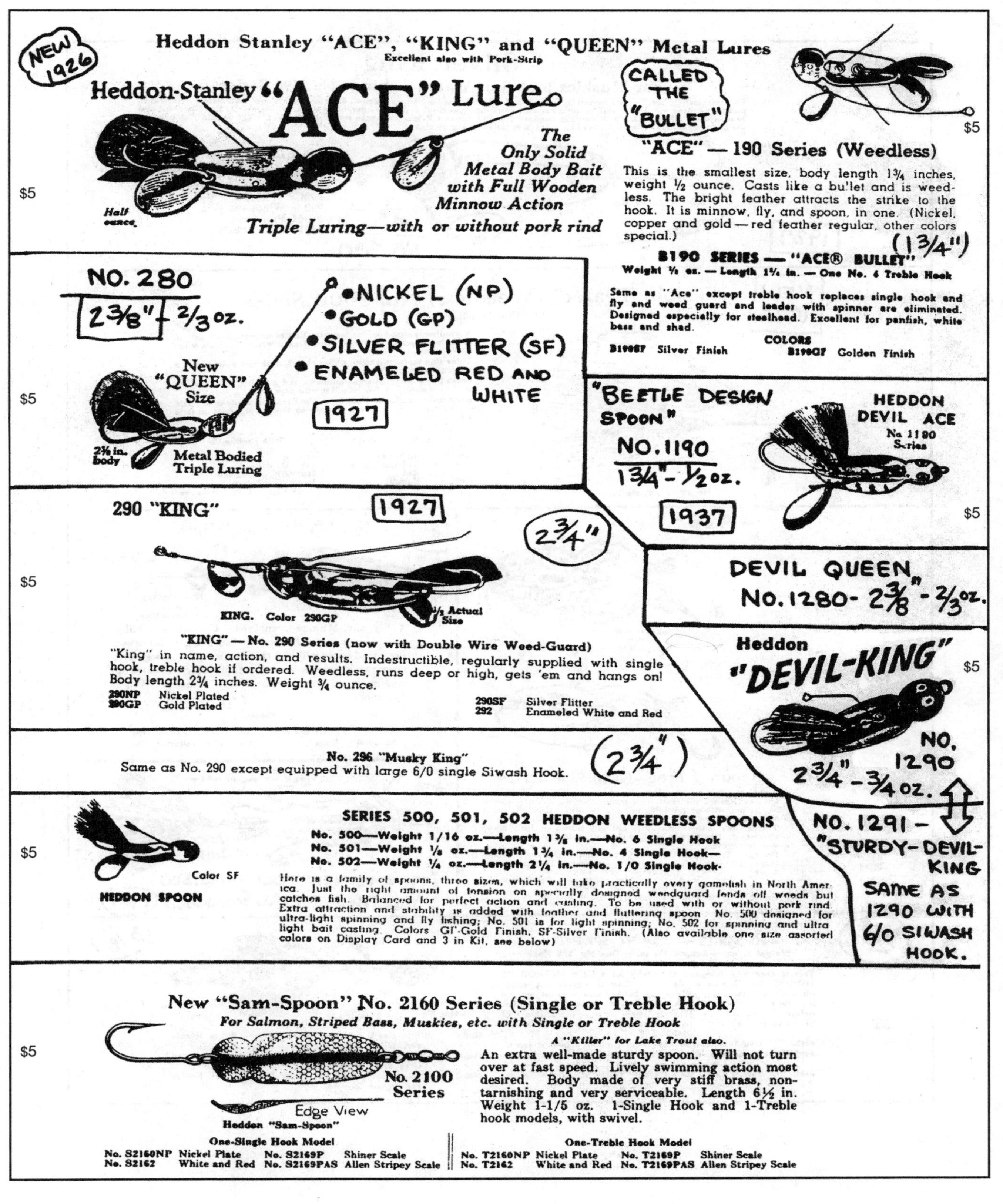

NEW 1926
Heddon Stanley "ACE", "KING" and "QUEEN" Metal Lures
Excellent also with Pork-Strip
Heddon-Stanley "ACE" Lure
The Only Solid Metal Body Bait with Full Wooden Minnow Action
Triple Luring—with or without pork rind
Half ounce.
$5
CALLED THE "BULLET"
$5
"ACE" — 190 Series (Weedless)
This is the smallest size, body length 1¾ inches, weight ½ ounce. Casts like a bullet and is weedless. The bright feather attracts the strike to the hook. It is minnow, fly, and spoon, in one. (Nickel, copper and gold — red feather regular, other colors special.)
(1¾")
B190 SERIES — "ACE® BULLET"
Weight ½ oz. — Length 1¾ in. — One No. 6 Treble Hook
Same as "Ace" except treble hook replaces single hook and fly and weed guard and leader with spinner are eliminated. Designed especially for steelhead. Excellent for panfish, white bass and shad.
COLORS
B190SF Silver Finish
B190GF Golden Finish
NO. 280
2⅜" - ⅔ oz.
•NICKEL (NP)
•GOLD (GP)
•SILVER FLITTER (SF)
•ENAMELED RED AND WHITE
1927
New "QUEEN" Size
2⅜ in. body
Metal Bodied Triple Luring
$5
"BEETLE DESIGN SPOON"
NO. 1190
1¾" - ½ oz.
1937
HEDDON DEVIL ACE
No. 1190 Series
$5
290 "KING"
1927
2¾"
$5
KING. Color 290GP
½ Actual Size
"KING" — No. 290 Series (now with Double Wire Weed-Guard)
"King" in name, action, and results. Indestructible, regularly supplied with single hook, treble hook if ordered. Weedless, runs deep or high, gets 'em and hangs on! Body length 2¾ inches. Weight ¾ ounce.
290NP Nickel Plated
290GP Gold Plated
290SF Silver Flitter
292 Enameled White and Red
DEVIL QUEEN
No. 1280 - 2⅜" - ⅔ oz.
Heddon "DEVIL-KING"
$5
NO. 1290
2¾" - ¾ oz.
No. 296 "Musky King"
Same as No. 290 except equipped with large 6/0 single Siwash Hook.
(2¾")
NO. 1291 - "STURDY-DEVIL-KING"
SAME AS 1290 WITH 6/0 SIWASH HOOK.
$5
Color SF
HEDDON SPOON
SERIES 500, 501, 502 HEDDON WEEDLESS SPOONS
No. 500—Weight 1/16 oz.—Length 1⅜ in.—No. 6 Single Hook
No. 501—Weight ⅛ oz.—Length 1¾ in.—No. 4 Single Hook—
No. 502—Weight ¼ oz.—Length 2¼ in.—No. 1/0 Single Hook.
Here is a family of spoons, three sizes, which will take practically every gamefish in North America. Just the right amount of tension on specially designed weedguard fends off weeds but catches fish. Balanced for perfect action and casting. To be used with or without pork rind. Extra attraction and stability is added with feather and fluttering spoon. No. 500 designed for ultra-light spinning and fly fishing; No. 501 is for light spinning; No. 502 for spinning and ultra light bait casting. Colors GF-Gold Finish, SF-Silver Finish. (Also available one size assorted colors on Display Card and 3 in Kit, see below)
$5
New "Sam-Spoon" No. 2160 Series (Single or Treble Hook)
For Salmon, Striped Bass, Muskies, etc. with Single or Treble Hook
A "Killer" for Lake Trout also.
An extra well-made sturdy spoon. Will not turn over at fast speed. Lively swimming action most desired. Body made of very stiff brass, non-tarnishing and very serviceable. Length 6½ in. Weight 1-1/5 oz. 1-Single Hook and 1-Treble hook models, with swivel.
No. 2100 Series
Edge View
Heddon "Sam-Spoon"
One-Single Hook Model
No. S2160NP Nickel Plate
No. S2162 White and Red
No. S2169P Shiner Scale
No. S2169PAS Allen Stripey Scale
One-Treble Hook Model
No. T2160NP Nickel Plate
No. T2162 White and Red
No. T2169P Shiner Scale
No. T2169PAS Allen Stripey Scale

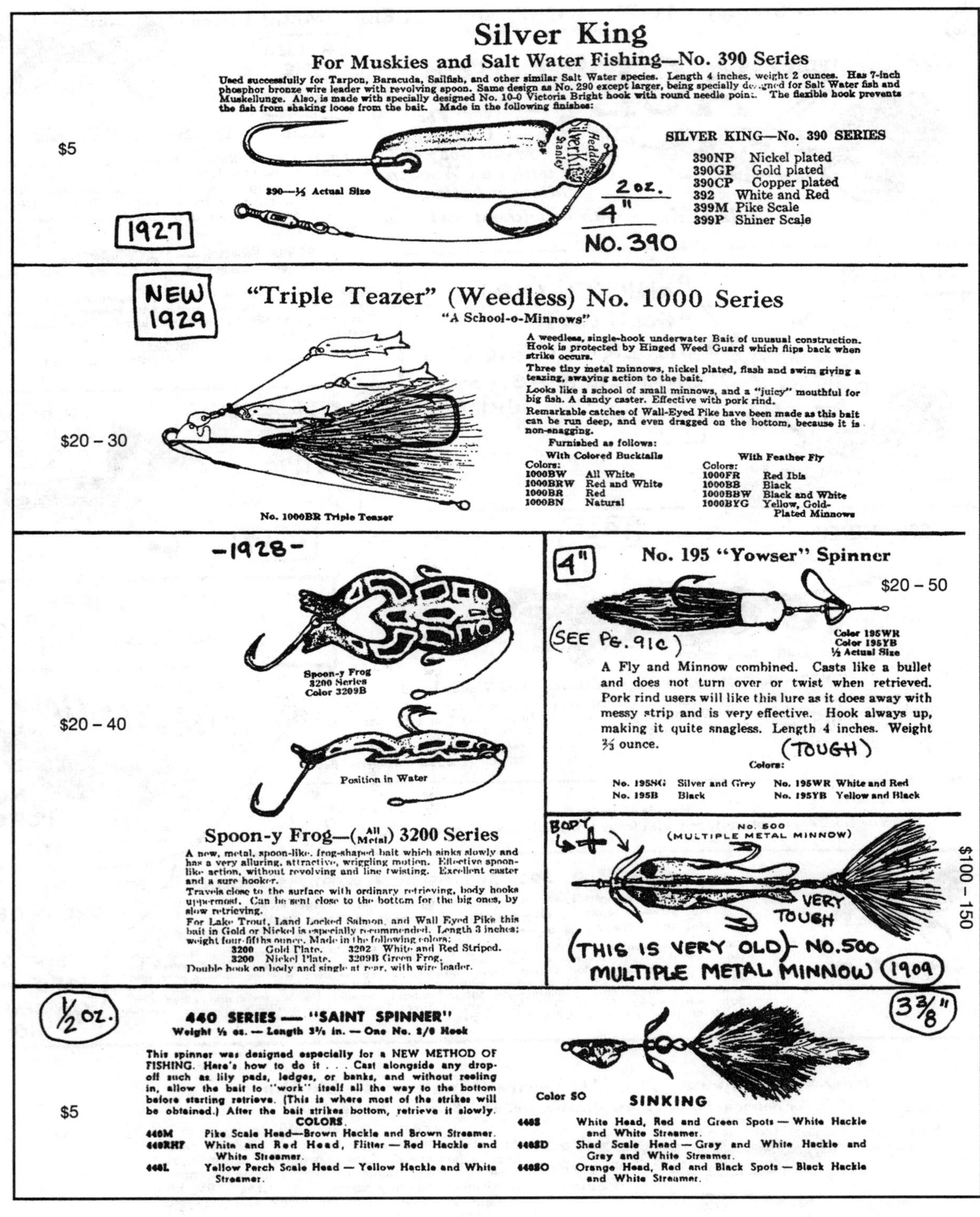

Silver King

For Muskies and Salt Water Fishing—No. 390 Series

Used successfully for Tarpon, Baracuda, Sailfish, and other similar Salt Water species. Length 4 inches, weight 2 ounces. Has 7-inch phosphor bronze wire leader with revolving spoon. Same design as No. 290 except larger, being specially designed for Salt Water fish and Muskellunge. Also, is made with specially designed No. 10-0 Victoria Bright hook with round needle point. The flexible hook prevents the fish from shaking loose from the bait. Made in the following finishes:

$5

Heddon
Silver King
Stanley

390—½ Actual Size

1927

2 oz.
4"
NO. 390

SILVER KING—No. 390 SERIES

390NP	Nickel plated
390GP	Gold plated
390CP	Copper plated
392	White and Red
399M	Pike Scale
399P	Shiner Scale

NEW 1929

"Triple Teazer" (Weedless) No. 1000 Series

"A School-o-Minnows"

$20 – 30

A weedless, single-hook underwater Bait of unusual construction. Hook is protected by Hinged Weed Guard which flips back when strike occurs.

Three tiny metal minnows, nickel plated, flash and swim giving a teazing, swaying action to the bait.

Looks like a school of small minnows, and a "juicy" mouthful for big fish. A dandy caster. Effective with pork rind.

Remarkable catches of Wall-Eyed Pike have been made as this bait can be run deep, and even dragged on the bottom, because it is non-snagging.

Furnished as follows:

With Colored Bucktails		With Feather Fly	
Colors:		Colors:	
1000BW	All White	1000FR	Red Ibis
1000BRW	Red and White	1000BB	Black
1000BR	Red	1000BBW	Black and White
1000BN	Natural	1000BYG	Yellow, Gold-Plated Minnows

No. 1000BR Triple Teazer

-1928-

Spoon-y Frog
3200 Series
Color 3209B

$20 – 40

Position in Water

Spoon-y Frog—(All Metal) 3200 Series

A new, metal, spoon-like, frog-shaped bait which sinks slowly and has a very alluring, attractive, wriggling motion. Effective spoon-like action, without revolving and line twisting. Excellent caster and a sure hooker.

Travels close to the surface with ordinary retrieving, body hooks uppermost. Can be sent close to the bottom for the big ones, by slow retrieving.

For Lake Trout, Land Locked Salmon, and Wall Eyed Pike this bait in Gold or Nickel is especially recommended. Length 3 inches; weight four-fifths ounce. Made in the following colors:

3200	Gold Plate.	3202	White and Red Striped.
3200	Nickel Plate.	3209B	Green Frog.

Double hook on body and single at rear, with wire leader.

4"

No. 195 "Yowser" Spinner

$20 – 50

(SEE PG. 91C)

Color 195WR
Color 195YB
½ Actual Size

A Fly and Minnow combined. Casts like a bullet and does not turn over or twist when retrieved. Pork rind users will like this lure as it does away with messy strip and is very effective. Hook always up, making it quite snagless. Length 4 inches. Weight ⅔ ounce.

(TOUGH)

Colors:

No. 195SG	Silver and Grey	No. 195WR	White and Red
No. 195B	Black	No. 195YB	Yellow and Black

BODY

No. 500
(MULTIPLE METAL MINNOW)

VERY TOUGH

$100 – 150

(THIS IS VERY OLD)- NO.500 MULTIPLE METAL MINNOW 1909

½ oz.

3⅜"

440 SERIES — "SAINT SPINNER"

Weight ½ oz. — Length 3⅜ in. — One No. 2/0 Hook

$5

This spinner was designed especially for a NEW METHOD OF FISHING. Here's how to do it . . . Cast alongside any drop-off such as lily pads, ledges, or banks, and without reeling in, allow the bait to "work" itself all the way to the bottom before starting retrieve. (This is where most of the strikes will be obtained.) After the bait strikes bottom, retrieve it slowly.

Color SO

SINKING

COLORS

440M	Pike Scale Head—Brown Hackle and Brown Streamer.
440RHF	White and Red Head, Flitter — Red Hackle and White Streamer.
440L	Yellow Perch Scale Head — Yellow Hackle and White Streamer.
440S	White Head, Red and Green Spots — White Hackle and White Streamer.
440SD	Shad Scale Head — Gray and White Hackle and Gray and White Streamer.
440SO	Orange Head, Red and Black Spots — Black Hackle and White Streamer.

NO. 9930

$5

No. 9930 Series

5/8 oz. HEDDON "STINGAREE" (Jointed-Sinking) 2½"

(ALSO IN MUSKIE SIZE) "Tiny Stingaree" (Sinking)

NO. 330

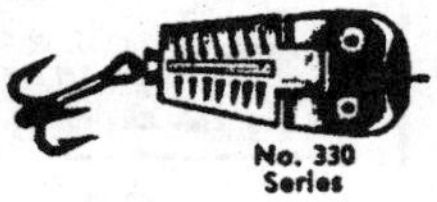

No. 330 Series

$5

No.	Length	Weight
330 Series	1½"	¼ oz.

Fidget Feather (Sinking)

$5

NO. 402

No. 402 Series

Weight 3/8 oz.

$5

No. 401 Series

FLUTED METAL TAIL.

Weight 3/8 oz.

Fidget Flasher

NO. 401

$5

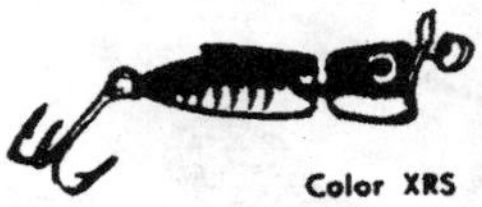

Color XRS

(SPOOK TAIL BODY)

"FIDGIT"

400 SERIES — "FIDGIT"

Wt. ⅜ oz. — Lgt. 2⅛ in. — One No. 6 Treble Hook

FLY ROD LURES

Heddon FAMOUS SPINNING LURES

"WHIS-PURR"

$5

• NO. 420 – 3" – ⅛ oz.

• NO. 425 – 3½" – ¼ oz.

1920's

Wilder-Dilg Lures

$10

All cuts one-half actual size

This cork and feather body combination closely imitates the action of a wounded minnow, causing bass to strike viciously.

NO. 910 *Bass Size.* Made in 12 exclusive patterns, No. 1 to No. 12. Each named for the celebrated fly fisherman who designed it. 6 light and 6 dark colors. Length, 3¼ inches. No. 1 Model Perfect Hook.

NO. 930 *Trout Size.* 3 light and 3 dark colors. Length, 2 inches. No. 6 Model Perfect Hook.

ALSO MADE IN SPOOK FINISHES

THIS LURE SERIES WAS NAMED AFTER 2 FISHING WRITERS IN THE 1920'S: W.H. DILG AND B.F. WILDER.

New! HEDDON FUZZI-BUG . .

Natural Fuzzy Finish!

$5 – 10

• BASS SIZE NO. 75

• SMALL SIZE NO. 74

$10 – 20

Heddon "POP-EYE FROG". No. 85 Series. (Fly Rod Lure)

There is something in the tantalizing stare of the downward-looking popping eyes that makes Mr. Bass really mad. "The Eyes have IT." Casts nicely, easy pick-up and never turns over. Equipped with effective weed-guard. Cork body, bucktail legs. Length 3½ in. Weight 1/20 oz.

85YF Yellow and Black Frog 85GF Green and Black Frog

$1

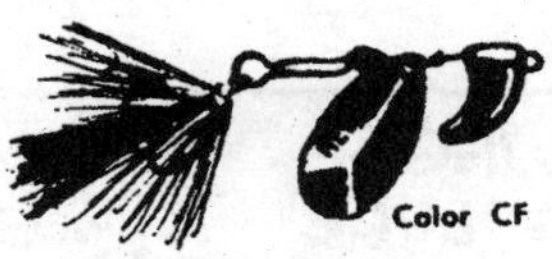

Color CF

"GAMBY" SPINNER

SERIES 421 AND 423 "GAMBY" SPINNERS

No. 421—Weight ⅛ oz.—Length 2¾ in.—One No. 8 Treble Hook—
No. 423—Weight ¼ oz.—Length 3¼ in.—One No. 6 Treble Hook—

This spinning lure features a spinner blade designed to start at a whisper and spin very close to its axis. Also, the body is keel-shaped to add extreme stability and prevent line twist. Couple these two features together and you have a deadly stream lure for trout and bass, as well as a most productive bait for all lake fish. Hooks are extra sharp for sure hooking even on light strikes. Excellent for trolling. Colors: SF-Silver Finish, GF-Gold Finish, CF-Copper Finish. (Also available one size assorted colors on Display Card and 4 in Kit, see below)

$1

Color GF

463 "HEP"

(1955)

SERIES 460, 461, 462, 463, 464 "HEP" SPINNERS

No. 460—Weight 1/16 oz.—Length 1¾ in.—One No. 10 Treble Hook—
No. 461—Weight ⅛ oz.—Length 2 in.—One No. 8 Treble Hook—
No. 462—Weight 3/16 oz.—Length 2⅜ in.—One No. 6 Treble Hook—
No. 463—Weight ¼ oz.—Length 2⅝ in.—One No. 6 Treble Hook—
No. 464—Weight ⅜ oz.—Length 2⅝ in.—One No. 2 Treble Hook—

Here is a scientifically designed lure with a spinner blade that works at any speed, even the slightest motion makes it deadly for trout, bass, walleyes, white bass, northern pike, crappies and large panfish. Special snap opener allows changing of hooks. Treble is super sharp, a sure hooker! Ideal for trolling. Colors: GF-Gold Finish, SF-Silver Finish. (Also available one size assorted colors on Display Card and 4 in Kit, see below)

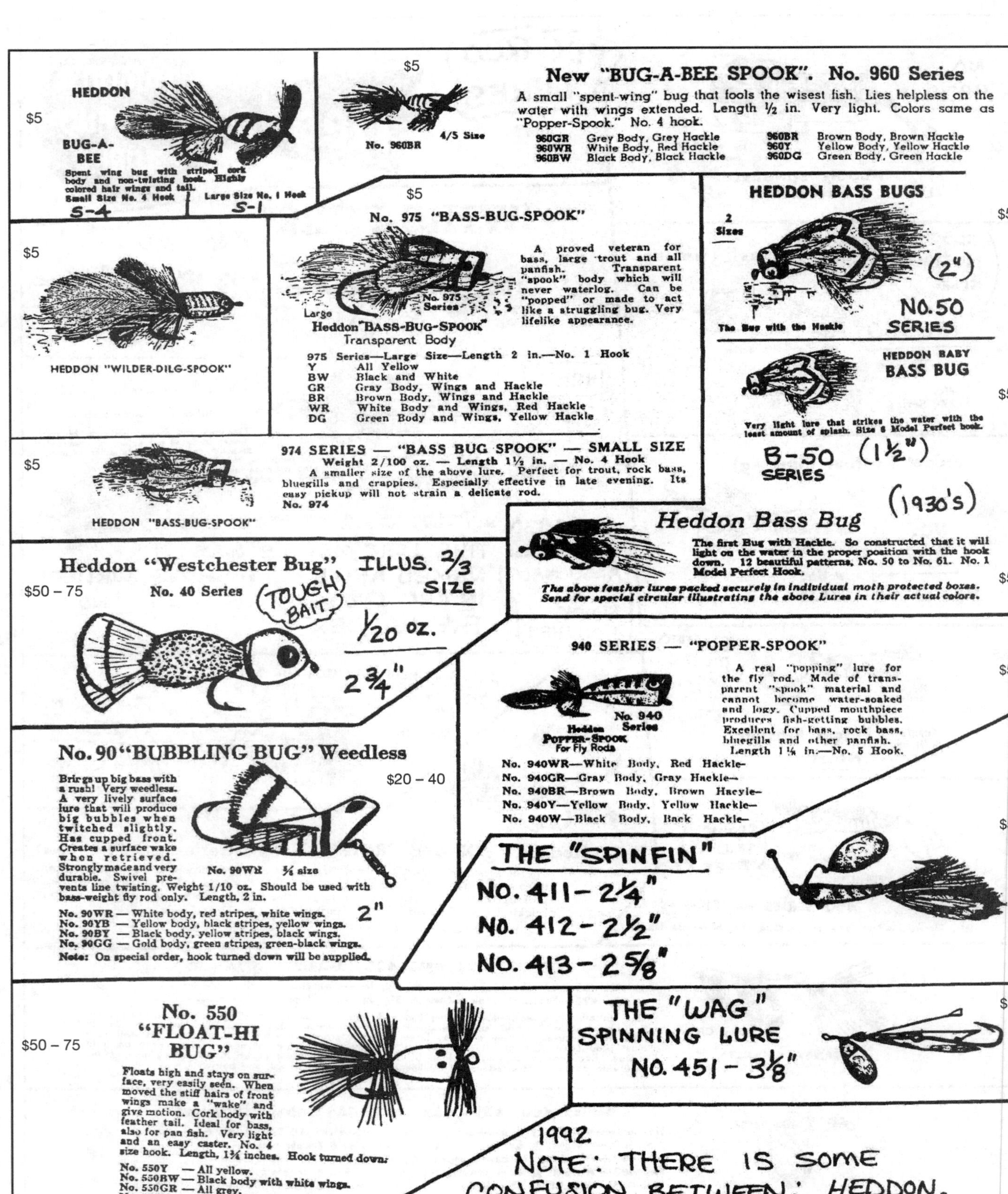

$5
HEDDON
BUG-A-BEE
Spent wing bug with striped cork body and non-twisting hook. Highly colored hair wings and tail.
Small Size No. 4 Hook S-4
Large Size No. 1 Hook S-1
$5
No. 960BR 4/5 Size
New "BUG-A-BEE SPOOK". No. 960 Series
A small "spent-wing" bug that fools the wisest fish. Lies helpless on the water with wings extended. Length ½ in. Very light. Colors same as "Popper-Spook." No. 4 hook.
960GR Grey Body, Grey Hackle
960WR White Body, Red Hackle
960BW Black Body, Black Hackle
960BR Brown Body, Brown Hackle
960Y Yellow Body, Yellow Hackle
960DG Green Body, Green Hackle
$5
HEDDON "WILDER-DILG-SPOOK"
$5
No. 975 "BASS-BUG-SPOOK"
No. 975 Series
Large Heddon "BASS-BUG-SPOOK" Transparent Body
A proved veteran for bass, large trout and all panfish. Transparent "spook" body which will never waterlog. Can be "popped" or made to act like a struggling bug. Very lifelike appearance.
975 Series—Large Size—Length 2 in.—No. 1 Hook
Y All Yellow
BW Black and White
GR Gray Body, Wings and Hackle
BR Brown Body, Wings and Hackle
WR White Body and Wings, Red Hackle
DG Green Body and Wings, Yellow Hackle
HEDDON BASS BUGS
$5
2 Sizes
(2")
NO. 50 SERIES
The Bug with the Hackle
HEDDON BABY BASS BUG
$5
Very light lure that strikes the water with the least amount of splash. Size 6 Model Perfect hook.
B-50 (1½") SERIES
$5
HEDDON "BASS-BUG-SPOOK"
974 SERIES — "BASS BUG SPOOK" — SMALL SIZE
Weight 2/100 oz. — Length 1½ in. — No. 4 Hook
A smaller size of the above lure. Perfect for trout, rock bass, bluegills and crappies. Especially effective in late evening. Its easy pickup will not strain a delicate rod.
No. 974
(1930's)
Heddon Bass Bug
The first Bug with Hackle. So constructed that it will light on the water in the proper position with the hook down. 12 beautiful patterns, No. 50 to No. 61. No. 1 Model Perfect Hook.
The above feather lures packed securely in individual moth protected boxes. Send for special circular illustrating the above Lures in their actual colors.
$5
Heddon "Westchester Bug"
ILLUS. 2/3 SIZE
$50 – 75
No. 40 Series
(TOUGH BAIT)
1/20 oz.
2¾"
940 SERIES — "POPPER-SPOOK"
$5
Heddon POPPER-SPOOK For Fly Rods
No. 940 Series
A real "popping" lure for the fly rod. Made of transparent "spook" material and cannot become water-soaked and logy. Cupped mouthpiece produces fish-getting bubbles. Excellent for bass, rock bass, bluegills and other panfish. Length 1¼ in.—No. 5 Hook.
No. 940WR—White Body, Red Hackle—
No. 940GR—Gray Body, Gray Hackle—
No. 940BR—Brown Body, Brown Hacyle—
No. 940Y—Yellow Body, Yellow Hackle—
No. 940W—Black Body, Back Hackle—
No. 90 "BUBBLING BUG" Weedless
$20 – 40
Brings up big bass with a rush! Very weedless. A very lively surface lure that will produce big bubbles when twitched slightly. Has cupped front. Creates a surface wake when retrieved. Strongly made and very durable. Swivel prevents line twisting. Weight 1/10 oz. Should be used with bass-weight fly rod only. Length, 2 in.
No. 90WR ¾ size
2"
No. 90WR — White body, red stripes, white wings.
No. 90YB — Yellow body, black stripes, yellow wings.
No. 90BY — Black body, yellow stripes, black wings.
No. 90GG — Gold body, green stripes, green-black wings.
Note: On special order, hook turned down will be supplied.
$5
THE "SPINFIN"
NO. 411 - 2¼"
NO. 412 - 2½"
NO. 413 - 2⅝"
No. 550 "FLOAT-HI BUG"
$50 – 75
Floats high and stays on surface, very easily seen. When moved the stiff hairs of front wings make a "wake" and give motion. Cork body with feather tail. Ideal for bass, also for pan fish. Very light and an easy caster. No. 4 size hook. Length, 1¾ inches. Hook turned down.
No. 550Y — All yellow.
No. 550BW — Black body with white wings.
No. 550GR — All grey.
No. 550W — White body with red hackle.
$5
THE "WAG" SPINNING LURE
NO. 451 - 3⅛"
1992
NOTE: THERE IS SOME CONFUSION BETWEEN: HEDDON, SO. BEND, HAYES BASS BUGS.

HEDDON COLOR CHART — With this many colors, through so many years, there is bound to be duplications, and other forms of confusion.......Good luck!

0	Green Cracked Back (Fancy Back), White Belly (Also GCB)
0S	White Body, Green & Red Spots
______	Black Cracked Back, White Belly
1	Rainbow, Green Back, Orange & Yellow Horiz. Stripes,White Belly
2 (old)	All White, Blended White, or Slate Back with White Belly (See 9W)
2 (new)	White Body, Red Head (RH)
2RET	White Body, Red Eyes & Tail
2M	White Body, Red Gills (Used on Salmon Plugs)
2LUM	White Luminous Body, Red Eyes & Tail
3	Aluminum (Also Silver Body with Green Back)
4	Red Body, Dark Green Blended Back. (Also Dark Red Back)
5	Yellow Body, Red & Green Spots
6	Gold
7 (old)	Fancy Sienna (Brown & Yellow Cracked Back)
7 (new)	White Body, Slate Back (See old 2)
8	White Body, Gold Specks (Flitter)
______	Yellow Body, Brown & Red Spots
______	Yellow Body, Green & Black Spots
______	Plain Green Back, White Belly
______	Red Body, Black Spots
______	Yellow Body, Fancy Mottled Back
______	Black Sucker (Used on No. 1300 only)
9	White Body, Silver Specks (Flitter)
9A	Yellow Perch, Yellow, Orange & Dark Greenish Slanted Stripes
9B	Green Spotted Frog
9BB	Meadow Frog
9BF	Bull Frog (New-1928)
9BK	Brook Trout
9BP	Blue Pearl
9BW	Black & White Crab
9BWH	Black Body, White Head
9C	Natural Crab (Used on Crab Wigglers)
9D	Green Scale (New-1917) I believe this was Heddon's first scale finish. The first vintage had a silver stripe back.
9E	White Body, Greenish Black Spots
9F	Yellow Body, Black Head
9G	All Black
9H	Red Scale (New-1919)
9I	?
9J	Frog Scale
9K	Gold Fish Scale
9L	Yellow Perch Scale
9LD	Light Green Scale
9M	Pike Scale (New-1921)
9MRH	Pike Scale Body, Red Head
9N	Red Dace Scale
9O	?
9P	Shiner Scale
9PAS	Allen Stripey, Shiner Scale Back, Red Head & Body Stripe
9PBH	Blue Herring Scale
9PG	Golden Shiner
9PL	Pearl
9PLB	Blue Pearl
9PRH	Shiner Scale Body, Red Head
9SH	Silver Herring
9SPRH	Spotted Body, Red Head
9SS	Silver Scale (Silver Flash)

O9R-(OLD) NATURAL SCALE

S (RED + GREEN SPOTS)

9T	Dark Green Back, Gold Specks
9U	?
9V	Orange Body, Black Spots (Also 9SO)
9W	All White (See 2)
9X	Blue Scale
9Y	All Yellow
9YBS	Yellow Body, Black Stripes
9YF	Yellow Body, Flitter
9YRH	Yellow Body, Red Head
9YS	Yellow Scale
9YXB	Yellow Body, Black Bone

RH	Red Head	SP	Sparkle
BH	Blue Head		
WH	White Head		

Wilbourn's Special — Red Back, Yellow Belly

GR	Grey
BR	Brown
GM	Grey Mouse
BM	Brown Mouse
SD	Green Shad

Crab Spook Only

NC	Natural Crab
GC	Green Crab
LC	Luminous Crab

Metal Finishes/Spoons

NP	Nickel Plate	CP	Copper Plate
GP	Gold Plate	B	Brass

Spook (Transparent Plastic) Finishes (I believe the Spook Series were new in 1930.)

NS	Natural Shrimp
S	Transparent Spook Body, Red & Green Spots
02XS	White & Red Shore Minnow
8RH	White Body with Gold Flitter, Red Head
9GW	Glow Worm (Luminous Paint)
9PLXB	Blue Pearl Shore Minnow
9PLXR	Pearl Shore Minnow
9XBW	Black & White Shore Minnow
9XGF	Greenfish Shore Minnow
9XRG	Green Shore Minnow (Glistening Green)
9XRS	Silver Shore Minnow
9XRW	Red & White Shore Minnow
9XRX	Blue Shore Minnow
9XRY	Yellow Shore Minnow
9XSK	Goldfish Shore Minnow

In 1935, the Shore Minnow Type Finish was called the X-Ray Finish.

Other Misc. Colors:

GFB	Goldfish, with Black
GFR	Goldfish, with Red
SFB	Silverfish, with Black
SFR	Silverfish, with Red
SRB	Silver, Red & Black Spots

(There's probably some more out there. If you know of them for sure, please let me know, and I'll include the information in the next supplement.

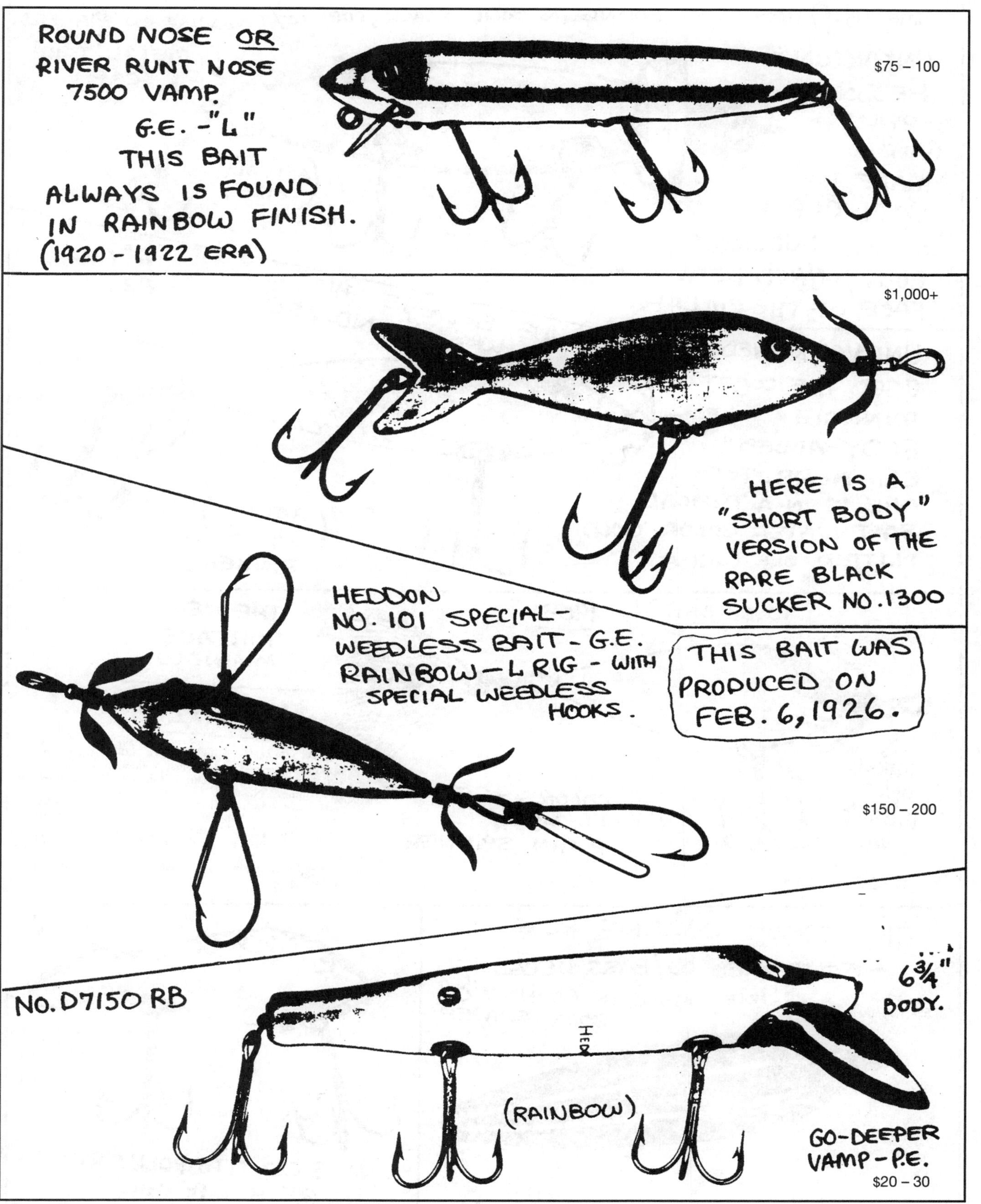

ROUND NOSE OR RIVER RUNT NOSE 7500 VAMP. G.E. -"L" THIS BAIT ALWAYS IS FOUND IN RAINBOW FINISH. (1920 - 1922 ERA)
$75 – 100
$1,000+
HERE IS A "SHORT BODY" VERSION OF THE RARE BLACK SUCKER NO.1300
HEDDON NO. 101 SPECIAL- WEEDLESS BAIT - G.E. RAINBOW - L RIG - WITH SPECIAL WEEDLESS HOOKS.
THIS BAIT WAS PRODUCED ON FEB. 6, 1926.
$150 – 200
NO. D7150 RB
6 3/4" BODY.
HED
(RAINBOW)
GO-DEEPER VAMP - P.E.
$20 – 30

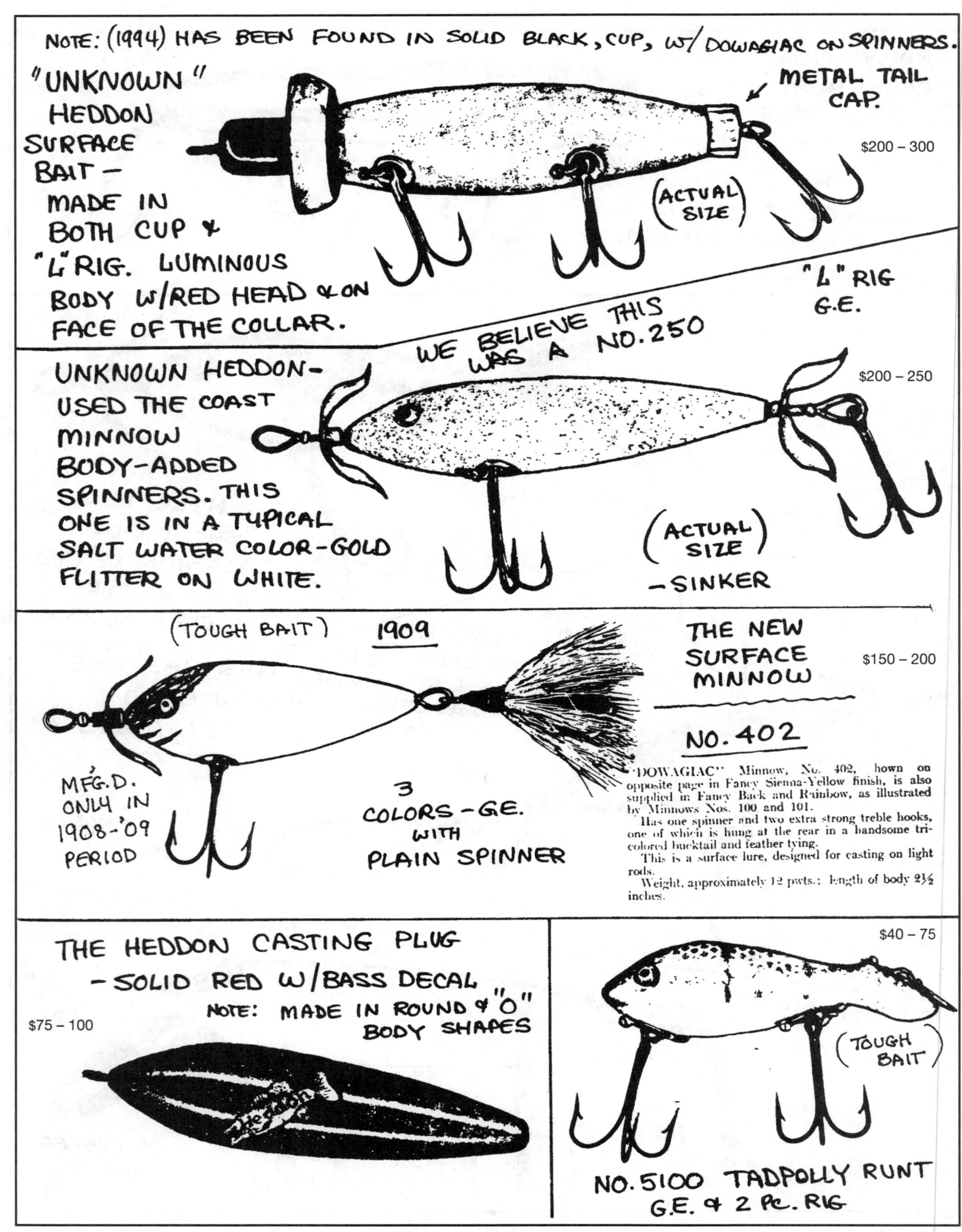
NOTE: (1994) HAS BEEN FOUND IN SOLID BLACK, CUP, W/DOWAGIAC ON SPINNERS.
"UNKNOWN" HEDDON SURFACE BAIT – MADE IN BOTH CUP & "L" RIG. LUMINOUS BODY W/RED HEAD & ON FACE OF THE COLLAR.
METAL TAIL CAP.
$200 – 300
(ACTUAL SIZE)
"L" RIG G.E.
WE BELIEVE THIS WAS A NO.250
UNKNOWN HEDDON – USED THE COAST MINNOW BODY – ADDED SPINNERS. THIS ONE IS IN A TYPICAL SALT WATER COLOR – GOLD FLITTER ON WHITE.
$200 – 250
(ACTUAL SIZE)
– SINKER
(TOUGH BAIT)
1909
THE NEW SURFACE MINNOW
$150 – 200
NO. 402
MFG.D. ONLY IN 1908-'09 PERIOD
3 COLORS – G.E. WITH PLAIN SPINNER
THE HEDDON CASTING PLUG – SOLID RED W/BASS DECAL
NOTE: MADE IN ROUND & "O" BODY SHAPES
$75 – 100
$40 – 75
(TOUGH BAIT)
NO. 5100 TADPOLLY RUNT
G.E. & 2 PC. RIG

"DOWAGIAC" Minnow, No. 402, hown on opposite page in Fancy Sienna-Yellow finish, is also supplied in Fancy Back and Rainbow, as illustrated by Minnows Nos. 100 and 101.

Has one spinner and two extra strong treble hooks, one of which is hung at the rear in a handsome tri-colored bucktail and feather tying.

This is a surface lure, designed for casting on light rods.

Weight, approximately 12 pwts.; length of body 2½ inches.

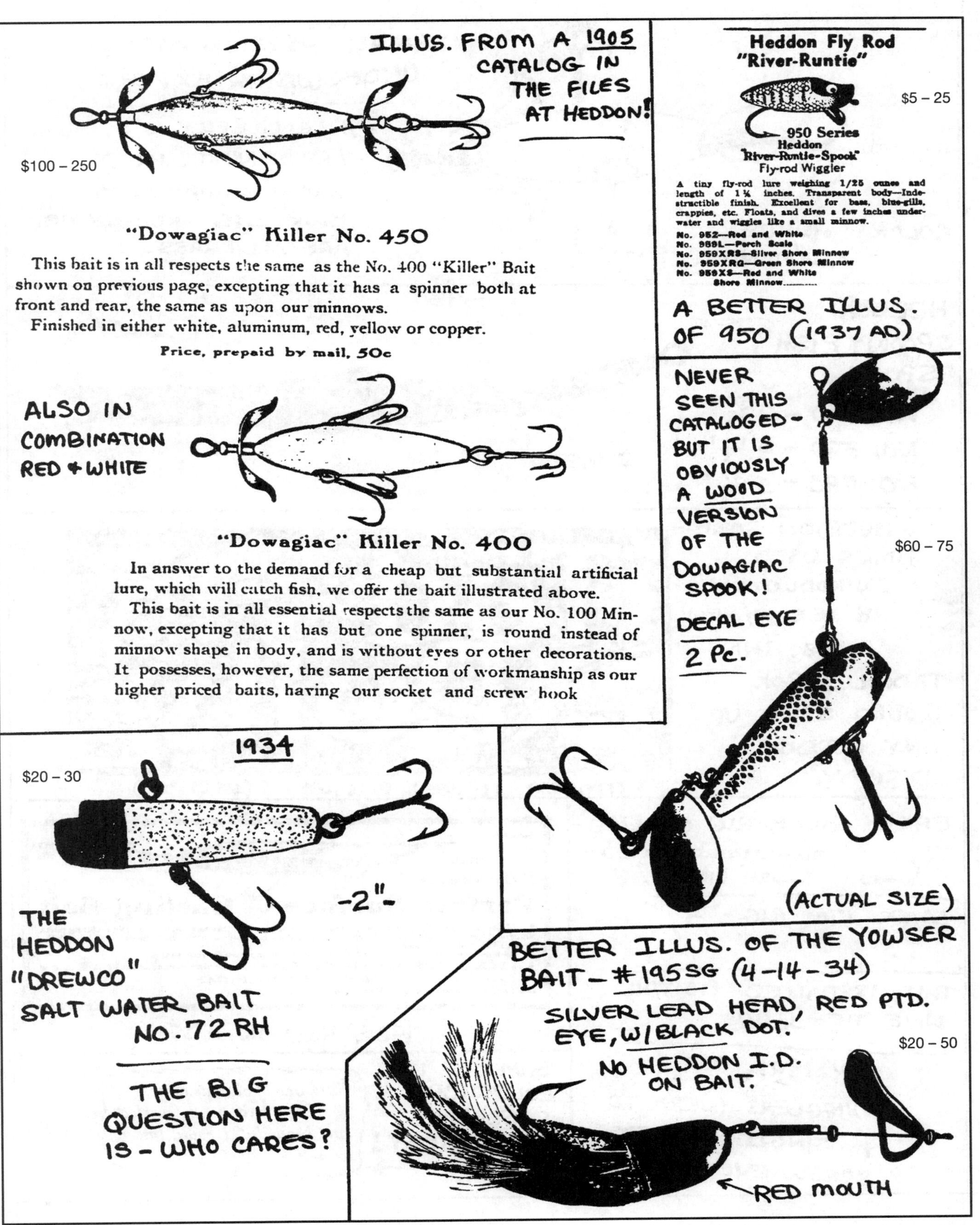

ILLUS. FROM A 1905 CATALOG IN THE FILES AT HEDDON!

$100 – 250

"Dowagiac" Killer No. 450

This bait is in all respects the same as the No. 400 "Killer" Bait shown on previous page, excepting that it has a spinner both at front and rear, the same as upon our minnows.

Finished in either white, aluminum, red, yellow or copper.

Price, prepaid by mail, 50c

ALSO IN COMBINATION RED & WHITE

"Dowagiac" Killer No. 400

In answer to the demand for a cheap but substantial artificial lure, which will catch fish, we offer the bait illustrated above.

This bait is in all essential respects the same as our No. 100 Minnow, excepting that it has but one spinner, is round instead of minnow shape in body, and is without eyes or other decorations. It possesses, however, the same perfection of workmanship as our higher priced baits, having our socket and screw hook

Heddon Fly Rod "River-Runtie"

$5 – 25

950 Series
Heddon
"River-Runtie-Spook"
Fly-rod Wiggler

A tiny fly-rod lure weighing 1/25 ounce and length of 1¾ inches. Transparent body—Indestructible finish. Excellent for bass, blue-gills, crappies, etc. Floats, and dives a few inches underwater and wiggles like a small minnow.

No. 952—Red and White
No. 959L—Perch Scale
No. 959XRS—Silver Shore Minnow
No. 959XRG—Green Shore Minnow
No. 959XS—Red and White Shore Minnow

A BETTER ILLUS. OF 950 (1937 AD)

NEVER SEEN THIS CATALOGED - BUT IT IS OBVIOUSLY A WOOD VERSION OF THE DOWAGIAC SPOOK!

DECAL EYE

2 Pc.

$60 – 75

(ACTUAL SIZE)

1934

$20 – 30

-2"-

THE HEDDON "DREWCO" SALT WATER BAIT NO. 72RH

THE BIG QUESTION HERE IS - WHO CARES?

BETTER ILLUS. OF THE YOWSER BAIT – #195SG (4-14-34)

SILVER LEAD HEAD, RED PTD. EYE, W/BLACK DOT.

NO HEDDON I.D. ON BAIT.

$20 – 50

RED MOUTH

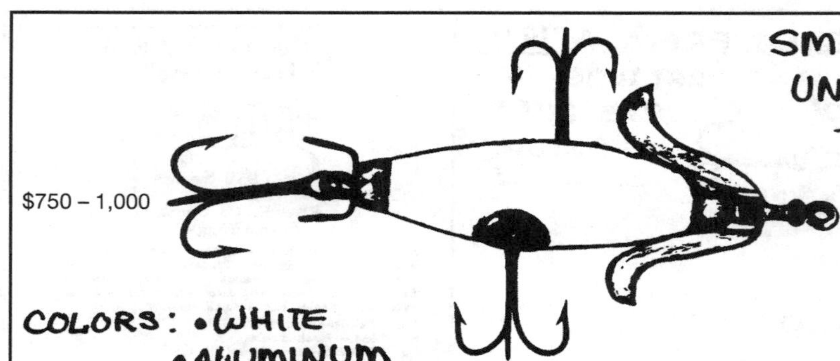

$750 – 1,000

SMALL VERSION OF THE UNDERWATER EXPERT

- 2 LEAD BELLY WTS.
- LARGE NICKEL PROP
- FRONT & REAR CAPS, HOOK CUPS, AND LINE TIE ARE ALL BRASS.

COLORS: • WHITE
• ALUMINUM

-1930-

HEDDON SPOONYFISH SPOON

$25 – 40

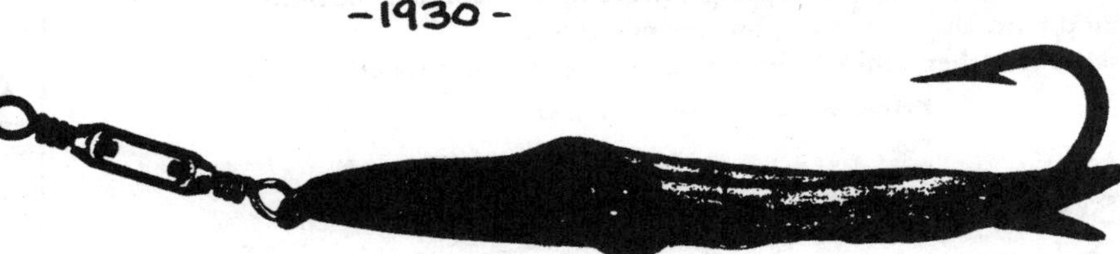

NO. 490 – 2 5/8"
NO. 590 – 4 1/4"
NO. 790 – 5 3/4"

- METAL -

HEDDON SOMETIMES USED INTRODUCTORY BOXES W/NEW PLUGS. THIS TADPOLLY BOX WOULD SPICE UP ANY HEDDON DISPLAY.

$50 – 75

"Tad Polly"

(FLOATS) (DIVES) (WIGGLES) (GETS 'EM)

EARLY HOOK RIG ON 1700 - SOMETIMES CALLED "INCH WORM".

LATER 1700 RIG -

THIS IS CALLED PIG TAIL LINE TIE -

BY 1921, THE WIGGLERS WERE TO A SINGLE LINE TIE SCREW EYE.

Principles All New
Nearly Every Strike a Kill
THE "Dowagiac"
Perfect Surface Casting Bait
You are losing fish and pleasure unless you use this new bass killer. No revolving parts. No twisted lines. Always right side up, insuring perfect hook presentment; casts easiest, reels beautifully; no other bait will attract bass so far.
An illustrated circular concerning baits and black bass in return for your address.
JAMES HEDDON & SON — Makers
DOWAGIAC, MICHIGAN
Don't put it off until tomorrow—Write Today.

1902 HEDDON AD!

SOME OF US COLLECTORS FEEL THIS WAY TODAY!

Said one of our customers:
"That bait is so perfect and beautiful I could bite it myself."

The Walter Harden Special **Harden's Star by Heddon**

Following is some information on Walter Harden, obtained by an interview with Charles Fox by Dick Healey.

Walter was catching alot of big bass on some modified Heddon baits, mostly modifications on the Old Zaragossa Wood Body. For awhile he was creditied with the world record smallmouth, but then it was found to be a strain of largemouth.

While he had that record, he went to Heddon and these two lures were put on the market. People were also trying to buy the baits right from him directly, so Heddon made some baits for him personally. On the boxes he sold, the ends were covered with brown paper tape, and on one end was typed "Walter Herden's Star" R/W. The other end said Connellsville, Pa.

A third bait that may be of his origin was the basic Heddon Vamp, with no lip attached.

(1) Harden's Star - Zaragossa Body, 2 SOS type light weight propellers, 3 trebles, two belly and one tail, G.E., 2 Pc. hook rigs, white with red detail on head, name stenciled in green on belly.

(2) Walter Harden Special - Zaragossa Body, 1 Heddon 150 type prop on the tail, none on the front. G.E. , 1-2 Pc. Rig belly hook and a tail treble, again white with red shading at head.

Harden ran ads in fishing magazines to promote his baits. (If you come upon one, zap me a copy for next supplement..thanks.)

(3) HARDEN'S WHIZ BY HEDDON

WAS A BABY VAMP WITH 2 SOS PROPS

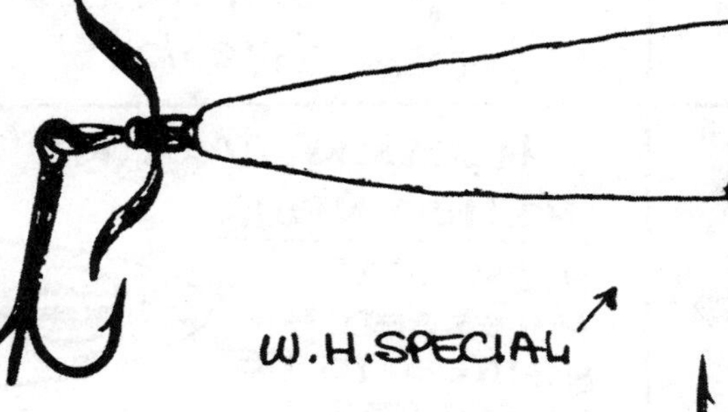
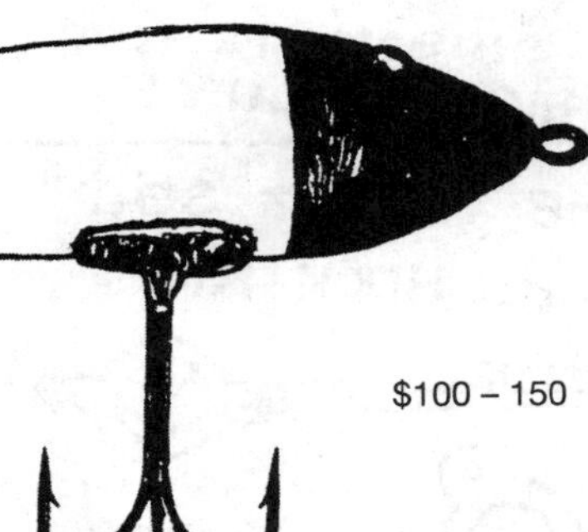

W.H.SPECIAL

$100 – 150

HEDDON
DOWAGIAC

THE EARLY TADPOLLYS HAD A "HEART" SHAPED HEAD PLATE.

WHEN YOU SEE THAT EARLY HEDDON PATENT DATE OF APRIL 1, 1902, IT WAS FOR THE PATENTS LISTED BELOW – NOT THE BAIT ITSELF.

The "Dowagiac" baits were patented April 1, 1902, the patented features being four in number, as follows:

FIRST, the angling collar, independent [that is, if used on any bait].

SECOND, the socket where hooks are held, independent.

THIRD, the open-eye screw-eye, independent.

FOURTH, the elevated fore-end, when used in combination with the angling collar, or any collar on any bait.

Any one making, selling or USING even one bait not made by or with the consent of the patentee, infringes the patent and will be promptly prosecuted in the United States courts for so doing.

A substantial reward will be paid to anyone furnishing evidence that will convict any party guilty of having violated the rights of this patent.

HEDDON'S LIT. NOW STATES PAT. NO. 696,433 WAS FILED ON JAN, 9, 1902, TO PROTECT: "NEW AND USEFUL IMPROVEMENTS IN FISH-BAITS

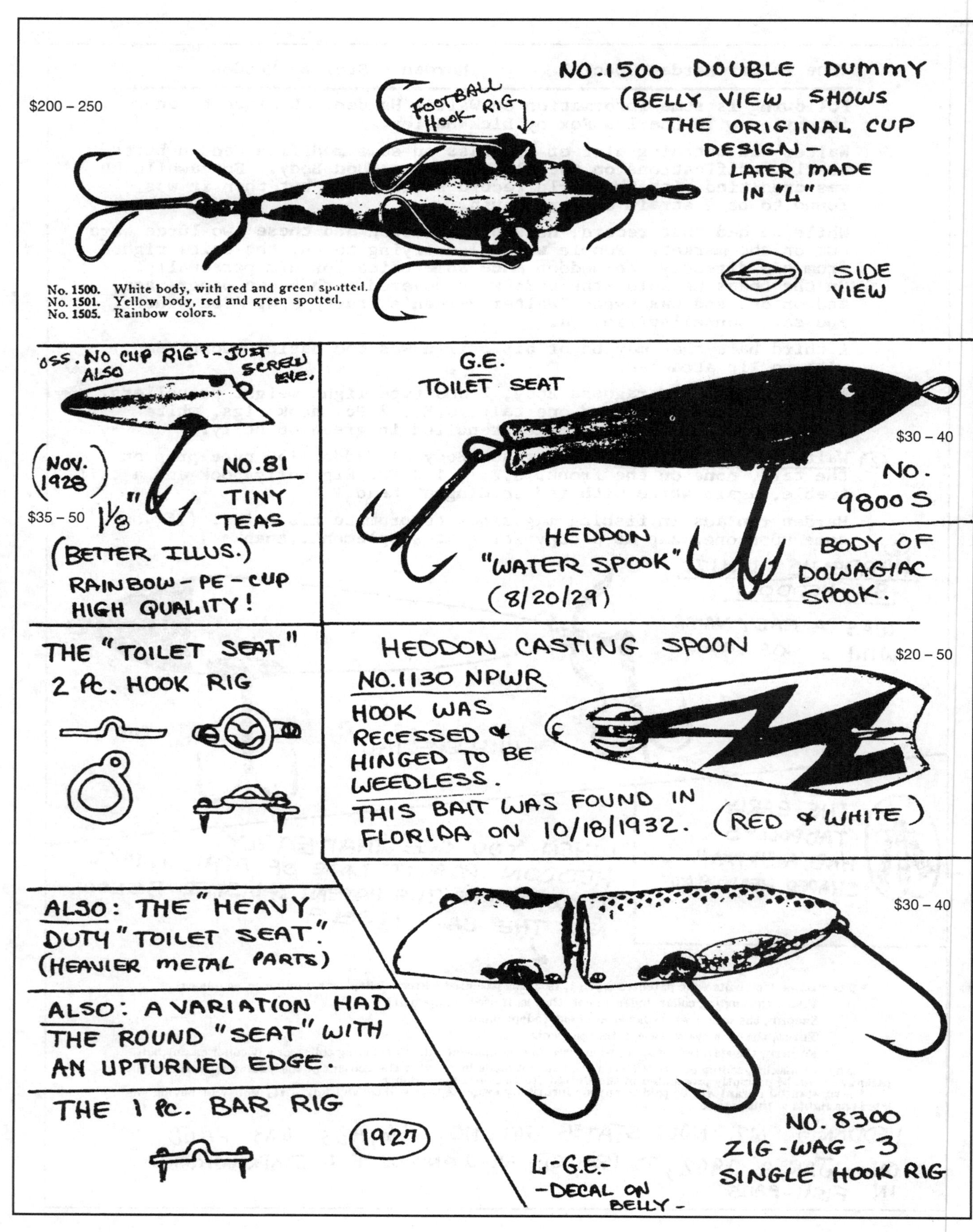

NO.1500 DOUBLE DUMMY
(BELLY VIEW SHOWS THE ORIGINAL CUP DESIGN - LATER MADE IN "L"
FOOTBALL HOOK RIG
$200 – 250
No. 1500. White body, with red and green spotted.
No. 1501. Yellow body, red and green spotted.
No. 1505. Rainbow colors.
SIDE VIEW
OSS. NO CUP RIG? - JUST SCREW EYE. ALSO
(NOV. 1928)
NO.81 TINY TEAS
$35 – 50
1 1/8"
(BETTER ILLUS.)
RAINBOW - PE - CUP
HIGH QUALITY!
G.E. TOILET SEAT
$30 – 40
NO. 9800 S
HEDDON "WATER SPOOK"
(8/20/29)
BODY OF DOWAGIAC SPOOK.
THE "TOILET SEAT" 2 Pc. HOOK RIG
HEDDON CASTING SPOON
NO.1130 NPWR
$20 – 50
HOOK WAS RECESSED & HINGED TO BE WEEDLESS.
THIS BAIT WAS FOUND IN FLORIDA ON 10/18/1932. (RED & WHITE)
ALSO: THE "HEAVY DUTY" TOILET SEAT". (HEAVIER METAL PARTS)
ALSO: A VARIATION HAD THE ROUND "SEAT" WITH AN UPTURNED EDGE.
THE 1 Pc. BAR RIG
1927
$30 – 40
L-G.E. - DECAL ON BELLY -
NO. 8300 ZIG-WAG - 3 SINGLE HOOK RIG

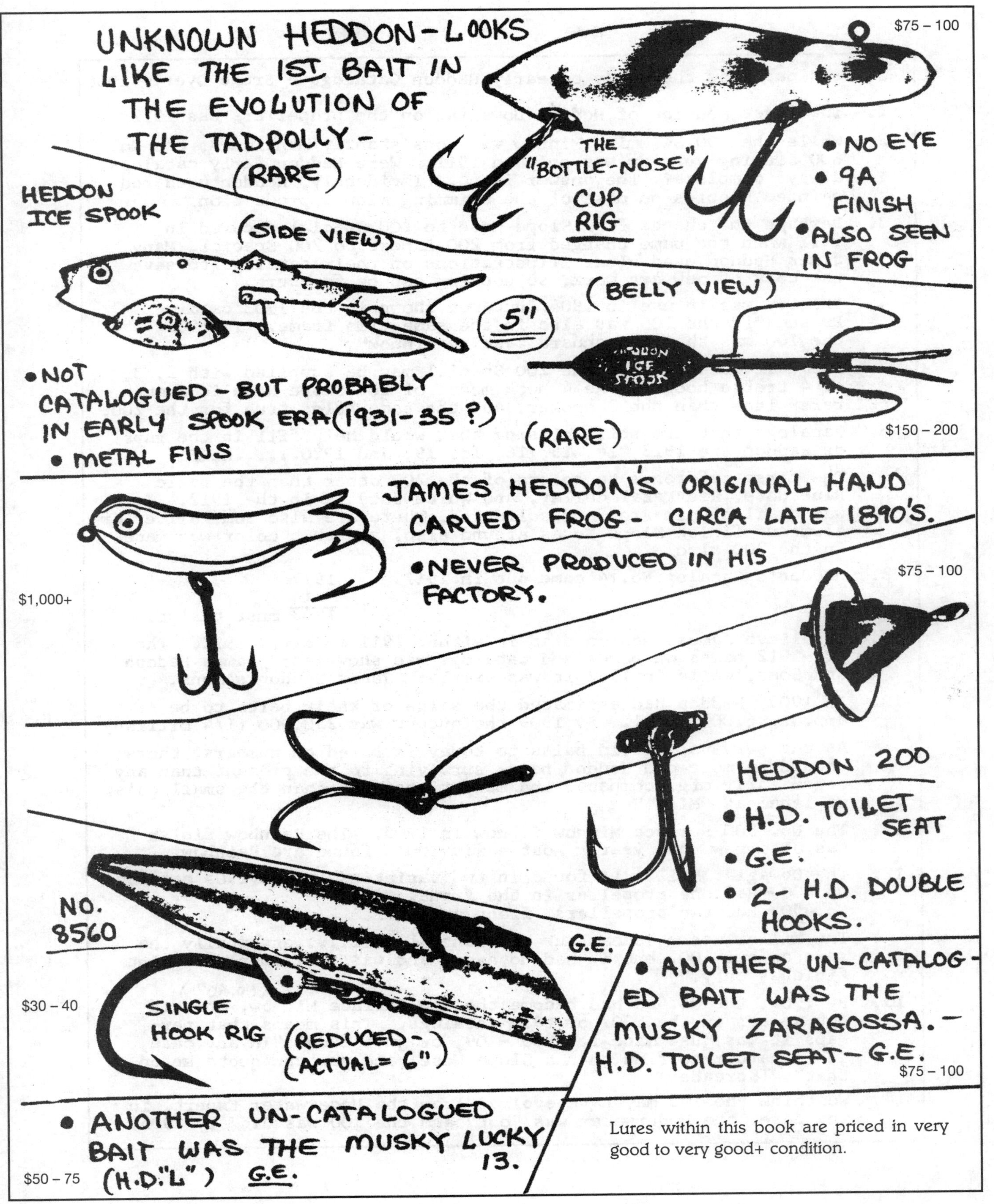
$75 – 100
UNKNOWN HEDDON - LOOKS LIKE THE 1ST BAIT IN THE EVOLUTION OF THE TADPOLLY - (RARE)
THE "BOTTLE-NOSE" CUP RIG
• NO EYE
• 9A FINISH
• ALSO SEEN IN FROG
HEDDON ICE SPOOK
(SIDE VIEW)
(BELLY VIEW)
5"
HEDDON ICE SPOOK
• NOT CATALOGUED - BUT PROBABLY IN EARLY SPOOK ERA (1931-35 ?)
• METAL FINS
(RARE)
$150 – 200
JAMES HEDDON'S ORIGINAL HAND CARVED FROG - CIRCA LATE 1890'S.
• NEVER PRODUCED IN HIS FACTORY.
$1,000+
$75 – 100
HEDDON 200
• H.D. TOILET SEAT
• G.E.
• 2 - H.D. DOUBLE HOOKS.
NO. 8560
G.E.
SINGLE HOOK RIG
(REDUCED - ACTUAL = 6")
$30 – 40
• ANOTHER UN-CATALOGED BAIT WAS THE MUSKY ZARAGOSSA. - H.D. TOILET SEAT - G.E.
$75 – 100
• ANOTHER UN-CATALOGUED BAIT WAS THE MUSKY LUCKY 13. (H.D."L") G.E.
$50 – 75

Lures within this book are priced in very good to very good+ condition.

Conclusions from the study of early Heddon Catalogs - Bruce Dyer - 1980

1. The first mention of Heddon Dowagiac on the propellers was 1912
2. While the 900 Swimming Minnow was consistantly mentioned, the No. 800 Sinking version was only in 1911. Were Heddon early catalogs always complete? The answer is no. Incidently, Heddon used red painted trebles on most of the swimming minnow production.
3. Perhaps the change from Slope Nose to 200 Special occured in 1911 when the name changed from 200 Expert to 200 Special. Many times Heddon used older illustrations on their catalogs to save the cost of new art work, so nothing can be for sure.
4. The 150 was in use in 1904, but not shown in the 1903 catalog. Presumably the 100 was also in the same time frame. In 1905, the 100 was their "standard casting minnow".
5. The 1912 catalog says the 200 Special may be supplied with 2, 3, or 4 treble hooks. The 4 hook model of the Slope Nose is a much rarer item than the 2 hooker, and the same holds true for the 200.
6. Catalogs that are still missing that would help fill in the gaps of Heddon are 1913, 14, 15, 16, 18, 19, and 1920......HELP!
7. The first reference to colors of the 200 other than the basic Blue Nose, Red Metal collar, and White body is in the 1912. It was available in Frog and solid Red. There are also some Silver or aluminum finish Slope Noses around also, and this color was made in the 200 also.
8. Heddon's Catalog No.14 came out in 1917.

   1917
   \- 14
   1903 must be 1st.
9. I believe James Heddon died in either 1911 or early 1912. The pre-1912 names on boxes and catalogs was shown as: James Heddon and Sons, while in 1912 it was simply: James Heddon's Sons.
10. In 1903, Heddon had estimated the sales of their baits to be approx. 6,000 total. By 1909 the output was 250,000 (1/4 million)

    As the survival of old baits to today is based on numbers, there should be more old Heddon baits surviving to the present than any other early mfg. company, and many times more than the small co's. we label as "Misc."
11. The No. 300 Surface Minnow is new in 1905. The Rainbow finish was also new that year. Most early 300's found are Rainbow.
12. The Dowagiac Killer is found in two varieties in the 1905 catalog.
    No.400 - Had one propeller in the front.
    No.450 - Had two propellers, front and rear.

    The Killer was a "cheap but substantial bait.....essentally the same as our 100, but it had no eyes, and was made in plain paint finishes only."
13. By 1909, the No.400 had become the New Surface Minnow, (No.402) and did not appear in the 1907 or 1910 catalogs. This means that perhaps it was just made in 1908 - 09, or just 1909! "In any case, it is harder to find than a Slope Nose, and you can quote me on that". (Streater)
14. We think the 100 may have evolved from the Underwater Expert. In any case, the Underwater was "out" and the 100 was "in" by 1905.

15. The No.20 Dowagiac Minnow is older than you might think. It is shown in the 1909 catalog. (Streater - I don't think the 20 was ever made in "L" rig, but was made as cup rig until the surface rigged, tack glass eye model appeared. Your best bet for the oldest models would be the paint finish)

16. Sizes varied for the same lure in different catalogs. Example: The 300 for 1907, 09, and 1910 was shown as 4". For 1911, 12, it was 3-1/2". In 1917 it was listed as 3-3/4".

17. The Multiple Metal Minnow, No.500 was shown in the 1909 catalog. The No.50 Artistic Minnow appears in just the 1907 & 1909 books.

18. The No.700 Muskollonge Minnow was first made in the 5 treble configeration, looking just like a king-sized 150, and was shown in the 1909, 1910 catalogs. The 3 treble 700 was 1st illustrated in 1911.

19. Heddon introduced 4 baits in 1912: No.0, No.00, No.10 & No.11. Because of item number one of this data, we can assume that all, or at least most, had Heddon Dowagiac on their propellers.

The following will be random comments and findings about Heddon from numerous sources. While I assume all are accurate, we are dealing with a subject of infinite variations. (Streater)

1. The Heddon Weight Buoy shown with the Artistic Minnow was also made in a red body with a black head.

2. Jim Heddon made one of his first baits from a corn cob, and used a modified bottle cap for a collar.

3. The Heddon Spoony Frog was invented and patented by: A. D. & D. M. Skelly, 18 Kingston Street, Lawrence, Mass. Patent date Aug. 3, 1926, No. 1,594,798. The back of the bait had the date stamped on it.

4. Heddon ordered some Oliver & Gruber "Glowurm" baits (double jointed lure) in 1922. O & G framed the check and put it on their wall. In 1923, Heddon came out with the Gamefisher (a double jointed lure) Coincidence?

5. Heddon made Vamps (& other baits) for Abbey & Imbrie. The A & I name was embossed on the lip instead of Heddon Dowagiac.

6. One way to date early Vamps (including the Vampire) is to check the center screw location below the lip......if the screw holding the "L" is also holding the lip, it is the early model.

7. The Heddon Flipper also came with Stanley type propellers. A hard to find model of this bait would be the trebles on the side, so it floated like the CCBCO Injured Minnow.

8. The "L" hook rig was first seen in a 1915 Crab Wiggler Ad.

9. The "Flat Nose" Crab Wiggler was also made in Green Scale. With Heddon's first scale finish (also Green Scale) in 1917, this would seem to indicate production of this lure at least until '17.

10. The "200" got its number because Jim Heddon caught 200 Bass on it in one day........man, that's fishin'.

11. The Heddon Chugger was made in wood also, not many though.

11.5 The Heddon "PAL" Series rods were introduced in 1933.

12. The Heddon Torpedo was also made with two side hooks and the tail hook, although I have never seen any cataloging.

13. The early spotted finishes were referred to as "Trouted Spots".

14. 1930 is the probable year for the introduction of the "Spook" finish baits. Heddon had problems with the stability of the early baits, a difference in formulation between Tenite I & II.

15. The wood Darting Zara No.6600 was introduced in 1933. There must have been a limited production, these are really hard to find. Oh yes, it's G.E.

16. Alot of wood No.110 Original River-Runts were made with cup hook rigs, even though they came after the "L" rig. It was a small bait, like the 20, so maybe there is a correlated reason.

17. Here is a list of Heddon Colors in 1908: White, Yellow, Red, Aluminum, Rainbow, Fancy Cracked Back (Green) & Fancy Sienna.

18. Heddon sometimes used "zinc" eyes in lieu of glass eyes. One bait I have seen with zinc is the No.260 Surface Minny.

19. The Zig-Wag Jr. was also made in "L" rig and a string tied, Salmon Plug rig. There sure are alot of 8300 Zig Wags around.

20. The 500 Multiple Metal Minnow was made in Nickel and Gold.

21. Rumor has it that Heddon made a Fly Rod Size Vamp. Confirmation?

23. A Double Dummy with just the side hooks would be authentic, it came that way from the factory, with an optional extra hook in the box but not attached, used as replacement or tail hook. The 1500 was new in 1913. A 1917 catalog showed the bait with a normal "L" hook rig, replacing the special rigging it was intro. with.

24. Refer back to 9. Heddon's 1st Green Scale Finish was called deluxe, and had a greenish silver streak down the back. Later it was replaced by a black stripe.

25. There seems to be an infinite number of possible combinations on Heddon baits, some of them were probably special order, and some were production items not cataloged. Examples would be a Walton Feathertail with no eye detail, and a Baby Vamp, 2 Pc. Hook Rig, with no lip. The Vamp Spook No.9750 was also made without a lip. Line tie on Baby Vamp was in point of nose.

26. One clue to the age of the No1000 Night Radiant Moonlight Bait (refer to Streater - page 66, and Dyer comment No.9, which puts the bait at 1911 or earlier. (James Heddon & Sons).

27. The No.260 Surface Minny was in the 1935 catalog, but not in the 1936. The No.350 Musky Surface was made in 1935 - 36.

28. Take the side fins off the Heddon 1600 Wiggler, put single line ties in the nose, and what do you have? A fatMoonlight Fish Spear!

29. The earliest models of Go-Deeper River Runt Spooks were 2 Pc. Rig.

30. The 370 Muskie S.O.S. was made in the 1928 - 29 era, and production must have been depressed by the depression, few exist today.

31. Some member has a "Musky" Zaragossa. I wish I could verify it.

32. In 1928, the 6" Musky Vamp was called the "Muskiteer".

33. The Zig-Wag bait lacked action with 3 trebles, so it was fixed (improved) by making just the 2 treble model No.8300 in 1928.

34. Here are the yearly production figures for the Heddon 900 Swimming Minnow:

Aug. 1, 1909 to Aug. 1, 1910		10,211
1910 to 1911		5,062
1911 to 1912		1,136
1912 to 1913		1,471
1913 to 1914		921
1914 to 1915		350
1915 to 1916	(Hmmmmm - bad year!)	45
1916 to 1917		1,498
	Total:	20,694

Just think, every time you find a 900, you are handling: $\frac{1}{20694}$ of the total production!!
Remember............You read it here first!

35. Rush Tango brought suit against the Crab Wiggler for infringement of its Tango patent.

36. In 1905 era, some of the 100's were shipped without the rear spinner.

37. Another scoop, or maybe two scoops: The Heddon Zaragossa has two stories as to how it got its' name:
    1. It was named after the "Zaragossa Sea" which is a huge mass of floating weeds.
    2. Originally called the Zaragossa of Florida in 1922, the name came from the wiggle action of the working girls' fannies in the red light district of Pensacola, Fla. on Zaragossa Street.

    (I like version number two the best, let's go with that one.)

38. The Lucky 13 was invented by Jack Welch in 1920. The testing of the prototype was done on Friday the 13th, thus the name.

39. Heddon introduced the Crazy Crawler in 1940 in the 2¼" and 3½" sizes, made of course, of wood. The plastic model intro. in '56.

40. The Shore Minnow Finish is credited to Lyell Wooster of Heddon.

41. The Artistic Minnow (1907 - 1909) may have been named after the Artistic Wood Turning Works of Chicago, Ill. who did the turning of large numbers of wood bodies for the bait co's of that era.

42. The 4200 "Munk-Mouse" not only had that strange reverse slant lip, but several have been seen with a Crab Wiggler type collar.

43. If you have a Heddon 150 with a funny steep slanted forehead and brass cups you have the earliest vintage.

44. The 9130 Torpedo Spook was originally made in wood by: J.C. Lockner of Clermont, Florida in 1928. It was called the "Kneedle Bait".

45. The earliest Spin Diver No.3000 may have been a version with a plain lip and no prop on the front.

46. The 5400 Gamefisher was also made later in 2 Pc. hook rig.

47. The 9850 Basser Spook made with just 2 trebles, both on belly.

48. 0 & 00 were made in cup and "L" rig, the "L" is more rare.

49. The Weedless Widow was new in 1928, called the Weedless Wizard which offended Pflueger, and Wizard was dropped for Widow.

50. The S.O.S. was new in 1928. SOS didn't mean "save our ship", nope, it meant: 1. "Swims-On-Side"
2. "Sells-On-Sight"
The 170 & 160 were introduced at the same time. The 1928 catalog made no mention of the 370 with these two. This same 1928 catalog showed as new the Little Luny and the Spoony Frog.

51. The Heddon Little Mary No.850 was shown as 2" in 1926, and 3" in 1927. This accounts for those small salt water Heddons that have been spotted around from time to time.

52. In the'what baits to use'in the 1917 catalog, it suggests the 1001 RH under the night fishing section. Apparently it was current enough to mention, even though it wasn't shown in '17. I assume this is the 1000 Moonlight Bait in Red Head finish.

53. The first Tadpollys had what we call a "heart shaped" metal lip, and came in a special introductory box. The later metal was furnished without this notch.

54. I've never seen one, but apparently Heddon made a "No-Snag" Vamp Spook.

55. While we're on the subject of abnormal Vamps, there's quite a few Baby Vamps around with 2 Pc. Rig and no lip detail.

56. Heddon made a Special Heavy Duty Rigged 8500 "Sinking" Basser.

57. What makes a Head-On Basser? Well, it says Head-On on the lip, but that isn't all. It was made in both cup & "L". Most of the ones I've seen have a thinner body, with a longer taper to the tail, and the lower lip was longer than on the later models. An even earlier version was RH/White - Cup - No Eyes - Long Lower Jaw - no metal lip.

58. In 1937, Joe Martin of Martin Tackle in Seattle sued Heddon on infringement on his patent on drop loose hook rigging for Salmon Plugs. Heddon lost and the settlement was $20,000.

59. Heddon made a Nickel Plated and a Gold Plated Color Series in their 9260 Zara Spooks. Some were solid metallic, and others were combined with other colors.

60. For you Heddon Basser Fans, here's a tidbit of information:
The 1933 catalog showed two different No. 9850 Basser-Spooks.
The 3 treble model was called simply - "Basser-Spook".
The 2 treble model was called the- "Sea-Basser Spook".

61. The 1933 catalog mentioned that special models of Bassers, Zig-Wags, and Lucky 13's were available-slightly larger-with extra heavy hooks and fasteners. This would be the heavy "L" I believe as the 2 pc. was phased in mainly in 1934.

62. On the Musky Type Baits during the 2 pc. era, they almost always had the heavy duty toilet seat rigs, not the standard 2 pc. rig.

63. The 1933 catalog also showed the River Runt Spook as "NEW".

64. Here is the assumed development sequence of the Dowagiac Spook:
(1930) 3-3/4" - 1 oz. - G.E. - Toilet Seat
(1931) 3-1/4" - 3/4 oz. - G.E. - 2 Pc.
(1949) 3-3/8" - 3/4 oz. - P.E. - Surface Rig

65. On the jointed Vamp Spook, No.9730 was introduced in 1933, 2 Pc. An interesting item was probably produced a few years before, the No.9300 (?) G.E. Jtd. Vamp Spook, had toilet seat belly hook and an "L" rig tail hook.

66. Some comments on the Luny Frog. In 1926 - 27, the Luny had a treble as a belly hook, and a single hook on the tail. From 1928 on it was equiped with a double hook on the belly and a single on the tail. The most common hook rig is the one Pc. bar. The latter stages of production had the legs of the bait solid or closed. This was to strengthen against breakage. Hard to find color for this bait was the Red Head/White. The Luny was made for 7 years.

67. The 1400 Single Hook Minnow had a new hook rig - the staple rig. I've never seen it so I can't draw it for you, maybe next time.

68. To summarize the Coast Minnow Sizes, arrived at by actual measurements. 2-3/8, 2-1/2, 3, 3-1/2, 4, 4-1/2, 5, and 5-1/4". I must put in a good word for the oft-neglected Coast Minnows. These baits are olde and rare, and should be higher rated than they currently are. Many times a advanced collection will have only one size of Coast Minnow.

69. The description on a Heddon Box extolling the virtues of the new Spook Baits listed: "Water Spook" - "Spinner Spook" and the "Shrimpy".

70. James Heddon did die in 1912 as I alluded to earlier. His son Charles then became president, and then John Heddon, Charles' son, ran the company. There was also a Will Heddon, which I think was John's brother who didn't participate in running the company, but did alot of fishing (field testing) with the baits.

71. The design of the Gamefisher may have been aquired, rather than developed internally. There are 2 known gamefisher-like lures, 1 double-jointed and 1 single jointed with the reg. gamefisher lip, except that it says "Vampir" on them. They had V-shaped joints. My thoughts are that Heddon bought the rights to this plug, along with the name. Then renamed the lure the gamefisher and stuck the name "Vampire" on the brand new Vamp they were getting ready to market also.

72. Add another developmental stage to my page 62 on the 200. Let's call this Stage C½. It would be "L" rig, still retaining the tail cap. The collar was still pin attached.

73. Another stage to add to page 62 would be Stage D½, which would be the 200 in 2 Pc. Toilet Seat.

74. Stage F½ for the 210 would be 2 Pc. Rig, with no eye detail.

W H E W !!!!!!!

Well, that concludes a really in depth summary of things we have found out about, and surmised about, Heddon. Small details come together to paint a full picture. I trust you all will contribute more, or start to contribute details about all the manufactured baits in our hobby.

Again, I'll plug the Kodak 150 Ektaprint Copier, with which I made most all of the exact size reproductions in this supplement. Without the availability of such a high quality machine, it would be better to send the bait to me for reproduction. Send it insured, and I will send it back the same way. One alternative would be to locate the Kodak machine somewhere near you, and make a trip once every 6 months or so, to get good copies. Some of you have sent me just awful gray, blurred images, that I just can't use, and the time involved to re-draw, let alone the ability, is just not available.

HOWE'S VACUUM BASS BAIT.

PAT'D. OCT. 5, 1909

$40 – 50

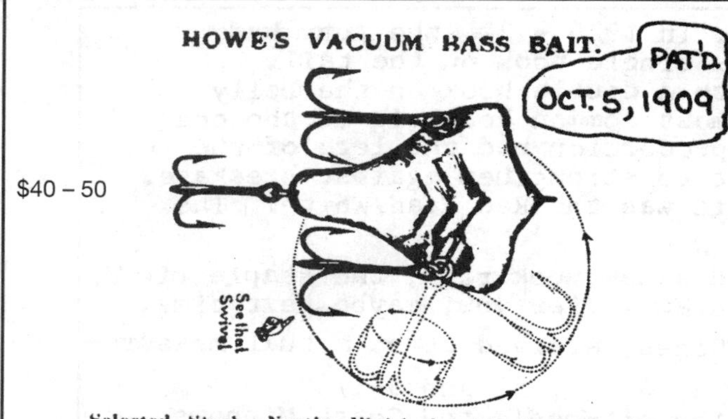
See that Swivel

Selected Stock, Neatly Finished with Eight Coats of Special White Horn Enamel, Red Striping, Waterproof, Nickel Plated Brass Metal Parts.
Howe's Vacuum Bait—With Three Best Imported Treble Hooks on Patent Swivels.....

(BY PROFESSOR HOWE)
VACUUM BAIT CO. - 307 WALNUT ST.
NORTH MANCHESTER, INDIANA

LATER IT WAS PRODUCED BY SO. BEND BAIT CO. IN TWO SIZES, + GLASS EYES.

"THE BOOSTER BAIT"
BY J. G. HENZEL - CHICAGO, ILL.

1907

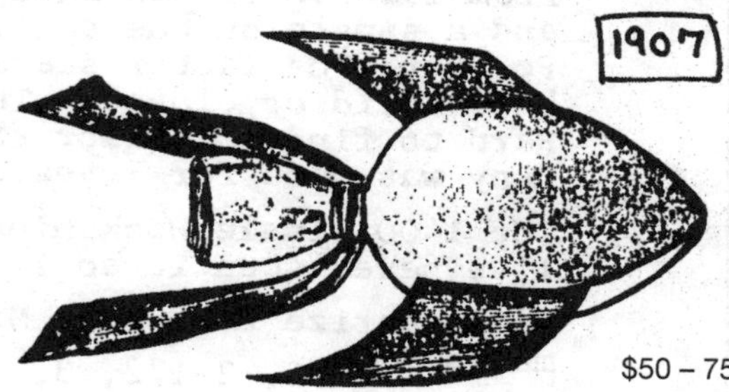

$50 – 75

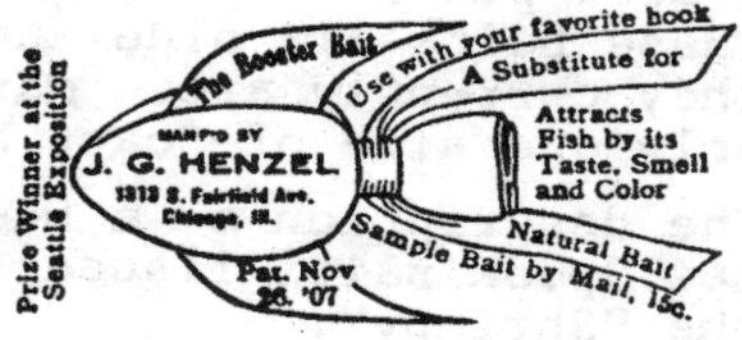
Prize Winner at the Seattle Exposition
The Booster Bait
Use with your favorite hook
A Substitute for
Natural Bait
MANF'D BY
J. G. HENZEL
S. Fairfield Ave.
Chicago, Ill.
Attracts Fish by its Taste, Smell and Color
Pat. Nov 26. '07
Sample Bait by Mail, 15c.

FILL THE BAIT WITH EDIBLE MATTER WHEN IN THE WATER, IT DISSOLVES, THROWING OFF A STRONG TASTE AND SMELL. IT MAY BE USED WITH ANY TYPE HOOK.

$10

1953

No. 2 HAWK LURE

½ ounce, 2 inch. Deep runner.

HAWK FISH LURE CO.
ST. LOUIS, MO.

HOLZWARTH
IT CATCHES FISH.

Its life-like movements in the water attracts game fish of all kinds. Specially good for large and small mouth Black Bass. Animated and irrestible.

The "HOLZWARTH" Minnow

is a beautifully made and durable artificial bait that will catch more fish than live bait. Superior to all others. Try one and you'l throw away your minnow bucket. By mail, post-paid,

WRITE FOR CATALOGUE E

J. C. HOLZWARTH, ALLIANCE, O.

$100 – 150

"HOOKZEM"

1921

The Latest Scientific Invention in Artificial Lures

FOR CASTING OR TROLLING

The first automatic weedless bait ever perfected has a unique and peculiar wiggle that attracts all game fish. The "HOOKZEM" travels about eight inches below the surface when in action, floats at rest and always keeps its upright position.

A Weedless Lure at Last Absolutely WEEDLESS, this feature removes the principal objection to the use of artificial bait. The hooks are so concealed and guarded that the weeds pass directly over them.

Every Strike a Catch The moment the fish makes a strike the hooks automatically spring from their concealed position and are forced deep in the fish's mouth. If your dealer cannot supply you, we will send direct.

$50 – 75

DEALERS: There will be a big demand for "HOOKZEM" this season. See that you are supplied.

Hookzem Bait Co., 3443 N. Harding Ave., Chicago, Ill.

"EXPERT"
Wooden Minnow

1904

An Artificial Bait
that will
Positively Catch More Fish than Live Bait.

Do not class the "Expert" with other cheap baits. It is in a class by itself. REFERENCE: Any business man or bank in Alliance, Ohio; in Duns or Bradstreets, see Spring. Holzwarth & Co.

Sent to any address in U. S. or Canada for postage prepaid. Address,

J. C. HOLZWARTH,
Alliance, Ohio.

F. B. HAMILTON MFG.
PASADENA, CALIF.

• NO. 1 – ½ OZ.
• NO. 2 – ¾ OZ.
2 SIZES

NOTE: SMALLER SIZE IS TOUGHER TO FIND.

$50 – 75

MEDLEY'S WIGGLY CRAWFISH

1920

2 Pc. HOOK RIGS

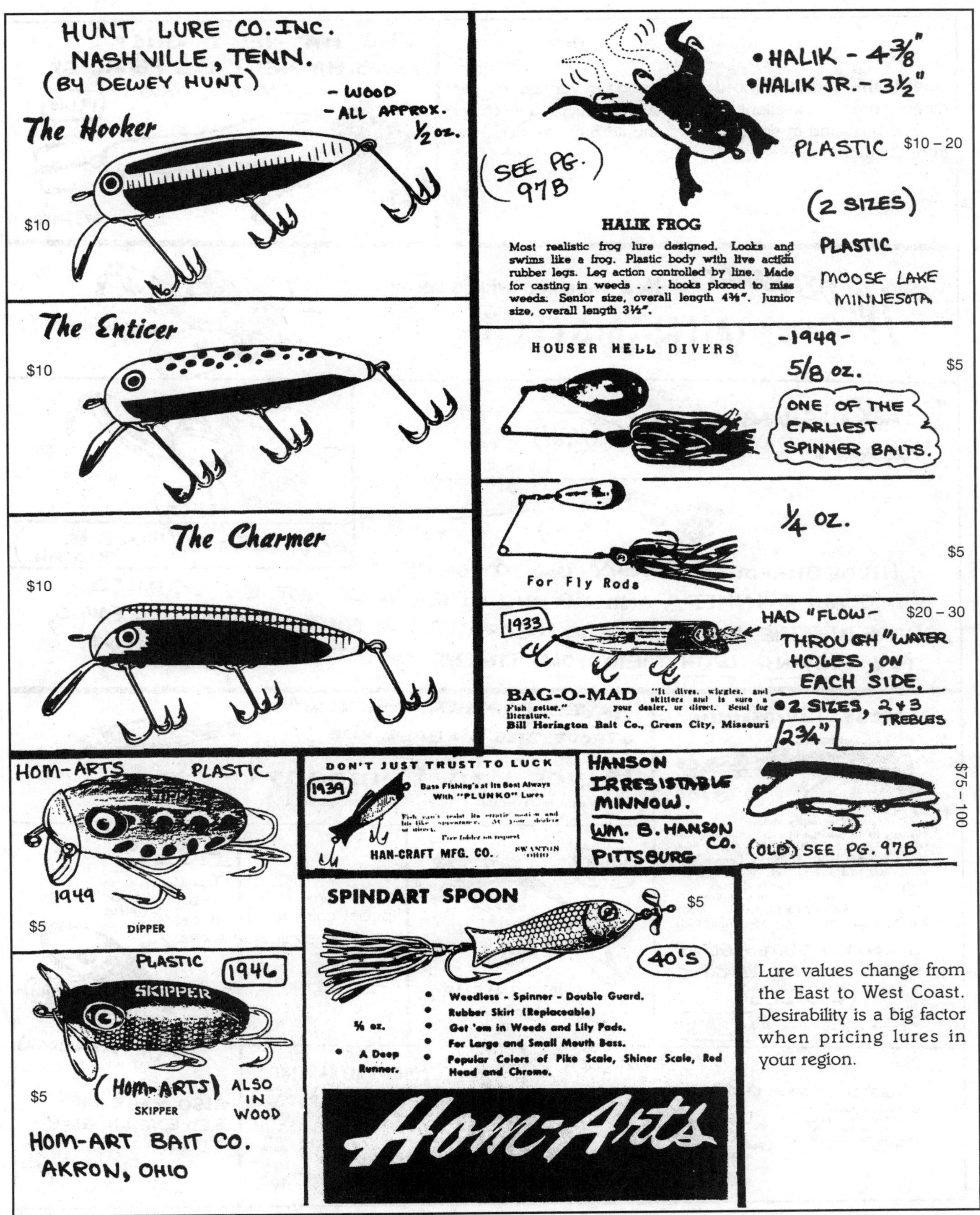
HUNT LURE CO. INC.
NASHVILLE, TENN.
(BY DEWEY HUNT)
- WOOD
- ALL APPROX. 1/2 OZ.
The Hooker
$10
The Enticer
$10
The Charmer
$10
• HALIK - 4 3/8"
• HALIK JR. - 3 1/2"
PLASTIC
$10 – 20
(SEE PG. 97B)
(2 SIZES)
HALIK FROG
Most realistic frog lure designed. Looks and swims like a frog. Plastic body with live action rubber legs. Leg action controlled by line. Made for casting in weeds . . . hooks placed to miss weeds. Senior size, overall length 4 3/8". Junior size, overall length 3 1/2".
PLASTIC
MOOSE LAKE MINNESOTA
HOUSER HELL DIVERS
-1949-
5/8 OZ.
$5
ONE OF THE EARLIEST SPINNER BAITS.
1/4 OZ.
$5
For Fly Rods
1933
HAD "FLOW-THROUGH" WATER HOLES, ON EACH SIDE.
$20 – 30
BAG-O-MAD
"It dives, wiggles, and skitters and is sure a Fish getter." your dealer, or direct. Send for literature.
Bill Herington Bait Co., Green City, Missouri
• 2 SIZES, 2 + 3 TREBLES
2 3/4"
HOM-ARTS
PLASTIC
1949
$5
DIPPER
DON'T JUST TRUST TO LUCK
1939
Bass Fishing's at Its Best Always With "PLUNKO" Lures
Free folder on request
HAN-CRAFT MFG. CO.
SWANTON OHIO
HANSON IRRESISTABLE MINNOW.
WM. B. HANSON CO.
PITTSBURG
(OLD) SEE PG. 97B
$75 – 100
PLASTIC
1946
SKIPPER
(HOM-ARTS) ALSO IN WOOD
$5
SKIPPER
HOM-ART BAIT CO.
AKRON, OHIO
SPINDART SPOON
$5
40'S
Weedless - Spinner - Double Guard.
Rubber Skirt (Replaceable)
Get 'em in Weeds and Lily Pads.
For Large and Small Mouth Bass.
Popular Colors of Pike Scale, Shiner Scale, Red Head and Chrome.
5/8 oz.
A Deep Runner.
Hom-Arts

Lure values change from the East to West Coast. Desirability is a big factor when pricing lures in your region.

Lures in this book are priced in very good to very good+ condition. Lures in excellent to mint condition, lures in correct original box, and in special colors should have a price quote from the authors.

THE HAYNES MAGNET
W.B. HAYNES - 275 PEARL ST.
AKRON, OHIO. (1908)

$75 – 100

HILDEBRANDT -- New weighted wiggle spoon

WIG-WAG (3 SIZES)

$5

• 3½W

(¼ OZ.)

"BLACK" WIG-WAG
FOR PORK RIND

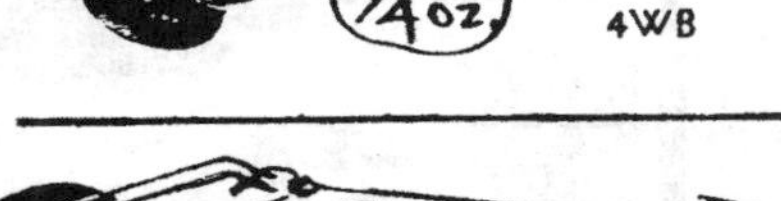

(¼ OZ.) 4WB

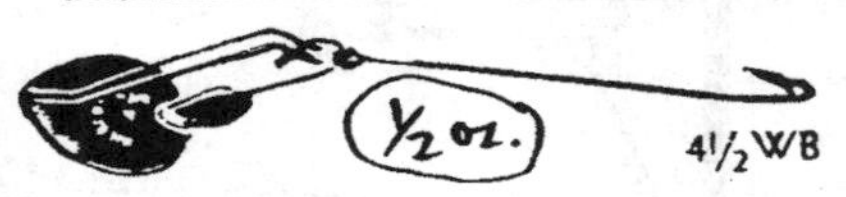

$5

(½ OZ.) 4½WB

$5

• 4½W

(½ OZ.)

•6 W – ⅝ OZ. (NICKEL OR GOLD FIN.)

HILDEBRANDT IS A VERY OLD MFG. OF QUAL. SPINNERS AND SPOONS. THEY WILL NOT BE DETAILED HEREIN – THE ABOVE ARE ILLUSTRATED SO THAT IF THEY ARE FOUND, TRY FISHING WITH THEM! OLD TIMERS SAY THEY ARE DEADLY!

Haas' Liv-Minno

$50 – 75

"It actually swims"

The only REAL imitation of a live minnow ever developed. A lure you can ALWAYS depend upon

No. 1 Length 4 in. wt. ½ oz. Tail & 1 body hinge. | No. 2 Length 5 in. wt. ⅝ oz. Tail & 2 body hinges.

If your dealer can't supply you send direct to

HAAS TACKLE CO.

8-10 N. Poplar St. Sapulpa, Okla.

JOINTED LURE – GLASS EYES – CLEAR PLASTIC LIP – (2 SIZES)
4" – 5" (1930's)

"HAYES FEATHER MINNOW"
•TROUT SIZE •BASS SIZE

(1923)

$5

Hayes Bait Company

156 Virginia Avenue Indianapolis, Ind. (2 SIZES)

(1949)

PLASTIC

$5

(HOLDENLANE)

CIRCLE H "SOURPUSS"

Special color lures have higher values.

2 SIZES

YELLOW, RED, BLACK, GREEN } AND WHITE

$5

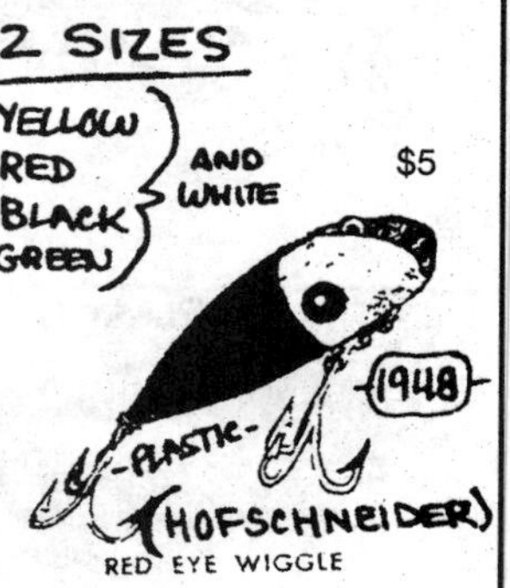

PLASTIC

(1948)

(HOFSCHNEIDER)

RED EYE WIGGLE

-ALSO MADE THE RED EYE WIGGLER SPOON.

$20 – 25

(SEE WILSON)

HASTINGS WEEDLESS RUBBER FROGS

Soft rubber body; two weedless hooks. Length of frog, 3½ inches. Nicely painted to imitate a frog. Weight, ½ oz.

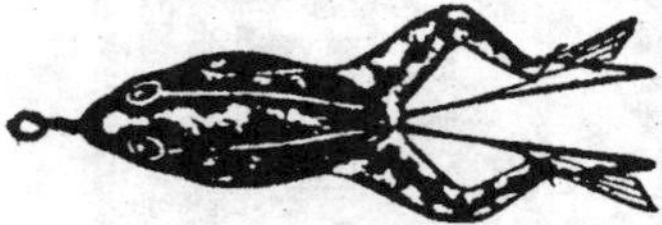

30,000 BAITCASTING,

SO CALIFORNIANS can't be wrong! Having tried and proven the WEEDLESS, REALISTIC, EASIEST CASTING DEADLY KILLING HOOT SPINNER. Simplicity personified. 100% handmade! Functions automatically. subercating. postpaid HOOT SPINNER. Dept. F-4629 Kingswell Ave., Hollywood, Calif.

HOOT SPINNER $5 – 10

$5

HELIN'S FLATFISH

FLY ROD FLATFISH

THE WORLD'S BEST SELLER! (MADE IN MANY STYLES AND SIZES.)

1ST FLATFISH – SEPT. 12, 1933.
INVENTED BY CHARLES HELIN.

The New Helin Swimmerspoon

(Patent Applied For)

$5

HISTORY'S FIRST SWIMMING SPOON

W/ PLASTIC INSERTS

FIRST PROTOTYPES MADE IN 1942.
1ST PRODUCTION SOLD: APRIL 19, 1960.

SWIMMERSPOON

Models	Bait Length	Weight
125	1¼"	1/12 oz.
150	1½"	⅛ oz.
175	1¾"	⅙ oz.
200	2"	⅕ oz.
225	2¼"	⅓ oz.
250	2½"	3/7 oz.
275	2¾"	⅜ oz.
300	3"	⅔ oz.
325	3¼"	¾ oz.
350	3½"	1 oz.
*600	6"	3 oz.

• ALSO MADE IN SALMON MODEL WITH SINGLE HOOK.

The Flatfish Is Manufactured Exclusively By

HELIN TACKLE COMPANY

4099 Beaufait Detroit 7, Mich.
Corner of Gratiot Ave. (U.S. 25)

FISHCAKE

HELIN'S SURFACE POPPER
The FISHCAKE

Model No.	Hooking	Lgth.	Wght.
7, spinning	2 gang only	1¾"	¼ oz.
9, reg. casting	3 or 4 gang	2¼"	⅜ oz.
11, large cast.	3 or 4 gang	2¾"	⅝ oz.

Choice of red or black spinners,
Red spins left; black spins right.

MADE IN 12 COLORS

OR, orange. LO, light orange. YE, yellow. FR, frog. BL, black. WH, white. WR, white, red. SI, silver. BSS, black, silver specs. SS, silver scale. RYF, red and yellow fluorescent. SCW, scale, white belly.

NO. 7 $5

NO. 9 $5

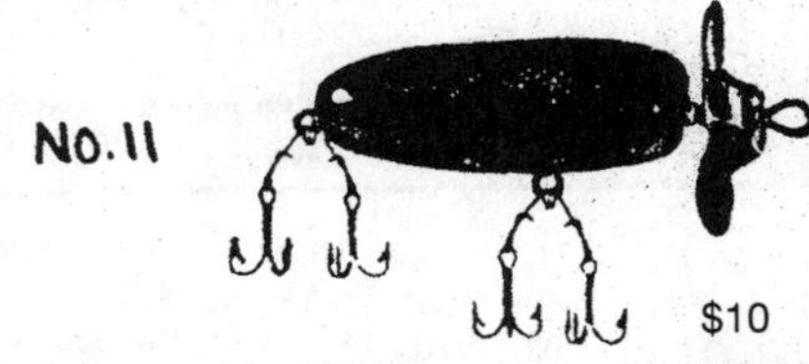

NO. 11 $10

Lure collecting is fun, tell a friend.

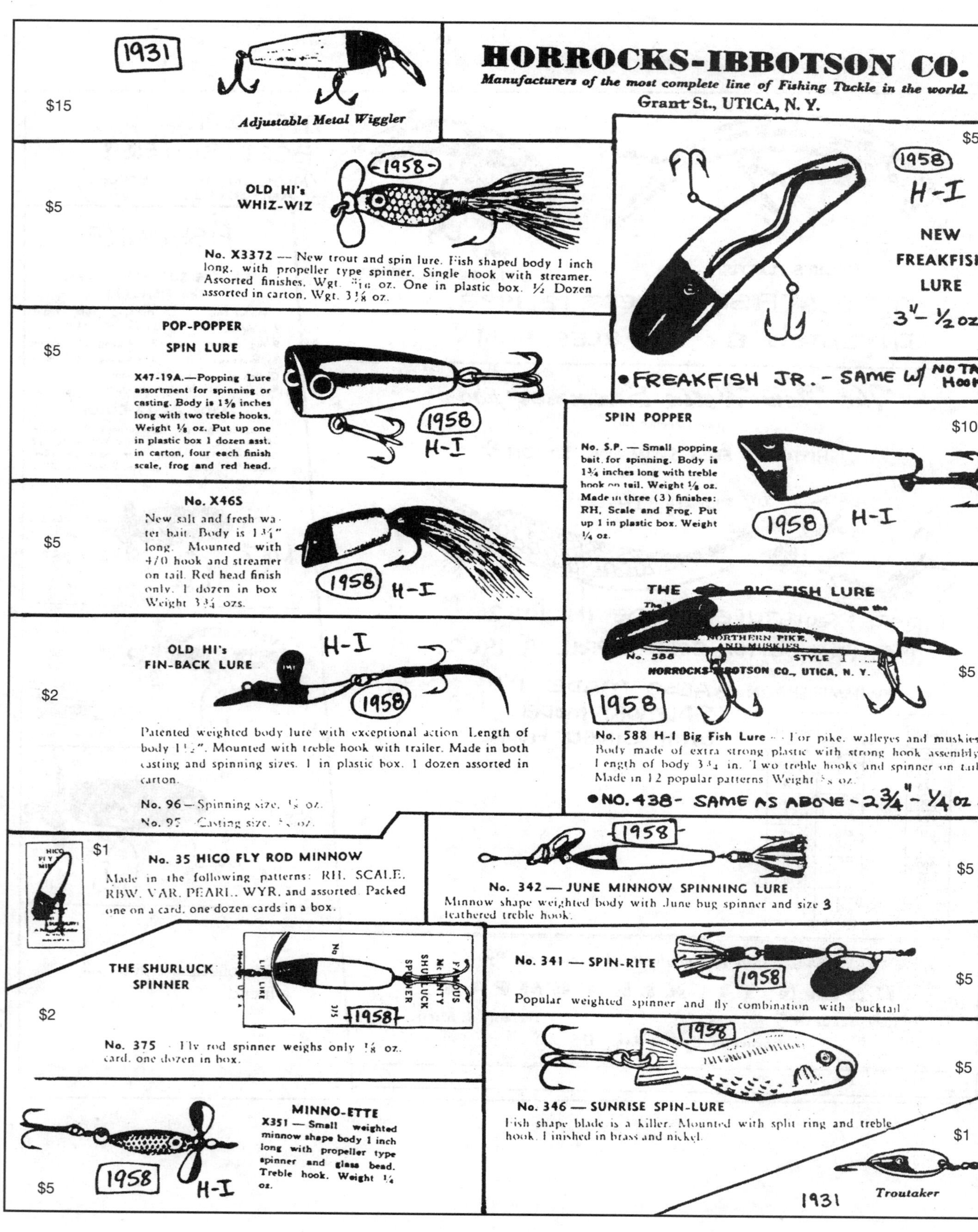

1931
Adjustable Metal Wiggler
$15
HORROCKS-IBBOTSON CO.
Manufacturers of the most complete line of Fishing Tackle in the world.
Grant St., UTICA, N. Y.
$5
1958
H-I
NEW FREAKFISH LURE
3" - 1/2 oz
• FREAKFISH JR. - SAME W/ NO TAIL HOOK
1958
OLD HI's WHIZ-WIZ
$5
No. X3372 — New trout and spin lure. Fish shaped body 1 inch long, with propeller type spinner. Single hook with streamer. Assorted finishes. Wgt. 3/16 oz. One in plastic box. 1/2 Dozen assorted in carton. Wgt. 3 1/8 oz.
POP-POPPER SPIN LURE
$5
X47-19A.—Popping Lure assortment for spinning or casting. Body is 1 3/8 inches long with two treble hooks. Weight 1/8 oz. Put up one in plastic box 1 dozen asst. in carton, four each finish scale, frog and red head.
1958
H-I
SPIN POPPER
$10
No. S.P. — Small popping bait for spinning. Body is 1 3/4 inches long with treble hook on tail. Weight 1/8 oz. Made in three (3) finishes: RH, Scale and Frog. Put up 1 in plastic box. Weight 1/4 oz.
1958
H-I
No. X46S
$5
New salt and fresh water bait. Body is 1 3/4" long. Mounted with 4/0 hook and streamer on tail. Red head finish only. 1 dozen in box Weight 3 3/4 ozs.
1958
H-I
THE BIG FISH LURE
NORTHERN PIKE
No. 588
STYLE
HORROCKS-IBBOTSON CO., UTICA, N. Y.
$5
1958
No. 588 H-I Big Fish Lure — For pike, walleyes and muskies Body made of extra strong plastic with strong hook assembly Length of body 3 3/4 in. Two treble hooks and spinner on tail Made in 12 popular patterns Weight 5/8 oz.
• NO. 438 - SAME AS ABOVE - 2 3/4" - 1/4 oz.
OLD HI's FIN-BACK LURE
H-I
1958
$2
Patented weighted body lure with exceptional action Length of body 1 1/2". Mounted with treble hook with trailer. Made in both casting and spinning sizes. 1 in plastic box. 1 dozen assorted in carton.
No. 96 — Spinning size. 1/8 oz.
No. 95 — Casting size. 3/8 oz.
$1
No. 35 HICO FLY ROD MINNOW
Made in the following patterns: RH, SCALE, RBW, VAR, PEARL, WYR, and assorted. Packed one on a card, one dozen cards in a box.
1958
$5
No. 342 — JUNE MINNOW SPINNING LURE
Minnow shape weighted body with June bug spinner and size 3 feathered treble hook.
THE SHURLUCK SPINNER
FAMOUS McCARTY SHURLUCK SPINNER
1958
$2
No. 375 — Fly rod spinner weighs only 1/8 oz. card, one dozen in box.
No. 341 — SPIN-RITE
1958
$5
Popular weighted spinner and fly combination with bucktail
1958
$5
No. 346 — SUNRISE SPIN-LURE
Fish shape blade is a killer. Mounted with split ring and treble hook. Finished in brass and nickel.
MINNO-ETTE
X351 — Small weighted minnow shape body 1 inch long with propeller type spinner and glass bead. Treble hook. Weight 1/4 oz.
1958
H-I
$5
$1
1931
Troutaker

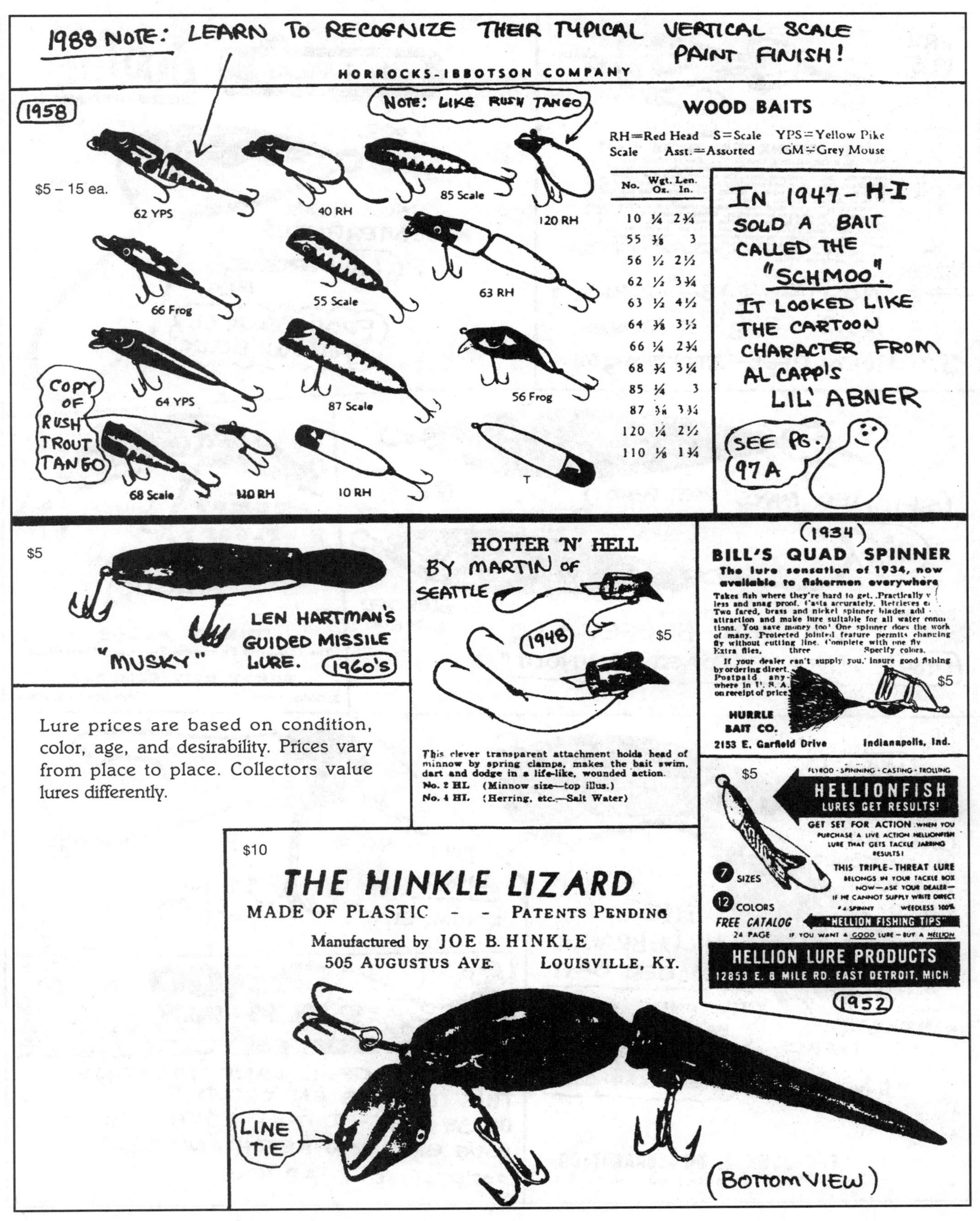
1988 NOTE: LEARN TO RECOGNIZE THEIR TYPICAL VERTICAL SCALE PAINT FINISH!
HORROCKS-IBBOTSON COMPANY
1958
NOTE: LIKE RUSH TANGO
$5 – 15 ea.
62 YPS
40 RH
85 Scale
120 RH
66 Frog
55 Scale
63 RH
64 YPS
87 Scale
56 Frog
COPY OF RUSH TROUT TANGO
68 Scale
120 RH
10 RH
T
WOOD BAITS
RH=Red Head S=Scale YPS=Yellow Pike Scale Asst.=Assorted GM=Grey Mouse
IN 1947 - H-I SOLD A BAIT CALLED THE "SCHMOO". IT LOOKED LIKE THE CARTOON CHARACTER FROM AL CAPP'S LIL' ABNER
SEE PG. 97A
$5
LEN HARTMAN'S GUIDED MISSILE "MUSKY" LURE. 1960's
HOTTER 'N' HELL
BY MARTIN OF SEATTLE
1948
$5
This clever transparent attachment holds head of minnow by spring clamps, makes the bait swim, dart and dodge in a life-like, wounded action.
No. 2 HL (Minnow size—top illus.)
No. 4 HL (Herring, etc.—Salt Water)
(1934)
BILL'S QUAD SPINNER
The lure sensation of 1934, now available to fishermen everywhere
Takes fish where they're hard to get. Practically w... less and snag proof. Casts accurately. Retrieves e... Two faced, brass and nickel spinner blades add attraction and make lure suitable for all water condi tions. You save money too! One spinner does the work of many. Protected jointed feature permits changing fly without cutting line. Complete with one fly Extra flies, three Specify colors.
If your dealer can't supply you, insure good fishing by ordering direct. Postpaid anywhere in U. S. A. on receipt of price.
$5
HURRLE BAIT CO.
2153 E. Garfield Drive Indianapolis, Ind.
$5
FLYROD · SPINNING · CASTING · TROLLING
HELLIONFISH
LURES GET RESULTS!
GET SET FOR ACTION WHEN YOU PURCHASE A LIVE ACTION HELLIONFISH LURE THAT GETS TACKLE JARRING RESULTS!
THIS TRIPLE-THREAT LURE BELONGS IN YOUR TACKLE BOX NOW—ASK YOUR DEALER— IF HE CANNOT SUPPLY WRITE DIRECT
#4 SPINNY WEEDLESS 100%
7 SIZES
12 COLORS
FREE CATALOG 24 PAGE
"HELLION FISHING TIPS"
IF YOU WANT A GOOD LURE – BUY A HELLION
HELLION LURE PRODUCTS
12853 E. 8 MILE RD. EAST DETROIT, MICH.
1952
$10
THE HINKLE LIZARD
MADE OF PLASTIC - - - PATENTS PENDING
Manufactured by JOE B. HINKLE
505 AUGUSTUS AVE. LOUISVILLE, KY.
LINE TIE
(BOTTOM VIEW)

No.	Wgt. Oz.	Len. In.
10	¼	2¾
55	⅜	3
56	½	2½
62	½	3¾
63	½	4½
64	⅜	3½
66	¼	2¾
68	¾	3¼
85	¼	3
87	5/16	3¾
120	¼	2½
110	⅛	1¾

Lure prices are based on condition, color, age, and desirability. Prices vary from place to place. Collectors value lures differently.

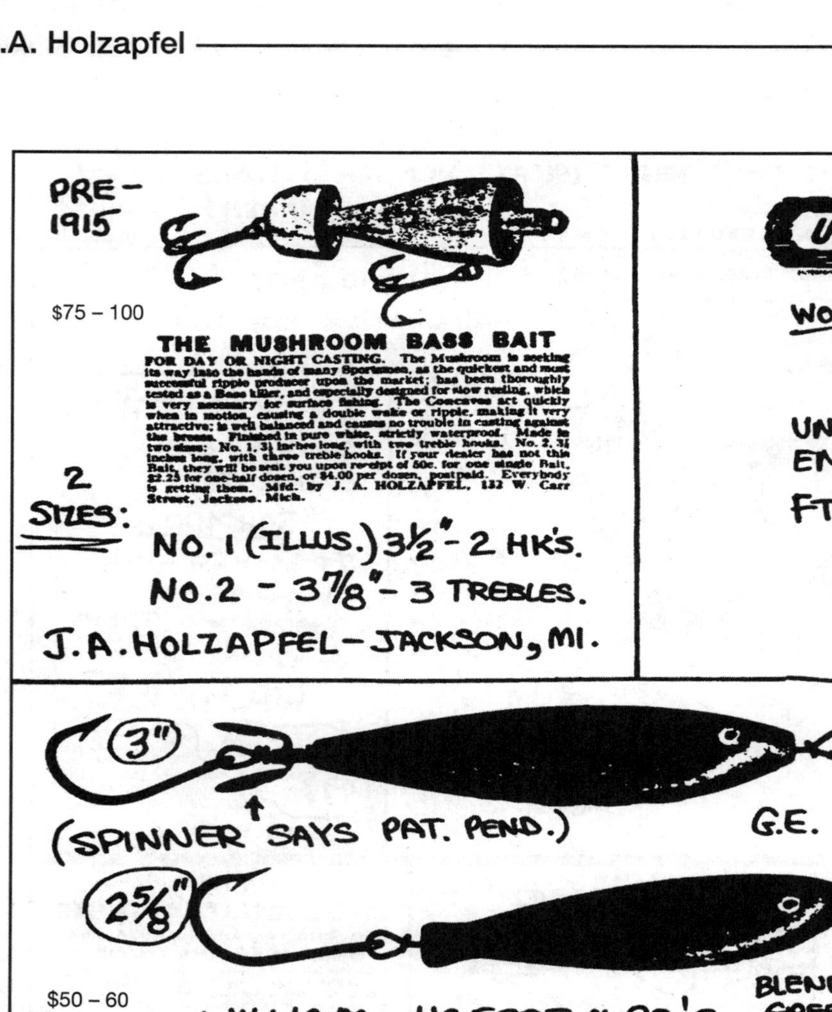
PRE-
1915
THE MUSHROOM BASS BAIT
FOR DAY OR NIGHT CASTING. The Mushroom is seeking its way into the hands of many Sportsmen, as the quickest and most successful ripple producer upon the market; has been thoroughly tested as a Bass killer, and especially designed for slow reeling, which is very necessary for surface fishing. The Concaves act quickly when in motion, causing a double wake or ripple, making it very attractive; is well balanced and causes no trouble in casting against the breeze. Finished in pure white, strictly waterproof. Made in two sizes: No. 1, 3½ inches long, with two treble hooks. No. 2, 3⅞ inches long, with three treble hooks. If your dealer has not this Bait, they will be sent you upon receipt of 50c. for one single Bait, $2.25 for one-half dozen, or $4.00 per dozen, postpaid. Everybody is getting them. Mfd. by J. A. HOLZAPFEL, 132 W. Carr Street, Jackson, Mich.
2 SIZES:
NO. 1 (ILLUS.) 3½" - 2 HK'S.
NO. 2 - 3⅞" - 3 TREBLES.
J.A. HOLZAPFEL - JACKSON, MI.
3"
(SPINNER SAYS PAT. PEND.)
G.E.
2⅝"
BLENDED GREEN
WILLIAM HOEGEE & CO'S
"NORTH COAST MINNOW"
1909

$75 – 100

$50 – 60

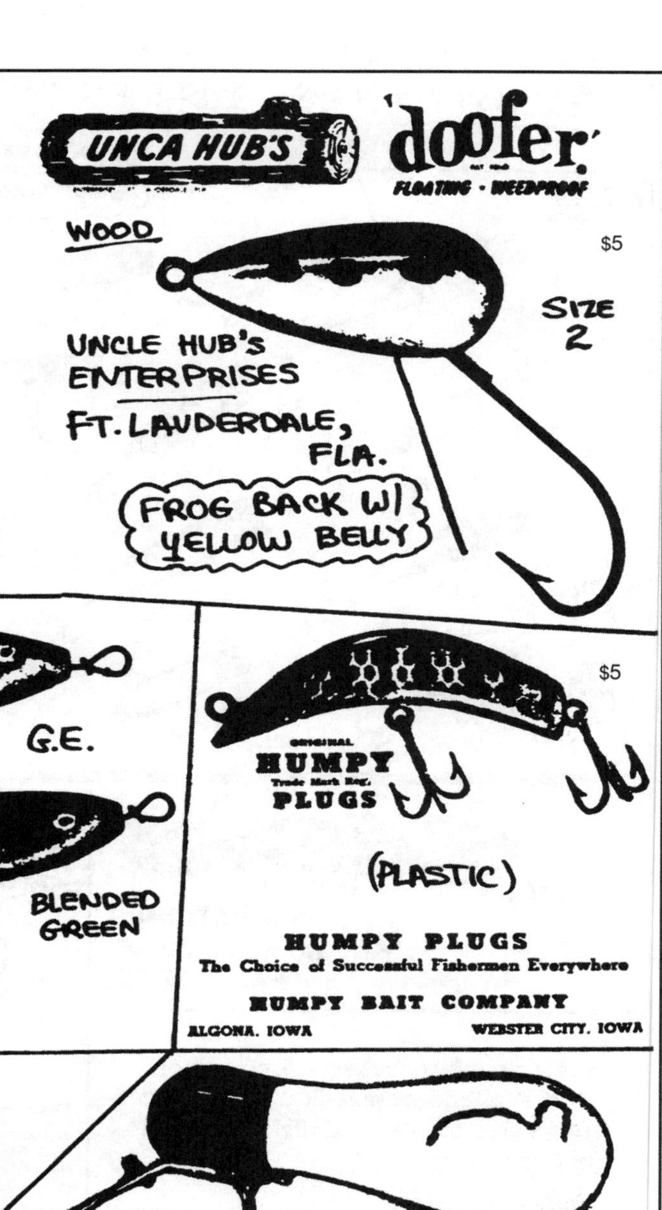
UNCA HUB'S
'doofer'
FLOATING · WEEDPROOF
WOOD
SIZE 2
UNCLE HUB'S ENTERPRISES
FT. LAUDERDALE, FLA.
FROG BACK W/ YELLOW BELLY
HUMPY PLUGS
(PLASTIC)
HUMPY PLUGS
The Choice of Successful Fishermen Everywhere
HUMPY BAIT COMPANY
ALGONA, IOWA
WEBSTER CITY, IOWA

$5

$5

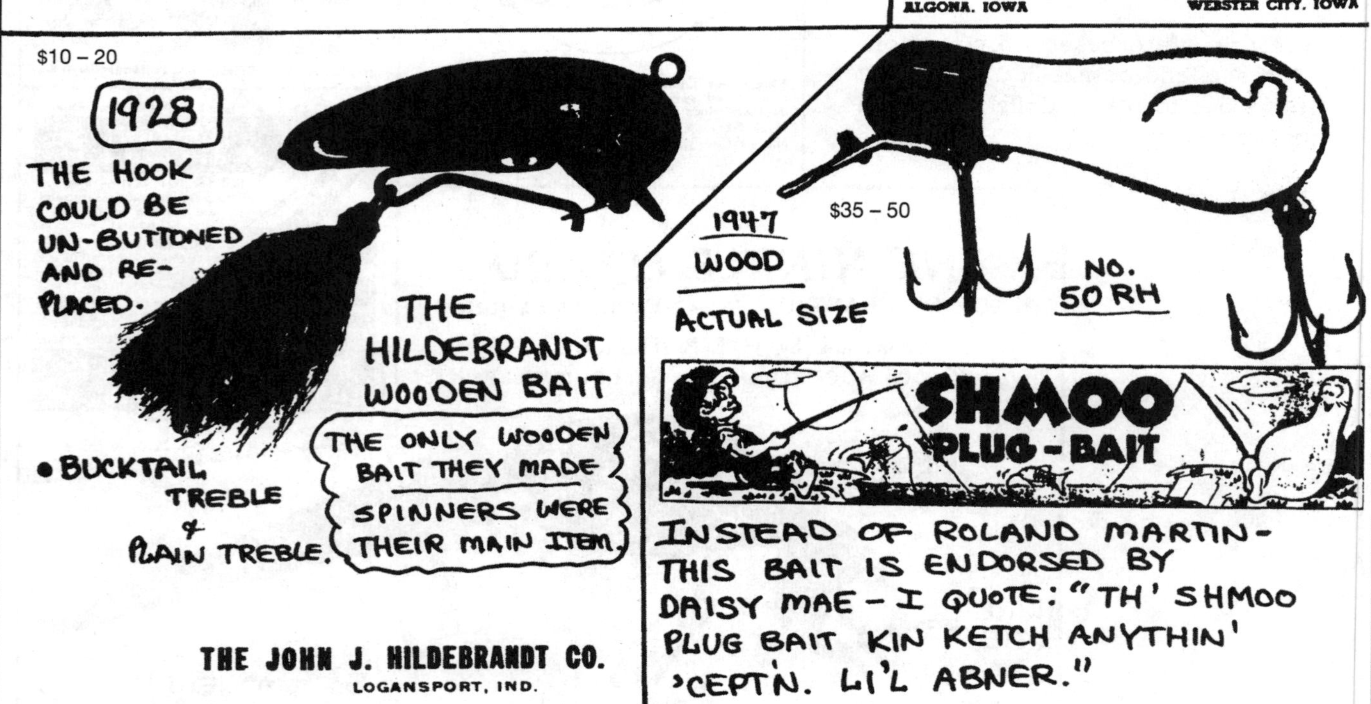
1928
THE HOOK COULD BE UN-BUTTONED AND RE-PLACED.
THE HILDEBRANDT WOODEN BAIT
THE ONLY WOODEN BAIT THEY MADE
SPINNERS WERE THEIR MAIN ITEM.
• BUCKTAIL TREBLE & PLAIN TREBLE.
THE JOHN J. HILDEBRANDT CO.
LOGANSPORT, IND.
1947
WOOD
ACTUAL SIZE
NO. 50 RH
SHMOO PLUG-BAIT
INSTEAD OF ROLAND MARTIN - THIS BAIT IS ENDORSED BY DAISY MAE - I QUOTE: "TH' SHMOO PLUG BAIT KIN KETCH ANYTHIN' 'CEPT'N. LI'L ABNER."

$10 – 20

$35 – 50

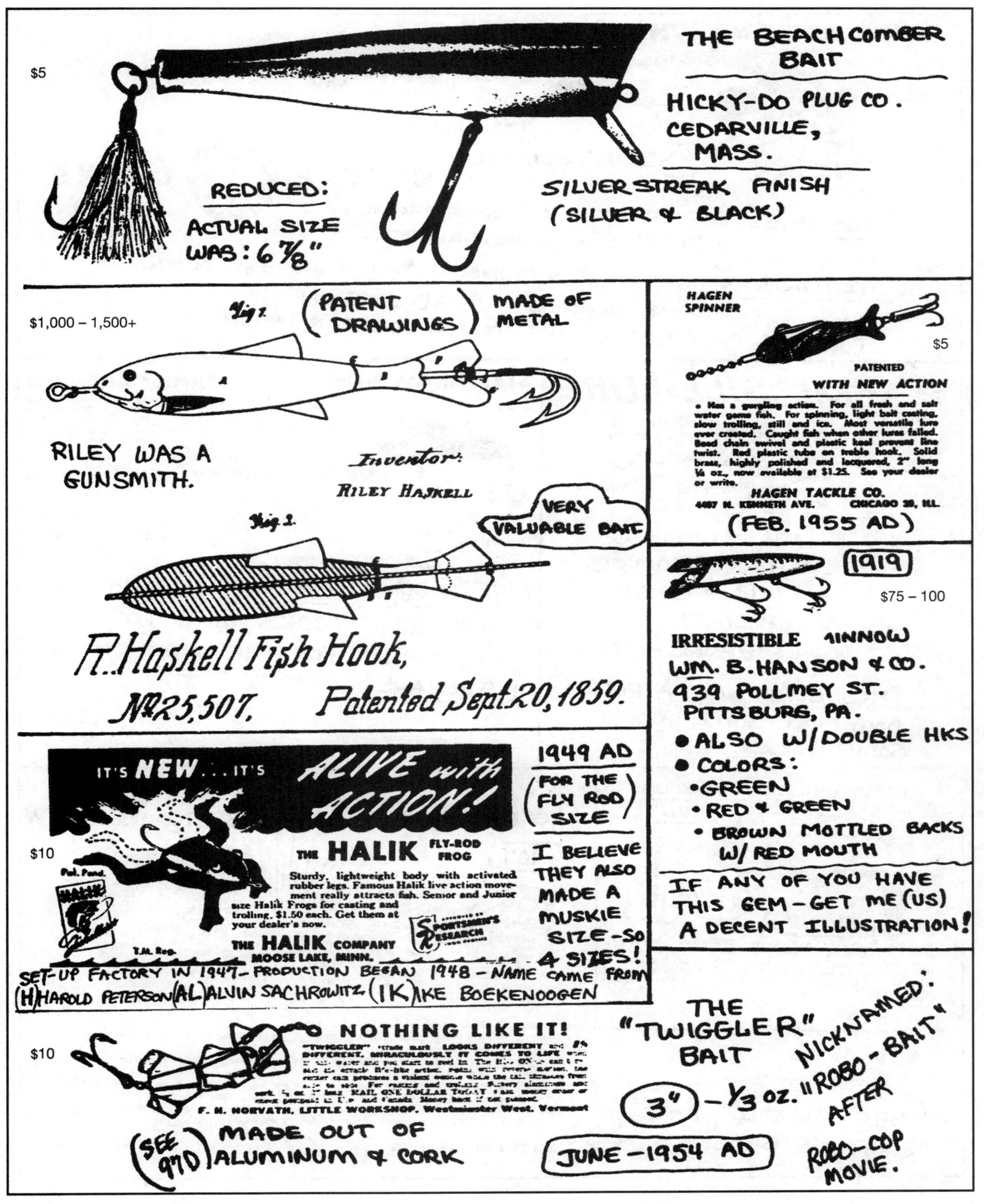
$5
THE BEACHCOMBER BAIT
HICKY-DO PLUG CO.
CEDARVILLE, MASS.
REDUCED:
ACTUAL SIZE WAS: 6 7/8"
SILVERSTREAK FINISH (SILVER & BLACK)
$1,000 – 1,500+
Fig 1.
(PATENT DRAWINGS)
MADE OF METAL
RILEY WAS A GUNSMITH.
Inventor:
RILEY HASKELL
Fig 2.
VERY VALUABLE BAIT
R. Haskell Fish Hook,
No 25,507. Patented Sept. 20, 1859.
HAGEN SPINNER
$5
PATENTED
WITH NEW ACTION
• Has a gurgling action. For all fresh and salt water game fish. For spinning, light bait casting, slow trolling, still and ice. Most versatile lure ever created. Caught fish when other lures failed. Bead chain swivel and plastic keel prevent line twist. Red plastic tube on treble hook. Solid brass, highly polished and lacquered, 2" long ¼ oz., now available at $1.25. See your dealer or write.
HAGEN TACKLE CO.
CHICAGO 38, ILL.
(FEB. 1955 AD)
1919
$75 – 100
IRRESISTIBLE MINNOW
WM. B. HANSON & CO.
939 POLLMEY ST.
PITTSBURG, PA.
• ALSO W/DOUBLE HKS
• COLORS:
• GREEN
• RED & GREEN
• BROWN MOTTLED BACKS W/ RED MOUTH
IF ANY OF YOU HAVE THIS GEM – GET ME (US) A DECENT ILLUSTRATION!
IT'S NEW... IT'S ALIVE with ACTION!
$10
Pat. Pend.
THE HALIK FLY-ROD FROG
Sturdy, lightweight body with activated rubber legs. Famous Halik live action movement really attracts fish. Senior and Junior size Halik Frogs for casting and trolling, $1.50 each. Get them at your dealer's now.
T.M. Reg.
SPORTSMEN'S RESEARCH
THE HALIK COMPANY
MOOSE LAKE, MINN.
1949 AD
(FOR THE FLY ROD SIZE)
I BELIEVE THEY ALSO MADE A MUSKIE SIZE – SO 4 SIZES!
SET-UP FACTORY IN 1947 – PRODUCTION BEGAN 1948 – NAME CAME FROM
(H)HAROLD PETERSON (AL)ALVIN SACHROWITZ (IK)IKE BOEKENOOGEN
$10
NOTHING LIKE IT!
"TWIGGLER" trade mark LOOKS DIFFERENT and IS DIFFERENT. MIRACULOUSLY IT COMES TO LIFE
MAIL ONE DOLLAR TODAY
F. H. HORVATH, LITTLE WORKSHOP, Westminster West, Vermont
(SEE 97D) MADE OUT OF ALUMINUM & CORK
THE "TWIGGLER" BAIT
3" – 1/3 OZ.
JUNE – 1954 AD
NICKNAMED: "ROBO-BAIT" AFTER ROBO-COP MOVIE.

RED AND WHITE SPECIAL

T.M. REG. U.S. PAT. OFF. 1937.

wt. ⅝ oz.

$5 each

¾ actual size

Death on bass. Fine as all-purpose lure.

SOURPUSS 606-F (floater, smooth) 3" body
BUTCH 756-S (sinker, ribbed) 2¾" body

HOLDENLINE Co. Cleveland 13, Ohio

(TENITE)

CIRCLE  LURES

(1937)

TWO TYPES: • SOURPUSS – 3" (FLOATER) SMOOTH.
• BUTCH – 2¾" (SINKER) RIBBED.

SIX COLORS: • RED & WHITE • RAINBOW TROUT • MOONEYE SHINER
• SHORE MINNOW • SHAD • PERCH

COLOR OF BAIT WAS ON THE INSIDE SO CLEAR LAYER ON OUTSIDE

40's – **MISSILE-LURE**
50's

$5

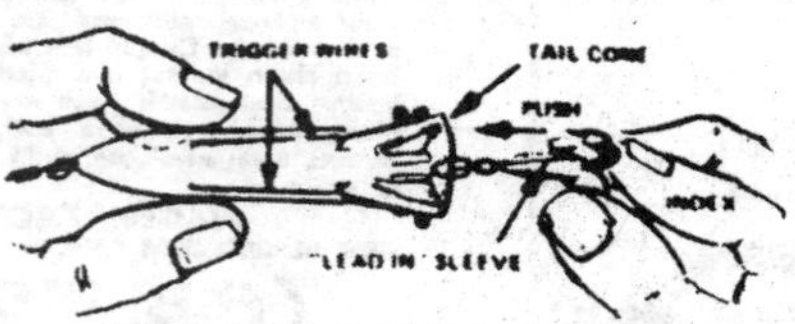
TRIGGER WIRES
TAIL CONE
PUSH
LEAD IN SLEEVE

HOLD LIKE THIS TO "LOAD"

HOLIDAY PRODUCTS
4117-W. 49th ST.
AMARILLO, TX
A.M. GIBBONS – PRES.

THIS LURE WAS A FLOP – AND COST SOME PEOPLE SOME BUCKS.

STARTLINGLY NEW AMAZINGLY DIFFERENT

The original Hall-Lure, the fishing lure with the sliding hooks Pre-tested in lakes and streams has proven a phenomenal fish getter. Compare its action with any other lure you now have. You'll see why thousands of fishermen say it's the Greatest Fish Fooler ever. The Hall-Lure darts—dives—wiggles—goes on its side—loops over. All due to a new principle of action, the Sliding Hooks, that throw the lure off balance as it is being retrieved All action controlled by speed of the retrieve.

FOR BASS, PIKE, MUSKY, BIG TROUT AND WALLEYE.

Colors spotted.
Green Body Black Spotted
Black Body Orange Spotted
Orange Body Black Spotted
Yellow Body Red Spotted
Red Body Black Spotted

COLORS
All White Bodies
Red Head Black Head
Green Head Orange Head

Pat. Pending

FLYROD SIZE .... $1.25 (No Eyes)
CASTING ROD .... $1.35 (With Eyes)

At Your Dealers or Order Direct

WILLIAM C. HALL
3630 Eoff St.
Wheeling, W. Va.

Can be fished any depth by putting split shot on slide wire on underside of front.

(1952 AD) • FLY ROD • CASTING

THIS BAIT LOOKS LIKE THE PROTO-TYPE FOR THE SUPER SONIC AIRPLANE.

(1952)

$5

HOOKZEM AUTOMATIC WEEDLESS WOBBLER

$50 – 75

(1922)

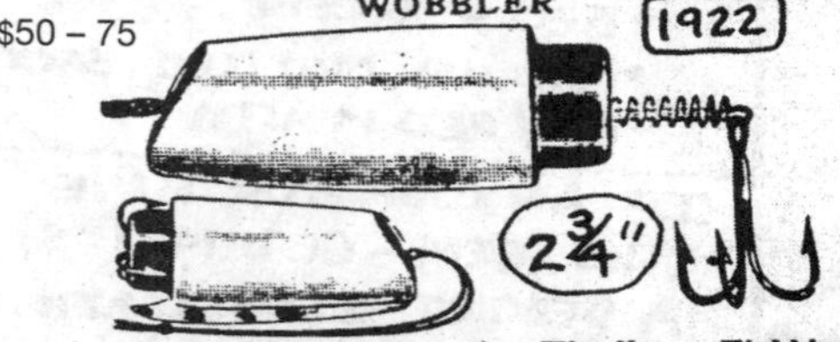

(2¾")

K434. Hookzem Automatic Weedless Wobblers. The only automatic fish bait perfected. When the fish strikes the hooks are forced into its mouth. When ready to use the hooks are held so closely that the bait will pass through all weeds without snagging. Color: White, red head; length 2¾ inches.

$50 – 75

The Haynes Pearl Casting Minnow

(1907)

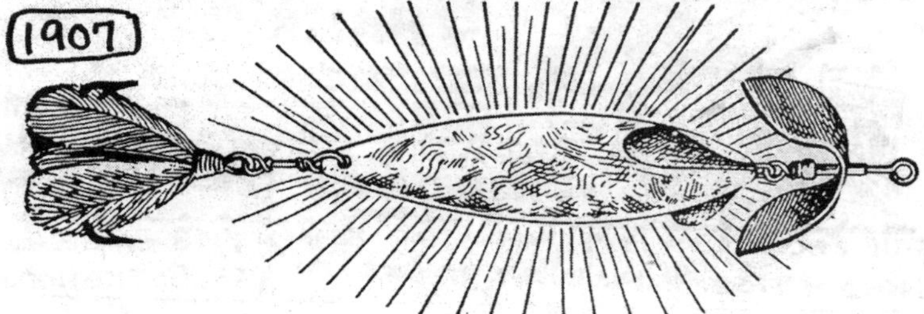

At Last. The ideal casting minnow for bass. **Why?**

BECAUSE: The pearl body throws out a shimmering ray in the water and game fish will strike it when no other bait tempts them.

BECAUSE: The pearl body stays bright and attractive all season, unlike painted casting baits that are disfigured in an hour's casting.

BECAUSE: There is only one feathered treble hook necessary instead of a dozen or so that break and tangle up and spoil your casts, and also catch in clothes and landing nets.

BECAUSE: The German Silver side gills keep it right side up without the use of a weight. No twisted lines.

Send me one dollar, paper money or postal order. I will mail you one prepaid.

Fraternally yours,

274 Park St., Akron, Ohio **W. B. Haynes**

SEE PAGE 6, A & I, DOERING BAIT.

$10 – 20

1932

BAG-O-MAD

(SEE PG. 93)

NOTE: ONLY 1 EXIT HOLE ON 1 SIDE!!

ACTUAL SIZE

(MADE IN 2 SIZES)

A sensational new bait, introduced in June, 1932 has been producing record catches all over the country and is REALLY something NEW in the plug line.

The passage of water through the holes in the head and out of the hole on the side gives the plug an action that really looks and acts like a live minnow, and you will get STRIKES, brother—you will get STRIKES.

Reel the plug slow to get best results, and a depth of 3 to 4 feet; for a top-water bait reel fast, and the plug comes up and skitters over the surface.

Try casting, allowing your bait to lie still on the surface for a slow count of 5 then give the rod a quick jerk: this will cause the plug to emit a "plop," and will many times result in a strike when the usual methods fail.

A gut leader tied to a plug will often fool the "BIG BOYS" you are after.

There are five colors of the BAG-O-MAD that are standard for Musky, Pike, Bass and other game fish.

No. 122. Red Head and White Body.
No. 133. Black Head and Yellow Body.
No. 144. Red Head and Yellow Body.
No. 155. Black Head and White Body.
No. 166. Solid Black.

Ask your dealer for BAG-O-MAD, or direct, 75c.

• BAG O'MAD JUNIOR – $2\frac{3}{4}$"

BILL HERINGTON BAIT CO.
GREEN CITY, MISSOURI

MISC. "H" FACTS & DATA:

- J.M. HERBERT OF SHREVEPORT, LA. WAS THE INVENTOR OF THE "HERB'S DILLY."
- THE HUMPHREY BAIT CO. OF JASONVILLE, IND. RE-INTRODUCED THE CARTERS BESTEVER BAITS AS "RED'S OLD TIMERS" – 2 SIZES, WITH PRESSED EYES – WOOD.
- LIVINGSTON S. HINCKLEY OF NEWARK, N.J. IS CREDITED WITH THE INVENTION OF THE NEW JERSEY ALUMINUM PHANTOM (SEE PAGE 43). THERE SEEMS TO BE QUITE A FEW OF THIS VERY OLD CLASSIC SURVIVING TO THIS DAY.

$10

1955

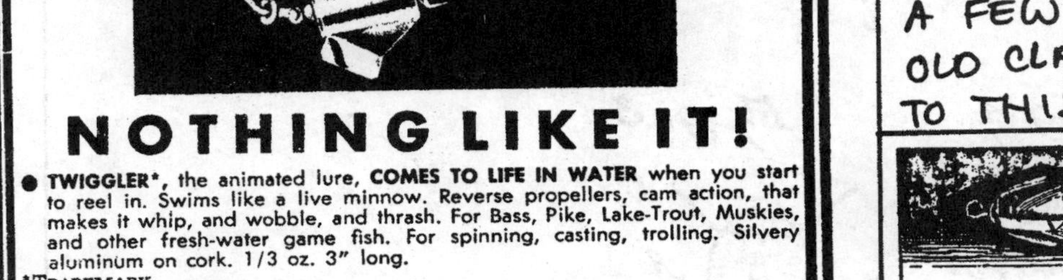

NOTHING LIKE IT!

• TWIGGLER*, the animated lure, COMES TO LIFE IN WATER when you start to reel in. Swims like a live minnow. Reverse propellers, cam action, that makes it whip, and wobble, and thrash. For Bass, Pike, Lake-Trout, Muskies, and other fresh-water game fish. For spinning, casting, trolling. Silvery aluminum on cork. 1/3 oz. 3" long.

*TRADEMARK

• IF YOUR FAVORITE TACKLE SHOP hasn't got it, mail one dollar (or $1.35 for the brilliant Red-Head TWIGGLER) cash, Money order or check. Postpaid in U. S. and Canada. Naturally your money back if not pleased.

F. H. HORVATH, Little Workshop
Westminster West Vermont

THE FISHERMAN'S HANDBOOK FOR 1955

(I THOUGHT THE "TWIGGLER" DESERVED ANOTHER ILLUS.)

1903 AD

LOOKS LIKE A 3 BLADE PROP?

FISHERMAN.

Have you ever used the Harkauf Wooden Minnow. Why not try one? Once used, no other you'll use, because it catches more and larger Black Bass and Pickerel than live minnows. It has the most perfect resemblance of a live minnow. With its glistening silver belly it attracts the fish from a greater distance. Sample sent postpaid to any address on receipt of 35 cents, three assorted baits for One Dollar.
Send for free circular explaining all about it.

H. C. KAUFFMAN & COMPANY,
No 2645 N. Colorado St., Phila., Pa.

THIS SHOWS THE RARE "HARKAUF" WOOD MINNOW.

$150 – 200

THE JAMISON "COAXER" PATENT. THIS WAS A TRULY "LANDMARK" BASS BAIT. William J. Jamison (Smiling Bill) and Anson Decker had a classic one on one bass competition on a private lake in mid-June, 1910. Congress Lake of Canton, Ohio was the site, with Jamison's Coaxer winning a decisive victory. He used the contest in his ads after that, and no doubt sold alot of baits because of it. Coaxers are moderately easy to find, with Red & White the dominant color....tough colors are Frog and Red/Aluminum.

No. 779,083. **PATENTED JAN. 3, 1905.**

W. J. JAMISON.

ARTIFICIAL BAIT.

APPLICATION FILED APR. 18, 1904.

Fig. 1.

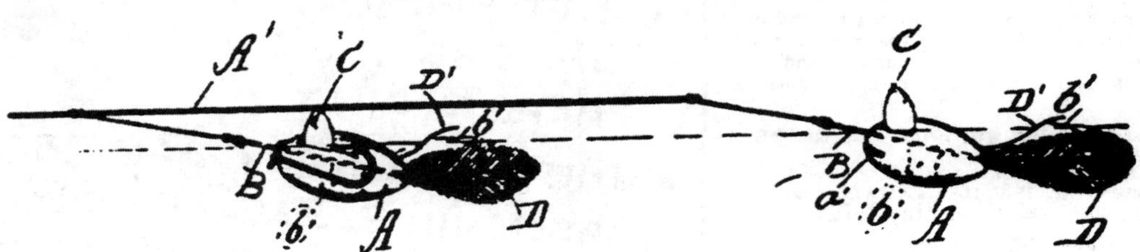
A'
C
D'
b'
B
b
A
D
a

Fig. 2

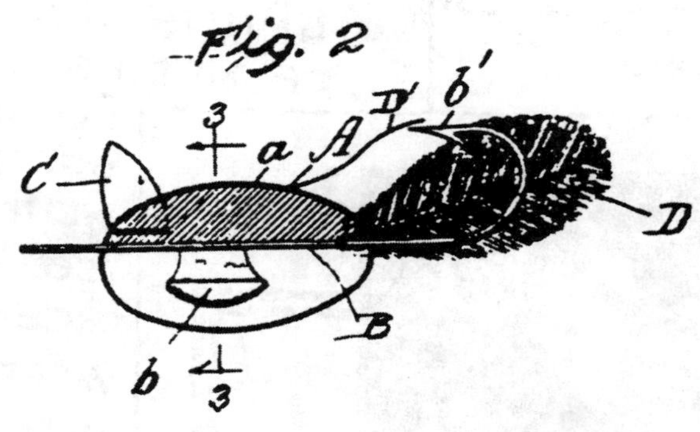
3
a
A
D'
b'
C
D
B
b
3

Fig. 4. Fig. 3

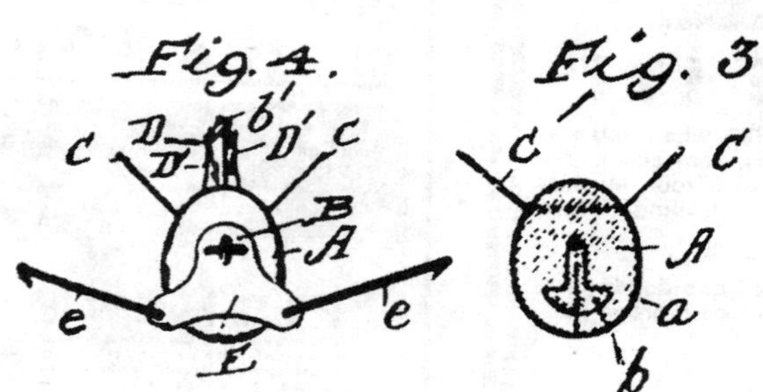
D
b'
D'
C
B
A
e
E
a
b

Witnesses: Inventor

Harry P. Bchule William J. Jamison,

Ray White By Charles M. Hill Atty.

JAMISON'S COAXERS

Original Cork Body Floating Fly

No. 1 Weedless "Coaxer"

LENGTH OVERALL- 3½"

A Floating Bait for Bass and Pickerel.

$10 – 30

1⅞" (WIDE BODY.)

The above is full size reproduction in natural colors of the No. 1 Weedless "Coaxer" Surface Bait. This bait is intended for all-round black bass and pickerel fishing. It is very attractive and exceedingly lively and life-like, and in spite of its open hook it will go through any and all kinds of weeds or lilies without snagging. It is easy to cast and can be used for skittering and trolling as well. It is made on strictly scientific principles, and is undoubtedly the most satisfactory bait ever devised, being not only a splendid killer but is the most humane bait on the market. No angler should be without a "Coaxer" if he wishes to be successful in black bass and pickerel fishing.

No. 1 "Coaxer," put up in handsome box,

Jamison's No. 1 Weedless Bucktail Coaxer

The "Coaxer" Floating Bass Fly.

$10

No. 1 Convertible "Coaxer"

Can be Changed to Weedless in Two Seconds.

$10 – 20

This cut shows the new No. 1 Convertible "Coaxer" or "X" style, designed to meet the demand for a "Coaxer" Bait with more hooks than is used on the regular weedless style. We believe this bait to be the greatest killer ever offered the angler. It can be made strictly weedless by simply removing the double hook from bottom of the bait, which is the work of but a second or two, and it goes back on just as easily. This gives you the choice of a weedless or non-weedless in one bait with a minimum amount of trouble. We heartily recommend this bait to all anglers desiring a sure killer.

No. 1 Convertible "Coaxer" Surface Bait,

No. 2 Weedless "Coaxer"

These baits are quite striking as to color and design, the bodies are made of cork and are enameled white, the wings are made of red felt, the tail is composed of a number of red feathers. The baits are heavy enough to cast very nicely from a free-running reel, they will always float right side up.

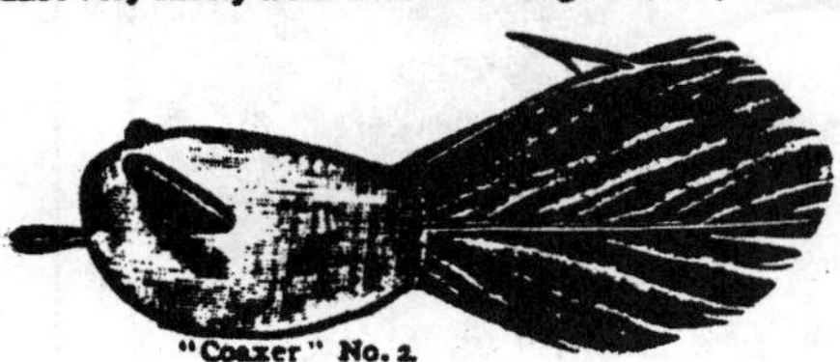

"Coaxer" No. 2.

1⅝"-MEDIUM BODY

A Floating Bait for Bass and Pickerel.

$10 – 20

The No. 2 Weedless "Coaxer" Surface Bait has a somewhat different shape from No. 1, but is constructed on the same general lines and is a very fine bait for either bass or pickerel fishing. This bait is the exact size and color of above illustration. While it is considerably smaller than No. 1 "Coaxer," it is easy to cast and is a great favorite with expert fishermen for both bass and pickerel. It has all the attractiveness and weedless qualities of No. 1 "Coaxer" and is considered by many to be a better killer, owing to its smaller size. Can be used for casting, skittering or trolling.

No. 2 "Coaxer," put up in handsome box,

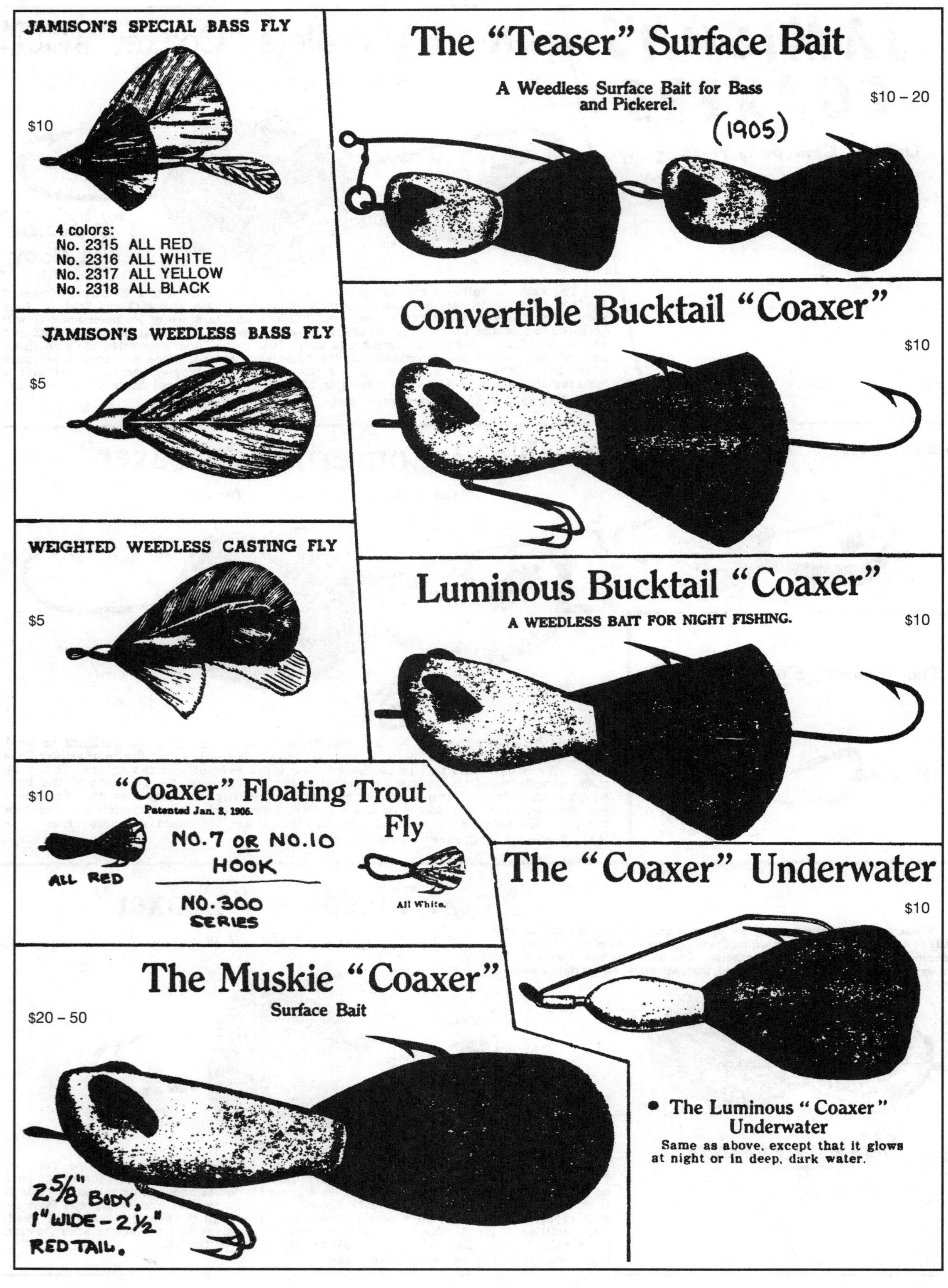
JAMISON'S SPECIAL BASS FLY
$10
4 colors:
No. 2315 ALL RED
No. 2316 ALL WHITE
No. 2317 ALL YELLOW
No. 2318 ALL BLACK
The "Teaser" Surface Bait
A Weedless Surface Bait for Bass and Pickerel.
$10 – 20
(1905)
JAMISON'S WEEDLESS BASS FLY
$5
Convertible Bucktail "Coaxer"
$10
WEIGHTED WEEDLESS CASTING FLY
$5
Luminous Bucktail "Coaxer"
A WEEDLESS BAIT FOR NIGHT FISHING.
$10
$10
"Coaxer" Floating Trout Fly
Patented Jan. 3, 1906.
ALL RED
NO.7 OR NO.10 HOOK
NO.300 SERIES
All White.
The "Coaxer" Underwater
$10
The Muskie "Coaxer"
Surface Bait
$20 – 50
2 5/8" BODY, 1" WIDE – 2 1/2" RED TAIL.
• The Luminous "Coaxer" Underwater
Same as above, except that it glows at night or in deep, dark water.

Bill's Bass Getter

A Humane Barbless Hook Bait

Floating, Near-Surface, Weedless

$20 – 30

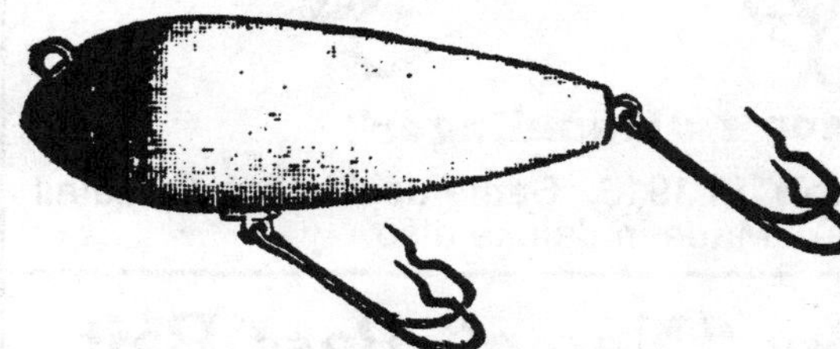

The BASS GETTER was NEW in 1929. It was furnished with Barbless-Single, Double (Illus) and Treble. Just a thought: with the depression setting in folks would want barbs to help landing the fish to eat!

$20 – 25

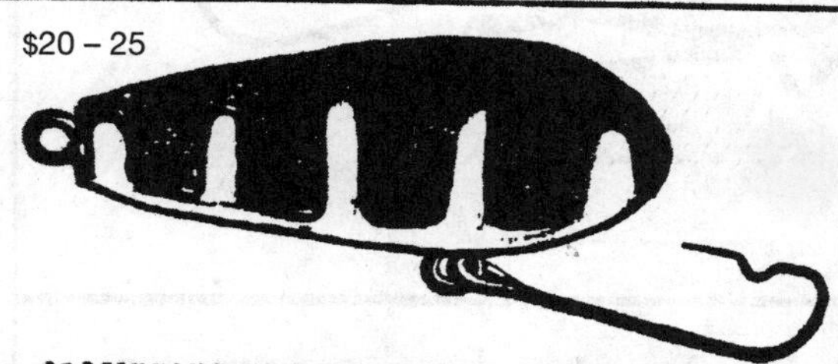

JAMISON'S SURFACE WIGGLER (Weedless)

This 2-3/4" Wood Bait was furnished with either a single or double hook (Weedless)

$20 – 25

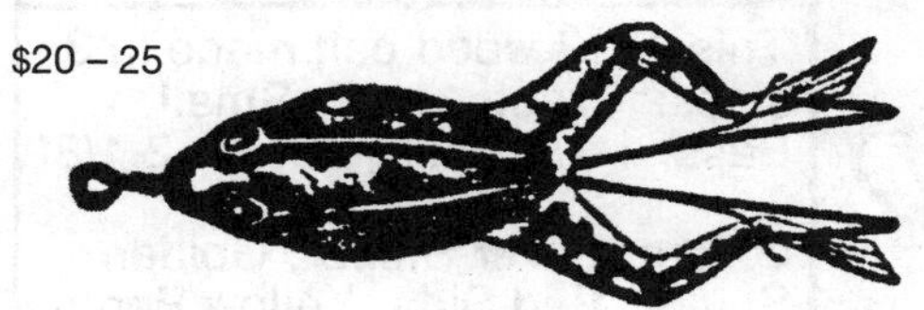

Jamison-Hastings

Soft Rubber Hollow Frog

Weedless

No. 5010 Green Meadow Frog Color Regular and Barbless Weedless Hooks

THE "MASCOT" WEEDLESS BAITS

Wobble, Dive, Float, Surface or Under

$20 – 30

THE WEEDLESS "MASCOT" - Near Surface or Surface Colors: Red Head/White, All White, All Red, All Yellow. This Wood bait was new in 1916 - 4"

$20 – 30

WEEDLESS No. 1 WINGED MASCOT - 4" - Same Colors as above, would run to around five feet deep.

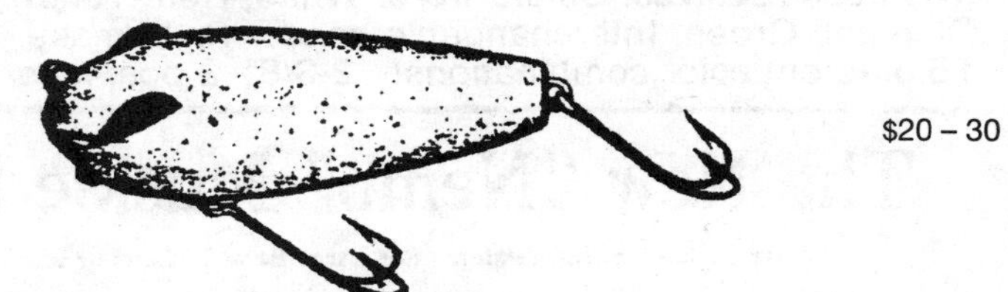

$20 – 30

JAMISON'S WEEDLESS No. 2 WINGED MASCOT Colors: Red Head/White & Luminous 2-3/4"

JAMISON'S WEEDLESS MUSCALLONGE MASCOT 5-1/2" - 2 HD 5/0 Double Hooks on Belly, 1 - 7/0 HD Double Hook on tail. (1917)

$40 – 50

JAMISON NEW DELUXE STYLE BAITS: Made for a few years with a "superfine" scale finish and glass eyes. Made in MASCOTS, HUMDINGERS and CHICAGO WOBBLERS. (1918)

$30 – 50

JAMISON'S WIG-WAG—

$25 – 40

Wood Baits, G.E. Made in two sizes: Bass Size - 4-1/2" No. 2400 Series, and Musky - 6-1/2" No. 2450 Series. Colors: 0 = Red Head/White, 1 = Black Head/Silver, 2 = Yellow Head & Body with Brown Back. Note: GEP also marketed these two baits....no ID on either.

$20 – 30

Jamison's Struggling Mouse

Also made with 2 trebles. The metal "wing" could be removed and turned over to change from surface to underwater. Note: Double Line Tie. Colors: Mouse, Crab, Frog, & Red Head/White (1919)

$25 – 30

Jamison's "Humdinger"

Shown as "New" in 1916. Same double line tie detail as the mouse. Made in deluxe also.

The New "Nemo" Bass Bait

Either Surface or Underwater. For Bass or Pickerel.

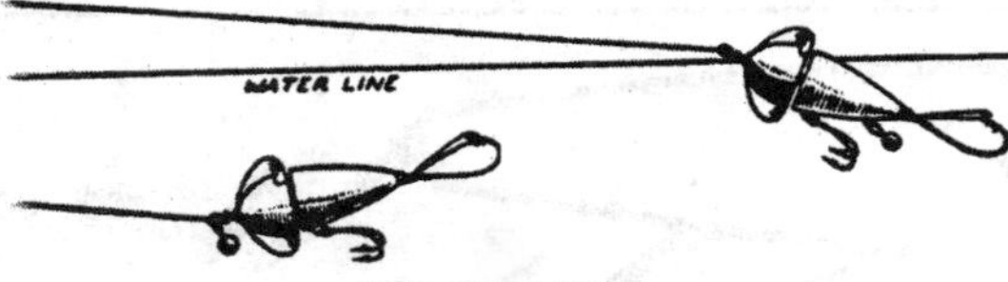
WATER LINE

The Nemo Bait.

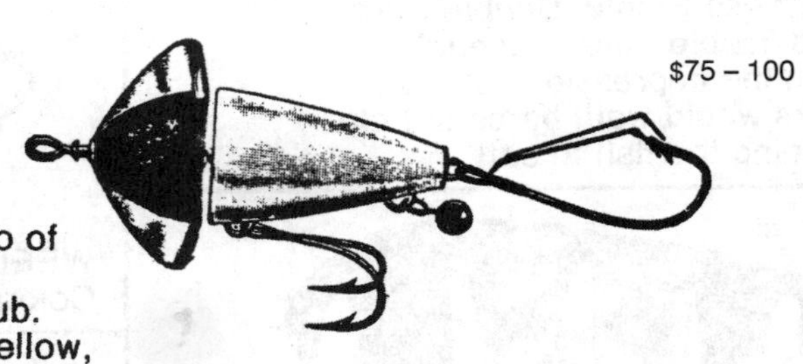

$75 – 100

New in 1911, The Nemo came from Capt. Nemo of Jules Vernes classic novel: "Twenty Thousand Leagues Under The Sea"& his atom powered sub. The head revolves. Colors were: White, Red, Yellow, Blue and Green. Interchangable heads would make 25 different color combinations! 2-3/8" 2 pos. lead

The New "Nemo" Muskie Bait

Either Surface or Underwater. For Large Bass, Pickerel or Muskies.

Same features as Bass Size. Came with extra double hooks and extra weights. Size 4" Made of Spanish Cedar, with 9 coats of paint.

$100 – 150

(1912)

This 1918 wood bait made in 3 sizes: Trout 1-1/4", Small Bass 1-3/4", Large Bass 2-1/8"

Colors: Silver Shiner, Golden Shiner, Red Side, Yellow Perch Red Head/White, White, Yellow, and Red.

Chicago Wobbler

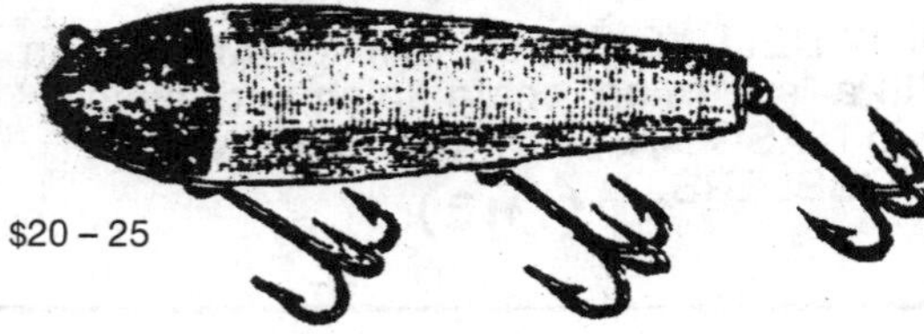

$20 – 25

COLORS

No. 1 Red Head/White
No. 2 All White
No. 3 All Yellow
No. 4 All Red

JAMISON'S

FLY ROD WIGGLER

$15

LOOKS LIKE A FISH
ACTS LIKE A FISH

4 Pack Vest Pocket Box

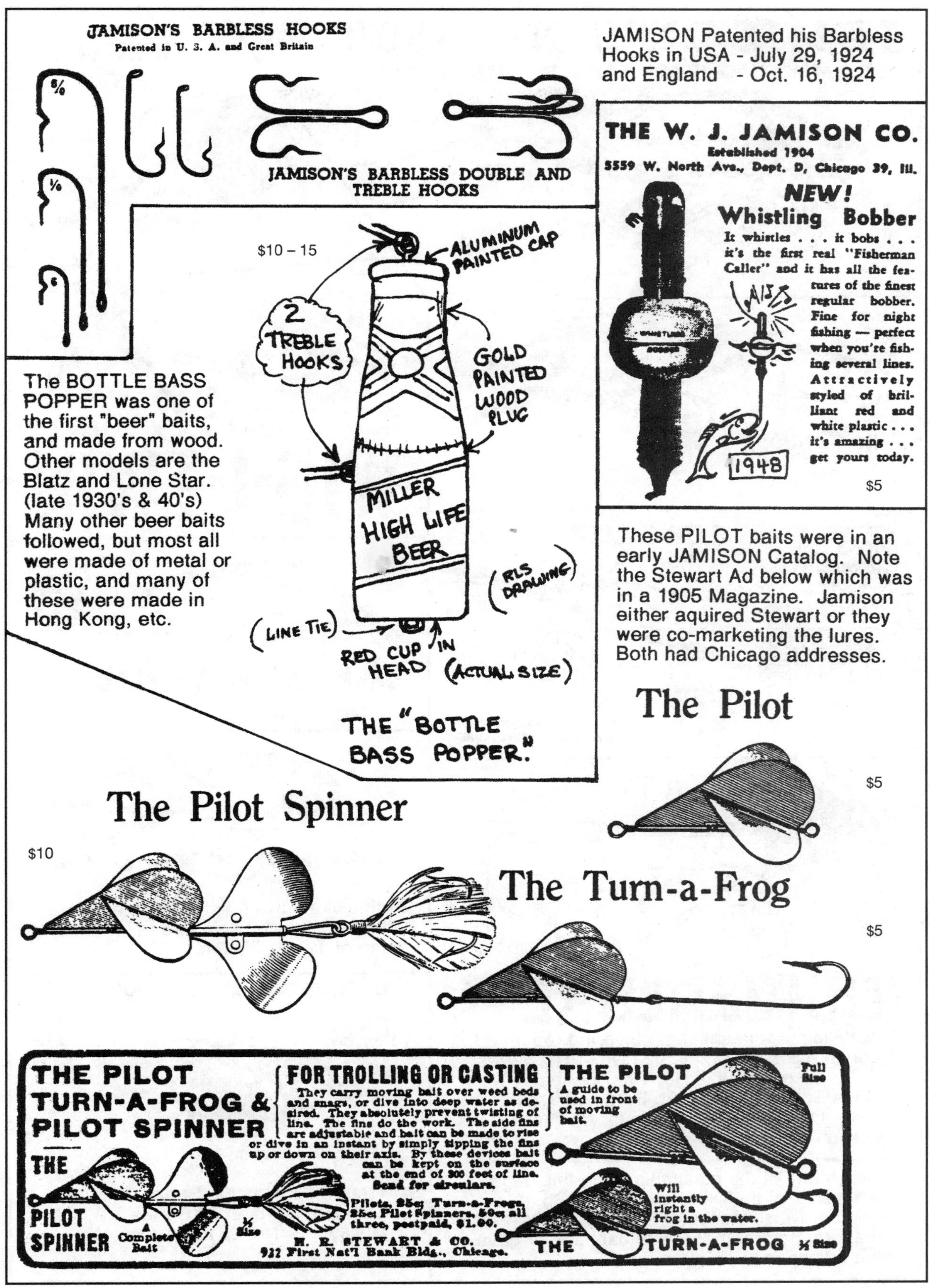
JAMISON'S BARBLESS HOOKS
Patented in U. S. A. and Great Britain
8/0
1/0
6
JAMISON'S BARBLESS DOUBLE AND TREBLE HOOKS
JAMISON Patented his Barbless Hooks in USA - July 29, 1924 and England - Oct. 16, 1924
THE W. J. JAMISON CO.
Established 1904
5559 W. North Ave., Dept. D, Chicago 39, Ill.
NEW!
Whistling Bobber
It whistles . . . it bobs . . . it's the first real "Fisherman Caller" and it has all the features of the finest regular bobber. Fine for night fishing — perfect when you're fishing several lines. Attractively styled of brilliant red and white plastic . . . it's amazing . . . get yours today.
1948
$5
$10 – 15
ALUMINUM PAINTED CAP
2 TREBLE HOOKS
GOLD PAINTED WOOD PLUG
MILLER HIGH LIFE BEER
(RLS DRAWING)
(LINE TIE)
RED CUP IN HEAD
(ACTUAL SIZE)
THE "BOTTLE BASS POPPER."
The BOTTLE BASS POPPER was one of the first "beer" baits, and made from wood. Other models are the Blatz and Lone Star. (late 1930's & 40's) Many other beer baits followed, but most all were made of metal or plastic, and many of these were made in Hong Kong, etc.
These PILOT baits were in an early JAMISON Catalog. Note the Stewart Ad below which was in a 1905 Magazine. Jamison either aquired Stewart or they were co-marketing the lures. Both had Chicago addresses.
The Pilot
$5
The Pilot Spinner
$10
The Turn-a-Frog
$5
THE PILOT TURN-A-FROG & PILOT SPINNER
FOR TROLLING OR CASTING
They carry moving bait over weed beds and snags, or dive into deep water as desired. They absolutely prevent twisting of line. The fins do the work. The side fins are adjustable and bait can be made to rise or dive in an instant by simply tipping the fins up or down on their axis. By these devices bait can be kept on the surface at the end of 300 feet of line. Send for circulars.
Pilots, 25c; Turn-a-Frogs, 25c; Pilot Spinners, 50c; all three, postpaid, $1.00.
H. R. STEWART & CO.
932 First Nat'l Bank Bldg., Chicago.
THE PILOT
A guide to be used in front of moving bait.
Full Size
THE PILOT SPINNER
A Complete Bait
½ Size
Will instantly right a frog in the water.
THE TURN-A-FROG
½ Size

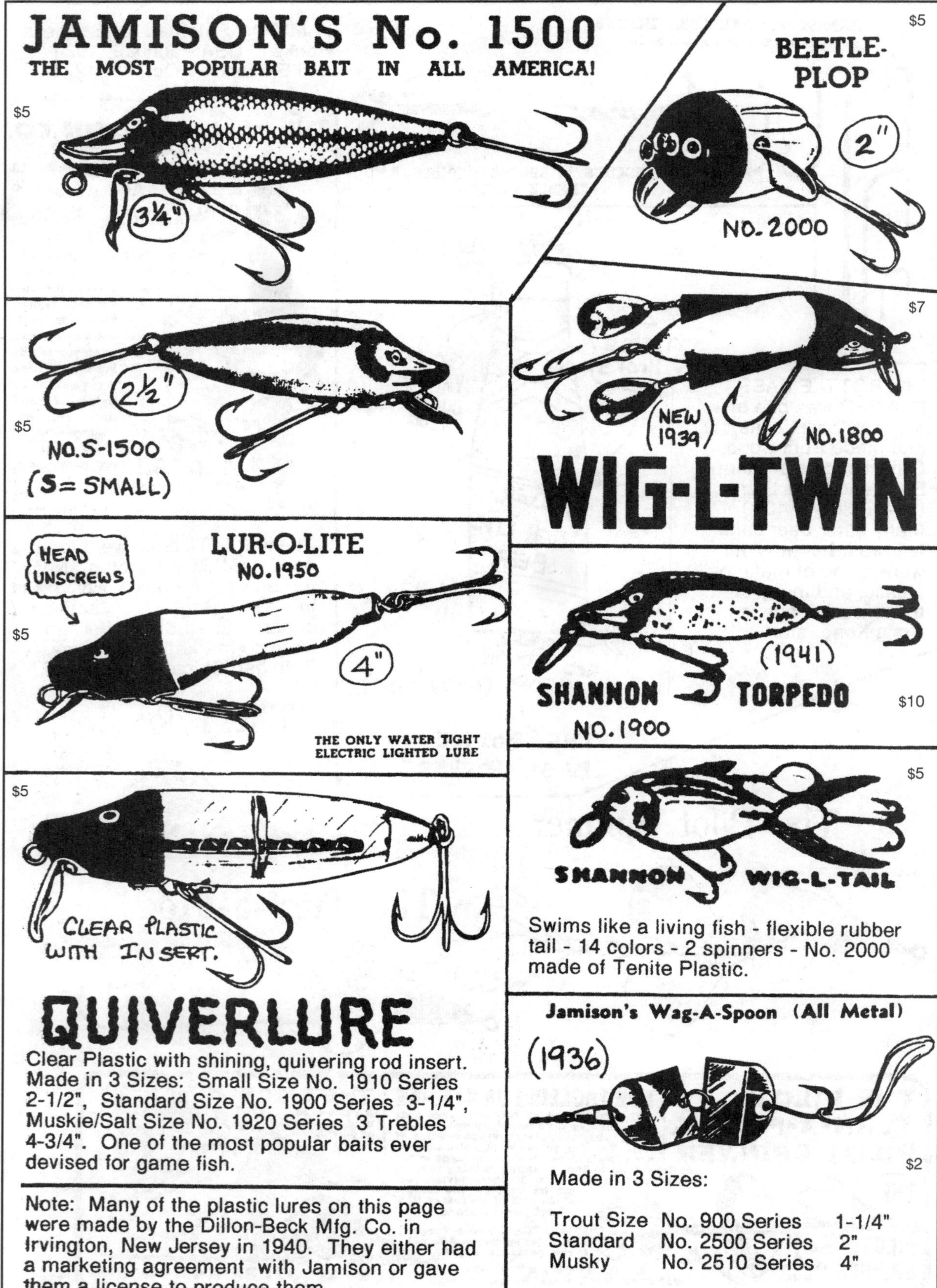
JAMISON'S No. 1500
THE MOST POPULAR BAIT IN ALL AMERICA!
$5
3¼"
$5
BEETLE-PLOP
2"
NO. 2000
$7
$5
2½"
NO. S-1500
(S= SMALL)
NEW 1939
NO. 1800
WIG-L-TWIN
HEAD UNSCREWS
LUR-O-LITE
NO. 1950
$5
4"
THE ONLY WATER TIGHT ELECTRIC LIGHTED LURE
(1941)
SHANNON
TORPEDO
$10
NO. 1900
$5
$5
CLEAR PLASTIC WITH INSERT.
SHANNON
WIG-L-TAIL
Swims like a living fish - flexible rubber tail - 14 colors - 2 spinners - No. 2000 made of Tenite Plastic.
QUIVERLURE
Clear Plastic with shining, quivering rod insert. Made in 3 Sizes: Small Size No. 1910 Series 2-1/2", Standard Size No. 1900 Series 3-1/4", Muskie/Salt Size No. 1920 Series 3 Trebles 4-3/4". One of the most popular baits ever devised for game fish.
Jamison's Wag-A-Spoon (All Metal)
(1936)
$2
Made in 3 Sizes:
Trout Size No. 900 Series 1-1/4"
Standard No. 2500 Series 2"
Musky No. 2510 Series 4"
Note: Many of the plastic lures on this page were made by the Dillon-Beck Mfg. Co. in Irvington, New Jersey in 1940. They either had a marketing agreement with Jamison or gave them a license to produce them.

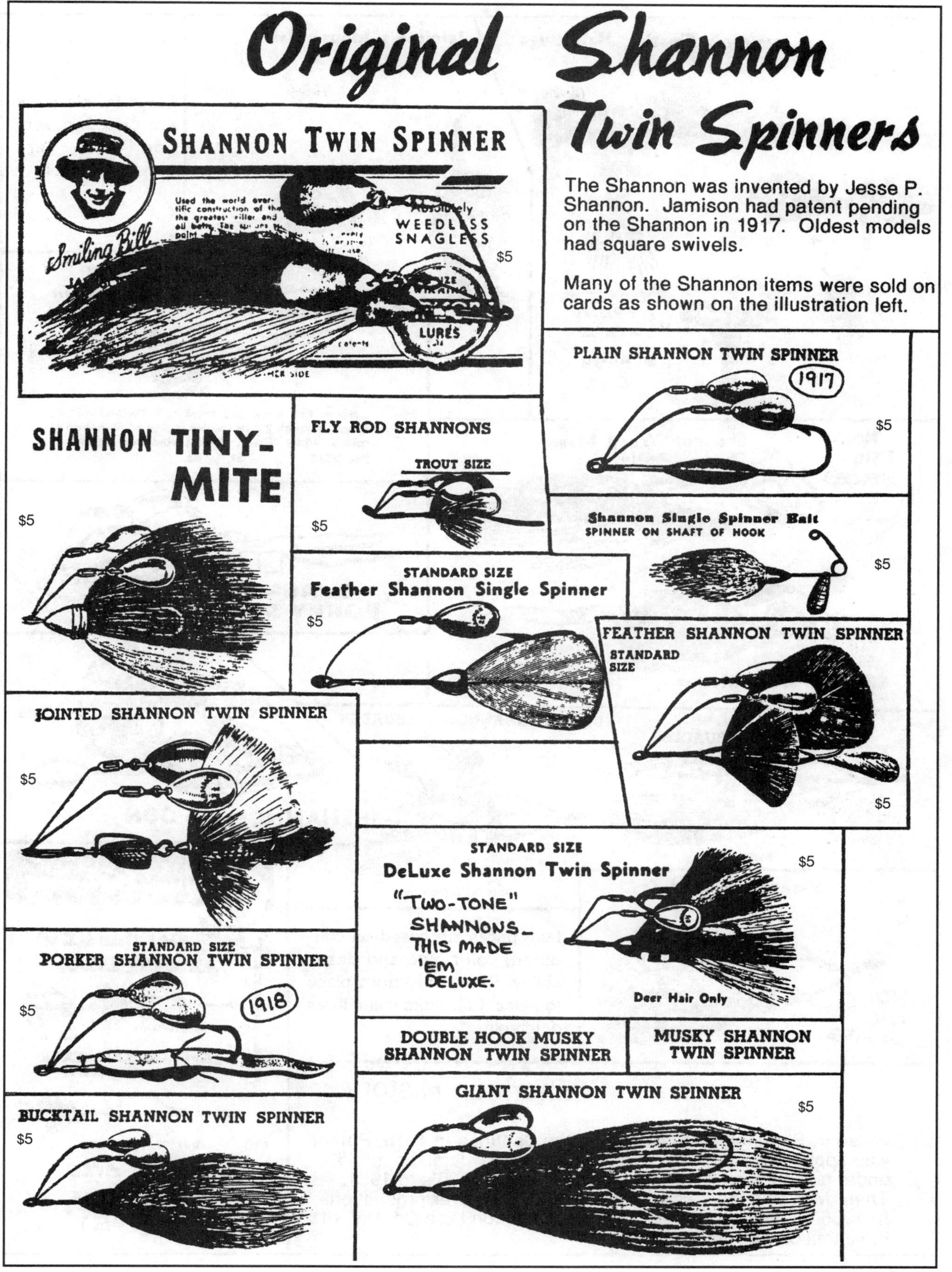
Original Shannon
Twin Spinners
The Shannon was invented by Jesse P. Shannon. Jamison had patent pending on the Shannon in 1917. Oldest models had square swivels.
Many of the Shannon items were sold on cards as shown on the illustration left.
SHANNON TWIN SPINNER
WEEDLESS
SNAGLESS
Smiling Bill
LURES
$5
PLAIN SHANNON TWIN SPINNER
1917
$5
SHANNON TINY-MITE
$5
FLY ROD SHANNONS
TROUT SIZE
$5
Shannon Single Spinner Bait
SPINNER ON SHAFT OF HOOK
$5
STANDARD SIZE
Feather Shannon Single Spinner
$5
FEATHER SHANNON TWIN SPINNER
STANDARD SIZE
$5
JOINTED SHANNON TWIN SPINNER
$5
STANDARD SIZE
DeLuxe Shannon Twin Spinner
"TWO-TONE" SHANNONS_ THIS MADE 'EM DELUXE.
Deer Hair Only
$5
STANDARD SIZE
PORKER SHANNON TWIN SPINNER
1918
$5
DOUBLE HOOK MUSKY SHANNON TWIN SPINNER
MUSKY SHANNON TWIN SPINNER
GIANT SHANNON TWIN SPINNER
$5
BUCKTAIL SHANNON TWIN SPINNER
$5

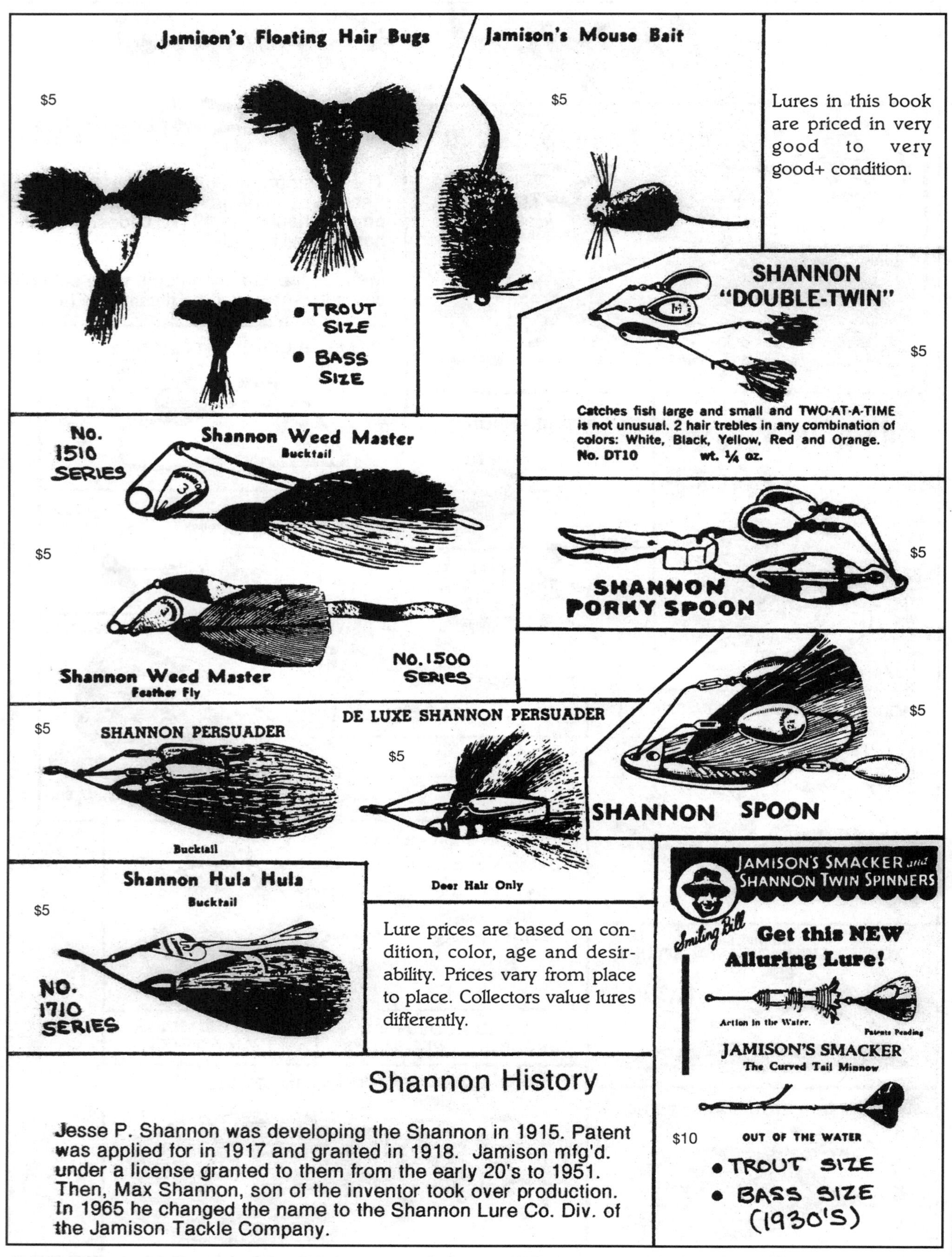
Jamison's Floating Hair Bugs
$5
• TROUT SIZE
• BASS SIZE
Jamison's Mouse Bait
$5
Lures in this book are priced in very good to very good+ condition.
SHANNON "DOUBLE-TWIN"
$5
Catches fish large and small and TWO-AT-A-TIME is not unusual. 2 hair trebles in any combination of colors: White, Black, Yellow, Red and Orange.
No. DT10 wt. 1/4 oz.
No. 1510 SERIES
Shannon Weed Master
Bucktail
$5
Shannon Weed Master
Feather Fly
No. 1500 SERIES
SHANNON PORKY SPOON
$5
$5
SHANNON PERSUADER
Bucktail
DE LUXE SHANNON PERSUADER
$5
Deer Hair Only
$5
SHANNON SPOON
Shannon Hula Hula
Bucktail
$5
NO. 1710 SERIES
Lure prices are based on condition, color, age and desirability. Prices vary from place to place. Collectors value lures differently.
JAMISON'S SMACKER and SHANNON TWIN SPINNERS
Smiling Bill
Get this NEW Alluring Lure!
Action in the Water.
Patents Pending
JAMISON'S SMACKER
The Curved Tail Minnow
OUT OF THE WATER
$10
• TROUT SIZE
• BASS SIZE
(1930'S)

Shannon History

Jesse P. Shannon was developing the Shannon in 1915. Patent was applied for in 1917 and granted in 1918. Jamison mfg'd. under a license granted to them from the early 20's to 1951. Then, Max Shannon, son of the inventor took over production. In 1965 he changed the name to the Shannon Lure Co. Div. of the Jamison Tackle Company.

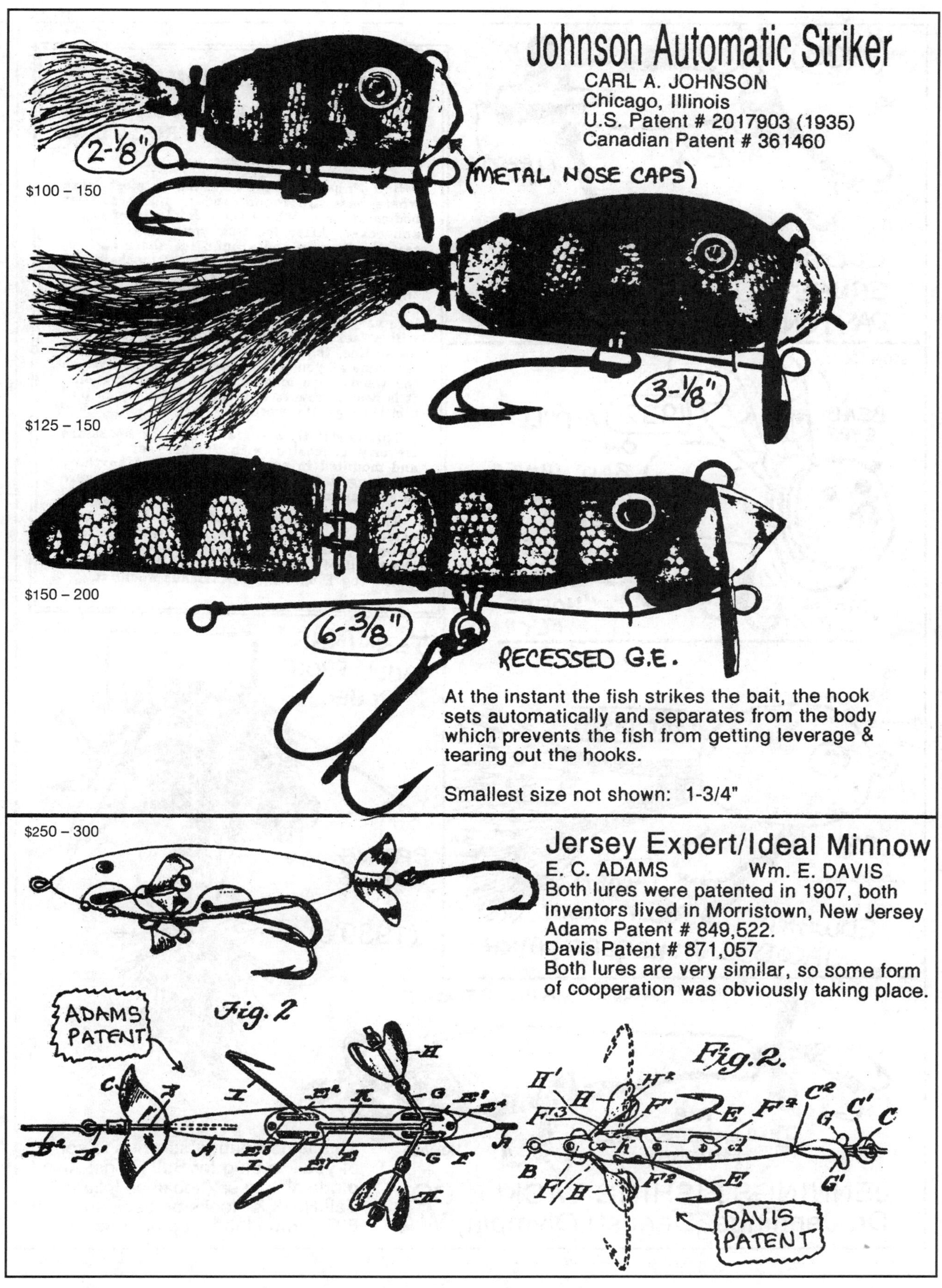
2-1/8"
(METAL NOSE CAPS)
$100 – 150
3-1/8"
$125 – 150
$150 – 200
6-3/8"
RECESSED G.E.
$250 – 300
ADAMS PATENT
Fig. 2
Fig. 2.
DAVIS PATENT

Johnson Automatic Striker

CARL A. JOHNSON
Chicago, Illinois
U.S. Patent # 2017903 (1935)
Canadian Patent # 361460

At the instant the fish strikes the bait, the hook sets automatically and separates from the body which prevents the fish from getting leverage & tearing out the hooks.

Smallest size not shown: 1-3/4"

Jersey Expert/Ideal Minnow

E. C. ADAMS Wm. E. DAVIS
Both lures were patented in 1907, both inventors lived in Morristown, New Jersey
Adams Patent # 849,522.
Davis Patent # 871,057
Both lures are very similar, so some form of cooperation was obviously taking place.

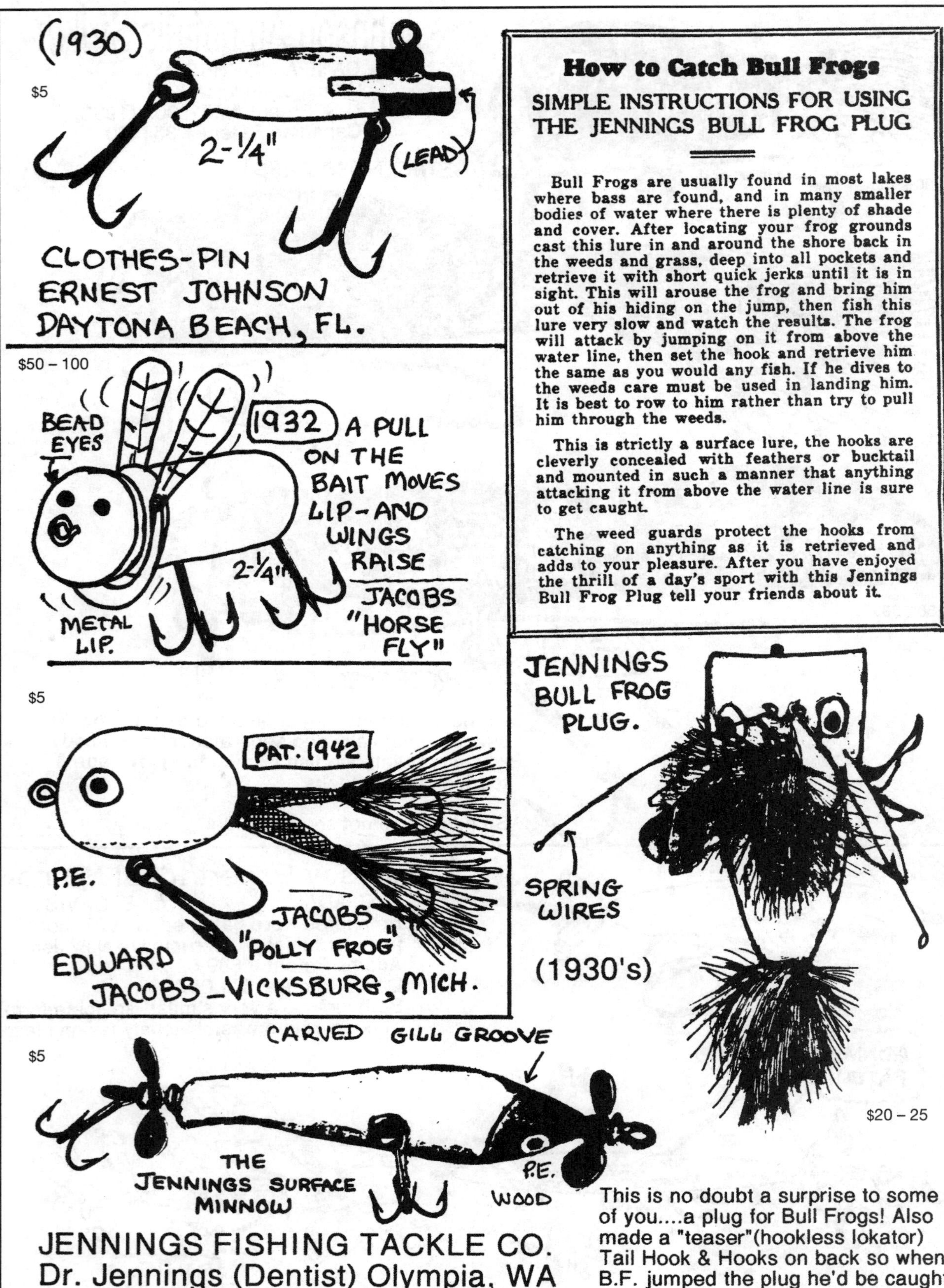
(1930)
$5
2-¼"
(LEAD)
CLOTHES-PIN
ERNEST JOHNSON
DAYTONA BEACH, FL.
$50 – 100
BEAD EYES
1932
A PULL ON THE BAIT MOVES LIP-AND WINGS RAISE
2-¼"
METAL LIP.
JACOBS "HORSE FLY"
$5
PAT. 1942
P.E.
JACOBS "POLLY FROG"
EDWARD JACOBS_VICKSBURG, MICH.
JENNINGS BULL FROG PLUG.
SPRING WIRES
(1930's)
$20 – 25
CARVED GILL GROOVE
$5
THE JENNINGS SURFACE MINNOW
P.E.
WOOD
JENNINGS FISHING TACKLE CO.
Dr. Jennings (Dentist) Olympia, WA

How to Catch Bull Frogs

SIMPLE INSTRUCTIONS FOR USING THE JENNINGS BULL FROG PLUG

Bull Frogs are usually found in most lakes where bass are found, and in many smaller bodies of water where there is plenty of shade and cover. After locating your frog grounds cast this lure in and around the shore back in the weeds and grass, deep into all pockets and retrieve it with short quick jerks until it is in sight. This will arouse the frog and bring him out of his hiding on the jump, then fish this lure very slow and watch the results. The frog will attack by jumping on it from above the water line, then set the hook and retrieve him the same as you would any fish. If he dives to the weeds care must be used in landing him. It is best to row to him rather than try to pull him through the weeds.

This is strictly a surface lure, the hooks are cleverly concealed with feathers or bucktail and mounted in such a manner that anything attacking it from above the water line is sure to get caught.

The weed guards protect the hooks from catching on anything as it is retrieved and adds to your pleasure. After you have enjoyed the thrill of a day's sport with this Jennings Bull Frog Plug tell your friends about it.

This is no doubt a surprise to some of you....a plug for Bull Frogs! Also made a "teaser"(hookless lokator) Tail Hook & Hooks on back so when B.F. jumped the plug he'd be caught.

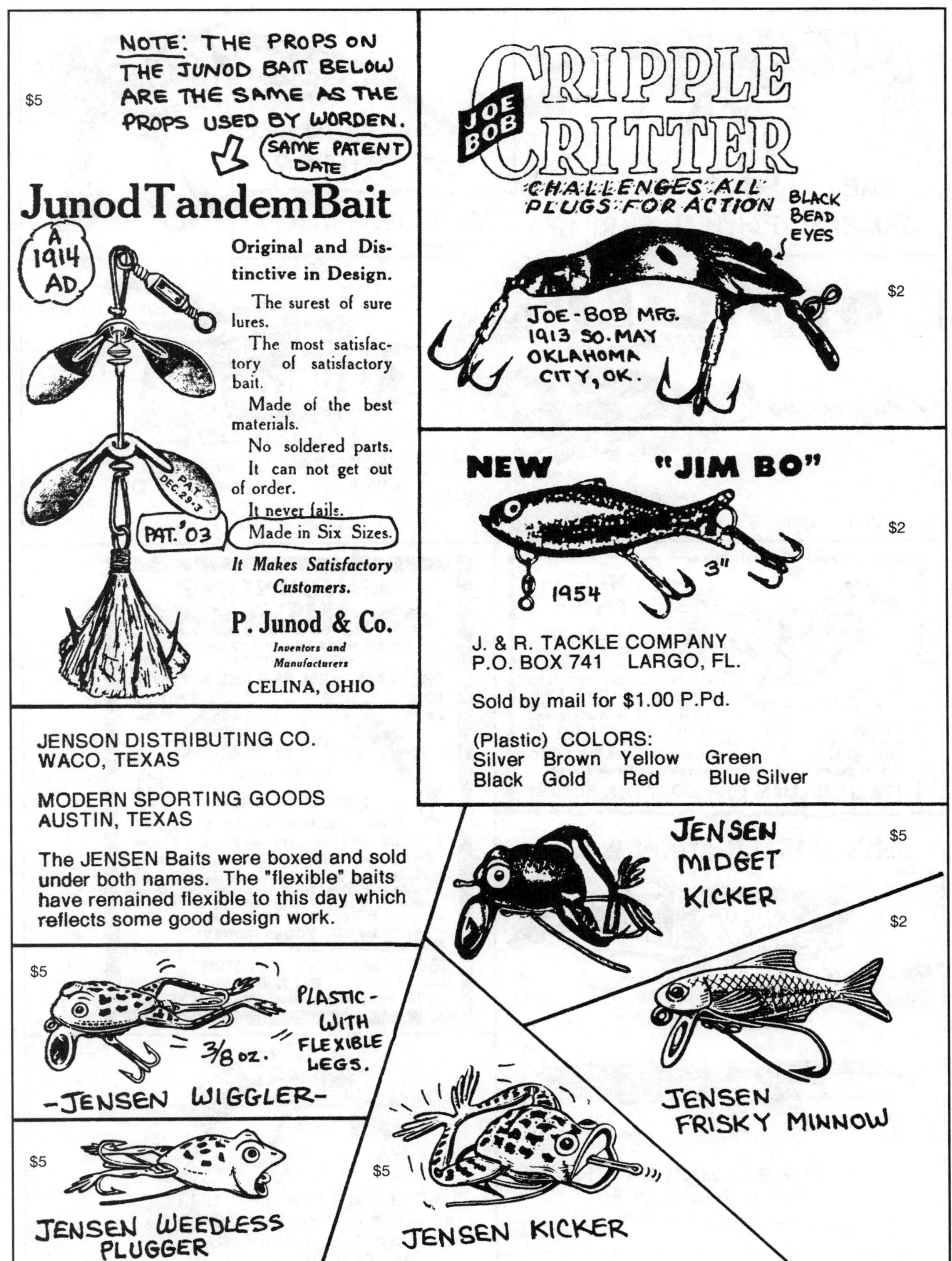
$5
NOTE: THE PROPS ON THE JUNOD BAIT BELOW ARE THE SAME AS THE PROPS USED BY WORDEN.
SAME PATENT DATE
Junod Tandem Bait
A 1914 AD
Original and Distinctive in Design.
The surest of sure lures.
The most satisfactory of satisfactory bait.
Made of the best materials.
No soldered parts.
It can not get out of order.
It never fails.
Made in Six Sizes.
PAT. '03
PAT. DEC. 29-3
It Makes Satisfactory Customers.
P. Junod & Co.
Inventors and Manufacturers
CELINA, OHIO
JOE BOB
CRIPPLE CRITTER
CHALLENGES ALL PLUGS FOR ACTION
BLACK BEAD EYES
JOE-BOB MFG.
1913 SO. MAY
OKLAHOMA CITY, OK.
$2
NEW "JIM BO"
3"
1954
$2
J. & R. TACKLE COMPANY
P.O. BOX 741 LARGO, FL.
Sold by mail for $1.00 P.Pd.
(Plastic) COLORS:
Silver Brown Yellow Green
Black Gold Red Blue Silver
JENSON DISTRIBUTING CO.
WACO, TEXAS
MODERN SPORTING GOODS
AUSTIN, TEXAS
The JENSEN Baits were boxed and sold under both names. The "flexible" baits have remained flexible to this day which reflects some good design work.
$5
JENSEN MIDGET KICKER
$2
$5
PLASTIC - WITH FLEXIBLE LEGS.
3/8 oz.
-JENSEN WIGGLER-
JENSEN FRISKY MINNOW
$5
JENSEN WEEDLESS PLUGGER
$5
JENSEN KICKER

THE
JENSEN FLIPPER SHRIMP

$2

JENSEN
ZIPPER
2-7/8"

$2

2 More Jensens(Tx)

JACK'S
RIP•L•LURE
For All Game Fish
Noisy Topper

$2

(Also Jointed 3-3/4") (1948)

Plastic Bait - 3" - Pin Eyes - Lip "Flip-Flops"

- SPOON -

3 Sizes, 6 Colors

HAVE YOU TRIED A
WIG-A-LURE
THEY SAY IT'S THE BEST

JACK'S TACKLE MFG. CO.
Box 4304 Oklahoma City, OK

$10 – 15

NEW! Flying Tempter

1938

Patent Pending

Here's a fly rod lure that's entirely new and different from anything you've ever seen. Two revolving wings spin and flutter as the lure settles to the water. When retrieved it flutters and struggles like a living, wounded, winged insect, in a most amazing, tantalizing manner that gets 'em when all else fails. A sensational, proven fish getter.

1/0 Bass Size 90c postpaid. Free Folder

JEWELL GILLIAM LURE CO., Wingo, Kentucky

ANNOUNCING JUDAS

TRADE MARK REG. U.S. PAT. OFF.
PATENTS PENDING

THE SENSATIONAL NEW FISH BETRAYER

BULL FROG — SPOTTED FROG

Wt. 5/8 oz
3¾ in. Long

PRICE $1.35 Postpaid
With Weedless Hooks $1.45
LIFELIKE APPEARANCE—DIVING ACTION
SEND FOR FREE ILLUSTRATED FOLDER

No longer do you have to depend on hard-to-get live frogs for catching those wise old BASS and WALLEYES who refuse all ordinary baits.

ORDER YOURS TODAY!
Money Order or Check Only — No C.O.D.s

1947

SPORTING INDUSTRIES
DEPT. 6
5912 N. Harlem Av., Chicago 31, Ill.

$20 – 30

Jeff's MASTER MINNOW

$2

Jeff's REAL EEL

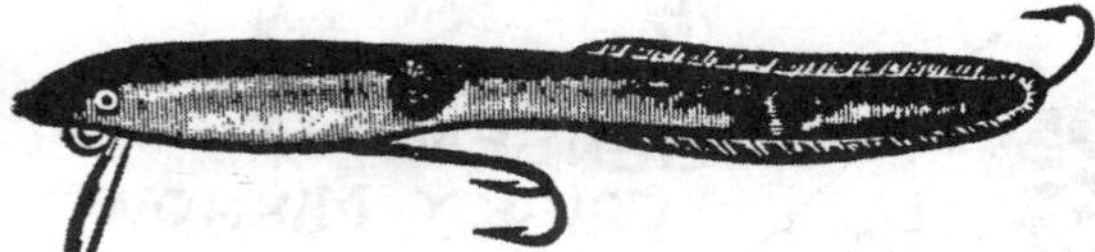

JEFFERS & BAILEY, INC.
5575 Air Terminal Dr. E
Fresno, Calif. 93727

$2

Doo-Dad Bait (Aluminum) 1948
Luhr Jensen, Hood River, OR.
Note: Do not confuse with So. Bend's Peach-Oreno.

Isle Royale Baits

OLD TIME FAVORITES

For All Game Fish

THEIR REGISTERED TRADE-MARK was "IRCO".
Made in: Jackson, Michigan

Note: They made some baits for SHAKESPEARE CO. during the 1942 - 1948 time period.

They apparently made quite a few baits, probably sold under various private labels and catalog sales.

$10 – 20 each

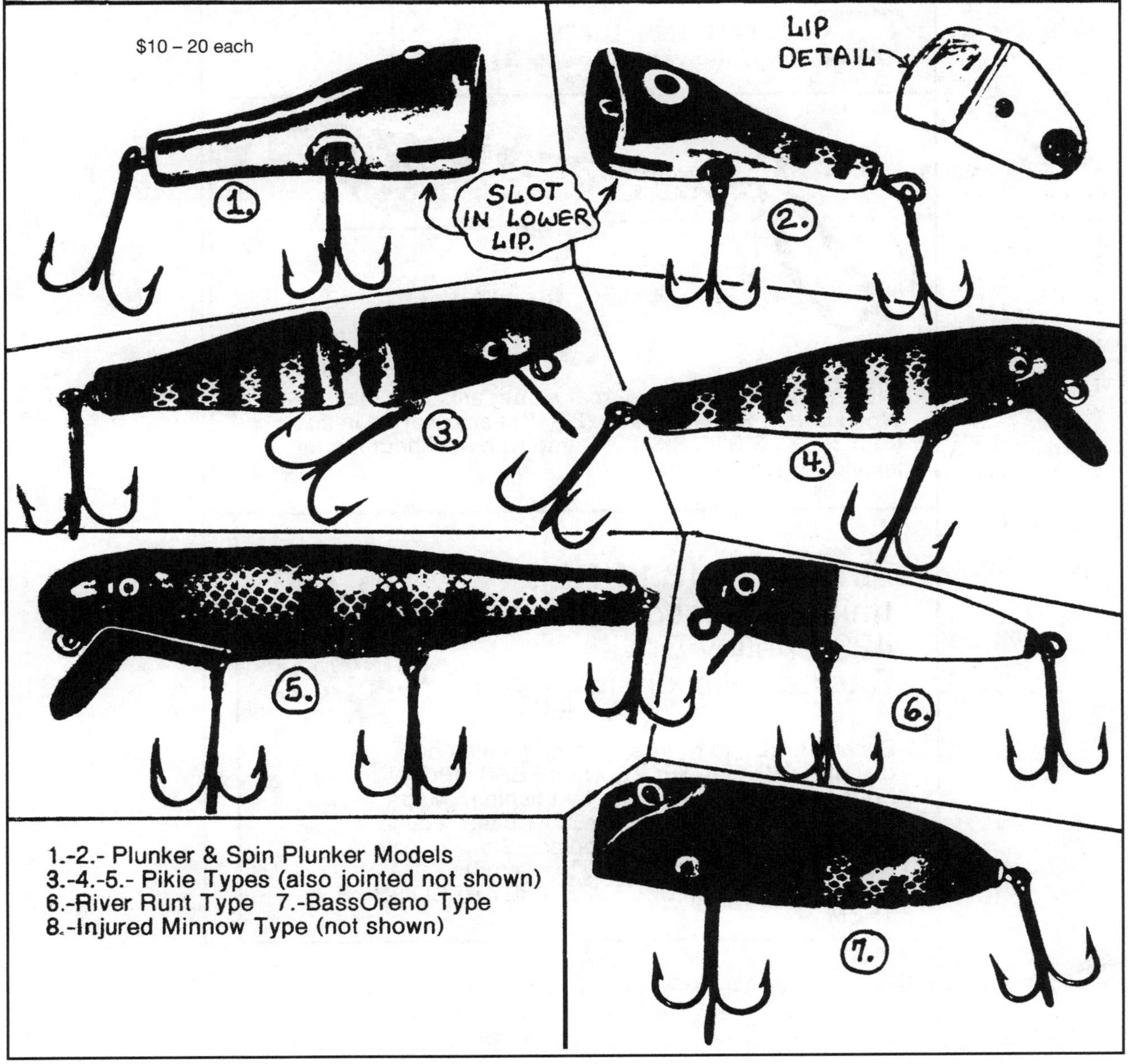

LIP DETAIL

1. SLOT IN LOWER LIP. 2.

3. 4.

5. 6.

7.

1.-2.- Plunker & Spin Plunker Models
3.-4.-5.- Pikie Types (also jointed not shown)
6.-River Runt Type 7.-BassOreno Type
8.-Injured Minnow Type (not shown)

WEEDLESS
OR YOUR MONEY BACK!

PATENTED

The Weeder

1952

$10

IT'S NEW! REVOLUTIONARY!

VICIOUS ACTION! NEVER MISSES!

Get the big ones in thick weeds, lily pads or around logs! Guaranteed Weedless. Patented spring protects hooks so they positively won't snag. But when a fish strikes—then bingo—both hooks set for the kill . . . there's no escape. Hooks are moulded in Flashy Plastic body. 5/8 ounce. 9 color patterns—red head, pikie finish, black scale, or orange dot, frog finish, etc. Representatives wanted.
If dealer can't supply, send $1.35, and state color preference.

IDEEL FISH LURES
6934 South Stewart, Chicago 21, Ill.

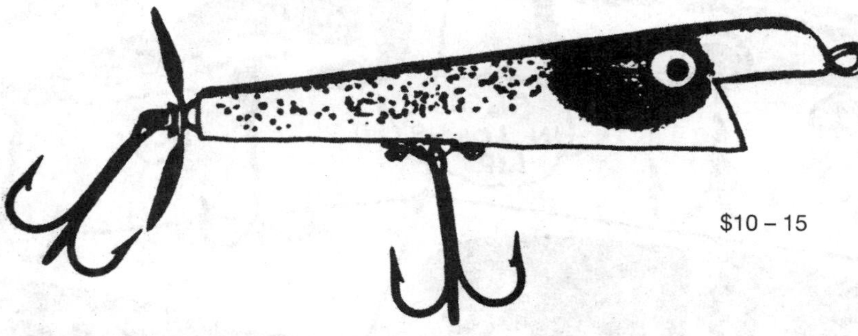

$10 – 15

INSTANT BASS LURE - Great name, unknown maker Wood Bait, 2 Sizes: Small - 2-3/4", Large-varied in size from 3-1/2", 3-5/8", 3-3/4". Came with & without the tail spinner.

FLY FISHING LURES
Imitation Insect Laboratory
423 Shelley Drive
Racine, Wisconsin

1951

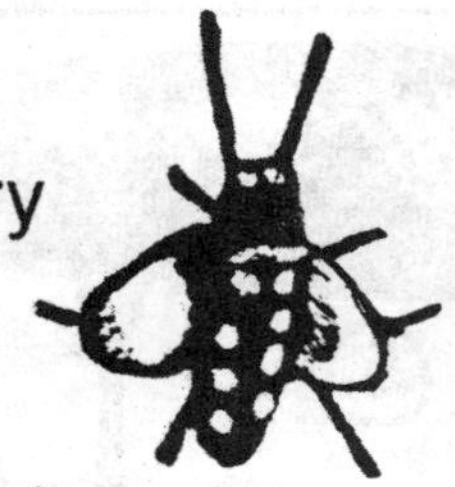

Second ONLY to Nature. Startling imitations of THE LIVING INSECTS FISH FEED UPON. Equally good for surface or bait fishing. Made of a specially compounded rubber base. Tough hollow non-collapsible air bodies. Shapes, colors sizes like the living models,. (patented) "FISH TAKE THEM BECAUSE THEY RECOGNIZE THEM."

$5 – 15

KEELING'S
FRED C. KEELING
ROCKFORD ILLINOIS

$10 – 25

DOUBLE WING PAT'D. 7-6-20

(The Lifelike Wiggler)

$30 – 50

COLORS

D. R. Dark Back, Red Belly.
G. W. Green Back, White Belly.
G. S. Green Body, Bronze Speckled.
A. R. H. Aluminum Body, Red Head.
G. R. H. Gold Body, Red Head.
W. R. H. White Body, Red Head.
R. W. Dr. Back, Red Sides, Wh. Belly.

PAT'D. — 7-6-20

- RAINBOW STRIPED
- YELLOW - WITH RED AND GREEN SPOTS.
- BLACK/WHITE HEAD
- YELLOW/BLACK HEAD

KEELING'S TOM THUMB
(The Little Underwater Wiggler)

EARLY BABY TOM HAD GLASS EYES.

(3 COLORS:)
- ALUMINUM
- COPPER
- WHITE

1917

KEELING'S
TOM THUMB
THE WIGGLER FOR BASS AND PIKE

PAT. 7-6-20
2 INCH
BABY TOM
2½ INCH
LITTLE TOM

— MADE IN 12 COLORS —
THE BAIT THAT BEAT FROGS 2 TO 1 - PORKRIND 3 TO 1
— TRY IT WHEN OTHER LURES FAIL —
AT DEALERS OR DIRECT
FRED C. KEELING - ROCKFORD, ILL.

Keeling's Tom Thumb Wiggler

$30 – 50

• BABY TOM 2 INCH	2"		$30 – 50
• LITTLE TOM 2½ INCH	2½"		$30 – 50
• PIKE TOM 2¾ INCH	2¾"		$30 – 50
• BIG TOM 3 INCH	3"		$30 – 50
• Surface Tom 3¼ INCH	3¼"		$30 – 50

Keeling's Surf-Kee-Wig

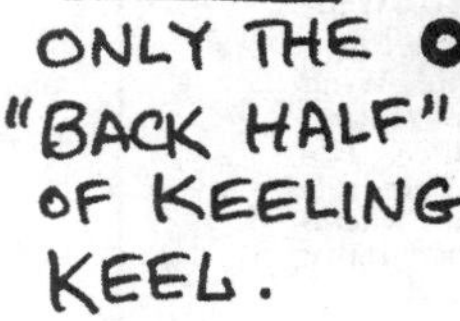
3½"
ONLY THE "BACK HALF" OF KEELING KEEL.

$30 – 40

The "Surf-Kee-Wig" is a surface bait which wiggles on top of the water creating a commotion with the back wing. It resembles some small animal swimming. Muskies and Bass will strike this bait even after dark. For best results reel slow and give a series of very short jerks. After jerk let bait rest a moment. This style of bait is best for early morning or evening when fish are near shore. It's a killer for Bass and Muskies if used as directed.

$20 – 40

Keeling's Tip-Top

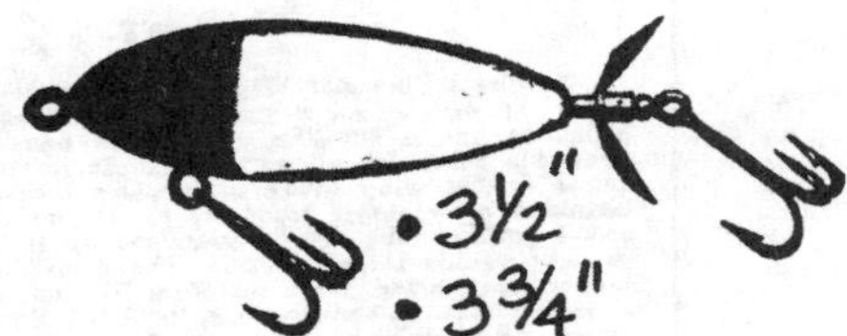
• 3½"
• 3¾"

This bait runs on the surface, churning the water with the spinner on the back. The spinner on the back gives better action than one on the front. This is a popular bait but lacks the life-like wiggling motion of the Surf-Kee-Wig which we consider the ideal surface bait.

Colors same as the Tom Thumb.

AN OBSERVATION ON COLLECTING KEELING LURES

Keeling started production around 1914, and ended around 1938. As I was updated the Keeling section of this book, I soon realized that everything could not be included. Keeling used his body shapes and sizes with keels, with props, with lips, with and without eye detail and on & on. A Keeling researcher came out with a reference.......totaled 94 Pages !!!

He stated it was the first attempt, and more info will surface.

KEELING'S RED WING
(The Wiggler with a Spinner)

The attractive spinner, the wiggling motion, are combined in the Red Wing. "That's all," we have to say. "That's Plenty," to a fisherman. We knew it was a winner, so worked months to perfect it.

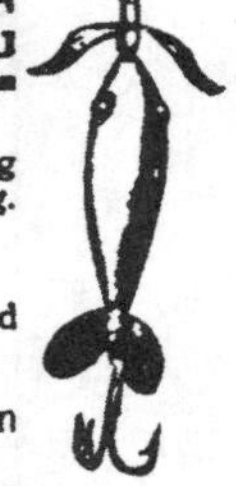

COLORS: White, Copper, Aluminum

G.E. (1917) 3" Soldered Lip on rear hook hanger & belly weight.

$50 – 60

KEELING'S

$30 – 50

Keeling's Bass-Kee-Wig

3"
G.E. & N.E.

Keeling's Bass-Kee-Wig is practically the same as the Big Tom Thumb excepting the larger front wing causes it to dive deeper if reeled fast, while with the Tom Thumb the faster you reel the higher it comes in. If fishing in deep water or at a time of the year when fish will not strike near the surface the Bass-Kee-Wig would be best, but if in shallow water or when fish are striking high use the Tom Thumb. They both have that wonderful wiggle that excites the admiration of fishermen and induces fish to strike when other lures fail. It is a good bait for Bass or Salt Water Trout.

Keeling's Trout-Kee-Wig 2½"

For Casting for Salt Water Trout in deep water. It is the same as the Little Tom Thumb, 2½ inches long, but has the Kee-Wig Wing, making a better bait for Trout when they are in the deep holes. This bait will stand fast reeling and jerking at the same time which produces the motion that catches the Trout. It is equally as good for Bass.

3 3/8"

$30 – 60

KEELING'S SCOUT

FOR
MUSCALLONGE
BASS AND
SALT WATER TROUT

Keeling's Scout is the result of months of experimenting to produce a floating minnow that would dart and cut up in an erratic way would not pull hard or dive deep. A bait for casting or trolling in shallow or weedy waters. We unhesitatingly offer Keeling's Scout to the expert or beginner as a remarkable bait for bass or Muskalonge, and one that will deliver the goods. It is especially good in early morning or evening fishing.

TOM THUMB or SCOUT COLORS

WHITE REDHEAD—GREEN SPECKLED
ALUMINUM REDHEAD—ALUMINUM
GOLD REDHEAD—COPPER

Keeling's Pike-Kee-Wig

3⅞"

$30 – 60

NOTE: 2 DIFF. NOSES

Keeling's Pike-Kee-Wig is as the name indicates, a bait for Pike. It wiggles on a slow pull and does not roll on a fast pull. It has a life-like appearance and a motion that has proved a killer for all game fish. It floats at rest. The patented double wing gives a wiggling motion that can not be obtained by a single front wing. If you doubt this try them out together. We refund your money if any minnow on the market equals it in motion. The Kee-Wig Wigglers have a larger front wing than the Tom Thumb, so will dive deeper if reeled fast. Used trolling for Wall Eye Pike, Big Florida Bass and Red Fish, attach a sinker about a foot above the bait if needed to go deep as a slow moving bait gives best results. Used casting for Muscallonge, Great Northern Pike, Rovalia, Mackerel and Salt Water Trout best results are obtained by a series of short jerks as it gives the bait an erratic fast darting and wiggling motion that brings them out when they will turn away from a live minnow. The Pike-Kee-Wig can be used this way in quite shallow water over weeds, oyster bars, etc.

$30 – 60

Keeling's Pike-Kee-Wig

The liveliest Wiggler that ever wiggled down the pike. Floats at rest and dives when reeled. A fine lure to use trolling for Wall Eye Pike as it has a fast wiggle on a slow pull. The patent Double Wing gives the Keeling baits the motion that a single wing cannot produce. It's a killer for any game fish. Made in 2 sizes. Pike-Kee-Wig 4½ inches with 3 Treble Hooks, Price 85 cents. Baby Pike-Kee-Wig 3½ inches, 75 cents.

- (BABY) PIKE-KEE-WIG - 3½"
- (STANDARD) - 4½"
- (MUSKY) - H.D. 4½" AND 6½"

KEELING'S MUSK-KEE-WIG

A floating Kee-Wig equipped with larger hooks than the Pike-Kee-Wig. It can be handled in the same manner as the Pike-Kee-Wg. A good bait for trolling or casting for Muskie, Bass, Rovalia, etc.

The Pike-Kee-Wig and Musk-Kee-Wig are made in the following colors:

COLORS

G. A. Dark Back, Aluminum Belly.
G. W. Green Back, White Belly.
R. W. Dark Back, Red Sides, White Belly.
W. R. H. White, Red Head.
A. R. H. Aluminum, Red Head.

THE EXPERT

KEELING MINNOWS

MARCH OFFER N—3 for $1.00

1—Keeling "Expert" St. Johns Wiggle Minnow
2—Keeling Underwater Minnows

If you order OFFER N we prepay these. Two have same kind of hooks other houses use. One has our Patent Detachable Treble Hooks, the only one on the market that can be put on and taken off with the fingers only. We equip with Detachable Doubles and Singles that stay in position, if desired.

FRED C. KEELING & CO., Rockford, Ill. ← (MARCH-1917 AD)

$75 – 100

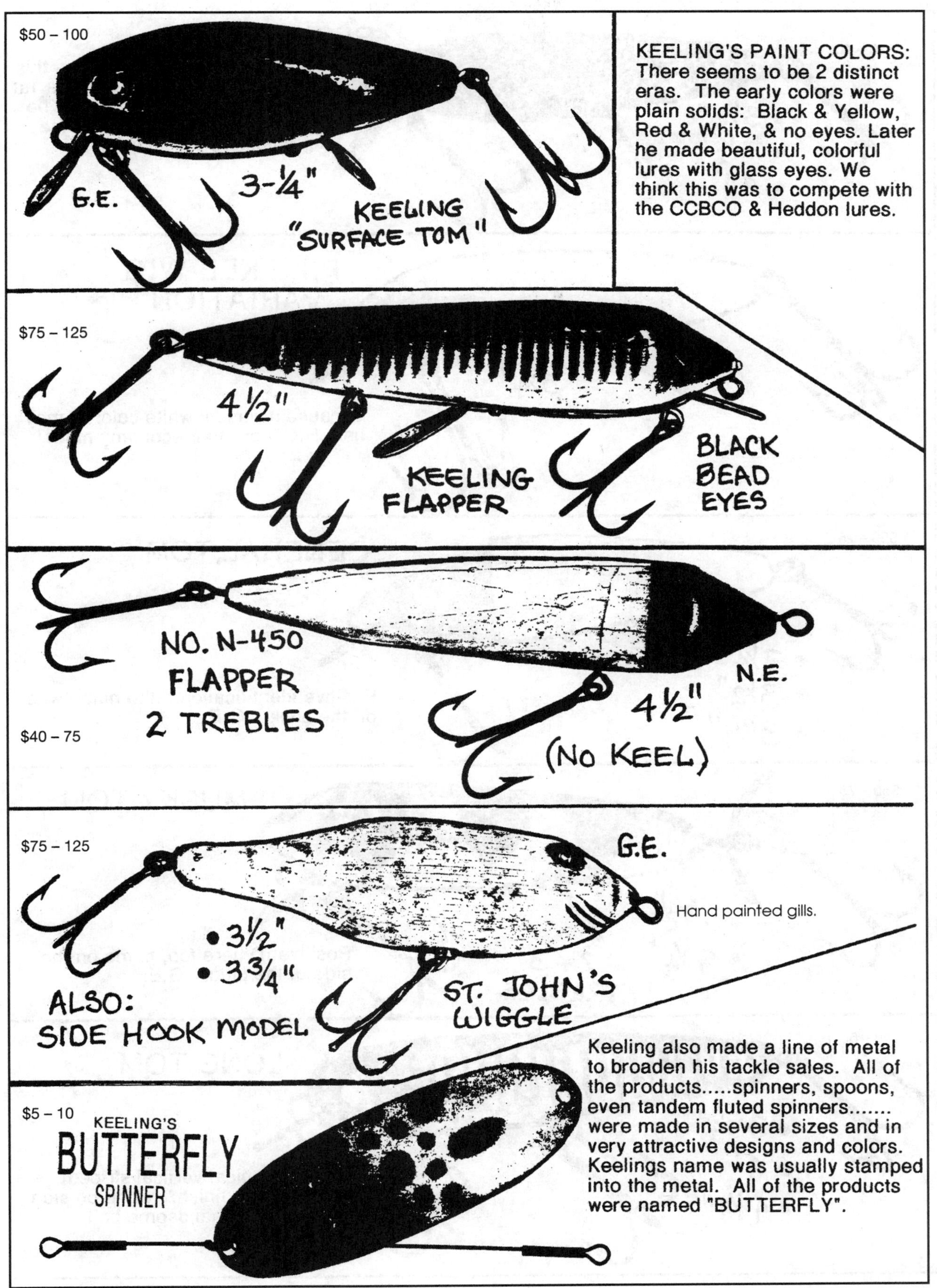

$50 – 100
G.E.
3-¼"
KEELING
"SURFACE TOM"
KEELING'S PAINT COLORS: There seems to be 2 distinct eras. The early colors were plain solids: Black & Yellow, Red & White, & no eyes. Later he made beautiful, colorful lures with glass eyes. We think this was to compete with the CCBCO & Heddon lures.
$75 – 125
4½"
KEELING FLAPPER
BLACK BEAD EYES
NO. N-450
FLAPPER
2 TREBLES
N.E.
4½"
(NO KEEL)
$40 – 75
$75 – 125
G.E.
Hand painted gills.
• 3½"
• 3¾"
ALSO:
SIDE HOOK MODEL
ST. JOHN'S WIGGLE
Keeling also made a line of metal to broaden his tackle sales. All of the products.....spinners, spoons, even tandem fluted spinners....... were made in several sizes and in very attractive designs and colors. Keelings name was usually stamped into the metal. All of the products were named "BUTTERFLY".
$5 – 10
KEELING'S
BUTTERFLY
SPINNER

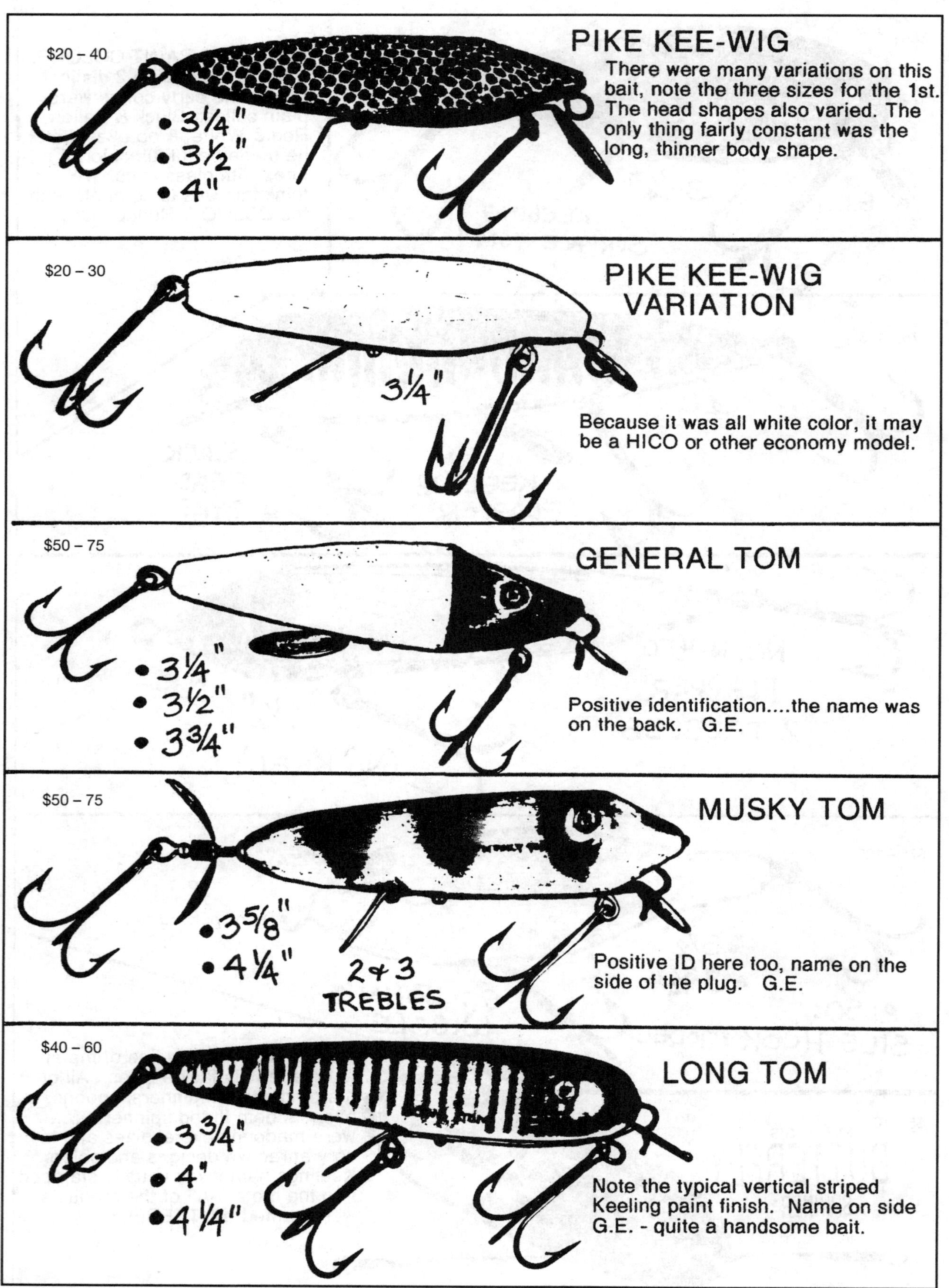
$20 – 40
PIKE KEE-WIG
There were many variations on this bait, note the three sizes for the 1st. The head shapes also varied. The only thing fairly constant was the long, thinner body shape.
• 3¼"
• 3½"
• 4"
$20 – 30
PIKE KEE-WIG VARIATION
3¼"
Because it was all white color, it may be a HICO or other economy model.
$50 – 75
GENERAL TOM
• 3¼"
• 3½"
• 3¾"
Positive identification....the name was on the back. G.E.
$50 – 75
MUSKY TOM
• 3⅝"
• 4¼"
2 & 3 TREBLES
Positive ID here too, name on the side of the plug. G.E.
$40 – 60
LONG TOM
• 3¾"
• 4"
• 4¼"
Note the typical vertical striped Keeling paint finish. Name on side G.E. - quite a handsome bait.

KEELING'S KING-BEE

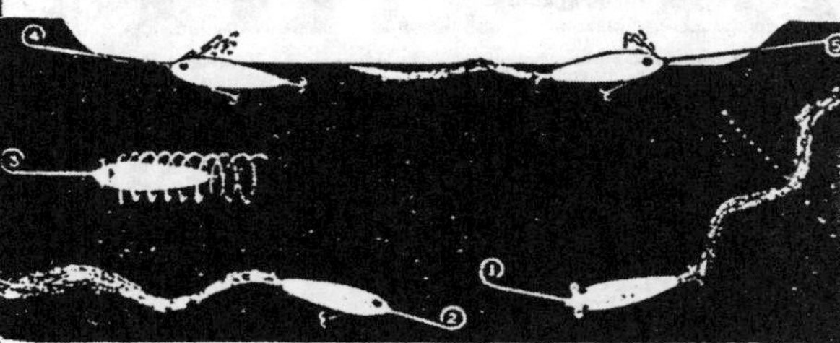

The minnow with 5 movements — fingers only tools needed. 1. Wiggles 1 or 20 feet deep. 2. Up and down jump motion. 3. Spins like spoon hook for trolling. 4. Throws spray on surface. 5. Wounded minnow surface wobble for bass. We bar no make of minnow when we say return and get your money back if anything on the market equals it in action. We offer copper colored minnows this year. Next year others will, as they are great for bass and muskie. In the meantime a copper Keeling expert will help you bring home some fish when other baits fail. For dark water we find aluminum or white best. Woods' patent the only detachable treble hook is part of our equipment. Special hooks used where laws allow 3 barbs only. You save by buying a set and get assorted colors, sizes also if you wish, as the King-bee small is only 2 inches long. Some little wiggler. Colors, copper, aluminum, white. Price, 75c prepaid. Set of three $2.00 prepaid.

FRED C. KEELING
128 N. First Street ROCKFORD, ILL.

OUTERS MAGAZINE AD - MAY, 1916

$50 – 75

Made in 4 Sizes: 2" - 2-1/2" - 3" - 3-1/2" (1916 - 1920) with belly weight, some with gills, and G.E. Similar to Pepper's Revolving Minnow.

1928 AD →

A BROADCASTING INVITATION
TOM THUMB
A TRUE SPORTSMANS BAIT
DRESS SUIT
BABY-TOM
THE BASS BAIT
LITTLE-TOM
FOR ANY GAME FISH
PIKE-TOM
SURFACE-TOM
AT DEALERS-25¢-OR DIRECT
FRED C. KEELING-ROCKFORD, ILL.

The name "TOM THUMB" sort of rang a bell with me so I looked it up in my "Webster's Collegiate Dictionary". It's definition: a legendary ENGLISH dwarf. I believe the name was also used as an act in the Ringling Brothers, Barnum & Bailey Circus.

H.P.G.M.
HAND PAINTED
GILL MARKS
(an early detail)
FISH TAILS

$60 – 100

$20 – 40

The "FISH TAIL" version of Keeling's baits is a detail seen mostly on General Toms and Tom Thumbs. It's a rare feature and a great find !

KODAK COPIERS

The two detail rich illustrations were made on a KODAK Copier. It is the only copier I have used that eliminates all the shadows and copies the lures with depth not a problem. They also have the clear advantage of ACTUAL SIZE copies.

THE HICO BAITS - As did other the

other makers of that era, Keeling sold baits to HORROCKS - IBBOTSON CO. of Utica, NY. This could result in more unusual baits with combinations of Keeling Features or Paint finishes. As an aside, some collectors have nicknamed the cheaper H - I as "Horrible - Ibbotson", for their low end quality.

A very early color used on their swimming baits was a mottled copper and gold.....it was created to imitate a goldfish or golden shiner minnow.

The Patent Date of 7-6-20 that is stamped on many of the Keeling "Belly Keels" is the date of the patent of that metal part, not the date of the bait itself. (This is true for other makers such as CCBCO and Heddon.

THE EXPERTS

The HOLZWARTH EXPERT

The WOODS EXPERT

The CLARK EXPERT

The SCHAFFER EXPERT

The KEELING EXPERT

The HOLZWARTH EXPERT

J. C. (JIM) HOLZWARTH had the Holzwarth Dry Goods Store in Alliance, Ohio. He was a local fisherman, and did some selling and marketing of the original Experts. He ran an ad inviting anglers to throw away their minnow buckets and use the Expert instead. They could order by mail, postpaid.. The dry goods store remained until the 1950's.

HOLZWARTH
IT CATCHES FISH.
Its life-like movements in the water attracts game fish of all kinds. Specially good for large and small mouth Black Bass. Animated and irresistible.
The "HOLZWARTH" Minnow
is a beautifully made and durable artificial bait that will catch more fish than live bait. Superior to all others. Try one and you'll throw away your minnow bucket. By mail, post-paid.
Write for Catalogue E
J. C. HOLZWARTH. ALLIANCE, O.

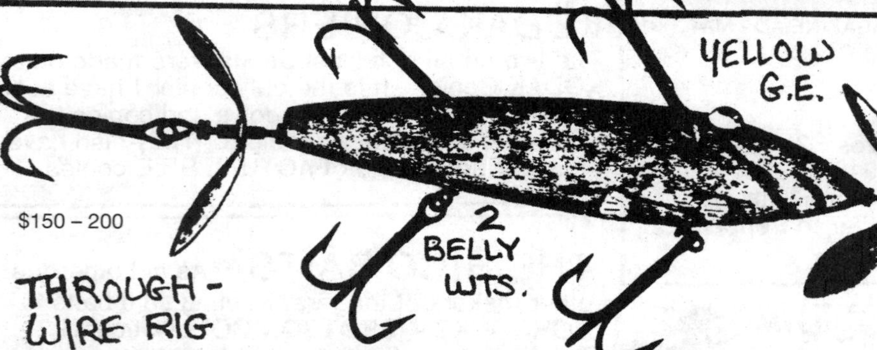
YELLOW G.E.
BLENDED GREEN TO GOLD BELLY.
HOLZWARTH NAME ON SIDE.
2 BELLY WTS.
THROUGH-WIRE RIG
NO PROP HOLES

$150 – 200

The SCHAFFER EXPERT

No. 723,045. PATENTED MAR. 17, 1903.
C. C. SHAFFER.
ARTIFICIAL BAIT.
APPLICATION FILED NOV. 8, 1901.
NO MODEL.
Fig. 1.

$150 – 250

Charles C. Shaffer obtained the original patent for the Expert in 1903. For some unknown reason he did not want to market under his name, so he linked up with Franklin C. Woods and the Expert took the Woods name the same year. Woods obtained two more patents for the double and the treble removable hooks, and the props went from rounded edges to the pointed type.

Ads promoting the sale of the EXPERT were in the 1901 Editions of Outers Mag.

The "MANHATTAN MINNOW" was a private label like Holzwarth.

The WOODS EXPERT

(TOP OF WOODS-"WOOD" BOX)

The "Expert" Wooden Minnow

PATENTED MAR. 17 AND DEC 22, '08.
MADE BY
F. C. WOODS & CO., ALLIANCE, OHIO.

DETACHABLE HOOKS. PERFORATED SPINNERS.
HOOKS WILL NOT TANGLE.

THE ORIGINAL WOODEN MINNOW

THE "EXPERT"

The "EXPERT"

Price, 75 cents.

We are the Pioneers of the Wooden Minnow. Been making them for ten years and know how to make them just right.

Patented March 17, '08.

"THE BEST IS NONE TOO GOOD FOR A FISHERMAN."

DETACHABLE HOOKS. PERFORATED SPINNERS.

When you want the VERY BEST, insist on the "EXPERT."

Send for our booklet, "A CATCHING THING."

F. C. WOODS & CO., Alliance, Ohio.

This 1905 Ad said they had been making wooden minnows for ten years. (1905 - 10 = 1895 ???) Note: The prop holes & detachable hooks are in the ad.

$100 – 150

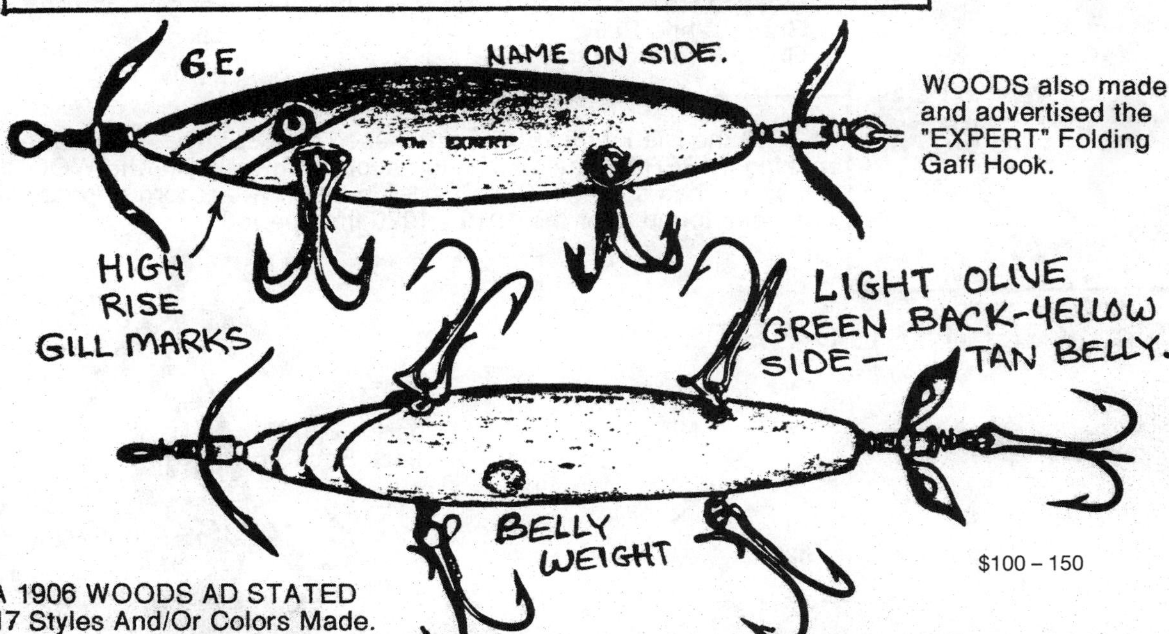
G.E.
NAME ON SIDE.
The EXPERT
HIGH RISE GILL MARKS
LIGHT OLIVE GREEN BACK-YELLOW SIDE- TAN BELLY.
BELLY WEIGHT

WOODS also made and advertised the "EXPERT" Folding Gaff Hook.

$100 – 150

A 1906 WOODS AD STATED 17 Styles And/Or Colors Made.

The CLARK EXPERT

J. L. (John Lewis) CLARK was the owner of a hardware company located in Rockford Illinois. His son Lewis Harold Clark was in the business with him, and together they bought the Shaffer/Woods patents in the 1907 - 08 time frame and started making the CLARK EXPERTS.

The Clark baits were upgraded in quality and the 4th Gill Mark was added to their standard production. Note: No other Experts had four gill marks.

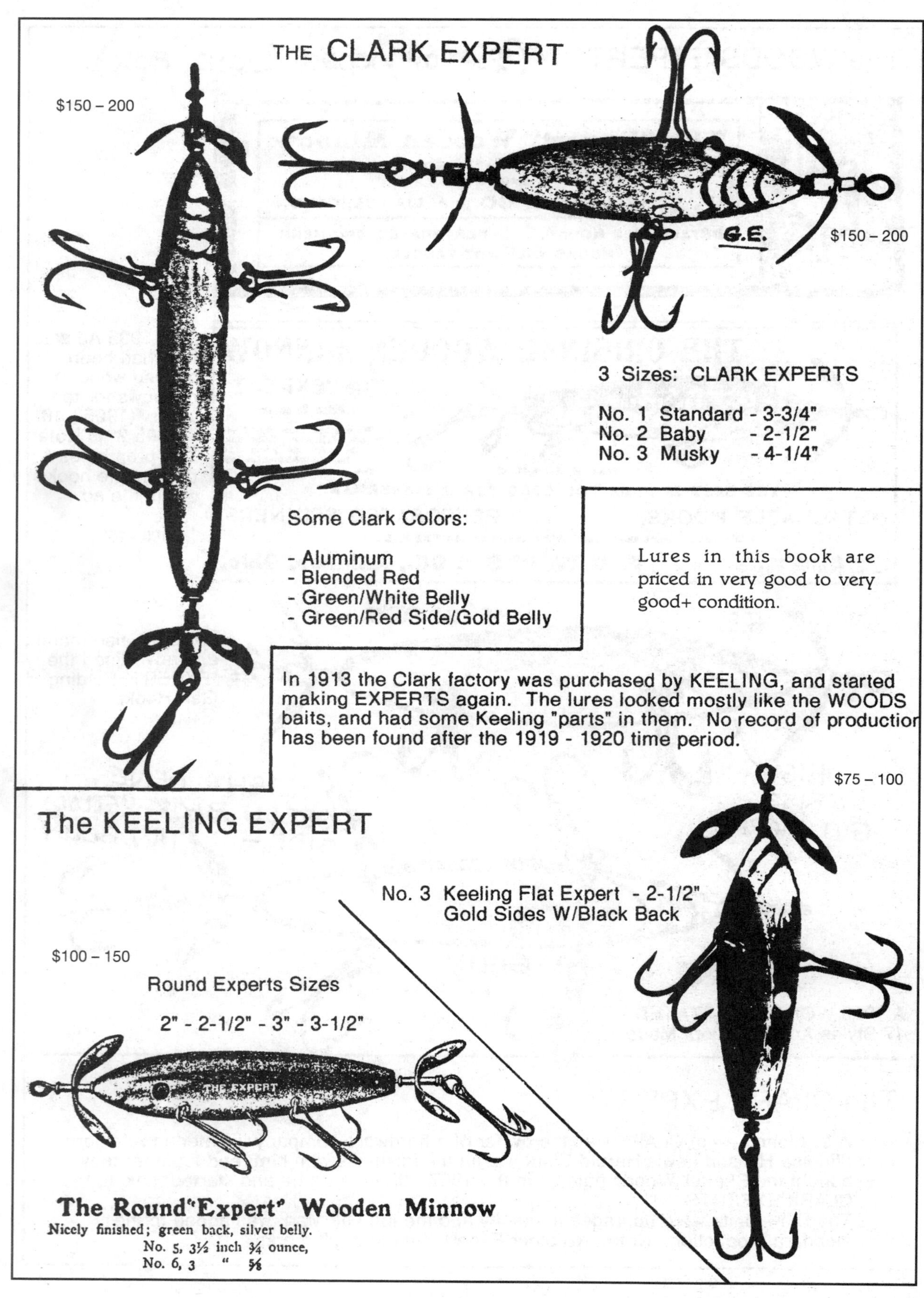
THE CLARK EXPERT
$150 – 200
G.E.
$150 – 200
3 Sizes: CLARK EXPERTS
No. 1 Standard - 3-3/4"
No. 2 Baby - 2-1/2"
No. 3 Musky - 4-1/4"
Some Clark Colors:
- Aluminum
- Blended Red
- Green/White Belly
- Green/Red Side/Gold Belly
Lures in this book are priced in very good to very good+ condition.
In 1913 the Clark factory was purchased by KEELING, and started making EXPERTS again. The lures looked mostly like the WOODS baits, and had some Keeling "parts" in them. No record of production has been found after the 1919 - 1920 time period.
$75 – 100
The KEELING EXPERT
No. 3 Keeling Flat Expert - 2-1/2"
Gold Sides W/Black Back
$100 – 150
Round Experts Sizes
2" - 2-1/2" - 3" - 3-1/2"
THE EXPERT
The Round "Expert" Wooden Minnow
Nicely finished; green back, silver belly.
No. 5, 3½ inch ¾ ounce,
No. 6, 3 " ⅝

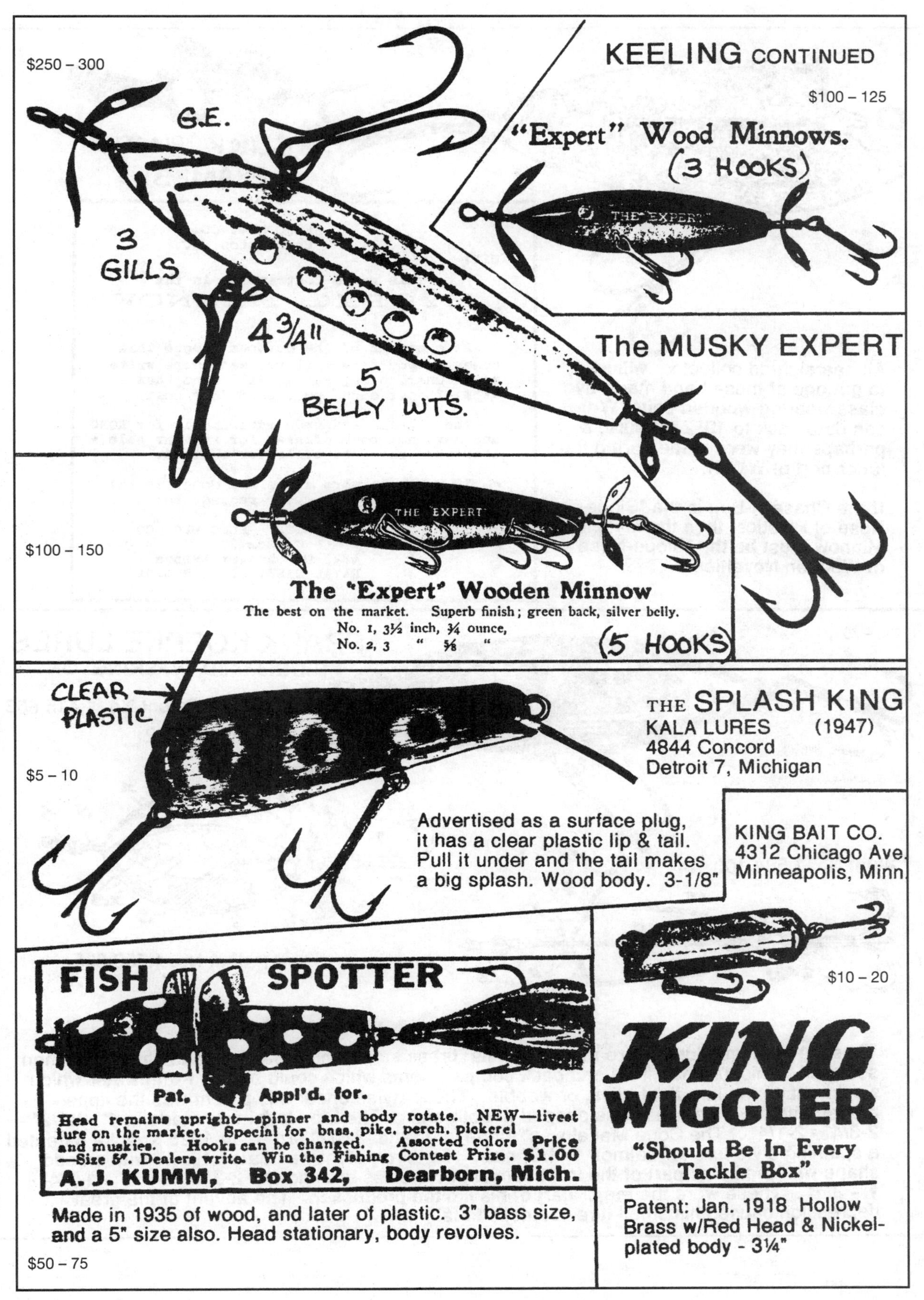
$250 – 300
G.E.
3
GILLS
4 3/4"
5
BELLY WTS.
KEELING CONTINUED
$100 – 125
"Expert" Wood Minnows.
(3 HOOKS)
THE EXPERT
The MUSKY EXPERT
$100 – 150
THE EXPERT
The "Expert" Wooden Minnow
The best on the market. Superb finish; green back, silver belly.
No. 1, 3½ inch, ¾ ounce,
No. 2, 3 " ⅝ "
(5 HOOKS)
CLEAR
PLASTIC
$5 – 10
THE SPLASH KING
KALA LURES (1947)
4844 Concord
Detroit 7, Michigan
Advertised as a surface plug,
it has a clear plastic lip & tail.
Pull it under and the tail makes
a big splash. Wood body. 3-1/8"
KING BAIT CO.
4312 Chicago Ave.
Minneapolis, Minn.
$10 – 20
FISH SPOTTER
Pat. Appl'd. for.
Head remains upright—spinner and body rotate. NEW—livest lure on the market. Special for bass, pike, perch, pickerel and muskies. Hooks can be changed. Assorted colors Price —Size 5". Dealers write. Win the Fishing Contest Prize. $1.00
A. J. KUMM, Box 342, Dearborn, Mich.
Made in 1935 of wood, and later of plastic. 3" bass size,
and a 5" size also. Head stationary, body revolves.
$50 – 75
KING
WIGGLER
"Should Be In Every
Tackle Box"
Patent: Jan. 1918 Hollow
Brass w/Red Head & Nickel-
plated body - 3¼"

BLACK PLASTIC
FRAMES

$50 – 75

KONO MFG. CO.
Charleston, SC

HEY!

This weird Contraption is the

MYOPIC MINNOW

As a member of the Octopus League this comes to you free - if you want more write me in Charleston, and we will send them at $1.25 per each, post paid (our cost)

These baits are made exclusively for KONO and have not been offered for regular sale - therefore they are collector's items.

If you want more shove the dough in the envelope and address your request to:

ED. SMITH - KONO MFG. CO
P.O. Box 27
4845 Dorchester Avenue
NAVAL BASE, SO. CAROLINA

All nearsighted collectors will want to get one of these hand made-eye glass wearing-wooden baits. We can date back to 1952 for sure, & perhaps they were made during the latter part of WW II.

If the Chase-A-Bug is the "Slope-Nose of Plastics, then the Myopic Minnow must be the "Slope-Nose" of Wooden Novelties!

$50 – 75

FRANK KOEPKE LURES

RIDGEFIELD, WASHINGTON

Bass Lure Patent No. 1,415,653
May 9, 1922

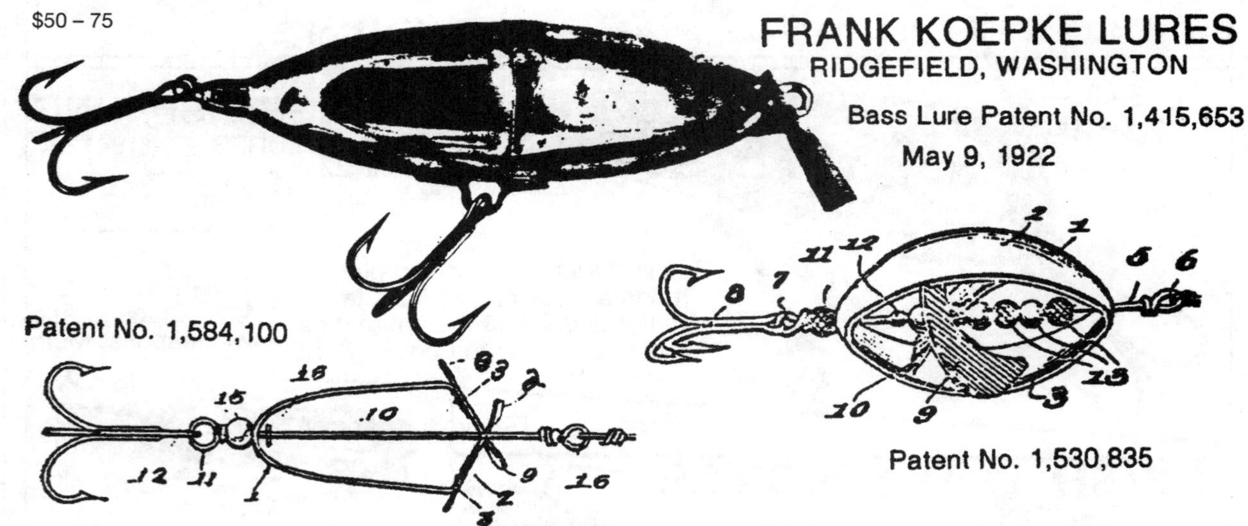

Patent No. 1,584,100

Patent No. 1,530,835

These very unique lures were made from flat brass stock which was rolled to shape and then soldered. This lure had front and back compartments which could be filled with water which would make the lure float, dive, or wobble. The 2 styles under this patent was the lipped model, and the other was cone shaped at both ends. The Lip Model was made in 4" -3-1/2" - 2-3/4" - 2-1/4" . The Cone Model was made in 4" and 3-1/2" sizes. In 1925 Koepke patented a spinning style lure for salmon 1-1/2" size. His third patent was dated 1927, with an odd shape with the lip as part of the front section. Five sizes are known: 2-3/4' - 1-1/2" - 1-1/4" - 1' - 3/4" . These were the major part of his limited production. The advent of the great depression caused his small lure business to fail.

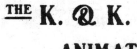

THE K. & K.

ANIMATED MINNOWS

$100 – 150

"THE MINNOW THAT SWIMS"

K. & K. MFG. CO.
TOLEDO, OHIO.

THE WRIGGLER

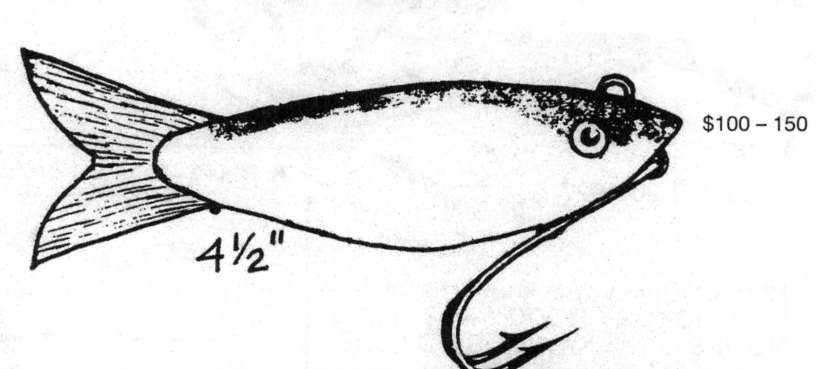
4½"

$100 – 150

THE GHOST

$150 – 175

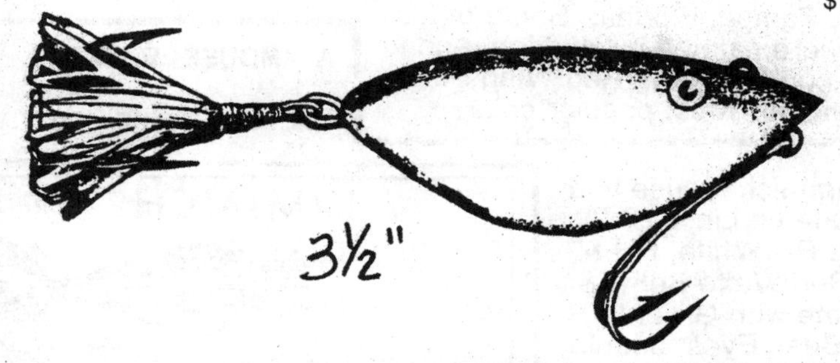
3½"

The K. & K. Baits were patented by J. D. Kreisser in June of 1907. He is given the credit for the first jointed ("animated") bait.
Colors:
Rainbow, All White, Gold, Silver, White W/ Red Stripe, Black & Red, Black & Silver, & "Red Devil" (Red & Gold Back & Side W/ Silver Belly) Green Back W/White or Silver Belly. Note: Most baits are found with severe paint loss.

The "model" for the animated minnow was the Golden Shiner Minnows commonly used in live bait fishing.

Baits Not Illustrated:
"MINNOETTE" - Jointed 3" Body (for small fish) 3 double hooks
"MUSCALONGE/SEA BASS" - 5-1/2" Male Body, 3 Double Hooks

Their numbering system was confusing at best. Here are some descriptions: 2 body styles -long & thin body (male type) fatter body (female type) Both Sinkers and Floaters were made.

A MINNOW THAT SWIMS

A "live" bait that you can carry in your tackle-box—the K & K Animated Minnow.

$150 – 200

Actually **swims** with all the life-like movement of a real minnow. No lures, no spinners — simply an artificial minnow jointed to produce the genuine action and lively "wiggle." Rights itself in water **instantly.** When bass strikes, the minnow pulls away from the fish. Splendid for casting, or still fishing—stream or lake. **Sent prepaid** if your dealer doesn't handle it; bass size, **$1.00**; for large sea bass or muscalonge, **$1.50.** WRITE TO-DAY for catalog and order one to try.

K & K MFG. CO., 109 St. Clair St., TOLEDO, O.

OUTING MAGAZINE AD - JUNE - 1908

No. 857,883.

$50 – 75

J. D. KREISSER.
ARTIFICIAL MINNOW FISHING BAIT.
APPLICATION FILED JAN. 8, 1906.

Fig. 1.

This copy of the original patent shows two joints but none have been found. Patent was obviously on the "hinging detail".

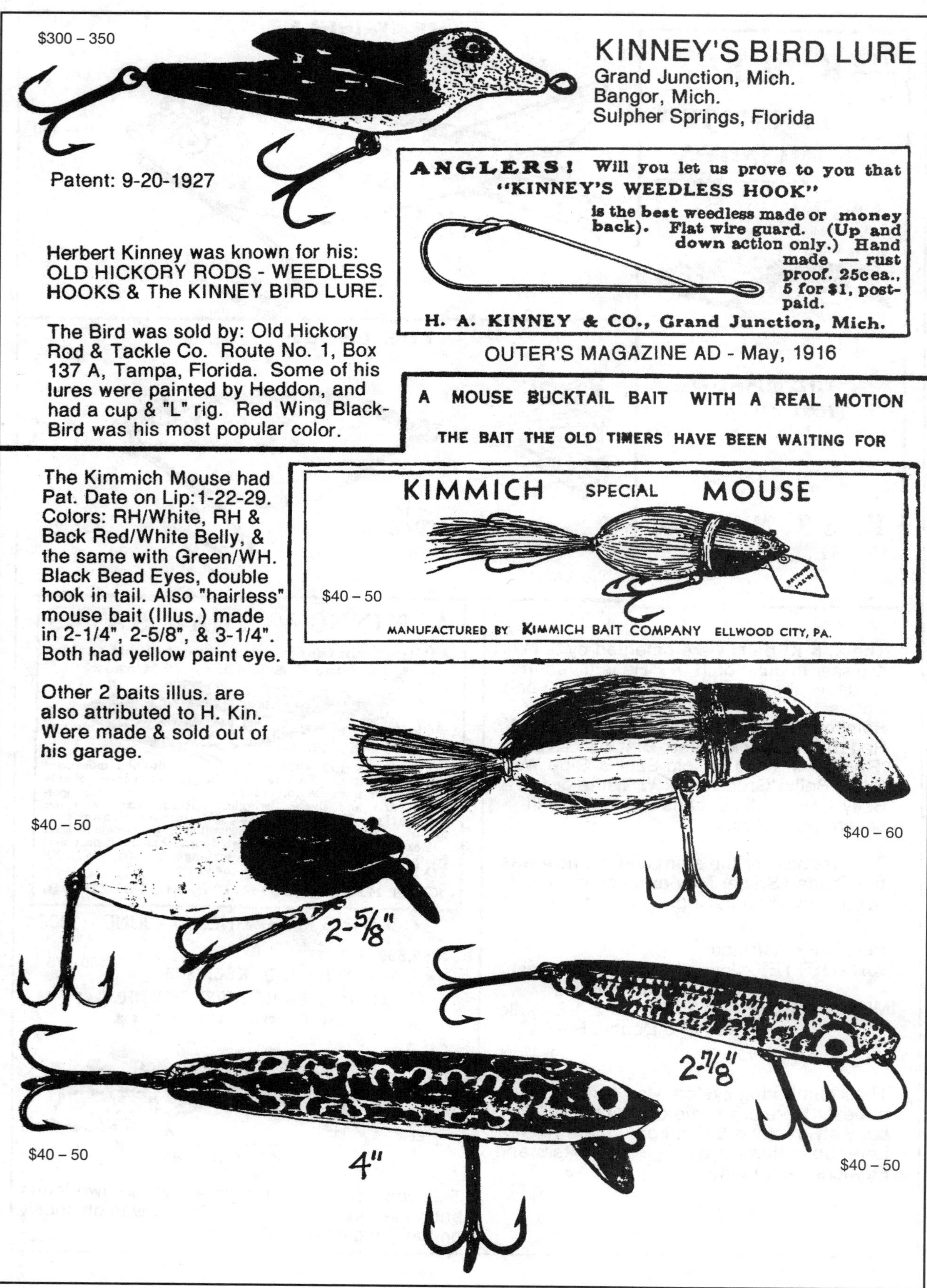
$300 – 350
KINNEY'S BIRD LURE
Grand Junction, Mich.
Bangor, Mich.
Sulpher Springs, Florida
Patent: 9-20-1927
ANGLERS! Will you let us prove to you that "KINNEY'S WEEDLESS HOOK" is the best weedless made or money back). Flat wire guard. (Up and down action only.) Hand made — rust proof. 25c ea., 5 for $1, post-paid.
H. A. KINNEY & CO., Grand Junction, Mich.
OUTER'S MAGAZINE AD - May, 1916
Herbert Kinney was known for his: OLD HICKORY RODS - WEEDLESS HOOKS & The KINNEY BIRD LURE.
The Bird was sold by: Old Hickory Rod & Tackle Co. Route No. 1, Box 137 A, Tampa, Florida. Some of his lures were painted by Heddon, and had a cup & "L" rig. Red Wing Black-Bird was his most popular color.
A MOUSE BUCKTAIL BAIT WITH A REAL MOTION
THE BAIT THE OLD TIMERS HAVE BEEN WAITING FOR
KIMMICH SPECIAL MOUSE
$40 – 50
MANUFACTURED BY KIMMICH BAIT COMPANY ELLWOOD CITY, PA.
The Kimmich Mouse had Pat. Date on Lip:1-22-29. Colors: RH/White, RH & Back Red/White Belly, & the same with Green/WH. Black Bead Eyes, double hook in tail. Also "hairless" mouse bait (Illus.) made in 2-1/4", 2-5/8", & 3-1/4". Both had yellow paint eye.
Other 2 baits illus. are also attributed to H. Kin. Were made & sold out of his garage.
$40 – 60
$40 – 50
2-5/8"
2-7/8"
$40 – 50
4"
$40 – 50

TRAIL-A-BAIT

THE COMPLETE LURE!

You can't miss with TRAIL-A-BAIT...the lure that has "built-in" every feature known to catch fish! PROVED sensational results in spinning, plugging, all lake and stream fishing.

Red, black, yellow, pink, green, grey
1/12 oz. $1.00
3/8 oz. $1.25

$10 – 20

- Luminous plastic body
- Balanced lip for fast action
- Flexible insect legs
- Channel for roe, eggs, cheese or odor lure
- Trailer attachment for bait or fly
- Belly ring for attaching added weight
- Use with large or small hooks

At your dealer or direct from

KRINGFISHER COMPANY, INC.
155 El Camino Real • Mountain View, California

FIELD & STREAM MARCH 1957

Plastic Bait - Hollow section on top for insertion of bait attractant/eggs, cheese

2 Sizes: Flyrod/Spinning and Bass.

THE KELLEY "FLIRT"

AT LAST A PERFECT PORK RIND LURE

Kelley Bait Company
915 Wilson Avenue
Chicago 40, Illinois

2 Sizes:
Bass Size
Muskie Size

This bait is different from most all Pork Rind Lures as it uses 2 Pork Strips which slip through the slots and snap on the buttons giving a two leg swimming action.

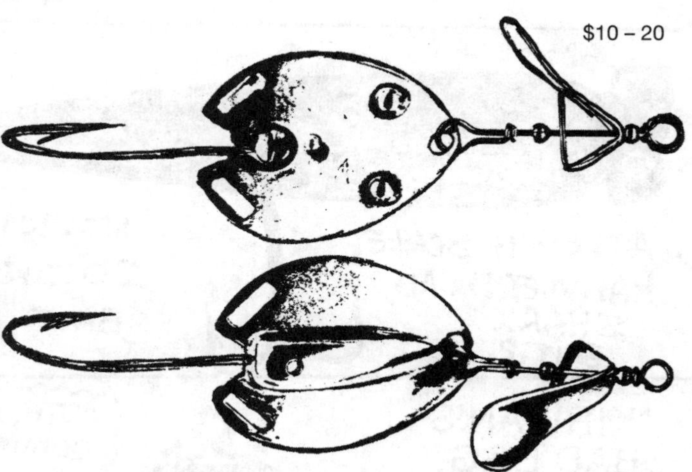

$10 – 20

Chautauqua Trolling Bait

A. J. Krantz and G. E. Smith
Jamestown, New York 3-1/2" (Pat. 8-31-1909)

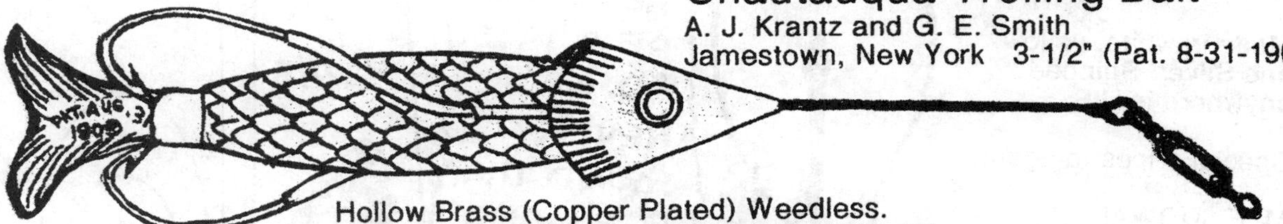

PAT. AUG. 3 1909

Hollow Brass (Copper Plated) Weedless.
Hooks are held inside the tail, when fish strikes they spring out. Scales, eyes, gills are stamped.

$2,000+

VERMILION MEADOW MOUSE

$40 – 60

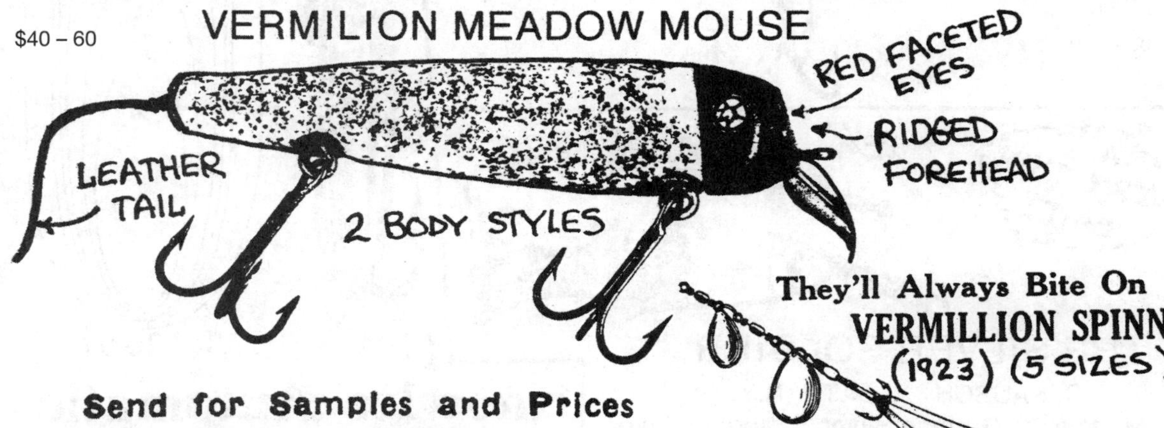
RED FACETED EYES
RIDGED FOREHEAD
LEATHER TAIL
2 BODY STYLES

They'll Always Bite On
VERMILLION SPINNERS
(1923) (5 SIZES)

Send for Samples and Prices

FRANK K. KNILL, Mfr.
Vermillion, Ohio

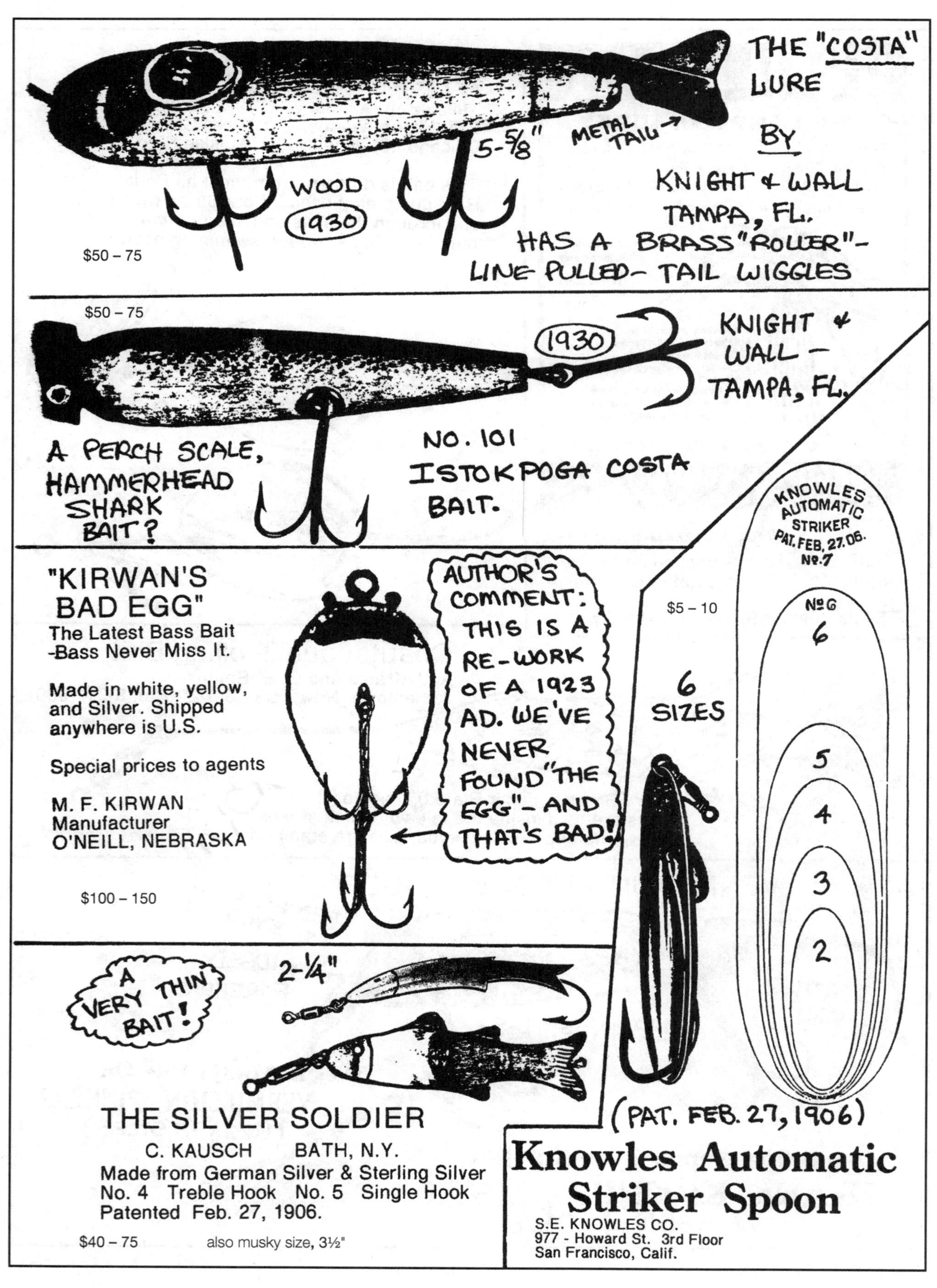
THE "COSTA" LURE
BY
KNIGHT & WALL
TAMPA, FL.
5-5/8"
METAL TAIL
WOOD
1930
HAS A BRASS "ROLLER" - LINE PULLED - TAIL WIGGLES
$50 – 75
$50 – 75
1930
KNIGHT & WALL - TAMPA, FL.
A PERCH SCALE, HAMMERHEAD SHARK BAIT?
NO. 101
ISTOKPOGA COSTA BAIT.
"KIRWAN'S BAD EGG"
The Latest Bass Bait -Bass Never Miss It.
Made in white, yellow, and Silver. Shipped anywhere is U.S.
Special prices to agents
M. F. KIRWAN
Manufacturer
O'NEILL, NEBRASKA
$100 – 150
AUTHOR'S COMMENT: THIS IS A RE-WORK OF A 1923 AD. WE'VE NEVER FOUND "THE EGG" - AND THAT'S BAD!
KNOWLES AUTOMATIC STRIKER PAT. FEB. 27.06. No.7
No 6
6
5
4
3
2
$5 – 10
6 SIZES
A VERY THIN BAIT!
2-1/4"
THE SILVER SOLDIER
C. KAUSCH BATH, N.Y.
Made from German Silver & Sterling Silver
No. 4 Treble Hook No. 5 Single Hook
Patented Feb. 27, 1906.
$40 – 75
also musky size, 3½"
(PAT. FEB. 27, 1906)
Knowles Automatic Striker Spoon
S.E. KNOWLES CO.
977 - Howard St. 3rd Floor
San Francisco, Calif.

$5 – 10

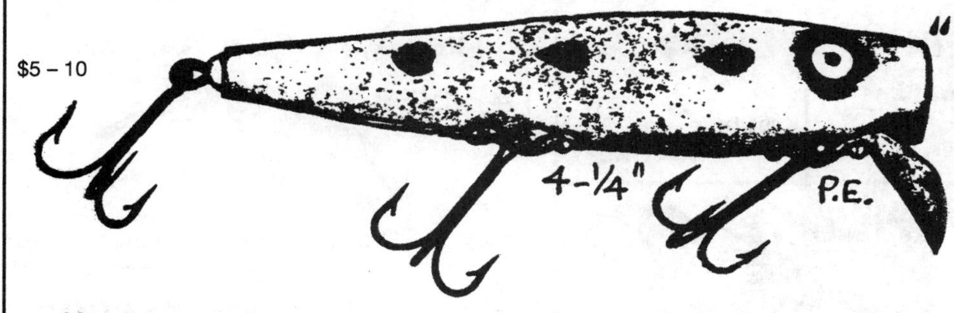
4-1/4"
P.E.

"K & M JET"
K & M TACKLE CO.
45 Lawrence Road
Salem Depot, N.H.

Six Colors;
Rainbow
X-Mas Tree
Silver Flash
Silver Scale
Blue Mullet
Frog

Mouth has an "intake" hole and water flows through and out the sides.
Moving Line Tie.

$10

2-1/2"
METAL CAP

WOOD

King Spiral Lure

KING SPIRAL CO.
1410 - W. WARREN AVE.
DETROIT, MICH.

INVENTOR:
L.J. ROSE

$5

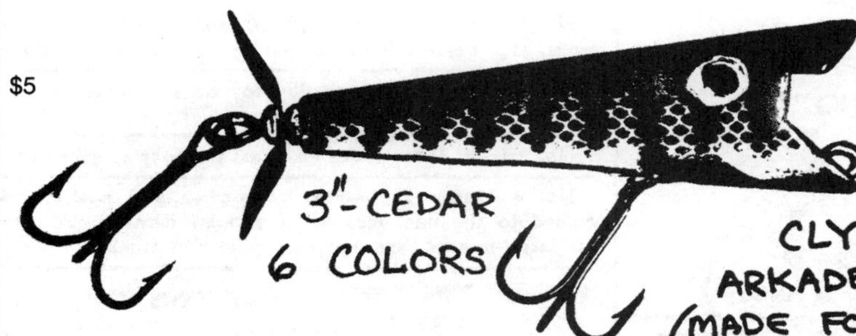
3"- CEDAR
6 COLORS

Glutton Dibbler

CLYDE E. KEY
ARKADELPHIA, ARKANSAS
(MADE FOR HIM BY A
GRASSY LAKE, MICHIGAN CO.)

$5

FISH GO FOR IT!
—so do fishermen
clear plastic spoon
with minnow
lamination.
Only the
minnow
shows
1946
Length
2½ in.
4 "
5 "
See Your
Dealer
PACIFIC ARROW MFG. CO.

3 SIZES:
2½"-4"-5"
237-YALE AVE. NO.
SEATTLE 9, WASH.

1932

S—SILVER
G—GOLD
B—BROWN
• 1-7/8"
• 3-1/2"
• 7"

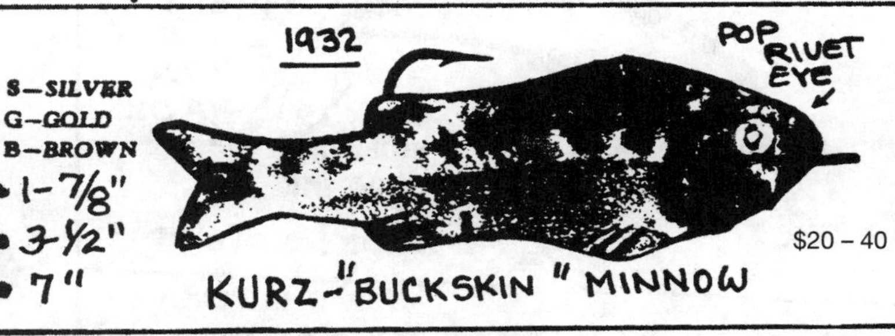
POP
RIVET
EYE

$20 – 40

KURZ-"BUCKSKIN" MINNOW

"Fish Call"

Keys & Jones
Manufacturing Co. LTD.
MOUNTAIN HOME, ARK.

$5 – 10

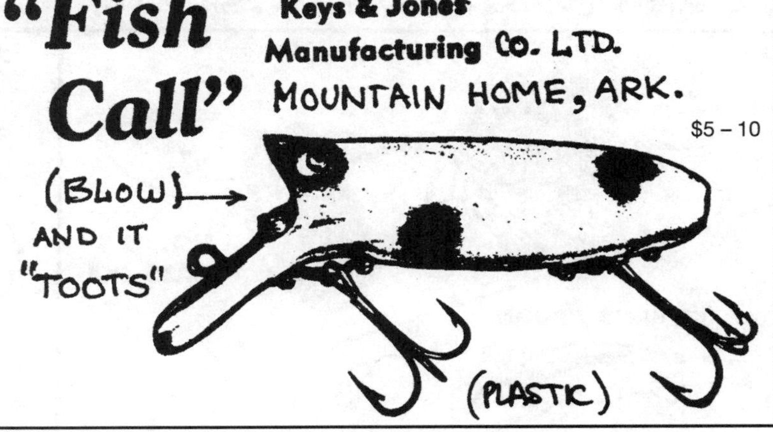
(BLOW)
AND IT
"TOOTS"
(PLASTIC)

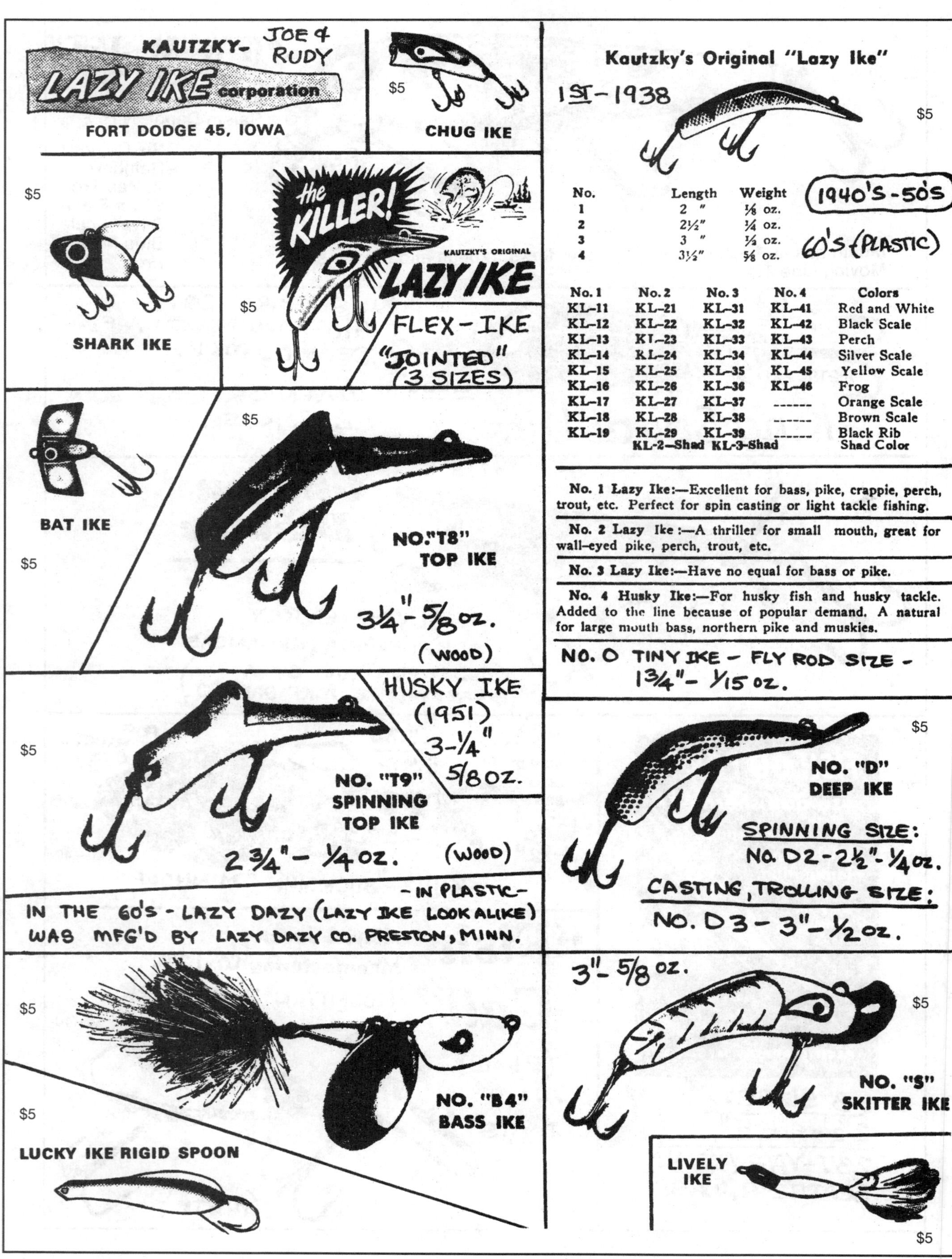
KAUTZKY- JOE & RUDY
LAZY IKE corporation
FORT DODGE 45, IOWA
$5
CHUG IKE
Kautzky's Original "Lazy Ike"
1ST-1938
$5
$5
SHARK IKE
the KILLER!
KAUTZKY'S ORIGINAL LAZY IKE
$5
FLEX-IKE "JOINTED" (3 SIZES)
No. Length Weight
1 2" 1/8 oz.
2 2½" 1/4 oz.
3 3" 1/2 oz.
4 3½" 5/8 oz.
1940'S-50'S
60'S (PLASTIC)
No. 1 No. 2 No. 3 No. 4 Colors
KL-11 KL-21 KL-31 KL-41 Red and White
KL-12 KL-22 KL-32 KL-42 Black Scale
KL-13 KL-23 KL-33 KL-43 Perch
KL-14 KL-24 KL-34 KL-44 Silver Scale
KL-15 KL-25 KL-35 KL-45 Yellow Scale
KL-16 KL-26 KL-36 KL-46 Frog
KL-17 KL-27 KL-37 ------ Orange Scale
KL-18 KL-28 KL-38 ------ Brown Scale
KL-19 KL-29 KL-39 ------ Black Rib
KL-2-Shad KL-3-Shad Shad Color
No. 1 Lazy Ike:—Excellent for bass, pike, crappie, perch, trout, etc. Perfect for spin casting or light tackle fishing.
No. 2 Lazy Ike:—A thriller for small mouth, great for wall-eyed pike, perch, trout, etc.
No. 3 Lazy Ike:—Have no equal for bass or pike.
No. 4 Husky Ike:—For husky fish and husky tackle. Added to the line because of popular demand. A natural for large mouth bass, northern pike and muskies.
NO. 0 TINY IKE - FLY ROD SIZE - 1¾"- 1/15 oz.
$5
BAT IKE
$5
NO. "T8" TOP IKE
3¼"-5/8 oz.
(WOOD)
HUSKY IKE (1951) 3-1/4" 5/8 oz.
$5
NO. "T9" SPINNING TOP IKE
2¾"-1/4 oz. (WOOD)
$5
NO. "D" DEEP IKE
SPINNING SIZE: NO. D2-2½"-1/4 oz.
CASTING, TROLLING SIZE: NO. D3-3"-1/2 oz.
- IN PLASTIC -
IN THE 60'S - LAZY DAZY (LAZY IKE LOOK ALIKE) WAS MFG'D BY LAZY DAZY CO. PRESTON, MINN.
3"-5/8 oz.
$5
$5
NO. "B4" BASS IKE
$5
NO. "S" SKITTER IKE
LUCKY IKE RIGID SPOON
LIVELY IKE
$5

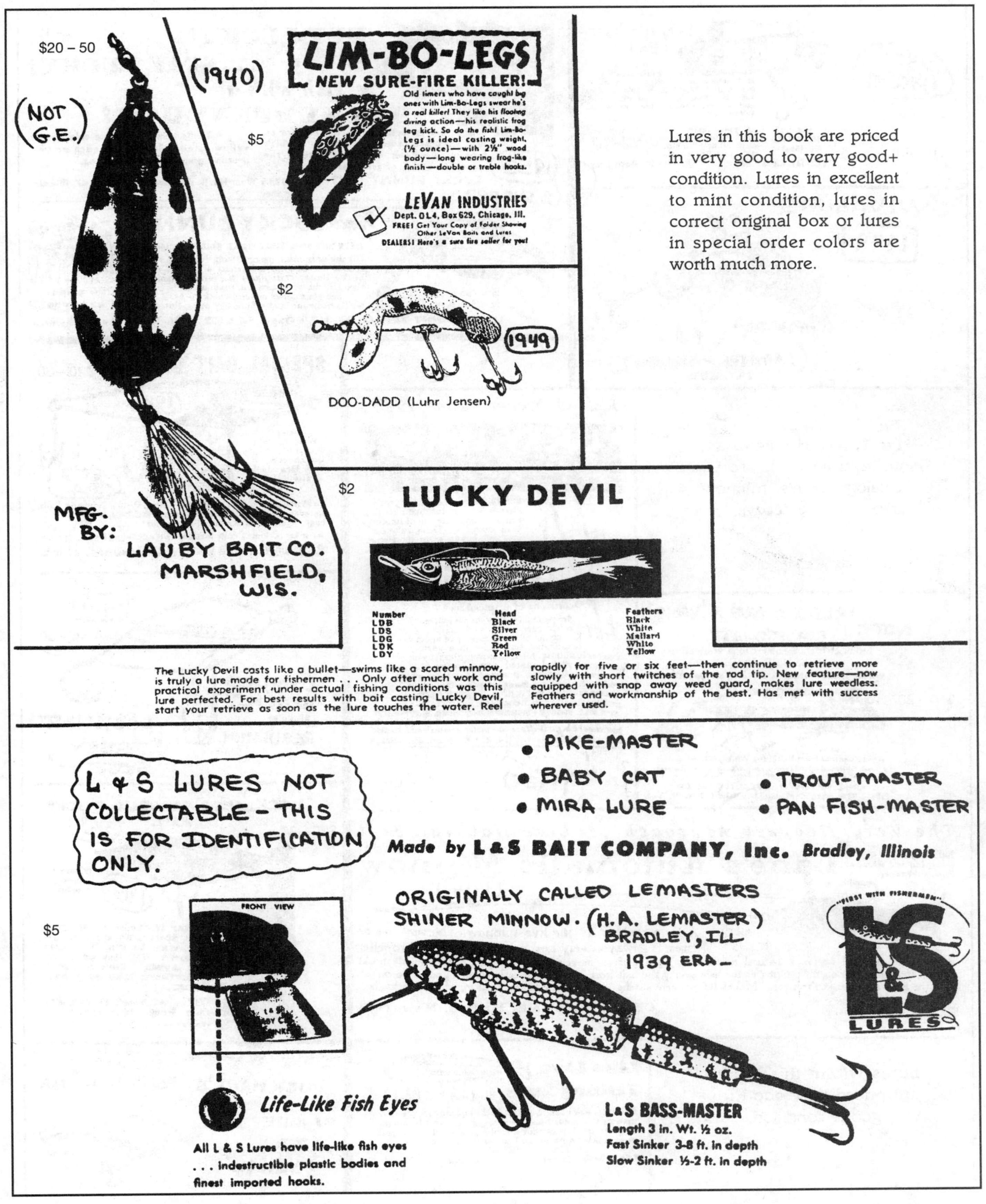
$20 – 50
(NOT G.E.)
(1940)
LIM-BO-LEGS
NEW SURE-FIRE KILLER!
Old timers who have caught big ones with Lim-Bo-Legs swear he's a real killer! They like his floating diving action—his realistic frog leg kick. So do the fish! Lim-Bo-Legs is ideal casting weight, (½ ounce)—with 2½" wood body—long wearing frog-like finish—double or treble hooks.
LeVAN INDUSTRIES
Dept. OL4, Box 629, Chicago, Ill.
FREE! Get Your Copy of Folder Showing Other LeVan Baits and Lures
DEALERS! Here's a sure fire seller for you!
$5
Lures in this book are priced in very good to very good+ condition. Lures in excellent to mint condition, lures in correct original box or lures in special order colors are worth much more.
$2
1949
DOO-DADD (Luhr Jensen)
MFG. BY: LAUBY BAIT CO. MARSHFIELD, WIS.
$2
LUCKY DEVIL
Number LDB LDS LDG LDK LDY
Head Black Silver Green Red Yellow
Feathers Black White Mallard White Yellow
The Lucky Devil casts like a bullet—swims like a scared minnow, is truly a lure made for fishermen . . . Only after much work and practical experiment under actual fishing conditions was this lure perfected. For best results with bait casting Lucky Devil, start your retrieve as soon as the lure touches the water. Reel rapidly for five or six feet—then continue to retrieve more slowly with short twitches of the rod tip. New feature—now equipped with snap away weed guard, makes lure weedless. Feathers and workmanship of the best. Has met with success wherever used.
L & S LURES NOT COLLECTABLE - THIS IS FOR IDENTIFICATION ONLY.
• PIKE-MASTER
• BABY CAT
• MIRA LURE
• TROUT-MASTER
• PAN FISH-MASTER
Made by L&S BAIT COMPANY, Inc. Bradley, Illinois
ORIGINALLY CALLED LEMASTERS SHINER MINNOW. (H.A. LEMASTER) BRADLEY, ILL 1939 ERA –
$5
FRONT VIEW
Life-Like Fish Eyes
All L & S Lures have life-like fish eyes . . . indestructible plastic bodies and finest imported hooks.
L&S BASS-MASTER
Length 3 in. Wt. ½ oz.
Fast Sinker 3-8 ft. in depth
Slow Sinker ½-2 ft. in depth
FIRST WITH FISHERMEN
L&S LURES

1921 PATENT

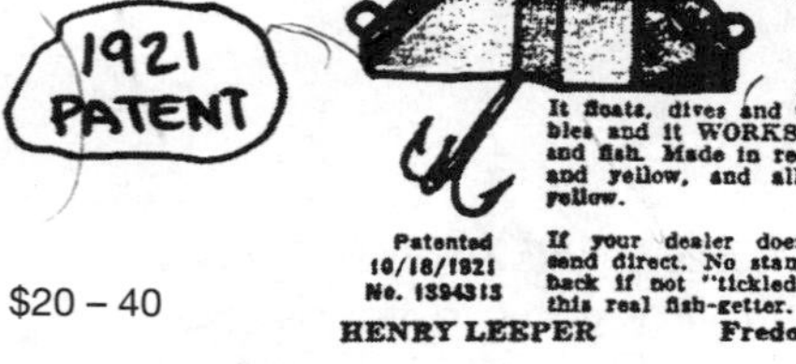

Leeper's Bass Bait

A Sure Fish Getter

It floats, dives and wiggles. It wobbles and it WORKS. It gets strikes and fish. Made in red and white, red and yellow, and all red, white or yellow.

If your dealer does not carry it, send direct. No stamps. Your money back if not "tickled to death" with this real fish-getter.

Patented 10/18/1921 No. 1394313

HENRY LEEPER   Fredonia, Kentucky

$20 – 40

GET LUCKY! ...STAY LUCKY!

Fish with a LUCKY BUNNY BAIT!

A new idea in lures...a deadly bait for all fish. An omen of luck—a genuine rabbit's foot with a hook. More life-like in the water than 99% of artificial lures.

• Tenite head. 3 flashing colors—red, yellow, green. Buy one of each at your sporting goods store. Wt. ½ oz.

LUCKY BUNNY BAIT CO., 3256 West North Avenue • Chicago 47, Illinois

$5 – 10

1953

(2 SIZES)

$5

***New* LUCKY BUNNY**

GETS BIG FISH THAT GRAB SMALL ANIMALS

It's the only spinning or casting lure with a real animal fur body. Made from a rabbit's foot. Lucky Bunny casts like a bullet and scampers through the water like a *live* rabbit.

See your dealer or send check or M.O. and we'll send your Lucky Bunny at once, Postpaid.

⅛ oz. Spinning . .
½ oz. Bait Casting

1,000 guides CAN'T be wrong!!!

LUCKY BUNNY BAIT COMPANY • Dept. F-74, 3256 W. North Ave., Chicago

SWIVALURE

1949

-PLASTIC-

(LAMOTHE-STOKES)

SWIVALURE

$10 – 20

SPECIAL BAIT OFFER $20 – 30

1914

Wobbler Wizard, one of Lockhart's WW Brand Baits

4¼"

To effectively introduce our line of Floating, Diving, Swimming Baits, we offer the above, having red breast and head, white body, yellow flutes or grooves, prepaid for ....

Write for booklet of baits that float, dive or swim at will of operator

E. J. LOCKHART, : Galesburg, Mich.

Pre-1950 tackle items are collectible reels, rods, catalogs, creels, minnow traps, and ice decoys.

Field & Stream—June, 1934

LUCKY LURES

Make 'em yourself

It's here! The chance you've always longed for! Add to the fun of fishing, the fun of making your own bait. Design the lure you've always wanted. Prove your skill and fishing knowledge with bait you've made yourself. ***Save Money.***

A COMPLETE KIT—Four Baits Postpaid

Containing materials and equipment for building an assortment of artificial bait.

Imagine!—You even get— several choice grained streamline cedar plugs; a supply of special fast-drying bait paint in a variety of colors including filler; life-like glass eyes; rust-proof nickel-plated gang hooks; lead shot for weighting; assorted sand paper, brushes, etc.—***and best of all***—elaborate working drawings suggesting designs for popular lures together with complete instructions.

IT'S ALL THERE—THERE'S NOTHING LEFT OUT

Send only • —we ship complete postpaid

You must be satisfied—or your money refunded

S. W. LAWRENCE, Dept. 1010, 221 N. LaSalle St., Chicago

(1934) $5 – 10

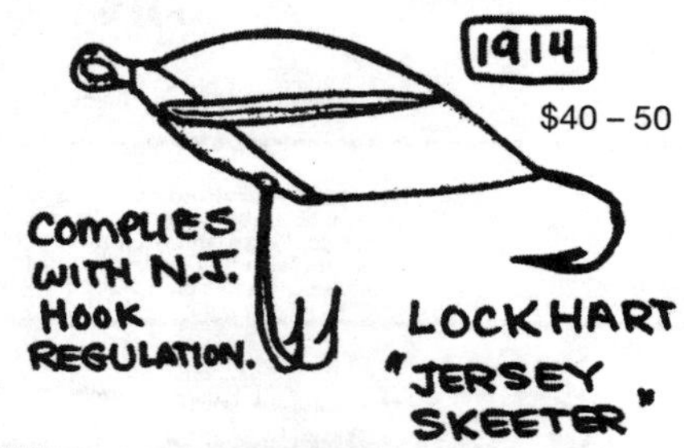

1914

$40 – 50

COMPLIES WITH N.J. HOOK REGULATION.

LOCKHART "JERSEY SKEETER"

NOTE: ALSO MADE A "VAMP"

FLASH-O-LITE finish, which means Light Reflection

FLASHER LURES which means natural motion, shape, color!

$10 – 20

BASS FLASHER No. 1 Red Head, White Body—

4 Fresh Water and 4 Salt Water types, available in six color combinations. At your dealer's, or order direct. Circular on request.

LONG ISLAND MANUFACTURING CO.
29-16 38th Ave., Dept. B, Long Island City, N. Y.

The Very Nearest Approach to Live Natural Bait

Pat. July 29, 1913. Canadian and other Patents pending.

Lane's Automatic Minnow

1914

A twin brother to the live minnow. Never dies or tires. Always lively and active. The tail propeller operates the pectoral fins in a natural manner, giving a perfect movement to the bait. The double hooks release and swing free on the striking of the fish, saving the bait from injury. Perfectly colored and proportioned, gets the big wary ones you're after. Makes 100 per cent catches. You'll find it the treasure of your tackle box.

CHAS. W. LANE, Madrid, New York

$250 – 300

LOCKHART'S "WAGTAIL WITCH" BAIT.

$20 – 30

3½"

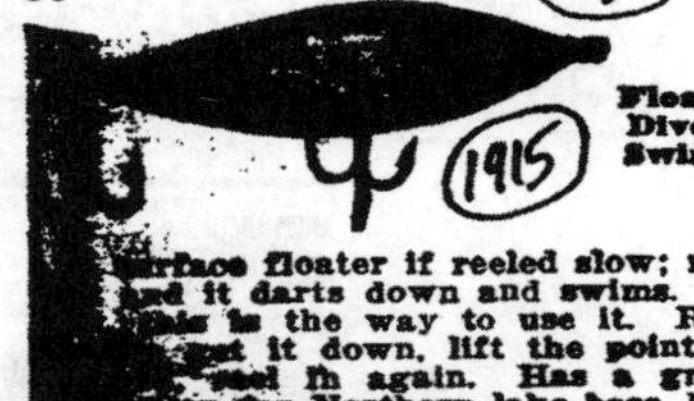

Floats Dives Swims

1915

...rface floater if reeled slow; reel ...d it darts down and swims. In ... is the way to use it. Reel ... it down, lift the point of ... reel in again. Has a great ... for Northern lake bass, bait ... trolling.

...—White with red throat, 3½ ... inches long, two treble ....

Lures within this book are priced very good to very good+ condition.

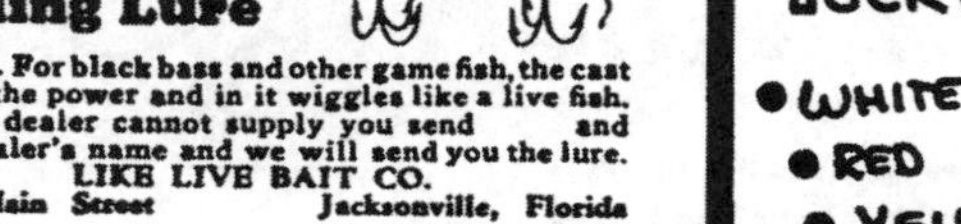

Like Live Fishing Lure

It floats. For black bass and other game fish, the cast throws the power and in it wiggles like a live fish. If your dealer cannot supply you send and your dealer's name and we will send you the lure.

LIKE LIVE BAIT CO.
1643 Main Street   Jacksonville, Florida

$10 – 15

$20 – 30

LOCKHART'S "POLLYWOG" BA...

• WHITE
• RED
• YELLOW

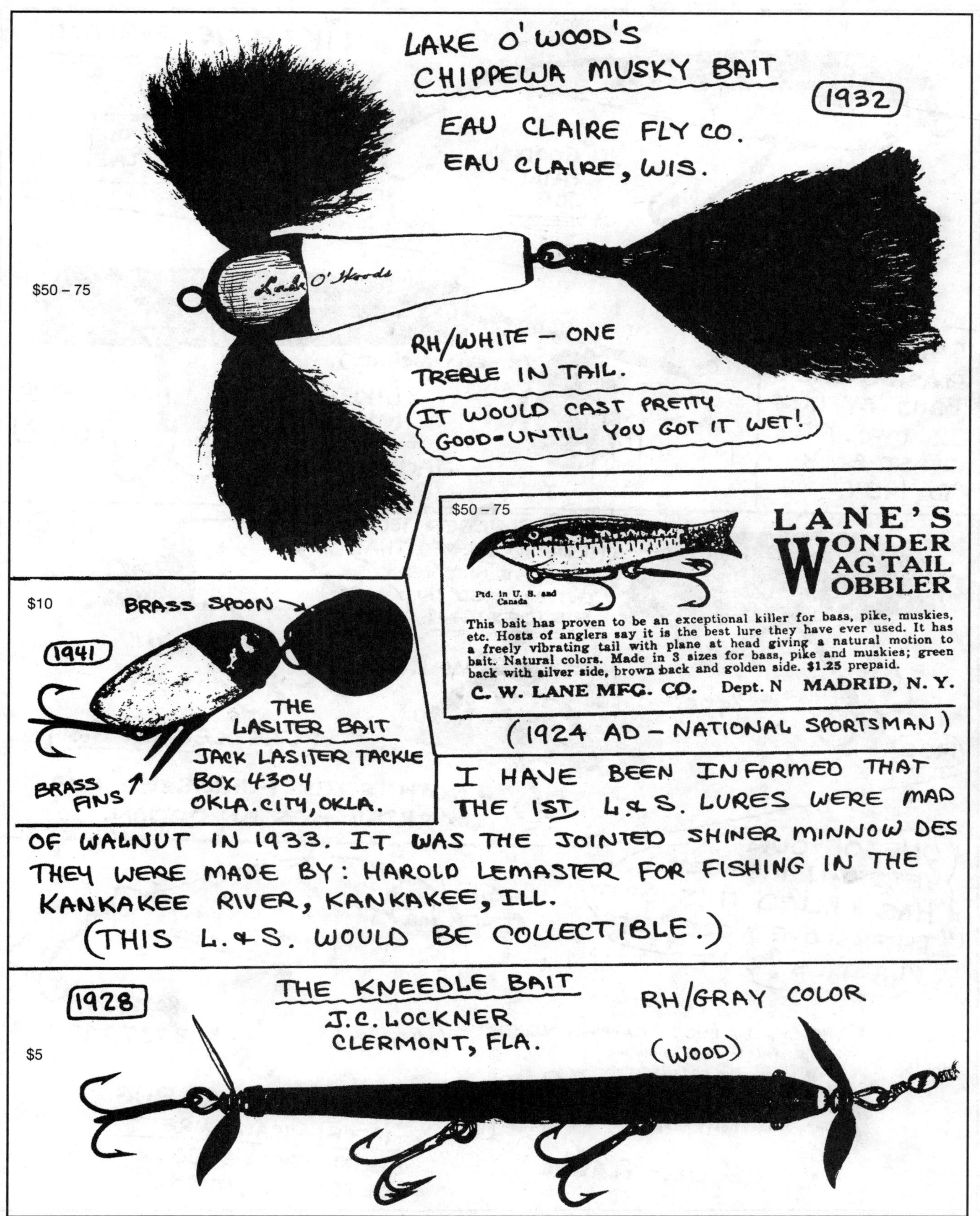
LAKE O' WOOD'S
CHIPPEWA MUSKY BAIT
1932
EAU CLAIRE FLY CO.
EAU CLAIRE, WIS.
Lake O'Woods
$50 – 75
RH/WHITE – ONE
TREBLE IN TAIL.
IT WOULD CAST PRETTY
GOOD – UNTIL YOU GOT IT WET!
$50 – 75
LANE'S
WONDER
WAGTAIL
WOBBLER
Ptd. in U. S. and Canada
This bait has proven to be an exceptional killer for bass, pike, muskies, etc. Hosts of anglers say it is the best lure they have ever used. It has a freely vibrating tail with plane at head giving a natural motion to bait. Natural colors. Made in 3 sizes for bass, pike and muskies; green back with silver side, brown back and golden side. $1.25 prepaid.
C. W. LANE MFG. CO. Dept. N MADRID, N. Y.
(1924 AD – NATIONAL SPORTSMAN)
$10
BRASS SPOON
1941
THE
LASITER BAIT
JACK LASITER TACKLE
BOX 4304
OKLA. CITY, OKLA.
BRASS
FINS
I HAVE BEEN INFORMED THAT
THE 1ST L.&S. LURES WERE MAD
OF WALNUT IN 1933. IT WAS THE JOINTED SHINER MINNOW DES
THEY WERE MADE BY: HAROLD LEMASTER FOR FISHING IN THE
KANKAKEE RIVER, KANKAKEE, ILL.
(THIS L.&S. WOULD BE COLLECTIBLE.)
1928
THE KNEEDLE BAIT
J.C. LOCKNER
CLERMONT, FLA.
RH/GRAY COLOR
(WOOD)
$5

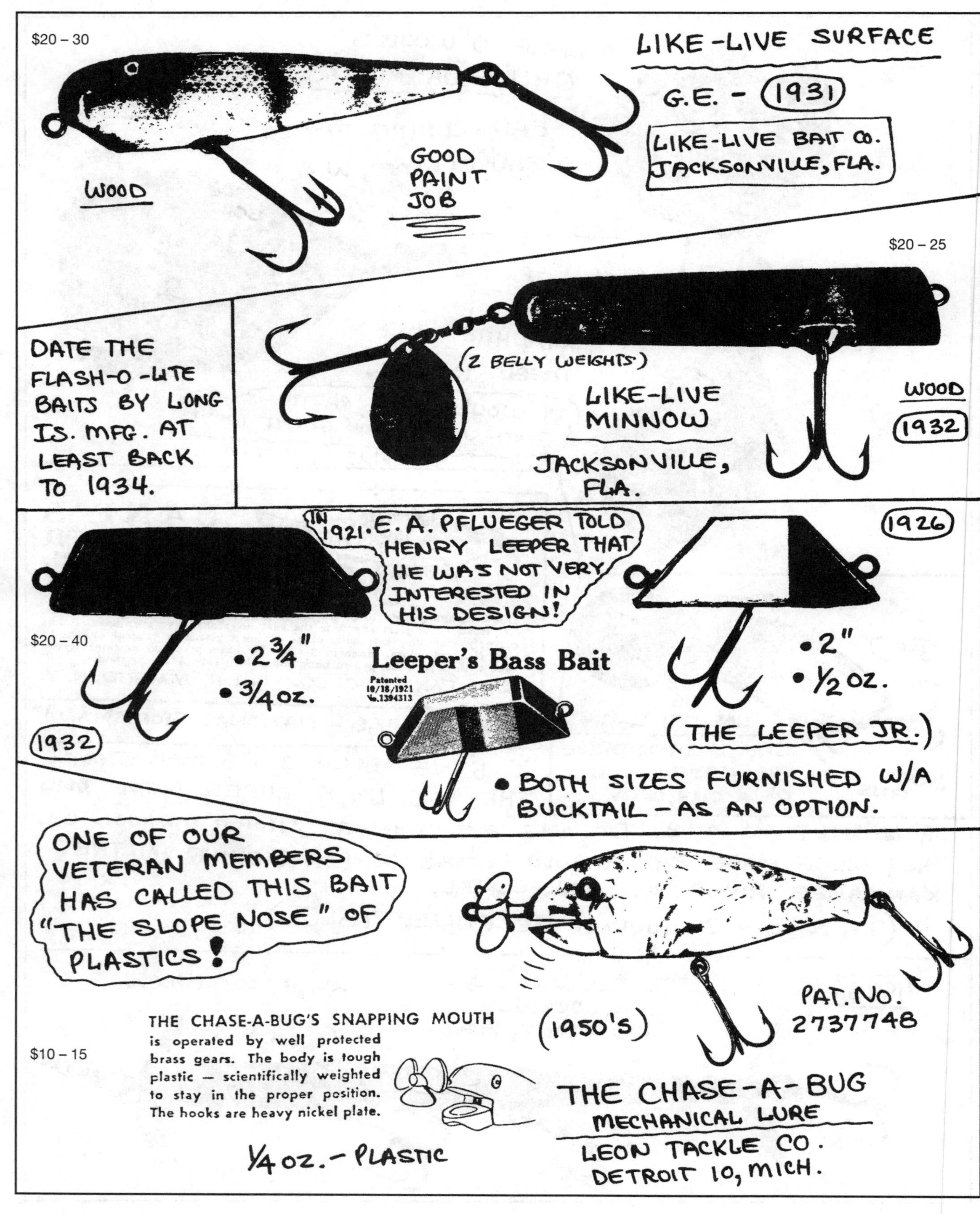

$20 – 30
LIKE-LIVE SURFACE
G.E. - 1931
LIKE-LIVE BAIT CO.
JACKSONVILLE, FLA.
GOOD PAINT JOB
WOOD
$20 – 25
DATE THE FLASH-O-LITE BAITS BY LONG IS. MFG. AT LEAST BACK TO 1934.
(2 BELLY WEIGHTS)
LIKE-LIVE MINNOW
JACKSONVILLE, FLA.
WOOD
1932
IN 1921, E.A. PFLUEGER TOLD HENRY LEEPER THAT HE WAS NOT VERY INTERESTED IN HIS DESIGN!
1926
$20 – 40
• 2 3/4"
• 3/4 OZ.
Leeper's Bass Bait
Patented 10/18/1921 No.1394313
• 2"
• 1/2 OZ.
1932
(THE LEEPER JR.)
• BOTH SIZES FURNISHED W/A BUCKTAIL - AS AN OPTION.
ONE OF OUR VETERAN MEMBERS HAS CALLED THIS BAIT "THE SLOPE NOSE" OF PLASTICS!
PAT. NO. 2737748
(1950'S)
THE CHASE-A-BUG'S SNAPPING MOUTH is operated by well protected brass gears. The body is tough plastic — scientifically weighted to stay in the proper position. The hooks are heavy nickel plate.
$10 – 15
THE CHASE-A-BUG
MECHANICAL LURE
LEON TACKLE CO.
DETROIT 10, MICH.
1/4 OZ. - PLASTIC

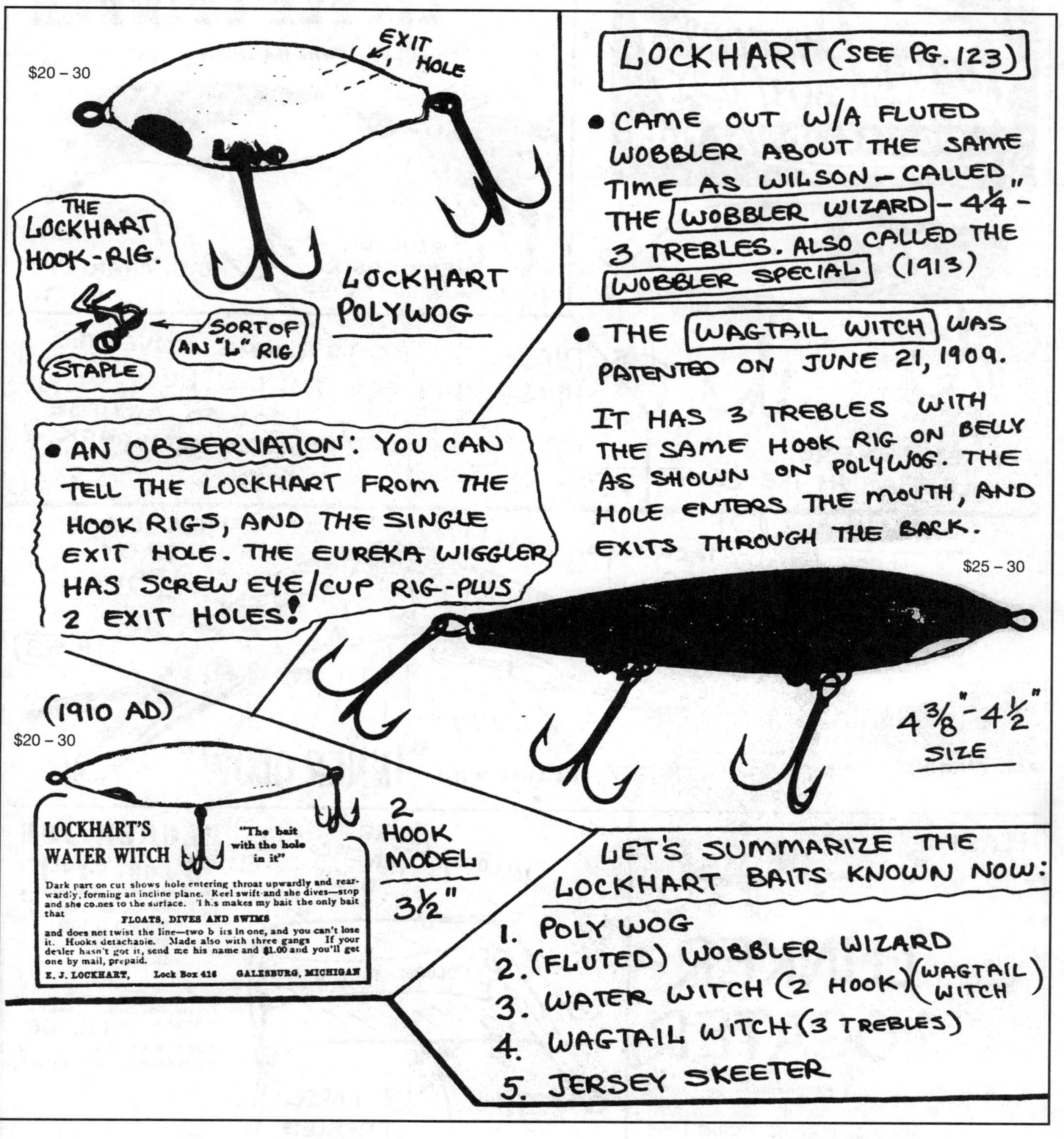
$20 – 30
EXIT HOLE
LEAD
THE LOCKHART HOOK-RIG.
SORT OF AN "L" RIG
STAPLE
LOCKHART POLYWOG
LOCKHART (SEE PG. 123)
• CAME OUT W/A FLUTED WOBBLER ABOUT THE SAME TIME AS WILSON – CALLED THE WOBBLER WIZARD – 4¼" – 3 TREBLES. ALSO CALLED THE WOBBLER SPECIAL (1913)
• AN OBSERVATION: YOU CAN TELL THE LOCKHART FROM THE HOOK RIGS, AND THE SINGLE EXIT HOLE. THE EUREKA WIGGLER HAS SCREW EYE/CUP RIG-PLUS 2 EXIT HOLES!
• THE WAGTAIL WITCH WAS PATENTED ON JUNE 21, 1909.
IT HAS 3 TREBLES WITH THE SAME HOOK RIG ON BELLY AS SHOWN ON POLYWOG. THE HOLE ENTERS THE MOUTH, AND EXITS THROUGH THE BACK.
$25 – 30
4⅜"-4½" SIZE
(1910 AD)
$20 – 30
LOCKHART'S WATER WITCH
"The bait with the hole in it"
Dark part on cut shows hole entering throat upwardly and rearwardly, forming an incline plane. Keel swift and she dives—stop and she comes to the surface. This makes my bait the only bait that
FLOATS, DIVES AND SWIMS
and does not twist the line—two baits in one, and you can't lose it. Hooks detachable. Made also with three gangs If your dealer hasn't got it, send me his name and $1.00 and you'll get one by mail, prepaid.
E. J. LOCKHART, Lock Box 416 GALESBURG, MICHIGAN
2 HOOK MODEL
3½"
LET'S SUMMARIZE THE LOCKHART BAITS KNOWN NOW:
1. POLY WOG
2. (FLUTED) WOBBLER WIZARD
3. WATER WITCH (2 HOOK) (WAGTAIL WITCH)
4. WAGTAIL WITCH (3 TREBLES)
5. JERSEY SKEETER

Fancy-Dancer
OH BOY!
ACTION! ACTION! ACTION!

$10

• WOOD
• EMBOSSED EYE
• HOLE THROUGH THE BODY

We Call It a

LITTLE STINKER

"With the Built-in Wiggle"

$10

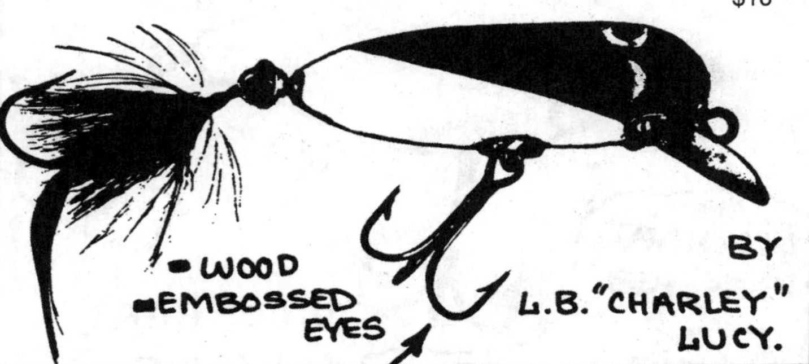
• WOOD
• EMBOSSED EYES
BY
L.B. "CHARLEY" LUCY.

THESE 2 BAITS WERE INVENTED 1948 – 1949 ERA BY: L.B. LUCY
1001 - SO. MONROE
LITTLE ROCK, ARK.

$5

MFG'D. BY:
LUCKY LADY TACKLE CO.
130 N. AVE. 50
LOS ANGELES 42, CALIF.
(PLASTIC)
THE LUCKY LADY BAIT
1953
WEIGHTS
1/10 oz. flyrod ......
1/8 oz. fly-spin .....
1/5 oz. spin ....
1/4 oz. spin-bait cast
5/8 oz. bait cast-troll
PAT. PENDING
THE LURE WITH "INNER GLOW"

• PLASTIC
• 3"

$5

LUNKER-LOCATER

PAT. PEND.

NEW ALL - PURPOSE FISHING LURE

LASSITER LURE COMPANY
Box 1082, Bryan, Texas

$5 – 10

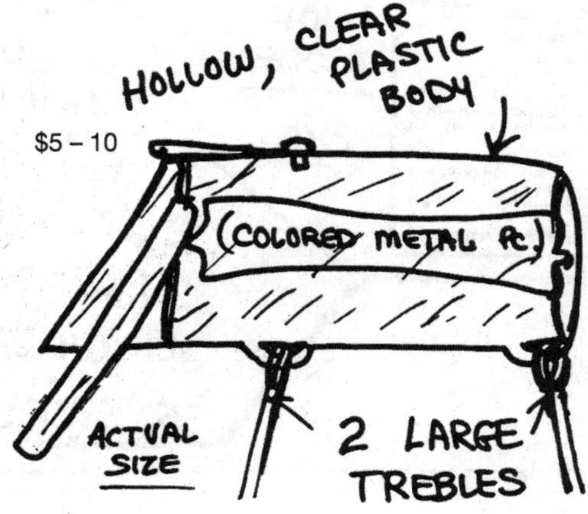
HOLLOW, CLEAR PLASTIC BODY
(COLORED METAL PC.)
ACTUAL SIZE
2 LARGE TREBLES

PLUGER JOE

3 LURES-IN-1

The most amazing fish-getter on the market. Each Pluger Joe has three interchangeable spinners.

• RED AND YELLOW
• RED AND WHITE
• SILVER

If your dealer cannot supply you order direct . . . today!

LYNX MFG. CO.
1689 PICCADILLY ROAD
PHOENIX, ARIZONA

5/8 oz.

$5

BASS
BITE on
KENTUCKY
LEADER LURES

Handmade, ¼ ounce wood plugs.
Casting or spin size.

Spin Lure — Casting Lure

Choice of white, yellow or green basic colors.

Send check or money order only. COD's accepted. Money back guarantee.

LEX BAITS
P. O. BOX 813
LOUISVILLE 1, KY.

1955

$15

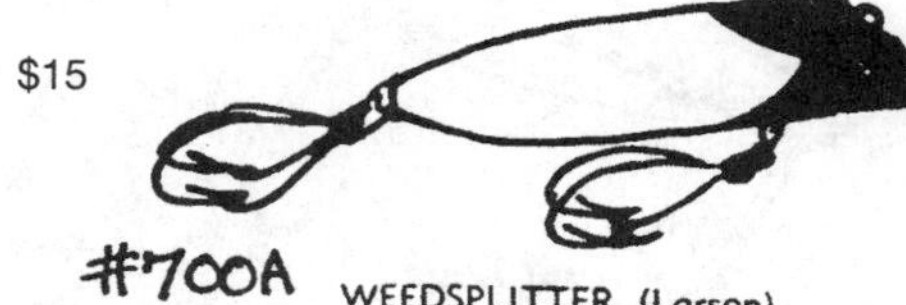

#700A WEEDSPLITTER (Larson)

LARSON BAIT CO.
AITKIN, MN.
ALSO MADE THE
FISHTRAP SPOON

Lure prices are based on condition, color, age, and desirability. Prices vary from place to place. Collectors value lures differently.

NEW LIGHTED PIRATE

Gets the Big Ones when other baits fail

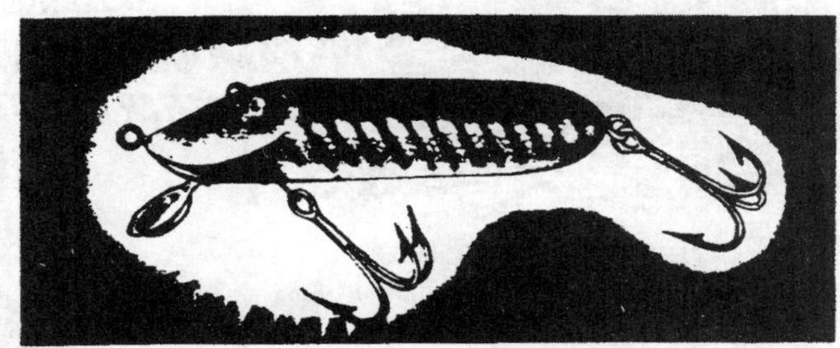

$10 – 15

Adds Extra Fishing Hours

Here is another **MUST** for your tackle box . . . a remarkably efficient lure that will stretch out the fishing hours of your vacation and bring results where other baits would be useless!

Once you use the new LIGHTED PIRATE you will know why it has won the enthusiastic endorsement of veteran sportsmen everywhere. One glance will tell you why fish simply can't resist its dazzling allure. . it's natural body action.

The new LIGHTED PIRATE is a colorful, hollowed, artificial minnow with illuminated red head. Made of transparent, durable Pryalin. Contains easily renewable pencil battery and bulb. Yet amazingly light in weight.

Picture the extra hours of fishing pleasure that will be yours earlier in the morning and later in the evening with the new LIGHTED PIRATE: Ideal for murky waters, on dark days and in early morning or late evening fishing, this unique bait will enable you to go after the big ones at a time of the day when the fish are striking the best!

Order yours today and thrill to its marvelous performance! You'll find the new LIGHTED PIRATE worth many times its low cost in the extra hours of fishing pleasure and better results it gives you!

LLOYD & CO. 3406 NORTH LINCOLN AVENUE, CHICAGO, ILLINOIS

$75 – 100

1939

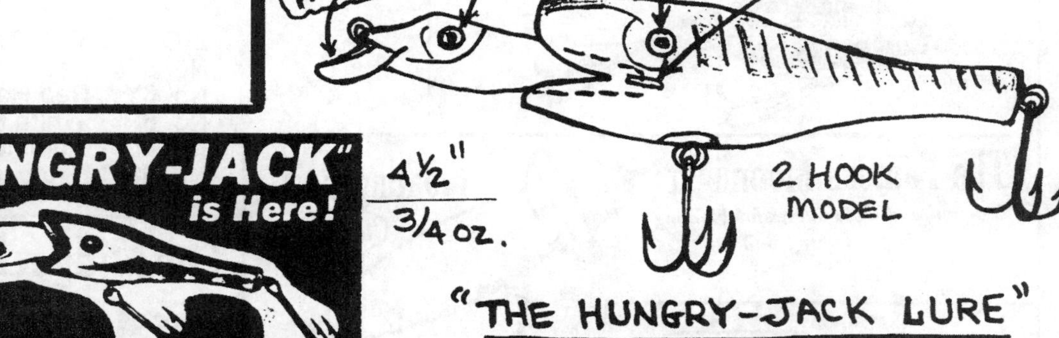
PAW PAW TYPE LIP
GLASS EYES
HINGED
"HUNGRY-JACK"
is Here!
4½"
3/4 OZ.
2 HOOK MODEL

"THE HUNGRY-JACK LURE"

IMPORTANT!

Simulate the action of one fish swallowing another by wiggling rod tip at intervals. This gives Hungry-Jack a gulping effect which arouses observing fish to action and will increase your catch. Write us your experiences. Best letter each week wins a LLOYD Lighted Pirate Lure free.

LLOYD & CO.

IF THIS LURE WAS STILL MADE— IT COULD BE SOLD BY "JACK-IN-THE-BOX REST.

1988 NOTE – 1 OF THEIR ADS SHOWS A 3-HOOKER MODEL WITH THE 3rd TREBLE IN SMALL FRONT MINNOW. (MAY-1939)

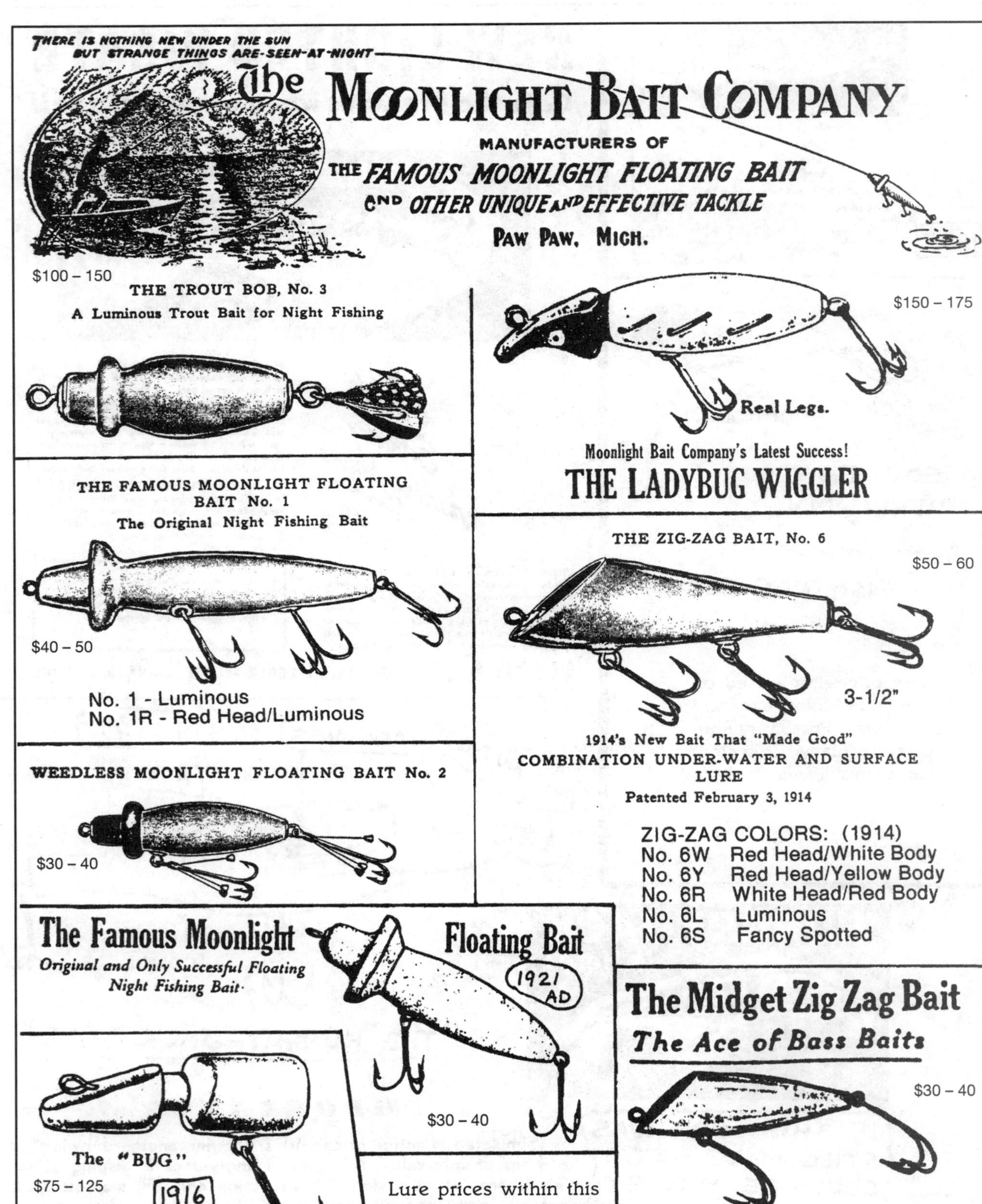
THERE IS NOTHING NEW UNDER THE SUN BUT STRANGE THINGS ARE-SEEN-AT-NIGHT
The MOONLIGHT BAIT COMPANY
MANUFACTURERS OF
THE FAMOUS MOONLIGHT FLOATING BAIT
AND OTHER UNIQUE AND EFFECTIVE TACKLE
PAW PAW, MICH.
$100 – 150
THE TROUT BOB, No. 3
A Luminous Trout Bait for Night Fishing
$150 – 175
Real Legs.
Moonlight Bait Company's Latest Success!
THE LADYBUG WIGGLER
THE FAMOUS MOONLIGHT FLOATING BAIT No. 1
The Original Night Fishing Bait
$40 – 50
No. 1 - Luminous
No. 1R - Red Head/Luminous
THE ZIG-ZAG BAIT, No. 6
$50 – 60
3-1/2"
1914's New Bait That "Made Good"
COMBINATION UNDER-WATER AND SURFACE LURE
Patented February 3, 1914
ZIG-ZAG COLORS: (1914)
No. 6W Red Head/White Body
No. 6Y Red Head/Yellow Body
No. 6R White Head/Red Body
No. 6L Luminous
No. 6S Fancy Spotted
WEEDLESS MOONLIGHT FLOATING BAIT No. 2
$30 – 40
The Famous Moonlight Floating Bait
Original and Only Successful Floating Night Fishing Bait
1921 AD
$30 – 40
The "BUG"
$75 – 125
1916
Lure prices within this book are for very good to very good+ condition.
The Midget Zig Zag Bait
The Ace of Bass Baits
$30 – 40
The "Wonder Bait" of 1921. (2-1/2")
Red, White, Yellow, Rainbow, Lum.
No tackle box complete without both.

$75 – 100

PAW PAW FISH SPEAR, No. 5

Combination Under-water and Surface Lure.
A "TWO-IN-ONE WIGGLER"

FISH SPEAR COLORS: (1914)
No. 5W Red Head/White
No. 5Y Red Head/Yellow
No. 5R White Head/Red
No. 5S Fancy Spotted

$100 – 125

MOONLIGHT

LADY BUG WIGGLER

No. M 800 Series 2-1/2" (1928)
M 801 Yellow Wings, Black Spots
M 803 Green Wings, White Spots
M 804 Red Wings, Black Spots
M 810 Black Wings, Red Spots
M 811 Black Wings, Yellow Spots

$40 –

Little Wonder
2100 Series
LITTLE WONDER

No. M 200 Series 3" (1920's)
M 213 Green Scale
M 214 Red Head/ White Body
M 217 Gold Scale

Also musky size, see p. 31.

$40 – 50

TROUT—EAT US

A very Attractive Fly Rod Lure; Wood Body with One Double Hook; Weight Each, 1/6 oz.; Weight per Dozen, 5/6 lb.

—Trout-Eat-Us
500 Series—

Nos.	Color
M53	Green Scale
M54	White Body, Red Head
M57	Gold Scale

Paw Paw Folding Boat Chair

$25 – 50

No fishing outfit is complete without the PAW PAW FOLDING BOAT CHAIR. It can be instantly attached to any boat seat and will last a lifetime. Easily taken apart and folds into a small space.
The chair is made of round steel frame, handsomely japanned. Seat and back trimmed with good grade of imitation leather, and is practically indestructible.

When used in connection with "MOONLIGHT" Brand Baits, you are assured of "all there is in fishing."

Authors comment: This would be one great piece to add to any Moonlight Collection!

The Moonlight Bait Company
Paw Paw, Michigan

The "1913 Special"

FOR UNDER WATER FISHING

$100 – 150

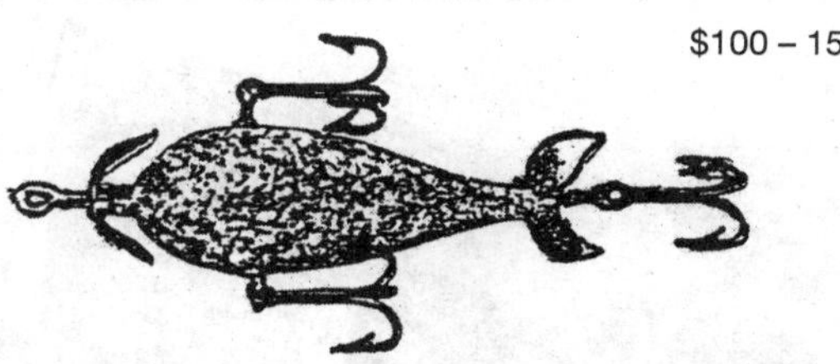

A very unique and attractive lure for under water fishing. It is made in correct casting weight and is fitted with forward and rear spinners and three treble hooks. Our specially prepared water proof coating gives it a sparkling effect when under water.

This bait was thoroughly tried out during 1912, and the result was such that we are making a special feature of the bait for 1913. To insure a "catch"be sure to have the "1913 Special" included in your tackle.

Light Bait Casting Feather Minnow

$75 – 100

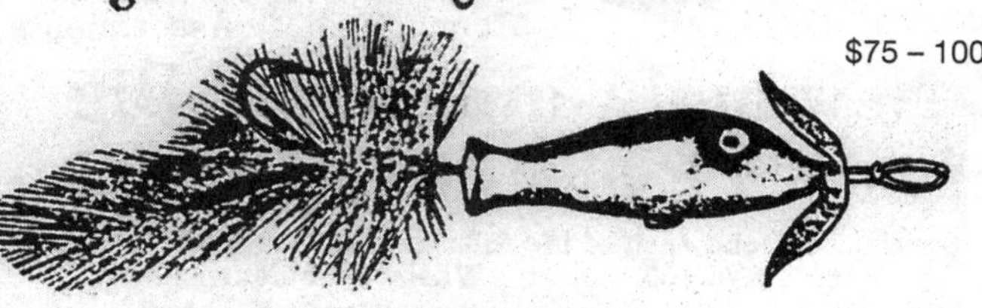

No. 1400 Series (1920 - 1926) 1-3/4"
Solid Colors with eye shadow detail
White - Red - Yellow - Gray - Orange - Brown

Moonlight Bait
1920's BOX

The Original Moonlight

Always Gets Fish

$150 – 200

No. 1200 Series

Casting Baits

$100 – 150

No. 1100 Series

These 2 Baits were in 1924 Catalog -They look like Underwaters, but the catalog said they were "floaters" and suggested a Dipsey sinker up the line about 6" for underwater use.

Colors: 01 - Yellow, 02 - Rainbow, 03 - Moss Back, 04 - White Body/Red Stripes, 06 - White Body/Black Stripes 07 - Yellow Body/Black Stripes, 08 - All White, 09 - Yellow Perch, 10 - Horned Ace

Author's comment: I found a 5 hooker in Seattle. The props were N.O.P. Heddon Dowagiac. What does that tell us?

$500+

PAW PAW PEARL WOBBLER, No. 7

2-3/4" $40 – 60

Several Bait Makers put out "Six-Paks" of their best selling lures. They make a great centerpiece for any collection. Illustrated are 5 different Paks that Moonlight made.

SILVER CREEK ASSORTMENT NO. 550
Best and Most Up-to-date Line of Bass Baits on the Market. The very latest models and popular priced

Moonlight Bait Assortments

New and Going Over Big Everywhere!

Special Six—one each of the following series: 2600, 1000, 600, 100, 50, and Wilson Wobbler....

Weedless Assortment—a selection of 99% Weedless Lures..............................

Bass Seeker Assortment—contains three of most popular colors in each of the two sizes...

2900 Series—real fish getters—one of each color.

Moonlight Brand Baits

$500+

The Moonlight Bait & Novelty Works

PAW PAW MICHIGAN

Canadian Representative

United Distributors, Ltd., Montreal, Que.

Most of the literature on Moonlight indicate a start-up of 1909. A 1915 catalog stated that they had been in business for "about 8 years" so 1915 - 8 = 1907, but I think they were referring to baits being made and sold just locally for those 2 years. The formal start of Moonlight Bait Company was the signing of an agreement on December 30, 1908 by the two principals, Horace E. Ball and Charles E. Varney. Varney provided funds and Ball was the Maker/Inventor. The Moonlight factory was located in the basement of the local court house where Ball was the janitor.

In the 1923 era, Moonlight absorbed another local bait maker - "The Silver Creek Novelty Works". They were the original makers of the PIKAROON, POLY WOG and SILVER CREEK WIGGLER. Schoenfeld- Gutter of New York were also marketing their baits under their tradename - SEA GULL. These baits can be identified by their use of just a screw eye hook rig, and most had glass eyes.

The Early Moonlight lures had regular metal cup hook rigs. Painted cups came with the change over to the Paw Paw Bait Co. who used Painted Cups.

The PIKAROON Baits had upturned noses. The POLLY-WOG baits had the fat throats and straight noses. The rarest Polly-wog had a "notched" mouth detail.

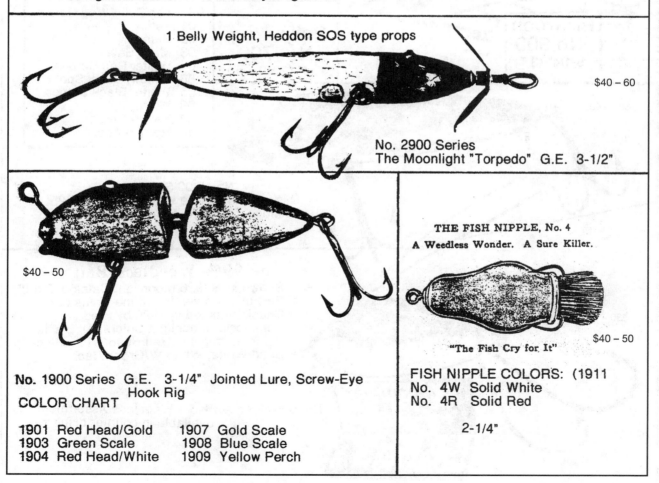

1 Belly Weight, Heddon SOS type props

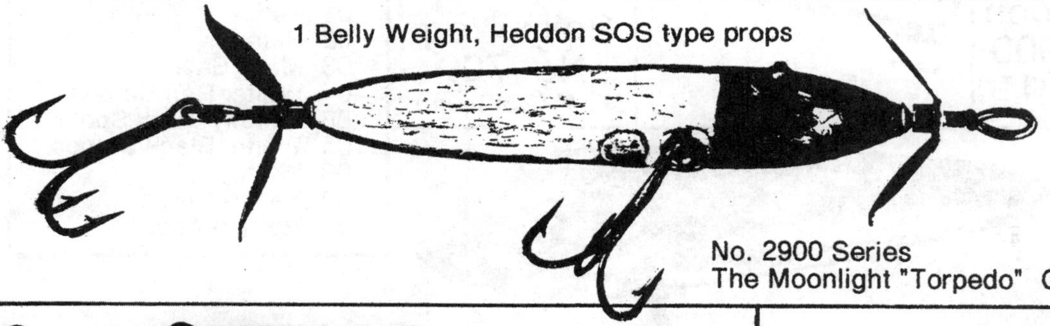

$40 – 60

No. 2900 Series
The Moonlight "Torpedo" G.E. 3-1/2"

$40 – 50

No. 1900 Series G.E. 3-1/4" Jointed Lure, Screw-Eye Hook Rig

COLOR CHART

1901 Red Head/Gold
1903 Green Scale
1904 Red Head/White
1907 Gold Scale
1908 Blue Scale
1909 Yellow Perch

THE FISH NIPPLE, No. 4
A Weedless Wonder. A Sure Killer.

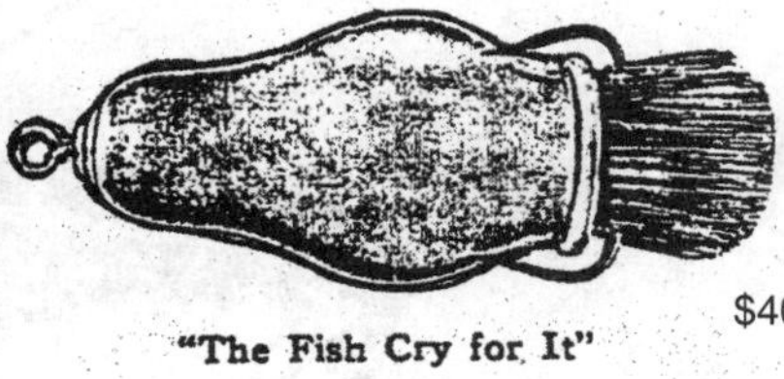

$40 – 50

"The Fish Cry for It"

FISH NIPPLE COLORS: (1911
No. 4W Solid White
No. 4R Solid Red

2-1/4"

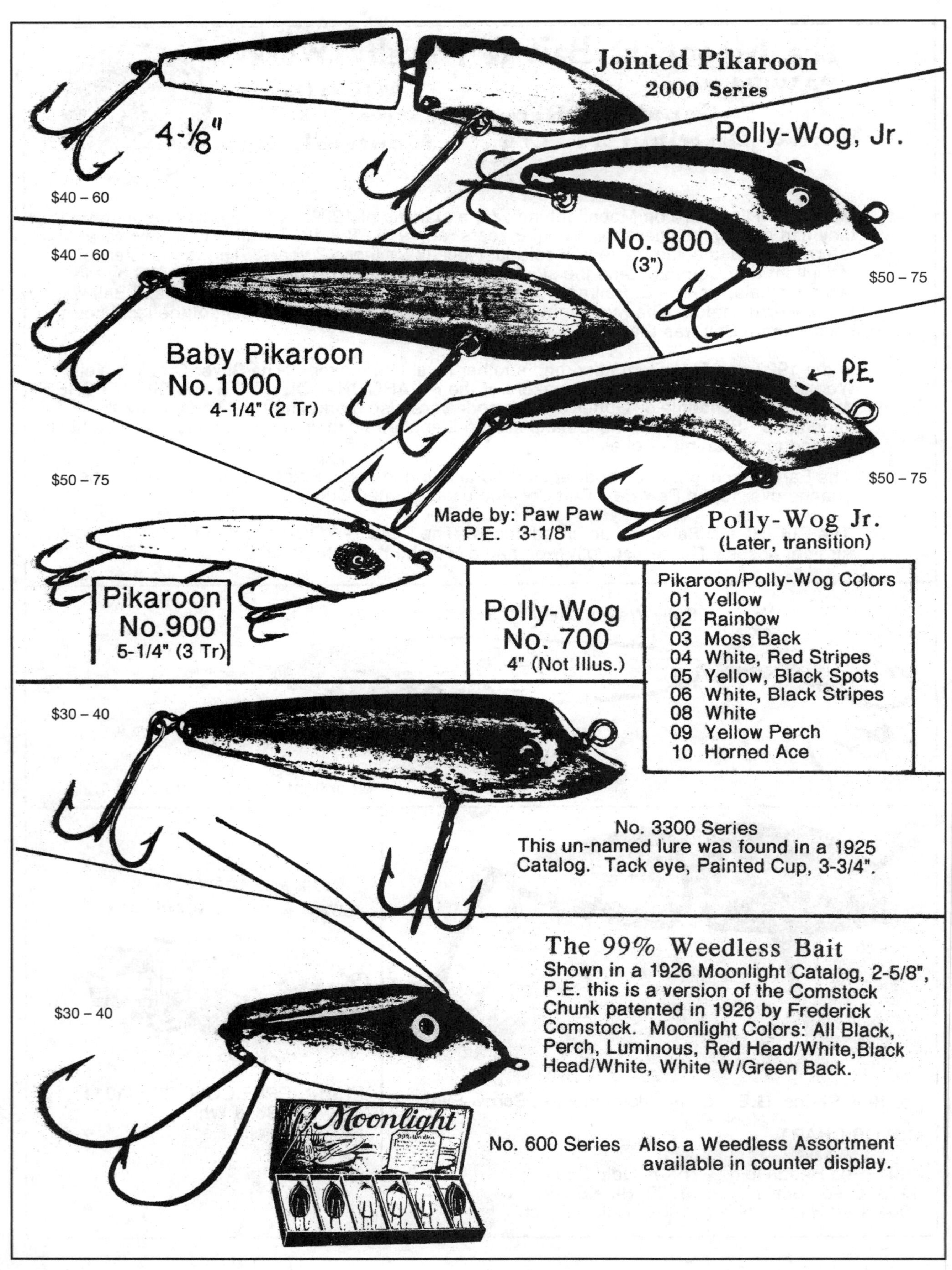
Jointed Pikaroon
2000 Series
4-1/8"
$40 – 60
Polly-Wog, Jr.
No. 800
(3")
$50 – 75
$40 – 60
Baby Pikaroon
No.1000
4-1/4" (2 Tr)
← P.E.
$50 – 75
$50 – 75
Made by: Paw Paw
P.E. 3-1/8"
Polly-Wog Jr.
(Later, transition)
Pikaroon
No.900
5-1/4" (3 Tr)
Polly-Wog
No. 700
4" (Not Illus.)
Pikaroon/Polly-Wog Colors
01 Yellow
02 Rainbow
03 Moss Back
04 White, Red Stripes
05 Yellow, Black Spots
06 White, Black Stripes
08 White
09 Yellow Perch
10 Horned Ace
$30 – 40
No. 3300 Series
This un-named lure was found in a 1925 Catalog. Tack eye, Painted Cup, 3-3/4".
The 99% Weedless Bait
Shown in a 1926 Moonlight Catalog, 2-5/8", P.E. this is a version of the Comstock Chunk patented in 1926 by Frederick Comstock. Moonlight Colors: All Black, Perch, Luminous, Red Head/White, Black Head/White, White W/Green Back.
$30 – 40
Moonlight
No. 600 Series Also a Weedless Assortment available in counter display.

PAW PAW UNDERWATER MINNOW (BUCKTAIL)

No. 6 1913 Catalog

3 COLORS
No. 6W All White
No. 6R All Red
No. 6Y All Yellow

$200 – 250+

$150 – 200

PAW PAW UNDERWATER MINNOW No. 7

Basically the same bait as No. 6 without the Bucktail. Same three colors.

$40 – 50

Bass Seeker
2600 Series

3 Trebles 4-1/8"
T.E. Scoop Nose

Bass Seeker Junior
2700 Series

2 Trebles 3-1/2"
T.E. Scoop Nose

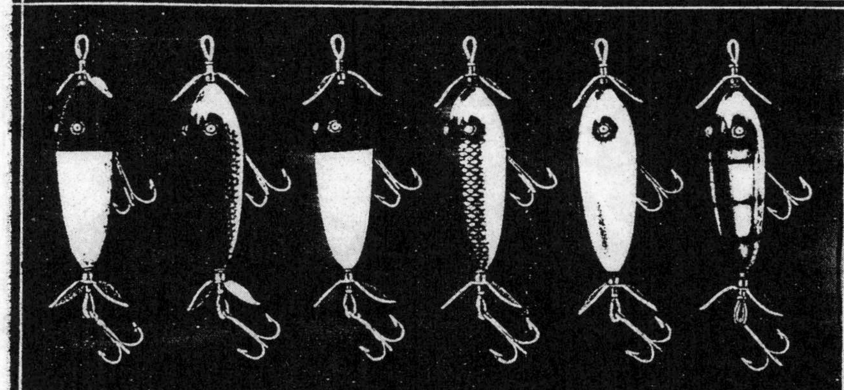

No. 3000 Series

In 1926 Catalog - G.E. - A Surface Bait-2-3/4"-6 Colors

$50 – 60

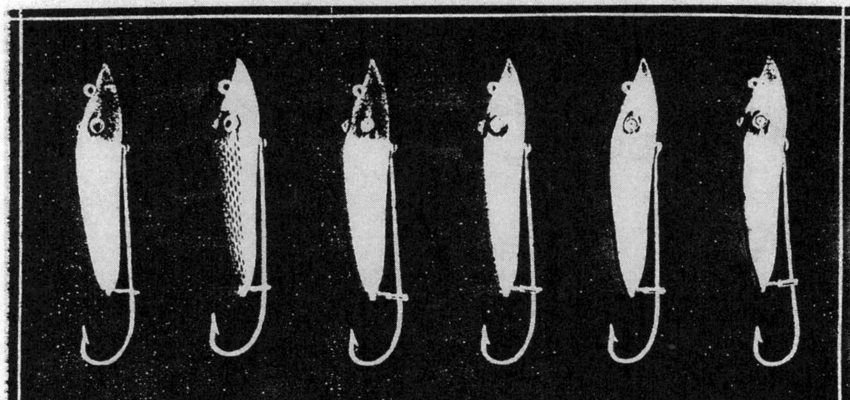

No. 2500 Series

This bait was made for Pike & Pickerel. 4-1/4", G.E. , In 1926 Catalog. A No. 7 hook fastened to the body on a sliding swivel that allows a swinging action.

$75 – 125

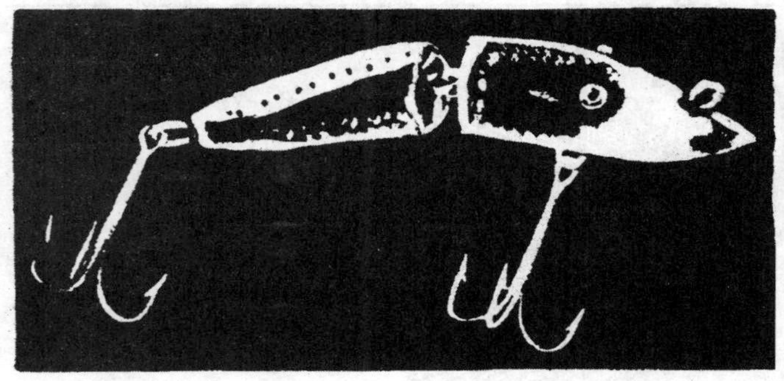

$75 – 100

Musky Special
No. 3100 Series

LARGE SIZED "JOINTED PIKAROON" for "MUSKY", also salt water fishing—has the same wiggling and swimming movement as our 2000 series, but much larger—has extra strong hooks. Made in two colors:

3103 Green Scale
3104 White, Red Head.

1926 Catalog - 1st Model had 2 screw eye joint - 6' - G.E.

1600 Series
Feather Minnow

$50 – 75

Light casting Feather Tail Minnow, with single hook in combination with a spinner that gives the tail an excessive wiggling movement—very effective when used in the lily pads and weeds.

Made in six colors:

1401	Yellow	**1409**	Orange
1404	Red	**1410**	Brown
1408	White	**1413**	Gray

1800 Series
Feather Minnow

$40 – 60

A wonderfully effective fly rod lure for Bass that can be used with bait casting rod. Closely imitates the movement of a wounded minnow—it rides on the surface of the water and makes a wake that is so real to life that the fish can't help but strike it.

1801	Yellow	**1809**	Orange
1803	Red	**1810**	Brown
1808	White	**1813**	Gray

THE DREADNOUGHT

(1912 - 1918) - 4" - N.E. - also it was called "The Fish Pirate" and the "Battleship". 2 Colors:

$250 – 350+ Red & White
Black & White

Moonlight made the claim in 1913 that they were unable to supply the demand for this bait after it's debut.

$40 – 60

Moonlight FLY ROD BAIT
(No. and Size not known)

Babe-Eat-Us

$20 – 30

No. 400 Series - P.E. - 2-1/2" - 3/8 Oz.

$30 – 50

No. 50 MOONLIGHT MOUSE
(1926) T.E. 2-3/8", thin metal lip, Ears usually broken/ chipped.
Colors: White Head/Black, Red & White, Mouse, Spotted

Bass-Eat-Us

$20 – 40

No. 300 Series - P.E. - 3" - 1/2 Oz.

Color Chart for No.300 & No.400

301/401	Yellow	306/406	Green Head/White
302/402	Rainbow	307/407	Black Head/Yellow
303/403	Moss Back	308/408	Blue Head/White
304/404	Red Head/White	309/409	Yellow Perch
305/405	Red Head/Yellow	310/410	Horned Ace

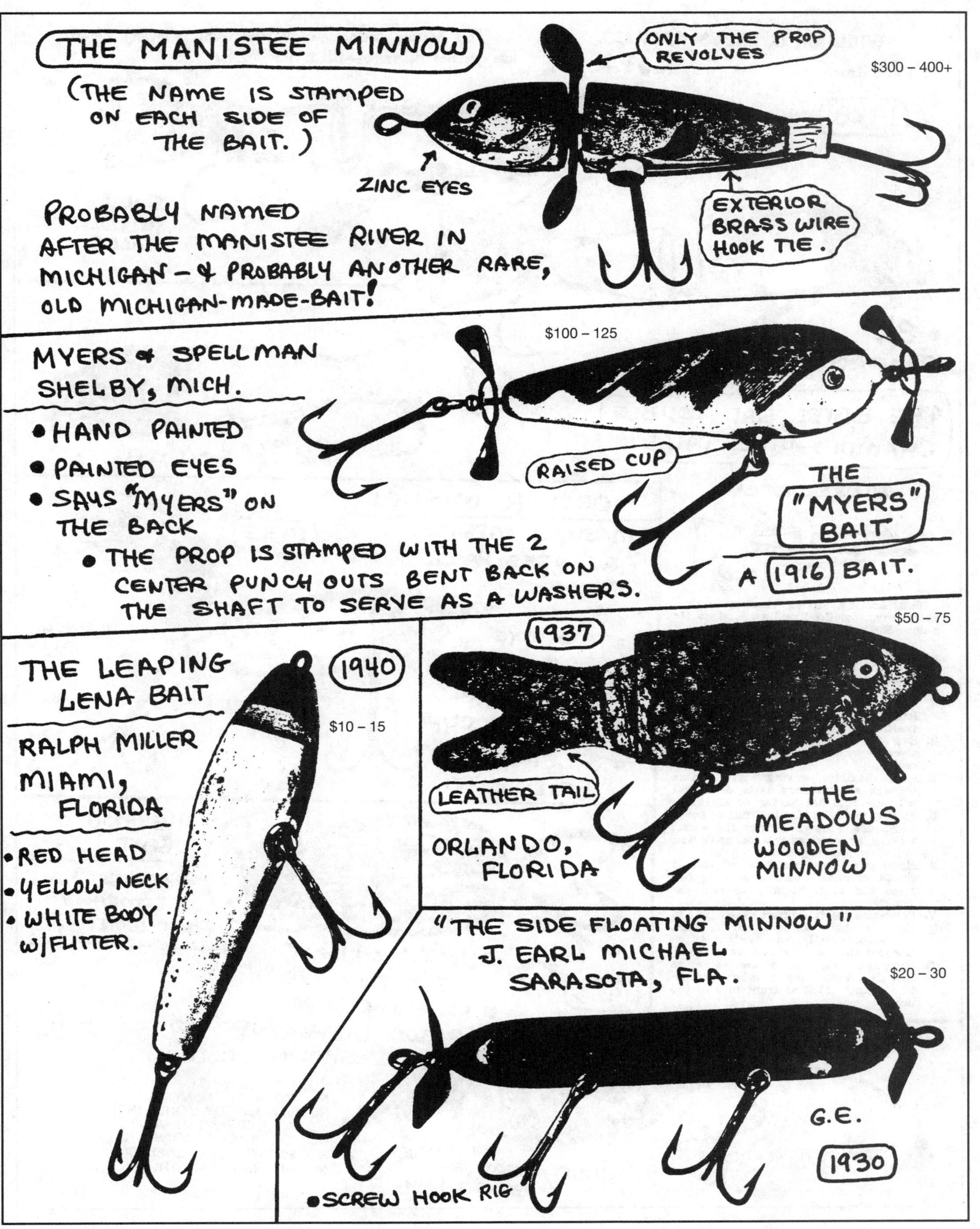
THE MANISTEE MINNOW
(THE NAME IS STAMPED ON EACH SIDE OF THE BAIT.)
ONLY THE PROP REVOLVES
$300 – 400+
ZINC EYES
EXTERIOR BRASS WIRE HOOK TIE.
PROBABLY NAMED AFTER THE MANISTEE RIVER IN MICHIGAN – & PROBABLY ANOTHER RARE, OLD MICHIGAN-MADE-BAIT!
$100 – 125
MYERS & SPELLMAN
SHELBY, MICH.
• HAND PAINTED
• PAINTED EYES
• SAYS "MYERS" ON THE BACK
• THE PROP IS STAMPED WITH THE 2 CENTER PUNCH OUTS BENT BACK ON THE SHAFT TO SERVE AS A WASHERS.
RAISED CUP
THE "MYERS" BAIT
A 1916 BAIT.
THE LEAPING LENA BAIT
1940
$10 – 15
RALPH MILLER
MIAMI, FLORIDA
• RED HEAD
• YELLOW NECK
• WHITE BODY W/FLITTER.
1937
$50 – 75
LEATHER TAIL
ORLANDO, FLORIDA
THE MEADOWS WOODEN MINNOW
"THE SIDE FLOATING MINNOW"
J. EARL MICHAEL
SARASOTA, FLA.
$20 – 30
G.E.
1930
• SCREW HOOK RIG

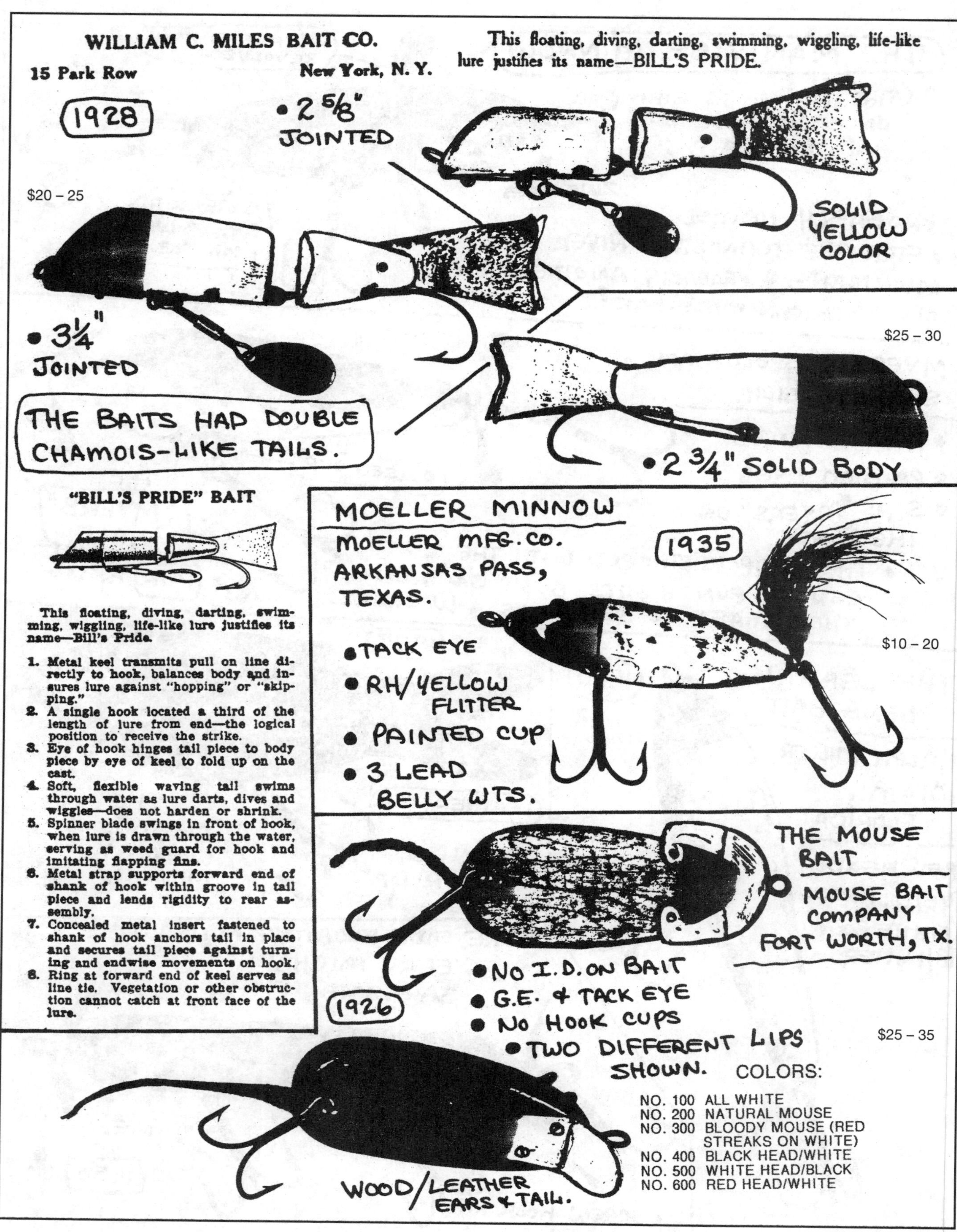

WILLIAM C. MILES BAIT CO.

15 Park Row **New York, N. Y.**

This floating, diving, darting, swimming, wiggling, life-like lure justifies its name—BILL'S PRIDE.

"BILL'S PRIDE" BAIT

This floating, diving, darting, swimming, wiggling, life-like lure justifies its name—Bill's Pride.

1. **Metal keel transmits pull on line directly to hook, balances body and insures lure against "hopping" or "skipping."**
2. **A single hook located a third of the length of lure from end—the logical position to receive the strike.**
3. **Eye of hook hinges tail piece to body piece by eye of keel to fold up on the cast.**
4. **Soft, flexible waving tail swims through water as lure darts, dives and wiggles—does not harden or shrink.**
5. **Spinner blade swings in front of hook, when lure is drawn through the water, serving as weed guard for hook and imitating flapping fins.**
6. **Metal strap supports forward end of shank of hook within groove in tail piece and lends rigidity to rear assembly.**
7. **Concealed metal insert fastened to shank of hook anchors tail in place and secures tail piece against turning and endwise movements on hook.**
8. **Ring at forward end of keel serves as line tie. Vegetation or other obstruction cannot catch at front face of the lure.**

1928
• 2 5/8" JOINTED
SOLID YELLOW COLOR
$20 – 25
• 3 1/4" JOINTED
THE BAITS HAD DOUBLE CHAMOIS-LIKE TAILS.
$25 – 30
• 2 3/4" SOLID BODY
MOELLER MINNOW
MOELLER MFG. CO.
ARKANSAS PASS, TEXAS.
1935
• TACK EYE
• RH/YELLOW FLITTER
• PAINTED CUP
• 3 LEAD BELLY WTS.
$10 – 20
THE MOUSE BAIT
MOUSE BAIT COMPANY
FORT WORTH, TX.
• NO I.D. ON BAIT
• G.E. & TACK EYE
• NO HOOK CUPS
• TWO DIFFERENT LIPS SHOWN.
1926
$25 – 35
COLORS:
NO. 100 ALL WHITE
NO. 200 NATURAL MOUSE
NO. 300 BLOODY MOUSE (RED STREAKS ON WHITE)
NO. 400 BLACK HEAD/WHITE
NO. 500 WHITE HEAD/BLACK
NO. 600 RED HEAD/WHITE
WOOD/LEATHER EARS & TAIL.

MOUSE BAIT - This is the most inventive, creative mouse bait we've ever seen. Leather ears and tail, bead eyes, spinners to simulate swimming legs, gray colors all went into this bait. We would be interested in learning more about the maker. This is the first time it has been published so perhaps someone knows more.

Made by:

Anton F. Hornyak
Grand Rapids, Mich.
(B 1-17-1919) (D 5-4-1982)

$50 – 60

(1912)
MARBLE'S
TROUT NIPPERS
One hand only needed—snap! Mr Speckled Beauty is fast till you let him go Can't lose him. No matter how much he struggles he
Can't Wiggle Out
They fit your pocket or hang over shoulder—always ready for emergencies—weigh only 4 ounces. Made of steel and heavily nickeled. Will last you many seasons. They'll tickle you. Get a pair!
If not at your dealer's we'll send direct.
Write for free catalog of Marble's Game Getter Gun and 60 Outing Specialties.
MARBLE ARMS & MFG. CO.
572 Delta Ave., Gladstone, Mich.
CAUGHT NIBBLING
(1912)
MARVEL BAIT
makes fish bite any season and when they bite our Marvel Automatic Fish Hook lands them every time. We give free a can of Marvel bait if you will help us introduce them in your locality, also 3 Marvel Automatic fish hooks, one of each size—small, medium and large. Write us today.
Japanese Novelty Co.,
Department 97, Clinton, Iowa
MOUSE BAIT

$30 – 40

$20 – 40

In 1909, Abercrombie & Fitch Co. sold a Mouse Bait made with a base of rubber & covered with real skin. 2" 2 colors:
Gray Mouse w/Black Tail
White Mouse w/Pink Tail

$30 – 40

THE MIRROR BAIT (1916)

ARTIFICIAL FISH BAIT.
APPLICATION FILED APR. 23, 1915.

1,180,753. Patented Apr. 25 1916.

FIG. 1.

FIG. 2.

$50 – 75

UNITED STATES PATENT OFFICE

ARTIFICIAL FISH-BAIT

1,180,753 Specification of Letters Patent Patented Apr. 25, 1916

Application filed April 23, 1915. Serial No. 23,351

. . . My invention relates more particularly to artificial baits for trawling, and its primary objects are to make the bait more attractive to the fish, to secure its proper position in the water, to provide a convenient and effective hanging of the hooks, and to generally improve the structure and operation of trawling baits. . . .

The attractiveness of the bait for the fish is increased by making the disks 6 and 9 of highly polished metal. The glitter and flashing lights occasioned by these and by the mirror are well known attractives; but the mirror 5 is an additional feature that insures the effectiveness of the bait in the following manner: A male fish seeing his image upon looking therein will appear to see another fish approach it from the opposite side with the intent to seize the bait, and this will not only arouse his warlike spirit, but also appeal to his greed, and he will seize the bait quickly in order to defeat the approaching rival. In case the fish is suspected of cowardice I may make the mirror of convex form, as shown at 5ª, in order that the rival or antagonist may appear to be smaller. In the case of a female fish the attractiveness of a mirror is too well known to need discussion. Thus the bait appeals to the ruling passion of both sexes, and renders it very certain and efficient in operation.

First time published...we hope it serves to ID some unknowns out there. Read the wild claims about this bait, especially on male & female fish.

LURES OF PROVEN QUALITY
Martin
U.S. PATENT NO. 2110382
CANADIAN PAT. NO. 384520
Trade Mark
FISH LURE CO.
2121 SECOND AVENUE
SEATTLE 1, WASHINGTON
FOR FRESH OR SALT WATER FISHING
PERCH SCALE

$10 – 20

TROUT PLUG

Neat Little Plug - made G.E. P.E. Plain & Feathered Hooks 2 Sizes: 1-1/2" & 1-3/4"- Bass & Trout size hooks.

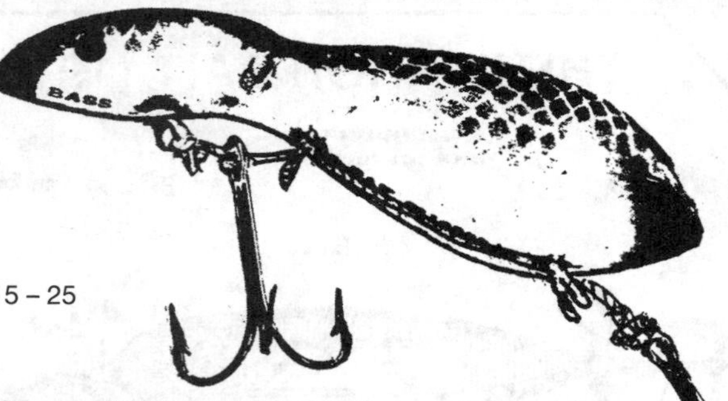
BASS

$15 – 25

Martin "TAD" (Tadpolly)string-tie rig, but says "Bass" on chin. P.E. 3-1/2".

Jointed "Tad" - Much Less Common than the standard model. Same rigs & colors.

$5 – 10

WESTERN BASS PLUG - 3-1/4" - G.E. & pressed eye, DLT, Bass Colors. Personal note - this plug was named after my bass club...The Western Bass Club of Seattle, WA. It is the oldest pure bass club in the U.S. - founded by Ed T. Fredrich in 1938!

$5 – 10

INJURED MINNOW - G.E. PL.E. P.E. 3-1/2", made in at least 18 colors, maybe more. Best seller of bass series.

$5 – 10

MARTIN SALMON PLUGS - Joe Martin won a lawsuit on Heddon using their string tie pull out hook rig patent. G.E. P.E. sizes all the way from 3" up to commercial sizes of 7".

Martin closed up in 1990. They made a very diverse line of lures for many different markets.

East Coast Striper Plugs. Ex. "Flaptail"

Bottom Salt Water. Ex. 7" & 13" Jtd. Ling Cod Plugs.

Offshore. 11" Teasers Skirted Marlin Trolling Plug.

$15 – 20

MARTIN BASS PLUG - G.E. P.E. 3-1/4" - basically their small salmon plug body with screw eye hook rigs & bass colors. Other Bass Plugs they made in limited quantities:

"DARTER"(3 Tr.) "JOINTED PIKIE"

(1925) A. J. Koshallek started Bass Hound Bait Co. in Stevens Point, Wis. (1929) Marathon Battery bought Bass Hound & changed name to Marathon Bait Co.(2 Shops located in Stevens Point and Wausau). (1967) Gould Battery buys Marathon and (1968) sells tackle operation to Ray Knetter. (1970) He moves operations to Mosinee, Wis. (1974) Corporate name was changed to Marathon Tackle, Inc.

MARATHON made a full line of Spinners, Spoons, and Bucktails, including the original MUSKY-HOUN Bait. For now at least, we will leave that research to the metal collectors.

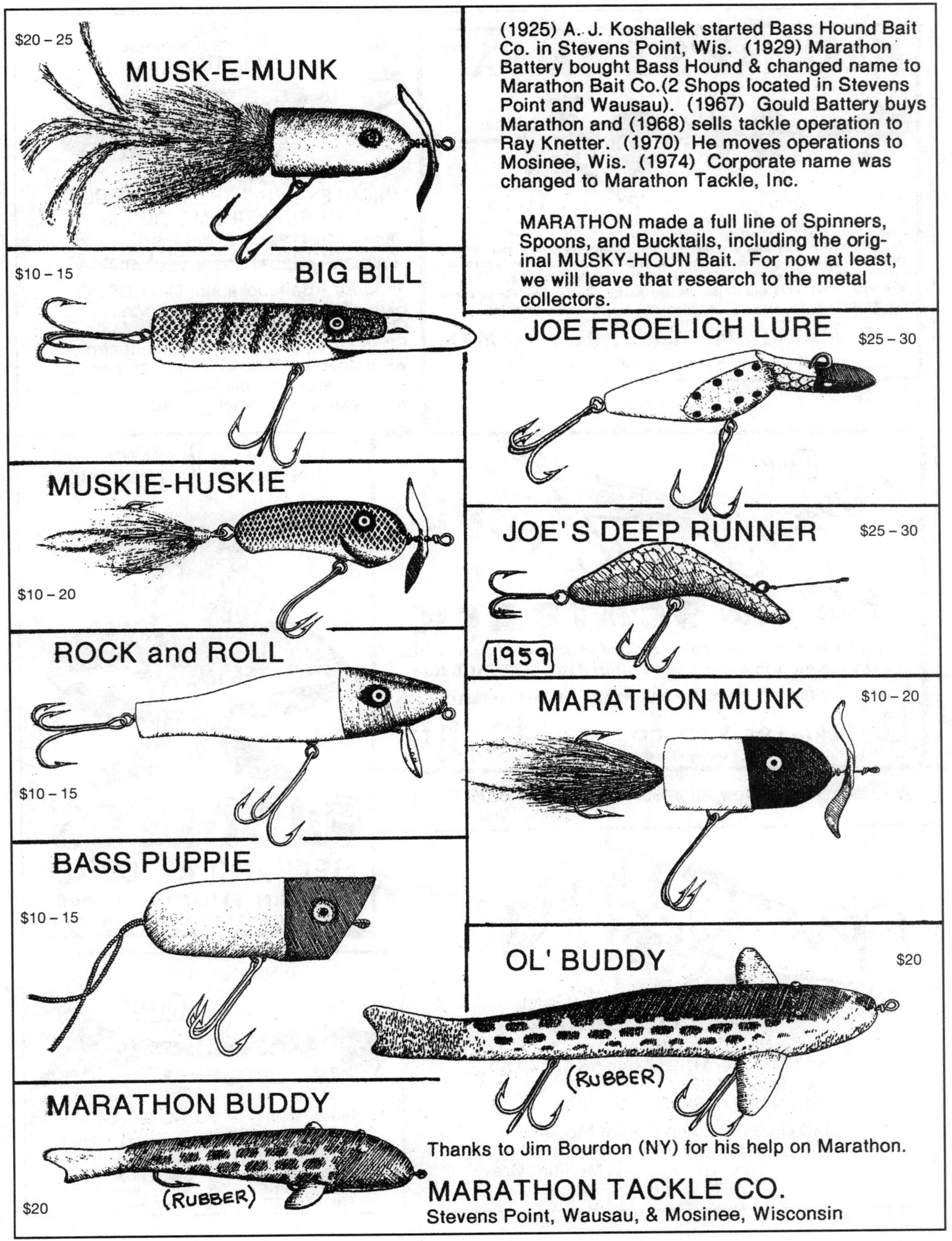
$20 – 25
MUSK-E-MUNK
$10 – 15
BIG BILL
MUSKIE-HUSKIE
$10 – 20
ROCK and ROLL
$10 – 15
BASS PUPPIE
$10 – 15
MARATHON BUDDY
(RUBBER)
$20
JOE FROELICH LURE
$25 – 30
JOE'S DEEP RUNNER
$25 – 30
1959
MARATHON MUNK
$10 – 20
OL' BUDDY
$20
(RUBBER)

Thanks to Jim Bourdon (NY) for his help on Marathon.

MARATHON TACKLE CO.

Stevens Point, Wausau, & Mosinee, Wisconsin

MARKHAM'S BALL BAIT

$40 – 50

1913

Something new and attractive. Something they will rise for and never go back. A surface bait that is life-like and active. It creates a ripple in the water and is an ideal bait for trolling and casting. The balls alternate in color red and white. Scientifically made and evenly balanced. A sure catch and a winner. Send today. Price 75 cents, prepaid.

C. E. MARKHAM, Manfr., Jackson, Mich.

Maker of Burgess Weedless Hooks.

"HOOTENANNA"

$5 – 10

"HOOTENANNA" THE FAMOUS OLD TIME TOPPER BASS TAKER!

MONTPELIER BAIT CO.

Montpelier, Ohio - Phone 495J

1939 Ad -(Bait looks alot like CCBCO Skipper) was made by Mr. & Mrs. Ozmun in a 1 car garage on E. Main St. in Montpelier, OH. The paint circles were done by Mrs. with wooden pencils with the erasers hollowed out First box was orange with black printing.

1948

ACTION!
FUSS!!!

$5 – 10

***the new* SCATBACK**

gives you the unbeatable team of *Action and Fuss,* with a zig-zag motion never before offered in a SURFACE lure.

FROG • PERCH • REDHEAD • SCALE • YELLOW

MERMADE BAIT CO. 2 SIZES { ½ oz. . $1.25 / 1⅛ oz. . $1.60

12015 Ashbury • Cleveland 6, Ohio

A 1949 AD Gave New Address: MERMADE BAIT CO. Inc. Platteville, Wisc.

PULL THE LINE TIE — WATCH THE LEGS "KICK"

$10 – 15

FROGLEGS

MECHANICAL LURE

MODERN SPORTING GOODS

AUSTIN - TEXAS

$5 – 10

MARTIN SHRIMP

MARTIN BAIT COMPANY (1950)
P.O. BOX 1928
AMARILLO, TEXAS

Made in 3 Joint and 4 Joint Models

Colors: Black & White, Red & White, Pale Green, Medium Grey, Pink & White, Amber

MOOSE MINNOWS

1926

HAND MADE FLEXIBLE RUBBER BAIT
(unknown)

$5 – 10

BLACK SUCKER	10"	Treble Hook
BLACK SUCKER	10"	Single Hook
DARK SHINER	5"	Single Hook
LIGHT SHINER	5"	Single Hook
TROUT SIZE	1-1/2"	Single Hook

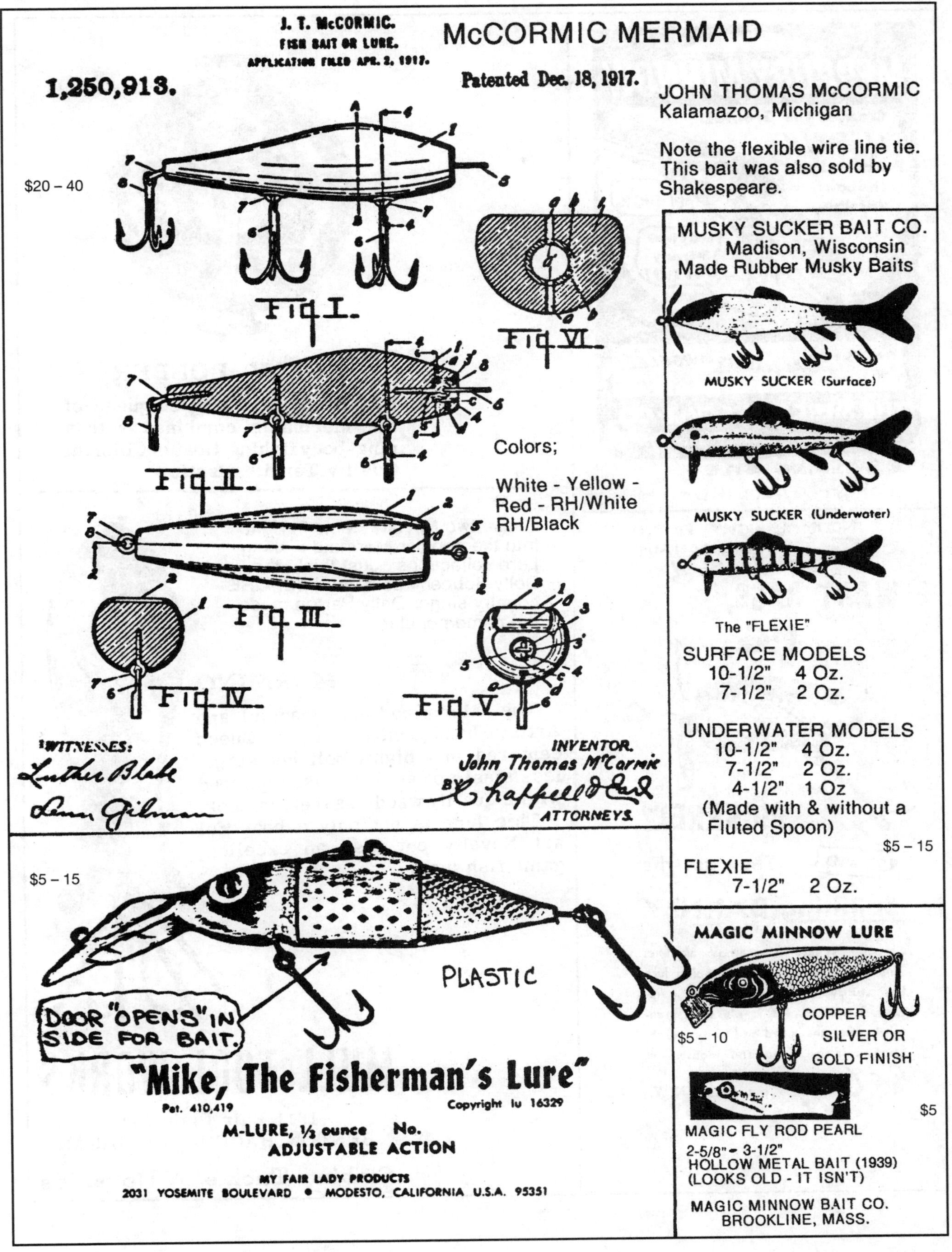
J. T. McCORMIC.
FISH BAIT OR LURE.
APPLICATION FILED APR. 2, 1917.
1,250,913.
Patented Dec. 18, 1917.
FIG I.
FIG II.
FIG III.
FIG IV.
FIG V.
FIG VI.
WITNESSES:
Luther Blake
Lenn Gilman
INVENTOR.
John Thomas McCormic
BY Chappell & Earl
ATTORNEYS.
MUSKY SUCKER (Surface)
MUSKY SUCKER (Underwater)
The "FLEXIE"
PLASTIC
DOOR "OPENS" IN SIDE FOR BAIT.
"Mike, The Fisherman's Lure"
Pat. 410,419
Copyright lu 16329
M-LURE, 1/3 ounce No.
ADJUSTABLE ACTION
MY FAIR LADY PRODUCTS
2031 YOSEMITE BOULEVARD • MODESTO, CALIFORNIA U.S.A. 95351
MAGIC MINNOW LURE

McCORMIC MERMAID

$20 – 40

JOHN THOMAS McCORMIC
Kalamazoo, Michigan

Note the flexible wire line tie. This bait was also sold by Shakespeare.

Colors;

White - Yellow - Red - RH/White RH/Black

MUSKY SUCKER BAIT CO.

Madison, Wisconsin
Made Rubber Musky Baits

SURFACE MODELS
10-1/2" 4 Oz.
7-1/2" 2 Oz.

UNDERWATER MODELS
10-1/2" 4 Oz.
7-1/2" 2 Oz.
4-1/2" 1 Oz
(Made with & without a Fluted Spoon)

$5 – 15

FLEXIE
7-1/2" 2 Oz.

$5 – 15

COPPER
SILVER OR
GOLD FINISH

$5 – 10

$5

MAGIC FLY ROD PEARL
2-5/8" - 3-1/2"
HOLLOW METAL BAIT (1939)
(LOOKS OLD - IT ISN'T)

MAGIC MINNOW BAIT CO.
BROOKLINE, MASS.

MERCURY MINNOW
Creates the Greatest
LIFE-LIKE
Action Ever
Thought
Possible
1940's
MOVING
Mercury
Does It!
DARTS • DIVES • CLIMBS • WIGGLES!
THE MERCOY TACKLE CO.
1359 Hollywood, Grosse Pointe 30, Mich.

●SPINNING SIZE –
● CASTING/TROLLING –

$5

$10 – 20

DOLLY BOBBER

Beautifully hand painted queen of the Mermaids combined with a ring-bouy fishing float of Colorful Quality Tennite plastic.

NOTE: BOUGHT PATENT FROM DONALY

WANT BASS, PIKE,

$5 – 10

PICKEREL?

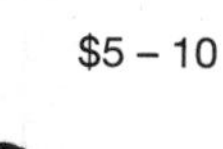
1953 AD

Then get the

Spinning BARNEY

. . . newest lure in a famous old line. This easy action surface popping lure has sturdy aluminum propeller, imported Mustad #2 treble hook, tantalizing finishes in red and white, perch, black, rainbow, frog and mouse.

McCagg Mt. Kisco, N. Y.

$10 – 20

These two Novelty Items fit right into the popular Mermaid Fishing Lure collections. Just think, the Dolly Bobber was named BEFORE country singer Dolly Parton made the name popular.

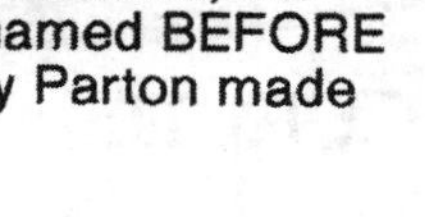

MERMINO

The "Mermino" is a graceful and Artistic hand painted mermaid Queen centered in a highly polished stainless steel spoon. It is also equipped with a quality weedless trebble hook.

This lure is not only a beautiful art Novelty but also an excellent game fish lure.

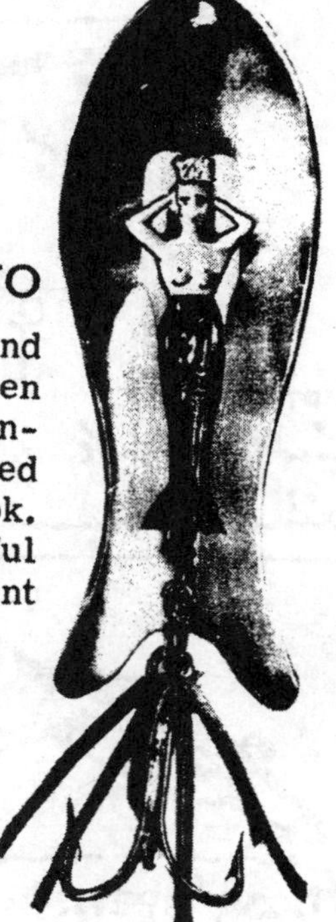

MULL TOOL WORKS

1811 Fair Plain Ave.
BENTON HARBOR, MICHIGAN

Fishing Tackle Novelties

HERB MILLS FISHING TACKLE CO.
PIQUA, OHIO, U. S. A.

Herb Mills Fishing Tackle

CHIEF TEAZUM SURFACE MINNOW

A Heap Good Bait

A Proven Fish Getter

More game fish have been taken on this type lure than on any other. Many old fishermen will use nothing else.

Don't Fail To Try This One

No. 711-P—Yellow Body, Brown Head
No. 711-Y—Jet Black Finish
No. 711-A—Aluminum Finish
No. 711-R. W.—Red Head, White Body

$5 – 15

Weedless THE CRAWDAD Luminous

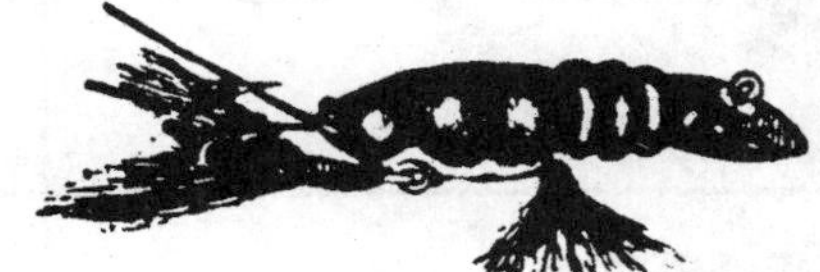

Wgt. ⅝ oz.

$5 – 15

So closely resembles the real, live soft Crawdad that even the highly educated old bass is so badly fooled that he soon finds himself on your stringer.

Natural Bucktail Pinchers tied on No. 3/0 double hook, hung in natural position of Pinchers. Natural Bucktail Legs. Snappy black eyes and realistic silk feelers. Special waterproof, permanent luminous paint needs no charging in light, and makes a very effective night bait.

No. 100 Crawdad Finish Only

FAVORITE Top or Bottom MINNOW

Surface or Deep

At times game fish will strike nothing but deep running lures. The Top or Bottom minnow goes down deep after them and invariably brings them to your stringer.

Reverse mouthpiece and you have a surface minnow that can't be beat. Swims like a real lively minnow. Weight, ⅝ oz.

No. 102-P—Yellow Body, Brown Head
No. 102-Y—Jet Black Finish
No. 102-A—Aluminum Finish
No. 102-R. W.—Red Head, White Body

$5 – 15

THE GENUINE OLD TIMERS' FAVORITE SPOON HOOK

Nothing can compare with the Fish-Getting qualities of the Old Timers' favorite spoon hook. Equally effective for bass, pike, pickerel or musky.

$5

Built just the right weight to cast nicely and the spoon has that slow, life-like wobbling spin that the big ones can't resist.

Equipped with No. 2/0 Feather Treble Hook, nickle, brass or copper spoon.

No. 99

ACROBAT SURFACE MINNOW

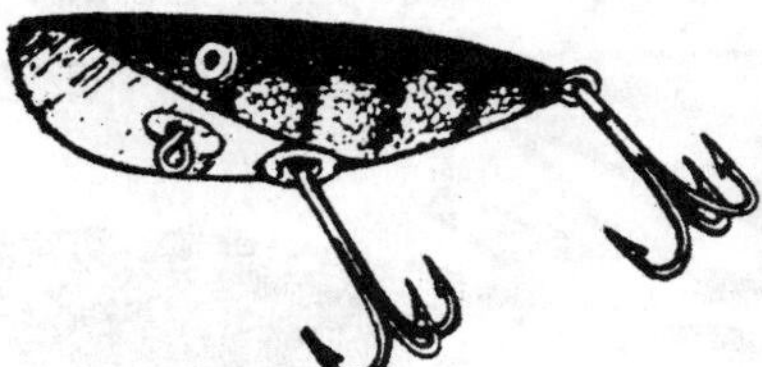

Does Everything That Makes All Game Fish Want to KILL IT

No Charleston Dancer can ever hope to imitate the wiggles, wobbles, dives and shimmeys that are easy for this bait. And no bass or any other game fish can resist taking a smash at it. **Don't Miss This One.**

Weight ⅝ oz.—Just right for casting.

No. 101-P—Yellow Body, Brown Head
No. 101-Y—Jet Black Finish
No. 101-A—Aluminum Finish
No. 101-R. W.—Red Head, White Body

$5 – 15

PIQUA SPECIAL SPINNER SPOON

--- Something New ---

$5

The good fish-getting qualities of both the spoon hook and tandem spinner are combined in this lure, and the results obtained with it have surpassed the anglers' fondest dreams of a perfect lure.

Under side of spoon luminous, with red diagonal stripe and sprinkled with brilliant metallics, making the most attractive lure that it is possible to manufacture.

Equipped with No. 2/0 Bucktail Treble Hook in black, white, yellow or red bucktail.

Brass, copper or nickel spoon and spinner.

A Safe Bet No. 103 Price

Huge production on a standardized line of tackle enable us to sell at the popular prices.

MILL RUN PRODUCTS COMPANY

1360 WEST 9th ST., CLEVELAND 13, OHIO

$5

"WONDER MOUSE"

WEEDLESS

Spoon length: 1¾"; Weight ⅝ oz.

$5

"MOUSIE SPOON"

DOUBLE HOOK

Spoon Size: 1¾"; Weight ½ oz.

$5

"SILVER SHINER"

WEEDLESS

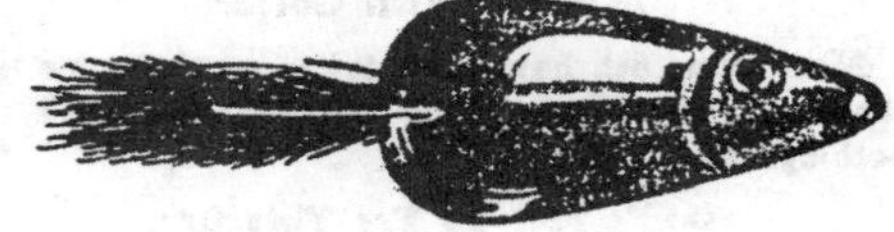

Spoon length: 2¼"; Weight ½ oz.

$5

"MOUSIE SPOON"

WEEDLESS

Spoon length 1¾"; Weight ½ oz.

"SILVER FROG"

WEEDLESS

$5

Body Size: 1¼"; Weight ⅝ oz.

$5

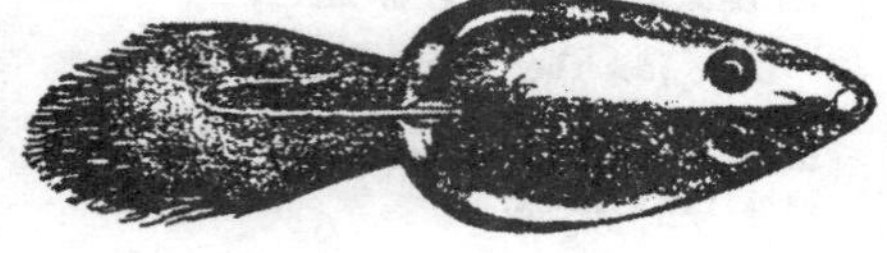

BABY MOUSIE—WEEDLESS

Effective in weedy waters—its flashing wig-wag action and wiggling bucktail has Fish Appeal. Fish it with or without Fly Rod Pork Rind impaled on point of hook.

Spoon Size: 1¼" long, ¾" wide. Weight: ¼ oz.

"CRAWFISH CRAWLER"

WEEDLESS

$5

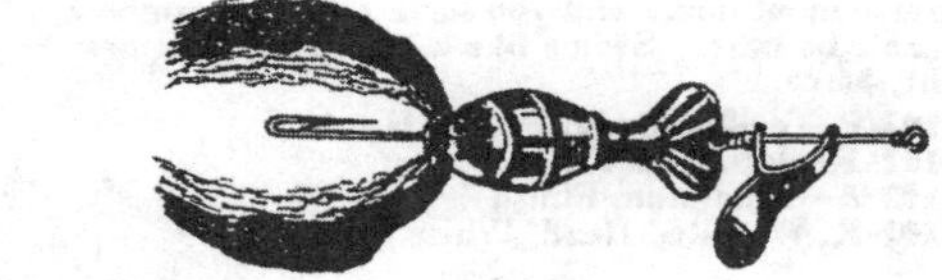

Body Size: 1⅝"; Weight ⅛ oz.

Lure Design by Charles P. Schilpp (Ex. Al Foss & True Temper Designer)

McDONALD WATER CRAWLER

SOLID PLASTIC

RUST-PROOF HARDWARE

½oz.

$10 – 20

$20 – 40

"The Mizzouri Bug Wobbler"

This 1923 Bait claimed it was - 3 Baits In One.
Wooden Minnow, Pork Bait, and Bucktail
The wings are white rubber

MIZZOURI BAIT CO.
ST. LOUIS, MISSOURI

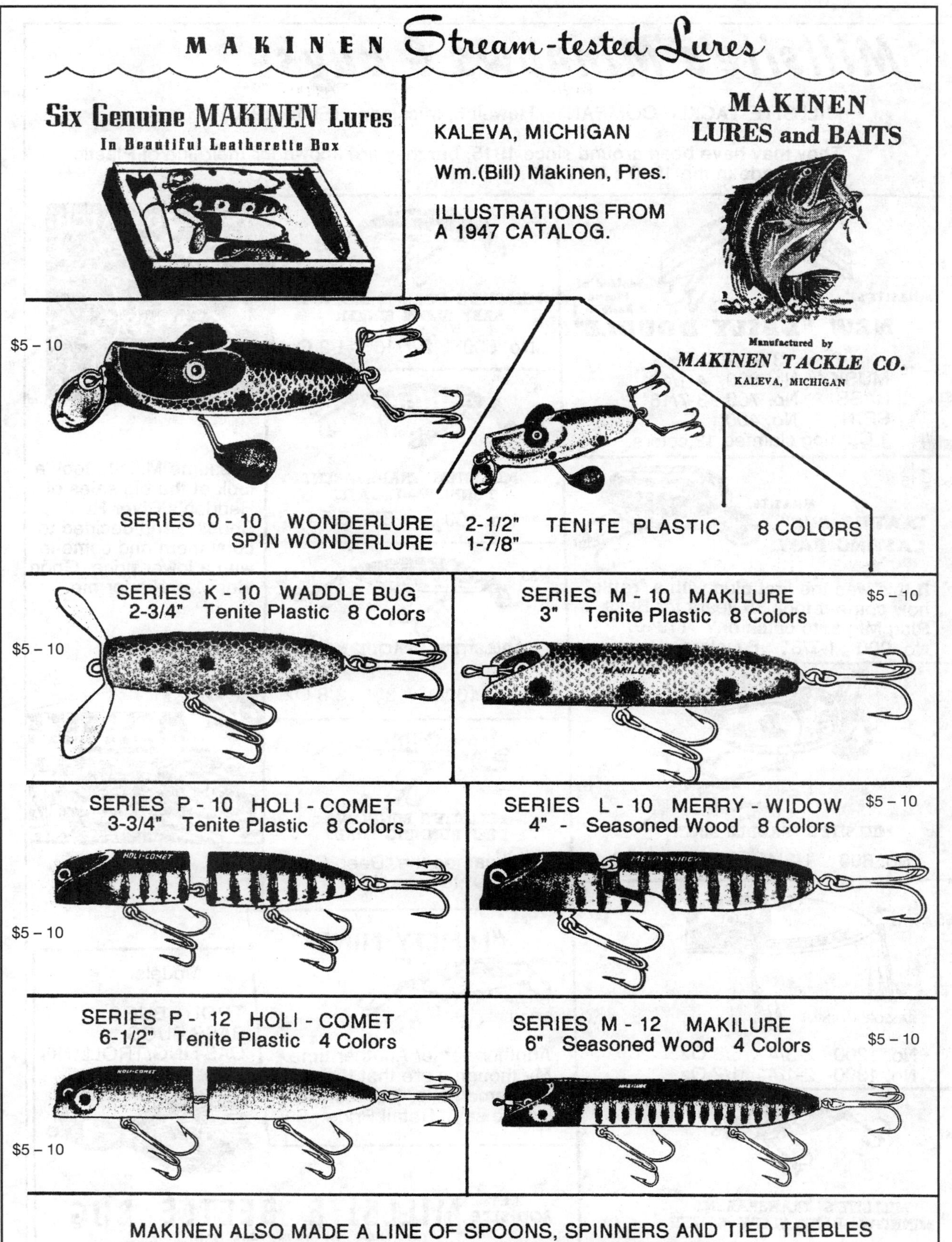
MAKINEN Stream-tested Lures
Six Genuine MAKINEN Lures
In Beautiful Leatherette Box
KALEVA, MICHIGAN
Wm.(Bill) Makinen, Pres.
ILLUSTRATIONS FROM A 1947 CATALOG.
MAKINEN LURES and BAITS
Manufactured by
MAKINEN TACKLE CO.
KALEVA, MICHIGAN
$5 – 10
SERIES 0 - 10 WONDERLURE 2-1/2" TENITE PLASTIC 8 COLORS
SPIN WONDERLURE 1-7/8"
SERIES K - 10 WADDLE BUG
2-3/4" Tenite Plastic 8 Colors
$5 – 10
SERIES M - 10 MAKILURE
3" Tenite Plastic 8 Colors
$5 – 10
MAKILURE
SERIES P - 10 HOLI - COMET
3-3/4" Tenite Plastic 8 Colors
$5 – 10
HOLI-COMET
SERIES L - 10 MERRY - WIDOW
4" - Seasoned Wood 8 Colors
$5 – 10
MERRY-WIDOW
SERIES P - 12 HOLI - COMET
6-1/2" Tenite Plastic 4 Colors
$5 – 10
SERIES M - 12 MAKILURE
6" Seasoned Wood 4 Colors
$5 – 10
MAKINEN ALSO MADE A LINE OF SPOONS, SPINNERS AND TIED TREBLES
For Purpose of this reference, we have elected not to detail them.

Millsite's Minnows & Bugs

MILLSITE TACKLE COMPANY Howell 5, Michigan (Since 1915)

They may have been around since 1915, but they are known for their line of Plastic Baits made in the 1940's & 1950's.

MILLSITE'S NEW "DAILY DOUBLE" Molded of Plastic 2 Baits in 1

3 SIZES:

$5 – 10 MUSKY No. 800 4-1/16"
$5 BASS No. 700 3-7/16"
$5 SPIN No. 400
1 Catalog claimed 12 colors.

$5 – 15

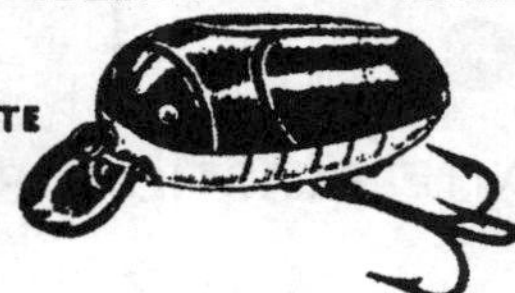

MILLSITE "RATTLE BUG" CASTING BAIT

If this was the first plug with a "rattle" how come it took 35 years for Bass Plug Mfg's. to catch on? (1940)
No. 900 1-7/8" 6 Colors

$5

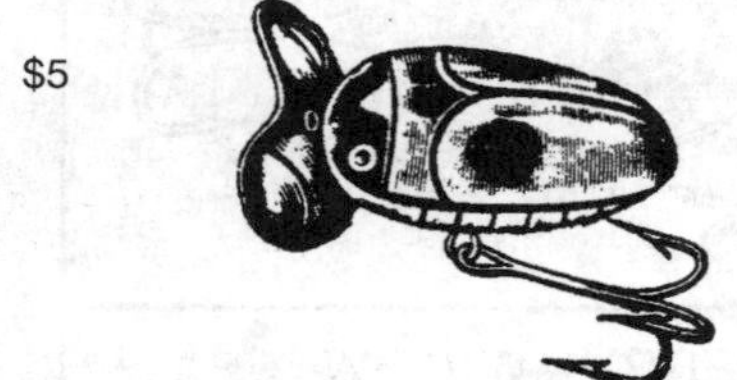

MILLSITE'S "PADDLE BUG"

No. 600 1-3/4" 6 Colors

$5

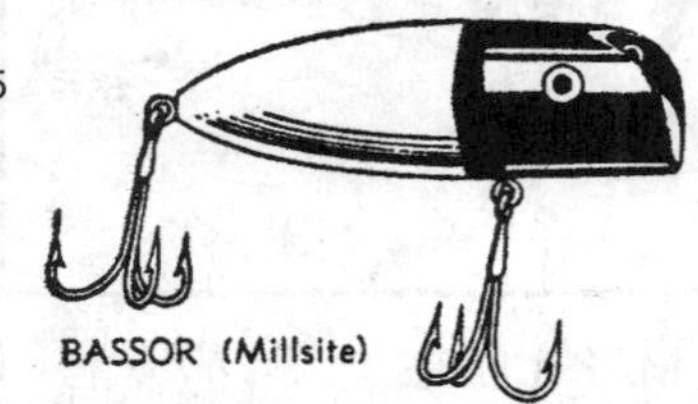

BASSOR (Millsite)

No. 1200 2-3/4" 5/8 Oz.
No. 1300 2-1/4" 1/2 Oz.

$5

MILLSITE'S TRANSPARENT MINNOW—BABY SLOW SINKER

No. 500T 2-7/16" 1/2 Oz.

$5

MILLSITE'S OPAQUE MINNOW BABY SLOW SINKER

No. 500M 2-7/16" 1/2 Oz.

$5

MILLSITE'S TRANSPARENT MINNOW—FLOATER

No. 100T 3" 3/5 Oz.

$5

MILLSITE'S OPAQUE MINNOW FLOATER

No. 100M 3" 3/8 Oz.

$5

MILLSITE'S MINNOW DEEP RUNNING LURE

Nicknamed the "Deep Creep"
Add "D" to Lure No.

WANT TO CATCH FISH?
use a MILLSITE DAILY DOUBLE

I assume Millsite took a look at the big sales of Heddon's River Runt Spooks, and decided to copy them and come in with a lower price. Good idea....works for me.

Buy MILLSITE FISHING TACKLE

"NINETY NINER"

$5 – 10

Another name/ Another time. My thoughts are that they are the same baits, just a clever way to say: Retail Price -.99¢

3 Models:

TROUT BUGS
BASS BUGS
CASTING/TROLLING BUG

FLY ROD SIZE MILLSITE BEETLE BUG

TRY THESE ON YOUR NEXT TRIP.

$5

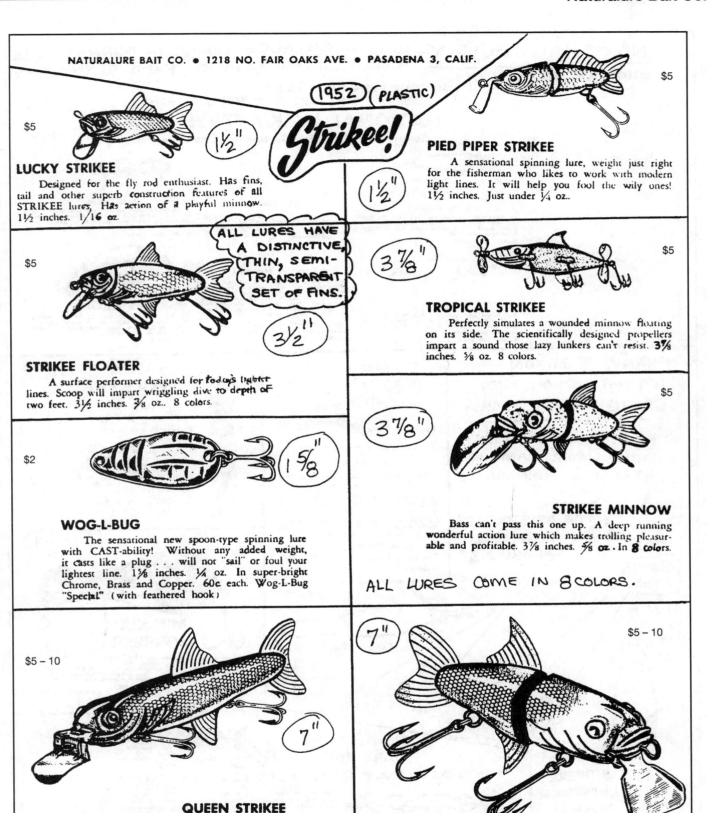

NATURALURE BAIT CO. • 1218 NO. FAIR OAKS AVE. • PASADENA 3, CALIF.

(1952) (PLASTIC)

Strikee!

$5

1½"

LUCKY STRIKEE

Designed for the fly rod enthusiast. Has fins, tail and other superb construction features of all STRIKEE lures, Has action of a playful minnow. 1½ inches. 1/16 oz.

$5

1½"

PIED PIPER STRIKEE

A sensational spinning lure, weight just right for the fisherman who likes to work with modern light lines. It will help you fool the wily ones! 1½ inches. Just under ¼ oz..

ALL LURES HAVE A DISTINCTIVE, THIN, SEMI-TRANSPARENT SET OF FINS.

$5

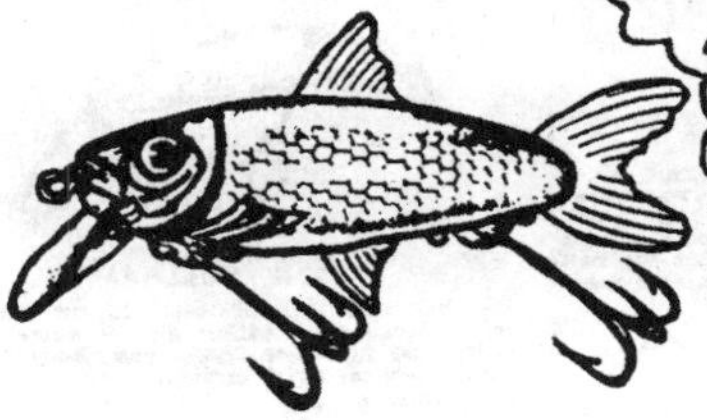

3½"

STRIKEE FLOATER

A surface performer designed for today's lighter lines. Scoop will impart wriggling dive to depth of two feet. 3½ inches. ⅜ oz.. 8 colors.

$5

3⅞"

TROPICAL STRIKEE

Perfectly simulates a wounded minnow floating on its side. The scientifically designed propellers impart a sound those lazy lunkers can't resist. 3⅞ inches. ⅝ oz. 8 colors.

$2

1⅝"

WOG-L-BUG

The sensational new spoon-type spinning lure with CAST-ability! Without any added weight, it casts like a plug . . . will not "sail" or foul your lightest line. 1⅝ inches. ¼ oz. In super-bright Chrome, Brass and Copper. 60c each. Wog-L-Bug "Special" (with feathered hook)

$5

3⅞"

STRIKEE MINNOW

Bass can't pass this one up. A deep running wonderful action lure which makes trolling pleasurable and profitable. 3⅞ inches. ⅝ oz. In 8 colors.

ALL LURES COME IN 8 COLORS.

$5 – 10

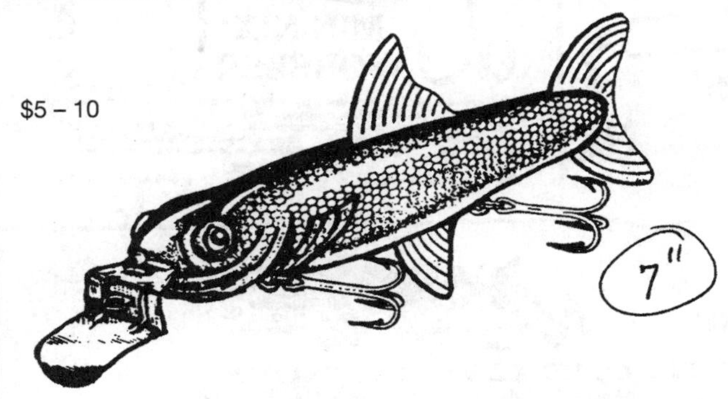

7"

QUEEN STRIKEE

A brand new surface lure, designed for Stripers, White Sea Bass, etc. Wonderful off kelp beds. Great for Salmon and Muskies. 7 inches. 3 oz. 12 colors.

$5 – 10

7"

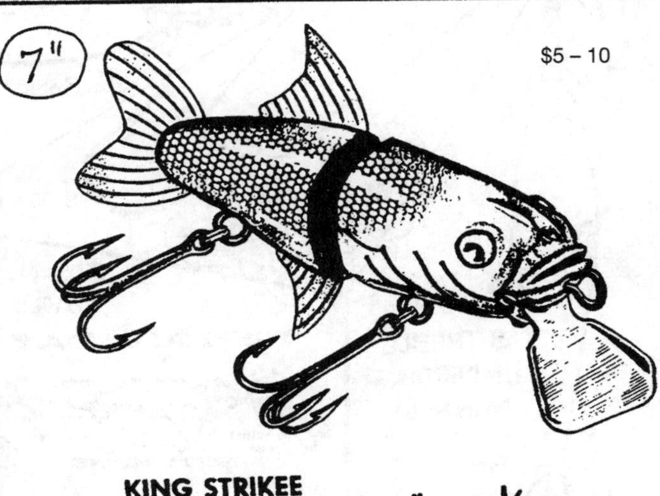

KING STRIKEE

(JOINTED)

7"– 3½ oz.

NATIONAL SUPPLY – WAS A CATALOG HOUSE IN MINNEAPOLIS SOLD PAW PAW & OTHERS – HARD TO IDENTIFY.
- SIMILAR TO GATEWAY -

FISH COME FROM OTHER LAKES
TO TAKE THESE NATIONAL BAITS . . . . .

NATIONAL LUCKY SEVEN BAITS

Seven Sure-Fire Fish-Getters at One Low Price

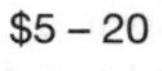
$5 – 20

RIVER SNOOPER

An unbeatable wall eyed pike bait. Just the right size—3¼" long. Just the right weight—⅝ oz. The bright metal lip increases action and attraction. A medium deep diver.

A-1412—Silver Scale........................

$5 – 20

THE RED HEAD

One of the most successful bass lures that ever pulled a fish out of a lake. The scoop head and protruding lip do the work. Equipped with 1/0 rustproof hooks. Body 4" long.

A-2004—Red Head................

$10 – 30

DARTING PLOPPER

Here is one of the real "Old Timers." Made originally for the crack bass caster who knows how to drop them in the lily pads and "plop" them into the eagerly waiting mouth of the hungry bass. Short, quick jerks cause the bait to jump, dive and dart in a most teasing manner. Try all three finishes.

A-2504—Red Head........................
A-2512—Silver Scale....................
A-2503—Green Back......................

$5 – 20

BASS SEEKER

A combination pike, pickerel and bass bait. It is 4¼" long. Rides just below the surface. Improved deflector lip under head causes it to take an erratic, zigzagging action.

A-1604—Red Head..........................

$10 – 30

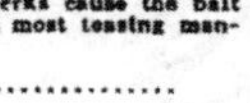

THE BULLHEAD

The bait that is different. Its twisting, rolling action deceives the wiliest fish. It whets their curiosity and fills your frying pan. Body is 4" long with a quarter twist turning.

A-3504—Red Head.........

FRANK T. NIXON
107 MT. VERNON AVE.
GRAND RAPIDS, MICH.

NIXON'S PERSIAN IVORY UNDER-WATER CASTING & TROLLING MINNOW.

1914

"THE ARISTOCRAT"
BODY: 3¼"
OVERALL: 4¼"

GLASS EYES

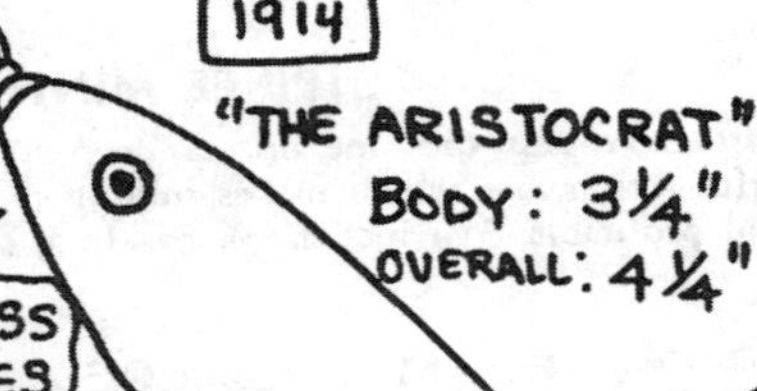

$100 – 150

ALL 3 BAITS IN AN IVORY-WHITE FINISH.

3 TREBLE UNDERWATER MINNOW.
BODY: 3"

$100 – 150

HERE IT IS! $5

THE NEW LAUREL BAIT

1928

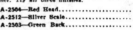

The Fish-Gettingest Lure of the Age

For all game fish, Guaranteed. *Read this.*

An all metal unbreakable lure. Every fisherman who likes to cast an easy casting bait with a wonderfully attractive action should have one of these WONDERFUL NEW LURES.

There is no question about its fish-getting qualities either casting or trolling. Our positive guarantee with every lure.

ASK YOUR DEALER OR ORDER DIRECT

The NEW LAUREL BAIT CO., INC.
Kalispell Mont.

$75 – 125

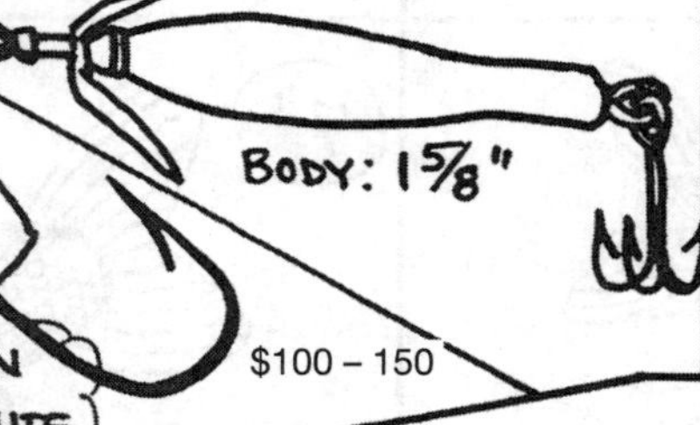

BODY: 1⅝"

1952 $10 – 15

"SAM-BO"

A Lure For Fishing & Fun

Every tackle Box Should Have one
Catch Bass, Pickerel, Pike, Walleyes and all Game Fish. SAM-BO Gives You Laughs and Fun. Makes an ideal gift for your fishermen friends.
If your dealer can not supply, send for "SAM-BO" post paid to

Novelty Lure Co.
Box 164 Lincoln, Nebr.

(SPOON)

$5 – 10

MIN-NIX

MIN-NIX WOBBLER

The greatest killer for bass, pickerel, pike, trout and muscallonge. Imitates live bait perfectly.
No. 1, in heavy weight German Silver, or No. 1a, heavy weight Polished Brass, No. 1b, heavy German Silver and Gold inside, prepaid. *Special prices to dealers ordering early.*

R. G. NIXON
905 South Avenue Rochester, N. Y.

JOS. NESS CO. - MPL'S. MN.

$75 – 150

½ actual size
PATENTED

FISH ALL DAY WITH ONE LIVE MINNOW
IN A
NIFTY MINNE

⅓ actual size
PATENTED DEC. 9-1913

1913

A Practical, permanent, live fish bait for salt or fresh water fishing. Minnow, frog, grasshopper or other bait enclosed in patented, non-breakable, transparent case. Inlet and outlet holes allow water to flow through slowly, keeping minnow alive. No child's toy. No glass to break. Nickel plated fittings. Hooks interchangeable. Weight 1 oz. Success demonstrated for three seasons. For sale by all dealers or sent parcels postpaid in U. S., Canada Made only by

JOS. M. NESS CO. E-740 Plymouth Building MINNEAPOLIS, MINN.

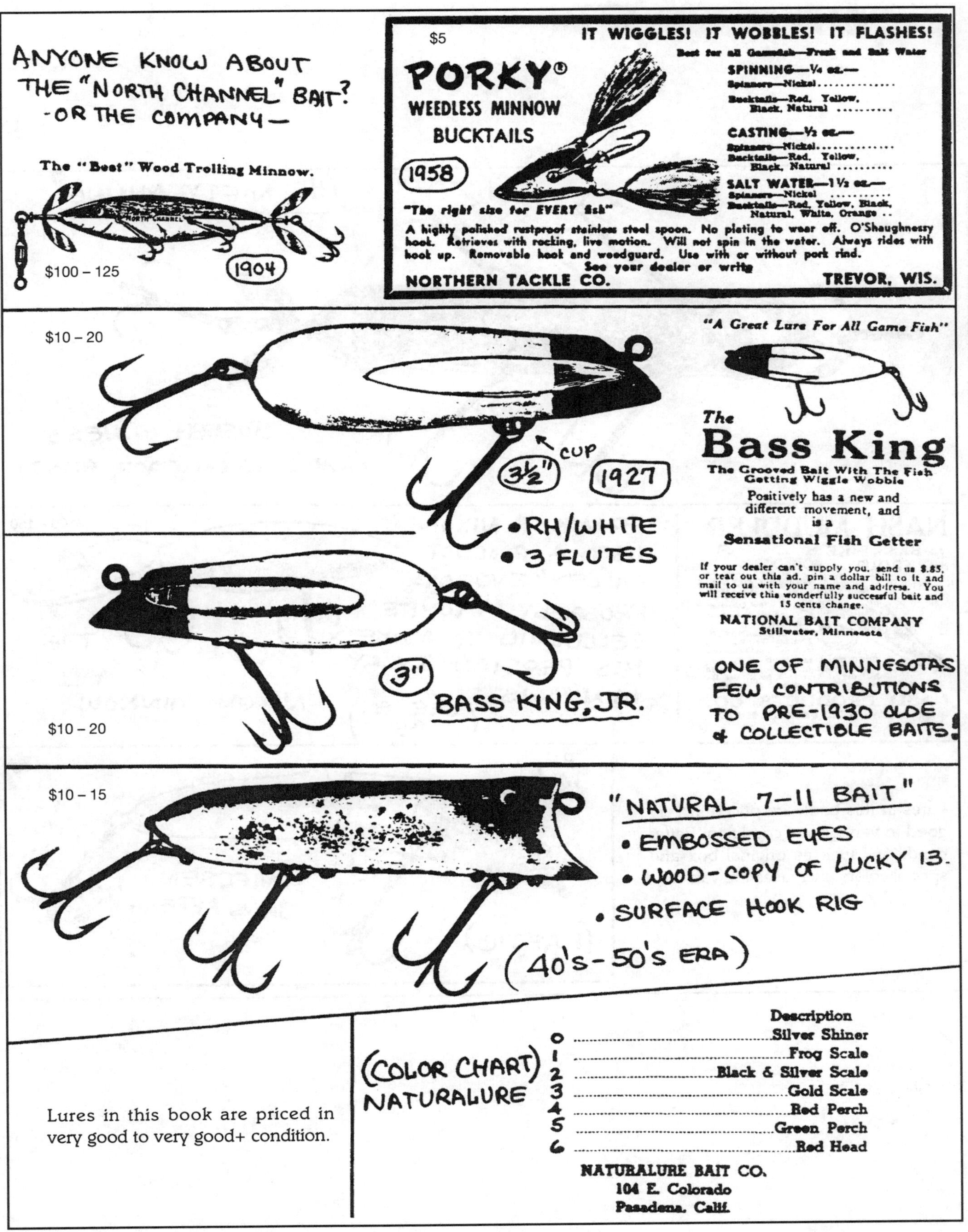
ANYONE KNOW ABOUT THE "NORTH CHANNEL" BAIT? -OR THE COMPANY-
The "Best" Wood Trolling Minnow.
$100 – 125
1904
$5
IT WIGGLES! IT WOBBLES! IT FLASHES!
SPINNING—¼ oz.—
CASTING—½ oz.—
SALT WATER—1½ oz.—
Natural, White, Orange
PORKY®
WEEDLESS MINNOW
BUCKTAILS
1958
"The right size for EVERY fish"
A highly polished rustproof stainless steel spoon. No plating to wear off. O'Shaughnessy hook. Retrieves with rocking, live motion. Will not spin in the water. Always rides with hook up. Removable hook and weedguard. Use with or without pork rind.
See your dealer or write
NORTHERN TACKLE CO.
TREVOR, WIS.
$10 – 20
CUP
3½"
1927
• RH/WHITE
• 3 FLUTES
"A Great Lure For All Game Fish"
The
Bass King
The Grooved Bait With The Fish Getting Wiggle Wobble
Positively has a new and different movement, and is a
Sensational Fish Getter
If your dealer can't supply you, send us $.85, or tear out this ad, pin a dollar bill to it and mail to us with your name and address. You will receive this wonderfully successful bait and 15 cents change.
NATIONAL BAIT COMPANY
Stillwater, Minnesota
3"
BASS KING, JR.
$10 – 20
ONE OF MINNESOTAS FEW CONTRIBUTIONS TO PRE-1930 OLDE & COLLECTIBLE BAITS!
$10 – 15
"NATURAL 7-11 BAIT"
• EMBOSSED EYES
• WOOD-COPY OF LUCKY 13.
• SURFACE HOOK RIG
(40's-50's ERA)
(COLOR CHART) NATURALURE
Description
0 Silver Shiner
1 Frog Scale
2 Black & Silver Scale
3 Gold Scale
4 Red Perch
5 Green Perch
6 Red Head
NATURALURE BAIT CO.
104 E. Colorado
Pasadena, Calif.

Lures in this book are priced in very good to very good+ condition.

$150 – 200

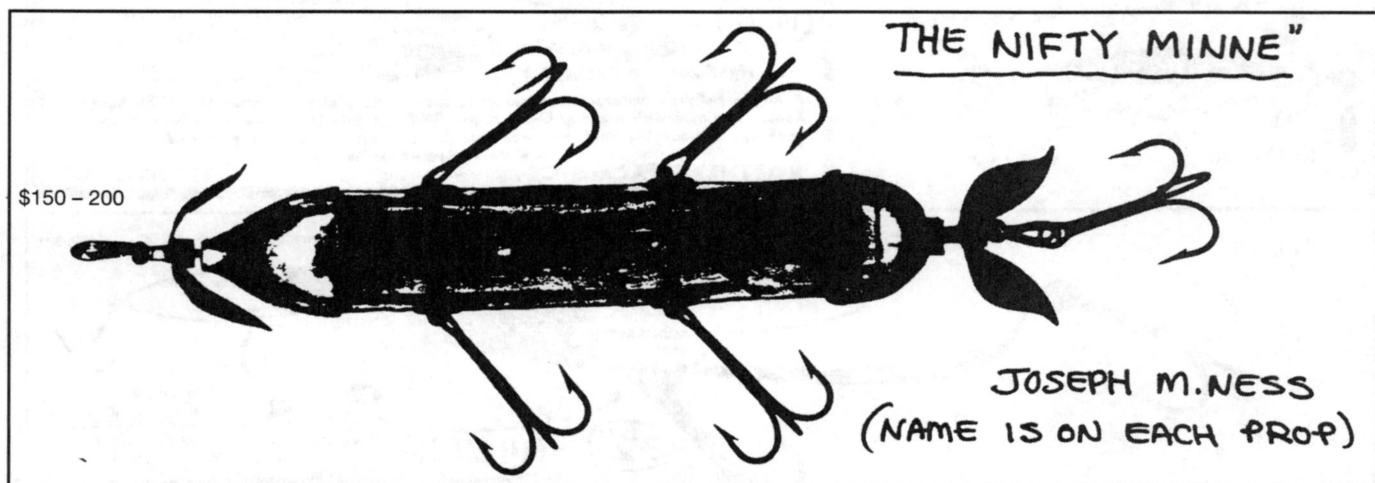
THE NIFTY MINNE"
JOSEPH M.NESS
(NAME IS ON EACH PROP)

$5 – 10

NASH MUDDLER
for BASS, PIKE and TROUT
1925
"No fisherman should be without this bait."
L. C. MANNETH,
President West Michigan
Game & Fish. Prot. Asso.
RESULTS: 2 bass, 5 pike in 2½ hrs.; 1 bass, 1 pike in 10 min.; 35 trout in half day; 7 bass in 3 hours. See the Nash Muddler at your dealer's or send direct to us.
NASH PRODUCTS CO.
12301 ILENE AVE., DETROIT, MICH.

$100 – 150

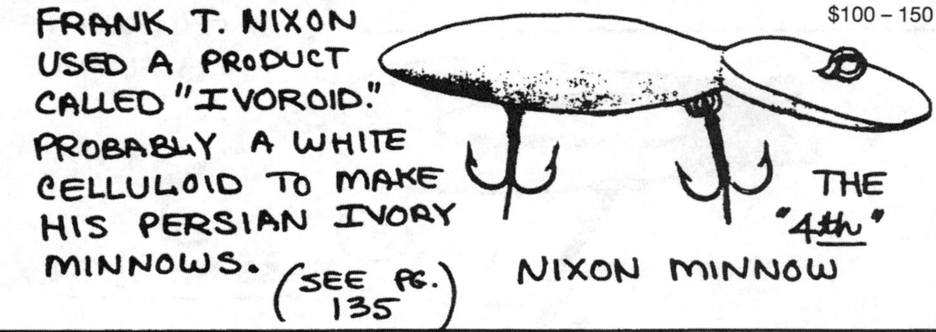

FRANK T. NIXON USED A PRODUCT CALLED "IVOROID." PROBABLY A WHITE CELLULOID TO MAKE HIS PERSIAN IVORY MINNOWS. (SEE PG. 135)

THE "4th" NIXON MINNOW

Lures in this book are priced in very good to very good+ condition. Better condition, such as original box and special colors, increases the value.

$5

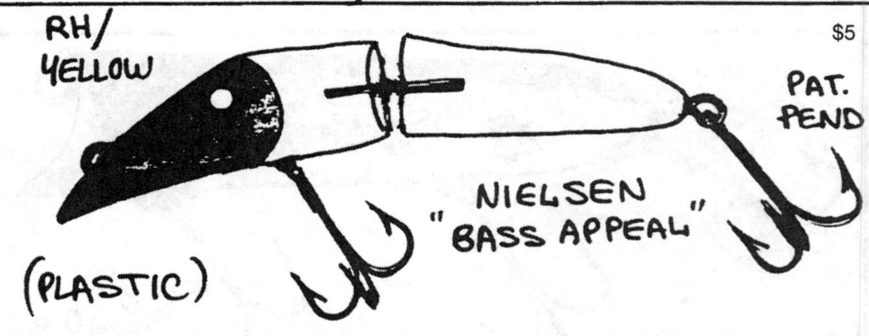
RH/
YELLOW
PAT.
PEND
NIELSEN
"BASS APPEAL"
(PLASTIC)

Outing Mfg. Co. **Elkhart, Indiana**

OUTING MFG. CO.
Elkhart-Indiana

Made of Hollow Bronze *Celluloid Colored*

GOOD OUTING GOODS

Manufacturers of Sporting Specialties including the "Getum" line of lures, "Durabilt" Tackle and Fly Boxes, folding camp furniture and Dewey's folding metal Bird Decoys.

$30 – 50

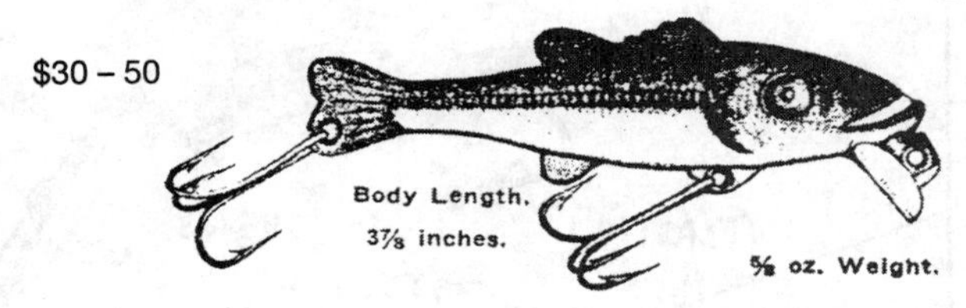
Body Length, 3⅞ inches.
⅝ oz. Weight.

1200 SERIES BASSY GETUM
Six Colors, ⅝ oz.

$30 – 50

No. 400 Series Outing's Floater Getum.
Four Colors, ¾ oz.

(COMES MOUNTED ON ALUMINUM RULE TO MEASURE FISH.)

3 SIZES

$5 – 10

PORKY GETTUM

No. 500 Series Outing's Porky Getum.
Four Colors, ½, ⅝ and ¾ oz.

(3 SIZES)

$5 – 10

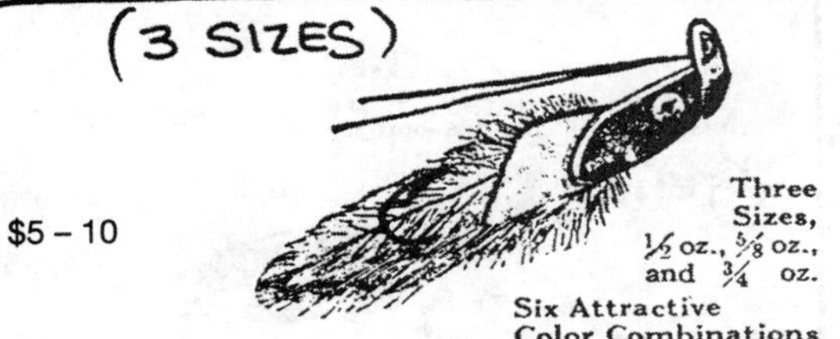
Three Sizes, ½ oz., ⅝ oz., and ¾ oz.
Six Attractive Color Combinations

"Feather Getum"

The "Feather Getum" is the original metal bodied lure—the big brother of the entire Dewey line. Has hackle feather tail, and colored rubber fins.

(METAL COVERED WITH CELLULOID) (3 SIZES)

$5 – 10

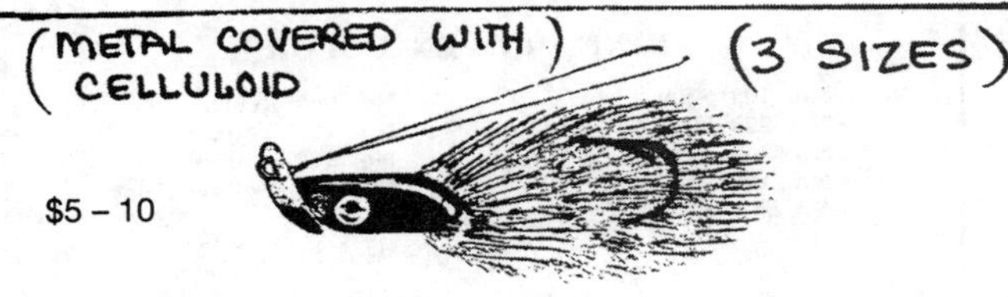

No. 800 Series Outing's Bucky Getum.
Six Colors, ½, ⅝ and ¾ oz.

$30 – 50

Body Length, 3⅜ inches ½ oz. Weight.

(Supplied with treble, double or single hooks)

1000 SERIES PIKY GETUM
Nine Colors, ½ oz.

DU-GETUM

$30 – 50

3⅛"
2¾"

NEW 1925

2 SIZES

700 AND 750 SERIES DU-GETUM
¾ and ½ oz. Six colors.

Our DU-GETUM was born of necessity and is the result of years of more or less patient experimenting to make a lure that is almost wholly weedless, a good hooker, and with an action on the surface. The biggest fish are almost always in the weeds where other lures won't hook fish. They get strikes all right, we don't claim a monopoly on strikes, but to successfully hook fish in weeds, the lure must be constructed so that the body will ward off weeds and yet with the hooks placed just right to hook fish, whether a nippin' short striker, or the big boy that wants to swallow the lure.

(GRASS FROG – BULL FROG – FIELD MOUSE – ALUMINUM/RED – WHITE/RED – BLACK)

$10 – 20

HEDDON BOUGHT OUT OUTING IN 1927

HEDDON OUTING

(AND QUIT MAKING THE METAL LURES.)

No. 105 and No. 108 Winona Reels.

This is the only line of hollow metal bodied lures in America. Colored with celluloid enamel. This combination gives you lures that last. They won't chip, swell, splinter, or split. They strike the water with less noise and disturbance than wooden body lures.

REEL ILLUS. FOR YOU REEL COLLECTOR TYPES

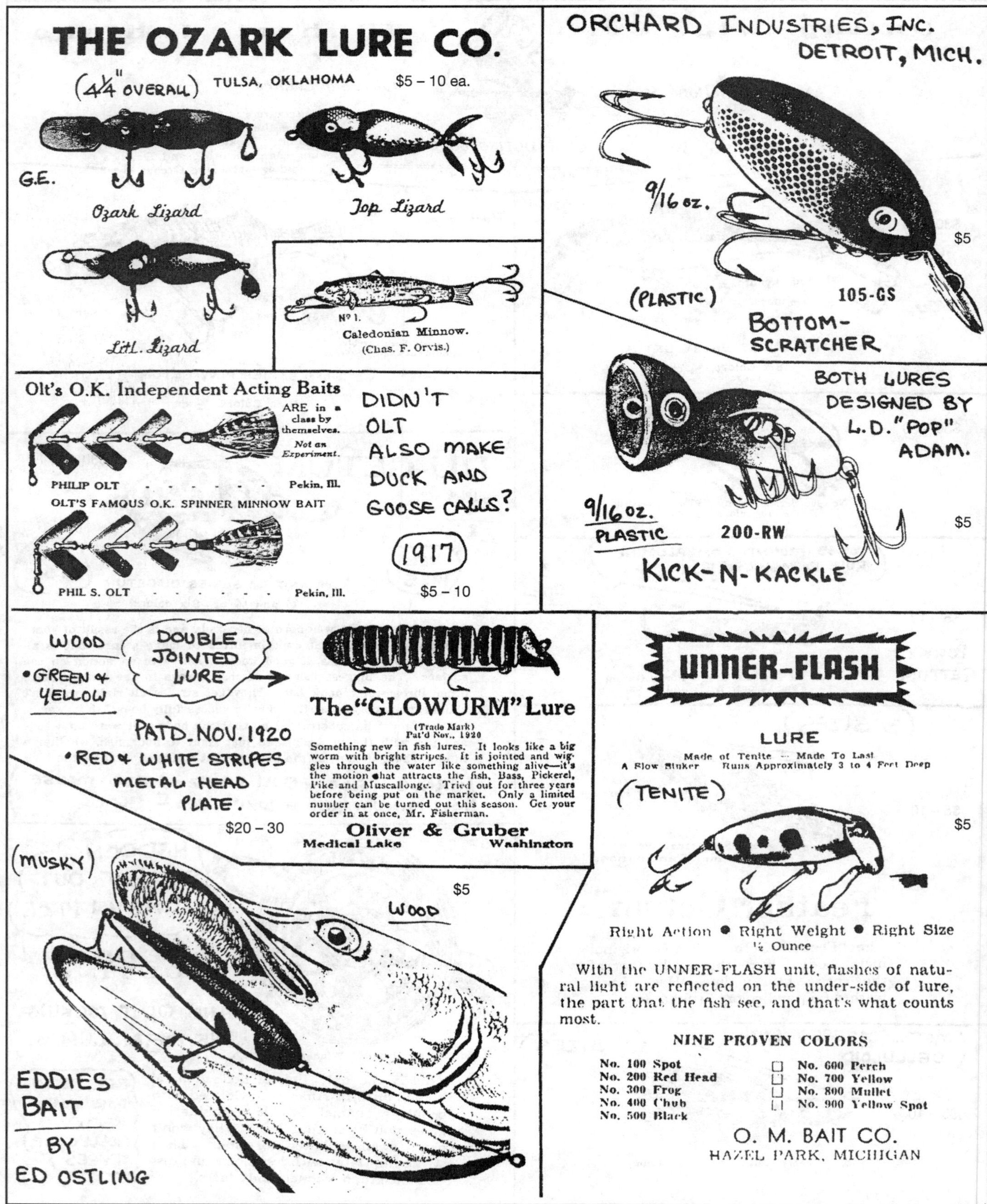
THE OZARK LURE CO.
(4¼" OVERALL) TULSA, OKLAHOMA $5 – 10 ea.
G.E.
Ozark Lizard
Top Lizard
Litl. Lizard
Nº 1.
Caledonian Minnow.
(Chas. F. Orvis.)
ORCHARD INDUSTRIES, INC.
DETROIT, MICH.
9/16 oz.
$5
(PLASTIC)
105-GS
BOTTOM-SCRATCHER
BOTH LURES DESIGNED BY L.D. "POP" ADAM.
9/16 oz.
PLASTIC
200-RW
$5
KICK-N-KACKLE
Olt's O.K. Independent Acting Baits
ARE in a class by themselves.
Not an Experiment.
PHILIP OLT Pekin, Ill.
OLT'S FAMOUS O.K. SPINNER MINNOW BAIT
PHIL S. OLT Pekin, Ill.
DIDN'T OLT ALSO MAKE DUCK AND GOOSE CALLS?
1917
$5 – 10
WOOD
• GREEN & YELLOW
DOUBLE-JOINTED LURE
PATD. NOV. 1920
• RED & WHITE STRIPES
METAL HEAD PLATE.
$20 – 30
The "GLOWURM" Lure
(Trade Mark)
Pat'd Nov., 1920
Something new in fish lures. It looks like a big worm with bright stripes. It is jointed and wiggles through the water like something alive—it's the motion that attracts the fish, Bass, Pickerel, Pike and Muscallonge. Tried out for three years before being put on the market. Only a limited number can be turned out this season. Get your order in at once, Mr. Fisherman.
Oliver & Gruber
Medical Lake Washington
UNNER-FLASH
LURE
Made of Tenite — Made To Last
A Slow Sinker Runs Approximately 3 to 4 Feet Deep
(TENITE)
$5
Right Action • Right Weight • Right Size
½ Ounce
With the UNNER-FLASH unit, flashes of natural light are reflected on the under-side of lure, the part that the fish see, and that's what counts most.
NINE PROVEN COLORS
No. 100 Spot
No. 200 Red Head
No. 300 Frog
No. 400 Chub
No. 500 Black
No. 600 Perch
No. 700 Yellow
No. 800 Mullet
No. 900 Yellow Spot
O. M. BAIT CO.
HAZEL PARK, MICHIGAN
(MUSKY)
$5
WOOD
EDDIES BAIT
BY
ED OSTLING

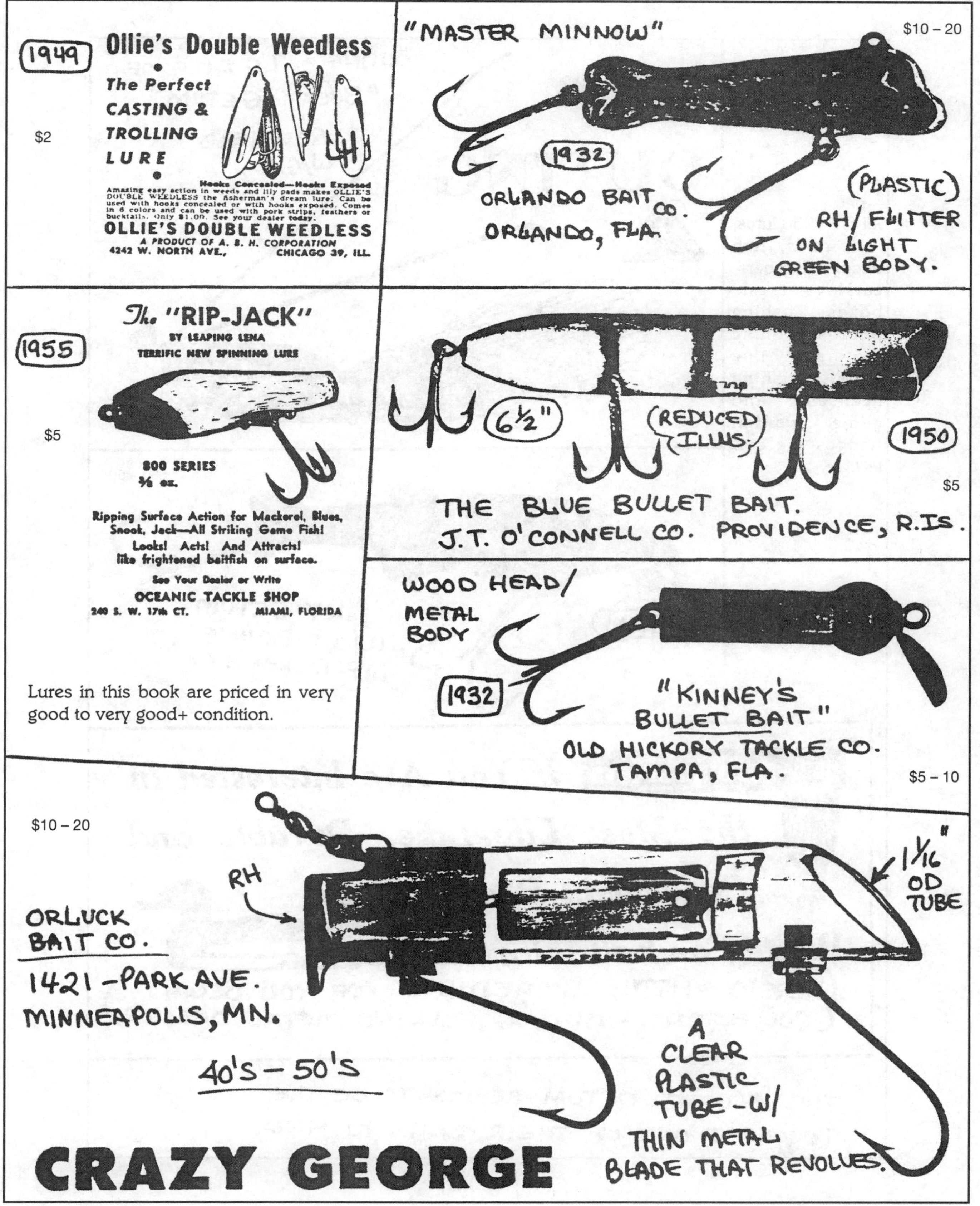
1949
Ollie's Double Weedless
The Perfect
CASTING &
TROLLING
LURE
$2
Hooks Concealed—Hooks Exposed
Amazing easy action in weeds and lily pads makes OLLIE'S DOUBLE WEEDLESS the fisherman's dream lure. Can be used with hooks concealed or with hooks exposed. Comes in 6 colors and can be used with pork strips, feathers or bucktails. Only $1.00. See your dealer today.
OLLIE'S DOUBLE WEEDLESS
A PRODUCT OF A. B. H. CORPORATION
4242 W. NORTH AVE., CHICAGO 39, ILL.
"MASTER MINNOW"
$10 – 20
1932
ORLANDO BAIT CO.
ORLANDO, FLA.
(PLASTIC)
RH/FLITTER
ON LIGHT
GREEN BODY.
The "RIP-JACK"
BY LEAPING LENA
TERRIFIC NEW SPINNING LURE
1955
$5
800 SERIES
⅜ oz.
Ripping Surface Action for Mackerel, Blues, Snook, Jack—All Striking Game Fish!
Looks! Acts! And Attracts!
like frightened baitfish on surface.
See Your Dealer or Write
OCEANIC TACKLE SHOP
240 S. W. 17th CT. MIAMI, FLORIDA
6½"
(REDUCED ILLUS.)
1950
$5
THE BLUE BULLET BAIT.
J.T. O'CONNELL CO. PROVIDENCE, R.IS.
WOOD HEAD/
METAL
BODY
1932
"KINNEY'S
BULLET BAIT"
OLD HICKORY TACKLE CO.
TAMPA, FLA.
$5 – 10
Lures in this book are priced in very good to very good+ condition.
$10 – 20
RH
ORLUCK
BAIT CO.
1421-PARK AVE.
MINNEAPOLIS, MN.
40'S – 50'S
1 1/16"
OD
TUBE
A
CLEAR
PLASTIC
TUBE-W/
THIN METAL
BLADE THAT REVOLVES.
CRAZY GEORGE

All pre-1950 lures, rod, reels, fish decoys, bobbers, catalogs, tackle boxes, fishing photos, trolling motors, line spools, fishing licenses, and game warden badges are collectible.

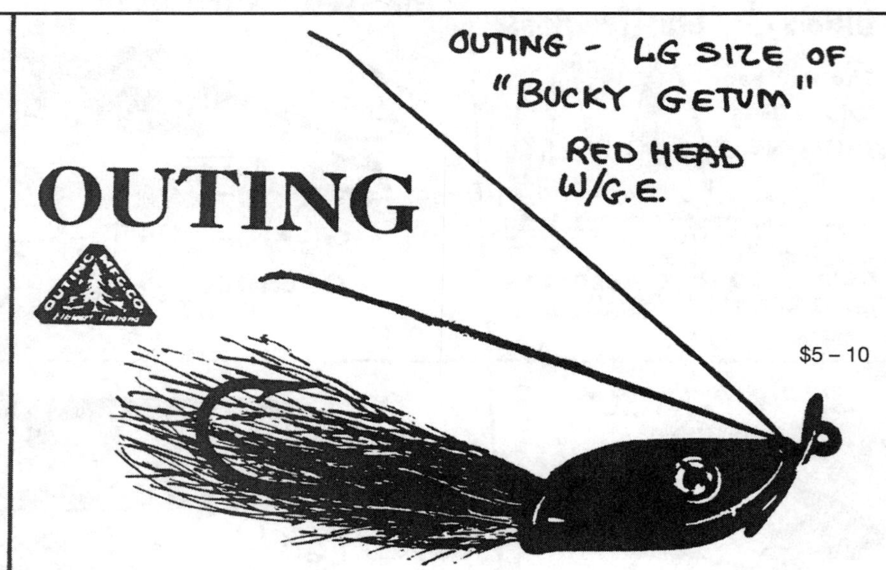
OUTING
OUTING - LG SIZE OF "BUCKY GETUM"
RED HEAD W/G.E.

$5 – 10

THIN
PIKY GETUM W/OUT DIVING LIP- (SURFACE?)

$30 – 50

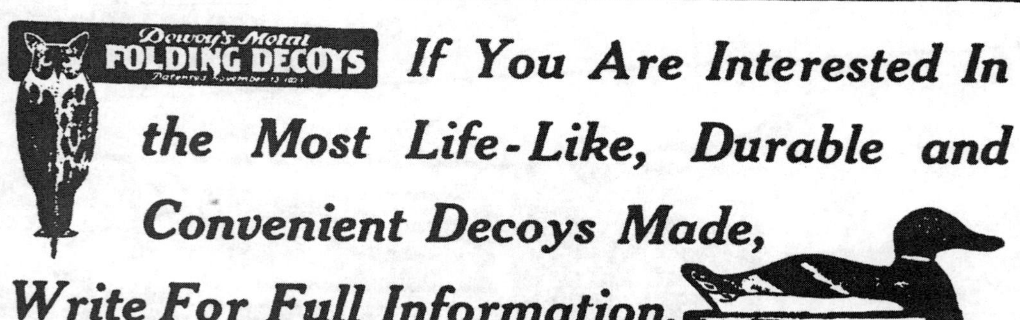
Dewey's Metal
FOLDING DECOYS
If You Are Interested In the Most Life-Like, Durable and Convenient Decoys Made,
Write For Full Information.
(HERE'S ALITTLE SOMETHING FOR YOU DECOY COLLECTORS - OUTING FOLDING METAL DECOYS)

THE FLOATER GETUM SEEMS TO BE THE TOUGHEST ONE OF THEIR BAITS TO FIND.

Established 1864
PFLUEGER
PRONOUNCED "FLEW-GER"
The Oldest and Largest Manufacturer of Fishing Tackle in the United States.

THE AMERICAN FISH HOOK CO. (ESTABLISHED 1864) WAS AN ANCESTOR OF THE AKRON FISHING TACKLE WORKS WHICH BECAME THE ENTERPRISE MFG. CO. - WHICH BECAME PFLUEGER, (THUS 1864.)

NOTE SURFACE HOOK RIG ILLUS.

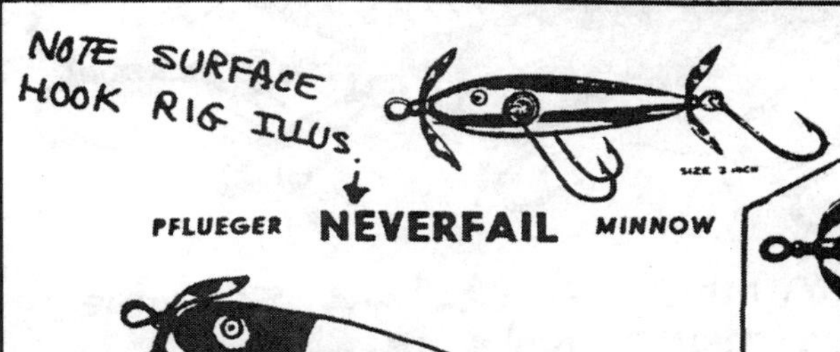

PFLUEGER **NEVERFAIL** MINNOW

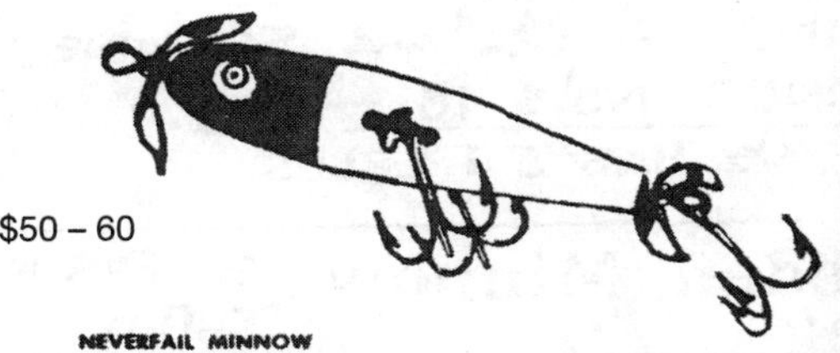

$50 – 60

NEVERFAIL MINNOW

One of the finest underwater baits made. It is highly recommended when necessary to go down deep for fish at certain times of the year.

No			Minnow Size—inch 2½	3¼
3106	Natural Perch—Scale finish	Color 06		
3169	White—Red—Yellow and Black Spots	Color 69		
3173	Rainbow	Color 73		
3185	Green Cracked Back	Color 85		
3193	Yellow Perch	Color 93		
3196	White Body, Red Head	Color 96		

LATER MODELS WERE 2½" and 3¼" – WITH PAINTED EYES.

PFLUEGER NEVERFAIL MINNOW

Trade Marks Reg. U. S. Pat. Office

Underwater or Sinking Minnow

$75 – 150

Size 3 Inch

Size 3⅝ Inch

	Minnow Size, Inches	3	3⅝
Length of Body	Inch	3	3⅝
Treble Hook, Ringed—On Tail	Sizes	1	1
Treble Hook, Ringed—On Side	Sizes	1	1
Fishing Weight of Minnow	Ounce	¾	1

Neverfail Minnow is one of the very best underwater or sinking baits on the market and is recommended when necessary to go down deep for the fish which is required at certain times and seasons of the year. Every angler should carry an assortment of these minnows in his tackle kit. Luminous Minnows are equally as effective for day as for evening or night fishing and are especially suited for deep or roily waters and cloudy days. Expose to either day or artificial light before using.

No.	Minnow Size, Inches	3	3⅝
3170	Luminous Enamel—Gold Spots		
3105	Natural Frog—Scale Finish		
3106	Natural Perch—Scale Finish		
3107	Natural Chub—Scale Finish		
3165	White Enamel—Frog Back		
3169	White Enamel—Green and Red Spots		
3173	Rainbow		
3174	Yellow Enamel—Red and Green Back		
3181	Red Enamel Complete		
3185	Green Cracked Back		
3193	Yellow Perch		
3196	White Enamel—Red Head		

PFLUEGER CRAWFISH BAIT

Trade Mark Reg. U. S. Pat. Office

(RUBBER)

$5 – 15

Actual Size

NO. 761

PFLUEGER METALIZED MINNOW

Trade Mark Reg. U. S. Pat. Office—Patented April 12, 1910 — Oct. 24, 1911

Under Water or Sinking Minnow

$100 – 150

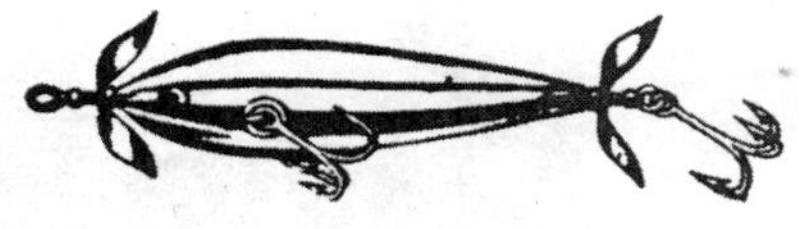

No. 2887—Size 3 Inch

Polished Nickel Over All

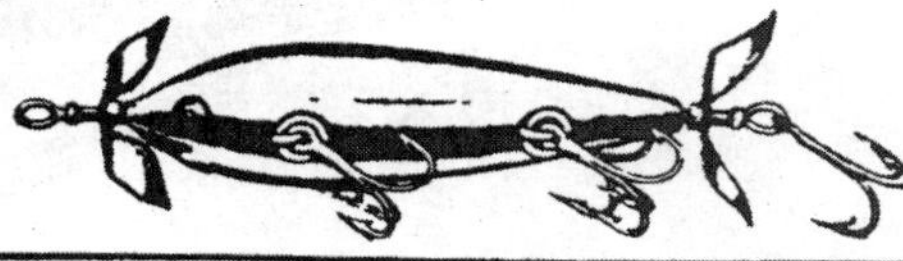

No. 2887 Size 3⅝ Inch

Polished Nickel Over All

$5 – 15

PFLUEGER SHRIMP BAIT

Trade Mark Reg. U. S. Pat. Office

(ACTUAL SIZE)

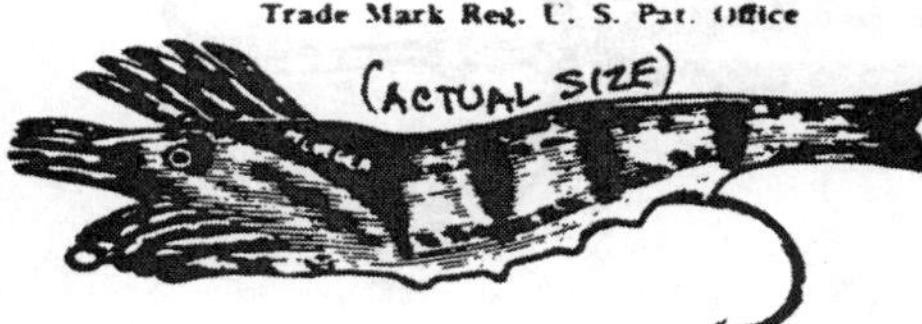

Actual Size

(RUBBER)

NO. 773

PFLUEGER RED DEVIL SPINNER

Trade Marks Reg. U. S. Pat. Office

No. 2700

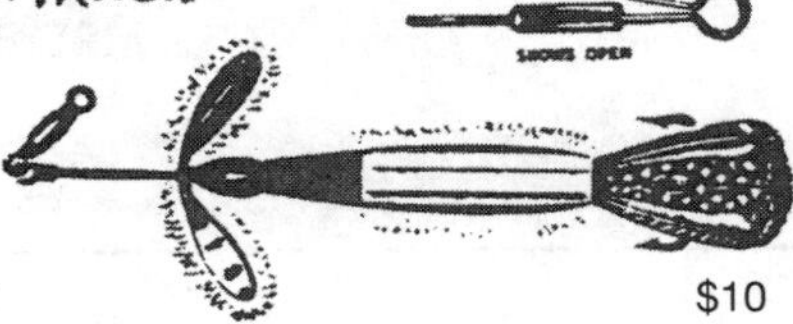

SLIDING SLEEVE HOOK CONNECTION
SHOWS OPEN

$10

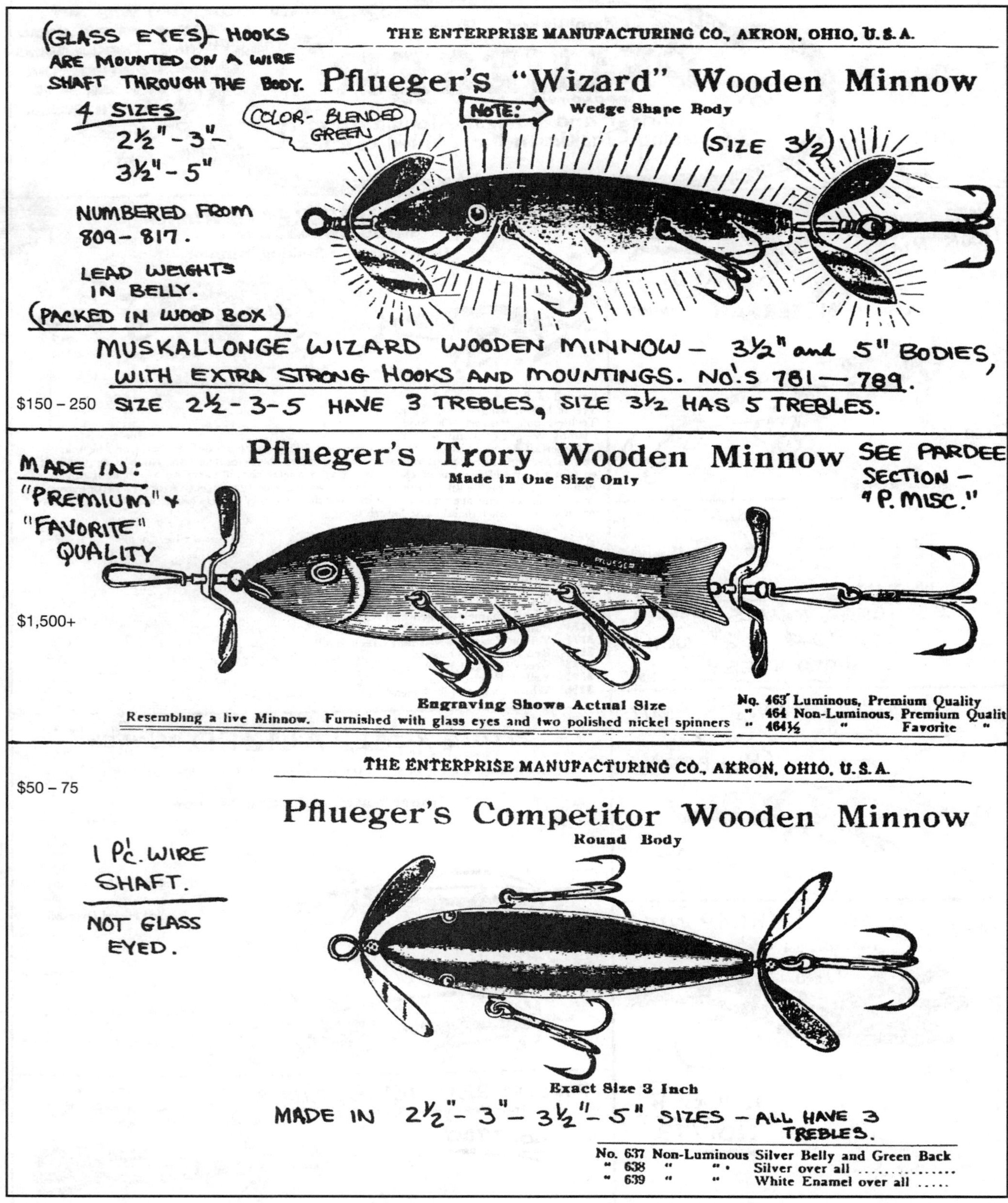
(GLASS EYES) HOOKS ARE MOUNTED ON A WIRE SHAFT THROUGH THE BODY.
THE ENTERPRISE MANUFACTURING CO., AKRON, OHIO, U.S.A.
Pflueger's "Wizard" Wooden Minnow
4 SIZES
2½" - 3" - 3½" - 5"
COLOR- BLENDED GREEN
NOTE:
Wedge Shape Body
(SIZE 3½)
NUMBERED FROM 809- 817.
LEAD WEIGHTS IN BELLY.
(PACKED IN WOOD BOX)
MUSKALLONGE WIZARD WOODEN MINNOW - 3½" and 5" BODIES, WITH EXTRA STRONG HOOKS AND MOUNTINGS. NO'.S 781 — 789.
SIZE 2½-3-5 HAVE 3 TREBLES, SIZE 3½ HAS 5 TREBLES.
Pflueger's Trory Wooden Minnow
Made in One Size Only
SEE PARDEE SECTION - "P. MISC."
MADE IN: "PREMIUM" & "FAVORITE" QUALITY
Engraving Shows Actual Size
Resembling a live Minnow. Furnished with glass eyes and two polished nickel spinners
No. 463 Luminous, Premium Quality
" 464 Non-Luminous, Premium Qualit
" 464½ " Favorite "
THE ENTERPRISE MANUFACTURING CO., AKRON, OHIO, U.S.A.
Pflueger's Competitor Wooden Minnow
Round Body
1 Pc. WIRE SHAFT.
NOT GLASS EYED.
Exact Size 3 Inch
MADE IN 2½" - 3" - 3½" - 5" SIZES - ALL HAVE 3 TREBLES.
No. 637 Non-Luminous Silver Belly and Green Back
" 638 " " Silver over all
" 639 " " White Enamel over all

$150 – 250

$1,500+

$50 – 75

No. 463. Luminous ......
No. 464. Non-Luminous

THE TRORY MINNOW

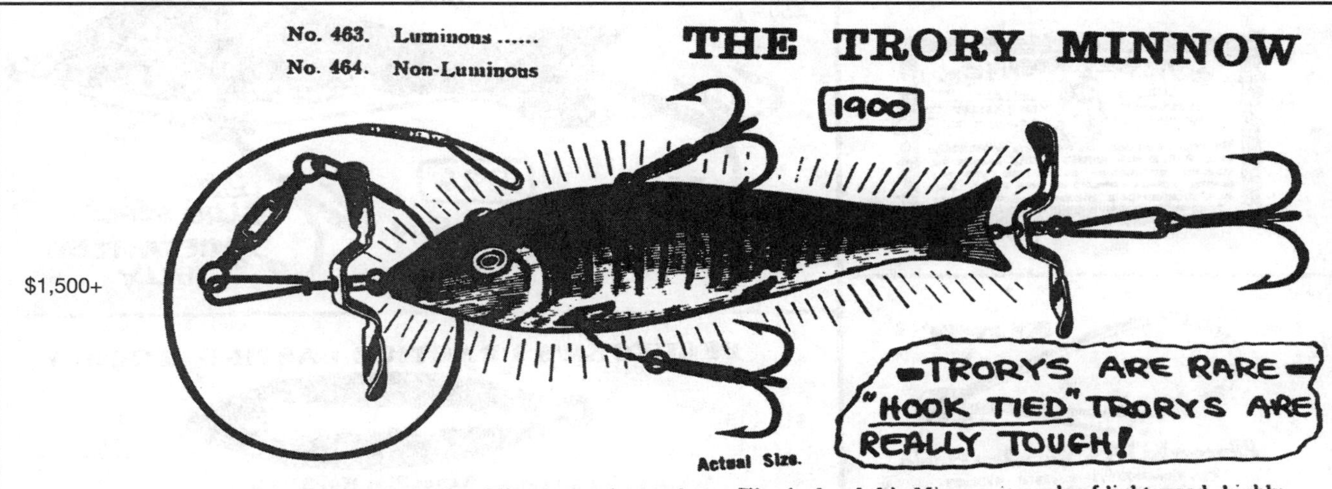
1900
—TRORYS ARE RARE—
"HOOK TIED" TRORYS ARE
REALLY TOUGH!

$1,500+

Actual Size.

More durable than any other Minnow on the market. The body of this Minnow is made of light wood, highly decorated, very buoyant, and is so weighted and balanced with lead that the instant it strikes the water, it swims upright with the head leaning slightly down. Both Spinners work freely, and very materially add to the attraction.

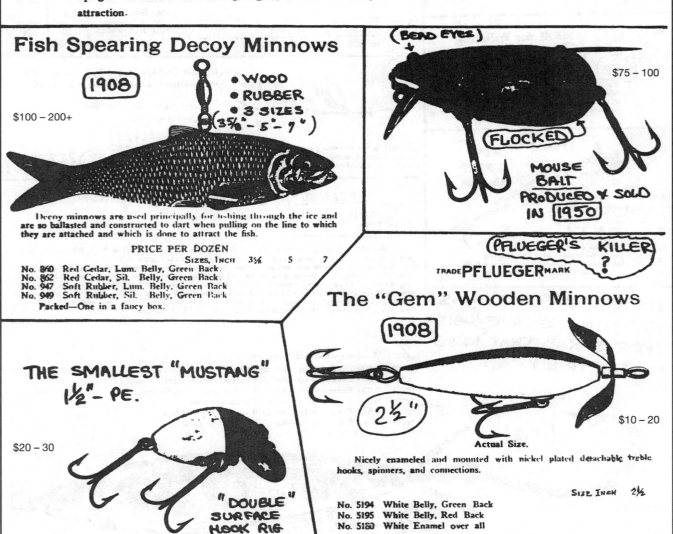

Fish Spearing Decoy Minnows

1908

• WOOD
• RUBBER
• 3 SIZES
(3⅝" - 5" - 7")

$100 – 200+

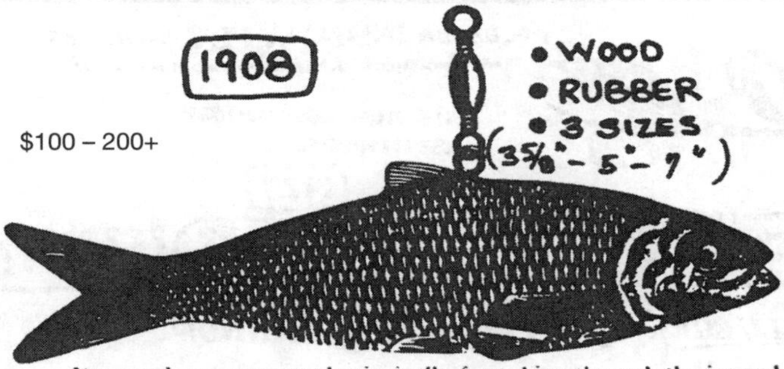

Decoy minnows are used principally for fishing through the ice and are so ballasted and constructed to dart when pulling on the line to which they are attached and which is done to attract the fish.

PRICE PER DOZEN

	Sizes, Inch	3⅝	5	7
No. 860	Red Cedar, Lum. Belly, Green Back.			
No. 862	Red Cedar, Sil. Belly, Green Back.			
No. 947	Soft Rubber, Lum. Belly, Green Back			
No. 949	Soft Rubber, Sil. Belly, Green Back			

Packed—One in a fancy box.

(BEAD EYES)

$75 – 100

FLOCKED

MOUSE BAIT
PRODUCED & SOLD
IN 1950

(PFLUEGER'S KILLER?)

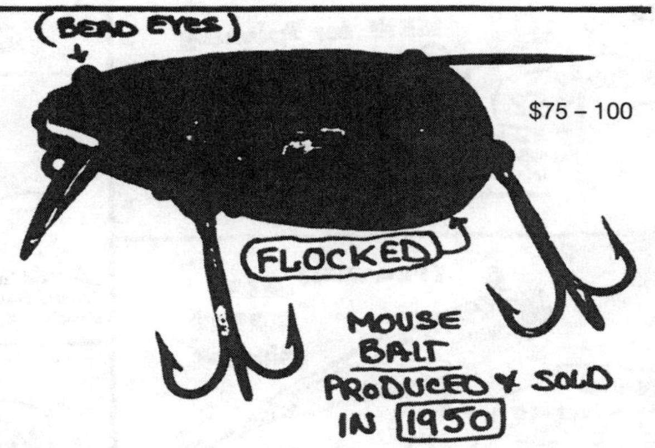

TRADE PFLUEGER MARK

The "Gem" Wooden Minnows

1908

2½"

$10 – 20

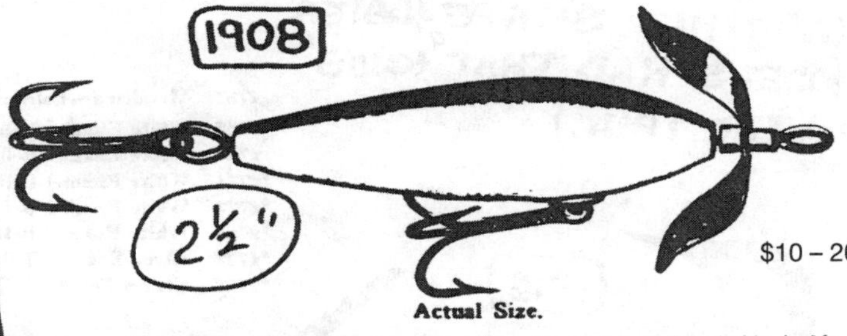

Actual Size.

Nicely enameled and mounted with nickel plated detachable treble hooks, spinners, and connections.

		Size, Inch 2½
No. 5194	White Belly, Green Back	
No. 5195	White Belly, Red Back	
No. 5180	White Enamel over all	

THE SMALLEST "MUSTANG"
1½" - PE.

$20 – 30

"DOUBLE" SURFACE HOOK RIG

OUR GUARANTEE
WITHOUT TIME LIMIT
We hereby guarantee the purchaser of Pflueger Bull Dog brand fishing tackle against all defective workmanship or material and will promptly repair or replace the same free of cost when such defect is brought to our attention

$50 – 75

1926
MODEL PAKRON MINNOW
•G.E.
•BLUE SCALE
•METALIZED BELLY

$2

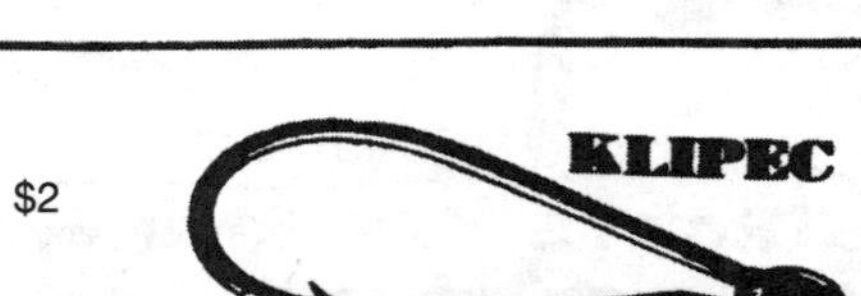
KLIPEC

Pflueger KLIPEC Weedless Hook

Pat. Nos. 1573553—1617318—1730383
One size—5/0. Tin plated
Price 15c each

Rides easily over weeds without becoming snagged, yet offers no resistance to the strike.

PFLUEGER'S PRACTICE CASTING MINNOW

$10 – 15

Exact Size No. 2

Made of wood and enameled white. Ballasted with lead on one end and equiped with a brass eye on the other. Made in two weights as follows:

	Size No.	1	2
	Weight, Ounces	¼	½
No. 880 Practice Casting Minnow			

$2

NEW for Spinning
NIFTEE
SPINNER
NEW - 1952

Weighs only 1/5 oz.—ideal for spin-casting. 4 color combinations. Size 4 hook. 65c

PFLUEGER INDIANA FLY SPINNERS

Trade Mark Reg. U. S. Pat. Office-Patent No. 480132

$2

SINGLE OR DOUBLE SPINNERS

1927

Supplied in the following patterns: Professor, Rube Wood, Silver Doctor, White Miller, Black Gnat, Coachman, Cow Dung.

COW DUNG? ????????

$5

(FLOATER)
NEW
JERKIT
Minnow
NEW - 1952

Jerk the line, it darts left—jerk again, it darts right. Here's the friskiest little bait that ever hit water. Get it now and catch more fish this summer. In 4 colors. 2¾" long. $1.00

PFLUEGER CATALINA MINNOW

4½" - 5"

Patented April 12, 1910

Especially designed for Bass, Pike, Muskallonge, Pickerel, Yellow Tail, Barracuda, Skipjacks, Bonita, Albacore and many other fresh and saltwater game fish.

Bodies are made of selected red cedar, beautifully blended with our special elastic indestructible waterproof porcelain enamels and metallic nickel and sufficiently weighted to ride "*right side up*" at any speed—mounted with extra stout, finest quality tinned Catalina O'Shaughnessy Hooks, brightly polished nickel plated spinners and with a square phosphor bronze shaft running clear through the same which prevents the Body from turning and holds the hook "*point up*," the very best position to receive the strike of the fish.

THE EARLY CATALINAS HAD THIS SHAPE. (LATER MODELS HAD THAT "KNOB" ON THE TAIL.)

No.		Sizes, Inches 4½	5
2787	Metalized—Polished Nickel over all	...	...
*2766	White Enamel Belly—Blended Gold Back	...	
2769	White Enamel Belly—Blended Green and Red Spots	...	...
*2771	White Enamel Belly—Blended Yellow and Green Back	...	
*2773	White Enamel Belly—Blended Rainbow Back	...	
2785	White Enamel Belly—Blended Green Cracked Back	...	
*2777	Silver Enamel Belly—Blended Dark Blue Back	...	
*2793	Yellow Perch	...	

5"

1916
NO. 2769 - 4½"

$100 – 150+

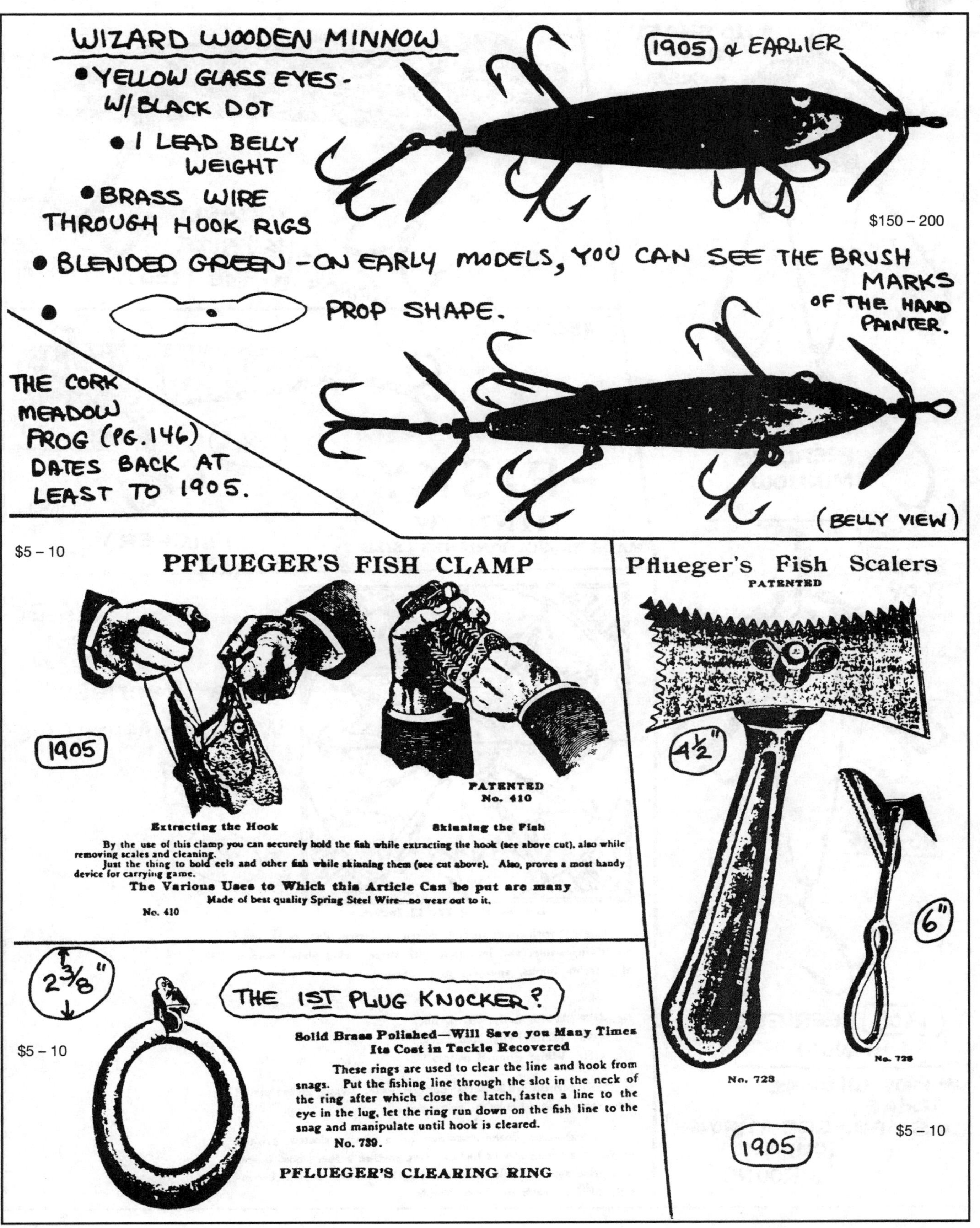
WIZARD WOODEN MINNOW
•YELLOW GLASS EYES - W/BLACK DOT
• 1 LEAD BELLY WEIGHT
•BRASS WIRE THROUGH HOOK RIGS
• BLENDED GREEN - ON EARLY MODELS, YOU CAN SEE THE BRUSH MARKS OF THE HAND PAINTER.
• PROP SHAPE.
1905 & EARLIER
$150 – 200
THE CORK MEADOW FROG (PG.146) DATES BACK AT LEAST TO 1905.
(BELLY VIEW)
$5 – 10
PFLUEGER'S FISH CLAMP
1905
PATENTED
No. 410
Extracting the Hook
Skinning the Fish
By the use of this clamp you can securely hold the fish while extracting the hook (see above cut), also while removing scales and cleaning.
Just the thing to hold eels and other fish while skinning them (see cut above). Also, proves a most handy device for carrying game.
The Various Uses to Which this Article Can be put are many
Made of best quality Spring Steel Wire—no wear out to it.
No. 410
Pflueger's Fish Scalers
PATENTED
4½"
6"
No. 728
No. 723
1905
$5 – 10
2⅜"
THE 1ST PLUG KNOCKER?
$5 – 10
Solid Brass Polished—Will Save you Many Times Its Cost in Tackle Recovered
These rings are used to clear the line and hook from snags. Put the fishing line through the slot in the neck of the ring after which close the latch, fasten a line to the eye in the lug, let the ring run down on the fish line to the snag and manipulate until hook is cleared.
No. 739.
PFLUEGER'S CLEARING RING

$5 – 10

• NO SHAFT PROP
• SCREW EYE HOOKS
• ROUND
• CHEAP PAINT
THE 1929 PEERLESS MINNOW
BRASS PROP
NO. 4195
1908 PEERLESS MINNOW
• PROP W/ BRASS SHAFT
• SMALL-"SEE THROUGH" CUPS.
• ROUND

$10

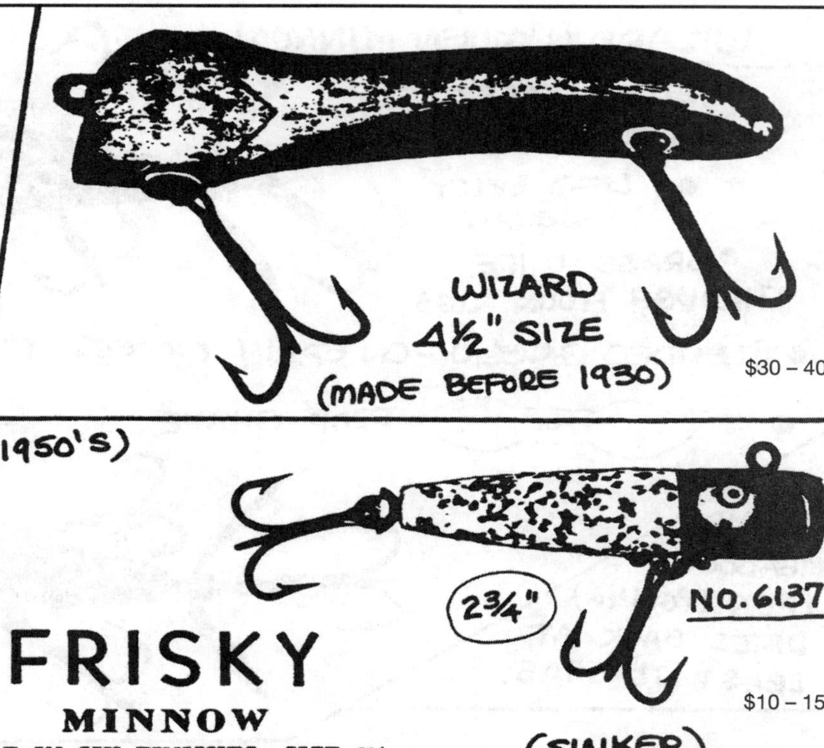
WIZARD
4½" SIZE
(MADE BEFORE 1930)
(1950'S)
2¾"
NO. 6137
FRISKY
MINNOW
MADE IN SIX FINISHES - SIZE 2¾
(SINKER)

$30 – 40

$10 – 15

$1,500+

PEERLESS
PEERLESS
PEERLESS
PEERLESS

Display Card 12 x 12 Inches.

The "Peerless" Wooden Minnows

1908

2½"

Coated with our special elastic indestructible waterproof porcelain enamel and mounted with three nickel plated detachable treble hooks, spinners and connections.

	Size, Inch 2½
No. 4194 White Belly, Green Back	
No. 4195 White Belly, Red Back	
No. 4180 White Enamel over all	

Will furnish with special pattern, extra strong nickel plated detachable single hooks at same price.

Packed—One dozen minnows on a heavy, slotted, printed display card, size 12 x 12 inches. One card in a fancy box, unless otherwise specified will send our regular assortment which consists of four each of above blends.

PFLUEGER'S CELEBRATED WOODEN MINNOWS

—MANUFACTURED BY—

THE ENTERPRISE MANUFACTURING COMPANY AKRON, OHIO, U. S. A.

We are the original Manufacturers of Wooden Minnows and they immediately found ready favor with the Angler, as a Lure for Bass and game fish; generally they have few equals. The Minnows for both "Surface" and "Under Water" fishing are furnished in a large variety of plain and blended colors. "Pflueger's Minnows" are made of selected stock, carefully shaped, and coated with from eight to twelve coats of a Special Elastic, indestructable and water proof, Porcelain Enamel, made from our own formula which has met all the severe tests usually put upon baits of this kind. Each Minnow is mounted with Nickel Plated detachable hooks, spinners and connections. The highly polished spinner blades revolving opposite to each other not only creates a great attraction, but prevents the bait turning and the necessity of using a swivel. The bodies are ballasted in such a manner that they will at all times ride with perfect balance in the water, and present the hooks at the best possible angle for the attack of the fish.

Pflueger's "Simplex" Minnow

For Under Water Fishing

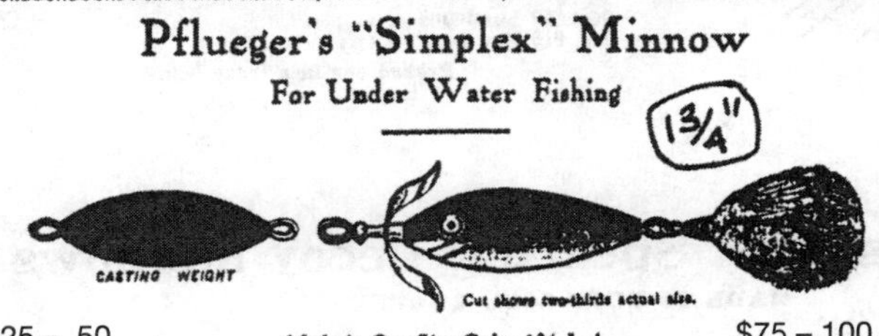
1¾"
CASTING WEIGHT

Cut shows two-thirds actual size.

$25 – 50 Made in One Size Only, 1¾ Inch $75 – 100

Treble Hooks are tied with genuine Buck Tail in colors. Casting weight furnished on both Premium and Favorite Qualities, to facilitace casting. Spinners and connections are gold plated on the Premium Quality, and Nickel Plated on the Favorite Quality, and are made only in the following colors:

STOCK No.	SIZE	LIST PRICES 1¾
No. 2475, Yellow Enamel Belly, Premium Quality, Price per Dozen Blended Brown Back.		
No. 2470, Gold Enamel Belly, Premium Quality, Price per Dozen Blended Dark Green Back.		
No. 2077, Silver Enamel Belly, Favorite Quality, Blended Dark Green Back.		

PLUEGER'S "MONARCH" MUSKALLONGE MINNOWS

For Under Water Fishing

4⅛"
3⅝"
5"

Cut shows two-thirds actual size.

$300 – 450+

Cut Shows Two-thirds Actual Size of 3¾ Inch Minnow

Mounted with extra Strong Treble Hooks and Connections, and is especially designed for not only the Muskallonge but all other heavy game fish. Each bait is mounted with detachable Nickel Plated Hooks, Spinners and Connections, and perfectly adapted for heavy fishing.

STOCK No.	SIZES	LIST PRICES 3¾	5
No. 2271, White Belly, Blended Green Back, Premium Quality, Per Doz.			
No. 2272, " " " Slate " " " " "			
No. 2273, " " " Rainbow " " " " "			
No. 2275, Yellow " " Brown " " " " "			
No. 2270, Red " " Brown " " " " "			

THE ENTERPRISE MANUFACTURING CO., AKRON, OHIO, U.S.A.

Pflueger's Muskallonge Minnow

$150 – 200

Cut shows two-thirds actual size.

MADE OF PURE SOFT RUBBER
MOUNTED EXTRA STRONG
PAINTED TRUE TO NATURE

THE MUSKALLONGE MINNOW

No. 818 Luminous ....
No. 819 Non-Luminous ....

Packed one in a fancy box.

Pflueger's Fish Spearing Decoy Minnows

MADE OF PURE SOFT RUBBER

Sizes........	2	2½	3	7
No. 947 Luminous Soft Rubber, Decorated........................				
" 948 " " " Plain Silver....................				
" 949 Non-Luminous, Soft Rubber, Decorated				
" 950 " " " " Plain Silver....				

Packed—Sizes 2, 2½ and 3 inch, one dozen in a box, 7 inch one in a box.

MADE OF CEDAR WOOD, WATERPROOFED

Sizes	3½	5
No. 860 Luminous, Cedar Wood, Decorated		
" 861 " " " Plain Silver....		
" 862 Non-Luminous, Cedar Wood, Decorated...		
" 863 " " " " Plain Silver...		

Packed—Size 3½ inch, one dozen in a box, 5 inch one in a box.

The above scene represents a fisherman in his movable "dark house" in the act of spearing fish through the ice, using a Decoy Minnow. The Decoy is painted true to life, and being weighted and balanced with a lead core it dances merrily by simply pulling on the line to which it is tied. It furnishes great sport to those that indulge in this class of fishing.

PRE-1900

AKRON, OHIO. ST. PAUL, MINN.

THE ENTERPRISE MANUFACTURING CO.

- Rubber Muskallonge Minnows (SEE PAGE 141) THIS BAIT WAS INVENTED BY ADRIAN HOLBROOK AND WAS NEW IN 1892 PATENT ASSIGNED TO ENTERPRISE. MADE IN LUMINOUS & NON-LUMINOUS FROM THE OUTSET.

FROM 1892 CATALOG - IMAGINE FINDING SOME SHOO-FLY-"IN-THE-BOX!"

Put up in hinge-cover metal boxes, handsomely lithographed.
Packed one dozen boxes in a Cartoon.

Price per dozen boxes, $3.00.

For Repelling Black Flies, Midges, Mosquitoes and Other Insects

This preparation is a decided improvement over all others. It contains no tar or animal fats, leaves no *stain*, is clean, easily applied, washes off readily *without the use of soap*, leaves the skin soft, smooth and free from irritation so common with other preparations. It relieves inflammation and pain from sunburn, and if used in time will prevent the burning.

USE
PFLUEGER'S Perfumed.
SHOO FLY CREAM.
"GREAT SCOT"
"PFLUEGER'S SHOO FLY CREAM WILL KEEP 'EM OFF
USE PFLUEGER'S LUMINOUS BAIT.

THE HANDWRITTEN COST FIGURES WERE MADE BY E.F. PFLUEGER (AS HIS PERSONAL COPY WAS XEROXED!)

PFLUEGER'S FISH SPEARING DECOY MINNOWS.

1892

Price per Dozen.

			Luminous	Non-Luminous
		Nos.	198	199
2	inch	2.00.	$ 4.00	$ 3.50
2¼	"	.350.	5.00	4.50
3	"	.300.	6.00	5.40
7	"	.750	15.00	12.00

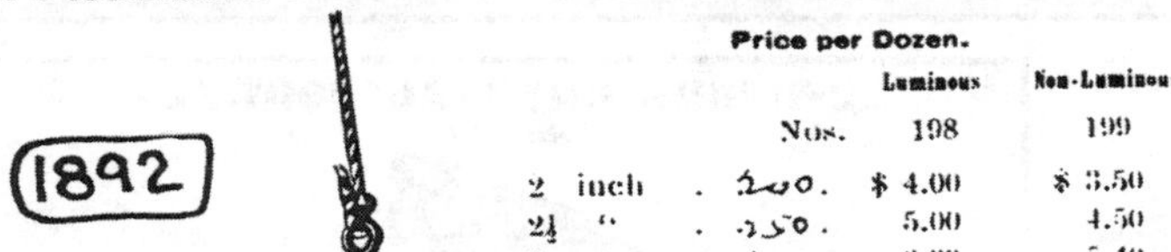

$100 – 250

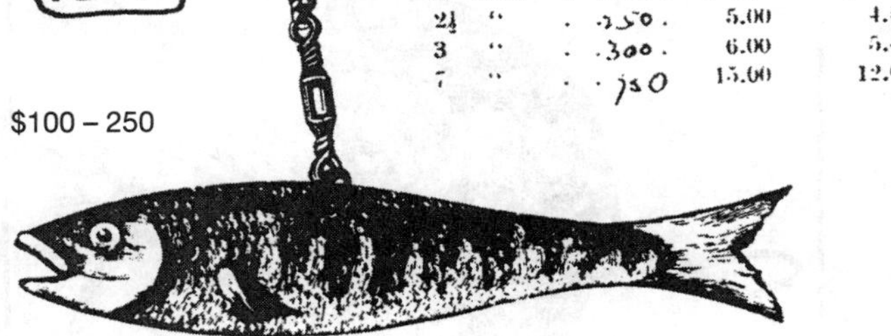

Size of 2½ in.

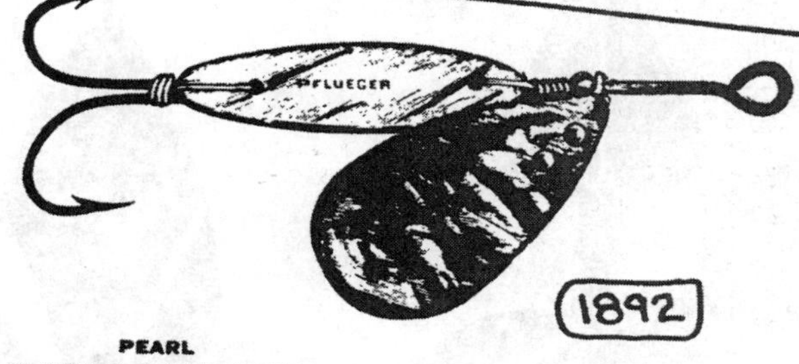
PFLUEGER

1892

PEARL
FLORIDA BASS BAIT.
No. 166.

$50 – 60

1892

THE "ADMIRAL" BAIT.

No. 995–Soft Rubber Minnow and Spoon Combined.

$20 – 50+

NO. 7- 2"
8- 2½" 9-3"

Exact Size No. 7.

SPOONS (FINISHES)
- BRASS
- COPPER
- OREIDE
- NICKEL PLATE
- GOLD- .15¢ EXTRA

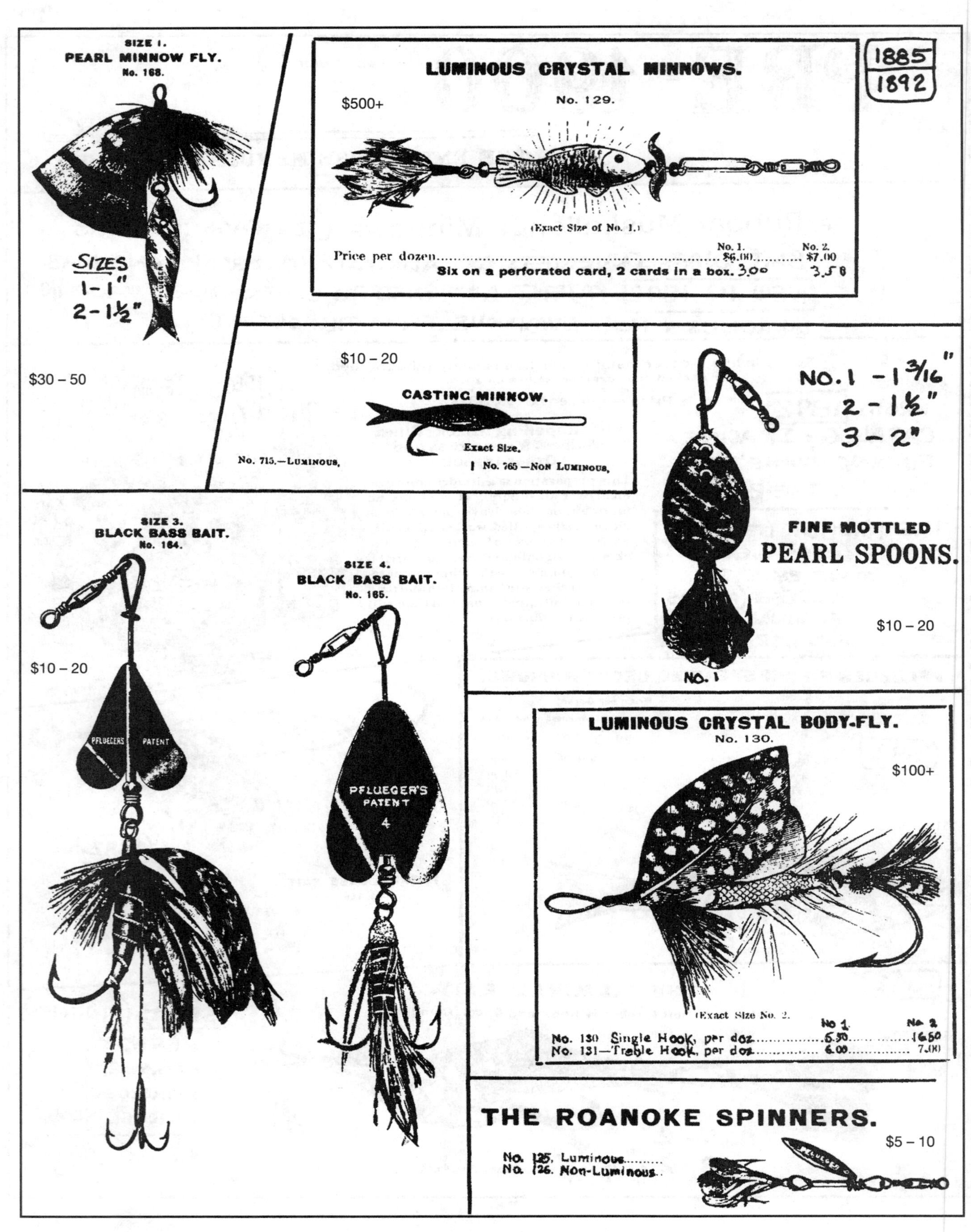
SIZE 1.
PEARL MINNOW FLY.
No. 168.
SIZES
1-1"
2-1½"
$30 – 50
LUMINOUS CRYSTAL MINNOWS.
No. 129.
$500+
1885
1892
(Exact Size of No. 1.)
No. 1. No. 2.
Price per dozen $6.00 $7.00
Six on a perforated card, 2 cards in a box. 3.00 3.50
$10 – 20
CASTING MINNOW.
Exact Size.
No. 715.—Luminous,
No. 765 —Non Luminous,
NO. 1 - 1 3/16"
2 - 1½"
3 - 2"
FINE MOTTLED
PEARL SPOONS.
$10 – 20
NO. 1
SIZE 3.
BLACK BASS BAIT.
No. 164.
$10 – 20
PFLUEGERS PATENT
SIZE 4.
BLACK BASS BAIT.
No. 165.
PFLUEGER'S PATENT
4
LUMINOUS CRYSTAL BODY-FLY.
No. 130.
$100+
(Exact Size No. 2.
No 1 No 2
No. 130 Single Hook, per doz 6.50 16.50
No. 131—Treble Hook, per doz 6.00 7.00
THE ROANOKE SPINNERS.
$5 – 10
No. 125, Luminous
No. 126. Non-Luminous
PFLUEGER

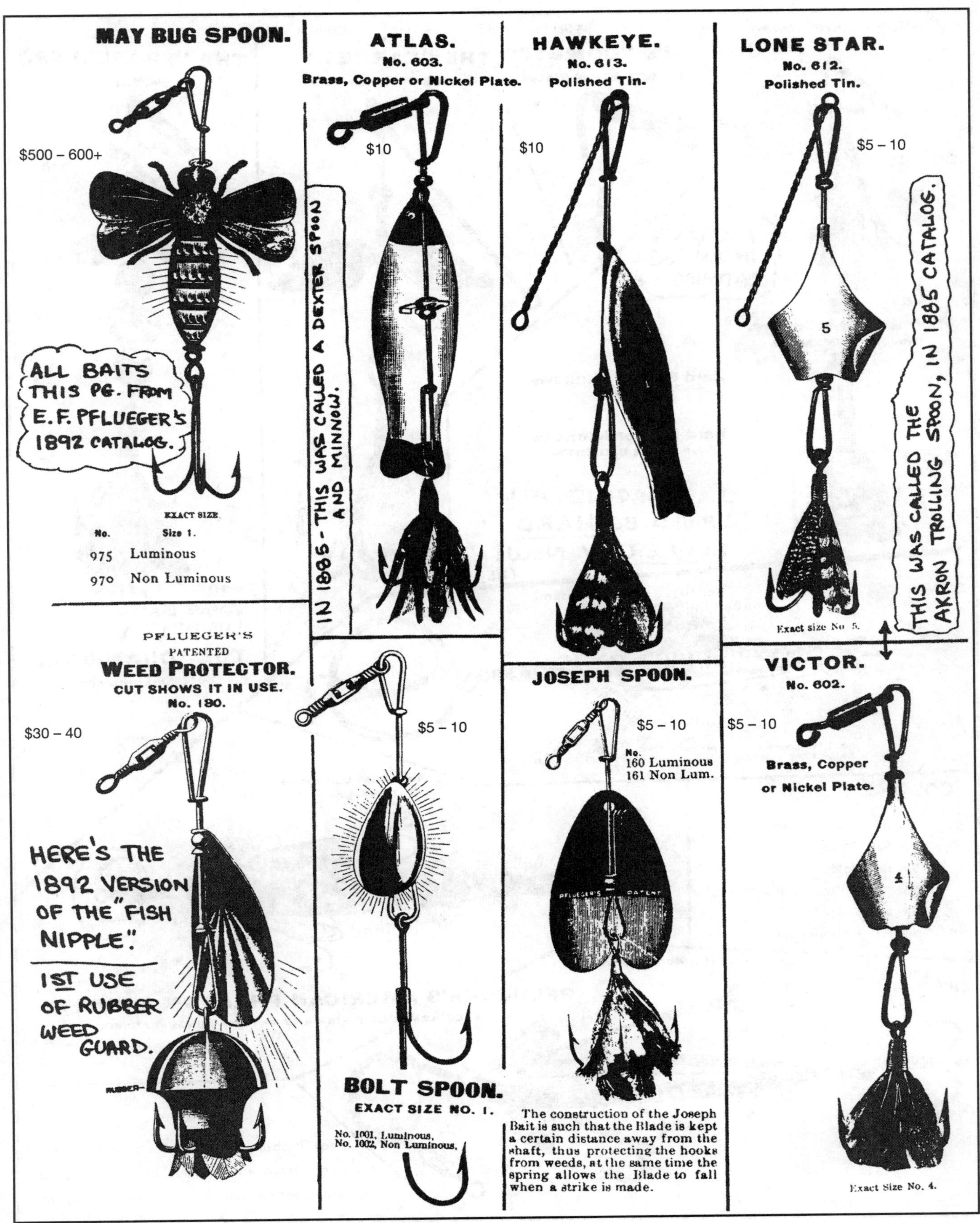
MAY BUG SPOON.
$500 – 600+
ALL BAITS THIS PG. FROM E.F. PFLUEGER'S 1892 CATALOG.
EXACT SIZE.
No. Size 1.
975 Luminous
970 Non Luminous
ATLAS.
No. 603.
Brass, Copper or Nickel Plate.
$10
IN 1885 - THIS WAS CALLED A DEXTER SPOON AND MINNOW.
HAWKEYE.
No. 613.
Polished Tin.
$10
LONE STAR.
No. 612.
Polished Tin.
$5 – 10
5
Exact size No. 5.
THIS WAS CALLED THE AKRON TROLLING SPOON, IN 1885 CATALOG.
PFLUEGER'S
PATENTED
WEED PROTECTOR.
CUT SHOWS IT IN USE.
No. 180.
$30 – 40
HERE'S THE 1892 VERSION OF THE "FISH NIPPLE."
1ST USE OF RUBBER WEED GUARD.
RUBBER
$5 – 10
BOLT SPOON.
EXACT SIZE NO. 1.
No. 1001, Luminous,
No. 1002, Non Luminous,
JOSEPH SPOON.
$5 – 10
No.
160 Luminous
161 Non Lum.
PFLUEGER'S PATENT
The construction of the Joseph Bait is such that the Blade is kept a certain distance away from the shaft, thus protecting the hooks from weeds, at the same time the spring allows the Blade to fall when a strike is made.
VICTOR.
No. 602.
$5 – 10
Brass, Copper or Nickel Plate.
4
Exact Size No. 4.

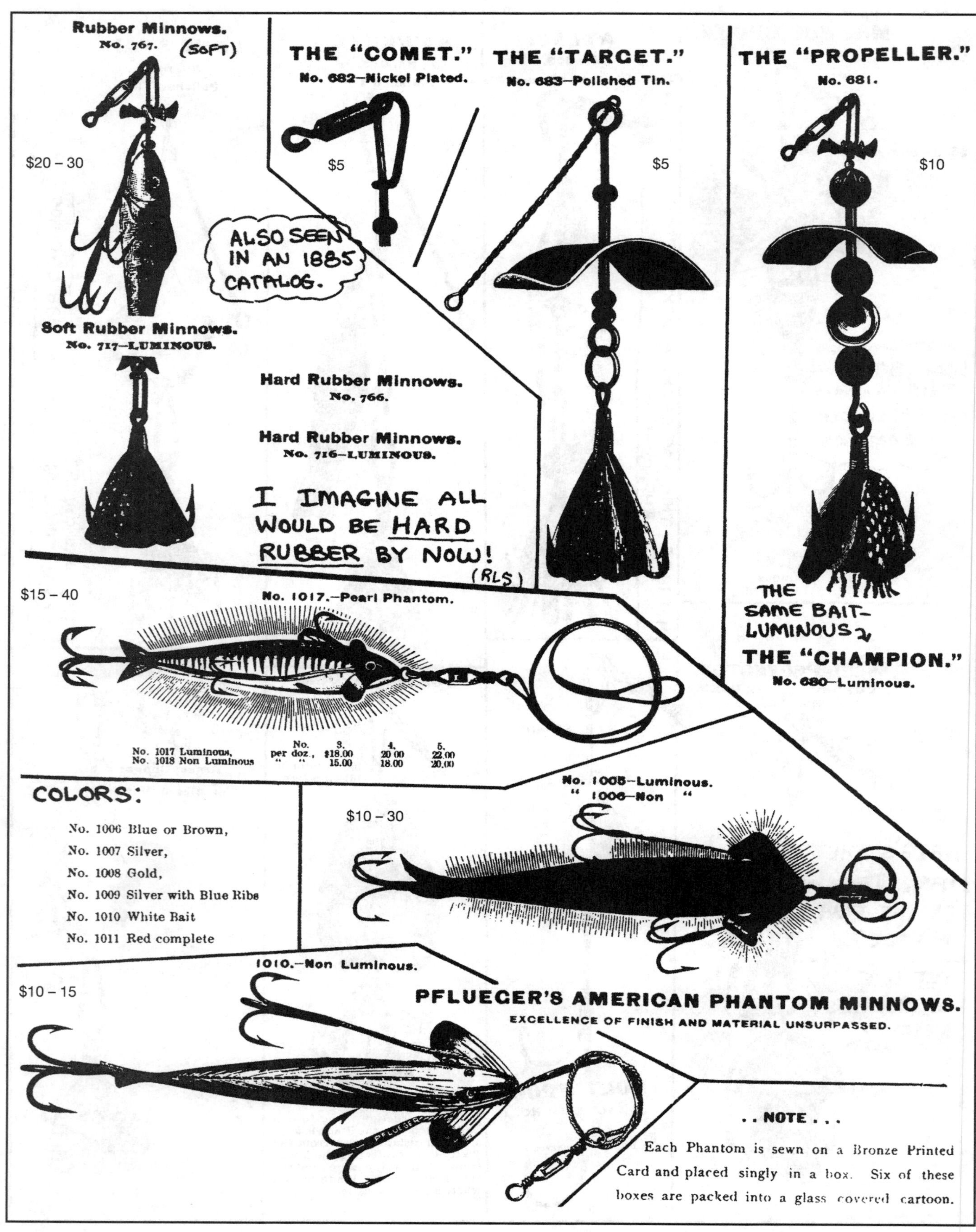
Rubber Minnows.
No. 767.
(SOFT)
$20 – 30
Soft Rubber Minnows.
No. 717—LUMINOUS.
THE "COMET."
No. 682—Nickel Plated.
$5
THE "TARGET."
No. 683—Polished Tin.
$5
THE "PROPELLER."
No. 681.
$10
ALSO SEEN IN AN 1885 CATALOG.
Hard Rubber Minnows.
No. 766.
Hard Rubber Minnows.
No. 716—LUMINOUS.
I IMAGINE ALL WOULD BE HARD RUBBER BY NOW! (RLS)
THE SAME BAIT-LUMINOUS
THE "CHAMPION."
No. 680—Luminous.
$15 – 40
No. 1017.—Pearl Phantom.
No. 1017 Luminous, per doz., No. 3. $18.00 4. 20.00 5. 22.00
No. 1018 Non Luminous " " 15.00 18.00 20.00
COLORS:
No. 1006 Blue or Brown,
No. 1007 Silver,
No. 1008 Gold,
No. 1009 Silver with Blue Ribs
No. 1010 White Bait
No. 1011 Red complete
No. 1005—Luminous.
" 1006—Non "
$10 – 30
1010.—Non Luminous.
$10 – 15
PFLUEGER'S AMERICAN PHANTOM MINNOWS.
EXCELLENCE OF FINISH AND MATERIAL UNSURPASSED.
PFLUEGER
. . NOTE . . .
Each Phantom is sewn on a Bronze Printed Card and placed singly in a box. Six of these boxes are packed into a glass covered cartoon.

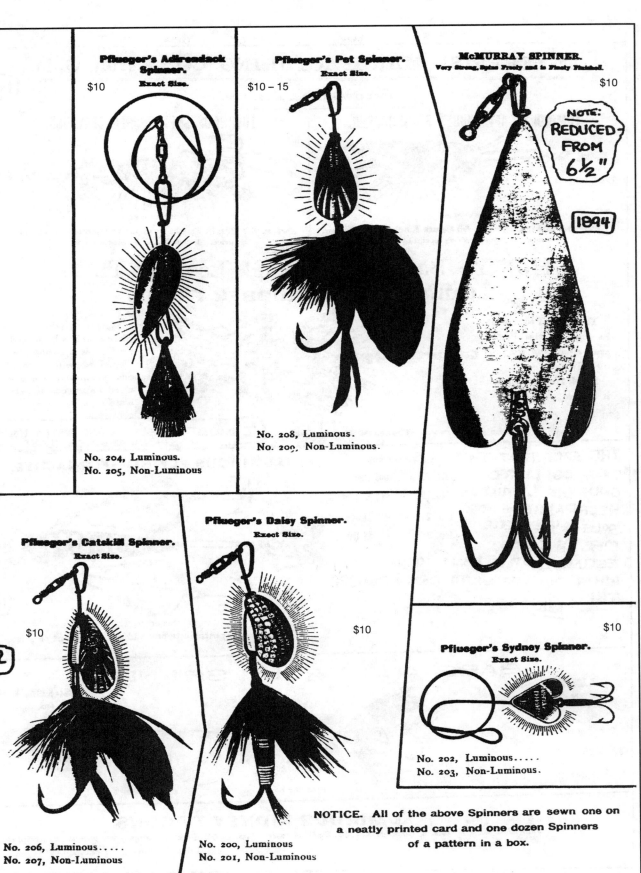

Pflueger's Adirondack Spinner.
Exact Size.

$10

No. 204, Luminous.
No. 205, Non-Luminous

Pflueger's Pet Spinner.
Exact Size.

$10 – 15

No. 208, Luminous.
No. 209, Non-Luminous.

McMURRAY SPINNER.
Very Strong, Spins Freely and is Finely Finished.

$10

NOTE: REDUCED FROM 6½"

1894

Pflueger's Catskill Spinner.
Exact Size.

$10

1892

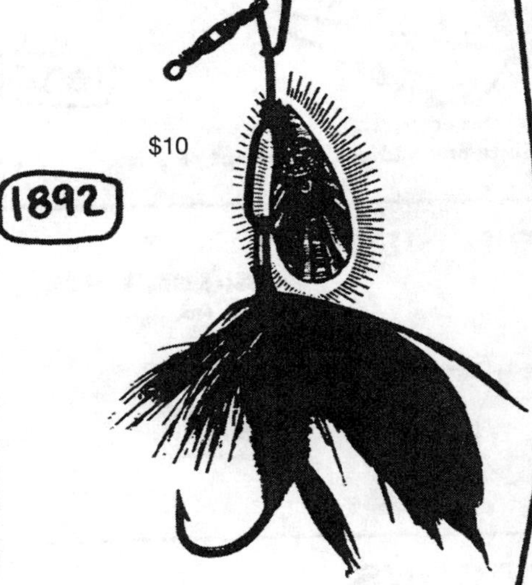

No. 206, Luminous.....
No. 207, Non-Luminous

Pflueger's Daisy Spinner.
Exact Size.

$10

No. 200, Luminous
No. 201, Non-Luminous

$10

Pflueger's Sydney Spinner.
Exact Size.

No. 202, Luminous.....
No. 203, Non-Luminous.

NOTICE. All of the above Spinners are sewn one on a neatly printed card and one dozen Spinners of a pattern in a box.

ENTERPRISE MANUFACTURING CO., Akron, Ohio.

1885

PFLUEGER'S PATENTS.

LUMINOUS SOFT RUBBER GRASSHOPPER.

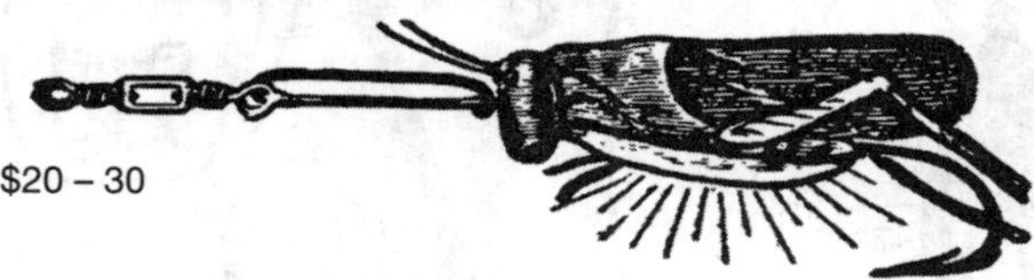

$20 – 30

EXACT SIZE.

Assorted Colors. Price, 60 Cents Each. Samples sent postpaid to any address on receipt of price.

LUMINOUS SOFT RUBBER CRAWFISH.

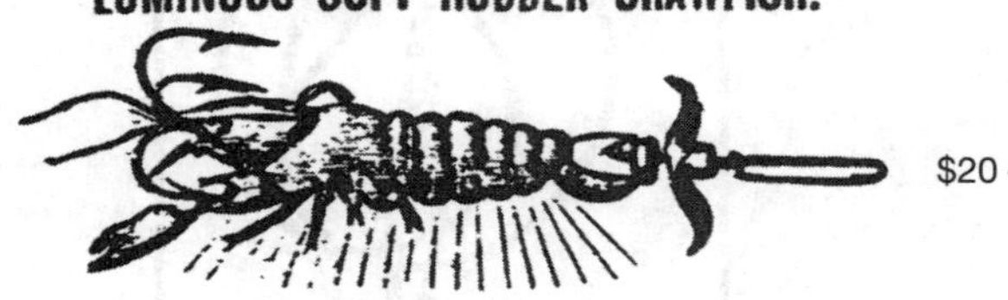

$20 – 30

EXACT SIZE.

Price, 60 Cents Each. Samples sent postpaid on receipt of price. Either Treble or Single Hook.

Ho! Ye Bass Fishermen! Look at This!

LUMINOUS SOFT RUBBER FROGS.

The only Frog made having a Treble Feathered Hook, and working on a Swivel.

Single Hooks furnished if desired.

Making it easy to replace a broken Hook, and the Bait is a lasting one. Combined with Luminous qualities, it is a decided improvement over live Frogs.

$20 – 40

EXACT SIZE.

Green and Brown. Price, 60 Cents Each.

I DOUBT IF ANY OF THE ABOVE HAVE SURVIVED SINCE 1885!

LUMINOUS FLYING HELGRAMITE.

Price Each.	
No. 0, -	80 Cents.
No. 1, -	85 Cents.
No. 2, -	90 Cents.
No. 3, - -	$1.00.

THE FACT THAT THIS CATALOG LISTED ONLY THE LUMINOUS HELGRAMITE – FOR SALE BY ENTERP. MFG. IS INTERESTING – BUT I DON'T KNOW WHAT CONCLUSION TO DRAW FROM THIS. RLD

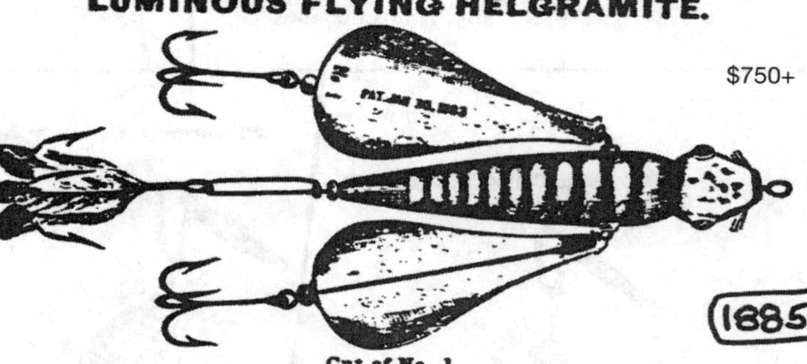

$750+

1885

Cut of No. 1.

Samples sent postpaid to any address, on receipt of price.

BASS AND TROUT SPINNERS.

LUMINOUS. No. 127.

NON-LUMINOUS. No. 128.

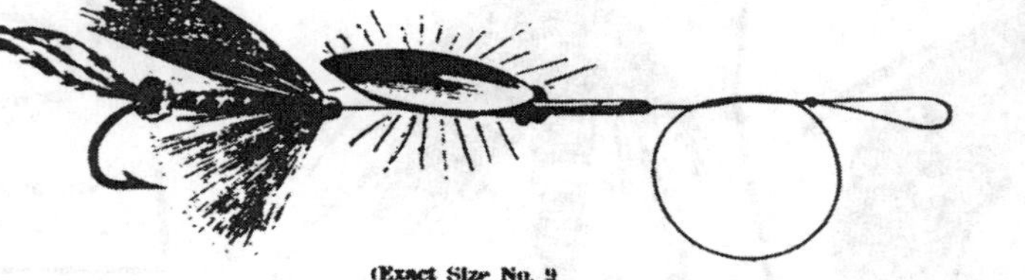

$20 – 25

1892

(Exact Size No. 9

LUMINOUS KIDNEY SPOONS.

Regular Sizes: No. 1, 50 Cents. No. 2, 55 Cents. No. 3, 60 Cents. Samples sent postpaid on receipt of price.

1885

Pflueger's "Monarch" Minnows

For Under Water Fishing

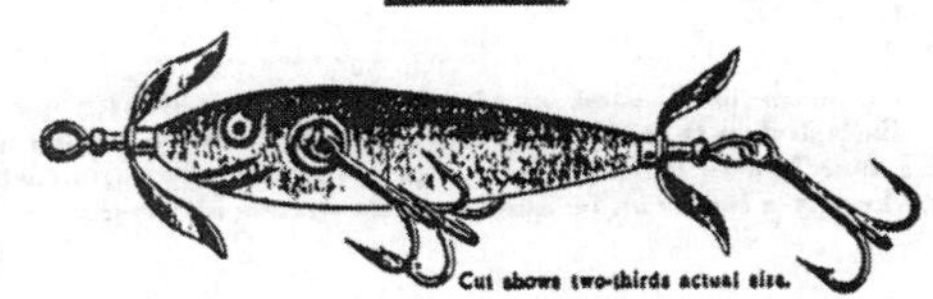
Cut shows two-thirds actual size.

$50 – 150

Cut Shows Two-thirds Actual Size of 2¾ Inch Minnow

Cut shows two thirds actual size.

Cut Shows Two-third Actual Size of 3⅝ Inch Minnow

For all around fishing this Minnow is especially adaptable. Made in a large variety of colors as follows:

STOCK No.	SIZES	LIST PRICES 2¾	3⅝
No. 2171, White Enamel Belly, Blended Green Back, Favorite Quality, Per Doz.			
No. 2172, " " " " Slate " " " "			
No. 2173, " " " " Rainbow " " " "			
No. 2174, Yellow " " " Red & Green " " " "			
No. 2175, " " " " Brown " " " "			
No. 2176, Red " " " Brown " " " "			
No. 2177, Silver, " " " Dark Blue " " " "			
No. 2178, " " " " Olive Green " " " "			
No. 2179, Gold " " " Dark Green " " " "			
No. 2180, White Enamel Over Entire Body " " " "			
No. 2181, Red " " " " " " "			
No. 2182, Silver " " " " " " "			

Size 2¾ has 2 Side Treble Hooks and 1 Tail Treble Hook Plain

Size 3⅝ " 4 " " " 1 " " "

Packed—One Bait in a Wooden Slide Cover Box, 12 Boxes Nested in a Carton.

Pflueger's "Monarch" Minnows

For Surface Fishing

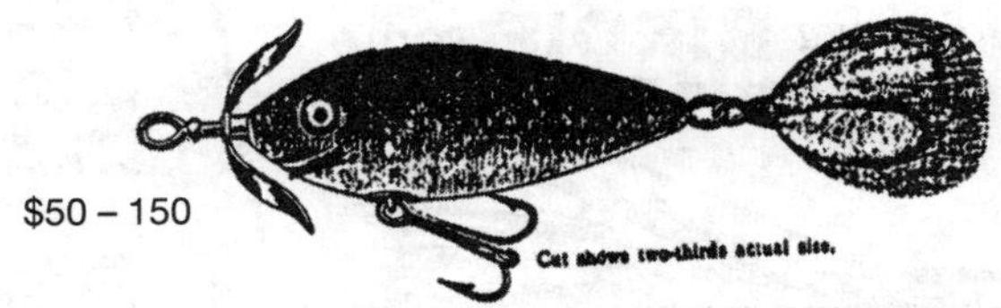
Cut shows two-thirds actual size.

$50 – 150

Cut Shows Two-thirds Actual Size of 2¾ Inch Minnow

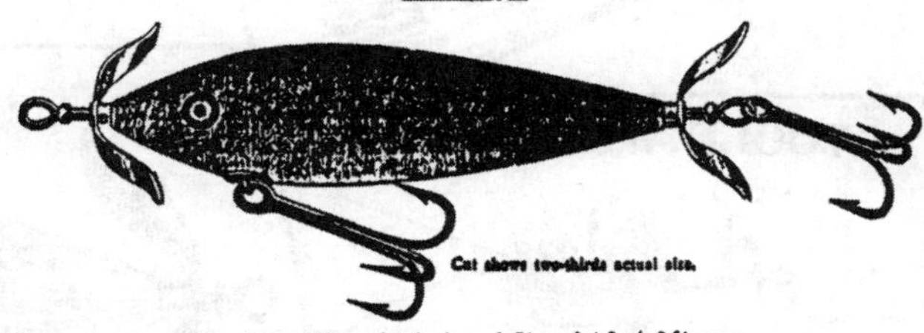
Cut shows two-thirds actual size.

Cut Shows Two-thirds Actual Size of 4 Inch Minnow

This Minnow, sometimes called a "Floater," is excellent for surface fishing. It is sufficiently buoyant at all times to set well in the water, even with the weight of the fishing line attached.

Made in the following colors only:

STOCK No.	SIZE	LIST PRICES Tail 2¾	Plain 4
No. 2371, White Enamel Belly, Blended Green Back, Favorite Quality, Per Doz.			
No. 2372, " " " Slate " " " " "			
No. 2373, " " " Rainbow " " " " "			
No. 2375, Yellow " " " Brown " " " " "			
No. 2376, Red " " " Brown " " " " "			
No. 2377, Silver " " " Dark Blue " " " " "			

Size 2¾ Inch is regularly furnished with a Buck Tail Treble Hook and Plain Treble Belly Hook.

Size 4 inch is regularly furnished with a Plain Treble Tail and Belly Hook.

Packed—One Bait in a Wooden Slide Cover Box and 12 Boxes Nested in a Carton.

PFLUEGER **TANTRUM** MINNOW

$10 – 15

4"
TANTRUM MINNOW
NO. 8400

PFLUEGER **BIRDIE** SQUID

Trade Marks Reg. U. S. Pat. Office

$5 – 10

WOOLE WORM SPINNER

$2 – 10

Trout—Size 8 Hook

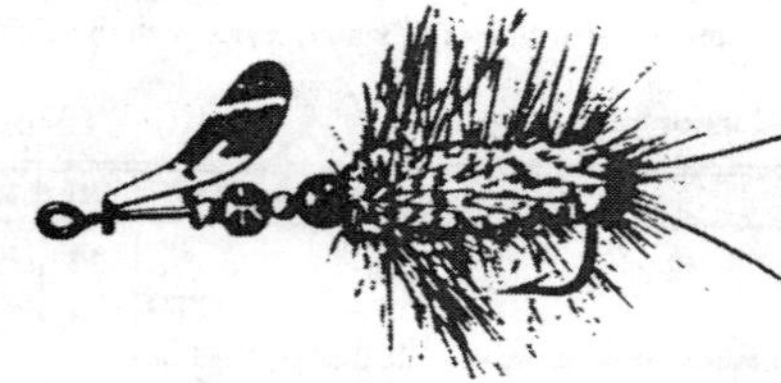

Bass—Size 2 Hook

$2 – 10

Harp SPINNER

WITH PORK RIND ATTACHMENT

$2 – 10

PFLUEGER PILOT FLY

• BASS SIZE

• TROUT SIZE

PFLUEGER **BEARCAT** MINNOW

Trade Mark Reg. U. S. Pat. Office—Patented June 6, 1922

Under Water or Sinking Minnow

$50 – 100

No. 6461

4¼"

	Minnow Size, Inch	4¼
Length of Body	Inch	4¼
Treble Hook Ringed—On Tail	Size	2/0
Treble Hook Ringed—On Belly	Size	2/0

Pflueger Bearcat Minnow is made of selected wood and heavily coated with our Flexible Enamel which will not peel. Ballasted so that the body will ride "Belly Down" under all conditions. Bright nickel plated Treble Hooks Ringed, sizes as per chart above and attached with our Patented Hook Fastener whereby a hook can be quickly and conveniently replaced.

No.
6403 Natural Mullet—Scale Finish
6461 White Enamel—Red Throat
6471 White Enamel—Yellow and Green Back

ELECTRIC WOODEN MINNOWS.

1921

$75 – 150

Made from carefully selected cedar, perfectly shaped and ballasted, always keeping minnow in proper position, will not revolve and twist the line; therefore, swivels are unnecessary. Before applying the required number of coats brilliant waterproof porcelain enamel, the cedar is especially treated to prevent the absorption of water, so that the enamel will not peel or flake off. Large glass eyes, fine propeller shaped spinners, polished nickel both sides, mounted on easy bearings turned from solid brass. Spinners made rights and lefts so as to revolve in opposite directions, being a great advantage in attracting fish from a distance. Detachable treble hooks heavily nickel-plated to prevent rusting if used in salt water.

The 2¾ inch Minnow is mounted with 3 Treble Hooks. The 3⅝ inch Minnow is mounted with 5 Treble Hooks.

D 53-821—2¾ inch. Blended Rainbow Back, White Belly
D 54-831—2¾ inch. Blended Olive Green Back, Aluminum Belly
D 55-833—2¾ inch. Cracked Green or Fancy Back, White Belly
D 56-821—3⅝ inch. Blended Rainbow Back, White Belly
D 57-831—3⅝ inch. Blended Olive Green, White Belly
D 58-833—3⅝ inch. Fancy Green Back, White Belly

2 SIZES
• 2¾"
• 3⅝"

PFLUEGER **FLILITE** BASS BUG

Trade Marks Reg. U. S. Pat. Office—Patent No. 1905567

ALSO WITH SINGLE HOOK

Cork Body—Floating Bug

Detachable Hook—Accidental damage to hook does not necessitate buying a new lure. Natural cork bodies beautifully enameled to which buck tail and squirrel tail hair including feathers are tied by a method which positively prevents pulling out. Our famous Tandem Spinner blade adds greatly to the attraction—a breath will spin it. Bright Tin Plated. Double hook, size 6, mounted points down.

$10 – 40

BETTER ILLUSTRATION OF THE 1916 MAGNET. THEY WERE PACKED IN A WOOD BOX.

ALSO COLOR NO. 3697 AVAILABLE ON SPECIAL ORDER: RH/LUM.

I THINK THESE ARE THE 4 LEVELS OF QUALITY ON PFLUEGER UNDERWATER BAITS:

1. MONARCH AND/OR ELECTRIC
2. NEVERFAIL
3. CHAMPION
& 4. PEERLESS

THE ENTERPRISE MANUFACTURING CO., AKRON, OHIO

TRADE PFLUEGER MARK

THE "MAGNET" WOODEN BAITS

A FLOATER OR SURFACE BAIT

Patent No. 272317

$10 – 25

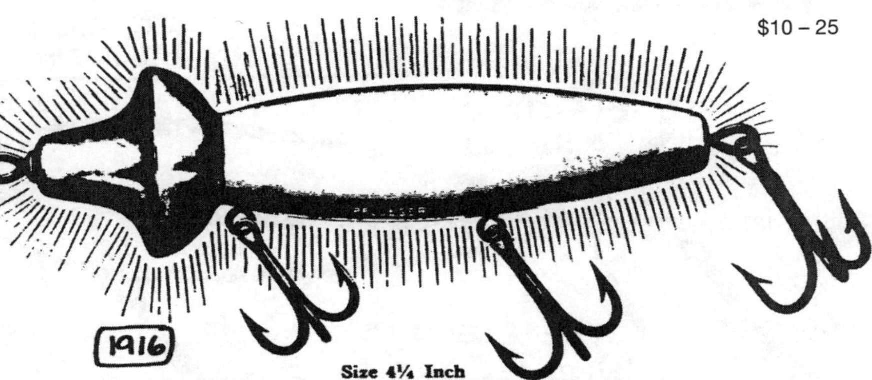
PFLUEGER

1916

Size 4¼ Inch

Made of selected Red Cedar and heavily coated with our special elastic indestructible waterproof porcelain enamel. Joint on the screw eye at head is soldered to prevent line from slipping out. The Luminous bait is especially attractive for night fishing and also very effective during the day. Expose the Luminous enamel to either day or artificial light before using—the enamel absorbs the light and emits it approximately in proportion to the length of time exposed.

Mounted with three Treble Hooks.

No. 3670	Luminous Enamel Over All	Per Dozen	$5.80
No. 3680	White Enamel Over All	Per Dozen	5.26
No. 3696	White Enamel Body with Red Head	Per Dozen	5.26

Packed—Each Bait is wrapped in silver tissue paper, one in a wood box, and twelve boxes in a carton.

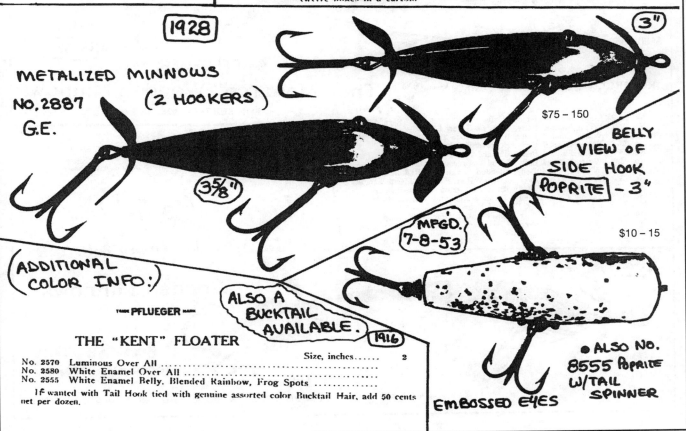

1928

METALIZED MINNOWS (2 HOOKERS)

NO. 2887

G.E.

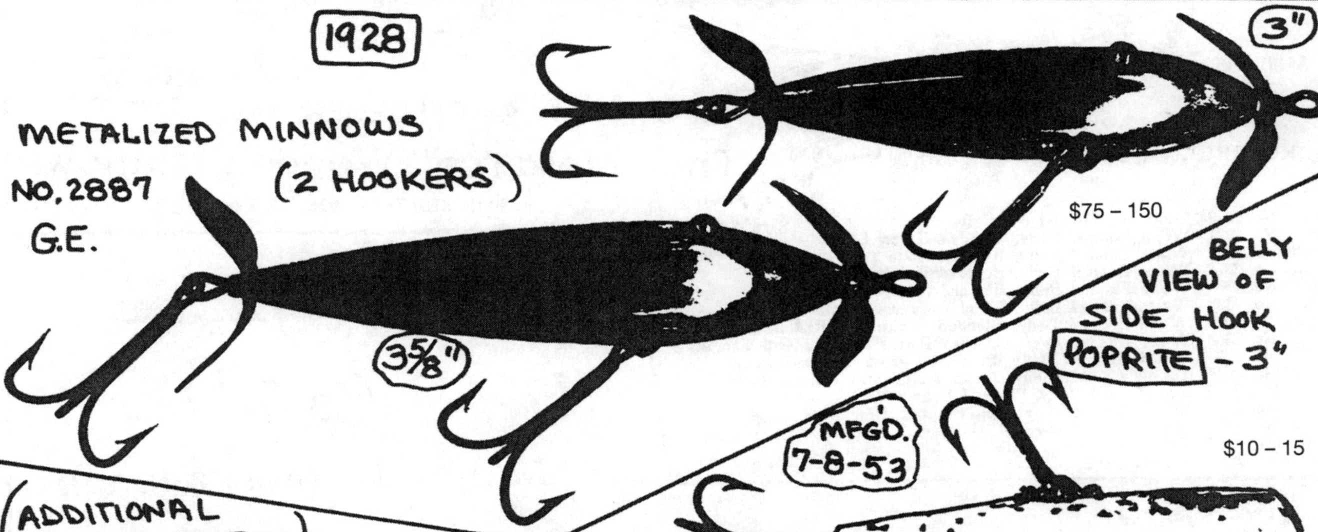

3"

3⅝"

$75 – 150

BELLY VIEW OF SIDE HOOK POPRITE - 3"

MFGD. 7-8-53

$10 – 15

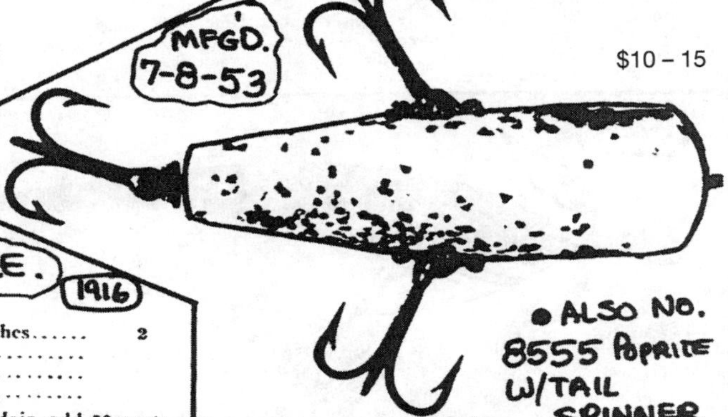

● ALSO NO. 8555 POPRITE W/TAIL SPINNER

EMBOSSED EYES

(ADDITIONAL COLOR INFO:)

ALSO A BUCKTAIL AVAILABLE.

TRADE PFLUEGER MARK

THE "KENT" FLOATER

1916

		Size, inches	2
No. 2570	Luminous Over All		
No. 2580	White Enamel Over All		
No. 2555	White Enamel Belly, Blended Rainbow, Frog Spots		

If wanted with Tail Hook tied with genuine assorted color Bucktail Hair, add 50 cents net per dozen.

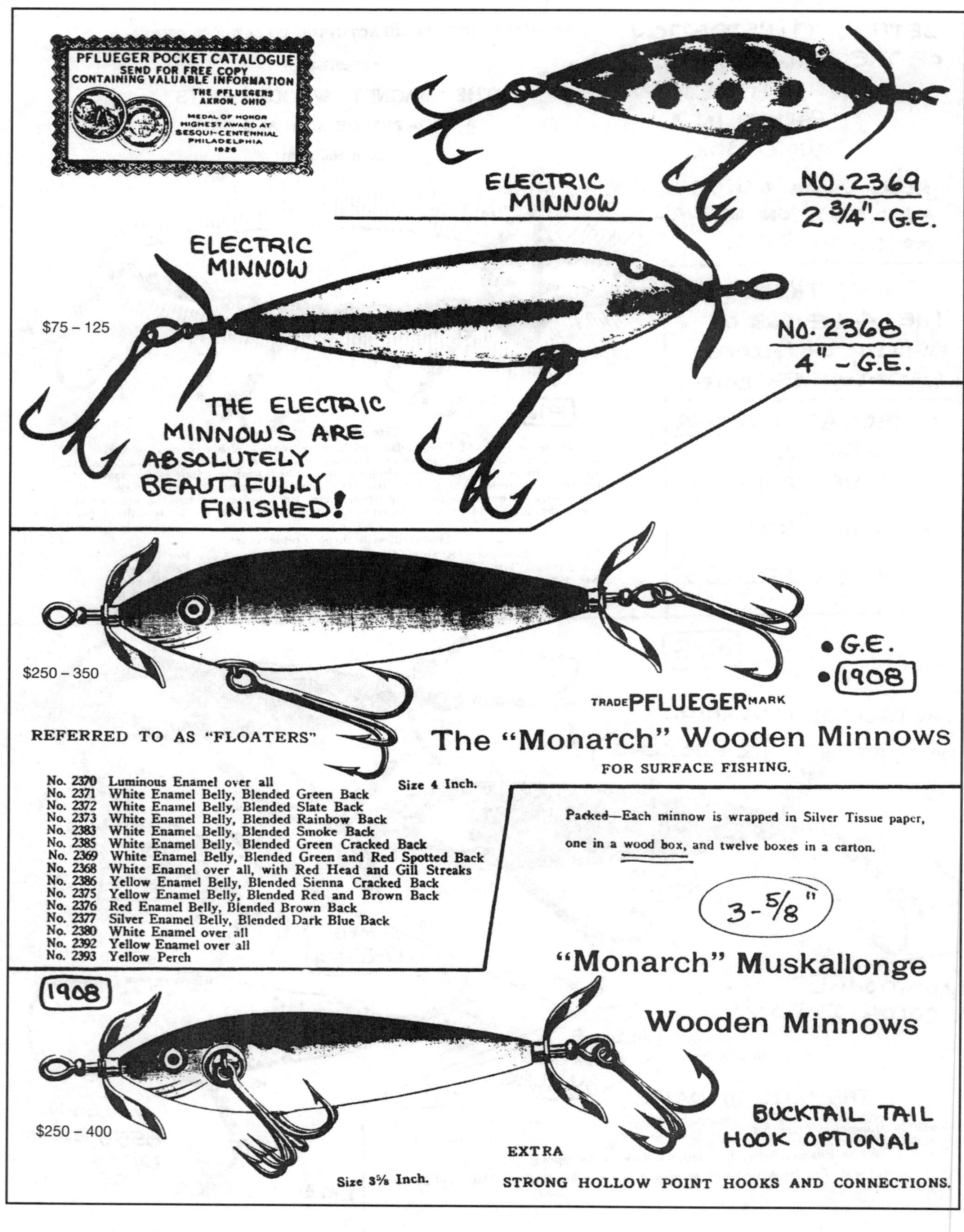

PFLUEGER POCKET CATALOGUE
SEND FOR FREE COPY
CONTAINING VALUABLE INFORMATION
THE PFLUEGERS
AKRON, OHIO
MEDAL OF HONOR
HIGHEST AWARD AT
SESQUI-CENTENNIAL
PHILADELPHIA
1926

ELECTRIC MINNOW

NO. 2369
2 3/4"-G.E.

ELECTRIC MINNOW

$75 – 125

NO. 2368
4" - G.E.

THE ELECTRIC MINNOWS ARE ABSOLUTELY BEAUTIFULLY FINISHED!

$250 – 350

• G.E.
• 1908

TRADE PFLUEGER MARK

REFERRED TO AS "FLOATERS"

The "Monarch" Wooden Minnows

FOR SURFACE FISHING.

Size 4 Inch.

No. 2370 Luminous Enamel over all
No. 2371 White Enamel Belly, Blended Green Back
No. 2372 White Enamel Belly, Blended Slate Back
No. 2373 White Enamel Belly, Blended Rainbow Back
No. 2383 White Enamel Belly, Blended Smoke Back
No. 2385 White Enamel Belly, Blended Green Cracked Back
No. 2369 White Enamel Belly, Blended Green and Red Spotted Back
No. 2368 White Enamel over all, with Red Head and Gill Streaks
No. 2386 Yellow Enamel Belly, Blended Sienna Cracked Back
No. 2375 Yellow Enamel Belly, Blended Red and Brown Back
No. 2376 Red Enamel Belly, Blended Brown Back
No. 2377 Silver Enamel Belly, Blended Dark Blue Back
No. 2380 White Enamel over all
No. 2392 Yellow Enamel over all
No. 2393 Yellow Perch

Packed—Each minnow is wrapped in Silver Tissue paper, one in a wood box, and twelve boxes in a carton.

3-5/8"

"Monarch" Muskallonge Wooden Minnows

1908

$250 – 400

BUCKTAIL TAIL HOOK OPTIONAL

Size 3⅝ Inch.

EXTRA STRONG HOLLOW POINT HOOKS AND CONNECTIONS.

PFLUEGER

PRONOUNCED "FLEW-GER"

FISHING TACKLE

Leaders Since 1864

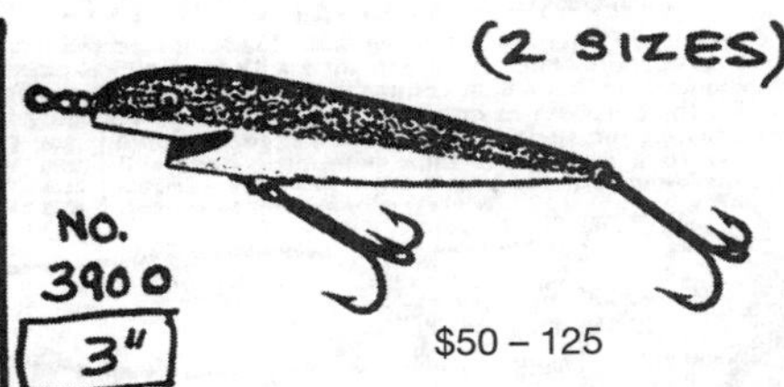
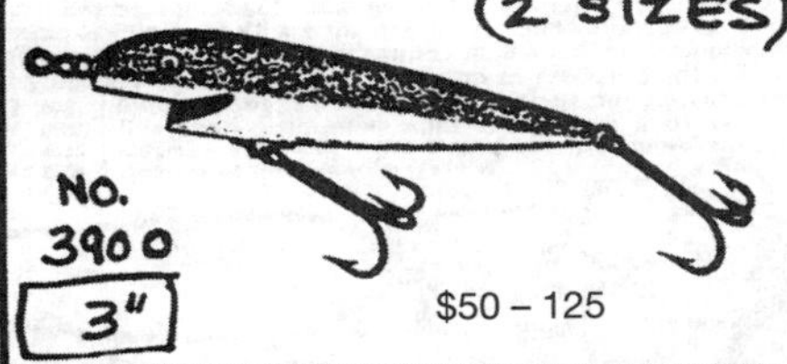
(2 SIZES)
NO. 3900
3"

$50 – 125

PFLUEGER TNT MINNOW
3¼"

$20 – 40

Trade Marks Reg. U. S. Pat. Office—Pat. Nos. 1418326-1750604—Pat. Pending

All Metal Body, Dives Deep, Wiggles and Wobbles

The T. N. T. is an all-metal body minnow especially constructed to dive deep and with a wiggle and wobble irresistible to game fish such as Bass, Pike, Muskallunge, Wall Eyes, etc.

The Spotlite with near gold diving plane is a most attractive finish never before offered in a similar lure.

Mounted with Bright Tin Plated Treble Hooks, size 1/0.

Our patented fastener prevents hooks tangling, and affords a quick and convenient means for detaching.

No.	Fishing weight, 1-1/10 oz.	Price Each Minnow, Size 3¼ In.
6904	Natural Pike—Scale Blend	
6906	Natural Perch—Scale Blend	
6936	White Body with Gold Sparks and Red Head	
6938	Spotlite Finish with Gold Plane	
6973	Rainbow Blend	
6987	Polished Nickel	

NEW-1930

$100 – 200

PFLUEGER KENT FROG *FLOATER*

Trade Marks Reg. U. S. Pat. Office—Patent No. 1418326

Floating or Surface Bait

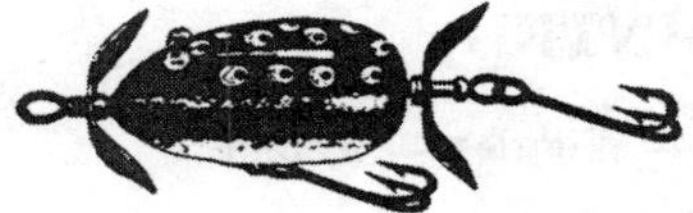

Made of selected cedar.

Rides on the surface and the churning of the highly polished nickel plated spinners, one turning to the right and the other to the left, produces a struggling and swimming effect. Bright Tin Plated Double Hooks Ringed, size 2/0.

No.	Fishing Weight, ¾ oz.
2555	Meadow Frog Finish

2"

(1920 NAME WAS THE "KENT CHAMPION FLOATER")

$10 – 25

PFLUEGER MERIT *BAIT*

4¼"

Trade Marks Reg. U. S. Pat. Office

Floating or Surface Bait

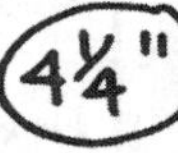

Rides on the surface and the collar produces a "wake" in the water. Bright Tin Plated Treble Hooks Ringed, size 1. Length of body 4¼ in.

Luminous Enamel—Red Head. Expose to either day or artificial light before using.

No.	Fishing Weight, ⅝ oz.	Bait Size, Inch 4¼
3697	Luminous Enamel—Red Head	

PFLUEGER MAGNET *BAIT*

1926

NO. 3600

Trade Mark Reg. U. S. Pat. Office—Patented Oct. 24, 1911—Also Patent No. 272317

Floating or Surface Bait

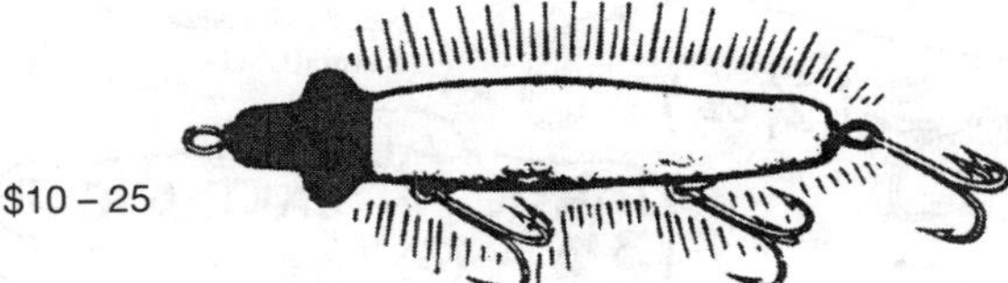

Bait Size, Inch	4¼
Length of Body .... Inch	4¼
Treb. Hook Rgd—On Tail . . Size	1
Treb. Hook Rgd—On Belly . . Size	1
Fishing Weight of Bait . . . Ounce	⅝

$10 – 25

4 BROTHERS 4

FOUR BROTHERS "SURPRISE" MINNOW

Patented Oct. 24, 1911. Also Patents No. 272317, 468361, 564839. Other Patents Pending.

Surface Bait that will Float, Dive and Wiggle

(4" - ⅝ oz.)

EARLY EYES WERE JUST HOLES

Size, 4-inch.

ASK THE MAN WHO HAS ONE

It Does the Trick and Gets the Fish

It will dive and wiggle like a live minnow—at proper fishing speed it will maintain a depth from 12 to 15 inches under the surface. The greater the speed, the deeper it will dive—stop reeling and the Bait will come to the surface, a very desirable feature when untangling *"Back Lashes"* and avoiding snags—Detachable Nickel Plated Hooks.

Made in Seven Blends as follows:

No. 3914	Luminous Enamel over all—Red Throat.
No. 3915	White Enamel over all—Red Throat.
No. 3916	White Enamel Belly—Rainbow Back, Red Throat.
No. 3917	White Enamel Belly—Green Cracked Back, Red Throat.
No. 3918	White Enamel Belly—Green and Red Spots, Red Throat.
No. 3919	White Enamel Belly—Green Back, Red Throat.
No. 3920	Yellow Perch—Red Throat.

All Patents Controlled and Manufactured Exclusively by

THE ENTERPRISE MFG. CO., AKRON, OHIO, U. S. A.

RAZEM *MINNO*

Minnow Sizes, Inch	2	2½	3
Hook Sizes	2/0	4/0	6/0
Fishing Weight, Ounce	⅝	¾	⅞

A combination of rubber minnow and spinner with features recognized as most attractive and very effective for all game fish—Bass, Pike, Muskallunge, etc.

The patented keel at head, a special feature, imparts a crippled minnow

NEW-1930

$10 – 20

UNO PHANTOM

$10

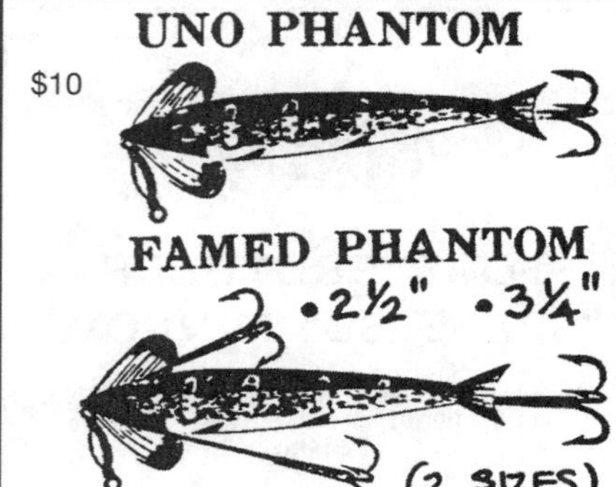

FAMED PHANTOM

•2½" •3¼"

(2 SIZES)

PFLUEGER "ALL-IN-ONE" MINNOW

Patented Oct. 24th, 1911, March 30th, 1915
Patent No. 272317

A Combination Floater and Underwater Bait. Made of selected red cedar and heavily coated with our special indestructible waterproof porcelain enamels. Furnished with four nickel-plated planes which are fastened to the head of the minnow with a very simple device which is durable and holds the planes firmly in the proper position and permits of instant interchanging for the purposes as indicated on illustration. By using the different planes the minnow will make a rotary motion, will stay on the surface and cause a life-like ripple similar to a natural surface swimming bait, will dive shallow or deep, and wiggle and wobble like a frightened crippled minnow as desired.

3570 Luminous Enamel over all
3580 White Enamel over all
3585 White Enamel Belly—Blended Green Cracked Back
3573 White Enamel Belly—Blended Rainbow Back
3565 White Enamel Belly—Frog Back
3569 White Enamel Belly—Green and Red Spots,

$150 – 300

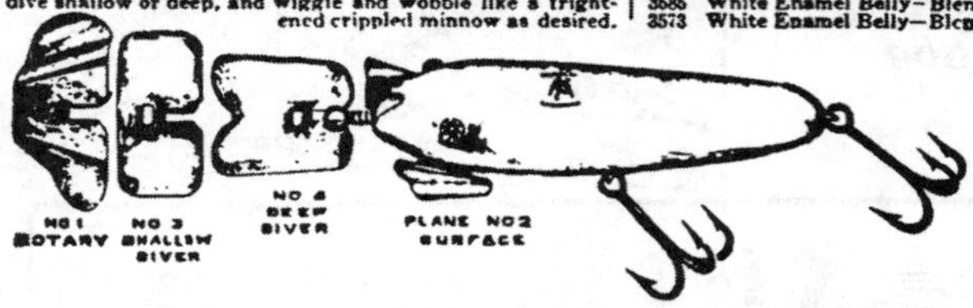

No 1 Rotary — No 3 Shallow Diver — No 4 Deep Diver — Plane No 2 Surface

Ask your dealer to show you the Pflueger "All-in-One" Minnow. If he will not supply you, remit price to us and we will guarantee delivery, charges prepaid.

THE ENTERPRISE MANUFACTURING CO.
Dept. 6 Akron, Ohio

Send 25c in stamps or coin for our big 100-page Fishing Tackle Catalog, some pages being in beautiful lithograph colors.

PATENT DATES: OCT. 24, 1911 AND MARCH 30, 1915.

PFLUEGER BREAKLESS DEVON MINNOW

Trade Mark Reg. U. S. Pat. Office—Patent No. 1756260

(1920'S—) (Detachable Keel)

$10

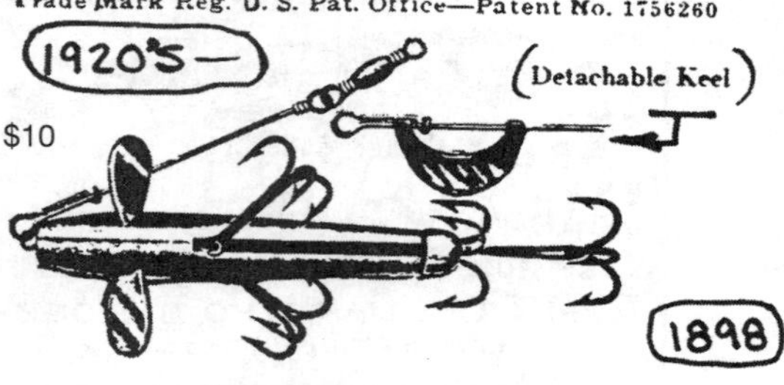

(1898)

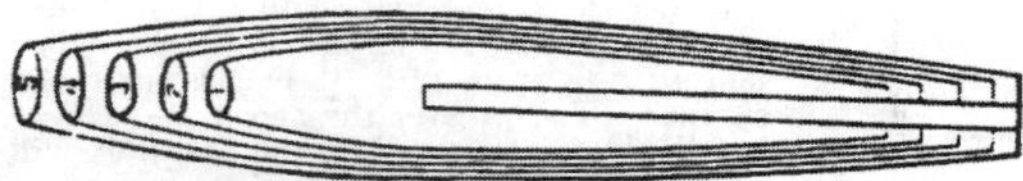

Minnow, Sizes	1	2	3	4	5
..........Inch	2	2¼	2½	2¾	3
.........Sizes	8	5	4	4	3
.........Sizes	7	4	3	3	2

Wire Frame is practically indestructible and permits quick interchange of hooks if necessary.

Bronzed Treble Hooks, Brass Barrel Swivels and Piano Wire Leaders Tinned. Mounted with Tandem Treble Tail Hook. (Both hooks brazed together on one shank.)

To avoid twisting line we provide two swivels, one inside of the body and the other on the leader, also a keel that can be attached to leader as shown above.

No.	
289	Polished Nickel Complete .
290	Polished Copper Complete .

PFLUEGER PAL-O-MINE MINNOW

(FLEW-GER)

Trade Marks Reg. U. S. Pat. Office—Patent Nos. 1418326-1615803

Floats — Dives — Wiggles — Wobbles

(1928) $25 – 35

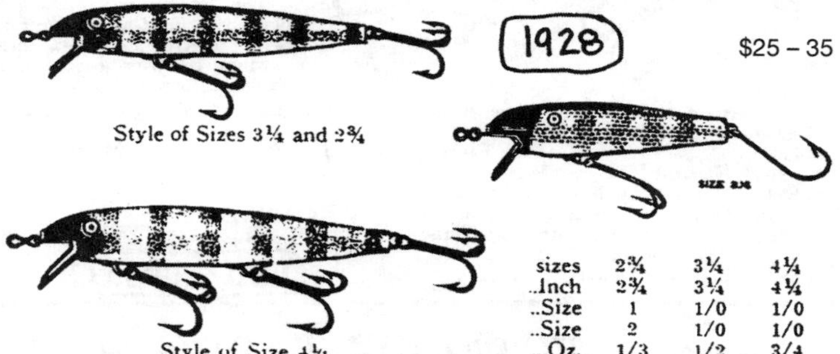

Style of Sizes 3¼ and 2¾

Style of Size 4¼

sizes	2¾	3¼	4¼
..Inch	2¾	3¼	4¼
..Size	1	1/0	1/0
..Size	2	1/0	1/0
...Oz.	1/3	1/2	3/4

JOINTED

(1932) $25 – 35

Floats — Dives — Wiggles — Wobbles

Style of Size 4¼

Style of Size 3¼

	Minnow, size	3¼	4¼
Length of Body	Inch	3¼	4¼
Treble Hooks, Bright Tin Plated	Hook size	1/0	1/0
Fishing Weight of Minnow	Ounce	5/8	3/4

PFLUEGER VICI PHANTOM

(1898)

$10

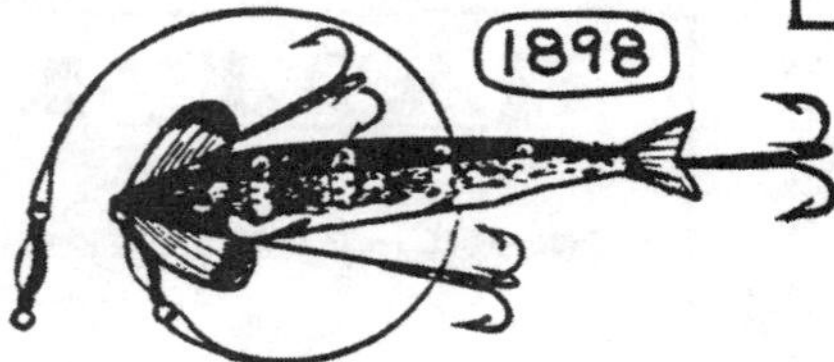

Blended oil colors on strong waterproof ribbed cloth.

PFLUEGER
Trade Mark Reg. U.S. Pat. Off.
O'BOY
MINNOW

Patented May 10, 1921
June 6, 1922
Other Patents Pending

Floats—Dives—Wiggles—Wobbles

(PAT'D. MAY 10, 1921)

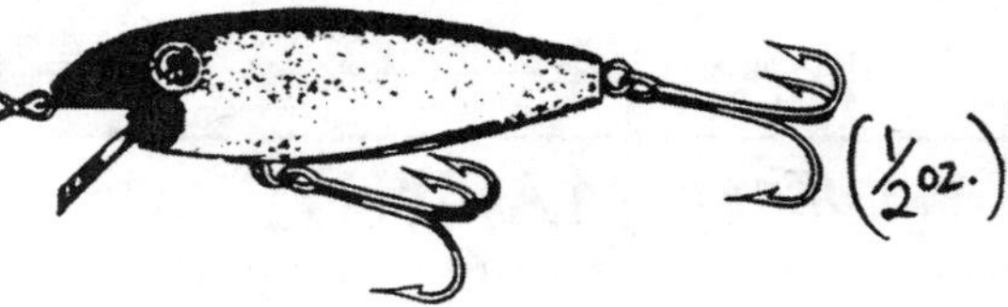

(½ oz.)

No. 5401—Size 2¾ Inch
GoldenShiner—ScaleFinish

$30 – 50

(¾ oz)

No. 5407—Size 3½
Natural Chub

ALSO MADE A SALT WATER 3½" —@ ⅞ oz.

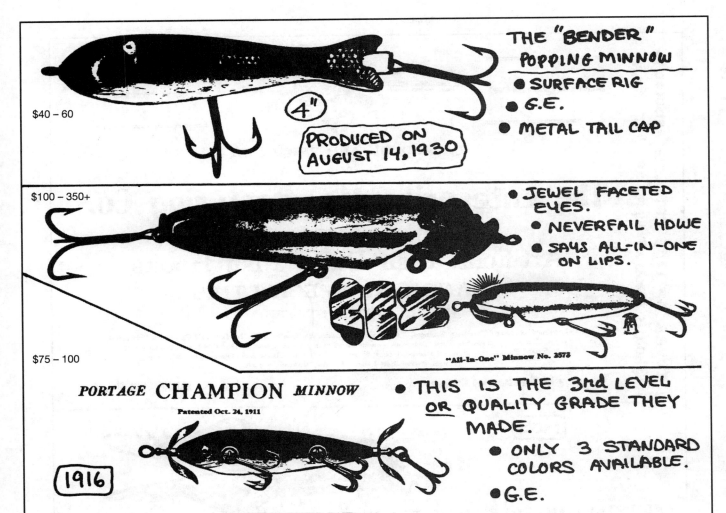

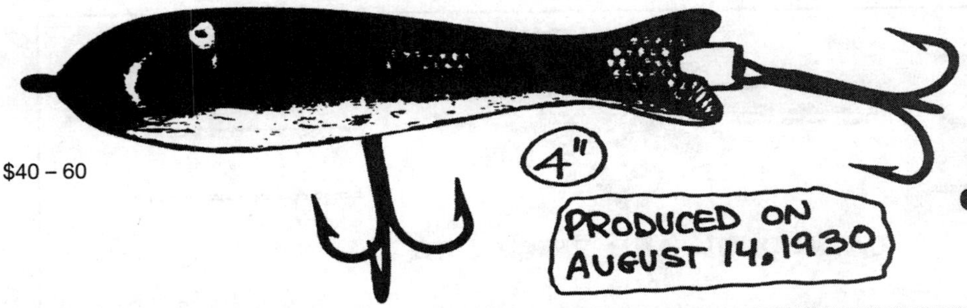

THE "BENDER" POPPING MINNOW

- SURFACE RIG
- G.E.
- METAL TAIL CAP

4"

PRODUCED ON AUGUST 14, 1930

$40 – 60

$100 – 350+

- JEWEL FACETED EYES.
- NEVERFAIL HOWE
- SAYS ALL-IN-ONE ON LIPS.

"All-In-One" Minnow No. 3573

$75 – 100

PORTAGE CHAMPION MINNOW

Patented Oct. 24, 1911

- THIS IS THE 3rd LEVEL OR QUALITY GRADE THEY MADE.
- ONLY 3 STANDARD COLORS AVAILABLE.
- G.E.

1916

A UNDER WATER BAIT

These Minnows are exceptionally well made for their grade and are the best competitive Baits offered by any one.

Wooden bodies are well coated with our special waterproof porcelain enamels and mounted with best quality bright Spear Point Treble Hooks ringed, sizes as follows:

Minnows size 2¾-inch with three Treble Hooks, size 2.

Minnows size 3⅝-inch with five Treble Hooks, size 2.

The side hooks can be attached and detached instantly with our patented nickel plated Hook Fastener, the simplest, strongest and best made.

Polished nickel plated Spinners, revolving in opposite directions and bodies ballasted so that they will ride "*Belly Down*" at all times and will present the hooks at the best possible angle to receive the strike of the fish.

ALSO WITH A BUCKTAIL

For tying genuine Bucktail Hair on the tail treble hooks, add 50 cents net per dozen.

2 3/4" – 3 5/8"

PRICE EACH

No.	Sizes, Inches	2¾	3⅝
6180	White Enamel over all		
6194	White Enamel Belly—Blended Green Back		
6195	White Enamel Belly—Blended Red Back	.30	.40
*6172	White Enamel Belly—Blended Slate Back		
*6156	White Enamel Belly—Blended Dark Blue Back		
*6157	White Enamel Belly—Blended Brown Back		

Packed—One in a card box and twelve boxes in a carton.

NOTICE—This mark * preceding the Stock Number, Name, Size or Price of the article indicates goods NOT carried in stock, but will be made to order.

COVER OF 1905 CATALOG (REDUCED) - SHOWS PRODUCT LINE OF THAT YEAR. →

Season of 1905 and 1906

No. F. 24

CATALOGUE AND PRICE LIST

OF

The Enterprise Manufacturing Co.

LARGEST MANUFACTURERS OF

Artificial Fish Baits, Fish Hooks

AND ANGLERS' SPECIALTIES

IN THE UNITED STATES

All sizes and styles of Trolling Spoons, American Spinners, Hard and Soft Rubber and Phantom Minnows, Frogs, Crawfish, Grasshoppers, Dobsons, Insects and every variety and pattern of Bass, Salmon and Trout Flies; also Ringed Hooks, Reels, Hooks to Gut and Gimp, Line Spreaders, Minnow Gangs, Furnished Lines, Floats, Sinkers, &c., &c.

The Enterprise Manufacturing Company - - - - - AKRON, OHIO, U. S. A.

1905

$20 – 30

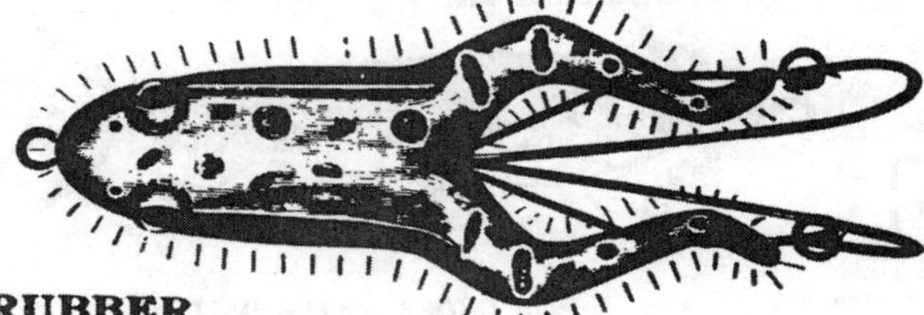

PFLUEGER'S IMPROVED SOFT RUBBER WEEDLESS FROG

Exact Size

The Spring Guards over the hooks are a very effective protection against weeds, rushes, etc, Very neatly decorated in Imitation of the Live Bait.

No. 866 Luminous
No. 867 Non-luminous

1905

$75 – 100

PFLUEGER'S RUBBER PRACTICE CASTING FROG

TOUGH FROG!

Exact Size No. 2

Made of Pure Rubber, Enameled White, as nearly indestructible as is possible to make it. Adopted by all the large Bait Casting Clubs in the country as the official Casting Frog. Made in two weights as follows:

Size No.	1	2
Weight, Ounces	¼	½
No. 780 Practice Casting Frog............		

PFLUEGER KORMISH FROGS

Trade Mark Reg. U. S. Pat. Office

Pure Soft Rubber

$5 – 15

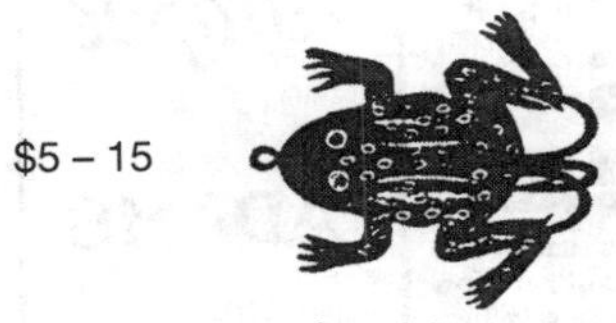

Actual Size 1/0

$5 – 15

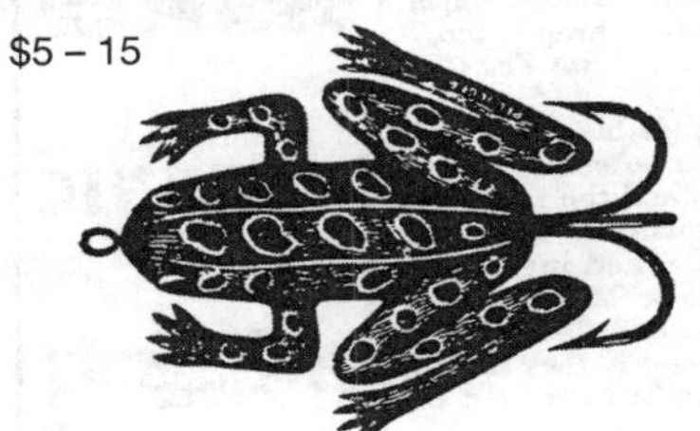

Actual Size 1

$5 – 15

Actual Size 2

ALL ARE MADE FROM "FLEXO" COATED RUBBER GREEN FROG COLOR.

JUSRITE MINNOW

Trade Mark Reg. U. S. Pat. Office

Pure Soft Rubber

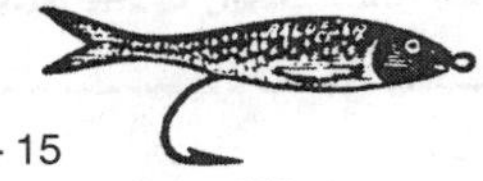

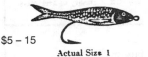

$5 – 15

Actual Size 1

Actual Size 3

Moulded with scales and fins in exact imitation of the natural Minnow.

Minnows size 1 are mounted with Hollow Point Sproat Hooks Ringed, size 6, and Minnows size 3 are mounted with Hollow Point Sproat Hooks Ringed, size 1.

No.
148 Silver Enamel Belly—Blended Green Back.
149 Silver Enamel Over All ....

PFLUEGER CONRAD FROGS

Trade Mark Reg. U. S. Pat. Office

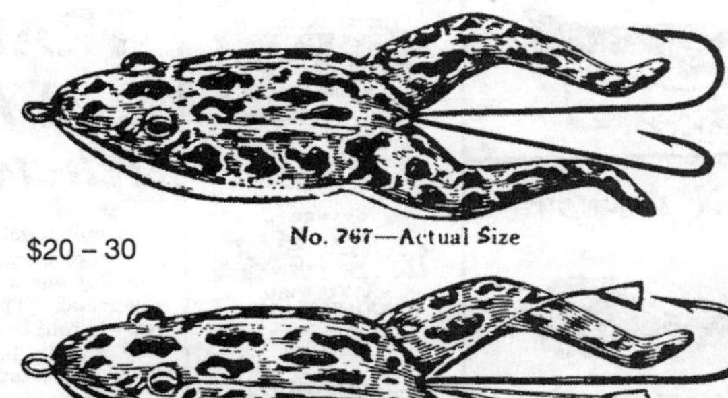

No. 767—Actual Size

$20 – 30

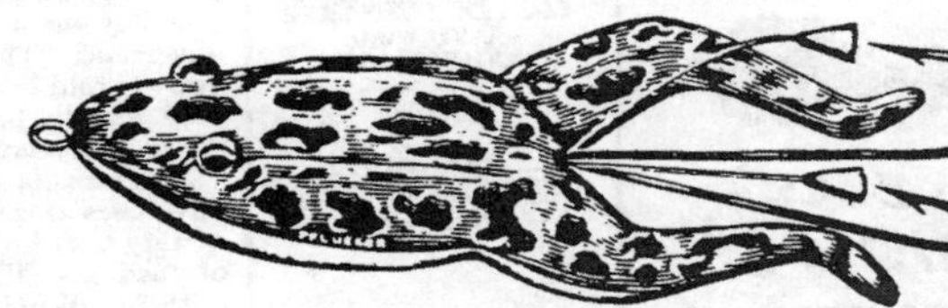

Weedless No. 867—Actual Size

Pure Soft Rubber

Keep the frog on the move continually and strike the instant you feel the fish. Very effective when cast among the spatter docks, weeds and lily pads. Painted and decorated with our special formula "FLEXO," the most scientifically perfect material ever invented and applied to rubber baits. It is as flexible as the rubber itself, waterproof, indestructible and will not crack or peel.

Mounted with extra stout Bright Tin Plated Aberdeen Hooks, Ringed hand filed out points, size 3/0. Weed Guards are made with best quality rust proof steel piano wire with brass cones designed to shed weeds and grass without interfering with hooking the fish.

No.
767 Conrad Frog, Green—Pure Soft Rubber..............
867 Conrad Frog, Green and Weedless—Pure Soft Rubber.

PFLUEGER MEADOW FLOATING FROGS

Trade Mark Reg. U. S. Pat. Office

1905

Satin Cork

$30 – 40

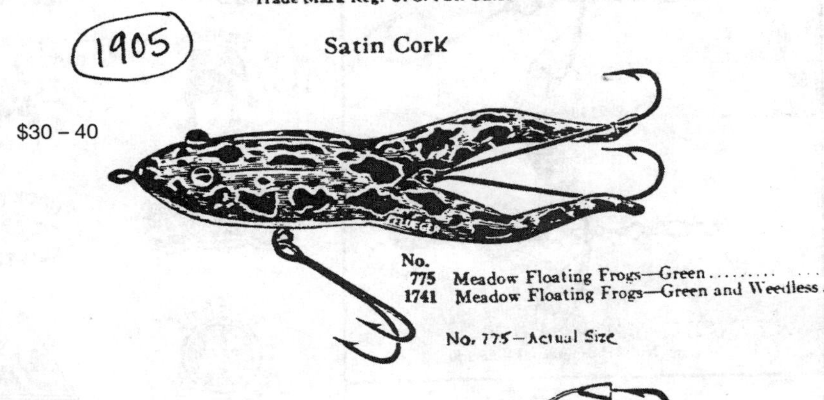

No.
775 Meadow Floating Frogs—Green..........
1741 Meadow Floating Frogs—Green and Weedless.

No. 775—Actual Size

$35 – 45

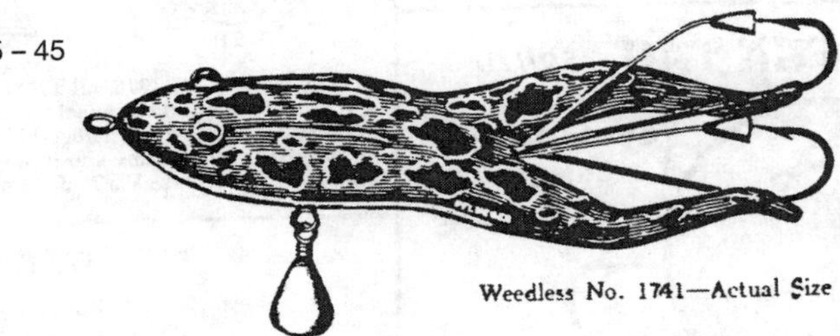

Weedless No. 1741—Actual Size

Meadow Floating Frogs are made of satin cork and ballasted so will float "*Belly Down*" and in the natural position of a swimming frog with the head slightly elevated out of the water.

Keep the frog on the move continually and strike the instant you feel the fish. Very effective when cast among the spatter docks, weeds and lily pads.

With our spring coil fastener on the belly of the frog the double hooks and sinkers can be instantly attached or detached.

Frogs No. 776 are mounted with Bright Tin Plated Double Hooks, hand filed out points, size 1, and Bright Tin Plated Aberdeen Hooks, Ringed hand filed out points, size 3/0.

Frogs No. 1741 are mounted with a lead belly weight and with Bright Tin Plated Aberdeen Hooks, Ringed hand filed out points size 3/0. Weed Guards are made of best quality rust proof steel piano wire with brass cones designed to shed weeds and grass without interfering with the hooking of the fish.

Painted and decorated with our special formula "FLEXO" which is as flexible as rubber and will not chip, crack or peel.

VANITIE *MINNOW*

$5 – 15

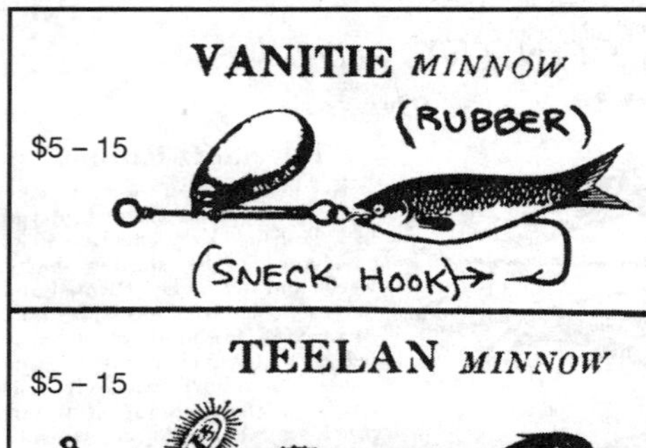
(RUBBER)
(SNECK HOOK)

TEELAN *MINNOW*

$5 – 15

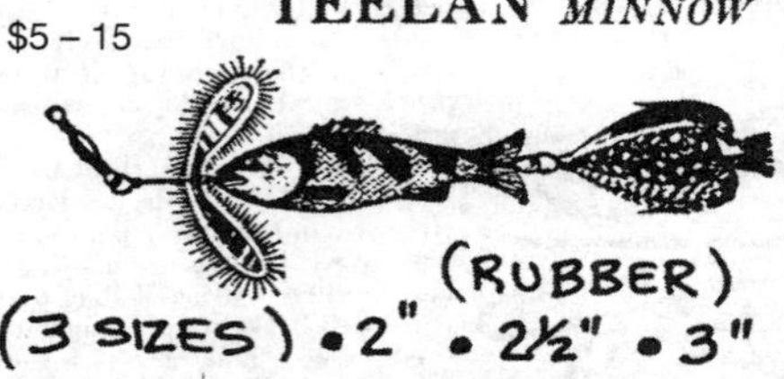
(RUBBER)
(3 SIZES) • 2" • 2½" • 3"

WHIRL-I-GIG *SPINNER*

$5

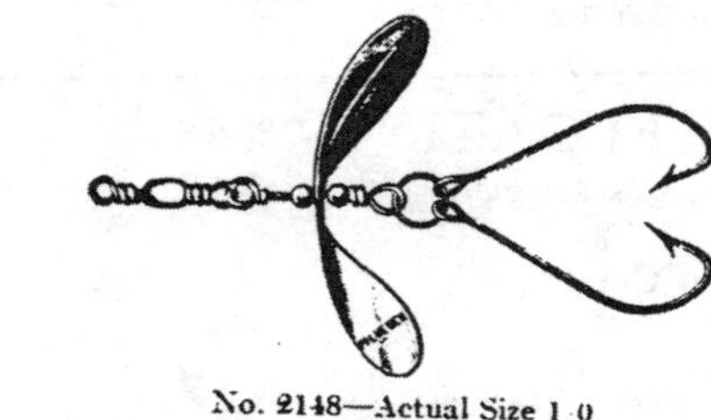

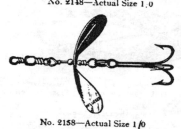

No. 2148—Actual Size 1/0

No. 2158—Actual Size 1/0

FAN-TAIL *SQUID*

$5

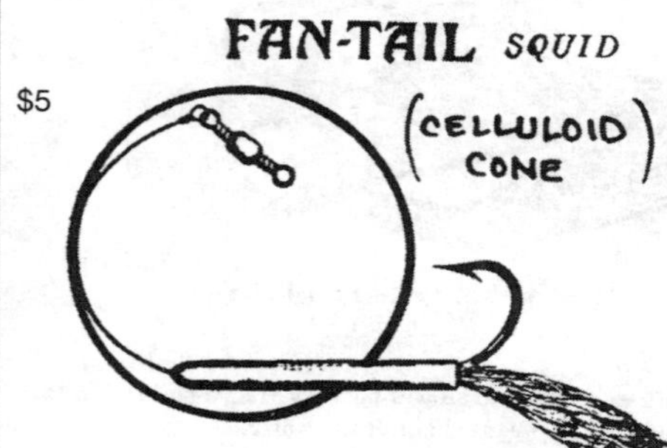
(CELLULOID CONE)

MACTAM *SPINNER*

$5

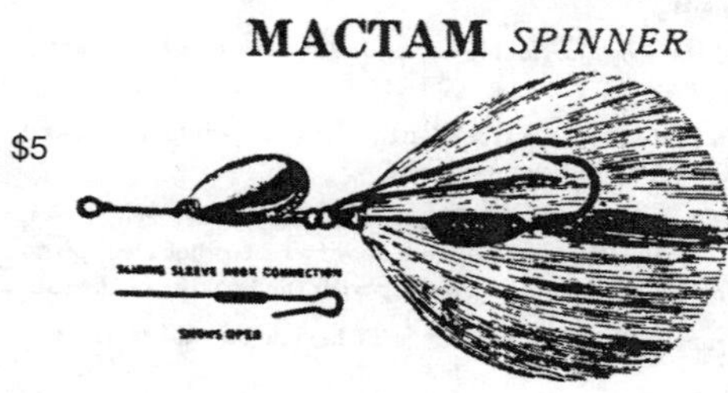

TRADE-MARKS
FAMOUS
Wherever Men Fish

Here is what these trade marks mean to you; merchandise of dependable quality. You are more certain of lasting satisfaction when you buy an article that is trade marked and advertised. The quality of merchandise which you are told is "just as good, and cheaper, too," may actually be just as good . . . *But You Can Never Be Certain of It.*

The manufacturer who brands his goods and advertises them world wide is so sure of their quality that he is willing to stand the full force of possible criticism and complaints. Put your faith in advertised merchandise and invariably you will be better satisfied. The Manufacturer of such merchandise must stand behind his articles and "make good" to you if they fail to satisfy . . . or be will quickly be forced out of business.

TANDEM

Pflueger Supreme Level Winding Anti-Back-Lash

Atlapac

PFLUEGER
SUMMIT
FISHING REEL
LEVEL WIND
ANTI-BACK-LASH

ADAMS

TEMPLAR

Fishing Akron Reel Level Wind

OCEANIC

Wizard

Pflueger PAL-O-MINE Minnow

Superex
AUTOMATIC

ALPINE

MEDALIST

PFLUEGER
(1915)
TRADE MARK

W.T.J. LOWE
L
REG. U.S. PAT. OFF.

TRADE MARK
P
REGISTERED

W.T.J. LOWE
REG. U.S. PAT. OFF.

PELICAN
TRADE MARK REG. U.S. PAT. OFF.

W.T.J. LOWE TRADE MARK BUFFALO, N.Y.

4 BROTHERS 4

Trade Mark
3/A
Reg. U.S. Pat. Off.

1/A
REG. U.S. PAT. OFF.

3X
TRADE MARK

2/X
REG. U.S. PAT. OFF.

On January 25, 1916, all TRADE MARK RIGHTS and good will of W. T. J. Lowe, Buffalo, N. Y., inventor and manufacturer of the Celebrated Lowe Star and Buffalo Baits, except Canada, were transferred to the Pfluegers, operating The Enterprise Mfg. Co., of Akron, Ohio, who will continue to manufacture and supply these Baits in the same high standard of quality as heretofore furnished by the late W. T. J. Lowe.

W. T. J. LOWE, Buffalo, N. Y.

Born July 2, 1840; died September 27, 1915.
Inventor and manufacturer of the celebrated

LOWE STAR AND BUFFALO BAITS

Business established 1883

On January 25, 1916, all TRADE MARK RIGHTS and good will of the business, except Canada, were transferred to the Pfluegers, operating The Enterprise Mfg. Co., of Akron, Ohio, who will continue to manufacture and supply these Baits in the same high standard of quality as heretofore furnished by the late W. T. J. Lowe.

+ EDITION OF JANUARY 1. 1892. +

ELEVEN YEARS OF SUCCESS.

Construction of Pflueger's Superior Trolling Baits.

BY a perusal of these pages the reader will find our line comprises the most complete assortment of styles and sizes of Trolling Spoons ever placed before the Trade. You will note we make most patterns of Spoon Bait in four different grades, thereby enabling the dealer to suit all classes of people in price, from the laborer to the capitalist. While we use different grades of metal, plating, and finish, according to the price of goods, we do not build any bait but what will give satisfaction.

Our First quality is unsurpassed for finish and grade of material used.

Our Second quality will compare favorably with some goods sold for "first."

Our Third quality we claim to be fully as good as other manufactures' so-called "second."

Our Fourth quality are goods that have a big run among the Hardware, Notion and Fancy Goods jobbers for country trade.

The Enterprise Manufacturing Co.

1892
−11
1881

(IN 1892 THEY WERE MAKING 4 DIFFERENT QUALITY LEVELS!)

PORTAGE **REFLEX** BAIT

Patented Oct. 24, 1911 ← (PATENTED: 1911)

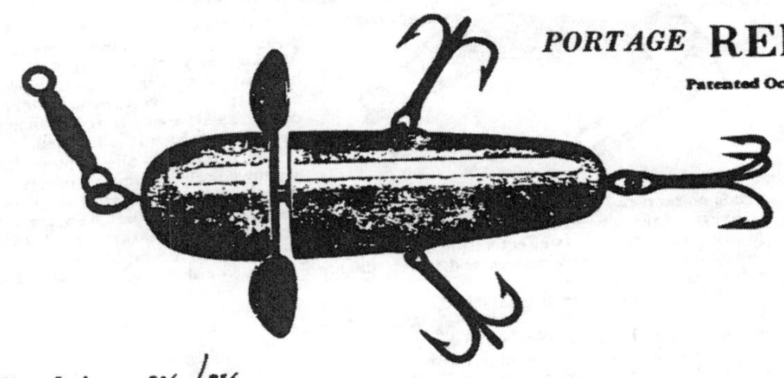

THE 1916 VERSION OF THE PFLUEGER GLOBE CALLED THE "PORTAGE REFLEX"

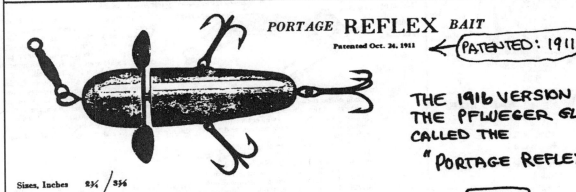

Sizes, Inches 2¾ / 3⅝

SIZE 2¾ INCH

A FLOATER OR SURFACE BAIT

1916

$5 – 20

Baits are well made and serviceable and as competitive baits are the best on the market.

Wooden bodies are well coated with our special waterproof indestructible porcelain enamels. Both sizes of baits are mounted with three best quality bright Spear Point Treble Hooks ringed, size 2. The side hooks can be attached or detached instantly with our patented nickel plated Hook Fastener, the simplest, strongest and best made. The polished spinner screwed to the head revolves the same very freely on hard brass bearings.

2 SIZES: 2¾" – 3⅝"

No.	
3880	White Enamel over all................
3896	White Enamel Body with Red Head....
3850	Yellow Enamel over all with Gold Spots.
*3898	Mouse Color Enamel over all...........

$5 – 20

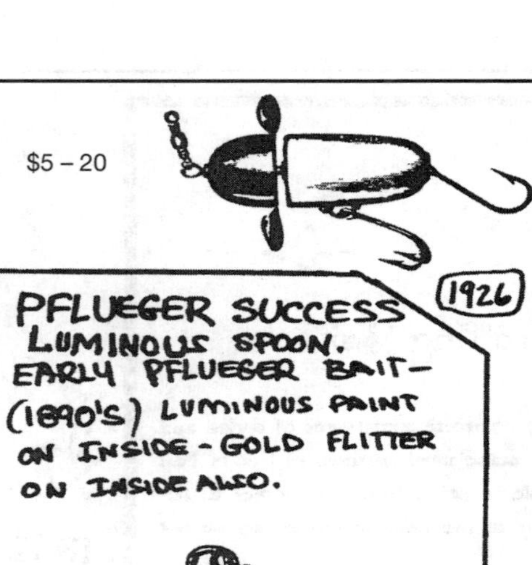

PFLUEGER **GLOBE** BAIT (3 SIZES)

Globe Bait is made of selected cedar and heavily coated with our flexible enamel which will not peel. The propeller blades are made of strong spring metal highly polished and attached firmly, spinning the head in a manner that produces a disturbance or struggling effect as if made by a drowning insect or swimming mouse.

Bait Size, Inch		2¾	3⅝	5¼
Length of Body	Inch	2¾	3⅝	5¼
Treble Hook, Tail	Sizes	1/0	2/0	3/0
Treble Hook, Belly	Sizes	1/0	2/0	4/0
Fishing Weight	Ounce	⅝	¾	1½

Bait sizes 2¾ and 3⅝—the tail hook secured to the body with a strong screw eye in and through a nickel plated socket eyelet. The ring on the hook is sufficiently submerged in the eyelet to prevent cocking or locking with the belly hook. Brass barrel swivels, nickel plated.

PFLUEGER SUCCESS LUMINOUS SPOON. (1926) EARLY PFLUEGER BAIT— (1890's) LUMINOUS PAINT ON INSIDE - GOLD FLITTER ON INSIDE ALSO.

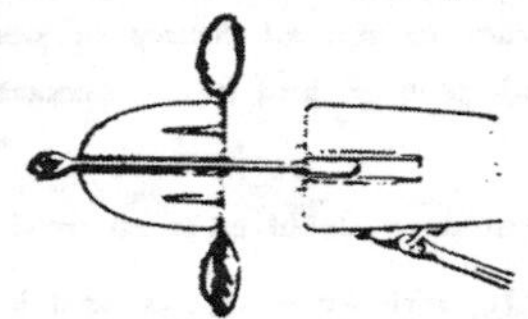

Improved Design Patent Pending Permits Separating Head and Body for Quick Removal of Weeds, etc., as Shown in Diagram (1935)

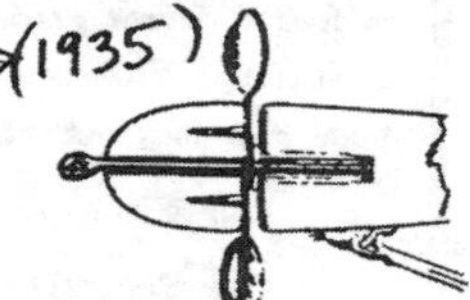

Bait size 5¼ is designed for Muskies, Pike, and salt water game fish—strong brass wire shaft of a *continuous length through the body* to which the tail hook is attached. No swivel.

Belly Hook is secured to the body with our patented hook fastener preventing the belly hook becoming entangled with the tail hook or spinner blades.

Bright Tin Plated Treble Hooks Ringed, sizes as per chart above.

Luminous Minnow No. 3770 is equally as effective for day as for evening or night fishing and is especially suited for deep or roily waters and cloudy days.

For Globe Baits with THREE HOOK POINTS see page 53

No.	
3770	Luminous Enamel—Gold Spots
3750	Yellow Enamel—Gold Spots
3796	White Enamel—Red Head
3704	Natural Pike—Scale Finish—Red Head
3706	Natural Perch—Scale Finish—Red Head

$5 – 15

3 SIZES

BASS SIZE.
Nos. 2, 3, 4, 5, 6.

MUSKELLUNCE SIZE.
Nos. 9 and 10.

PIKE AND PICKEREL SIZE.
Nos. 7 and 8.

No. 4707 Size 3½
No. 4773 Size 1¾
No. 4785 Size 3
No. 4796 Size 1½
No. 4705 Size 2¼
No. 4706 Size 3½

PFLUEGER *Wizard* WIGGLER

Trade Marks Reg. U. S. Pat. Office—Patent Nos. 1418326-1409680-1537261

Floats—Dives—Wiggles—Wobbles

6 SIZES!

$15 – 30

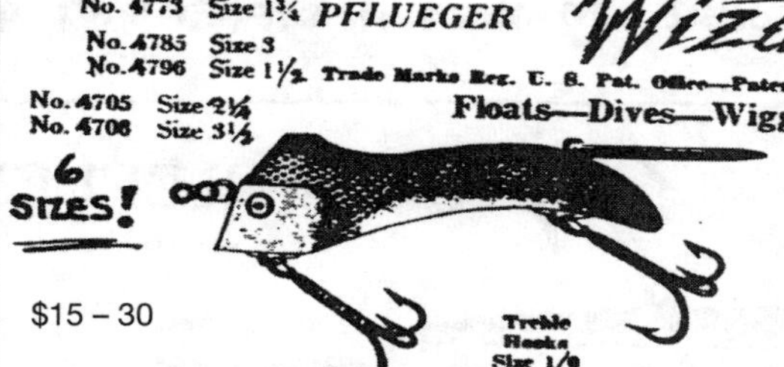
Treble Hooks Size 1/0

It is unsurpassed as a general purpose lure for the taking of Bass, Pike, Muskies and other game fish. Very buoyant, the Wizard can be worked as a top water bait, or will travel as deeply as desired, in accordance with the way in which it is handled.

The Wizard has a most powerful and snappy wiggle, resulting from its unique and scientifically designed shape—it depends on no metal attachments which might become bent or damaged and affect the action.

Every angler should carry an assortment of these minnows in his tackle kit. Luminous Minnows are equally as effective for day as for evening or night fishing and are especially suited for deep or roily waters and cloudy days. Expose to either day or artificial light before using.

Fly Rod Wizard, see page 100.

Fishing Weight ½ oz. Wiggler Size 3

No.	
4706	Natural Perch—Scale finish
4754	Black—Silver Lightning Flash
4759	Luminous—Red Lightning Flash
4785	Green Cracked Back
4796	White Body—Red Head
4798	Grey Mouse

Wiggler Size, Inch	1½	1¾	2¼	3	3½
Inch	1½	1¾	2¼	3	3½

Patented May 10, 1921 — June 6, 1922 -

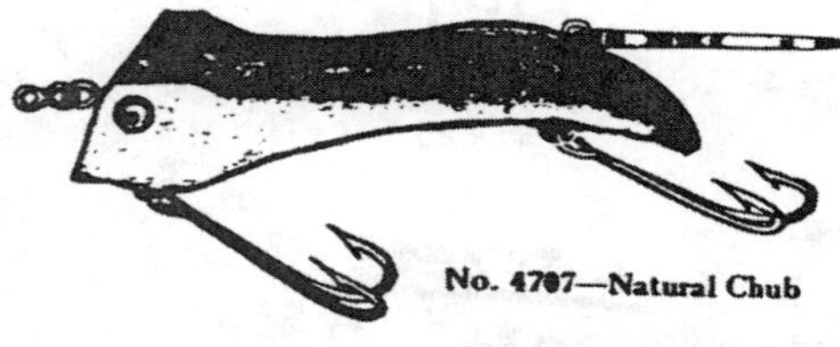

No. 4707—Natural Chub

DOUBLE HOOKS MODEL

$5 – 20

PFLUEGER (FLEW-GER) *Wizard* FLY ROD WOBBLER

Trade Marks Reg. U. S. Pat. Office—Patent No. 1499689

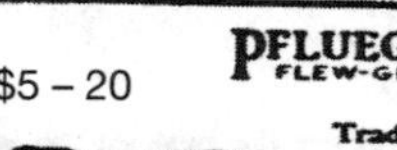

Floats—Dives—Wiggles—Wobbles

Length of body 1½ inch; Double Hook size 6; Fishing weight 1/20 ounce.

No.	
4706	Natural Perch—Scale Finish
4707	Natural Chub—Scale Finish
4769	White Enamel—Green and Red Spots
4770	Luminous—with Gold Spots
4773	Rainbow Blend
4796	White Body—Red Head

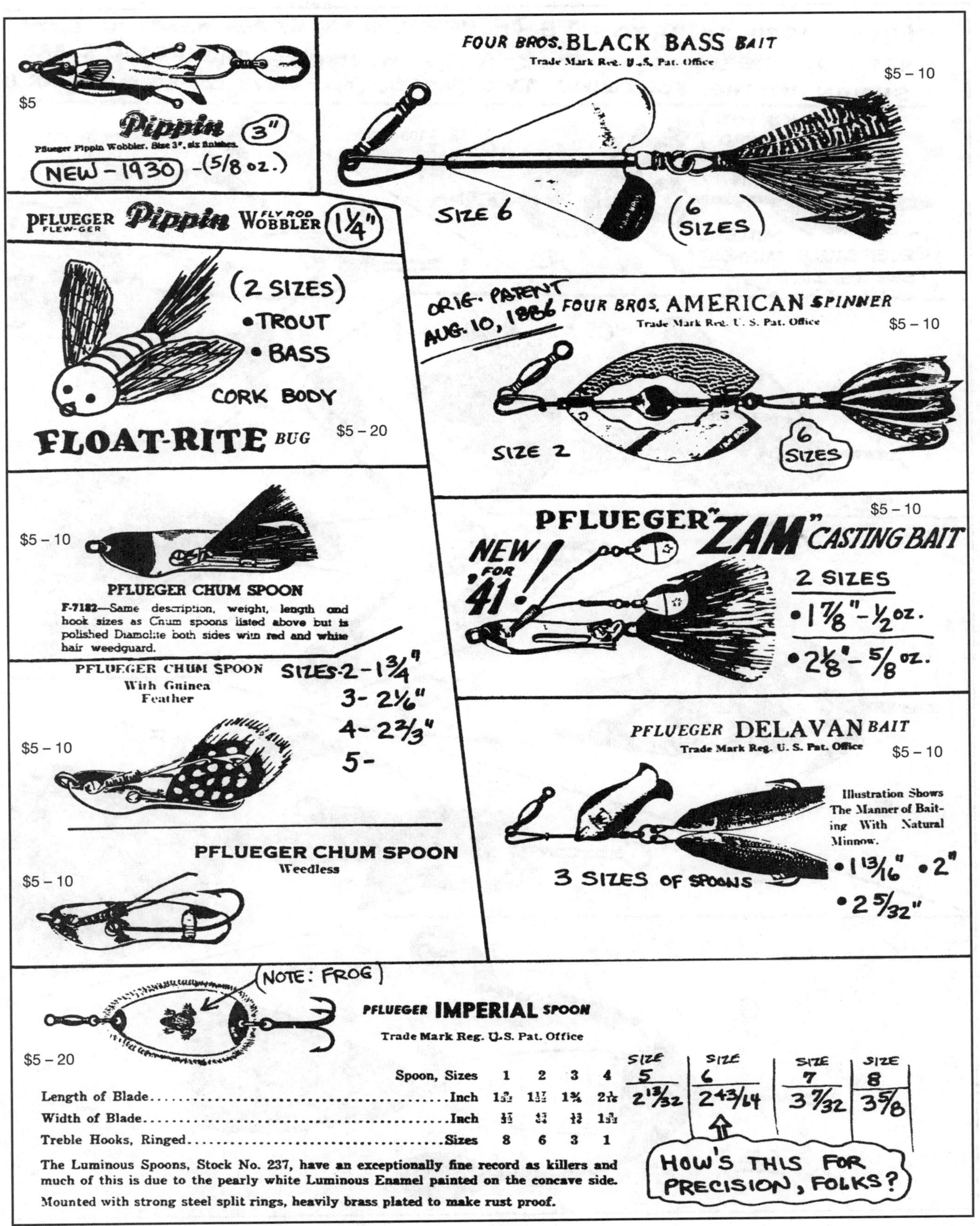
$5
Pippin
3"
Pflueger Pippin Wobbler. Size 3", six finishes.
NEW - 1930
-(5/8 oz.)
FOUR BROS. BLACK BASS BAIT
Trade Mark Reg. U.S. Pat. Office
$5 – 10
SIZE 6
(6 SIZES)
PFLUEGER FLEW-GER Pippin FLY ROD WOBBLER
1¼"
(2 SIZES)
•TROUT
•BASS
CORK BODY
FLOAT-RITE BUG
$5 – 20
ORIG. PATENT AUG. 10, 1886
FOUR BROS. AMERICAN SPINNER
Trade Mark Reg. U.S. Pat. Office
$5 – 10
SIZE 2
6 SIZES
$5 – 10
PFLUEGER CHUM SPOON
F-7182—Same description, weight, length and hook sizes as Chum spoons listed above but is polished Diamolite both sides with red and white hair weedguard.
$5 – 10
PFLUEGER "ZAM" CASTING BAIT
NEW FOR '41!
2 SIZES
•1⅞" - ½ oz.
•2⅛" - ⅝ oz.
PFLUEGER CHUM SPOON
With Guinea Feather
SIZES-2 - 1¾"
3 - 2⅙"
4 - 2⅔"
5 -
$5 – 10
PFLUEGER DELAVAN BAIT
Trade Mark Reg. U.S. Pat. Office
$5 – 10
Illustration Shows The Manner of Baiting With Natural Minnow.
3 SIZES OF SPOONS
•1 13/16" •2" •2 5/32"
PFLUEGER CHUM SPOON
Weedless
$5 – 10
NOTE: FROG
PFLUEGER IMPERIAL SPOON
Trade Mark Reg. U.S. Pat. Office
$5 – 20
Spoon, Sizes 1 2 3 4
Length of Blade.....Inch 1¾
Width of Blade.....Inch
Treble Hooks, Ringed.....Sizes 8 6 3 1
SIZE 5 2 13/32
SIZE 6 2 43/64
SIZE 7 3 7/32
SIZE 8 3⅝
The Luminous Spoons, Stock No. 237, have an exceptionally fine record as killers and much of this is due to the pearly white Luminous Enamel painted on the concave side.
Mounted with strong steel split rings, heavily brass plated to make rust proof.
HOW'S THIS FOR PRECISION, FOLKS?

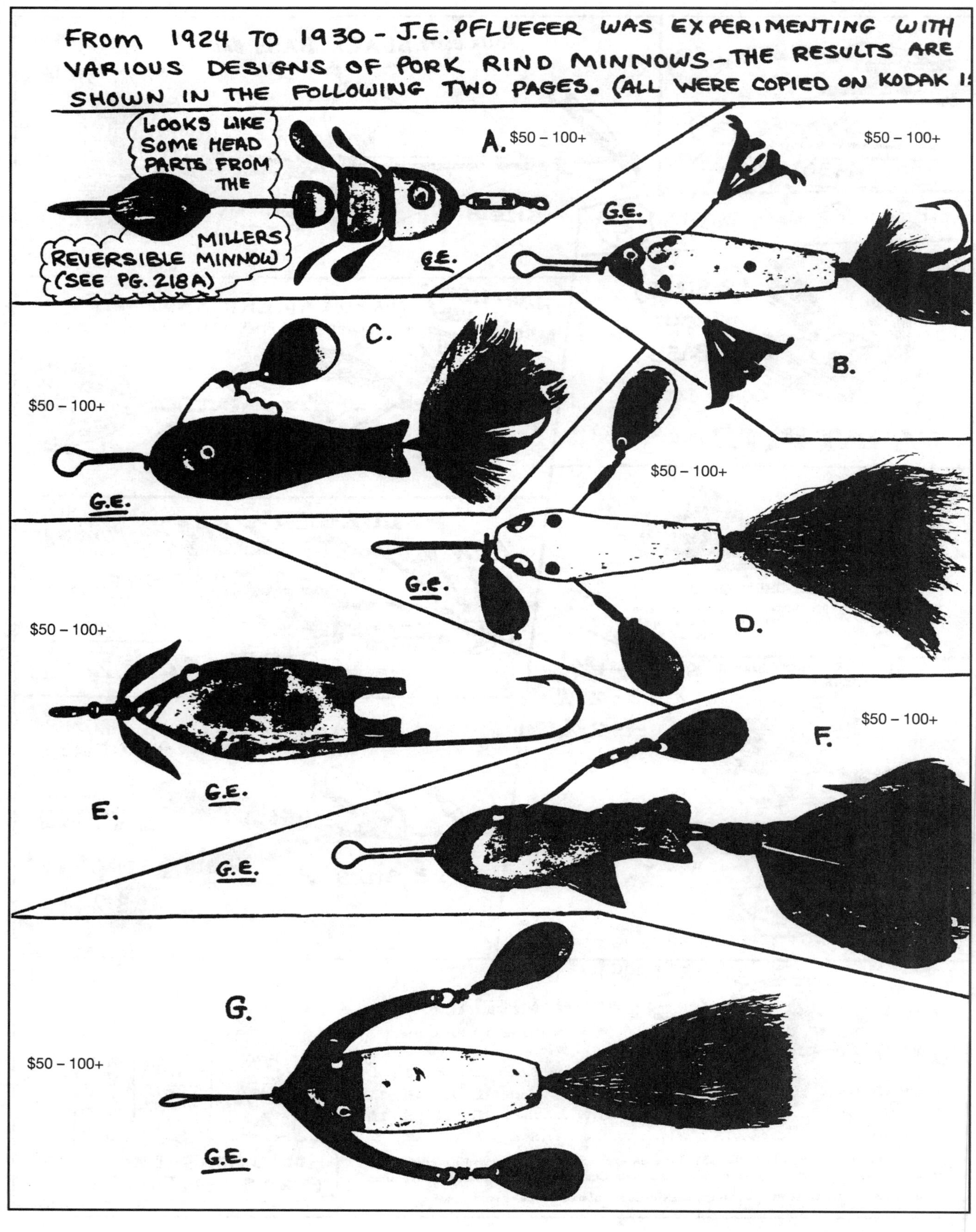
FROM 1924 TO 1930 - J.E. PFLUEGER WAS EXPERIMENTING WITH VARIOUS DESIGNS OF PORK RIND MINNOWS - THE RESULTS ARE SHOWN IN THE FOLLOWING TWO PAGES. (ALL WERE COPIED ON KODAK I
LOOKS LIKE SOME HEAD PARTS FROM THE MILLERS REVERSIBLE MINNOW (SEE PG. 218A)
A.
$50 – 100+
G.E.
$50 – 100+
G.E.
B.
C.
$50 – 100+
G.E.
$50 – 100+
G.E.
D.
$50 – 100+
G.E.
E.
$50 – 100+
F.
G.E.
G.
$50 – 100+
G.E.

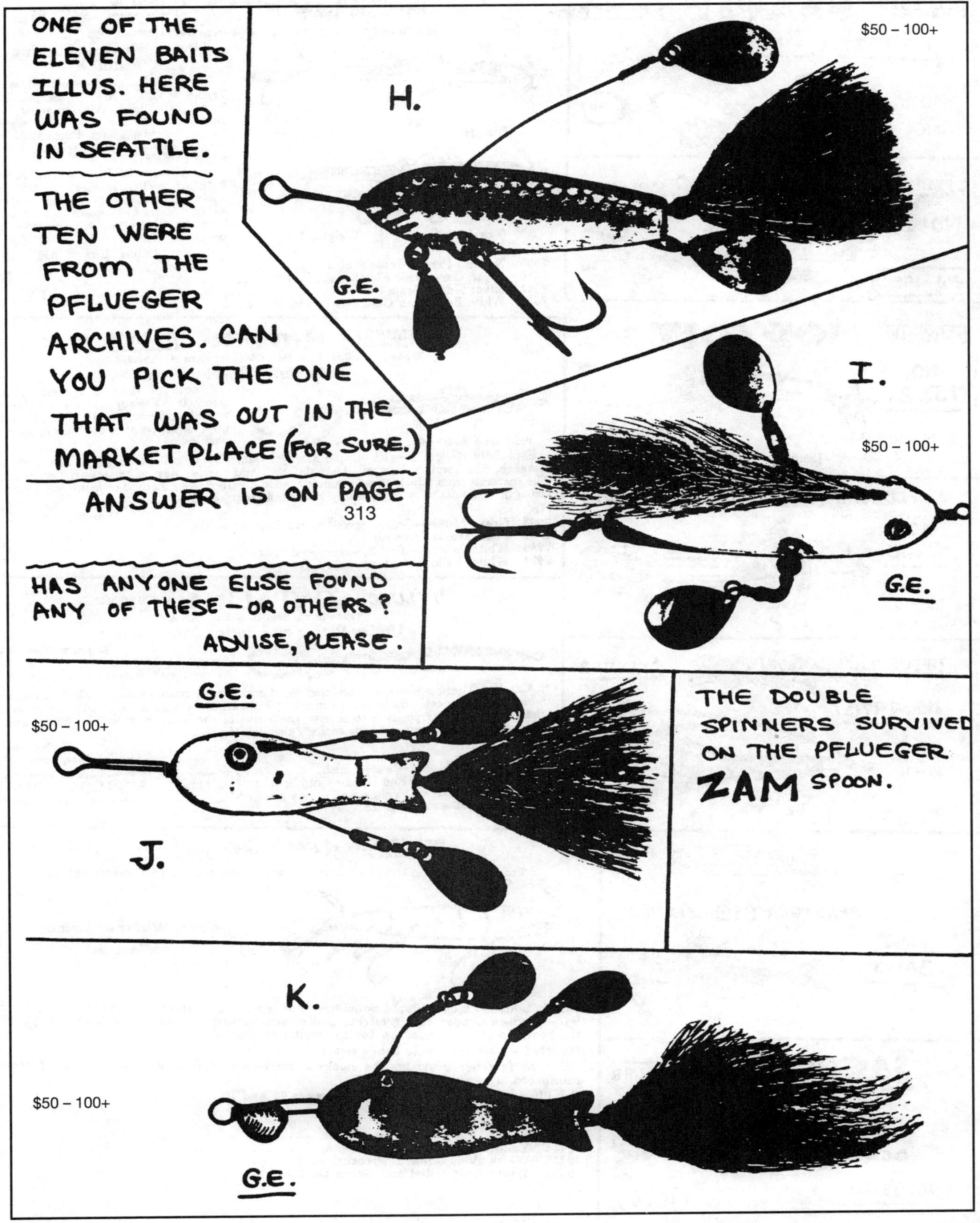
ONE OF THE ELEVEN BAITS ILLUS. HERE WAS FOUND IN SEATTLE.
THE OTHER TEN WERE FROM THE PFLUEGER ARCHIVES. CAN YOU PICK THE ONE THAT WAS OUT IN THE MARKET PLACE (FOR SURE.)
ANSWER IS ON PAGE 313
HAS ANYONE ELSE FOUND ANY OF THESE – OR OTHERS? ADVISE, PLEASE.
H.
G.E.
$50 – 100+
I.
$50 – 100+
G.E.
G.E.
$50 – 100+
J.
THE DOUBLE SPINNERS SURVIVED ON THE PFLUEGER ZAM SPOON.
K.
$50 – 100+
G.E.

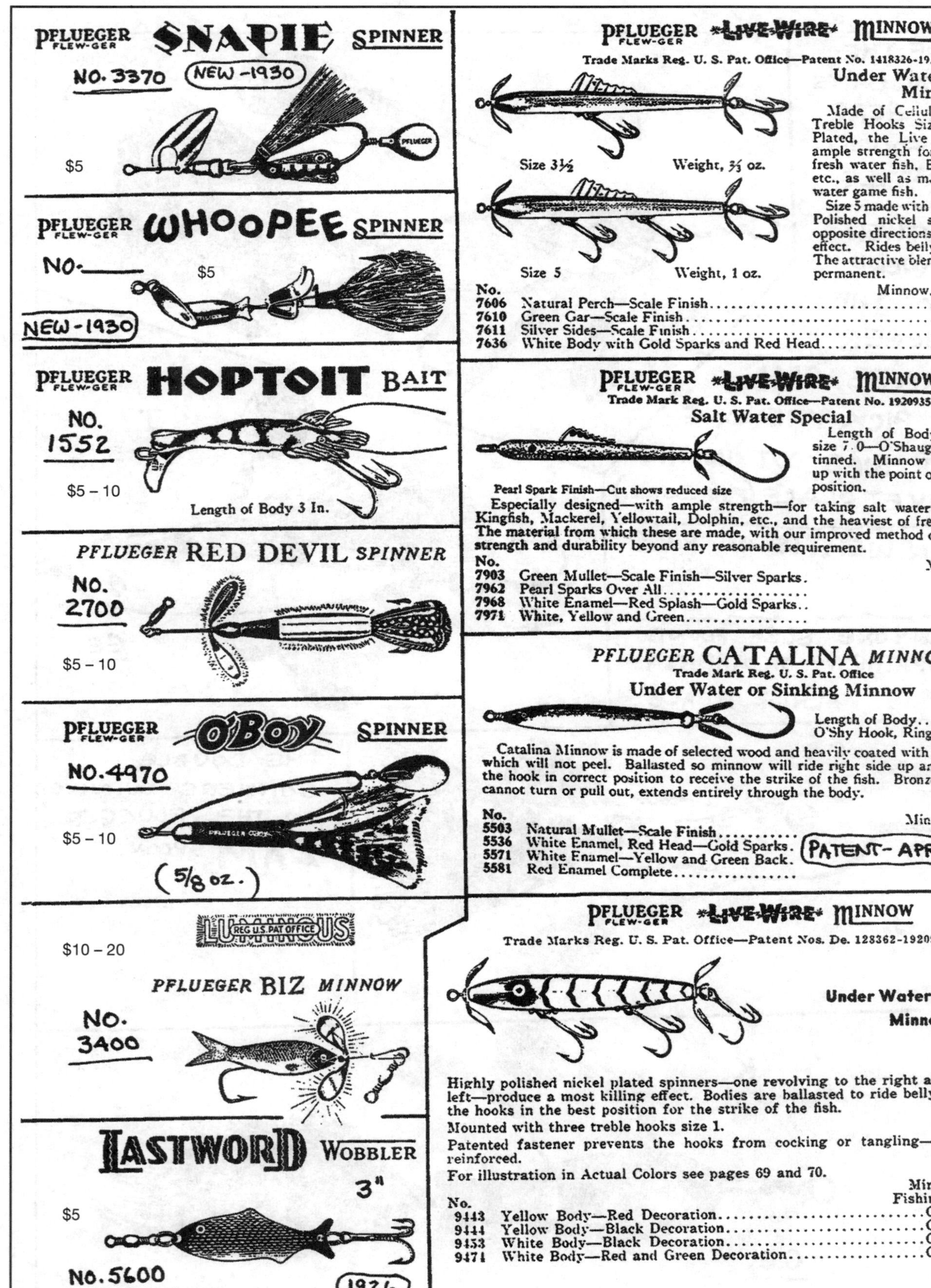

PFLUEGER FLEW-GER SNAPIE SPINNER

NO. 3370 (NEW-1930)

$5

PFLUEGER FLEW-GER WHOOPEE SPINNER

NO.—

$5

NEW-1930

PFLUEGER FLEW-GER HOPTOIT BAIT

NO. 1552

$5 – 10

Length of Body 3 In.

PFLUEGER RED DEVIL SPINNER

NO. 2700

$5 – 10

PFLUEGER FLEW-GER O'BOY SPINNER

NO. 4970

$5 – 10

(5/8 oz.)

LUMINOUS REG. U.S. PAT OFFICE

$10 – 20

PFLUEGER BIZ MINNOW

NO. 3400

LASTWORD WOBBLER

3"

$5

NO. 5600

(1926)

PFLUEGER FLEW-GER LIVE-WIRE MINNOW $20 – 30

Trade Marks Reg. U. S. Pat. Office—Patent No. 1418326-1920935

Under Water or Sinking Minnow

Size 3½ Weight, ⅔ oz.

Size 5 Weight, 1 oz.

Made of Celluloid—mounted with Treble Hooks Size 1/0, Bright Tin Plated, the Live Wire minnow has ample strength for taking the largest fresh water fish, Bass, Pike, Muskies, etc., as well as many varieties of salt water game fish.

Size 5 made with Extra Strong Hooks. Polished nickel spinners revolve in opposite directions, producing a killing effect. Rides belly down at all times. The attractive blends or colorations are permanent.

No.		Minnow, Size 3½	5
7606	Natural Perch—Scale Finish		
7610	Green Gar—Scale Finish		
7611	Silver Sides—Scale Finish		
7636	White Body with Gold Sparks and Red Head		

(1932)

PFLUEGER FLEW-GER LIVE-WIRE MINNOW $20 – 25

Trade Mark Reg. U. S. Pat. Office—Patent No. 1920935

Salt Water Special

Length of Body 5 Inches. Hook size 7/0—O'Shaughnessy short shank, tinned. Minnow will ride right side up with the point of the hook in correct position.

Pearl Spark Finish—Cut shows reduced size

Especially designed—with ample strength—for taking salt water game fish such as Kingfish, Mackerel, Yellowtail, Dolphin, etc., and the heaviest of fresh water game fish. The material from which these are made, with our improved method of mounting, insures strength and durability beyond any reasonable requirement.

No.		Price Each Minnow, Size 5
7903	Green Mullet—Scale Finish—Silver Sparks	
7962	Pearl Sparks Over All	
7968	White Enamel—Red Splash—Gold Sparks	
7971	White, Yellow and Green	

PFLUEGER CATALINA MINNOW $50 – 75

Trade Mark Reg. U. S. Pat. Office

Under Water or Sinking Minnow

Minnow, Size 4½
Length of Body..........Inch 4½
O'Shy Hook, Ringed.......Size 6/0

Catalina Minnow is made of selected wood and heavily coated with our Flexible Enamel which will not peel. Ballasted so minnow will ride right side up and with the point of the hook in correct position to receive the strike of the fish. Bronze Wire Shaft, which cannot turn or pull out, extends entirely through the body.

No.		Price Each Minnow Size, Inch 4½
5503	Natural Mullet—Scale Finish	
5536	White Enamel, Red Head—Gold Sparks	
5571	White Enamel—Yellow and Green Back	
5581	Red Enamel Complete	

(PATENT- APRIL 12, 1910)

PFLUEGER FLEW-GER LIVE-WIRE MINNOW $20 – 25

Trade Marks Reg. U. S. Pat. Office—Patent Nos. De. 128362-1920935-2001652

Under Water or Sinking Minnow

Highly polished nickel plated spinners—one revolving to the right and the other to the left—produce a most killing effect. Bodies are ballasted to ride belly down and preserve the hooks in the best position for the strike of the fish.

Mounted with three treble hooks size 1.

Patented fastener prevents the hooks from cocking or tangling—tail hook fastener reinforced.

For illustration in Actual Colors see pages 69 and 70.

No.		Minnow, Size 3¾ Fishing Weight ¾ oz.
9443	Yellow Body—Red Decoration	Color 43
9444	Yellow Body—Black Decoration	Color 44
9453	White Body—Black Decoration	Color 53
9471	White Body—Red and Green Decoration	Color 74

PFLUEGER FISHING TACKLE
FLEW-GER

PFLUEGER **BALLERINA** MINNOW

$10 – 20

4¼"
NO.5400

$10 – 20

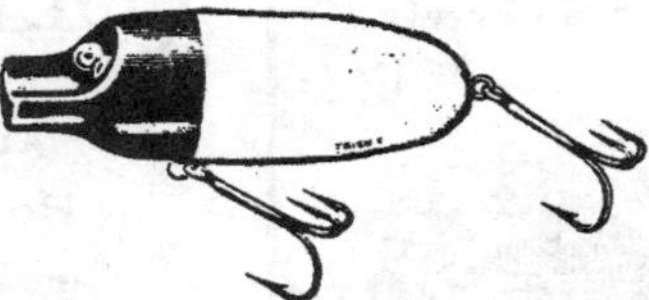

PORTAGE **FRISKY** MINNOW

Trade Marks Reg. U. S. Pat. Office—Patent No. 2036946

Floats — Dives
Wiggles — Wobbles

Minnow size 3 inches.

A minnow of unusual action—attractively finished—at a very low price. Mounted with bright treble hooks.

1934

No.	
8494	White, Green Back, Red Splash
8496	White Body, Red Head
8498	Mouse Color

PFLUEGER **POPRITE** MINNOW
FLEW-GER

Trade Marks Reg. U. S. Pat. Office—Patent Nos. 1418326-

$10 – 20

NO.8500 SERIES
3"- ½oz.
4"- ⅝oz.

PFLUEGER **SCOOP** MINNOW
FLEW-GER

NO.9300 SERIES

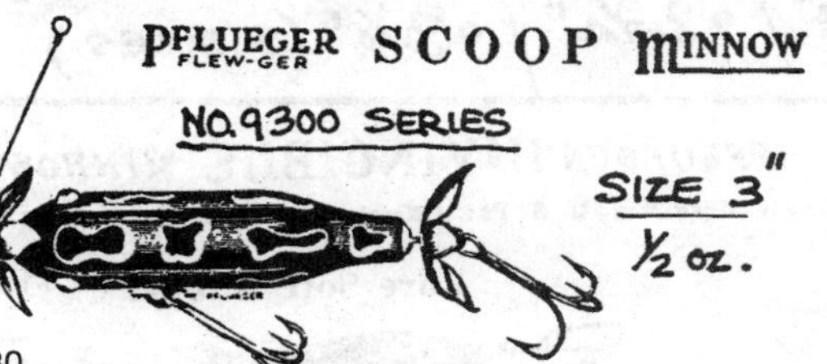

SIZE 3"
½ oz.

$10 – 30

SIZE 3⅝"
¾ oz.

(NOTE THE 3 BLADED PROPS.)

PFLUEGER FISHING TACKLE
FLEW-GER

PORTAGE **PEERLESS** MINNOW

Trade Mark Reg. U. S. Pat. Office

ALSO MADE IN 2" SIZE. NO.110

$10 – 20

Offered only in Assorted Packing

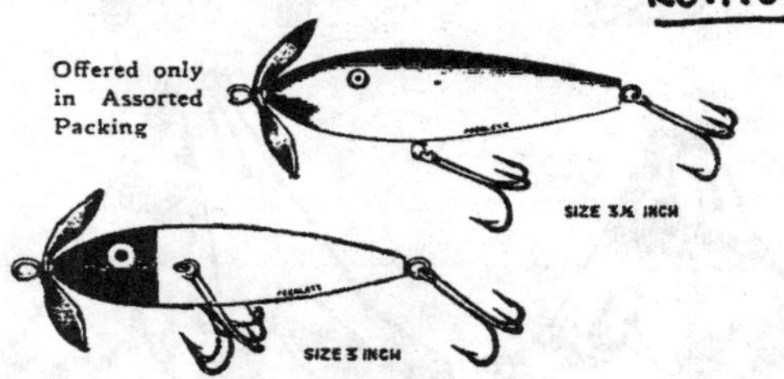
SIZE 3½ INCH
SIZE 3 INCH

The Peerless fills a demand for a wood minnow low in price but attractive and serviceable.

Comprises two styles of spinner type minnow.

Mounted with Bright Treble Hooks size 1.

Size 3½—Floating or top water minnow.

Size 3—Sinking or under water minnow.

PFLUEGER **Mustang** MINNOW
FLEW-GER

Trade Mark Reg. U. S. Pat. Office—Patent Nos. 2158037-2001652

$10 – 15

Dives—Wiggles—Wobbles

Designed and strongly built for heavy duty fishing, in either fresh or salt water. This bait is very effective for taking Pike, Muskallunge and Kingfish.

This slow sinking type bait is mounted with three extra heavy 3/0 treble hooks and has a polished nickel flasher plate attached to the body both top and bottom. These flasher plates add to the killing effect of the bait and to the protection of the body.

Size 5" -Weight 1½ oz. MUSKIE SIZE.

No.	
9596	White Enamel, Red Head.

PFLUEGER **PaKron** MINNOW

$20 – 35

NO. 7000

2¾"

1 oz.

The Pakron is an underwater bait designed particularly for salt water fish, such as Weakfish, Striped Bass, Roballo, etc.

The solid metal head provides sufficient weight to carry this minnow to the proper depth.

Lures in this book are priced in very good to very good+ condition.

ALSO MADE IN 4¼"

PFLUEGER **MUSTANG** MINNOW

8600-(SINKER)

Trade Mark Reg. U. S. Pat. Office—Patent No. 1,418,326, Patent Pending

Under Water Popping Minnow • 2½"

8900-(FLOATER)

$5 – 10

Especially designed for "pop casting" under conditions which require a slowly sinking minnow.

Metal diving plane, highly polished, is extra strength—not easily bent out shape—gives the body a sharp snappy wiggle. A slight twitch or pull of the rod is sufficient to operate the minnow successfully in "popping." Size 1 treble hooks.

Fishing weight ½ oz.

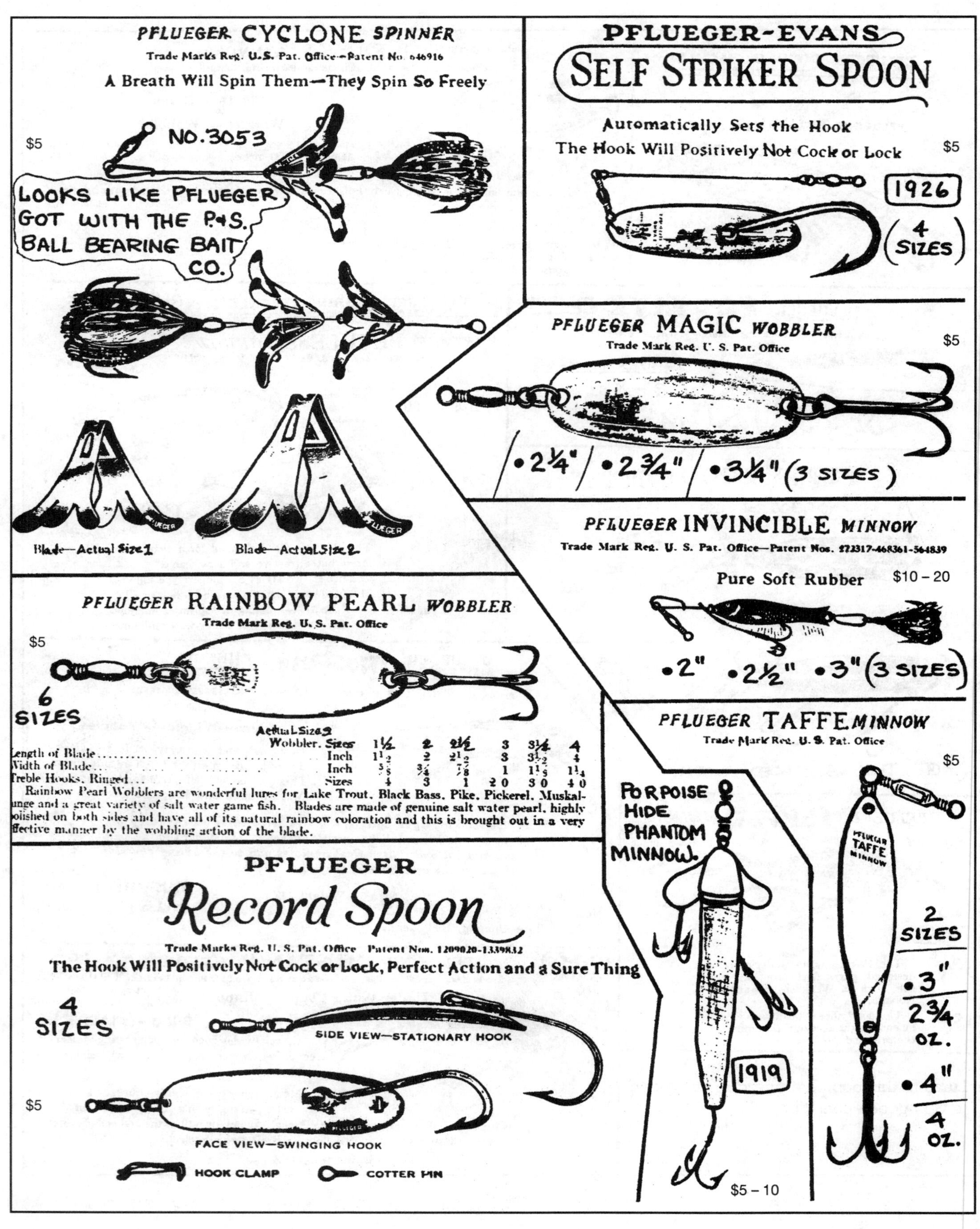
PFLUEGER CYCLONE SPINNER
Trade Marks Reg. U.S. Pat. Office—Patent No. 646916
A Breath Will Spin Them—They Spin So Freely
$5
NO. 3053
LOOKS LIKE PFLUEGER GOT WITH THE P&S. BALL BEARING BAIT CO.
Blade—Actual Size 1
Blade—Actual Size 2
PFLUEGER-EVANS
SELF STRIKER SPOON
Automatically Sets the Hook
The Hook Will Positively Not Cock or Lock
$5
1926
(4 SIZES)
PFLUEGER MAGIC WOBBLER
Trade Mark Reg. U. S. Pat. Office
$5
• 2¼" / • 2¾" / • 3¼" (3 SIZES)
PFLUEGER INVINCIBLE MINNOW
Trade Mark Reg. U. S. Pat. Office—Patent Nos. 873317-468361-564839
Pure Soft Rubber
$10 – 20
• 2" • 2½" • 3" (3 SIZES)
PFLUEGER RAINBOW PEARL WOBBLER
Trade Mark Reg. U. S. Pat. Office
$5
6 SIZES
Actual Size 2

		1½	2	2½	3	3¼	4
	Wobbler. Sizes	1½	2	2½	3	3¼	4
Length of Blade	Inch	1½	2	2½	3	3½	4
Width of Blade	Inch	⅝	¾	⅞	1	1⅛	1¼
Treble Hooks, Ringed	Sizes	4	3	1	2 0	3 0	4 0

Rainbow Pearl Wobblers are wonderful lures for Lake Trout, Black Bass, Pike, Pickerel, Muskalunge and a great variety of salt water game fish. Blades are made of genuine salt water pearl, highly polished on both sides and have all of its natural rainbow coloration and this is brought out in a very effective manner by the wobbling action of the blade.
PFLUEGER
Record Spoon
Trade Marks Reg. U. S. Pat. Office Patent Nos. 1209020-1339832
The Hook Will Positively Not Cock or Lock, Perfect Action and a Sure Thing
4 SIZES
SIDE VIEW—STATIONARY HOOK
$5
FACE VIEW—SWINGING HOOK
HOOK CLAMP
COTTER PIN
PORPOISE HIDE PHANTOM MINNOW.
1919
$5 – 10
PFLUEGER TAFFE MINNOW
Trade Mark Reg. U. S. Pat. Office
$5
PFLUEGER TAFFE MINNOW
2 SIZES
• 3" 2¾ OZ.
• 4" 4 OZ.

MUSKILL SPOONS

$5

PFLUEGER TANDEM SPINNERS

$5

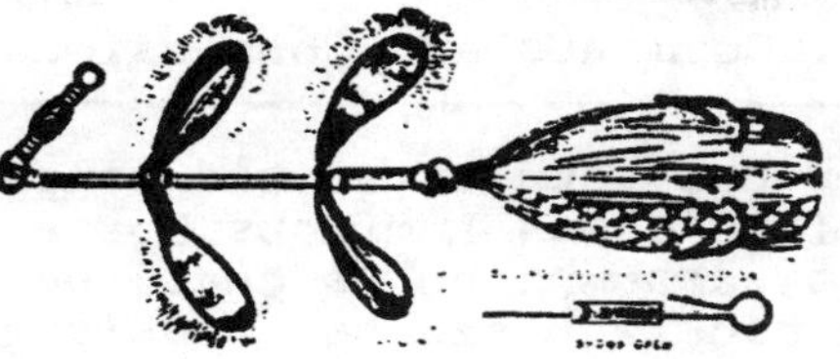

The "Luminous Tandem Spinner" is famous the world over, being equally as effective for day as for evening and night fishing. A great killer in deep water or on cloudy days. Mounted on long shank, with feathered treble hooks. The blades spin easily in opposite directions, one of the killing features of this lure.

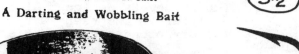

Size 3 2 1 1/0 2/0 3/0 4/0

NEW WEIGHTED TANDEM SPINNER

Many fishermen have in the past complained of the difficulty in casting the regular Tandem Spinner. We now offer this popular lure, with a weight between the blades, so that it casts easily. Runs a little deeper than the regular Shannon. Nickeled spinners with luminous reverse side.

$5

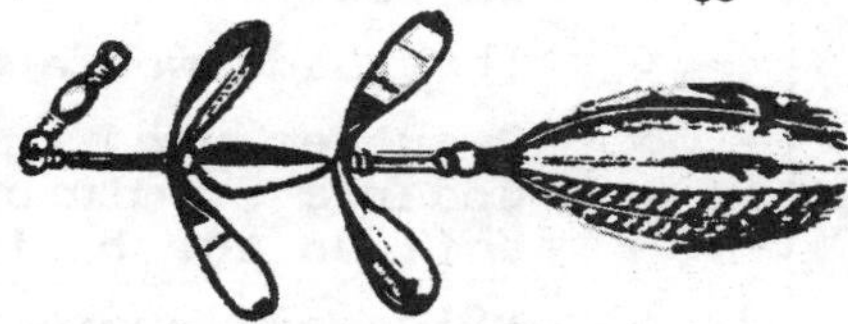

PFLUEGER BEARCAT SPINNER

$5

PFLUEGER SALAMO SPOON

Trade Mark Reg. U. S. Pat. Office

A Darting and Wobbling Bait

3½"

SIDE VIEW

$5

$5

PFLUEGER DRAGON SPINNER

1934

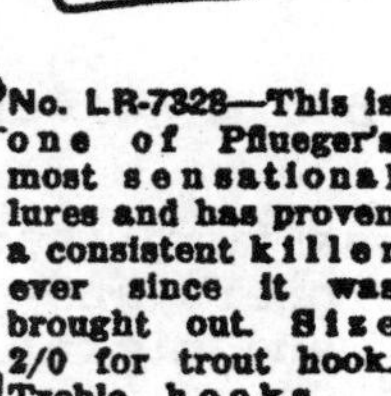

No. LR-7328—This is one of Pflueger's most sensational lures and has proven a consistent killer ever since it was brought out. Size 2/0 for trout hook. Treble hooks.

PFLUEGER GRASSHOPPER BAIT

Trade Mark Reg. U. S. Pat. Office

Pure Soft Rubber

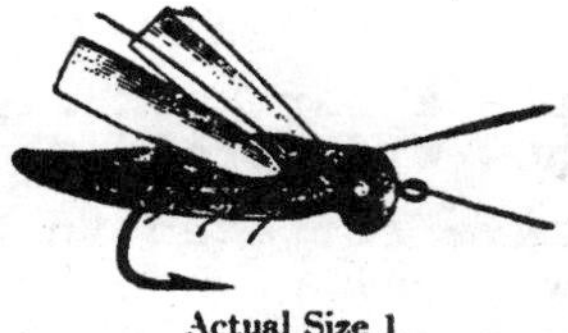

Actual Size 1

$5 – 10

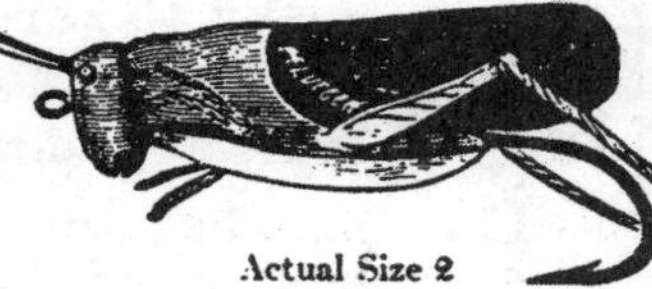

Actual Size 2

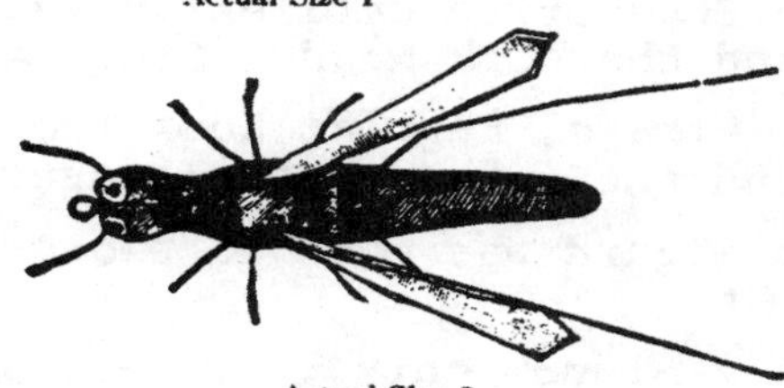

Actual Size 3

Good anywhere and always for Bass and Trout.

Painted and decorated a close imitation of the natural Green Grasshopper with our special formula "FLEXO," the most scientifically perfect material ever applied to rubber baits and is as flexible as the rubber itself. Positively will not crack or peel.

No.		Price Each		
760	Grasshopper Bait—Green. Grasshopper, Sizes	1	2	3

HELGRAMITE BAIT

Trade Mark Reg. U. S. Pat. Office

Pure Soft Rubber

$5

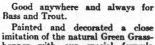

Actual Size 2

Actual Size 1/0

Actual Size 1

No. 759 Helgramite Bait

PFLUEGER (Enterprise)......Comments and Conclusions

153A

1. Ernest F. Pflueger was the founder of the company. Their big business in the late 1800's was Luminous Horse Collars and Harnesses. The logical assumption is that the automobile pushed them into the fishing tackle business on a large scale.
2. E. F. Pflueger is credited with the invention of the Luminous Bait.
3. The Enterprise Mfg. Co. was established in 1881, and incorporated in 1886.
4. They had two factories - Akron, Ohio and St. Paul, Minnesota.
5. Pflueger used the see through hook rigs for a time on their underwater minnows. They used a flat wire. Shakesp. stopped this on the basis of patent infringement. (Circa Mid-Teens)
6. Pflueger apparently used a few notched props, but they are not as noted for them as was So. Bend and Shakespeare.
7. Pfl. started using their surface hook rig approx. 1928.
8. The Pfluegers designed alot of the baits themselves. The main designer in the teens was: W. Adams. I looked through alot of factory prototypes, and his name was on most of them.
9. Pflueger was making rubber fish spearing decoys in sizes: 2", 2½", 3", & 7", in 1892.
10. The 4" Pfl. Surprise Minnow is relatively easy to find, but that little 3 incher is a toughie.
11. In 1910, Pflueger was offering their higher quality baits in wooden, top sliding, boxes.
12. The Portage Frisky Minnow - originally made by Charles G. Malecek, 5011 Pershing Ave. So., Cleveland, Ohio in 1931. Pflueger bought the patent in 1933.
13. Found another size of the Wizard Wiggler when going through the production records of Pflueger - 4½". I suppose this was the Musky Wizard?
14. Pflueger used a one piece bar hook rig on a Bearcat Minnow in 1925. I don't know how widespread the use of this rig was.
15. The Pakron seems to have surfaced in the late 20's, one ad said new in 1930, but it was being made before that.
16. Plugs in the Enterprise Catalog in 1900 were the Trory with tied hooks and the cork Meadow Frog, and the rubber Maskallonge.
17. In 1905, the Wizard, Regular hook Trory, the Competitor, and the Frogs, and the rubber Maskallonge.
18. In 1902, the Wizard was made in two qualities: 1st had a swivel, and 2nd didn't.
19. On the Simplex Minnow only.....The casting weight was furnished with both the Premium and Favorite Quality. The spinners and connections were gold plated on the premium quality and nickel plated on the Favorite. (1909-1910) Shipped in wood boxes.
20. The Metalized Minnows were available in both Polished Nickel and Polished Copper. The copper ones are hard to find, and must've been made in much smaller qu ntities.
21. Pflueger was using some of the P. & S. Spinners in 1900.
22. The Pflueger family was really involved in the business. From the founder E. F. I found reference to the following: E.A. in 1922, J.E. in 1926, and C.T. in the '30's.

23. I believe the date of the patent for E.F. Pflueger applying luminous paint to fishing spoons was Feb.13, 1883. Enterprise was first involved in luminous paint on the metal parts of horse harnesses.

24. The supposed dates of the neverfail hook hanger is 1911 - 1921

25. The Monarch therfore, came before the Neverfail.

26. To the illustrious Scoop family, add the Baby Scoop, 2¼", 2 bladed prop, No.9310.

27. Apparently in 1930, the Globe patent was revised to allow the head to be removed. There was no mention of this in the 1929 catalog. This was a feature that enabled "quick removal of weeds".

28. IN DOING THE RESEARCH FOR THE PFLUEGER/ENTERPRISE SECTION OF THIS SUPPLEMENT, IT BECAME APPARENT TO ME THAT THE CROWN THAT HEDDON WEARS AS THE FOUNDER OF THE MODERN TACKLE BUSINESS IS TENUOUS AT BEST. THE PFLUEGERS WERE DOING INNOVATIVE THINGS AND DEVELOPING A LINE OF BAITS WELL BEFORE HEDDON GOT CRANKED UP. BEING IN AKRON THEY HAD A GREAT DEAL OF RUBBER TECHNOLOGY AROUND THEM, THUS THE EARLY RUBBER BAITS. THE 1900 WOOD TRORY IS VERY ENLIGHTENING TO US HISTORIAN TYPES. (If you find one, call Joe Courcelle, collect)

PFLUEGER SALT WATER MINNOW (RUBBER)

REDUCED ILLUS. ACTUAL: 6½"

1932

$10 – 30

Pflueger's Muskallonge Wizard Wooden Minnow

Wedge Shaped Body

Mounted with Extra Strong Hooks and Mountings suitable in every respect for the class of fishing for which it is intended.

No.		Sizes......	3½	5 inch
781.	Luminous over all	Premium Quality, Price per Dozen		
782.	" belly and green back	" "	$15 78	$18 94
783.	" " silver back	" "		
784.	Non-luminous silver belly and green back	" "		
785.	" " over all	" "	12 62	15 16
786.	" white enamel over all	" "		
787.	" silver belly and green back	Favorite Quality, "		
788.	" " over all	" "	8 84	11 86
789.	" white enamel over all	" "		

I ESTIMATE THIS CATALOG SECTION TO BE 1908 OR BEFORE. IT SHOWS THE MFG. OF H.D. WIZARD WOODEN MINNOWS, BOTH WITH A SWIVEL, AND WITHOUT (PREMIUM VS. FAVORITE QUALITY) SHIPPED IN WOODEN BOXES.

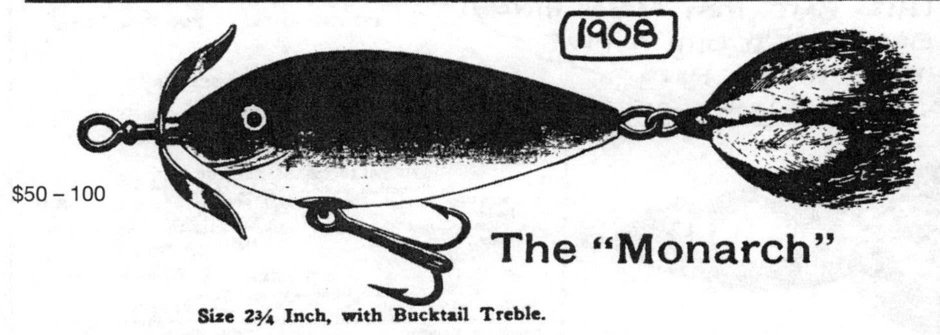
1908

$50 – 100

The "Monarch"

Size 2¾ Inch, with Bucktail Treble.

THE ANSWER TO THE QUESTION ON PAGE 307 IS: I.

Paw Paw Baits

NOTE: THE AD BELOW SHOWS THAT MOONLIGHT BAIT CO. BECAME PAW PAW.

Paw Paw Mouse Bait

$20 – 30

(2½")

There is no question but that the mouse bait in its various forms will attract Bass, Pike or Pickerel from the darkest depths. This "Paw Paw" mouse has a most erratic motion in the water and we guarantee that it will lure any fish that has the least bit of curiosity in its make-up. Length 2½ inches, weight ¾ oz. Stocked in two colors as listed.

No. 50PP. Regular mouse color. Each.........................

No. 56PP. Black with White Head. Each............

The Famous Paw Paw Flies

BUCKTAIL "FLIES"

No. 380—Bucktail. 4/0 Hook

$5 – 7 each

SPOONS (2 SIZES)

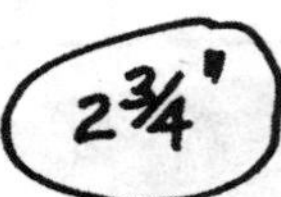
2¾"

WOBBLE-BOYS

No. 100
Length—2¾ inches
Weight—⅝ oz.

No. 200
Length—3½ inches
Weight—⅝ oz.

(3½")

(Packed 6 assorted colors on a card.)

PAW PAW BAITS

• 3¼"
• 4"

The Brilliant BASS SEEKER

Gamesters strike with a vicious smash when the darting, gleaming Metallic Bass Seeker slips into their favorite haunts. This dazzling new bait was a sensation with the old timers last season—not ever the hot listless days dulled its brilliant catches.

Four sparkling finishes. If your dealer can't supply you write us. Send today for the Angler's Guide. It's free.

Paw Paw Bait Co.
Formerly Moonlight Bait Co.
423 Center St., Paw Paw, Mich.

A PAW PAW LURE
Means fish for Sure

$5

COUSIN JACK RED TAIL

COUSIN JACK RED TAIL NO. 6900

$20 – 30

ALSO A JOINTED MODEL 3¼" 2T, TE

A PEARL FINISH PLUG

Length—4 in. Weight—¾ oz.

No. 2603—Green Scale
No. 2604—White, Red Head
No. 2605—Pearl Finish
No. 2607—Gold Scale
No. 2608—Frog Finish
No. 2609—Perch
No. 2612—Metallic

THIS BAIT MAY ALSO HAVE BEEN MFG'D WITH A FLAT NOSE AND A FIXED LINE TIE.

$25 – 50

NATURAL HAIR MOUSE

Length—3½ in. Weight—⅝ oz.

No. 60—Gray
No. 61—Yellow Head
No. 64—Red Head
No. 68—White

ALSO MADE FROM GENUINE DEER HAIR SKIN - WITH A NOSE PROP.

GOLD PLATED HEAD BASS SEEKER

Length 3¼ inches—Weight ¾ oz.

No. 4603—Green Scale
No. 4604—White, Gold Head
No. 4605—Rainbow
No. 4606—Silver Scale
No. 4607—Gold Scale
No. 4608—Frog Finish

METALLIC BASS SEEKER 3/4 oz.

Length 4 inches—Weight ¾ oz.

No. 2601Met—Red Head, Gold Body
No. 2602Met—Red Head, Green Body
No. 2603Met—Perch (Silver Side, Green Back)
No. 2604Met—Red Head, Silver Body

METAL FLAKES

BASS SEEKER

Length 4 inches—Weight ¾ oz.

No. 2603—Green Scale
No. 2604—White, Red Head
No. 2605—Rainbow
No. 2607—Gold Scale
No. 2608—Frog Finish
No. 2609—Perch

Dace Natural Minnow

$10 – 30

3½"

Ever use a Dace? Cut open the next big trout, bass, pike or other game fish you catch and you'll find the remains of a dace. These natural food minnows are found in streams and lakes from coast to coast and form the basis of nearly every game fishes diet. Natural Dace color. Length 3½", weight ½ oz.

Perch Caster

$10 – 30

No. 1877—One of our new "real fish" line of casting lures. So closely imitates the real thing that the big ones go for it as if they were starved! It has an enticing natural swimming action in the water that fools the wisest of old "sockdollogers." Made in natural perch finish, the best of all-around colors for bass, pike, pickerel, etc.

TROUT CASTER

$10 – 30

3½"

No. 1873—Did you ever see bass and trout in the same waters? You didn't for the simple reason that bass, pike, pickerel and steelhead will feed on trout to the exclusion of anything else as long as they can. You'll find this natural trout will make them hit at times when all other lures faill Length 3½", weight ½ oz. Color: natural trout.fry.

A RIVER GO GETTER

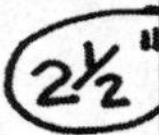
2½"

No. 1871 — It's one of those popular small river type of lures, only improved in form and finish over anything ever shown before, a moving shadow of irridescent pearl, one of the spookiest, most ghost-like lures on the market. Length 2½", weight ½ oz. Colors: bass, chub, dace, perch, shiner, trout.

$5 – 30

Baby Wobbler

$5 – 10

3"

No. 1870—A junior size in the standard groove head type of bass wobbler. Length 3", weight ½ oz. Colors: red head white body, silver scale, natural pike, rainbow.

NEW GROOVED HEAD BASS WOBBLER

$10 – 20

3¾"

No. 1800—Standard groove-head type of bass wobbler, the most widely used and most consistently successful bait ever designed. Often imitated but never equalled. This bait should be in every fisherman's kit. Length 3¾ in., weight ¾ oz. Carried in four popular colors: Yellow perch, red head white body, rainbow, natural pike.

Surface Minnow

$10 – 15

3¼"

No. 1879—The ever popular type of surface lure, revolving spinners and wriggling body, give the old-timers the idea that here is a free meal for the taking, and they hit it like Louis hit Schmeling! Length 3¼ in., weight ½ oz. Carried in four colors: Red head white body, natural pike, silver scale, or frog finish.

FLY ROD LURES

JUG HEAD

$5

1¾"

—Copied from one of the most successful bass plugs of all time, this new fly rod size jug-head has real fish getting ability built right into it. Length 1¾". Colors: red head white body, rainbow, or green spotted.

GROOVE HEAD

$5

1⅝"

—A fly rod size edition of the famous groove head wobbler. Deadly effective on the pan fishes, and a proven lure for brown, brook and native trout. Length 1⅝". Colors: red head white body, rainbow, or scale finish. Include 1c postage.

The CRIPPLED KILLER

$10 – 15

-A flat side floating minnow that imitates an injured minnow lying on the surface of the water. By reeling alternately slow and fast and by twitching the rod to give the bait the action of a wounded minnow the wise fisherman can tease even the smart old "lunkers" into taking a chance on this appealing bait. Colors: Yellow perch, white-red head, silver scale, natural pike.

$2

PAW PAW'S NEW SPINNER
with 6-inch wire leader
No. 1 Spoon—3¼ in.
Six on a card—
No. 2 Spoon—3½ in.

2 SIZES

McGINTY

$5

No. 1875—A spinner type wobbling lure, especially good for trout, bass and pickerel, has an unusual action, half flashing spinner and half wobbling plug, a combination that has proven successful in all parts of the country. Colors: red and white, rainbow trout, silver flitters.

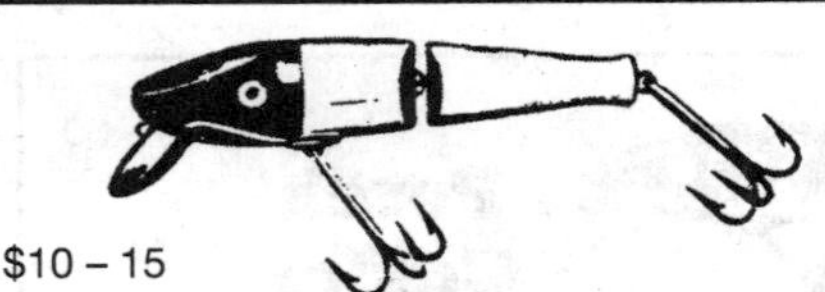

$10 – 15

BABY JOINTED PIKE

Jointed pike lure with a short, quick wobbling action. Weight ½ oz., length 3¼". In yellow perch and pike scale.

2100— 3¼"

$10 – 20

JUNIOR PIKE MINNOW

Underwater lure, medium size. Length 3¼ inches, weight ½ ounce. Four colors:

3¼"

No. 1401—Perch Scale.
No. 1404—White Body, Red Head.
No. 1407—Pike Scale.
No. 1412—Silver Flitters.

$5

PAW PAW'S JIG-A-LURE

Weight ⅜ oz., length 1-5/16" Assorted colors.

F-7100—

PAW PAW'S WOTTAFROG "He's a Honey"
GETS THE FISHERMEN — GETS THE FISH

• 2¼" - ½ oz.
• 3¼" - ⅝ oz.
• FLY ROD
4 SIZES
MUSKY

Legs are hinged to the body, permitting them to move in a kicking, swimming motion. Treble hooks are covered with hair — they look like feet. Body is bright grass-frog green speckled with black . . . true frog markings.

No. 73—Length 3¼ in., Weight ⅝ oz.

No. 72 — Length 2¼ in., Weight ½ oz. —

MADE WITH AND WITHOUT HAIR TREBLES

$10 – 20

$10

JUNIOR WOBBLER

A standard underwater lure that has taken many a bass. 3 inches long, weighs ½ ounce. Four colors:

3"

No. 4201—Perch Scale.
No. 4204—White Body, Red Head.
No. 4207—Pike Scale.
No. 4212—Silver Flitters.

3" 3/4 oz.

POPPING LURE

A surface lure, with that plunking action that has obtained such unusual results. 3 inches long, weighs ¾ ounce. Three colors:

No. 2201—Yellow Perch.
No. 2208—Frog Finish.
No. 2212—Silver Flitters.

$10 – 15

$10 – 15

SKIPPY MINNOW

A surface lure that really takes them. When retrieved rides just under the surface. 3¾ inches long, weighs ¾ ounce. Three colors:

No. 9208—Frog finish.
No. 9209—Yellow, Spotted.
No. 9212—Silver Flitters.

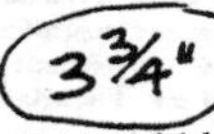
3¾"

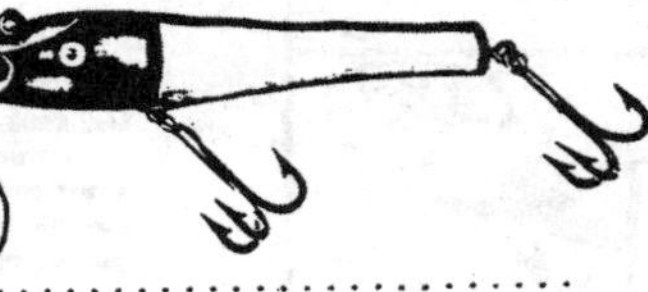

No. 1000
PIKIE OR PIKE
4½" 3/4 oz.

$10 – 20

$10 – 15

UNDER WATER MINNOW

2-3/8" ½ oz.

—An underwater type minnow with easy action front spinner and three strongly mounted treble hooks. A great favorite in all waters this minnow has proven especially effective as a trolling lure for pike, pickerel, bass and lake trout. Colors: rainbow, natural pike, silver scale, red head white body. Length 2⅜"; weight ½ oz.

PAW PAW SURFACE LURE

$10 – 15

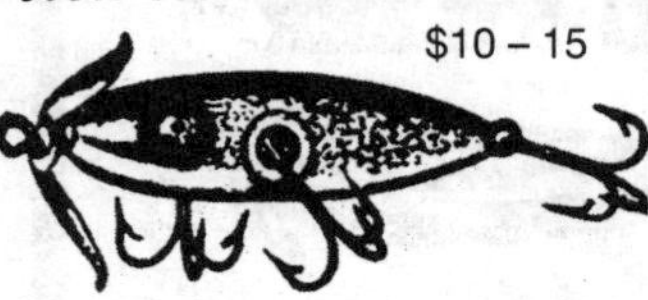

A smaller, compact and very lively swimmer—made extra strong to hold big fish. The spinner makes it unusually attractive for small-mouth bass, and the three treble hooks make it a "sure-hooker." Length 2⅜ in. Wt. ½ oz.

No. 3304— White, Red Head

2⅜"

No. 3311— All Black

ALSO MADE IN NO. 400 SERIES, WITH 2 TREBLES.
-ADDITIONAL COLORS WERE CHUB SCALE AND RAINBOW.

PAW PAW

$10

RED and WHITE CASTING LURE

A very serviceable plug that will give pleasing action.
No. 65—Spiner bait. Is a real "Go-Getter." Weight ½ oz. Length 2 ins. Treble.

2"

GETS 'EM BAIT. No. 66–
Length of body 2 ins.
Weight ½ ounce.

2" - ½ oz.

$5

$10 – 15

JOINTED PIKE

NO. 2000

4½"

real tantalizing action, you can't beat the darting, wobbling wiggle of this jointed pike—put together with a new type of stronger hinged joint, that gives free action to the tail section. This lure casts easily and wobbles easily even when retrieved at a slow rate of speed. Length 4½", weight ¾ oz. Colors: yellow perch, red and white, rainbow, natural pike.

Paw Paw Baits

$10 – 20

CRAWFISH

NO. 500 HAS RUBBER FEELERS.
2 3/4" - 3/4 oz.
- WOOD BODY

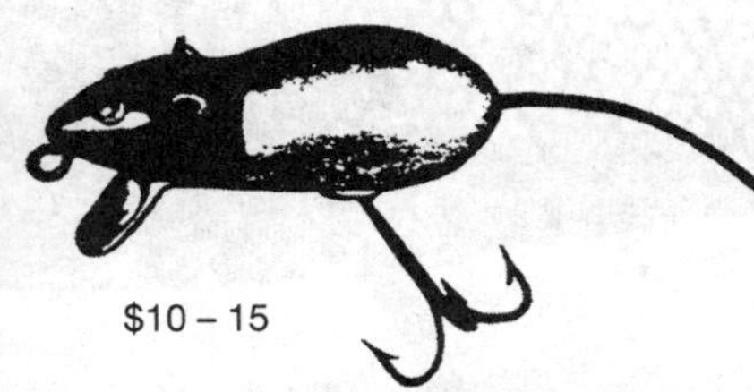

$10 – 15

PAW PAW MINNIE MOUSE

The natural food for bass; it floats, dives and swims. Nothing could be more natural than the fur finish. In brown fur finish and gray fur finish. Weight 5/8 oz., length 2½"

F-50— 5/8 oz. — 2½"

$5

1-5/16"

PAW PAW'S LITTLE JIGGER

A brilliant feather combination that gives it fine visibility and great fish-taking qualities. Assorted colors. Weight 5/8 oz., length 1-5/16"

F-7200—

PAW PAW MOUSE
All Pearl Finishes
Length—2½ in. Weight—5/8 oz.

No. 40—Brown	No. 47—Black
No. 44—White, Red Head	No. 48—White
No. 46—Black, White Head	No. 49—Gray

Paw Paw River Type

ALSO CALLED "THE CHUB"

$10

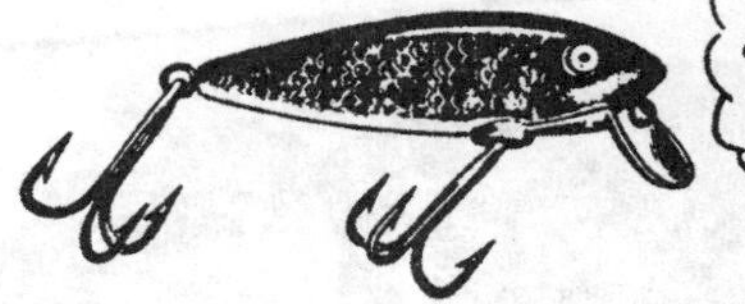

No.	Length	Weight
900 Series	2⅝"	½ oz.

No.	Colors	No.	Colors
901	Perch Scale	906	Silver Scale
903	Green Scale	907	Pike Scale
904	White, Red Head	908	Frog Scale
905	Rainbow	912	Silver Flitters

PAW PAW

ALSO CALLED THE "RIVER WOBBLER"
ALSO MADE IN JOINTED MODEL.

Paw Paw "Torpedo"

ALSO CALLED THE SLIM LINDY

4" - 5/8 oz.

No.
2400 Series

$10

No.	Colors	No.	Colors
2401	Yellow Perch	2407	Pike Scale
2403	Green, Gold Scale	2412	Silver Flitters
2406	Shad	2417	Black Serpentine

$10

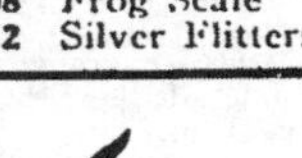

PAW PAW'S FLAT SIDE

Crippled minnow type lure. Weight ¾ oz., length 3½". Assorted colors.

F-2501— 3½"

$5

PAW PAW'S MIDGET

One of the newest of the smaller lures for all weather and all waters. Tenite body. Weight 3/8 oz., length 2½". Assorted colors.

F-3900— 2½"

(TENITE) NO. 3600 $5

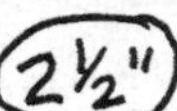

Flap Jack
the Sensation for 19
(1941)

MORE FUN!
MORE FISH!

If you fish for *fun* as well as for *fish* (we know you do) then you'll certainly want Flap Jack with you on your fishing trips this season. He's full of tantalizing tr that tease the big . . . darts, dives, sw . . . all the antics lively minnow. Beautiful, streamli TENITE body, str and durable — the right weight easy, accurate cast 13 popular patterns cluding "NITE-GL for night fishing. *Action gets the fis* Ask your dealer, or Write us.

WEEDLESS WOW
A fleshy, no-snag bait that stirs up plenty of ripples on the surface. Resembles a pork-chunk in shape but is far better because it floats. Can be cast into the big-fish "jungles" with safety . . . weeds, lily pads, logs—they're no bug-a-boo for WEEDLESS WOW.
6 colorful patterns

PAW PAW BA
Paw Paw, Michig

PAW PAW BAITS
. . . MADE FOR YOUR ENJOYMEN

NEW PAW PAW WOBBLER

$5

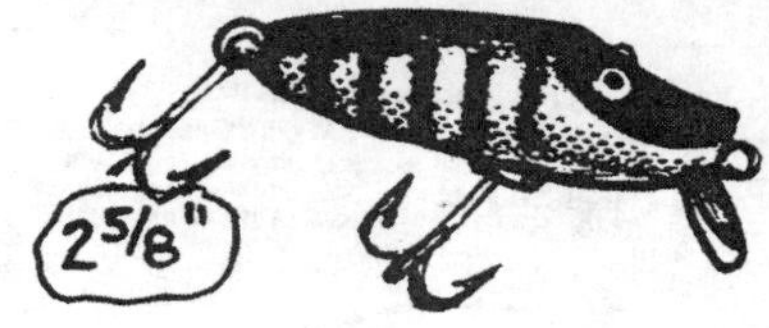

2 5/8"

No. 9101—Yellow Perch.
No. 9106—Silver Scale.
No. 9108—Frog Finish.
No. 9112—Silver Flitter.

3/8 oz.

$10

Paw Paw Casting Minnow

BAIT THAT CATCH FISH

Never before has any bait caused such a genuine sensation and received such acceptance by fishermen as this new combination feather lure. No game fish can resist it. Head length 2¼ in. Over-all 5¼ inches. Weight ½ oz.

No. 1207—Yellow Scale, Yellow Feathers
No. 1211—White and Black Head, Black and White Feathers

5¼ OVERALL
2¼"-BODY

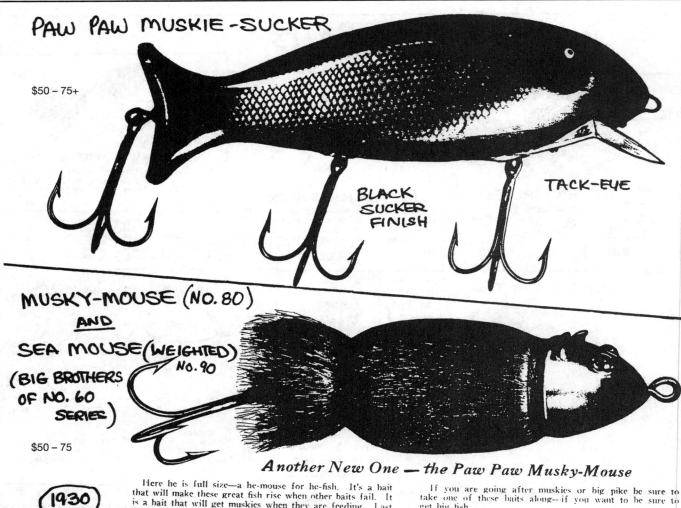

PAW PAW MUSKIE-SUCKER

$50 – 75+

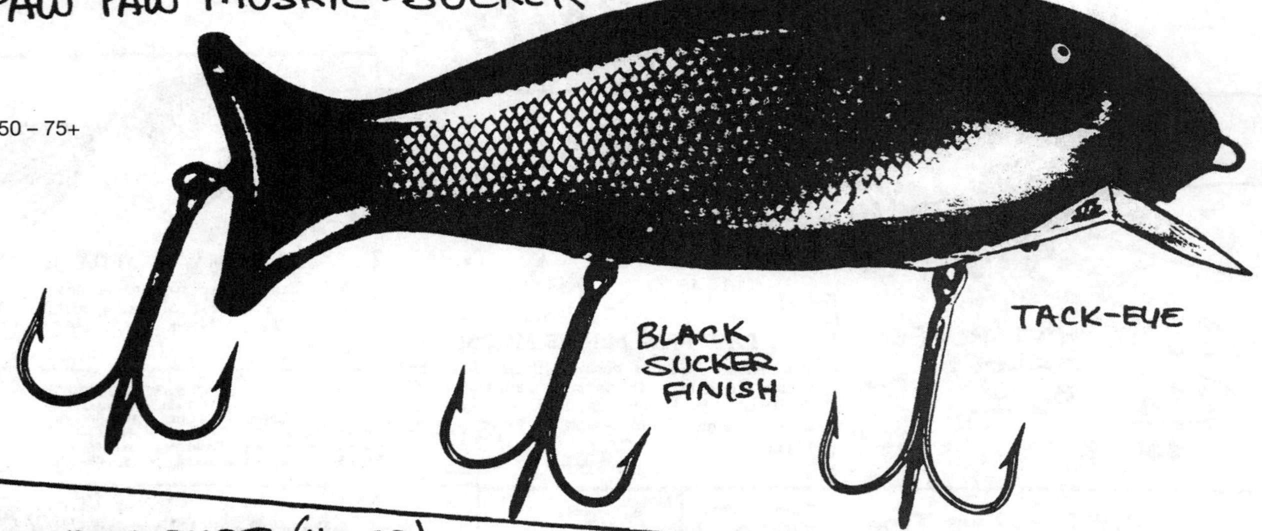

BLACK SUCKER FINISH

TACK-EYE

MUSKY-MOUSE (NO. 80) AND SEA MOUSE (WEIGHTED) NO. 90

(BIG BROTHERS OF NO. 60 SERIES)

$50 – 75

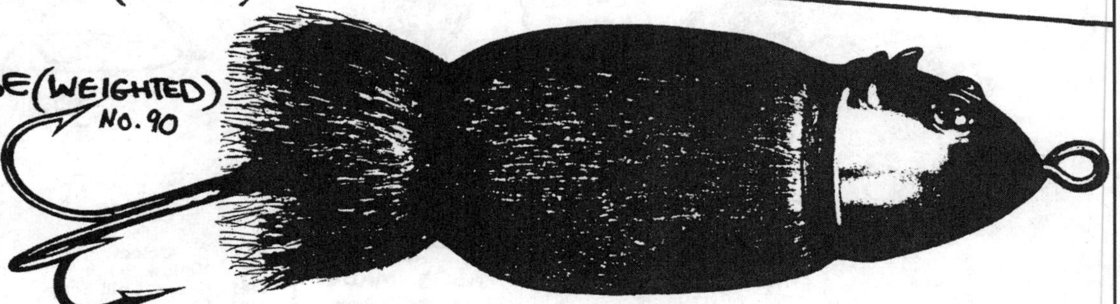

1930

Another New One — the Paw Paw Musky-Mouse

Here he is full size—a he-mouse for he-fish. It's a bait that will make these great fish rise when other baits fail. It is a bait that will get muskies when they are feeding. Last year the small size Paw Paw Hair Mouse was used and our angler friends found that muskies would strike hard, but the hooks were too small to hold the big fish. Here is a bait that will get attention and it will hold the fish. Cast it, let it lay on the water and s-l-o-w-l-y reel it away—no faster than a mouse would swim.

If you are going after muskies or big pike be sure to take one of these baits along—if you want to be sure to get big fish.

MUSKY MOUSE

For all big Game Fish.

No. 80—Gray
No. 81—Yellow Head
No. 84—Red Head
No. 88—White Head

SEA MOUSE

Weighted for salt water fishing.

No. 90—Gray
No. 91—Yellow Head
No. 94—Red Head
No. 98—White Head

1930

The Greatest Spearing Minnow

$25 – 50+

Looks just like a fat, juicy perch. It is weighted so it will hang in the water just like a perch. The slightest lift on your line will make it act like a swimming perch. It will nose around in the water, and can be made to dart quickly to the side from six to eight feet and slowly circle back to its original position. And its motion in the water, its colorings, etc., make it look as if really it were swimming down there under the ice.

No. 2800—Colored just like a perch.

And you'll say it is the finest spearing minnow you ever have used.

NO. 2800

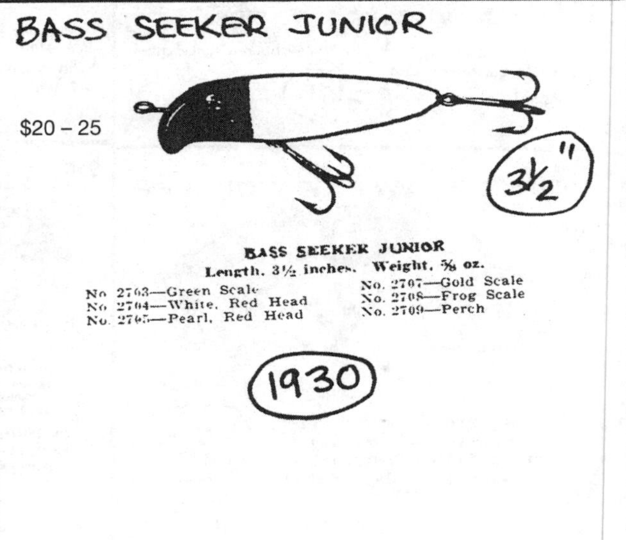

BASS SEEKER JUNIOR

$20 – 25

3½"

BASS SEEKER JUNIOR

Length, 3½ inches. Weight, ⅝ oz.

No. 2703—Green Scale
No. 2704—White, Red Head
No. 2705—Pearl, Red Head
No. 2707—Gold Scale
No. 2708—Frog Scale
No. 2709—Perch

1930

No.1 - 3¼"
No.2 - 2½"

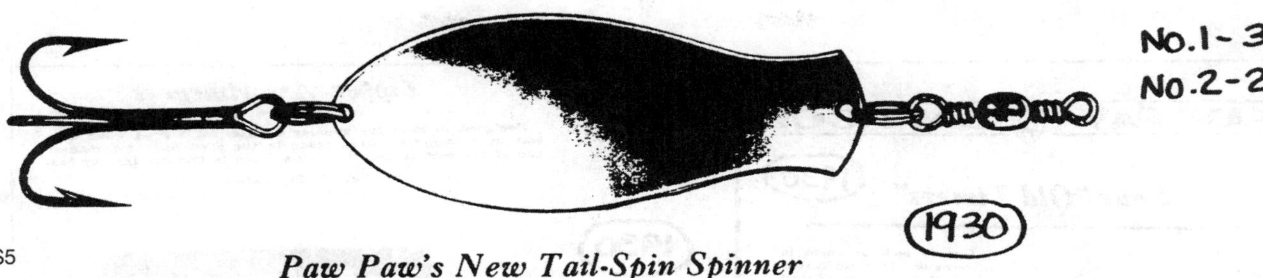

(1930)

$5

Paw Paw's New Tail-Spin Spinner

It's a wobble spoon—one of those erratic skip—dodge—dive—slither—kind of baits that bring out the pike and pickerel and get the hard smashes from fighting bass. It is a copper-nickel spoon that has plenty of light value and can be used in any water with good results. It is a spoon they've been using in northern lakes and streams to get the big fellows. It has the action of an injured minnow—which, of course, is enough to make it a great fish getter. Besides, it is a splendid caster; you'll like it the minute you use it. This is a great spinner for big trout.

No. 1 Spoon—3¼-inch—
No. 2 Spoon—2½-inch—

$10 – 15

PAW PAW BAIT CO.

No. 40 Mouse Series

The mouse bait has been brought out in various forms, but here is one that dives, floats and swims with a true to nature motion. The numbers 40 and 49 are in the new Paw Paw Pearl Finish.

Length, 2½ inches. Weight, ⅝ oz.

No. 40—Brown Pearl
No. 44—White, Red Head
No. 46—Black, White Head
No. 47—All Black
No. 48—All White
No. 49—Gray Pearl

(1930)

Paw Paw Bull Frog

G.E.

$20 – 40

Bait that has been used with telling results for a long time, you might find it to be just the thing for your lakes or streams, — why not try one, often.

No. 1704—White, Red Head
No. 1708—Bull Frog Finish

(1930)

G.E.

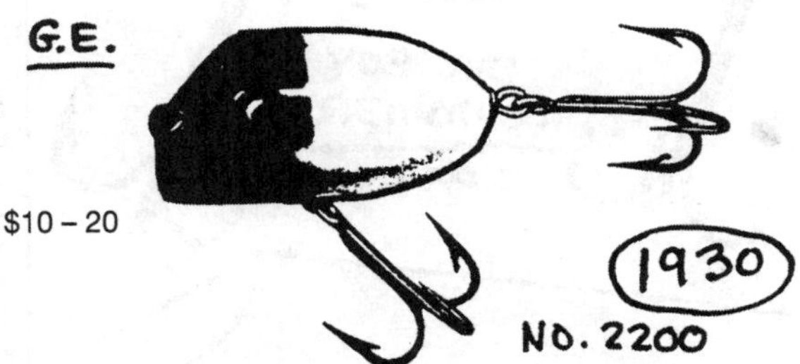

$10 – 20

(1930)

NO. 2200

The Plunker—A Great Performer

"One of the result-gettin -est baits we ever saw" is what one of the fishermen sent in with several fine strings of fish he and his partners took on different occasions—fish that would make any man's casting arm thrill.

This Plunker is the funniest looking thing you ever saw—a short fat plug with only the faintest shadow of a wiggle, but, Lordy! how the fish do go after it. Why they do we don't know, because it is like nothing that swims or flies—yet we have pictures from a dozen or more fishermen to prove that it gets BIG fish.

It is the result of a year's experimenting and we predict great things for it next season.

(2")

In These Finishes

No. 2200 Series—Length, 2 inches. Weight, ¾ oz.

No. 2201—Yellow
No. 2204—White, Red Head
No. 2206—Black, White Head
No. 2207—Silver
No. 2208—Frog
No. 2209—Perch

NOTE: THE GREAT INJURED MINNOW & THE BULLHEAD AND OTHERS MADE TE /GE.

A Pearl Finish Plug

Most Unusual Bait Ever Put On the Market

Nothing ever before brought out like it. It has a pearl shell finish with all the irridescence of sea pearl shell. It catches the light from every direction and reflects this light in many colors. The fish are sure to get the color value they want, for the Paw Paw Pearler gives off all the colors of the rainbow. It is a hard finish—will last longer than the average finish and will stand up longer under hard strikes.

We used it all last year experimenting under every condition with it in lakes and streams—dark days and sunshiny days and always caught fish with it. We punished it in every way we could and it came through Ace High. Try one and you'll never go out without it.

$20 – 40

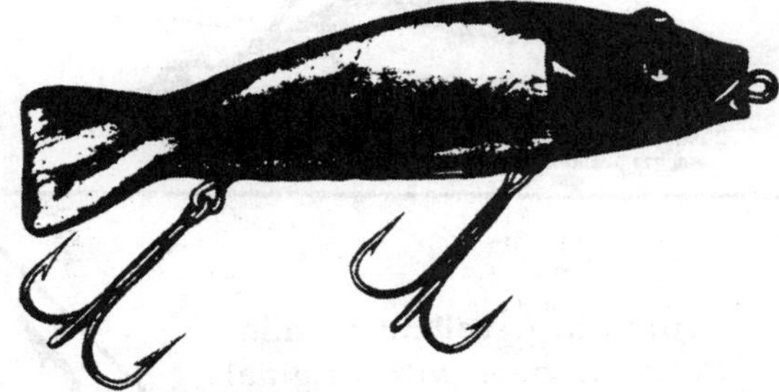

The finish is available now on the following numbers:

No. 3405—Injured Minnow . . . .
No. 2605—Bass Seeker . . . .
No. 2705—**Jr.** size, Bass Seeker . . . . .
No. 5505—Bullhead . . . .
No. 40 and **No.** 49—Mouse Series . . . .

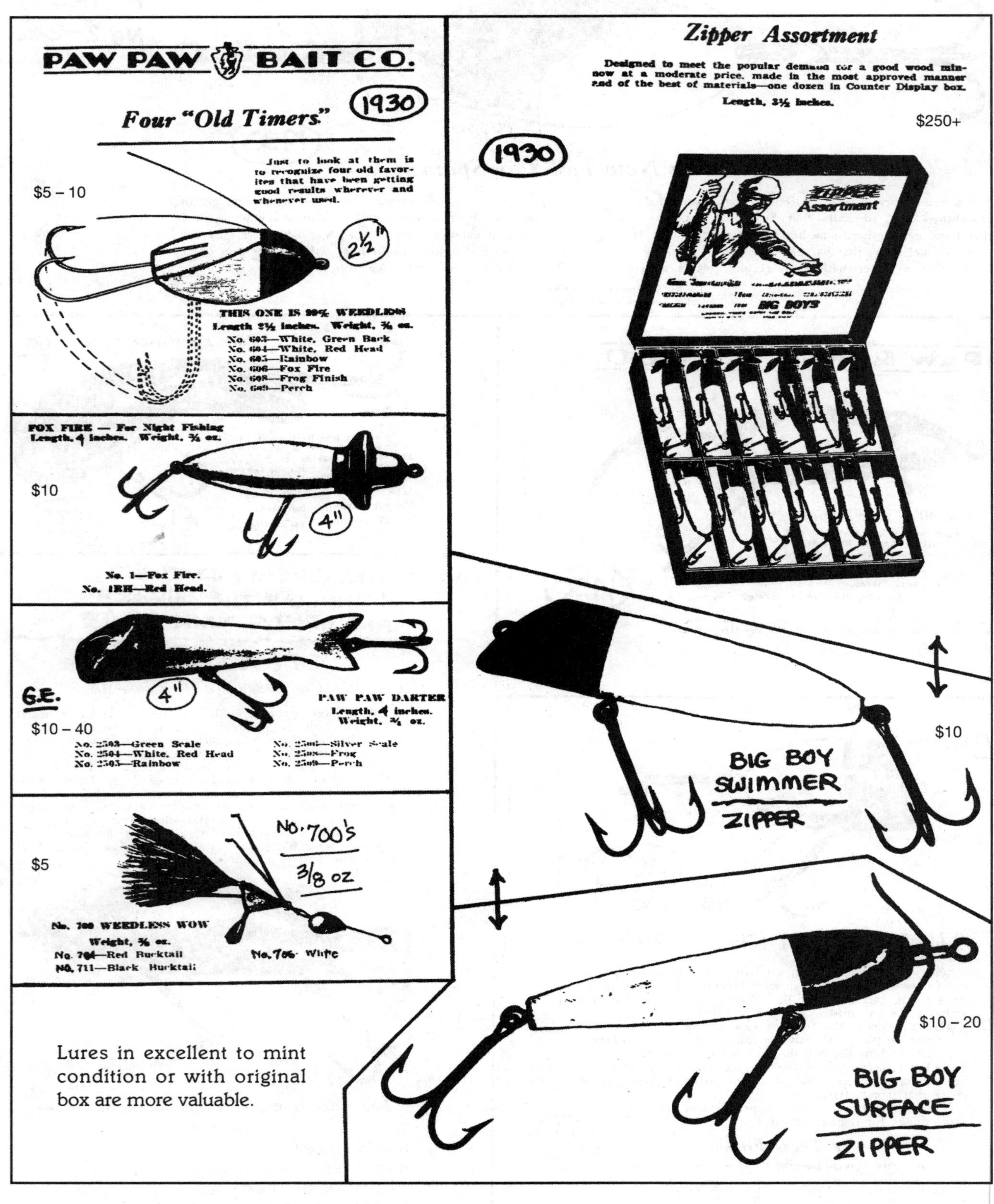
PAW PAW BAIT CO.
Four "Old Timers."
1930
Just to look at them is to recognize four old favorites that have been getting good results wherever and whenever used.
$5 – 10
2½"
THIS ONE IS 90% WEEDLESS
Length 2½ inches. Weight, ⅝ oz.
No. 603—White, Green Back
No. 604—White, Red Head
No. 605—Rainbow
No. 606—Fox Fire
No. 608—Frog Finish
No. 609—Perch
FOX FIRE — For Night Fishing
Length, 4 inches. Weight, ¾ oz.
$10
4"
No. 1—Fox Fire.
No. 1RH—Red Head.
4"
G.E.
$10 – 40
PAW PAW DARTER
Length, 4 inches.
Weight, ¾ oz.
No. 2503—Green Scale
No. 2504—White, Red Head
No. 2505—Rainbow
No. 2506—Silver Scale
No. 2508—Frog
No. 2509—Perch
$5
No. 700's
3/8 oz
No. 700 WEEDLESS WOW
Weight, ⅜ oz.
No. 704—Red Bucktail
No. 711—Black Bucktail
No. 706 White
Zipper Assortment
Designed to meet the popular demand for a good wood minnow at a moderate price, made in the most approved manner and of the best of materials—one dozen in Counter Display box.
Length, 3½ inches.
$250+
1930
Zipper
Assortment
BIG BOYS
$10
BIG BOY
SWIMMER
ZIPPER
$10 – 20
BIG BOY
SURFACE
ZIPPER

Lures in excellent to mint condition or with original box are more valuable.

PAW PAW BAIT CO.

$5

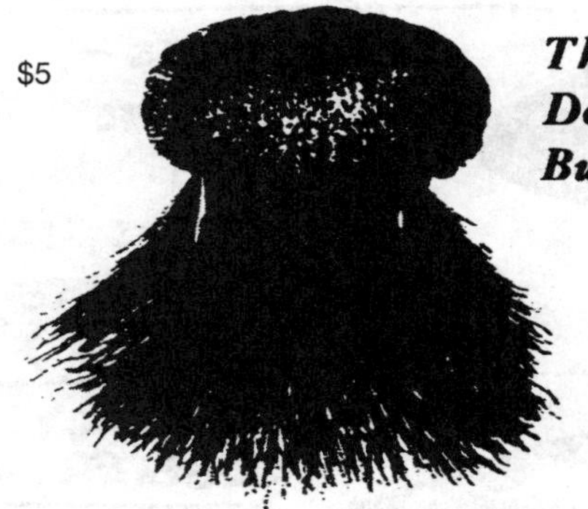

The Doodle Bug

We laughed at the sample of the Doodle Bug sent us by one of our angler friends, but we tried it with the fly-rod and when the rod was almost jerked out of our hand we looked at the Bug in puzzled amazement. We put *that* bass on our stringer and made another cast and got another bass —then we went back to the shop.

That Doodle Bug is like a big, fuzzy bug when it lights easily on the water. It's wiggly; it's crawly. It spreads out and when you twitch your rod it seems to shiver all over and the bass and other game fish just come up for a good juicy meal—and YOU get them.

If you fish fly rod—get one of these right away. ½ dozen assorted colors packed in carton.

No. 120.

NO. 120

Here's "The Moose"

PEACOCK FEATHERS & MOOSE HAIR!

Maybe we should call it the "Peacock - Moose" because it is a combination of peacock feathers and moose hair. Notice the bunch of moose hair in front of the hook—keeps it off the weeds and yet the fish will easily push it down on the strike.

This is a new bait with a June Bug spinner and it is getting mighty good results.

$10

The long moose hair gets soft in the water and has a sassy wiggle—and they are tough enough to stand a lot of abuse.

No. 270.

NO. 270

It Certainly Gets the Fish

It's a pearl wobbler—made of heavy iridescent pearl in the natural shell shape, it makes a splendid caster and has all the wobble action of a wounded fish trying hard to struggle through the water. You can have it in a number of different colors or color combinations; natural and red; natural; green and red; green, red, black and natural. These are great for ALL game fish, especially for pike, bass and big trout.

WOBBLE-BOYS

No. 100—Length, 2¾ inches. Weight, ⅜ oz.
No 200—Length, 3½ inches. Weight, ⅝ oz.

(Packed 6 assorted colors on a card.)

No. 100—
No. 200—

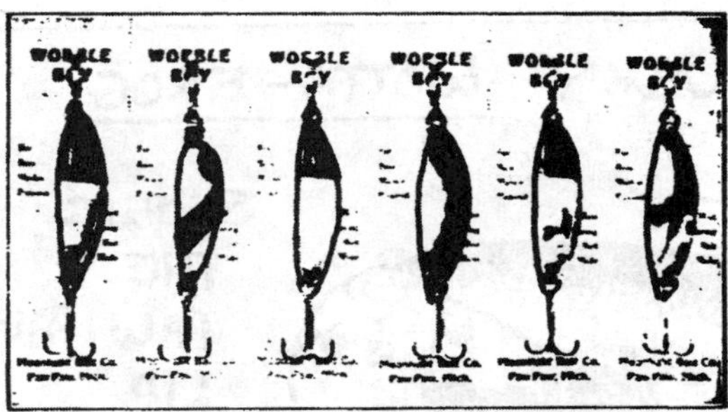
WOBBLE BOY
WOBBLE BOY
WOBBLE BOY
WOBBLE BOY
WOBBLE BOY
WOBBLE BOY

No. 100 - 2¾"
No. 200 - 3½"

NOTE: ALL THIS PAGE FROM 1930.

$5 – 10 each

$5

A Spinner

That's Catching Limit Catches

It's weedless, casts easily and doesn't tangle—one of those spinners that get fish in any waters and under most any kind of conditions. There is a lure in the bright colored feathers and the sassy tag that wiggles at the end of the hook. The flash of the whirling June Bug spinner brings the fish from far and near.

Instead of a wire weed guard we are using moose hair—you'll not miss so many strikes with this combination. The hair is stiff enough to keep your hook out of the weeds and soft enough to let the fish close down on the hook. There is a combination of colors all mounted on an attractive show card on your dealer's counter. Six on counter display card.

No. 230.

NO. 230

$10 – 20

Wilson Wobbler

Length, 4 inches.
Weight, ⅝ oz.

Known from one end of the country to the other and over in Canada as a great bait. Fishermen swear by it—and NEVER at it. It is one of those good baits that always will be good.

1-F—White, Red Flutes, 3 hooks.
4-F—Red, 3 hooks.
5-F—Yellow, 3 hooks.
2-F—Fox Fire, 3 hooks.
10-F—Rainbow, 3 hooks.
1-FS—White, Red Flutes, 2 hooks.
1-S—Super-Wobbler, 2 double hooks.

PAW PAW ALSO MADE THE SUPER WOBBLER NO. 1-S W/2 DOUBLE HOOKS.

IS YOUR WILSON WOBBLER A HASTINGS OR A PAW PAW?

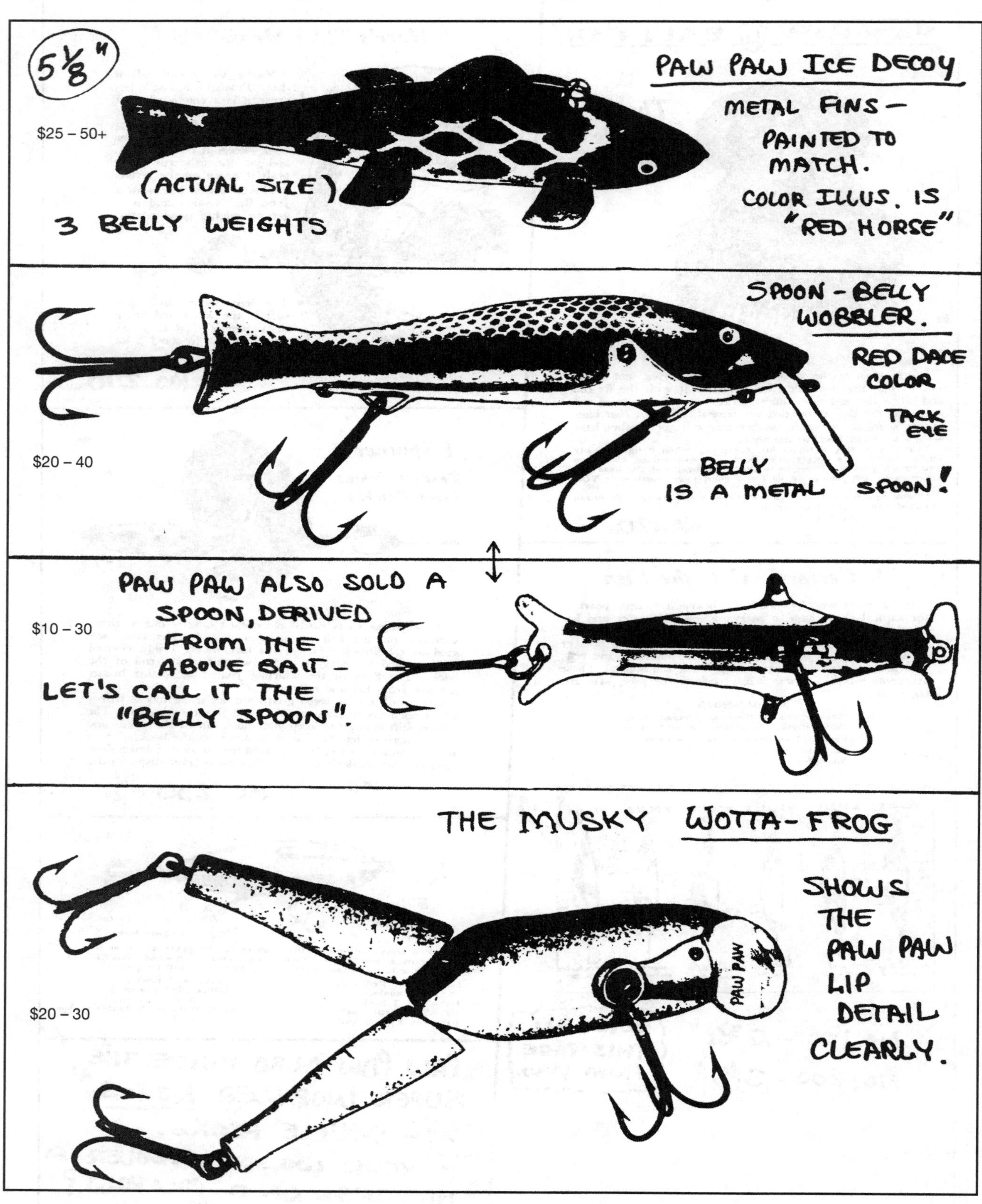
5 1/8"
PAW PAW ICE DECOY
METAL FINS —
PAINTED TO
MATCH.
COLOR ILLUS. IS
"RED HORSE"
$25 – 50+
(ACTUAL SIZE)
3 BELLY WEIGHTS
SPOON - BELLY
WOBBLER.
RED DACE
COLOR
TACK
EYE
$20 – 40
BELLY
IS A METAL SPOON!
PAW PAW ALSO SOLD A
SPOON, DERIVED
FROM THE
ABOVE BAIT —
LET'S CALL IT THE
"BELLY SPOON".
$10 – 30
THE MUSKY WOTTA-FROG
SHOWS
THE
PAW PAW
LIP
DETAIL
CLEARLY.
PAW PAW
$20 – 30

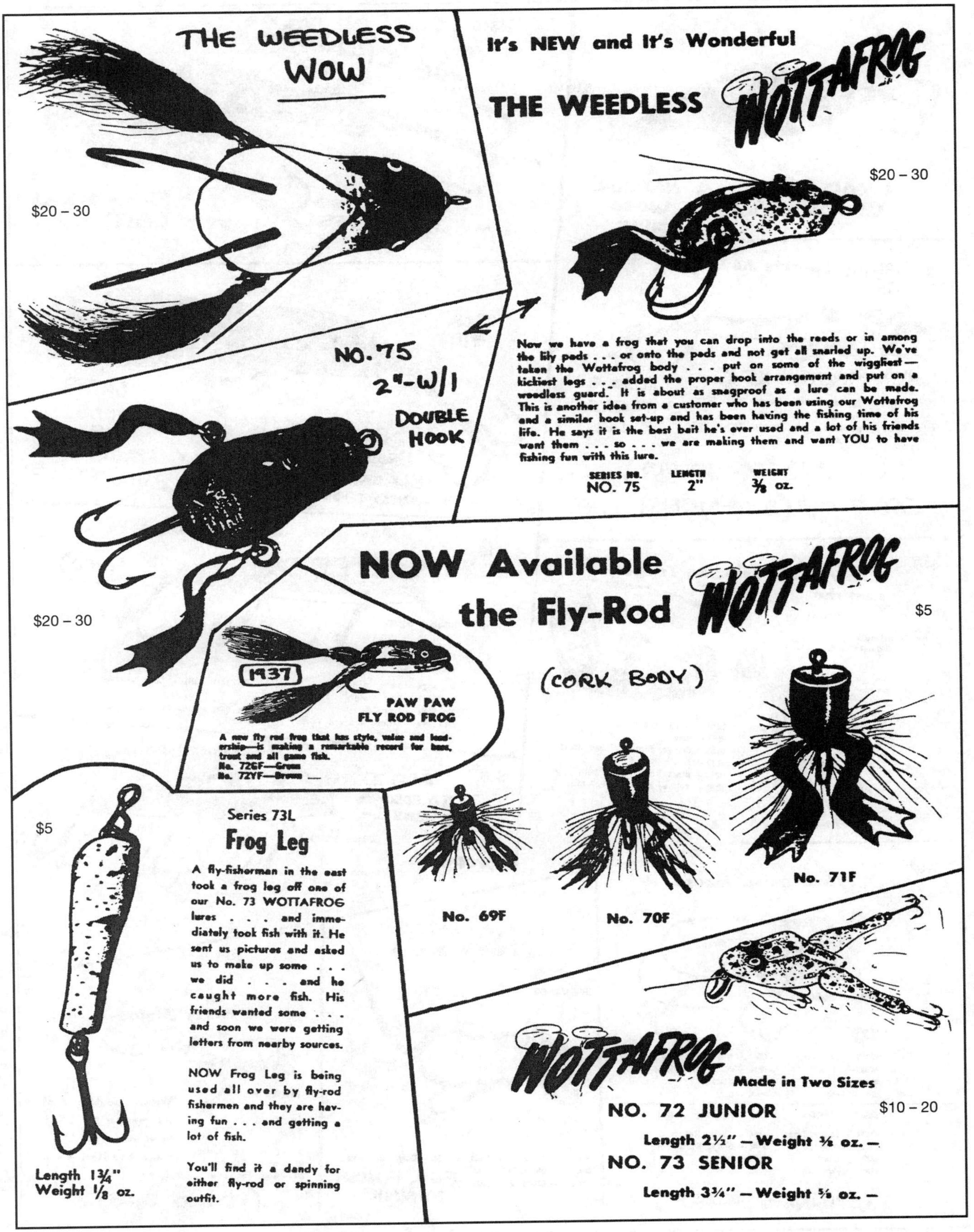
THE WEEDLESS WOW
$20 – 30
NO. 75
2"-W/1
DOUBLE HOOK
$20 – 30
It's NEW and It's Wonderful
THE WEEDLESS WOTTAFROG
$20 – 30
Now we have a frog that you can drop into the reeds or in among the lily pads . . . or onto the pads and not get all snarled up. We've taken the Wottafrog body . . . put on some of the wiggliest—kickiest legs . . . added the proper hook arrangement and put on a weedless guard. It is about as snagproof as a lure can be made. This is another idea from a customer who has been using our Wottafrog and a similar hook set-up and has been having the fishing time of his life. He says it is the best bait he's ever used and a lot of his friends want them . . . so . . . we are making them and want YOU to have fishing fun with this lure.
SERIES NO. NO. 75
LENGTH 2"
WEIGHT ⅜ oz.
NOW Available the Fly-Rod WOTTAFROG
$5
(CORK BODY)
1937
PAW PAW FLY ROD FROG
A new fly rod frog that has style, value and leadership—is making a remarkable record for bass, trout and all game fish.
No. 72GF—Green
No. 72YF—Brown
No. 69F
No. 70F
No. 71F
$5
Series 73L
Frog Leg
A fly-fisherman in the east took a frog leg off one of our No. 73 WOTTAFROG lures . . . and immediately took fish with it. He sent us pictures and asked us to make up some . . . we did . . . and he caught more fish. His friends wanted some . . . and soon we were getting letters from nearby sources.
NOW Frog Leg is being used all over by fly-rod fishermen and they are having fun . . . and getting a lot of fish.
You'll find it a dandy for either fly-rod or spinning outfit.
Length 1¾"
Weight ⅛ oz.
WOTTAFROG Made in Two Sizes
$10 – 20
NO. 72 JUNIOR
Length 2½" — Weight ⅜ oz. —
NO. 73 SENIOR
Length 3¾" — Weight ⅝ oz. —

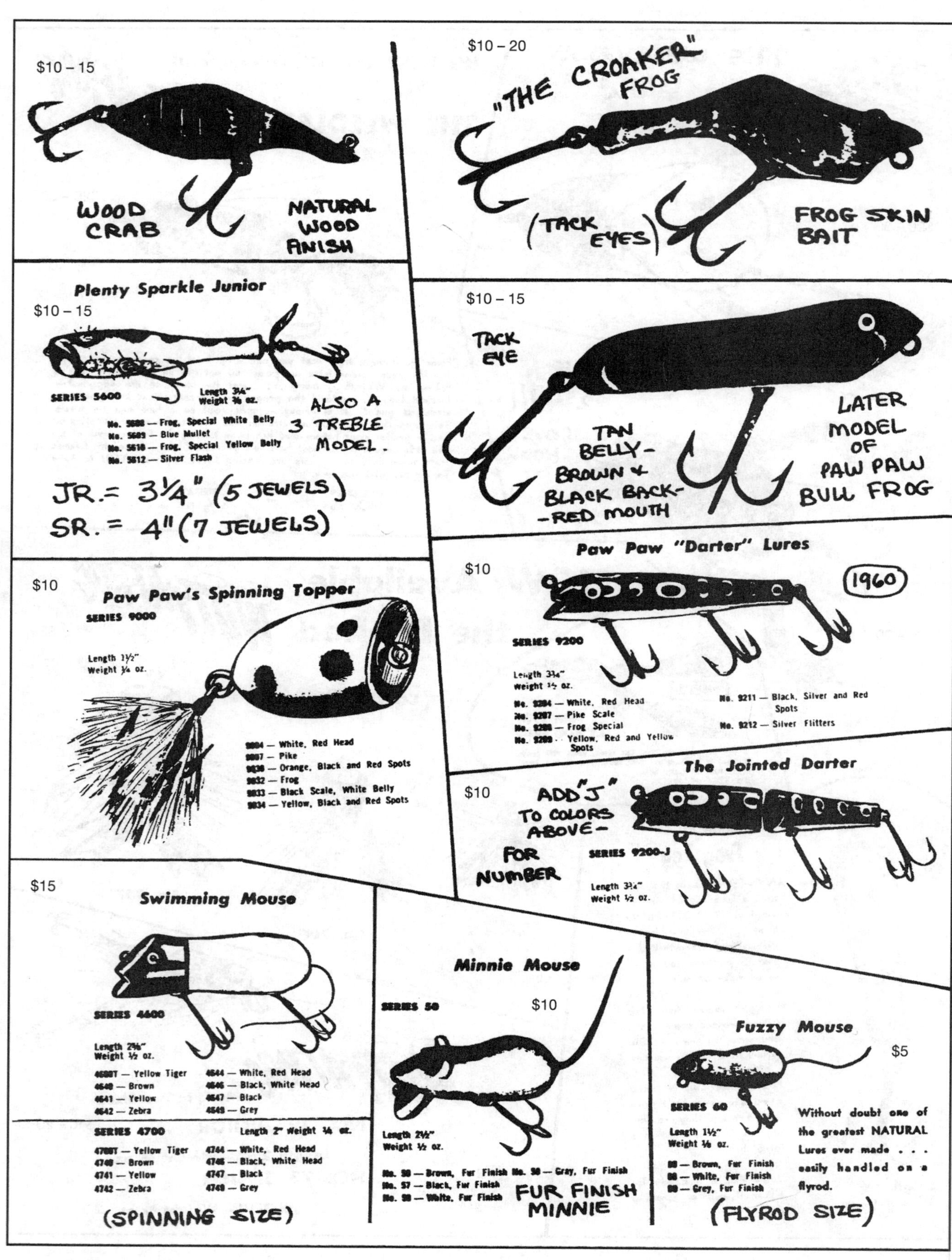
$10 – 15
WOOD CRAB
NATURAL WOOD FINISH
$10 – 20
"THE CROAKER" FROG
(TACK EYES)
FROG SKIN BAIT
Plenty Sparkle Junior
$10 – 15
SERIES 5600
Length 3¼"
Weight ⅜ oz.
No. — Frog, Special White Belly
No. 5603 — Blue Mullet
No. 5610 — Frog, Special Yellow Belly
No. 5612 — Silver Flash
ALSO A 3 TREBLE MODEL.
JR. = 3¼" (5 JEWELS)
SR. = 4" (7 JEWELS)
$10 – 15
TACK EYE
TAN BELLY - BROWN & BLACK BACK - RED MOUTH
LATER MODEL OF PAW PAW BULL FROG
$10
Paw Paw's Spinning Topper
SERIES 9000
Length 1½"
Weight ¼ oz.
— White, Red Head
— Pike
— Orange, Black and Red Spots
9032 — Frog
9033 — Black Scale, White Belly
9034 — Yellow, Black and Red Spots
Paw Paw "Darter" Lures
$10
1960
SERIES 9200
Length 3¾"
Weight ½ oz.
No. — White, Red Head
No. 9207 — Pike Scale
No. — Frog Special
No. — Yellow, Red and Yellow Spots
No. 9211 — Black, Silver and Red Spots
No. 9212 — Silver Flitters
The Jointed Darter
$10
ADD "J" TO COLORS ABOVE - FOR NUMBER
SERIES 9200-J
Length 3¾"
Weight ½ oz.
$15
Swimming Mouse
SERIES 4600
Length 2⅝"
Weight ½ oz.
4600T — Yellow Tiger
4640 — Brown
4641 — Yellow
4642 — Zebra
4644 — White, Red Head
4646 — Black, White Head
4647 — Black
4649 — Grey
SERIES 4700
Length 2" Weight ¼ oz.
4700T — Yellow Tiger
4740 — Brown
4741 — Yellow
4742 — Zebra
4744 — White, Red Head
4746 — Black, White Head
4747 — Black
4749 — Grey
(SPINNING SIZE)
Minnie Mouse
SERIES 50
$10
Length 2½"
Weight ½ oz.
No. — Brown, Fur Finish
No. 57 — Black, Fur Finish
No. — White, Fur Finish
No. — Gray, Fur Finish
FUR FINISH MINNIE
Fuzzy Mouse
$5
SERIES 60
Length 1½"
Weight ⅛ oz.
— Brown, Fur Finish
— White, Fur Finish
— Grey, Fur Finish
Without doubt one of the greatest NATURAL Lures ever made . . . easily handled on a flyrod.
(FLYROD SIZE)

THE GREATEST IMPROVEMENT SINCE THE SCALE FINISH!

1960

NEW *Bonehead* FINISH

(ON WOOD)

Spinning and Light Casting Sizes

When we named this the BONEHEAD LINE we did it because we wondered why we hadn't thought of it a long time ago. It is NEW . . . DIFFERENT from anything ever produced. It has an action and effect in the water that no other bait can produce. It forms air bubbles in its wake. Its corrugated sides give an effect that is enticing to every game fish. Brilliant Eyes flash with every wiggle . . . and can be seen from far distances. Its golden, spotted finish resembles a swamp minnow . . . a frog and many other forms of under-water life.

Bob Becker . . . famous sportsman, lecturer and writer, who tested this bait for us in many waters says, "This is something . . . it is new and unusual . . . I've taken lots of fish on it. It is a swamp minnow and many other things that attract fish. Why didn't you think of it long ago?"

It isn't a colorful, flashy bait to catch the eye of the angler . . . but it CERTAINLY CATCHES THE EYES OF THE FISH . . . judging by reports from all over the fishing world.

$10 – 20

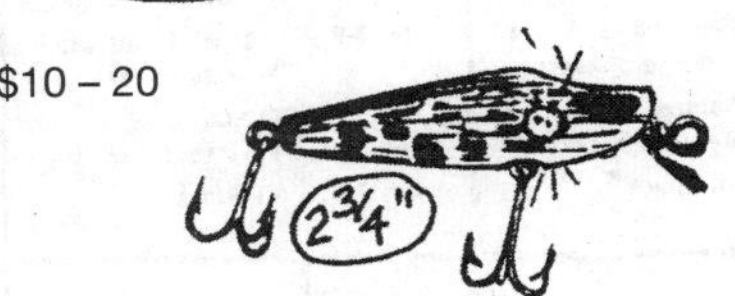
2 3/4"

SERIES 12-A
Length 2¾" — Weight ¼ oz. —

Miss Flatside $10 – 20

2"

SERIES 12-D
Length 2" — Weight ¼ oz. —

Wigglin' Minnie $10 – 20

2 3/4"

SERIES 12-G
Length 2¾" — Weight ¼ oz. —

Jointed Swamp Minnow $10 – 20

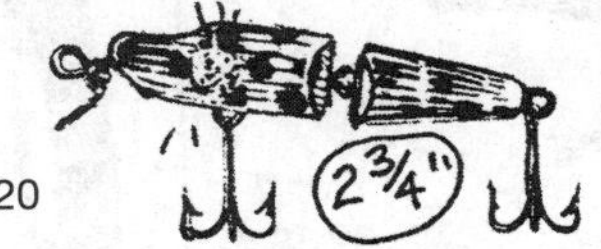
2 3/4"

SERIES 12-B
Length 2¾" — Weight ¼ oz. —

Tail Splasher $10 – 20

2"

SERIES 12-E
Length 2" — Weight ¼ oz. —

The Wobbler $10 – 20

3 1/4"

SERIES 12-N
Length 3¼" — Weight ½ oz. —

Bright-eyed Popper

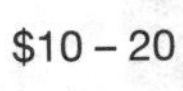
$10 – 20

2"

SERIES 12-C
Length 2" — Weight ¼ oz. —

Bonehead Wiggler $10 – 20

2 3/8"

SERIES 12-F
Length 2⅜" — Weight ¼ oz. —

Baby Splasher $10 – 20

1 7/8"

SERIES 12-S
Length 1⅞" — Weight ½ oz. —

Southern Swamp Minnow $10 – 20

4"

SERIES 8555
Length 4" — Weight ½ oz. —

Struttin' Sam $10 – 20

3 5/8"

SERIES 12-M
Length 3⅝" — Weight ⅜ oz. —

Southern Torpedo - Floater $10 – 20

4"

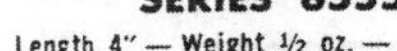

SERIES 2455
Length 4" — Weight ½ oz. —

Paw Paw's Hair Bodies Bass Bugs

$5

1937

PAW PAW'S BLUGILL BUSTER

$5

1937

THE BAIT I SAW IN THIS FINISH WAS GROOVED AND EMBOSSED IN BROWN—WITH A JEWEL EYE.

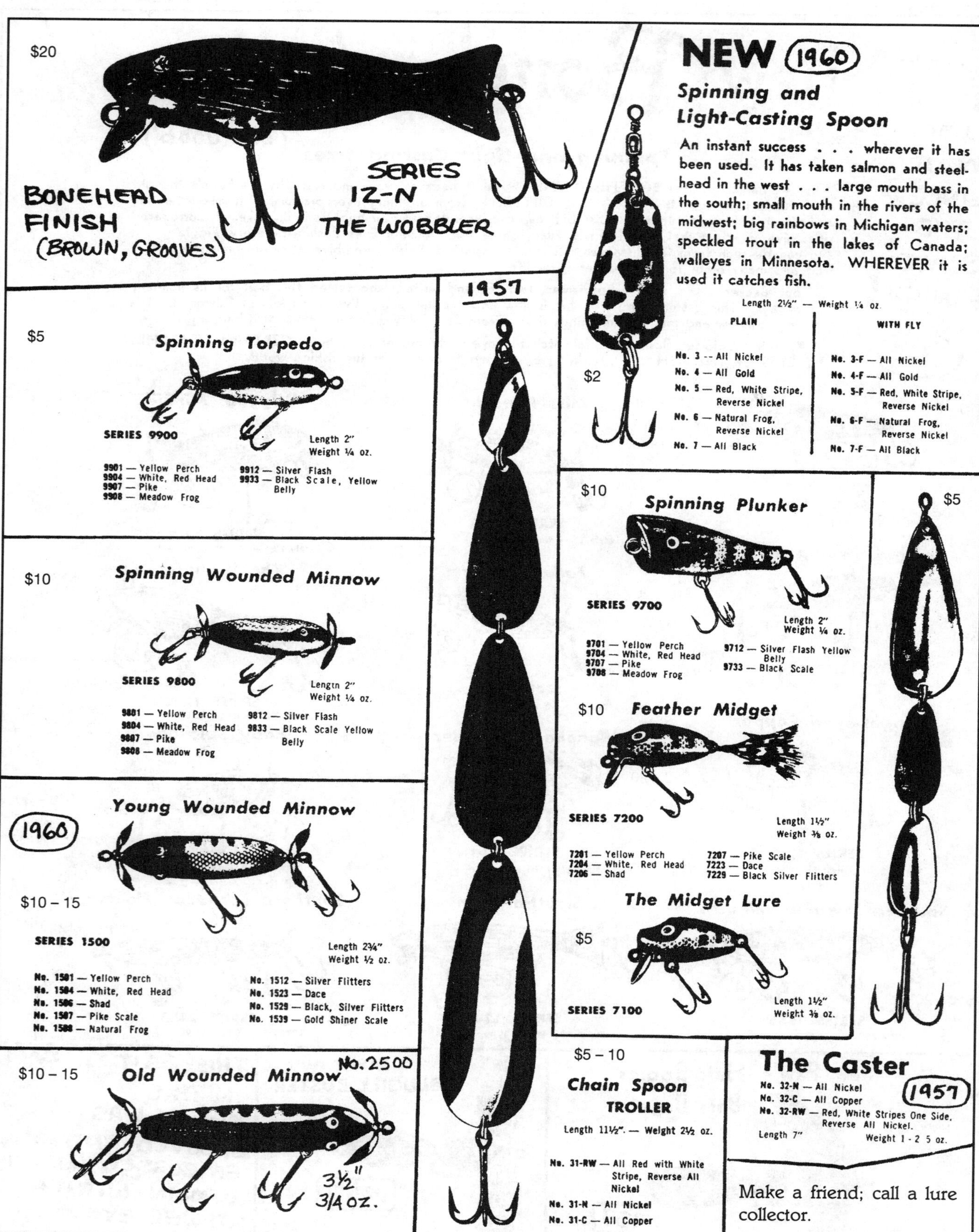
$20
BONEHEAD FINISH (BROWN, GROOVES)
SERIES 12-N THE WOBBLER
NEW 1960
Spinning and Light-Casting Spoon
An instant success . . . wherever it has been used. It has taken salmon and steelhead in the west . . . large mouth bass in the south; small mouth in the rivers of the midwest; big rainbows in Michigan waters; speckled trout in the lakes of Canada; walleyes in Minnesota. WHEREVER it is used it catches fish.
Length 2½" — Weight ¼ oz.
PLAIN
No. 3 -- All Nickel
No. 4 — All Gold
No. 5 — Red, White Stripe, Reverse Nickel
No. 6 — Natural Frog, Reverse Nickel
No. 7 — All Black
WITH FLY
No. 3-F — All Nickel
No. 4-F — All Gold
No. 5-F — Red, White Stripe, Reverse Nickel
No. 6-F — Natural Frog, Reverse Nickel
No. 7-F — All Black
$2
$5
Spinning Torpedo
SERIES 9900
Length 2" Weight ¼ oz.
9901 — Yellow Perch
9904 — White, Red Head
9907 — Pike
9908 — Meadow Frog
9912 — Silver Flash
9933 — Black Scale, Yellow Belly
1957
$10
Spinning Wounded Minnow
SERIES 9800
Length 2" Weight ¼ oz.
9801 — Yellow Perch
9804 — White, Red Head
9807 — Pike
9808 — Meadow Frog
9812 — Silver Flash
9833 — Black Scale Yellow Belly
$10
Spinning Plunker
SERIES 9700
Length 2" Weight ¼ oz.
9701 — Yellow Perch
9704 — White, Red Head
9707 — Pike
9708 — Meadow Frog
9712 — Silver Flash Yellow Belly
9733 — Black Scale
$5
$10
Feather Midget
SERIES 7200
Length 1½" Weight ⅜ oz.
7201 — Yellow Perch
7204 — White, Red Head
7206 — Shad
7207 — Pike Scale
7223 — Dace
7229 — Black Silver Flitters
Young Wounded Minnow
1960
$10 – 15
SERIES 1500
Length 2¾" Weight ½ oz.
No. 1501 — Yellow Perch
No. 1504 — White, Red Head
No. 1506 — Shad
No. 1507 — Pike Scale
No. 1508 — Natural Frog
No. 1512 — Silver Flitters
No. 1523 — Dace
No. 1529 — Black, Silver Flitters
No. 1539 — Gold Shiner Scale
The Midget Lure
$5
SERIES 7100
Length 1½" Weight ⅜ oz.
$10 – 15
Old Wounded Minnow
No. 2500
3½" 3/4 oz.
$5 – 10
Chain Spoon
TROLLER
Length 11½". — Weight 2½ oz.
No. 31-RW — All Red with White Stripe, Reverse All Nickel
No. 31-N — All Nickel
No. 31-C — All Copper
The Caster
1957
No. 32-N — All Nickel
No. 32-C — All Copper
No. 32-RW — Red, White Stripes One Side, Reverse All Nickel.
Length 7"
Weight 1 - 2 5 oz.

Make a friend; call a lure collector.

Paw Paw's Great Lures for SOUTHERN Fishing

These lures have done such a splendid job of fish catching for Southern fishermen that we are very proud to distribute them through the better dealers and jobbers. They have been tried and proven . . . they are built to take the hard usage of big fish and heavy catches.

Aristocrat Shiner

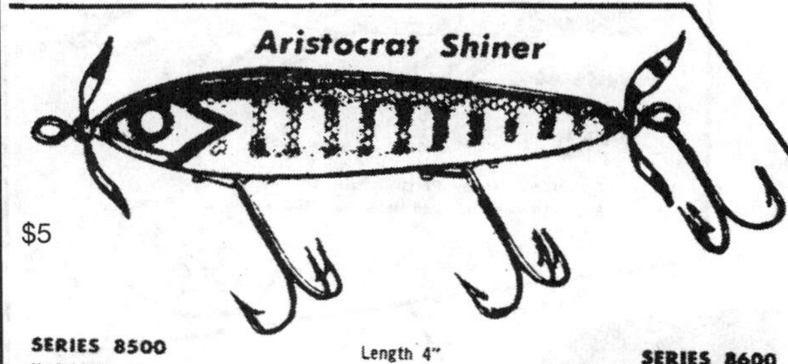

$5

SERIES 8500
Weight 1/2 oz.
FLOATER

Length 4"

SERIES 8600
Weight 3/4 oz.
SINKER

Southern Torpedo

$5 – 10

SERIES 500
Length 4"
Weight 5/8 oz.

The Little Shiner

$5

SERIES 8400
Length 2 3/4"
Weight 3/8 oz.

FLOATER

Aristocrat Torpedo

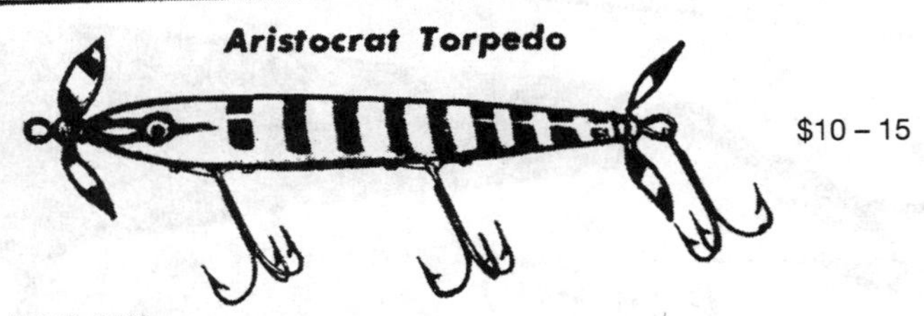

$10 – 15

SERIES 2400

2400-S
SINKERS
Length 4"
Weight 5/8 oz.

2400-F
FLOATERS
Length 4"
Weight 1/2 oz.

Made Especially for

Alabama
Arkansas
Florida
Georgia
Kentucky
Louisiana
Mississippi
North Carolina
South Carolina
Tennessee
Texas
Virginia
Missouri
Oklahoma

Spinning Sunfish

$5

SERIES 1300
Length 1 7/8" -- Weight 1/2 oz.

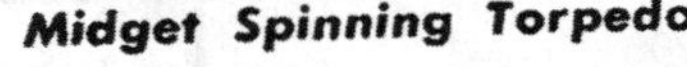

Midget Spinning Torpedo

SERIES 800
Length 1 7/8"
PRICE 85c

$5

SINKERS

FLOATERS

Spinning Top-Eye

$5

No. S-1300
Length 1 7/8" — Weight 1/2 oz.

(ACTUAL SIZE)

$10 – 15

PAW PAW
BAIT CO.

ON MARCH 24, 1960, MR. C.C. SINCLAIR (OWNER OF PAW PAW) BOUGHT FROM L.F. DOSTING, (PRES) AND D.R. ARNOLD (GEN'L. MGR) THE ARNOLD TACKLE CORP. – 100 COMMERCIAL AVE. – PAW PAW, MICH (ARNOLD STILL MADE ICE FISHING STUFF)

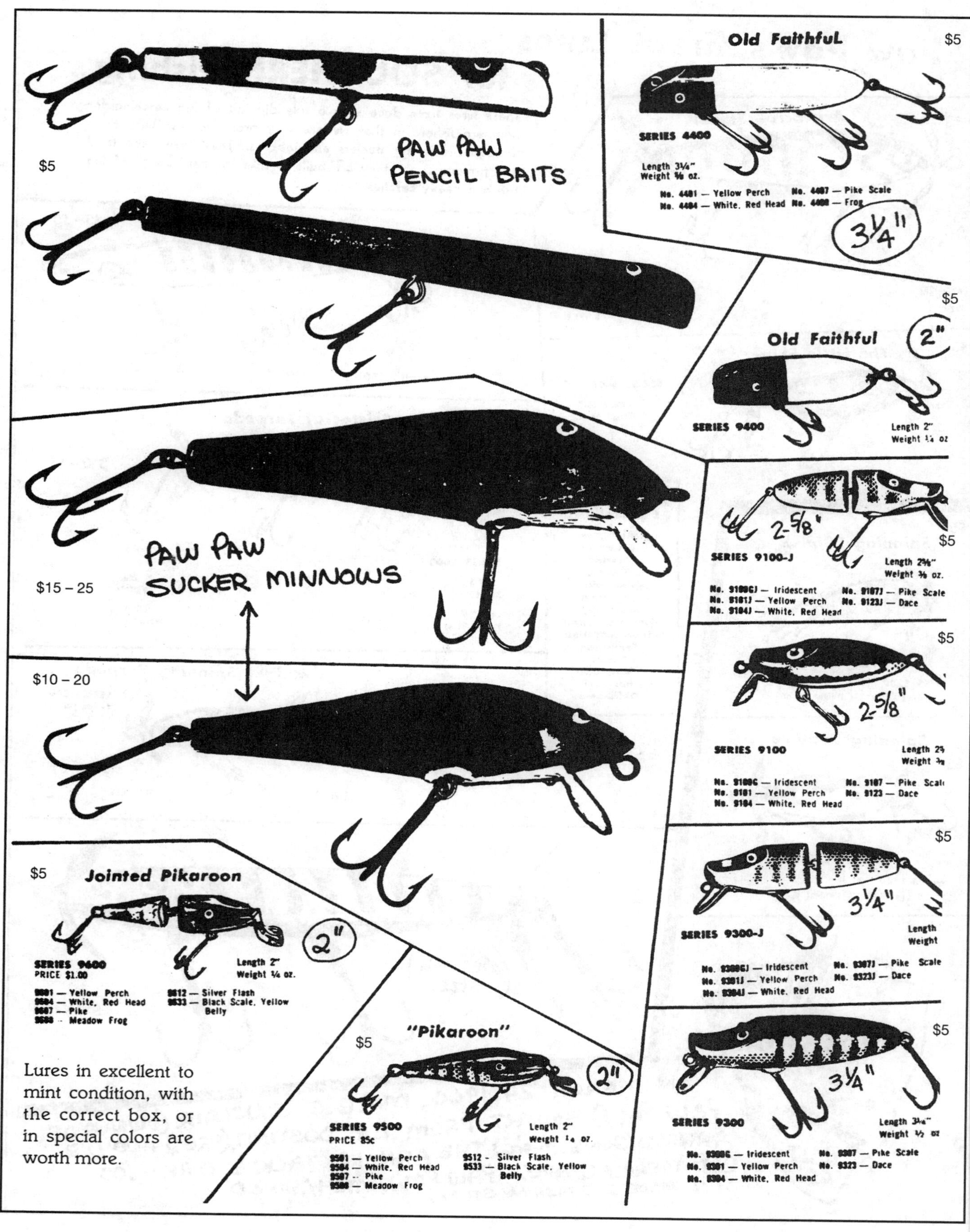
PAW PAW
PENCIL BAITS
$5
Old FaithfuL
$5
SERIES 4400
Length 3¼"
Weight ⅝ oz.
No. 4481 — Yellow Perch
No. 4484 — White, Red Head
No. 4487 — Pike Scale
No. 4488 — Frog
3¼"
$5
Old Faithful
2"
SERIES 9400
Length 2"
Weight ¼ oz
PAW PAW
SUCKER MINNOWS
$15 – 25
$10 – 20
2-5/8"
$5
SERIES 9100-J
Length 2⅝"
Weight ⅜ oz.
No. 9100GJ — Iridescent
No. 9101J — Yellow Perch
No. 9104J — White, Red Head
No. 9107J — Pike Scale
No. 9123J — Dace
$5
2-5/8"
SERIES 9100
No. 9100G — Iridescent
No. 9101 — Yellow Perch
No. 9104 — White, Red Head
No. 9107 — Pike Scale
No. 9123 — Dace
$5
Jointed Pikaroon
2"
SERIES 9600
PRICE $1.00
Length 2"
Weight ¼ oz.
— Yellow Perch
— White, Red Head
— Pike
Meadow Frog
— Silver Flash
— Black Scale, Yellow Belly
$5
3¼"
SERIES 9300-J
Length
Weight
No. 9300GJ — Iridescent
No. 9301J — Yellow Perch
No. 9304J — White, Red Head
No. 9307J — Pike Scale
No. 9323J — Dace
$5
"Pikaroon"
2"
SERIES 9500
PRICE 85c
Length 2"
Weight ¼ oz.
9501 — Yellow Perch
9504 — White, Red Head
9507 — Pike
9508 — Meadow Frog
9512 — Silver Flash
9533 — Black Scale, Yellow Belly
$5
3¼"
SERIES 9300
Length 3¼"
Weight ½ oz
No. 9300G — Iridescent
No. 9301 — Yellow Perch
No. 9304 — White, Red Head
No. 9307 — Pike Scale
No. 9323 — Dace

Lures in excellent to mint condition, with the correct box, or in special colors are worth more.

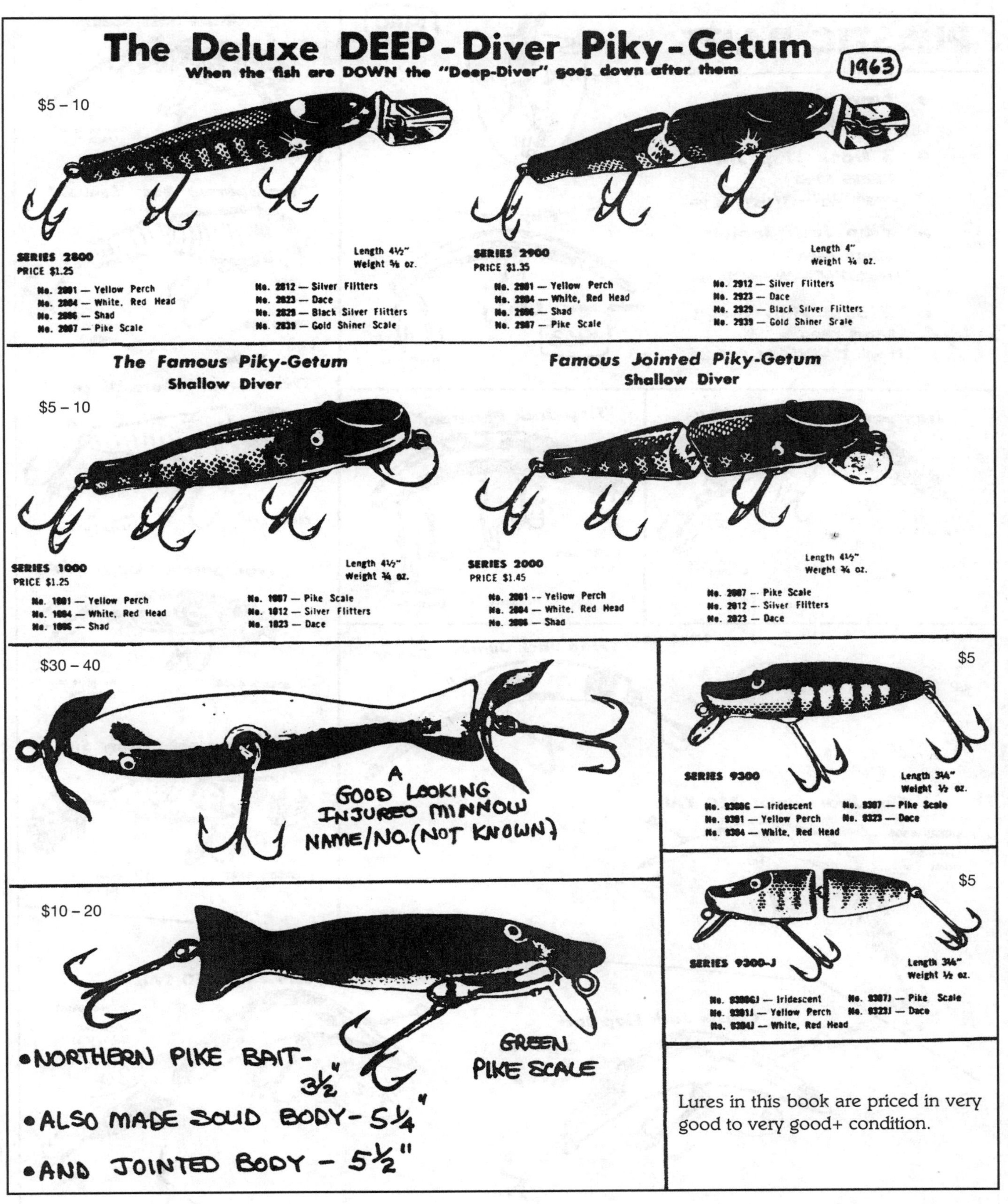
The Deluxe DEEP-Diver Piky-Getum
When the fish are DOWN the "Deep-Diver" goes down after them
1963
$5 – 10
SERIES 2800
PRICE $1.25
Length 4½"
Weight ⅝ oz.
No. 2801 — Yellow Perch
No. 2804 — White, Red Head
No. 2806 — Shad
No. 2807 — Pike Scale
No. 2812 — Silver Flitters
No. 2823 — Dace
No. 2829 — Black Silver Flitters
No. 2839 — Gold Shiner Scale
SERIES 2900
PRICE $1.35
Length 4"
Weight ¾ oz.
No. 2901 — Yellow Perch
No. 2904 — White, Red Head
No. 2906 — Shad
No. 2907 — Pike Scale
No. 2912 — Silver Flitters
No. 2923 — Dace
No. 2929 — Black Silver Flitters
No. 2939 — Gold Shiner Scale
The Famous Piky-Getum
Shallow Diver
$5 – 10
SERIES 1000
PRICE $1.25
Length 4½"
Weight ¾ oz.
No. 1001 — Yellow Perch
No. 1004 — White, Red Head
No. 1006 — Shad
No. 1007 — Pike Scale
No. 1012 — Silver Flitters
No. 1023 — Dace
Famous Jointed Piky-Getum
Shallow Diver
SERIES 2000
PRICE $1.45
Length 4½"
Weight ¾ oz.
No. 2001 — Yellow Perch
No. 2004 — White, Red Head
No. 2006 — Shad
No. 2007 — Pike Scale
No. 2012 — Silver Flitters
No. 2023 — Dace
$30 – 40
A GOOD LOOKING INJURED MINNOW
NAME/NO. (NOT KNOWN)
$5
SERIES 9300
Length 3¼"
Weight ½ oz.
No. 9300G — Iridescent
No. 9301 — Yellow Perch
No. 9304 — White, Red Head
No. 9307 — Pike Scale
No. 9323 — Dace
$5
SERIES 9300-J
Length 3¼"
Weight ½ oz.
No. 9300GJ — Iridescent
No. 9301J — Yellow Perch
No. 9304J — White, Red Head
No. 9307J — Pike Scale
No. 9323J — Dace
$10 – 20
GREEN PIKE SCALE
• NORTHERN PIKE BAIT - 3½"
• ALSO MADE SOLID BODY - 5¼"
• AND JOINTED BODY - 5½"
Lures in this book are priced in very good to very good+ condition.

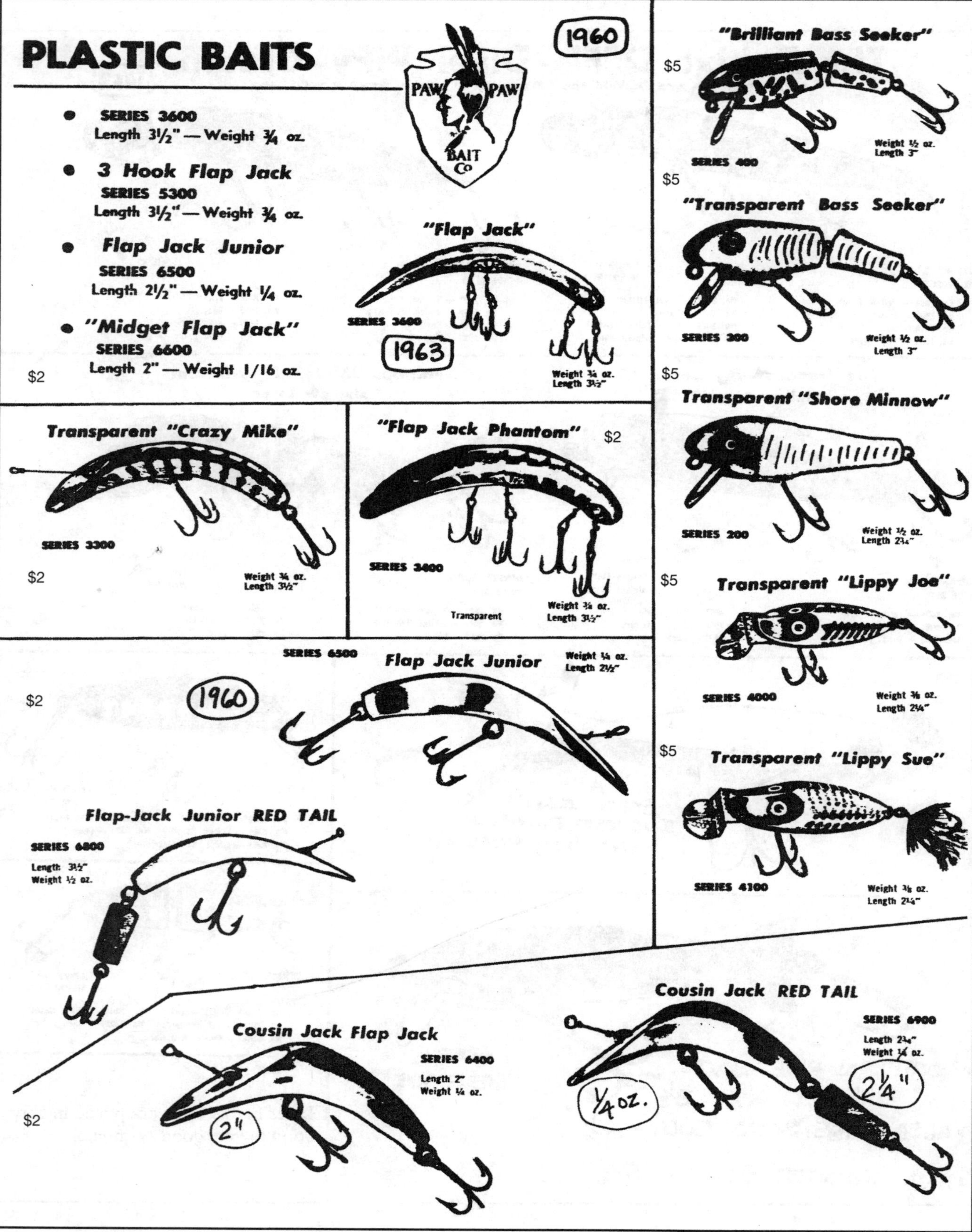

PLASTIC BAITS
1960
PAW PAW BAIT Co
SERIES 3600
Length 3½" — Weight ¾ oz.
3 Hook Flap Jack
SERIES 5300
Length 3½" — Weight ¾ oz.
Flap Jack Junior
SERIES 6500
Length 2½" — Weight ¼ oz.
"Midget Flap Jack"
SERIES 6600
Length 2" — Weight 1/16 oz.
$2
"Flap Jack"
SERIES 3600
1963
Weight ¾ oz.
Length 3½"
"Brilliant Bass Seeker"
$5
SERIES 400
Weight ½ oz.
Length 3"
$5
"Transparent Bass Seeker"
SERIES 300
Weight ½ oz.
Length 3"
$5
Transparent "Shore Minnow"
SERIES 200
Weight ½ oz.
Length 2¾"
Transparent "Crazy Mike"
SERIES 3300
$2
Weight ¾ oz.
Length 3½"
"Flap Jack Phantom"
$2
SERIES 3400
Transparent
Weight ¾ oz.
Length 3½"
$5
Transparent "Lippy Joe"
SERIES 4000
Weight ⅜ oz.
Length 2¼"
$5
Transparent "Lippy Sue"
SERIES 4100
Weight ⅜ oz.
Length 2¼"
SERIES 6500
Flap Jack Junior
Weight ¼ oz.
Length 2½"
$2
1960
Flap-Jack Junior RED TAIL
SERIES 6800
Length 3½"
Weight ½ oz.
Cousin Jack RED TAIL
SERIES 6900
Length 2¼"
Weight ¼ oz.
2¼"
¼ oz.
Cousin Jack Flap Jack
SERIES 6400
Length 2"
Weight ¼ oz.
$2
2"

PUT 1000 OF YOUR WARPATH
ZIGGER
3" LONG ½ OZ.
AT YOUR DEALER or POSTPAID
1.10
PAW PAW BAIT CO.
400 S. KALAMAZOO AVE. PAW PAW MICH.
(1948 AD)
WHOOPS!!!
THIS WAS MIS-I.D.'d AS A PAW-PAW.
IT IS: GLEN L. EVANS (IDAHO) HEXAGONAL PLUNKER KNOWN AS-"BLOOPER."
• BLENDED RED HEAD/WHITE, W/GOLD GLITTER.
• TACK EYES
(NOT PAW PAW)
$10 – 20
$5 – 10
SIDE VIEW
PAW PAW "PLATYPUS"
NO. 3524
(PLASTIC)
RAINBOW TROUT FIN.
$5
"Woggle Bug"
WB-900
Length 3" — Weight 5/8 oz.
WB-700
Length 2¼" — Weight ¼ oz.
2 SIZES
A PRODUCTIVE ERA ENDED ON MARCH 24, 1970 - WHEN SHAKESPEARE BOUGHT ALL RIGHTS AND EQUIPMENT OF THE PAW PAW BAIT CO.
PAW PAW BAIT CO.
BORN: 1906
DIED: 1970

PAW PAW

G.E. 7

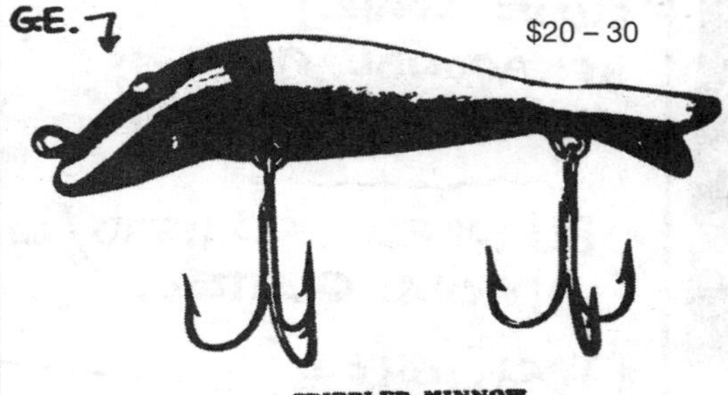

$20 – 30

CRIPPLED MINNOW

Length—4 in. Weight—⅝ oz.

No. 3403—Green Scale
No. 3404—White, Red Head
No. 3405—Pearl Finish
No. 3406—Silver Scale
No. 3408—Frog Finish

Paw Paw's Great Injured Minnow

Six Finishes

The NATURAL Food of All Game Fish

AN injured minnow in any water hasn't a chance if there are game fish around—and we have imitated the natural action—it doesn't wobble; it makes long frantic curves; it struggles to the surface and dives again to the bottom; you can make it jump from the water and dive back.

Fish simply can't resist its actions. It's the "fish gettin'est" plug bait you ever saw.

Send for Circu. v.

The Paw Paw Bait Company

ALSO TACK EYE

$5

(NEW-1953) SPOON

You're Sure with this LURE!

The NEW Lucky 7

Notice to Fishermen:

It's NEW...

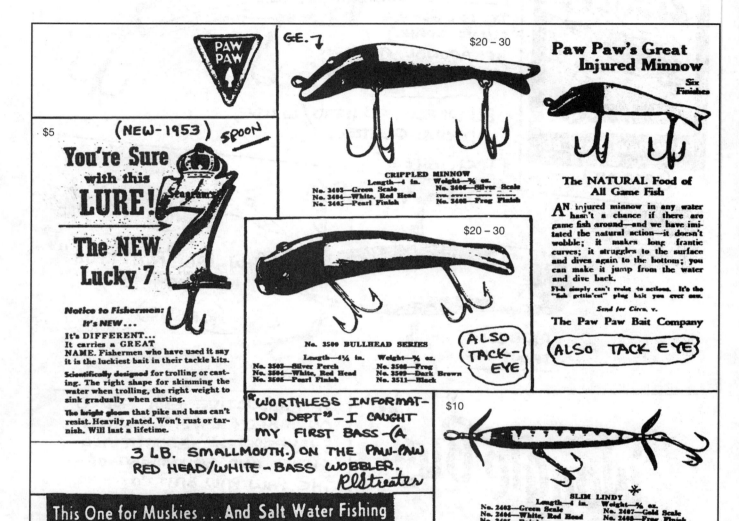

It's DIFFERENT...
It carries a GREAT NAME. Fishermen who have used it say it is the luckiest bait in their tackle kits.

Scientifically designed for trolling or casting. The right shape for skimming the water when trolling, the right weight to sink gradually when casting.

The bright gleam that pike and bass can't resist. Heavily plated. Won't rust or tarnish. Will last a lifetime.

$20 – 30

No. 3500 BULLHEAD SERIES

Length—4¼ in. Weight—⅝ oz.

No. 3503—Silver Perch
No. 3504—White, Red Head
No. 3505—Pearl Finish
No. 3508—Frog
No. 3509—Dark Brown
No. 3511—Black

ALSO TACK-EYE

*"WORTHLESS INFORMATION DEPT"—I CAUGHT MY FIRST BASS—(A 3 LB. SMALLMOUTH.) ON THE PAW-PAW RED HEAD/WHITE-BASS WOBBLER.

RLStreater

$10

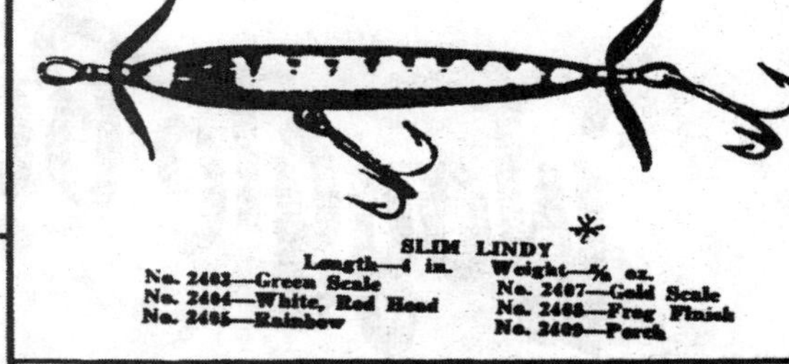

SLIM LINDY *

Length—4 in. Weight—⅝ oz.

No. 2403—Green Scale
No. 2404—White, Red Head
No. 2405—Rainbow
No. 2407—Gold Scale
No. 2408—Frog Finish
No. 2409—Perch

* REFERS TO LINDBERG, THE AVIATOR, WHO'S NICKNAME WAS "SLIM"

This One for Muskies . . . And Salt Water Fishing

For taking all salt water game fish—such as Kingfish, Mackerel, Yellow Tail, etc., and all the heaviest fresh water game fish. Brass wire shaft which cannot turn or pull out extends entirely through the body. Hooks are double extra strong, which cannot break or pull away. Extra heavy nose piece which produces that irresistible action. Length of body 6¼ in. 1⅜ in. diameter. Wt. 2⅜ oz. (Illustrated)

No. 5104—White Body, Red Head
No. 5107—Scale Finish

(6¼"- 2⅜ oz.)

For The Big Ones

● ALSO MADE IN A JOINTED MODEL (ADD "J") TO NUMBERS.

$10

$5

P & K SALT WATER LURES

1940's

LIPPY

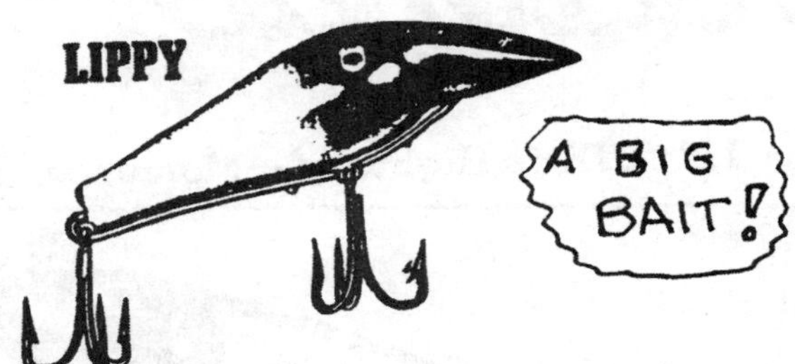
A BIG
BAIT!

For casting or trolling. A deep running lure. Hooks mounted on sturdy metal strip extending to head of plug for attaching line. Excellent for shore or boat fishing. Metal lip (not illustrated) protects leading edge from wear through bottom contacts.

No. 5/0 Belly Hook, No. 7/0 extra strong tail hook.
No. 63 RW (Red & White) **No. 63 B (Blue Scale)**
No. 63 BS (Brown Scale **No. 63 S (Silver)**
No. 63— **Weight 3½ oz.**

$5

5/8 oz.
2¼"

AMAZIN' MAIZIE

NO. 42 SERIES

Patent Applied For
(Made of Tenite)

(2 SIZES)

$5

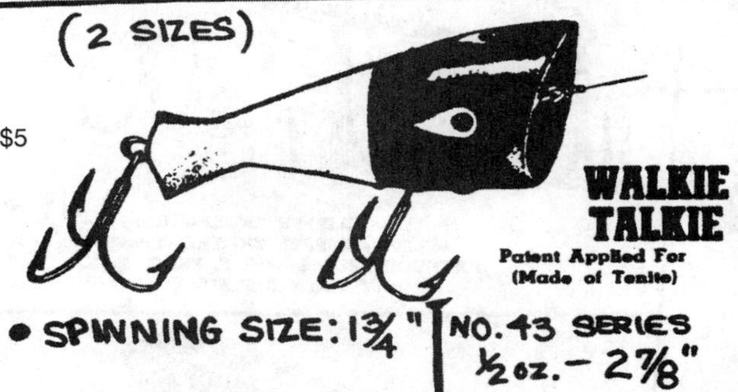

WALKIE TALKIE

Patent Applied For
(Made of Tenite)

• SPINNING SIZE: 1¾" | NO. 43 SERIES ½ oz. – 2⅞"

$2

P. & K. WHIRL-A-WAY

NEW-1942

3" — 5/8 oz.

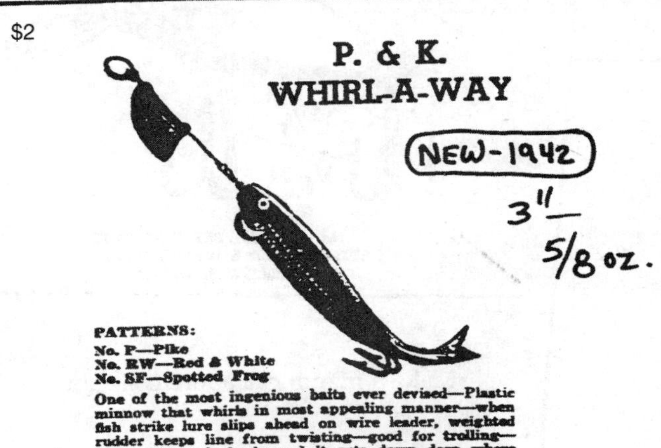

PATTERNS:
No. P—Pike
No. RW—Red & White
No. SF—Spotted Frog

One of the most ingenious baits ever devised—Plastic minnow that whirls in most appealing manner—when fish strike lure slips ahead on wire leader, weighted rudder keeps line from twisting—good for trolling—in casting reel slowly and, it gets down deep where the big fellows hang out. Good for Bass, Pickerel, Salmon, Trout.

Minnow 3" long, wire leader 3½", weight ⅝ oz.

THE SALT WATER WALKIE TALKIE

$5

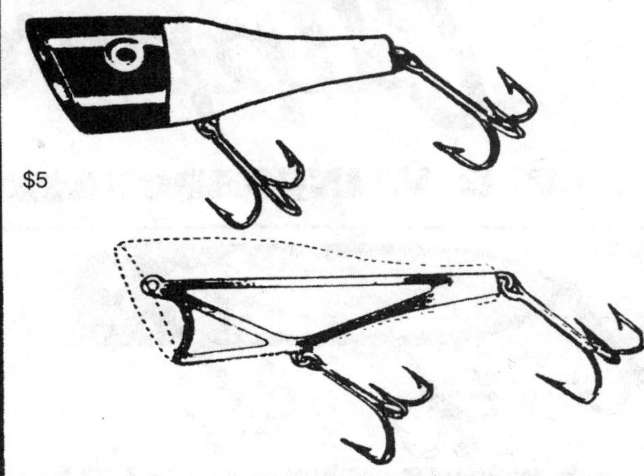

A new casting or trolling lure for salt water. Ideal for Striped Bass, Channel Bass (Red Fish), Mackerel, Barracuda, Kingfish, Tarpon, Snook (Robalo), Weakfish—also for fresh water Muskie, Northerns and Lake Trout. When surf casting, can be retrieved steadily—does away with jerk and wind—rod always in position to set hook on strike.

Made of durable wood, specially treated to protect against action of salt water, and moisture absorption. Reinforced brass hook holding device, riveted and cemented into body, makes it impossible for fish to tear hooks from lure.

No. 5/0 Belly Hook, No. 7/0 extra strong tail hook.
No. 62 RW (Red & White) **No. 62 B (Blue Scale)**
No. 62 BS (Brown Scale) **No. 62 S (Silver)**
No. 62— Price: **each. Weight 3½ oz. Length 5½ inches.**

$5

½ oz.
2¾"

BRIGHT EYES

NO. 44 SERIES

Patent Applied For
(Made of Tenite)

SPINNING MINNIE

(TENITE)

• FLY ROD SIZE: 1¼"

CASTING SIZE: • 3¼"

$5

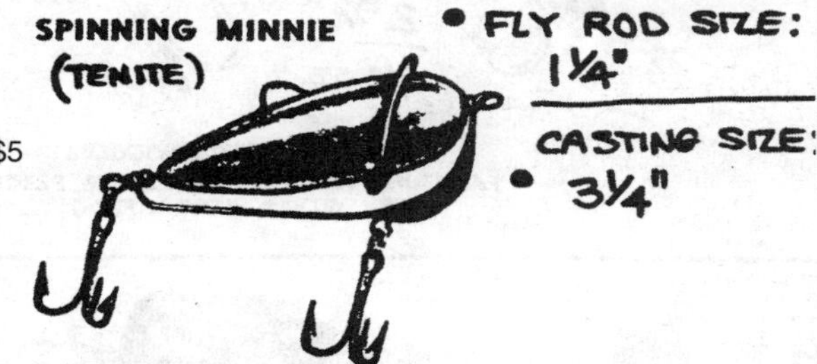

$5

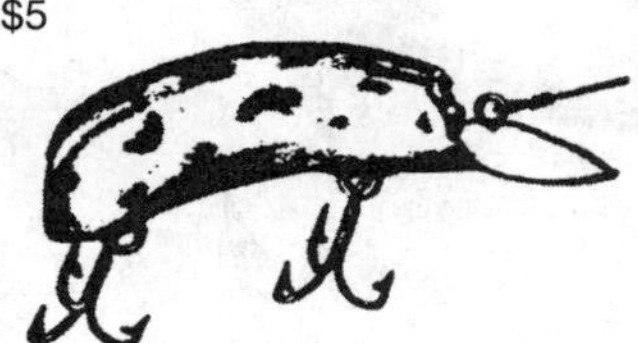

DEEP RUNNING BRIGHT EYES

Same as above, but has metal lip. Exceptionally deep runnin[g] —will not float!
Cat. No. DR44—Color code same as above.

NO. DR44 (SINKER)

Clipper Lures

P & K INCORPORATED – 122 N. Dixie Highway —Momence, Illinois

$5

No. 501 — CLIPPER BASS WOBBLER (Small) -2½"-½ oz.
No. 502 — CLIPPER BASS WOBBLER (Large) -3¾"-⅝ oz.
PATTERNS: RED & WHITE, YELLOW PERCH, PIKE, SILVER FLITTER

$5

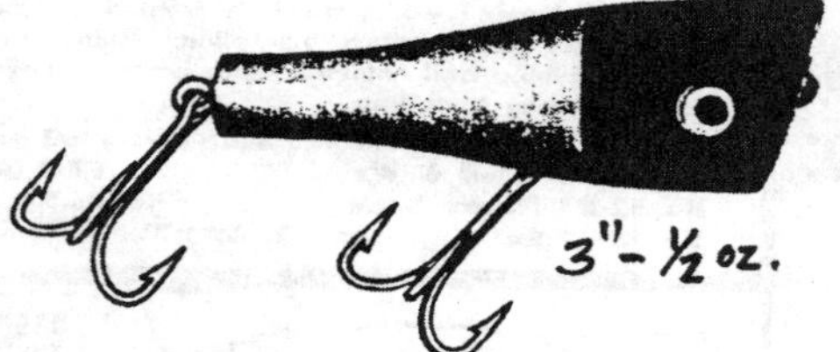
3"-½ oz.

No. 503 — CLIPPER TOP KICK
PATTERNS: RED & WHITE, YELLOW PERCH, PIKE, SILVER FLITTER, FROG

$5

2¾"
½ oz

No. 500 — CLIPPER WIGGLER
PATTERNS: RED & WHITE, YELLOW PERCH, PIKE, SILVER FLITTER, FROG

$5

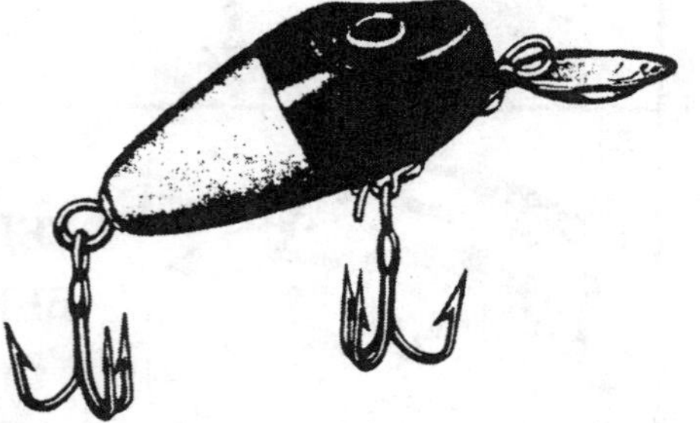

No. 511—CLIPPER WIGGLER (Small)
PATTERNS: RED & WHITE, FROG, PIKE

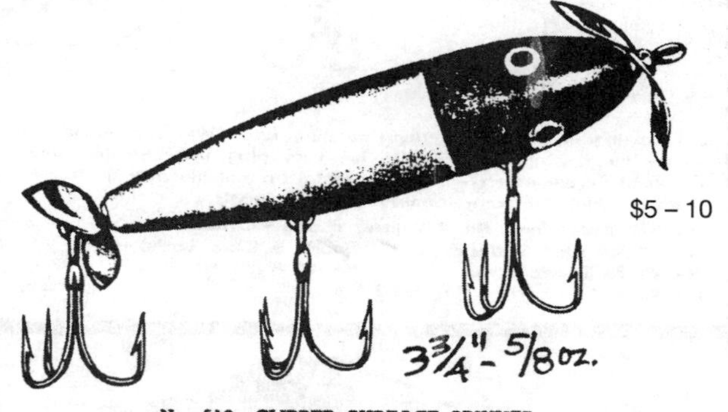
3¾"-⅝ oz.

$5 – 10

No. 512—CLIPPER SURFACE SPINNER
PATTERNS: RED & WHITE, FROG, PIKE

$5

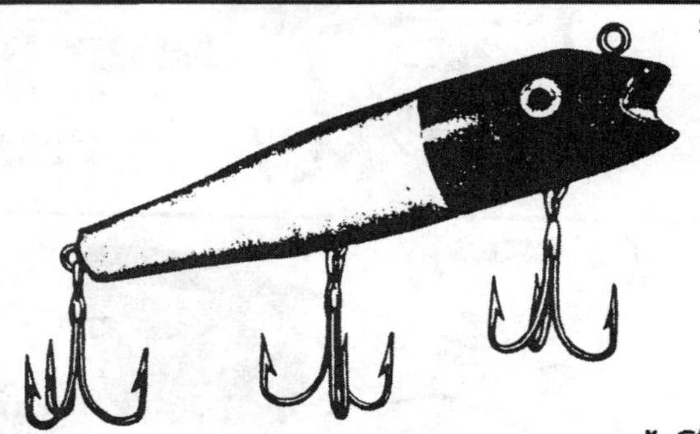

No. 508—CLIPPER ZIG-ZAG (Large) -4"-⅝ oz.
No. 509—CLIPPER ZIG-ZAG (Small) -3"-½ oz.
PATTERNS: RED & WHITE, FROG, PIKE, YELLOW & BLACK

$5

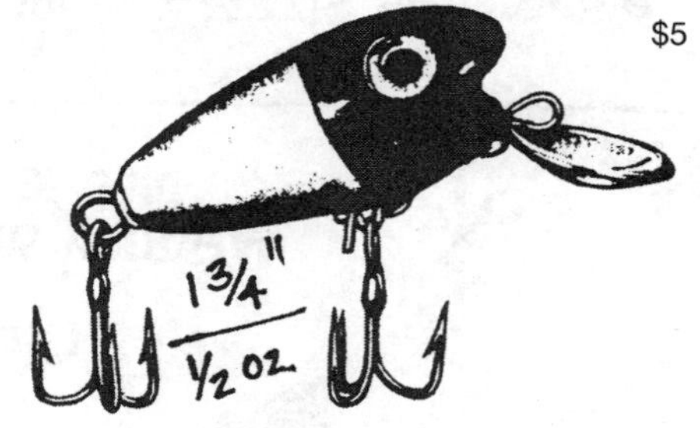
1¾"
½ oz.

No. 510—CLIPPER TINY MITE
PATTERNS: RED & WHITE, FROG, PIKE, YELLOW & BLACK

Make a friend; call a lure collector.

P & K LIVE RUBBER BAITS

$5

Spotty THE WONDER FROG

The only frog with knee action! Made of soft, tough, LIVE rubber and will last indefinitely. Absolutely natural in color. Always land right side up and can be fished in any water. Weedless.

No. 2—Fly rod size. 1/16 oz.

No. 201—Bait rod size. 5/8 oz.

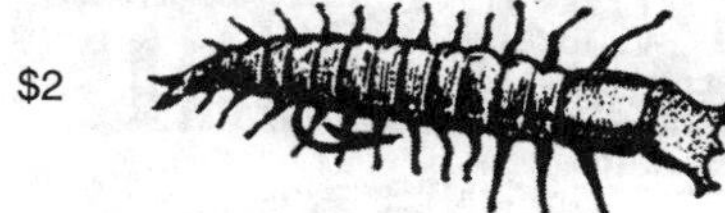

$2

HELLGRAMMITE

No more searching under rocks for this fellow. Here is a well made live rubber bait so real you can almost see him crawl.

No. 8, large. No. 1/0 hook. No. 801, small. No. 6 hook.

2 SIZES:

$5

FLY ROD RUBBER MOUSE. 2" – 1/16 oz.

$5

RUBBER MOUSE

Surface lure made of tough, live rubber that lasts indefinitely.

Looks and swims like a real live mouse. The cups on sides make ripples when retrieving that gives Mr. Bass visions of a good meal—but fish it slow, with pauses, and you'll be the one to eat. Best time early evening and nighttime. Best places among the lily pads.

Cat. No. 26-7—5/8 oz.,

(ALSO MADE WITH WEEDLESS TREBLE)

$2

SOFTY, THE WONDER CRAB

Ends your soft shell crab bait worries. The greatest of all P & K fishing aids yet introduced. Nothing else like it to be found. In color, form and appearance looks and feels like a real soft shell crab. Made of soft, tough, live rubber. Lasts indefinitely. Mounted on a high quality hook. Weedless. Faithful balance and design give Softy the natural wriggling action of a real live crab such as you've never seen before. In 4 sizes.

No. 103—Bait Rod—Weedless—5/8 oz.—No. 4/0 hook (4 SIZES)

No. 102—Medium—Weedless—1/2 oz.—No. 3/0 hook

Individually boxed. Shipping wgt., doz., 1 lb.

No. 101 Fly Rod No. 1/0 hook 1/16 oz.

No. 1 Midget Fly No. 8 single 1/32 oz.

$2

SHINER

Looks like, acts like, feels like and is a natural color, life like shiner. Plays no favorites. Catches them all. Will definitely outsell many other types of baits.

No. 401—Bait rod, weighs 5/8 oz., No. 1 Treble hook. Individually boxed. Shipping wgt., per doz., 1 lb., No 4—Fly rod, 1/32 oz., No. 1 hook.

RUBBER SHINER

$2

Looks, feels and swims like a real shiner, weedless, for casting or trolling. Cup on front end makes it dive and rise in a most natural manner. Length 4¼ inches.

$5

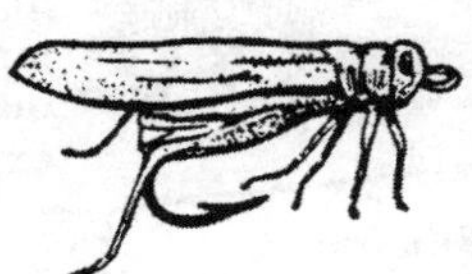

GRASSHOPPER

Another amazing reproduction of the real thing. Holding and looking at this live rubber reproduction in natural color makes one wonder how this life likeness can be attained. Every real fisherman will want this number once he sees it.

No. 6, large. 1/16 oz. No. 2 hook. No. 601, small. 1/32 oz. No. 6 hook.

Condition = value.

P & K POPPING FROG

$2

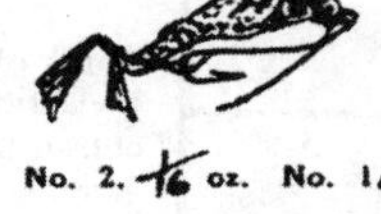

This old favorite P & K Lure has been newly designed. Realistic rubber frog, with hollow nose for use as popper. Has knee action.

No. 2. 1/16 oz. No. 1/0 Single hook.

Lures in this book are priced in very good to very good+ condition. Lures in the correct original box, lures in excellent to mint condition, and lures in special order colors are worth considerably more.

FOR A PERFECT DAY·USE P&K!

PACHNER & KOLLER, INC.

NOTE: 2 ADDRESSES & 2 NAMES.

PACHNER & KOLLER INC.
3444 ARCHER AVENUE
CHICAGO 8, ILLINOIS

P & K INCORPORATED 122 N. Dixie Highway Momence, Illinois

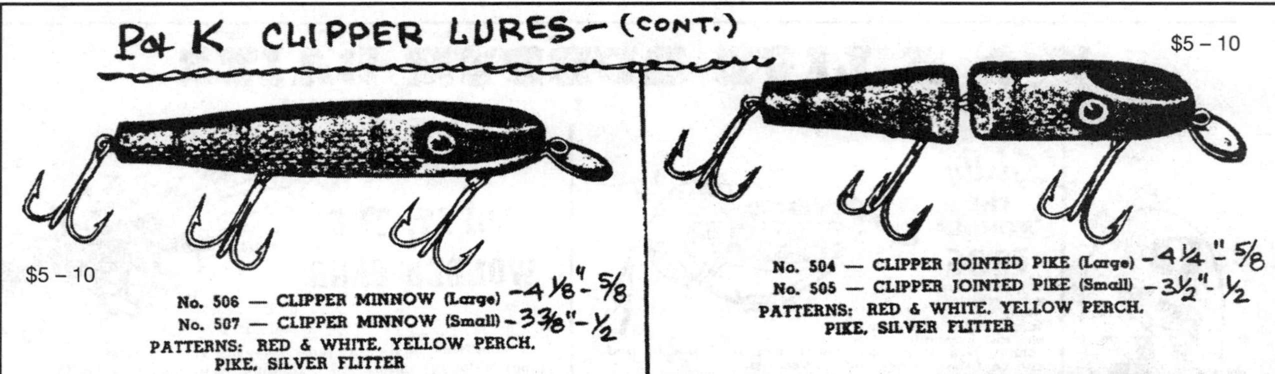
P&K CLIPPER LURES – (CONT.)
$5 – 10
$5 – 10
No. 506 — CLIPPER MINNOW (Large) -4 1/8" - 5/8
No. 507 — CLIPPER MINNOW (Small) - 3 3/8" - 1/2
PATTERNS: RED & WHITE, YELLOW PERCH, PIKE, SILVER FLITTER
No. 504 — CLIPPER JOINTED PIKE (Large) - 4 1/4" - 5/8
No. 505 — CLIPPER JOINTED PIKE (Small) - 3 1/2" - 1/2
PATTERNS: RED & WHITE, YELLOW PERCH, PIKE, SILVER FLITTER

PAUL BUNYAN
leads the way!
With lures that catch the big ones!

LOOK to Paul Bunyan for lures that have been catching fish for *years* . . . proved baits that bring up the big ones . . . baits that are not an experiment!

$5

Paul Bunyan
ARTFUL DODGER
No. 2100

ACTUAL SIZE

1 1/4" - 1/25 oz.

$2

Paul Bunyan
DINKY
No. 1000

A fly rod lure with a unique and tantalizing action. It's a wood lure and fly combination. Comes in four attractive colors. Weight 1/20 oz.

Paul Bunyan
TRANSPARENT DODGER
No. 900

$5

4"

This bait darts, wobbles, dives and has the action of a crippled minnow. Made of transparent Tenite, the ribs and spine give the bait a skeleton appearance. An attractive lure for Bass, Pike, etc.

Length, 4 inches
Weight, 5/8 oz
Size 1/0 Treble Hooks (1939)

Colors: 900 C—Clear Transparent
900 R—Ruby Transparent
900 A—Amber Transparent
900 G Green Transparent
900 WR—White Opaque with Red Head
900 B—Black

Paul Bunyan
GUARANTEED BAITS
No. 2900
3" - 3/4 oz
$2
Brand New

Flasheye Weedless

Get the BIG ONES with Paul Bunyan GUARANTEED BAITS

Proven Baits You'll Need

(2) 3 1/2" A 3/4"
$2
NO. 1600

BUNYAN RUBY-EYE SPOON

Nickel or copper finish, recessed light-reflecting back ruby eyes with brilliants; 2 0 detachable hooks; 3 1/2" long, wgt. 9 10 oz. Giant size, 4 3/4", wgt. 2 1/8 oz. (1941)

NO. 2700

$2

FLOATING
WEAVER
2 3/4"

New, sensational, top-water Paul Bunyan bait! Grand "weaving" action. Recesses on back multiply light. Four finishes: White, Pike scale, silver or yellow; length 2 3/4", weight 3/4 oz. Price . . . .

Your Sporting Goods or Hardware Dealer
Send for New Paul Bunyan Catalog

PAUL BUNYAN BAIT COMPANY
529 So. 7th, Minneapolis, Minn.

(BABY) (13/16") RUBY SPOON
No. 2400

$2

(1/25 oz.)

Lures within this book are priced in very good to very good+ condition.

66 LUCKY LURE (Bunyan)

$2

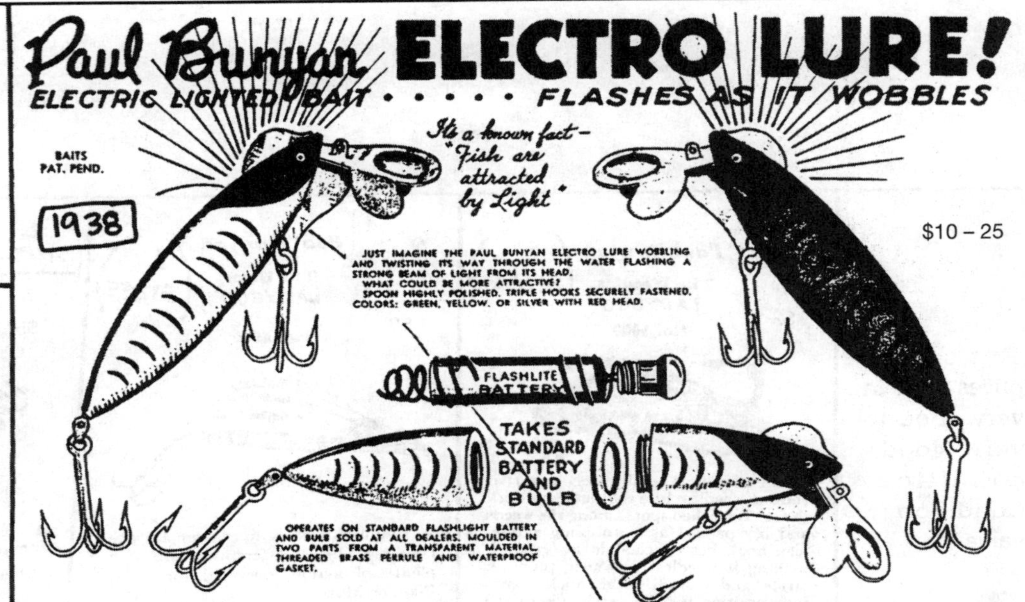

Paul Bunyan ELECTRO LURE!
ELECTRIC LIGHTED BAIT • • • • • FLASHES AS IT WOBBLES
BAITS PAT. PEND.
1938
It's a known fact — "Fish are attracted by Light"
JUST IMAGINE THE PAUL BUNYAN ELECTRO LURE WOBBLING AND TWISTING ITS WAY THROUGH THE WATER FLASHING A STRONG BEAM OF LIGHT FROM ITS HEAD. WHAT COULD BE MORE ATTRACTIVE? SPOON HIGHLY POLISHED. TRIPLE HOOKS SECURELY FASTENED. COLORS: GREEN, YELLOW, OR SILVER WITH RED HEAD.
FLASHLITE BATTERY
TAKES STANDARD BATTERY AND BULB
OPERATES ON STANDARD FLASHLIGHT BATTERY AND BULB SOLD AT ALL DEALERS. MOULDED IN TWO PARTS FROM A TRANSPARENT MATERIAL. THREADED BRASS FERRULE AND WATERPROOF GASKET.

$10 – 25

$5 – 10

Paul Bunyan

SILVER SHINER No. 1100
and
GOLD FISH No. 1200

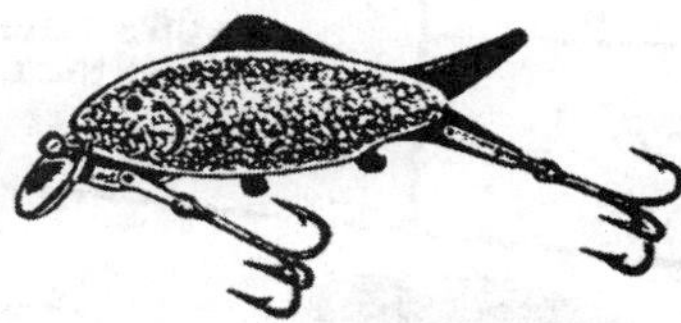

This bait is made of Pyrolin in attractive natural silver and gold colors which will not rust or tarnish. It floats half way out of water and maintains a perfect balance, but the scoop is so shaped that when bait is retrieved, it will cause it to travel at any depth desired. It's tops for Bass and surface fishing.

No. 1100—Silver Shiner
No. 1200—Gold Fish
Length, 3⅝ inches
Weight, 9/16 ounce
Size 1 Treble Hooks

$5 – 10

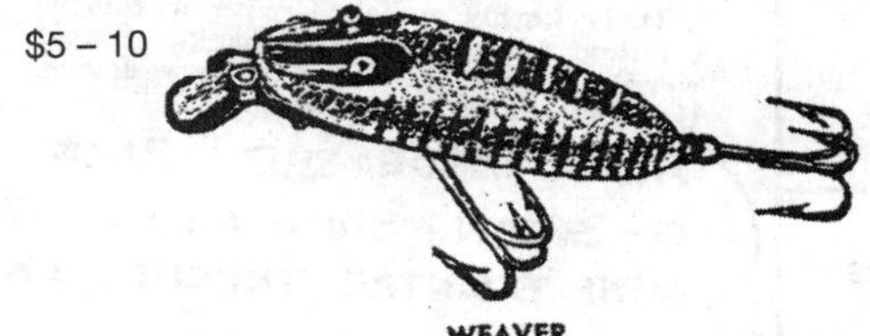

WEAVER

$5 – 10

Paul Bunyan
FLI SPOON
No. 3000

1¼" – 1/25 oz.

BABY SILVER SHINER AND GOLD FISH WITH SCOOP

$5 – 10

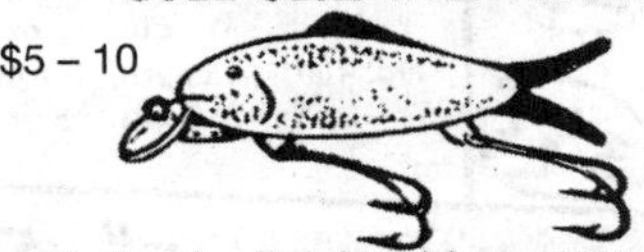

Made of celluloid with a natural silver or gold finish. Good for still fishing, casting, trolling and fly fishing. A larger double hook may be put in place of small front hook for larger fish.
Price ....
Length 1⅛". Weight ⅛ oz.
Two No. 8 Double Hooks.
Colors:
1800—Baby Silver Shiner.
2000—Baby Gold Fish.
1800 B—One No. 1 Double Hook.
2000 B—One No. 1 Double Hook.

(ALSO CAME WITH A WIRE LEADER & SINGLE SPINNER.)

THE PAUL BUNYAN MINNOW
No. 1250

$5 – 10

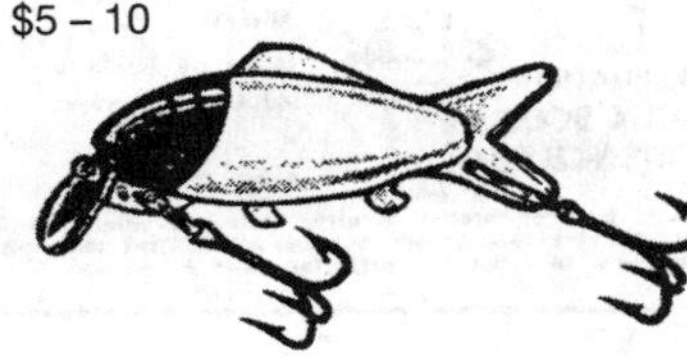

Made of Pyrolin and a real fish getter. This bait floats and has a perfect balance and natural swimming action in water, or will travel deeply according to the speed at which it is retrieved. Good for Bass, Pike, and all game fish.

No. 1250W—Minnow, white with red head
No. 1250P—Minnow, pikie finish

Length, 3⅝ inches 5/16 oz.

Paul Bunyan

MINNIE

No. 1600

$2 – 5

An amazing, life-like bait that ends forever the live minnow problem. Can be weighted for deep trolling or is equally effective as a surface lure. Made of wood, beautifully finished, complete with spinner.

Length, 2¼ inches
Weight, ⅛ ounce
Finish, 3 colors:
WR—White with red head
YS—Yellow with silver scale
BS—Black with silver scale

Paul Bunyan
PRESTO SINKER SET

$2

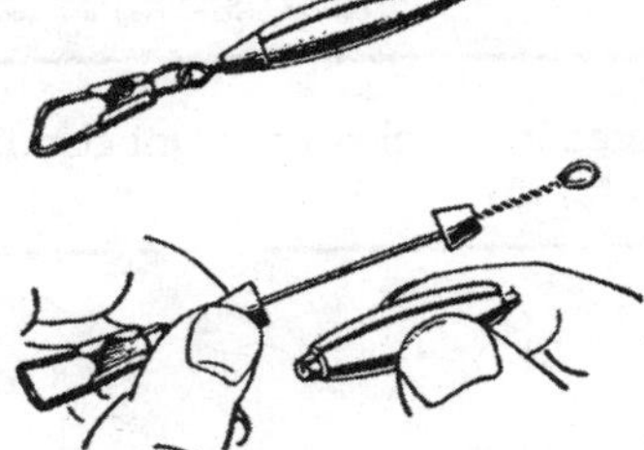

A must for every fisherman! Presto Sinker is the only changeable sinker on the market. At last, just what the fishermen have been looking for. To change sizes merely press the sinker against the spring and insert the desired size. (See illustration).

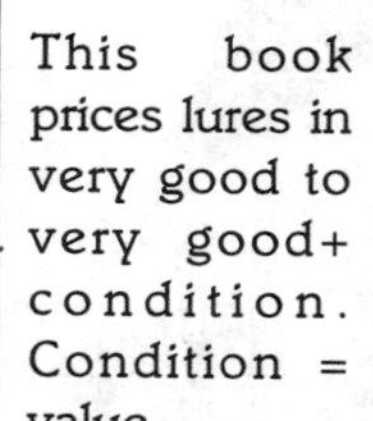
This book prices lures in very good to very good+ condition. Condition = value.

(2 SIZES)

Paul Bunyan

The Weedless LADYBUG

No. 5000

$2

This Ladybug is totally weedless. It is the one weedless lure that lets you work the seldom fished spots among the weeds and lily pads. Has a wobbling action. The hook lies couched in a "groove" making it weedless and snag proof. A strike and instantly the hook comes into position for the catch. (See cut.) Made of Tenite in the following sizes:

No. 5000—Length, 2½ inches (2½")
Weight, ½ oz.
Size 5/0 Hook

5001—Length, 3¼ inches (3¼")
Weight, ⅝ oz.
Size 6/0 Hook

Paul Bunyan

The Diver LADYBUG (2 SIZES)

No. 4000

$2

A Tenite bait that dives deep for the lazy, big fellows. A tempting lure with plenty of action, designed for Bass, Pike, or Muskies.

Equipped with a treble tail hook. Available in 2 sizes and 4 finishes.

No. 4000—Length, 2½ inches
Weight, ½ oz.

No. 4001—Length, 3¼ inches
Weight, ⅝ oz.

(2 SIZES)

Paul Bunyan

PAUL'S POPPER, Large

No. 1400

$5

A specially designed floating lure that can be made to pop and wobble. An excellent bait to use in shallow water and for night fishing. Should be retrieved in short jerks.

Length, 3½ inches
Weight, ¾ ounce

Finish, 4 Colors:
WR—White with red head
BS—Black with silver scale
YS—Yellow with silver scale
GF—Green Frog

Two Size 1 Treble Hooks
Packed—Individually Boxed.

Paul Bunyan

PAUL'S POPPER, Small

No. 1500

Same as above.
Length, 2¾ inches
Weight, [illegible] ounce

$2

CENTIPEDE SPINNER

5" – ⅝ oz.
METAL BAIT

CENTIPEDE SPINNER—"NEW AND DIFFERENT"
A BAIT WITH A CHANGE OF FACE. HAS A WONDERFUL TANTALIZING ACTION IN THE WATER. HEAD PIECE STANDS STILL AND ACTS AS A WEED DISPENSER AND LINE STABILIZER.
COLORS: NICKEL, COPPER, WHITE, PERCH, AND YELLOW. STATE COLOR

$5

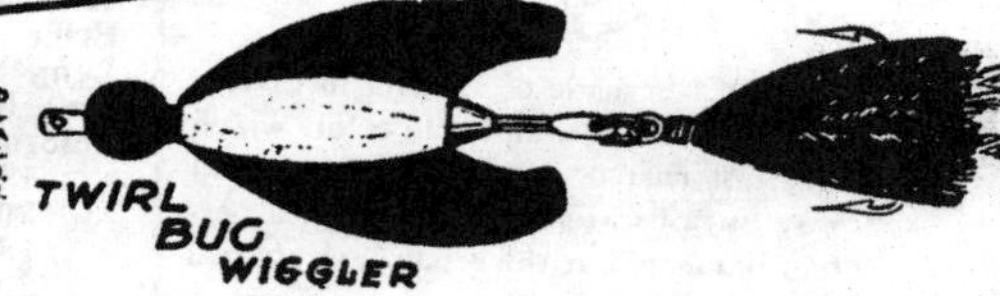

TWIRL BUG WIGGLER

TWIRL BUG WIGGLER
ATTRACTIVELY COLORED WINGS, TWIRL ON A MACHINED BEARING. HAS A WIGGLING, DARTING ACTION. COLORS: GOLD, PEARL, RED, AND SILVER.

$5

TRANS-LURE (TRANSPARENT)

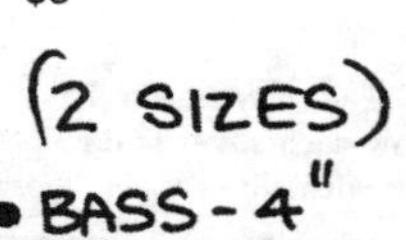
(2 SIZES)
• BASS - 4"
• PAN FISH
1¾"

FISH ALL DAY with One Bait That Houses Live and Artificial Bait

Trans-Lure Bass Size	INSERT-LIVE-BAIT OR 12 COMBINATION HEAD & BODY INSERTS INCLUDED	Trans-Lure Pan Fish Size
Length 4 In. Weight ⅞ Oz.		Length 1¾ In. Weight ¼ Oz.
Used as Casting or Trolling Lure		Used as Surface or Under-water Lure
S-BS --Trans-Lure		S-PS—Trans-Lure

Trans-Lure that houses live and artificial bait. Bait perforated to allow water to enter live bait living chamber. Lure has unseen air chamber to give lure proper balance when filled with water. Colored printed head and body inserts are included to make 144 artificial baits or spoons.

JEWEL WEEDLESS SPOON

$2

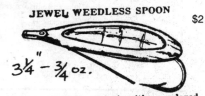

3¼" – ¾ oz.

It is highly polished with a colored celluloid raised inserted back. Single weedless hook, fastened by new device. Used with pork chunk or rind.

ALSO MADE THE "BUCK-O-SPOON – SAME AS ABOVE WITH BUCKTAIL TREBLE HOOK

Lures in excellent to mint condition or with original box have greater values.

$50 – 60

PEARL PLUG
1922

PEARL PLUG

A new and novel bait; head and tail end are red; centre of pearl fastened with two silver bands.

(THIS BAIT REMINDS ME OF A SALT & PEPPER SHAKER!)

$50 – 75

PAYNE BAIT CO.
3142 EDGEWOOD AVE.
CHICAGO, ILL.

1915

OPENS WHEN STRUCK

Payne's Woggle-Bug

Does not foul fish in body

Hooks all your strikes because the hooks are where the fish strikes, being held in the groove by an adjustable clip. Nearly impossible to foul fish in the body with the remaining hooks, while it is being played. Can be successfully used with weedless hooks, a set supplied

We make a specialty of Rod and Reel repairing. Send your Rods early before the rush of the Fishing Season.

$5

Phantom Minnows.

(Lengths given below include head and tail.)

Highest Quality Phantom Minnows.

No. 4.

Wherever live bait has been hard to get, anglers have for many years resorted to the Phantom Minnow as the most generally successful substitute for black bass trolling. Our **"Highest Quality"** Phantom Minnows are made of silk and rubber, with heavy twisted mist color gut trace. **When the fish is hooked, the Phantom slides up the trace.**

With bronzed treble hooks at tail, as illustrated above.
No. 4 (2¾ inches))
" 5 (3½ ") } ....
" 6 (4 "))

With large single O'Shaughnessy hook at tail. (Recommended for Southern waters.)
No. 5 (3¼ inches))
" 6 (4 ") } ....
" 7 (4¼ "))

Porpoise Hide Phantom Minnows—With Swivel.

Very durable and extra strong. Blue or Silver. For heavy fishing in Southern waters, such as Sea Trout, Crevalle, Red Drum, etc. Heavy treble hooks on 6-ply gut.

Nos.	5	6	7	8	9	10
Inches	3¼	4	4¼	4½	5¼	6

PHANTOMS ARE VERY OLD, (AND TO ME AT LEAST,) VERY DULL. THE ABOVE IS FROM A 1914 CATALOG. (THEY ORIG. CAME FROM ENGLAND.)

Look for pre-1950 fishing tackle.

-Hollow-
-Wood-
1949

PITT-KAN
LIVE ACTION
MINNOW

$5

The New
Helle's
Weedless
BALL
BAIT

$5 – 15

GUARANTEED
Weedless

ACTUAL SIZE

PROGRESSIVE
Tool & Mfg Co.
559 West Quincy St.
Chicago, U. S. A.

1927 LOOKS LIKE A TAKE OFF ON THE MOONLIGHT FISH NIPPLE?

PFEIFFER'S BAIT HOLDER

$100 – 250+

PAT. MARCH 3, 1914

"THE ORIGINAL TRANSPARENT BAIT HOLDER

MFG'D BY:
PFEIFFER LIVE BAIT HOLDER CO.
52 CLARK COURT
DETROIT, MICHIGAN

3 SIZES
- TROUT
- BASS
- MUSKIE

Lure collection is fun, tell a friend.

THE "P & S" Ball Bearing FLY-TROLL AND CASTING BAITS

THE "P AND S" BALL BEARING BAIT CO.
PRINCIPAL OFFICE
WHITEHALL, N.Y.
U.S.A.

FACTORY
SAYRE, PENN.
U.S.A.

1900 CATALOG

$5

STYLE M.

Upper spinner No. 1 nickel; and lower No. 2 polished brass, mounted on 4-ft. wire leader. Bright treble feathered hook. This bait is called *The King of all Baits*.

Trolling is a pleasure with P. & S. Baits.

Go slow and deep for success and big fish.

Examine our feathered hooks and those of other makes. No stiff quills to break.

NOTE: ONLY A FEW OF THEIR MANY STYLES ARE SHOWN HERE.

STYLE E.

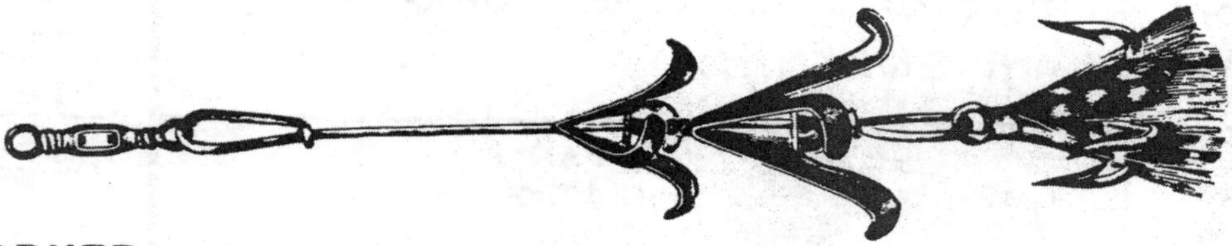

A LITTLE CORKER.

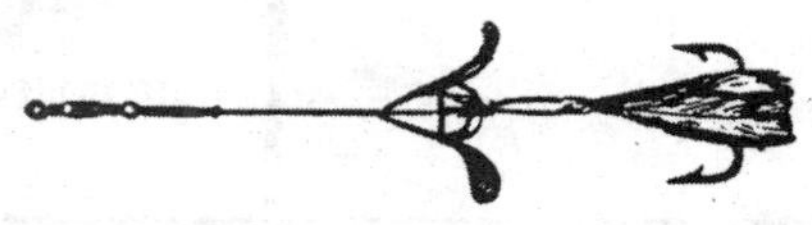

STYLE N.

This little bait is a winner for casting. Mounted with 0.size spinner and No. 1-0 treble hooks feathered.

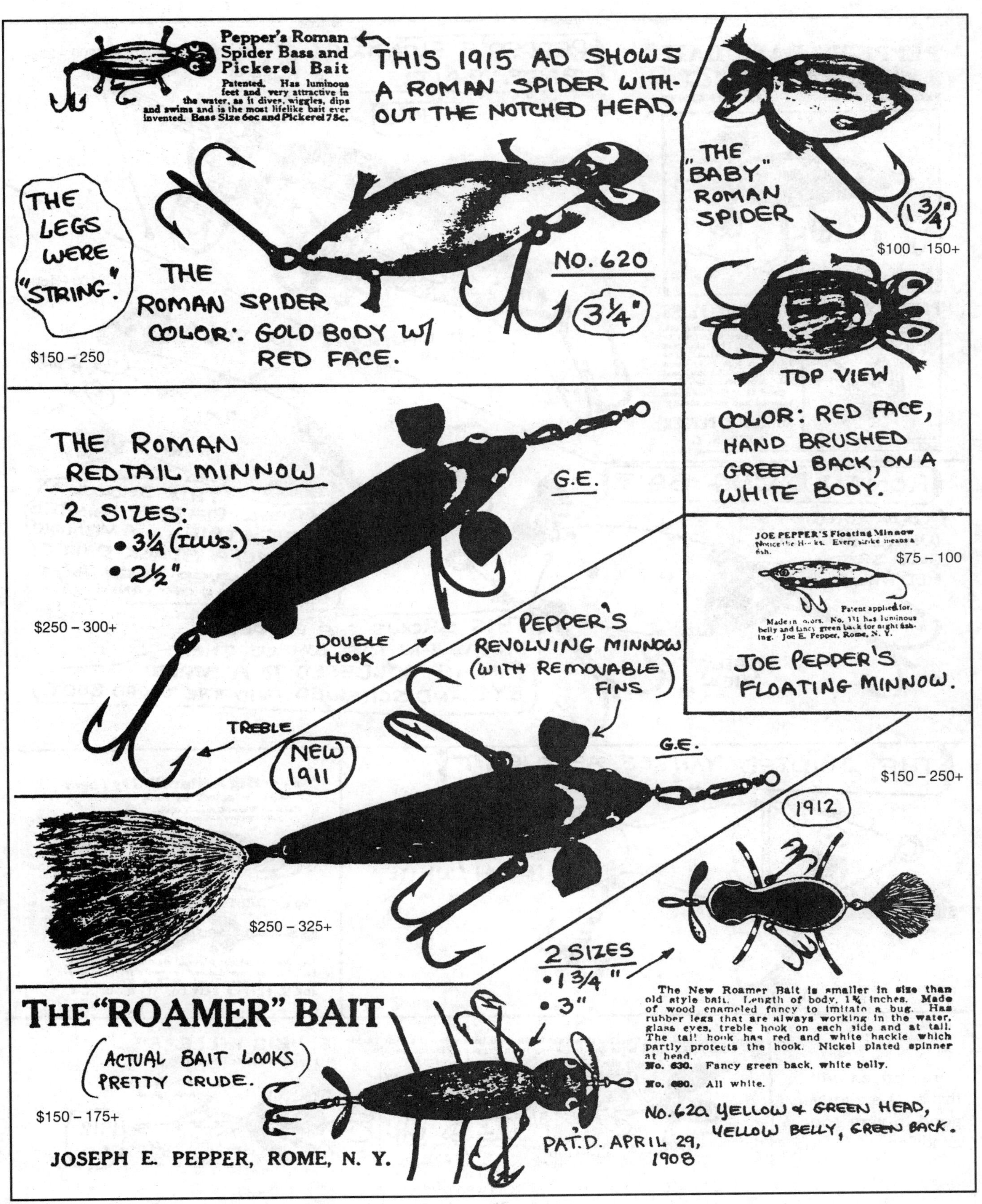
Pepper's Roman Spider Bass and Pickerel Bait
Patented. Has luminous feet and very attractive in the water, as it dives, wiggles, dips and swims and is the most lifelike bait ever invented. Bass Size 60c and Pickerel 75c.
THIS 1915 AD SHOWS A ROMAN SPIDER WITHOUT THE NOTCHED HEAD.
THE LEGS WERE "STRING".
THE ROMAN SPIDER
COLOR: GOLD BODY W/ RED FACE.
NO. 620
3¼"
$150 – 250
"THE "BABY" ROMAN SPIDER
1¾"
$100 – 150+
TOP VIEW
COLOR: RED FACE, HAND BRUSHED GREEN BACK, ON A WHITE BODY.
THE ROMAN REDTAIL MINNOW
2 SIZES:
• 3¼ (ILLUS.)
• 2½"
G.E.
$250 – 300+
DOUBLE HOOK
TREBLE
JOE PEPPER'S Floating Minnow
Every strike means a fish.
$75 – 100
Patent applied for.
Joe E. Pepper, Rome, N. Y.
JOE PEPPER'S FLOATING MINNOW.
PEPPER'S REVOLVING MINNOW (WITH REMOVABLE FINS)
NEW 1911
G.E.
$150 – 250+
$250 – 325+
1912
2 SIZES
• 1¾"
• 3"
THE "ROAMER" BAIT
(ACTUAL BAIT LOOKS PRETTY CRUDE.)
$150 – 175+
JOSEPH E. PEPPER, ROME, N. Y.
The New Roamer Bait is smaller in size than old style bait. Length of body, 1¾ inches. Made of wood enameled fancy to imitate a bug. Has rubber legs that are always working in the water, glass eyes, treble hook on each side and at tail. The tail hook has red and white hackle which partly protects the hook. Nickel plated spinner at head.
No. 630. Fancy green back, white belly.
No. 680. All white.
NO. 620 YELLOW & GREEN HEAD, YELLOW BELLY, GREEN BACK.
PAT.D. APRIL 29, 1908

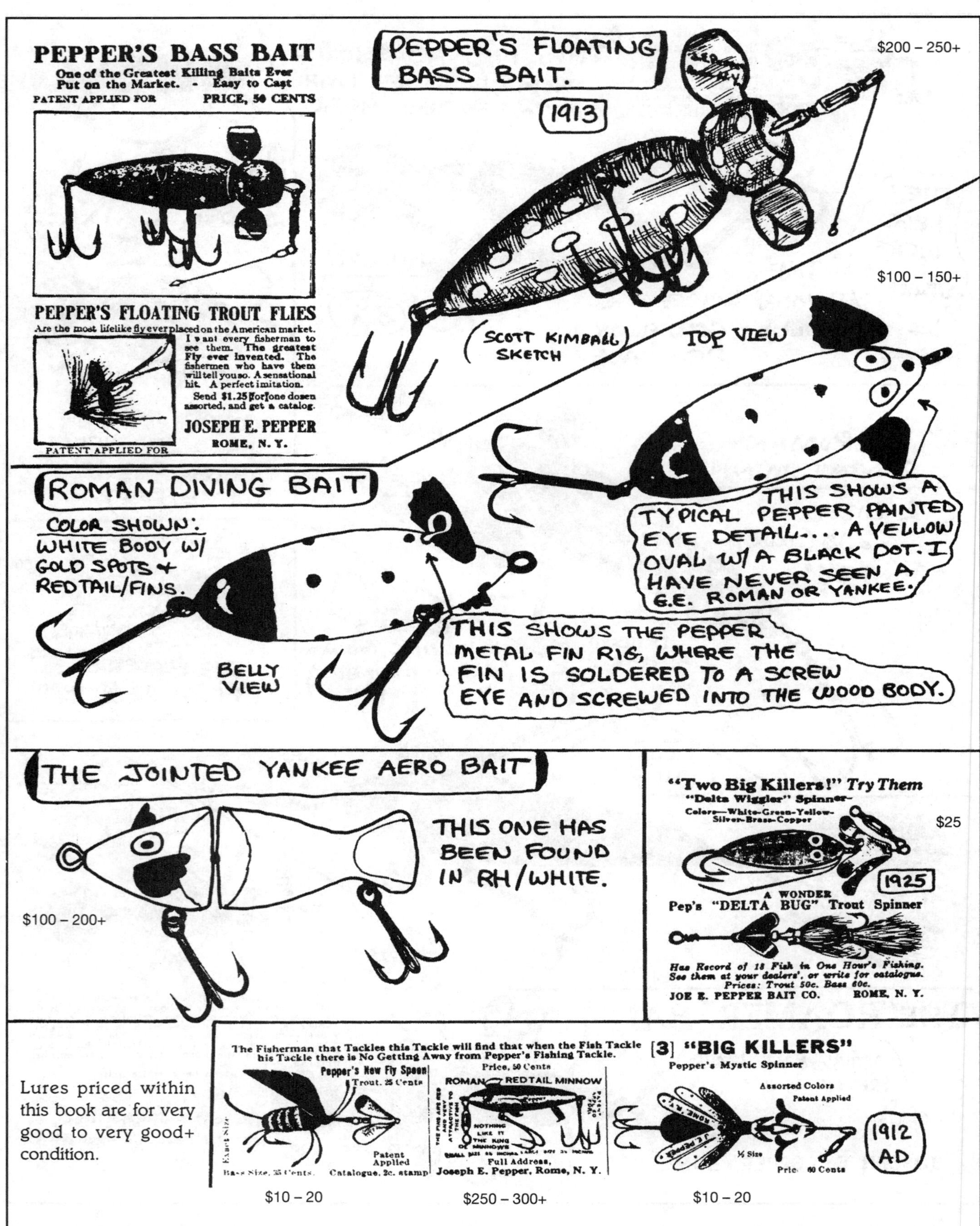
PEPPER'S BASS BAIT
One of the Greatest Killing Baits Ever Put on the Market. - Easy to Cast
PATENT APPLIED FOR
PRICE, 50 CENTS
PEPPER'S FLOATING TROUT FLIES
Are the most lifelike fly ever placed on the American market.
I want every fisherman to see them. The greatest Fly ever invented. The fishermen who have them will tell you so. A sensational hit. A perfect imitation.
Send $1.25 for one dozen assorted, and get a catalog.
JOSEPH E. PEPPER
ROME, N. Y.
PATENT APPLIED FOR
PEPPER'S FLOATING BASS BAIT.
1913
$200 – 250+
(SCOTT KIMBALL SKETCH)
$100 – 150+
TOP VIEW
THIS SHOWS A TYPICAL PEPPER PAINTED EYE DETAIL.... A YELLOW OVAL W/ A BLACK DOT. I HAVE NEVER SEEN A G.E. ROMAN OR YANKEE.
ROMAN DIVING BAIT
COLOR SHOWN: WHITE BODY W/ GOLD SPOTS + RED TAIL/FINS.
BELLY VIEW
THIS SHOWS THE PEPPER METAL FIN RIG, WHERE THE FIN IS SOLDERED TO A SCREW EYE AND SCREWED INTO THE WOOD BODY.
THE JOINTED YANKEE AERO BAIT
THIS ONE HAS BEEN FOUND IN RH/WHITE.
$100 – 200+
"Two Big Killers!" Try Them
"Delta Wiggler" Spinner
Colors—White-Green-Yellow-Silver-Brass-Copper
$25
1925
A WONDER
Pep's "DELTA BUG" Trout Spinner
Has Record of 18 Fish in One Hour's Fishing. See them at your dealers', or write for catalogue. Prices: Trout 50c. Bass 60c.
JOE E. PEPPER BAIT CO. ROME, N. Y.
Lures priced within this book are for very good to very good+ condition.
The Fisherman that Tackles this Tackle will find that when the Fish Tackle his Tackle there is No Getting Away from Pepper's Fishing Tackle.
Pepper's New Fly Spoon
Trout. 25 Cents
Exact Size
Patent Applied
Bass Size, 35 Cents.
Catalogue, 2c. stamp
Price, 50 Cents
ROMAN REDTAIL MINNOW
NOTHING LIKE IT
THE KING OF MINNOWS
Full Address,
Joseph E. Pepper, Rome, N. Y.
[3] "BIG KILLERS"
Pepper's Mystic Spinner
Assorted Colors
Patent Applied
½ Size
Price 60 Cents
1912 AD
$10 – 20
$250 – 300+
$10 – 20

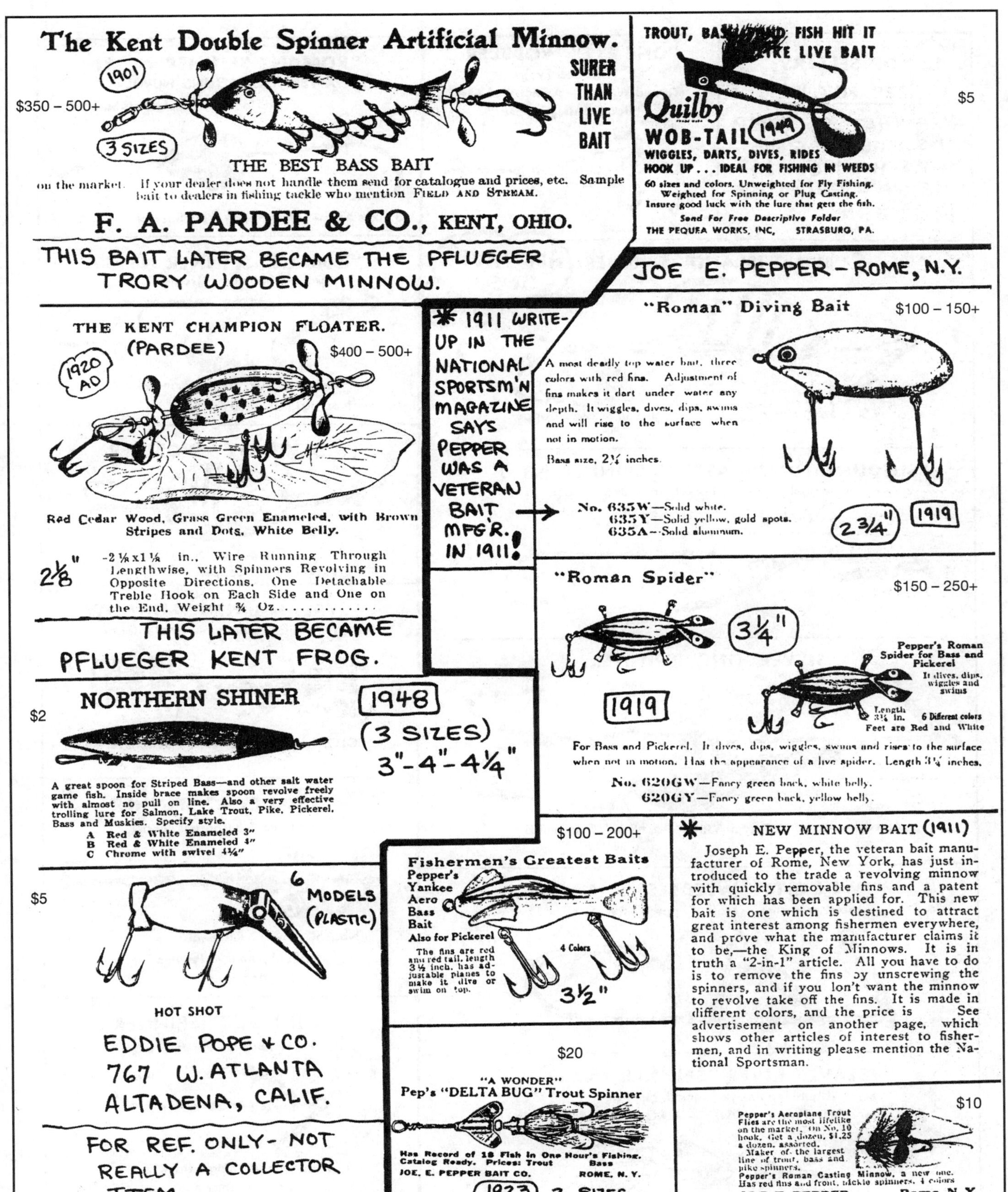
The Kent Double Spinner Artificial Minnow.
1901
$350 – 500+
3 SIZES
SURER THAN LIVE BAIT
THE BEST BASS BAIT
on the market. If your dealer does not handle them send for catalogue and prices, etc. Sample bait to dealers in fishing tackle who mention FIELD AND STREAM.
F. A. PARDEE & CO., KENT, OHIO.
THIS BAIT LATER BECAME THE PFLUEGER TRORY WOODEN MINNOW.
LIKE LIVE BAIT
$5
Quilby
WOB-TAIL
1949
WIGGLES, DARTS, DIVES, RIDES HOOK UP... IDEAL FOR FISHING IN WEEDS
60 sizes and colors. Unweighted for Fly Fishing. Weighted for Spinning or Plug Casting. Insure good luck with the lure that gets the fish.
Send For Free Descriptive Folder
THE PEQUEA WORKS, INC, STRASBURG, PA.
JOE E. PEPPER – ROME, N.Y.
THE KENT CHAMPION FLOATER.
(PARDEE)
$400 – 500+
1920 AD
Red Cedar Wood, Grass Green Enameled, with Brown Stripes and Dots, White Belly.
2⅛"
-2⅛x1⅛ in., Wire Running Through Lengthwise, with Spinners Revolving in Opposite Directions. One Detachable Treble Hook on Each Side and One on the End. Weight ¾ Oz.............
THIS LATER BECAME PFLUEGER KENT FROG.
* 1911 WRITE-UP IN THE NATIONAL SPORTSM'N MAGAZINE SAYS PEPPER WAS A VETERAN BAIT MFG'R. IN 1911!
"Roman" Diving Bait
$100 – 150+
A most deadly top water bait, three colors with red fins. Adjustment of fins makes it dart under water any depth. It wiggles, dives, dips, swims and will rise to the surface when not in motion.
Bass size, 2¼ inches.
No. 635W—Solid white.
635Y—Solid yellow, gold spots.
635A—Solid aluminum.
2¾"
1919
"Roman Spider"
$150 – 250+
3¼"
1919
Pepper's Roman Spider for Bass and Pickerel
It dives, dips, wiggles and swims
Length 3¼ in.
6 Different colors
Feet are Red and White
For Bass and Pickerel. It dives, dips, wiggles, swims and rises to the surface when not in motion. Has the appearance of a live spider. Length 3¼ inches.
No. 620GW—Fancy green back, white belly.
620GY—Fancy green back, yellow belly.
NORTHERN SHINER
$2
1948
(3 SIZES)
3"-4"-4¼"
A great spoon for Striped Bass—and other salt water game fish. Inside brace makes spoon revolve freely with almost no pull on line. Also a very effective trolling lure for Salmon, Lake Trout, Pike, Pickerel, Bass and Muskies. Specify style.
A Red & White Enameled 3"
B Red & White Enameled 4"
C Chrome with swivel 4¼"
$5
6 MODELS (PLASTIC)
HOT SHOT
EDDIE POPE & CO.
767 W. ATLANTA
ALTADENA, CALIF.
FOR REF. ONLY - NOT REALLY A COLLECTOR ITEM.
$100 – 200+
Fishermen's Greatest Baits
Pepper's Yankee Aero Bass Bait
Also for Pickerel
The fins are red and red tail, length 3½ inch, has adjustable planes to make it dive or swim on top.
4 Colors
3½"
* NEW MINNOW BAIT (1911)
Joseph E. Pepper, the veteran bait manufacturer of Rome, New York, has just introduced to the trade a revolving minnow with quickly removable fins and a patent for which has been applied for. This new bait is one which is destined to attract great interest among fishermen everywhere, and prove what the manufacturer claims it to be,—the King of Minnows. It is in truth a "2-in-1" article. All you have to do is to remove the fins by unscrewing the spinners, and if you don't want the minnow to revolve take off the fins. It is made in different colors, and the price is See advertisement on another page, which shows other articles of interest to fishermen, and in writing please mention the National Sportsman.
$20
"A WONDER"
Pep's "DELTA BUG" Trout Spinner
Has Record of 18 Fish in One Hour's Fishing. Catalog Ready. Prices: Trout Bass
JOE. E. PEPPER BAIT CO. ROME, N. Y.
1923 2 SIZES
$10
Pepper's Aeroplane Trout Flies are the most lifelike on the market. On No. 10 hook. Get a dozen, $1.25 a dozen, assorted.
Maker of the largest line of trout, bass and pike spinners.
Pepper's Roman Casting Minnow, a new one. Has red fins and front, nickle spinners. 4 colors
JOE. E. PEPPER Rome, N. Y.

12 TOP SELLERS

OFFERED FOR 1951

NOTE THAT JOE PEPPER WAS STILL MAKING BAITS IN 1951 – ALL THE WAY FROM PRE-1911 ERA.

"ONE-EYE" WOBBLER

(One Red-Eye)

(Turned Wings) — A Real Wobbler

Nickel, Brass, Copper

$5

Asst. to Doz.

"BLIND ISLAND" SPINNER

ALL ARE JOE PEPPER

$2

Kidney Shaped — Fluted

Nickel, Brass or Copper

"SUSQUEHANNA" CASTING SPINNER No. 7

Minnow Hook

Nickel, Brass and Copper

$2

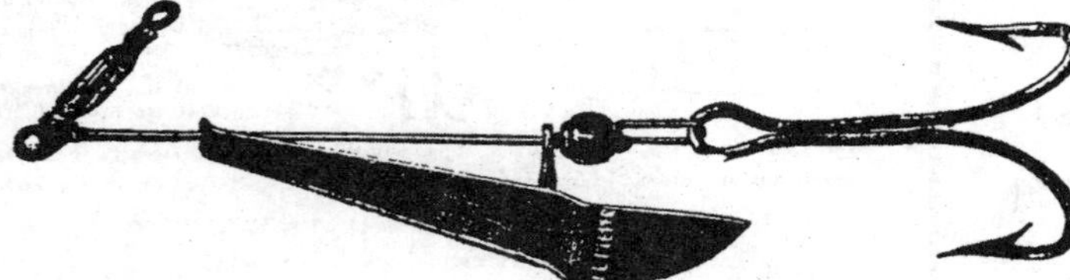

$2

"SILVER KING" SPINNER

All Nickel, Brass, Copper or White-Red, Nickel, Copper Tip

"TWIN CITY" WEEDLESS SPINNER

$2

Spinner in Nickel, Brass, Copper — RW Asst.

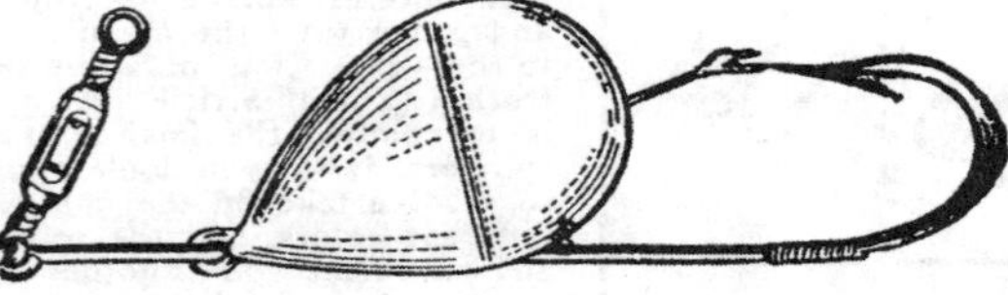

$2

"BEAVER RIVER" SPINNER No. 22

(Double spinner, one small, one large)

AN OLD TIME FAVORITE — A POPULAR SELLER

"ROMAN" SPINNER No. 71

A VERY FAST SELLING NUMBER

Single Hook — Nickel, Brass Spinner

$2

3 Sizes Asst. — Oval Shape, Very Special

"ROMAN" SPINNER No. 401

Double Spinner — Treble Hooks

$2

Nos. 301, 302, 303 — Minnow Hook

Nos. 401, 402, 403 Treble

"DEVIL-EYE" WOBBLER

$2

(Fluted) — Red-Eyes

Nickel, Brass, Copper

"STREAM-LINED" MINNOW

With Nickel Spinner — Treble Hooks

$5

COLORS: White, Red, Yellow-Red, Silver-Red

"RED-DEVIL" SPINNER

$2

(11 Red Transparent Beads)

No. 150 (Trout) 7 Red Beads

Nickel Spinner — Painted Eyes

No. 250

"JUNE BUG" SPINNER

Nickel, Brass, Copper — RW

$2

No. 1 (Small Spinner) Single Hook

No. 11 (Medium Spinner) Single Hook

No. 111 (Large Spinner)

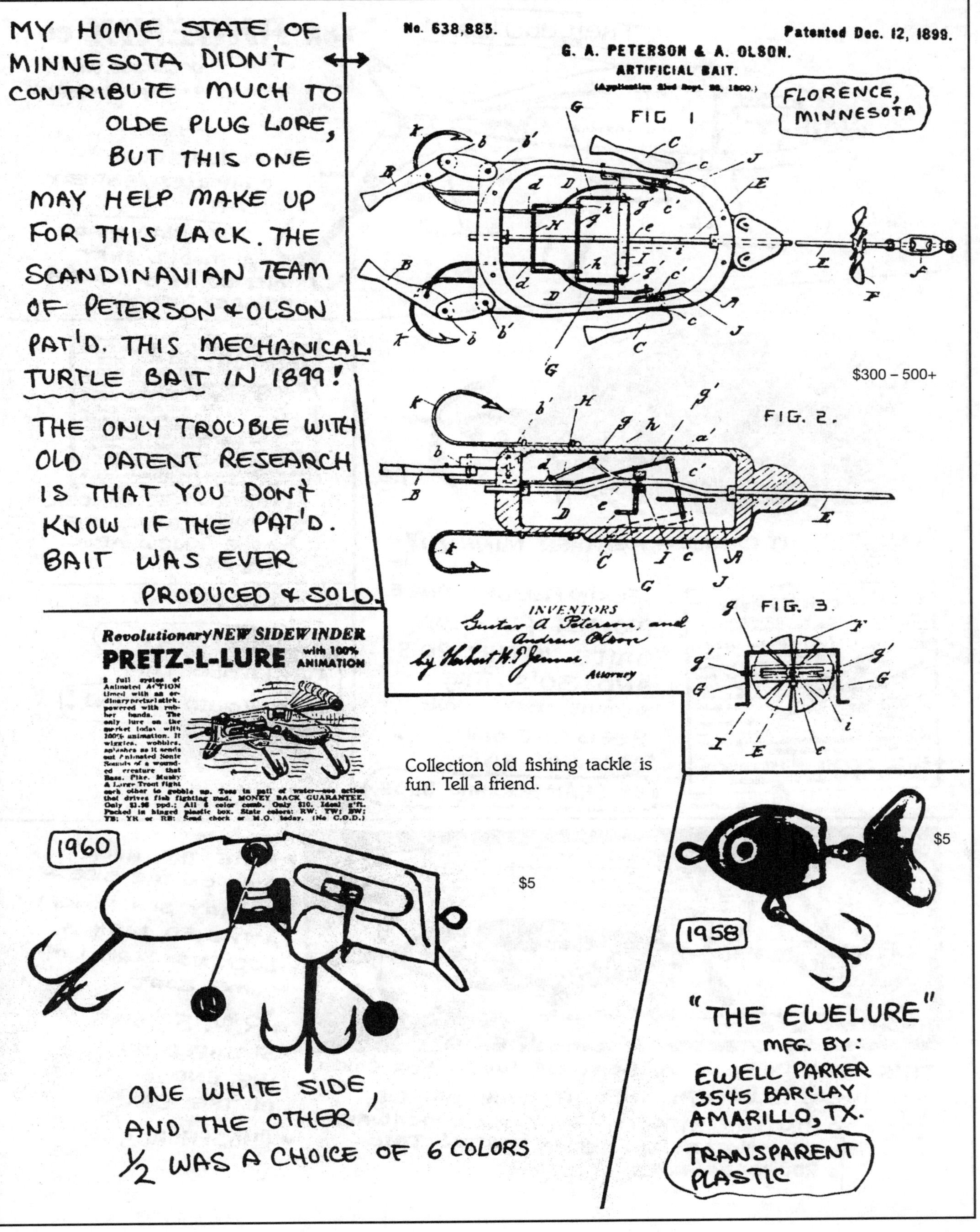
MY HOME STATE OF MINNESOTA DIDN'T CONTRIBUTE MUCH TO OLDE PLUG LORE, BUT THIS ONE MAY HELP MAKE UP FOR THIS LACK. THE SCANDINAVIAN TEAM OF PETERSON & OLSON PAT'D. THIS MECHANICAL TURTLE BAIT IN 1899!
THE ONLY TROUBLE WITH OLD PATENT RESEARCH IS THAT YOU DON'T KNOW IF THE PAT'D. BAIT WAS EVER PRODUCED & SOLD.
No. 638,885.
Patented Dec. 12, 1899.
G. A. PETERSON & A. OLSON.
ARTIFICIAL BAIT.
FLORENCE, MINNESOTA
FIG 1
FIG. 2.
FIG. 3.
INVENTORS
Gustav A. Peterson, and Andrew Olson
by Herbert W. Jenner
Attorney
$300 – 500+
Revolutionary NEW SIDEWINDER
PRETZ-L-LURE with 100% ANIMATION
2 full cycles of Animated ACTION timed with an ordinary pretzel stick, powered with rubber bands. The only lure on the market today with 100% animation. It wiggles, wobbles, splashes as it sends out Animated Sonic Sounds of a wounded creature that Bass, Pike, Musky & Large Trout fight each other to gobble up. Toss in pail of water—see action that drives fish fighting mad. MONEY BACK GUARANTEE. All 6 color comb. Only $10. Ideal gift. Packed in hinged plastic box. State colors: RW; YW; BW; YB; YR or RB: Send check or M.O. today. (No C.O.D.)
Collection old fishing tackle is fun. Tell a friend.
1960
$5
ONE WHITE SIDE, AND THE OTHER 1/2 WAS A CHOICE OF 6 COLORS
$5
1958
"THE EWELURE" MFG. BY: EWELL PARKER 3545 BARCLAY AMARILLO, TX.
TRANSPARENT PLASTIC

THE LULU BAIT

THE PHOENIX CO
OF CHICAGO, INC.
1913 N. Harlem Avenue • Chicago, Illinois 60635

$10

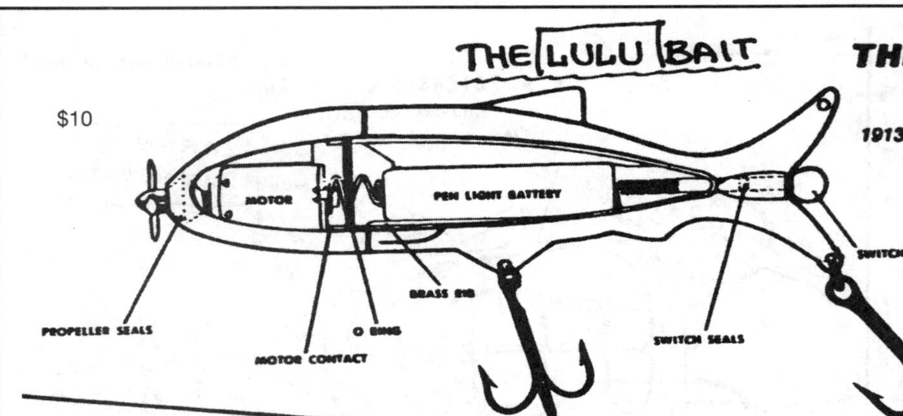
MOTOR
PEN LIGHT BATTERY
SWITCH
BRASS RIB
PROPELLER SEALS
O RING
MOTOR CONTACT
SWITCH SEALS

A MAIL ORDER PROPELLER/BATTERY BAIT.

THEY ALSO MADE A MODEL THAT OPENED TO BECOME A CIGARET LIGHTER.

$5

P.E.

"PECKS BAIT CASTING FEATHER MINNOW"

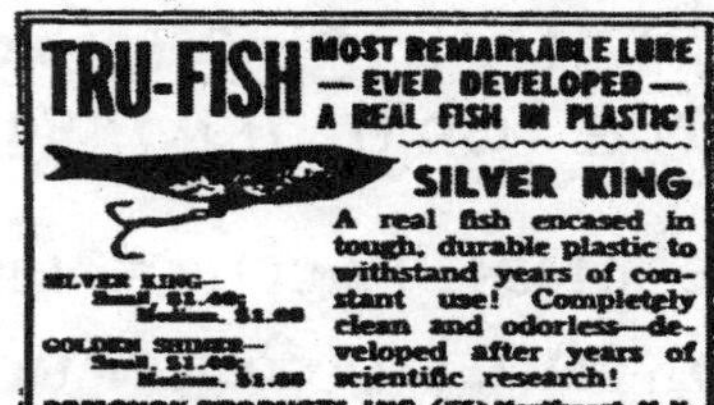
TRU-FISH
MOST REMARKABLE LURE — EVER DEVELOPED — A REAL FISH IN PLASTIC!
SILVER KING
A real fish encased in tough, durable plastic to withstand years of constant use! Completely clean and odorless—developed after years of scientific research!
POMONOK PRODUCTS, INC. (FS) Northport, N.Y.

$5

(1952 AD) I WONDER IF THE ACTUAL LURE PEOPLE KNEW ABOUT THIS?

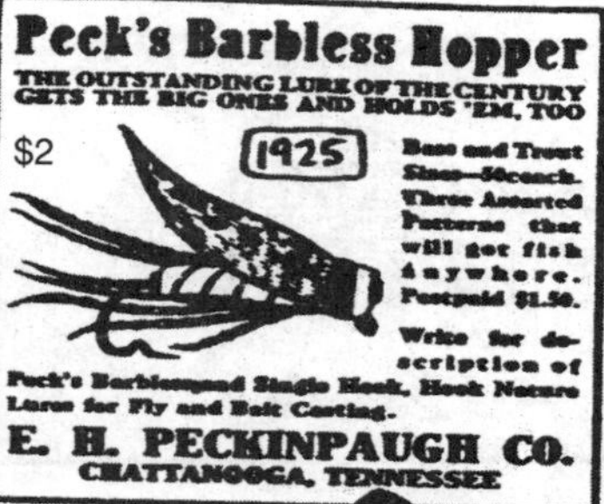
Peck's Barbless Hopper
THE OUTSTANDING LURE OF THE CENTURY
GETS THE BIG ONES AND HOLDS 'EM, TOO

$2

1925

Bass and Trout Sizes—50c each. Three Assorted Patterns that will get fish anywhere. Postpaid $1.50.

Write for description of Peck's Barbless and Single Hook, Hook Nature Lures for Fly and Bait Casting.

E. H. PECKINPAUGH CO.
CHATTANOOGA, TENNESSEE

PECKINPAUGH MADE MOSTLY FLY-ROD BAITS IN THE 20'S AND 30'S. THE ABOVE MAY HAVE BEEN THE ONLY "CASTING" BAIT.

34 CHAMBERLAIN BLDG.

THIS SPACE IS AVAILABLE FOR YOUR CONTRIBUTION!

PONTIAC MFG. CO.

THIS IS A COPY OF A BEAT-UP WOOD BOX COVER, BUT THERE IS ENOUGH INFO. TO MAKE AN I.D.

- PONTIAC MFG. CO.
- G.E. – ROTARY SIDE HKS.
- ROUNDED PROPS
- 5 HOOK UNDERWATER W/ BUCKTAIL TAIL HOOK.

- NOTE THE HOOK RIGS ON THE SIDE – (ROTARY SIDE HOOKS) ATTACHED WITH A LOCKING SCREW OF SOME SORT.
- "R.M.5." WAS STAMPED ON THE END OF THE BOX.
- PHOSPHORUS

$250 – 300+

STRI-PERT PLUGS

$1.80 EACH

POINT JUDE BAITS
POINT JUDITH, R.I

MADE H/DUTY STRIPER BAITS IN THE 60'S.

MADE:
- THE CUTLESS
- SWIM-A-LONG JOINTED
- WING-ADING SURFACE PLUG
- FLY-MITE SALT WATER FLYROD BAIT

(NEED MORE INFORMATION)

JIM PFEFFER
BOX 4164
ORLANDO, FLA.

$10 – 20

1952

JIM PFEFFER MIDGET SHINER

PFEFFER SUNFISH

$50 – 75+

PRE-1930

- 2 HOOK MODEL OF TOP SHINER – 2 5/8" – INS. MINO

$10 – 20

PFEFFER TOP SHINER

1952

PFEFFER STARTED MAKING LURES IN THE LATE 20'S. DENMARK SPORTING GOODS STORE (ORLANDO) SOLD THE ORIGINAL BAITS. THE FRESH-WATER SERIES WAS SHINER FINISHES – SILVER SPECKS ON A GREEN BACK W/ GOLD OR WHITE BELLY COLOR. PACKAGED IN A MANILLA ENVELOPE W/ "JIM PFEFFER, ORLANDO SHINER" ON IT. STOPPED PRODUCTION APPROX. 1960'S.

THE PEARL ROCKET BAIT

- TACK EYE
- FLUTED LIP
- LIP ATTACHED W/3 SCREWS

$10 – 15

WOOD

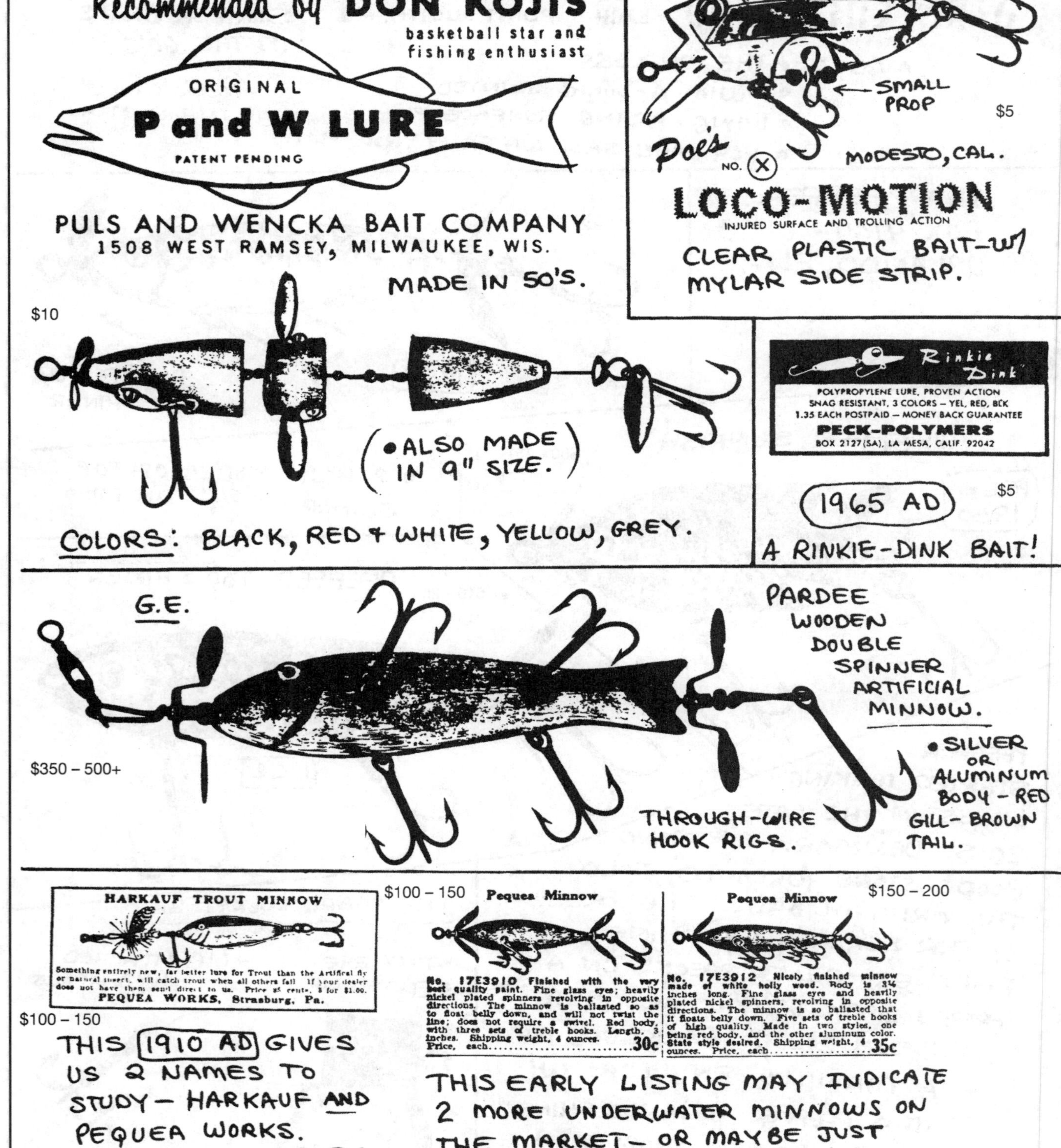
Recommended by DON KOJIS
basketball star and
fishing enthusiast
ORIGINAL
P and W LURE
PATENT PENDING
PULS AND WENCKA BAIT COMPANY
1508 WEST RAMSEY, MILWAUKEE, WIS.
MADE IN 50'S.
$10
(•ALSO MADE IN 9" SIZE.)
COLORS: BLACK, RED & WHITE, YELLOW, GREY.
MYLAR
SMALL PROP
$5
Poe's
NO. X
MODESTO, CAL.
LOCO-MOTION
INJURED SURFACE AND TROLLING ACTION
CLEAR PLASTIC BAIT-W/ MYLAR SIDE STRIP.
Rinkie Dink
POLYPROPYLENE LURE, PROVEN ACTION
SNAG RESISTANT, 3 COLORS – YEL, RED, BLK
1.35 EACH POSTPAID – MONEY BACK GUARANTEE
PECK-POLYMERS
BOX 2127(SA), LA MESA, CALIF. 92042
1965 AD
$5
A RINKIE-DINK BAIT!
G.E.
PARDEE WOODEN DOUBLE SPINNER ARTIFICIAL MINNOW.
$350 – 500+
•SILVER OR ALUMINUM BODY - RED GILL- BROWN TAIL.
THROUGH-WIRE HOOK RIGS.
HARKAUF TROUT MINNOW
Something entirely new, far better lure for Trout than the Artifical fly or natural insect, will catch trout when all others fail. If your dealer does not have them send direct to us. Price 35 cents, 3 for $1.00.
PEQUEA WORKS, Strasburg, Pa.
$100 – 150
$100 – 150
Pequea Minnow
No. 17E3910 Finished with the very best quality paint. Fine glass eyes; heavily nickel plated spinners revolving in opposite directions. The minnow is ballasted so as to float belly down, and will not twist the line; does not require a swivel. Red body, with three sets of treble hooks. Length, 3 inches. Shipping weight, 4 ounces. Price, each.........30c
Pequea Minnow
$150 – 200
No. 17E3912 Nicely finished minnow made of white holly wood. Body is 3¼ inches long. Fine glass eyes and heavily plated nickel spinners, revolving in opposite directions. The minnow is so ballasted that it floats belly down. Five sets of treble hooks of high quality. Made in two styles, one being red body, and the other aluminum color. State style desired. Shipping weight, 4 ounces. Price, each.........35c
THIS 1910 AD GIVES US 2 NAMES TO STUDY - HARKAUF AND PEQUEA WORKS.
DON'T KNOW IF RELATED TO THE PEQUEA MINNOWS →
THIS EARLY LISTING MAY INDICATE 2 MORE UNDERWATER MINNOWS ON THE MARKET - OR MAYBE JUST "JOBBING" SOME OTHER MFG.
EARLY COLORS - SOLID RED & ALUMINUM.

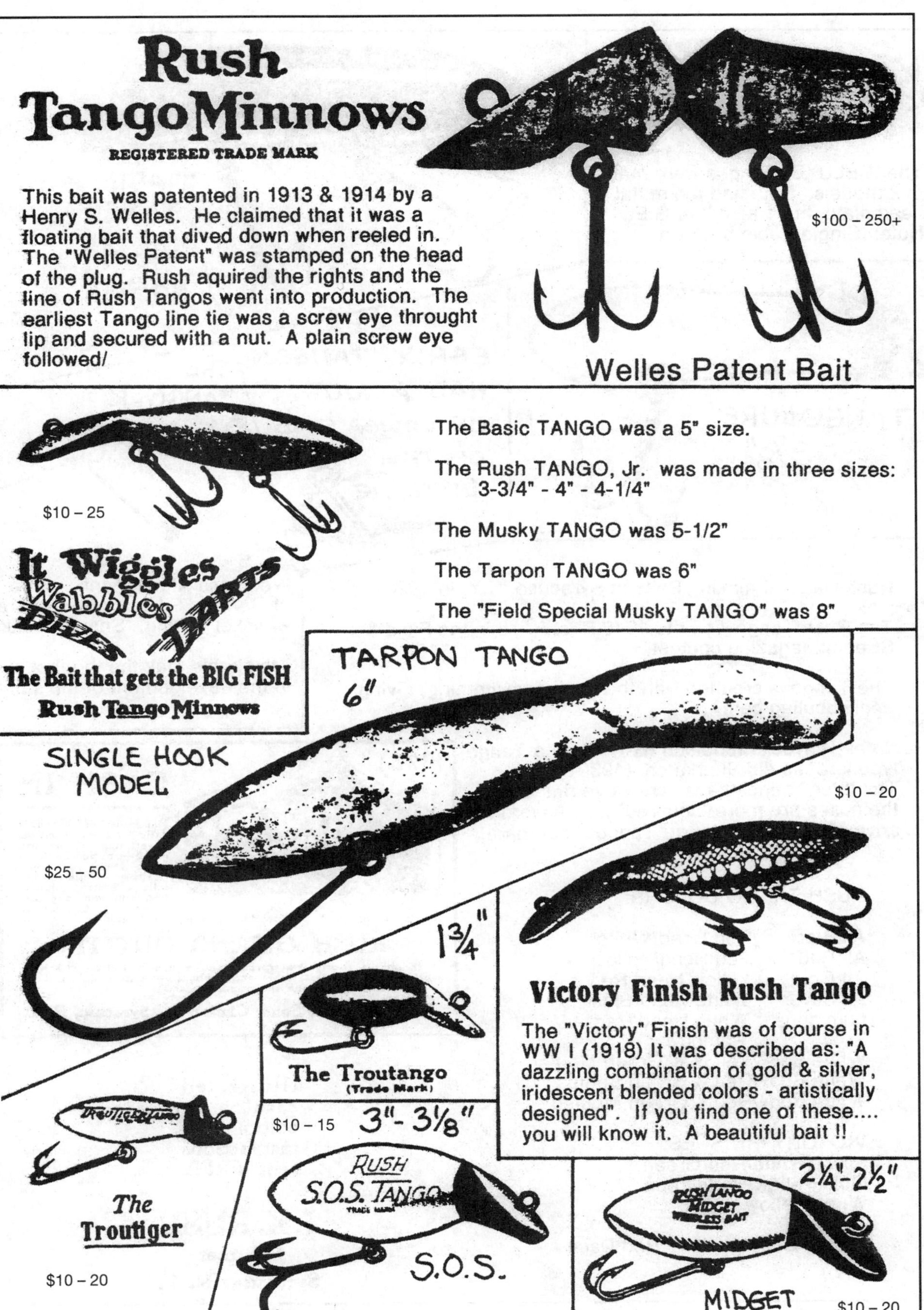

Rush
Tango Minnows
REGISTERED TRADE MARK
This bait was patented in 1913 & 1914 by a Henry S. Welles. He claimed that it was a floating bait that dived down when reeled in. The "Welles Patent" was stamped on the head of the plug. Rush aquired the rights and the line of Rush Tangos went into production. The earliest Tango line tie was a screw eye throught lip and secured with a nut. A plain screw eye followed/
$100 – 250+
Welles Patent Bait
$10 – 25
It Wiggles Wabbles Dives Darts
The Bait that gets the BIG FISH
Rush Tango Minnows
The Basic TANGO was a 5" size.
The Rush TANGO, Jr. was made in three sizes: 3-3/4" - 4" - 4-1/4"
The Musky TANGO was 5-1/2"
The Tarpon TANGO was 6"
The "Field Special Musky TANGO" was 8"
TARPON TANGO
6"
SINGLE HOOK MODEL
$10 – 20
$25 – 50
1¾"
The Troutango
(Trade Mark)
Victory Finish Rush Tango
The "Victory" Finish was of course in WW I (1918) It was described as: "A dazzling combination of gold & silver, iridescent blended colors - artistically designed". If you find one of these.... you will know it. A beautiful bait !!
$10 – 15
3"-3⅛"
RUSH
S.O.S. TANGO
The Troutiger
$10 – 20
S.O.S.
2¼"-2½"
RUSH TANGO MIDGET
MIDGET
$10 – 20

$50 – 75+

The "DELUXE" Tangos were made in 2 models. Both had the metal head plate, but 1 also had G.E. Note: Single treble hook rig.

TIGER
TANGO
3 7/8" - 4"
NO. 400

$10 – 25

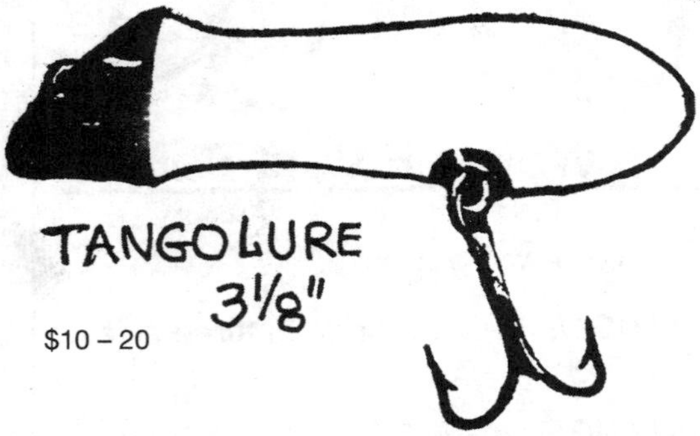

TANGO LURE
3 1/8"

$10 – 20

EARLY TANGOS HAD A NUT ON LOWER END OF THE LINE-TIE

THE TANGO-K

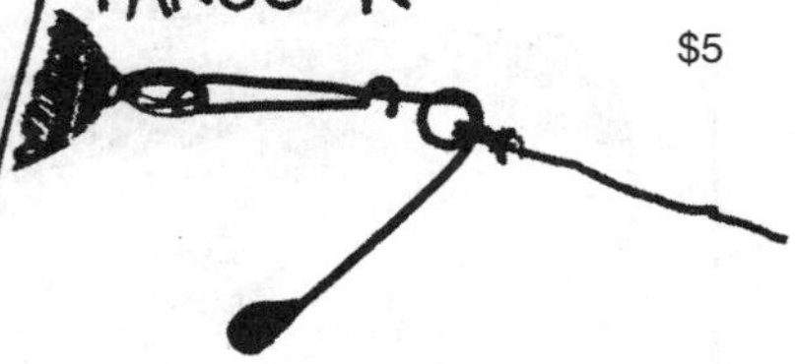

$5

Weedless Attachment - made of German Silver or Spring Brass w/nickel plating. "Snaps on Lure"

I think this may the the first step in the development of the safety pin lure.

Rush was still making Baits in Syracuse, N.Y. in 1928.

The Rush Tango won the 1916 First Prize in the Field & Stream Magazine contest,

The Tango is credited with the original swimming, diving, and wobbling bait.

Note: Horrocks Ibbotson (H-I) made a Tango type lure, as did Shurkatch. (1930's) The later Tangos have screw eye rigs and the noses are more "squared"........A word of advice......there's alot of "Tangos" out there.

RUSH TANGO COLORS:

All Black	Red Head/White
All Red	Red Head/Yellow
All Gold	Yellow Head/Red
All Silver	White Head/Black
Luminous	White Head/Red
	Rainbow

White Body/Yellow & Green Mottled
White Body/Red & Green Spots
White Body/Red & Green Mottled

VICTORY FINISHES:
Silver/White/Red/Green
Gold/Yellow/Red/Green
White/Yellow

Deluxe Scale Finish - Red Dace

(1923)

CASH IN

Hundreds of inquiries daily from our national advertising. There are many—probably hundreds from your own territory. Write for details of our co-operation and generous discounts on the most complete, compact, comfortable camping outfit—the

RUSH OUTING OUTFIT

4 in one—a roomy, waterproof tent, a double Deluxe bed with springs and mattress, table and cupboard—all in a 4 ft. x 1 ft. square trunk carried on the running board.

J. K. Rush, 640 South Clinton St., Syracuse, N. Y.

Illustrated catalog in colors with instructions sent FREE.

J. K. RUSH
F Street
Syracuse, N. Y.

Louis Rhead's NEW Nature Lures
For Trout, Bass, Pike, Pickerel and other Game Fishes of Fresh or Salt Water
Frogs that float and swim. Cannot float on its back. Made solid to last. Three kinds. Green leopard frog for eastern states. Brown pickeral frog for middle west. Red belly frog for Pacific coast states. True to life in form and color. Have a single powerful hook through the body. Small single hook under each hind leg. Floats with only head and shoulders above surface. Legs move like natural frog. Made under personal supervision and painted by inventor. None sent on approval, but money refunded promptly if dissatisfied and returned.
Sold for ONE DOLLAR EACH at
217 OCEAN AVENUE BROOKLYN, N. Y.
All unmarked lures, $50 – 100+ each
FLOATING DARTER MINNOW
FLOATING DARTER MINNOW
FOR BROWNS RAINBOWS AND BASS
$25
$25
LOUIS RHEAD'S
American Nature Flies
LOUIS RHEAD WAS A VERY INTERESTING PERSON
HE WAS:
Anti- Live Bait
Anti-Still Fishing
Anti-Treble Hooks
Anti-Wooden Chunks of Wood (Plugs)
Anti-Trolling
Anti-Rubber Lures
Anti-Sinking, Heavy Lures
Lamprey Eel - only "rubber" lure made by Rhead
Louis Rhead's New Artificial NATURE LURES
FOR TROLLING OR CASTING
Trout Minnows ....
Bass Minnows, large...
Bass Minnows, medium
"Shiny Devils" ....
Frogs ....
Crawfish ....
Helgamites ....
(1915-'20)
ILLUSTRATIONS ARE FROM L. RHEAD'S BOOK - FISHERMAN'S LURES and GAME - FISH FOOD
Schribner - N.Y. (1920)
$25

SOUTH COAST WOODEN MINNOW

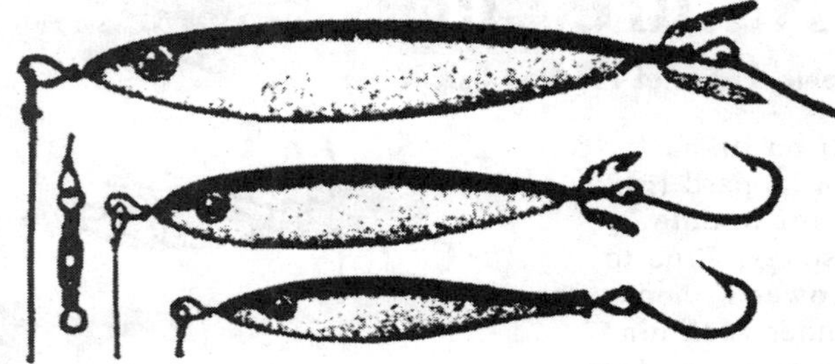

SOUTH COAST METAL MINNOW

$50 – 100 each

DR. H. C. ROYER'S SOUTH COAST MINNOWS (1908 - '12)

It is pretty well accepted that this bait was the forerunner to the Heddon Coast Minnow. His ads stopped about the time Heddon put their Coast Minnow into their line, name and body style are enuf clues for me at least.

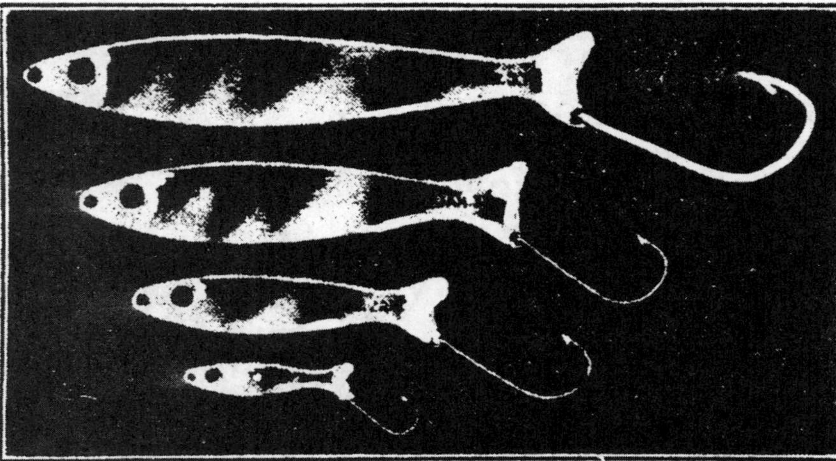

$20 – 25

The South Coast Minnow Co. has placed on the market in addition to the wooden minnow an all metal minnow made in 4 sizes, 4 inches, 3¼ inches, 2¼ inches and 1 inch, a Trout Size. The South Coast wood-n bait, is having a remarkable sale, and is classed by fishermen both inland and coast fishing as the best lure they have ever used. Dr. Royer the designer of these baits believes in simplicity and one hook. The South Coast baits has proven this correct. Now comes the South Coast Metal Minnow with less parts, more simple in design and will outcatch the South Coast Wooden Lure on dark days and in roily water and will hold it level any place. This metal minnow has a body and a hook. That's all. The body is nicely plated and catches fish that strikes a spoon or minnow. This minnow rides back up. No swivel or sinker used. The minnow does not turn over. Why? here comes the patented idea. By placing the hook below the horizontal center, in the lower point of tail the bait is kept in an upright position. The minnow is indestructible and gets the fish Last year we sold 4 wooden South Coast Minnows for $2.00. This Season we sell by mail 3 wooden South Coast Minnows, 3 sizes, and 4 metal South Coast Minnows, 4 sizes, making 7, all for $2.00, we believe this is the greatest value ever offered to fishermen, the Hooks are same as used on the wooden lure made and tempered for these baits specially at considerable expense, a most desirable hook, both as to shape and strength. 7 samely designed and well built for $2.00 or if you want a set of 3 wooden ones, 3 sizes, at $1.50, or 4 metal, 4 sizes, for $1.00. This is all I can do for you Brother Angler until I receive your order. Then I will send you these minnows by return mail postpaid. Send for Booklet and Folder. It will be sport for you to do it now, we have moved our Los Angeles office to our factory

Address, H. C. ROYER, Terminal Island, Los Angeles County, Calif.

Doing research is sometimes a thankless task, but every once in awhile up pops new information. Here is a May, 1912 Ad from Outer's Magazine showing that Royer was also producing the SOUTH COAST METAL MINNOW in 4 sizes. It also gave the new address of the factory. His previous address must have been his doctor's office at 335 Wilson Block, Los Angeles, California.

3"- WOOD-P.E.
HAND PAINTED

$20 – 30

R.B.Co. LURE

The Robinson Bait Co.

2888 So. Fern Creek Ave. Orlando, Fla.

Now! JINX New!
"SURFCASTER"

$5

MEDIUM & DEEP RUNNING MODELS 3X STRONG 2/0 TINNED TREBLES 1½ OZ. 5 IN.

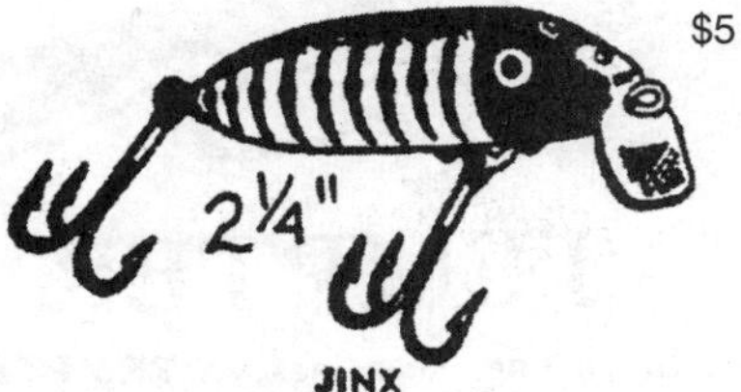
5"

FOR STRIPERS BLUES AND OTHER FRESH AND SALT WATER GAMEFISH SEE YOUR DEALER TODAY!

RINEHART TACKLE CO. Marietta Ohio

$5

2¼"

JINX

$5

4¾"

RINEHART MUSKIE JINX

Popular Plastic Lures from the 1940's and 1950's by Fred Rinehart, Marietta, Ohio.

$20

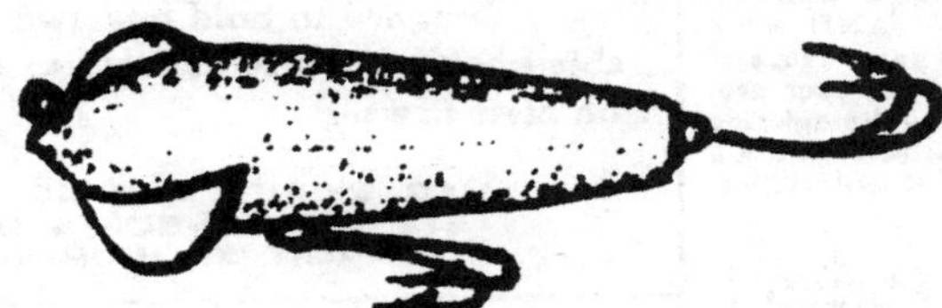

The Swan Lake WIGGLER

"Catch Fish Worth Fishing For"
Use the TEMPTER Bait

$30 – 45

It imitates a wounded, or injured minnow as it struggles and works from side to side. It's a sure killer. Get one and settle the bait question. postpaid, any color. A FREE prize to every angler. value write for full particulars.

J. W. Reynolds Decoy Factory Chicago, U. S. A.

TEMPTER

Patented

"Catches Fish Worth Fishing For"

J. W. Reynolds Decoy Factory Chicago, U. S. A.

(1920 AD)

THE REYNOLDS ADS APPEARED IN THE APRIL & JULY ISSUES OF 1915 OUTERS MAGAZINES. (Swan Lake Wiggler & Spike Tail Motion Baits)

$20

THE NEW WEEDLESS "SPIKE-TAIL MOTION BAIT No. 2."

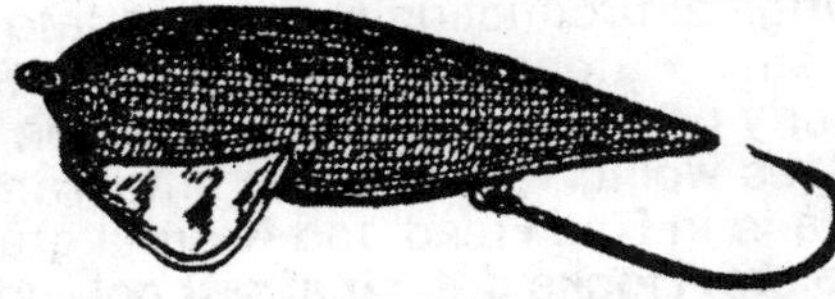

Tried out 1913. Patent allowed Sept., 1914.

FLOATS, DIVES, WOBBLES.

You can fish in the rushes and lilies without fouling, and best of all it lands the fish. Price 65 cents, postpaid. Your money back if not as represented. Write for descriptive matter of other "Spike-Tail Baits" and "Swan Lake Wigglers"

J. W. Reynolds Decoy Factory, Chicago, U. S. A.

IT FLOATS, DIVES, DARTS, WIGGLES. IT SWIMS
PAT.

FISHERMEN GET 'EM EASY!

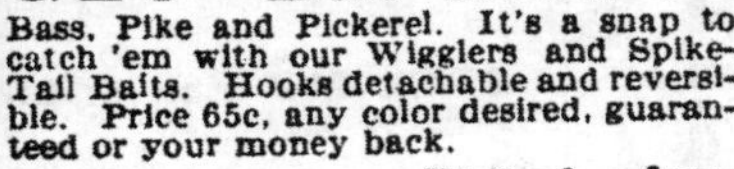

Bass, Pike and Pickerel. It's a snap to catch 'em with our Wigglers and Spike-Tail Baits. Hooks detachable and reversible. Price 65c, any color desired, guaranteed or your money back.

We make DECOYS

of the portable and compact kind, that are good wherever the water fowl flies. See cut of our "Automatic Duck Decoys", open and collapsed. Thousands sold annually in many parts of the world. You can't beat them. Write to us.

COLLAPSED.

Write for descriptive matter, etc.

J. W. REYNOLDS DECOY FACTORY - CHICAGO, U. S. A.

$50 – 75

TEMPTER FROG
1940's Version - 3-7/8"

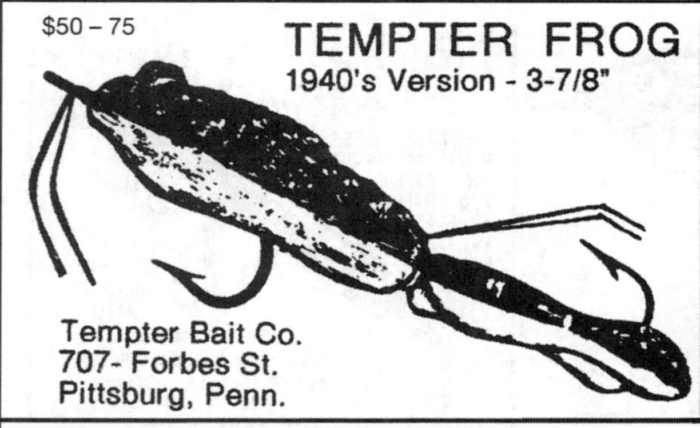

Tempter Bait Co.
707- Forbes St.
Pittsburg, Penn.

"PLASTIC MINNOW TUBE" (1947)

Live Lure PAT. APPLIED FOR

LIVE LURE
PAT. APPLIED FOR

$10

FOR BASS PIKE PICKEREL and OTHER GAME FISH

FOR CASTING or TROLLING LURE

WORLD'S LIVELIEST BAIT

Magnifies all live bait when placed inside transparent plug in water.

DIRECTIONS

1. Remove head.
2. Place live bait in place.
3. Put head back in place.

Hooks are threaded with 45 lb. test Monel Wire. (Rust Proof)

Plug is designed to hold one, two or three treble hooks, any size desired, to conform with State Laws.

MFG. BY RICE ENG. CO.
912 STEPHENSON BLDG.
DETROIT (2), MICHIGAN

$50 – 75

(Patent applied for) (1932)

TEMPTER

In one short season TEMPTER has taken the fishing world by storm. News of its killing prowess has spread like wild fire. Anglers everywhere are telling of its successes. Muskies, pike, pickerel, and bass have fallen before it by the score. AND WHY SHOULDN'T THEY! Frogs are a natural food for all game fish, and TEMPTER is the most accurate imitation of a live frog ever produced. It FLOATS naturally, SWIMS gracefully, and its coloring is perfect. Its white belly also makes it a clever night lure; and it's weedless. TEMPTER is NOT just another mechanical gadget, but a REAL plug, designed for REAL anglers.

With the medium size at $1.00 and the large size no kit should be without a supply.

If your dealer doesn't stock them send directly to

(2 SIZES)

ELMER E. RAWDON
(Well-known outdoor writer)
620 Phillips Ave. Akron, Ohio

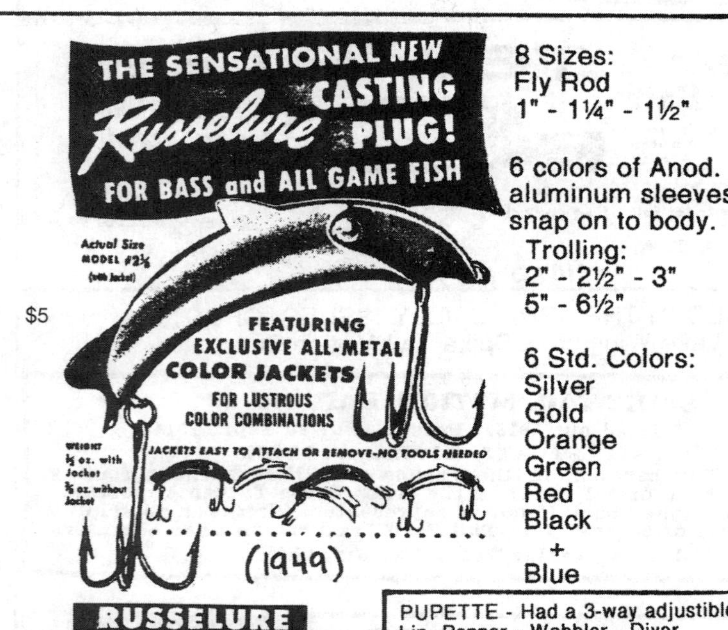
THE SENSATIONAL NEW
Russelure CASTING PLUG!
FOR BASS and ALL GAME FISH
FEATURING
EXCLUSIVE ALL-METAL
COLOR JACKETS
FOR LUSTROUS
COLOR COMBINATIONS
JACKETS EASY TO ATTACH OR REMOVE-NO TOOLS NEEDED

$5

(1949)

8 Sizes:
Fly Rod
1" - 1¼" - 1½"

6 colors of Anod. aluminum sleeves snap on to body.

Trolling:
2" - 2½" - 3"
5" - 6½"

6 Std. Colors:
Silver
Gold
Orange
Green
Red
Black
\+
Blue

RUSSELURE
MFG. CO., INC.

2514 - So. Grand Ave.
Los Angeles 7, Calif.

P. O. Box 537
Chico, CA

PUPETTE - Had a 3-way adjustible Lip, Popper - Wobbler - Diver

$5

2 7/8" (1949)

Natural Mud Puppy

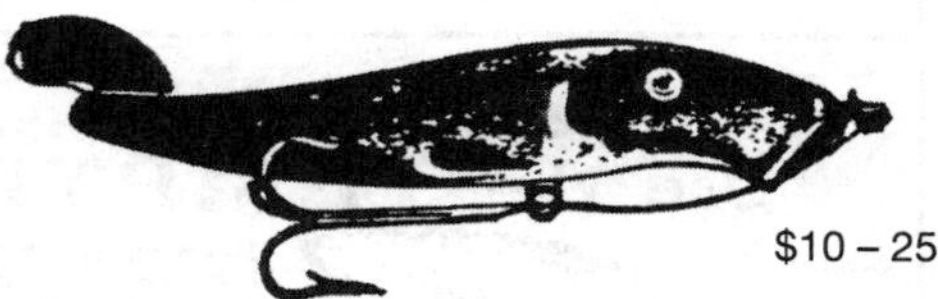

$10 – 25

Made in two sizes — **LITTLE MUD PUPPY 5½ inches, 1¼ oz.; MUD PUPPY 7 inches, 2 oz.**

Either size in Red Head or Natural finish.

C. C. ROBERTS
Mosinee, Wisconsin

Original production was in the late teens. Patent was granted in 1928. Early production had G.E. and the sizes would vary with the time frame Made in Red Head and Natural gray colors. Hooks detach after hook-up.

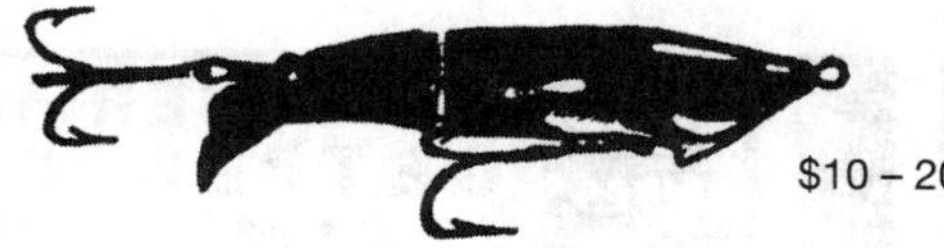

$10 – 20

RIVER PUP same as River Model but 4½" long, ¾ oz.

River Pup (4-1/2") & River Model (5"), the River Model had 3 fixed trebles.

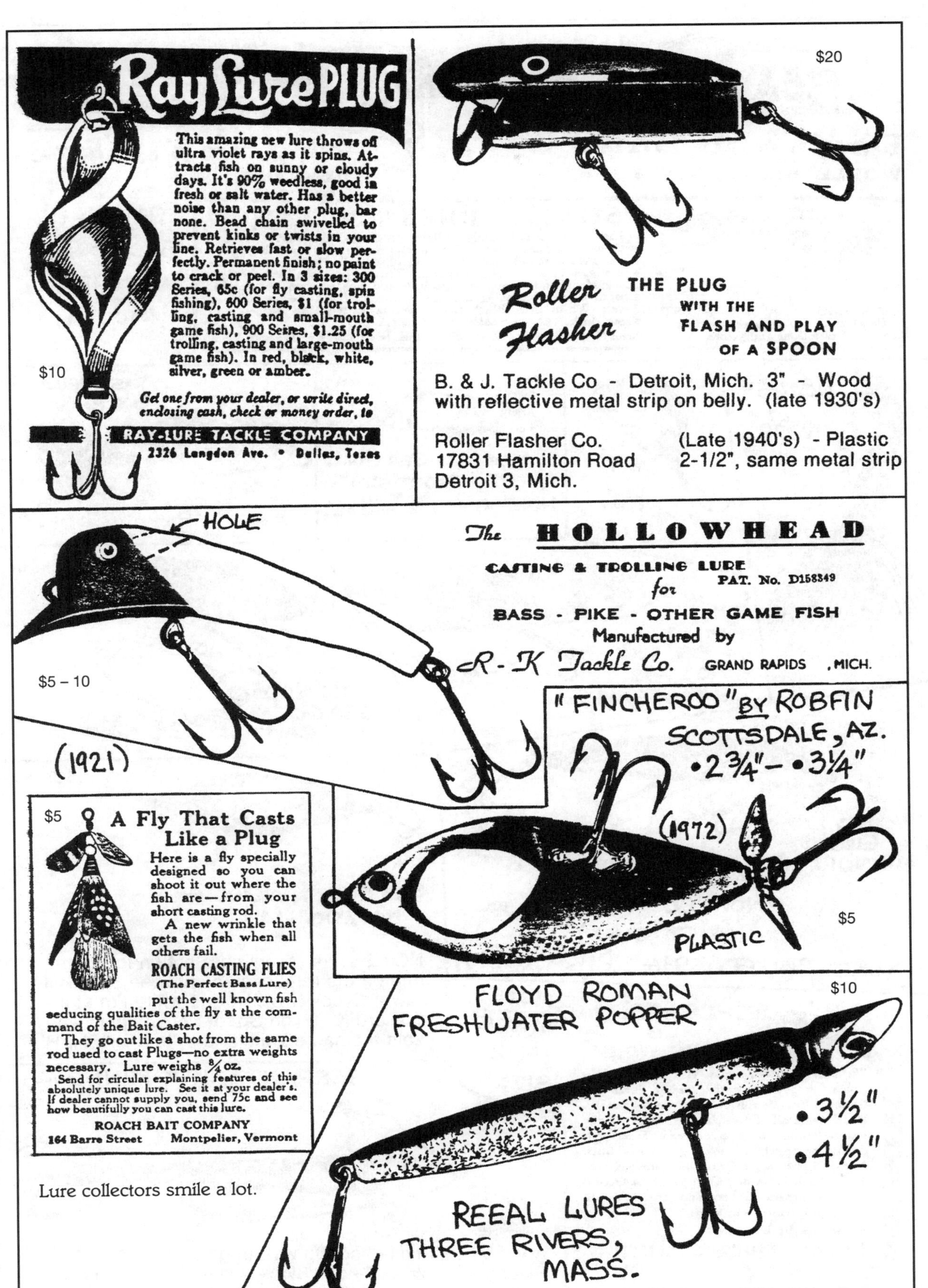
Ray Lure PLUG
This amazing new lure throws off ultra violet rays as it spins. Attracts fish on sunny or cloudy days. It's 90% weedless, good in fresh or salt water. Has a better noise than any other plug, bar none. Bead chain swivelled to prevent kinks or twists in your line. Retrieves fast or slow perfectly. Permanent finish; no paint to crack or peel. In 3 sizes: 300 Series, 65c (for fly casting, spin fishing), 600 Series, $1 (for trolling, casting and small-mouth game fish), 900 Seires, $1.25 (for trolling, casting and large-mouth game fish). In red, black, white, silver, green or amber.
Get one from your dealer, or write direct, enclosing cash, check or money order, to
RAY-LURE TACKLE COMPANY
2326 Langdon Ave. • Dallas, Texas
$10
$20
Roller Flasher
THE PLUG WITH THE FLASH AND PLAY OF A SPOON
B. & J. Tackle Co - Detroit, Mich. 3" - Wood with reflective metal strip on belly. (late 1930's)
Roller Flasher Co.
17831 Hamilton Road
Detroit 3, Mich.
(Late 1940's) - Plastic
2-1/2", same metal strip
HOLE
The HOLLOWHEAD
CASTING & TROLLING LURE
PAT. No. D158349
for
BASS - PIKE - OTHER GAME FISH
Manufactured by
R-K Tackle Co. GRAND RAPIDS, MICH.
$5 – 10
(1921)
"FINCHEROO" BY ROBFIN
SCOTTSDALE, AZ.
•2 3/4" - •3 1/4"
(1972)
PLASTIC
$5
$5
A Fly That Casts Like a Plug
Here is a fly specially designed so you can shoot it out where the fish are—from your short casting rod.
A new wrinkle that gets the fish when all others fail.
ROACH CASTING FLIES
(The Perfect Bass Lure)
put the well known fish seducing qualities of the fly at the command of the Bait Caster.
They go out like a shot from the same rod used to cast Plugs—no extra weights necessary. Lure weighs 3/4 oz.
Send for circular explaining features of this absolutely unique lure. See it at your dealer's. If dealer cannot supply you, send 75c and see how beautifully you can cast this lure.
ROACH BAIT COMPANY
164 Barre Street Montpelier, Vermont
FLOYD ROMAN
FRESHWATER POPPER
$10
•3 1/2"
•4 1/2"
REEAL LURES
THREE RIVERS,
MASS.

Lure collectors smile a lot.

(1922)
SEA GULL
Schoenfeld-Gutter, Inc.
Reels and Baits
WORLD BLDG., NEW YORK
MADE IN TWO SIZES
3¼" - ⅜ oz - NO. 800
Sea Gull Bait No. 801.
4" - ¾ oz. - NO. 700
G.E.
(GLASS EYES)
$20 – 35
"SILVER CREEK" POLLYWOG
Last year this bait made its debut in the anglers' world. It met with instantaneous favor. Those who used it say that they have never before struck such a successful killer. Has the dip, dive and wiggle of a real fish in action. Travels fourteen inches below the surface under moderate reeling and floats when not reeled. Length 4 in.; weight ¾ oz. Furnished in Solid Yellow, Yellow Perch, White with Black Spots, White with Black Stripes and Moss Back. At your dealer's or direct.....................$1.00
Send for Circular in Colors. Silver Creek Novelty Works, Dowagiac, Mich.
$75.00 GOLD PRIZE CONTEST
Send today for circular describing conditions and prizes
THIS AD SHOWS A "NOTCHED" MOUTH
NO. 654
1-5/8"
$10
$10
1½"
NO. 600
$10
NOTCH
SEA GULL TROUT BAIT
NO. 500 - 1¾" - ¼ oz.
SEA GULL FLY BAIT
$10
NO. 634
1-5/8"
NOTCH
$10
SEA GULL NO. 300 BASS BAIT
3" - ½ oz.
$10
NOTCHED
NO. 400 SEA GULL BASS BAIT
2½" - ⅜ oz.

$20 – 50

SEA GULL MINNOW
- NO. 900 5¼" - ⅝ oz.
- NO. 1000 4¼" - ½ oz. (2 TREBLES)

(ALSO CALLED THE PIKAROON)

$20 – 30

SEA GULL TROLLING BAIT
NO. 200 - 4"

NOTE: See Moonlight Section for more info on the relationship between Sea Gull-Silver Creek Novelty, and while I'm at it... Edward K. Tryon Co. of Philadelphia who sold the same baits under "KINGFISHER'

$5

WIGGLING WORM

The best bass lure made. Will take all other game fish down to and including Perch and Channel Cat. Beautiful action at all speeds. Hand painted fishy designs. Individually tested. Money back guarantee. From your dealer, or direct from me "With his address, Please." Five colors: Green and Green, Green and Yellow, Black and Orange. Three Greens and Red Brown, Cherry Red. Last two with segmentary spiral markings.
¼ oz. — ⅛ oz.

CLARENCE J. SMITH
R.F.D. 2, Box 109 Lewiston, Ill.

NOTE: MADE IN 2 SIZES.

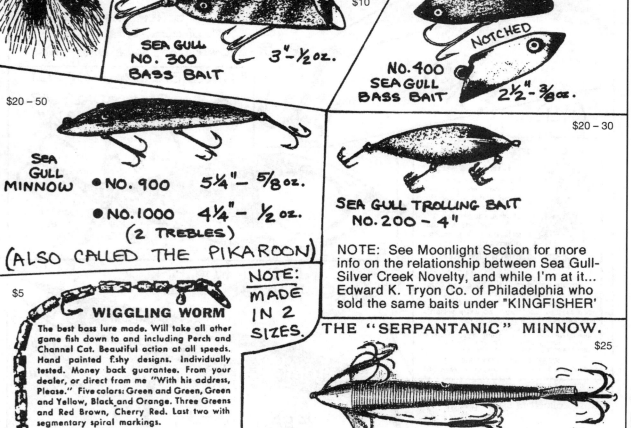

THE "SERPANTANIC" MINNOW.

$25

An 1899 Bait-coiled spring wire in gold, bronze, nickel
Sizes: 1" - 1½" - 2" - 3" - 3½" - 4" - 4½"

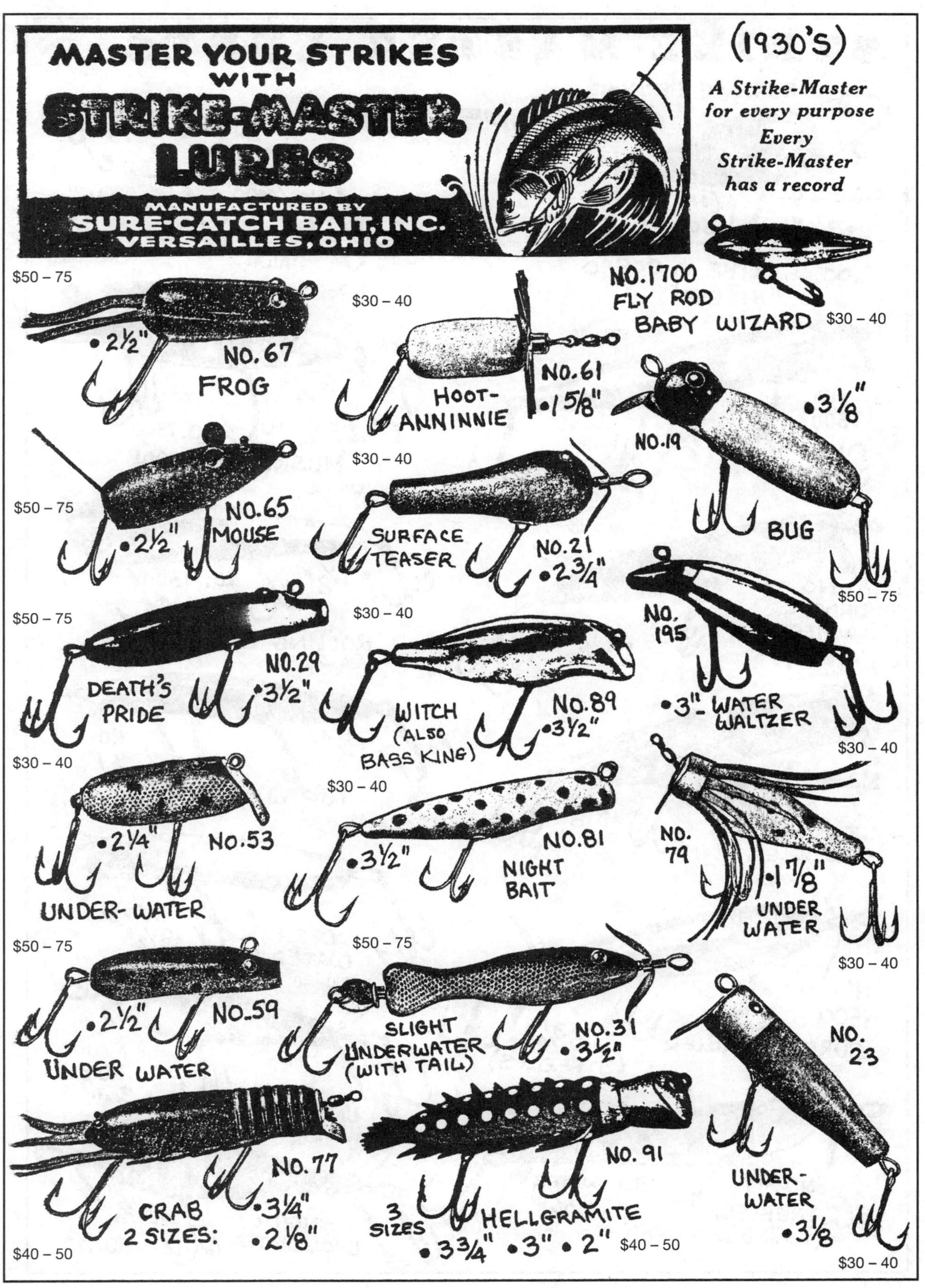
MASTER YOUR STRIKES
WITH
STRIKE-MASTER
LURES
MANUFACTURED BY
SURE-CATCH BAIT, INC.
VERSAILLES, OHIO
(1930'S)
A Strike-Master
for every purpose
Every
Strike-Master
has a record
NO. 1700
FLY ROD
BABY WIZARD
$30 – 40
$50 – 75
•2½"
NO. 67
FROG
$30 – 40
HOOT-
ANNINNIE
NO. 61
•1 5/8"
NO. 19
•3⅛"
BUG
$50 – 75
$30 – 40
$50 – 75
NO. 65
MOUSE
•2½"
SURFACE
TEASER
NO. 21
•2¾"
$50 – 75
$50 – 75
NO. 29
•3½"
DEATH'S
PRIDE
$30 – 40
WITCH
(ALSO
BASS KING)
NO. 89
•3½"
NO.
195
•3" – WATER
WALTZER
$30 – 40
$30 – 40
•2¼"
NO. 53
UNDER-WATER
$30 – 40
•3½"
NO. 81
NIGHT
BAIT
NO.
79
•1 7/8"
UNDER
WATER
$30 – 40
$50 – 75
•2½"
NO. 59
UNDER WATER
$50 – 75
SLIGHT
UNDERWATER
(WITH TAIL)
NO. 31
•3½"
NO.
23
UNDER-
WATER
•3⅛
$30 – 40
NO. 77
CRAB
2 SIZES:
•3¼"
•2⅛"
$40 – 50
NO. 91
3
SIZES
HELLGRAMITE
•3¾" •3" •2"
$40 – 50

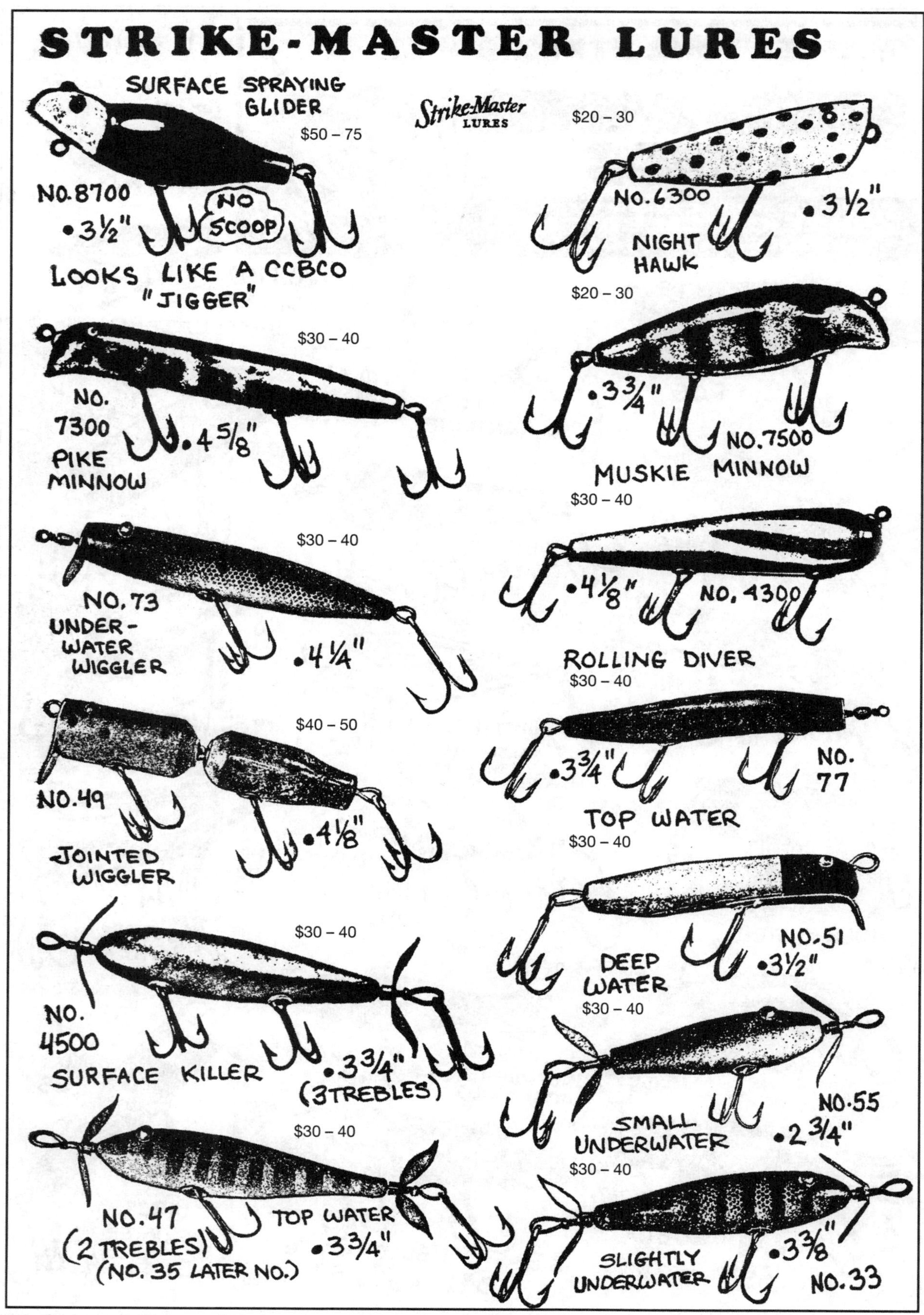
STRIKE-MASTER LURES
SURFACE SPRAYING GLIDER
Strike-Master LURES
$50 – 75
NO. 8700
•3½"
NO SCOOP
LOOKS LIKE A CCBCO "JIGGER"
$20 – 30
NO. 6300
•3½"
NIGHT HAWK
$30 – 40
NO. 7300
•4⅝"
PIKE MINNOW
$20 – 30
•3¾"
NO. 7500
MUSKIE MINNOW
$30 – 40
NO. 73
UNDER-WATER WIGGLER
•4¼"
$30 – 40
•4⅛"
NO. 4300
ROLLING DIVER
$40 – 50
NO. 49
•4⅛"
JOINTED WIGGLER
$30 – 40
•3¾"
NO. 77
TOP WATER
$30 – 40
NO. 4500
SURFACE KILLER
•3¾"
(3 TREBLES)
$30 – 40
DEEP WATER
NO. 51
•3½"
$30 – 40
NO. 47
(2 TREBLES)
(NO. 35 LATER NO.)
TOP WATER
•3¾"
$30 – 40
SMALL UNDERWATER
NO. 55
•2¾"
$30 – 40
SLIGHTLY UNDERWATER
•3⅜"
NO. 33

TURBULENT
FISHING LURE
MANUFACTURED BY
O. C. SCHAEFER
1610 Kearney Ave.
Racine, Wis.

Best for Wall-Eye Pike, Muskellunge, Bass, Pickerel, Great Northern Pike, Lake Trout, Salmon, Deep Sea Fishing, Sturgeon.

$20 – 30

PENETRATOR

Good for casting, trolling, for penetrating deep holes, deep sea fishing and fishing through holes in the ice. Raising and lowering the lure in deep holes gets the big ones. In weed beds, the revolving spinners push the weeds aside, making a clear path. It is an under water lure.

15 COLORS

BLACK YELLOW
BLACK WHITE
BLACK GREEN
BLACK DOTTED
WHITE GREEN
WHITE DOTTED
GREEN DOTTED
RED YELLOW
RED WHITE
RED BLACK
RED GREEN
RED DOTTED
YELLOW GREEN
YELLOW WHITE
YELLOW DOTTED

Turbulent Fishing Lures Best For

MUSKELLUNGE
WALL-EYE PIKE
GREAT NORTHERN PIKE
BASS
LAKE TROUT
SALMON
DEEP SEA FISHING

$20 – 30

PENETRATOR

TURBULENT
SURFACE $20 – 30

TURBULENT EXCITOR

$20 – 30

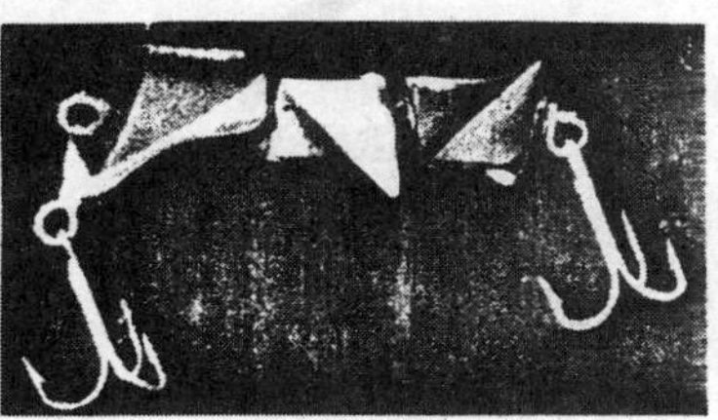

TURBULENT
DIVER $20 – 30

TURBULENT WHITE
$20 – 30 DOTTED
LUMINOUS DIVER

$20 – 30

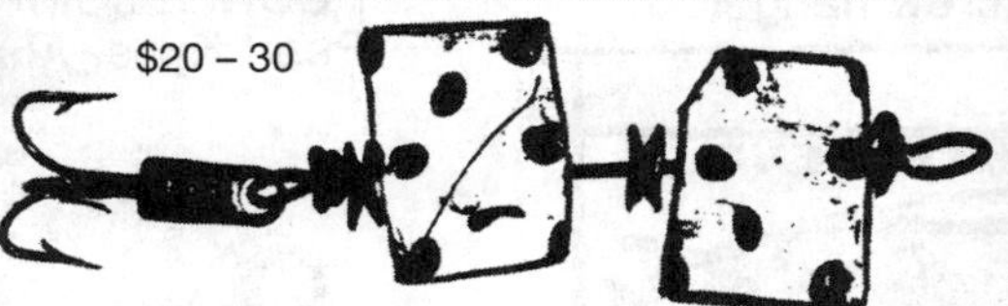

TURBULENT WET FLY

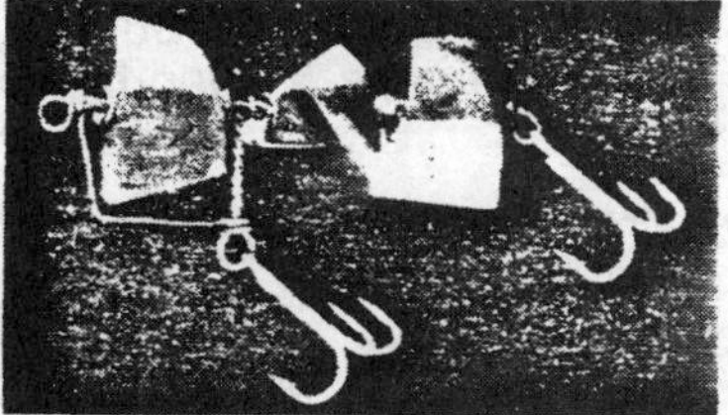

TURBULENT TIGER $20 – 30

Oscar Schaefer also made 4 lures for SALT WATER - DEEP SEA

They were called: TURBULENT GIANT LURES (W/Big Hooks)

1. TURBULENT GIANT SURFACE LURE
2. TURBULENT GIANT DIVER LURE
3. TURBULENT GIANT TIGER LURE
4. TURBULENT GIANT PENETRATOR LURE
   (only color was Red & White)

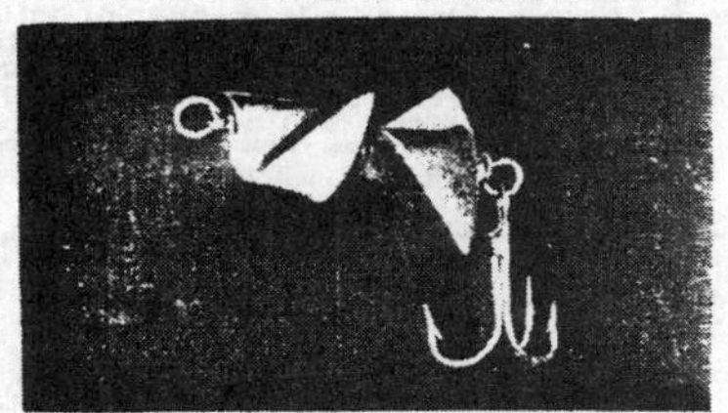

TURBULENT $20 – 30
HEADLESS

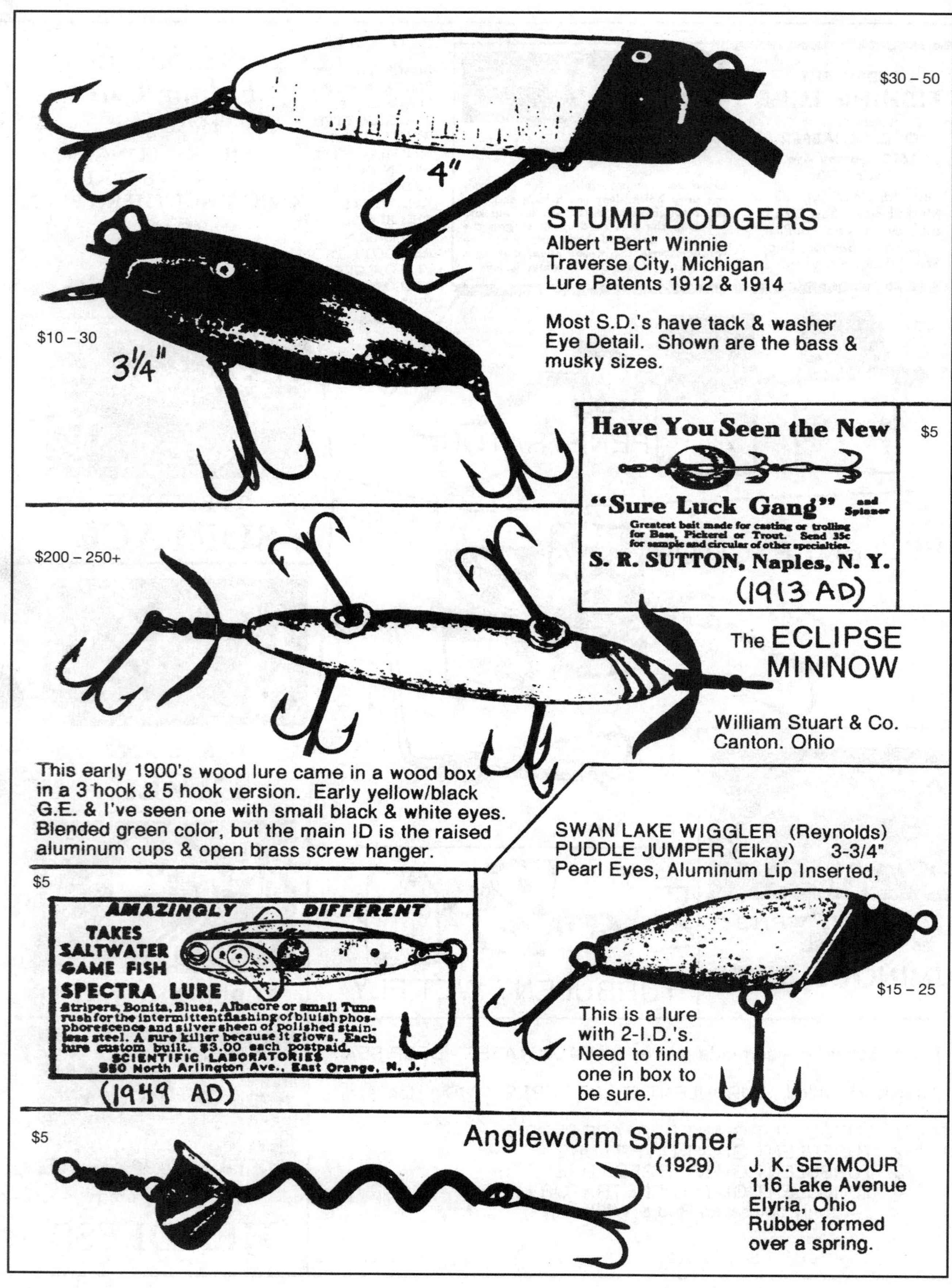
$30 – 50
4"
STUMP DODGERS
Albert "Bert" Winnie
Traverse City, Michigan
Lure Patents 1912 & 1914
Most S.D.'s have tack & washer Eye Detail. Shown are the bass & musky sizes.
$10 – 30
3¼"
Have You Seen the New
"Sure Luck Gang" and Spinner
Greatest bait made for casting or trolling for Bass, Pickerel or Trout. Send 35c for sample and circular of other specialties.
S. R. SUTTON, Naples, N. Y.
(1913 AD)
$5
$200 – 250+
The ECLIPSE MINNOW
William Stuart & Co.
Canton. Ohio
This early 1900's wood lure came in a wood box in a 3 hook & 5 hook version. Early yellow/black G.E. & I've seen one with small black & white eyes. Blended green color, but the main ID is the raised aluminum cups & open brass screw hanger.
SWAN LAKE WIGGLER (Reynolds)
PUDDLE JUMPER (Elkay) 3-3/4"
Pearl Eyes, Aluminum Lip Inserted,
$5
AMAZINGLY DIFFERENT
TAKES SALTWATER GAME FISH
SPECTRA LURE
Stripers, Bonita, Blues, Albacore or small Tuna rush for the intermittent flashing of bluish phosphorescence and silver sheen of polished stainless steel. A sure killer because it glows. Each lure custom built. $3.00 each postpaid.
SCIENTIFIC LABORATORIES
850 North Arlington Ave., East Orange, N. J.
(1949 AD)
$15 – 25
This is a lure with 2-I.D.'s. Need to find one in box to be sure.
$5
Angleworm Spinner
(1929)
J. K. SEYMOUR
116 Lake Avenue
Elyria, Ohio
Rubber formed over a spring.

"You can Really Catch Fish with the new WEED KING, the 100% Weedless Lure."

Patented WEED KING has no exposed hooks to snag or tangle. Always comes through clean. Three expanding hooks release only when fish strikes. Hooks are barbless and are easy to remove.

SEVDY AUTOMOTIVE ENTERPRISES
Worthington, Minnesota

$20 – 30

Springfield Novelty Mfg. Co.

MANUFACTURERS OF

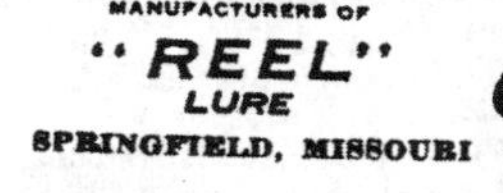

"REEL" LURE

SPRINGFIELD, MISSOURI

THE "REEL" LURE

— MADE IN SPRINGFIELD, MO. —

STANLEY MYERS and ADOLF KUNZ

(1933 - 1935)

$20 – 25

WEIGHT

ACTUAL SIZE (2 5/8")

A Sinking Minnow Made of Red Cedar, Nickel Silver Spinner & Wire.
Entire Body with Spiral Stripe Revolves
Casts Like a Bullet—Semi-Weedless.

The GOO GOO EYES

Get 'em!

$5

SALT WATER
BAIT LINE

12 different models-3/4Oz. to 3-1/4 Oz. Molded Plastic with really big, bulging eyes. They offered a sample 6" jointed bait - 1¼ Oz. for $2 postpaid in 1960.

STAMFORD PRODUCTS, Ltd.
P.O. Box 203
Stamford, Conn.

MADE OF MAHOGANY—

CRAWPAPPY

$10 –

New Bass Plug Really Gets The Big Ones

½ oz.
Made of Mahogany

(1951)

Natural color . . . life size. Perfect backwards action just like a real crawdad. Casts beautifully; trolls 2 to 2½ feet deep. Big success first year, 1951. Now available direct from maker at only Money refunded if not satisfied. Send check or M.O. Postage prepaid. Write today.

DEALERS WRITE FOR ATTRACTIVE OFFER

SMITH & YELTON CO.
Rural Route 5, Kansas City, Mo.

$20 – 50

WILL H. DILG, the Noted Fisherman and Writer, says:

"Winter's Weedless Surface Bait

is a wonderful bait-casting lure and will undoubtedly take plenty of fish."

Patent Applied For
1921

Continuing Mr. Dilg said, "Ever since the advent of the modern plug bait-casting bass fishermen with high ideals have hoped and prayed for a **one-hook plug and here it is at last!"**

Mr. Souther offered Mr. Dilg one of each of the four different colored patterns FREE, but he refused to take them for nothing and promptly dug into his pocket and pulled out four round dollars and paid cash.

Winter's Weedless Surface Bait has not been offered to the fishing tackle stores because the producers could not make them in time for this year's business. We can, however, deliver them now through the mails. **Send us a dollar at once and one of these baits will be mailed to your address.** You will find this new plug absolutely weedless and a good Fish Getter.

They are made in four patterns—Green, White and Red; Yellow, Red and Black; Tan, Red and White; White, Red and Black. We have a smaller plug, same pattern, for Trout Fishermen.

N. C. SOUTHER & CO., *Sales Distributors*
Suite 750, 220 S. Michigan Ave. CHICAGO, ILLINOIS

$300 – 400+

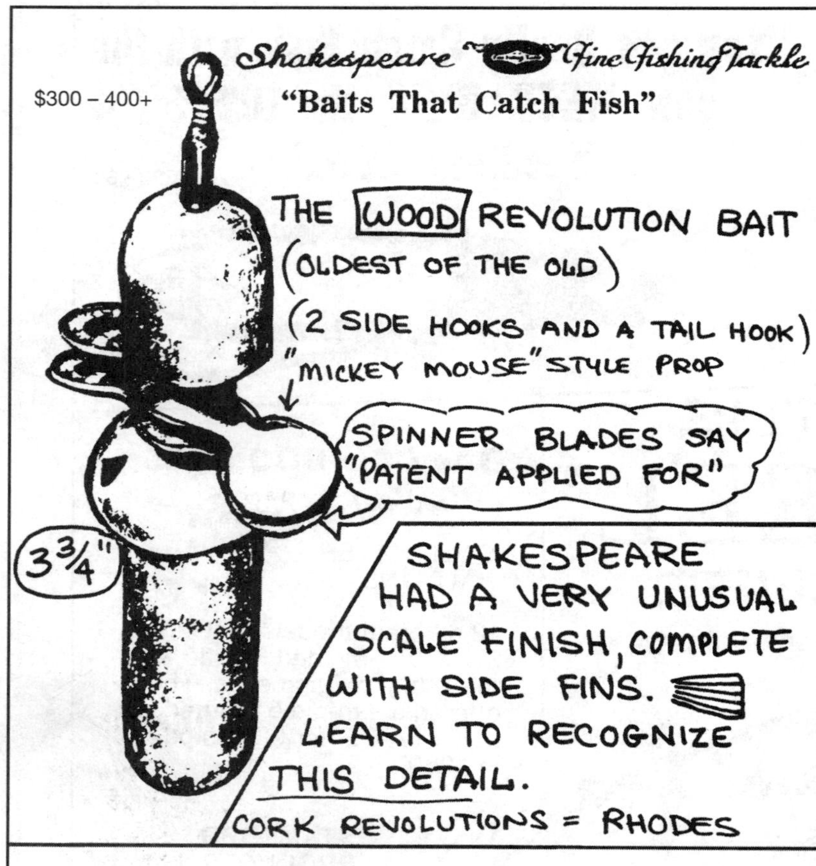
Shakespeare Fine Fishing Tackle
"Baits That Catch Fish"
THE WOOD REVOLUTION BAIT
(OLDEST OF THE OLD)
(2 SIDE HOOKS AND A TAIL HOOK)
"MICKEY MOUSE" STYLE PROP
SPINNER BLADES SAY "PATENT APPLIED FOR"
3¾"
SHAKESPEARE HAD A VERY UNUSUAL SCALE FINISH, COMPLETE WITH SIDE FINS.
LEARN TO RECOGNIZE THIS DETAIL.
CORK REVOLUTIONS = RHODES

$40 – 65

No. 6535

The Darting Shrimp resembles the live shrimp in both action and appearance and is designed for both salt and fresh-water fishing. It is jointed to permit a vertical action of the tail, created by a succession of sharp, quick turns of the reel handle, pausing between turns. A slight twitching of the rod will produce this action, which is forward and upward at each jerk, doubling up and slowly sinking when line is slack. Successful landing of the fish, even under severe strain, is insured by the use of the Shakespeare links which secure the belly hook and act as a hinge between sections. Very enticing to game fish such as Sea Trout, Red Fish, King and Mackerel in salt water and Pike, Wall-Eyed, Muskies and especially Black Bass in deep fresh water. Weight, 7/10 ounce.

No. 6535C—Copper sides, dark back, silver belly, red at throat.
No. 6535WRG—White, shaded red head, flecked with gold.
No. 6535F—Natural frog finish.

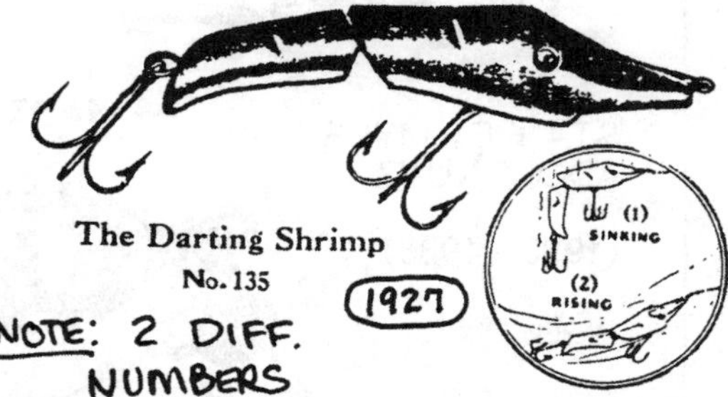
(1) SINKING
(2) RISING

The Darting Shrimp
No. 135

(1927)

NOTE: 2 DIFF. NUMBERS

The Hydroplane

No. 709—The Hydroplane bait was built at the suggestion of a great number of expert anglers who, from time to time, have asked us to manufacture a bait of this kind. It is thoroughly practical and in it are scientifically combined the best features of floating, slightly submerged and deeply submerged lures. A metal plane is inserted in the forward part of the bait and by use of this device a depth ranging from six to ten feet can be attained, according to the speed at which the line is retrieved.

Made in eight color combinations:

No.		No.	
709SW	—Solid white.	**709RW**	—Red and white.
709FG	—Fancy green.	**709GW**	—Rainbow.
709FB	- Frog back.	**709SR**	—Solid red.
709SS	—Spotted.	**709YP**	—Yellow perch.

No. 709—Length of body, 4½ in.; 2 treble belly and 1 treble tail hooks.
No. 709½—Same as above but smaller; body, 3 in. long.

HYDROPLANE

It swims on the surface or under water, as you wish

$30 – 50

2 SIZES
NO. 709 – 4½"
NO. 709½ – 3"

For Bass and Pickerel

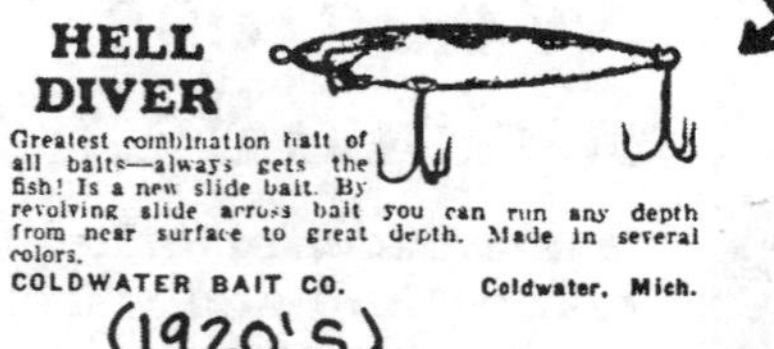
HELL DIVER

HELL DIVER

Greatest combination bait of all baits—always gets the fish! Is a new slide bait. By revolving slide across bait you can run any depth from near surface to great depth. Made in several colors.

COLDWATER BAIT CO. Coldwater, Mich.

(1920'S)

I DON'T KNOW IF THIS IS THE SAME BAIT AS THE HYDROPLANE OR NOT.
IT HAS AN ADJUSTABLE "SLIDE" (LIP)

$30 – 40

"Surface Wonder" No. 42WW

DISTINCTIVE HEAD SHAPE

OTHER COLORS: RED HEAD/YELLOW - FROG

4"
1910

Illustration
⅞ actual size

A floating bait that is a fish catcher of highest merit. Exceedingly popular with game-fish anglers throughout the country. The forward movement of the bait causes the peculiarly shaped head to throw up a very animated wake. Made in the best Shakespeare style. Has red head and white body.

$20 – 25

"Whirlwind Spinner"

$50 – 75

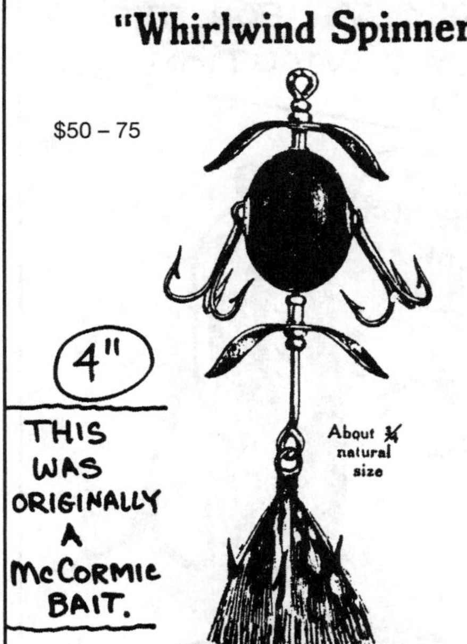
About ¼ natural size

4"

THIS WAS ORIGINALLY A McCORMIC BAIT.

No. 6SRW—Red body. No. 6SYW—Yellow body. No. 6SWW—White body.

Shakespeare Floating "Spinner"

1910

Illustration is actual size

2 SIZES

$30 – 50

No.4 3¼"

No.3 2⅞"

Many an angler relies on this floating bait for his largest catches. The head and spinners of this bait revolve together, in a manner apparently irresistibly attractive to game fish, while the body rides steadily, always presenting the hooks to the best advantage. Made in three styles, with Shakespeare thouroughness and finish.

No. 4RWS—Solid red head, solid white body.
No. 4SYS—Solid yellow head and body, decorated with gold spots.
No. 4SWS—Solid white head and body, decorated with gold spots.

Length of body, 3⅛ inches.

"Weedless Frog"

$20 – 40

No. 4WF

3¼"

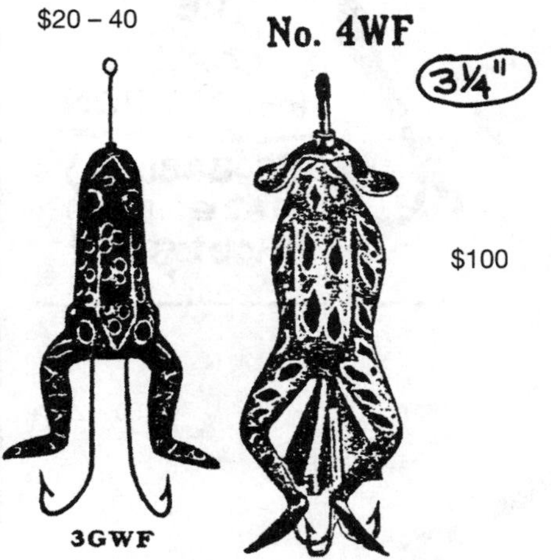
3GWF

$100

SOFT RUBBER BODY. THE TREBLE HOOK PROTECTED BY SOFT RUBBER GUARDS.

Shakespeare "Punkin-Seed" Minnow

$75 – 100+

Floating Bait

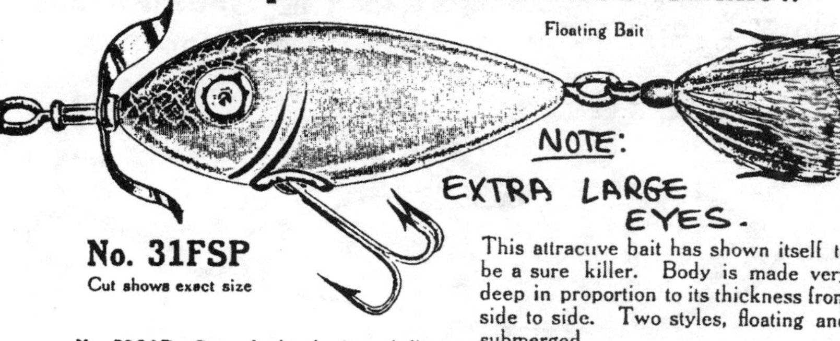

NOTE: EXTRA LARGE EYES.

No. 31FSP

Cut shows exact size

This attractive bait has shown itself to be a sure killer. Body is made very deep in proportion to its thickness from side to side. Two styles, floating and submerged.

No. 30GAP—Green back, aluminum belly.
No. 30GWP—Green back, white belly.
No. 30RAP—Red back, aluminum belly.
(Submerged style, without belly hook)

No. 31SWP—White, with red or green on head.
31GWP—Green back, white belly.
Two gangs.
No. 31FSP—Fancy sienna yellow with brown head.

"Sure Lure" Weedless Bait

1902

$200+

(RUBBER)

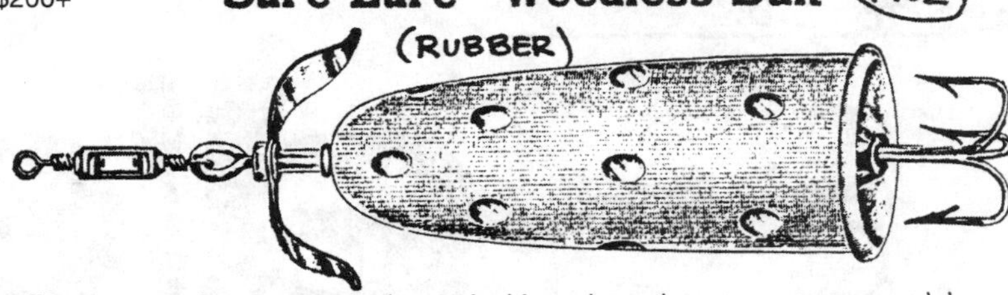

This bait can be cast among the reeds, lily pads, rushes, stumps moss and logs where the fish are lying, without danger of fouling. Made of pure soft rubber, which yields instantly when a strike occurs, permitting the treble hook to engage Bright aluminum color, trimmed with gold spots.

Made in one size and style only.

"Little Pirate" MINNOW

KAZOO QUALITY – (LIKE HEDDON NO. 20) 2½"

Two side gangs, one tail gang.

A wonderful example of effective economy. Made in red back, white belly, and green back, white belly.

NOSE SPINNER
-2 SIDE
-1 TAIL TREB.

IN A 1909 AD IN "THE SPORTING GOODS DEALER" – SHAKESP. CLAIMED 50 STYLES OF BAITS!

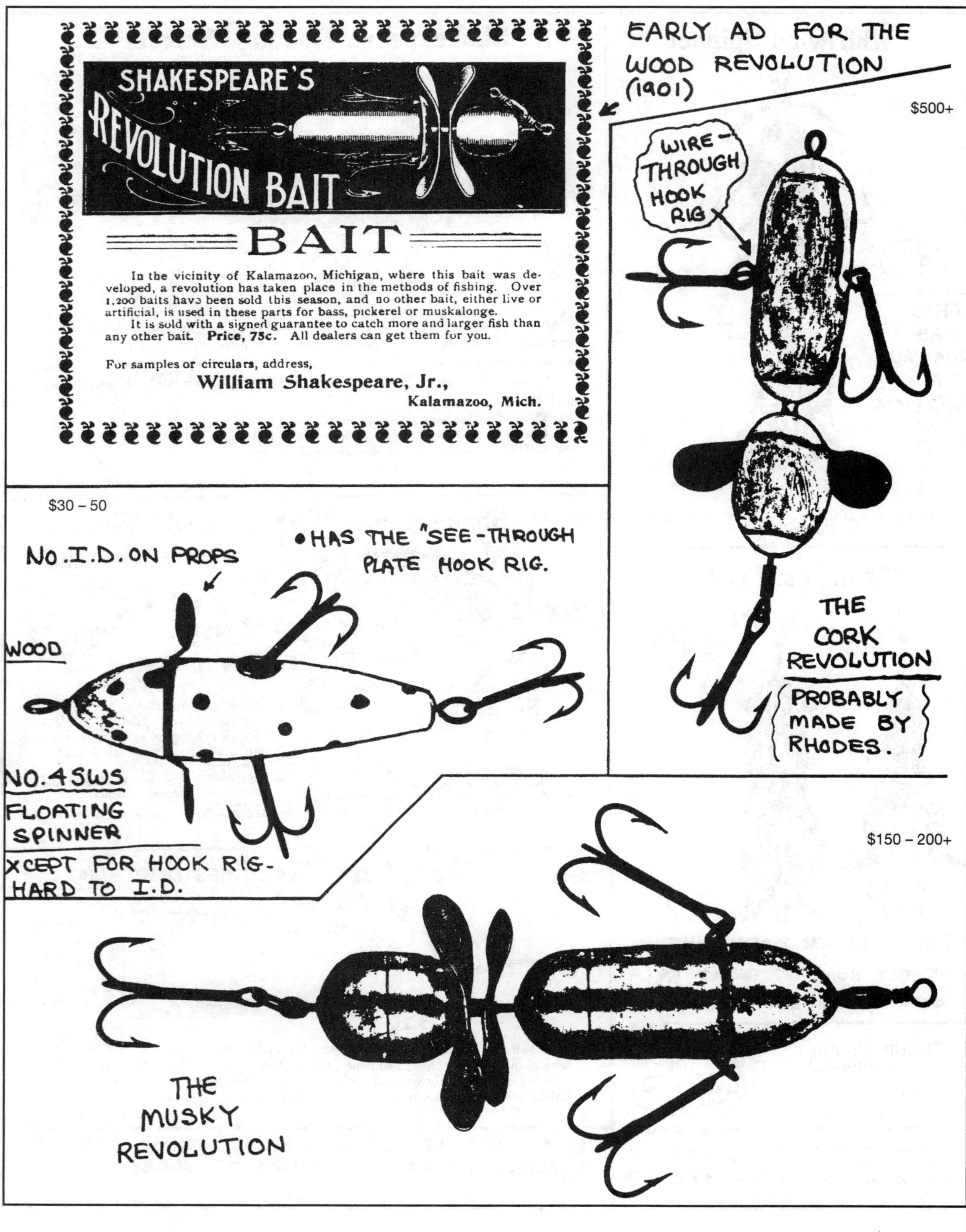
SHAKESPEARE'S
REVOLUTION BAIT
BAIT
In the vicinity of Kalamazoo, Michigan, where this bait was developed, a revolution has taken place in the methods of fishing. Over 1,200 baits have been sold this season, and no other bait, either live or artificial, is used in these parts for bass, pickerel or muskalonge.
It is sold with a signed guarantee to catch more and larger fish than any other bait. Price, 75c. All dealers can get them for you.
For samples or circulars, address,
William Shakespeare, Jr.,
Kalamazoo, Mich.
EARLY AD FOR THE WOOD REVOLUTION (1901)
$500+
WIRE-THROUGH HOOK RIG
THE CORK REVOLUTION
PROBABLY MADE BY RHODES.
$30 – 50
NO. I.D. ON PROPS
• HAS THE "SEE-THROUGH PLATE HOOK RIG.
WOOD
NO. 4SWS
FLOATING SPINNER
XCEPT FOR HOOK RIG- HARD TO I.D.
$150 – 200+
THE MUSKY REVOLUTION

Fred D. Rhodes - Rhodes was an early (1900's) inventor and innovator of fishing baits. Many of his patents and designs became part of the Shakespeare line, so I have elected to include his stuff under Shakesp. instead of "R" Misc. section. Club members have found many unknown baits in the Kalamazoo, Michigan area, where Rhodes lived and made his baits, baits showing experimentation and original ideas. The see-through wire hook hangers which became the "hook-link" construction was one of the Rhodes designs. The first "lip" on the front of a bait was Rhodes Diving Plane(1904). It is also assumed that the Cork Revolution was the 1st of the Revolution series, and that it was made by Rhodes. (Any further info. about Rhodes would be much appreciated, and will be included in future supplements.)

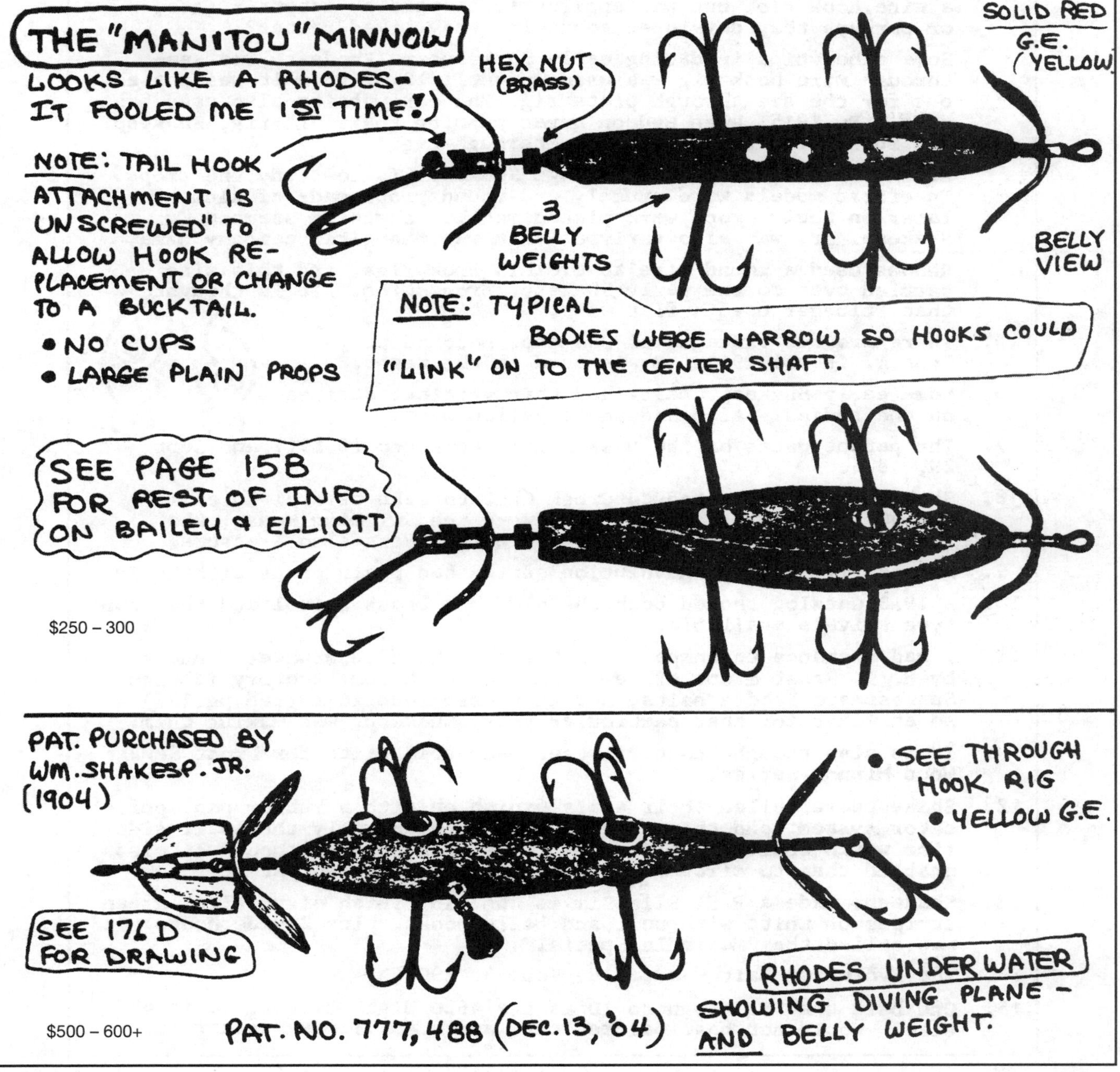
THE "MANITOU" MINNOW
LOOKS LIKE A RHODES-
IT FOOLED ME 1ST TIME!)
HEX NUT (BRASS)
SOLID RED G.E. (YELLOW)
NOTE: TAIL HOOK ATTACHMENT IS UNSCREWED" TO ALLOW HOOK RE-PLACEMENT OR CHANGE TO A BUCKTAIL.
• NO CUPS
• LARGE PLAIN PROPS
3 BELLY WEIGHTS
BELLY VIEW
NOTE: TYPICAL BODIES WERE NARROW SO HOOKS COULD "LINK" ON TO THE CENTER SHAFT.
SEE PAGE 15B FOR REST OF INFO ON BAILEY & ELLIOTT
PAT. PURCHASED BY WM. SHAKESP. JR. (1904)
• SEE THROUGH HOOK RIG
• YELLOW G.E.
SEE 176D FOR DRAWING
RHODES UNDERWATER
SHOWING DIVING PLANE - AND BELLY WEIGHT.
PAT. NO. 777,488 (DEC. 13, '04)

$250 – 300

$500 – 600+

SHAKESPEARE - Observations and Comments

1. The Shakespeare "ball" rear tail hook rig was used in the 1929 - 1931 era. (see illustration)
2. Shakesp. introduced pressed eyes on their wood baits in 1933.
3. The Revolution Bait and the Worden Bucktail Revolution were both made with Notch Props.An observant and diligent Shakesp. collector could have a display of just the variations of this series of baits that would number in the 12 to 16 area.
4. Pflueger used the see-through hook rig for a short time using a wire hook tie, but was apparently stopped by patent rights, or perhaps they developed something they liked better?

   Some other tips in dating early Shakespeare/Rhodes: The see-through wire hook rig was used up until 1910, when it was phased out for the see-through plate rig. The early baits also used brass cups. By 1915, when Heddon began pushing their "L" rig, Shakesp. was fully into their plate see-through rig.

   Another way to help date vintage Shakesp. is to study the props. The first models were crudely cut round props made of aluminum, later on their props were plated metal. Anything stamped Wm. Shakesp. Jr. was also early as that was the first company name.

   Rhodes used a round wire to tie his hook rigs, and this also carried over to the early Shakesp. production. It is thought that Pflueger used a flat wire.
5. There are two vintages of Shakesp. notched props. Type A. is pre-1910. B. is used in the teens.
6. Some early Shakesp. baits had thin vertical stripes on the bodies. Also had small yellow eyes.
7. The patent dates of the Bass-A-Lure were Dec.18,1917 and Sept. 29, 1925.
8. Shakespeare contracted to Creek Chub to make several lures in the 40's and 50's. Known lures were the Swimming Mouse, the Pup, and the Pop-Eye Frog. There were others also I assume.
9. Some early Shakesp. Revolution series had plain props with no ID.
10. A 1913 Catalog showed both the olde box brass swivel and the round type swivels available.
11. I had a chance to compare the "Senate" Wood Underwater Minnows by H. J. Frost & Co. of New York City with some factory labeled Shakespeare Rhodes baits, and they were identical (see pg.177) so at least for that particular year, Shakesp. was making them.

    It is also thought that Pflueger made some baits for Frost Senate Wood Minnow Series.
12. Shakespeare rolled their scale finish on with a rubber pad applicator system, and this enabled them to also apply the small side fins which couldn't be done by the screen/spray method. It also enabled them to circumvent the CCBCO scale finish patent.
13. Shakesp. made a P.E. Slim Jim in the old finish of vertical green stripes on white with tail and belly hooks, plus 2 side hooks. It was called the "McKinnie Special".
14. The Evolution Bait was pat'd. Feb. 5, 1901.
15. One bait that is tough to ID is the #680 Night Caster. It is 4" size. Would not have painted cups and a small nose washer.

SHAKESPEARE - Comments and Conclusions

16. For you color set fans, add color No.6555B to the Waukazoo Bait, Black Body W/Yellow Stripe.
17. It is assumed that Shakespeare had completely absorbed Fred Rhodes production by 1910. Many of Rhodes production baits came in wood boxes....one of these with the bait would be a great centerpiece for a Misc. or Shakesp. collection.
18. Shakesp. served as a jobber/distributor for other makers baits, and they were sometimes shown in the Shakesp. catalogs. (teens)
19. The No.3 Artificial Minnow Trolling Bait was seen in a 1903 catalog. I have a thought that this may be Shakesp. selling the Pflueger/Enterprise Rubber Muskallonge Minnow, although they did have rubber technology with the Evolution bait. It is shown on page 177 of my catalog.
20. The Shakesp. Hydroplane was 4-1/2" in length, as the most common model, the 3" length one is hard to find.

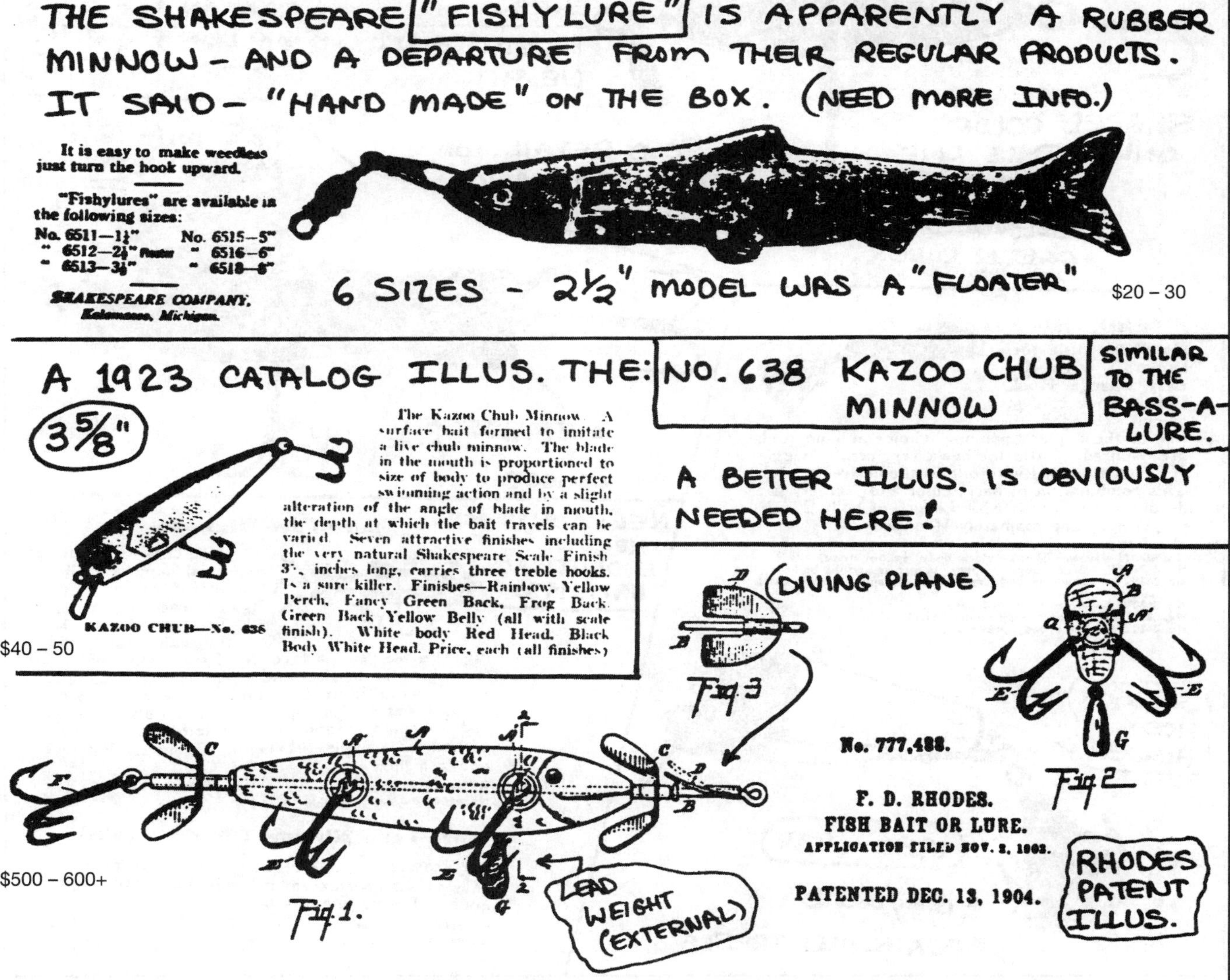

THE SHAKESPEARE "FISHYLURE" IS APPARENTLY A RUBBER MINNOW – AND A DEPARTURE FROM THEIR REGULAR PRODUCTS. IT SAID – "HAND MADE" ON THE BOX. (NEED MORE INFO.)
It is easy to make weedless just turn the hook upward.
"Fishylures" are available in the following sizes:
No. 6511—1½"
" 6512—2½" Floater
" 6513—3½"
No. 6515—5"
" 6516—6"
" 6518—8"
SHAKESPEARE COMPANY, Kalamazoo, Michigan.
6 SIZES – 2½" MODEL WAS A "FLOATER"
$20 – 30
A 1923 CATALOG ILLUS. THE: NO. 638 KAZOO CHUB MINNOW
SIMILAR TO THE BASS-A-LURE.
3⅝"
The Kazoo Chub Minnow. A surface bait formed to imitate a live chub minnow. The blade in the mouth is proportioned to size of body to produce perfect swimming action and by a slight alteration of the angle of blade in mouth, the depth at which the bait travels can be varied. Seven attractive finishes including the very natural Shakespeare Scale Finish 3½ inches long, carries three treble hooks. Is a sure killer. Finishes—Rainbow, Yellow Perch, Fancy Green Back, Frog Back, Green Back Yellow Belly (all with scale finish). White body Red Head, Black Body White Head. Price, each (all finishes)
KAZOO CHUB—No. 636
$40 – 50
A BETTER ILLUS. IS OBVIOUSLY NEEDED HERE!
(DIVING PLANE)
Fig 3
Fig 2
Fig 1.
LEAD WEIGHT (EXTERNAL)
No. 777,488.
F. D. RHODES.
FISH BAIT OR LURE.
APPLICATION FILED NOV. 2, 1903.
PATENTED DEC. 13, 1904.
RHODES PATENT ILLUS.
$500 – 600+

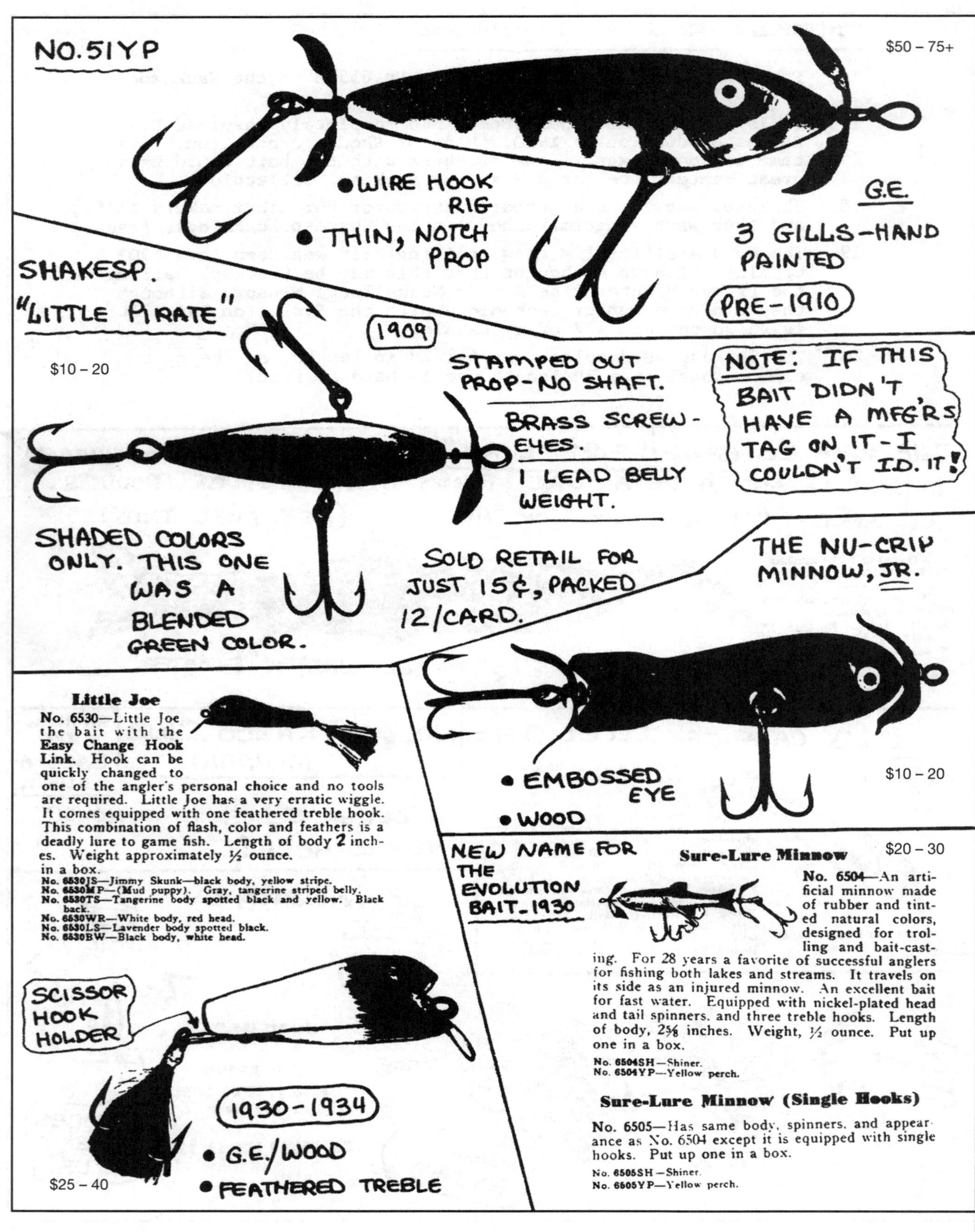
NO. 51YP
$50 – 75+
• WIRE HOOK RIG
• THIN, NOTCH PROP
G.E.
3 GILLS–HAND PAINTED
PRE-1910
SHAKESP. "LITTLE PIRATE"
1909
$10 – 20
STAMPED OUT PROP–NO SHAFT.
BRASS SCREW-EYES.
1 LEAD BELLY WEIGHT.
NOTE: IF THIS BAIT DIDN'T HAVE A MFG'R'S TAG ON IT – I COULDN'T I.D. IT!
SHADED COLORS ONLY. THIS ONE WAS A BLENDED GREEN COLOR.
SOLD RETAIL FOR JUST 15¢, PACKED 12/CARD.
THE NU-CRIP MINNOW, JR.
• EMBOSSED EYE
• WOOD
$10 – 20
SCISSOR HOOK HOLDER
1930-1934
• G.E./WOOD
• FEATHERED TREBLE
$25 – 40
NEW NAME FOR THE EVOLUTION BAIT_1930
$20 – 30

Little Joe

No. 6530—Little Joe the bait with the **Easy Change Hook Link.** Hook can be quickly changed to one of the angler's personal choice and no tools are required. Little Joe has a very erratic wiggle. It comes equipped with one feathered treble hook. This combination of flash, color and feathers is a deadly lure to game fish. Length of body 2 inches. Weight approximately ½ ounce.

in a box.

No. 6530JS—Jimmy Skunk—black body, yellow stripe.
No. 6530MP—(Mud puppy). Gray, tangerine striped belly.
No. 6530TS—Tangerine body spotted black and yellow. Black back.
No. 6530WR—White body, red head.
No. 6530LS—Lavender body spotted black.
No. 6530BW—Black body, white head.

Sure-Lure Minnow

No. 6504—An artificial minnow made of rubber and tinted natural colors, designed for trolling and bait-casting. For 28 years a favorite of successful anglers for fishing both lakes and streams. It travels on its side as an injured minnow. An excellent bait for fast water. Equipped with nickel-plated head and tail spinners, and three treble hooks. Length of body, 2⅝ inches. Weight, ½ ounce. Put up one in a box.

No. 6504SH—Shiner.
No. 6504YP—Yellow perch.

Sure-Lure Minnow (Single Hooks)

No. 6505—Has same body, spinners, and appearance as No. 6504 except it is equipped with single hooks. Put up one in a box.

No. 6505SH—Shiner.
No. 6505YP—Yellow perch.

Shakespeare
Fishing Tackle FREE On Trial

My Fishing Tackle is for sale by all first class dealers, but I want you to see it and try it for yourself. I will send you a complete outfit, express charges prepaid, for a free trial on your next fishing trip. I will also send you free my books on "How to Catch Bass," "The Art of Bait Casting," and my 100 page Catalog of Fine Fishing Tackle. Simply send your name and address and the name and address of a fishing tackle dealer in your city, and I will at once arrange for the free trial. Write at once to William Shakespeare, Jr., 438 Shakespeare Building, Kalamazoo, Michigan.

←APRIL, 1905 AD – (HE WAS CONFIDENT!)

IN 1924 – T. ROBB WAS THE LURE DESIGNER

$50 – 60

Barnacle Bill

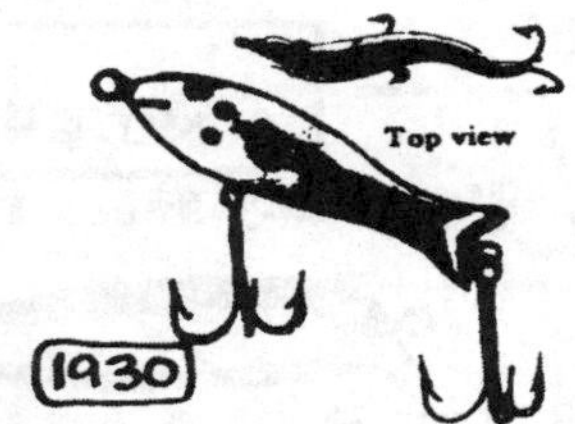
Top view
1930

No. 6529—Barnacle Bill is a tested lure for salt-water fishing, designed to imitate the movements of a minnow. A proven killer for salt-water trout and other species of small salt-water fish. Special shaped body adds an extremely lifelike action. Body wire is continuous through the body making it impossible to pull hooks out. Special plated hooks to resist rust in salt-water. Length of body 3 inches. Weight, 3/5 ounce. Made in the following true-to-nature patterns:

No. 6529WRG—White body, red head, gold flitters.
No. 6529S—White body spotted red, yellow and black. Gold flitters, black back.
No. 6529MP—(Mud puppy). Silver flitters.
No. 6529RN—Rainbow, blue, green, yellow, red and white.
No. 6529GF—Gold fish.
No. 6529W—White body, eyes and tail shaded black.

Shakespeare Company Fine Fishing Tackle Kalamazoo U.S.A.

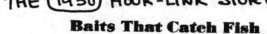

T. Robb Had To Quit Before Breakfast

It was the first day of the bass season, on just an ordinary Michigan Lake. Among the old timers assembled to observe opening day was T. Robb, designer for the Shakespeare Company.
All day long that lake was fished—with every known lure. At all hours of the day fishermen quit—some with one, many with none, some with two or three. Late in the day a meager few had filled their string of ten.
But before breakfast, when other fishermen were barely warmed to the sport, T. Robb and his companion were on their way to shore, each with his limit of ten. Secured on their lures in a few exciting hours.
These Shakespeare lures, Mouse, Bass-A-Lure and (T. Robb) Weedless Spinner are now available, three baits that you should have because "They Catch Fish."

SHAKESPEARE COMPANY, *Kalamazoo, Michigan*

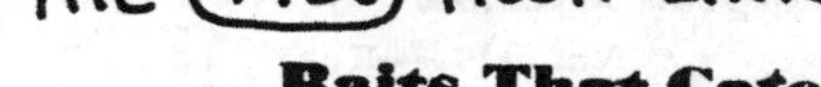

(THE 1930 HOOK-LINK STORY)

$20 – 30

Baits That Catch Fish

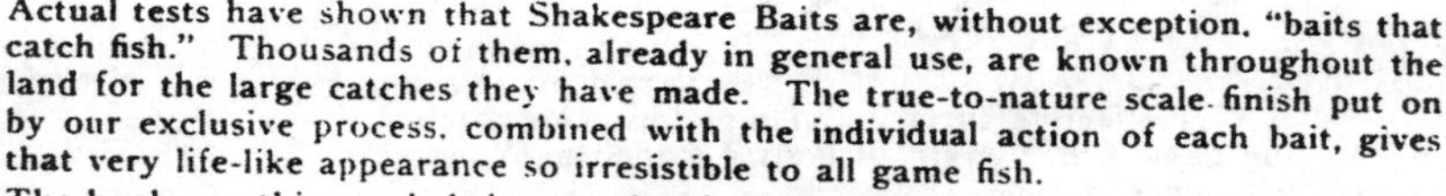

Actual tests have shown that Shakespeare Baits are, without exception, "baits that catch fish." Thousands of them, already in general use, are known throughout the land for the large catches they have made. The true-to-nature scale finish put on by our exclusive process, combined with the individual action of each bait, gives that very life-like appearance so irresistible to all game fish.
The hooks on this year's baits are plated with a new special rust-resisting material found only on Shakespeare hooks. This gives longer life to the hooks in salt-water as well as fresh-water.
The diagram at the right shows the method used in attaching the treble belly hooks on the Slim Jim, Bass-A-Lure, Kazoo Wobbler, Tantalizer, Sea Witch Midget, Tarpalunge, Striped Bass Wobbler, Barnacle Bill, Little Joe and Sure-Lure Minnow baits. This link or clevis arrangement makes it impossible for a large fish to pull out the hooks.

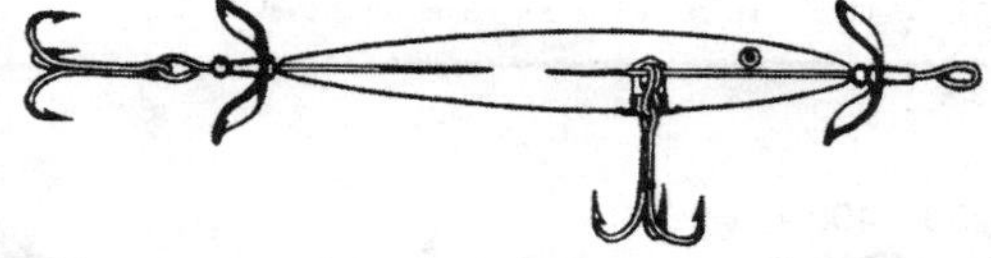

$40 – 50

Absolutely Weedless
Always Alive
Gets the Fish
Constantly Swimming and Kicking
CAME IN WOODEN BOX – IN THE EARLY PROD.

RHODES MECH. FROG PAT'D. OCT. 31, 1905. AND JULY 3, 1906.

$40 – 50

1921

(PRESSED EYE)

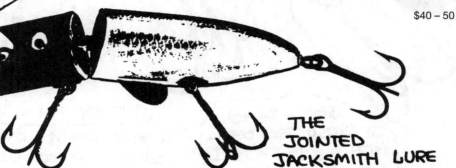

THE JOINTED JACKSMITH LURE

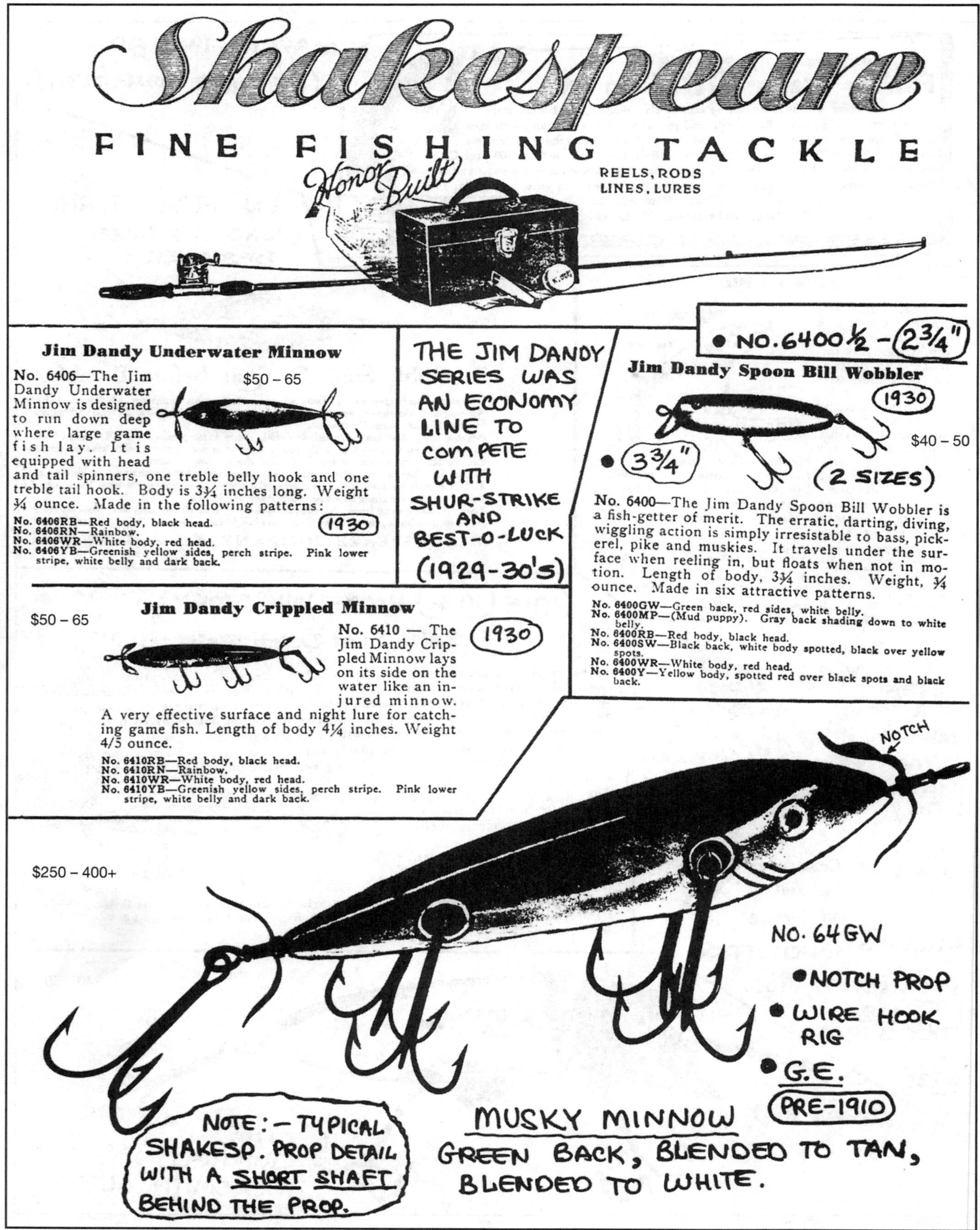
Shakespeare
FINE FISHING TACKLE
Honor Built
REELS, RODS
LINES, LURES
Jim Dandy Underwater Minnow
No. 6406—The Jim Dandy Underwater Minnow is designed to run down deep where large game fish lay. It is equipped with head and tail spinners, one treble belly hook and one treble tail hook. Body is 3¼ inches long. Weight ¾ ounce. Made in the following patterns:
No. 6406RB—Red body, black head.
No. 6406RN—Rainbow.
No. 6406WR—White body, red head.
No. 6406YB—Greenish yellow sides, perch stripe. Pink lower stripe, white belly and dark back.
$50 – 65
1930
THE JIM DANDY SERIES WAS AN ECONOMY LINE TO COMPETE WITH SHUR-STRIKE AND BEST-O-LUCK (1929-30'S)
• NO. 6400½ - 2¾"
Jim Dandy Spoon Bill Wobbler
1930
$40 – 50
• 3¾"
(2 SIZES)
No. 6400—The Jim Dandy Spoon Bill Wobbler is a fish-getter of merit. The erratic, darting, diving, wiggling action is simply irresistable to bass, pickerel, pike and muskies. It travels under the surface when reeling in, but floats when not in motion. Length of body, 3¾ inches. Weight, ¾ ounce. Made in six attractive patterns.
No. 6400GW—Green back, red sides, white belly.
No. 6400MP—(Mud puppy). Gray back shading down to white belly.
No. 6400RB—Red body, black head.
No. 6400SW—Black back, white body spotted, black over yellow spots.
No. 6400WR—White body, red head.
No. 6400Y—Yellow body, spotted red over black spots and black back.
Jim Dandy Crippled Minnow
$50 – 65
No. 6410 — The Jim Dandy Crippled Minnow lays on its side on the water like an injured minnow. A very effective surface and night lure for catching game fish. Length of body 4¼ inches. Weight 4/5 ounce.
1930
No. 6410RB—Red body, black head.
No. 6410RN—Rainbow.
No. 6410WR—White body, red head.
No. 6410YB—Greenish yellow sides, perch stripe. Pink lower stripe, white belly and dark back.
NOTCH
$250 – 400+
NO. 64GW
• NOTCH PROP
• WIRE HOOK RIG
• G.E.
PRE-1910
MUSKY MINNOW
GREEN BACK, BLENDED TO TAN, BLENDED TO WHITE.
NOTE: - TYPICAL SHAKESP. PROP DETAIL WITH A SHORT SHAFT BEHIND THE PROP.

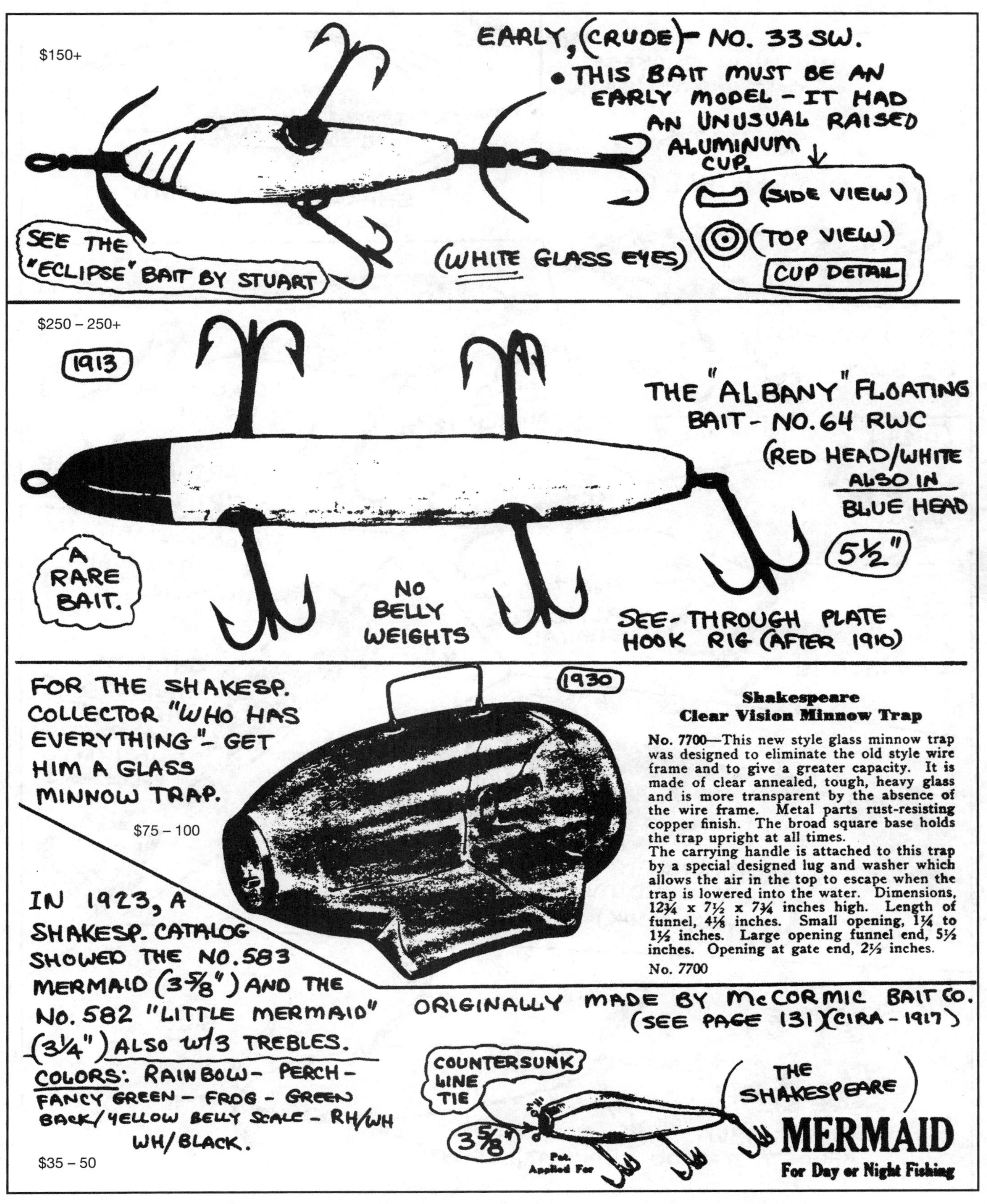
$150+
EARLY, (CRUDE) - NO. 33 SW.
• THIS BAIT MUST BE AN EARLY MODEL - IT HAD AN UNUSUAL RAISED ALUMINUM CUP.
(SIDE VIEW)
(TOP VIEW)
CUP DETAIL
SEE THE "ECLIPSE" BAIT BY STUART
(WHITE GLASS EYES)
$250 – 250+
1913
THE "ALBANY" FLOATING BAIT - NO. 64 RWC
(RED HEAD/WHITE
ALSO IN
BLUE HEAD
5½"
A RARE BAIT.
NO BELLY WEIGHTS
SEE-THROUGH PLATE HOOK RIG (AFTER 1910)
FOR THE SHAKESP. COLLECTOR "WHO HAS EVERYTHING" - GET HIM A GLASS MINNOW TRAP.
1930
$75 – 100
IN 1923, A SHAKESP. CATALOG SHOWED THE NO. 583 MERMAID (3-5/8") AND THE NO. 582 "LITTLE MERMAID" (3¼") ALSO W/3 TREBLES.
COLORS: RAINBOW - PERCH - FANCY GREEN - FROG - GREEN BACK/YELLOW BELLY SCALE - RH/WH WH/BLACK.
$35 – 50
ORIGINALLY MADE BY McCORMIC BAIT CO. (SEE PAGE 131) (CIRA - 1917)
COUNTERSUNK LINE TIE
3⅝"
Pat. Applied For
(THE SHAKESPEARE)
MERMAID
For Day or Night Fishing

Shakespeare
Clear Vision Minnow Trap

No. 7700—This new style glass minnow trap was designed to eliminate the old style wire frame and to give a greater capacity. It is made of clear annealed, tough, heavy glass and is more transparent by the absence of the wire frame. Metal parts rust-resisting copper finish. The broad square base holds the trap upright at all times.
The carrying handle is attached to this trap by a special designed lug and washer which allows the air in the top to escape when the trap is lowered into the water. Dimensions, 12¾ x 7½ x 7¾ inches high. Length of funnel, 4⅛ inches. Small opening, 1¼ to 1½ inches. Large opening funnel end, 5½ inches. Opening at gate end, 2½ inches.

No. 7700

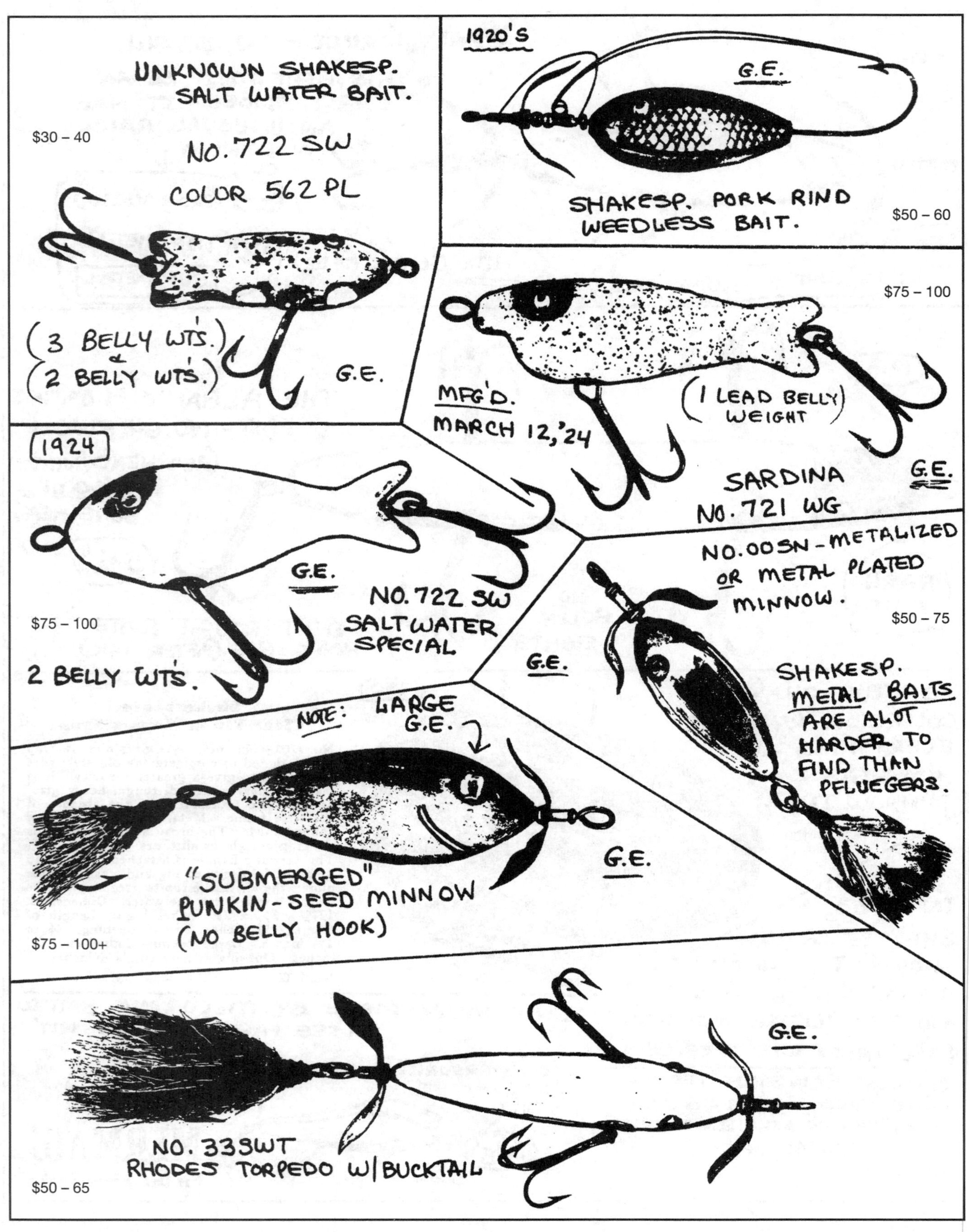

UNKNOWN SHAKESP. SALT WATER BAIT.
$30 – 40
NO. 722 SW
COLOR 562 PL
(3 BELLY WTS.) & (2 BELLY WTS.)
G.E.
1920'S
G.E.
SHAKESP. PORK RIND WEEDLESS BAIT.
$50 – 60
$75 – 100
MFG'D. MARCH 12, '24
(1 LEAD BELLY WEIGHT)
SARDINA NO. 721 WG
G.E.
1924
G.E.
NO. 722 SW SALTWATER SPECIAL
$75 – 100
2 BELLY WTS.
NO. 00SN - METALIZED OR METAL PLATED MINNOW.
$50 – 75
G.E.
SHAKESP. METAL BAITS ARE ALOT HARDER TO FIND THAN PFLUEGERS.
NOTE: LARGE G.E.
G.E.
"SUBMERGED" PUNKIN-SEED MINNOW (NO BELLY HOOK)
$75 – 100+
G.E.
NO. 33SWT RHODES TORPEDO W/BUCKTAIL
$50 – 65

"Shakespeare-Worden" Bucktail Bait

$50 – 100

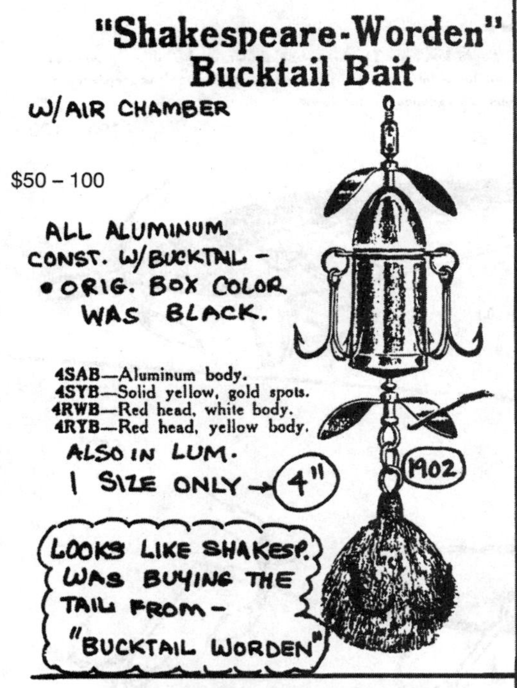
W/AIR CHAMBER
ALL ALUMINUM CONST. W/BUCKTAIL – • ORIG. BOX COLOR WAS BLACK.
4SAB—Aluminum body.
4SYB—Solid yellow, gold spots.
4RWB—Red head, white body.
4RYB—Red head, yellow body.
ALSO IN LUM.
1 SIZE ONLY → 4"
1902
LOOKS LIKE SHAKESP. WAS BUYING THE TAIL FROM – "BUCKTAIL WORDEN"

"Revolution" Bait

$50 – 100

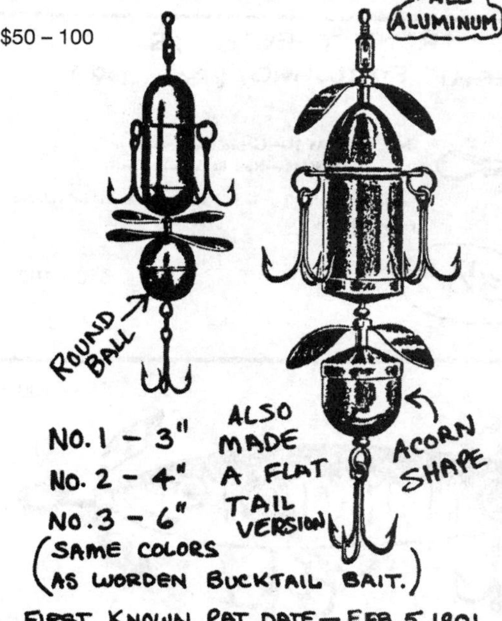
ALL ALUMINUM
ROUND BALL
ACORN SHAPE
NO. 1 – 3"
NO. 2 – 4"
NO. 3 – 6"
ALSO MADE A FLAT TAIL VERSION
(SAME COLORS AS WORDEN BUCKTAIL BAIT.)
FIRST KNOWN PAT. DATE – FEB. 5, 1901

NO. 680

$20 – 25

No. 680

Night Caster

SHAKESP. LUMINOUS FLOATING BAIT.

"Rhodes" Wooden Minnow

$50 – 100

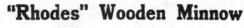

1910

No. 44 About 4-5 actual size

The "Rhodes" Wooden Minnows are made of exactly the same high grade materials and with the same first class finish as the "Shakespeare" Minnows They are identical in construction throughout except that the Rhodes baits have *round* instead of *shaped* bodies. The hook link shown in the illustration has now been discarded for a newer one, the same as depicted in the representations of the various "Shakespeare" Minnows.

No. 44 Length of body 3 3-4 in.

No. 44GWR—Green back, white belly.
No. 44RWR—Red back, white belly.
No. 44BWR—Brown back, white belly.
No. 44GWN—Green back, white belly, striped;
No. 44RWN—Red back, white belly, striped.
No. 44BWN—Brown back, white belly, striped-

NOTE—Bucktail on any of above baits, in place of tail hook, extra,

"Rhodes" Wooden Minnow

$50 – 100

No. 43

¾ actual size

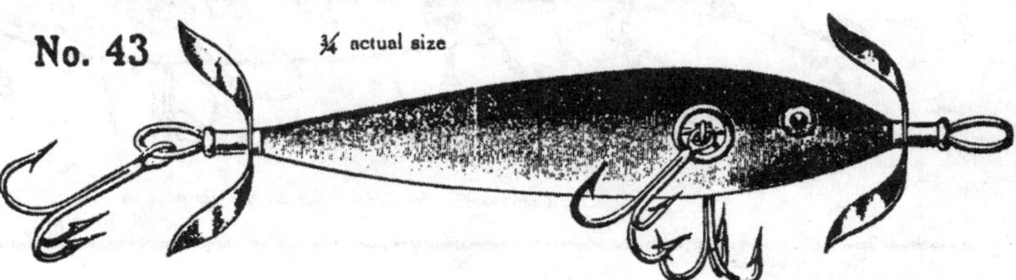

No. 43—Length of body 3 3-4 ins.

ALSO W/BUCKTAIL

No. 43GWR—Green back, white belly.
43RWR—Red back, white belly.
43BWR—Brown Back, white belly.

No. 43GWN—Green back, white belly, striped.
43RWN—Red back, white belly, striped.
43BWN—Brown back, white belly,

NOTE—Bucktail on any of above baits, in place of tail hook, extra,

No. 33—Length of body 3 inches

No. 33GWR—Green back, white belly.
33RWR—Red back, white belly.
33BWR—Brown Back, white belly.

No. 33SRR—Red, solid color,
33SYR—Yellow, solid color.
33SWR—White, solid color.

NO. 3

$50 – 75

No. 3—Artifical Minnow Trolling Bait.

"Rhodes" Casting Minnows

The "Rhodes" Wooden Minnows are made of exactly the same high grade materials and with the same first class finish as the "Shakespeare" minnows. They are identical in construction throughout except that the Rhodes baits have *round* instead of *shaped* bodies. The hook link shown in the illustration has now been discarded for a later model, the same as shown in the representations of the various "Shakespeare" minnows.

$50 – 100

No. 33GWR—Green back, white belly.
33RWR—Red back, white belly.
33GWN—Green back, white belly, striped.
33RWN—Red back, white belly, striped.

Length of body 3 in.; 2 spinners; 4 treble side, 1 treble tail hook.

Cut shows No. 33

3"

WE JUST LEARNED SOMETHING HERE - RHODES MINNOWS HAD ROUND, RATHER THAN SHAPED BODIES.

$50 – 100

Rhodes "Torpedo" Bait

This is a very striking and popular bait and a great fish getter. The construction is similar to that of the regular Rhodes minnows except that it has brass eyes. Furnished in eight color combinations, enameled in bright attractive shades.

No.	No.
33RWT—Red and white.	**33GWT**—Green and white.
33SWT—Solid white.	**33SRT**—Solid red.
33SYT—Solid yellow.	**33SAT**—Solid aluminum.
33RHT—Red head, white body.	**33RTT**—Red head and tail.

Length of body, 3 in.; 2 spinners; 2 treble side, 1 treble tail hook.

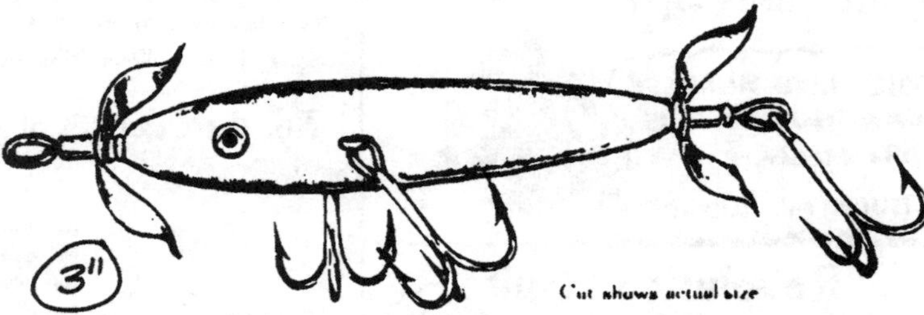

3"

Cut shows actual size

NOTE: ON SHAKESP. & SO. BEND 5 HOOKERS - FRONT TREBLE IS RIGHT FORWARD (FROM TOP)

No. 44GWR—Green back, white belly.
44RWR—Red back, white belly.

Length of body, 3¼ in.; 2 spinners; 4 treble side, 1 treble tail hook.

$50 – 100

3¼"

Cut shows No. 44GWR—About 4-5 actual size.

$50 – 100

No. 44GWN—Green back, white belly, striped.
44RWN—Red back, white belly, striped.

Length of body, 3¼ in.; 2 spinners; 4 treble side, 1 treble tail hook.

3¼"

Cut shows No. 44GWN—About 4-5 actual size.

FAVORITE IS TOUGH!

"Favorite" Floating Bait

NO. 41 3-5/8"

This is absolutely a surface floating bait with a hook arrangement that is right. The belly hook is held in position by a small pin, and the tail hook gets the strikes from behind. The shape of the body makes the bait ride properly in the water.

No. 41—Length of body, 3⅝ in.; 1 double belly hook, 1 treble tail hook.

No.	No.
41SRF—Solid red color.	**41SYF**—Solid yellow color.
41SWF—Solid white color.	**41FRF**—Imitation frog color

NOTE: BELLY PIN

$75 – 125

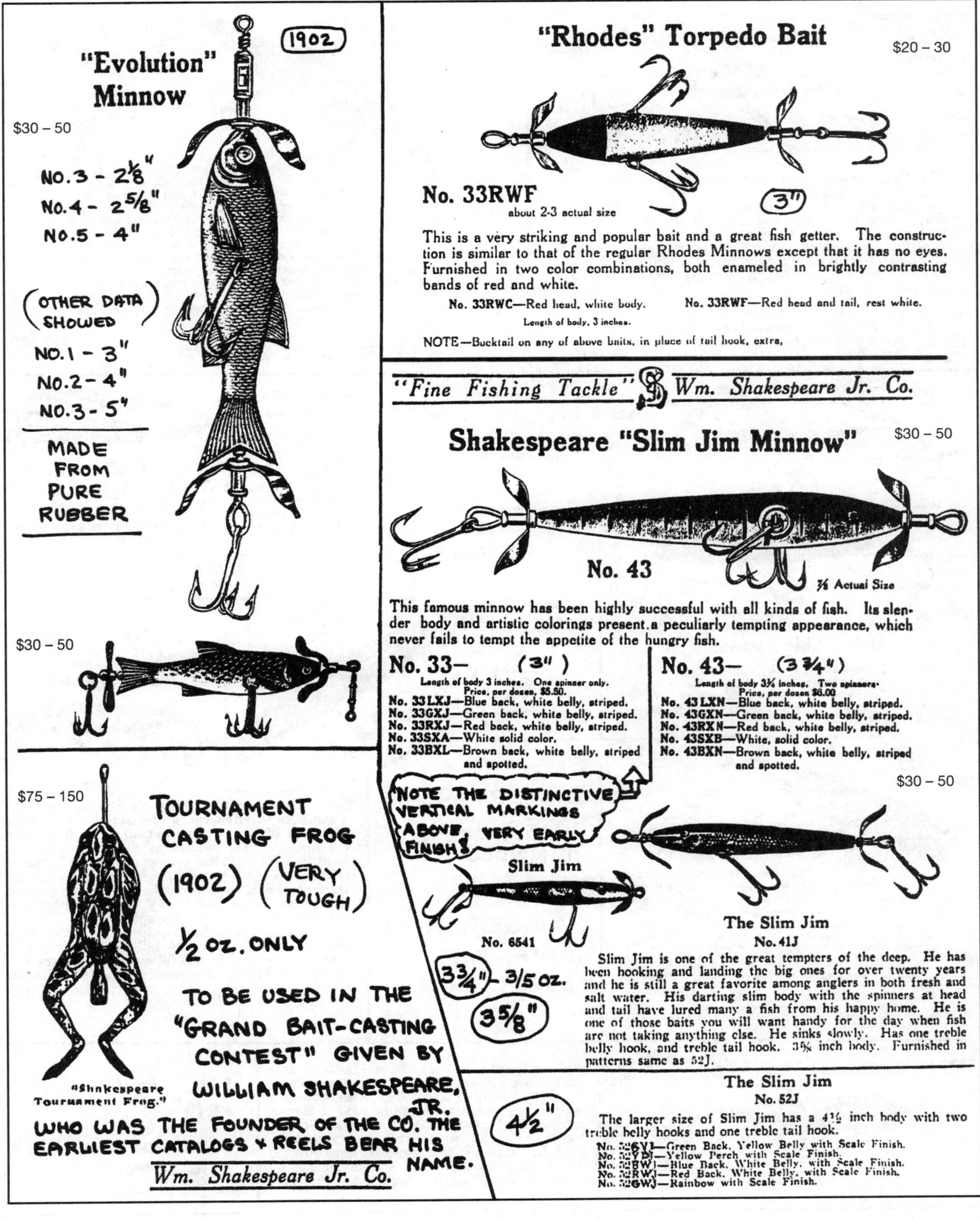
"Evolution" Minnow
(1902)
$30 – 50
NO.3 - 2 1/8"
NO.4 - 2 5/8"
NO.5 - 4"
(OTHER DATA SHOWED
NO.1 - 3"
NO.2 - 4"
NO.3 - 5"
MADE FROM PURE RUBBER
$30 – 50
$75 – 150
TOURNAMENT CASTING FROG
(1902) (VERY TOUGH)
1/2 OZ. ONLY
TO BE USED IN THE "GRAND BAIT-CASTING CONTEST" GIVEN BY WILLIAM SHAKESPEARE, JR. WHO WAS THE FOUNDER OF THE CO. THE EARLIEST CATALOGS & REELS BEAR HIS NAME.
"Shakespeare Tournament Frog."
Wm. Shakespeare Jr. Co.
"Rhodes" Torpedo Bait
$20 – 30
No. 33RWF
about 2-3 actual size
(3")
This is a very striking and popular bait and a great fish getter. The construction is similar to that of the regular Rhodes Minnows except that it has no eyes. Furnished in two color combinations, both enameled in brightly contrasting bands of red and white.
No. 33RWC—Red head, white body.
No. 33RWF—Red head and tail, rest white.
Length of body, 3 inches.
NOTE—Bucktail on any of above baits, in place of tail hook, extra.
"Fine Fishing Tackle" Wm. Shakespeare Jr. Co.
Shakespeare "Slim Jim Minnow"
$30 – 50
No. 43
3/4 Actual Size
This famous minnow has been highly successful with all kinds of fish. Its slender body and artistic colorings present a peculiarly tempting appearance, which never fails to tempt the appetite of the hungry fish.
No. 33— (3")
Length of body 3 inches. One spinner only.
Price, per dozen, $5.50.
No. 33LXJ—Blue back, white belly, striped.
No. 33GXJ—Green back, white belly, striped.
No. 33RXJ—Red back, white belly, striped.
No. 33SXA—White solid color.
No. 33BXL—Brown back, white belly, striped and spotted.
No. 43— (3 3/4")
Length of body 3 3/4 inches. Two spinners.
Price, per dozen $8.00
No. 43LXN—Blue back, white belly, striped.
No. 43GXN—Green back, white belly, striped.
No. 43RXN—Red back, white belly, striped.
No. 43SXB—White, solid color.
No. 43BXN—Brown back, white belly, striped and spotted.
NOTE THE DISTINCTIVE VERTICAL MARKINGS ABOVE, VERY EARLY FINISH!
$30 – 50
Slim Jim
No. 6541
3 3/4" - 3/5 oz.
3 5/8"
The Slim Jim
No. 41J
Slim Jim is one of the great tempters of the deep. He has been hooking and landing the big ones for over twenty years and he is still a great favorite among anglers in both fresh and salt water. His darting slim body with the spinners at head and tail have lured many a fish from his happy home. He is one of those baits you will want handy for the day when fish are not taking anything else. He sinks slowly. Has one treble belly hook, and treble tail hook. 3 5/8 inch body. Furnished in patterns same as 52J.
The Slim Jim
No. 52J
4 1/2"
The larger size of Slim Jim has a 4 1/2 inch body with two treble belly hooks and one treble tail hook.
No. 52GYJ—Green Back, Yellow Belly with Scale Finish.
No. 52YPJ—Yellow Perch with Scale Finish.
No. 52BWJ—Blue Back, White Belly, with Scale Finish.
No. 52RWJ—Red Back, White Belly, with Scale Finish.
No. 52GWJ—Rainbow with Scale Finish.

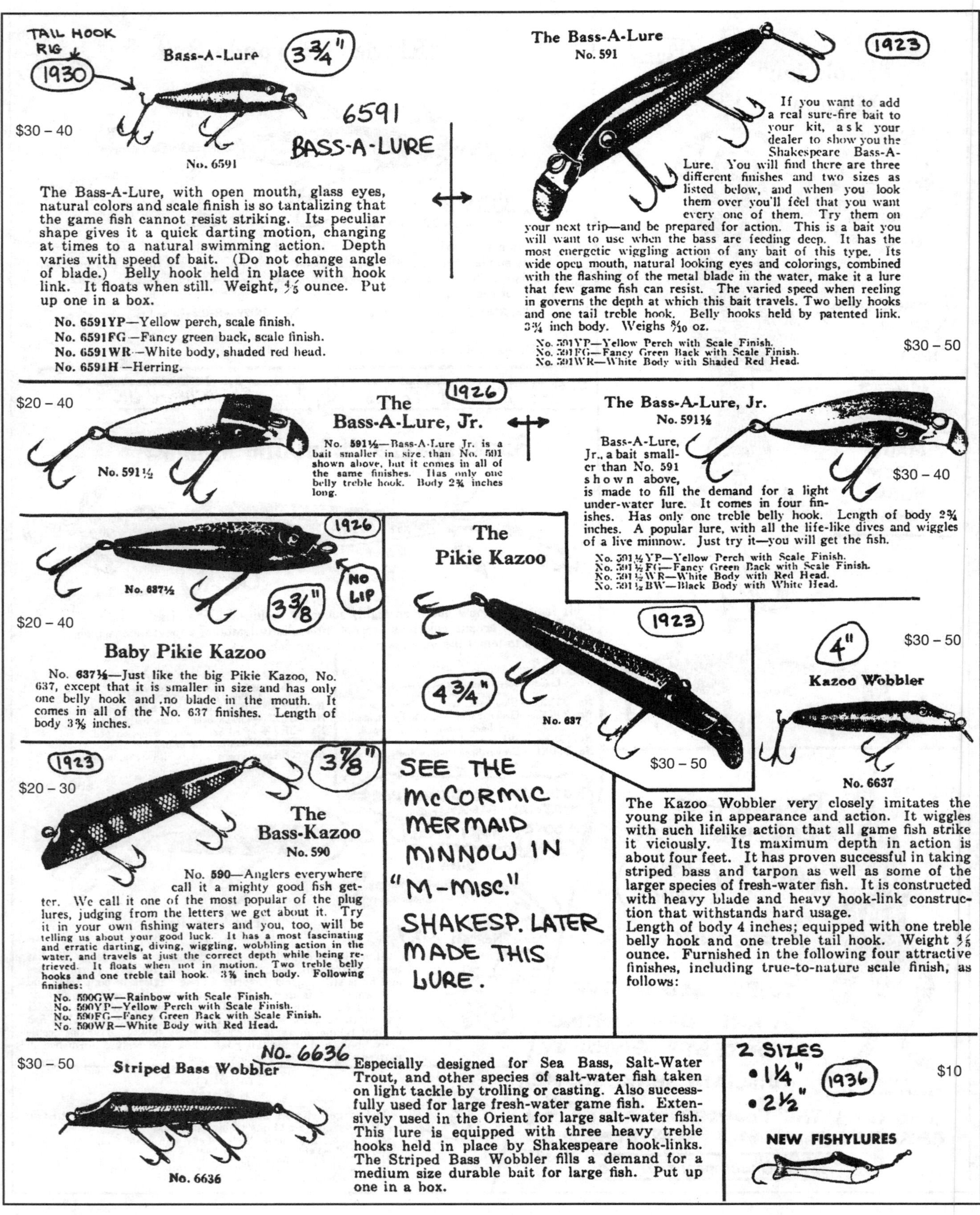
TAIL HOOK RIG
1930
3¾"
6591
BASS-A-LURE
1923
1926
1926
NO LIP
3⅜"
1923
4¾"
4"
1923
3⅞"
SEE THE McCORMIC MERMAID MINNOW IN "M-MISC." SHAKESP. LATER MADE THIS LURE.
NO. 6636
2 SIZES
• 1¼"
• 2½"
1936

$30 – 40

Bass-A-Lure

No. 6591

The Bass-A-Lure, with open mouth, glass eyes, natural colors and scale finish is so tantalizing that the game fish cannot resist striking. Its peculiar shape gives it a quick darting motion, changing at times to a natural swimming action. Depth varies with speed of bait. (Do not change angle of blade.) Belly hook held in place with hook link. It floats when still. Weight, ⅕ ounce. Put up one in a box.

No. 6591YP—Yellow perch, scale finish.
No. 6591FG—Fancy green back, scale finish.
No. 6591WR—White body, shaded red head.
No. 6591H—Herring.

The Bass-A-Lure
No. 591

If you want to add a real sure-fire bait to your kit, ask your dealer to show you the Shakespeare Bass-A-Lure. You will find there are three different finishes and two sizes as listed below, and when you look them over you'll feel that you want every one of them. Try them on your next trip—and be prepared for action. This is a bait you will want to use when the bass are feeding deep. It has the most energetic wiggling action of any bait of this type. Its wide open mouth, natural looking eyes and colorings, combined with the flashing of the metal blade in the water, make it a lure that few game fish can resist. The varied speed when reeling in governs the depth at which this bait travels. Two belly hooks and one tail treble hook. Belly hooks held by patented link. 3¾ inch body. Weighs 8/10 oz.

No. 591YP—Yellow Perch with Scale Finish.
No. 591FG—Fancy Green Back with Scale Finish.
No. 591WR—White Body with Shaded Red Head.

$30 – 50

$20 – 40

The Bass-A-Lure, Jr.

No. 591½

No. 591½—Bass-A-Lure Jr. is a bait smaller in size than No. 591 shown above, but it comes in all of the same finishes. Has only one belly treble hook. Body 2¾ inches long.

The Bass-A-Lure, Jr.
No. 591½

Bass-A-Lure, Jr., a bait smaller than No. 591 shown above, is made to fill the demand for a light under-water lure. It comes in four finishes. Has only one treble belly hook. Length of body 2¾ inches. A popular lure, with all the life-like dives and wiggles of a live minnow. Just try it—you will get the fish.

$30 – 40

No. 591½YP—Yellow Perch with Scale Finish.
No. 591½FG—Fancy Green Back with Scale Finish.
No. 591½WR—White Body with Red Head.
No. 591½BW—Black Body with White Head.

No. 637½

$20 – 40

Baby Pikie Kazoo

No. **637½**—Just like the big Pikie Kazoo, No. 637, except that it is smaller in size and has only one belly hook and no blade in the mouth. It comes in all of the No. 637 finishes. Length of body 3⅜ inches.

The Pikie Kazoo

No. 637

$30 – 50

$30 – 50

Kazoo Wobbler

No. 6637

The Kazoo Wobbler very closely imitates the young pike in appearance and action. It wiggles with such lifelike action that all game fish strike it viciously. Its maximum depth in action is about four feet. It has proven successful in taking striped bass and tarpon as well as some of the larger species of fresh-water fish. It is constructed with heavy blade and heavy hook-link construction that withstands hard usage.
Length of body 4 inches; equipped with one treble belly hook and one treble tail hook. Weight ⅘ ounce. Furnished in the following four attractive finishes, including true-to-nature scale finish, as follows:

$20 – 30

The Bass-Kazoo
No. 590

No. **590**—Anglers everywhere call it a mighty good fish getter. We call it one of the most popular of the plug lures, judging from the letters we get about it. Try it in your own fishing waters and you, too, will be telling us about your good luck. It has a most fascinating and erratic darting, diving, wiggling, wobbling action in the water, and travels at just the correct depth while being retrieved. It floats when not in motion. Two treble belly hooks and one treble tail hook. 3⅞ inch body. Following finishes:

No. 590GW—Rainbow with Scale Finish.
No. 590YP—Yellow Perch with Scale Finish.
No. 590FG—Fancy Green Back with Scale Finish.
No. 590WR—White Body with Red Head.

$30 – 50

Striped Bass Wobbler

No. 6636

Especially designed for Sea Bass, Salt-Water Trout, and other species of salt-water fish taken on light tackle by trolling or casting. Also successfully used for large fresh-water game fish. Extensively used in the Orient for large salt-water fish. This lure is equipped with three heavy treble hooks held in place by Shakespeare hook-links. The Striped Bass Wobbler fills a demand for a medium size durable bait for large fish. Put up one in a box.

$10

NEW FISHYLURES

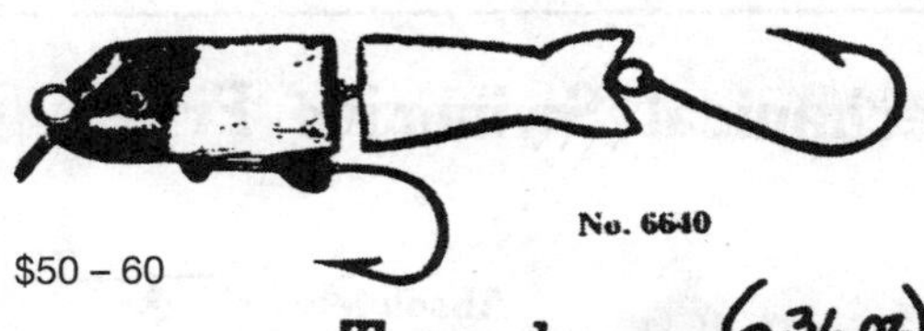

No. 6640

$50 – 60

Tarpalunge (2¾ oz)

Hook-Link Construction

MT'—Mullet.
SH'—Shiner.
WRS—Red and White; Silver Flitters.

$30 – 50

Strike-It (NO METAL LIP)

No. 6666

A shallow running jointed bait with the same natural swimming action as the deep running Shakespeare Tantalizer which is universally popular with anglers. This combination must be seen in action to be fully appreciated. It gets the fish when other baits fail. The Strike-It is easy to cast. The close joint allows the bait to bend just enough for ideal action but not enough to affect the accuracy of the cast. Put up one in a box. Weight, 4/5 ounce.

No. 6666H - Herring.
No. 6666MP - Light grey back and sides, red at throat.
No. 6666WR - White body, shaded red head.

1928

Tantalizer OLDER VINTAGE NO: NO. 638

$30 – 50

(4")

No. 6638

HEAVY DUTY RIG - 9/10 oz.

$30 – 50

NO. 6639 (4")

TANTALIZER, JR.

SMALLER SCALE VERSION OF 6638.

¾ oz.

6638WR—White body, shaded red head.
6638YP—Yellow perch with scale finish.
6638P—Pickerel.
6638H—Herring.

$30 – 40

NO. 6534

(2¾") - ½ oz.

SEA WITCH MIDGET

$75 – 100+

Shakespeare "Metal Plated" Minnows

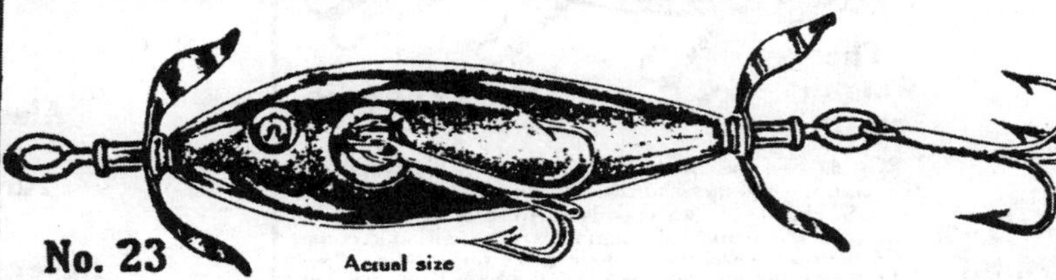

No. 23 Actual size

These baits are made by electroplating a regular Shakespeare Minnow with a heavy coating of nickel, gold or copper, placed directly over preparatory coats of special enamel. They are an unsurpassed success for deep water trolling and casting. The bright gleam of the polished metalic surface attracts the fish from a great distance.

No. 03—Length of body 1 3-4 inches

No. 03SC—Solid copper. No. 03SN—Solid nickel. No. 03SG—Solid gold.

No. 23—Length of body 2 1-2 inches

No. 23SC—Solid copper. No. 23SN—Solid nickel. No. 23SG—Solid gold.

(ALSO IN NO. 44) **No. 33—Length of body 3 inches**

No. 33SC—Solid copper. No. 33SN—Solid nickel. No. 33SG—Solid gold.

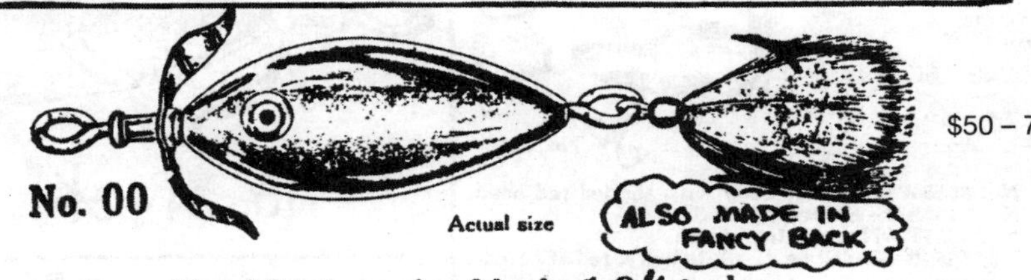

No. 00 Actual size

ALSO MADE IN FANCY BACK

$50 – 75

No. 00—Length of body 1-3/4 inches

No. 00SC—Solid copper. No. 00SN—Solid nickel. No. 00SG—Solid gold.

Shakespeare "Shiner" Minnow

(2 SIZES)

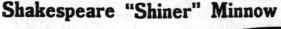

A very popular minnow made in immitation of a "shiner"—black back, white belly. Made in two sizes with fancy feathered bucktail. Furnished without bucktail if desired.

No. 23 4-5 actual size

$50 – 65

- No. 23BWS — Length of body, 2½ inches.
- No. 43BWS — Length of body, 3¾ inches.

NO. 6553 - SEA WITCH

SAME AS NO. 133 EXCEPT DOUBLE LINE TIE.

(3 5/16") - ½ oz.

(1928)

ALSO LATER AS NO. 6531 - (3¾")

(4") - ¾ oz.

The Sea Witch
No. 133

$40 – 50

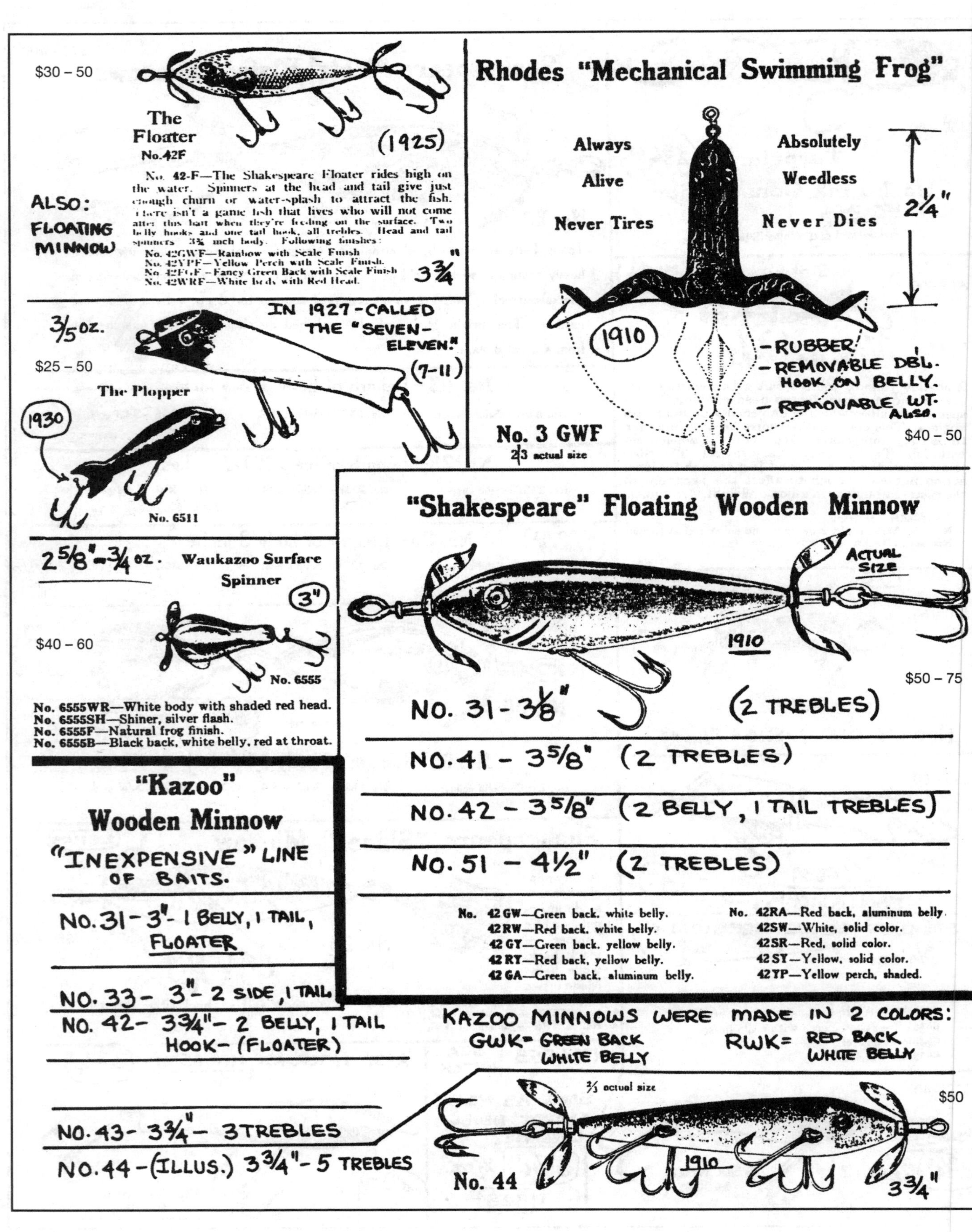

$30 – 50

The Floater
No.42F

(1925)

ALSO: FLOATING MINNOW

No. 42-F—The Shakespeare Floater rides high on the water. Spinners at the head and tail give just enough churn or water-splash to attract the fish. There isn't a game fish that lives who will not come after this bait when they're feeding on the surface. Two belly hooks and one tail hook, all trebles. Head and tail spinners 3¾ inch body. Following finishes:

No. 42GWF—Rainbow with Scale Finish
No. 42YPF—Yellow Perch with Scale Finish.
No. 42FGF—Fancy Green Back with Scale Finish
No. 42WRF—White body with Red Head.

3¾"

3/5 oz.

IN 1927 - CALLED THE "SEVEN-ELEVEN." (7-11)

$25 – 50

The Plopper

1930

No. 6511

2 5/8" – 3/4 oz.

Waukazoo Surface Spinner

3"

$40 – 60

No. 6555

No. 6555WR—White body with shaded red head.
No. 6555SH—Shiner, silver flash.
No. 6555F—Natural frog finish.
No. 6555B—Black back, white belly, red at throat.

Rhodes "Mechanical Swimming Frog"

Always Alive

Never Tires

Absolutely Weedless

Never Dies

2¼"

1910

- RUBBER
- REMOVABLE DBL. HOOK ON BELLY.
- REMOVABLE WT. ALSO.

No. 3 GWF
2/3 actual size

$40 – 50

"Shakespeare" Floating Wooden Minnow

ACTUAL SIZE

1910

$50 – 75

NO. 31 - 3 1/8" (2 TREBLES)

NO. 41 - 3 5/8" (2 TREBLES)

NO. 42 - 3 5/8" (2 BELLY, 1 TAIL TREBLES)

NO. 51 - 4½" (2 TREBLES)

No. 42 GW—Green back, white belly.
42 RW—Red back, white belly.
42 GY—Green back, yellow belly.
42 RY—Red back, yellow belly.
42 GA—Green back, aluminum belly.

No. 42RA—Red back, aluminum belly.
42SW—White, solid color.
42SR—Red, solid color.
42 SY—Yellow, solid color.
42 YP—Yellow perch, shaded.

"Kazoo" Wooden Minnow

"INEXPENSIVE" LINE OF BAITS.

NO. 31 - 3" - 1 BELLY, 1 TAIL, FLOATER

NO. 33 - 3" - 2 SIDE, 1 TAIL

NO. 42 - 3¾" - 2 BELLY, 1 TAIL HOOK - (FLOATER)

NO. 43 - 3¾" - 3 TREBLES

NO. 44 - (ILLUS.) 3¾" - 5 TREBLES

KAZOO MINNOWS WERE MADE IN 2 COLORS:
GWK = GREEN BACK WHITE BELLY
RWK = RED BACK WHITE BELLY

2/3 actual size

$50

1910

No. 44

3¾"

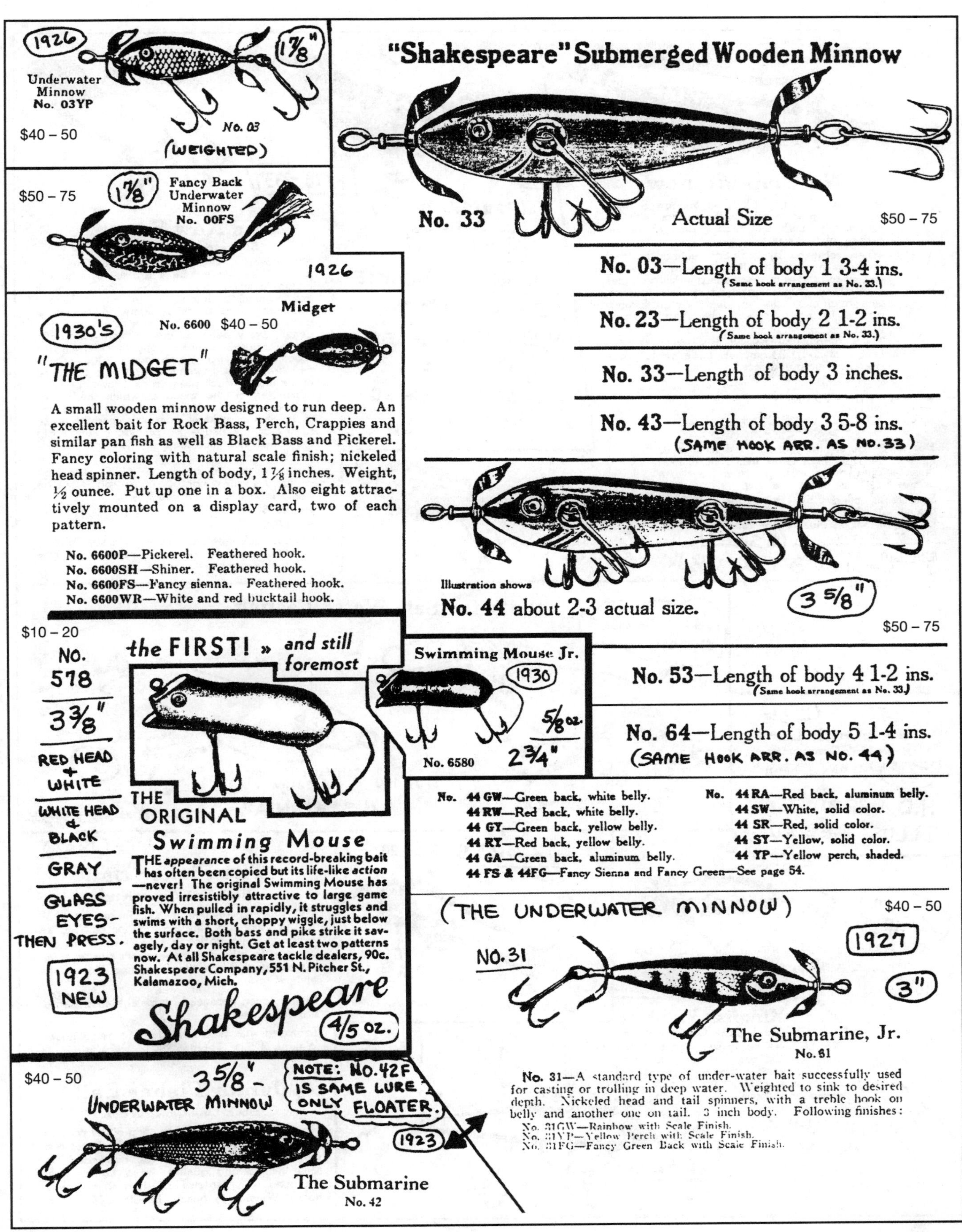

1926 — 1⅞"

Underwater Minnow No. 03YP

No. 03 (WEIGHTED)

$40 – 50

$50 – 75 — 1⅞"

Fancy Back Underwater Minnow No. 00FS

1926

"Shakespeare" Submerged Wooden Minnow

No. 33 — Actual Size — $50 – 75

No. 03—Length of body 1 3-4 ins. (Same hook arrangement as No. 33.)

No. 23—Length of body 2 1-2 ins. (Same hook arrangement as No. 33.)

No. 33—Length of body 3 inches.

No. 43—Length of body 3 5-8 ins. (SAME HOOK ARR. AS NO. 33)

Illustration shows No. 44 about 2-3 actual size. — 3 ⅝"

$50 – 75

No. 53—Length of body 4 1-2 ins. (Same hook arrangement as No. 33.)

No. 64—Length of body 5 1-4 ins. (SAME HOOK ARR. AS NO. 44)

No. 44 GW—Green back, white belly.
44 RW—Red back, white belly.
44 GY—Green back, yellow belly.
44 RY—Red back, yellow belly.
44 GA—Green back, aluminum belly.
44 FS & 44FG—Fancy Sienna and Fancy Green—See page 54.

No. 44 RA—Red back, aluminum belly.
44 SW—White, solid color.
44 SR—Red, solid color.
44 SY—Yellow, solid color.
44 YP—Yellow perch, shaded.

Midget

1930's — No. 6600 $40 – 50

"THE MIDGET"

A small wooden minnow designed to run deep. An excellent bait for Rock Bass, Perch, Crappies and similar pan fish as well as Black Bass and Pickerel. Fancy coloring with natural scale finish; nickeled head spinner. Length of body, 1⅞ inches. Weight, ½ ounce. Put up one in a box. Also eight attractively mounted on a display card, two of each pattern.

No. 6600P—Pickerel. Feathered hook.
No. 6600SH—Shiner. Feathered hook.
No. 6600FS—Fancy sienna. Feathered hook.
No. 6600WR—White and red bucktail hook.

$10 – 20

NO. 578 — 3⅜"

RED HEAD + WHITE

WHITE HEAD & BLACK

GRAY

GLASS EYES-THEN PRESS.

1923 NEW

the FIRST! » and still foremost

THE ORIGINAL Swimming Mouse

THE *appearance* of this record-breaking bait has often been copied but its life-like *action*—never! The original Swimming Mouse has proved irresistibly attractive to large game fish. When pulled in rapidly, it struggles and swims with a short, choppy wiggle, just below the surface. Both bass and pike strike it savagely, day or night. Get at least two patterns now. At all Shakespeare tackle dealers, 90c. Shakespeare Company, 551 N. Pitcher St., Kalamazoo, Mich.

Shakespeare — 4/5 oz.

Swimming Mouse Jr. — 1930

No. 6580 — ⅝ oz. — 2¾"

(THE UNDERWATER MINNOW) — $40 – 50

NO. 31 — 1927 — 3"

The Submarine, Jr.
No. 31

No. 31—A standard type of under-water bait successfully used for casting or trolling in deep water. Weighted to sink to desired depth. Nickeled head and tail spinners, with a treble hook on belly and another one on tail. 3 inch body. Following finishes:

No. 31GW—Rainbow with Scale Finish.
No. 31YP—Yellow Perch with Scale Finish.
No. 31FG—Fancy Green Back with Scale Finish.

$40 – 50

3⅝" - UNDERWATER MINNOW

NOTE: NO. 42F IS SAME LURE ONLY FLOATER.

1923

The Submarine
No. 42

$20 – 30

6510 SF

Nu-Crip Minnow

No. 6510—This new Crippled Minnow Surface Bait is designed to ride on the surface with approximately one half of each spinner above the surface of the water.

When retrieved by ordinary reeling the bait produces a very attractive wake in the water and when used with short, sharp jerks, produces a splashing, spluttering commotion on the surface which makes the bait ideal for night fishing, surface fishing over weed beds and inshore fishing.

The Nu-Crip is unsurpassed for taking black bass. Length of body, 3¾ inches; three treble hooks size 1X. Weight ⅝ ounces.

$10 – 25

6678 F

6680 WR

NEW – 1937

(PAINTED EYES)

3 SIZES

NO. 6679 – MUSKIE
3¾" – 1½ oz.
NO. 6678 – BASS
3¼" – 1 oz.
NO. 6680 – BASS
2⅞" – 7/10 oz.

The New Favorite

Shakespeare's Pad-ler Bait

Shakespeare's new Pad-ler has everything that is most likely to induce a fish to strike to kill. Picture a small rodent, scared almost to death and swimming frantically in an undecided course for some place of safety and you've a good idea of the life-like action of this new fish-getter. Every detail of construction contributes to its natural, life-like appearance from the spoons at the rear, which look like the rapidly paddling feet of a swimming animal to the shape of the throat which piles up or throws out water depending on the speed at which the bait is retrieved. There's no fear of getting "hung up" in the bass or pickerel hideouts among the reeds, rushes or lily pads—the position of the hooks see to that. Ask your dealer to show you this new favorite.

Available in two sizes. No. 6678 Bass size, length 3¼ in. Weight 1 oz. No. 6679 Muskie size, length 3¾ in. Weight 1½ oz.

No. 6678

No. 6679

No. 6680—A new and smaller bass size Pad-ler. Length 2⅞ inches. Weight .7 ounce. Hook size 1/0 double rust-proof.

Frog Skin Bait

No. 6505—Here's the world's best fish getter for bass and salt water game fish. Natural food finish acquired by stretching actual frogs skin over wood. Looks like a live frog.

Best results obtained by jerk and reel method of fishing. Available in two sizes. No. 6505L—Large size, 3¾ in. No. 6505S—Small size, 3 in. Specify size in ordering. (2 SIZES)

$30 – 40

• 3" • 3¾"

6505 L

$30 – 40

Baits for Salt Water Casting

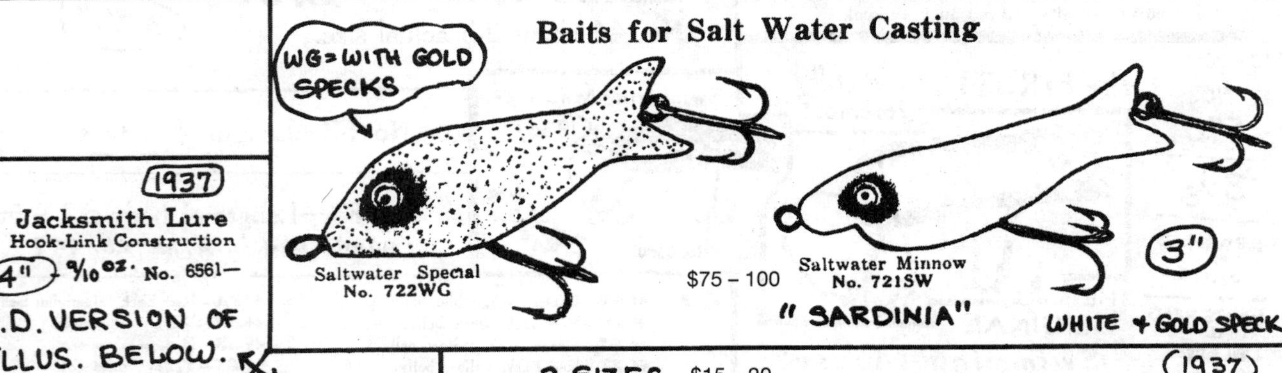
WG = WITH GOLD SPECKS
3"

Saltwater Special No. 722WG

$75 – 100

Saltwater Minnow No. 721SW

" SARDINIA"

WHITE + GOLD SPECK

(1937)

(1937)

Jacksmith Lure

Hook-Link Construction

4" – 9/10 oz. No. 6561—

H.D. VERSION OF ILLUS. BELOW.

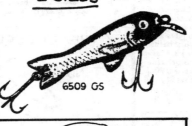

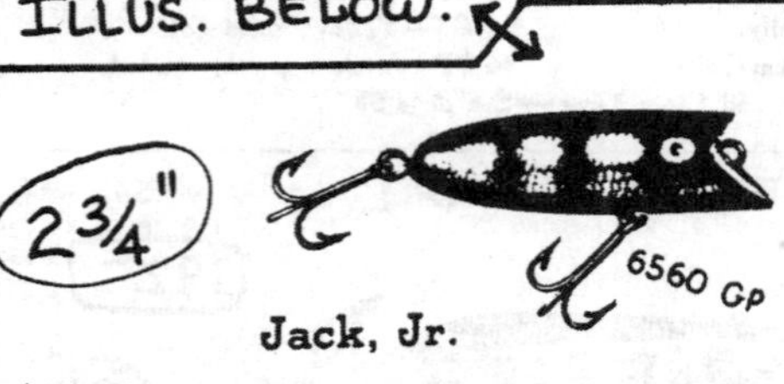
2¾"
6560 GP

Jack, Jr.

$10 – 20

2 SIZES $15 – 20

6509 GS

The Fisher Bait

(Hook-Link Construction)

No. 6509—Developed in the Shakespeare bait testing laboratory, this new Fisher bait has an action that fish go for in a big way. Floats and dives in an alluring manner that's sure to bring the big 'uns up from the deep holes. Floats while at rest.

Diving action produced by metal blade. A sure-fire fish getter.

Equipped with two, size 1, strong treble hooks. Weight: 3/5 oz. Length: 3¾ in.

Kingfish Wobbler

Hook-Link Construction

No. 6535—A heavy weighted bait strongly built with patented hook-link construction and special bright chromium plated back plate. This plate serves as an attractor for the fish. Its action is an energetic wobble.

4⅞" – 1¼ oz.

CHROME BACK PLATE

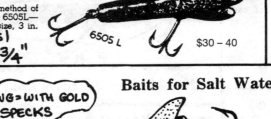

6535 WR

$30 – 60

2⅞" Junior Fisher Bait

Hook-Link Construction

No. 6508—A new smaller edition of the popular Fisher bait introduced last year. Developed particularly for fishermen who demanded the same fish getting qualities in a lighter lure. Equipped with two size 3X short shank treble hooks. Weight: ½ ounce, Length: 2⅞ inches.

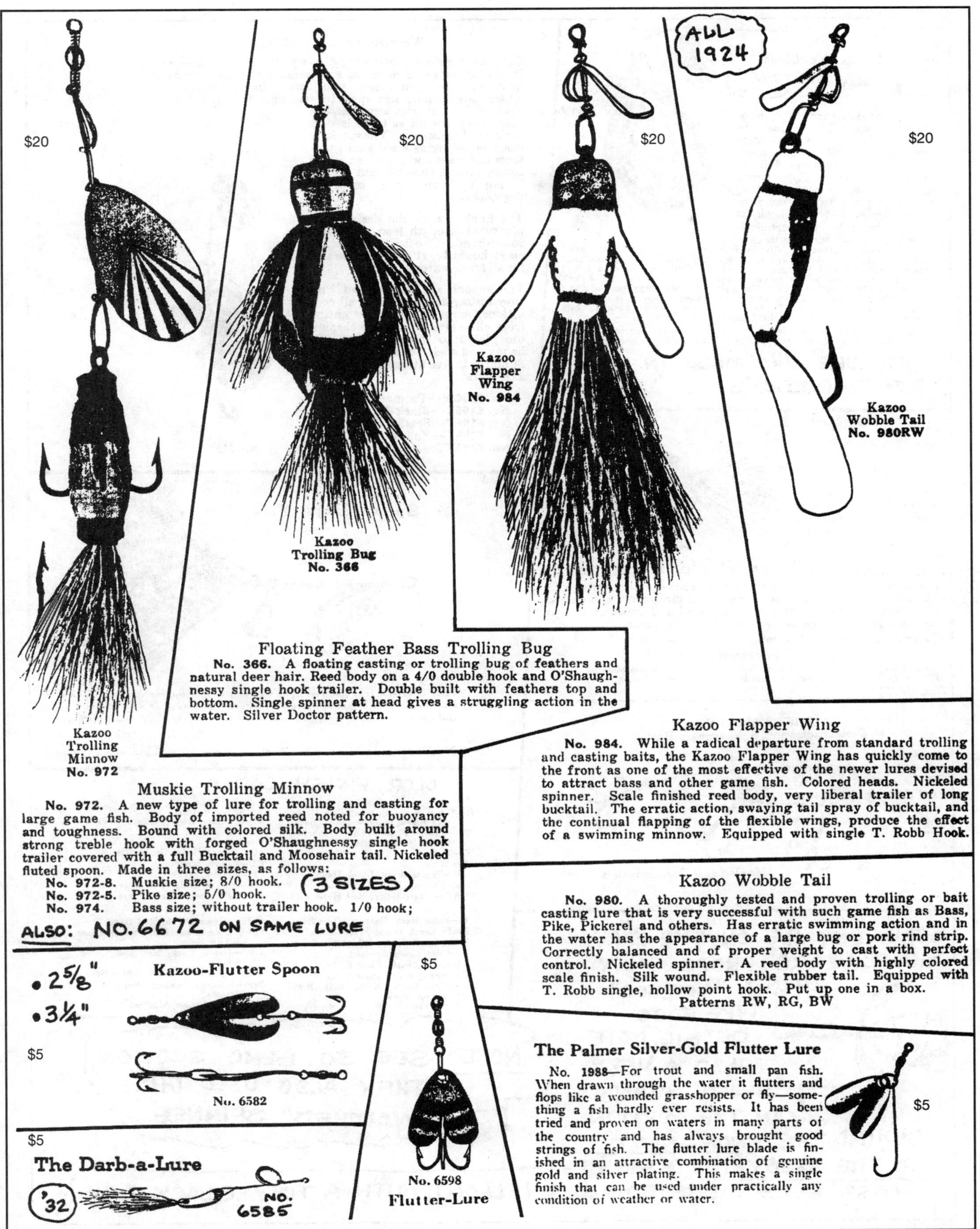

$20 $20 $20 $20

ALL 1924

Kazoo Trolling Minnow No. 972

Kazoo Trolling Bug No. 366

Kazoo Flapper Wing No. 984

Kazoo Wobble Tail No. 980RW

Floating Feather Bass Trolling Bug

No. 366. A floating casting or trolling bug of feathers and natural deer hair. Reed body on a 4/0 double hook and O'Shaughnessy single hook trailer. Double built with feathers top and bottom. Single spinner at head gives a struggling action in the water. Silver Doctor pattern.

Muskie Trolling Minnow

No. 972. A new type of lure for trolling and casting for large game fish. Body of imported reed noted for buoyancy and toughness. Bound with colored silk. Body built around strong treble hook with forged O'Shaughnessy single hook trailer covered with a full Bucktail and Moosehair tail. Nickeled fluted spoon. Made in three sizes, as follows:

No. 972-8. Muskie size; 8/0 hook. (3 SIZES)
No. 972-5. Pike size; 5/0 hook.
No. 974. Bass size; without trailer hook. 1/0 hook;

ALSO: NO. 6672 ON SAME LURE

Kazoo Flapper Wing

No. 984. While a radical departure from standard trolling and casting baits, the Kazoo Flapper Wing has quickly come to the front as one of the most effective of the newer lures devised to attract bass and other game fish. Colored heads. Nickeled spinner. Scale finished reed body, very liberal trailer of long bucktail. The erratic action, swaying tail spray of bucktail, and the continual flapping of the flexible wings, produce the effect of a swimming minnow. Equipped with single T. Robb Hook.

Kazoo Wobble Tail

No. 980. A thoroughly tested and proven trolling or bait casting lure that is very successful with such game fish as Bass, Pike, Pickerel and others. Has erratic swimming action and in the water has the appearance of a large bug or pork rind strip. Correctly balanced and of proper weight to cast with perfect control. Nickeled spinner. A reed body with highly colored scale finish. Silk wound. Flexible rubber tail. Equipped with T. Robb single, hollow point hook. Put up one in a box.
Patterns RW, RG, BW

Kazoo-Flutter Spoon

• 2 5/8"
• 3 1/4"

$5

No. 6582

$5

No. 6598
Flutter-Lure

The Palmer Silver-Gold Flutter Lure

No. 1988—For trout and small pan fish. When drawn through the water it flutters and flops like a wounded grasshopper or fly—something a fish hardly ever resists. It has been tried and proven on waters in many parts of the country and has always brought good strings of fish. The flutter lure blade is finished in an attractive combination of genuine gold and silver plating. This makes a single finish that can be used under practically any condition of weather or water.

$5

$5

The Darb-a-Lure

'32 NO. 6585

$10

T. Robb Weedless Bass Fly (1925)

The Shakespeare T. Robb Weedless Bass Fly is just the bait for fishing grounds where weedy shores and bottoms make fishing with other lures difficult. Designed by Mr. T. Robb, whose many years of successful fishing has enabled him to determine the shape, size of body and hook, as well as the right color combinations. Weighted for ease in casting into weeds, rushes and lily pads where the big game fish are found. Tied on imported, specially designed No. 5/0 long Shank, Hollow Point Central Draught Bass hooks. The hook is of a size, shape and thickness which makes it difficult for the fish to shake or pry it loose from his jaws. The comparatively large size of the hook is one of the proven features that have made this lure so generally successful. The T. Robb Weedless Fly is packed one in a box and may be had in the following four patterns:—

No. 196

No. 196W. Parmachene Belle.
No. 196B. Black Prince.
No. 196R. Scarlet Ibis.
No. 196Y. Yellow Sally.

THIS LURE WAS MADE IN MANY DIFF. VARIATIONS.

Weedless Flutter-Fly

$10

Cast the Weedless Flutter-Fly directly into the weeds—or in the lily pads—retrieve and as it mounts the obstructions dropping into open spaces, your lure is being presented where large game fish may be feeding. The Weedless Flutter-Fly is strictly weedless, will cast into the wind as there is very little wind resistance. The specially designed swinging weed-guard protects the hook and permits the fish to run with the line without getting "hung up" on weeds or other vegetation.

The hook is a special design with plenty of strength from the point to the bend. The fish once hooked, stays hooked. It is a suitable size for all fresh-water game fish.

The spoons are so designed that they flutter actively under all conditions; sure to attract attention from all angles. They are chromium plated to insure lasting brilliancy and wear. Weight ⅜ ounce. Supplied in five attractive patterns as follows:

No. 6196W—Parmachene Belle.
No. 6196B—Black Prince.
No. 6196R—Scarlet Ibis.
No. 6196Y—Yellow Sally.
No. 6196BT—Natural Bucktail.

No. 6196

$5

No. 6331

Shakespeare Wonder Bugs

No. 6331A—Air-tight hair body, rubber coated and covered with silk; rustproof O'Shaughnessy hooks set at the correct angle for a sure catch. Wonder Bugs are so balanced and constructed that they always land in the proper position on the water.

Two sizes in 6 assorted patterns on perforated card.

PATTERNS:

YS—Yellow Sally.
BP—Black Prince.
SI—Scarlet Ibis.
NB—Natural Buck.
WM—White Miller.
F—Frog Green.

Kalamazoo Spoon Bass Flies

$10

No. 2000— It is just the right size and weight for even those skillful casts into the pockets of pads and rushes. Furnished complete with nickeled spoon and dipsey sinker. Weighted, chenille covered body of fly tied with bucktail.

No. 2000½—Same as No. 2000 and has in addition a weed guard to hook.

A Word About the Construction of Shakespeare Baits

Hook-Link Construction

COLOR FINISH CODES

S—White Body, Spotted Red, Green and Black, Narrow Green Back.
SF—Silver Flitter Sides, Narrow Green Back, White Belly.
T—Tiger.
W—White.
WB—White Body, Black Head.
WR—White Body, Red Head.
WRS—White Body, Red Head with Silver Flitters.
WS—White Body, Black Wave Stripe
Y—Yellow.
YG—Yellow Body, Green Stripes
YJ—Yellow Jacket.
YP—Yellow Perch.
YR—Yellow Body, Red Head.
YS—Yellow with Black Spots.

B—Solid Black, Narrow White Belly.
BRI—Black Body, White Ribs.
BW—Black Body, White Head.
F—Frog, Green Spotted.
FW—Frog with White Belly.
FY—Frog with Yellow Belly.
G—Gray Body, White Belly, Black Down Back.
GP—Green Perch.
GPR—Green Perch, Red Head.
GS—Green Bronze Back, Silver Sides, White Belly.
GW—Green Back, Red and Green Sides.
LG—Light Gray Body, White Belly.
NP—Natural Pickerel—Vertical Stripes.
PL—Pearl Finish, Mottled.

SOME DETAILS ON THE EARLY SHAKESPEARE PROPS. THEY HAD A "NOTCHED" TYPE EDGE DETAIL. NOTE ALSO A VERY SHORT SHANK IN THE PORTION BEHIND THE PROP-NEXT TO THE BODY. THE EARLY GLASS EYES WERE SMALL & YELLOW, WITH A TINY BLACK DOT.

No. 5

4/5 actual size No. 5

NOTE: SEE SO. BEND SECTION, THEY ALSO USED THIS "NOTCHED" SPINNER.

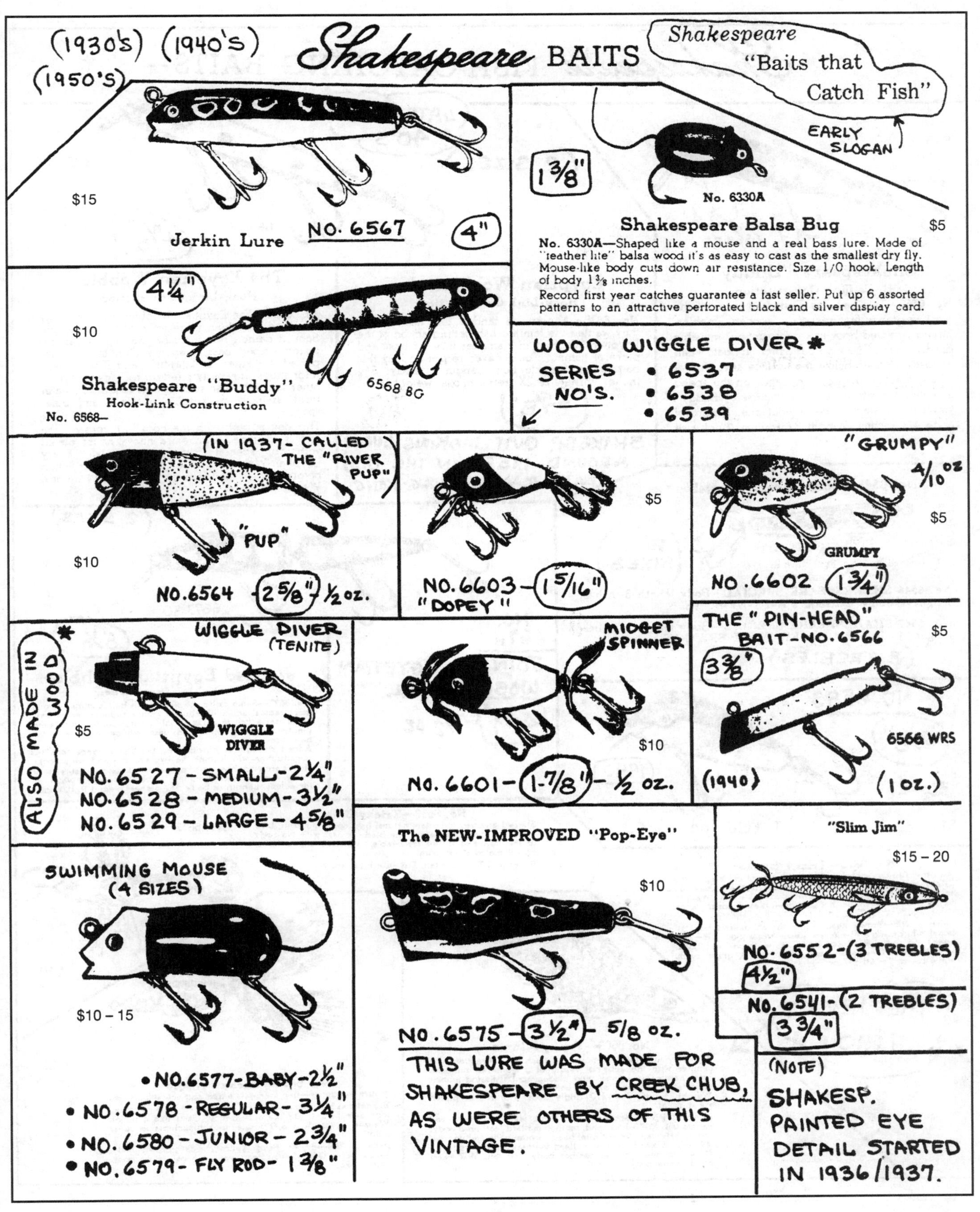
(1930's) (1940's)
(1950's)
Shakespeare BAITS
Shakespeare
"Baits that
Catch Fish"
EARLY
SLOGAN
$15
Jerkin Lure
NO. 6567
4"
1 3/8"
No. 6330A
Shakespeare Balsa Bug
$5
No. 6330A—Shaped like a mouse and a real bass lure. Made of "feather lite" balsa wood it's as easy to cast as the smallest dry fly. Mouse-like body cuts down air resistance. Size 1/0 hook. Length of body 1 3/8 inches.
Record first year catches guarantee a fast seller. Put up 6 assorted patterns to an attractive perforated black and silver display card.
4 1/4"
$10
Shakespeare "Buddy"
Hook-Link Construction
No. 6568—
6568 BG
WOOD WIGGLE DIVER *
SERIES NO'S.
• 6537
• 6538
• 6539
(IN 1937- CALLED THE "RIVER PUP")
"PUP"
$10
NO.6564 - 2 5/8" - 1/2 oz.
$5
NO.6603 - 1 5/16"
"DOPEY"
"GRUMPY"
4/10 oz
$5
GRUMPY
NO.6602 1 3/4"
*
ALSO MADE IN WOOD
WIGGLE DIVER (TENITE)
$5
WIGGLE DIVER
NO. 6527 - SMALL - 2 1/4"
NO. 6528 - MEDIUM - 3 1/2"
NO. 6529 - LARGE - 4 5/8"
MIDGET SPINNER
$10
NO. 6601 - 1-7/8" - 1/2 oz.
THE "PIN-HEAD" BAIT - NO. 6566
$5
3 3/8"
6566 WRS
(1940)
(1 oz.)
SWIMMING MOUSE (4 SIZES)
$10 – 15
• NO.6577 - BABY - 2 1/2"
• NO. 6578 - REGULAR - 3 1/4"
• NO. 6580 - JUNIOR - 2 3/4"
• NO. 6579 - FLY ROD - 1 3/8"
The NEW-IMPROVED "Pop-Eye"
$10
NO. 6575 - 3 1/2" - 5/8 oz.
THIS LURE WAS MADE FOR SHAKESPEARE BY CREEK CHUB, AS WERE OTHERS OF THIS VINTAGE.
"Slim Jim"
$15 – 20
NO. 6552 - (3 TREBLES)
4 1/2"
NO. 6541 - (2 TREBLES)
3 3/4"
(NOTE)
SHAKESP. PAINTED EYE DETAIL STARTED IN 1936/1937.

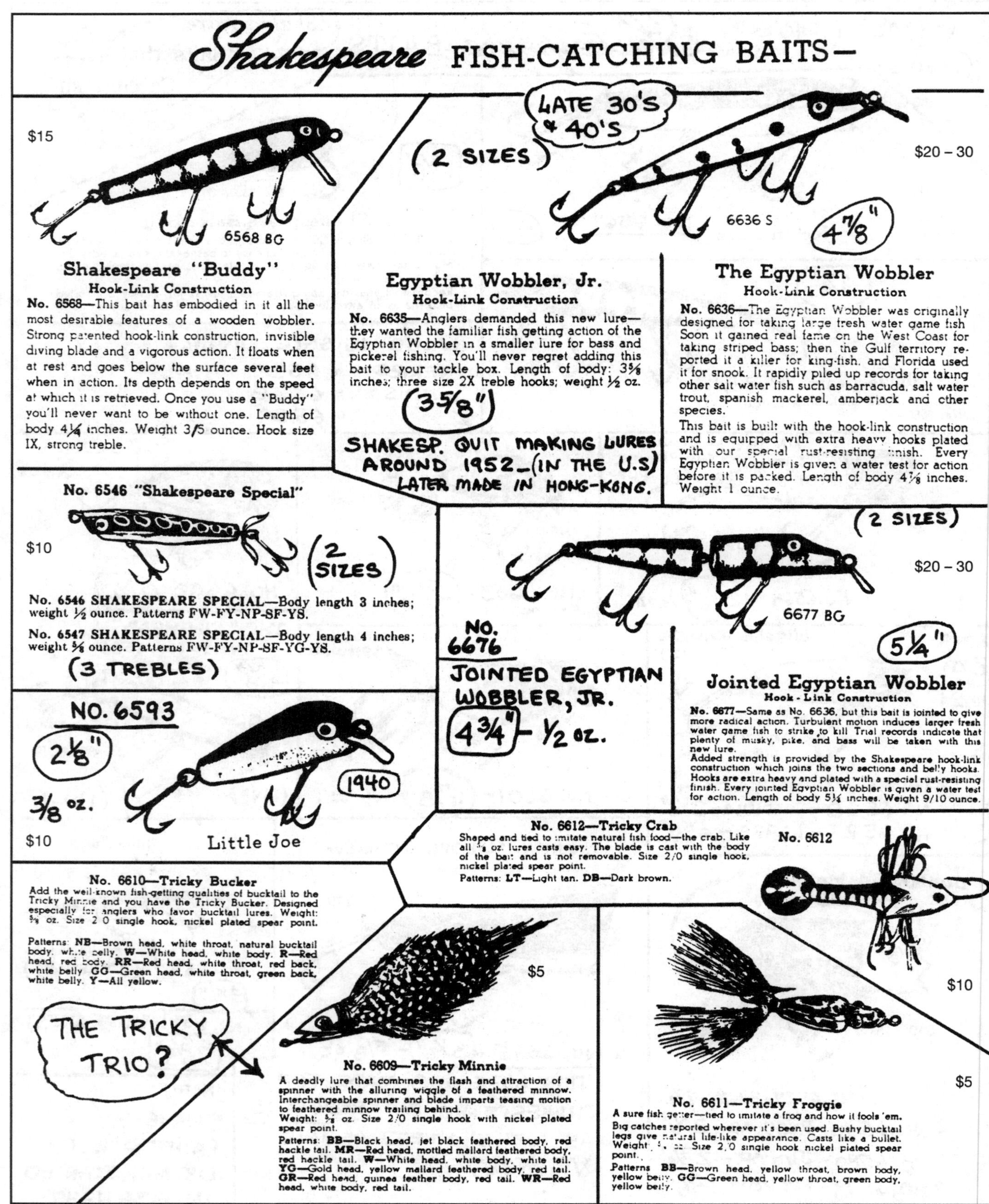

Shakespeare FISH-CATCHING BAITS—

$15

6568 BG

Shakespeare "Buddy"

Hook-Link Construction

No. 6568—This bait has embodied in it all the most desirable features of a wooden wobbler. Strong patented hook-link construction, invisible diving blade and a vigorous action. It floats when at rest and goes below the surface several feet when in action. Its depth depends on the speed at which it is retrieved. Once you use a "Buddy" you'll never want to be without one. Length of body 4¼ inches. Weight 3/5 ounce. Hook size IX, strong treble.

LATE 30'S & 40'S

(2 SIZES)

$20 – 30

6636 S

4⅞"

Egyptian Wobbler, Jr.

Hook-Link Construction

No. 6635—Anglers demanded this new lure—they wanted the familiar fish getting action of the Egyptian Wobbler in a smaller lure for bass and pickerel fishing. You'll never regret adding this bait to your tackle box. Length of body: 3⅝ inches; three size 2X treble hooks; weight ½ oz.

(3⅝")

SHAKESP. QUIT MAKING LURES AROUND 1952_(IN THE U.S) LATER MADE IN HONG-KONG.

The Egyptian Wobbler

Hook-Link Construction

No. 6636—The Egyptian Wobbler was originally designed for taking large fresh water game fish. Soon it gained real fame on the West Coast for taking striped bass; then the Gulf territory reported it a killer for king-fish, and Florida used it for snook. It rapidly piled up records for taking other salt water fish such as barracuda, salt water trout, spanish mackerel, amberjack and other species.

This bait is built with the hook-link construction and is equipped with extra heavy hooks plated with our special rust-resisting finish. Every Egyptian Wobbler is given a water test for action before it is packed. Length of body 4⅞ inches. Weight 1 ounce.

No. 6546 "Shakespeare Special"

$10

(2 SIZES)

No. 6546 SHAKESPEARE SPECIAL—Body length 3 inches; weight ½ ounce. Patterns FW-FY-NP-SF-YS.

No. 6547 SHAKESPEARE SPECIAL—Body length 4 inches; weight ⅝ ounce. Patterns FW-FY-NP-SF-YG-YS.

(3 TREBLES)

(2 SIZES)

$20 – 30

6677 BG

NO. 6676

JOINTED EGYPTIAN WOBBLER, JR.

(4¾")- ½ OZ.

5¼"

Jointed Egyptian Wobbler

Hook - Link Construction

No. 6677—Same as No. 6636, but this bait is jointed to give more radical action. Turbulent motion induces larger fresh water game fish to strike to kill. Trial records indicate that plenty of musky, pike, and bass will be taken with this new lure.

Added strength is provided by the Shakespeare hook-link construction which joins the two sections and belly hooks. Hooks are extra heavy and plated with a special rust-resisting finish. Every jointed Egyptian Wobbler is given a water test for action. Length of body 5¼ inches. Weight 9/10 ounce.

NO. 6593

2⅛"

3/8 OZ.

1940

$10

Little Joe

No. 6612—Tricky Crab

Shaped and tied to imitate natural fish food—the crab. Like all ⅝ oz. lures casts easy. The blade is cast with the body of the bait and is not removable. Size 2/0 single hook, nickel plated spear point.

Patterns: **LT**—Light tan. **DB**—Dark brown.

No. 6612

$10

No. 6610—Tricky Bucker

Add the well-known fish-getting qualities of bucktail to the Tricky Minnie and you have the Tricky Bucker. Designed especially for anglers who favor bucktail lures. Weight: ⅝ oz. Size 2/0 single hook, nickel plated spear point.

Patterns: **NB**—Brown head, white throat, natural bucktail body, white belly. **W**—White head, white body. **R**—Red head, red body. **RR**—Red head, white throat, red back, white belly. **GG**—Green head, white throat, green back, white belly. **Y**—All yellow.

THE TRICKY TRIO?

$5

No. 6609—Tricky Minnie

A deadly lure that combines the flash and attraction of a spinner with the alluring wiggle of a feathered minnow. Interchangeable spinner and blade imparts teasing motion to feathered minnow trailing behind.

Weight: ⅝ oz. Size 2/0 single hook with nickel plated spear point.

Patterns: **BB**—Black head, jet black feathered body, red hackle tail. **MR**—Red head, mottled mallard feathered body, red hackle tail. **W**—White head, white body, white tail. **YG**—Gold head, yellow mallard feathered body, red tail. **GR**—Red head, guinea feather body, red tail. **WR**—Red head, white body, red tail.

$5

No. 6611—Tricky Froggie

A sure fish getter—tied to imitate a frog and how it fools 'em.

Big catches reported wherever it's been used. Bushy bucktail legs give natural life-like appearance. Casts like a bullet. Weight: ⅝ oz. Size 2/0 single hook nickel plated spear point.

Patterns: **BB**—Brown head, yellow throat, brown body, yellow belly. **GG**—Green head, yellow throat, green body, yellow belly.

THIS IS IMPORTANT INFORMATION – (FROM 1920 CATALOG)

Introduction

SOME twenty years ago Mr. F. G. Worden of South Bend, Indiana started the small fishing tackle factory which bore his name. The growth of this factory was only mediocre, perhaps due to the fact that Mr. Worden was developing one particular kind of bait. This bait was the Buck-Tail and became so popular that its manufacturer was known throughout the Angling World at "Buck-Tail" Worden.

In the changes that took place during this twenty years, the old business incorporated by "Buck-Tail" Worden has grown into a large fishing tackle plant, now making a large variety of meritorious bait-casting lures. This new factory, now called the South Bend Bait Company, also produces the famous South Bend Anti-Back-Lash Reel.

The splendid tackle known throughout the country as Quality Fishing Tackle that is now being made in the new plant has given eminent satisfaction wherever it has been used; not only due to the fact that every article, no matter how small, is most carefully inspected, but due to the fact that the goods themselves are right and made to give satisfaction to anglers and fishermen. Our trade mark is a guarantee. If in spite of our care, you receive anything that shows defect either in workmanship or material we request that you allow us to examine the article and replace it.

We were fishermen first, then tackle manufacturers. Every article produced and offered by us has been tried out—they are not a lot of impossible contraptions.

We all know that correct design, highest grade materials and skilled experienced workmanship are the fundamental necessities in manufacturing any article. In our opinion these facts are even more pronounced in the manufacture of Fishing Tackle. It is our aim and policy at all times to render the best of service and produce meritorious fishing tackle that will give true satisfaction. It wins friendship and creates "boosters" that no manufacturer can afford to be without. We are happy to have this opportunity of thanking the thousands of fellow anglers whose boosting and patronage have attributed so much to our success as manufacturers of South Bend Quality Tackle.

Our products are sold by almost all responsible jobbers and dealers and we prefer that you patronize home dealers, who should be able to supply you as readily as we could and at the same price. In event our product is not handled by your dealer we shall be pleased to fill your order from our factory at catalgue prices, transportation prepaid by us.

SOUTH BEND
QUALITY TACKLE
BAIT COMPANY

South Bend Bait Co.
South Bend, Indiana. U.S.A.
QUALITY TACKLE

Three Treble Under-Water Minnows

$50 – 75

THE PANETELLA.

NOTE: NOTCHED PROPS ON THIS PAGE!

Style No. 903 RHTW

Style No. 904 W

NOTE: THIS PAGE SHOWS THAT So. BEND ALSO USED THE "NOTCHED" TYPE OF SPINNER BLADES - WHICH WERE THOUGHT TO BE ONLY EARLY SHAKESPEARE. THIS TYPE OF BLADE INDICATES THAT THE LURE IS OF AN "OLDER VINTAGE", BASICALLY IN THE TEENS AND EARLY TWENTIES.

THE SOUTH BEND MIN-BUCK.

A happy combination of an under water minnow with a Buck Tail Treble Hook. It has proved successful when all other minnows failed to get a strike.

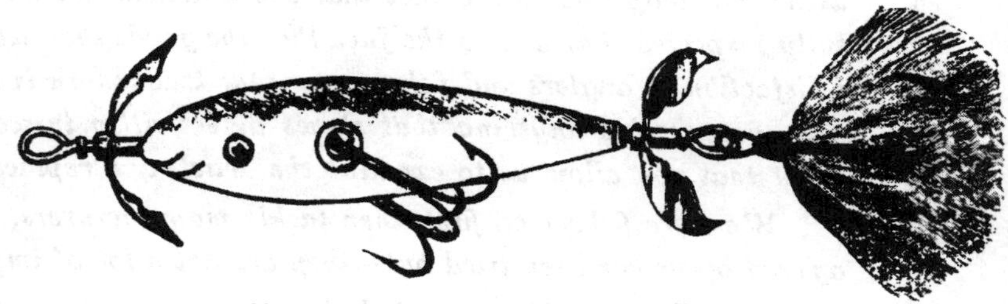

No. 943. Color: Red Cracked Back, White Belly.

Packed one in a box, one dozen boxes in a carton. Colors: Minnow—All Standard Colors; Buck Tail—White, White and Brown, White and Grey, White with Red Center

D 52 A–943—With Three Treble Hooks

D 52 B–945—With Five Treble Hooks. .

$50 – 75

Five Treble Under-Water Minnows

THE WORDEN COMBINATION MINNOW. Length of body 3⅝ inches. Weight approximately 1¼ ozs.

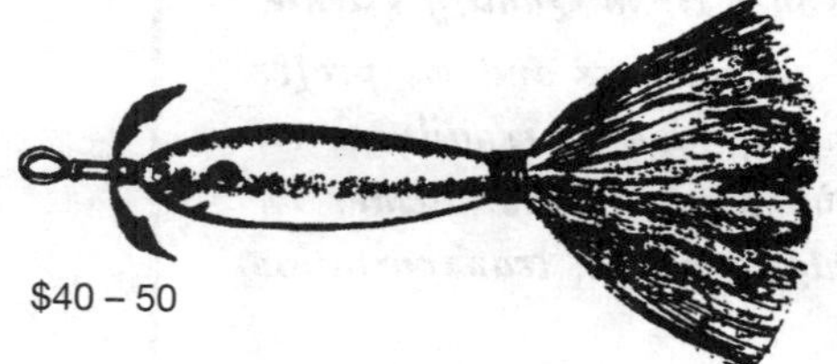

$40 – 50

Style No. 905 YP

$50 – 75

NOTE: THIS INDICATES So. BEND ALSO MFG. A HEXAGON LURE! (AT LEAST A PAINTED LOOK-ALIKE.)

Style No.

906W—White body, Red and green spotted decorations (hexagon shape effect) .

906Y—Yellow body, Red and green spotted decorations (hexagon shape effect) .

906R—Red body, Black spotted decorations (hexagon shape effect) . . . . .

905R—Rainbow color, Green back, red and yellow sides blending into white belly

905YP—Yellow Perch . . . . . .

905GCBW—Green Cracked Back, White Belly

Style No.

905SCBY—Sienna Cracked Back, Yellow Belly . . . .

905RCBY—Red Cracked Back, Yellow P

905SW—White body with dark shaded

905SR—Red body with dark shaded back

905W—Solid White color . . . .

905RHW—White body with Red Head . .

905RHTW—White body with Red Head and Tail . . . .

905SA—Solid Aluminum color . . . .

South Bend
FIVE TREBLE UNDERWATER MINNOWS

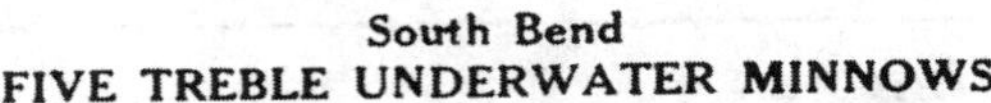

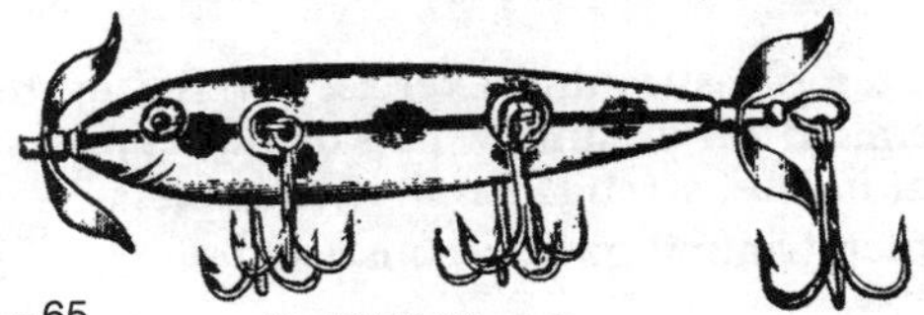

$40 – 65

No. 906W Minnow

(906W) (3 5/8") (1 1/4 oz.)

$20 – 35

South Bend
THREE TREBLE UNDERWATER MINNOWS

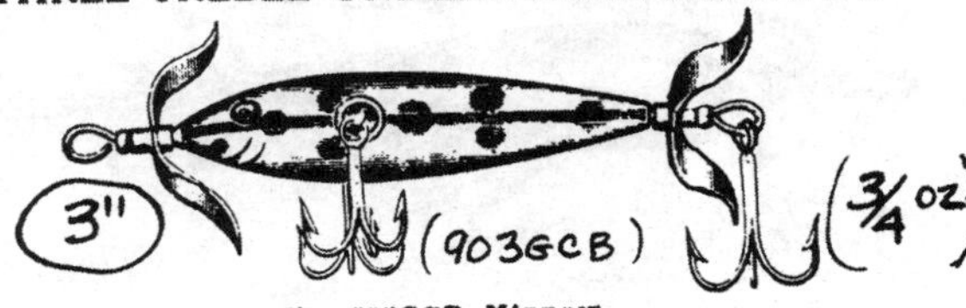

3" (903GCB) (3/4 oz.)

No. 903GCB Minnow

South Bend
MUSKELLUNGE TROLLING MINNOWS

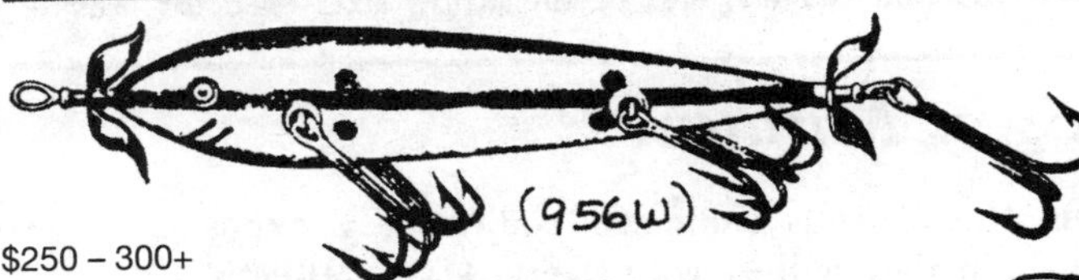

(956W)

$250 – 300+

No. 956W Muskie Minnow
(Illustration approx. ½ actual size)

5 1/4"

In general lines these minnows are the same as our five treble underwater baits excepting the size is much larger. Also the construction and trimmings throughout are super-strong, being well adapted to withstand the rushes of these vicious fighters. Body length 5¼ inches. Packed one in a box, a dozen in a carton. Furnished in the following colors:

South Bend
MIDGET UNDERWATER MINNOW

$20 – 30

(901SF) 2 1/2" 1/2 oz.

No. 901SF Midget Minnow
(Illustration approx. 3/5 actual size)

The Midget Minnow—another underwater minnow of the same general design as the standard South Bend Minnows, except being smaller. Equipped with a front spinner only, and three treble hooks. Body length is 2½ inches. Packed one in a box, a dozen in a carton. In the following colors:

$30 – 45 * (904SD) 3"

No. 904SD-W Minnow
(Illustration trifle over ½ actual size)

South Bend
PANETELLA MINNOW, FIVE TREBLE

$40 – 50

(915GCB) 4 1/4"

No. 915GCB Panetella Minnow
(Illustration almost 3/5 actual size)

ALSO MADE WITH CONVENT. 3 TREBLES, IN BELLY.

South Bend
PANETELLA MINNOW, THREE TREBLE

4 1/4" (9/10 oz.)

No. 913GCB Panetella Minnow
(Illustration almost 3/5 actual size)

$30 – 40

South Bend COMBINATION MINNOWS

Small underwater minnow; the buck-tail substantially tied on the minnow body. It is equipped with one treble hook which is masked by the buck-tail.

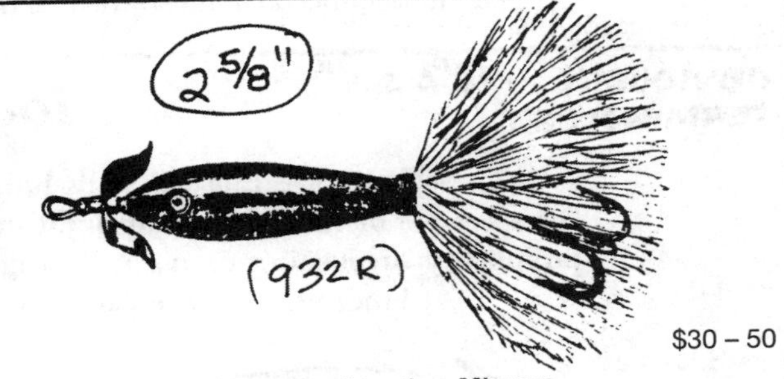

2 5/8" (932R)

$30 – 50

No. 932R Combination Minnow
(Illustration 3/5 actual size)

(933RAIN) 2 5/8"

No. 933RAIN Combination Minnow
(Illustration approx. 3/5 actual size)

No. 933 and 934 Combination Minnow is identical to No. 931 and 932, excepting hook equipment is two side trebles

(944W) 3"

South Bend MIN-BUCK MINNOW

No. 944W Min-Buck Minnow
(Illustration approx. ½ actual size)

$40 – 50

Muskie Casting Minnows

The fascination for casting combined with the greater pleasure and exercise offered by this method of angling has created a constantly growing demand for a minnow bait of this type. meet this we have developed a casting minnow bait, ideal in size, strength a.d effectiveness.

Hooks are very extra strong, hollow point. All other trimmings and construction are very substantial.

Packed one in a box, one dozen in a carton.
Three treble.
Length of body 3⅝ in. Weight approximately 1⅓ ozs.

NO. 953

Style No.
953W—White body, red and green spotted decorations (hexagon effect . .
953Y—Yellow body, red and green spotted decorations (hexagon effect) . . .
953R—Red body, black spotted decorations (hexagon effect) . . . .
953 Rainbow—Green back, red and yellow sides blending into white belly . .
953SW—White body with dark shaded back
953SR—Red body with dark shaded back .
953GCBW—Green Cracked Back, White Belly

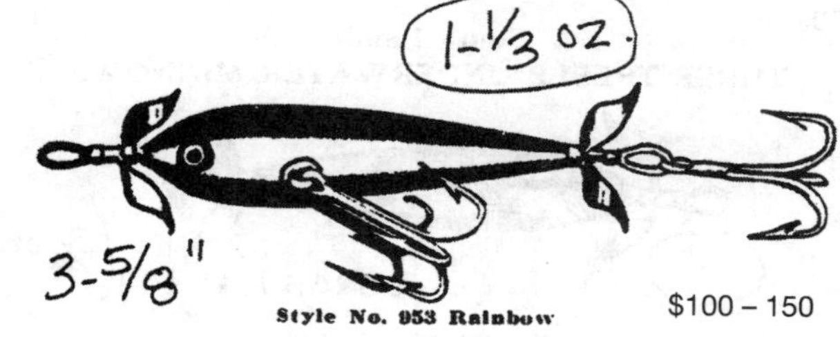
1-1/3 OZ.
3-5/8"
Style No. 953 Rainbow

$100 – 150

These Muskie Casting minnows also furnished equipped with single hooks at same price.
For description and illustration of spoons only and swivels, etc., of the larger sizes used for Muskie

OBVIOUSLY AN "OLDE" TERMINOLOGY.

Moonlight Minnows

These baits are finished with luminous phosphorous enameled bodies. By exposing for a couple of minutes to day-light or sun-light they will glow in the dark very effectively. popularity of evening or night fishing has grown rapidly as this class of fishing is generall, landing the large cautious bass.

$20 – 40

Style No. 922

$20 – 25

Style No. 924

Style No.
922—Solid white luminous color, body length 3½ inches, weight approximately ¾ oz. The size and shape of this minnow is the same as South Bend Floating Minnow, style No. 920

Style No.
924—White luminous body, with red head and collar. Body length 4½ inches, weight approximately 9-10 oz. The size and shape of this minnow is the same as Style No. 923 woodpecker.

NOTE: ON BOTH SO. BEND & SHAKESPEARE 5 HOOKERS - THE FRONT TREBLE IS ON RIGHT-SIDE FORWARD (FROM TOP)

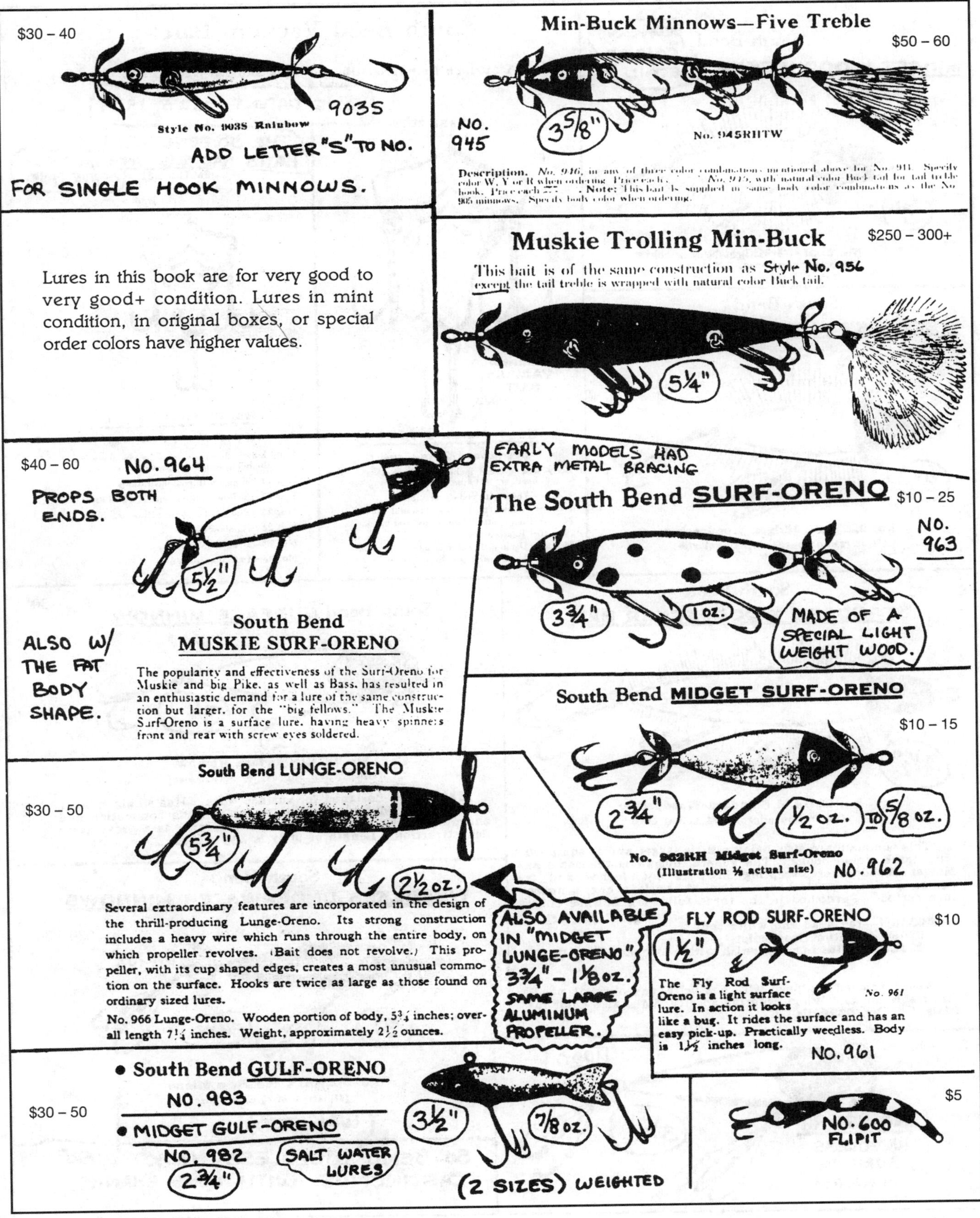
$30 – 40
9035
Style No. 903S Rainbow
ADD LETTER "S" TO NO.
FOR SINGLE HOOK MINNOWS.
Min-Buck Minnows—Five Treble
$50 – 60
NO. 945
3 5/8"
No. 945RHTW
Lures in this book are for very good to very good+ condition. Lures in mint condition, in original boxes, or special order colors have higher values.
Muskie Trolling Min-Buck
$250 – 300+
This bait is of the same construction as Style No. 956 except the tail treble is wrapped with natural color Buck tail.
5 1/4"
$40 – 60
NO. 964
PROPS BOTH ENDS.
5 1/2"
South Bend MUSKIE SURF-ORENO
ALSO W/ THE FAT BODY SHAPE.
The popularity and effectiveness of the Surf-Oreno for Muskie and big Pike, as well as Bass, has resulted in an enthusiastic demand for a lure of the same construction but larger, for the "big fellows." The Muskie Surf-Oreno is a surface lure, having heavy spinners front and rear with screw eyes soldered.
EARLY MODELS HAD EXTRA METAL BRACING
The South Bend SURF-ORENO
$10 – 25
NO. 963
3 3/4"
1 oz.
MADE OF A SPECIAL LIGHT WEIGHT WOOD.
South Bend MIDGET SURF-ORENO
$10 – 15
2 3/4"
1/2 oz. TO 5/8 oz.
No. 962RH Midget Surf-Oreno
(Illustration 1/2 actual size)
NO. 962
South Bend LUNGE-ORENO
$30 – 50
5 3/4"
2 1/2 oz.
Several extraordinary features are incorporated in the design of the thrill-producing Lunge-Oreno. Its strong construction includes a heavy wire which runs through the entire body, on which propeller revolves. (Bait does not revolve.) This propeller, with its cup shaped edges, creates a most unusual commotion on the surface. Hooks are twice as large as those found on ordinary sized lures.
No. 966 Lunge-Oreno. Wooden portion of body, 5 3/4 inches; overall length 7 1/4 inches. Weight, approximately 2 1/2 ounces.
ALSO AVAILABLE IN "MIDGET LUNGE-ORENO" 3 3/4" – 1 1/8 oz. SAME LARGE ALUMINUM PROPELLER.
FLY ROD SURF-ORENO
$10
1 1/2"
The Fly Rod Surf-Oreno is a light surface lure. In action it looks like a bug. It rides the surface and has an easy pick-up. Practically weedless. Body is 1 1/2 inches long.
No. 961
NO. 961
• South Bend GULF-ORENO
NO. 983
$30 – 50
• MIDGET GULF-ORENO
NO. 982
2 3/4"
SALT WATER LURES
3 1/2"
7/8 oz.
(2 SIZES) WEIGHTED
$5
NO. 600 FLIPIT

$10 – 15

South Bend
MIDGET WOODPECKER

CONCAVE COLLAR DETAIL

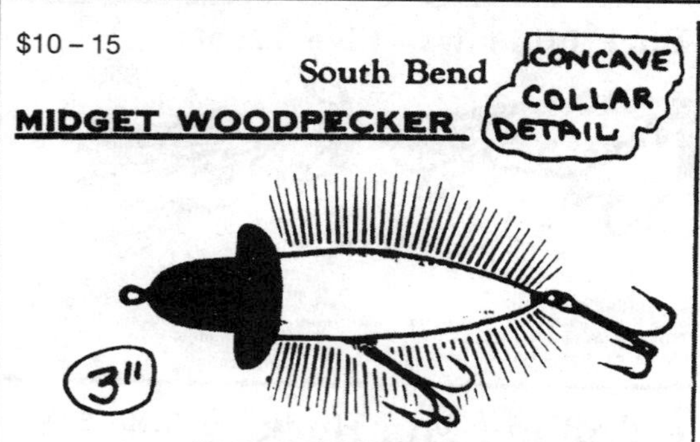
3"

No. 926LUM Midget Woodpecker
(Illustration approx. 3/5 actual size)

South Bend
WEEDLESS MIDGET WOODPECKER

$10 – 15

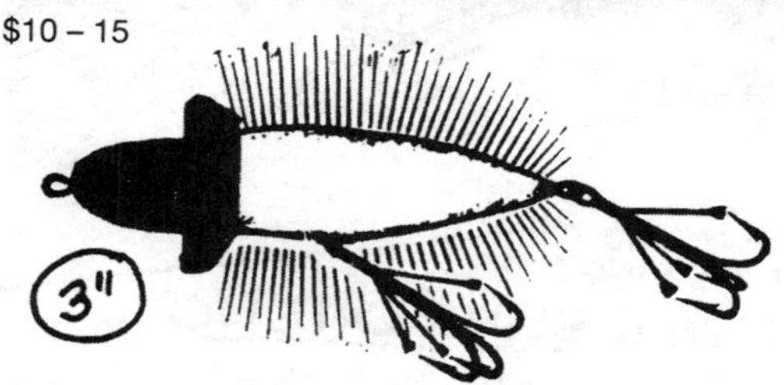
3"

No. 926Wdls Midget Woodpecker
(Illustration approx. 3/5 actual size)

South Bend Vacuum Bait

A Surface Bait Irrisistible to Bass and All Game Fish.

HOWE PATENT – OCT. 5, 1909

THE SO. BEND VAC. BAITS HAD G.E. – AT LEAST SOME OF THE TIME.

STANDARD SIZE

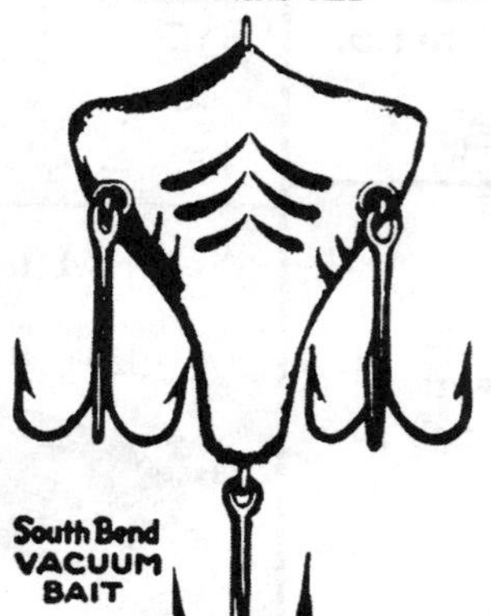
South Bend
VACUUM
BAIT

No. 1 Standard Vacuum

(Illustration 2/3 actual size)

Body length 2 3/8 inches by 2 inches wide at head, weight approximately ⅜ oz.

No. 1—White with red decorations.
No. 2—Yellow, spotted with red and green.
No. 3—Red, spotted with yellow and black.
No. 40—Rainbow color.
No. 50—Dragon fly color design.
No. 60—Imitation frog color.

SMALL SIZE

$30 – 50

No. 21 Small Vacuum

(Illustration ½ actual size)

Body length 2 inches by 1 5/8 inches wide at the head, weight approximately ½ oz.

No. 21—White with red decorations.
No. 22—Yellow, spotted with red and green.
No. 23—Red, spotted with yellow and black.
No. 24 Rainbow color.
No. 25—Dragon fly color design.
No. 26—Imitation frog color.

$10 – 20

South Bend
STANDARD WOODPECKER BAIT

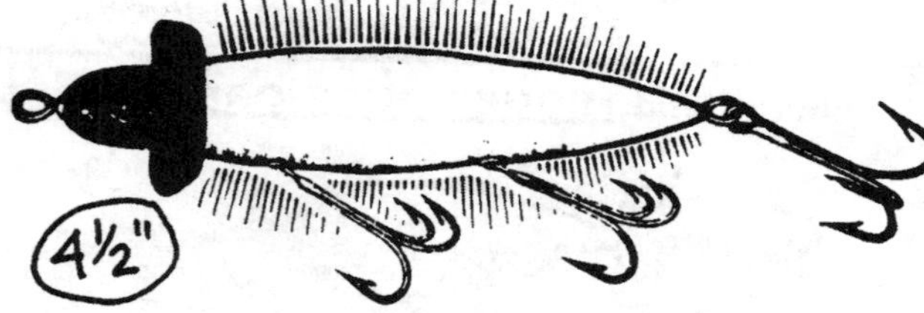
4½"

No. 924LUM Standard Woodpecker
(Illustration approx. 2/3 actual size)

This is a standard size, being a little larger and is equipped with three treble hooks. The general design is the same as Midget Woodpecker excepting body is 4½ inches and is equipped with 3 treble hooks. Packed one in a box, a dozen in a carton. Furnished in the three following finishes only:

No. 923RH—red head and white body,
923F—imitation frog color,
924LUM—Nite Luming finish with red head.

ALSO 2 TREBLES

Also furnished equipped with one belly, and one tail weedless treble hooks. When ordering specify Wdls. also color initials, i. e. No. 923Wdls-RH.

$20 – 40

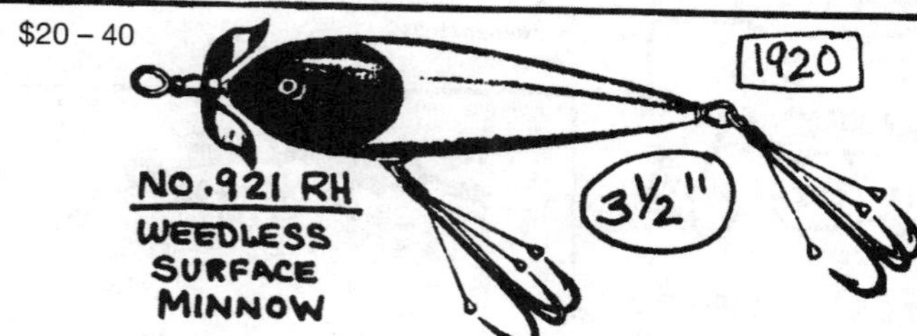
1920
NO. 921 RH
WEEDLESS
SURFACE
MINNOW
3½"

South Bend **SURFACE MINNOW**

$20 – 30

3½"

No. 921RH Surface Minnow
(Illustration approx. ½ actual size)

This bait is designed for surface work. Has single spinner at head. It rides high in the water and the commotion and churning of the water caused by the spinner is a great game fish attraction. Length of body is 3½ inches.

South Bend
WEEDLESS UNDERWATER MINNOWS

$20 – 30

No. 902
3"
¾ oz.

No. 902RAIN Weedless Minnow
(Illustration ½ actual size)

(WEIGHTED)

SO. BEND WEEDLESS HOOKS WERE DISTINCTIVE WITH LONG SHANKS.

$20

(1929)
South Bend PLUNK-ORENO
G.E.
3 3/4"
5/8 oz.
No. 929

For Classes 1F-2F See page 3

The Plunk-Oreno is the stand-by of many anglers who know the results obtained from using it. Its action is different—its weight is just enough so you can place it accurately.

Body length, 3 3/4 inches. Weight, approximately 5/8 ounce. Equipped with two extra-strong treble hooks, highly nickel-plated. The tail hook being slightly larger, elevates the head to the ideal plunking position.

NOTE: CHANGED DESIGN IN 1939.

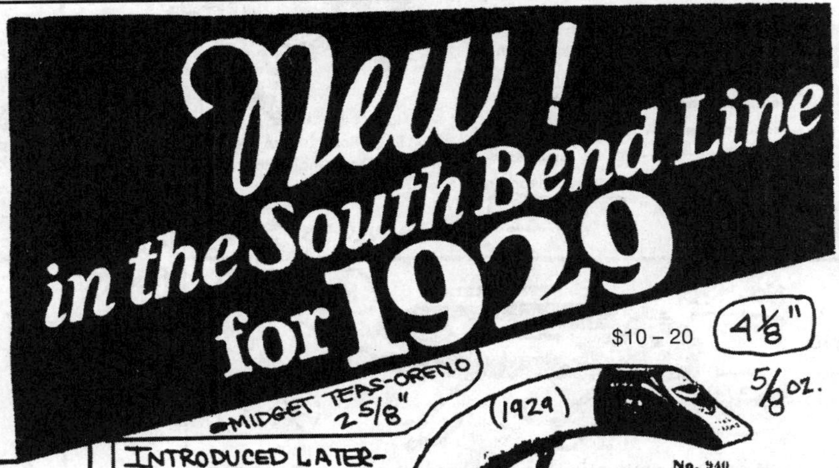
New!
in the South Bend Line
for 1929
MIDGET TEAS-ORENO 2 5/8"
(1929)

$10 – 20 (4 1/8") 5/8 oz.

INTRODUCED LATER- THE BABY TEAS-ORENO No. 939 (3 1/4") (1/2 oz.) -NOT ILLUSTRATED-

No. 940 Teas-Oreno

The (3 SIZES) TEAS-ORENO

* An entirely new bait sensation. Radically *different* in shape *very different* in action.

Teas-Oreno is a surface lure. Has a wiggling, side-slipping, crawling action entirely its own. Weight and size are ideal for accuracy in casting. Six favorite finishes. Sell

We know what Teas-Oreno will do. It's had a full season's testing among nearly a thousand fishing "bugs." It's going to be 1929's bait sensation.

$30 – 45

WOOD FLOAT
5/8 oz.
No. 935 Whirl-Oreno (NEW)
(1929)
3 1/2" L
3" W

The WHIRL-ORENO

The WHIRL-ORENO, an attractive bass or pickerel mouthful, rides atop the water. In action its riffle and swirling on the surface invites game fish in an unfailing manner. 1-TREBLE HOOK

To read the test reports on WHIRL-ORENO is to realize its fish-taking qualities. It's a winner.

Consists of a hook masked in a gay hackle and buck-tail combination headed by a propeller-like enameled float. Three standard combinations to sell

NO. 935 (ALSO A BABY WHIRL-ORENO?)

STAINLESS STEEL

The South Bend Bait Company takes the initiative in inaugurating the use of Stainless Steel for fishing tackle. It is a new metal alloy, extremely hard and durable and has the characteristic of retaining its brilliance more than any other known metal. Head plates for the three Pike-Orenos and the No. 949 Mouse-Oreno are made of this metal. The Nos. 597, 598 and 599 in addition to the propeller on the Lunge-Oreno are also of stainless Steel.

3"
1 oz.
1927-NEW
FLASH ORENO

No. 506 Flash-Oreno

The FLASH-ORENO

To look at this bait is to realize its effective action wobbling, side-slipping, rolling. Withal it does not revolve.

Flash-Oreno is a flashy metal spoon attractive to every game fish species. Equally good for casting or trolling. Comes in the new iridescent pearl, frog, and red and white striped enamel finish, also silvery chromium, copper, and red head, white body. *Sells*

$5 – 10

WEEDLESS PLUG-ORENO

NO. 959

No. 959 (2") (5/8 oz.)

A surface lure with slight wobbling action that dodges lily-pads, logs, snags and vegetation. Effectively used with Wiggletail Pork Rind. Body, 2 inches long. Weight, 5/8 ounce. Equipped with two extra-strong single hooks. No. 959

$50 – 75

$10 – 20

CRIPPLED MINNOW

3 1/4"
5/8 oz.
No 965

The big ones will get mad when they see the crippled minnow, seemingly injured with strength almost spent, lying on its side with just a little life-like action. There's something in the way it acts that brings on that mad rush. No. 965—Length, 3 1/4 inches. Weight, 5/8 ounce. Spinners at head and tail. Two treble hooks. Supplied in 6 finishes: RH-RB-LUM-SF-MS-SS silver speckled, brown blend

G.E.—SO. BEND ON PROPELLERS.

$5

NO. 543
(NEW-1927)
3 1/2"
1/2 oz.
No. 545 Dart-Oreno
4 1/4"
3/4 oz.

The DART-ORENO

A highly polished metal body—a masked hook of bright hackle and bucktail—a quivering, sweeping pork rind riding over the hook. That's the Dart-Oreno the liveliest pork-rind wiggler made.

It is a semi surface lure—practically weedless. Comes in silvery chromium, copper or brass finish metal body, with six varied hackle and buck-tail combinations. The new Dart-Oreno, 3-4 oz. size, ideal for casting, sells

1ST TEAS-ORENOS DID NOT HAVE THIS RIG. *

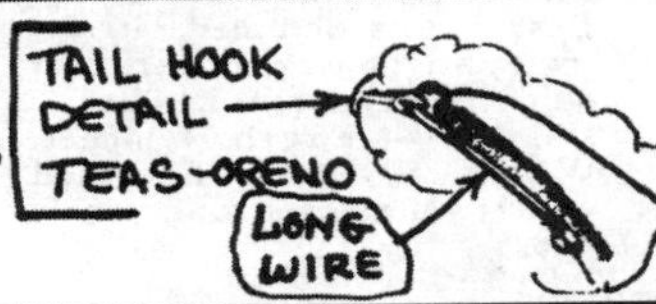
TAIL HOOK DETAIL
TEAS-ORENO
LONG WIRE

No. 991 ENTICE-ORENO

Entice-Oreno derived its name from its amazing, darting, fluttering action when retrieved, regardless of whether slow or fast. "enticing" action seems irresistible to about all fresh water game fish and a great many varieties of the smaller salt water species. Stainless steel headplate adds an extra "flash." 1939

$5 – 10

No. 991—Body length 2⅝ inches; weight ½ ounce. Two treble hooks.

2⅝"

STAINLESS STEEL HEAD-PLATE (SALT WATER BAIT)

The Deep Diving Fish-Oreno

The Fish-Oreno is a sure winner—for Bass, Walleyes, Pike, Pickerel, Muskie, Lake Trout and many others. Specially designed to travel deep, it is perfect for deep trolling when the big ones are down in the cool waters. Its bright metal head-plate adds flash to its typical Bass-Oreno action. Length 3½ inches, weight ⅝ ounce; two No. 1/0 treble hooks. Patterns: RH-YP-SSY.

No. 953

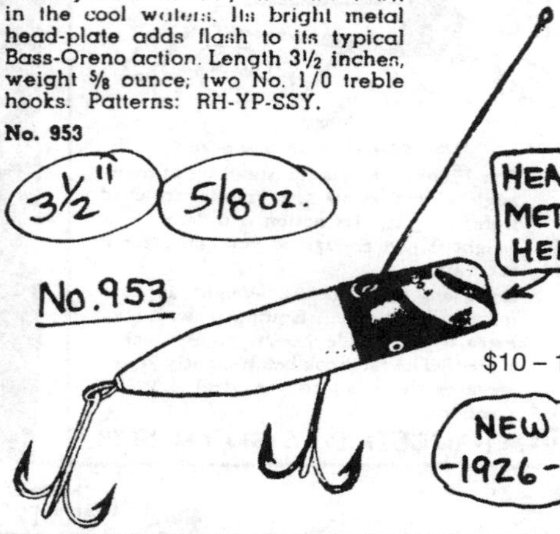

3½" 5/8 oz.

HEAVY METAL HEAD

No. 953

$10 – 15

NEW -1926-

No. 975 TWO-ORENO

NEW-1937

$10 – 20

3¾" 3/4 oz.

A bait with dual action—two lures in one that may be fished from either end. With line fastened to the end on which the head plate is mounted, it will travel deep with the action of the well known Pike-Oreno. Fishing it from the other end it has the darting, diving action of the famous Bass-Oreno. Length, 3¾ in. Weight, ¾ oz. Carried in colors: RW, F, YP and SF.
T13425 Price, each ....

ALSO AVAILABLE IN BABY TWO-ORENO 3" - ½ oz. NO. 974

No. 936 New Truck-Oreno

1939

9" 5 oz.

$200 – 250

No. 936—Truck-Oreno—Designed according to specificatior mitted by authorities on muskie fishing. Attracts Muskie Northern Pike because of the commotion created on surface. . inch propeller-like head revolves churning water. Overall length 9 inches with extra strong 1/0 treble muskie hook, in center. Spinner ahead of size 7/0 feathered treble hook. Heavy wire extending completely through lure gives extra strength. Supplied in finishes: RH—red head and white body with red and white feathered treble; F—frog color with red and white color feathered treble, and BY—butterfly color yellow with black stripe, black and red dots, red and white color feathered treble. Weight approximately 5 ounces.

No. 1973 BASS-OBITE

3¼" 5/8 oz

$5 – 10

TENITE PLASTIC

All the erratic diving and darting actions of the famous Bass-Oreno have been incorporated in this lure of molded Tenite. Care has been exercised to achieve, in addition, extreme strength and durability. Belly hooks are attached by a stainless steel pin, easily removed for replacing with cadmium plated hooks to prevent rusting. Two sizes, each carried in colors: P, RW, F, SF, YP and Lum.
No. 1973 Length, 3¼ in. Weight, ⅝ oz.
No. 1972 Length, 2⅞ in. Weight, ½ oz.

• BABY BASS-OBITE - 2⅞" - ½"

THE BETTER BASS-ORENO

(2 SIZES)

NEW 1934

$5 – 20

A bait of better design, better construction and greater durability. The aluminum plate which has been cemented and riveted in the White Cedar body makes a direct connection between the line and the hooks, as both are attached to it. The old style screw eye fastening has been entirely eliminated. It is a much finer lure throughout, with all the realistic zigzag, darting, diving action of the old style. This action is much more uniform. Length, 3½ in. Weight, ⅝ oz. Carried in colors: RW, SF, YP, P, F and Lum.
T13418 ....

• BETTER BABE-ORENO - 2¾" - (ALUM. PLATE)

NO. 912 South Bend NEW SLIM-ORENO

$30 – 40

3¾" ½ oz.

Color Chart opposite page 1

A slender underwater minnow of light weight. Easily, instantly revolving spinners work constantly. Effective for fresh water species and also used successfully for a variety of smaller salt water fish. Sinks slowly. Body length 3¾ inches, weight approximately ½ ounce. No. 912 Slim-Oreno made in following finishes:

No. 999 MINNOW

5/8 oz.

1931 No. 999 4"

A slender enticer that dives, darts and then floats lazily. Best results obtained retrieving by slight jerks or series of quick turns of reel handle.
No. 999—Length, 4 inches. Weight, ⅝ ounce. Equipped with two extra-strong treble hooks.

$20 – 35

South Bend PORK-ORENO

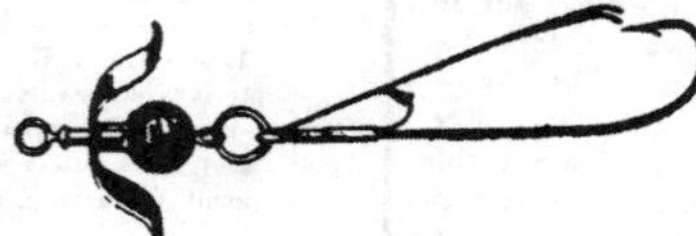

An excellent lure for the pork-rind angling enthusiast. Consists of our Jersey Spinner attachment and a size 3/0 weedless tandem hook. Used with a Jack's pork-rind frog or strip, it's a winner for casting or trolling

No. 413, Pork-Oreno.

The Jersey spinner attachment at forward end may be had separately, for use with any treble or single hook.

$2

South Bend WEEDLESS SPINNER HOOK

NO. 553

A weighted, weedless spinner hook, with swivel at forward end. Used with Jack's pork strips or frogs, it's most effective. Great for trolling or casting.
In two sizes, 3/0 and 5/0 hook No. 553

$2

1931

No. 30 Oreno June Bug Spinner Fly

$2

A casting lure consisting of a nickel June Bug Spinner with gold tip and a fancy feathered 1/0 size inverted wing fly. The spinner shank is weighted at proper place to prevent fouling when casting. The spinner revolves freely between red glass beads. The fly can be quickly detached for substituting different pattern fly. Mounted one on a card in cellophane envelope. Packed one dozen in a container. Weight, ¾ pound per dozen. Supplied in six standard patterns as follows:

Style No.		Style No.	
30RI	Red Ibis	30BG	Black Gnat
30CF	Col. Fuller	30McG	McGinty
30SD	Silver Doctor	30PB	Parama-cheene Belle

No. 30 Oreno June Bug Spinner

THE
BeBop
"Terrific" NEW
Salt Water
Bait
NEW
1950
No. 903 Be Bop
¾ oz., 4½ in.
9 finishes,
No. 902 Be Bop
½ oz., 3¾ in.
9 finishes,

$5 – 10

Spinner Attachments

$2

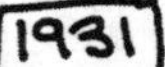
1931

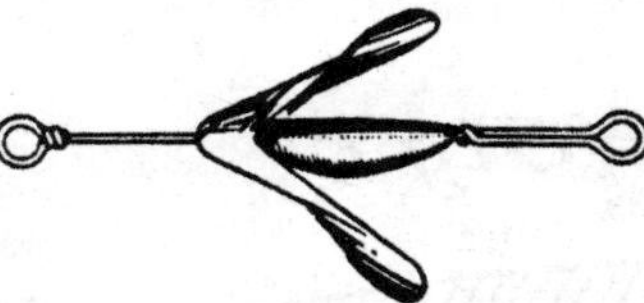

A wonderfully effective nickel-plated, polished spinner of strong construction. Revolves freely the instant reeled. Mounted on piano wire with snap arrangement, permitting the quick attachment of any fly or hook. Weight approximately ½ ounce. Mounted one on a card twelve cards connected. Packed one dozen in a container.

No. 363 Spinner attachment, weighted

No. 958 South Bend New Big Pike-Oreno

The Big Pike-Oreno is destined to be one of the greatest Muskie lures ever designed.

$15 – 20

5 3/8"

STAINLESS STEEL

The South Bend Bait Company takes the initiative in inaugurating the use of Stainless Steel for fishing tackle. It is a new metal alloy, which is extremely hard and durable and has the characteristic of retaining its original brilliance more than any other known metal. Headplates for all Pike-Orenos are made of this new metal.

1932

No. 958RH

• NO. 960 – GIANT JOINTED PIKE-ORENO – 7" – 2 1/8 OZ.

• NO. 969 – BIG JOINTED PIKE ORENO – 6"

South Bend Jersey Spinner Attachment

$2

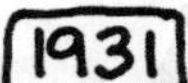
1931

Consisting of ball weight with nickel spinner at forward end, and steel split ring for hook connection at opposite end. Attached to any buck-tail treble or single hook it makes a most effective lure. Weight is ½ ounce.

Packed one dozen in a container. Weight ½ pound per dozen.

No. 365 Jersey Spinner Attachment.

June Bug Spinner Set

$10

NO. 89

SOUTH BEND
JUNE BUG SPINNER SET
SOUTH BEND BAIT COMPANY
SOUTH BEND, INDIANA, U. S. A.

(1931)

The June Bug Spinner, combined with the effectiveness of a South Bend Squirrel-Oreno or Fuzz-Oreno, has no equal for casting or trolling. June Bug has nickel finish with gold tip. Lures are interchangeable.
No. 89 June Bug Spinner Set

THE ORIGINAL PATENT OF THE BASSORENO TO: J.S. OLDS OF MICHIGAN. (WHERE ELSE?)

HE 1ST TRIED TO SELL IT TO SHAKESP. & HEDDON, AND THEY BOTH SAID "NO". (WE ALL MAKE MISTAKES) HE THEN ASSIGNED THE PATENT TO SOUTH BEND.

UNITED STATES PATENT OFFICE.

JAMES S. OLDS, OF BENTON HARBOR, MICHIGAN, ASSIGNOR TO SOUTH BEND BAIT COMPANY, OF SOUTH BEND, INDIANA, A CORPORATION OF INDIANA.

FISH BAIT OR LURE.

1,209,641. Specification of Letters Patent. Patented Dec. 19, 1916.

Application filed June 28, 1915. Serial No. 36,755.

Fig. 1. 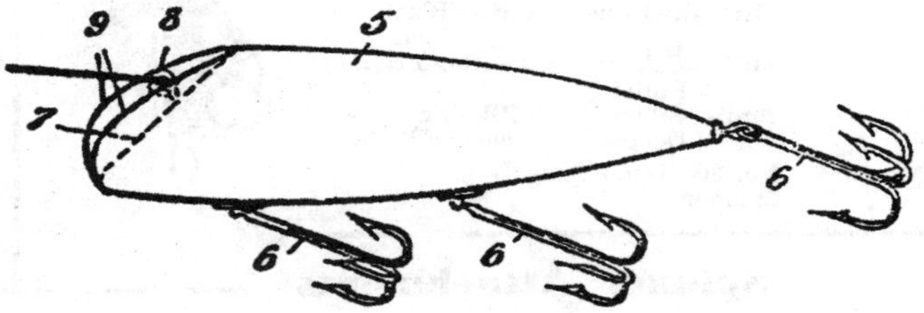
9
8
5
7
6
6
6
Fig. 2. 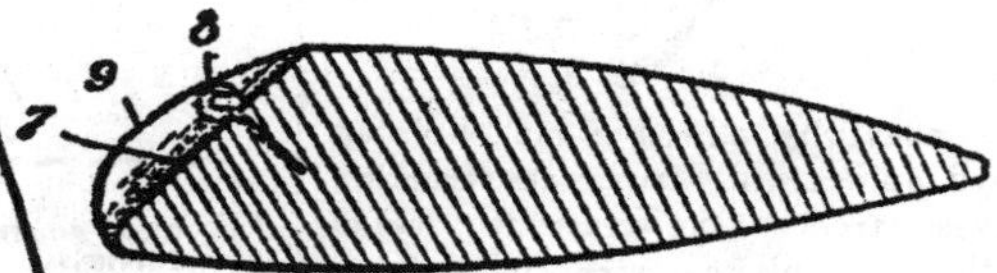
8
9
7
Fig. 3.
5
8
7
9
9

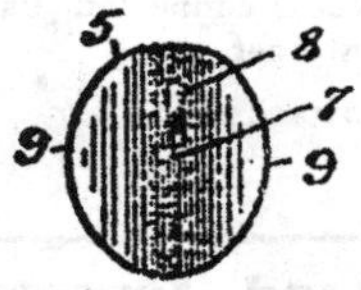

SO. BEND NO. 560 FROG - ORENO

1940

$10

ORIG. ROCKHOPPER!

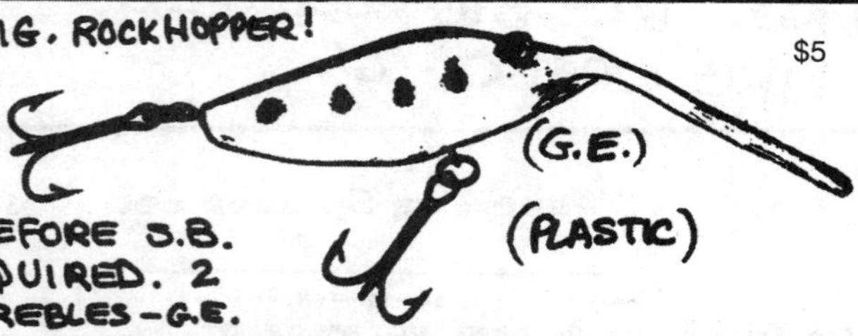

(G.E.)

(PLASTIC)

BEFORE S.B. AQUIRED. 2 TREBLES - G.E.

$5

ROCK HOPPER*

SIZES AND COLOR PATTERNS AVAILABLE

No. 675 Wt. 1/6 Oz. No. 676 Wt. 1/4 Oz.

NO. 999M

NOTE KNOB

RED

1929

4 1/8"

G.E.

$20 – 40

SOUTH BEND
SOUTH BEND
QUALITY TACKLE
BAIT COMPANY
Fishing Tackle of all kinds
Rods-Reels-Lines-Baits

(INVENTED BY: JAMES S. OLDS)

BASS-ORENO BAITS

(INTRO. 1915)

(PATENT DATE: DEC. 19, 1916)

$5 – 25

973 RW
3¾"

No. 973 Bass-Oreno

The original and genuine world-famous South Bend Bass-Oreno—for more than a generation the world's greatest game fish lure and the most widely imitated bait ever designed. Its record of consistent results has created for the Bass-Oreno a reputation famous in the angling world. Its darting, diving Bass-Oreno action never fails to lure and land the big ones. Length 3¾ inches, weight ¾ ounce. Three No. 1 treble hooks. Patterns RW-YP-P-F-LUM and SF. Packed 12 in container. Weight per container 1½ pounds.

972 RW
2¾"

No. 972 Babe-Oreno

A small size Bass-Oreno weighing ½ ounce, perfect for use with the popular light action rods. One of the most effective small lures ever created. Has that irresistibly alluring Bass-Oreno action. Length 2¾ inches, weight ½ ounce. Two No. 1 treble hooks. Patterns RW-YP-F-SF. Packed 12 in container. Weight per container 1¼ pounds. This bait should be in every tackle box.

$5

968RW
2¼"

No. 968 Midg-Oreno

The smallest casting lure of the Bass-Oreno type made by South Bend. Weighing but ⅜ ounce, it casts beautifully with a six foot light action rod, 9 or 12-pound test Black-Oreno line and either a No. 60 or No. 760 South Bend reel. Length 2¼ inches, weight ⅜ ounce. Two No. 5 bronze treble hooks. Patterns RW-YP-P and SF. Packed 12 in container. Weight per container 1¼ pounds.

$5

THE OLDEST BASS-ORENO HAD A SHALLOW CUPPED HEAD AND NO EYES.

1⅝"
971 RW

No. 971 Trout-Oreno

The Trout-Oreno is extremely strong, yet light in weight—easy to cast and easy to pick up. A very popular and dependable lure for a great variety of fish, including trout, bass and panfish. An aluminum plate, cemented into the body, connects hook and line. Length 1⅝ inches, weight 1/10 ounce. Packed one on a card, four connected, three cards per container. Weight per container 6 ounces. Supplied in choice of following patterns: RW-YP-F-SF and Y.

NOTE: LATER MADE A "SPIN-ORENO."

1⅛" 970RW

$5

No. 970 Fly-Oreno

Constructed along the same lines and having the same wobbling, diving, zigzag action as the Trout-Oreno. An aluminum plate connects line tie with hook and runs through body of lure, thereby eliminating any possibility of losing fish because of loosened hooks or line tie. Very light weight (1/20 ounce) and easy to cast. Length 1⅛ inches. Packed one on a card, four connected, three cards per container. Weight per container 5 ounces. Patterns: RW-YP and F.

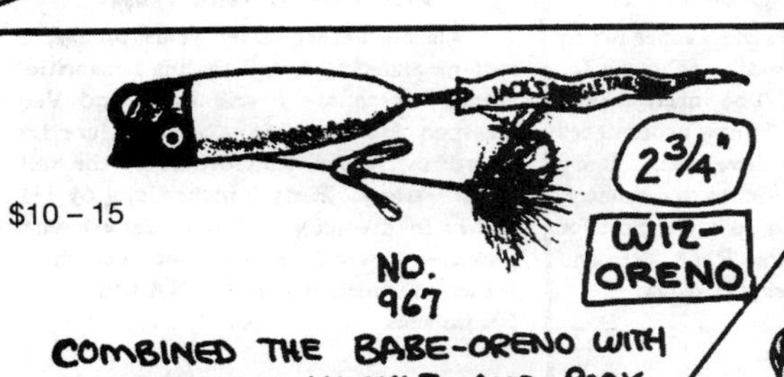
JACK'S SINGLE TAIL
2¾"
WIZ-ORENO

$10 – 15

NO. 967

COMBINED THE BABE-ORENO WITH A SPINNER, HACKLE, AND PORK RIND. ONE LONG SHANK 5/0 SNECK HOOK.

ALSO G.E. + 3¾"

3½"

South Bend Salt Water BASS-ORENO

The salt water Bass-Oreno has been brought out as the result of innumerable demands by salt water anglers for a bait just like the famous Bass-Oreno, only heavier equipped.

It is the same excepting it has but one belly treble with the tail treble, and both trebles are super strong to meet the smashes and vicious fights of striped bass, rockfish, kingfish, grouper, red fish, weakfish, and other salt water species.

Also has been used with wonderful success on large, fresh-water fish such as muskie and northern pike.

No. 977

Body length is 3½ inches. Standard equipment, one super-strong belly treble and tail treble. No. 977 Salt water Bass-Oreno supplied in four colors: RH-RAIN-SF-RSF. (See color chart, page 46.)

$5 – 10

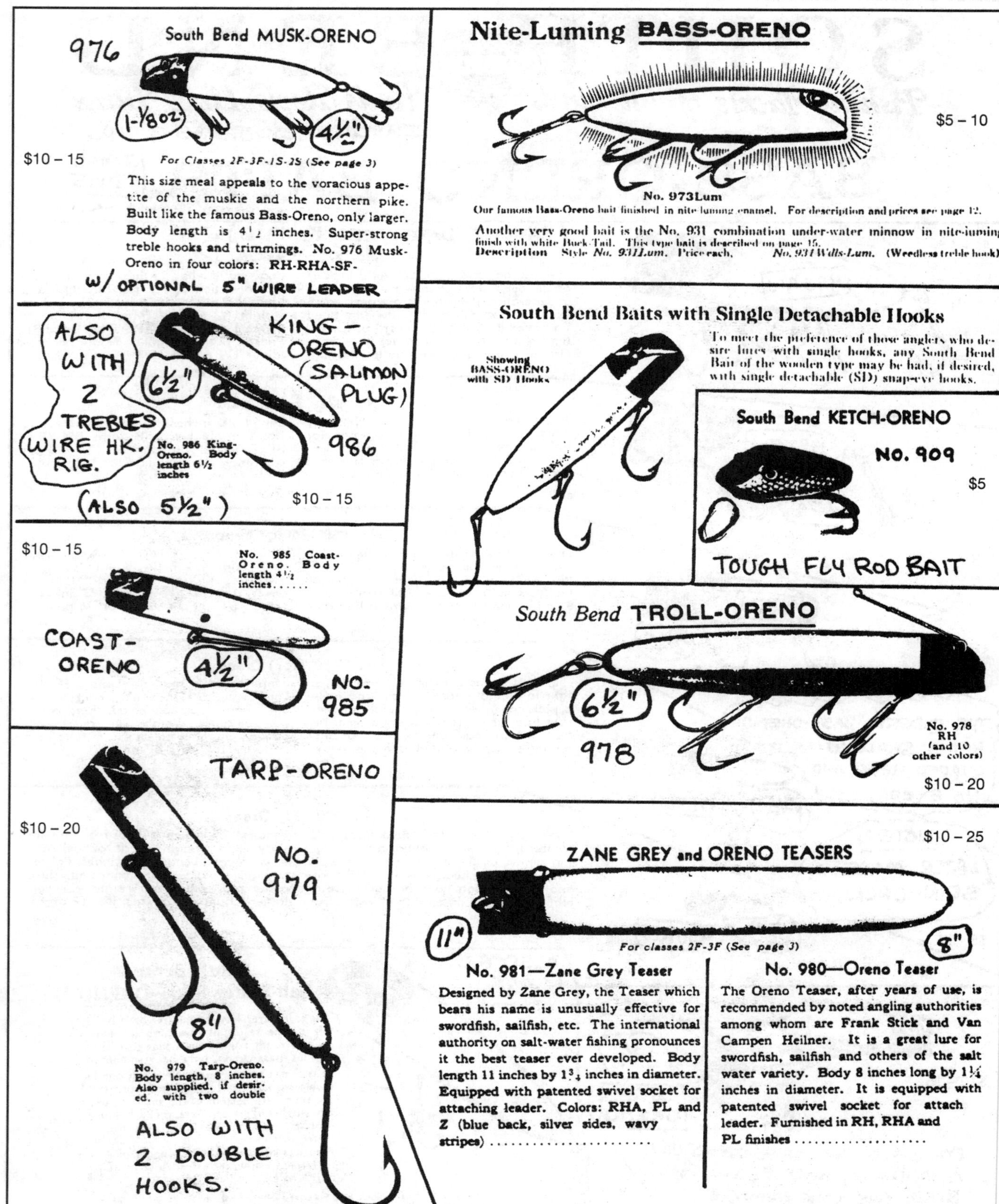

South Bend MUSK-ORENO

976

1-1/8 oz

4½"

$10 – 15

For Classes 2F-3F-1S-2S (See page 3)

This size meal appeals to the voracious appetite of the muskie and the northern pike. Built like the famous Bass-Oreno, only larger. Body length is 4½ inches. Super-strong treble hooks and trimmings. No. 976 Musk-Oreno in four colors: RH-RHA-SF-

W/ OPTIONAL 5" WIRE LEADER

Nite-Luming BASS-ORENO

$5 – 10

No. 973Lum

Our famous Bass-Oreno bait finished in nite-luming enamel. For description and prices see page 12.

Another very good bait is the No. 931 combination under-water minnow in nite-luming finish with white Buck-Tail. This type bait is described on page 15.

Description Style *No. 931Lum.* Price each. *No. 931 Wdls-Lum.* (Weedless treble hook).

KING-ORENO (SALMON PLUG)

ALSO WITH 2 TREBLES WIRE HK. RIG.

6½"

No. 986 King-Oreno. Body length 6½ inches

986

(ALSO 5½")

$10 – 15

South Bend Baits with Single Detachable Hooks

Showing BASS-ORENO with SD Hooks

To meet the preference of those anglers who desire lures with single hooks, any South Bend Bait of the wooden type may be had, if desired, with single detachable (SD) snap-eye hooks.

South Bend KETCH-ORENO

NO. 909

$5

TOUGH FLY ROD BAIT

$10 – 15

No. 985 Coast-Oreno. Body length 4½ inches......

COAST-ORENO

4½"

NO. 985

South Bend TROLL-ORENO

6½"

978

No. 978 RH (and 10 other colors)

$10 – 20

TARP-ORENO

$10 – 20

NO. 979

8"

No. 979 Tarp-Oreno. Body length, 8 inches. Also supplied, if desired, with two double

ALSO WITH 2 DOUBLE HOOKS.

$10 – 25

ZANE GREY and ORENO TEASERS

11"

8"

For classes 2F-3F (See page 3)

No. 981—Zane Grey Teaser

Designed by Zane Grey, the Teaser which bears his name is unusually effective for swordfish, sailfish, etc. The international authority on salt-water fishing pronounces it the best teaser ever developed. Body length 11 inches by 1¾ inches in diameter. Equipped with patented swivel socket for attaching leader. Colors: RHA, PL and Z (blue back, silver sides, wavy stripes) ....

No. 980—Oreno Teaser

The Oreno Teaser, after years of use, is recommended by noted angling authorities among whom are Frank Stick and Van Campen Heilner. It is a great lure for swordfish, sailfish and others of the salt water variety. Body 8 inches long by 1¼ inches in diameter. It is equipped with patented swivel socket for attach leader. Furnished in RH, RHA and PL finishes ....

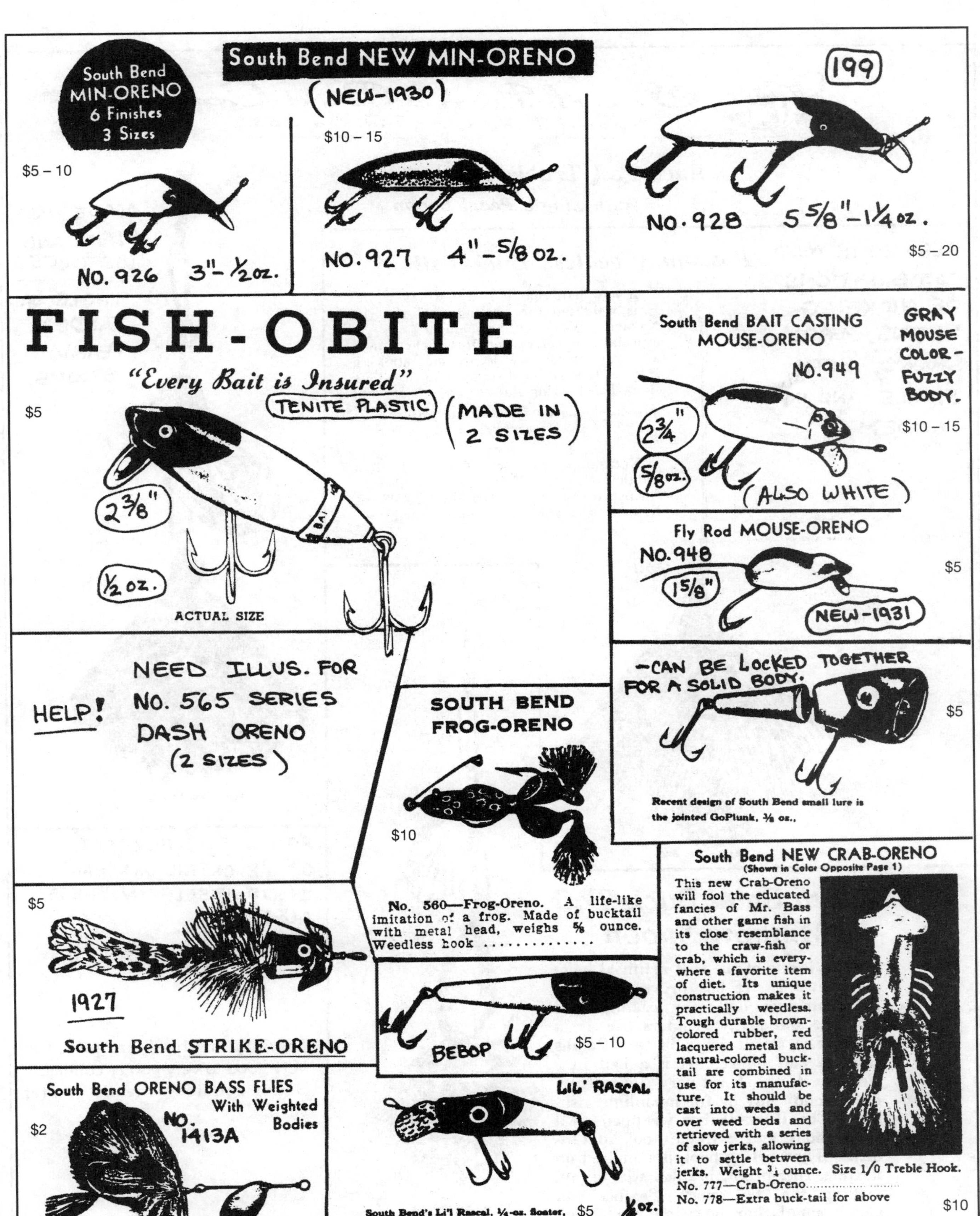
South Bend MIN-ORENO
6 Finishes
3 Sizes
South Bend NEW MIN-ORENO
(NEW-1930)
199
$5 – 10
NO. 926 3"-½oz.
$10 – 15
NO. 927 4"-5/8 oz.
NO. 928 5 5/8"-1¼oz.
$5 – 20
FISH-OBITE
"Every Bait is Insured"
TENITE PLASTIC
(MADE IN 2 SIZES)
$5
2 3/8"
½ oz.
ACTUAL SIZE
South Bend BAIT CASTING MOUSE-ORENO
NO. 949
GRAY MOUSE COLOR - FUZZY BODY.
2 3/4"
5/8 oz.
(ALSO WHITE)
$10 – 15
Fly Rod MOUSE-ORENO
NO. 948
1 5/8"
NEW-1931
$5
NEED ILLUS. FOR NO. 565 SERIES DASH ORENO (2 SIZES)
HELP!
SOUTH BEND FROG-ORENO
$10
-CAN BE LOCKED TOGETHER FOR A SOLID BODY.
$5
Recent design of South Bend small lure is the jointed GoPlunk, 3/8 oz.,
No. 560—Frog-Oreno. A life-like imitation of a frog. Made of bucktail with metal head, weighs 5/8 ounce. Weedless hook ....
$5
1927
South Bend STRIKE-ORENO
BEBOP
$5 – 10
South Bend NEW CRAB-ORENO
(Shown in Color Opposite Page 1)
This new Crab-Oreno will fool the educated fancies of Mr. Bass and other game fish in its close resemblance to the craw-fish or crab, which is everywhere a favorite item of diet. Its unique construction makes it practically weedless. Tough durable brown-colored rubber, red lacquered metal and natural-colored buck-tail are combined in use for its manufacture. It should be cast into weeds and over weed beds and retrieved with a series of slow jerks, allowing it to settle between jerks. Weight ¾ ounce. Size 1/0 Treble Hook.
No. 777—Crab-Oreno..................
No. 778—Extra buck-tail for above
$10
South Bend ORENO BASS FLIES
With Weighted Bodies
NO. 1413A
$2
LIL' RASCAL
South Bend's Li'l Rascal, ¼-oz. floater,
$5
¼ oz.

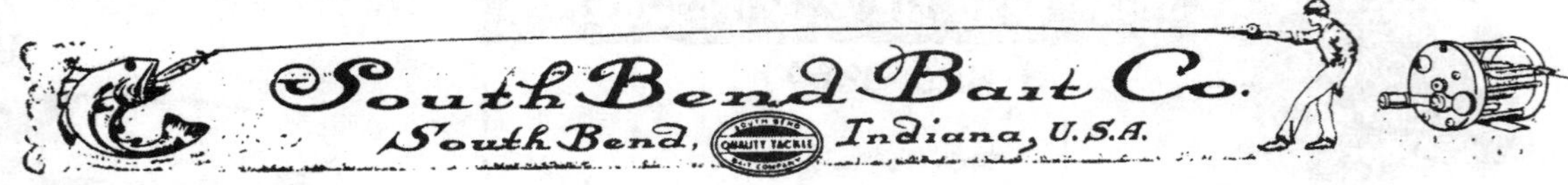
South Bend Bait Co.
South Bend, Indiana, U.S.A.

Buck-Tail Treble Hook

With Single Pearl Spoon

MADE IN PLAIN AND WEEDLESS.

SINGLE OR TANDEM PEARL SPOONS.

ALSO WITH MANY COMBINATIONS OF NICKELED SPOONS, PEARL SPOONS, BOTH SINGLE AND IN TANDEM.

Possum Weedless Buck-Tail

A new bait that is really worth while. It is weighted for casting and has the Navarre Weedless attachment. It is especially effective for Bass when they are lying in the weeds and not striking freely. It is an ideal single hook weedless Buck-Tail Casting Bait.

Mounted one on a card, one dozen in a carton.

Colors

Natural Color Buck-Tail with Red Feather Center. If desired can also be furnished at 5c each extra in Pure White, Red, or Red and White hair mixed.

$2

824

Style No. 824

703C

$2

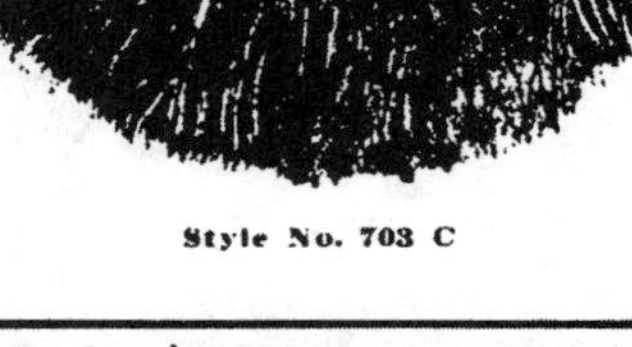

Style No. 703 C

$5

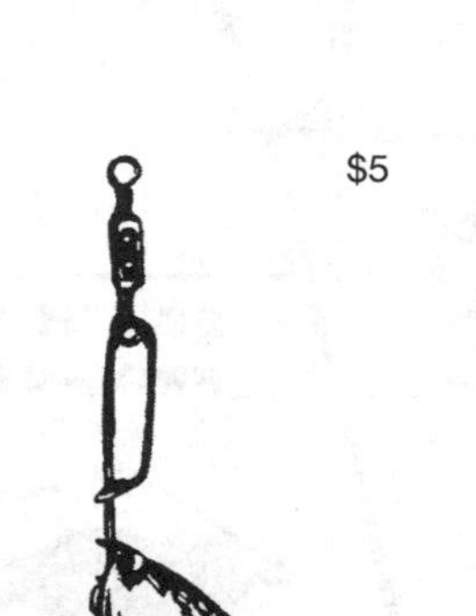

801A

Style No. 801 A

South Bend Buck-Tail Minnow Spoon

This is one of the best artificial baits ever devised. It has proven wonderfully effective both for casting and trolling, and many Anglers use it in preference to all other baits. Weighs about a half ounce. It is a bait in a class by itself. Used very successfully on a cloudy day or for moonlight fishing. The Buck-Tail is wrapped on a single hook and a treble hook in tandem. The trailing hook is mounted on flexible, rust-proof, braided wire gimp, making the tail very flexible and closely simulating the swimming motion.

AGAIN, THE HERITAGE OF "BUCKTAIL WORDEN" SHOWS ITSELF IN THESE LURES.

Lures in this book are priced in very good to very good+ condition. Better condition means greater value.

South Bend Buck-Oreno

$2

1932

Furnished in

Style No.	Description
888-R	Red Buck-tail—White Hackle
888-W	White Buck-Tail—Red Hackle
888-Nat.	Natural Buck-tail—Red Hackle

Special Muskie Spoon

$2

Old-timers thoroughly familiar with the appetites of Muskie, Great Northern Pike and big Lake Trout in "Lake of the Woods" region recognize this new Special Spoon as the "world's best" for these fighters in northern waters. The brass shank, snap and swivel are of extra heavy construction. Red buck-tail tied very full on treble hook. Spoon is red head, white enamel finished. **Packed one-half dozen in a container.** Weight per container, 13 ounces.

Style No.	Finish	Hook Size	Spoon Size	Length, Inches
1323A—RH—Red Head		8/0	9	3
1324A—RH—Red Head		10/0	12	3⅝

1932

Buck-Tail Trolling Spoon

$2

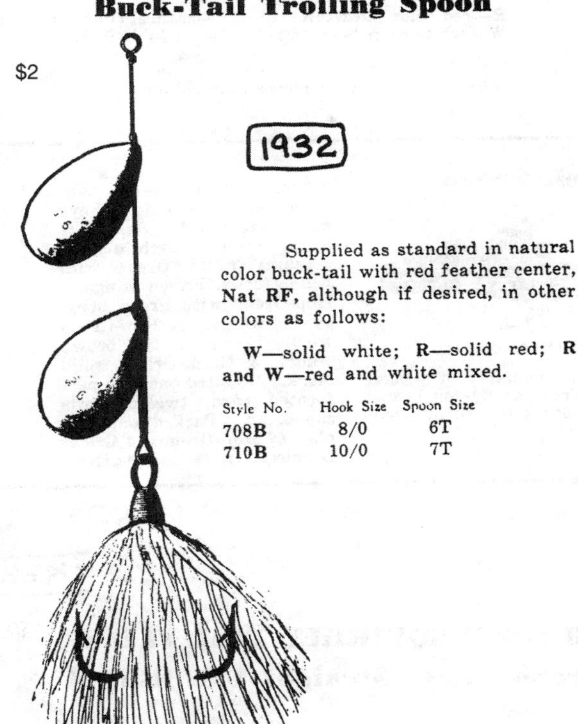

1932

Supplied as standard in natural color buck-tail with red feather center, **Nat RF,** although if desired, in other colors as follows:

W—solid white; R—solid red; R and W—red and white mixed.

Style No.	Hook Size	Spoon Size
708B	8/0	6T
710B	10/0	7T

Large Trolling Spoon

$2

No. 1319A

A recognized standard trolling lure for large fresh-water game fish such as Muskie, Great Northern Pike, Lake Trout, etc. The brass shank, snap and swivel are of extra heavy construction. Feathered treble hooks are tied with red, white and fancy guinea feathers on high-grade imported hooks. The spoon is supplied in three standard finishes:

N—Highly buffed, mirror nickel finish.

P—Lustrous iridescent pearl finish.

RH—White body with red head, both convex and concave.

Mounted one on a card. **Packed one-half dozen in a container.** Weight, 3½ pounds per dozen. Supplied in following two standard sizes and three finishes:

Style No.	Finish	Hook Size	Spoon Size	Length, Inches
*1319A-N	Nickel	7/0	9	3
*1319A-P	Pearl	7/0	9	3
*1319A-RH	Red Head	7/0	9	3
*1322A-N	Nickel	8/0	12	3⅝
*1322A-P	Pearl	8/0	12	3⅝
*1322A-RH	Red Head	8/0	12	3⅝

1932

Rubber Pork Rind

$2

No. 248 Rubber Pork Rind

An imitation of pork rind made of rubber strips. Has white body and red head, with "groove" for attaching to hook. Made in Fly Rod and Bass sizes, and for the No. 594 Trix-Oreno lure. **Packed one dozen strips in an envelope, one dozen envelopes in a container.**

Style No.		Per Doz. Envelopes
247	Rubber Pork Rind (2¼ inches long)	--
248	Rubber Pork Rind (3½ inches long)	--
244	Rubber Pork Rind (1¾ in. long) all white, for No. 594 Trix-Oreno.	

1932

1932

$10

ORENO
PORK RIND
NO. 262 BASS SIZE
SOUTH BEND BAIT CO.
SOUTH BEND, IND. MADE IN U.S.A.

All pre-1950 lures, rods, reels, fish decoys, bobbers, catalogs, tackle boxes, fishing photos, trolling motors, line spools, fishing licenses, and game warden badges are collectible.

South Bend Double Spin-Oreno

Nite-Luming

$3

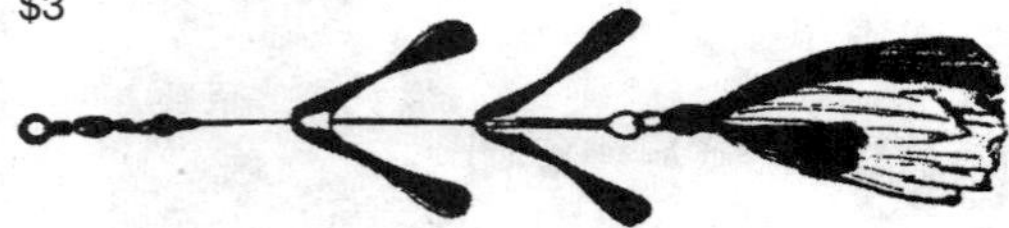

No. 1380 Double Spin-Oreno

No. 1375 Double Spin-Oreno

The Double Spin-Oreno is for casting, trolling or spatting for Bass and other game fish. Consists of a double spinner with swivel at forward end and a long shank, ringed treble hook, wrapped full with red, white and fancy genuine feathers. Spinners are nickel-plated bell shaped having nite-luming tip. The spinners revolve in opposite directions.

Mounted one on a card, six cards connected. **Packed one dozen in a container.** Weight, ¾ pound per dozen.

Style No.	
1380	Length over all, 6 inches; No. 1 hook
1375	Length over all, 4¼ inches; No. 6 hook

1932

South Bend Weedless Spinner Hooks

Buck-Tail or Feathered

1932

THIS IS A NEW BODY SHAPE - SEE PAGE 206 FOR 1920'S MODEL.

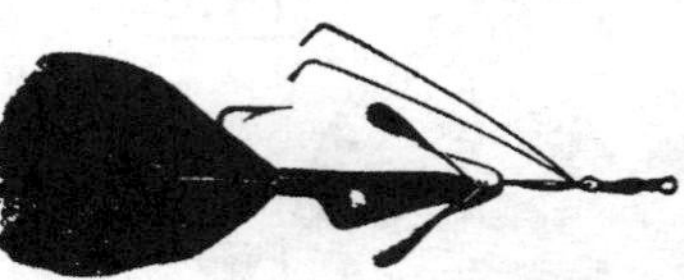

No. 565RI Weedless Spinner Hook

This combination either in buck-tail or feathered is a most effective casting or trolling lure, especially when used with pork-rind strip.

The hook is Sneck hollow point, with keel-shaped weighted shank. Spinner is nickel-plated, swivel size is No. 5. Strong construction and of such design that spinner starts revolving the very instant the bait is moved. It is weedless, permitting casting into thickest of weeds and rushes.

Mounted one on a card, six cards connected. **Packed one dozen in a container.** Weight, 1 pound per dozen. Supplied in three colors of buck-tail and one feathered pattern as follows. Supplied in assorted colors unless otherwise specified.

R—red color buck-tail
W—white color buck-tail
N—natural color buck-tail
RI—red ibis feathered

Style No.	Hook Size
565	5/0 in above four colors

South Bend Hop-Oreno and Crick-Oreno

$2

1932

The Hop-Oreno and Crick-Oreno contained in the displays illustrated below are most perfect reproductions in form and action of both the grasshopper and the cricket, known bass delicacies. Their design combines feathers and either buck-tail or peacock herl into a lifelike resemblance of wings and crawlers. In addition to being excellent for Bass and Trout as fly-rod lures, they are most effective for Crappies, Perch and Bluegills, either trolled or used with a cane pole.

(Trout Size) (Bass Size)

Tied over a non-slip cork body on a turn-down eye hook, size 1/0 for Bass, size 8 for Trout. Each display contains 3 Hop-Oreno with yellow body, brown wings, 3 Hop-Oreno with green body, green wings, 3 Hop-Oreno with brown body, brown wings, 3 Crick-Oreno, solid black. Mounted one on a perforated card, twelve cards connected. **Packed one display (9 Hop-Orenos, 3 Crick-Orenos) in a container.**

WORDEN'S COMBINATION BAIT

(Wooden Minnow and Buck Tail)
Patent Spinner.

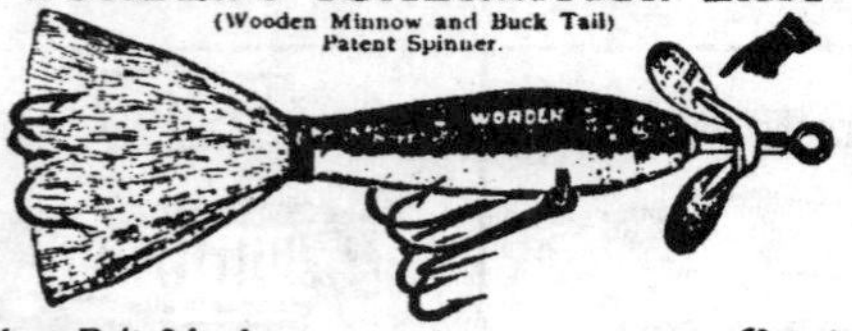

Above Bait, 3 hooks	60 cents
Wooden Minnows, 5 hooks	75 cents
Buck Tail Carting Spoons	40 cents
Weedless, Weighted Hooks (3)	25 cents
Weedless Frog Spinner, Patent	30 cents
Buck Tail Gangs	40 cents
Buck Tail "Muski" Spoons	$1.00

24-Page Illustrated "Facts and Fish Stories" 4c. stamps. Mention your dealer

WORDEN BUCK TAIL MFG. CO., South Bend, Ind.

THIS 1905 AD SHOWS SOME OR ALL OF "BUCK-TAIL WORDENS" PRODUCT LINE AT THAT TIME.

$100 – 150

1932

$3

SOUTH BEND SQUIRREL TAIL FLIES

Sqr'l-Oreno Flies—Straight Eye Ringed

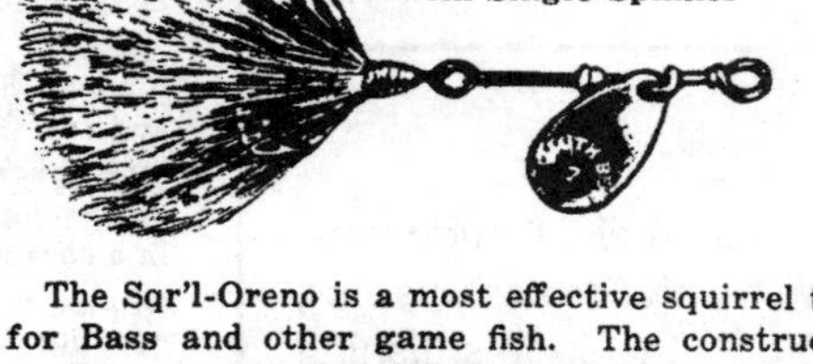

No. 1436A Sqr'l-Oreno with Single Spinner

No. 1431 Sqr'l-Oreno Fly

The Sqr'l-Oreno is a most effective squirrel tail lure for fly rod casting for Bass and other game fish. The construction is of the same high quality as our buck-tail flies, tied with genuine silk on straight eye-ringed hollow point highest grade hooks, bronzed finish.

Mounted one on a card, twelve cards connected. **Packed one dozen in a container.** Weight, ¾ to 1½ pounds per dozen. Unless otherwise specified will be supplied assorted in following three standard colors:

Red Fox—Grey Squirrel—Black Squirrel.

SOUTH BEND TREBLE HOOKS---WITH FLUTED SPOON

$2

Treble Buck-tail Fluted Casting Spoon No. 734

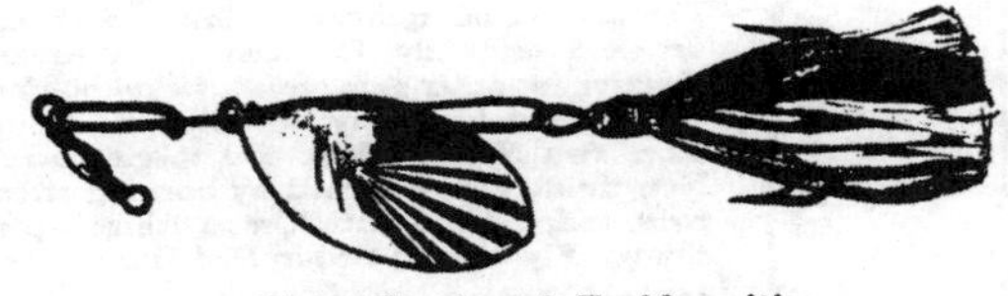

Plain Feathered Treble with Fluted Spoon No. 1312A

South Bend ORENO-BASS FLY

Weighted Body

$2

1929

NO. 1413

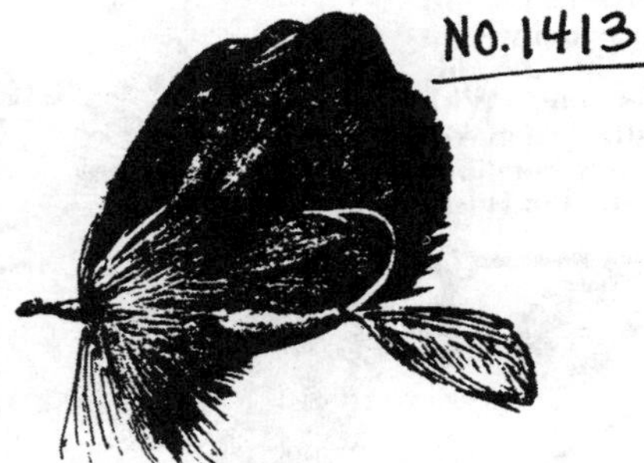

No. 1413 Oreno-Bass Fly
(Illustration ¾ actual size)

Oreno Bass Flies are tied on extra strong, hollow point, bronzed, ringed eye Sproat hooks with heavy tied inverted wings and enameled, waterproofed weighted bodies. Used with a single or double spinner and Jack's pork rind, it presents a well proven, irresistible lure.

Mounted one on a card, six cards connected. **Packed one dozen in a container.** Weight ½ pound per dozen. Supplied in six standard patterns as follows: (Unless otherwise specified supplied in assorted fly patterns.)

RI—Red Ibis
YM—Yellow May
WM—White Miller
BG—Black Gnat
MB—March Brown
PB—Parmacheene Belle

South Bend ORENO-BASS FLY

NO. 1425

Weedless— Weighted Body

1929

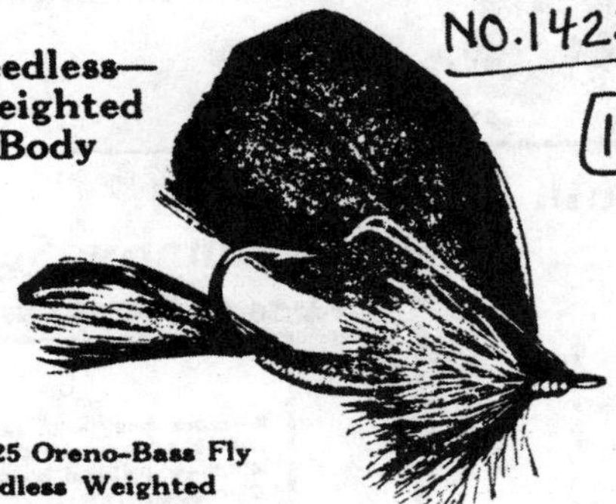

No. 1425 Oreno-Bass Fly
Weedless Weighted
(Illustration ¾ actual size)

Oreno-Bass Flies are furnished equipped with double weed guards as illustrated above. Mounted one on a card, six cards connected. **Packed one dozen in a container.** Weight ¾ pound per dozen. Supplied in same six colors as listed in opposite column. (Unless otherwise specified assorted patterns supplied.)

Showing Actual Sizes of Fluted Spoons

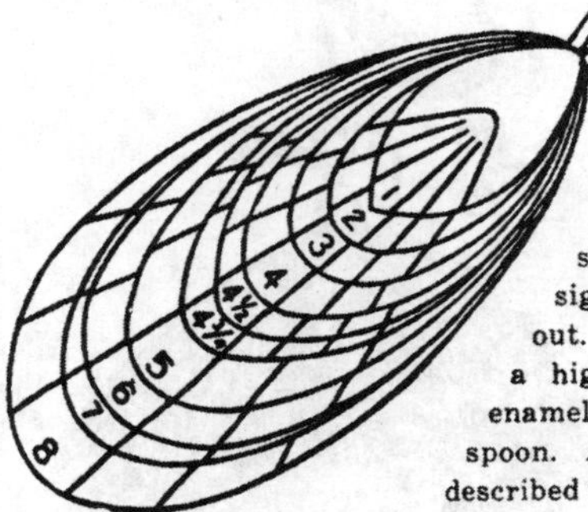

1
2
3
4
4½
5
6
7
8

Chart shows the exact sizes of fluted spoon blades. These spoons are built substantially and are carefully designed and constructed throughout. They are made of brass with a high nickel-plated finish. Red enamel on back. Lug is soldered on spoon. Also supplied in the RH finish described above.

NO. 579 CASTING SPOON

HAS "RAISED" EYES.

2⅛"

$2

(NEW–1951)

$2

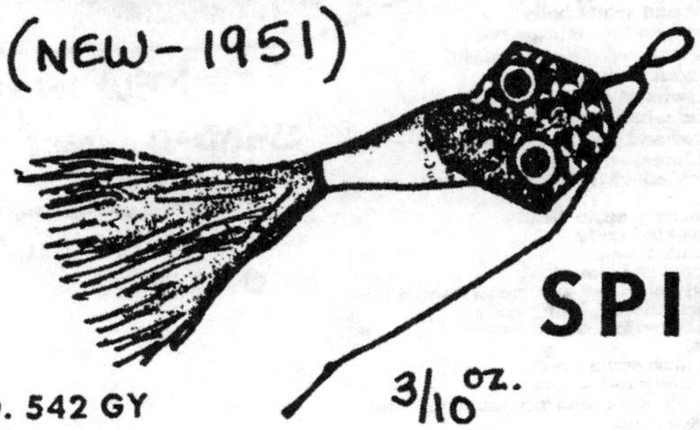

• ALSO MADE "ITSADUZY"– 5/8 oz.

SOUTH BEND

SPIN-I-DUZY

FOR SPINNING

NO. 542 GY

3/10 oz.

NEW–1951 (PLASTIC)

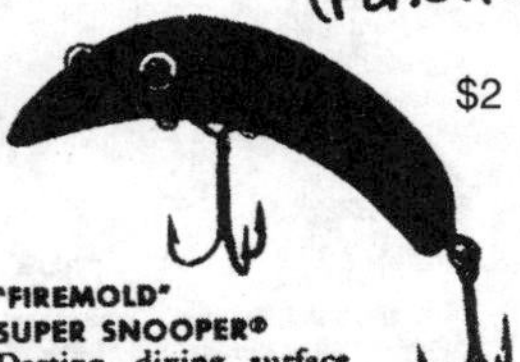

$2

"FIREMOLD" SUPER SNOOPER® Darting, diving surface bait. Fluorescent "Fire-powder" molded in plastic body. Wt. 1/2 oz.

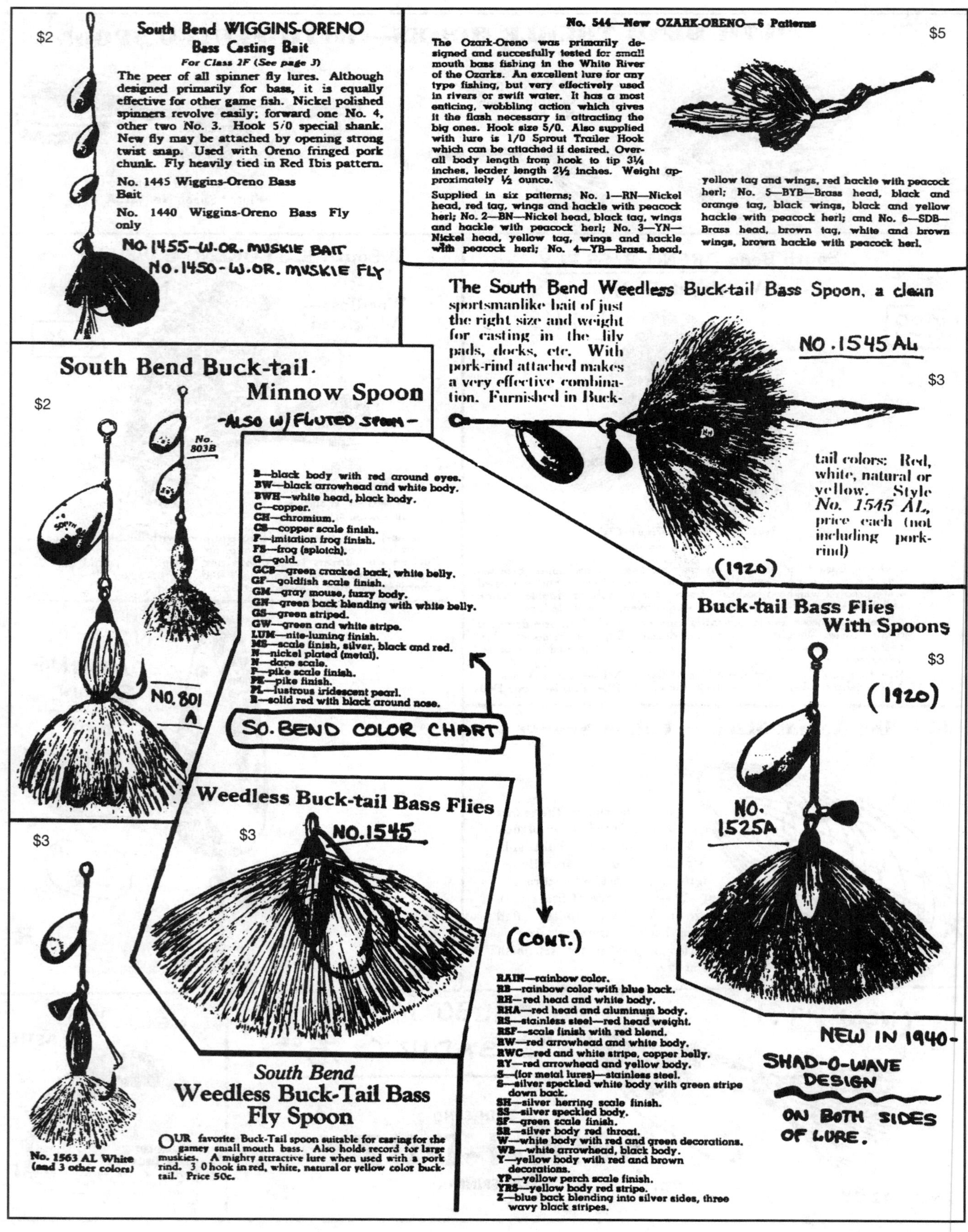
$2
South Bend WIGGINS-ORENO
Bass Casting Bait
For Class 2F (See page 3)
The peer of all spinner fly lures. Although designed primarily for bass, it is equally effective for other game fish. Nickel polished spinners revolve easily; forward one No. 4, other two No. 3. Hook 5/0 special shank. New fly may be attached by opening strong twist snap. Used with Oreno fringed pork chunk. Fly heavily tied in Red Ibis pattern.
No. 1445 Wiggins-Oreno Bass Bait
No. 1440 Wiggins-Oreno Bass Fly only
NO. 1455-W.OR. MUSKIE BAIT
NO. 1450-W.OR. MUSKIE FLY
No. 544—New OZARK-ORENO—6 Patterns
$5
The Ozark-Oreno was primarily designed and succesfully tested for small mouth bass fishing in the White River of the Ozarks. An excellent lure for any type fishing, but very effectively used in rivers or swift water. It has a most enticing, wobbling action which gives it the flash necessary in attracting the big ones. Hook size 5/0. Also supplied with lure is 1/0 Sprout Trailer Hook which can be attached if desired. Overall body length from hook to tip 3¼ inches, leader length 2½ inches. Weight approximately ½ ounce.
Supplied in six patterns; No. 1—RN—Nickel head, red tag, wings and hackle with peacock herl; No. 2—BN—Nickel head, black tag, wings and hackle with peacock herl; No. 3—YN—Nickel head, yellow tag, wings and hackle with peacock herl; No. 4—YB—Brass head, yellow tag and wings, red hackle with peacock herl; No. 5—BYB—Brass head, black and orange tag, black wings, black and yellow hackle with peacock herl; and No. 6—SDB—Brass head, brown tag, white and brown wings, brown hackle with peacock herl.
The South Bend Weedless Buck-tail Bass Spoon, a clean sportsmanlike bait of just the right size and weight for casting in the lily pads, docks, etc. With pork-rind attached makes a very effective combination. Furnished in Buck-tail colors: Red, white, natural or yellow. Style No. 1545 AL, price each (not including pork-rind)
NO. 1545 AL
$3
(1920)
South Bend Buck-tail Minnow Spoon
-ALSO W/FLUTED SPOON-
$2
No. 803B
NO. 801 A
B—black body with red around eyes.
BW—black arrowhead and white body.
BWH—white head, black body.
C—copper.
CH—chromium.
CS—copper scale finish.
F—imitation frog finish.
FS—frog (splotch).
G—gold.
GCB—green cracked back, white belly.
GF—goldfish scale finish.
GM—gray mouse, fuzzy body.
GN—green back blending with white belly.
GS—green striped.
GW—green and white stripe.
LUM—nite-luming finish.
MS—scale finish, silver, black and red.
N—nickel plated (metal).
N—dace scale.
P—pike scale finish.
PK—pike finish.
PL—lustrous iridescent pearl.
R—solid red with black around nose.
SO. BEND COLOR CHART
(CONT.)
RAIN—rainbow color.
RB—rainbow color with blue back.
RH—red head and white body.
RHA—red head and aluminum body.
RS—stainless steel—red head weight.
RSF—scale finish with red blend.
RW—red arrowhead and white body.
RWC—red and white stripe, copper belly.
RY—red arrowhead and yellow body.
S—(for metal lures)—stainless steel.
S—silver speckled white body with green stripe down back.
SH—silver herring scale finish.
SS—silver speckled body.
SF—green scale finish.
SR—silver body red throat.
W—white body with red and green decorations.
WB—white arrowhead, black body.
Y—yellow body with red and brown decorations.
YP—yellow perch scale finish.
YRS—yellow body red stripe.
Z—blue back blending into silver sides, three wavy black stripes.
Buck-tail Bass Flies With Spoons
$3
(1920)
NO. 1525A
NEW IN 1940-
SHAD-O-WAVE DESIGN
ON BOTH SIDES OF LURE.
Weedless Buck-tail Bass Flies
$3
NO.1545
$3
No. 1563 AL White (and 3 other colors)
South Bend
Weedless Buck-Tail Bass Fly Spoon
OUR favorite Buck-Tail spoon suitable for casting for the gamey small mouth bass. Also holds record for large muskies. A mighty attractive lure when used with a pork rind. 3 0 hook in red, white, natural or yellow color buck-tail. Price 50c.

TO FURTHER COMPLICATE THINGS FOR US COLLECTORS - SO. BEND PUT OUT THE LOW COST LINE OF "BEST-O-LUCK" LURES IN THE '30'S AND 40'S. I WOULD ASSUME THEY USED LESS EXPENSIVE HOOK RIGS, AND FEWER COATS OF PAINT.

No. 941 WEIGHTED WOBBLER

$10

Weighted wobbler witn nickel plated head-plate. Two treble hooks. Length 2⅝ inches. Weight ½ ounce. Made in RH, GS (green striped), S (silver speckled), RB (rainbow color), PL, P, N (red dace scale) and YP finishes

No. 921 PANATELLA WOBBLER

$10

Panatella wobbler with nickel plated head-plate. Two treble hooks. Length 4 inches. Weight ⅝ ounce. Made in RH, RHA and GS (green striped finishes

Nos. 577-579-580-581 METAL WOBBLERS

Style No.	Length	Weight
577	1¼ in.	
579	2¼ in.	⅜ oz.
580	2⅞ in.	⅝ oz.
581	3½ in.	1 oz.

$2 each

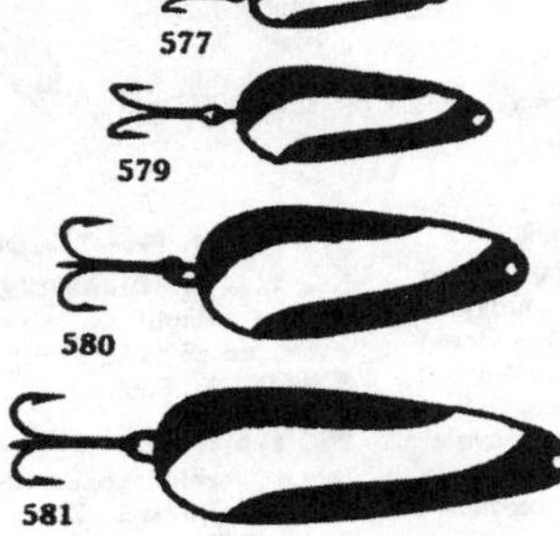
577
579
580
581

$10 – 20 each

BEST-O-LUCK BAITS

Because of the low price of Best-O-Luck baits, they will not carry our customary guarantee. They are, we believe, exceptional values.

No. 916 SURFACE LURE

Surface lure with spinner at front. Two treble hooks. Length 2¾ inches. Weight ¾ ounce. Made in RH and F finishes

No. 950 SURFACE LURE

Surface lure with spinner at front. Two treble hooks. Length 3¼ inches. Weight ½ ounce. Made in RH, GN (green back, white belly), SR (silver body, red throat) and YRS (yellow body, red stripe down back) finishes

No. 914 BABY WOUNDED MINNOW

For use with light weight casting rod. Flat sides. Spinners at front and back. Two treble hooks. Length 2¾ inches. Weight, ½ ounce. Made in RH, SS (silver speckled body), PK (pike color) and YP finishes

No. 907 BABY PIKE LURE

Baby pike lure with nickel plated head-plate. Two treble hooks. Length 3¼ inches. Weight ½ ounce. Made in RH, PK (pike color), GS (green striped), S (silver speckled), YP, RB (rainbow color), SF and P finishes

No. 930 PIKE LURE

Pike lure with nickel plated headplate. Two treble hooks. Length 4⅜ inches. Weight ⅝ ounce. Made in RH, PK (pike color), GS (green striped), S (silver speckled), YP, RB (rainbow color), SF and P finishes

No. 942 BABY WOBBLER

Baby grooved-head wobbler. Two treble hooks. Length 2¾ inches. Weight ½ ounce. Made in RH, GS (green striped), PK (pike color), SF, P and YP finishes

No. 920 WOUNDED MINNOW

Flat sides, floating minnow. Spinners at front and back. Three treble hooks. Length 3⅝ inches. Weight ¾ ounce. Made in RH, SS (silver speckled body), PK (pike color), and YP finishes

No. 918 WEIGHTED UNDERWATER LURE

Weighted underwater lure with spinner at front. Two treble hooks. Length 3 inches. Weight ⅝ ounce. Made in RH, RB (rainbow color) and PK (pike color) finishes

No. 910 WEIGHTED UNDERWATER LURE

Weighted underwater lure with spinner at front. Three trebles. Length 3 inc Weight ⅝ ounce. Made in RH, (green back, white belly), YRS (yellow body, red stripe down back) and SR (silver body, red throat) finishes

No. 908 BABY JOINTED PIKE LURE

Baby jointed pike lure with nickel plated headplate. Two treble hooks. Length 3½ inches. Weight ⅛ ounce. Made in RH, PK (pike color), GS (green striped), S (silver speckled), YP, RB (rainbow color), SF and P finishes

No. 931 JOINTED PIKE LURE

Standard jointed pike lure with nickel plated headplate. Two treble hooks. Length 4½ inches. Weight ⅝ ounce. Made in RH, PK pike color), GS (green striped), S (silver speckled) YP, RB (rainbow color), SF and P finishes

No. 943 STANDARD WOBBLER

Standard grooved-head wobbler. Three treble hooks. Length 3¾ inches. Weight ⅝ ounce. Made in RH, GS (green striped), PK (pike finish), SF, P and YP finishes

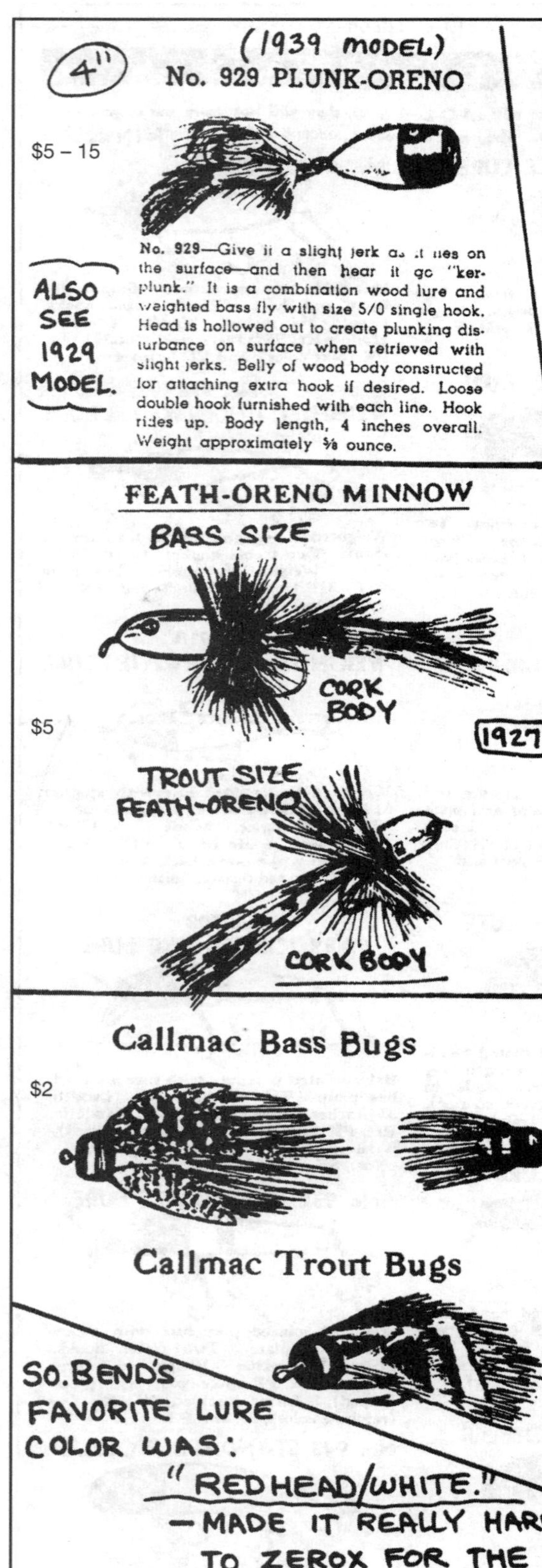

(1939 MODEL)

4"

No. 929 PLUNK-ORENO

$5 – 15

No. 929—Give it a slight jerk as it lies on the surface—and then hear it go "ker-plunk." It is a combination wood lure and weighted bass fly with size 5/0 single hook. Head is hollowed out to create plunking disturbance on surface when retrieved with slight jerks. Belly of wood body constructed for attaching extra hook if desired. Loose double hook furnished with each line. Hook rides up. Body length, 4 inches overall. Weight approximately ⅝ ounce.

ALSO SEE 1929 MODEL.

FEATH-ORENO MINNOW

BASS SIZE
CORK BODY
TROUT SIZE FEATH-ORENO
CORK BODY

$5

1927

Callmac Bass Bugs

$2

Callmac Trout Bugs

SO. BEND'S FAVORITE LURE COLOR WAS: "RED HEAD/WHITE." —MADE IT REALLY HARD TO ZEROX FOR THE BOOK.

PEACH-ORENO BAITS

ALL METAL LURE

$10 – 15

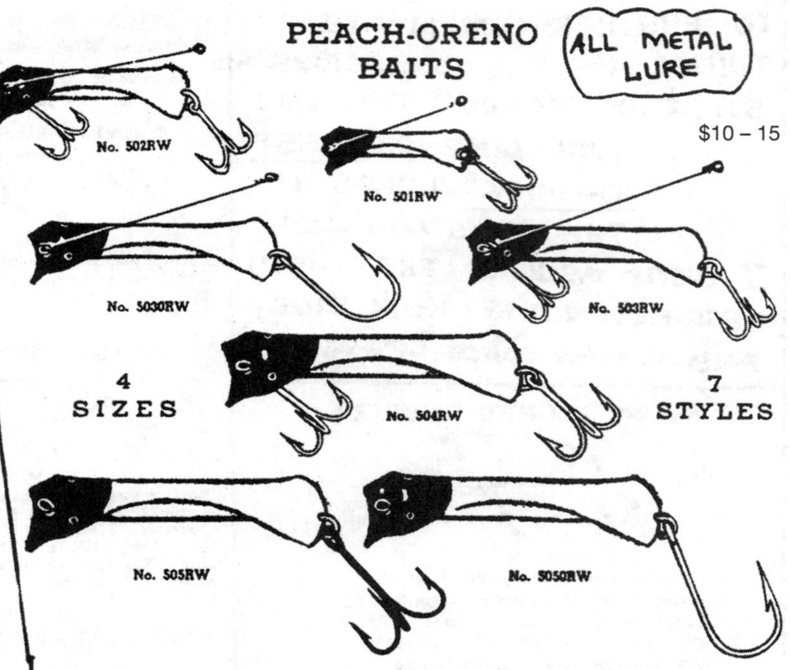

No. 502RW
No. 501RW
No. 5030RW
No. 503RW
4 SIZES
No. 504RW
7 STYLES
No. 505RW
No. 5050RW

No. 501 Peach-Oreno—The smallest of the Peach-Oreno series—extremely energetic in action and a sure attracter. Length 2½ inches, weight ½ ounce, one No. 1 treble hook. Equipped with piano wire leader Patterns: CH, G, YP, FS, RW, SH, SF, RB. Each ....

No. 502 Peach-Oreno—The popular ¾ ounce model with an action indescribably tempting. Length 3¼ inches; equipped with two 1/0 treble hooks and piano wire leader. Patterns: CH, G, YP, FS, RW, SH, SF, RB. Each ....

No. 503 Peach-Oreno—This is the medium large size which has proved so resultful in taking Muskellunge, large Great Northern Pike, Salmon and other of the bigger fresh water and salt water fish. Primarily a trolling lure, it can be easily handled with "heavy" or Muskie action bait casting rods. Length 4⅛ inches, weight 1⅛ ounces. Two No. 1/0 Muskie extra heavy treble hooks and piano wire leader Patterns: CH, G, YP, FS, RW, SH, SF, RB. Each ....

No. 5030 Peach-Oreno—Similar to No 503 except equipped with one 7/0 single Siwash hook for Lake Trout and salt water use. Each ....

No. 504 Peach-Oreno—The largest of the Peach-Oreno series, designed and developed for the biggest Lake Trout, Pacific Salmon, Muskellunge, and salt water use. Length 4⅞ inches, weight 2 ounces. Two No. 5/0 extra heavy treble hooks. Patterns: CH, G, YP, FS, RW, SH, SF, RB. Each ....

No. 505 Peach-Oreno—Similar to No. 504 except equipped with one No. 7/0 extra heavy treble hook. Each ....

No. 5050 Peach-Oreno—Similar to No. 504 except equipped with one No. 10/0 extra heavy single Siwash hook. Each ....

$5

No. 996—TEX-ORENO FLOATER

Designed originally for trout fishing in the Houston-Corpus Christi Gulf waters, news of the exceptional catches made by the Tex-Oreno spread rapidly until within a few months it was being used for a number of species of fish in many waters. Tested for fresh water fishing, Tex-Oreno produced the same amazing fish-getting results. There are two models—one a sinker and the other a floater.

No. 995—TEX-ORENO SINKER

No. 995—Tex-Oreno Sinker—Body length 2¾ inches; weight ⅝ ounce. Two treble hooks, cadmium plated. Eight finishes: RW-W-RB-PL-S-MS-RY-N. Each ....

No. 996—Tex-Oreno Floater—Body length 2¾ inches; weight ½ ounce. Two treble hooks, cadmium plated. Eight finishes: RW-W-RB-PL-S-MS-RY-N. Each ....

MANY OF THE "MODERATELY OLD" SO. BEND LURES DID NOT HAVE GLASS EYES, BUT A PAINTED NAIL EYE.

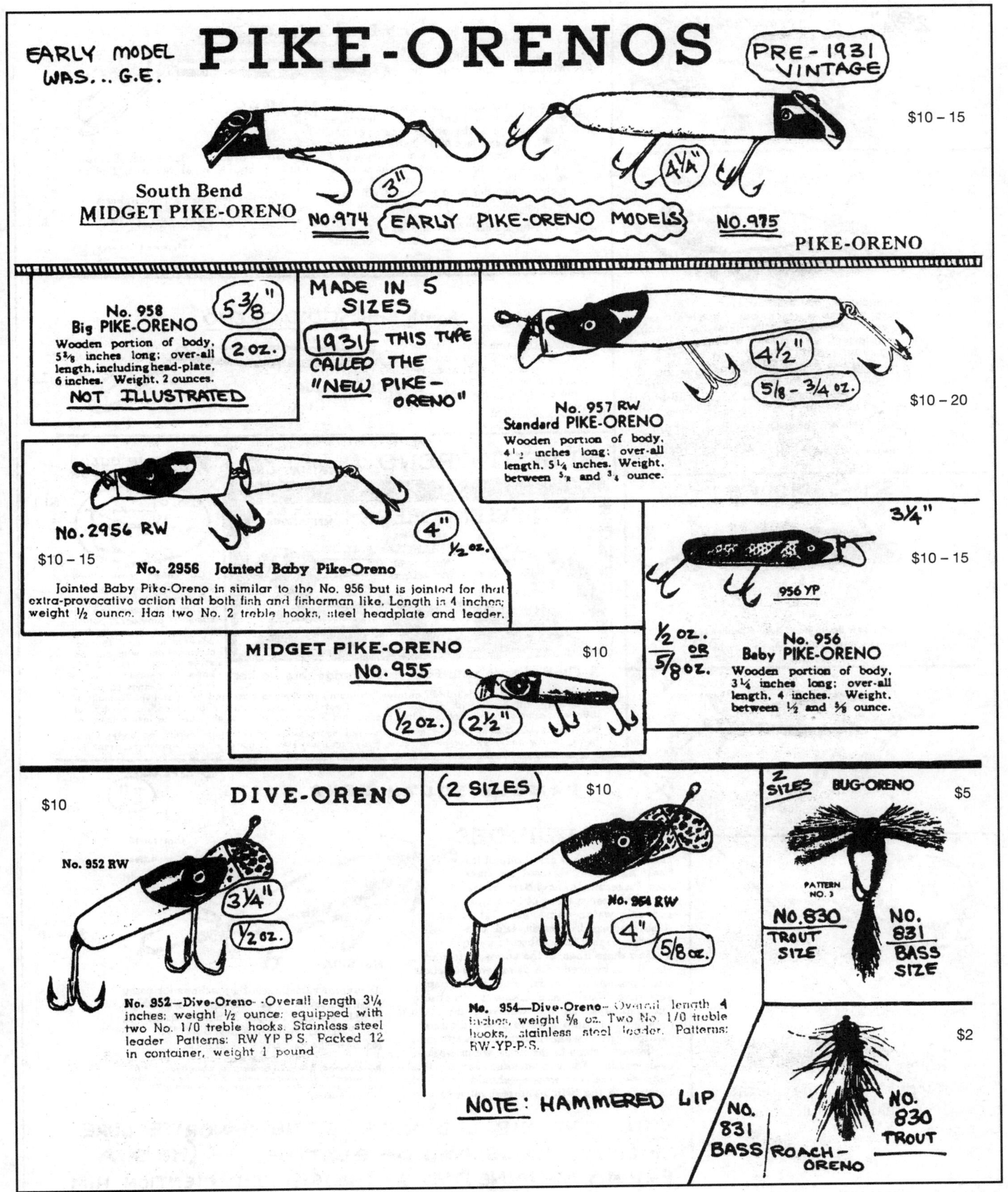
EARLY MODEL WAS... G.E.
PIKE-ORENOS
PRE-1931 VINTAGE
$10 – 15
South Bend
MIDGET PIKE-ORENO
3"
4¼"
NO.974
EARLY PIKE-ORENO MODELS
NO.975
PIKE-ORENO
No. 958
Big PIKE-ORENO
Wooden portion of body, 5⅜ inches long; over-all length, including head-plate, 6 inches. Weight, 2 ounces.
5⅜"
2 oz.
NOT ILLUSTRATED
MADE IN 5 SIZES
1931 - THIS TYPE CALLED THE "NEW PIKE-ORENO"
4½"
5/8 - 3/4 oz.
$10 – 20
No. 957 RW
Standard PIKE-ORENO
Wooden portion of body, 4½ inches long; over-all length, 5¼ inches. Weight, between ⅝ and ¾ ounce.
No. 2956 RW
4"
½ oz.
$10 – 15
No. 2956 Jointed Baby Pike-Oreno
Jointed Baby Pike-Oreno is similar to the No. 956 but is jointed for that extra-provocative action that both fish and fisherman like. Length is 4 inches; weight ½ ounce. Has two No. 2 treble hooks, steel headplate and leader.
3¼"
$10 – 15
956 YP
MIDGET PIKE-ORENO
NO. 955
$10
½ oz.
2½"
½ oz. OR ⅝ oz.
No. 956
Baby PIKE-ORENO
Wooden portion of body, 3¼ inches long; over-all length, 4 inches. Weight, between ½ and ⅝ ounce.
DIVE-ORENO
(2 SIZES)
$10
$10
No. 952 RW
3¼"
½ oz.
No. 952—Dive-Oreno—Overall length 3¼ inches; weight ½ ounce; equipped with two No. 1/0 treble hooks. Stainless steel leader Patterns: RW YP P S. Packed 12 in container, weight 1 pound
No. 954 RW
4"
⅝ oz.
No. 954—Dive-Oreno—Overall length 4 inches, weight ⅝ oz. Two No. 1/0 treble hooks, stainless steel leader. Patterns: RW-YP-P-S.
NOTE: HAMMERED LIP
2 SIZES
BUG-ORENO
$5
PATTERN NO. 3
NO.830
TROUT SIZE
NO. 831
BASS SIZE
$2
NO. 831
BASS
ROACH-ORENO
NO. 830
TROUT

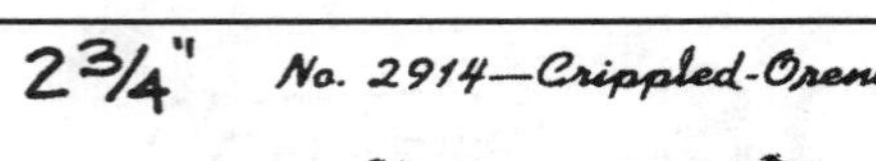
2¾"
No. 2914—Crippled-Oreno

$10 – 20

$10 – 20

No. 2920—Crippled-Oreno

3⅝"

minnow in distress, able to make a brief fuss on the surface but unable to swim away. Work it by alternately retrieving a couple feet, then allowing it to rest, repeating until retrieved. Made in two sizes.

No. 2914 Crippled-Oreno—Body length 2¾ inches, weight ½ ounce, two No. 1 treble hooks. Patterns: RW-FS-YP-SSY-SB-SSS-N-SH. Each . . . .

No. 2920 Crippled-Oreno—Body length 3⅝ inches, weight ¾ ounce, three No. 1/0 treble hooks. Patterns: RW-FS-YP-SSY-SB-SSS-N-

South Bend TUN-ORENO

A salt-water trolling lure. Moulded from pure tin. Both eyes swivel in the body, preventing the line from kinking and twisting and also preventing the fish from getting a leverage. The tube runs the entire length of the squid. The eyes are much harder to break off than the eyes on the ordinary squid or even on other types of loose-hook squids. This is the same patented swivel socket which has been so successfully used for years on South Bend salt-water wooden plugs. Used *successfully* for Tuna, Bluefish, Bonita, Albacore and Dolphin along the New Jersey coast. Irresistible for Grey Grouper, Barracuda, Spanish Mackerel and King Mackerel in Florida waters.

NO. 989

$2

Weight approximately 5½ ounces, length 5 inches. Equipped with one extra strong special double hook. Furnished in natural polished tin body with enameled red head.

No. 989, price $1.50 each

South Bend SQUID-ORENO

This is the same construction as the Tun-Oreno except that the body is triangular and the motion is somewhat more erratic. **No. 991, price $1.50 each**

NO. 991

$2

SELECT-ORENO 16 COLOR COMBINATIONS • SHOWN IN COLOR ON BACK COVER

$10

SOUTH BEND SELECT-ORENO 16 COLOR COMBINATIONS
From These
INTERCHANGEABLE BODIES
NO. 1950
PATENT NO. 2,220,

Cut shows construction

Select-Oreno lures come in assortments of four interchangeable bodies and two special "pin-hooks" which slip through the body. It is possible to create 16 color combinations with one assortment of Select-Oreno baits. No need to untie the leader to change lures! It's

A Fly Rod Lure with Four Interchangeable Bodies

a surface lure that "pops" and "gurgles," bringing up the big bass and big pan-fish. To make it a "sinker," fill body with water. The "Pin-Hook" chassis permits substitution, in a jiffy, of different patterns. Select-Oreno bodies are molded of plastic, with air chambers to insure floating.

No. 1950 Select-Oreno—Packed four lures—red head, white body; white head, red body; black head, yellow body; yellow head, black body; and two special hooks in box with transparent lid.

SPIN-I-DIDDEE

$5

Deadly new South Bend Spin-I-Diddee is a top-water lure. It weighs ⅜ oz.

$5

WEE-NIPPEE

$5 FIN-DINGO

-3 SIZES- (3")

FAMOUS SOUTH BEND BAITS

The NIP-I-DIDDEE

. . . . . that terrific semi-weedless surface bait!

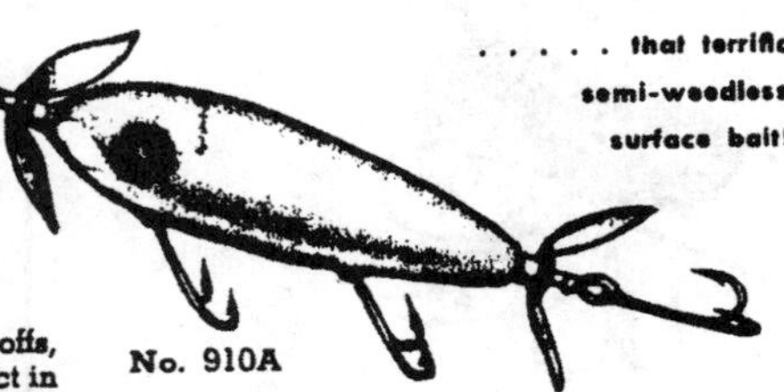

No. 910A

$5 – 10

The Nip-I-Diddee is rated one of the finest baits ever devised for Bass, Pike, Pickerel, Channel Bass, Weakfish and other species of both fresh and salt water game fish. It is semi-weedless in design and construction so that in addition to using it along shore lines, at the edges of drop-offs, etc., it can be used with devastating effect in weed pockets and beds. Fore and aft spinners give "flash" and create a tantalizing disturbance during the retrieve at the same time that they help to serve as weed guards. Two forward hooks are designed and attached to "retract" close to the body when worked over weeds. For utmost effectiveness, this bait—especially in weeds—should be fished slowly with the twitch-and-rest retrieve and its several variations. Suggestions for using included in bait box. Equipped with three double hooks. Length 3 inches; weight ⅝ oz. Patterns: A-RW-RWA-WB-RY-YP.

No. 910—Each . . . .

Color Key

A—aluminum; RW—red arrowhead, white body; RWA—red arrowhead, aluminum body; WB—white arrowhead, black body; RY—red arrowhead, yellow body; YP—yellow perch scale.

NOTE: THE NIP-I-DIDDEE IS THE FAVORITE LURE OF CHUCK CLEVELAND OF SEATTLE, (HE'S A FRIEND OF MINE, SO I THOUGHT I'D MENTION HIM.)

Rods, reels, catalogs, fish decoys, and other items have value for collectors.

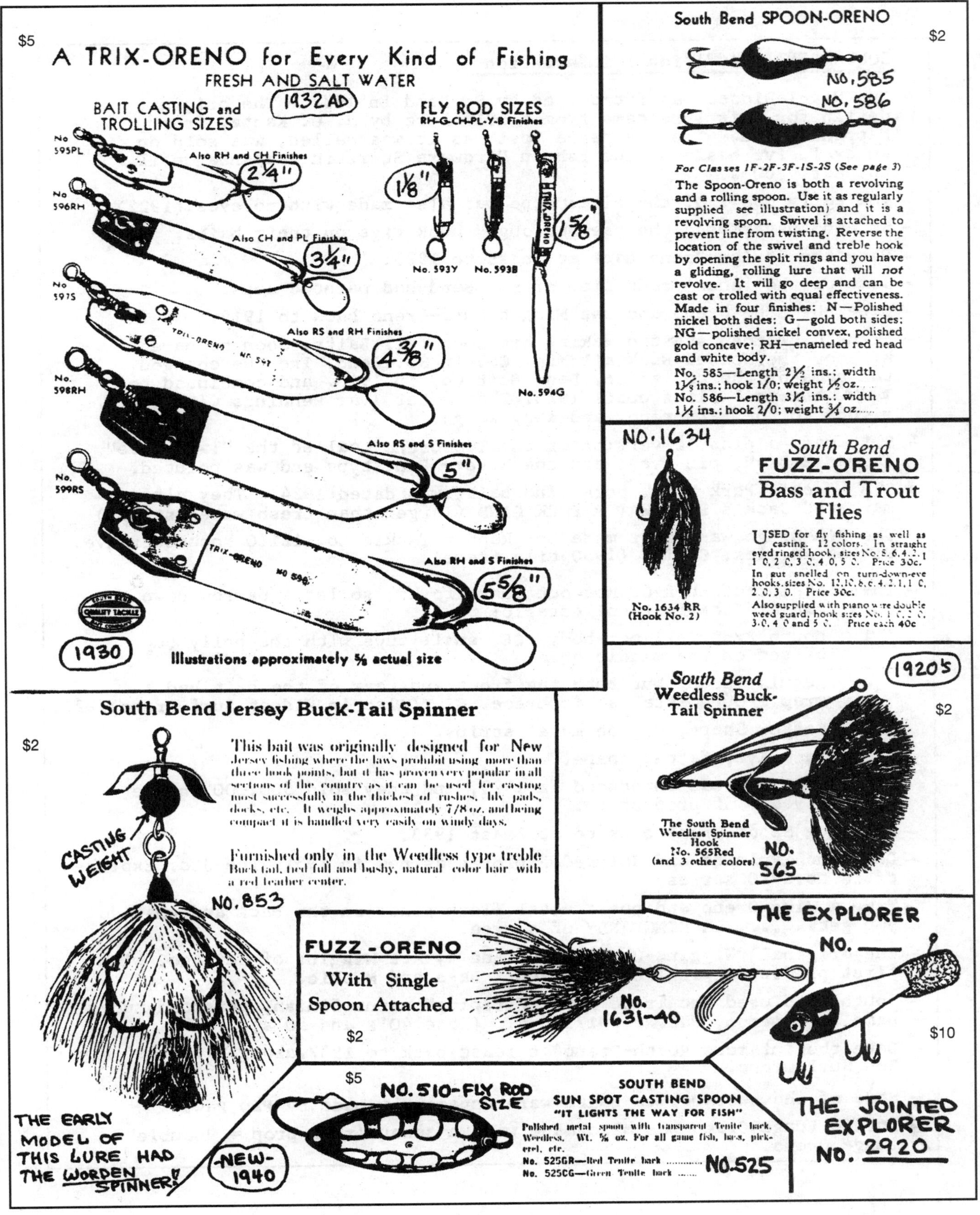
$5
A TRIX-ORENO for Every Kind of Fishing
FRESH AND SALT WATER
1932 AD
BAIT CASTING and TROLLING SIZES
FLY ROD SIZES
RH-G-CH-PL-Y-B Finishes
No 595PL
Also RH and CH Finishes
2¼"
No 596RH
Also CH and PL Finishes
3¼"
No 597S
TRIX-ORENO NO 597
Also RS and RH Finishes
4⅜"
No. 598RH
Also RS and S Finishes
5"
No. 599RS
TRIX-ORENO NO 599
Also RH and S Finishes
5⅝"
1⅛"
No. 593Y
No. 593B
1⅝"
TRIX-ORENO
No. 594G
1930
Illustrations approximately ⅝ actual size
South Bend SPOON-ORENO
$2
NO. 585
NO. 586
For Classes 1F-2F-3F-1S-2S (See page 3)
The Spoon-Oreno is both a revolving and a rolling spoon. Use it as regularly supplied see illustration) and it is a revolving spoon. Swivel is attached to prevent line from twisting. Reverse the location of the swivel and treble hook by opening the split rings and you have a gliding, rolling lure that will not revolve. It will go deep and can be cast or trolled with equal effectiveness. Made in four finishes: N—Polished nickel both sides; G—gold both sides; NG—polished nickel convex, polished gold concave; RH—enameled red head and white body.
No. 585—Length 2½ ins.; width 1⅓ ins.; hook 1/0; weight ½ oz.
No. 586—Length 3¼ ins.; width 1¼ ins.; hook 2/0; weight ¾ oz.
NO. 1634
South Bend
FUZZ-ORENO
Bass and Trout Flies
USED for fly fishing as well as casting. 12 colors. In straight eyed ringed hook, sizes No. 5, 6, 4, 2, 1, 1 0, 2 0, 3 0, 4 0, 5 0. Price 30c.
In gut snelled on turn-down-eye hooks, sizes No. 12, 10, 8, 6, 4, 2, 1, 1 0, 2 0, 3 0. Price 30c.
Also supplied with piano wire double weed guard, hook sizes No. 1 0, 2 0, 3 0, 4 0 and 5 0. Price each 40c
No. 1634 RR (Hook No. 2)
South Bend Jersey Buck-Tail Spinner
$2
This bait was originally designed for New Jersey fishing where the laws prohibit using more than three hook points, but it has proven very popular in all sections of the country as it can be used for casting most successfully in the thickest of rushes, lily pads, docks, etc. It weighs approximately 7/8 oz. and being compact it is handled very easily on windy days.
Furnished only in the Weedless type treble
Buck tail, tied full and bushy, natural color hair with a red leather center.
CASTING WEIGHT
NO. 853
THE EARLY MODEL OF THIS LURE HAD THE WORDEN SPINNER!
South Bend Weedless Buck-Tail Spinner
1920's
$2
The South Bend Weedless Spinner Hook No. 565Red (and 3 other colors)
NO. 565
FUZZ-ORENO
With Single Spoon Attached
NO. 1631-40
$2
THE EXPLORER
NO. ____
$10
THE JOINTED EXPLORER
NO. 2920
$5
NO. 510-FLY ROD SIZE
-NEW- 1940
SOUTH BEND
SUN SPOT CASTING SPOON
"IT LIGHTS THE WAY FOR FISH"
Polished metal spoon with transparent Tenite back. Weedless. Wt. ⅝ oz. For all game fish, bass, pickerel, etc.
No. 525GR—Red Tenite back
No. 525CG—Green Tenite back
NO.525

SOUTH BEND - Additional Information

- The Nip-I-Diddee was introduced by So.Bend in 1932. The original design for this lure came from a 1915 lure by J. O. Kantz, from Nappanee, Ind. The "Nappanee Ypsi" as it was called, was sold on an exclusive basis by the Lehman Hardware Store in Nappanee until the early 60's.
- The early model of the Pike-Oreno was also made with no eyes.(1922)
- So.Bend never used the "see through" hook rigs on their baits.
- Date the Strike-Oreno back at least to 1923.
- Some of the later production of So. Bend had painted cups.
- Date the Babe-Oreno and the Midget Surf-Oreno back to 1919.
- Frank G. Worden started making his Buck Tail Baits. Soon he named his co. the Worden Bucktail Mfg. Co. in So. Bend, Ind. He changed the name of the co. to So. Bend Bait Co. in 1910, and continued to make bucktail flies until 1916. Then enter Ivar Hennings with the rights to the Bassoreno, and away we go.
- S.B. made a plastic version of the Two-Oreno, called the "Two-Obite". It was 2-3/4", pin eyes, and the River- Runt type end was pointed.
- S.B. Jack's Pork Frog, pork rind bait, was dated 1924. They also marketed Jack's SALT WATER PORK RIND (larger than fresh water strips)
- The Fin-Dingo was first made by: Ropher Tackle Co. 12110 Rochester Ave. W. Los Angeles, Calif. (1950 time frame)
- There's alot of Surf-Orenos out there folks, so let's narrow down the ones that are the most collectable:
    1. Notch Prop, slimmer body, GE, small cups with the belly cup offset on the middle one.
    2. Regular prop, but both the front and rear of the bait had a wrap around metal strip brace. GE. (Also in Midget Surf-Oreno)1922.
    3. Fatter Shape, GE, no metal strips.
    4. Tack Eye, fatter shape.
- The Trix-Oreno was intoduced in 1929, and they sold 300,000 in the first 3 years of production.
- Date the Spoon-Oreno back to at least 1933.
- Date the Explorer and Jointed Explorer as new in 1951. The Jtd. Explorer is No.2920 series.
- Take a King-Oreno and put a metal flash plate on the back and what do you get.........A KING ANDY of course.
- The original "Wiggins-Oreno" was made by Art Wiggins of Chicago, with first production in 1903. 2 sizes: Bass and Muskie.
- South Bend used the Trade Mark "Fireplug" paint finish, patented under name of Gantron, Pat.No.2417383-4. (late 40's and 50's).
- Date the infamous Roach-Oreno at least back to 1937,along with the Fly Rod Surf Oreno.
- Some of the Best-O-Luck baits were apparently made by Paw Paw.
- No.966 Lunge Oreno was also made with a second/rear prop = "Double" Lunge Oreno.

EARLY SO. BEND
SURFORENO – NOTCH
PROP – GE – (NOTE THE
OFF-SET MIDDLE
BELLY HOOK). THIS
IS ALSO AN EXAMPLE
OF THE SLIMMER BODY STYLE.
SOLID
YELLOW
NO. 963
$20 – 30

SO. BEND NO. 919 RH
"BEST-O-LUCK" BAIT.

- TACK EYE
- PAINTED CUP

IN 1933, THESE BAITS SOLD TO THE JOBBER AT $2.31/DOZEN!

SCREW
EYE
W/WASHER
CUP
(PAINTED)

$5 – 10

"BEST-O-LUCK" NO. 950 YRS

$10

- BLACK PAINTED EYE, W/YELLOW DOT.
- BASIC SCREW-EYE HOOK RIG
- PROP IS LOOSE ON SCREW EYE.
- JOBBER PRICE: $1.55/DOZEN.

1935

TO MATCH THE HEDDON "O" AND "OO", SO. BEND PAINTED THEIR BAITS WITH THIS DESIGN.

$20 – 50

SOUTH BEND SPOTTED MINNOW, HEXAGON EFFECT

No. 904. Colored in rich enamel blendings. Very attractive and effective lure. An under water bait. On cloudy days, when they bite fast, this lure has proven the one that gets the big fellows. White, yellow or red body.

SO.BEND - additional information

- In the 1916 - 1920 era, S.B. made a real humungous BassOreno - 10½" long, 2½" in diameter, 3 swivel type hook hangers with 3 #10/0 Hooks.
- There is a smaller third size of the Dive-Oreno - 2-3/4", overall, body length only = 2-1/4".
- South Bend diverted much of its production during WW II to making airplane parts.
- The Truck-Oreno was made in 2 body styles, 1 was the Surf-Oreno Body, and the other (& older) was a body designed just for it.

THE STANLEY SMELT.

(Invented by Fish Commissioner Henry O. Stanley, of Dixfield, Me.)

$10 – 20

Is the Most Natural Artificial Bait.

A New, Attractive, and KILLING LURE for LAND-LOCKED SALMON, TROUT, PICKEREL and BASS. No. 1, large, 75 cents. No. 2, small, 65 cents. Made of solid Aluminum.

The line, as shown by cut, draws from a pin near the center, and the bait darts from side to side as the bars at the head of bait allow.

Manufactured and sold by (1908)

STANLEY & CHAPMAN,

P. O. Box 1390, - - Boston, Mass.

Sent, postpaid, on receipt of price.

(SOLID ALUMINUM)

G.E.

$5

GET SOME LAYFIELD LURES—

America's

No. 1 Basser!

This little Texas lure was patented back in 1938 by Lester L. Layfield. The bait was made by the Sunnybrook Lure Company, Box 104-X, Tyler, Texas. Patent No. 2179641

Colors:

No. 101 Red Eyed Pearl
No. 102 Red Head/White
No. 103 Black, White & Dots
No. 104 Solid Black
No. 105 Black, White Dots
No. 106 Yellow
No. 107 Yellow/Black Scales
No. 109 Clear Translucent
No. 110 White Head/Black
No. 111 Pearl, Black Stripe
No. 112 Green Scale

$5 – 10

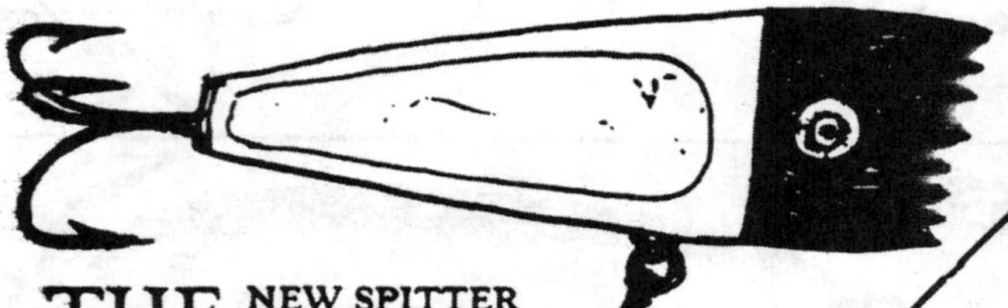

THE NEW SPITTER BASS GETTER

Patented 1932 by:
Francis P. Sumner
F. F. Schwanbeck

G.E. - Sculptured Sides Like a CCBCO PLunker except for the 20 teeth on the perimeter.

THE SUNCO QUICKSILVER BAIT

Quicksilver is another name for Mercury, so this is another form of....Mercury Minnow.

The name is on the inside of the plastic neck of bait. There is a mercury blob in the chamber of the bait. Color: Clear/Red.

$10 – 20

Scooterpooper

$20

Scientifically designed to make a sound under water, Scooterpooper creates a vibration heard 200 feet! Fish, attracted, bite. Bass fishermen have long begged for such a lure. Immediate delivery.

BASS STRIKE

THE SCOOTERPOOPER

SCOOTERPOOPER SALES, INC.

1911 Blossom St. Columbia. S. C.

(1948)

Scooterpooper Sales, Inc.

$40 – 75
G.E.
1924
2 3/4"
(BELLY) VIEW
THE STANDARD MINNOW
Probably a "private label" bait, I cannot locate any more info. Brass washer & hardware. Brown Back/Yellow Belly. A well made underwater bait.
$10 – 20
ANNOUNCING
JUDAS
TRADE MARK REG. U.S. PAT. OFF.
PATENTS PENDING
THE SENSATIONAL NEW FISH BETRAYER
BULL FROG
SPOTTED FROG
Wt. 3/8 oz
3¾ in. Long
(1947)
With Weedless Hooks
LIFELIKE APPEARANCE—DIVING ACTION
SEND FOR FREE ILLUSTRATED FOLDER
No longer do you have to depend on hard-to-get live frogs for catching those wise old BASS and WALLEYES who refuse all ordinary baits.
ORDER YOURS TODAY!
Money Order or Check Only — No C.O.D.s
SPORTING INDUSTRIES
DEPT. F
5912 N. Harlem Av., Chicago 31, Ill.
1949
NEW!
LIFE-LIKE CRYSTAL-CLEAR PLASTIC SHINER
Catches MORE Fish!
SPINALURE
SADILURES
6724 - Florence Blvd.
Omaha 11, Nebraska
"A Clear Plastic Chippewa Bait"
$5
(1946)
OPEN
$5 – 10
BLACK BEAD EYES
CLOSED
THE SAFE-T LURE
Safe-T-Lure Company
Cleveland, Ohio
Note: You can put this baby in your pocket !
THE VIRGIN MERMAID
Stream-Eze, Inc.
1916 So. Main
So. Bend, Ind.
Hair Colors:
Blonde
Red Head
Black
Many variations out there with more than one maker. Also made a very deluxe model with an Indian Type Headdress as a "lip called Lloyd's Mermaid Queen
Some had belly and back hooks.
No. M-1500S (Surface)
No. M-1500U (Underwater)
2 rare colors: Gold Plated & Luminous
Fly Rod Mermaids by:
Hughes Tool & Mfg. Co.
Benton Harbor, Michigan
$10 – 25
SWANBERG
METALIVE BAIT
IT'S NEW!
THE METAL BAIT ALIVE
No. 1 2-1/2"
No. 2 3-1/4"
No. 3 4-1/8"
No. 4 4-3/4"
$5 – 15
Chrome Plated (1939)
JULIUS SWANBERG
5124 N. Kildare Ave.
Chicago, Illinois

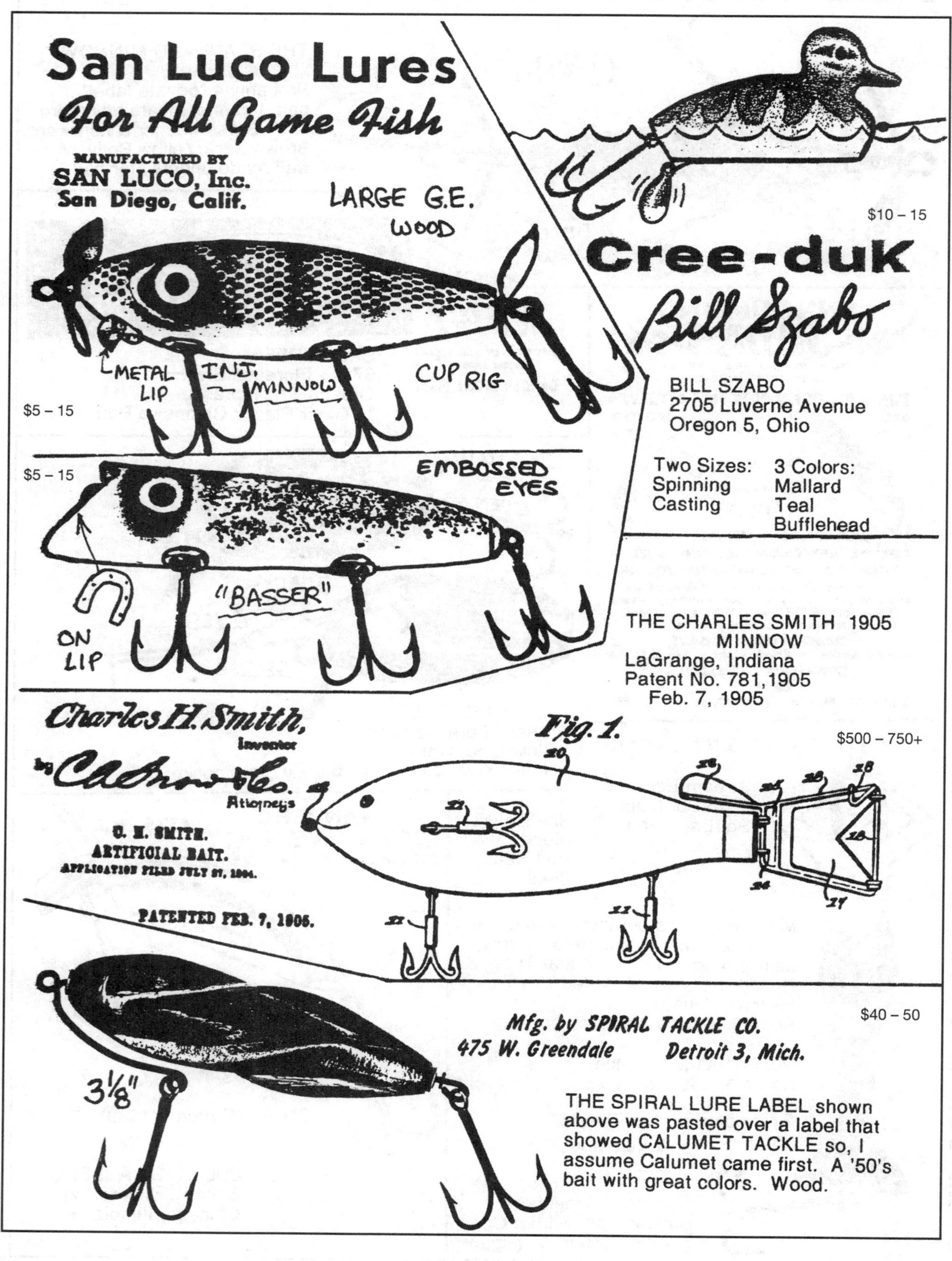
San Luco Lures
For All Game Fish
MANUFACTURED BY
SAN LUCO, Inc.
San Diego, Calif.
LARGE G.E.
WOOD
METAL LIP
INJ. MINNOW
CUP RIG
$5 – 15
$5 – 15
EMBOSSED EYES
"BASSER"
ON LIP
$10 – 15
Cree-duk
Bill Szabo
BILL SZABO
2705 Luverne Avenue
Oregon 5, Ohio
Two Sizes: Spinning Casting
3 Colors: Mallard Teal Bufflehead
THE CHARLES SMITH 1905 MINNOW
LaGrange, Indiana
Patent No. 781,1905
Feb. 7, 1905
Charles H. Smith, Inventor
Attorneys
C. H. SMITH.
ARTIFICIAL BAIT.
APPLICATION FILED JULY 27, 1904.
PATENTED FEB. 7, 1905.
Fig. 1.
$500 – 750+
Mfg. by SPIRAL TACKLE CO.
475 W. Greendale Detroit 3, Mich.
$40 – 50
3 1/8"
THE SPIRAL LURE LABEL shown above was pasted over a label that showed CALUMET TACKLE so, I assume Calumet came first. A '50's bait with great colors. Wood.

(1938) Philip Morris & Co. NASHUA N. H. STRIPER PLUGS

FISHMASTER SUCCESSFUL SALT WATER LURES

Action and depth of this plug can be varied by adjusting the monel mouthpiece. Size 7/0 Extra Heavy Mustad Double Hooks are held close to the body in proper striking position and will release when fish is hooked. Hooks are also set to allow 360° swiveling.

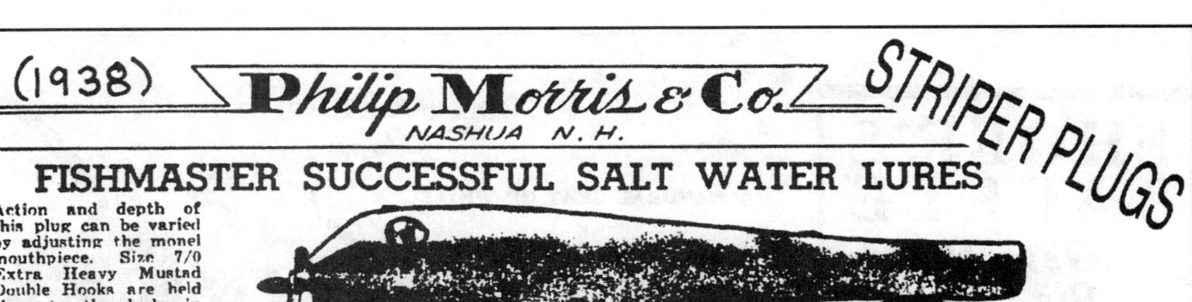

HEAVYWEIGHT NO. H.W.

$5 – 10

Length 8 in. Weight 3¾ oz. Colors: Blue Mullet, Red and White, Silver Streak. Specify color.

HEAVYWEIGHT TARPON: NO. H.W.T. Same style and colors as No. HW. Heavyweight plug but with size 8/0 Pflueger Sobly hooks. Specify color.

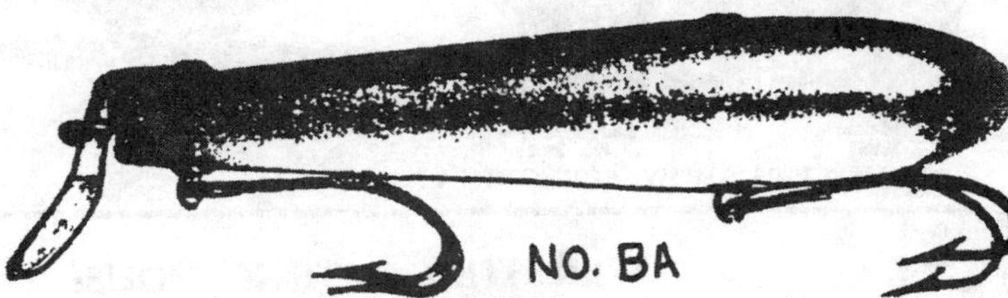

NO. BA

BASS-AQUA

$5 – 10

A new plug and unique in design which permits easier and longer casts even against the wind. The monel diving fin is adjustable to control action and depth. Length 6¾ in. Weight 3¾ oz. 7/0 Extra Heavy Mustad hook. Colors: Blue Mullet, Red and White, Silver Streak.

A famous surface lure that has taken many record fish. Action is built right in plug. Swiveled flap-tail causes loud commotion and shower of spray while lure is retrieved. Length 9½ in. Weight 3¼ oz. 5/0 Heavy Mustad Treble Hooks. Colors: Blue Mullet, Pike Finish, Red and White.

JERRY SYLVESTER'S MULLET

NO. J

$5 – 10

JERRY SYLVESTER'S JOINTED PLUG

NO. JJ

$5 – 10

A deep running lure that dives deep and has lively wiggly action that really stirs 'em up. Monel and brass nickel plated fittings. Length 7⅜ in. Weight 2½ oz. 5/0 Mustad Treble Hooks. Colors: Blue Mullet, Pike Finish, Red and White.

POPPER

NO. JP

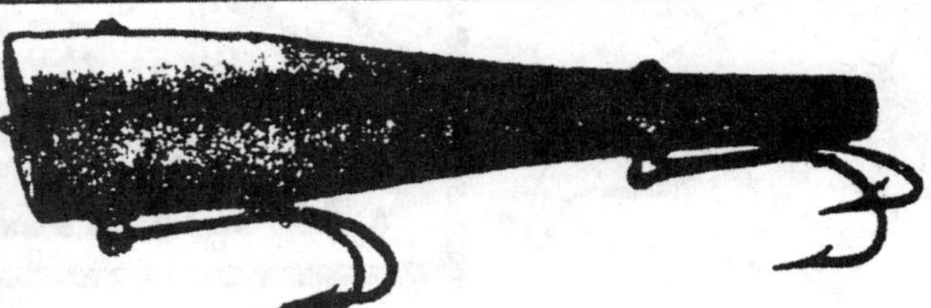

$5 – 10

Designed to pop and splash and is particularly effective in bringing them right up off the bottom to strike. Length 7 in. Weight 3¾ oz. 7/0 Extra Heavy Mustad Double Hooks. Hooks will release from body when fish is hooked. Colors: Squid Red, Black, Silver Streak.

AUTHOR'S EDITORIAL COMMENT: SOMEBODY FROM THE EAST COAST HAS TO STEP UP TO BAT AND WRITE A **STRIPER PLUG REFERENCE BOOK!!** The West Coast Troops have done some preliminary Salmon Plug Work, more to come.

SHOFF'S
TACKLE
Gets the
Big Ones!

SHOFF'S MICE $10 – 20 each
(Patented)

NATURAL GRAY OR WHITE

$5

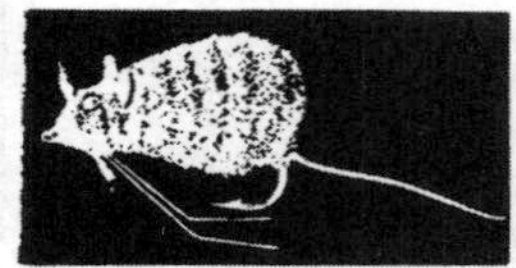

WEEDLESS FLY ROD MICE

Baby Mouse No. 300B

Small Mouse No. 300S

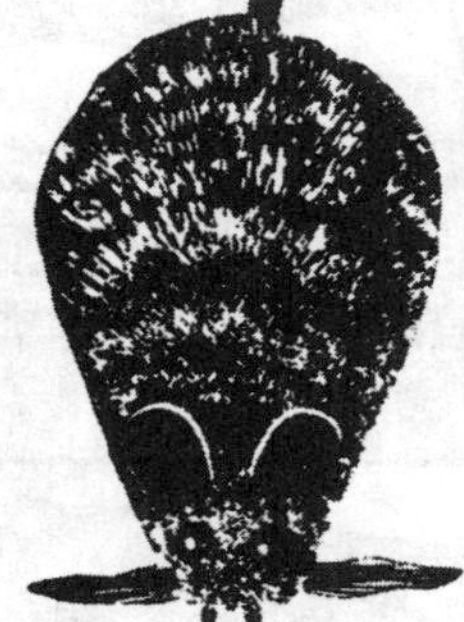

Large Mouse No. 300L

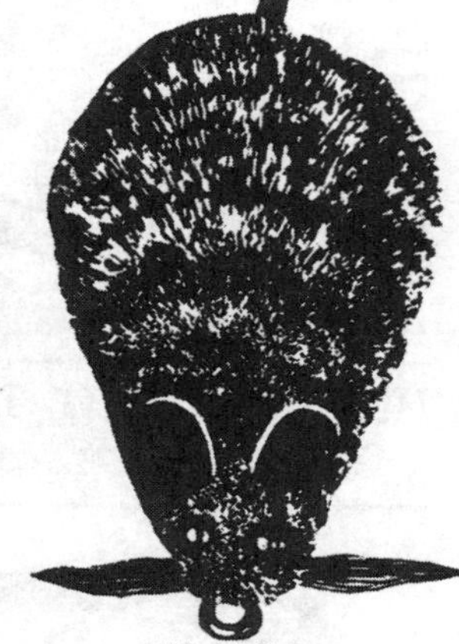

Musky Mouse No. 300M

ABOVE CUTS SHOW APPROXIMATE SIZES

No. 300BW. Baby Mouse. Weedless. Size 4 hook.
No. 300SW. Small Mouse. Weedless. Size 1/0 hook.
No. 300LW. Large Mouse. Weedless. Size 3/0 hook.
No. 300MW. Musky Mouse. Weedless. Size 6/0 hook.

$10 – 20

WEIGHTED CASTING MOUSE

They float and are Weedless. Packed one bait to a box.
No. 300CL. For Bass, size 4/0 hook. ½ oz. weight. Each....$1.00
No. 300CM. For Muskies. Size 6/0 hook. ¾ oz. weight. Ea. 1.25

In Memory of
Clarence H. Shoff
Date of Birth
April 30, 1894
Passed Away
May 24, 1975

SHOFF MICE PATENTS:
U.S. No. 1953692
CAN. No. 363795

Shoff's Wagtails
Killer For Pike, Pickerel and Bass
No. 298

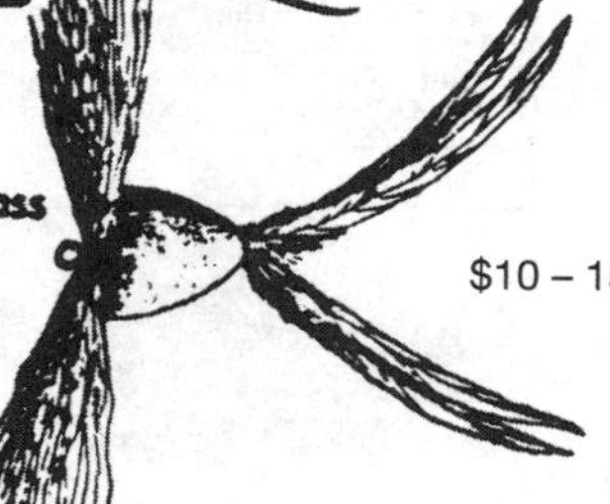

$10 – 15

April 1, 1930. A. J. SOBECKI 1,752,706
FISH LURE
Filed Aug. 16, 1928

$20 – 50

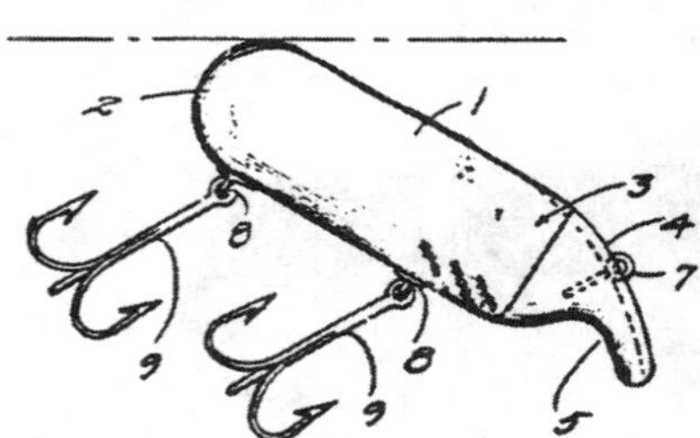
Fig. 1.
2
1
3
4
7
8
9
8
9
5

A SURE CATCH!
Use a "1929 Wiggler" and be sure of a good catch. Fish just can't resist it. Always brings them in—even when other baits fail. Send for yours NOW. Take it on your next fishing trip and get a good catch. Ask your dealers, or send $1 direct.
ANTON SOBESKI
223 E. La Salle St. So. Bend, Ind.

A "Blow-Up" of this 1929 Ad reveals that they spelled the inventor's name wrong...... SOBESKI instead of SOBECKI. The lure is: 3-5/8", and has been found only in Red Head/White and used cup and screw eye hook mounts. Anton J. Sobecki lived in South Bend, Indiana.

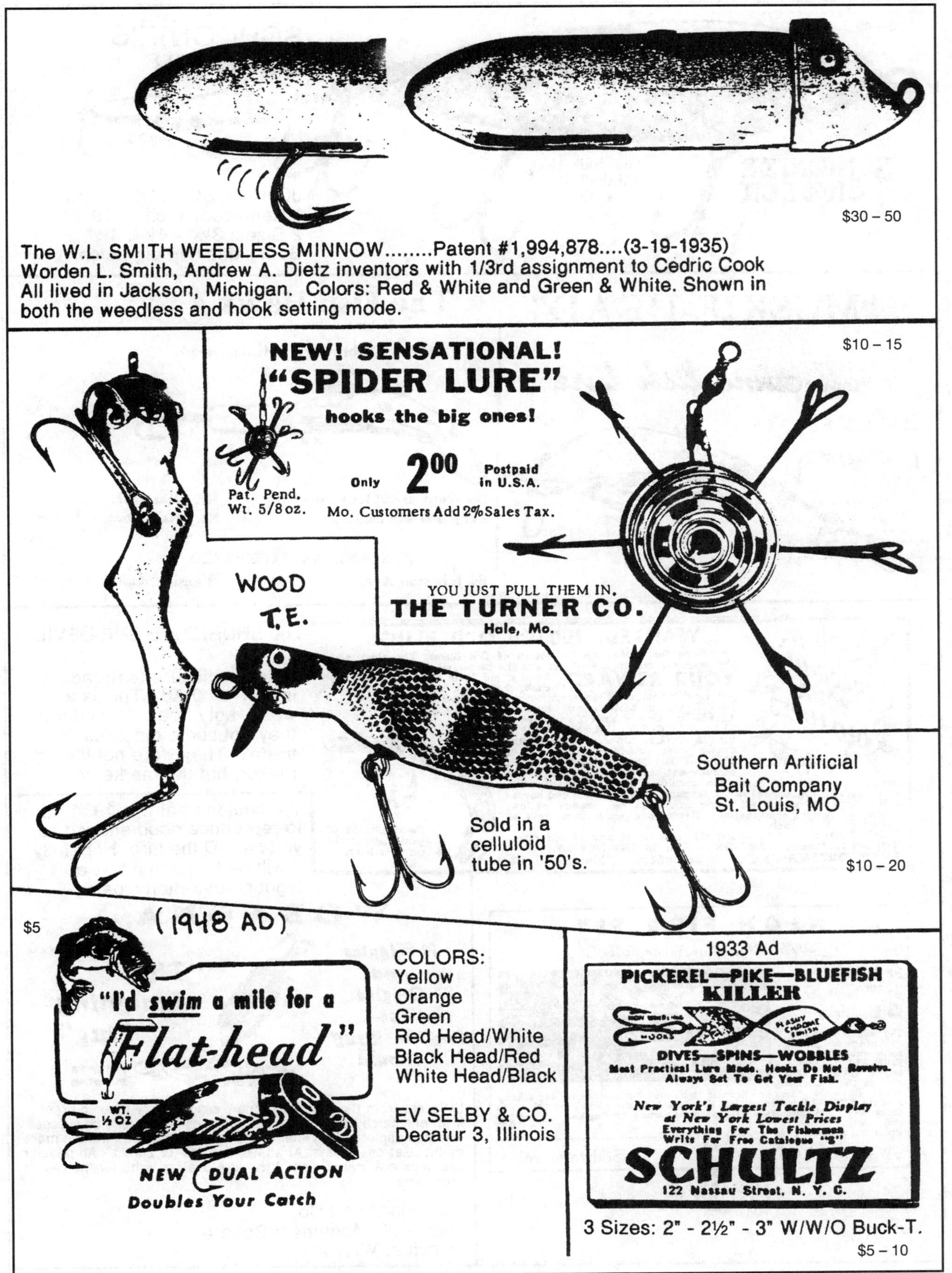
$30 – 50
The W.L. SMITH WEEDLESS MINNOW........Patent #1,994,878....(3-19-1935)
Worden L. Smith, Andrew A. Dietz inventors with 1/3rd assignment to Cedric Cook
All lived in Jackson, Michigan. Colors: Red & White and Green & White. Shown in both the weedless and hook setting mode.
$10 – 15
NEW! SENSATIONAL!
"SPIDER LURE"
hooks the big ones!
Only 2.00 Postpaid in U.S.A.
Pat. Pend.
Wt. 5/8 oz.
Mo. Customers Add 2% Sales Tax.
YOU JUST PULL THEM IN.
THE TURNER CO.
Hale, Mo.
WOOD
T.E.
Southern Artificial Bait Company St. Louis, MO
Sold in a celluloid tube in '50's.
$10 – 20
$5
(1948 AD)
"I'd swim a mile for a Flat-head"
WT. ½ OZ
NEW DUAL ACTION
Doubles Your Catch
COLORS:
Yellow
Orange
Green
Red Head/White
Black Head/Red
White Head/Black
EV SELBY & CO.
Decatur 3, Illinois
1933 Ad
PICKEREL—PIKE—BLUEFISH KILLER
DIVES—SPINS—WOBBLES
Most Practical Lure Made. Hooks Do Not Revolve. Always Set To Get Your Fish.
New York's Largest Tackle Display at New York Lowest Prices
Everything For The Fisherman
Write For Free Catalogue "S"
SCHULTZ
122 Nassau Street, N. Y. C.
3 Sizes: 2" - 2½" - 3" W/W/O Buck-T.
$5 – 10

$20 – 40

SCHOONIE'S SCOOTER

"SCHOONIE'S SKOOTER"
The bait that "thinks" its a fish.
(TOP)

JOHN R. SCHOONMAKER
Kalamazoo, Mich. (1916)
2 Sizes: 3½" - 4¼", 4½"
Both sides had big notch

"MUSKIE-HEAD"

all-game fish lure

$5

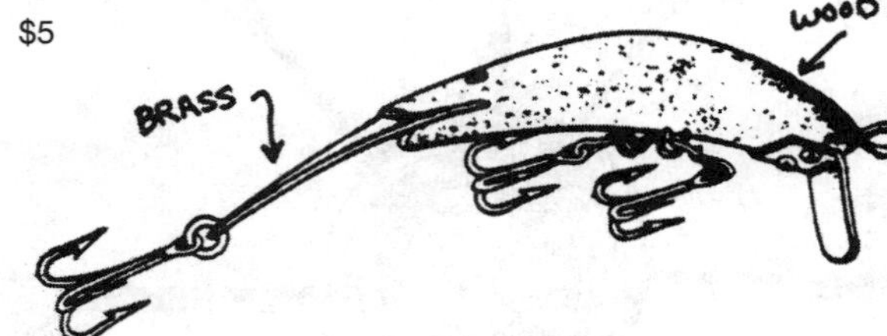
WOOD
BRASS

The Fish Hawk

Patent

The Fish-Hawk is brother to Muskie-Head

$5

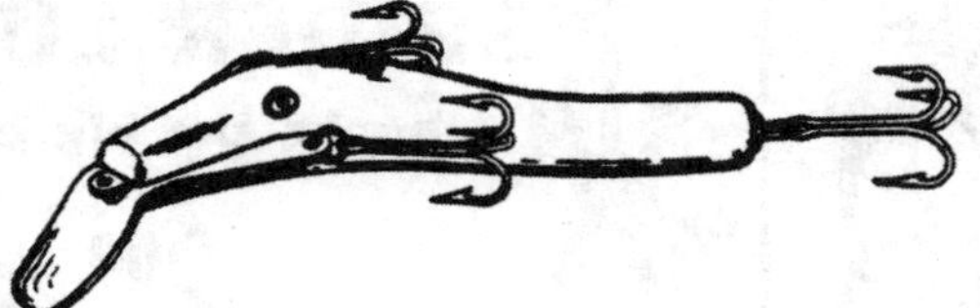

Standard size 3" long ...... **No. 4 Hks. ¼ oz.**
Large size 3½" long .... **No. 3 Hks. ⅜ oz.**

A. SAARIMAA TACKLE CO.
64 Johnston Ave. **Lansing, Ont.**

TRADE-IN YOUR OLD LURES

WANTED: 100,000 OLD PLUGS

or spoons for a Museum Collection of Old Lures. The older and the more chewed-up these lures are the better we like 'em.

YOUR REWARD: Send 2 old lures and one dollar in cash, check or money order, and you will receive postpaid 2 famous Minnow-Actioned SHE-DEVIL plastic bait-casting plugs worth $2.50 (Trade-In Value of Your Two Lures Is $1.50). No COD's. U.S. &. POSSESSIONS ONLY. Offer will be withdrawn when collection is completed. SHE-DEVIL: Colorful, banana-shaped, minnow-actioned plastic lure that has caught thousands of game fish including bass, northern pike, walleyes, muskies, big rainbows, tarpon, snook, bonefish and barracuda. Comes in nearly all colors . . . frog, red, orange, yellow, black and various combinations. Name your preferences. Sells at dealers for $1.25 each.
SEND TODAY . . . $1 and 2 old lures or $5 and 10 old lures. You get (postpaid) 2 SHE-DEVILS or 10 SHE-DEVILS.

Send photos of your fish caught on this lure.

THE SPORTSMAN'S CO. Box 468. Chicago 90, Ill.

The SHUREBITE SHE-DEVIL

This plastic lure featured in this 1950 Ad. This is a weird, ugly lure....I wonder if they got some old lures in trade? They were not the maker, but the marketer.

We couldn't get this 1924 Ad to reproduce good enough so you can ID the lure. Hopefully it will be found in a box or bigger illustration/catalog.

NEON FIRE FLY

"The Glow that Never Fails"

No Batteries
No Wires
No Electricity

The slightest tipping, spinning or jerking movement causes the FIRE FLY to emit a bright, life-like glow even in clear, shallow water. In cloudy waters and down in those deep holes where the big fellows lurk the FIRE FLY is irresistible. For Bass, Pike and all fighting fish which strike deep under the surface. Designed for casting, trolling and still fishing.
Order this attractive and mystifying lure today........................ $1.85 Post Paid

ST. CROIX BAIT CO. Stillwater, Minn.

$15 1939 AD

WOBAHNA

$15 – 20

It Wiggles and Giggles as Reg'lar "Stuff" Should

PATENTS PENDING

"The Laughing Plug"

Different from the rest. Has a new wiggle every time you reel it in, and catch fish - Boy, how it catches 'em. Used by success oriented anglers everywhere, and selling as fast as we can make them. Get one today. At all live dealers or Direct All popular colors except scale finish. Live-wire dealers write for the real proposition.

Standard Bait Co.
530 - W. Monument Square
Racine, Wisconsin

See What GETS HIM?
He can't resist it—he's a game fish—a natural born fighter. He resents intrusion—challenges, investigates, every unfamiliar object that appears in his favorite haunts and feeding places —and at once attacks, if not satisfied that "all is well." SKVOR'S QUICK, INTER-CHANGEABLE BAIT arouses him —he can't ignore the "rapid-fire" changes —the intermingling of peculiar colors that flash before him—in combative mood, he strikes at this bait. Then—he's HOOKED —you've GOT HIM.
The Attractor is the feature of this remarkable bait—it lures game fish to strike, whether hungry or not. No need for you to move—or cut or tie your line; just stand still and try one after another of these 36 instantaneous color combinations, in quick succession. One of them will land your fish, and you'll enjoy all the thrills and satisfaction of the true sportsman, in producing just the right one. Outfit in handsome case, 4 in. x 6 in. x ½ in.—weighs only 4 ounces—carry in coat or hip-pocket—complete, for any kind of fish, any time, anywhere, casting or trolling. Guaranteed satisfactory. PRICE $2.50 PREPAID. If your dealer does not sell these real "fish-getters," send your order to us or write for particulars and handsome booklet, free.
Skvor's Patent Attractor
invented and perfected by a successful fisherman.
Skvor & Co., 102 First Ave., W., Cedar Rapids, Ia.
OUTER'S MAGAZINE AD - May, 1913

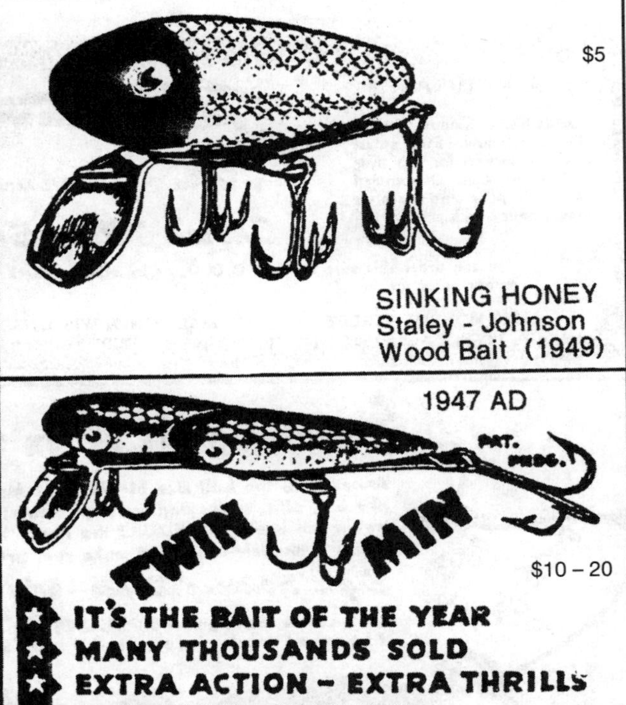
PAT. PEND.
TWIN MIN
IT'S THE BAIT OF THE YEAR
MANY THOUSANDS SOLD
EXTRA ACTION – EXTRA THRILLS
FLOATERS – SINKERS
EXCELLENT FOR BIG CATCHES
NO OTHER BAIT LIKE IT
Manufactured by-
STALEY-JOHNSON MFG. CO. INC.
FORT WAYNE, INDIANA
GET A TWIN-MIN TO-DAY

$5

SINKING HONEY
Staley - Johnson
Wood Bait (1949)

1947 AD

$10 – 20

Stanley Perfection Weedless Hook

The Only Open Weedless Hook That's Really Weedless

Tackle can't be tangled up in rushes, lily pads or weed beds because **The Stanley Perfection Weedless Hook** is so constructed that it assures an unobstructed barb for the strike of the fish and fully protects the point of the hook against entanglement of weeds, etc., when casting or trolling. It is the only open Weedless Hook of proved merit as testified to by thousands of enthusiastic fishermen.

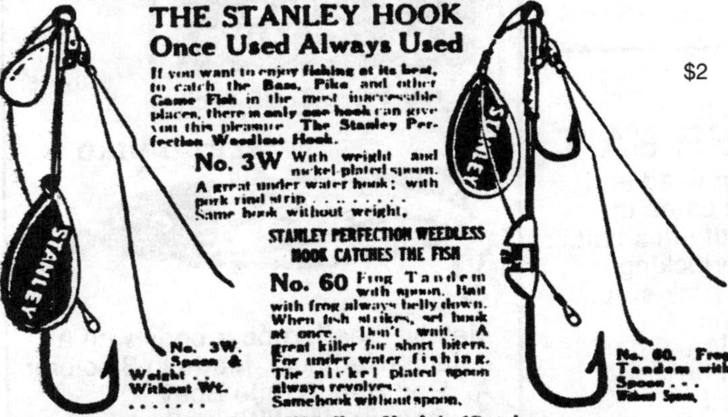

THE STANLEY HOOK
Once Used Always Used

If you want to enjoy fishing at its best, to catch the Bass, Pike and other Game Fish in the most inaccessible places, there is only one hook can give you this pleasure. The Stanley Perfection Weedless Hook.

No. 3W With weight and nickel plated spoon. A great under water hook; with pork rind strip . . . .
Same hook without weight.

STANLEY PERFECTION WEEDLESS HOOK CATCHES THE FISH

No. 60 Frog Tandem with spoon. Bait with frog always belly down. When fish strikes, set hook at once. Don't wait. A great killer for short biters. For under water fishing. The nickel plated spoon always revolves. . . . .
Same hook without spoon.

No. 3W. Spoon & Weight . . Without Wt. . . . .

No. 60. Frog Tandem with Spoon . . Without Spoon.

$2

The Stanley Perfection Open Weedless Hook in 17 styles. Every Hook Guaranteed. Money back if not satisfied. Insist upon the **Stanley Perfection Weedless Hook** from your dealer. If he cannot supply you we will ship direct on receipt of **Money Order.**

Write Us for Free Illustrated Price List

WM. STANLEY & CO., 1217 E. 55th St., CHICAGO, ILL.

STANLEY WAS BOUGHT BY HEDDON

$5

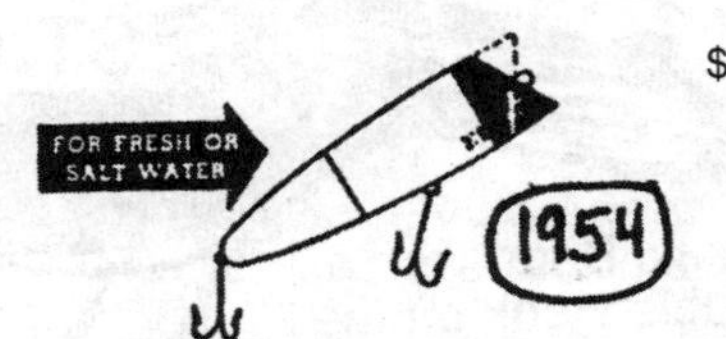
FOR FRESH OR SALT WATER
1954

The New ALL new All Purpose Plug
"ALLPUR"
GRAND MASTER
The Lure all America is Talking About

Convertible from surface to Underwater
4 Reversible and Interchangeable Heads 4
Heads and Bodies in four Colors
(all parts are interchangeable)
Red, Green, Yellow and White
A luminous Model for Dark or Deep Water
Highest Quality Detachable Hooks
Easily changed for a larger or Dull Hook
Each in Durable Plastic Case
One color body and four heads..
ALL four colors, Bodies & Heads..
At all dealers or sent direct if not stocked
Insured and postpaid-Give Dealer's name
Specify if luminous and color desired

SILVER BAITS, Inc.
218 Augustine St. Rochester, N. Y.
Send a dime stamps or coin for Engraved Den Decorator and Circulars.

$5 – 10

A NATURAL!

Looks like a minnow. Swims like a minnow. Even smart fish are suckers for this durable plastic bait. Guaranteed to catch pike and bass or your money back.

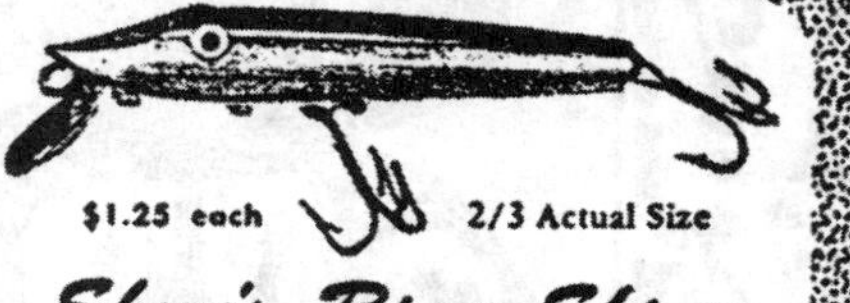

$1.25 each 2/3 Actual Size

Shore's River Shiner

$5 – 15 You can order this sure fire bait C. O. D. or by sending check or money order to:

1717 MONROE STREET MADISON 5, WISCONSIN

FISH Where You Could Never Fish Before

WEEDPLANE IS WEEDPROOF

1940

Is there an old whopper lurking in the deep weeds where you have never been able to fish? Weedplane will get him. No weedy retreat is safe from Weedplane. It's in a class by itself, a proven fish getter for Bass, Pike, Pickerel, Musky.

If your dealer cannot supply you, order direct.

SEALAND MANUFACTURING CO.

25-4th Street, North St. Petersburg, Florida

Something *NEW* on the BURRELLINE!

$5

Announcing the *bait size* BURRELLURE Minnow. 5½ inches long with life-like fins, gills, scales and eyes—plus the remarkable WIGLIT*—make this treble tail hook BURRELLURE the finest 'killer' for big ones yet! See this lure and marvel—use it and make your grandest fishing dreams come true!

***Eight 'Striking' Types*—only $1.65 ea.**

Purchase this exciting new BURRELLURE from your dealer. If he cannot supply you send us his name and address.

HERRING
GOLDEN SHINER
GOLDFISH
LUMINNOW (Luminous Body)
SHINER
PERCH
SALMON
PIKEY (Luminous Belly)

A 1947 Ad For this plastic bait pushed their WIGLIT oscillating lip. 8 Colors 5-1/2"

Burrellure

***WIGLIT—Exclusive Burrellure patented oscillating device which causes absolute fish-like movements.**

BURRELLURES—made exclusively by SMITHCRAFT PRODUCTS CO. · KENVIL, NEW JERSEY

ST.CROIX "SNIPE"

Plastic Boat with a Double Hook on the brass tail spinner. 2-5/8" Name on side

$5 – 10

The Swimming Motion of

STREICH'S FLEX-O-MINO

Retail Price $1.25 each

$10 – 15

FLEX-O-MINO

Metallic head, rubber body with a detachable hook. Made in 3 colors:

A. Red Head/White Body
B. Copper Head/White Body
C. Nickel Head/White Body

STREICH BAIT WORKS
708 W. Jasper Street
Joliet, Illinois

Patent: March 4, 1924

SCHALLER'S THREE BAGGER BAIT

We found this really small ad and enlarged it but couldn't come up with much help to identify this bait. 3-1/2" detachable interlocking hooks. Snap swivel for pork strip.

Colors:

Red Head/White	Red Head/Yellow
Red Head/Black	Black Head/White
Black Head/Yellow	Black Head/Red
All Red	All Black
All Yellow	All White

$20 – 30

SCHALLER BAIT COMPANY
(Not Incorporated)
Dept. 21
Mendota, Illinois

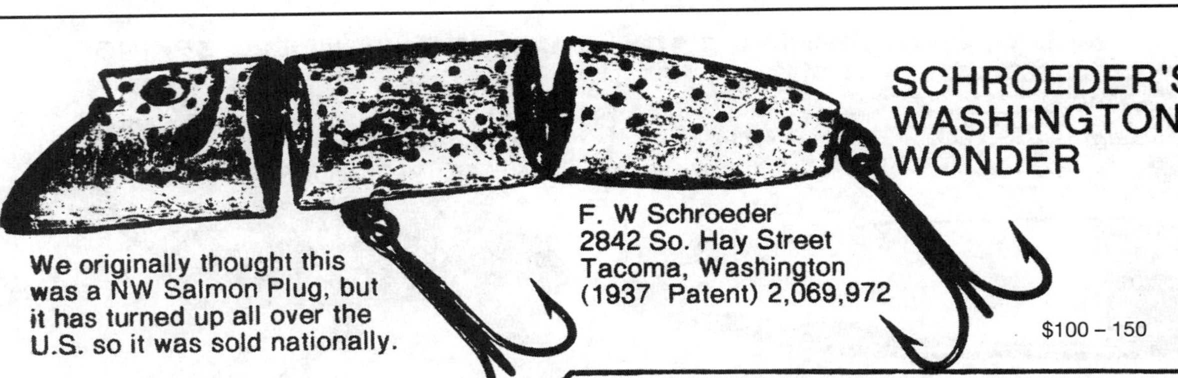

SCHROEDER'S WASHINGTON WONDER

F. W Schroeder
2842 So. Hay Street
Tacoma, Washington
(1937 Patent) 2,069,972

We originally thought this was a NW Salmon Plug, but it has turned up all over the U.S. so it was sold nationally.

3 diff. models: G.E.
Double Jointed
Single Jointed (Baby)
Solid Body

$100 – 150

BASS
Fight For
STEELS WIGGLEFROG

Looks, Acts, Feels
(1949) Like a Live Frog!

Floats at rest but dives and swims with fast-wiggling action a foot under water on retrieve. Soft plastic body. Invisible plastic lip. Nylon action feet. Wt. ⅝ oz. Casts like tournament plug. Weedless. Hooks 90% of strikes. Designed by Frank R. Steel, world's record fisherman and famous outdoor writer.

FRANK STEEL, Inc. 176 W. Adams, CHICAGO 3, ILL.

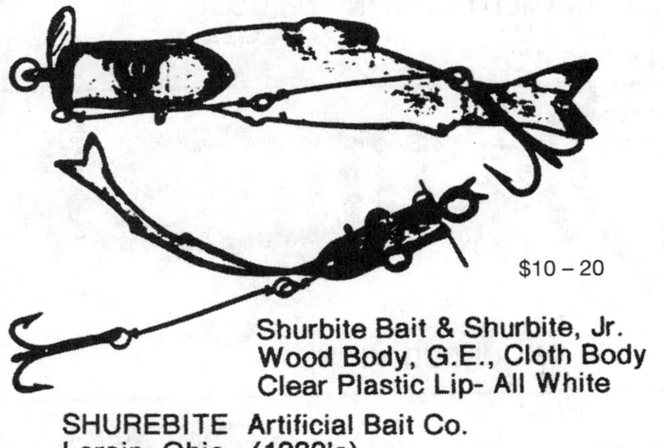

$10 – 20

Shurbite Bait & Shurbite, Jr.
Wood Body, G.E., Cloth Body
Clear Plastic Lip- All White

SHUREBITE Artificial Bait Co.
Lorain, Ohio (1930's)

GLASS
EYES
For All Purposes
(1923)
Minnow and Duck Decoy
Eyes a Specialty
G. SHOEPFER
221 West 33rd Street
New York City

SCOOTIN' ANNIE

A sensational new BASS, PIKE, MUSKIE and LAKE TROUT killer —Casts beautifully— Gets them near the surface or way down deep.

$1.25 Each

Through your dealer, or direct. A guaranteed lure of wholly new designs and truly amazing action. Handsomely finished. One size. One color. One price.

(1930)

LUCKY CAMERON
(of Northern Ontario)
1505 Clark Bldg Pittsburgh, Pa.

$20 – 40

Plastic Lure

$5 – 15

SHUREBITE
Trade Mark

SKATE

Patent Pending
SHUREBITE, Inc.
Bronson, Michigan

SEND ME TEN CENTS

And I will mail you postpaid, one of my INTRODUCTION MINNOWS

$20 – 50

1915

Colored in Rich Enamel Blendings. Red shaded to white; Green shaded to white; all white. Can be used for Casting or Trolling. A very effective and attractive lure for Bass, Pike or Pickerel.

I will also send you one of my 72-page catalogues which will save you money in buying tackle.

BOB SMITH, Sporting Goods
79 Federal St. - - - Boston, Mass.

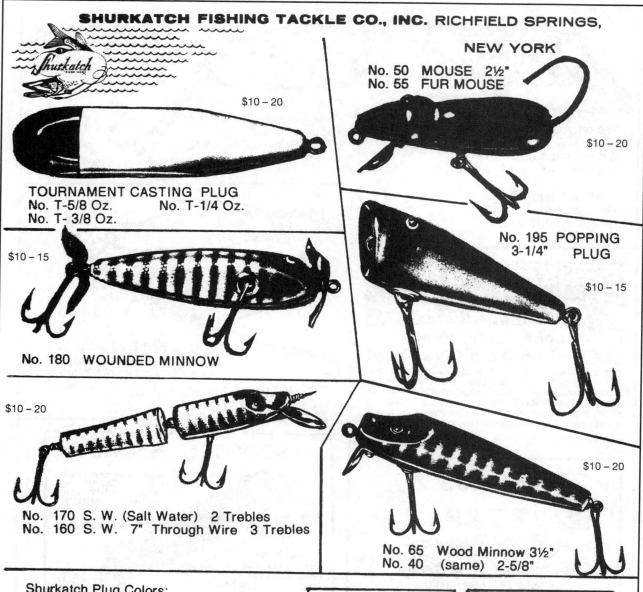

SHURKATCH FISHING TACKLE CO., INC. RICHFIELD SPRINGS, NEW YORK

Shurkatch TRADE MARK

$10 – 20

TOURNAMENT CASTING PLUG
No. T-5/8 Oz. No. T-1/4 Oz.
No. T- 3/8 Oz.

No. 50 MOUSE 2½"
No. 55 FUR MOUSE

$10 – 20

$10 – 15

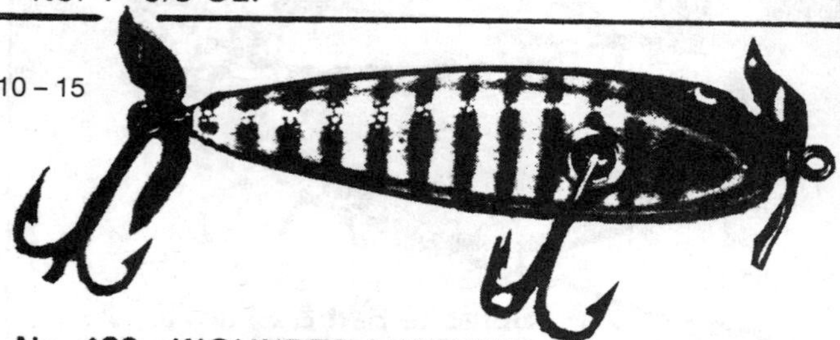

No. 180 WOUNDED MINNOW

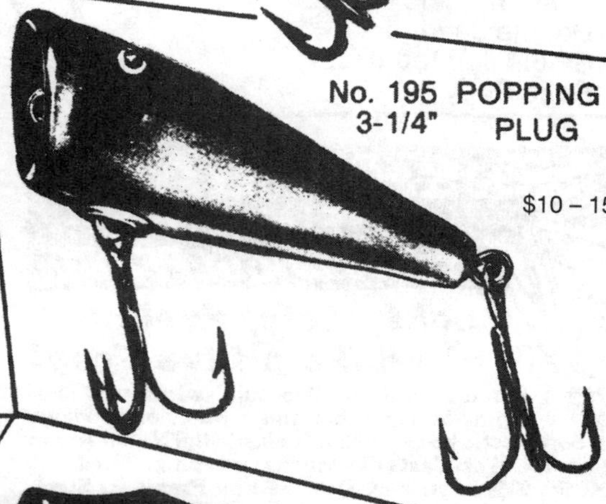

No. 195 POPPING PLUG 3-1/4"

$10 – 15

$10 – 20

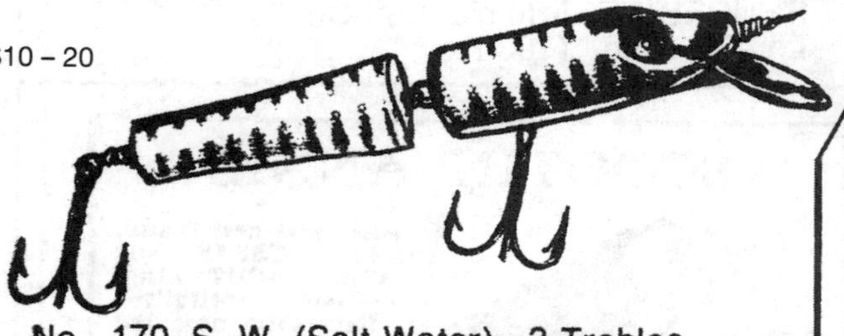

No. 170 S. W. (Salt Water) 2 Trebles
No. 160 S. W. 7" Through Wire 3 Trebles

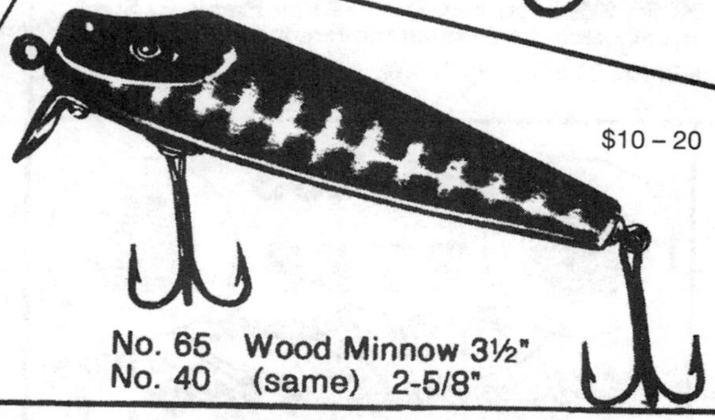

$10 – 20

No. 65 Wood Minnow 3½"
No. 40 (same) 2-5/8"

Shurkatch Plug Colors:

RH Red Head
FR Frog
YPS Yellow Perch Scale
SHS Silver Herring Scale
SP Scale Perch
GS Green Scale
BS Blue Scale

The LULU BAIT
(1941)

SHURKATCH was a low end maker with ties to H - I, They made baits similar to the popular baits of the day such as Pikies & BassOrenos. It is interesting that they made a line of through-wire Musky & Salt plugs, and their mouse at least deserves being identified. (1940's - 1960's)

SHURKATCH
No. 110
A Deadly Lure for Trout and Smallmouth Bass
Made in U.S.A.

$10 – 20

SHURKATCH
FLY ROD
MINNOW
No. 140
ACTION
DURABILITY
A Proven Fish Catcher
By SHURKATCH
MADE IN U. S. A.

$10 – 20

$100 – 150

The Hartford Minnow Float.

THE GREAT MINNOW LIFE SAVER. The Most Noiseless, Lightest Running Float Ever Hitched to a Boat. Most Perfect and Practical Bait Receptacle Ever Invented.

THE HARTFORD is torpedo-shaped, with conical ends and cylindrical body, the forepart of which is a still-water chamber, wherein the minnows are protected from the lashing of the water while the float is being towed or when the wind causes the water to be rough. The rear of the body is perforated all around to allow a constant flow of fresh water to preserve the minnow. There are air chambers in each end, so arranged as to keep it afloat, *always right side up*, allowing a free circulation of fresh air as well as fresh water at all times.

Pulls Easy and Never Catches Weeds. With its conical ends and cylindrical body it will glide lightly through the water and not retard the rowing in the least. It will also pass through the lily pads and rushes, never catching weeds or making any noise to scare away the fish. It has a ballast at the bottom to keep it from rotating and is also submerged in the water to a proper depth, to preserve the minnow by reaching cool water.

There is a handle which serves a two-fold function: you hold this in one hand, while with the other you operate a noiseless sliding cover and take out bait when wanted, and it will, when suspended by the handle, retain enough water to preserve the minnows. Get the HARTFORD and you will never lose your minnow. The best bait on earth to catch game fish with is live minnows, small fish being the natural food for large fish.

Keeps Minnows Alive and Fresh. The HARTFORD is guaranteed to keep minnows alive throughout a day's fishing and when unused will preserve them for days if the float be kept in fresh water, such as minnows require before capture. A dead minnow is not much better than artificial bait. Why does the inventor of artificial bait try to represent the minnow? Because he knows the minnow is the best bait to use. Isn't it a fact, Mr. Fisherman, that live minnows are better than dead ones? Get the HARTFORD MINNOW FLOAT, which is guaranteed to keep your minnows alive. It is made of galvanized iron, 28 inches long. 7 inches in diameter, weighs 8¼ pounds. The inner walls are perfectly smooth, which is necessary to preserve minnows. Beware of the old pail and bucket with the wire crate inside, wherein more minnows have been destroyed from the effects of the wire than were ever used on the angler's hook. If the HARTFORD fails to do what we say it will, return it to us and we will refund your money. Price, $2.50.

A Boon for Resort Keepers. The HARTFORD STORAGE FLOAT, which is made on the same principle as the small fishing float, is 7 feet, 6 inches long, 18 inches in diameter, and will hold 2,000 minnows. It can be anchored out in the lake or stream where the water is always cool and fresh. With its conical end it will always point to the wind and waves. In the still-water chamber, in the forepart, the minnows are protected from the lashing of the water. The wind may blow and the waves may toss, but in the HARTFORD STORAGE FLOAT the minnows are secure. The storage float will pay for itself in a month. (Mention Sports Afie d.)

Manufactured and sold by the **SHINNERS-RUSSELL CO., Hartford, Wis.**

This 1907 Ad shows in detail the No. 1 MINNOW FLOAT/MINNOW BUCKET for all tackle collectors....The Hartford Minnow Float. Every once in awhile one of these turns up and is added to someone's collection.

Now, read the last part of the ad ....A BOON FOR RESORT OWNERS...they made a giant size HARTFORD STORAGE FLOAT that will hold 2,000 minnows, 7'-6' in length, and the same shape. I doubt if any of these survived to today, but if they did the place to display it would be the Freshwater Fishing Hall of Fame in Hayward, Wisconsin, not my tackle room!

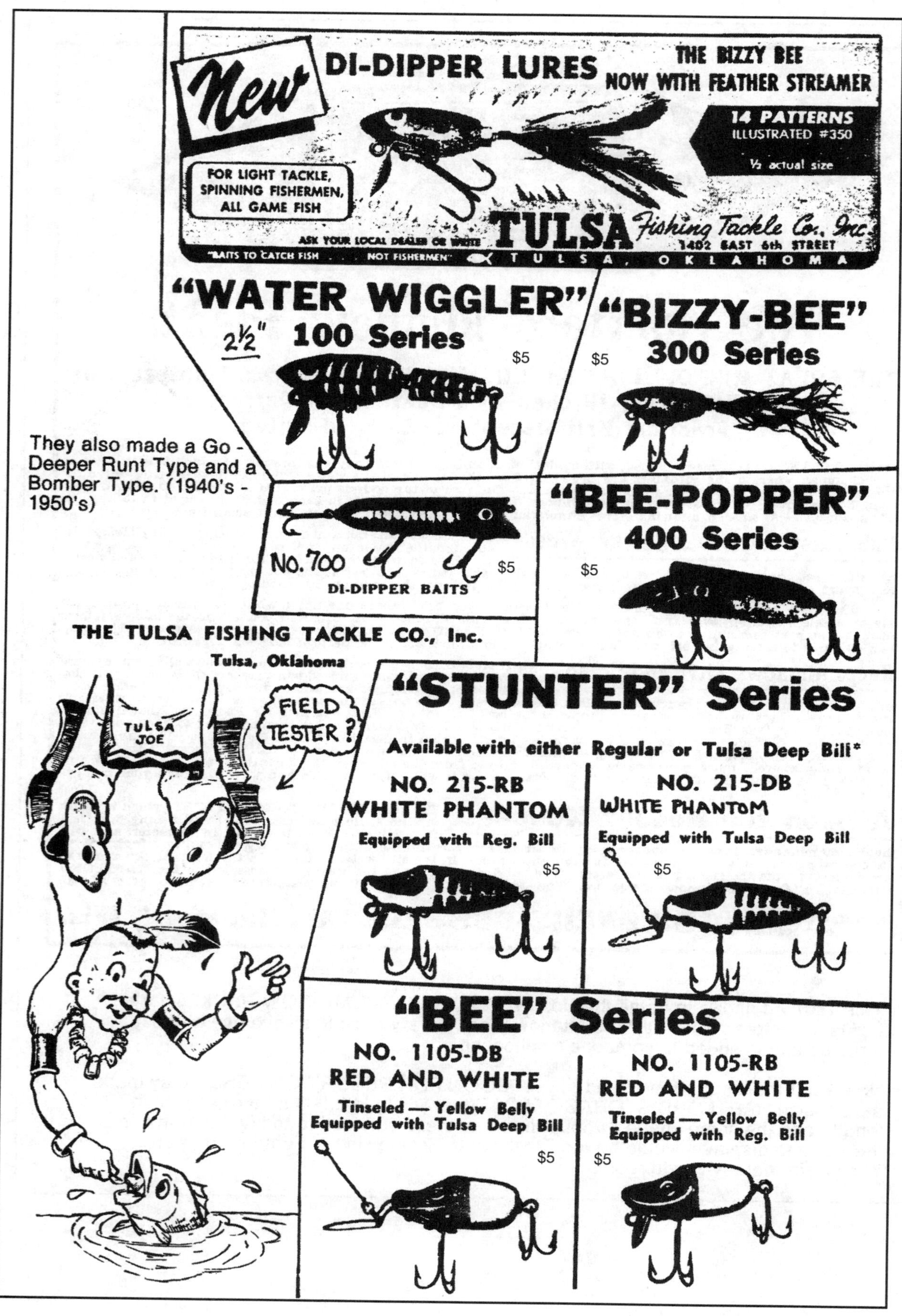
New
DI-DIPPER LURES
THE BIZZY BEE NOW WITH FEATHER STREAMER
14 PATTERNS
ILLUSTRATED #350
½ actual size
FOR LIGHT TACKLE, SPINNING FISHERMEN, ALL GAME FISH
ASK YOUR LOCAL DEALER OR WRITE
TULSA Fishing Tackle Co., Inc.
1402 EAST 6th STREET
"BAITS TO CATCH FISH . . . NOT FISHERMEN"
TULSA, OKLAHOMA
"WATER WIGGLER"
2½" 100 Series
$5
"BIZZY-BEE"
300 Series
$5
No. 700
DI-DIPPER BAITS
$5
"BEE-POPPER"
400 Series
$5
THE TULSA FISHING TACKLE CO., Inc.
Tulsa, Oklahoma
TULSA JOE
FIELD TESTER?
"STUNTER" Series
Available with either Regular or Tulsa Deep Bill*
NO. 215-RB
WHITE PHANTOM
Equipped with Reg. Bill
$5
NO. 215-DB
WHITE PHANTOM
Equipped with Tulsa Deep Bill
$5
"BEE" Series
NO. 1105-DB
RED AND WHITE
Tinseled — Yellow Belly
Equipped with Tulsa Deep Bill
$5
NO. 1105-RB
RED AND WHITE
Tinseled — Yellow Belly
Equipped with Reg. Bill
$5

They also made a Go - Deeper Runt Type and a Bomber Type. (1940's - 1950's)

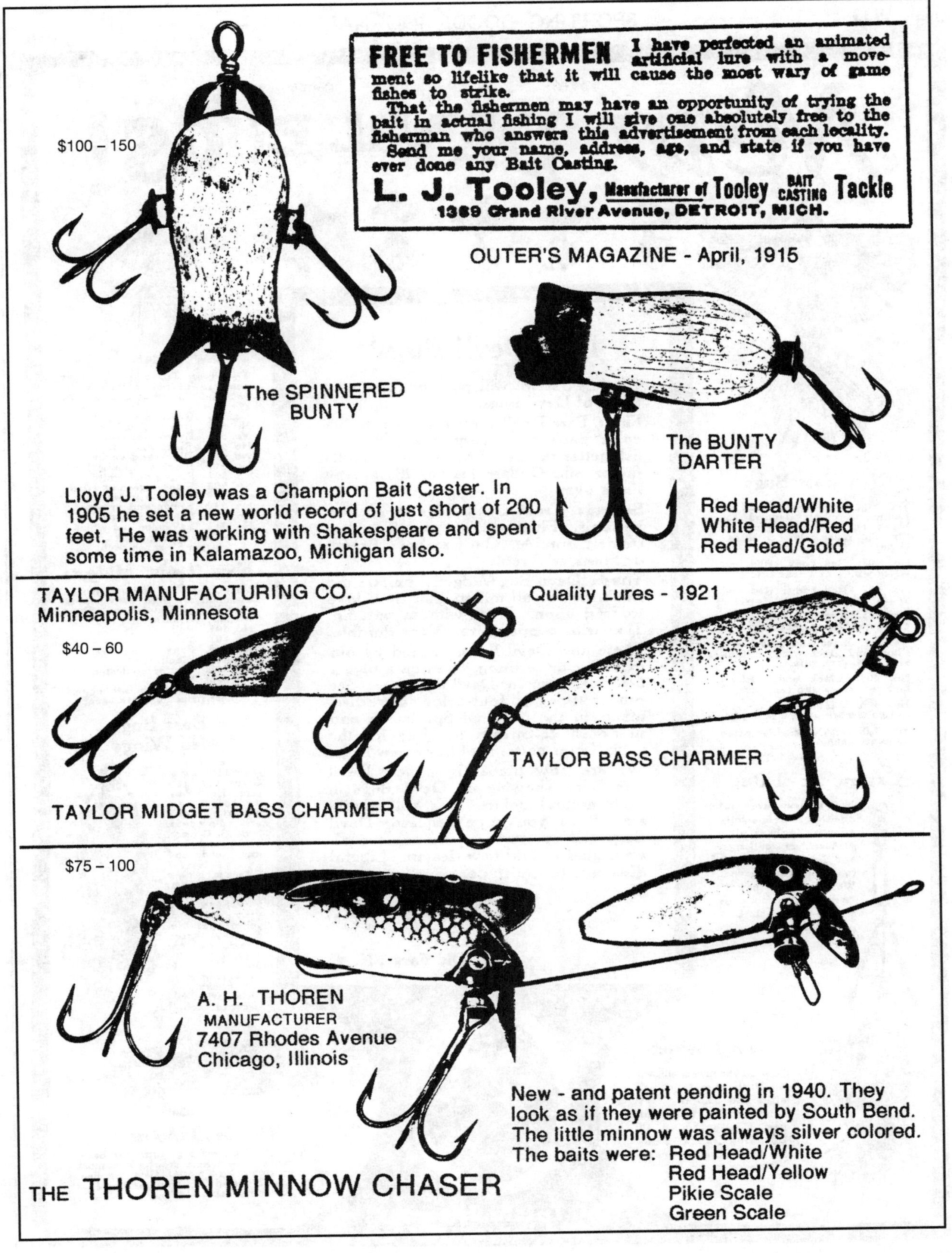

FREE TO FISHERMEN I have perfected an animated artificial lure with a movement so lifelike that it will cause the most wary of game fishes to strike.
That the fishermen may have an opportunity of trying the bait in actual fishing I will give one absolutely free to the fisherman who answers this advertisement from each locality.
Send me your name, address, age, and state if you have ever done any Bait Casting.
L. J. Tooley, Manufacturer of Tooley BAIT CASTING Tackle
1369 Grand River Avenue, DETROIT, MICH.

OUTER'S MAGAZINE - April, 1915

$100 – 150

The SPINNERED BUNTY

The BUNTY DARTER

Lloyd J. Tooley was a Champion Bait Caster. In 1905 he set a new world record of just short of 200 feet. He was working with Shakespeare and spent some time in Kalamazoo, Michigan also.

Red Head/White
White Head/Red
Red Head/Gold

TAYLOR MANUFACTURING CO.
Minneapolis, Minnesota

Quality Lures - 1921

$40 – 60

TAYLOR BASS CHARMER

TAYLOR MIDGET BASS CHARMER

$75 – 100

A. H. THOREN
MANUFACTURER
7407 Rhodes Avenue
Chicago, Illinois

New - and patent pending in 1940. They look as if they were painted by South Bend. The little minnow was always silver colored.

The baits were: Red Head/White
Red Head/Yellow
Pikie Scale
Green Scale

THE THOREN MINNOW CHASER

June, 1923 SPORTING GOODS JOURNAL $5 – 25 each

New DEVIL BUGS!

New Devil Bugs!

On July 1st we will put out three new kinds of Devil Bugs.

First: Bass Devil Bugs with wings. Six color patterns. Every one proved a fish-getter in use. Float without paraffin or oil. Outlast feather flies many times over.

Second: Trout Devil Bugs in 12 new patterns. Float without paraffin. Extremely durable. Get Rainbow, Brown or Speckled Trout.

Third: Devil Bug Midgets. Imitate the small moths and millers that trout love to feed upon. Float without paraffin. Tied with copper wire. Very durable.

These new Devil Bugs, backed by our extensive advertising, open up a bigger field than ever for Devil Bug sales. See our full-page, four-color advertisements in the National Sportsman and in Forest & Stream for July for the actual color patterns of these new bugs. We are now preparing a new Devil Bug book showing all Devil Bugs in their natural colors. We will gladly send it to you upon request. Devil Bugs sell everywhere and we are always glad to add new dealers. Liberal discounts to the trade.

O C Tuttle

Old Forge, N. Y.

New Bass Bugs

The biggest killing fly rod or trolling lure yet devised for black bass, pike or pickerel. Six different color combinations:

No. 401. Red body. Red and white wings and rear tuft.

No. 402. Red body. Red and yellow wings and rear tuft.

No. 403. Red body. Red and green wings and rear tuft.

No. 404. Black and gray body. Black and green wings. Black and gray rear tuft.

No. 405. Black body. Black and red wings and rear tuft.

No. 406. Black body. Black and yellow wings and rear tuft.

Size 1/0 ring hook. List price 60 cents each.

Casting Devil Bug

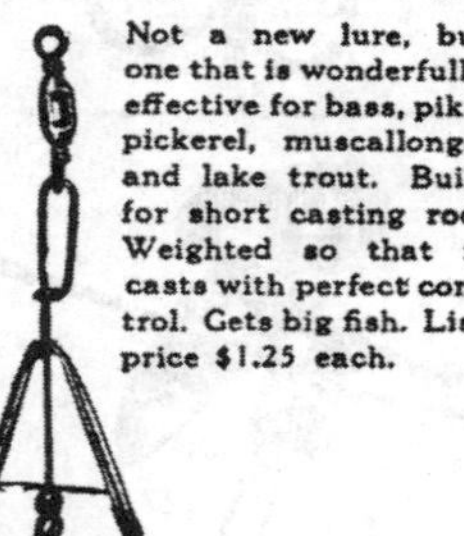

Not a new lure, but one that is wonderfully effective for bass, pike, pickerel, muscallonge, and lake trout. Built for short casting rod. Weighted so that it casts with perfect control. Gets big fish. List price $1.25 each.

New Booklet

Now on the press. Shows all Devil Bugs in actual sizes and colors. Gives complete description for use. Copies free to all Devil Bug dealers. Sample copies upon request. Write for it.

New Trout Bugs

The new Trout Devil Bugs come in 12 new color combinations. All tried and proved effective.

No. 501. Red and white
No. 502. Red and yellow
No. 503. Green and red.
No. 504. Black and red
No. 505. Black and yellow
No. 506. Black and Green
No. 507. Purple and white
No. 508. Black, green and red
No. 509. Brown and white
No. 510. Brown and green
No. 511. Gray and white
No. 512. Lavender and white

Size No. 8 ring hooks. List price 50 cents each.

New Trout Midgets

Very small to imitate moths and millers. Tied with copper wire like all Devil Bugs. Float without paraffin.

No. 601. Red
No. 602. Yellow
No. 603. Gray
No. 604. Black
No. 605. White, red design
No. 606. Brown

Ring or snell No. 14 hooks. List price 50 cents each.

Bass Bugs No Wings

The original Devil Bugs. Great fish getters. No. 1 Red, yellow eyes. Yellow, black and yellow eyes. No. 3 Gray, black and yellow head and eyes. No. 4 Black, gray body design, yellow eyes. No. 5 White and gray, red head, yellow eyes. No. 6 Gray, green head, yellow eyes. Sizes No. 3, 6, or 8 ring snell hooks. List price 60 cents each.

The Devil Mouse

A wonderful lure for big trout, for bass, pike, pickerel and lake trout. The most popular single lure made. Gets big fish. Size Nos. 2/0 and 3/0 ring hooks. List price 75 cents each.

O.C.Tuttle, Inventor
Old Forge, N.Y.

The advertiser appreciates your mentioning SPORTING GOODS JOURNAL

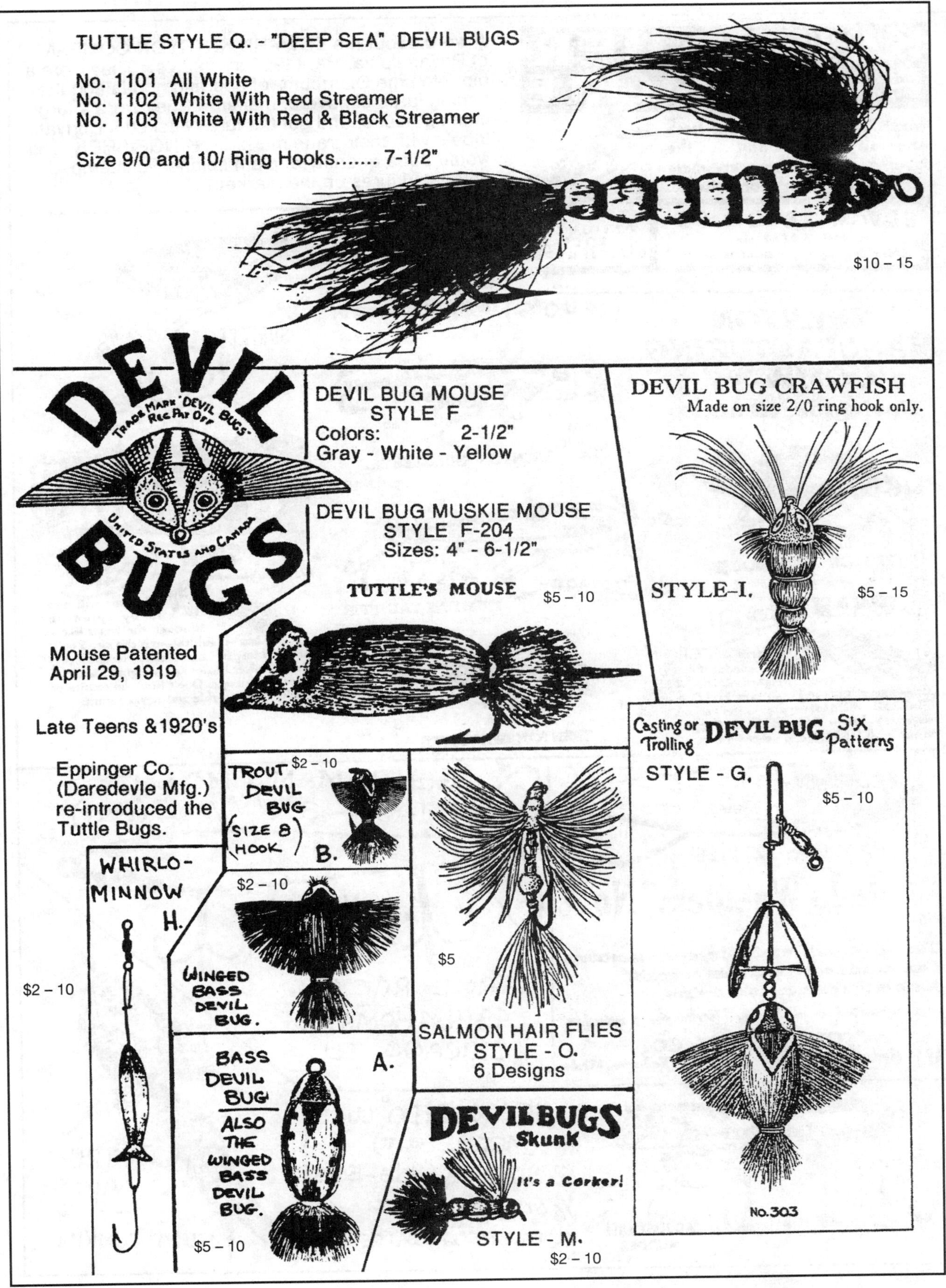
TUTTLE STYLE Q. - "DEEP SEA" DEVIL BUGS
No. 1101 All White
No. 1102 White With Red Streamer
No. 1103 White With Red & Black Streamer
Size 9/0 and 10/ Ring Hooks....... 7-1/2"
$10 – 15
DEVIL BUGS
TRADE MARK "DEVIL BUGS" REG PAT OFF
UNITED STATES AND CANADA
DEVIL BUG MOUSE
STYLE F
Colors: 2-1/2"
Gray - White - Yellow
DEVIL BUG MUSKIE MOUSE
STYLE F-204
Sizes: 4" - 6-1/2"
TUTTLE'S MOUSE
$5 – 10
DEVIL BUG CRAWFISH
Made on size 2/0 ring hook only.
STYLE–I.
$5 – 15
Mouse Patented
April 29, 1919
Late Teens &1920's
Eppinger Co.
(Daredevle Mfg.)
re-introduced the
Tuttle Bugs.
TROUT DEVIL BUG
(SIZE 8 HOOK)
B.
$2 – 10
Casting or Trolling DEVIL BUG Six Patterns
STYLE - G.
$5 – 10
WHIRLO-MINNOW
H.
$2 – 10
$2 – 10
WINGED BASS DEVIL BUG.
$5
SALMON HAIR FLIES
STYLE - O.
6 Designs
BASS DEVIL BUG
ALSO THE WINGED BASS DEVIL BUG.
A.
$5 – 10
DEVILBUGS
Skunk
It's a Corker!
STYLE - M.
$2 – 10
No.303

KINGFISHER
FISHING TACKLE

Meets all requirements for fresh and salt water fishing . . . the favorite of fishermen everywhere .. at your dealer's, or write us.

EDW K TRYON CO.
PHILADELPHIA
Oldest Sporting Goods House in America

DESIGNERS · SOLE · DISTRIBUTORS

A word about the EDWARD K. TRYON COMPANY of Philadelphia, PA. (1900's - 1920's) They were a big, old time Distributor of sporting goods and the fishing lures of several makers. They were a large catalog house, and got the lures packed for private labels with their trade mark.......KINGFISHER. This would put a quantity of plain spinner, unstamped, unlabeled lures on the market........oh joy!

$2

3/8 oz. 5"

(1940'S) TRENTON SPIN-TWIN

$5

SURFACE 2 7/8"

doodler

TRENTON MANUFACTURING COMPANY

Covington, Kentucky

5/8 oz
WOOD
3 1/4"

$5

TRENTON GURGLEHEAD

trenton

$5 – 10

2 3/4" - 1/2 oz.

TRENTON MAD MOUSE

$10 – 15

5/8 oz - WOOD - 4 5/8"

TRENTON TAIL SPIN

SPIN doodler

This one will lure you by spinning through the water like a buzz-bomb through the air. You'll know him by the flashy, eccentrically-shaped offset blades and weighted hook of improved design. Don't hook on to him or you'll go for a ride and never return.

$5

$5

WHAM! doodler

Wanted—for killing Ol' Grandpa Pike. Gramp weighed 42 lbs. 2 ozs.—biggest caught in '46 says FIELD & STREAM! WHAM! doodler wears various disguises—bright Stainless Steel, Copper, White with Red Head, 4 other finishes.

$5 – 10

4"
3/4 oz.

TRENTON SPIN DIVER

PAT. MAY 12, 1925

"Toledo Weedless" No. 2

$10 – 20

The famous bait wanted by every sportsman. Guaranteed not to catch grass or weeds. Made in five different color designs.

Agents wanted in all States. Write for particulars.

TOLEDO BAIT CO.
1944 Broadway Toledo, Ohio

"GENTLEMAN JIM" BAIT
TENITE - 3 3/4" - 1/2 oz. (1947)

$5

NO. 500
LUMINOUS

TROLL-RITE CO.
4814 THOMAS ST.
CHICAGO, ILL.

$2 – 10

TRUE ART'S

SUM PUNKIN

ADJUSTABLE RUDDER

THE "TORPEDO" LURE
(METAL BAIT)
3 SIZES: (40's-50's
1/6 oz - 1/4 oz - 3/8 oz.
GOLD - RED - WHITE

$10 – 20

Doodle Bug
REG. U.S. PAT. OFFICE

THE ONE CASTING BAIT ALL GAME FISH TAKE

(1937)
40¢ AT YOUR DEALER OR DIRECT

Looks like a Bug, with the action of a Bug; Game Fish go "bugs" over it. Thoroughly Tested, Perfected and proven in the past seven years in taking all inland-water Game Fish. TROUT (Brook, Brown and Rainbow, Wall-eyes, Bass, Pickerel and Perch. Made in two colors, the Yellow Ace and the Green Deuce. All over size 1¼"x2⅛". Weight ¼ oz. — Thru popular request from the Fly Fishermen we have created the BABY or Fly Rod size for Trout, Bass, and all Pan fish. Weight 20 grs. Has same action.

Twin-City Bait Co., MARINETTE, WISCONSIN

TRANS - LURE BAIT CO.
Merchandise Mart Chicago

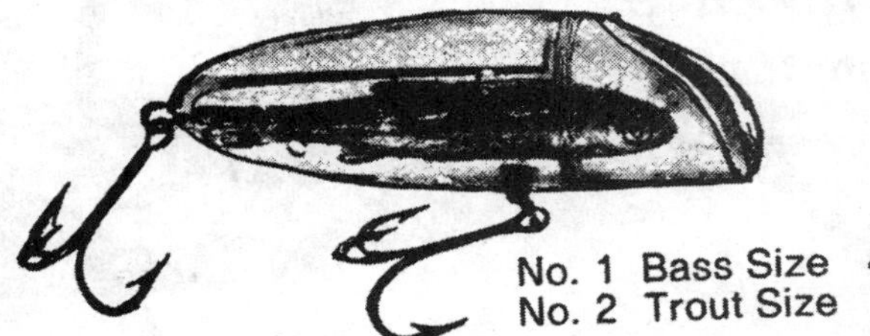

No. 1 Bass Size 4"
No. 2 Trout Size 1-3/4"

Showing Trans-Lure No. 1 with live minnow inserted

Head Insert Colors:	Body Insert Colors:
Red	
Black	(Same)
Green	
White	
Red Stripe	

Colors Inserted In Lure

$5 – 10

25 BAITS IN ONE
For
CASTING - TROLLING - SURFACE
or
UNDERWATER FISHING

$5 – 10

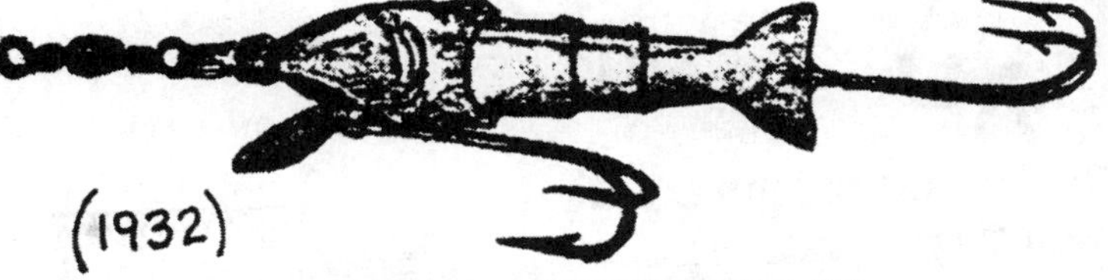

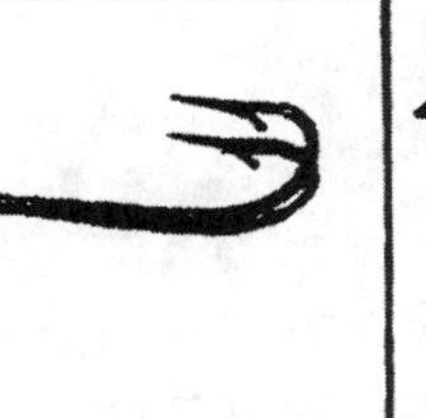

(1932)

THE FLEX-ZIT BAIT

A swimming bait for Black Bass. The body of fish is composed of four moveable parts. Made in three colors—nickel, brass or copper. Length of body 2⅜ inches.

Price .... $1.00 Each

TRADEWINDS, INC. P. O. Box 1191-SA TACOMA 1, WASH.
SIZES: 1½"- 2"- 3"- 4"- 4½"- 5"

$2 – 5

SPIN-IN-HERRY

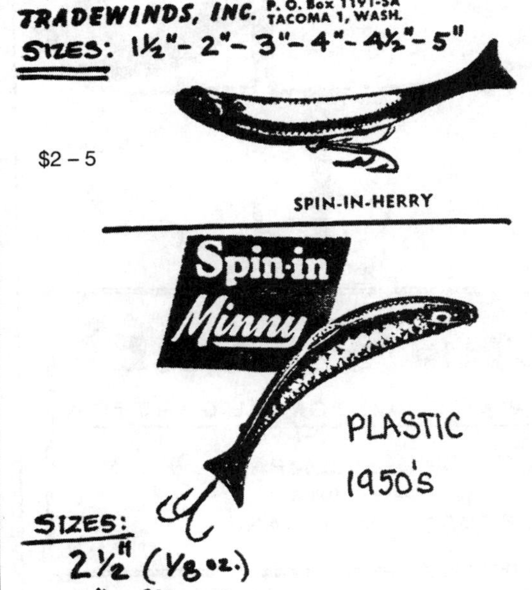
Spin-in
Minny
PLASTIC
1950's
SIZES:
2½" (1/8 oz.)
3" (1/4 oz.)
4" (3/8 oz.)
Built-in Flash!
Fluoro Colors!

$2 – 5

SOLID COLOR PLASTIC

"GET A "GIZMO"

Write for Our Free Catalog

THE SENSATIONAL BAIT OF '48

Tom BAIT COMPANY
MATTOON, ILLINOIS

(1948)

A SOLID PLASTIC SPOON → THE "SHINEROO"

$2 – 5

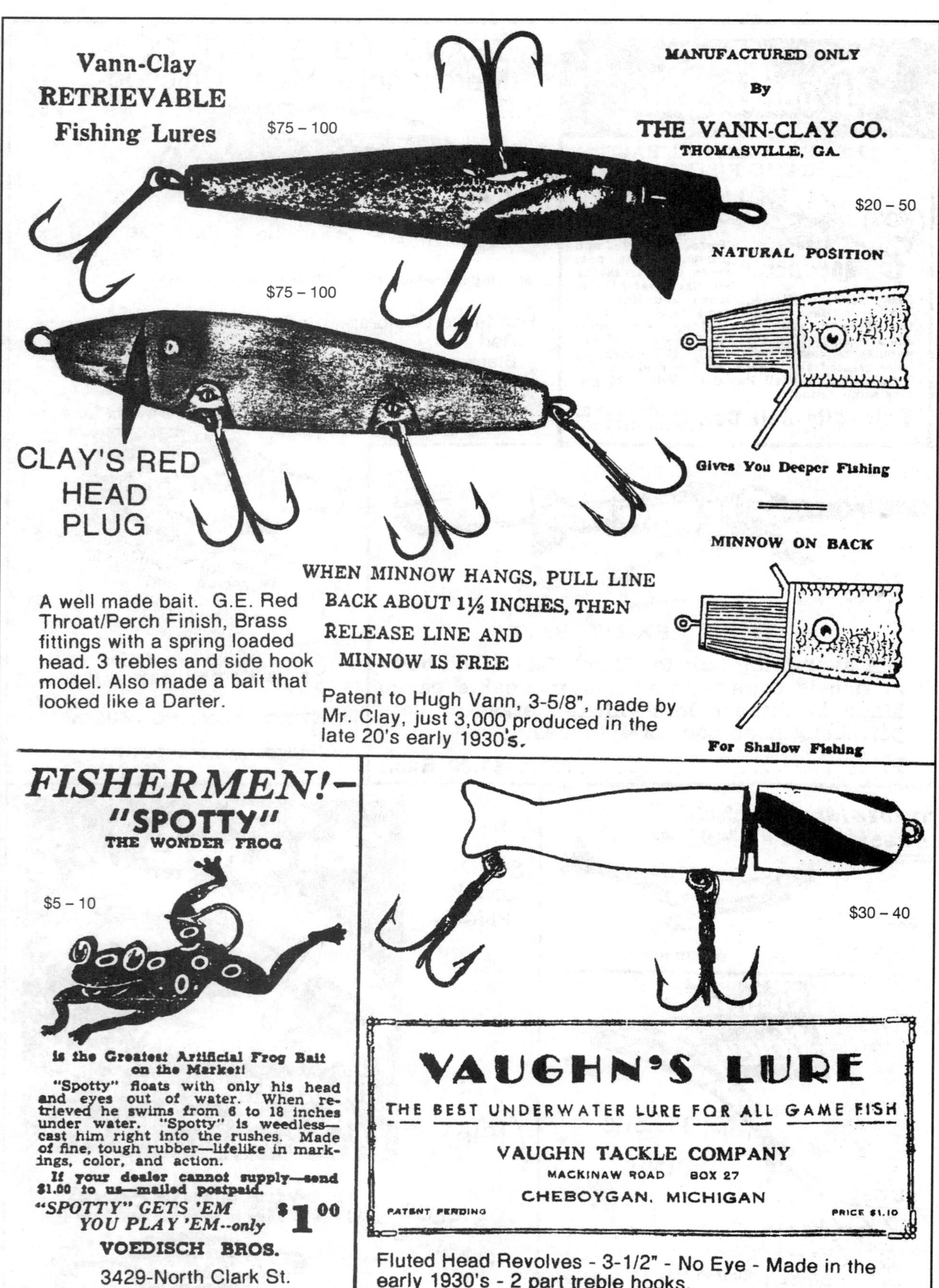
Vann-Clay
RETRIEVABLE
Fishing Lures
MANUFACTURED ONLY
By
THE VANN-CLAY CO.
THOMASVILLE, GA.
NATURAL POSITION
Gives You Deeper Fishing
MINNOW ON BACK
For Shallow Fishing
WHEN MINNOW HANGS, PULL LINE
BACK ABOUT 1½ INCHES, THEN
RELEASE LINE AND
MINNOW IS FREE
FISHERMEN!—
"SPOTTY"
THE WONDER FROG
is the Greatest Artificial Frog Bait on the Market!
"Spotty" floats with only his head and eyes out of water. When retrieved he swims from 6 to 18 inches under water. "Spotty" is weedless—cast him right into the rushes. Made of fine, tough rubber—lifelike in markings, color, and action.
If your dealer cannot supply—send $1.00 to us—mailed postpaid.
"SPOTTY" GETS 'EM
YOU PLAY 'EM--only
$1.00
VOEDISCH BROS.
VAUGHN'S LURE
THE BEST UNDERWATER LURE FOR ALL GAME FISH
VAUGHN TACKLE COMPANY
MACKINAW ROAD BOX 27
CHEBOYGAN, MICHIGAN
PATENT PENDING
PRICE $1.10

$75 – 100

$75 – 100

$20 – 50

CLAY'S RED HEAD PLUG

A well made bait. G.E. Red Throat/Perch Finish, Brass fittings with a spring loaded head. 3 trebles and side hook model. Also made a bait that looked like a Darter.

Patent to Hugh Vann, 3-5/8", made by Mr. Clay, just 3,000 produced in the late 20's early 1930's.

$5 – 10

3429-North Clark St.
Chicago, Illinois

$30 – 40

Fluted Head Revolves - 3-1/2" - No Eye - Made in the early 1930's - 2 part treble hooks.

THE BOHANAN ARTIFICIAL MINNOW

This minnow retains the natural position of a live minnow in the water, can not be made to turn on its side or back. The rear hooks are connected by a wire reaching from the rear running through the fish and out at the mouth to the line, making it impossible for hooks to pull out.

They are painted in seven attractive natural colors and made in three styles and five sizes. Price $1.00 post paid. Send for descriptive catalog to

F. S. VANDERSLOOT **Farmington, Illinois**

FIVE SIZES

3 STYLES

7 NATURAL COLORS

$10 – 20

PATENTED.

This ad was found in a May Issue of OUTER'S BOOK from 1911. Note the described through wire construction. It also shows that the lure was patented.

The VEX BAIT

VEX BAIT COMPANY
1921 - Main Street
Dayton, Ohio

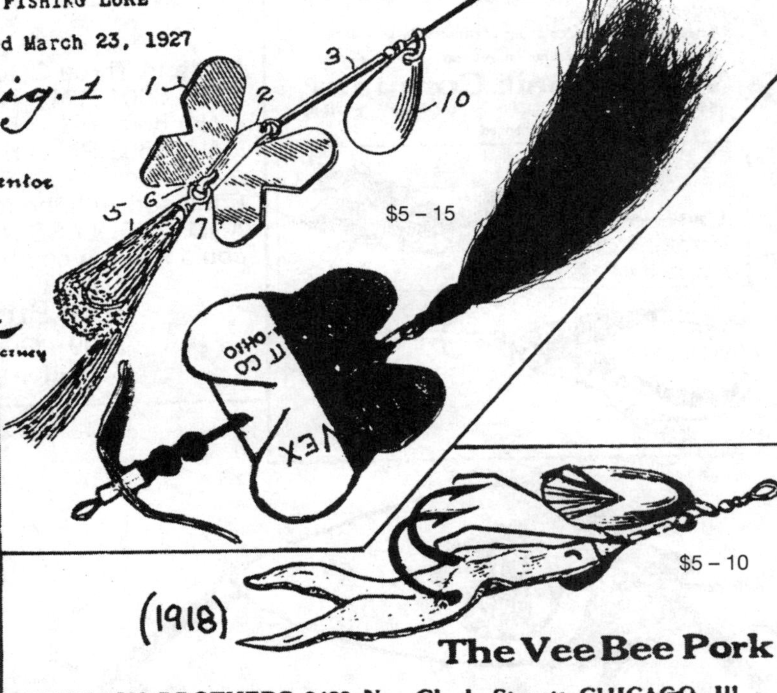

1,738,617 Dec. 10, 1929.
C. H. SCHARRER
FISHING LURE
Filed March 23, 1927
Fig. 1
Inventor
Carl H. Scharrer
By F. L. Walker
Attorney
VEX

$5 – 15

"THE VACUUM" is a Prize Winner

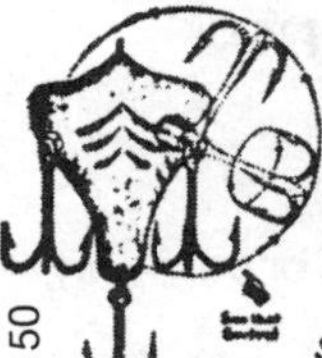

Hartwel's 8-lb. large-mouth was landed with this bass killer.

100 other baits on the market, but only one Vacuum. It's entirely different—casts perfectly—very attractive and a sure hooker.

One of the most successful surface lures. Equally good day or night.

Ask for circular.

Sold by all dealers, or mailed postpaid on receipt of 75 cents.

VACUUM BAIT CO.

307 Walnut Street North Manchester, Indiana

$20 – 50

(1912 Ad) Note:
Also see So. Bend Vacuum Bait & Howe's Vacuum Bait.

(1918)

The Vee Bee Pork

VOEDISCH BROTHERS 3429 No. Clark Street, CHICAGO, Ill

$5 – 10

Another Old Tackle Distributor:
Von Lengerke & Antoine
Chicago, ILL. (since 1891)

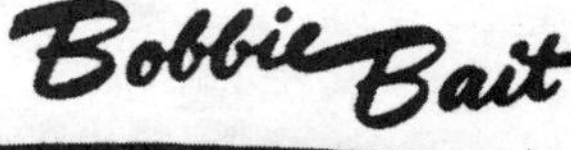

Bobbie Bait

Mfg'd. by:
Robert Vander Velden

$5

A popular wooden Muskie Bait from the 1950's and 1960's. The metal tail could be bent to change the action. Size: 8" - 9". Also made a "Bobbie" Jr. about 6-1/2". Gray Back/White.

TWO IN ONE
DIVING OR SURFACE

$1.35

$20 – 40

Patented

Trade **VESCO** Mark

BAITS AND SPOONS

Made of **DU PONT PYRALIN**

THE 24 colors and combinations show that Smooth, Slimy, Fishy Glint.

Baits have an erratic wiggle and the wounded minnow roll. Hooks single or treble. Instantly attached or removed without tools.

PYRALIN SPOONS have **Pyralin** non-matting Feathered Hooks — practically indestructible and moth-proof.

Material, finish and coloring permanently guaranteed.

Circular on request

VESCO Bait Company
154 West 18th St. NEW YORK

Patented

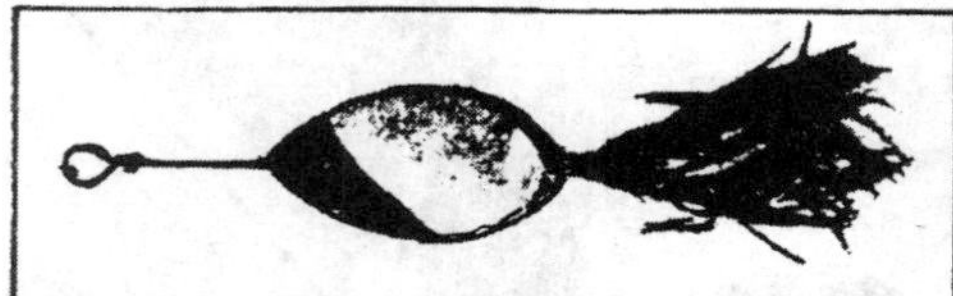

$10

(1922)

VAL-LURE

10 Proven Lures
In One Bait

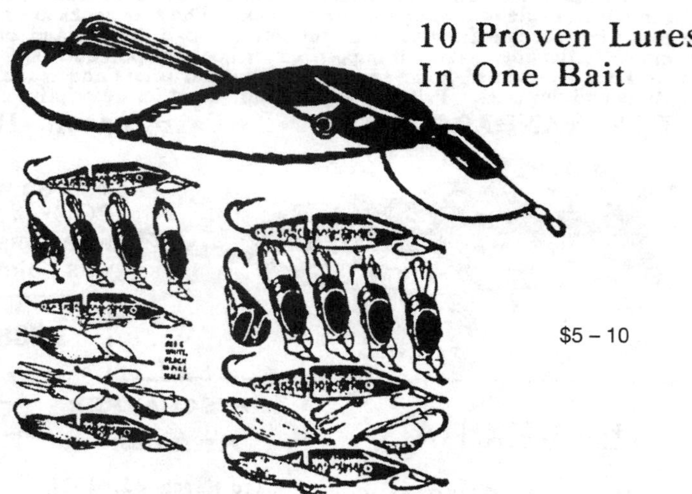

$5 – 10

Made In Three Colors:

No. 6601 RW	Red & White
No. 6602 PR	Perch Scale
No. 6603 PK	Pike Scale

(1936)

Equipped with the famous "VAL SNAG PROOF AND WEEDLESS NOSE GUARD". The Val Lure Set could make a combination of 10 different lures.

Val Products
7239 - Greenleaf Ave.
Chicago, Illinois

The Spinno Minno

Pecos River Tackle Co.
Carlsbad, New Mexico
&
Uniline Manufacturing Corporation
Dallas 5, Texas

Plastic Lure with a revolving metal Spinner. (1945 - 1950's) Very colorful box, and a color collector's delight with around 20 different colors over the life of the bait.

$5 – 15

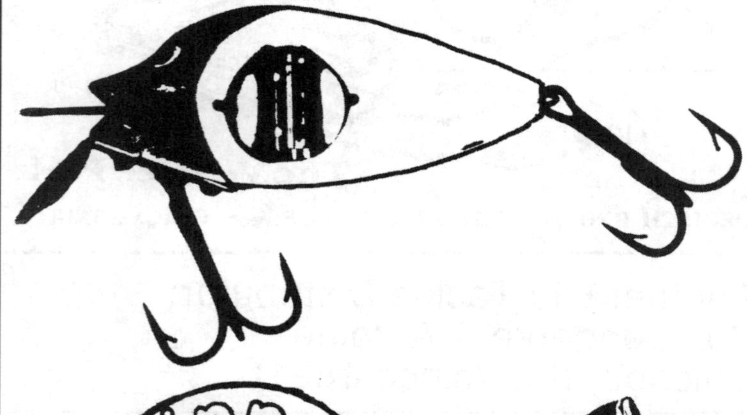

Spinno
Minno

KETCHALL WOBBLER
No. F-606—White Body—Red Head.
United States Athletic Company
327 North Wells Street
Chicago, Ill. :: U. S. A.

$30 – 40

This copy of the box top is the only clue we have to ID this bait. It looks like - but is not - a Bite-Em Wiggler.

$2

U. B. FROG HARNESS.

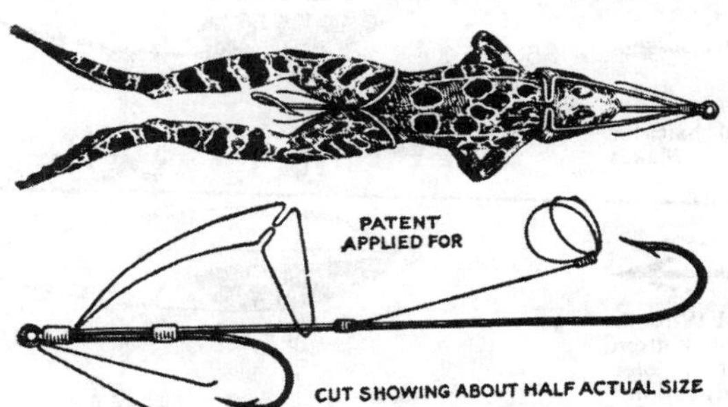
PATENT APPLIED FOR
CUT SHOWING ABOUT HALF ACTUAL SIZE

The **Live Frog Harness** holds the frog perfectly, and **keeps it alive.** The frog is so held **without hooking,** that it has free use of every part of its body, and is always in natural position. An unlimited number of casts may be made with the **Live Frog Harness without injury to frog.**

Place the frog in the harness by drawing its hind leg through the saddle loops and place its head in the yoke with the vertical wires just back of the jaws. The loops are made of annealed wire and may be bent to fit the frog.

U - B also made the U-B Spin - Fly Bait. Jamison (also in Chicago) bought rights to the U-B and sold it as their own.

Unkefer & Bradley
91 Dearborn Street
Chicago, Illinois

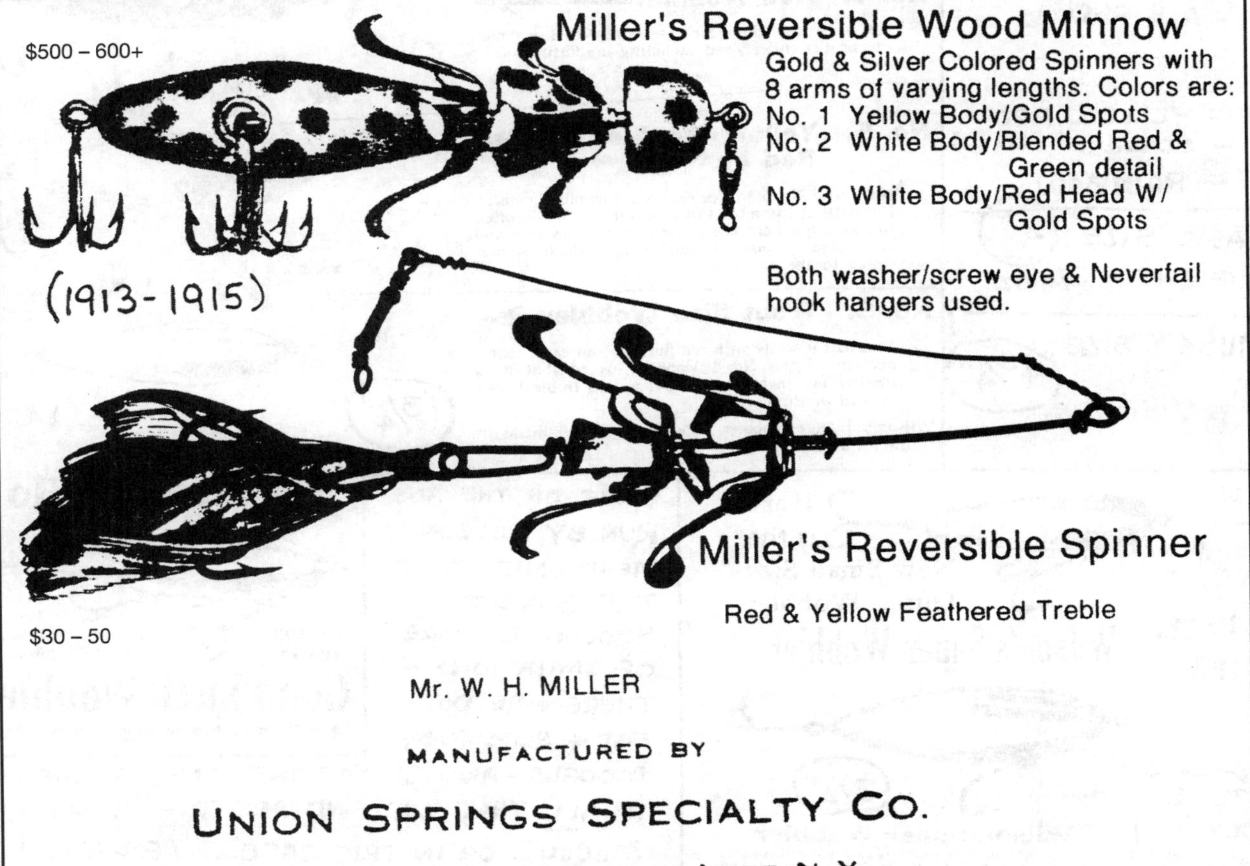
(1913-1915)

Miller's Reversible Wood Minnow

$500 – 600+

Gold & Silver Colored Spinners with 8 arms of varying lengths. Colors are:

No. 1 Yellow Body/Gold Spots
No. 2 White Body/Blended Red & Green detail
No. 3 White Body/Red Head W/ Gold Spots

Both washer/screw eye & Neverfail hook hangers used.

Miller's Reversible Spinner

Red & Yellow Feathered Treble

$30 – 50

Mr. W. H. MILLER

MANUFACTURED BY

UNION SPRINGS SPECIALTY CO.

UNION SPRINGS-ON-CAYUGA LAKE. N. Y.

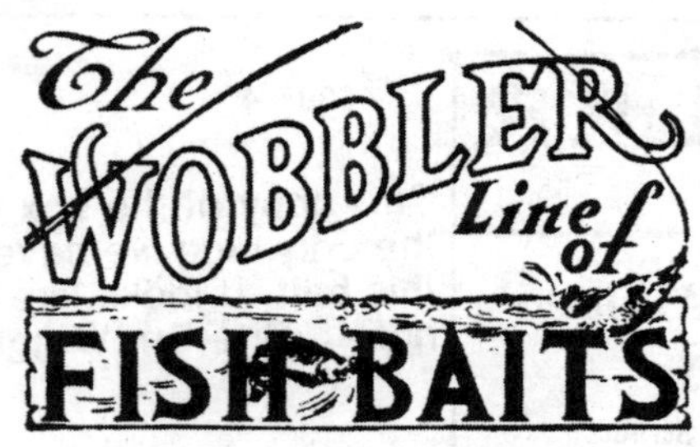
The
WOBBLER
Line of
FISH BAITS

The Bait That Gets 'Em

HASTINGS
SPORTING GOODS COMPANY
418 Michigan Ave. HASTINGS, MICH.

DESIGNED BY: ART WILSON.

THE FIRST WOBBLER WAS INTRODUCED ABOUT 1912. (PAT'D. MAY, 1913.)

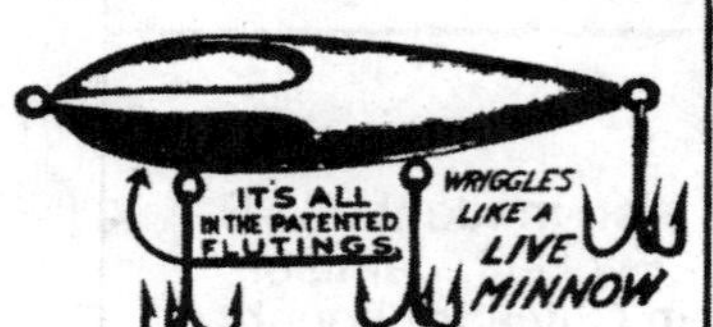
IT'S ALL IN THE PATENTED FLUTINGS
WRIGGLES LIKE A LIVE MINNOW

No. 1. White, with Red Flutings

WILSON'S FLUTED WOBBLER

COLORS

1F - WHITE, RED FLUTES
2F - LUMINOUS
- ALL RED

5F - YELLOW, RED FLUTES
- SCALE
10F - RAINBOW

BASIC SIZE: 4"
WEIGHT - 3/4 OZ.

• MUSKY SIZE: 4 3/4"

WILSON'S FLUTED WOBBLERS

No. 2. Luminous Wobbler → For Night Fishing $5 – 15

Glows brightly in the dark. The ideal bait for night fishing. **Gets 'em** every time. Makes night fishing a great sport.

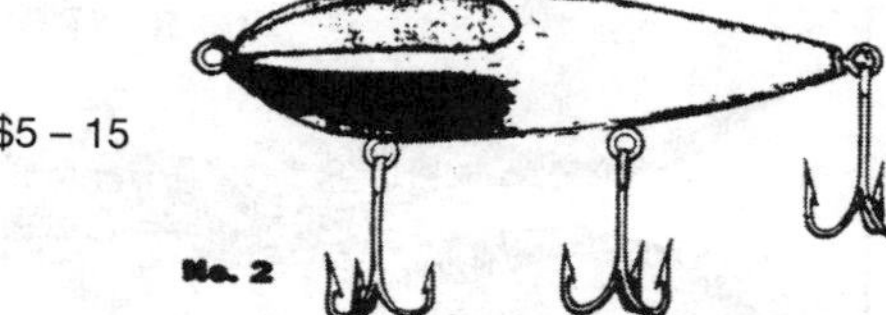

No. 2

No. 3. Sinking Wobbler → $5 – 15

White with red flutings, same as the No. 1 Wilson's Fluted Wobbler. This bait sinks to the bottom when not in motion, while the regular wobbler floats when not in motion. This is the only sinking bait we make. To be used when you have to go deep for them.

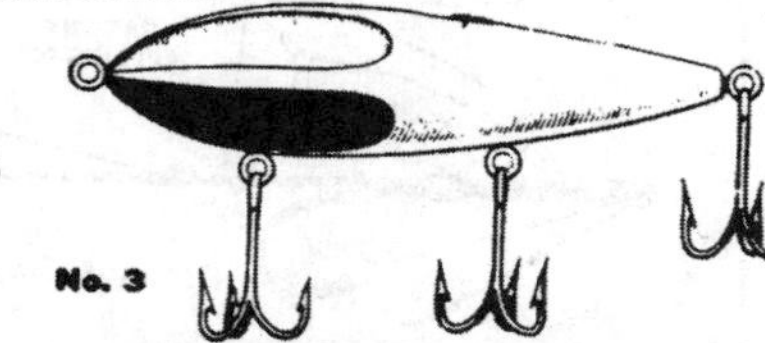

No. 3

No. 4. Red Wobbler → $5 – 15

No. 4 is just the same as the No. 1 wobbler, except it is entirely red, including the flutings.

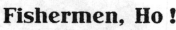

No. 5. Yellow Wobbler → Red Flutings $5 – 15

No. 4 and No. 5 are for dark days or muddy water. Put both of these baits in your kit. One will often suit exactly where the other would be useless, and vice versa. You can quickly tell which is best suited to the day and water.

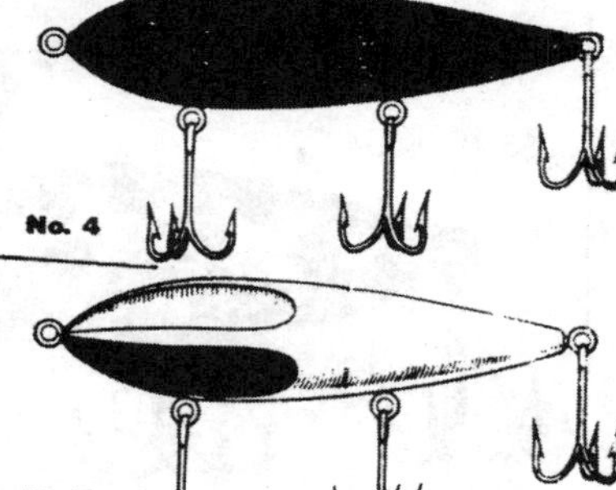

No. 4

No. 5

No. 6. Trout Size Wobbler → $5 – 10

This bait is white with red flutings—an exact reproduction of the No. 1 wobbler, except that it is smaller (1¾ inch long) and has two treble hooks instead of three.

1 3/4"

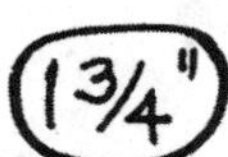

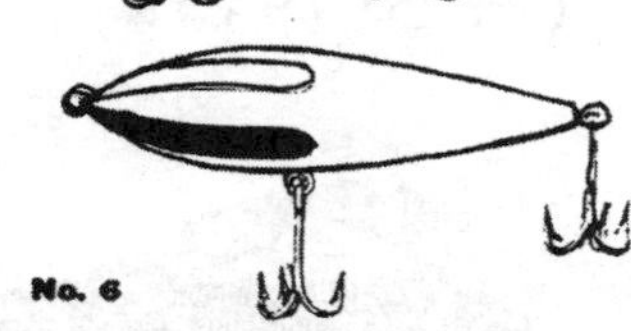

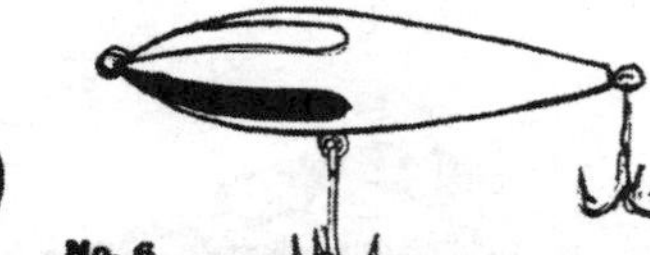

No. 6

Wilson's Flange Wobbler, shown on page 5, made in all of above styles.

$5 – 15

NEW - 1919

NO. 1S OR 1FS

Here is the New Small Size Fluted Wobbler

Wilson's Super-Wobbler

(Patented)

3 1/2"

Wilson Super Wobbler

Double hook in the center acts as a pivot making an unusually lively worker. Hooks can be turned up for use among weeds and lily pads. Finish White, Luminous, Rainbow and Scale finish.

NOTE 2 BODY SHAPES.

SOME OF THE ADS RUN BY WILSON MENTIONED THAT THE BUYERS SHOULD BEWARE OF IMITATIONS - THERE ARE BOTH FAT & SLIM BODY MODELS - AND I FOR ONE, AM NOT SURE IF ALL THAT WE FIND ARE THE "REAL McCOY" OR IN THIS CASE...."REAL WILSON."

Fishermen, Ho!

Are You Wise to

"Wriggles Like a Live Minnow"

Good Luck Wobblers

(Wilson's Patents, formerly known as Wilson's Wobblers)

WILSON'S FLUTED WOBBLERS

This bait is individually boxed. We also furnish a display box containing one dozen baits with every order for one dozen or more. This box contains a printed

$250 +

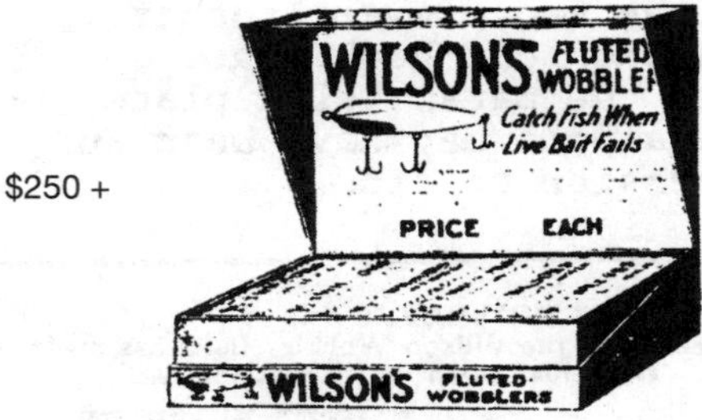

WILSONS FLUTED WOBBLER
Catch Fish When Live Bait Fails
PRICE EACH
WILSON'S FLUTED WOBBLERS

description of the bait and its uses. Your jobber can supply you. Nationally advertised in all the following magazines:

Saturday Evening Post
Outdoor World and Recreation
Outdoor Life
Outersbook
Hunter, Trader & Trapper
National Sportsman
Field & Stream
Outing
Rod & Gun
Sportsman's Review
Sporting Life

Thousands now in use.

Hastings Sporting Goods Works
Hastings, Mich.

$100 – 150

The Staggerbug

VERY FEW OF THESE HAVE BEEN FOUND!

A new creation in artificial lures. This new bait has the same alluring motion which has made the Wobbler Family famous.

By reeling slow the bait wobbles directly on the surface making an ideal lure for night fishing. At the ordinary speed of reeling it travels to a depth of ten or twelve inches.

The Staggerbug will give you new sensations in bait casting and it is backed by the reputation of the Wobbler Family as a fish getter.

Furnished in white with red shading on the head, or other Wilson Wobbler colors on special order.

Meet new people. Call a lure collector today!

WILSON COLORS:

- RED BODY/MOTTLED SPOTS
- FANCY GREEN BACK/WHITE BELLY
- SOLID RED
- SOLID YELLOW
- SOLID WHITE (ALSO WHITE LUMINOUS)
- SOLID GREEN
- BROWN SCALE
- RAIN BOW
- YELLOW/RED FLUTES

$40 – 50

Wilson's Six-In-One Wobbler

ADJ. LIP

This lure is made with an adjustable diving guide which may be set at any one of six different positions. One position will cause the bait to skim on the surface of the water, the other positions will cause the bait to travel in the water at various depths, ranging to a maximum of six feet. Each different change in the position of the diving guide not only causes the bait to travel at a different depth, but with a different wobbling movement.

No. 1S. White, red head.
No. 11S. Light green crackle back.
No. 12S. Red stripes on green back.

Lure values change from time to time and from place to place. Condition, color, and boxes add value.

WILSON WOBBLERS

- The metal Sizzler bait came in a second and larger size: 3-1/4"
- Wilson Wobblers were made in the late 20's and 30's by Moonlight, and then by Paw Paw. This would be a hard variation to pick out in the red & white colors, but some of the more exotic colors are no doubt of these two later manufacturers.Also painted cups are later.
- In my opinion, the hardest Wilson bait to find is the Staggerbug.
- Do not confuse Wilson with a manufacturer and distributor named: "Thos.E. Wilson & Co." of New York, Chicago, and San Francisco.
- A recent discovery of the actual tackle box of Franklin A. Alger will give us alot more information about this early tackle pioneer. He was marketing the Getsem Bait himself, under an address of 819 Lafayette Ave. S.E. Grand Rapids, Michigan. He made several other baits plus a small "Michigan Trout Spinner, and some hook rigs. There are two models of the Getsem, one with the metal belly plate, and one with a wood belly only. The non-metal one may have been an "economy" model, and is by far the harder version to find.

Fishermen—
Another new one!

$15 – 20

ALGER'S
GETSEM
Weedless Bait

THIS 1915 AD SHOWS THAT HASTINGS ADDED THE ALGER'S GETSEM IN 1915.

- THE WILSON "SIX-IN-ONE" WAS NEW IN 1915.

THE
HIGH
SIGN

ORIGINAL WILSON'S FLUTED WOBBLER

FREE, *Bait Casting* Booklet and Tackle Folder. Address *Dept. B*
HASTINGS SPORTING GOODS WORKS
Hastings, Michigan

WILSON'S WOBBLERS

The escaping minnow movement of the Wilson Wobbler Baits has made them the sensation in artificial lures. They float when not in motion.

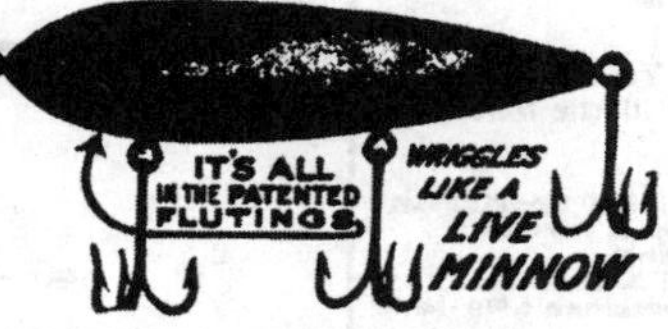
IT'S ALL IN THE PATENTED FLUTINGS
WRIGGLES LIKE A LIVE MINNOW

FLUTED WOBBLER
Wriggles Like an Escaping Minnow
Three Gangs Treble Hooks

No. IFW/58. White body, red flutings; size ⅞x4 inches.
No. IFR/58. Red body, red flutings; size ⅞x4 inches.
No. IFY/58. Yellow body, red flutings; size ⅞x4 inches.
No. IFSF/58. Silver finish body, red flutings; size ⅞x4 inches.
One in a box; weight, per dozen, 24 ounces.

Fluted—Small Size

Fluted Weedless

FLUTED—SMALL SIZE
Two Gangs Treble Hooks

No. 1FS/58. White body, red flutings; size ⅞x3½ inches; one in a box; weight, per dozen, 24 ounces.

FLUTED WEEDLESS
Two Gangs Treble Weedless Hooks

No. 1FWW/81. White body, red flutings; size ⅞x4 inches.

THIS AD SHOWS:
- SMALL SIZE 3 HOOKER—(3½")
- SOLID RED COLOR
- WEEDLESS HOOK MODEL.

$10 – 20

Lures in this book are valued very good to very good+ condition. Excellent to mint conditions bring greater value.

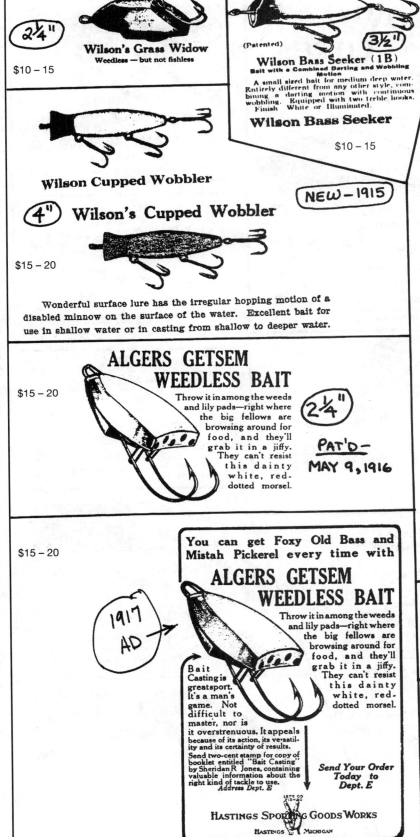

2¼"

Wilson's Grass Widow

Weedless — but not fishless

$10 – 15

(Patented) 3½"

Wilson Bass Seeker (1B)

Bait with a Combined Darting and Wobbling Motion

A small sized bait for medium deep water. Entirely different from any other style, combining a darting motion with continuous wobbling. Equipped with two treble hooks. Finish White or Illuminated.

Wilson Bass Seeker

$10 – 15

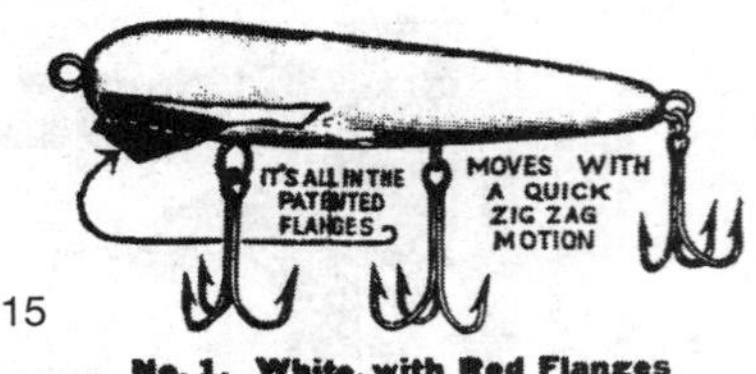
IT'S ALL IN THE PATENTED FLANGES
MOVES WITH A QUICK ZIG ZAG MOTION

$10 – 15

No. 1. White, with Red Flanges

Wilson Cupped Wobbler

NEW—1915

4" **Wilson's Cupped Wobbler**

$15 – 20

Wonderful surface lure has the irregular hopping motion of a disabled minnow on the surface of the water. Excellent bait for use in shallow water or in casting from shallow to deeper water.

WILSON'S FLANGE WOBBLER

(PAT'D— JAN. 13, 1914.)

The patented flanges on this bait give it a quick zig-zag motion through the water and also make the bait weedless to a certain extent. Cannot be considered an absolutely weedless bait, but the flanges part the weeds and, in most cases, allow the hooks to glide by without being caught. By bending the rear of the flanges upward the bait sinks deeper. Bend them downward and the bait rises. Floats when not in motion. The flanges are finished red. Made in all different styles and colors, same as the Fluted Wobbler

4"

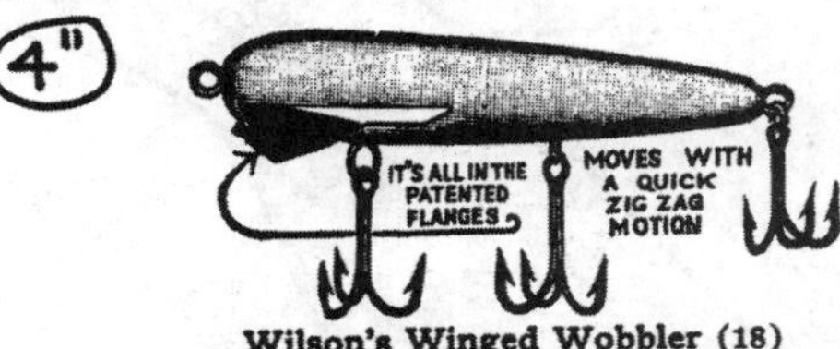
IT'S ALL IN THE PATENTED FLANGES
MOVES WITH A QUICK ZIG ZAG MOTION

Wilson's Winged Wobbler (18)

No. 1W. White with Red Wings.

Its patented wings gives it a quick zig-zag motion in the water and also makes it weedless to a certain extent. It will travel to a depth of six feet when being reeled in, yet will float when not in motion. We recommend it for deep water fishing.

NOTE: CALLED BOTH FLANGE AND WINGED WOBBLER.

$15 – 20

ALGERS GETSEM WEEDLESS BAIT

Throw it in among the weeds and lily pads—right where the big fellows are browsing around for food, and they'll grab it in a jiffy. They can't resist this dainty white, red-dotted morsel.

2¼"

PAT'D— MAY 9, 1916

$15 – 20

1917 AD

You can get Foxy Old Bass and Mistah Pickerel every time with

ALGERS GETSEM WEEDLESS BAIT

Throw it in among the weeds and lily pads—right where the big fellows are browsing around for food, and they'll grab it in a jiffy. They can't resist this dainty white, red-dotted morsel.

Bait Casting is great sport. It's a man's game. Not difficult to master, nor is it overstrenuous. It appeals because of its action, its versatility and its certainty of results.

Send two-cent stamp for copy of booklet entitled "Bait Casting" by Sheridan R Jones, containing valuable information about the right kind of tackle to use.

Address Dept. E

Send Your Order Today to Dept. E

LET'S GO FISHING

HASTINGS SPORTING GOODS WORKS

HASTINGS MICHIGAN

Wilson's Bassmerizer

Bait shown on the left is a combination bait. Dives and wobbles—or with lines attached to other end becomes a surface bait with a good husky wiggle.

$10 – 20

$5 – 15

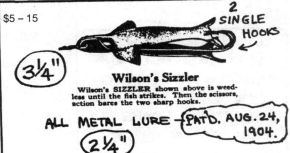

2 SINGLE HOOKS

3¼"

Wilson's Sizzler

Wilson's **SIZZLER** shown above is weedless until the fish strikes. Then the scissors, action bares the two sharp hooks.

ALL METAL LURE — PAT'D. AUG. 24, 1904.

2¼"

© W.M.Co. 1950

EAGLE CLAW LURES

Trade Mark Reg U S Pat. Off.

Manufactured by
WRIGHT & McGILL CO.
Denver Colorado

$5

2 3/8"

No. 303 SERIES

BUG-A-BOO

EAGLE CLAW "BUG-A-BOO"

Weight ½ oz.; length 2⅜". A bass attractor—has peculiar erratic diving, wiggling motion. Plastic body. 12 assorted colors.

MIRACLE Trade **MINNOW** Mark

$5

466W SERIES

Length ....1¾ inches
Weight ....⅝ ounce

1948
MIRACLE MINNOW
No. 305 SERIES
½ oz.
3"

$5

EAGLE CLAW "MIRACLE MINNOW"

Medium size; weight ½ oz. Floats at rest. On retrieve goes into a dive, wiggling and darting like a live minnow. Its curved shape gives the balance needed for perfect control in casting. Plastic body. 12 assorted colors.

BUG-A-BOO
Trade-Mark

Series No. 467W
Series No. 600

$5

467W SERIES

Length ....1¾ inches 467w—
Weight ....⅝ ounce 467w—

NOTE: "W" MEANS WEIGHTED OR SINKER.

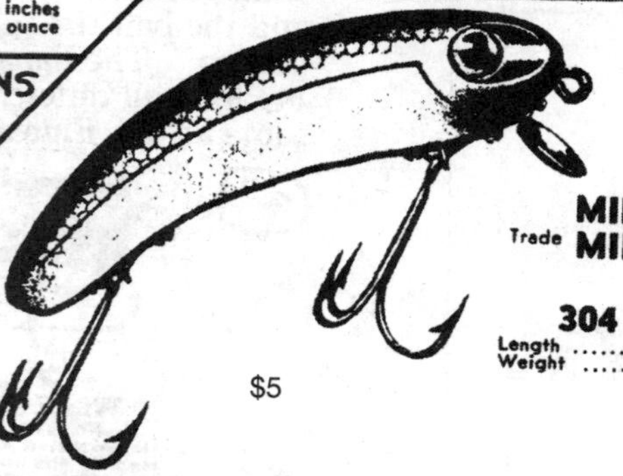

MIRACLE Trade **MINNOW** Mark

304 SERIES

Length ....3¾ inches
Weight ....⅝ ounce

$5

$5

JOINTED

MIRACLE MINNOW

Length 2½ in.
Weight ⅝ oz.

No. 472-J SERIES
WRIGHT & McGILL

MIRACLE Trade **MINNOW** Mark

$5

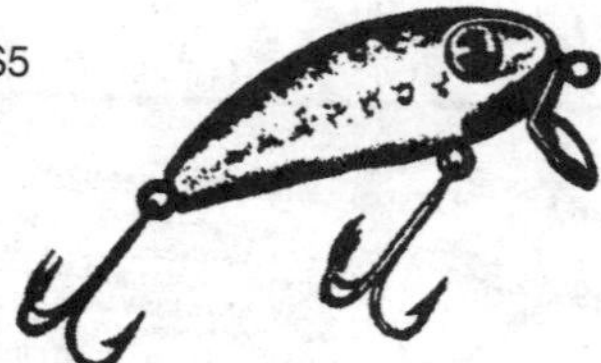

601 SERIES

Length ....1¾ inches
Weight ....⅛ ounce

MIRACLE Trade **MINNOW** Mark

$5

SILVER BELLY PLATE

470W SERIES

Length ....1¾ inches
Weight ....⅝ ounce

NO. 471 W- GOLD PLATED HOOKS (SINKER)

1948
HIJACKER
No. 302 SERIES

$5

EAGLE CLAW "HIJACKER"

Weight ⅝ oz.; length 3½". Rides on surface until retrieved, then dives and swims with a life-like wiggle. Plastic body. 12 assorted colors.

BASSKIL
Trade-Mark
301 SERIES

Length ....3 inches
Weight ....½

$5

IT HAS BEEN ASSUMED THAT W. & McG. QUIT MAKING LURES, SO THEY COULD SELL THEIR HOOKS TO THE OTHER MFG'S.

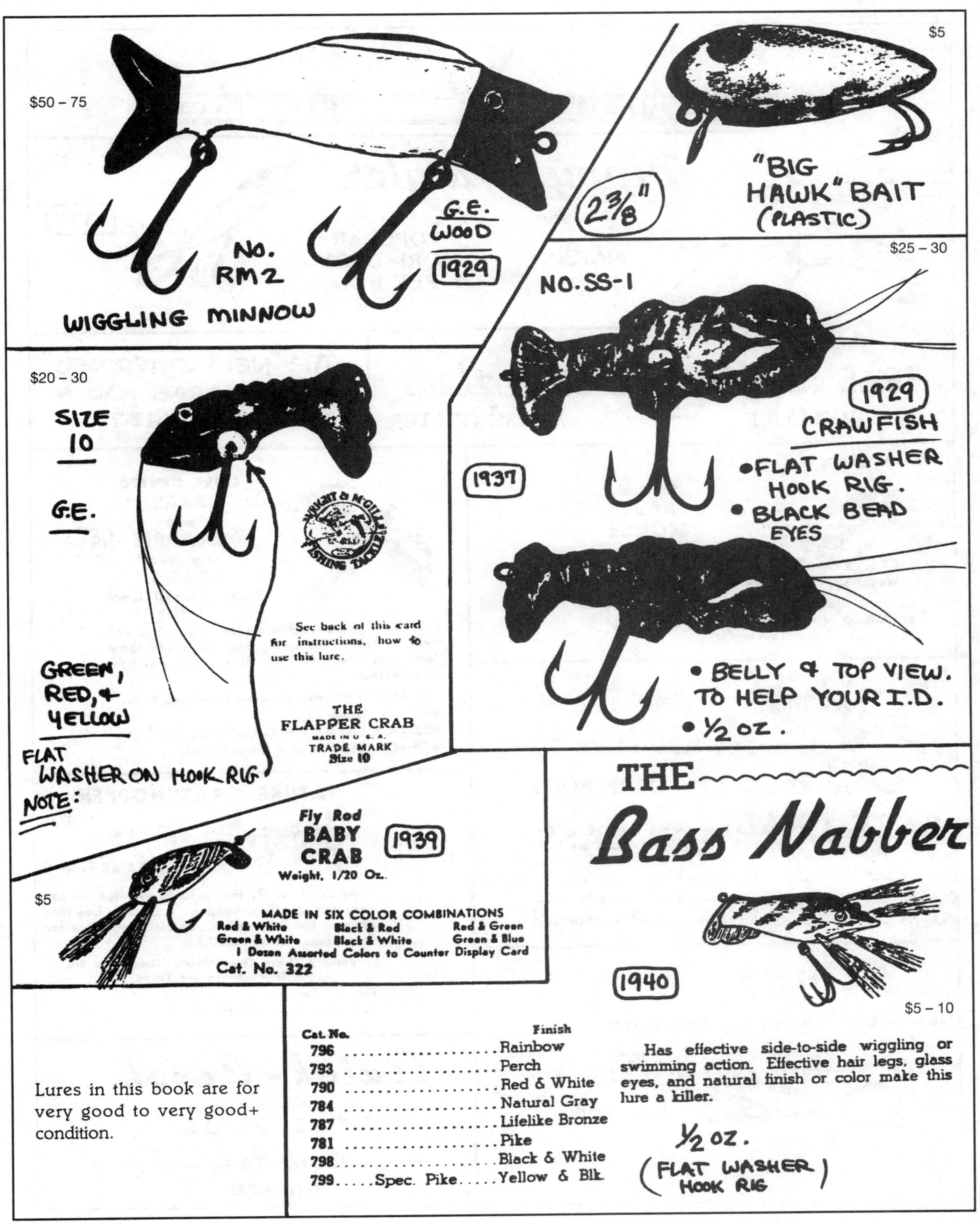
$50 – 75
G.E.
WOOD
1929
NO.
RM2
WIGGLING MINNOW
$5
2 3/8"
"BIG
HAWK" BAIT
(PLASTIC)
$25 – 30
NO. SS-1
1929
CRAWFISH
•FLAT WASHER
HOOK RIG.
•BLACK BEAD
EYES
1937
• BELLY & TOP VIEW.
TO HELP YOUR I.D.
• 1/2 OZ.
$20 – 30
SIZE
10
G.E.
See back of this card for instructions, how to use this lure.
THE
FLAPPER CRAB
MADE IN U. S. A.
TRADE MARK
Size 10
GREEN,
RED, &
YELLOW
FLAT
WASHER ON HOOK RIG
NOTE:
Fly Rod
BABY
CRAB
1939
Weight, 1/20 Oz.
$5
MADE IN SIX COLOR COMBINATIONS
Red & White
Black & Red
Red & Green
Green & White
Black & White
Green & Blue
1 Dozen Assorted Colors to Counter Display Card
Cat. No. 322
THE
Bass Nabber
1940
$5 – 10
Cat. No. Finish
796 .... Rainbow
793 .... Perch
790 .... Red & White
784 .... Natural Gray
787 .... Lifelike Bronze
781 .... Pike
798 .... Black & White
799 .....Spec. Pike..... Yellow & Blk.
Has effective side-to-side wiggling or swimming action. Effective hair legs, glass eyes, and natural finish or color make this lure a killer.
1/2 OZ.
(FLAT WASHER
HOOK RIG)
Lures in this book are for very good to very good+ condition.

WRIGHT & McGILL
FISHING TACKLE

$5

Dippy Wiggler

Trade Mark

NO. 304

POPULAR CORK BODY FLY ROD LURE

(1937)

$5

NO. 303

HERE IS *Peppy Wiggler*

A FLY ROD LURE — Trade Mark — A FISH GETTER

THE "NEW IMPROVED" FLAPPER CRAB HAD A CORK BODY – 1937.

$30 – 40

Fly Rod
BABY MOUSE
For
BASS, TROUT and ALL GAME FISH

Weight 1/20 of an Ounce

No.	Finish
307	Black with White Head . . .
317	Natural finish Silver Gray.

(1939)

$2

CORK CENTER
BASS
and
CRAPPIE
Fly Rod
BUGS
Hand Turned Cork Bodies

(1939)

Wound with attractive colors. Hair wings and tails, twitching line or jiggling rod made these lures very effective. They float and are as light as a feather.

Made in Six Attractive Colors—1 Dozen Lures to Box

No.	Hooks
802	Bass Size on 1/0 Ringed Hook.
804	Crappie Size on 4 Ringed Hook.

$5

FLY ROD LURE

IT FLOATS—CORK BODY

BABY CRAB FOR BASS

Trade Mark

Cat. No. 322 White body, Red head
Cat. No. 323 Green and Red—White underside
Cat. No. 324 Gray and black body—Yellow underside

NATURE GRASSHOPPER

$5

For

ALL GAME FISH

At Last! A Fly that actually imitates the appearance of a Grasshopper. A durable lure that attracts the fish, and is especially effective for Trout, Bass, and all pan fish.

Boxed ½ Dozen, Three Assorted Colors to a Box. Brown, Green and Yellow

No.	Size
927	Size 4, 6, or 8 Hooks

$5

Skippy

New Light-Weight Fly-Rod Lure

Weighs 1/20 Ounce

(1939)

NO. D340

Quick-Catch

Trade Mark

BASS BUGS

Cork-Body

NO. 820

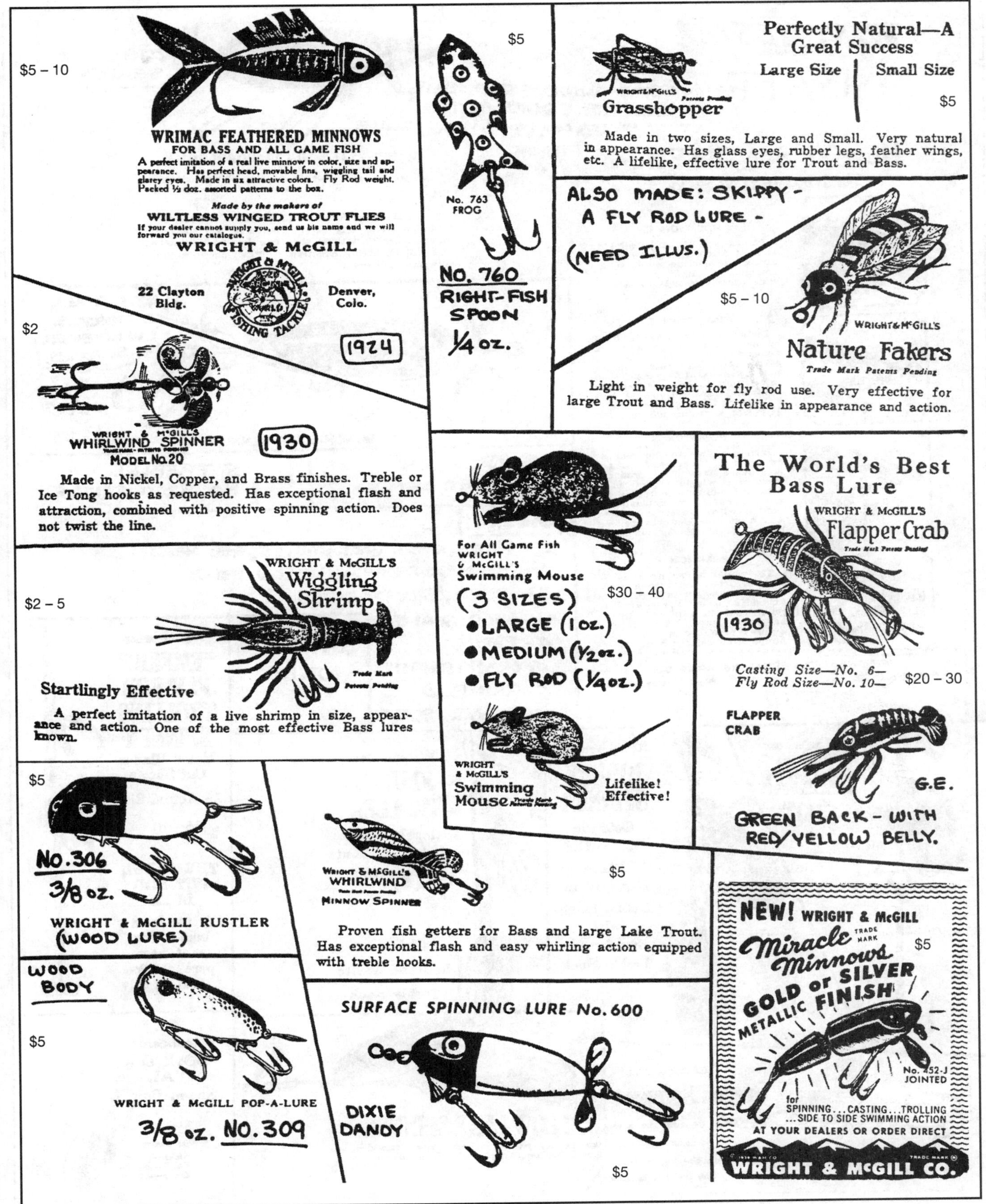
$5 – 10
WRIMAC FEATHERED MINNOWS
FOR BASS AND ALL GAME FISH
A perfect imitation of a real live minnow in color, size and appearance. Has perfect head, movable fins, wiggling tail and glassy eyes. Made in six attractive colors. Fly Rod weight. Packed ½ doz. assorted patterns to the box.
Made by the makers of
WILTLESS WINGED TROUT FLIES
If your dealer cannot supply you, send us his name and we will forward you our catalogue.
WRIGHT & McGILL
22 Clayton Bldg.
Denver, Colo.
1924
$5
No. 763 FROG
NO. 760
RIGHT-FISH SPOON
¼ oz.
Perfectly Natural—A Great Success
Large Size
Small Size
$5
WRIGHT & McGILL'S Grasshopper
Patents Pending
Made in two sizes, Large and Small. Very natural in appearance. Has glass eyes, rubber legs, feather wings, etc. A lifelike, effective lure for Trout and Bass.
ALSO MADE: SKIPPY - A FLY ROD LURE -
(NEED ILLUS.)
$5 – 10
WRIGHT & McGILL'S
Nature Fakers
Trade Mark Patents Pending
Light in weight for fly rod use. Very effective for large Trout and Bass. Lifelike in appearance and action.
$2
WRIGHT & McGILL'S
WHIRLWIND SPINNER
MODEL No. 20
1930
Made in Nickel, Copper, and Brass finishes. Treble or Ice Tong hooks as requested. Has exceptional flash and attraction, combined with positive spinning action. Does not twist the line.
For All Game Fish
WRIGHT & McGILL'S
Swimming Mouse
(3 SIZES)
● LARGE (1 oz.)
● MEDIUM (½ oz.)
● FLY ROD (¼ oz.)
$30 – 40
WRIGHT & McGILL'S
Swimming Mouse
Lifelike! Effective!
The World's Best Bass Lure
WRIGHT & McGILL'S
Flapper Crab
Trade Mark Patents Pending
1930
Casting Size—No. 6—
Fly Rod Size—No. 10—
$20 – 30
FLAPPER CRAB
G.E.
GREEN BACK - WITH RED/YELLOW BELLY.
$2 – 5
WRIGHT & McGILL'S
Wiggling Shrimp
Trade Mark Patents Pending
Startlingly Effective
A perfect imitation of a live shrimp in size, appearance and action. One of the most effective Bass lures known.
$5
NO. 306
3/8 oz.
WRIGHT & McGILL RUSTLER
(WOOD LURE)
WRIGHT & McGILL'S
WHIRLWIND
MINNOW SPINNER
$5
Proven fish getters for Bass and large Lake Trout. Has exceptional flash and easy whirling action equipped with treble hooks.
WOOD BODY
$5
WRIGHT & McGILL POP-A-LURE
3/8 oz. NO. 309
SURFACE SPINNING LURE No. 600
DIXIE DANDY
$5
NEW! WRIGHT & McGILL
Miracle Minnows
TRADE MARK
$5
GOLD or SILVER
METALLIC FINISH
No. 452-J
JOINTED
for SPINNING...CASTING...TROLLING
...SIDE TO SIDE SWIMMING ACTION
AT YOUR DEALERS OR ORDER DIRECT
WRIGHT & McGILL CO.

WINCHESTER TRADE MARK

BAIT

NOTE
• SOME WINCHESTER BAITS HAD THE EQUIV. OF THE SHAKESPEARE LITHO SCALE FINISH.

No. 9200 SERIES

$50 – 75

WINCHESTER MULTI-WOBBLER

By slight adjustments of the planes of this bait it can be made to dive, dart or wobble.

There are four principal adjustments. See directions on back. A little experience will disclose many other variations that can be made readily and will be highly effective. When not in action this bait will float.

How To Set The Planes

ON THE MULTI-WOBBLER

POSITION 1.

Planes set about parallel to body of bait. This gives a deep diving and darting motion which combines a slight roll with a wide dart from side to side.

POSITION 2.

Incline planes towards front of bait to make an angle of about 60 degrees with the body of the bait. This results in the bait traveling at less depth than in position 1 and gives an entirely different action—the bait quivers and jumps from side to side like a frightened minnow.

POSITION 3.

Incline planes to the rear at angle of 75 degrees from the lengthwise axis. This produces a surface wiggle typical of a wounded minnow, scurrying for shallow water. Particularly effective when water is smooth and a surface disturbance can be seen from considerable depth.

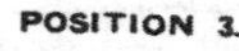

POSITION 4.

Tip planes at an angle of 45 degrees from lengthwise axis This gives a bait of high value for days when the water is rough and you want to keep the bait on surface. Bait throws a spray to either side and also jumps from side to side.

WINCHESTER REPEATING ARMS CO.
Form No. C-543. New Haven, Conn.

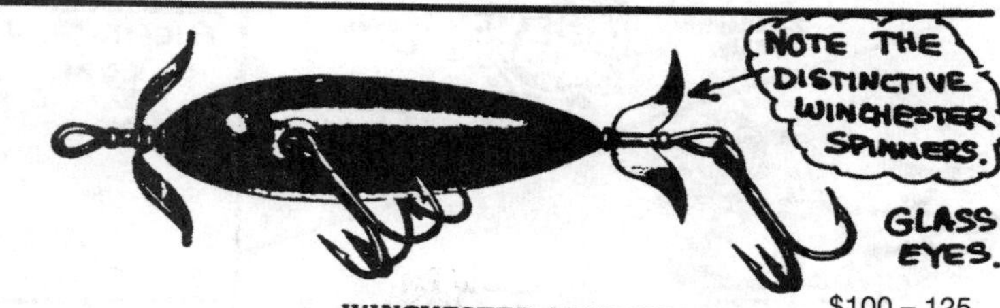
NOTE THE DISTINCTIVE WINCHESTER SPINNERS.
GLASS EYES.

WINCHESTER MINNOW

$100 – 125

3 TREBLES
• NO. 9010 SERIES

5 TREBLES
• NO. 9210 SERIES

COLORS:
0 - WHITE, GREEN BACK STRIPES, RED HEAD.
1 - GREEN/GOLD BACK, YELLOW BELLY.
2 - GREEN/SILVER SIDES
3 - GOLD SCALE
4 - RED
5 - CRACKLEBACK
6 - RAINBOW
7 - SILVER SCALE

1920'S ONLY

Winchester
"EMERIC" FLY ROD TROLLING SPINNER
Has 3 Blades Cut Shows
½ Actual Size

$5 – 10

THE IDEAL FLY ROD LURE
For use from a boat— for trout, bass, perch, pickerel, etc.

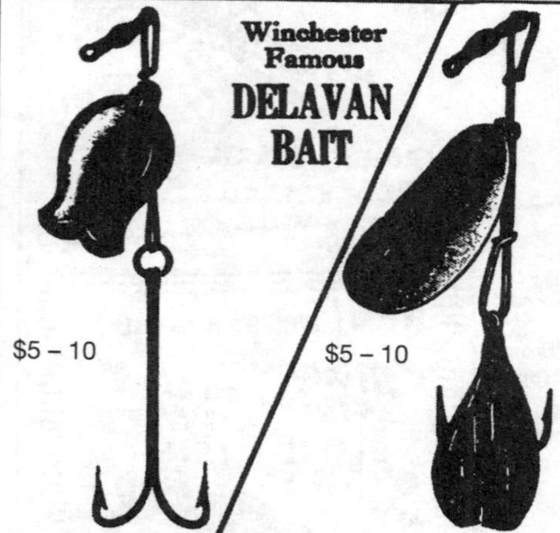

Winchester Famous
DELAVAN BAIT

$5 – 10

Winchester
KIDNEY SPINNER
Gets the BIG ONES
Blade 1⅛x9/16 in.
Nickel finish with Feathered Treble Hook

$5 – 10

Winchester
FLUTED TROLLER
Nickel Convex
Nickel and Red Concave

$5 – 10

Red and White Treble Hook

Winchester
Oregon Spinners
One of the most popular of baits.
Size 20—2¼ in. Blade
Size 00—3¼ in. Blade

Nickel Finish Double Hook

$5 – 10

WILLOW LEAF SPINNER
One of the greatest spinners ever designed—Small, Medium, Large, Extra Large Sizes.

$5 – 10

Winchester
SOUND OVAL Spoon Bait

Nickel Finish
No. 1—1⅞ in.
No. 2—2¼ in.
No. 3—2¾ in.

$5

WINCHESTER-(CONT.)

THEY MADE A LINE OF TACKLE —INCLUDING REELS, FOR A SHORT TIME IN THE 1920'S. THESE ITEMS ARE SOUGHT AFTER BY BOTH TACKLE AND WINCHESTER COLLECTORS. THEY ALSO MADE ICE SKATES, KNIVES, LANTERNS, ETC. WHEN THE DEPRESSION HIT—THEY SOLD OUT ALL THEIR "SIDE-LINES."

Winchester
SEATTLE TROUT SPOONS
Every Fisherman knows what a great killer this bait is on big fish 1 size only—1⅞x6 inches.
Nickel Finish

$5

Winchester
LAKE TAHOE SPOONS
Famous for its big fish catching abilities. Good for bass, lake trout, pike, pickerel, muskies and all salt water fishing. One size only—3⅝x6 inches. Nickel finish.

$5

Winchester
WILLOW LEAF TROLLER
3 Blade
14" long

$5 – 10

5 Blade
23" long

Nickel Blades with snap fasteners.
A Real Fish Getter

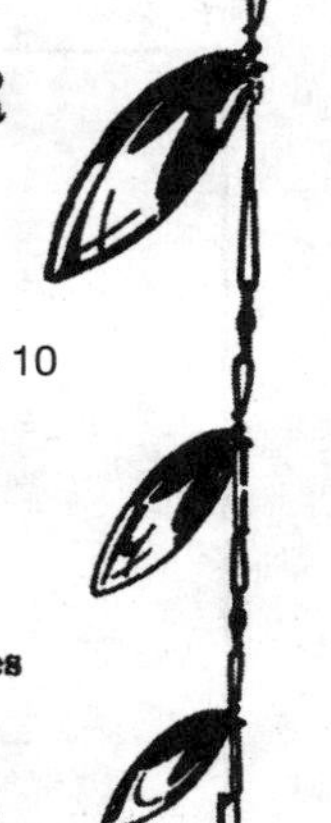

ALSO MADE IN A MUSKY SIZE

$10 – 20

1915

"JIM-DANDY" FISH BAIT

The 1915 Sensation

Has Startled the Whole Country

The wobbling, wiggling, laboring motion of "Jim Dandy" hypnotizes fish and captivates fishermen. Regardless of what luck you have had—no matter what kind of bait or equipment is your present hobby—no matter how skeptical you are—no matter if you have been "stung" a hundred times and absolutely "bait wise"—*Jim Dandy Fish Bait* will revolutionize your fishing.

Thousands upon thousands of fishermen have adopted Jim Dandy, and unanimously—to a man—they agree that it is the World's Greatest Fish Bait. *Go to your Dealer* and pay him for one of these baits and *do it today* if you want more fish and better sport.

If your dealer can't supply you, order from us direct.

"JIM-DANDY"

See that Notch and Concave Face

DEALERS
Write for our big special offer — 3 "JIM DANDY" baits absolutely FREE.

2¼"

• Regular Size
• Muscallonge Size

WISE SPORTSMAN'S SUPPLY CO.
Dept. D. 22 W. Jackson, Chicago

2 SIZES

COLORS: (ALL WHITE) NO.101 — (RED FACE/WHITE) NO.102 — (GREEN SPOTTED) NO.103 (FROG)

I DON'T THINK THE WORTH PLUGS ARE WORTH MUCH! →

$5 THE WORTH PLUG. 2½"

WORTH FLY ROD PLUG 1½" NO. 707

$5

$5 – 10

WHIR-LI-GIG 1947 LURE.

-WOOD

WOODS & WATERS-VICKSBURG, MICH

Have fun, collect old fishing tackle items.

LATER BECAME THE YAKIMA BAIT CO. GRANGER WASH.

NOTE: DO NOT CONFUSE THIS WORDEN WITH "BUCKTAIL" WORDEN-WHO WAS IN THE EARLY 1900'S AND PART OF THE START OF THE SO. BEND COMPANY.

1943

WORDEN'S BONEFISH

1934

FLYING LURES

PATENTS PENDING

$5

New Fly-Rod Lures
that flutter and fly real as life. Variety of colors in four sizes. Trout, 40c each, three for $1. Bass, 50c each three for $1.25. Wholesalers and dealers wanted. Free circulars. Satisfaction guaranteed. Worden Floating Spinner Company, Granger, Washington.

"W" Misc.

One of the past writings about old plugs mentioned a Winchester Mouse bait. I have never heard of or seen such a bait.

Winchester went into receivership in 1929, and sold off their sidelines including tackle, so it's easy to date the age of their baits. It is not known at this time whether they made the baits, or had them made for them by others.

One member has seen the Shakespeare patented scale finish on a Winchester 5 hooker minnow, which might give us a clue.

....

There is another, lesser known "Winchester" - that is the Winchester Bait & Mfg. Co. Winchester, Ind. They made a line called the "Lucky Hit" baits. The No. 1940 Diving Beauty Bait is shown below. They also made the jointed diving beauty, and the earliest known date on these baits is 1931. I believe they also made a cheapo bait like the Heddon 100 with 2 side trebles and a tail treble. It was a No. 9014 and had Winchester stamped on the front prop. There was no rear prop, and was blended green to white color. Screw eye hook rig.

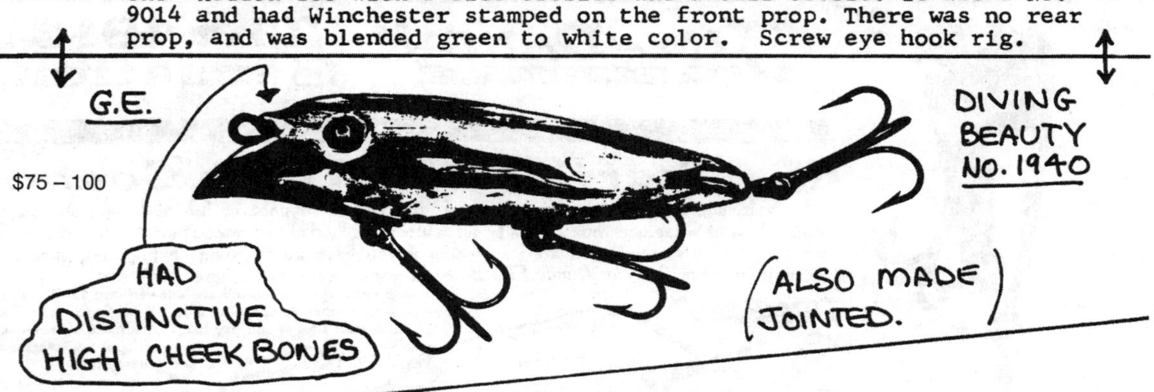

G.E.

$75 – 100

HAD DISTINCTIVE HIGH CHEEK BONES

DIVING BEAUTY NO. 1940

(ALSO MADE JOINTED.)

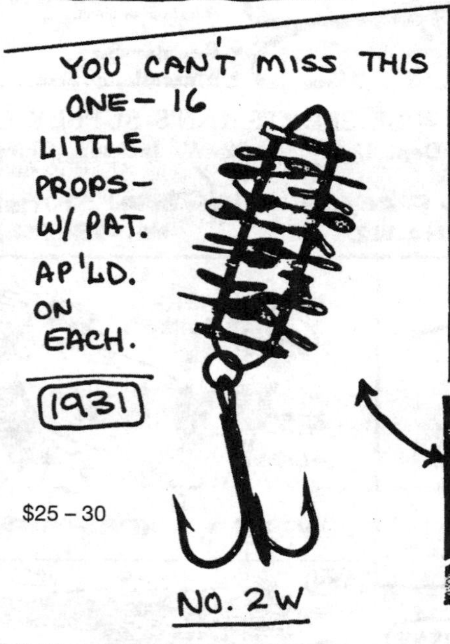

YOU CAN'T MISS THIS ONE – 16 LITTLE PROPS – W/ PAT. AP'LD. ON EACH.

1931

$25 – 30

NO. 2W

WATCH'EM SMACK OLE SHRIMP-BACK!

HE'S RESISTLESS! • RUSTLESS! • NON-SHEDDIN'! USE WITH OR WITHOUT SPINNER — HOOK IS FLAT EYED.

1951

$2

Note the plastic BODY

Streamers and shrimp-back hackle are hardened right into body! Note Z Nickel rustless hook! And, above all, note how the mackerel, stripers, weaks, blues, tarpon, pollock, snook, etc. fall for it!

The WAPSI CO. DEPT. 25 INDEPENDENCE, IOWA direct if not available locally. Dealers write

SPEED BAIT

MAKES 'EM BITE QUICK

THE only bait constructed scientifically! For trolling, casting, dipping. 3 sizes—trout (casting), bass, muskies. Tests prove Speed Bait, with its 16 flashing spinners, effective where others fail. Positively noisy. Tested to maximum pulls. Silver or copper. Trout or bass, $1.00, musky, $1.50. Dealers—*Write for Offer*

WALTON PRODUCTS CO., 77 South Ave., Rochester, N.Y.

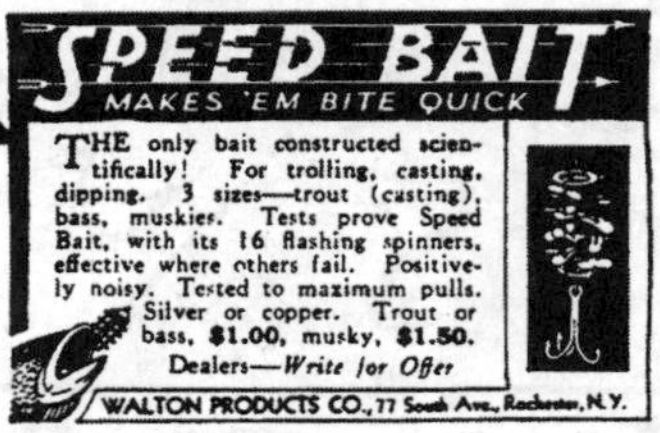

WALTON PRODUCTS 77 SOUTH AVE. ROCHESTER, N.Y.

I DON'T THINK THIS IS THE LEGENDARY ISSAC WALTON.

PLASTIC

(ACTUAL SIZE)

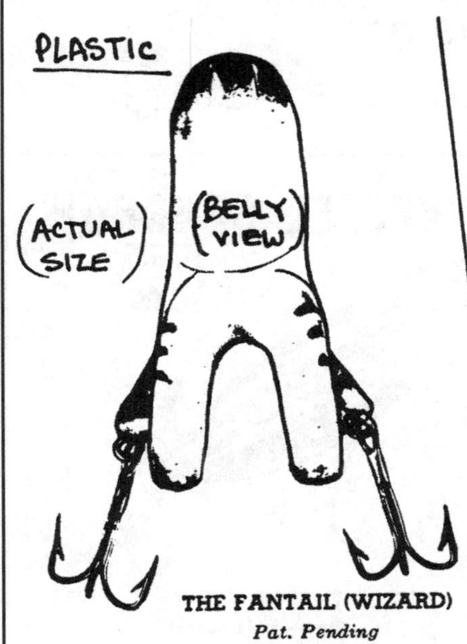
(BELLY VIEW)

THE FANTAIL (WIZARD)

Pat. Pending

WIZARD LURE MFG. CO.
BOX 5
GAMBIER, OHIO

- WOOD BODY
- 3 SINGLE HOOKS
- 40'S-50'S
- NO EYES

Twirling Twirp

ORIGINAL

3 BLADE

Revolving Lure

WATT TACKLE CO.
Manufacturer

8500 NORTHLAWN—DETROIT 4, MICH.

$5

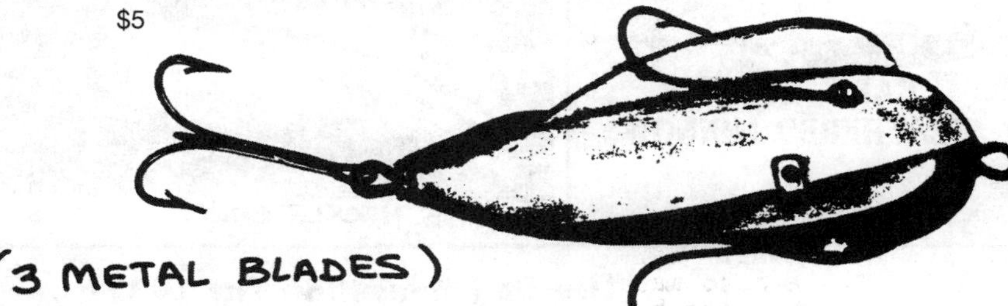

(3 METAL BLADES)

$5

1927

J. L. WILCOX

"CLOTHES PIN BAIT"

- 3 COLOR PAINTED EYE- RED/YELLOW/BLACK
- YELLOW HEAD W/ RED BACK & WHITE BELLY.

ROY WHITEHEAD

MANUFACTURER OF FINE PLUGS FOR SALT WATER GAME FISH

$5

1947

FINISHES:
Blue Mullet
Green Mullet
Yellobelly
Mackerel
Shiner
Frost Fish
Silver Herring
Niteswimmer
Red and White

Originator of famous TIDERUNNER SLAPTAIL PLUG, Genuine Massachusetts Popping Plugs (1946 Sensation!), SLAPTAIL POPPING PLUGS.

Word to the wise, order now, guaranteed satisfaction or money back, $2.00 each, 4 for $7.00

ROY WHITEHEAD 2899 Kingsbridge Ter. BRONX, NEW YORK

"THE TIDEWATER SLAPTAIL PLUG."

$30 – 50+

Acts Like a Live Minnow

The Wiggle Tail is the only artificial minnow that faithfully reproduces the motions of a live one. Tail always in motion. Better than live minnows because it's always "alive." Costs less. No trouble. Lasts for years. Get one quick. $1 postpaid—and money back if not satisfied.

THE WIGGLE TAIL MINNOW COMPANY
Dept C, 162 W. Canfield Avenue, Detroit, Michigan

THIS IS A 1912 BAIT! (NEED AN ACTUAL ILLUS.)

$20 – 30

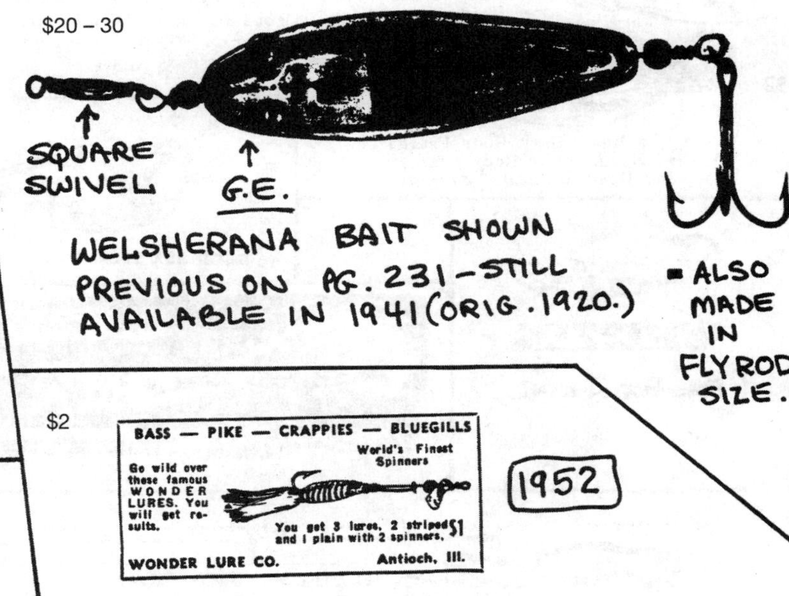
SQUARE SWIVEL
G.E.
BASS — PIKE — CRAPPIES — BLUEGILLS
World's Finest Spinners
Go wild over these famous WONDER LURES. You will get results.
You get 3 lures, 2 striped and 1 plain with 2 spinners. $1
WONDER LURE CO. Antioch, Ill.

WELSHERANA BAIT SHOWN PREVIOUS ON PG. 231-STILL AVAILABLE IN 1941 (ORIG. 1920.)

- ALSO MADE IN FLYROD SIZE.

$2

1952

CISCO KID LURES MADE BY WALLSTEN TACKLE CHICAGO - SINCE 50'S (NOT COLLECTIBLE)

The Weezel Bait Company

MANUFACTURERS

3506 Columbia Parkway — Cincinnati 26, Ohio, U. S. A.

FLY ROD- 1/20 oz.

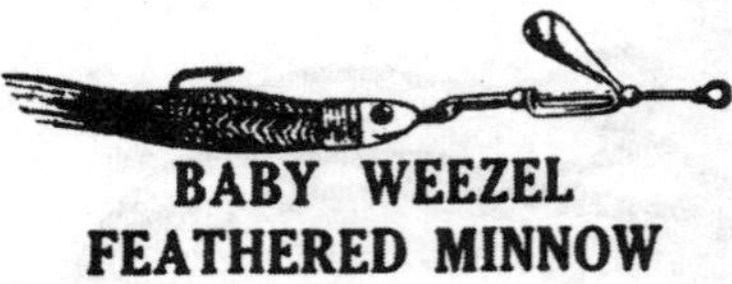

BABY WEEZEL FEATHERED MINNOW

$2

HACKLE 5/8 oz.

(WHITE HACKLE ONLY)

$2

WEEZEL SPARROW

NEW 1948

$10 – 15

1/2 oz.

$2

MEDAL-MINNOW

The Bait Sensation For 1937 . . .

WESSNER'S FEATHERED MINNOW WEEZEL

1935

USING THE WOBBLER

2 Lures for the Price of One

Choice of 4 Color Combinations

$2

USING THE SPINNER

Oh, Boy . . . What a Lure! That's What the Users of the Weezel Say . . . And You Get 2 Lures for the Price of 1.

The Weezel is an original and genuine spinning, wobbling feathered minnow lure. Supplied with a spinner and wiggle disc, giving the fisherman two distinctive baits, both with weed guard attached. Best grade fancy feathers tied to head by special process, will not pull loose or out. Imported hollow point hooks used.

When the fish don't bite on ordinary lures, use a Weezel and get them.

Weight 5/8 oz. Size 3/0 Hook.

No.	Color Head	Color Feathers
A-WW1	Red	Black, White Spotted....
A-WW3	Red	Gray with White Tail....
A-WW5	Red	All White..............
A-WW9	Red	Brown with White Tail..

1ST USED HAIR/BUCK-TAIL IN 1941.

The Pioneer Manufacturers of THE FAMOUS REX SPOON

Introduce the new

Sensational

WEEZEL SPARROW

Manufactured under U.S. Patent Number 2,365,502.

A revolutionary new idea in top water plugs. It looks and acts like a wounded sparrow fluttering on the surface of the water. This is a proven fish getter and made its record in five years of experiment and testing, from Florida to Canada. Built of the best possible materials, covered with brown Mallard feathers. Weight 1/2 oz. Another champion in the famous line of Weezel lures.

1 OZ.

WEEZEL MUSKIE — SALT WATER
Showing use of Spinner and Wiggle Disc. Weight 1 Oz. Length 9" With Spinner.

WEESNER'S MUSKIE WEEZEL

Results with this lure were very good in 1939. Weighs slightly over 1 ounce. Positive weed guard. 8/0 hook. Three colors:

$2

1939

M2—Silver Head, Gray Body Feathers..
M5—Red Head, White Body Feathers...
M11—Red Head, Guinea Body Feathers.

$2

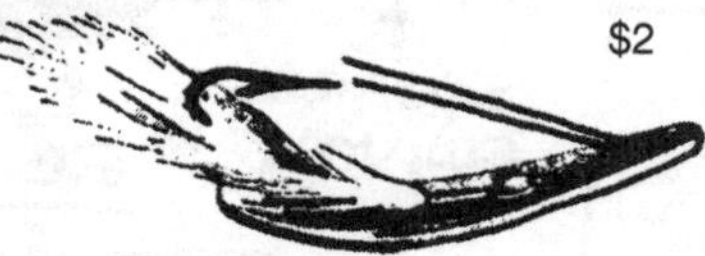

JUNIOR REX SPOON wgt. 1/4 oz.

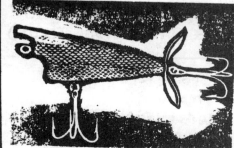

$2

WHIZZER

(FOR PORK RIND)

Rex Spoon

7/8 oz. = 4" LENGTH = STAINESS STEEL

$2

BOPPER

1/2 oz.

$5

$2

7 1/2"

FLY Rod WEEZEL

WEEZEL STRIPER (FOR WHITE BASS)

Weller
Classic
Minnow

ERWIN WELLER COMPANY
Sioux City, Iowa

STILL MORE THRILLS

MASTER BAITS WITH PLENTY OF NATURAL ACTION
A JUICY LOOKING MEAL FOR ANY GAME FISH

SEMI-SURFACE
See All Your Strikes

BLUE DEVIL (BLUE HEAD)

FINISHES: The "Classic" is made in four finishes at present — PIKO, PERCH, CHUB, and RED DEVIL (Red Head, White Body).

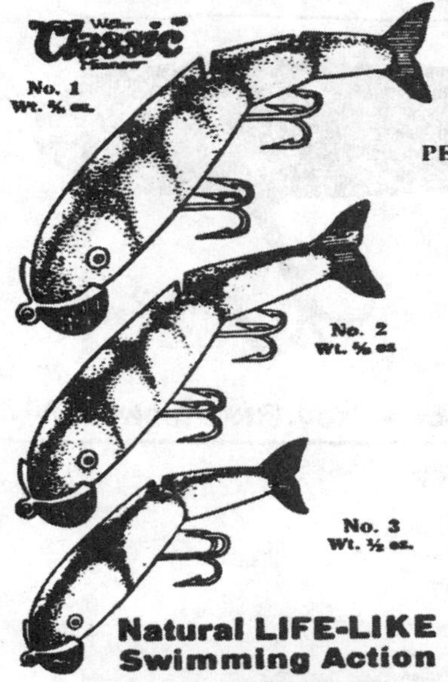
Weller
Classic
Minnow
No. 1
Wt. ⅝ oz.
No. 2
Wt. ⅝ oz.
No. 3
Wt. ½ oz.

Natural LIFE-LIKE Swimming Action

—1925— RUBBER OR FEATHER TAIL

(3 SIZES)

$10 – 25

NEW! NEW!

Weller "MOUSE"

Just what you have been wishing for!

—A BAIT THAT REALLY LOOKS AND ACTS LIKE A MOUSE!

Weighs ⅓ Ounce

Action? Oh Boy!

1928

$10 – 20

It is a wiggly, lively-acting Mouse, and above all, it has the feature that all ardent fishermen have wished for—a real, honest-to-goodness, wiggly, waving, "Feather Tail." NO OTHER BAIT HAS THIS FEATURE. A double hook is hidden among the feathers.

This "Weller Mouse" acts so natural, waves the feather tail so life-like, that all game fish strike is fiercely, including Bass, Pike, Pickerel, Muskies, Crappies and large trout.

It is a semi-surface bait, a wonderful lure for casting with light tackle and catches fish when most other baits fail to get them. In fact, this "Weller Mouse" is a fitting companion to our famous "Classic" Minnow lures and every angler should have one or more in his tackle box.

FINISHES: Gray, Red and White, All White with Pink Eyes, and All Black.

Note: On special order, these baits can be fitted with single hook instead of the regular double hook. Also supplied in a strictly "Surface" bait which stays on top of the water when used with light tackle. Unless otherwise specified, we ship the regular semi-surface style, with double hook.

THE WEBER CO.
STEVENS POINT, WIS.

$2

WEBER LIFE-LIKE PLUGAKLE
New hair and feather image of large wood lures yet airy light for Fly Rod. Use wet or on surface. White or fawn body, red or black head, [illegible] in. with size 1/0 hook.

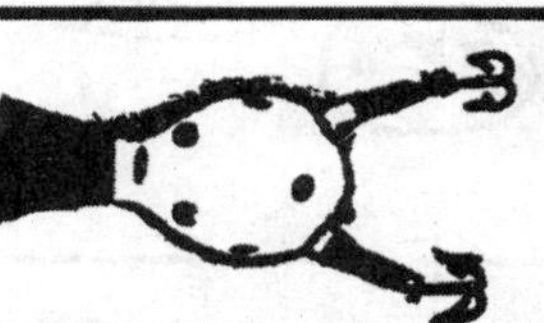

WEBER FLIP-FROG

$5

$2

Sensational New Spinning Lure . . . by
Weber
Big Shot
wt. ¼ oz.
FOR FRESH OR SALT WATER FISHING
INDESTRUCTIBLE . . . made of durable TENITE II plastic . . .

(1954)

$5

Weber
STEVENS POINT
"SN2"
SPINNING LURE
It Floats.. Dives.. Swims!
Rigged backward, swims backward . . . but there's nothing backward about the way it catches fish. Rides high at rest . . . squirms like a demon on retrieve. Indestructible Tenite II body . . . 12 patterns . . . gold treble hook.
The Weber Lifelike Fly Co., Stevens Point, Wis.

$5

NO. WSG — STREAMER
Spinning Lure — 85¢
NO. SLG — SHINERAKLE
Spinning Lure — 85¢
THE WEBER LIFELIKE FLY CO. Stevens Point, Wis.
if Weber makes it a fish takes it

$5

NO 1.
Black

Bob Becker's
Sensational
"POP-N-WIGL"
Fly Rod Lure

A Wonderful Wiggler **Weller Ozark Minnow** No. 6 Weight ½ oz.

$10 – 15

G.E.
2½"

This little bait is a marvel for action—it was originally designed for Small Mouth Bass Fishing in the lakes and streams of the Ozarks but has since then proven itself a sure killer for all kinds of game fish including Crappies, Bass, Pike, Pickerel and large trout.

It is well constructed and beautifully finished. Wiggles all the time, at any speed, slow or fast. It sinks slowly when at rest and swims several feet under water when reeling. Length of bait body, 2½ inches.

No. 6 Series—

No. 640 Brown Piko
No. 641 Green Piko
No. 642 Perch
No. 643 Chub
No. 644 Red and White
No. 645 Yellow, Black Head
No. 648 Black, White Head

ERWIN WELLER COMPANY

SIOUX CITY, IOWA

WELLER WOULD REPLACE THE RUBBER TAIL FOR 15¢ IF YOU MAILED THE BAIT BACK TO THEM.
G.E.
NO.2

$10 – 20

MOST WELLERS YOU FIND TODAY- NEED TAILS!

SIMPLEX WIGGLER

CATCHES

Bass, Pike, Pickerel and Other Game Fish

A good bait of proven quality, strong and well finished. For casting or trolling. Floats when at rest.

No. 1040 Brown Piko
No. 1041 Green Piko
No. 1042 Perch
No. 1043 Chub
No. 1044 White-Red Head
No. 1045 Yellow-Black Head
No. 1048 Black-White Head

$10 – 20

G.E.
3¼"
NO. 10

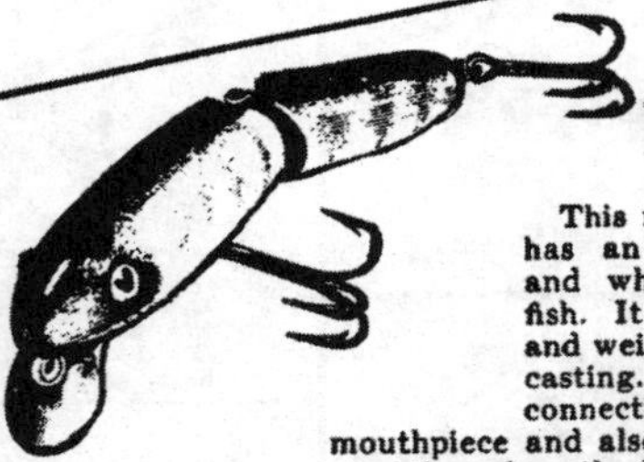

NEW!!

G.E.

This new "Classic" Minnow has an entirely new action and what a killer on game fish. It is just the right size and weight for good all 'round casting. The jointed feature in connection with this new mouthpiece and also a new balanced construction gives the bait a real wiggle that fish can't resist. Floats when at rest but swims under water when reeling. Beautiful finishes.

No. 4 Series—

No. 440 Brown Piko. No. 441 Green Piko. No. 442 Perch. No. 443 Chub. No. 444 Red and White

$10 – 20

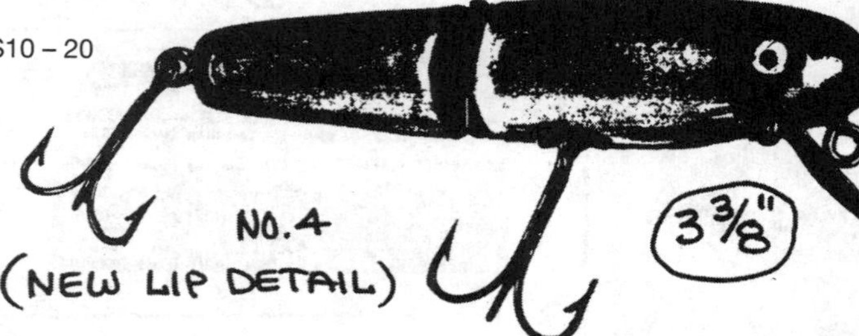
NO.4
(NEW LIP DETAIL)
3⅜"

$10 – 20

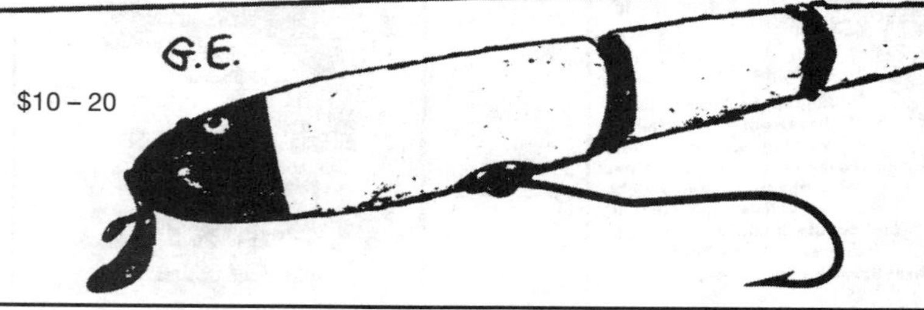
G.E.

WELLER CLASSIC -(SINGLE HOOK MODEL)- "RED DEVIL" COLOR = RH AND RED IN EACH JOINT. "BLUE DEVIL" ALSO.

—*OL' SKIPPER

(1946 – 1953)

•LUCKY TAIL GRAN' POPPA IS SERIES 1000.

WOODEN BAITS WITH PLASTIC COATING.

Lucky Tail JOINTED-WOBBLER

A special jointed design — with all of the Exclusive WOBBLER features . . . . $1.40 each

$5

ALSO AVAILABLE —
LEG "Jointed-Wobbler" (no tail or hackle) .
PLAIN "Jointed-Wobbler" (no tail or legs) .

NO. 600

The Streamer "POPPA"

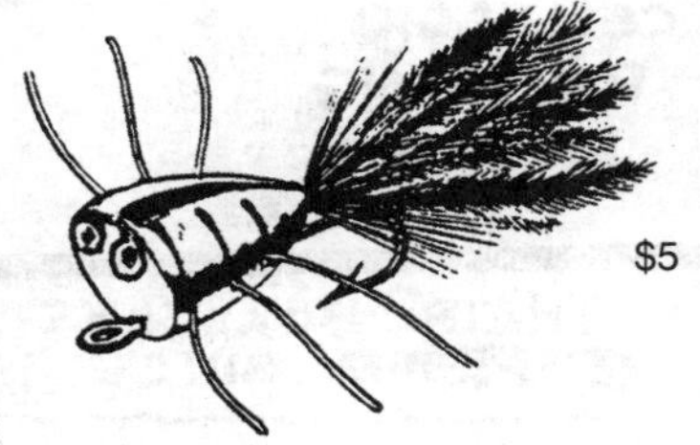

$5

$5

the Lucky Tail WOBBLER

KING SIZE

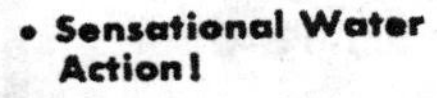

- Sensational Water Action!
- The Proven Lucky Tail!
- Twitching Rubber Legs!
- 6 "Fish-luscious" Colors!
- "DIP-KOTE" Plastic Finish!

King Size WOBBLER is also available in two other models:

1. The Leg WOBBLER—with the twitching, life-like rubber legs . . .
2. The Plain WOBBLER—the conventional type plug—Has the DIP-KOTE plastic finish and the WOBBLER Gravity-Balance.

Lucky Tail "POPPA"

NO. 500

$5

Lucky Bug Plug

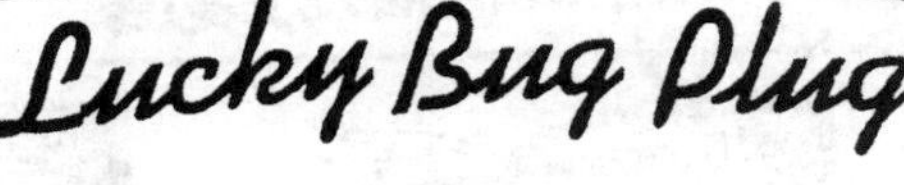

$5

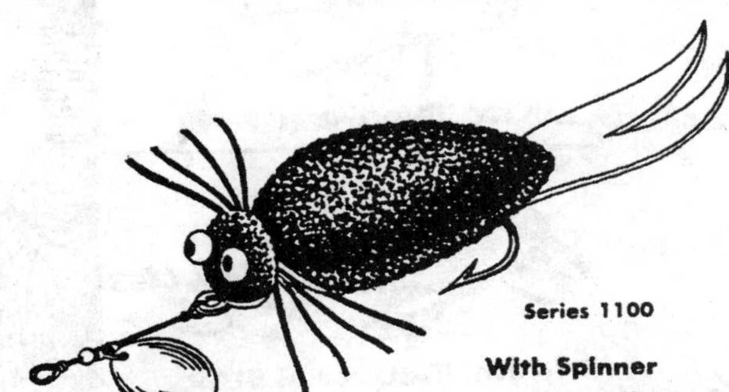

Series 1100

With Spinner
Without Spinner

The Lucky Bug

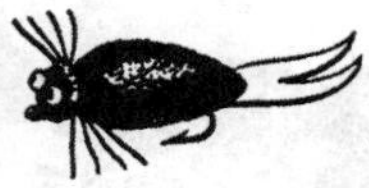

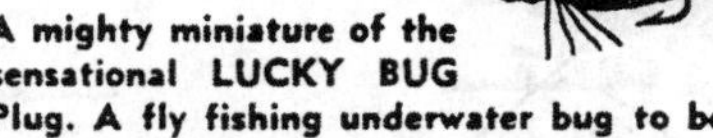

A mighty miniature of the sensational LUCKY BUG Plug. A fly fishing underwater bug to be used with or without a spinner. A luscious lure for all bug loving game fish. Comes in 4 body colors.

$5

201 Red
202 Black
203 Gray
204 Cream

Sizes 1 - 1/0 - 2/0

Sizes 4 6

PERCY WADHAMS NATURE BAITS

TROUT

SMELT

A series of artificial lures which are a most life-like imitation of the fish they represent. They are practically indestructible, as the colors cannot be scratched or rubbed off. The weight has been carefully considered and varies according to size. The lighter the weight used the more natural the motion in the water. They are direct copies from "nature" and will be found a very attractive bait for trout and black bass. Made in five patterns: gudgeon, smelt, trout, dace and goldfish.

No. 1½. Percy Wadhams, for trout, 1½ in.
No. 2. Percy Wadhams, for trout, 2 in....
No. 3. Percy Wadhams, for trout, 3 in....

CELLULOID (1920'S)

Percy Wadham's Nature Baits

GUDGEON

TROUT

DACE

SMELT

NATURE BAITS

The most natural ever made. Very light, transparent and colored perfectly true to life, colors are on the inside, practically indestructible. In species Trout and Smelt.

1	2	3	4	5
1½	2	2½	3	3½ inches

6 SIZES

SMALLEST IS THE "TIT-BIT" – 1¼" (1-SMALL TREBLE) CELLULOID REVOLVING MINNOW.

– GUDGEON
– TROUT
– DACE
– SMELT

$5

THEIR BOX SAYS THEY'VE BEEN CRAFTSMEN SINCE 1889!

(WOOD)

WYNNE PRECISION CO.

$5

2¼" NO. 1300

LUCKY TAIL WOBBLER "CHUBBY"

$5

LUCKY TAIL JOINTED WOBBLER

$5

LUCKY TAIL GRAN' POPPA

$5

RUBBER LEGS

SPINNA-TAIL WOBBLER
(ALL HAD RUBBER LEG FEELERS)

■ PLASTIC
■ SINKER

$5 – 10

ACTUAL SIZE

THE NEW CRAB CRAWLER

INDESTRUCTIBLE INDISPENSABLE

ED. WOOD BAIT

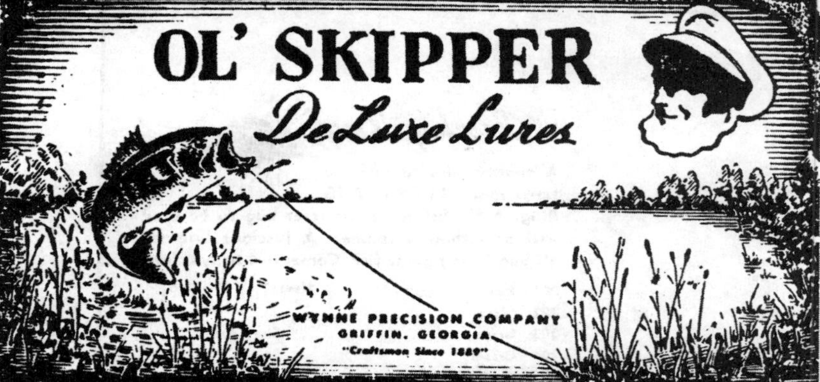
OL' SKIPPER
DeLuxe Lures
WYNNE PRECISION COMPANY
GRIFFIN, GEORGIA
"Craftsmen Since 1889"

$5 – 10

1936

The WEED QUEEN is a non-floating lure, a little heavier to give you more distance and accuracy. When the fish strikes, two spring hooks release with double the spread of a three-prong hook.

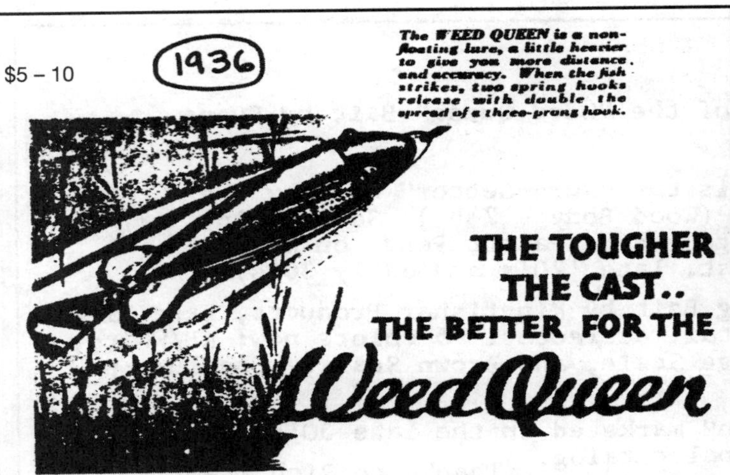
THE TOUGHER
THE CAST..
THE BETTER FOR THE
Weed Queen

The new concealed hook bait that you can cast into the toughest and most likely spots where the "big ones" are hiding, with no fear of catching a snag. Cast with confidence over logs and sticks, through weeds, grass, mud and all kinds of tangles; and the WEED QUEEN will slip through like an eel and return to you minus the souvenirs.

The WEED QUEEN is a combination spoon and plug that's a real fish getter! It comes in six popular colors of Pearl, Perch, Mullet, Pike, Frog, and Red Head.

The ideal all-purpose bait for BASS, PIKE, PICKEREL, MUSKIE, and LARGE TROUT

EVANS WALTON CO.
DETROIT, MICHIGAN

Catch Fish Day or Night With
Will-O'-the Wisp (PLASTIC)

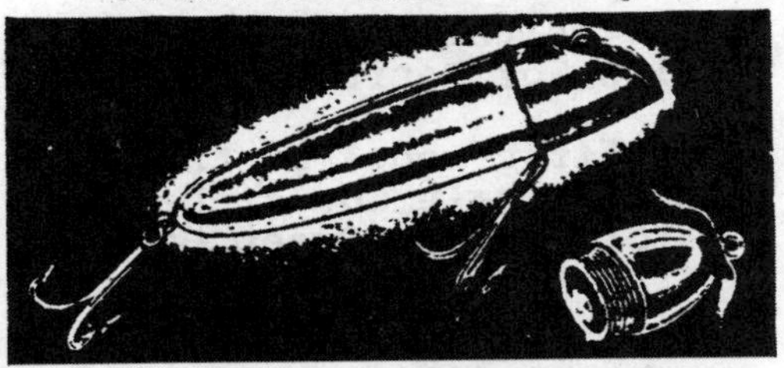

Completely Illuminated ELECTRIC BAIT for Trolling or Casting

Heads and bodies interchangeable, without tools. You simply unscrew one head and replace it with another of the type and color you wish. Lighted by a tiny electric bulb which glows brightly through a body of colorful translucent material, completely illuminating the lure. By admitting varying amounts of water into its body-chamber, you can fish at any level you wish. The lighting unit in this bait consists of a standard flashlight bulb and fountain pen size battery. One of these batteries costing 5c lasts up to 3 hours if used intermittently, or about 45 minutes if used continuously. (Complete with 1 head.)

No. 101—Red and White Wobble Head Style..............
No. 102—Red and White Spinning Head Style ....
No. 133—Extra black head only. Wobble style
No. 134—Extra black head only. Spinning style

$5 – 10

JUST RIGHT

ARTIFICIAL MINNOW

Great Killer for Bass and Pickerel

Beautifully enameled in attractive colors.

1911

$20 – 50

H. G. WRIGHT

26 W. Washington St., Chicago, Ill.

CLINTON WILT MFG. CO.
SPRINGFIELD, MO.

$100 – 150

PATENT APPLIED FOR: AUG. 26, 1911.

PATENTED SEPT. 16, 1913.

NO. 70 The Little Wonder Bait. 2⅛"

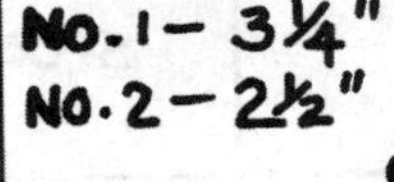
No. 1 – 3¼"
No. 2 – 2½"

$20 – 40

"WESTCHESTER KING"

Wooden casting bait with large spinner at head that revolves; the bait does not revolve. Furnished either yellow, mouse colored or white, single or treble hooks.
No. 1 - 3¼ inches
No. 2 - 2½ inches

(SEE DONALY)

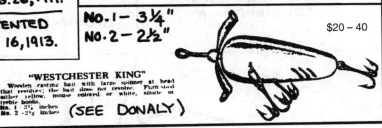

NO. 50 The Champion Bait. 3¼"

$150 – 200

COLORS

1 – WHITE/RED STRIPES
3 – ORANGE/RED STRIPES
5 – GOLD/RED STRIPES
7 – WHITE/GREEN STRIPES
9 – ORANGE/GREEN STRIPES
11 – GOLD/GREEN STRIPES
13 – RED/GREEN STRIPES
15 – GREEN/ORANGE STRIPES

"Water Witch"

A deadly lure for trout, salmon, pike, etc., and suitable for river, sea or lake. It is composed of a series of graduated metal balls, each a separate unit, revolving on a single metal bar running through the center of the bait. The fins, or head of the bait, spin quite separately from the body, which is a distinct innovation as compared with other patterns now offered to the public. Supplied in gold only.

Size bodies	1	2	3	4
Length, inches	1¼	1½	2	2½

No. 2095—

$5

FULL SIZE
NO. 2095

W - Misc.

Here is the possible history of the "Weed Queen" Bait by Evans Walton of Detroit, Mich.

The first model of this lure is the "Sure-Getter" made by the Neptune Bait Co. of Detroit. (Wood Body - 2½") Solid paint colors only: Green Head/Orange Body. Patent Pend. on metal belly w/no tail attractor. (est. late '20's and early 30's)

Stage two is the Weedless King Bait by Kingfisher Products, Base Line, Mich. 2-5/8" Length w/metal tail attractor. 5 colors now: RH/White, Blue Scale, Green Scale, Orange Scale, and Brown Scale. The lure now has Patent No.1994169 (1935).

Stage three is the "Weed Queen" marketed in the late 30's. This was shown on page 229 of my original catalog. (Thanks to Rich Treml)

The Croaker Bass Bait Company (DIDN'T KNOW JUST WHERE TO PUT THIS GEM.)

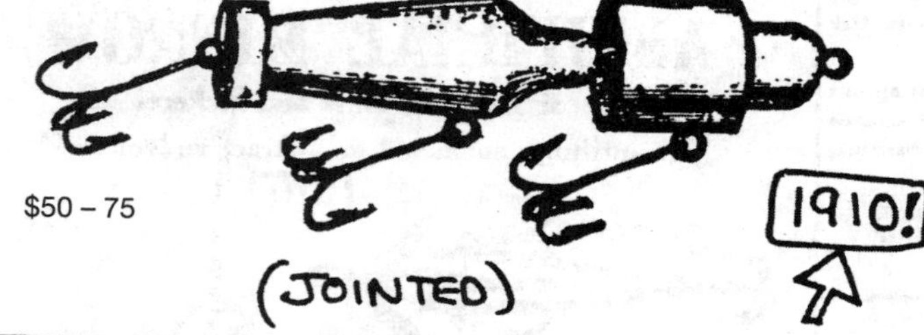

$50 – 75

(JOINTED)

1910!

THE EAMONS "CROAKER" BASS BAIT MFGD. BY L.A. WIFORD & SON JACKSON, MICH.

MAX WEESNER'S BUCK SPINNER

IT'S NEW! WEEZEL CRAB

Shaped like a crab—wiggles like a crab and catches more fish than any other crab on the market. Length 3¾ inches. Weight ⅝ ounces. Extra rubber creepers offered with each bait. $1.00 value.
No. C1—Nickel Finish
No. C2—Copper Finish
No. C5—Brass Finish

1937

SPOON- W/ RUBBER

MAX WEESNER'S CASTING SPINNER

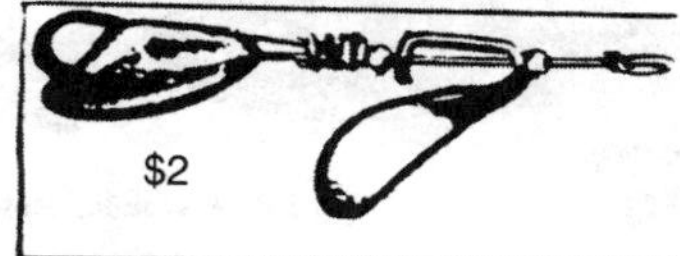

$2

$2

1906 No. 1

We make 8 different styles of hooks that will hold minnows, frogs or crawfish for bait casting.
If you want the best, send post card with address for descriptive folder.
WEST WEEDLESS HOOK CO., • Council Bluffs, Iowa

$2

1951

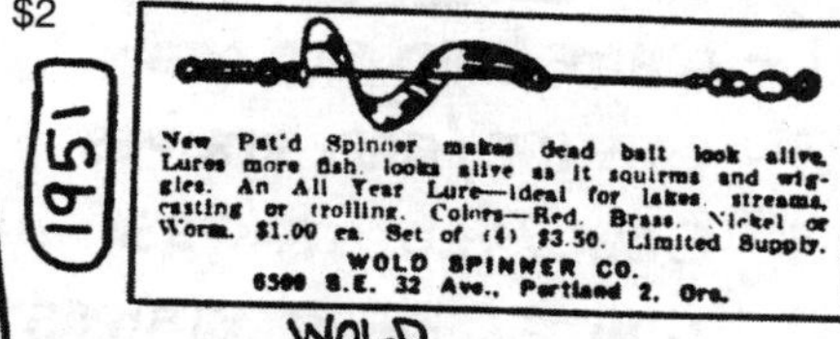

New Pat'd Spinner makes dead bait look alive. Lures more fish, looks alive as it squirms and wiggles. An All Year Lure—ideal for lakes, streams, casting or trolling. Colors—Red, Brass, Nickel or Worm. $1.00 ea. Set of (4) $3.50. Limited Supply.
WOLD SPINNER CO.
6500 S.E. 32 Ave., Portland 2, Ore.

WOLD

$5

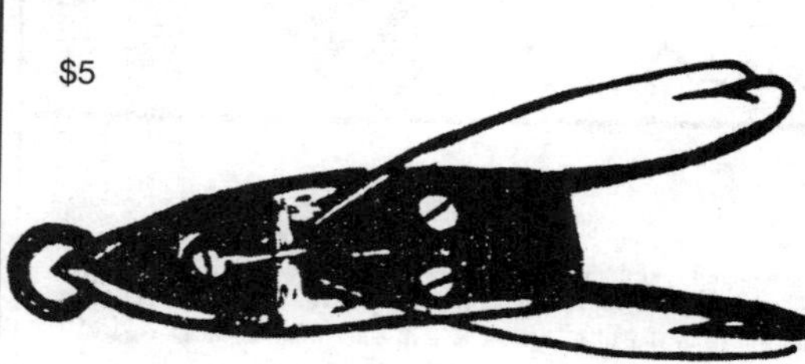

ALUMINUM BAIT

PELICAN
WEEDLESS PORK RIND BAIT

Manufactured by WHEELER-LUNBECK MFG. CO.
VALPARAISO, IND.

$5

WHITMAN ALL METAL BAIT

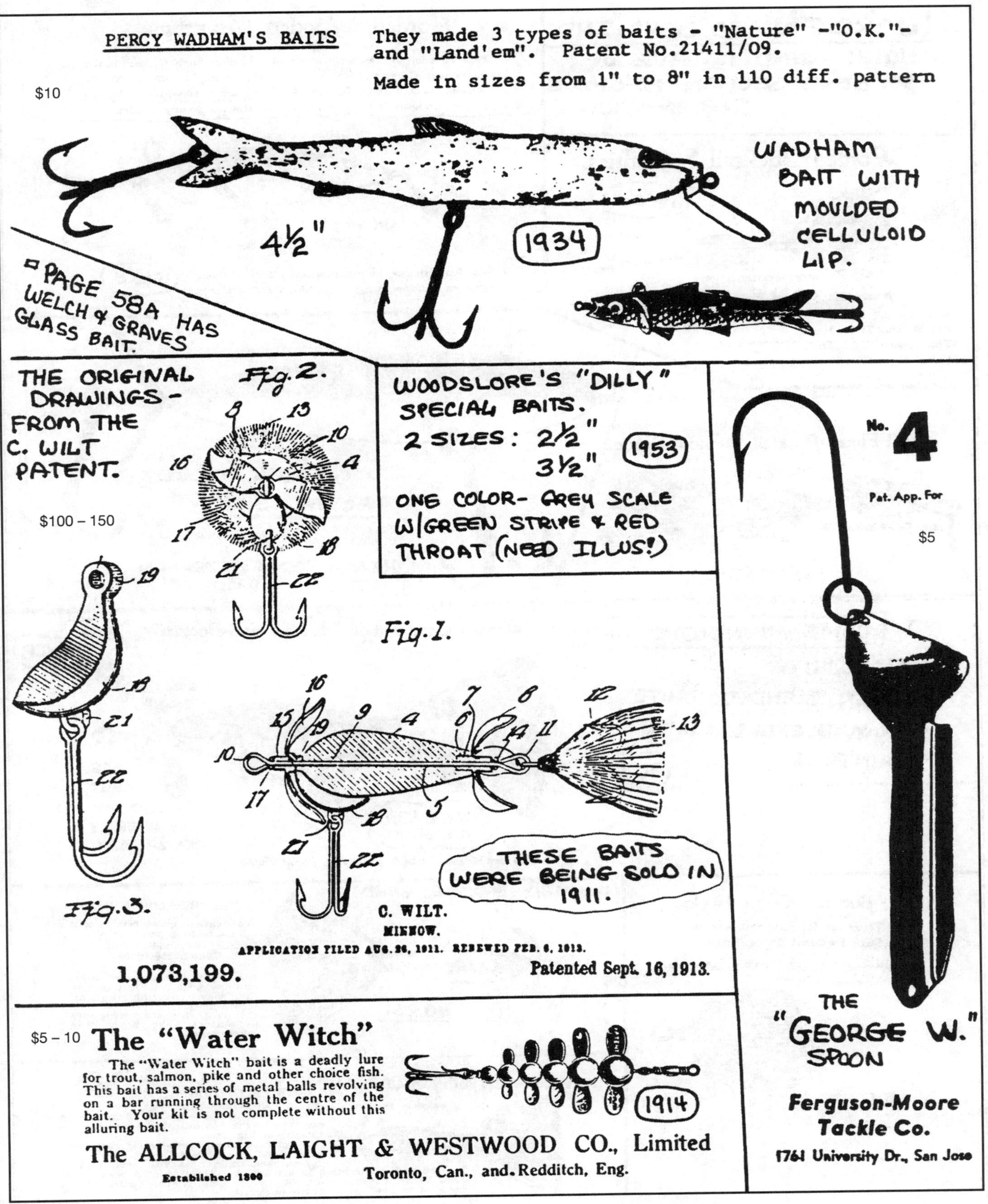
PERCY WADHAM'S BAITS
They made 3 types of baits - "Nature" -"O.K."- and "Land'em". Patent No.21411/09.
Made in sizes from 1" to 8" in 110 diff. pattern
$10
WADHAM BAIT WITH MOULDED CELLULOID LIP.
4½"
1934
PAGE 58A HAS WELCH & GRAVES GLASS BAIT.
THE ORIGINAL DRAWINGS - FROM THE C. WILT PATENT.
$100 – 150
Fig. 2.
Fig. 1.
Fig. 3.
WOODSLORE'S "DILLY" SPECIAL BAITS.
2 SIZES: 2½" 3½"
1953
ONE COLOR- GREY SCALE W/GREEN STRIPE & RED THROAT (NEED ILLUS!)
No. 4
Pat. App. For
$5
THESE BAITS WERE BEING SOLD IN 1911.
C. WILT.
MINNOW.
APPLICATION FILED AUG. 26, 1911. RENEWED FEB. 6, 1913.
1,073,199.
Patented Sept. 16, 1913.
THE "GEORGE W." SPOON
Ferguson-Moore Tackle Co.
1761 University Dr., San Jose
$5 – 10
The "Water Witch"
The "Water Witch" bait is a deadly lure for trout, salmon, pike and other choice fish. This bait has a series of metal balls revolving on a bar running through the centre of the bait. Your kit is not complete without this alluring bait.
1914
The ALLCOCK, LAIGHT & WESTWOOD CO., Limited
Established 1800
Toronto, Can., and Redditch, Eng.

WORDEN - SO. BEND, IND.

NOTE: READ 1ST PAGE OF SO. BEND SECTION FOR MORE INFORMATION.

Worden Wooden Minnows.

These Wooden Minnows are made of red cedar, finely finished in the following colors; Green and Red with "cracked back," Green and White with "cracked back." Red. White, Yellow. All are fitted with new Patent Spinner, the strongest and best spinner ever attached to any wooden bait.

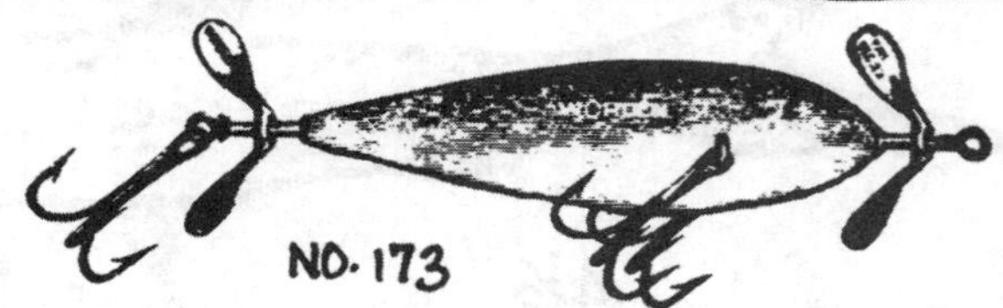

NO. 173

$75 – 100

Nos.
173 Wooden Minnow; length 3 inches, 3 Treble Hooks
75 Wooden Minnow; length 5 inches, 5 Treble Hooks

1900'S

Worden Bucktail Specialties.

1900's

$2

BUCK TAIL CASTING SPOON

A sure killer for Bass, Pickerel and other game fish.

Size ....
With Bucktail Treble Hook ....
With Bucktail Single Hook ....
With Bucktail Weedless Single Hook

(5 SIZES)

$50 – 75

2 HOOK MODEL
ACTUAL SIZE

COLOR – RED SPATTER ON WHITE

$5

Nickel Fluted Bucktail Minnow Spoon.

BUCK TAIL MINNOW SPOON

COMB. MINNOW COLORS

- ALL WHITE
- GREEN, BLENDED WHITE
- GRAY, BLENDED WHITE
- RAINBOW

1903

$75 – 125

Worden Combination Minnow and Bucktail.

BIG SPINNER

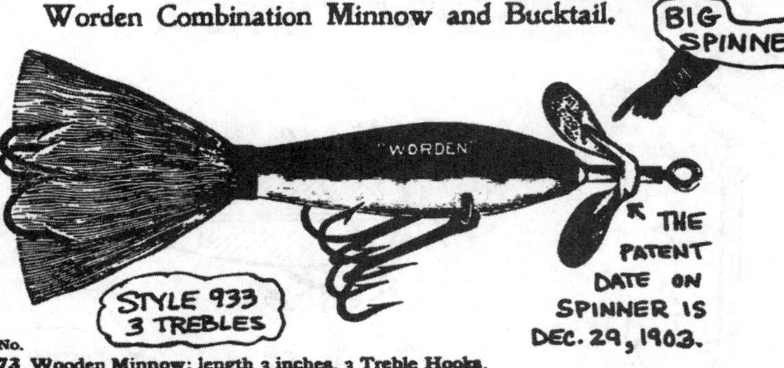
"WORDEN"

THE PATENT DATE ON SPINNER IS DEC. 29, 1903.

STYLE 933
3 TREBLES

No.
73 Wooden Minnow; length 3 inches, 3 Treble Hooks.

Bucktail Treble Hooks.

These are far more alluring than the ordinary feathered Treble Hooks.

Size.... 1 1/0 2/0 3/0 4/0

$2

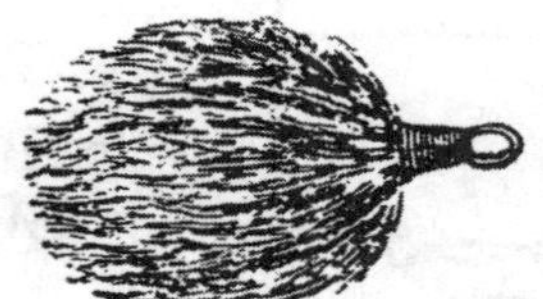

(PROBABLY EARLY SO. BEND)

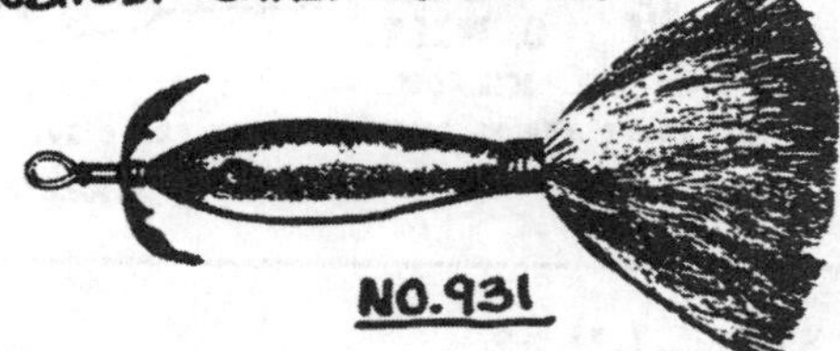

NO. 931

The "Bucktail" Killer.

When other baits fail, it will be sure to attract the fish.

Length of body (Rainbow Color), 2½ inches.

A small under-water wood minnow with bucktail tied to the body, covering the tail treble hook.

It is a very successful lure in waters that have been much fished.

$50 – 75

(NOTE WORDEN SPINNER)

NO. 715

WHITE BUCKTAIL MINNOW.

A Surface Bait and a Remarkably Successful One.

Try it along the edge of rushes, moss, etc., where the big ones hide—has a reputation for big ones.

A splendid night lure—try it some time after dark. Reel slow.

A nickel spinner at the head making just enough commotion to attract the attention of a bass; white oven baked enamel body, 2¾ inches long, a fine quality, treble hook concealed in a white bucktail.

-1915-

$50 – 75

$200 – 300+

1915

BAIT CASTERS ATTENTION!

Dr. Wasweyler's Marvelous Electric Glow Casting Minnow

Each bait a complete light plant, containing a dry cell and bulb. No wires, no phosphorous. Light is positive—turned on and off—a beautiful rich glow. Any color. Absolutely weedless. Can be used as a surface or under-water bait. Wonderfully efficient at dawn, twilight and at night. Has been successfully tried out by experienced and practical baitcast ers Every bait guaranteed or money refunded

Endorsed and Approved of by the Wisconsin State Game and Fish Warden

Do not delay! We are now selling them as fast as we can make them. Order at once so that you get yours in time.

Bait With 3 Batteries,

DR. C. S. WASWEYLER

455 Mitchell Street - - Milwaukee, Wis.

2 SIZES – FLYROD/CASTING

THE FAMOUS **X-RAY** BAIT -- more flash and glisten than any other bait

$15 – 25

-1920-

Pat applied for

Finished in six colors: No. 1, Amber, No. 2, Frog Green, No. 3, Orange No 4 Red: No. 5, Gold Scale Finish: No. 6, Silver Scale Finish.

TO CATCH THE BIG ONES USE

THE WELSHERANA TRANSPARENT BAIT

for Bait Casting and Trolling—It floats, wobbles and dives

1920's

Live baits only rival The X-Ray bait gives the true chromatic flashes of the live minnow, due to wonderful light refraction. An addition to the famous Telarana Nova family A killer for Bass, Pike, Trout and Musky. You can cast 25 yards farther than with ordinary baits, due to sinker shape and less wind resistance. Weight, ¾ oz. Also special fly-rod model, feather weight.

State color, and whether you want Bait or Fly, rod model.

STEWART WELSH **Pasadena, California**

THIS 1915 BAIT GETS MY VOTE AS THE MOST IMAGINARY NAME IN THIS BOOK...... "DR. WASWEYLER'S MARVELOUS ELECTRIC GLOW CASTING MINNOW."

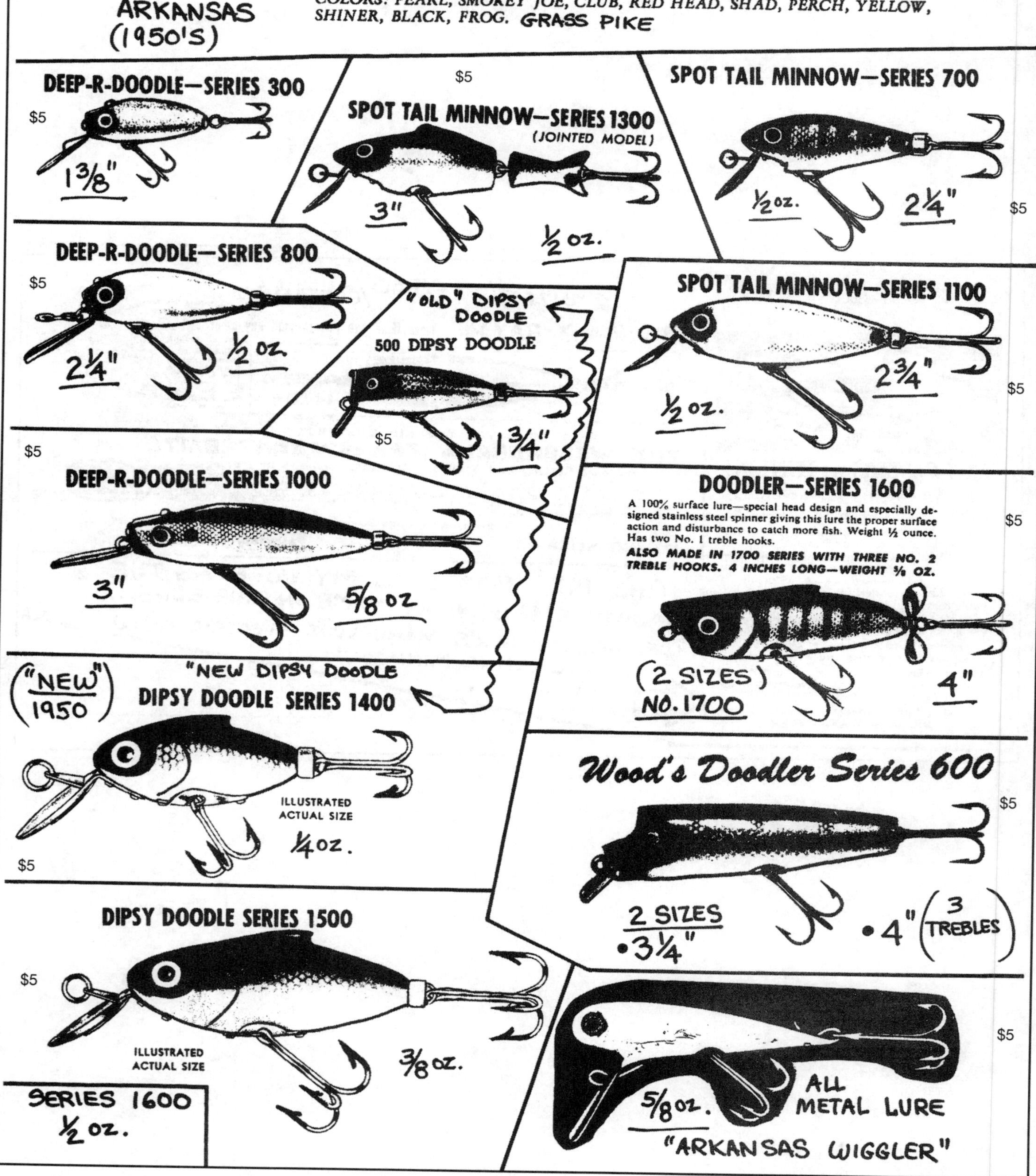
EL DORADO AND CONWAY - ARKANSAS (1950'S)
Wood "Stream-Tested" Lures
WOOD LURES ARE MADE OF MOLDED PLASTIC IN TEN PRACTICAL COLORS: PEARL, SMOKEY JOE, CLUB, RED HEAD, SHAD, PERCH, YELLOW, SHINER, BLACK, FROG. GRASS PIKE
DEEP-R-DOODLE—SERIES 300
$5
1 3/8"
$5
SPOT TAIL MINNOW—SERIES 1300
(JOINTED MODEL)
3"
1/2 oz.
SPOT TAIL MINNOW—SERIES 700
1/2 oz.
2 1/4"
$5
DEEP-R-DOODLE—SERIES 800
$5
2 1/4"
1/2 oz.
"OLD" DIPSY DOODLE
500 DIPSY DOODLE
$5
1 3/4"
SPOT TAIL MINNOW—SERIES 1100
2 3/4"
1/2 oz.
$5
$5
DEEP-R-DOODLE—SERIES 1000
3"
5/8 oz
DOODLER—SERIES 1600
A 100% surface lure—special head design and especially designed stainless steel spinner giving this lure the proper surface action and disturbance to catch more fish. Weight 1/2 ounce. Has two No. 1 treble hooks.
ALSO MADE IN 1700 SERIES WITH THREE NO. 2 TREBLE HOOKS. 4 INCHES LONG—WEIGHT 5/8 OZ.
$5
(2 SIZES) NO. 1700
4"
("NEW" 1950)
"NEW DIPSY DOODLE
DIPSY DOODLE SERIES 1400
ILLUSTRATED ACTUAL SIZE
1/4 oz.
$5
Wood's Doodler Series 600
$5
2 SIZES
•3 1/4"
•4" (3 TREBLES)
DIPSY DOODLE SERIES 1500
$5
ILLUSTRATED ACTUAL SIZE
3/8 oz.
SERIES 1600
1/2 oz.
$5
5/8 oz.
ALL METAL LURE
"ARKANSAS WIGGLER"

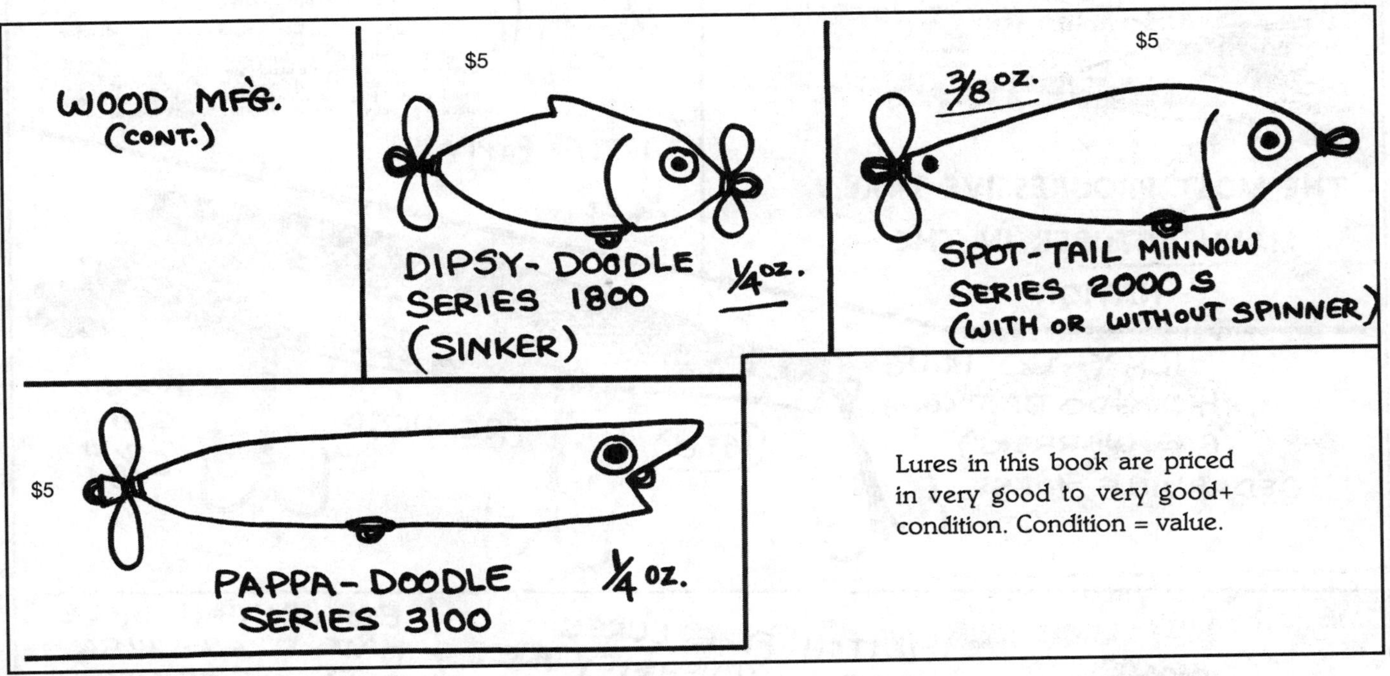

WOOD MFG.
(CONT.)
$5
DIPSY-DOODLE
SERIES 1800
(SINKER)
1/4 OZ.
$5
3/8 OZ.
SPOT-TAIL MINNOW
SERIES 2000 S
(WITH OR WITHOUT SPINNER)
$5
PAPPA-DOODLE
SERIES 3100
1/4 OZ.

Lures in this book are priced in very good to very good+ condition. Condition = value.

THE EARLY DIPSY-DOODLE WAS 1947.

THE 3100 SERIES OF THE POPPA-DOODLE WAS MADE OF WOOD.

Exact Size
As Shown
4 Inches
all
wooden
body
BRAND NEW BIG POPPA
Sharp short rod tip action causes a loud GULP sound—can be heard 100 feet at surface. On steady retrieve depth can be controlled by retrieve speed —lure darts very actively. (Don't copy boys, this lure is Registered.)
4"
1/2 ounce
12 COLORS
No. 3000
See Your Dealer or Write
WOOD MANUFACTURING CO. Conway, Ark.

$5

$2

Doodle-Socker—SERIES 5000 (5/8 oz.) CASTING
—SERIES 5100 (1/2 oz) SPINNING

A guaranteed spinner-type lure created and designed by one of our nation's foremost fishing authorities exclusively for WOOD. Available in two sizes, 5/8 and 1/2 oz., the DOODLE-SOCKER has proven itself to be the VERY BEST early spring and summer lure now on the market with a record of over 3,000 bass caught by its designer during a 2-month trial period. It will operate at any depth and spinner blade *will* turn while sinking or even on the slowest retrieve. With the Colorado spinner blade creating vibrations and its *rubber* skirt wiggling as it moves through the water, fish cannot and do not resist its tantalizing action. Available in the following rubber skirt colors.

● 5/8 oz. ● 1/2 oz.

THE MOST PROGRESSIVE LURE MANUFACTURER IN THE NATION

$5

Little Poppa—SERIES 3200

Lure weighs 1/4 oz. and is ideal for spin-casting. An exceptional lure for all pan fish and bass, both black and white. Retrieve slowly with erratic rod-tip action and this lure will prove its worth to you. Retails for $1.25. Available in attractive colors: Chub ● Red Head ● Blue Shad ● Perch ● Green Shad Black. ● See your dealer for other Wood's famous Lures.

"LITTLE POPPA" 1/4 OZ.

$5

HICKY-DO PLUG
HICKY-DO BAIT CO.
(R.E. WARREN)
CEDARVILLE, MASS.

1950

(REDUCED)

ACTUAL SIZE $6\frac{7}{8}$"

WITCH FIRE LURES
2550 UNIVERSITY AVE.
MADISON, WIS.

(FLUORESCENT AND PHOSPHORESCENT LURE.)

$5

GOGGLE EYES
BLACK BODY
1 PC. WIRE

• PLASTIC-
• TREBLE OR SINGLE HOOK MODELS
• SOME WITH BELLY SPINNERS

ED WYMAN MADE HAIR FLIES - 4456 SIDNEY AVE. - CHICAGO
1919

Old DAD WATSON'S
SECRET LURE

was invented by Dad Watson 32 years ago, out in the Puget Sound country, where the big 40- and 50-pound Silver Salmon fight like hell.

Old Dad's perfected Lure is now manufactured by his youngest son "Jim" and his partner Sam Scheldt (under firm name of Watson-Scheldt) at Everett, Washington. It is furnished in

THREE SIZES

No. 3, outer spoon length, 1⅞ inches
No. 5, outer spoon length, 2⅜ inches
No. 7, outer spoon length, 3 inches

SIZE 5H

SEATTLE, WA

$2

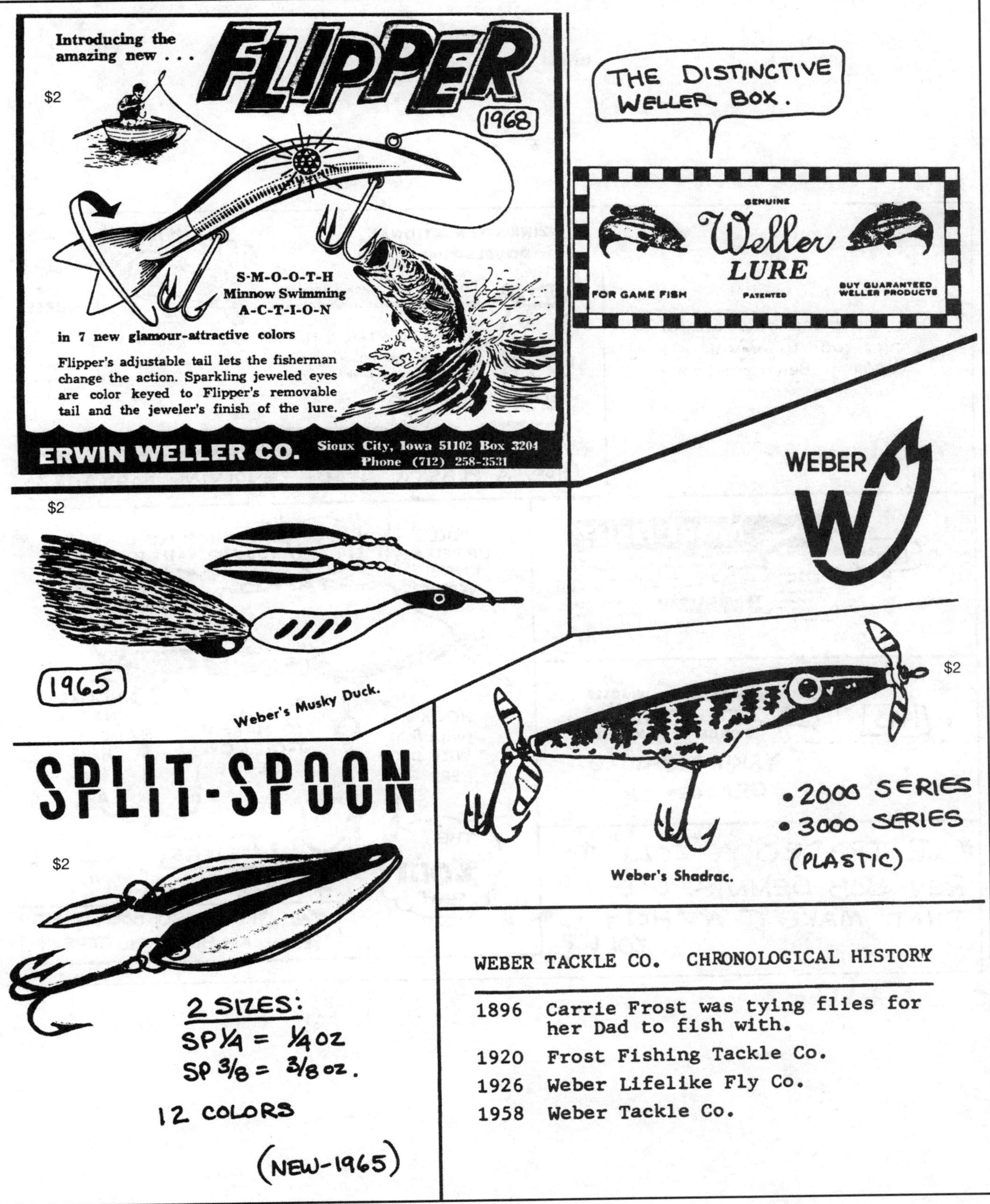
Introducing the amazing new . . .
FLIPPER
$2
1968
S-M-O-O-T-H
Minnow Swimming
A-C-T-I-O-N
in 7 new glamour-attractive colors
Flipper's adjustable tail lets the fisherman change the action. Sparkling jeweled eyes are color keyed to Flipper's removable tail and the jeweler's finish of the lure.
ERWIN WELLER CO.
Sioux City, Iowa 51102 Box 3204
Phone (712) 258-3531
THE DISTINCTIVE WELLER BOX.
GENUINE
Weller
LURE
FOR GAME FISH
PATENTED
BUY GUARANTEED WELLER PRODUCTS
WEBER
W
$2
1965
Weber's Musky Duck.
SPLIT-SPOON
$2
2 SIZES:
SP 1/4 = 1/4 OZ
SP 3/8 = 3/8 OZ.
12 COLORS
(NEW-1965)
$2
• 2000 SERIES
• 3000 SERIES
(PLASTIC)
Weber's Shadrac.

WEBER TACKLE CO. CHRONOLOGICAL HISTORY

1896	Carrie Frost was tying flies for her Dad to fish with.
1920	Frost Fishing Tackle Co.
1926	Weber Lifelike Fly Co.
1958	Weber Tackle Co.

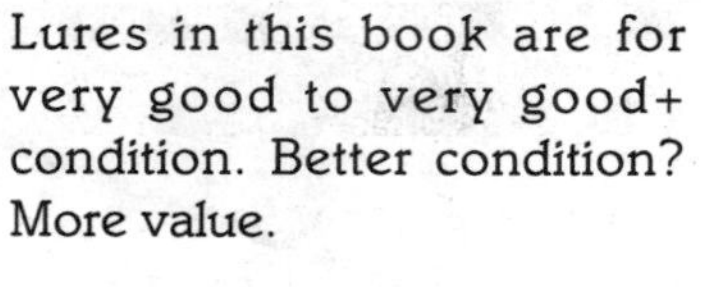
Lures in this book are for very good to very good+ condition. Better condition? More value.

$5 – 15

ZINK'S SENSATIONAL
DOUBLE-PURPOSE

"SCREWTAIL"
LURES
Pat. Pending

The world's only instantly convertible (under water-surface) lure.

1. Fins adjusted for under water.
2. Fins set for surface retrieve.

The SCREWTAIL Is Not Just Another Plug With Hooks—

It's a specially designed lure with built-in action—(It spins, darts and wobbles). Has a proven record for all types of game fish. Casts like a bullet. Choice 4 colors.

These lures are now available. If your dealer cannot supply you, write Dept. A

WRITE for FOLDER

ZINK ARTIFICIAL BAIT CO.
DIXON, ILLINOIS

(HAS A PLASTIC HEAD - REVOLVING BODY) 1946

$2

1954

MORE FISH?
*Yankee Doody—new lure for bass, steelhead, salmon, muskies, other game fish.
Darts and wiggles like crippled minnow—may double your catch!
*TRADE MARK PAT. PEND.
1/2 SIZE
Money refunded if not satisfied.
YANKEE SPORTS GOODS CO.
To June 30, 1954:—

$2

1943
WIGGLES
DARTS
FLOATS
WORDEN'S BONEFISH
YAKIMA BAIT CO.
GRANGER, WA.

$5

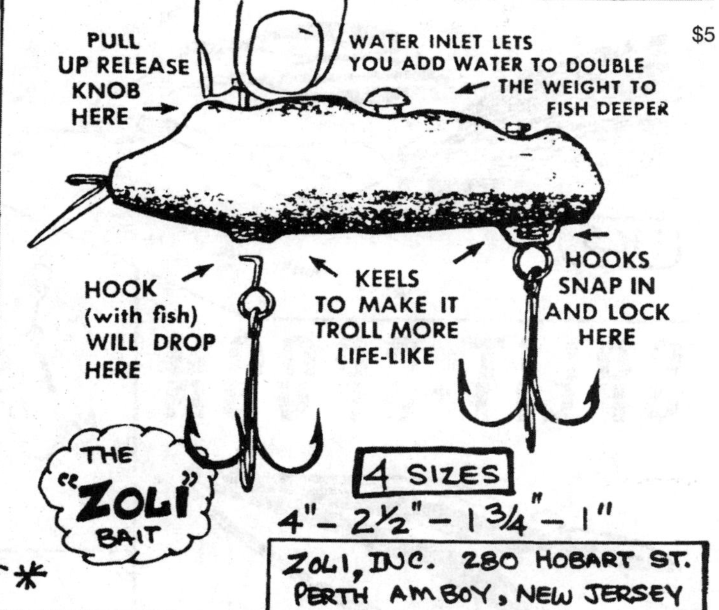
PULL UP RELEASE KNOB HERE
WATER INLET LETS YOU ADD WATER TO DOUBLE THE WEIGHT TO FISH DEEPER
HOOK (with fish) WILL DROP HERE
KEELS TO MAKE IT TROLL MORE LIFE-LIKE
HOOKS SNAP IN AND LOCK HERE
THE "ZOLI" BAIT
4 SIZES
4" – 2½" – 1¾" – 1"
ZOLI, INC. 280 HOBART ST.
PERTH AMBOY, NEW JERSEY

* I TRADED A "ZOLI" TO REV. BOB DENNIS. DID THAT MAKE IT A "HOLY ZOLI"? *

About the Authors

Dudley Murphy

Growing up in a family of fishermen, it was only natural for Dudley Murphy to develop a healthy interest in fishing. His father, Dudley C. Murphy, Sr., manufactured one of the early vibrating lures of the 1950s — Murph's Irish Shad. His grandfather, Dudley A. Murphy, was a conductor on the L&N Railroad who whittled fine examples of folk art which often included fishing lures. But it was his grandfather, Frank D. Royce, who presented him at age 13 with a gift of old Heddon, Jamison, and Clark lures that led Dudley to become a lifelong collector. As one of the original three founders of the National Fishing Lure Collector's Club, Dudley is an active collector with a variety of interests, including fishing.

Currently an artist teaching graphic design and directing the visual communication program at Drury College in Springfield, Missouri, Dudley designs and edits the *NFLCC Magazine* and pursues a secondary career as a songwriter and member of the popular bluegrass band, Radio Flyer.

Dudley, his wife Deanie, and their children, Quinn and Jennifer, enjoy life in the beautiful Missouri Ozarks.

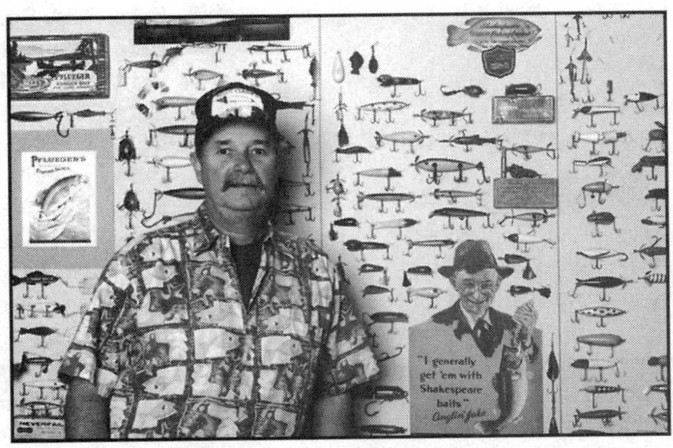
"I generally get 'em with Shakespeare baits."

Rick Edmisten

Born in California, Rick Edmisten was introduced to fishing at age 12 by his father. By the time he was 18, he had developed a keen interest in collecting lures and old tackle. After viewing the Heddon Company's traveling display of antique lures in 1979, Rick began to collect lures seriously, haunting antique shops and flea markets, advertising in newspapers, and displaying at sportmen's shows and tackle shops.

For the last 14 years Rick has hosted a very successful fishing tackle collectible show in North Hollywood, California, and searches widely for old lures via his network of collectors.

In November of 1989 Rick was invited to tape a segment of the nationally aired television program "Missing Reward," one of the most popular episodes in the season.

Recognized as an authority on old tackle, Rick is often asked to appraise estates and collections. He hopes someday to open a fishing tackle museum.

Rick continues a proud 87-year-old California family real estate tradition with his wife Diane and children Gable, Jim, and Krista, their beloved golden retriever Cooper, and three cats, Maggie, Laurel, and J.B.

NOTE: The authors are always interested in seeing, photographing, and often in purchasing old fishing lures for their collections. Persons wishing to contact the authors about old lures may do so by calling (818) 763-9406; by writing P.O. Box 686, North Hollywood, California 91603; or by e-mail www.flc.com.

Index

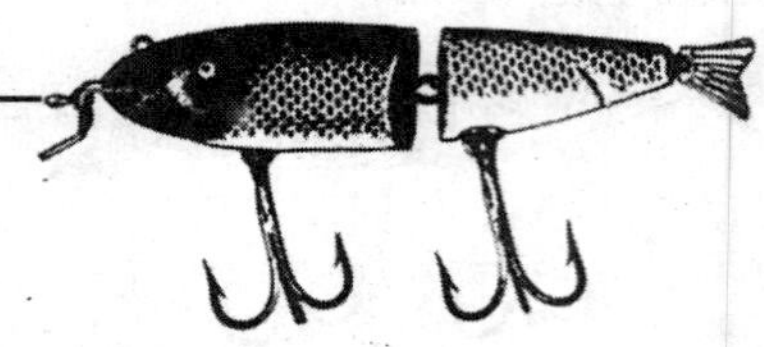

Numbers as primary identification:

COLLECTOR BOOKS

Informing Today's Collector

For over two decades we have been keeping collectors informed on trends and values in all fields of antiques and collectibles.

DOLLS, FIGURES & TEDDY BEARS

4707	A Decade of **Barbie** Dolls & Collectibles, 1981–1991, Summers	$19.95
4631	**Barbie** Doll Boom, 1986–1995, Augustyniak	$18.95
2079	**Barbie** Doll Fashion, Volume I, Eames	$24.95
4846	**Barbie** Doll Fashion, Volume II, Eames	$24.95
3957	**Barbie** Exclusives, Rana	$18.95
4632	**Barbie** Exclusives, Book II, Rana	$18.95
4557	**Barbie,** The First 30 Years, Deutsch	$24.95
5252	The **Barbie** Doll Years, 3rd Ed., Olds	$18.95
3810	**Chatty Cathy Dolls**, Lewis	$15.95
1529	Collector's Encyclopedia of **Barbie** Dolls, DeWein	$19.95
4882	Collector's Encyclopedia of **Barbie** Doll Exclusives and More, Augustyniak	$19.95
2211	Collector's Encyclopedia of **Madame Alexander Dolls**, Smith	$24.95
4863	Collector's Encyclopedia of **Vogue Dolls**, Izen/Stover	$29.95
3967	Collector's Guide to **Trolls,** Peterson	$19.95
5253	Story of **Barbie,** 2nd Ed., Westenhouser	$24.95
1513	**Teddy Bears & Steiff** Animals, Mandel	$9.95
1817	**Teddy Bears & Steiff** Animals, 2nd Series, Mandel	$19.95
2084	**Teddy Bears, Annalee's & Steiff** Animals, 3rd Series, Mandel	$19.95
1808	Wonder of **Barbie,** Manos	$9.95
1430	World of **Barbie** Dolls, Manos	$9.95
4880	World of **Raggedy Ann** Collectibles, Avery	$24.95

TOYS, MARBLES & CHRISTMAS COLLECTIBLES

3427	**Advertising Character** Collectibles, Dotz	$17.95
2333	Antique & Collector's **Marbles,** 3rd Ed., Grist	$9.95
4934	**Breyer Animal** Collector's Guide, Identification and Values, Browell	$19.95
4976	**Christmas** Ornaments, Lights & Decorations, Johnson	$24.95
4737	**Christmas** Ornaments, Lights & Decorations, Vol. II, Johnson	$24.95
4739	**Christmas** Ornaments, Lights & Decorations, Vol. III, Johnson	$24.95
4649	Classic Plastic **Model Kits,** Polizzi	$24.95
4559	Collectible **Action Figures,** 2nd Ed., Manos	$17.95
3874	Collectible Coca-Cola Toy **Trucks,** deCourtivron	$24.95
2338	Collector's Encyclopedia of **Disneyana,** Longest, Stern	$24.95
4958	Collector's Guide to **Battery Toys,** Hultzman	$19.95
5038	Collector's Guide to **Diecast Toys & Scale Models,** 2nd Ed., Johnson	$19.95
4651	Collector's Guide to **Tinker Toys,** Strange	$18.95
4566	Collector's Guide to **Tootsietoys,** 2nd Ed., Richter	$19.95
5169	Collector's Guide to **TV Toys** & Memorabilia, 2nd Ed., Davis/Morgan	$24.95
4720	The Golden Age of **Automotive Toys**, 1925–1941, Hutchison/Johnson	$24.95
3436	Grist's Big Book of **Marbles**	$19.95
3970	Grist's Machine-Made & Contemporary **Marbles,** 2nd Ed.	$9.95
5267	**Matchbox** Toys, 1947 to 1998, 3rd Ed., Johnson	$19.95
4871	**McDonald's Collectibles**, Henriques/DuVall	$19.95
1540	**Modern Toys** 1930–1980, Baker	$19.95
3888	**Motorcycle** Toys, Antique & Contemporary, Gentry/Downs	$18.95
5168	Schroeder's Collectible **Toys,** Antique to Modern Price Guide, 5th Ed.	$17.95
1886	Stern's Guide to **Disney** Collectibles	$14.95
2139	Stern's Guide to **Disney** Collectibles, 2nd Series	$14.95
3975	Stern's Guide to **Disney** Collectibles, 3rd Series	$18.95
2028	**Toys**, Antique & Collectible, Longest	$14.95

FURNITURE

1457	American **Oak** Furniture, McNerney	$9.95
3716	American **Oak** Furniture, Book II, McNerney	$12.95
1118	Antique **Oak** Furniture, Hill	$7.95
2271	Collector's Encyclopedia of **American** Furniture, Vol. II, Swedberg	$24.95
3720	Collector's Encyclopedia of **American** Furniture, Vol. III, Swedberg	$24.95
1755	Furniture of the **Depression Era,** Swedberg	$19.95
3906	**Heywood-Wakefield** Modern Furniture, Rouland	$18.95
1885	**Victorian** Furniture, Our American Heritage, McNerney	$9.95
3829	**Victorian** Furniture, Our American Heritage, Book II, McNerney	$9.95

JEWELRY, HATPINS, WATCHES & PURSES

1712	Antique & Collector's **Thimbles** & Accessories, Mathis	$19.95
1748	Antique **Purses,** Revised Second Ed., Holiner	$19.95
1278	Art Nouveau & Art Deco **Jewelry,** Baker	$9.95
4850	Collectible **Costume Jewelry,** Simonds	$24.95
3875	Collecting Antique **Stickpins,** Kerins	$16.95
3722	Collector's Ency. of **Compacts, Carryalls & Face Powder Boxes,** Mueller	$24.95
4854	Collector's Ency. of **Compacts, Carryalls & Face Powder Boxes,** Vol. II	$24.95
4940	**Costume Jewelry**, A Practical Handbook & Value Guide, Rezazadeh	$24.95
1716	Fifty Years of Collectible **Fashion Jewelry,** 1925–1975, Baker	$19.95
1424	**Hatpins** & Hatpin Holders, Baker	$9.95
1181	100 Years of Collectible **Jewelry,** 1850–1950, Baker	$9.95
4729	**Sewing Tools** & Trinkets, Thompson	$24.95
4878	Vintage & Contemporary **Purse Accessories**, Gerson	$24.95
3830	Vintage **Vanity Bags & Purses,** Gerson	$24.95

INDIANS, GUNS, KNIVES, TOOLS, PRIMITIVES

1868	Antique **Tools,** Our American Heritage, McNerney	$9.95
1426	**Arrowheads** & Projectile Points, Hothem	$7.95
4943	Field Guide to **Flint Arrowheads & Knives** of the North American Indian	$9.95
2279	**Indian Artifacts** of the Midwest, Hothem	$14.95
3885	**Indian Artifacts** of the Midwest, Book II, Hothem	$16.95
4870	**Indian Artifacts** of the Midwest, Book III, Hothem	$18.95
5162	Modern **Guns,** Identification & Values, 12th Ed., Quertermous	$12.95
2164	**Primitives,** Our American Heritage, McNerney	$9.95
1759	**Primitives,** Our American Heritage, 2nd Series, McNerney	$14.95
4730	Standard **Knife** Collector's Guide, 3rd Ed., Ritchie & Stewart	$12.95

PAPER COLLECTIBLES & BOOKS

4633	**Big Little Books,** Jacobs	$18.95
4710	Collector's Guide to **Children's Books,** 1850 to 1950, Jones	$18.95
1441	Collector's Guide to **Post Cards,** Wood	$9.95
2081	Guide to Collecting **Cookbooks,** Allen	$14.95
5271	Huxford's **Old Book** Value Guide, 11th Ed.	$19.95
2080	Price Guide to **Cookbooks & Recipe Leaflets,** Dickinson	$9.95
3973	**Sheet Music** Reference & Price Guide, 2nd Ed., Pafik & Guiheen	$19.95
4654	**Victorian Trade Cards,** Historical Reference & Value Guide, Cheadle	$19.95
4733	**Whitman Juvenile Books,** Brown	$17.95

GLASSWARE

4561	Collectible **Drinking Glasses,** Chase & Kelly	$17.95
4642	Collectible **Glass Shoes,** Wheatley	$19.95
4937	Coll. **Glassware from the 40s, 50s & 60s,** 4th Ed., Florence	$19.95
1810	Collector's Encyclopedia of **American Art Glass,** Shuman	$29.95
4938	Collector's Encyclopedia of **Depression Glass,** 13th Ed., Florence	$19.95
1961	Collector's Encyclopedia of **Fry Glassware,** Fry Glass Society	$24.95
1664	Collector's Encyclopedia of **Heisey Glass,** 1925–1938, Bredehoft	$24.95
3905	Collector's Encyclopedia of **Milk Glass,** Newbound	$24.95
4936	Collector's Guide to **Candy Containers**, Dezso/Poirier	$19.95
4564	**Crackle Glass,** Weitman	$19.95
4941	**Crackle Glass,** Book II, Weitman	$19.95
4714	**Czechoslovakian Glass** and Collectibles, Book II, Barta/Rose	$16.95
5158	**Elegant Glassware** of the Depression Era, 8th Ed., Florence	$19.95
1380	Encyclopedia of **Pattern Glass,** McCain	$12.95
3981	Evers' Standard **Cut Glass** Value Guide	$12.95
4659	**Fenton** Art Glass, 1907–1939, Whitmyer	$24.95
3725	**Fostoria,** Pressed, Blown & Hand Molded Shapes, Kerr	$24.95
4719	**Fostoria**, Etched, Carved & Cut Designs, Vol. II, Kerr	$24.95
3883	**Fostoria Stemware,** The Crystal for America, Long & Seate	$24.95
4644	**Imperial Carnival Glass,** Burns	$18.95
3886	**Kitchen Glassware** of the Depression Years, 5th Ed., Florence	$19.95
5156	Pocket Guide to **Depression Glass,** 11th Ed., Florence	$9.95